ENCYCLOPEDIA OF

CHRISTIAN THEOLOGY

VOLUME 2

ENCYCLOPEDIA OF
CHRISTIAN THEOLOGY

VOLUME 2

JEAN-YVES LACOSTE
EDITOR

G-O

ROUTLEDGE
New York • London

Published in 2005 by
Routledge
270 Madison Avenue
New York, NY 10016

Published in Great Britain by
Routledge
2 Park Square
Milton Park, Abingdon
Oxon, OX14 4RN

Originally published as *Dictionnaire critique de théologie (Nouvelle Edition),* edited by Jean-Yves Lacoste (Paris: Presses Universitaires de France, 1999), ISBN 2–13–048825–0
©Presses Universitaires de France, 1998 and 1999

Published with the participation of the *Ministère français chargé de la Culture–Centre National du Livre* (French Ministry of Culture–National Book Center)

10 9 8 7 6 5 4 3 2 1

Library of Congress Cataloging-in-Publication Data

Dictionnaire critique de théologie. English.
  Encyclopedia of Christian theology / Jean-Yves Lacoste, editor.
      p. cm.
    Includes bibliographical references and index.
      ISBN 1–57958–250–8 (set: alk. paper)—ISBN 1–57958–236–2 (v. 1: alk. paper)—ISBN 1–57958–239–7 (v. 2: alk. paper)—ISBN 1–57958–332–6 (v. 3: alk. paper) 1. Theology—Encyclopedias. I. Lacoste, Jean-Yves. II. Title.
  BR95.D5313 2004
  230'.03—dc22
  2004004150

Printed in the United States of America on acid-free paper.

Contents

Foreword

A reader about to venture into a thick reference work (especially one dealing with theology) has the right to ask for additional mercy from its editor: that is, that the editor specifies the aim and use of the work. A few glosses about the title will answer this request. First and foremost, this is an encyclopedia of theology, meaning, in a restrictive sense that is also a precise sense, the massive amount of discourse and doctrines that Christianity has assembled about God and its experience of God. There are other discourses on God, and theology was often the first to champion their rationality. By selecting one term to refer to one practice (historically circumscribed) of the logos and one call (historically circumscribed) in the name of God, we do not pretend to deny the existence or the rationality of other practices or calls—we are only offering to make use of *theological* to name the fruits of a kind of covenant between the Greek logos and the Christian restructuring of the Jewish experience. When the philosopher discusses God, it rarely appears that his interest is theological, in the fixed sense of the term. Because Judaism was able to tie in the richest things it had to say without pillaging the theoretical legacy of classical antiquity, it is also unlikely that *theological* needs to be applied to its doctrines. Likewise, because the Islamic Kalam itself follows some rather original structuration rules, it is inadequate to baptize it "Islamic theology," unless one accepts a certain vagueness. As for the rigorous comparative study of all the discourses in which the signifier *God* (whether its intervention be that of name, concept, or other) appears, it is still in its infancy.

Second, this is an encyclopedia, by which we mean an academic tool serving knowledge. It is one thing to produce knowledge and another to transmit it. Thus, we will not expect from this collegiate effort, which the present foreword concludes, that it was a work of creation. In the organized disorder presided over by the alphabetical order of the entries, its ambition was modest: to provide readers with a starting point for the main theological objects. Events, doctrines, contributors, theories and metatheories, over five hundred objects are to be found within the pages of this encyclopedia. The reader who wants to browse through the pages following a question will always find stand-alone entries and the point about the question. The reader who prefers long explorations can rely on the navigational tools provided to learn, one entry after another, for example, about Biblical theology in general or about medieval theology or about Lutheran theology or more. For want of a consensus among scholars, which cannot be found anywhere, this work is expected to keep the promises inherent to its scientific genre: legibility, intellectual honesty, and historical precision.

Last, this intends to be a critical work, which doesn't bound its fate to some deconstructing temerity but rather emphasizes the native condition of any academic endeavor at the service of truth. The first task of critical reasoning is to criticize itself. Although it was critical of the objects it inherited from tradition, the reason of the Enlightenment was less critical of itself, its powers, duties, and agents. One demand remains, which we owe and of which we should not be afraid: we will expect from the "critical" history of the doctrines or from the "critical" presentation of the theological traditions that they wanted to identify their own objects so that they appear as they are, in all their diachronic or synchronic complexity, sometimes in all indecision. Theology concerns itself mostly with phenomena that never demand intellection without also demanding adhesion, and the historical work of discernment that the encyclopedia undertook will not deprive anybody of the necessity to forge a personal opinion. One never believes, however, without knowing slightly. If one wants to forge a straight opinion, then it is best to know critically rather than precritically.

The editor has one pleasant remaining task: that of giving thanks. Firstly, he wishes to thank the 250 contributors, from about one hundred institutions and representing about fifteen nationalities. They made this encyclopedia and accepted the many constraints imposed by such an exercise. All graciously complied with the editorial goal of global cohesiveness, and their good will allowed the work to be more than a collection of stand-alone entries. All used their own voice, however, and this allows the work to let its authors speak with the accents peculiar to their cultural and scientific traditions.

Secondly, the editor wishes to thank all colleagues and friends who, flying to the rescue at the last minute, helped fill gaps, update bibliographies, refine translations, and verify thousands of references. I thus burn the incense of my gratitude to Daniel Bourgeois, Rémi Brague, Michel Cagin, Olivier de Champris, Michel Corbin, Michel Gitton, Jérôme de Gramont, Yves-Jean Harder, Max Huot de Longchamp, Goulven Madec, Thaddée Matura, Cyrille Michon, Bruno Neveu, Jacqueline de Proyart, and Daniel de Reynal. The members of the editorial board know how dear their collaboration was to me as well as the pleasure I had working with them. It is fair that the reader should know about them, too. My thanks turn superlative for Marie-Béatrice Mesnet, who bore the final responsibility of the French manuscript, from disks to proofs, including the organization of the bibliographies, cross-references, and abbreviations: I fear to think what we would have published without her help. As for Jacqueline Champris, she allowed for this work to be published while its editor was alive, or that its editor would not die in the process: each reader will judge its merit.

Our first French edition owed its index to Georges Leblanc, and we kindly remember Edith Migo providing us with secretarial help early on. The logistical support from Franços de Vorges and Didier Le Riche greatly eased the work of the editorial board. Françoise Muckensturm and Renza Arrighi also provided their biblical knowledge. The published work bore the mark of their labors.

Some members of the editorial board and the like spent more time than others in compiling the second French edition: my hat off thus to Paul Beauchamp, Olivier Boulnois, Vincent Carraud, Irène Fernandez, Marie-Béatrice Mesnet, Oliver O'Donovan, and Françoise Vinel as well as to the knowledgeable and devoted editor of the encyclopedia. As with the first, the second edition also had many benefactors who wrote entries in a few days, suggested useful amendments, and published encouraging notices. I cannot name them all, but I do want to name Cyrille Michon, Hervé Barreau, Rémi Brague, Claude Bressolette, Yves Delorme, Henri de L'Éprevier, Bernard de Guibert, Dominique Le Tourneau, Roger Pouivet, Émile Poulat, Michel Sales, Yves Tourenne, and Claude Villemot. The first French edition was honored by the Académie des Sciences Morales et Politiques, which awarded it the Chanoine Delpeuch Prize. As for Tabatha, finally, she knows what we owe her: a lot.

Jean-Yves Lacoste

Introduction

The *Dictionnaire critique de théologie* was first published in French in 1998. When in 1999 work began on an anglophone presentation, the U.S. publishers had at their disposal the French additions and modifications to the original text undertaken with a view to its second edition. The present work is a translation of the second edition of the French original.

Users of the *Encyclopedia of Christian Theology*, whether chiefly interested in consulting it for specific information or in browsing more widely, may well wish to begin with the index. The French editorial committee and the editorial director have achieved the not inconsiderable feat of containing very nearly all the material falling within the ambit of a critical work of theology, as those terms are defined in the foreword, within some five hundred entries.

Theology remains the rationally structured discussion of the Christianized experience of Hebrew monotheism, as it was originally elaborated with the help of Greek philosophical categories and considerations familiar to the early Christian Greek-speaking world and subsequently developed during two millennia of Christian thought.

This has meant paying little more than passing attention to other important aspects of Christian life as it developed. Its liturgies, its widely diverging spiritualities, its administrative hierarchy, and its noncore teaching even about important moral and social issues occurring in response to the often political constraints that arose in the course of history are not central to its theology as here understood. Attention is concentrated on such matters as Trinitarian theology, Christology, the Incarnation, the Redemption, revelation, ecclesiology, and the understanding of the workings of the divine plan for humanity. The definition also excludes formal consideration of eastern religions and even of Islam, immensely powerful in its own right and also the vehicle for carrying the thought of Aristotle, heavily contaminated by Neoplatonism, to the Christian scholastic theologians of the High Middle Ages.

Philosophy itself, as an intellectual discipline, does not fall within the ambit of the reference function of the *Encyclopedia*, but its exclusion poses more difficult problems. As the editor of the French original, Jean-Yves Lacoste, points out in his own entry on philosophy, it is still possible in the twentieth century with Barth or Heidegger to conduct philosophical discussion without reference to any theological position. In fact, however, the possibility of the autonomous conduct of philosophical investigation, although it is not discussed in the *Encyclopedia*, looks today increasingly fragile.

Christian theology as a discipline, particularly on account of the Greco-Roman legacy still woven into it, is much more difficult to insulate from its philosophical substructure. In many of its entries, the *Encyclopedia*, having expounded the theology with which they are concerned, concludes them with philosophical considerations. Philosophically speaking, Christian theology has for centuries relied on a *philosophia perennis,* drawing its categories and premises largely from Aristotelian and Platonist traditions.

Certain aspects of that traditional substructure, notably its anthropology, its epistemology, and its ontology, are no longer generally considered useful and at least in non-English-speaking Europe have been replaced by a newer tradition. In the *Encyclopedia,* no attempt has been made to diminish the reliance on philosophical reflections developed from the mainstream European, mostly German-language tradition as it has emerged from Kant and the German idealists and subsequently been developed by Hegel, Husserl, and Heidegger, and from more recent variations of an essentially phenomenological approach to the subject such as appear also in the work of some modern theologians like Karl Rahner.

The content of the work, as indicated in the foreword, is laid out alphabetically, and anglophone readers will have no difficulty finding the keyword for many of the most important themes, events, people, and topics discussed. There is an elaborate system of cross-referencing, but, as the relative length of the entries and the bibliographies makes clear, a format of relatively long entries and essays, still within the scope of what is known as a *dictionnaire* in French, has been chosen rather than that of a high number of short entries generally denoted by the word *dictionary* in English.

Some of the new entries, like that for Moses, fill lacunae in the original text, and very few important topics will be found to have been altogether neglected, although to locate the several treatments of such themes as transsubstantiation or of theologians as important as Melanchthon, it is necessary to refer first to the index. It is even possible that certain readers will feel that occasionally, like the original eighteenth-century French *Encyclopédie*, this *Encyclopedia* advances views or developments that it purports merely to transmit or that it gives an acceptably ecumenical doctrinal spin to the historical record by omitting to dwell on or even to note some of the harsher reactions perceivable in the decrees of the council of Trent or of Vatican I or in the decisions of the Pontifical Biblical Commission. Theologians of the last fifty years are not unreasonably accorded a prominence that implies a value judgment about their work, which is inevitably less certain to endure than judgments made about theologians from centuries earlier than the twentieth whose historical contribution to the development of today's theology cannot be challenged.

It will not be difficult for users to identify the corporate viewpoint of the editorial committee of the *Encyclopedia.* It is, however, as the third paragraph of the foreword makes clear, important to preserve the work's intellectual integrity. That means identifying and acknowledging what its point of view is, especially on account of the probability that here and there the more speculative essays may seem to be urging Catholic theology to develop in a particular direction and the further probability that any such direction will be one with which the original French readership may feel more at ease than theologians brought up in some of the traditions at present current in different degrees in the various anglophone regions of the globe.

The university level that determines the amount and type of information contained in the *Encyclopedia* requires its content to be not only historically accurate, deep enough for university-level reflection, and well enough written to be readily intelligible but also useful in a university context, that is, one in which reasonably ample library resources are available. Users wishing to follow up references to patristic works, the scholastics, or modern books and articles will often require the bibliographic resources normally found only in theological colleges or in large, general academic institutions.

Because the *Encyclopedia* is intended also to serve outside a formal university context as an initial guide to the state of theological discussion on all major topics covered by its definition of theology, the references to reviews, editions, and relatively small-circulation journals are included simply for the convenience of those who wish to pursue further research. Further investigation into most of the topics covered is likely to require access to good editions of the Fathers of the Church and, where there are any, of the scholastics, as well as to more recent theologians from the nineteenth and twentieth centuries. The entries are written with a view to being easily intelligible even where there is no immediate access to the cited sources.

Some topics, like the Dead Sea Scrolls, have primarily been discussed only in languages other than English and chiefly in specialist journals. In such instances, the *Encyclopedia* attempts primarily to do service as a handbook or guide to the present state of discussion, giving only pointers in its references to places or sources where the discussion has been further developed or on which advocates of different views have relied. In all cases, and in spite of its inevitable point of view, the *Encyclopedia* attempts an objective exposition of the facts and arguments, without bias, prejudice, or any viewpoint that could be interpreted as sectarian.

The *Encyclopedia* does not aspire to be historical in that it does not undertake to cover the history of the theology of the topics that it includes except incidentally, in order to explain and contextualize them, and except insofar as the sources for contemporary theological views are necessarily grounded in the historic sources of the Christian revelation. The method adopted is, however, critical. At every point it goes out of its way to confront doctrines and views with the sources and traditions on which they rely, and it is relentless in its pursuit of theological truth as warranted by the sources and the historical facts. This criticism is not destructive of anything but falsehood, although when applied as rigorously as it is here to the legitimacy of some of the emphases of medieval theology, it produces results that are likely to surprise many brought up on a precritical tradition. The critical account of the tradition reveals, for instance, that the notion of an individual judgment at the moment of death appeared only relatively late in eastern theology and shows that the virginity of Mary has a less strong scriptural basis than is often assumed.

Without a doubt, the critical expertise of the theologians on whom the editorial committee has drawn for the entries is where this work's serious theological interest primarily lies. Whatever services may be rendered by the utility of its reference function, the most significant achievement of the entries in the work consists overwhelmingly in the critical acumen applied by its authors to their subject matter, invariably through a rigorous treatment of the sources and tradition underlying the historical and contemporary theological discussion of all theology's major issues. To this critical treatment of the tradition is often appended a more speculative section, as in the entry on being, pointing to tasks remaining to be accomplished and to directions in which theological discussion appears to be moving.

The critical method used is essentially based on a balanced appraisal of the theological sources that time, tradition, and individual religious spiritualities, such as those developed within the great religious orders or outside them by popular devotion, have inevitably tended to obscure. By confronting patterns of Christian religious belief and behavior with the sources of the Christian revelation and with the major developments in theological tradition, the *Encyclopedia* no doubt implicitly calls for a reevaluation of some views and attitudes that may at different periods have been too uncritically, and perhaps wrongly, assumed to have been dictated by fundamental theological dogma. The critical function of the *Encyclopedia* lies not in criticizing them but in confronting them with a more authentic understanding of the Christian revelation, leaving it to individuals to mold the moral and religious commitments that best both fulfil their own spiritual needs and accord with the revelation. Insofar as the *Encyclopedia* fulfils the task it has taken on itself, it must promote a pluralism of religious attitudes, both moral and devotional, capable of fulfilling the individual hunger for spiritual nourishment on the basis of a critical understanding of genuine theological truth.

It is difficult to think of any earlier attempt to produce a comprehensive critical theological handbook in the sense in which the *Encyclopedia* defines theology. There are no doubt historical reasons why this should be so, and the appearance of the *Encyclopedia* marks an important stage in the diminution of sectarian slants on theological discussion as well as a hope that a point has been reached when all those whose experience is enhanced by a spirituality situated within the Judeo-Christian religious tradition can look forward to agreeing on the theology that lies at its center. The *Encyclopedia,* in giving, however succinctly, a fully critical account of that tradition, is a product of progress already made as well as a pointer to what questions still urgently await their resolution and an indicator of the most promising paths to be followed. It summarizes the present state of theological discussion without dwelling on what has recently been achieved or laying down firm paths for the future. It may well constitute a milestone in the progress toward a truly critical theology and therefore also toward promoting a religious awareness and providing the basis for an intelligently reflective religious commitment without laying down new orthodoxies. Its task is to present the critical summary of Judeo-Christian theology necessary to further the personal and corporate attitudes of those who seek to live by the norms it promotes.

Anthony Levi

Alphabetical List of Entries

Abbreviations

A. Usual Abbreviations

a.	articulus
ACFEB	Association catholique française pour l'étude de la Bible
adv.	adversus
anath.	anathema
anon.	anonymous
Apos. Const.	Apostolic Constitution
ap.	*apud* (according to)
ARCIC	Anglican-Roman Catholic International Commission
arg.	argumentum
art.	article
BHK	Biblia Hebraica, ed. Kittel
BHS	Biblia Hebraica Stuttgartensia
bibl.	includes a bibliography
c.	circa
CADIR	Centre pour l'analyse du discours religieux, Lyon
can.	canon
CEPOA	Centre d'étude du Proche-Orient ancien, Louvain
ch(ap).	chapter
COE	Conseil œcuménique des Églises (see WWC)
col.	column
coll.	collection
comm.	*Commentum,* commentary
concl.	conclusio
d.	distinctio
Decr.	Decretal
diss.	dissertatio
dub.	dubium
ed.	edidit, editio
ed.	editor
ep.	epistula(e), letters
f	next verse (biblical citations)
ff	two following verses (biblical citations)
FS	Festschrift
GA	Gesamtausgabe
gr.	Greek
GS	Gesammelte Schriften
GW	Gesammelte Werke
hb, hebr.	Hebrew
hom.	homily
l.	*liber*
lat.	latin
lect.	*lectio*
MA	Middle Ages
ms.	manuscript
mss	manuscripts
n.	note/*numerus*
NT	New Testament
O.P.	Order of Preachers (Dominicans)
O.S.B.	Order of Saint Benedict (Benedictines)
OC	Œuvres complètes; Complete Works
Op.	*Opera* (Works)
OT	Old Testament
par.	parallel passages (in synoptic gospels)
Ps.-	Pseudo-
q.	quaestio
qla	quaestiuncula
quod.	quodlibet
quod sic	videtur quod sic
resp.	responsio, solutio
sess.	session
SIDC	Société internationale de droit canonique
S.J.	*Societatis Jesu* (Jesuits)
Sq	*sequen(te)s,* and following
SW	Sämtliche Werke
syr.	syriac
tract.	tractatus
v.	verse
Vulg.	Vulgate, Latin version latine of the Bible, by Jerome
vv.	verses
WWC	World Council of Churches
WW	Werke
Ia IIae	Thomas Aquina, Summa Theologiae,

	prima secundae, first part of the second part
IIa Iiae	*Ibid., secunda secundae,* second part of the second part
LXX	Septuagint, Greek version of the Hebrew Bible

B. Biblical Texts

The Hebrew and Greek transcription of biblical texts come from the *Concordance de la Traduction œcuménique de la Bible.*

Biblical References

Colon(:) between chapter and verse. For example, Dt 24:17 refers to Deuteronomy, chapter 24:verse 17.

Hyphen: indicates the verses. For example, Dt 24:17–22 (from v. 17 to 22).

The letter *f* next to a verse refers to this verse and the following one. For example, Dt 24:17f (chapter 24:verses 17 and 18).

The letters *ff* refers to the verse and the following two. For example, Dt 24:17ff (chapter 24:verses 17, 18, and 19).

Acts	Acts of the Apostles
Am	Amos
Bar	Baruch
1 Chr	1 Chronicles
2 Chr	2 Chronicles
Col	Colossians
1 Cor	1 Corinthians
2 Cor	2 Corinthians
Dn	Daniel
Dt	Deuteronomy
Eccl	Ecclesiastes
Eph	Ephesians
Est	Esther
Ex	Exodus
Ez	Ezekiel
Ezr	Ezra
Gal	Galatians
Gn	Genesis
Hb	Habakkuk
Heb	Hebrews
Hg	Haggai
Hos	Hosea
Is	Isaiah
Jas	James
Jb	Job
Jdt	Judith
Jer	Jeremiah
Jgs	Judges

Jl	Joel
Jn	John
Jon	Jonah
Jos	Joshua
1 Jn	1 John
2 Jn	2 John
3 Jn	3 John
Jude	Jude
1 Kgs	1 Kings
2 Kgs	2 Kings
Lam	Lamentations
Lk	Luke
Lv	Leviticus
1 Macc	1 Maccabees
2 Macc	2 Maccabees
Mal	Malachi
Mi	Micah
Mk	Mark
Mt	Matthew
Na	Nahum
Neh	Nehemiah
Nm	Numbers
Ob	Obadiah
Phil	Philippians
Phlm	Philemon
Prv	Proverbs
Ps	Psalms
1 Pt	1 Peter
2 Pt	2 Peter
Rev	Revelation
Rom	Romans
Ru	Ruth
Sg	Song of Songs
Sir	Sirach
1 Sm	1 Samuel
2 Sm	2 Samuel
Tb	Tobit
1 Thes	1 Thessalonians
2 Thes	2 Thessalonians
Ti	Titus
1 Tm	1 Timothy
2 Tm	2 Timothy
Wis	Wisdom
Zep	Zepaniah

C. Writings from Ancient Judaism

a) Qumran Writings

11QT	The Temple Scroll
1QH	Hodayot, Hymns
1Qisa	Great Isaiah Scroll (Is 1–66)
1Qisb	Qumran Scroll of Isaiah
1QM	Serekh ha-Milhamah, The War Rule

1QpHab	Pesher on Habakkuk (Commentary)
1QS	Serek ha-Yachad, the Rule of the Community
1Qsa	The Rule of the Congregation
4QapMess	Messianic Apocrypha (= 4Q521)
4QDeutero-Ez	Deutero-Ezekiel (= 4Q385)
4Qenastr	Astronomical fragment from the Book of Enoch
4Qflor	Pesharim, 4Qflorilegium (= 4Q174)
4QMMT	Miqsat ma'ase ha-torah (= 4Q394–399)
4Qps-Danc	Pseudo-Daniel, ms c (= 4Q245)
4QtestQah	Testament of Qahat
4QtgJob	Targum de Job
4QviscAmrf	Visions of Amram
CD	Ciaro Damascus Document

(The numeral preceding the letter "Q" indicates the Grotto number)

b) Other Writings

Ant	Antiquitates judaicae (Flavius Josephus)
Ap	Contra Apionem (Id.)
2 Ba	Syriac Apocalypse of Baruch
Bell	De bello judaico (Flavius Josephus)
3 Esd/4 Esd	3rd/4th book of Esdras
Hen	Henoch
Lib Ant	*Biblical Antiquities* (Pseudo-Philo)
Or Sib	*Sibylline Oracles*
Ps Sal	*Psalm of Solomon*
T	Targum
TB	Talmud of Babylon
TJ	Talmud of Jerusalem
Test	Testament
Test XII	*Testaments of the Twelve Patriarchs*
Test Zab	*Testament of Zebulon*
Vita	Vita Josephi (Flavius Josephus)

D. Documents from the Second Vatican Ecumenical Council

AA *Apostolicam Actuositatem,* decree on the apostolate of the laity, November 18, 1965

AG *Ad Gentes,* decree on the mission activity of the Church, December 7, 1965

CD *Christus Dominus,* decree concerning the pastoral office of bishops in the Church, October 28, 1965

DH *Dignitatis Humanae,* declaration on religious freedom, December 7, 1965

DV *Dei Verbum,* dogmatic constitution on divine revelation, November 18, 1965

GE *Gravissimum Educationis,* declaration on Christian education, October 28, 1965

GS *Gaudium et Spes,* pastoral constitution on the Church in the modern world, December 7, 1965

IM *Inter Mirifica,* decree on the media of social communication, December 4, 1963

LG *Lumen Gentium,* dogmatic constitution on the Church, November 21, 1964

NA *Nostra Aetate,* declaration on the relation of the Church to non-Christian religions, October 28, 1965

OE *Orientalium Ecclesiarum,* decree on the Catholic Churches of the Eastern rite, November 21, 1964

OT *Optatam Totius,* decree on priestly training, October 28, 1965

PC *Perfectae Caritatis,* decree on the adaptation and renewal of religious life, October 28, 1965

PO *Presbyterorum Ordinis,* decree on the ministry and life of priests, December 7, 1965

SC *Sacrosanctum Concilium,* constitution on the sacred liturgy, December 4, 1963

UR *Unitatis Redintegratio,* decree on ecumenism, November 21, 1964

E. Editions, Collections, and Classic Works

The journal and collections abbreviations are from *Abkürzungsverzeichnis* from the *TRE* (rev. ed. 1994).

AA	Kant, Akademie Ausgabe
AAS	Acta apostolicae sedis, *Vatican City, 1909 (ASS, 1865–1908)*
AAWLM	Abhandlungen der Akademie der Wissenschaften und der Literatur in Mainz, Mainz
AAWLM.G	—Geistes- und Sozialwissenschaftliche Klasse, 1950–
ABAW	Abhandlungen der (k.) bayerischen Akademie der Wissenschaften, Munich
ABAW. PH	—Philosophisch-historische Abteilung, NS, 1929–
ABAW. PPH	—Philosophisch-philologische und historische Klasse, 1909–1928
ABC	Archivum bibliographicum carmelitanum, Rome, 1956–1982
ABG	*Archiv für Begriffsgeschichte,* Bonn, 1955–
ACan	*L'Année canonique,* Paris, 1952–
ACar	Analecta Cartusiana, Berlin, etc., 1970–1988; NS, 1989–
ACHS	American Church History Series, New York, 1893–1897
Aci	*Analecta Cisterciensa,* Rome, 1965–

ACO	*Acta conciliorum œcumenicorum,* Berlin, 1914–
Adv. Haer.	Irenaeus, *Adversus Haereses* (Against Heresies)
AF	*Archivio di filosofia,* Rome, 1931–
AFH	*Archivum Fransciscanum historicum,* Florence, 1908–
AFP	*Archivum Fratrum Praedicatorum,* Rome, 1930–
AGJU	Arbeiten zur Geschichte des antiken Judentums und des Urchristentums, Leiden, 8, 1970–15, 1978
AGPh	*Archiv für Geschichte der Philosophie und Soziologie,* Berlin, 1888–
AHC	*Annuarium historiae conciliorum,* Amsterdam, etc., 1969–
AHDL	*Archives d' histoire doctrinale et littéraire du Moyen Age,* Paris, 1926/1927–
AHP	*Archivum historiae pontificiae,* Rome, 1963–
AISP	*Archivio italiano per la storia della pietà,* Rome, 1951–
AkuG	*Archiv für Kulturgeschichte,* Berlin, 1903–
ALKGMA	Archiv für Literatur- und Kirchengeschichte des Mittelalters, Berlin, etc., 1885–1900
Aloi.	Aloisiana, Naples, 1960–
ALW	*Archiv für Liturgiewissenschaft,* Ratisbonne, 1950–
AmA	*American Anthropologist,* Menasha, Wis., 1888–1898; NS, 1899–
AnBib	Analecta biblica, Rome, 1952–
AncBD	*Anchor Bible Dictionary,* New York: Doubleday, 1992
AnCl	*Antiquité classique,* Bruxelles, 1932–
Ang.	*Angelicum,* Rome, 1925–
AnGr	Analecta Gregoriana, Rome, 1930–
ANRW	*Aufstieg und Niedergang des römischen Welt,* Berlin, 1972–
Anton.	*Antonianum,* Rome, 1926–
AphC	*Annales de philosophie chrétienne,* Paris, 1830–1913
Apol.	Luther, *Apologia confessionis Augustanae* (Apology of the Augsburg Confession)
Aquinas	*Aquinas. Revista internazionale de filosofia,* Rome, 1958–
ARMo	*L'actualité religieuse dans le monde,* Paris, 1983–
ArPh	*Archives de philosophie,* Paris, 1923–
AsbTJ	*The Asbury Theological Journal,* Wilmore, Ky, 1986–
ASCOV	*Acta synodalia sacrosancti Concilii Œcumenici Vaticani II,* Vatican City, 1970–1983
ASEs	*Annali di storia dell' esegesi,* Bologna, 1984–
ASI	*Archivio storico italiano,* Florence, 1852–
ASOC	*Analecta Sacri Ordinis Cisterciensis,* Rome, 1945–1964 (= *ACi,* 1965–)
ASS	*Acta sanctae sedis,* Rome, 1865–1908
ASSR	*Archives de sciences sociales des religions,* Paris, 1973–
A-T	Descartes, *Œuvres* (Works), eds. C. Adam and P. Tannery
ATA	Alttestamentliche Abhandlungen, Munich, 1908–1940
Ath	*L'année théologique,* Paris, 1940–1951
AthA	*Année théologique augustinienne,* Paris, 1951–1954 (= *REAug,* 1955–)
AThANT	Abhandlungen zur Theologie des Alten und Neuen Testaments, Zurich, 1944–
Aug.	*Augustinianum,* Rome, 1961–
Aug(L)	*Augustiniana,* Louvain, 1951–
AUGL	*Augustinus-Lexicon,* edited by C. Mayer, Basel, etc., 1986–
AugM	*Augustinus Magister,* Année théologique. Supplement, 3 vols., Paris: Études augustiniennes, 1954–1955
BAug	Bibliothèque augustinienne, Paris, 1936–
BBB	Bonner biblische Beiträge, Bonn, 1950–
BBKL	Biographish-bibliographisches Kirchenlexicon, edited by F. W. Bautz, Hamm, 1970–
BCG	Buchreihe der Cusanus-Gesellschaft, Münster, 1964–
BCNH	Bibliothèque copte de Nag Hammadi, Quebec.
BCPE	*Bulletin du Centre protestant d' études,* Geneva, 1949–
BEAT	Beiträge zur Erforschung des Alten Testaments und des antiken Judentums, Frankfurt, 1984–
BEL.S	Bibliotheca (Ephemerides Liturgicae), Subsidia, Rome 1975–
BEM	COE, Foi et Constitution, *Baptême, eucharistie, ministère. Convergence de la foi* (Lima, January 1982), Paris, 1982

BEThL	Bibliotheca ephemeridum theologicarum Lovaniensium, Louvain, 1947–
BevTh	Beiträge zur evangelischen Theologie, Munich, 1940–
BGLRK	Beiträge zur Geschichte und Lehre der reformierten Kirche, Neukirchen, 1937–
BGPhMA	Beiträge zur Geschichte der Philosophie (1928) und Theologie des Mittelalters, Münster, 1891–
BHK	Biblia Hebraica, ed. R. Kittel. Stuttgart, 1905/1906; 16th ed., 1973
BHS	Biblia Hebraica Stuttgartensia, Stuttgart, 1969–1975; 2nd ed., 1984
BHSA	*Bulletin historique et scientifique de l'Auvergne.* Clermont-Ferrand, 1881–
BHTh	Beiträge zur historischen Theologie, Tübingen, 1929–
Bib	*Biblica.* Commentarii periodici ad rem biblicam scientifice investigandam, Rome, 1920–
BICP	*Bulletin de l'Institut catholique de Paris,* Paris, 2nd ser., 1910–
Bidi	Bibliotheca dissidentium, Baden-Baden, 1980–
BIHBR	*Bulletin de l'Institut historique belge de Rome,* Rome, etc., 1919–
Bijdr	*Bijdragen.* Tijdschrift voor philosophie en theologie, Nimègue, etc., 1953–
BIRHT	*Bulletin de l'Institut de recherche et d'histoire des textes,* Paris, 1964–1968 (= RHT, 1971–)
BJ	*La Bible de Jérusalem* (Jerusalem Bible)
BJRL	*Bulletin of the John Rylands Library,* Manchester, 1903–
BLE	*Bulletin de littérature ecclésiastique,* Toulouse, 1899–
BN	Catalogue général des livres imprimés de la bibliothèque nationale, Paris, 1897 (General catalog of printed works from the Bibliothèque Nationale in Paris)
BN	*Biblische Notizen. Beiträge zur exegetischen Diskussion,* Bamberg, 1976–
BPhM	*Bulletin de philosophie médiévale,* Louvain, 1964–
Br	Pascal, Blaise. *Pensées.* Brunschvig.
BS	*Bibliotheca sacra,* London, 1843 (= *BSTR,* Andower, Mass.; 1844–1851 = *BSABR*; 1851–1863 = BS, Dallas, etc. 1864–)
BSFP	*Bulletin de la Société française de philosophie,* Paris, 1901–
BSGR	*Bibliothek der Symbole und Glaubensregeln der Alten Kirche,* edited by A. and C. L. Hahn, Breslau, 1842; reprinted 1962, Hildesheim
BSHPF	*Bulletin de la Société d'histoire du protestantisme français.* Paris, 1852–
BSKORK	*Bekenntnisschriften und Kirchenordnungen der nach Gottes Wort reformierten Kirche,* edited by W. Niesel, Zollikon, etc., 1937–1938; 2nd ed., 1938 (etc.) (*CCFR,* Geneva, 1986)
BSLK	*Bekenntnisschriften der evangelisch-lutherischen Kirche,* Göttingen, 1930; 10th ed., 1986; 11th ed., 1992 (FEL, Paris-Geneva, 1991)
BSS	*Bulletin de Saint-Sulpice.* Revue internationale de la Compagnie des prêtres de Saint-Sulpice, Paris, 1975–
BSSV	*Bollettino della Società di studi Valdesi,* Torre Pellice, 1934–
BSt	Biblische Studien. Neukirchen, 1951–
BT.B	Bibliothèque de théologie. 3rd ser. Théologie biblique, Paris, 1954–
BTB	*Biblical Theology Bulletin,* New York, 1971–
BTB(F)	—French ed.
BThom	*Bulletin thomiste,* Étiolles, etc., 1924–1965
BThW	*Bibeltheologisches Wörterbuch,* Graz, etc., 1–2, 19673 (Eng. Ed. *EBT*)
BTT	Bible de tous les temps, Paris, 8 vol., 1984–1989
BullFr	*Bullarium Franciscanum,* Rome, etc., 1929–1949
BWANT	Beiträge zum Wissenschaft vom Alten und Neuen Testament, Stuttgart, 1926 (= BWAT, 1908–1926)
BWAT	*Beiträge zum Wissenschaft vom Alten Testament,* Stuttgart, 1908–1926
Byz	*Byzantion,* Bruxelles, 1924–
BZ	*Biblische Zeitschrift,* Paderborn, etc., 1903–1938; NF 1957–
BZAW	Beihefte zur Zeitschrift für die alttestamentliche Wissenschaft, Berlin, 1896–
BZNW	Beihefte zur Zeitschrift für die neutestamentliche Wissenschaft, Berlin, etc., 1923–
BZRGG	Beihefte der Zeitschrift für Religions- und Geistesgeschichte, Leyden, 1953–
CA	*Confession of Augsburg*

CAG	Commentaria in Aristotelem Graeca, Berlin, 1883
CAR	Cahiers de l'actualité religieuse, Tournai, 1954–1969 [Continued after 1969 as *Cahiers pour croire aujourd'hui*]
CAT	Commentaire de l'Ancien Testament, Neuchatel, 1963
Cath (M)	*Catholica. Jahrbuch für Kontroverstheologie,* Munster, etc. 1932–39, 1952/53–
Cath	*Catholicisme. Hier, aujourd'hui, demain,* Paris, 1948–
CBFV	Cahiers bibliques de *Foi et Vie,* Paris, 1936–
CBiPA	Cahiers de Biblia Patristica, Strasbourg, 1987–
CBQ	*Catholic Biblical Quarterly,* Washington, DC, 1939–
CCEO	*Codex Canonum ecclesiarum orientalium.* Rome, 1990
CCFR	Confessions et catéchismes de la foi reformée, ed., Oliver Fatio, Geneva, 1986 (*BSKORK,* Zollikon)
CCG	Codices Chrysostomi Graeci, Paris, 1968–
CChr	Corpus Christianorum, Turnhout
CChr.CM	—Continuatio mediaevalis, 1966
CChr.SA	—Series Apocryphorum, 1983–
CChr.SG	—Series Graeca, 1977
CChr.SL	—Series Latina, 1953
CCist	*Collecteana Cisterciensia,* Westmalle, Forges, etc. 1934–
CCMéd	*Cahiers de civilisation médiévale. X^e–XIIe siecles,* Poitiers, 1958–
CDTor	*Collationes Diocesis Tornacensis,* Tournai, 1853–
CEC	*Catéchisme de l'Eglise catholique (Catechism of the Catholic Church),* Paris, 1992 (Typical Latin text, Vatican City, 1992; rev. ed., 1997.
CEv	Cahiers évangile, Paris, 1972–
CFan	Cahiers de Fangeaux, Fanjeaux, etc., 1966–
CFi	Cogitatio fidei, Paris, 1961
CFr	Collecteana franciscana, Rome, etc.,1931–
CG	*Summa Contra Gentiles*
CGG	*Christlicher Glaube in moderner Gesellschaft,* Fribourg, 1981–1984
CHFMA	Classiques de l'histoire de France au Moyen Age, Paris, 1923–
ChGimG	see *CGG*
ChH	*Church History,* Chicago: American Society of Church History, 1932–

ChPR	*Chroniques de Port-Royal,* Paris, 1950–
CIC	*Codex iuris canonici,* Rome, 1917 and Rome, 1983
CIC(B).C	*Corpus iuris civilis,* ed. P. Krueger, T. Mommsen, Berlin, -2. *Codex Iustianus,* 1874–1877; 2nd ed., 1880, etc.
CIC(L)	*Corpus iuris canonici,* ed. E. Friedberg, Leipzig, 1837–1839; Graz, 1955 (reprint)
CILL	Cahiers de l'Institut de linguistique de Louvain, Louvain, 1972–
Cîteaux	*Cîteaux: commentarii cistercienses,* Westmalle, 1959–
Citeaux, SD	—*Studia et documenta,* 1971–
COD	*Conciliorum oecumenicorum Decreta,* eds. Albergio and Jedin, Bologna, 3rd ed., 1973 (*DCO,* 1994)
Com(F)	*Communio. Revue catholique internationale,* Paris, 1975/76–
Com(US)	*Communio. International Catholic Review,* Spokane, Wash., 1974–
Con	*Contemporain,* Paris, 1866–
Conc(D)	*Concilium. Internazionale Zeitschrift für Theologie,* Einsiedeln, 1965–
Conc(F)	*Concilium. Revue internationale de théologie,* Paris, 1965–
Conc(US)	*Concilium. Theology in the Age of Renewal,* New York, 1965–
ConscLib	*Conscience et Liberté,* Paris, 1971–
Corp IC	see *CIL (L)*
CPG	Clavis Patrum Graecorum, Turnhout, 1974– (= CChr.SG)
CPIUI	*Communio. Pontificium Institutum Utriusque Juris,* Rome, 1957–
CPPJ	Cahiers de philosophie politique et juridique, Caen, 1982–
CR	Corpus reformatorum, Berlin, 1834–
CRB	Cahiers de la *Revue Biblique,* Paris, etc., 1964–
CrSt	*Cristianesimo nella storia,* Bologna, 1980–
CR.Th.Ph	*Cahiers de la Revue de théologie et de philosophie,* Geneva, 1977–
CSCO	Corpus scriptorum Christianorum orientalum, Rome, etc., 1903–
CSEL	Corpus scriptorum ecclesiasticorum Latinorum, Vienna, 1866–
CT	*Concilium Tridentinum. Diarium, actorum, epistularum, tractatum nova collectio,* Fribourg, 1901–1981
CTh	Cahiers théologiques, Neuchâtel, etc., 27, 1949– (= CthAP, 1923–1949)
CTh.HS	—*Hors série,* 1945– (Special edition)

CTJ	*Calvin Theological Journal,* Grand Rapids, Mich, 1966–		crétariat de la Conférence des évêques de France, Paris, 1965–
CUFr	Collection des Universités de France (Les Belle Lettres), Paris, 1920–	*DOP*	*Dumbarton Oaks Papers,* Cambridge, Mass., 1941–
DA	*Deutsches Archiv für Erforschung des Mittelalters,* Marburg, etc., 1937–	*DOPol*	*Dictionnaire des oeuvres politiques,* Paris, 1986
DACL	*Dictionnaire d'archéologie chrétienne et de liturgie,* Paris, 1924–53	*DPAC*	*Dizionario patristico e di antichità cristiane,* edited by A. di Berardino,
DAFC	*Dictionnaire apologétique de la foi catholique,* Paris, 1889; 4th ed., 1909–1931		Casale Monferrato, 1–3, 1983–1988 (French trans. *DECA*)
DB	*Dictionnaire de la Bible,* Paris, 1895–1928	*DPhP*	*Dictionnaire de philosophie politique,* eds. Ph. Raynaud and St. Rials, Paris, 1997
DBS	*Dictionnaire de la Bible. Supplément,* Paris, 1928–	*DR*	*Downside Review,* Bath, 1880–
DBW	*Dietrich Bonhoeffer, Werke,* ed. E. Bethge *et al.,* Munich, 1986–	*DS*	*Enchiridion Symbolorum,* eds. H. Denzinger and A. Schönmetzer, Freiburg, 36th ed., 1976
DC	*Documentation Catholique,* Paris: 1919–	*DSp*	*Dictionnaire de spiritualité ascétique et mystique,* Paris, 1932–1995
DCO	*Conciliorum oecumenicorum Decreta; Les Conciles Oecuméniques,* II, 1 and 2. *Les Décrets.* ed. Albergio, Paris, 1994 (trans. of *COD*)	*DT*	*Divus Thomas. Jahrbuch für Philosophie und spekulative Theologie,* Fribourg, 1914–1953
DCTh	*Dictionnaire critique de théologie.* ed. Jean-Yves Lacoste, Paris, 1998; 2nd revised ed., 1999	*DT(P)*	*Divus Thomas. Commentarium de philosophia et theologia,* Plaisance, 1880–
DDC	*Dictionnaire de droit canonique,* Paris, 1924–1965	*DTF*	*Dizionario di Teologia Fondamentale,* eds. R. Latourelle et R. Fisichella, Assisi, 1990. (*Dictionnaire de Théologie Fondamentale,* Paris, 1992)
DEB	*Dictionnaire encyclopédique de la Bible,* Turnhout, 2 vols., 1956–1987	*DThC*	*Dictionnaire de Théologie Catholique,* Paris, 1–15, 1903–1950 + tables 1–3, 1951–1972
DECA	*Dictionnaire encyclopédique du christianisme ancien.* ed. A. di Bernardino, Paris, 2 vols., 1990. (Trans. of *DPAC*)	Dumeige	*La Foi Catholique,* G. Dumeige, Paris, 1975
DEPhM	*Dictionnaire d'éthique et de philosophie morale,* edited by M. Canto Sperber, Paris, 1996	*DViv*	*Dieu Vivant,* Paris, 1945–1955
		EAug	Études augustiniennes, Paris, 1954– (Studies on Augustine)
DH	*Enchiridion Symbolorum. Eds. H. Denzinger and P. Hunerman, Fribourg, 37th ed., 1991*	*EBT*	*Encyclopedia of Biblical Theology,* London, 1970, etc. (Eng. ed. of *BThW*)
DHGE	*Dictionnaire d'histoire et de géographie ecclésiastiques.* Paris, 1912–	*ECQ*	*Eastern Churches Quarterly,* Ramsgate, 1936–1964 (= *OiC,* 1965–)
DHOP	Dissertationes historicae. Institutum historicum FF. Praedicatorum, Rome, etc., 1931–	*ECR*	*Eastern Churches Review,* Oxford, 1966–1978
DJD	*Discoveries in the Judean Desert,* Oxford, 1955–	EdF	Erträge der Forschung, Darmstadt, 1970–
DK	*Die Fragmente der Vorsokratiker,* eds. H. Diels and W. Kranz, Berlin, 1903; 13th ed., 1972 (= *FVS*)	EE	Estudios ecclesiásticos, Madrid, 1922–
DMA	*Dictionary of the Middle Ages,* ed. R. Strayer, New York, 1982–	*EeT*	*Église et théologie,* Paris, 1958–1962 (= *BFLTP,* 1934–1958)
DoC	*Doctor Communis,* Rome, 1948–	EETS	Early English Text Society, London, 1864–
Doc.-épisc.	*Documents-épiscopat,* Bulletin du se-	*EFV*	*Enchiridion fontium valdensium,* Torre Pelice, 1958

EI(F)	*Encyclopedia of Islam,* French ed, Leyden. 1913–1936; new ed. 1954–
EJ	*Encyclopaedia Judaica,* Jerusalem 1–16, 1971; 17, 1982–
EKK	Evangelisch-katholischer Kommentar zum Neuen Testament, Neukirchen, 1975–
EKL	*Evangelisches Kirchenlexikon,* Göttingen, 1956–1961; 2nd ed., 1961–1962; 3rd ed., 1986–1997
EN	*Ethica nicomachea* Aristotle
En. Ps.	*Enarrationes in Psalmos,* Augustine
EnchB	*Enchiridion Biblicum,* Rome, 1927; 4th ed., 1961
EnchP	*Enchiridion patristicum,* M.J. Rouët de Journel, Fribourg, 1911; 25th ed., 1981
EncProt	*Encyclopédie du Protestantisme,* edited by P. Gisel, Paris-Geneva, 1995
EncRel(E)	*The Encyclopedia of Religion,* edited by M. Eliade, New York, 1–16, 1987
EncRel(I)	*Enciclopedia delle religioni,* edited by M. Gozzini, Florence, 1970–1976
Enn.	*Enneads,* Plotinus
EO	*Ecclesia orans.* Periodica de scientiis liturgicis, Rome, 1984–
EOr	*Échos d'Orient,* Bucharest, 1897/1898–1942/1943 (= *EtByz,* 1943–1946; *REByz,* 1946–)
Eos	Eos. Commentarii societatis philologae Polonorum, Wroclaw, etc., 1894–
Eph	*Études philosophiques,* Paris, 1927–
EPRO	Études préliminaires aux religions orientales dans l'Empire romain, Leyden, 1961–
ER	*Ecumenical Review,* Lausanne, 1948–
ErIs	*Eretz Israel,* Jerusalem, 1951–
EstB	*Estudios biblicos,* Madrid, 1929–
EStL	*Evangelisches Staatslexikon,* Stuttgart, 3rd ed., 1987
EstLul	*Estudios lulianos,* Palma de Mallorca, 1957–
EtB	Études bibliques, Paris, 1903–
EtCarm	*Études carmélitaines,* Paris, 1911–1964
Eth. à Nic.	*Ethica nicomachea,* Aristotle (Éthique à Nicomaque; Nichomachean Ethics)
Éthique	*Éthique. La vie en question,* Paris, 1991–1996 (22 issues)
EthL	*Ephemerides theologicae Lovanienses,* Louvain, etc., 1924–
EtMar	*Études mariales,* Paris, 1947–
ETR	*Études théologiques et religieuses,* Montpellier, 1926–
EU	*Encyclopaedia Universalis,* Paris, 1968–1986, 1985–1988
EvTh	*Evangelische Theologie,* Munich, 1934–1938; NS, 1946/1947–
EWNT	*Exegetisches Wörterbuch zum Neuen Testament,* Stuttgart, etc., 1–3, 1980–1983
FEL	La foi des Églises luthériennes: confessions et catéchismes, eds. A. Birmele and M. Lienhard, Paris-Geneva, 1991 (*BSLK* Göttingen)
FOP	Faith and Order Paper(s), World Council of Churches, Geneva, NS, 1949–
FKTh	*Forum katholische Theologie,* Aschaffenburg, 1985–
FRLANT	Forschungen zur Religion und Literatur des Alten und Neuen Testaments, Göttingen, 1903–
FrSA	*Fransciscan Studies Annual,* St. Bonaventure, NY, 1963– (= *FrS,* 1924–1962)
FS	Franziskanische Studien, Münster, etc., 1914–
FS.B	—Beiheft, 1915–
FSÖTh	Forschungen zur systematischen und ökumenischen Theologie, Göttingen, 1962–
FThSt	Freiburger theologische Studien, Fribourg, 1910–
FTS	Frankfurter theologische Studien, Frankfurt, 1969–
FV	*Foi et Vie,* Paris, 1898–
FVS	*Die Fragmente der Vorsokratiker,* eds. H. Diels and W. Kranz, Berlin, 1903; 13th ed., 1972 (= *DK*)
FZPhTh	*Freiburger Zeitschrift für Philosophie und Theologie,* Freibourg (Switzerland), 1954–
GCFI	*Giornale critico della filosofia italiana,* Florence, etc., 1920–
GCS	Die griechischen christlichen Schriftsteller der ersten drei Jahrhunderte, Berlin, 1897–
GNO	*Gregorii Nysseni Opera,* ed. Werner Jaeger, Berlin then Leiden (= Jaeger), 1921
GOTR	*Greek Orthodox Theological Review,* Brookline (Mass.), 1954–
Gr	*Gregorianum,* Rome, 1920–
GRBS	Greek, Roman and Byzantine Studies, Cambridge, Mass., 1958–

Grundfr. syst. Th.	*Grundfragen systematischer Theologie,* W. Pannenberg, Göttingen, 1967, vol 2, 1980
GS	Germanische Studien, Berlin, etc., 1919–
GuV	*Glauben und Verstehen, Gesammelte Aufsätze,* R. Bultmann, 4 vol., Tübingen, 1933–1965
GVEDL	Die geltenden Verfassungsgesetze der evangelisch-deutschen Landeskirchen, edited by Emil Friedberg, Fribourg, 1885 and suppl. 1–4, 1888–1904
HadSt	*Haddock Studies,* Moulinsart, 1953–
Hahn	see *BSGR*
HBT	*Horizons in Biblical Theology,* Pittsburg, Pa, 1979–
HCO	*Histoire des conciles œcuméniques,* ed. G. Dumeige, Paris, 1962–
HDG	*Handbuch der Dogmengeschichte,* edited by M. Schmaus, A. Grillmeier, *et al.,* Fribourg, etc., 1951–
HDThG	*Handbuch der Dogmen- und Theologiegeschichte,* edited by C. Andresen, Göttingen, 1982–1984
HE	*Historia ecclesiastica.* Eusebius
Hermes	*Hermes. Zeitschrift für klassische Philologie,* Wiesbaden, 1866–1944, 1952–
HeyJ	*Heythrop Journal,* Oxford then London, 1960–
HFTh	*Handbuch der Fundamentaltheologie,* edited by W. Kern *et al.,* 4 vol., Fribourg, 1985–1988
Hier. eccl.	*Hiérarchie ecclésiastique (Ecclesiastica hierarchia)*
HistDog	*Histoire des dogmes,* Paris, 1953–1971 (unfinished trans. by *HDG*)
HJ	*Historisches Jahrbuch der Görresgesellschaft,* Munich, etc., 1880–
HKG(J)	*Handbuch der Kirchengeschichte,* edited by H. Jedin, Fribourg, etc., 1962–1979
HMO	*Handbook of Metaphysics and Ontology,* eds. H. Burkhardt and B. Smith, Munich-Philadelphia-Vienna, 1991
HST	*Handbuch systematischer Theologie,* Gütersloh, 1979–
HThK	Herders theologisches Kommentar zum Neuen Testament, Fribourg, 1953–
HThR	*Harvard Theological Review,* Cambridge, Mass., 1908–
HThS	Harvard Theological Studies, Cambridge, Mass., 1916–
HTTL	*Herders theologisches Taschenlexikon,* edited by K. Rahner, 8 vol., Fribourg, 1972–1973
HUCA	*Hebrew Union College Annual,* Cincinnati, Ohio, 1924–
HWP	*Historisches Wörterbuch der Philosophie,* Basel-Stuttgart, 1971–
HZ	*Historische Zeitschrift,* Munich, etc., 1859–
IDB	*The Interpreter's Dictionary of the Bible,* New York, 1/4, 1962 +suppl., 1976
IkaZ	*Internationale katholische Zeitschrift Communio,* Frankfurt, 1972–
IKZ	*Internationale kirchliche Zeitschrift. Revue Internationale ecclésiastique. International Church Review,* Berne, 1911–
In Sent.	*Commentary on the Sentences*
Inst.	*Institutes of the Christian Religion,* Calvin
Irén	Irénikon, Chèvetogne, etc., 1926–
Ist	*Istina,* Boulogne-sur-Seine, etc., 1954–
JAAR	*Journal of the American Academy of Religion,* Boston, Mass., etc., 1967–
JAC	*Jahrbuch für Antike und Christentum,* Münster, 1958–
JAC.E	—*Ergänzungsband,* 1964–
Jaeger	*Gregorii Nysseni Opera,* ed. W. Jaeger, Berlin then Leyden (= *GNO*), 1921–
JBL	*Journal of Biblical Literature,* Philadelphia, Pa., 1890–
JCSW	*Jahrbuch für christliche Sozialwissenschaften,* Münster, 1968–
JEH	*Journal of Ecclesiastical History,* London, etc., 1950–
JES	*Journal of Ecumenical Studies,* Philadelphia, etc., 1964–
JHI	*Journal of the History of Ideas,* New York, etc., 1940–
JJS	*Journal of Jewish Studies,* London, 1948–
JLW	*Jahrbuch für Liturgiewissenschaft,* Münster, 1921–1941
JÖBG	*Jahrbuch der österreichischen byzantinischen Gesellschaft,* Vienna, etc., 1951–1968 (= *JÖB*, 1969–)
JRE	*Journal of Religious Ethics,* Waterloo, Ont., etc., 1973–
JSNTSS	*Journal for the Study of the New Testament,* Supplement series, Sheffield, 1980–

JSOT	*Journal for the Study of the Old Testament,* Sheffield, 1976–
JSOT.S	—Supplements Series, 1976–
JSPE.*S*	Journal for the Study of the Pseudepigrapha. Supplement series, Sheffield, 1987–
JThS	*Journal of Theological Studies,* Oxford, etc., 1899–1949; NS, 1950–
KD	*Die Kirchliche dogmatik,* K. Barth, Zollikon-Zurich, vol. I to IV, 1932–1967 + Index, 1970 (*Dogmatique,* 26 vol., Geneva, 1953–1974, + Index, 1980)
KiKonf	Kirche und Konfession, Göttingen, 1962–
Kirch	*Enchiridion fontium historiae ecclesiasticae,* ed. C. Kirch, Freibourg, 1910; 6th ed., 1947
KKD	*Kleine Katholische Dogmatik,* edited by J. Auer and J. Ratzinger, Ratisbonne, 1978–1988
KJ	*Kirchliches Jahrbuch für die Evangelische Kirche in Deutschland,* Gütersloh, 1900– (= *ThJb,* 1873–1899)
KL	*Kirchenlexikon oder Encyklopädie der katholischen Theologie und ihrer Hilfswissenschaften,* edited by H. J. Wetzer and B. Welte, Fribourg, 1847–1860; 2nd ed., 1882–1903
Kotter	*Die Schriften des Johannes von Damaskus,* ed. B. Kotter, Berlin, 1969–
KrV	*Kritik der reinenVErnunft,* Kant
KSA	*Kritische Studienausgabe,* Nietzsche; edited by Colli and Montinari, ed. minor
KuD	*Kerygma und Dogma,* Göttingen, 1955–
Lat	Lateranum, Rome, NS, 1935–
LCL	Loeb Classical Library, London, 1912–
LeDiv	Lectio divina, Paris, 1946–
Leit	*Leiturgia. Handbuch des evangelischen Gottesdienstes,* Kassel, 1952–1970
Liddell-Scott	*A Greek-English Lexicon,* Liddell-Scott-Jones, Oxford
LJ	*Liturgisches Jahrbuch,* Münster, 1951–
LNPh	*Les notions philosophiques,* edited by S. Auroux, vol. II of the *Encyclopédie philosophique universelle,* edited by A. Jacob, Paris, 2 vol., 1990
LO	Lex orandi, Paris, 1944–
LouvSt	*Louvain Studies,* Louvain, 1966/1967–
LR	*Lutherische Rundschau,* Stuttgart, etc., 1951–1977
LSEO	Libri symbolici Ecclesiae orientalis, ed. E. J. Kimmel, Iéna, 1843; 2nd ed., 1850
LThK	*Lexikon für Theologie und Kirche,* Fribourg-Basel-Vienna, 1930–1938; 2nd ed., 1957–1967; 3rd ed., 1993
LTP	*Laval théologique et philosophique,* Quebec, 1944/1945–
LuJ	*Luther-Jahrbuch,* Leipzig, etc., 1919–
LV(L)	*Lumière et vie,* Lyon, 1951–
LWF.R	*Lutheran World Federation Report,* 1978–
Mansi	*Sacrorum conciliorum nova et amplissima collectio,* edited by J. D. Mansi, Florence, 1759–1827; Paris-Leipzig, 1901–1927
Mar.	*Marianum. Ephemerides Mariologiae,* Rome, 1939–
Maria	*Maria. Études sur la Sainte Vierge,* edited by H. du Manoir, 8 vol., Paris, 1949–1971
MCS	Monumenta christiana selecta, Tournai, etc., 1954–
MD	*La Maison-Dieu. Revue de pastorale liturgique,* Paris, 1945–
MDom	*Memorie Domenicane,* Florence, etc., NS, 1970–
MethH	*Methodist History,* Lake Junaluska, NC, 1962–
MF	*Miscellanea francescana,* Rome, etc., 1936– (= *MFS,* 1886–1935)
MFEO	Monumenta fidei Ecclesiae orientalis, ed. H. J. C. Weissenborn, Iéna, 1850
MFCG	Mitteilungen und Forschungsbeiträge der Cusanus-Gesellschaft, Mainz, 1961–
MGH	Monumenta Germaniae historica inde ab a. C. 500 usque ad a. 1500, Hanover, etc.
MGH.Conc	—Concilia, 1893–
MGH.Ep	—Epistolae, 1887–
MGH.L	—Leges, 1835–1889
MHP	*Miscellanea historiae pontificae,* Rome, 1939–
MHSJ	Monumenta historica Societatis Jesu, Rome, etc., 1894–
MiHiEc	*Miscellanea historiae ecclesiasticae,* Congrès… de Louvain, 1960–
ML.T	Museum Lessianum. Theological section, Bruxelles, 1922–

MM	Miscellanea mediaevalia, Berlin, etc., 1962–
MS	Mediaeval Studies, Toronto, 1939–
MSR	Mélanges de science religieuse, Lille, 1944–
MSSNTS	Monograph Series. Society for New Testament Studies, Cambridge, 1965–
MThZ	Münchener theologische Zeitschrift, Munich, etc., 1950–1984
MySal	Mysterium Salutis, Grundriß heilsgeschichtlicher Dogmatik, vol. I to V, edited by J. Feiner and M. Löhrer, Einsiedeln, etc., 1965–1976 + supplements, 1981, etc. (Dogmatique de l'histoire du salut, vol. I–III/2 and IV/1 (p. 457–599), 14 vol., 1969–1975)
NBL	Neues Bibel-Lexikon, Zurich, 1991
NCE	New Catholic Encyclopaedia, New York, 1967–1979
NHThG	Neues Handbuch Theologischer Grundbegriffe, edited by P. Eicher, 2nd ed. augm., Freibourg-Basel-Vienna, 1991
Not	Notitiae. Commentarii ad nuntia et studia de re liturgica, Vatican City, 1975–
NRTh	Nouvelle revue théologique, Louvain, 1869–1940; 1945–
NSchol	New Scholasticism, Washington D.C., 1927–
NStB	Neukirchener Studienbücher, Neukirchen, 1962–
NT	Novum Testamentum, Leyden, 1956–
NTA	Neutestamentliche Abhandlungen, Münster, 1908–
NTS	New Testament Studies, Cambridge, 1954–
NTTS	New Testament Tools and Studies, Leyden, 1960–
Numen	Numen. International Review for the History of Religions, Leyden, 1954–
NV	Nova et vetera, Geneva, 1926–
OBO	Orbis biblicus et orientalis, Fribourg (Switzerland), 1973–
OCA	Orientalia christiana analecta, Rome, 1935–
OCP	Orientalia christiana periodica, Rome, 1935–
Oec.	Œcumenica. Jahrbuch für ökumenische Forschung, Gütersloh, etc., 1966–1971/1972
ODCC	Oxford Dictionary of the Christian Church, edited by F. L. Cross, London,

	1957; 2nd ed., 1974 (F. L. Cross and E. A. Livingstone); 3rd ed. rev. and augm., 1997 (by E. A. Livingstone)
OED	The Oxford English Dictionary
OGE	Ons geestelijk erf, Anvers, etc., 1927–
OiC	One in Christ, London, 1965–
OR	L'Osservatore romano, Vatican City, 1849–
ÖR	Ökumenische Rundschau, Stuttgart, 1952–
Or.	Orientalia, Rome, 1920–
OrChr	Oriens Christianus, Rome, 1901–
OrChrA	see OCA
OrChrP	see OCP
OS	Ostkirchliche Studien, Würzburg, 1952–
OstKSt	Ostkirchliche Studien, Würzburg, 1952–
ÖTh	Ökumenische Theologie, Zurich, etc., 1978–
OTS	Oudtestamentische Studien, Leyden, etc., 1942–
Par.	Paradosis. Études de littérature et de théologie ancienne, Fribourg (Switzerland), 1947–
PAS	Proceedings of the Aristotelian Society, London, 1887; NS, 1900/1901–
PatSor	Patristica Sorbonensia, Paris, 1957–
PG	Patrologia Graeca, ed. J.-P. Migne, Paris, 1857–1866
PGL	Patristic Greek Lexicon, ed. G. W. H. Lampe, Oxford, 1961–1968
Ph	Philologus. Zeitschrift für das klassische Altertum, Wiesbaden, etc., 1846–
Phil.	Philosophy, London, 1916–
PhJ	Philosophisches Jahrbuch der Görres-Gesellschaft, Fulda, etc., 1888–
PiLi	Pietas liturgica. Studia, St. Ottilien, 1983–
PL	Patrologia Latina, ed. J.-P. Migne, Paris, 1841–1864
PLS	Patrologiae Latinae supplementum, Paris, 1958–1970
PO	Patrologia Orientalis, Paris, etc., 1907–
POC	Proche-Orient chrétien, Jerusalem, 1951–
PosLuth	Positions luthériennes, Paris, 1953–
PoTh	Point théologique, Institut catholique de Paris, 1971–
PPR	Philosophy and Phenomenological Research, Buffalo, NY, 1940/1941–
PRMCL	Periodica de re morali, canonica, liturgica, Rome, 1907–

PuN	*Pietismus und Neuzeit,* Göttingen, 1974–
PTS	Patristische Texte und Studien, Berlin, 1964–
QD	Quaestiones Disputatae, Fribourg-Basel-Vienna, 1958–
QFRG	*Quellen und Forschungen zur Reformationsgeschichte,* Gütersloh 1921–, includes *QGT*
QGT	*Quellen zur Geschichte der Taüfer,* Gütersloh 1951–
QRT	*Quaker religious Thought,* New Haven, Conn., 1959–
Qschr	*Quartalschrift,* Milwaukee, Wis., 1947–
QuLi	*Questions liturgiques,* Louvain, 1910–
RAC	*Reallexikon für Antike und Christentum,* Stuttgart, 1950–
RAM	*Revue d'ascétique et de mystique,* Toulouse, 1920–1971
RB	*Revue biblique,* Paris, 1892–1894; NS, 1915–
RBen	*Revue bénédictine de critique, d'histoire et de littérature religieuses,* Maredsous, 1890–
RDC	*Revue de droit canonique,* Strasbourg, 1951–
RDCCIF	Recherches et débats du Centre catholique des intellectuels français, Paris, 1948–1952; NS, 1952–1980
RdQ	*Revue de Qumrân,* Paris, 1958–
RE	*Realencyklopädie für protestantische Theologie und Kirche,* Gotha, 3rd ed., 1896–1913
REAug	*Revue des études augustiniennes,* Paris, 1955– (= *AThA,* 1951–1954)
REByz	*Revue des études byzantines,* Paris, 1946–
RECA	*Real-Encyclopädie der classischen Altertumswissenschaft,* edited by A. Pauly, Stuttgart, 1839–1852
RechAug	*Recherches augustinien*nes, Paris, 1958–
RechBib	Recherches bibliques, Bruges, etc., 1954–
RecL	*Revue ecclésiastique de Liège,* Liège, 1905–1967
REG	*Revue des études grecques,* Paris, 1888–
REL	*Revue des études latines,* Paris, 1923–
RelSt	*Religious Studies,* London, etc., 1965/1966–
RET	*Revista española de teología,* Madrid, 1940–
RevBib	*Revista biblica,* Buenos Aires, 1939–
RevPhil	*Revue de philosophie,* Paris, 1900–1940
RevSR	*Revue des sciences religieuses,* Strasbourg, 1921–
RFNS	*Rivista di filosofia neoscolastica,* Milan, 1909–
RGG	*Die Religion in Geschichte und Gegenwart,* Tübingen, 1909–1913; 2nd ed., 1927–1932; 3rd ed., 1956–1965
RH	*Revue historique,* Paris, 1876–
RHDF	*Revue historique de droit français et étranger,* Paris, 1855–1869; 1922–
RHE	*Revue d'histoire ecclésiastique,* Louvain, 1900–
RHEF	*Revue de l'histoire de l'Église de France,* Paris, 1910–
RHMo	*Revue d'histoire moderne,* Paris, 1926–1940 (= 1899–1914, 1954–, *RHMC*)
RHMC	*Revue d'histoire moderne et contemporaine,* Paris, 1899–1914, 1954– (= 1926–1940, *RHMo*)
RHPhR	*Revue d'histoire et de philosophie religieuses,* Strasbourg, etc., 1921–
RHR	*Revue de l'histoire des religions,* Paris, 1880
RHSp	*Revue d'histoire de la spiritualité,* Paris, 1972–1977
RHT	*Revue d'histoire des textes,* Paris, 1971– (= *BIRHT*)
RICP	*Revue de l'Institut catholique de Paris,* Paris, 1896–1910 (= *BICP,* 1910–)
RIPh	*Revue Internationale de Philosophie,* Bruxelles, 1938–
RITh	*Revue internationale de théologie,* Berne, 1893–1910
RivBib	*Rivista biblica,* Rome, 1953–
RLT	*Rassegna di letteratura tomistica,* Naples, 1966–
RMAL	*Revue du Moyen Age latin,* Paris, etc., 1945–
RMM	*Revue de métaphysique et de morale,* Paris, 1893–
ROC	*Revue de l'Orient chrétien,* Paris, 1896–1936
RPFE	*Revue Philosophique de la France et de l'étranger,* Paris, 1876–
RPL	*Revue philosophique de Louvain,* Louvain, etc., 1946–
RSF	*Rivista di storia della filosofia,* Rome, 1946; NS, 1984–

RSHum	*Revue des sciences humaines,* Lille, NS, 45, 1947–
RSLR	*Rivista di storia e letteratura religiosa,* Florence, 1965–
RSPhTh	*Revue des sciences philosophiques et théologiques,* Paris, 1907–
RSR	*Recherches de science religieuse,* Paris, 1910–
RThAM	*Recherches de théologie ancienne et médiévale,* Louvain, 1929–
RThom	*Revue thomiste,* Bruges, etc., Toulouse, 1893–
RThPh	*Revue de théologie et de philosophie,* Lausanne, 1868–1911; 3rd ser., 1951–
RTL	*Revue théologique de Louvain,* Louvain, 1970–
RTLu	*Revue théologique de Lugano,* Facoltà di teologia di Lugano, 1996–
Sal	*Salesianum,* Turin, 1939
SBAB	Stuttgarter biblische Aufsatzbände, Stuttgart, 1988–
SBi	Sources Bibliques, Paris, 1963–
SBS	Stuttgarter Bibelstudien, Stuttgart, 1965–
SC	Sources Chrétiennes, Paris, 1941–
ScC	*Scuola Cattolica,* Milan, 1873, 6th ser., 1923–
SCA	Studies in Christian Antiquity, Washington, D.C., 1941–
SCE	*Studies in Christian Ethics,* Edinburgh, 1988–
ScEc	*Sciences écclesiastiques: Revue philosophique et théologique,* Bruges, 1948–1967 (= *ScEs,* 1968–)
ScEs	*Science et esprit,* Bruges, 1968–
SCH(L)	Studies in Church History, London, 1964–
Schol.	*Scholastik. Vierteljahresschrift für Theologie und Philosophie.* Fribourg, 1926–1965 (= *ThPh,* 1966–)
Schr.zur Th.	*Schriften zur Theologie,* K. Rahner. Einsiedeln-Zürich-Cologne, 1954–1983
SE	*Sacris erudiri,* Steenbrugge, etc., 1948–
SecCent	*The Second Century.* Abilene, Tex., 1981
SémBib	*Sémiotique et Bible,* Lyon, 1975–
Semeia	*Semeia.* An Experimental Journal for Biblical Criticism. Atlanta, Ga, 1974–
SemSup	Semeia Supplements. Philadelphia, Pa., etc., 1975–
Sent.	*Sententiarum Libri IV,* Peter Lombard
SESJ	Suomen Eksegeettisen Seuran julkaisuja. Helsinki, 1966–
SHCSR	*Spicilegium historicum Congregationis SSmi Redemptoris.* Rome, 1953–
SHCT	Studies in the History of Christian Thought. Leyden, 1966–
SJP	*Salzburger Jahrbuch für Philosophie und Psychologie,* Salzburg, 1957–
SJTh	*Scottish Journal of Theology.* Edinburgh, 1948–
SKG	Schriften der Königsberger Gelehrten Gesellschaft. Halle
SKG.G	—Geisteswissenschaftliche Klasse, 1924–1944
SM (D)	*Sacramentum Mundi. Theologisches Lexikon für die Praxis.* ed. K. Rahner. Fribourg, 1967–1969
SM (E)	*Sacramentum Mundi. An Encyclopedia of Theology.* New York, 1968–1970
SO	Symbolae Osloenses. Oslo, 1923–
Sob	*Sobornost.* London, 1979–
Sommervogel	Bibliothèque de la Compagnie de Jésus, new edition by C. Sommervogel, Bruxelles, 1890–1930; 3rd ed., 1960–1963
SOr	Sources orientales. Paris, 1959–
SPAMP	Studien zur Problemgeschichte der antiken und mittelalterlichen Philosophie, Leyden, 1966–
SpOr	Spiritualité orientale, Bégrolles-en-Mauges, 1966–
SSL	Spicilegium sacrum Lovaniense, Louvain, 1922–
SST	*Studies in Sacred Theology.* Washington, D.C., 1895–1947; 2nd ser. 1947–
ST	*Summa Theologica,* Thomas Aquinas
StA	*Werke in Auswahl* (Studien Ausgabe), P. Melanchthon, edited by R. Stupperich, Gütersloh, 1951–1955
StAns	Studia Anselmiana. Rome, 1933–
StANT	Studien zum Alten und Neuen Testament. Munich, 1960–1975
StCan	*Studia Canonica,* Ottawa, 1967–
StEv	Studia Evangelica, Berlin, 1959–1982 (= TU 73, etc.)
StGen	*Studium Generale,* Berlin, 1947–1971
STGMA	Studien und Texte zur Geistesgeschichte des Mittelalters, Leyden, 1950–
StMed	*Studi medievali,* Turin, etc.; NS, 1960–
StMiss	*Studia missionalia.* Rome, 1943
StMor	*Studia moralia,* Rome, 1963–

STMP	Studia theologiae moralis et pastoralis, Salzburg, 1956–
StPatr	Studia patristica, Berlin, 1957–
StPh	*Studia philosophica,* Basel, 1946–
STPIMS	Studies and texts, Pontifical Institute of Mediaeval Studies, Toronto, 1955–
Strom.	*Stromata,* Clement of Alexandria
StSS	Studia scholastico-scotistica. Rome, 1968–
StT	Studi e testi, Biblioteca Apostolica Vaticana, Vatican City, 1900–
StTom	Studi tomistici, Vatican City, 1974– MMMM
StZ	*Stimmen der Zeit,* Fribourg, 1914–
SVF	*Stoicorum Veterum Fragmenta,* ed. J. von Arnim, Stuttgart. 3 vol. + index, 1903–1924, etc.
SVTQ	*St. Vladimir's Theological Quarterly,* New York, 1969–
Symb. Ath.	Symbol of Athanasius
TAPhS	*Transactions of the American Philosophical Society,* Philadelphia, Pa, 1769–1809; NS, 1818–
TDNT	*Theological Dictionary of the New Testament,* Grand Rapids, Mich., 1964–1977 (trans. of *ThWNT*)
TEH	Theologische Existenz heute, edited by K. Barth *et al.,* Munich, 1933–1941; NS, 1946–
TFil	*Tijdschrift voor filosofie.* Louvain, 1962– (= *TPh,* 1939–1961)
THAT	*Theologisches Handwörterbuch zum Alten Testament,* ed. E. Jenni and C. Westermann, Munich, 1971–1976
Theos. H.	*Theosophical History.* A Quarterly Journal of Research, London, 1985–1989; Fullerton, Calif., 1990–
ThGl	*Theologie und Glaube,* Paderborn, 1909–
ThH	Théologie historique, Paris, 1963–
ThJb	*Theologisches Jahrbuch,* Gütersloh, 1873–1899 (= *KJ,* 1900–)
ThJb(L)	*Theologisches Jahrbuch.* Leipzig, 1957–
ThLZ	*Theologische Literaturzeitung,* Leipzig, 1876–
Thom	*Thomist,* Washington, D.C., 1939–
ThPh	*Theologie und Philosophie,* Fribourg, 1966–
THPQ	*Theologisch-praktische Quartalschrift,* Linz, 1848–
ThQ	*Theologische Quartalschrift,* Tübingen, etc., 1819– (1960–1968 = *TThQ*)
ThR	*Theologische Rundschau.* Tübingen, 1897–1917; NF 1929–
ThSt(B)	Theologische Studien, edited by K. Barth *et al.,* Zurich, 1938–
ThTo	*Theology Today.* Princeton, N.J., etc., 1944/1945–
ThW	*Theologische Wissenschaft,* Stuttgart, etc., 1972–
ThWA	*Theorie Werkausgabe,* Hegel, Frankfurt, 1970, 20 vols.
ThWAT	*Theologisches Wörterbuch zum Alten Testament,* edited by G. J. Botterweck and H. Ringgren, Stuttgart, etc., 1973–
ThWNT	*Theologisches Wörterbuch zum Neuen Testament,* edited by G. Kittel, Stuttgart, 1933–1979
ThZ	*Theologische Zeitschrift,* Basel, 1945–
TKTG	Texte zur Kirchen und Theologiegeschichte, Gütersloh, 1966–
TOB	Traduction oecuménique de la Bible
TPh	*Tijdschrift voor philosophie,* Louvain, 1939–1961 (= *Tfil,* 1962–)
Tr	Traditio. Studies in Ancient and Medieval History, Thought and Religion, New York, etc., 1943–
TRE	*Theologische Realenzyklopädie,* edited by G. Krause and G. Muller, Berlin, 1976–
Trin	*De Trinitate,* Augustine
TS	*Theological Studies,* Woodstock, Md., etc., 1940–
TSTP	Tubinger Studien zur Theologie und Philosophie, Mainz, 1991–
TTh	*Tijdschrift voor theologie,* Nimègue, 1961–
TThQ	*Tübinger theologische Quartalschrift,* Stuttgart, 1960–1968 (= *ThQ*)
TThZ	*Trierer Theologische Zeitschrift,* Trier, 1947–
TTS	Tübinger theologische Studien, Mainz, 1973–1990
TU	Texte und Untersuchungen zur Geschichte der altchrislichen Literatur, Berlin, 1882–
TuG	Theologie und Gemeinde, Munich, 1958–
UB	Urban-Bücher, Stuttgart, 1953–
UnSa	Unam Sanctam, Paris, 1937–
VC	*Verbum Caro. Revue théologique et ecclésiastique œcuménique,* Taizé, etc., 1947–1969
VerLex	*Deutsche Literatur des Mittelalters. Verfasserlexikon,* Berlin, etc, 1933–1955; 2nd ed., 1978–

VetChr	*Vetera Christianorum,* Bari, 1964–
VieCon	*Vie consacrée,* Bruxelles, 1966–
VigChr	*Vigiliae Christianae,* Amsterdam, 1947–
VS	*Vie spirituelle,* Paris, 1946–
VT	*Vetus Testamentum,* Leyden, 1951–
VT.S	*—Suppl.,* 1953–
VThB	*Vocabulaire de théologie biblique,* edited by X. Léon-Dufour, Paris, 1962; 2nd ed., 1970
WA	*Werke. Kristiche Gesamtausgabe,* Luther (Weimarer Ausgabe), 1883–
WA.B	*—Briefwechsel,* 1930–
WA.DB	*—Deutsche Bibel,* 1906–
WA.TR	*—Tischreden,* 1912–
WBS	Wiener byzantinistische Studien, Graz, etc., 1964–
WdF	Wege der Forschung, Darmstadt, 1956–
Weischedel	*Werkausgabe,* Kant, edited by W. Weischedel, Frankfurt, 1958–1964
WMANT	Wissenschaftliche Monographien zum Alten und Neuen Testament, Neukirchen, 1960–
WSAMA.T	Walberger Studien der Albertus-Magnus-Akademie, Mainz, Theologische Reihe, 1964–
WUNT	Wissenschaftliche Untersuchungen zum Neuen Testament, Tübingen, 1950–
WuW	*Wort und Wahrheit,* Vienna, etc., 1946–1973
ZAW	*Zeitschrift für die alttestamentliche Wissenschaft und die Kunde des nach-biblischen Judentums,* Berlin, 1881–
ZDP	*Zeitschrift für deutsche Philologie,* Berlin, etc., 1869–
ZDPV	*Zeitschrift des deutschen Palästina-Vereins,* Wiesbaden, 1978–
ZevKR	*Zeitschrift für evangelisches Kirchen-recht,* Tübingen, 1951–
ZKG	*Zeitschrift für Kirchengeschichte,* Stuttgart, 1877–
ZKTh	*Zeitschrift für katholische Theologie,* Vienna, etc., 1877–
ZNW	*Zeitschrift für die neutestamentliche Wissenschaft und die Kunde der äl-teren Kirche,* Berlin, etc., 1900–
ZSRG.K	*Zeitschrift der Savigny-Stiftung für Rechtsgeschichte. Kanonistische Abteilung,* Weimar, 1911–
ZPE	*Zeitschrift für Papyrologie und Epigraphik,* Bonn, 1967–
ZThK	Zeitschrift für Theologie und Kirche, Tübingen, 1891–

Frankfurt = Frankfurt am Main
Fribourg = Fribourg-en-Brisgau
Fribourg-Paris = Fribourg (Switzerland)—Paris
A hyphenated date (1963–) means that the publishing is not complete or that the collection or journal is still ongoing.

G

Gadamer, Hans Georg. *See* **Hermeneutics**

Gallicanism

Even though it wrongly suggests the existence of a uniform doctrine, "Gallicanism" is a useful term of reference for a series of distinctively French attitudes toward ecclesiastical power, and the principles on which they were based. Its unifying principle was a resistance on both political and ecclesiastical grounds to maximalist interpretations of pontifical primacy, as exemplified by ultramontanism*. However, the bedrock of Gallicanism was primarily political: it represented the concept of what would come to be called the "separation of powers," the total division of the spiritual from the temporal.

1. History
The foundations of all future Gallicanism were probably laid by the juridical counselors who developed the principle of this separation during the conflict between Pope Boniface VIII and the French King Philip the Fair (1303), and also by the clerics* who simultaneously developed its dogmatic* aspects (Jean de Paris, 1302). References to the original Gallicanism, which brought into play a typically medieval conception of society*, would have a long life, but its interpretations would be rereadings and updatings. Another founding element of a "Gallican" conception was the prospect of an internal reform of the Church*, to be carried out by the General Council (Durand de Mende, 1312), and the Schism* of the West made this prospect seem quite real and imminent. By proclaiming the superiority of the Council as the representative of the Church militant, the Council of Constance* (1414–17) marked an important turning point. And although French authors held a central place in the elaboration of the Council's theses, it was not only on account of their proposal of an ecclesiology* of a mystico-corporative type (Gerson, d'Ailly), but also because of their arguments against the defenders of papal power, a rationale based often on an ancient ecclesiastical right of which only France was supposed to have preserved the traces—the *Freedoms of the Gallican Church,* of which the monarchy was the protector. The *Pragmatic Sanction* of Bourges (1438), an adapted acceptance of the Council of Basel*'s decrees, reinforced these abstract references and tendentious reconstructions.

Never put into effect, this text would become an idealized reference; in 1516, a concordat between France and the Holy See replaced it. While moderating the wording, the concordat upheld certain of the demands of the *Pragmatic Sanction* with regard to Roman interventions, but suppressed elections to benefices, entrusting these appointments to the sovereign, with a right of ratification being reserved to the pope himself. From that date onward, the French sovereign assumed the role of mediator between the Gallican demands of the juridic counselors and theologians, who were preoccupied with preserving a participatory ecclesial model, and the most extreme of the Roman theorists. The Reformation was to make the situation more complex. By forcing French Catholics to choose between fidelity to Rome* or rejection of Rome, it could only weaken Gallican attitudes in those who wanted to remain faithful to Rome. On the other hand, the wish to preserve the kingdom's integrity also encouraged a more "political" attitude, which favored dialogue with the Protestants and a search for union. One French response to the Council of Trent* would make these elements clear. At the close of this Council, two forms of Catholicism* confronted each other in France, both manipulated by the monarch, who was trying in this way to control them more easily. On one side were ranged a party of "Romans" or ultramontanes, anxious to reform the Church according to the Tridentine model and the wishes of the papacy; on the other side, the "Gallicans," whom reasons of national unity (but also ideological motives) drove to reject this conception, which they countered with the principles of the ancient Church. Thus it was that the *Libertés de l'Eglise gallicane* was published in a collection designed to supply *proofs* of a different practice, that is, its authorized precedents (Pithou, 1598; Dupuy, 1639). At this stage, the Gallican resistance came just as much from parliamentary circles as from the ranks of the theologians.

In this matter the works of Edmond Richer (1559–1631), syndic of the Faculty of Theology in Paris, took on particular importance. By publishing Gerson's writings and those of the more extreme conciliarist authors, Richer really adopted the stance of a redrafter of ecclesiological Gallicanism. He set himself apart from Gerson's democratic conception (his 18th-century disciples would return to it) in order to bend it toward "sacerdotalism." In particular he added a political component to it by expounding a systematic regalism in his short *Libellus de ecclesiastica et politica potestate* (1612). Richer was condemned at the Synod* of Sens in 1612, and the clergy rejected an article proposed to the Etats Généraux in 1614, which shows that these ideas were not majority views. It was not until almost the end of the century that editions and re-editions of the syndic's works would exert a real influence. But under Louis XIII, the Gallicanism of both the politicians and the ecclesiastics consisted above all in upholding national independence by maintaining a prudent relationship with Rome, on which Spanish influence was feared. The example of Richelieu, who used the Gallican arguments as a means of applying pressure or even of blackmailing, confirms the pragmatism of this attitude.

Of course, by asking the papacy to intervene in the Jansenist* question, France gave it the opportunity to assert its supremacy. Nonetheless, the French prelates were anxious to put into effect the reception of the papal bull *Cum Occasione* (1653) by adding their own interpretation. This effort, of which the archbishop of Toulouse, P. de Marca was the guiding spirit, simultaneously went against the varied strands of Gallicanism, the first successes of a renewal of the Catholic theology of the episcopacy, and the influence of historical works devoted to the great examples of the past. The successive interventions of popes concerning the Jansenist question and the difficulties to which it gave rise encouraged a more vigorous assertion of papal infallibility*. In theological circles strained relations resulted, and this tension soon took a political turn with the conflict between Louis XIV and Pope Alexander VII (1662). On that occasion the Faculty of Theology in Paris was "invited" to expound its doctrine on the points of contention. It obeyed in six articles (1663). The first three expressed the doctrine of the "separation of powers"; of the independence of royal power; and of the duty to obey. The other three contained an acknowledgment of Gallican liberties; a denial of papal supremacy over the Council; and a denial of infalibility. These prudently written proposals were taken up again, in part, in the *Quatre articles du clergé de France* of 1682.

The occasion which brought the latter into being was a new conflict between France and the papacy, this time about the right to regalia, that is, the king's prerogative to draw revenues from vacant abbacies, which had been extended to the whole of the kingdom. To put pressure on Innocent XI, the king and his ministers convoked a meeting of the clergy that produced a declaration in four articles. These articles, drafted by Bossuet, who instilled into them a patristic spirit, presented a codification of what until then had been simply a cluster of convergences:

1) In temporal matters, kings and sovereigns are subject to no ecclesiastical power within the order established by God. They cannot be deposed, either directly or indirectly, by invoking the authority* of the leaders of the Church. That same authority cannot dispense their subjects from the

submission and obedience which they owe them, nor absolve these subjects from the oath of fidelity.

2) The total power that the Apostolic See and the successors of Peter*, vicars of Jesus Christ, hold over spiritual matters is such that the decrees of the ecumenical Council of Constance nonetheless retain their full force.

3) The exercise of apostolic authority should be modeled on the canons created by the Spirit of God and be confirmed by the general respect of all. The rules, customs, and constitutions accepted in the kingdom and in the Gallican Church must retain their full force and traditional usages must remain unchanged.

4) The pope has the chief role in matters of faith*, and his decrees concern all the churches and each church individually. However, his judgment is not final without the consent of the Church.

This declaration truly constituted Gallicanism, that is, a doctrine peculiar to France, since it was ordered to be taught throughout the kingdom. And since, rather than condemn it explicitly (Alexander VIII's apostolic constitution, *Inter multiplices* [1690], dealt more with the process of promulgation than its content [DS 2281–85]), Rome preferred to encourage refutations, commentaries and defenses were published that contributed to the deeper examination and circulation of Gallican ideas. Far from resolving the conflict with Innocent XI, the declaration aggravated it, and the pope refused to grant investiture to the bishops chosen from among the members of that assembly. In 1688 Louis XIV had an appeal drawn up to the future General Council, thereby adding a dangerous precedent to the Gallican arsenal. A compromise was negotiated with Innocent XII: the bishops appointed had to disavow the declaration and Louis XIV had to agree that it would not be taught. The king did not keep his word, and the teaching of the articles of 1682 remained obligatory during the whole of the Ancien Régime—which is what gave the 18th century French church its seeming Gallican homogeneity.

Anxious to control the religious situation in France, Louis XIV again approached Rome, which he asked to intervene in the issues raised by Quietism* (which the pope did in the 1699 bull *Cum alias*), then again on the question of Jansenism (*Vineam Domini*, 1705; *Unigenitus,* 1713). On those occasions the bishops insisted on verifying the pontifical judgment before giving their agreement (which they did in the assemblies of the clergy in 1700, 1705, and 1714). This insistence heralded the component of the long conflict with the papacy that would centre on *Unigenitus*. It was a multiform component moreover, since the "authoritative Gallicanism" of the bishops and the monarchy was joined by more extreme interpretations, inspired (through Richer, whose works were beginning to be rediscovered) by the conciliarist authors. The appeal to the Council, in 1717, was the culminating point of this "participatory Gallicanism" since it provoked the joint opposition of the pope and the king.

From that time onward two Gallicanisms existed in France and they also exerted an influence on the whole of European Catholicism. The two models persisted until the French Revolution, when they came into conflict on the subject of the Civil Constitution of the Clergy (1790). The constitutional Church and its defenders (Grégoire, Tabaraud) marked the end of this conception inspired by Richer; the episcopacy and many refractory members of the clergy demonstrated the continued presence of the other position.

The restoration of Catholicism under Napoleon was accomplished with the agreement of a papacy whose authority was very clearly on display, and it marked the end of the Gallican Church. Survivals of Gallicanism could be seen, but these were primarily matters of tradition and cast of mind: they represented above all a cultural continuity, via treatises of theology and history*, or of liturgical practices. One could also note the presence of an administrative Gallicanism, facilitated by the constitutional articles added to the Concordat of 1801, which had been anxious to control religious activity and also to orient it. These elements, and especially these attitudes, revived ultramontanism, which led to a reaction by several bishops and theologians in favor of a moderating episcopalism. A neo-Gallicanism can therefore be observed, which preferred to place itself in the tradition of Gerson and of Bossuet, but which was above all a response to ultramontane excesses (Mgr. Darboy, Mgr Maret). Vatican* I permitted a major debate on these questions. In addition to the proclamation of papal infallibility, the confirmation of the primacy of the pope and the unchallengeable nature of his judgments marked the definitive end of Gallicanism.

2. Chief Characteristics

The above historical overview emphasizes the pragmatic character of the Gallican position. It represented a reaction to particular conditions, and more generally to direct or indirect strains in relations with papal authority. A dialectical element is associated with it, so it is important to resist too rigid a definition. In this sense, Gallicanism can be seen as a series of reactions to the demands of ultramontanism (both terms were coined in the 19th century), which indeed points to an ideological view.

Gallicanism was opposed to ultramontanism on the question of a "separation of powers," since it denied the papacy any right to intervene in temporal matters, and even rejected, in addition to the demands of Boniface VIII's bull *Unam sanctam* (1302), the theory of an indirect authority. It opposed ultramontanism by defending episcopal jurisdiction* (in particular on everything that concerned the exempt religious orders) and by placing collegial action in the foreground. It denied papal infallibility in favor of ecclesiastical consensus; it relativized primacy; and above all it submitted the pope's Magisterium* to a process of active interpretation that considerably restricted its authority.

This resistance and opposition were based on a historicizing argument that drew from the past the elements that allowed it to reconstruct an ideal ecclesiological model. From that time onward, not one but multiple Gallicanisms existed, according to both the practical and utopian ecclesiological model that each particular individual or author constructed by manipulating his references.

3. Gallican Models

a) Two Constants. The first constant was a legal concept inherited from the Middle Ages, which adhered to the constitutional character of a Church ruled by the canons; that was the meaning of the *Libertés de l'Eglise gallicane.* It based itself on references to Antiquity— the mirror of the Church in its early period—allied to a reformist preoccupation, in order to rediscover the original purity. This view was stimulated by the wish to restore Christian unity* and heal the schism of the Reformation, the damage caused by which was felt on the national level. It drew on a static view that idealized the early Church and rejected any evolution in doctrine or in ecclesiastical* discipline. On the other hand, it approved of communion*, expressed by the joint action of the bishops united to the Holy See. It saw in the synods, the provincial and national councils, as well as in the ideal general council, events that formed part of the ordinary running of the Church.

The second constant was the national conception of the relations between Church* and State. The role of the monarchy was not perceived in the same way by the politicians and by the ecclesiastics, but they all agreed to acknowledge a secular power's right of regulation and of "protection," principally in its relations with the Apostolic See. In the ultimate Jansenist variation, it was agreed to transfer the powers of the monarchy to the nation, represented by its elected officials.

b) Two Models. These constants made possible the development of quite different ecclesiological models, founded on two conceptions of society. On the one side stood a participatory Gallicanism, and on the other, an authoritarian one. The former emerged from a medieval substrate founded on Aristotle's *Politics,* and it developed a democratic model centered on the ideas of interpretation and representation. It understood representation to be a process of definition of truth*, which starts from the base and rises through levels of authority to be expressed at the most elevated level. Reception, meanwhile, was viewed as an inverse process of adhesion that confirms and authenticates the decision. This was the conception held by parliamentary and university circles, and the one that the opponents of *Unigenitus* would adopt. As for authoritarian Gallicanism, it adapted the hierarchized Tridentine model to the interests of the monarchy and of the episcopacy. It would speak of regalism and episcopalism.

Many of the concepts circulated by the ecclesiologies of the Gallican type belong to the orthodox core, such as the principle of communion, given new vigor in recent decades. Their polemical use provoked condemnations, and the condemnations elicited necessary clarifications.

- E. Puyol (1876), *Edmond Richer, Étude historique et critique sur la rénovation du g. au commencement du XVIIe siècle,* Paris.
- V. Martin (1919), *Le gallicanisme et la réforme catholique,* Paris.
- V. Martin (1929), *Le gallicanisme politique et le Clergé de France,* Paris.
- E. Préclin (1930), "Edmond Richer (1539–1631), Sa vie, son œuvre, le richérisme," *RHMo* 55, 241–69, 321–36.
- F. Gacquère (1932), *Pierre de Marca (1594–1662): sa vie, ses œuvres, son gallicanisme,* Paris.
- J. Lecler (1932–34), "Qu'est-ce que les Libertés de l'Église gallicane?", *RSR* 23, 385–410, 542–68; 24, 47–87.
- V. Martin (1939), *Les origines du gallicanisme,* Paris.
- J. Orcibal (1949), *Louis XIV contre Innocent XI: Les appels au futur concile de 1688 et l'opinion française,* Paris.
- A.-G. Martimort (1953), *Le gallicanisme de Bossuet,* Paris.
- R. Thysman (1957), "Le gallicanisme de Mgr Maret et l'influence de Bossuet," *RHE* 52, 401–65.
- J.R. Palanque (1962), *Catholiques libéraux et gallicans en France face au concile du Vatican, 1867–1870,* Aix-en-Provence.
- G. de Lagarde (1963), *La naissance de l'esprit laïque à la fin du Moyen Age,* Louvain and Paris.
- R. Duchon (1970), "De Bossuet à Febronius," *RHE* 55, 375–422.
- A.-G. Martimort (1973), *Le gallicanisme,* Paris.
- L.B. Pascoe (1973), *Jean Gerson's Principles of Church Reform,* Leyden.
- H.J. Sieben (1988), *Die Katholische Konzilidee von der Reformation bis zur Aufklärung,* Paderborn.
- J.M. Gres-Gayer (1991), "Le gallicanisme de L. Ellies Du Pin," *Lias* 18, 37–82.
- P. Blet (1995), *Le clergé du Grand Siècle en ses assemblées, 1615–1715,* Paris.
- J.M. Gres-Gayer (1995), "Le gallicanisme d'Antoine Arnauld: Éléments d'une enquête," *ChPR* 44, 31–51.
- J. Bergin (1996), *The Making of the French Episcopate,* New Haven and London.

JACQUES M. GRES-GAYER

See also **Conciliarism; Jansenism; Ultramontanism**

Gattungsgeschichte. *See* **Literary Genres in Scripture**

Gautier of Saint-Victor. *See* **Saint-Victor, School of**

Gehenna. *See* **Hell**

Gentiles. *See* **Paganism; Universalism**

Gerdi, Hyacinthe Sigismond. *See* **Ontologism**

Gilbert de la Porree (Gilbertus Porretanus/Gilbert of Poitiers). *See* **Chartres, School of**

Gilson, Etienne. *See* **Thomism**

Glory of God

---

a) Old Testament. Whereas the Greek *doxa* suggests reputation, fame, the Hebrew *kâvôd* (adj. *kâvéd*) expresses the weight, the value of a person (Gn 13:2) or of a city (Is 62:2). The term is chosen to designate possessions (see Ps 49:17; Jb 19:9; 29:20)—such as those of Abraham (Gn 13:2) and of Jacob (31:1)—and the "weight" or "importance" (TOB) of Joseph in the heart of Pharaoh. Glory is what characterizes the king, whether he is divine (Ps 24) or human (Prv 25:2).The glory of one at prayer may be God* himself (Ps 3:4; 57:9; 62:8). The glory of the flesh is perishable (Is 40:6; see 17:4 in the Septuagint). The glory of God ("glory of the Lord"—the phrase appears 53 times in Psalms) is associated with his name* (Ex 33:19; *see* Ps 29:2; 72:19; 79:9; 96:2f., 7f.; 102:16; 113:3f.; 115:1; 145:5), with his splendor (*tife'ârâh*: Is 63:12, 14). It is present in the cloud (Ex 40:34f.; 2 Macc 2:8), in the ark (1 Sm 4), in the temple* (1 Kgs 8:10), and in Zion (*see especially* Is 4:5; 24:23; 60; 62:2; 66). If holiness* defines God in himself, glory is his radiance (Is 6:3). It is God communicating about what he is by what he does.

It is because God creates by the Word* (Gn 1:1–2:4a) that the heavens "speak" in recounting his glory (Ps 19:1), that he is celebrated in reply (Ps 104:31–34; 147:12). The cosmos* (Sir 43:1, 9, 12, 44) and man (Sir 44:2) attest to the permanence of his glory. Theophanies* assume cosmic aspects (Jb 38:31–38); those psalms* that are called psalms "of the King of glory" (Ps 24; 29; 96; 97; 145) glorify God as creator and eschatological judge. The theophanies of the covenant* give full prominence to the theme of glory (Ex 24:15bff.). Once Moses has been made aware of this glory, even and especially after the idolatry* of the golden calf (contrast "glory/idol": Ps 106:20; Jer 2:11; *see* Rom 1:23), he can only aspire to see it again (Ex 33:20), although it is not now linked to a cosmic phenomenon. Moses' face "shone" (Ex 34:29f., 35), which the Septuagint renders as *doxazesthai,* "to be glorified."

Ezekiel, while having as a priest an acute sense of the glorious presence of the Lord in the temple, also perceives (and it is all one) how divine glory overflows the site of its manifestation. The same glory that appears in personal form to the prophet* (Ez 1:28; 8:2, 4) is present in the temple, but not restricted to that place (10:18f.).It accompanies the people* of God into exile (11:22f.) and on their return from exile (43:4). Glory and Spirit interpenetrate in a conception that develops that of the new covenant according to Jeremiah 31:31 (*see* Ez 36:26). Prophet of the glory of YHWH, Ezekiel is also, and correlatively, the prophet of his Spirit. The description of the future temple, once again inhabited by glory, prepares for the apocalyptic continuations (also evoked by Hg 2:3, 9; Zec 2:9).

The literary sources most in harmony with the theme of glory are those that emanate from circles close to the temple (priests, psalmists); they help to describe the great theophanies of Sinai (Ex 24:40; Lv 9:6, 23; Nm 14:10). In the late period of the Old Testament, the wisdom writings see in Wisdom* the divine manifestation that gradually encompasses all the others. They link it to the theme of glory (Sir 24:17), and emphasize its parallel with the glory of the cult* (Sir 45; 50:5–13). Wisdom itself is "the radiance of the glory of the All-Powerful" (Wis 7:25; *see* 9:11).

b) New Testament. *Doxa,* in the theological sense, is very frequent in the New Testament (appearing more than 200 times). The complex meaning of *kaukhasthai* ("to glorify oneself, display one's pride") should not be overlooked. It is, for example, characteristic of the Pauline* corpus (where it is found more than 50 times), expressing the way in which human beings are given prestige, either vainly (Rom 3:27; Gal 6:13), or in God, in Christ* (Rom 5:11) and his cross (Gal 6:14), and particularly in the community of the apostle Paul's disciples (1 Cor 15:31; 2 Cor *passim*).

The continuity between the glory of the temple and the new glory is attested by the hymn of Luke 2:29–32; it is in the temple that Simeon recognizes in the child Jesus* the "glory of Israel." The same jubilation recurs throughout the other gospel authors.

2 Corinthians 3:4–5:6, the *locus classicus* of Pauline theological aesthetics (Balthasar* 1969), closely ties together the themes of glory, the "new covenant," and the Holy Spirit, on the basis of an echo of Exodus 32 and 34. The glory of God in Christ is communicated to the community of believers by the integration of the Torah, the prophets (repetition of Jeremiah), the wisdom books (theme of "reading": 2 Cor 3:15), and apocalyptics* (2 Cor 3:13—the *telos*). In John, the glory of the Son in the flesh culminates in his final prayer* (Jn 17:5), which presents a synthesis of the theme: the one of whom "we have seen his glory"(Jn 1:14) has shown it in many signs (Jn 2:11) until it reiterates Isaiah's vision of that glory (Jn 12:41). He has not however obtained the personal union of "belief." The rejection is interpreted as a preference for the glory that comes from human being over the glory given by God (Jn 12:43). Conversely, Jesus exalts the communication of glory between the Father*, himself, and his disciples. He shows its nature in this way: "The glory that you have given me I have given to them, that they may be one even as we are one" (Jn 17:22). To be sure, it was necessary to wait for the cross, the Passion*, and the Resurrection* for a total manifestation of that glory to the disciples. But for John 13:31f., it is from eternity to eternity, so that, through the prologue, the perspective extends to the entire history* of mankind.

When it comes to the revelation of glory, a special place is reserved in the synoptic tradition for the transfiguration (Mt 17:1–8 and parallel passages). The substance of this episode is reflected back onto the narrative* of the baptism* of Jesus (Mt 3:3–17 and parallel passages) and forward onto that of his agony in Gethsemane (Mt 26:36–46 and parallel passages). The entire life of Jesus is thus permeated by his glory.

By "doxologies" is understood the formulas (preserved in all the "glory to"s of Christian liturgies*) by which God and his Christ are glorified. Their frequency in the Pauline writings (Rom 1:25; 9:5; 11:36; 16:25ff.; 2 Cor 1:20; 4:15; Gal 1:5; Eph 3:21; Phil 4:20) shows that this homage of praise held the principal place in the prayers of the earliest communities. Indeed, glory is the end of all things (Eph 1:6, 14), those of God and those of man, who in the end are one. The Book of Revelation illustrates this in its doxologies (1:6; 5:12f.; 19:1) and in the picture (inscribed in traditional visions) of Jerusalem* illuminated by the glory of God, toward which flows the "glory of the nations" (Rev 21).

● H. U. von Balthasar (1969), *Herrlichkeit* III/2, Einsiedeln.
Y. Simoens (1981), *La gloire d'aimer: Structures stylistiques et interprétatives dans le Discours de la Cène (Jn 13–17)*, An-Bib 90, Rome.
M. Weinfeld (1982–84), "*Kabôd*," *ThWAT* 4, 23–40.
Y. Simoens (1997), *Selon Jean*, 1. *Une traduction*, 2. *Une interprétation*, Brussels, 29–77.
F. J. Moloney (1998), *The Gospel of John* (Sacra Pagina Series 4), Collegeville, 33–48.

YVES SIMOENS

See also **Holy Spirit; Name; Praise; Temple; Theophany; Wisdom; Word**

Gnosis

a) Gnosis and Gnosticism.   At the beginning of the Christian era the term *gnosis,* meaning knowledge, signified exclusively a particular type of knowledge having to do with the essence of things, such as the mysteries of the divine world and celestial beings. The term went beyond simple *pistis* (faith*). The "gnostic" who was initiated into this knowledge was guaranteed salvation. The concept was susceptible to orthodox theological use. Thus Clement of Alexandria, followed by other fathers* of the church, proposed the ideal of the "true gnostic" as a perfect Christian who allows himself or herself to be transformed by "knowledge" in such a way as to live in harmony with God*. The term *gnosticism,* then, is better suited than *gnostic* to signify the religious movement that developed, over the first centuries of Christianity, into a multitude of sects that shared the same conception of gnosis, a conception the Church* fought against and rejected. This movement is known to us first through the polemics of the heresiologists, who often distorted it in their descriptions, and more lately through an increasingly rich collection of rediscovered original texts, the most important being the Coptic library found at Nag-Hammadi.

b) The Characteristics of Christian Gnosticism. It is impossible for a single definition to encompass gnosticism as a whole because of the variety of its theories, but its principal distinctive traits can be described as follows: 1) A dualistic factor tends to dissociate creation* from redemption, just as it tends to separate completely the material world, dominated by evil or limited powers, from the spiritual world, the domain of the transcendent and "unknown" God. It is from this latter world that human souls* emanate, souls of spiritual essence, prisoners of this world on earth. It is from the spiritual world, too, that the Savior descends in order to bring back to the higher world the souls of the elect—those who possess *gnosis*. This dualism can be explained by the anguished priority given to the problem of evil—of its origins and why it exists. It attempts to disengage the human soul from any personal responsibility. 2) A privileged knowledge, transmitted through secret, unveils the mysteries of the celestial world. 3) Speculation, which explores the plenitude of the divine (or *Pleroma*), tries to discover the entities (or *aeons*) of which it is formed in a manner that tends toward mythologizing. 4) A form of anti-Judaism sees in the "god of the Jews" only a demiurge, creator of the universe.

c) The Great Gnostics of the Second Century. Not including Marcion*, who is not a gnostic in the strict sense of the word, Basilides and Valentinus are the most important gnostics of the second century. Basilides's system is not well known. It seems to have philosophical resonances and includes a negative conception of being*; the "unknown" God becomes, for Basilides, "non-existent" and produces a seed, a sort of primitive chaos, in which is enclosed all future evolution*. His eschatology* is marked by pessimism, with everything in this world returning to a state of cosmic forgetfulness. Valentinus, whose sect flourished with great success, is more important. Metaphysician and mythmaker, he is the author of a system dominated by the notion of the *syzygy* (conjunction) of male and female entities. Starting from the Father* (who is Void and Silence) the Valentinian *Pleroma* is

deployed by successive emanations of pairs of *aeons*. The last *aeon*, Sophia, is at the origin of the production of the material world by the demiurge. Humanity is divided into three categories: carnal people, psychic people, and spiritual people. It is only to these last that certain salvation is promised through the *aeon* Jesus*, Savior, fruit of the *Pleroma*. Valentinus found justification for his system in the Old and New Testaments and used a particular exegetical method in which allegory played a large role. His theological concepts stimulated the thinking of the fathers of the church and resulted in their elaboration of the dogma of the Trinity*. The sect of Valentinus developed into two schools, the Italianate and the Oriental, with doctrinal and exegetical variations. Several Nag-Hammadi documents (notably the *Gospel of Truth*) contributed to a better knowledge of Valentinianism and of the stages of its evolution.

d) The Origins of Christian Gnosticism. The extremely difficult problem of the origins of gnosticism has not yet been satisfactorily solved. The fathers of the church perceived gnosticism to be an internal deviation from Christianity due to its contamination by philosophy, particularly by Platonism. This is generally corroborated by the explanation of Adolf von Harnack, who wrote of the "chronic Hellenization of Christianity." This thesis is simplistic, however, and recent research considers the gnostic phenomenon rather as an intellectual or spiritual attitude with universal influence and scope. The tendency is to ascribe the gnosticism of the first centuries of Christianity to the development of religious syncretism that issued from Alexander's conquests (especially the influence of Persian dualism). Mention must also be made of the existence of a pre-Christian gnostic (Simon of Samaria) and especially of a Jewish gnosticism (gnostic elements are present in some of the intertestamentary writings). Resurgences of an Egyptian religious mentality must not be excluded either.

● E. de Faye (1913), *Gnostiques et gnosticismes,* Paris.
S. Pétrement (1947), *Le dualisme chez Platon, les gnostiques et les manichéens,* Paris.
F.-M. Sagnard (1947), *La gnose valentinienne et le témoignage de saint Irénée,* Paris.
G. Quispel (1951), *Gnosis als Weltreligion,* Zurich.
H. Jonas (1958), *The Gnostic Religion,* Boston (Rev. Ed. 1970).
R. M. Wilson (1958), *The Gnostic Problem,* London.
J. Doresse (1958–1959), *Les livres secrets des gnostiques d'Égypte,* Paris.
A. Orbe (1958–1966), *Estudios valentinianos,* Rome.
G. G. Scholem (1960), *Jewish Gnosticism, Merkabah, Mysticism and Talmudic Tradition,* New York.
R. M. Grant (1964), *La gnose et les origines chrétiennes,* Paris.
Coll. (1967), *The origins of Gnosticism,* Colloque de Messine, Leyden.

M. Tardieu (1974), *Trois mythes gnostiques...*, Paris.
The Nag Hammadi Library in English (1977), Leyden.
H.-C. Puech (1978), *En quête de la gnose*, 2 vols, Paris.
M. Tardieu, J.-D. Dubois (1986), *Introduction à la littérature gnostique* I, Paris.
Ch. Markschies (1992), *Valentinus Gnosticus?*, Tübingen.
M. Simonetti (1993), *Testi gnostici in lingua greca e latina*, Milan.
W. A. Löhr (1996), *Basilides und seine Schule,* Tübingen.

K. Rudolph (1996), *Gnosis und spätantike Religionsgeschichte: Gesammelte Aufsätze,* Tübingen.

RENÉ BRAUN

See also **Alexandria, School of; Fathers of the Church; Heresy; Intertestament; Judaism; Manicheanism; Platonism, Christian; Scripture, Senses of**

God

A. Theological Problematics

I. Biblical Theology

In its more normative occurrences (those of the burning bush and of the *Shema' Yiserâél*), the biblical naming of God, *YHWH 'Elohîm*, is a double naming. *YHWH* (conventionally rendered as "Yahweh" when the vowels omitted in Hebrew orthography are added) records a unique and indispensable historical revelation, while *'Elohîm* refers just as much to what the pagans call "God," even when an idol is designated. This bipolarity continues into the New Testament, whose message cannot be conveyed without the association of the word that names Jesus* and the one that, in any language, names God.

1. The Old Testament

a) How Does the Biblical God Make Himself Known? The Book* cannot be understood as a direct and immediate communication from God. It conveys in written narrative form the fact that certain people, especially in the beginning, heard God speak to them, directly or not. Sometimes God showed himself: this event was exceptional (Ex 24:10; Is 6:1; Am 9:1), or was reported with reservations and corrections (Dt 5:24ff.; Nm 12:6ff.), or even denied completely (Dt 4:15; Ex 33:20; Jgs 13:22). The recipients of the divine communication were usually individuals, chosen to address their communities.

b) The Object of Divine Communication. God behaves in the same way as humans do, in the sense that God reveals less what he is than what he likes and what he feels. What pleases him is declared to the people* through the law* of Moses and through the prophets*. It is especially through the latter that what he feels is shown, the intensity of divine pathos even going so far as to give himself up to be read in the bodily history of his messengers (Is 8:1–4, 18; Hos 1:1–3; Jer 16:1–9; Ez 24:15–27). Wisdom* transmits the word along with life itself, from parents to children, and it enables both to go back to their divine origin (Prv 1–9).

c) God's Identity. The message is authenticated by God's signature, which is the Name*. This name, YHWH, refers back to history. It is linked to the Mosaic Law: the burning bush next to Sinai (Ex 3).

The word YHWH is formed of two components: the subject (third person: "He") and the verb *to be,* in the third person. As it stands, the narrative* interprets YHWH as derived from the verb in the *first* person, for first of all God utters it in this form in Exodus 3:14 (adopted in Hos 1:9, in the negative form in the Hebrew!). Here the Vulgate—*Ego sum qui sum* (Ex 3:14a: "I am who I *am,*" not retained in 14b, despite the Hebrew)—is more faithful to the Hebrew than the Septuagint's *ho ôn* ("the being").

God's name makes him known as subject: it is in the act of speaking that his essence of being is given, by his signing of a promise*. For this reason he calls out, he is called to, he is announced, without ever losing the link that ties him to the founding event (Ex 3:15 ab). The covenant* can be considered the authorization and foundation of the exchange of words between God and humanity. Committed to a covenant that cannot proceed without controversy, the biblical God exposes himself to history*. One of the biblical epithets that best sums up the divine manifestations is that of "living" (1 Kgs 18:15; 2 Kgs 2:2; 3:14; Jer 10:10; 23:36). God is living, although immortal. Correlatively, the idol is a god who is not living.

d) Transfers. "The Lord our God, the Lord is one" (Dt 6:4). Now, biblical monotheism* has two aspects: its exclusiveness, and its capacity for infusing with YHWH's identity those manifestations of the divine that, in olden times, did not claim to be His: according to Exodus 6:3, if the patriarchs did not know YHWH, it was because he appeared to them under another name. According to a different tradition*, Abraham was able to recognize YHWH in the "God Most High" (Gn 14:22) whom the kings of Canaan worshipped (14:18). To oblige the people to choose either Baal or Yahweh (1 Kgs 18:21) was also to displace onto YHWH some of Baal's characteristics (Hos 2:18b). These kinds of connections did not necessarily spring from a spirit of annexation. Rather than a wish to conquer the surrounding surface, the narrative aimed to conquer time*—from before Israel* up to its origins. More than others, the narrative encountered other cultures and religions along the way: it did not suppress these interferences. The fact that a journey so attracted toward the Unique one has left such visible traces of its vicissitudes is worth mentioning. It should be added that fidelity to the one God was not originally focused on the number (*mono*theism): it was part of an effort not to confuse him with what might be another god, even under his name.

e) Ambivalences. God has spoken "at many times and in many ways" (Heb 1:1): this variety is also characteristic of his actions. Some of them unfold in a mixture of light and darkness whose ambivalence the narrator stresses or does not manage to hide. There are moments of dread when a humano-divine being becomes Jacob's enemy (Gn 32:23–33), or when YHWH (Ex 2:24ff., MT; LXX: his Angel) tries to kill Moses's son (or Moses himself?). There is a crucial moment, at the heart of this history, when the division of roles between God and the "destroyer" (Ex 12:23.27) is still not clear, in the extermination of the first-born of Egypt. God already ratified the violence* of the whole mass of humanity after the flood (Gn 9:2). Ezekiel's temerity in having God say: "I gave them statutes that were not good" (Ez 20:25) is a unique example. With regards to the enormous cultual amount of bloody sacrifices*, however, the uncertainty is not lifted: did God want them (Jer 7:22; Am 5:25; Ps 15:18ff., but v. 21) or did he not?

The biblical narrative reveals precisely what will later become its crises: that is, where the irrepressible rather than the intended character of its truth* is revealed. The texts are in no way eager to show God dissociating himself from the darkness. The opacity of these texts also lends them weight. God strangely assumes humanity's darkness, as if he could heal humanity from darkness only by accompanying it through. The most convincing aspect of the process is its slowness, because God's purpose is that the whole human city* becomes a holy society*. That is why he is called king, one of his most remarkable titles (Nm 23:21; Is 6:5; 44:6; Ps 24:7ff.; 48:3).

f) Holiness and Love. "I am holy," says God (Lv 11:44ff.; 19:2; 20:26; 21:8). Thus is expressed that property of God which is his insofar as he is the only one to *be* God; a property, nonetheless, which is able to touch human beings (Lv 21:8) as the burning coal touched Isaiah (Is 6:6–7). This characteristic pervades the whole ethical domain from further back, from his founding. It ensures him his position as one who respects the singular, of the proper name that, within the network of kinships, designates the sanctuary of each being (Lv 18). The communication of what is unique can be called love*: God loves Israel (Dt 4:37; 7:8; Hos 11:1) and calls on Israel to love him. The encounter with the holiness of the biblical God is a test, a shock, a "fear*." There is no reason to be surprised that it is in continuity with the experience* of God's love.

g) Divine Paternity. God speaks as subject. God is alive. God is holy. God loves. His position as speaker already places God in a contradictory position with respect to himself. And he speaks to himself ("Let us make.") before making man in his image. The fact that in his image he makes man masculine and feminine could tell us something about what he is, the nearest deduction being that he contains a difference. Genesis 1:27 does not call the Creator "Father" (despite Gn 5:3). According to Proverbs 8:22 from the beginning God engenders eternal Wisdom. This introduction of a God who engenders Wisdom points toward the identity between divine speech and divine life, toward a God who is father of life and truth. This God is indeed invoked in the texts, although sparingly, under the name of Father*. To call him so had been the privilege of the king (Ps 2:7; 89:27; *see* 2 Sm 7:14).

Since Israel has the role of the mother and sons (Hos 2:4), God is sometimes featured as her spouse (Hos 1–3) and as her father (Hos 11:1), or as her spouse and creator (Is 54:5; Is 62:5 [?]). Maternal feelings are not alien to him. The implication of God in the couple's relationship supplies the Song of Songs with its full meaning. His implication in the genealogies, illustrated particularly in Genesis, is always assumed. The intersection of nuptial language and the political register (e.g. Jgs 9:3; 2 Sm 5:1; 19:13f., and Gn 2:23) is not a justification for conflating them, but indicates a decisive *locus* of the divine manifestation.

h) A God of Excess. The law maintains evil* as well as good* within boundaries. Transgression of the law is only remedied and healed by excess, heralded by certain prophecies inspired by the upheaval of the exile (Is 54–55; 59:21; Jer 31:31–34; Ez 16:59–63; 20:44; 36:16–32; Joel 3:1–5). To his people who will break the covenant, God will respond by giving it more than he had already given; more than the renewal of the covenant, he will give his people the ability to be faithful to it, which their awareness of sin* will make possible. Where biblical anthropomorphism is principally transcended is perhaps in this excess of forgiveness: "I will not execute my burning anger (...) for I am God and not a man" (Hos 11:9). Jer (31:31) calls it the "new covenant." Israel then wonders about God's compassion toward its rightful sufferers.

2. The New Testament

The God of the New Testament makes himself known through the voices of those who spread the "good news" (gospel), which is destined first of all for Israel (Rom 1:16), then for the whole of humankind. The announced novelty consists in the fact that God gives himself entirely to his Son Jesus. Now, this gift has further repercussions: "How will he not also with him [his Son] graciously give us all things?" (Rom 8:32).

a) Difference in God. Jesus' relationship with God can be understood in the difference. Jesus has taken his place among the Jews who worship God. When called "good," Jesus points out that only God is good. Dying, he cries out: "My God, My God" (see Jn 20:17b). In reply (Heb 5:7) the Father (designated as "God") raises Jesus from the dead (Acts 3:14ff.), exalts him (Acts 5:31), makes him Lord and Christ (Acts 2:36), and makes him Leader and Savior (Acts 5:31; *see* Rom 1:4 "proved that Jesus is the powerful Son of God").

b) Divine Unity and Unicity. This difference is that between a "Father" and a "Son." The character of Jesus' filiation* is unique (monogenesis*). In Jesus, God has "his own Son" (Rom 8:32), his beloved Son. No other expression of the relationship between God and Jesus has been so widely turned into a theme as that of their paternity-filiation: the life given by God is the life received by Jesus. It is only Jesus' way of being that fully reveals what the condition of son of God is, and thus "equal with God" (Phil 2:6). To be son is not to be slave. The synoptic Gospels make this visible already through of the Son's regal style: "But I tell you" (Mt 5), his liberating "authority*" (Mt 7:29; Mk 1:27), his daring to absolve sinners, the biblically unprecedented calls to suffer "because of me" (Mt 5:11). John takes it all up schematically: "No man ever spoke like this man" (7:46). Those who hear the speech see the actions: "Whoever has seen me has seen the Father" (Jn 14:9). The Son can reveal the Father without reserve because the Father, this God without jealousy, "shows him all that he himself is doing" (Jn 5:20). "All that I have is yours, and all that you have is mine" (Jn 17:10); this authorizes the New Testament's most radical statements, such as "I and the Father are one" (Jn 10:30) or the "My Lord and my God" (Jn 20:28), addressed to the risen Jesus. A hymn borrowed by Paul puts the name of Jesus alongside the name formerly revealed to Moses: "above every name" (Phil 2:9). The divine essence, by remaining attached to a narrative series, confirms its own unicity, symbolized by the theme of the name: "...your name, which you have given me," says the Son (Jn 17:12; *see* Jn 6:27: the "seal" of the Father).

c) The Work of the Son. God is not fully known as long as the ambivalence is not resolved, the veil lifted with which he had wished to cover himself during the time of his "forbearance" (Rom 3:26). The era of biblical slowness is over: Jesus does indeed follow the rhythm that tells him his "hour" has come, but this hour precipitates the victory of the light and tears the veil. In his son, God himself does more than pardon: he delivers himself without resistance into the hands of sinners, experiencing the evil that he heals. The Pauline teachings will show that the cross reveals with shattering clarity the way in which sin and death* have made use of the law for their own benefit. As can already be discerned in the Old Testament, God's way of experiencing human history continues right to the end. Darkness can only be vanquished by being walked through. The excess which tears the veil of the old law is also the very one that the whole Old Testament heralded. It is in the forgiveness that turns the instrument of malediction, the cross, into an instrument of salvation* destined first of all for those who have desired it, that God definitively reveals who he is, without need for any later additions.

d) "All who are led by the spirit of God are sons of God" (Rom 8:14). The hour of Jesus draws brothers into the filiation that is his own. The specific nature of the gift of the Holy* Spirit offered to human beings signifies that "brothers" are at the same time "children" (*tekna*: Jn 13:33; *paidia*: Heb 2:13f.); but also something other than simply Jesus' heirs or continuators during the course of history, and more than disciples (Jn 6:45; 16:12f.): they breathe the same life-truth that Jesus had received, it is through liberty* that they share the condition of son that belongs to this Jesus whom they call "Master and Lord" (Jn 13:13). This still incomplete expansion of the filial condition gives, or will give, its full magnitude to the divine work.

God does not withdraw from time. The capacity of the biblical God to reveal himself as having been there already will also apply to the Father of Jesus Christ. For that to come about, an era of patience reopens. The discursive undertaking of a rereading which relates the two Testaments to each other makes possible the broad propagation of the gospel message, and above all ensures its penetration in depth. This message not only wins adherents to a new religion, it discloses its prehistory. The Gospel* of John recounts in particular how the coming of the Word* made flesh reveals the work that the Father was doing, before that advent of the Word, among the "children of God who are scattered abroad" (Jn 11:52), in every human group that is "not of this fold" (Jn 10:16): "Everyone who is [already] of the truth listens to my voice" (Jn 18:37; *see* 3:21). The bipolarity, which the Old Testament had outlined, between the God of a singular series and the God of all people is adopted again as a promise.

● W. Thüsing (1986), Per Christum in Deum. D*as Verhältnis der Christozentrik zur Theozentrik*, 3rd Ed., Münster.
J. Schlosser (1987), *Le Dieu de Jésus: Étude exégétique*, Paris.
H. Cazelles (1989), *La Bible et son Dieu*, Paris.
H. Niehr (1990), *Der Höchste Gott*, BZAW 190.
J. Briend (1992), *Dieu dans l'Écriture*, Paris.
A. de Pury, "Le Dieu qui vient en adversaire: De quelques différences à propos de la perception de Dieu dans l'Ancien Testament", in R. Kuntzmann (Ed.) (1995), *Ce Dieu qui vient*, 45–68, Paris.
J. Schreiner (1995), *Theologie des alten Testaments*, Würzburg.

PAUL BEAUCHAMP

See also **Anthropomorphism; Father; Monotheism; Name; Theophany; Word of God**

II. Patristic Theology

1. Preliminary Remarks
The theology* of the fathers* of the church was organized at first as a discourse on God the Father of Jesus Christ, to become with Augustine* a theory of God the Trinity. God is of course the God of the Jews (Justin, *Dialogue* 11, 1) and of the pagans, but he is known in a new way (Tertullian*, *Adversus Praxean* 31, 2; Clement of Alexandria, *Stromata* VI, 5, 41–42). There is a central paradox: God is both alone and not alone,

single and multiple (Tertullian, *Adversus Praxean* 5, 2; Hippolytus, *Contra Haeresin Noeti* 10). The Father cannot be named without also naming along with him his Son and his Holy Spirit, which are like his "two hands" (Irenaeus*, *Adversus Haereses* IV, 7, 4; 20, 2). The Son, in his turn, cannot be named without the world and human beings entering into the theme: for "God is love*" (1 Jn 4:8, 1 Jn 4:16), and loving human beings constitutes his "distinguishing characteristic" (Gregory of Nyssa, *Catechetical Orations* 15).

The Christian God is both like and unlike the Absolute known by paganism*. In pagan thought there reigns an absolute transcendence with which one can only communicate through mediators, within a hierarchical system. But the Christian God is a personal God, whose transcendence does not forbid proximity and who appears in history as "Emmanuel," "God with us." In paganism, moreover, the Absolute—Plotinus's "the One," for instance—necessarily engenders, "like an overflowing crater" (Gregory of Nyssa, *Catechetical Orations* 29, 4; *see Enneads* V, 1, 6), or more precisely he does not engender but radiates (this is, the second hypostasis which "engenders" the Forms or the Ideas: *see* P. Hadot in Plotinus, *Treatise* 38, 1987). He gives nothing, and above all does not give "himself." By contrast, the God who is Father of Jesus is the bearer in himself of a mystery* of donation and of alterity in which is rooted another type of alterity, the creation*. In this, theology very early recognized a new sign of transcendence (creation *ex nihilo*: Hermas, *The Shepherd* 26, 1 [Mand. 1]; *see* G. May, *Schöpfung aus dem Nichts,* Berlin, 1978). In order to be understood, the church fathers' expositions on God must not be separated from a double context: the name of "God" applies to the Father, the Son, and the Holy Spirit, and "theology," which is the contemplation* of God in God, is inseparable from the "economy" in which God manifests his love for human beings, his *philanthrôpia* (Titus 3:4).

2. Before Nicaea I
God was spoken about in the daily life of the Church, in its catechetical and cultural experience, before he was discussed in the works of theologians: therefore the oldest language* (and a language that theologians would be able to use almost permanently) was that of the Easter kerygma, of doxology, of the baptismal liturgies* associating Father, Son, and Holy Spirit. But since the goal of Christian language was not only to allow believers to testify to and verify as a community what they believed, but was also a language aimed at non-Christians, Christianity would not be able to avoid using the words and arguments that seemed the most universal, those of philosophy*. The Apostolic* Fa-

thers already casually employed a lexicon imbued with a philosophical tone (Clement of Rome, *Correspondence*, 20 and 24, 5; Ignatius of Antioch, *Polyc.* 3, 2; *Eph.* 7, 2). Begun in fact before the Christian era (by thinkers such as Philo of Alexandria), the confrontation of biblical faith* with Greek rationality became necessary among the fathers with the advent of the apologists*. Thus, Justin commended the practice of idolatry for the sake of a purer conception of God, of whom he saw traces among the pagans themselves (*Apol.* I, 5 and 46; II, 8–11). Moreover, he transferred certain features of the God of late Greek philosophy onto the God of Jesus Christ: God receives the titles of unbegotten (*agennètos*) and of impassible, and is placed at a distance from the world. It becomes unthinkable that the unbegotten "should have left the super-celestial regions in order to appear in a corner of the world" (*Dial.* 60 and 127). It is not him but his Word who appeared in the Old Testament (*Dial.* 60–61; 127–128; *Apol.* I, 63). When the apologists state that God possesses a creative power that allows him to come into contact with what is not him, they are therefore making almost the same statement as the philosophers—but by identifying this power with Jesus of Nazareth (Daniélou 1961), they simultaneously distance themselves as far as possible from philosophy's conceptual framework.

If it had to be proved that there is no ambivalence between the Christian and the philosophical naming of God, it also had to be proved that the God known in Jesus Christ was a God already known in the Old Testament. To counter Marcionite and Gnostic dualism, Irenaeus of Lyons stated forcibly that the same God is creator and savior, the God of Israel and the Father of Jesus, God both just and good, uniting in himself superficially irreconcilable attributes*. No other God stands above him, for he encompasses and dominates everything (*Adv. Haer.* II, i, 1–4). Here we stand at the origins of the first affirmation of the symbols of the faith ("I believe in one God, the Father, the Almighty," *see* Irenaeus, ibid. I, 10, 1, *Apostolic Tradition* 85 [SC 11 *bis*, p. 85]; *DS* 1–15, 125, 150). In addition to its anti-Judaism, Gnosticism represented a second challenge for theology: it claimed specifically to have a knowledge of God (a "gnosis") superior to faith. In Irenaeus's terms, the gnosis claimed to know God *according to his greatness* and thus came to a deadlock, for no one can see God thus and live (Ex 33, 20). On the other hand, *according to his love*, God is "seen by man, by those he chooses, when he chooses, and how he chooses" (*Adv. Haer.* IV, 20, 5): it is in the element of faith that he is known then, through the "various divine economies" which he chooses in order to allow himself be known (ibid. I, 10, 3; II, 28, 1–3; IV, 20, 5–7).

Among the pre-Nicene fathers it fell to Origen* to make the most systematic and speculative propositions, and perhaps also to use simultaneously the most philosophical as well as the most biblical language. Origen borrowed from Clement of Alexandria (for instance *Strom.* V, 12–13) a necessary insistence on God's unknowability. He also shared the Greek understanding according to which the infinite* is unthinkable as such, unthinkable without a determination. But since the divine paternity stands foremost in his axiomatics, to speak of the Father "without limits" (*apeiros, aperigraphos*) is only possible by speaking simultaneously of the Son who is his "delimitation" (*perigraphè*) and thus makes him knowable and shareable (*see* Irenaeus, *Adv. Haer.* IV, 4, 2; IV, 6, 6; *see* the Gnostic theories, ibid., I, 2, 2, Daniélou 1961; and Crouzel, SC 253). The concepts are metaphysical, but they are in keeping with a historical framework within which the contemplation of the Son's sufferings authorizes even Origen to challenge the Greek dogma* of divine impassibility: "We must dare to say that Christ's goodness has seemed greater and *more divine* and *truly in the image of the Father* when he abased himself, making himself obedient even unto death, and unto death on the cross." (*Com. in Jo.* I, 32, §119)

A reconciliation of divine unity and the multiplicity of the created, such as the mystery of Christ, allows it to be understood (ibid. I, 20 §119); a reconciliation of divine incomprehensibility and the revelation in Jesus Christ of God's paternal secret—it is very clear in Origen that theology cannot speak of God and of his relationship with man without developing a trinitarian discourse. Even if Origen's trinitarian theology suffers from a certain subordinationism* (for instance ibid. XIII, 25, §151–53)—which would be reinforced later by Eusebius of Caesarea and even more so by Arius— in any event, the language used is Christian through and through.

3. After Nicaea I

It fell to Athanasius* of Alexandria, the greatest of the Nicene theologians, to develop a trinitarian discourse that could not fall back into the old ruts of modalism* or into subordinationism, and that could refute the Arian conception of the intermediary, of the Son that God produced in order to produce the world (*Contra Arianos II*, 24, PG 26, 200A). The Son is not a son in order to be a demi-god: "Even if God had thought it well not to create the world, nonetheless he would have had his Son" (ibid. II, 31). The trinitarian mystery of God is, moreover, a shareable mystery: "Not only has God created men, but even more so he has also called them 'sons,' in the sense that he has engendered them" (ibid. II, 39). One cannot speak about God in a Christian context without also speaking about man, because it is in the christological unity of the human and the divine that the divine can be most fully apprehended. What is more, it is of all human beings that one must speak when speaking about God, for the divine relationship between Father and Son is an open relationship, in which room is made for a "filial adoption" that realizes an assumption of the created within the Trinity.

Nicene theology was to extend and refine itself in the theology of the Cappadocian Fathers, to whom first of all we owe the refinement of the trinitarian vocabulary: unicity of the divine *substance,* triplicity of the *hypostases.* These expressions would govern all the affirmations of divine unity. The classic questions about knowledge and participation had to undergo a similar refinement in the controversy with Eunomius. According to the latter, in fact, man can know God as God knows himself (Socrates, *Hist. eccl.* IV, 7, PG 67 B; *see* SC 28 *bis,* nn. 4, 12), but no one, not even the Son, can share in him. Gregory of Nyssa's response first of all made it possible for him to formulate a theory of grace* that makes thinkable the participation of the created in the uncreated through the Son's mediation. Furthermore, it allowed him to maintain the absolute unknowability of the being* of God (of his *ousia*), while at the same time conferring a positive meaning to the confrontation between man and divine infinity. In fact the infinity of the *ousia* corresponds to a desire to which the divinity of God opens a limitless field: that is why Moses, "having set his feet on the ladder at the top of which stood God, does not stop climbing, for each rung which he reaches in the heights always opens onto a beyond" (*Life of Moses* II). Thus, theological science has always to be accompanied by a certain nescience. But if God's grandeur is the gauge of our scanty knowledge, God's grace and condescension contain the conditions for a fortunate knowledge and relationship, in the eschatological perspective of man's eternal ecstasy toward God.

Augustine's speculation began in the context of Neoplatonism, the schema of "exit" *(proodos),* of "conversion*" *(epistrophè)* and of "dwelling" *(monè)* in God thus providing the framework for a consideration of the ascent toward God, of anagogy. All the same, post-Nicene demands soon forced him to have recourse to a consideration of analogy* (O. du Roy, *L'intelligence de la foi en la Trinité selon Saint Augustin,* 1966), in which man's spiritual life* is the complete image of divine life, in such a way that it becomes possible to speak about God in the terms that rational psychology uses to speak about human beings. Moreover, making a distinction, with regard to God, between the "absolute" names which are suitable for the three divine persons* and the "relative" names which characterize each of them in their relation to the

two others, Augustine imposed a theory of relation, coordinated in his case with a notion of the divine substance, a notion destined to dominate Western theology. He also had to distance himself from Plotinus's conceptualizations by making a major decision: unlike Plotinus, he would no longer place above everything an Absolute which was "beyond being"; rather, in line with a metaphysics of "degrees of being," doubtless inspired by Porphyry, he would place above everything the God-Trinity identified with the Supreme Good and with Being (*Sermon* 7; *Civ. Dei* XI, 28; *see* du Roy 1966; Madec, *La patrie et la voie,* Paris, 1989; Solignac, *Les Confessions,* BAug).

The tradition of Plotinus, received in the context of thinking in terms of "exit" and " return," *exitus* et *redditus* (Proclus), was to find in Dionysius* the Pseudo-Areopagite its most remarkable sphere of influence. Theology divides at this point: on the one hand into a theology of affirmation (cataphatic), which sets out the manifestations of God with regard to human beings; and on the other hand into a theology of negation (apophatic), in which human beings go beyond the content of what they understand in order to strain in ecstasy toward union with God. Richer than the affirmative way, the apophatic path differs from the former notably in that it has far less to do with any kind of discursive-conceptual practice than with an experience. Whether apophatic knowledge is considered as Pseudo-Dionysius's last word (Lossky 1944), or whether it is understood as a stage on the way toward a third moment, that of going beyond by means of eminence (Puech, *En quête de la gnose I,* 1978), or whether going beyond by means of eminence itself is based on the mystery of Christ taken in its integral aspects (Corbin, *RSPhTh* 69, 65–75), one aspect of the Dionysian contribution remains primary and incontestable: in short, if one can "speak about God," exactness demands an admission that one is speaking about the "mystery of God"; and if therefore theology proves itself adapted to its object by making itself a "mystic" theology, it is to experience*—to the experience of the one who allows himself to be initiated into the mystery—that God offers himself, and for this experience, God is not the one about whom it speaks but the one whom it "honors in silence."

The end of the patristic era and of Byzantine theology would see confirmed in a few great creative syntheses the work of the previous centuries. For Maximus* the Confessor the paradox of the Christian God appeared even stronger in the light of Chalcedonian Christology*: God shows himself to be still more God not only because he is both one and triune, but also because in Christ comes to pass the union without confusion or separation of the one and the multiple (*Quest. ad Thal* 60; *Letter* 44; *Quaestiones et* *dubia* q. 173, CCG 10). God appears in Christ in total truth, as the trinitarian lord of the universe. Man appears in Christ in total truth, as the adoptive son existing in the image of the eternal Son. One problem still remains, that of the real condition of the divinization, *theôsis,* that God proposes to man as his absolute future. How could the unsharable be shared? Pseudo-Dionysius contented himself with naming the problem: "It is shared unsharably." In the twilight of Byzantine history, Gregory* Palamas would try to solve the problem by applying to it in a new way a distinction already known by the Greek Fathers: a distinction between the divine essence, which remains strictly unsharable, and the "uncreated energies," which divinize the one who shares in them. Doubtless the theory's originality is less important than the permanence of the preoccupations to which it responds. Patristic thought, and the thinking to which it gave rise, never ceased to meditate on God's transcendence except to meditate on a condescension that they knew to be just as great: trinitarian theology, Christology, the theory of divinization, all the patristic discourses aim to express the necessity of this double meditation, as it is imposed by knowledge of a God who is recognized as Father in the Son who became one among human beings.

● J. Lebreton (1928), *Histoire du dogme de la Trinité,* vol. 2, Paris.
G.L. Prestige (1936), *God in Patristic Thought,* London (2nd Ed. 1952).
Vl. Lossky (1944), *Théologie mystique de l'Église d'Orient,* Paris.
J. Daniélou (1961), *Message évangélique et culture hellénistique,* Paris (2nd Ed. 1990).
A.H. Wolfson (1964), *The Philosophy of the Church Fathers,* 2nd Ed., Cambridge, MA.
R.M. Grant (1966), *The Early Christian Doctrine of God,* Charlottesville.
R.A. Norris (1966), *God and the World in Early Christian Theology,* London.
A.H. Armstrong (Ed.) (1967), *The Cambridge History of Later Greek and Early Medieval Philosophy,* Cambridge.
W. Pannenberg (1967), "Die Aufnahme des philosophischen Gottesbegriffes als dogmatisches Problem der frühchristlichen Theologie", *Grundfr. syst. Th.,* 196–346.
J. Pelikan (1971), *The Christian Tradition,* vol. 1, Chicago.
C. Stead (1977), *Divine Substance,* Oxford.
C. Stead (1994), *Philosophy in Christian Antiquity,* Cambridge.

JOSEPH WOLINSKI

See also **Dionysius the Pseudo-Areopagite; Gregory Palamas; Negative Theology; Platonism, Christian**

III. Medieval Theology

1. The Name

In the Middle Ages the name of "God" (God = *theos*) was associated with two origins: *theorô* ("I see:": Pseudo-Dionysius, *Divine Names XII,* 2, 969 C) to re-fer to the coincidence between the divine vision and the creative act; or *theô* ("I run"), to indicate the cosmogonic course of the Word touching all beings to give them life (John the Scot Eriugena, *De divisione naturae*). God's unicity, revealed by the Bible* as well as by the Koran and confirmed by Neoplatonic speculations, renders problematical the use of the name in the plural: God is a proper name; it is improper, idolatrous, meaningless, to speak about several "gods" (William of Auxerre, *Summa aurea*). But is it the name that is most proper to God himself? Under the influence of Maimonides this status came to be reserved for the name YHWH, the only name that is but God (Bonaventure*, *Sentences* I), that human beings cannot utter, and that God alone knows. God can be named only by God, that is why he reveals himself in the Scriptures* by names whose multiplicity compensates for this partial approach. Following Augustine, a primary distinction is made between the "name of substance" ("whose name is 'I am'," Ex 3:14) and the "name of mercy*" ("the God who was worshipped by Abraham, Isaac, and Jacob," Ex 3:16), thus coordinating divine economy and theology.

2. Knowledge and Revelation

Knowledge* of God is a response to divine revelation. But God does not reveal himself in the Holy Scriptures alone. He also reveals himself in his work, the "book of the world" (Hugh of Saint Victor, PL 176, *De arca Noe morali* II, 12; *Didascalicon* VII, 3, 814 B). Creatures are "mystical likenesses," making possible the contemplation of their author (Baldwin of Canterbury, *De sacramento altaris,* PL 204, 744 D). Thus a symbolic theology unfolds, for which nature* is a system of correspondences that expresses the glory* of God. The very structure of the theology articulated around the opposition between things and signs (Peter Lombard, *Sententiae I,* Grottaferrata, 1971, d. 1) makes God the Signified par excellence in all creation. The medieval encyclopedias shared in this work of listing and understanding the divine works, in order to better know their author.

For Augustinian tradition it was by retreating inside his soul* that man could best reach the one of whom he was the image: through the image, he would glimpse the original (Augustine*). Socrates's injunction, "Know thyself," thus became the way to know God (Courcelle 1975). God is therefore in the depths of the soul, more elevated than the soul, but reached through its highest point. Union with God can be achieved through two of the soul's faculties, intellect or love (intellectualism*, voluntarism*). "Charity itself is the eye by which God is seen" (William of Saint Thierry, *La nature et la dignité de l'amour*). In a more veiled but fundamental way, God is also reached in an ethical and emotional dimension, as the one who is the object of the desire for God, or of the fear of him. Adopted in a theological context, these qualities imply that he is present and knowable through fraternal love: "Fraternal love is God," said Peter Lombard (*Sententiae* I).

Knowledge of God culminates in the admission of his unknowability: he surpasses any image (William of Saint Thierry, *Meditativae orationes*), he is incomprehensible (Alexander of Hales, *Summa theologica* I), inaccessible (Bonaventure, *Hexaemeron*). But formulating this unknowability remains the only way of understanding it; to think about God is not only to think about something greater than all else (*majus omnibus*), but to test the unthinkable (*quo maius cogitari nequit*, Anselm*), to know God as unknown (Thomas* Aquinas).

For this *learned ignorance* (Nicholas* of Cusa), the highest speculation about God attains the same object as does the simple believer's faith. However, it implies a survey of inappropriate positions, and a critique of naive, magical, or anthropological elements. It is theology's task, therefore, to separate the concept of God from the metaphors, the narrative interlacings, and the textual contradictions. Thus, the *translatio in divinis* never ceases to test human language, submitting it to logical rules in order to reach in a fitting way God's nature and attributes (Boethius*). Several "paths" intended to purify our knowledge of its finite imperfections and to raise them to a pure perfection converge at their summit: it is necessary to sort out what is said about God without truth and what is said about him with truth, even if the latter be denied with more truth (Pseudo-Dionysius, *Divine Names*, I, 3). A distinction must be made between: the image of God and what is only its trace* (its more or less erased vestiges); proper names and names that are metaphorical, foreign, or improper; and the absolute perfections (*simpliciter*) that are better than their negations, and which can be attributed to God ("better than everything which is not him," according to Anselm), and mixed perfections, which can be attributed to certain beings, but not to God (analogy*). These paths are integrated in several ways, sometimes by stressing God's unknowable transcendence, beyond every perfection (Rhineland*-Flemish mysticism, Nicholas of Cusa), sometimes by stressing the constitution of a transcendental concept applicable to God envisaged as the maximum of perfections (John Duns* Scotus: "We do not love negations in a sovereign way," *Ordinatio* I).

3. Principle, Middle, and End

According to a Platonic schema, God is often characterized as principle, mediator, and end of the universe as he is of human existence. "What then is God? For the universe, the end; for choice*, salvation*; for himself, he knows what." (Bernard* of Clairvaux, *De consideratione, Opera omnia*)

The ultimate end, God is the one who can only be enjoyed *(frui)* and never exhausted as a means *(uti)*, the one toward whom the whole cosmos* and all human action reach, he is beatitude*, glimpsed here below through shadowy sketches, and which will be fully grasped only in the celestial homeland. As principle, God is creator, such that his capacity to create and to preserve the world suffices to reveal his nature. "Whatever creature comes along, if they make such a heaven and such an earth, I shall say they are God" (Peter Lombard, *Sententiae*). God's nature is studied first in a reflection on the Trinity, essential in the confrontation with Judaism* and Islam: the unity of the essence that, following Augustine and Boethius, is distinguished from the trinity of persons, makes possible a speculation on God's existence and his nature. If God is said to be "substance," it is in a sense that transcends the limits of this category, since it cannot lend itself to accidents. Of a spiritual nature, he is characterized as life, sovereign good, perfection, and above all, charity: by essence, God loves himself and all things, the good he does and not the evil that we do. Thus, his attributes are truth*, immutability*, simplicity*, such that all that is in God is God, including his operations: prescience (divine knowledge*), providence*, omnipresence*, predestination* (justice* and mercy*), omnipotence*, and will (in the order given in Peter Lombard's *Sententiae,* and their commentaries). His relationship with the world presents the problem of non-reciprocal relations between eternity and time*: although God is in himself "Lord" of all eternity, he is not the "ruler of the world" until after the creation (Alexander of Hales, *Summa theologica*).

As mediator, God wills the salvation of human beings, and he alone can restore them to the image of God. The history of salvation is thus marked by long stages, and is understood according to a trinitarian rhythm, following Joachim* of Fiore and Bonaventure*: a reign of the Father (creation, revelation), of the Son (incarnation), of the Holy Spirit (in grace* and in the sacraments*). The questions then become: can one say that "God is [a] man," or is it only the person of the Word who unites himself with humanity? (Peter Lombard, *Sententiae*). Can God suffer? Is he really present in the Eucharist*? The autonomous development of a theology of essence made these questions all the more pressing.

4. Birth of a Natural Theology

Scholasticism* assimilated the philosophical theology of Antiquity (Proclus, *Elements of Theology*) and found itself confronting Jewish and Islamic theology (Maimonides and Avicenna respectively). After its confrontation with the logic and grammatical disciplines, Scholasticism turned theology into a scientific discipline. The possibility of a philosophical theology, then of a theological philosophy, is founded on Romans 1:20, interpreted by Peter Lombard's *Gloss* (PL 191, 1327). Natural theology gradually separated itself from the economy of salvation and from speculation about the Trinity to acquire its own autonomy. From the 13th century onward, knowledge through faith became detached from the Scriptures and the world, setting up a third form of revelation (Alexander of Hales, in I *Sent.*).

This move was characterized by the constitution of "God" in a concept, distinct from everyday, natural, and religious usages. In the first place, he is often replaced by a proper term developed by the theologian in his speculation on God. This trend is visible as early as Anselm *(Monologion),* with the concepts of *summa essentia, summus spiritus, ipsum bonum.* Each theologian would thus deploy his own proper name for God, allowing him to contemplate God's existence, nature, and main attributes: *ipsum esse* in Thomas Aquinas's case, *Necesse esse* for Henry of Ghent, *ens infinitum* for John Duns Scotus (*De primo principio,* Bonaventure), and, more idiosyncratically, *maximum et minimum,* "Non-other," or even the untranslatable *possest,* in Nicholas of Cusa *(Trialogus de possest).* A series of calls to order countered this trend of specialization in infinite scission: Bernard of Clairvaux denounced Abelard*'s use of logic, Bonaventure thundered against the masters of arts, Gerson demanded the return to current vocabulary ("Letter to Pierre d'Ailly"). These theologians thus emphasized that the God of the believers possessed attributes unknown to the philosophers, such as liberty, love, and omnipotence (Damian, *Letter on Divine Omnipotence,* SC 191). The concept constructed by philosophical reason alone diverged increasingly from the God known through revelation.

Secondly, this plurality of divine names was confronted by the ontological affirmation of God. Since God's names must transcend the limits of the finite meanings of being, they are acceptable only to the extent that they express the attribute transcendentally. Thus, the Augustinian school favors the True; a Pseudo-Dionysian trend prefers to speak about God as Good, rather than as Being (Bonaventure, *Itinerarium Mentis in Deum*); another, Proclusian, school of thought named him as One (Dietrich of Freiburg, Berthold of Moosburg); yet another, blending Aristotelianism and Platonism*, would speak about Being itself (Thomas Aquinas). But they all ran the risk of being reduced to the existing (*ens*) in general, even if it were distinguished as infinite (John Duns Scotus). One way of transcending the transcendental itself was then to imagine God as nothingness* (John the Scot Eriugena, *De Divisione Naturae,* Hadewijch of Antwerp, Eckhart, Suso, Angela di Foligno).

Thirdly, scholastic theology increasingly constructed a priori the philosophical name of God, to the point of forming a true natural* theology: reason* alone possesses the principles that make it possible to demonstrate God's existence and nature. While Thomas Aquinas's five paths left to faith the job of acknowledging the unity of their five respective goals, and their identity with "what everyone calls God" (*ST* Ia, q.2, a, 3), Henry of Ghent stressed the necessity of starting from a previous concept that implied a priori "God's" unicity and singularity. With Henry, then with John Duns Scotus, the a posteriori proof simply verified the existence of a term corresponding to the concept. God is reached metaphysically, independently from all cosmology, as the "first principle" in conformity with his concept. John Duns Scotus's *Tractatus de Primo Principio* (c. 1308) completed this journey by presenting the first autonomous metaphysical treatise about God. Nicholas of Cusa brought out its implications: the thought of God becomes a conception of the Concept (*Idiota de sapientia, Opera omnia* V), and God is absorbed into the thought that engenders him. Ockham (*Quodlibeta septem, Opera theologica IX*), Bonaventure, then the Nominalists* would deny that the proof of God reached the one God—thus confirming the split between theology and philosophy.

● J. Kilgenstein (1898), *Die Gotteslehre des Hugo von St Viktor,* Würzburg.

M. Chossat (1911), "Dieu (connaissance naturelle de)," *DThC* 4/1, 756–874.

S. Guichardan (1933), *Le problème de la simplicité divine, en Orient et en Occident au XIVe et au XVe siècle: Grégoire Palamas, Duns Scot, Georges Scholarios,* Lyon.

M. Schmaus (1935), "Die Gotteslehre des Augustinus Triumphus nach seinem Sentenzenkommentar," in Albert Lang, Joseph Lechner, and Michael Schmaus (Ed.), *Aus der Geisteswelt des Mittelalters: Studien und Texte Martin Grabmann zur vollendung des 60. Lebensjahres von Freunden und Schülern gewidmet,* Münster, 896–935.

J. Déchanet (1945), "Amor ipse intellectus est", *RMAL* 1, 350–374.

H. de Lubac (1956), *Sur les chemins de Dieu,* Paris.

J. Leclercq (1956), *L'amour des lettres et le désir de Dieu,* Paris.

Vl. Lossky (1960), *Théologie négative et connaissance de Dieu chez Maître Eckhart,* Paris.

A. Lang (1962), *Die Entfaltung des apologetischen Problems in der Scholastik des Mittelalters,* Friburg.

E. Gössmann (1964), *Metaphysik und Heilsgeschichte: Eine theologische Untersuchung der Summa Halensis,* Munich.

U. Horst (1964), *Die Trinitäts- und Gotteslehre des Robert von Melun,* Mainz.

A.C. Pegis (1968 *Sq*), "Toward a New Way to God: Henry of Ghent", *MS* 30, 226–247; 31, 93–116; 33, 158–176.

E. Gössmann (1971), *Glaube und Gotteserkenntnis im Mittelalter*, Friburg.

K. Flasch (1974), "Gott VI. Mittelalter," *HWP* 3, 741–748.

L. Oeing-Hanhoff (1974), "Gotteserkenntnis im Licht der Vernunft und des Glaubens nach Thomas von Aquin," in L. Oeing-Hanhoff (Ed.), *Thomas von Aquin, 1274–1974,* Munich, 97–124.

P. Courcelle (1975), *"Connais-toi toi-même": de Socrate à saint Bernard,* Paris.

P. Vignaux (1976), *De saint Anselme à Luther,* Paris.

E. Zum Brunn, Z. Kaluza, A. de Libera et al. (1984), *Maître Eckhart à Paris: une critique médiévale de l'ontothéologie,* Paris.

É. Gilson (1932), *L'esprit de la philosophie médiévale,* Paris.

A. B. Wolter (1990), *The Philosophical Theology of John Duns Scotus,* Ithaca.

S. T. Bonino (Ed.) (1995), "Saint Thomas et l'onto-th.," RThom 95/1.

OLIVIER BOULNOIS

See also **Aristotelianism; Deity; Existence of God, Proofs of; Negative Theology; Rhineland-Flemish Mysticism; Scholasticism**

IV. Reformation and Modern Theology

1. From Luther to the Protestant Orthodoxies

The theological controversies sparked off by the Reformation had no effect on the content of the trinitarian and christological confession: in these areas Luther* took over in its totality the legacy of patristic and medieval theology. All the same, the seamless continuity of a confession of faith cannot lead to neglect of the fact that the order of reasons was subjected to profound upheavals. In fact it was Christology, and more particularly the theology of the cross, that provided Luther with a focus for theological organization. God is indeed firstly the transcendent lord of history, the omnipotent and sovereign will on whom everything depends, and in whose hands creatures are mere "puppets." But if there is a theology that assigns itself the mission of speculating on the inaccessible lord of creation—a *theologica gloriae*—this theology suffers from a deficit: it cannot know God's love, and it can only acknowledge that the Almighty is also, christologically, the All-Near. Now, it is indeed charity and the nearness of God that matter when theology is articulated as the "theology of the cross," *theologica crucis.* The God revealed through his opposite on the cross of Christ, the God to whom only faith gives access, it was this "burning furnace filled with love" that Luther experienced, and it was its paradoxical manifestation that he thematized. All natural knowledge is excluded: it is in Christ, and nowhere else, that God entrusts his promises, proves his fidelity, and reveals his trinitarian secret. Not only is theology alone able to speak about God, but it can also only do so by basing itself on a christological contemplation.

A shared fundamental agreement about the faith confessed by the Church, together with a new outline of theology's path, was also encountered in Calvin*— and this new outline did not always meet the Lutheran path. Divine majesty and glory were the key concepts. Calvin's God was primarily the one who had created everything for his glory, and whose glory, in conformity with the doctrine of double predestination (and in opposition to Lutheran indeterminism), revealed itself as much in the election of some as in the reprobation of others. Divine proximity was therefore absent from this theology; and it would be one of Calvinism*'s constant tasks, faced with Lutheranism*, to propose a Christology in which, in the name of the founding principle that wanted the finite to be incapable of harboring the infinite *(finitum non capax infiniti),* God would reveal himself in any event as the Almighty. Here again, the thought is strictly theological, and natural reason can only attain fruitless knowledge. But it was undeniably another image of God that was provided. Such a theocentrism was present in Zwingli*, where it was additionally fed by humanist influences. As for Bucer's theology, first structured as a theology of the Holy Spirit, it would evolve later toward a christocentrism.

The Reformers' primordial intuitions had to undergo a certain marginalization from the second half of the 16th century onward. Melanchthon's *Loci*—the first of the Protestant dogmatics—exhibit, during the course of their redevelopments, a return to favor of the theoretical moves that Luther and Calvin had excluded. The proofs of the existence* of God regained there a rightful theological place; Luther's insistence on the "hidden God" was recalled, but exerted no strong influence; lastly, the systematic scaffolding tended to obfuscate Luther's primarily existential interests. Later, Protestant theology would turn into a new Scholasticism, which certainly owed its confession of faith to the Reformers, but which also owed a good part of its conceptual trappings to post-Tridentine Catholic theology, and to Suarez* principally, while at the same time it marked a new chapter in the history of Christian Aristotelianism*.

2. The God of the Enlightenment

Although at the dawn of modern theology God appeared as omnipotence and love, classical rationalism* did not fail to influence theology in its own turn. From Descartes* to Leibniz* and Wolff, the God of the philosophers did not experience any great metamorphosis with regard to his classical or medieval forms, when he was conceived as supreme power or supreme reason. Nonetheless, this God, who is also God the warrantor of a perfect mathematization of the real (he is also Newton's God) would enter theology without any part of his concept being thought through again. Enlightenment theology was very willing to be *theologica more geometrico demonstrata;* its God would borrow more than one major trait from the God of theism (deism*). The notion of God's omnipotence in creation therefore tended to overshadow any sense of a historical revelation. Divine love was largely interpreted in terms of a universal benevolence, which itself tended logically to preclude any possibility of divine wrath. In the face of the avowed reality of evil, the question of providence acquired an urgency that it had never had before: and if it was a matter of admiring the universe, as science revealed it, it was just as much a matter of acquitting a God being tried by human suffering. Natural knowledge of God ended up by becoming the focus of theology—and even more so in Protestantism* than in Catholicism*. From "physico-theology" to "neology" and to strict "rationalism," an exemplary path thus envisaged the theological crowning of the God of pure reason—a God who was perhaps nothing more than the apotheosis of the enlightened intellectual.

3. The God of Feeling

The 17th and 18th centuries were not only an age of pure reason and of theological rationalism*. As early as the mid-17th century the divorce pronounced by Pascal* between the "God of Abraham, Isaac, and Jacob" and the "God of the philosophers and scholars" was pregnant with a theological task that relaunched the Reformation's initial impulses. This task was to define itself steadily, and doubtless be diverted, when Pietism* arose to ask theology to speak to it of a God "felt in the heart" (soul*-heart-body). Beyond confessional barriers, the "emotional transposition of doctrines" (Pelikan) is thus the exact counterweight of a rationalism to which the Enlightenment, nevertheless, cannot be reduced. Here the merciful Savior counters the all-powerful Creator, the sorrowful face on the cross counters an almost faceless God; and the establishment of a close link between theological work and the spiritual experience of "regenerated" man counters a practice of theology where only the scientific/rational is of significance. Thus God intervenes as the one who moves man's emotions: once again he is that "furnace of love" of which Luther spoke, and the in-self of the divinity is important only because of what it is for me. These strains are noticeable in the work of the greatest Anglo-Saxon theologian of the century, Jonathan Edwards*, and they certainly find their most compelling (and conclusive) expression in Schleiermacher*'s work. In his *Reden über die Religion* (1799), the latter had striven to give credit to religion

from the perspective of a somewhat Rousseauist contemplation of the universe. His *Dogmatik* (1821) went considerably further. It proposed a condition for access to God, the "feeling of absolute dependence," in which man abdicates any claims to absolute autonomy: "God" acquires his meaning in the element of feeling, of the *Gefühl.* Even more importantly, everything that is said about God is only said about him obliquely, and informs us only of what feeling grasps according to its own logic. The in-self of the divinity then vanishes; and those doctrines that the theologian does not manage to topple under the influence of feelings cannot help but be marginalized—thus trinitarian theology is relegated to an appendix of the work.

4. The God of Ethics

If it was necessary for Schleiermacher to have recourse to feeling, this was because pure reason, in its use of metaphysics, no longer seemed to permit access to God. To the growing Pietism, the God of reason did not seem quite capable of inspiring piety. But Kant* had intervened between this Pietism and Schleiermacher, and after the demolition of the proofs of God's existence that was undertaken in the *Critique of Pure Reason,* the God of reason had disappeared to make way for the God of practical reason, at once moral legislator, sovereign Good, and eschatological judge. With religion reduced to morality, the result obtained by Kant could not but be accepted by rationalism, and in fact accompanied it until its disappearance, when the quarrel between rationalism and supranaturalism ended and the theological world's interest was captured by the episodes of Hegel*'s legacy. The moral God was to reappear, perhaps even more strongly, in the middle of the 19th century, when A. Ritschl (1822–89) started his polemics against "metaphysical idols." He based his theology on Christology and on the concept of love, the latter being reduced to its ethical content. Kant's God would be the God of liberal Protestantism: he was therefore the God whose death would be announced by Nietzsche*.

5. The Absolute and the Spirit

The God of pure reason certainly did not die as a result of Kant's critique, and the philosophies of German idealism were to give him currency. Thought of as "Absolute," "Absolute Idea," "Absolute Spirit," or "Lord of being," the God of Fichte, Hegel, and Schelling* is in each case the God of metaphysics, a God whose manifestation *ad extra* ("economy") requires him to be deciphered on the basis of the moment of "immanence" of the divine life, and a God who remains unknown in the realm of feelings. On the one hand, the a priori requirements of reason are once again honored: thus,

Hegel proposes an ample defense and illustration of the proofs of God's existence. On the other hand, however, Hegel's and Schelling's God (but not Fichte's) is indeed the God of Abraham, Isaac, and Jacob who has entered philosophy; a redefinition of the "philosophical" in its relations with the "theological" is at work here, and represents what is perhaps the most important intellectual event in the theology of the 19th century. All the same, Hegel had to wait until the 20th century for a theological hearing that would respect the aims and the actual contents of his texts, and the theological reception of Schelling's late texts has only begun. The history of 19th century Schellingianism is one of a strongly influential school of thought (*see* Wolf, *PhJ*, [98] 1991, 145–160), but one which almost fell into oblivion. And the history of Hegelianism* presents the pathetic spectacle of faithful and not very talented heirs (the "old Hegelians"), incapable of preventing the "young Hegelians" from proceeding to a total secularization* of the master. The same would happen to the protest made by Kierkegaard* against Hegel in the name of a subjectivity that sought the Absolute, not in history*, but in an experiential logic of faith (a protest that, moreover, should not mask the fact that both thinkers exhibited the same contempt for the classically defined boundaries of the philosophical and the theological!), with the result that it would not be properly heard until the 20th century. The 19th century remains the century of Schleiermacher.

- W. Gass (1854–64), *Die Geschichte der protestantischen Dogmatik in ihrem Zusammenhange mit der Theologie überhaupt,* 4 vols., Berlin.
K. Barth (1947), *Die protestantische Theologie im 19. Jh.,* Zurich.
E. A. Dowey (1952), *The Knowledge of God in Calvin's Theology,* New York.
Th. L. Parker (1952), *The Doctrine of the Knowledge of God: A Study in the Theology of John Calvin,* London.
E. Hirsch (1954), *Geschichte der neuern evangelischen Theologie,* 5 vols., Gütersloh.
W. A. Neuser (1957), *Der Ansatz der Theologie Philipp Melanchthons,* BGLRK 9/1, Neukirchen.
G. Ebeling (1964), *Luther: Einführung in sein Denken,* Tübingen (4th Ed. 1981).
K. H. Ratschow (1964–66), *Lutherische Dogmatik zwischen Reformation und Aufklärung,* 2 vols., Gütersloh.
J. Pelikan (1966–68) (Ed.), *Makers of Modern Theology,* 5 vols., New York.
A. Peters (1969), "Die Trinitätslehre in der reformatorischen Christenheit", *ThLZ* 94, 561–570.
U. Asendorf (1971), *Gekreuzigt und Auferstanden: Luthers Herausforderung an die moderne Christologie,* Hamburg.
R. Stauffer (1978), *Dieu, la création et la providence dans la prédication de Calvin,* Bern.
A. I. C. Heron (1980), *A Century of Protestant Theology,* Guildford.
J. Pelikan (1984, 1989), *The Christian Tradition,* vol. 4 and 5, Chicago.
J. Wallmann (1990), *Der Pietismus,* Göttingen.

See also **Being; Deism and Theism; Descartes, René; Hegel, Georg Wilhelm Friedrich; Kant, Immanuel; Kierkegaard, Soren Aabye; Luther, Martin; Pietism; Schelling, Friedrich Wilhelm Joseph von; Schleiermacher, Friedrich Daniel Ernst**

V. Contemporary Theology

1. The God of Crisis

The inaugural act of contemporary theology was unquestionably to break away from Schleiermacher and his heirs, and the manifesto of this rupture was Barth*'s *Römerbrief* (1919), a plea for divine transcendence and alterity, for faith as the only element of a just affirmation of God, and for a strict theological theocentrism. Whatever the names given to this reorientation by Barth ("dialectic theology," "crisis theology"), the return to a pure Calvinist conception of divine majesty was undeniable. "God" intervenes here as judge and critical authority in relation to what man could say about him that he has not said about himself; he intervenes as the one par excellence who cannot be appropriated, denouncing the "religious" constructions that make him a god tailored to human needs or a god measured by human experiences *(Erlebnisse)*. Thus, a hermeneutics* of feeling in its religious function (Schleiermacher) is opposed on the one hand by the Word in which God expresses himself objectively, and on the other hand by a divine inaccessibility that dooms to failure any self-transcendence of man toward God. The demolition of any anthropocentric base would be pursued methodically, and in a manner independent of all the changes of direction that Barth's thought would later take—thus his trinitarian theology would avoid the concept of person, because of the weight of anthropological reference with which modernity had loaded it, and would have recourse instead to the concept of the "mode of being," *Seinsweise*. This purification of theological language also led to a rejection of any form of natural* theology and to a fierce polemic against the concept of *analogia entis,* which was viewed as "an invention of the Anti-Christ." Only divine liberty and divine love open the field to a knowledge of God and to a discourse about God. Several thematics arising from the early Barth would live on vigorously through the course of the century, and would often cut across confessional boundaries.

a) God's unavailability, relayed by the criticism of the objectifying language provided by Heidegger* in his *Being and Time,* would supply an organizing concept to all the theologies anxious to free God from the clutches of metaphysical thought. Whether it was a matter of writing a theology of the Crucified Christ "between theism and atheism*" (Jüngel); of thinking of God as existing "without being" (J. L. Marion); of setting up the "trial of God's objectivity" (Colette et al., CFi 41); or still of thinking of God as "ever greater," or as a "God ever more God" (M. Corbin), the desire to let God alone say who God is remained a common preoccupation despite the diverse approaches.

b) *The unknowability* of God outside of faith is a classical theme of the Reformation, but it has taken on a new urgency in the wake of Barth. This theme is linked to the one above: natural theology is criticized for having boarded God for inspection by the world and by man. Nonetheless, the theme becomes complicated insofar as God's unavailability is tied here to a theology of revelation occupied with freeing the term "God" from all meanings and references other than Christian ones. Whether through a criticism of conceptual "idols" (Marion), through a challenge to "religious" language in the name of a non-religious reading of the biblical texts (Bonhoeffer*), or through the redevelopment of an integrally theological ontology (Dalferth), the debt to Barth is clear, whether it is acknowledged or not.

c) Barth was not without precursors. E. Schaeder had already protested theological anthropocentricism, and the Kantian phenomenology of the sacred developed by R. Otto (*Das Heilige,* 1917) had prepared the way for an exaggerated affirmation of divine alterity. This second reference is paradoxical, however, for reticence before the "sacred" is a characteristic sign of Barth's influence in theology. E. Levinas would provide a useful conceptual couple when, in a context outside that of Christian theology, he would distinguish the "sacred" from the "holy": this distinction goes to the heart of Barthian and post-Barthian criticism of the "religious." One then realizes that the theologies of secularization* (Van Buren) or the theologies of the world (Metz) have perhaps fed on crumbs from Barth's table—if the enchantments of the sacred in fact reveal a divine that is not God, then the disenchantment (Weber) of the world is an event worthy of applause.

2. The God of History
Another path was opening up to whoever wanted to have done with both moral and emotional theological anthropocentrism, the path of a particular understanding of Hegel. To the Barthian theme of a divine eternity as the judge of time, W. Pannenberg and J. Moltmann opposed the theme of a universal history with which the divine manifestation is strictly co-

extensive, and the theme of a God who is craftsman of history and craftsman of the future. Contemplation of the "infinite qualitative difference" that separates the Creator from the creature then yields to an essentially "economic" theology, busy deciphering the traces of a divine interest in the history of man; the God of crisis cedes place to the God of the eschatological promises that have already been proleptically realized (Pannenberg), and whose complete fulfillment is history's secret (Moltmann). Thus God enters theological discourse as the one who *has* come. Whether the traces of his passage are readable by any kind of historiography (Pannenberg's extremist position) or whether their interpretation requires a hermeneutic based on faith (Cullmann), theology's first task remains the same: to identify a divine signature in the facts of the world. And to the extent that these attempts are contemporaneous with the "new research on the Jesus* of history," launched by E. Käsemann in 1953, it is hardly surprising that the question of God is first asked there in a christological context and that the trinitarian perspective only reveals itself at a later stage. For the looming of eternity over the present time (Barth) is thus substituted an appeal for direction coming from the end, an appeal for eschatological accomplishment to loom over history. Waiting for the Parousia*, therefore, becomes a substitute to the *memoria Dei in Christo;* God is the one who *will* come. At the time of writing, the best textbook on Catholic theology to have been published for a very long time, *Mysterium Salutis* (1965–75), also presents itself as a broad reading of the "history of salvation." And even the most speculative of the Catholic theologies of the period, that of H. U. von Balthasar, adheres to this logic—a logic that Vatican II also made its own.

3. The God of Subjectivity and the Lord of Existence
Although the publication of Barth's *Römerbrief* should be considered Kierkegaard's first theological victory, subjectivity, existence, and the existing influenced other theories than crisis theology; and they did not do it under Kierkegaard's aegis alone.

a) Thus it was in the line of a certain Kantianism (from the Post-Kantian Thomism arising from P. Scheuer and J. Maréchal) that K. Rahner*'s transcendental theology was organized—a theology in which the historical (the "categorial") reveals nothing, or almost nothing that is not deducible a priori ("transcendentally") in the interpretation of the spiritual dynamisms of subjectivity or the lacunae that affect it.

Theological anthropology* thus becomes once again the matrix of the whole theology. Rahner was to make a terminological proposal close to Barth's by suggesting that "person" in trinitarian theology be replaced by the concept of "mode of subsisting," *Subsistenzweise,* and he did it for the same reason, to avoid anthropomorphism*. Nonetheless, his viewpoint is the opposite: Barth's starting point was the eruption of a word of truth into the human world; Rahner's was an ontological/existential qualification which makes man a "hearer of the Word" even before it has been uttered.

b) It was under the influence of Heidegger that Bultmann, the young Barth's fellow traveler, was led to express the question of God in an existential way. Here history is not forgotten in favor of the transcendental, but in favor of the eschatological, itself imagined in terms of "authentic" existence wrested by faith from the daily misfortunes of being-in-the-world. On *(über)* God himself, theology cannot speak; it can only speak of *(von)* him; and of him, it can only confess in faith his grace and his mercy. The historical reference therefore vanishes even before Bultmann's exegetical skepticism* has led him to brand with unknowability the facts that the theology of the history of salvation invoked. Only God counts, in Bultmann's view—the God who saves me today. Fichte can be paraphrased: it is the existential, and not the historical, that gives beatitude*.

c) Heidegger's influence (but this time the influence of his philosophy of language) is also highly visible in the hermeneutical theologies of E. Fuchs and G. Ebeling, and to some extent in that of E. Jüngel. Yet again, the present is central: it is *now* that the Word must be heard and accepted, because it is now that the text of Scripture becomes a Word for me. And because theological interpretation aims to be existential, speaking about God is only possible with the presupposition, already adopted in Bultmann, that God is involved in the very structures of existence. The spoken Word, welcomed in the present where it is uttered, is a word understood beforehand.

4. The Death of God

Although Christianity is perfectly equipped to understand that even at the moment of death* God can find a place in himself, it fell to the 20th century to think of an Easter Saturday that is followed by no Easter joy banishing the darkness. The concept of "Christian atheism*" may indicate first of all, in a provocative way, a refusal to let the logic of theism put pressure on the confession of the God of Jesus Christ—and understood thus, almost the whole of living theology in the century shares this refusal. The "theology of the death of God," however, has more than that to say. It says no less and proposes (in the case, for instance, of J. A. T. Robinson) to take leave from an onto-theological God. But it aims

to proclaim such a concentration of the divine in Jesus that on Good Friday it is indeed the whole divinity who dies on the cross, without anyone being able to resurrect him. The "gospel of Christian atheism" (Altizer) is thus the good news of a transfer in meaning: what "God" meant has passed entirely into man's history. Chapters on theology may still have to be written after the death of God (Sölle), but this death is real, and the God who dies in the Hegelian sense of the definition *remains* dead in the Nietzschian sense of the definition: what was said about him must then be found to be said about another, or must also die. A generation later, the post-modern "atheologies" would adopt the majority of the themes of the theology of the death of God, by transposing them in a hermeneutical and grammatological perspective inspired by J. Derrida (Taylor etc.) and often by placing their "deconstruction" efforts under the aegis of classical negative theology. Lastly, without belonging to the movement—an Anglo-Saxon one above all—of the Death Of God Theology, H. Braun treads the same waters when he attributes to the term "God" only the quality of being "a certain form of interpersonality," *eine Art Mitmenschlichkeit.*

There have certainly been other discourses in the 20th century. As responses to theological criticism of theism there have been efforts to defend and to illustrate the God of Scholasticism (e.g. Mascall); there have been strictly metaphysical redevelopments (e.g. Swinburne, or God as the "foundation of being" of Macquarrie); in contemporary orthodox theology there are trinitarian discourses which are careful not to compromise themselves with talk of the divine "essence" or "substance" (e.g. Zizioulas). Moreover, this critique is intensified in Process* theology, with its renewed challenge to divine absoluteness and the shifts it makes in the concept of divine eternity. It is intensified, in the same way, in the various readoptions of the theopaschite theme—without there being any unified school, K. Kitamori's God escapes from the conceptualities of classical theism as much as does the God of F. Varillon or W. M. Thomson. One point at least is abundantly clear: whether it is a question (in the majority of attempts) of taking a definitive leave of him, or of making a new covenant with him (Rahner), the God of the philosophers is always present in contemporary theology, in the wings or on the stage.

● H. Zahrnt (1966), *Die Sache mit Gott: Die protestantische Theologie im 20. Jahrhundert,* Munich.
H. Vorgrimler and R. Vander Gucht (1969–70), *Bilanz der Theologie im 20. Jh.,* 4 vols., Friborg-Basel-Vienna.
J. Macquarrie (1981), *Twentieth-Century Religious Thought,* Rev. Ed., London.
P. Lønning (1986), *Der begreiflich Unergreifbare: Sein Gottes und modern-theologische Denkstrukturen,* Göttingen.

R. Gibellini (1992), *La teologia del XX secolo*, Brescia.
E. Vilanova (1992), *Historia de la teología cristiana*, vols. 3, Barcelona.
K. Blaser (1995 a), *La théologie au XXe siècle*, Lausanne.
K. Blaser (1995 b), *Les théologies nord-américaines*, Geneva.

See also **Barth, Karl; Being; Christ and Christology; Eschatology; Heidegger, Martin; Language, Theological**

VI. Systematic Theology

Informed by almost 20 centuries of the Christian utterance of God's name, and whatever might be the multiplicity of contemporary expressions, whose coordination is extremely difficult, a systematic discourse could be organized according to the following currents of thought.

1. Christological Reduction

Christian Theology's first words are a christological confession: *Kurios ho Ièsous,* Jesus is lord/Lord, and its first task is to associate God with the specificity of Jesus' fate. God's name is certainly not utterable exclusively with regard to the "event of Jesus Christ." Nevertheless, the New Testament requires an assertion that this horizon is at least the only adequate one. No one has ever seen God, but the one who is closest to the bosom of the Father has made him known (Jn 1:18); whoever has seen Jesus has seen the Father (Jn 14:9). And based on the developments that these affirmations received during the early centuries of Christianity, christological mediation seems to be theology's identifying principle: "For in him the whole fullness of deity dwells bodily" (Col 2:9). The paradoxical coherence of Christian discourse requires therefore that everything that can be stated about God should hang on a christological interpretation. Theology only speaks about God by basing itself on a divine authorization: whether it uses the concept or not, it lives in order to make a constant appeal to a revelation, to a divine self-revelation; in Jesus' destiny it sees the perfect image of this unveiling. Therefore, it is first of all a matter of setting aside all the contents of the meaning of the word "God" that are not acquired or integrated christologically. The primordial element of the Christian naming of God is therefore memory. God is not primarily the one who *is,* but the one who *has* come: his "immanent" divinity is only strictly confessable when his "economic" divinity has first been confessed. It is a certain hermeneutics of a certain history that gives its exact meaning to the word "God"; the God who is discussed theologically is a God who gave rise to himself and gave himself a face.

2. The Trinitarian Unfolding

If theological reason is a reason certified by memory, it must also be stated at once that the God known in Jesus Christ is not an Absolute who has placed himself at the disposal of human beings by assuming their humanity, that God has not died in his divinity (in his transcendence, in his "highness") in order to give himself, in Jesus, a being-in-the-world. The christological economy of revelation, in fact, absolutely forbids a reduction in what we say about God to what we can say about Jesus: it is precisely christo-logical, which is more than Jesus-logical, because Jesus is recognized as Christ, as one signed with a messianic anointing that does not come from himself. Only a trinitarian hermeneutic can do justice to the "event of Jesus Christ" in such a way that the "opposition of relationship" between Jesus and the one he calls Father (and between Jesus and the Holy Spirit that he gives to his disciples) does not contradict the strict unity claimed by the Johannine Christ, and in such a way that it is necessary to speak about God simultaneously in the plural and in the singular (*hèn esmen, unum sumus,* Jn 10:30). The concept of self-revelation should therefore be defined. Jesus is not Lord as a revelation of *himself,* but as revealed by the Father and by the "unknown beyond the Word" (Balthasar). Speaking about God thus requires the use of a double language: both the language of *subsistence,* according to which God dwells in Jesus, and the language of *iconicity,* according to which Jesus is "the image of the invisible God" (Col 1:15; *see* 2 Cor 4:4) and "the radiance of his glory" (Heb 1:3). The one who *comes* is indeed the one who *is;* and in saying this we are not referring to the faceless being of a substance or divine essence, but to the "mystery" (*mustèrion*) par excellence, to which the "Jesus Christ event" yields itself in order to initiate (*muein*) reason, that of a divine life that is communion*. Jesus' resurrection*, then, is only the first word in Christology (Pannenberg, Moingt et al.) by being the first word in trinitarian theology. What God shows himself to be in the life, death, and resurrection of Jesus ("economically"), so he is still (in an "immanent" way). Whether "God," *theos,* names the Father (in the New Testament) or the triad of persons (from Nicaea I onward), the christological faith cannot in any case unfold except in a trinitarian mode.

3. The God of Jesus Christ, the God of Israel

God expresses himself and shows himself in Jesus. Nevertheless, the christological "fullness of time" (Gal 4:4) cannot be interpreted as the first occurrence of divine word. The God of Jesus Christ is not a God immured in his own transcendence until the time of condescension has come—he is the God of Israel, already known, being already linked to humanity through a covenant. For this reason Old Testament pre-comprehensions are not optional in a hermeneutic of New Testament texts and of the confession of Christian faith. The first great theoretical debate into which the primitive Church had to enter was the debate provoked by Gnosticism and Marcionism*: a debate led by theologians announcing another God and abrogating the experience of Israel. If it has to be conceded that Christianity speaks about God differently than does biblical (and post-biblical) Judaism, the lesson from this debate is indeed that a Christianity that would disqualify the God of Israel would deprive itself *ipso facto* of the semantic, metaphorical, and symbolic resources necessary for the structuring of a christological affirmation. The discourse of alterity ("God otherwise") cannot be maintained here without being tied dialectically to a discourse of continuity, and therefore without the formulation of a project for a christological reading of the Old Testament. When the curtain of the temple* is torn (Mt 27:51) and God is no longer present in the world except *sub contrario,* on the cross of Jesus, displacement and discontinuity are warded off—the God of Jesus Christ "scandalizes" Israel (1 Cor 1:23). Yet discontinuity cannot be imagined except in the light of an equally strong continuity. Post-biblical Israel can (or should) try to de-Judaize Jesus ("on his lips, we do not recognize our own verses"—Levinas) in order to contradict any Christian claim to continuity, but the pagano-Christian Church must itself maintain with all its might the homogeneity of the same speech act which fashioned Israel's experience, and which makes possible the—difficult—recognition of the God of Jesus Christ as the God of Abraham, Isaac, and Jacob.

4. A Universal Meaning

If "God alone speaks properly of God" it is inevitable that theological statements systematically make their initial reference to the history in which the Absolute pitched his tent among human beings. Nevertheless, the provincial specificity of the "history of salvation" cannot all the same obscure the fact that God's name is not just uttered within the confines of Israel and the Church. This has to be taken into account at several levels.

a) First of all, the God of Israel only takes his place among human beings, in the specificity of a culture, and subject to the accidents of language, by identifying himself at the same time as lord of the whole cosmos*; and what is more, as lord integrating all that is within the sphere of the covenant. The God of the covenant is God the creator and not one of those gods who would share between themselves the sovereignty of the world and its peoples. But, reciprocally, God the creator is also the God of the covenant, and this (at least) means that there could be no question of man without God himself also coming into question. It is certainly "more natural" (Jüngel) for theology to organize itself christologically and in a trinitarian way than to make an appeal to meanings taken on by the word "God" in other spheres of experience than those of Israel and the Church. But the fact that that name is not theology's exclusive property is itself a major theological fact; between what theology says about God and what non-biblical cultures and religions say about him, there could not exist a pure and simple ambivalence.

b) The importance of universality of a meaning and of a reference has a strongly attested place in philosophical rationality. It matters little here whether God entered philosophy so that his name might be sanctified in it or his divinity finally forgotten in it. The only thing that matters is the intersubjective agreement on what the words mean; and the service that can be asked of them here, and that they undeniably perform, is to prevent any referential errors. After all, such an ill-famed concept as that of *causa sui* has only God as possible referent. Its extreme poverty can be granted. But it must also be agreed that it refers to God without any ambivalence. Looking at it this way, the "God of the philosophers" is not the other of the "God of Abraham, Isaac, and Jacob." Some other terms are undeniably naming procedures, and names may be different, but the one that they name is the same. Doubtless God is misunderstood wherever the historical conditions of his manifestation are not admitted and considered. Nonetheless, that is not to say that God is unknown there, or unknowable.

c) Therefore it must be proposed that the God of Jesus Christ cannot be expressed if he has not already been pre-expressed; and if the pre-diction has the faith of Israel as its favored modality, it is also realized in the expectation of the nations. Although first in the order of systematizing reasons, Christology and trinitarian theology do not have the first word; their discourse is only audible because God has already been spoken about. And in whatever way one gives theological status to the expectation of the nations (in patristic terms of the theory of the "evangelical preparation," or in J. S. von Drey's of a theory of the "originating revelation," etc.), it is important to note that God is never spoken about christologically/trinitarily without this language being partially receivable because it is partially pre-understood.

5. Word and Liturgy

Theology speaks about God and constructs propositional sequences with the same structure as the sequences constructed for any other body of knowledge. But whatever it says about God, we cannot say it without confessing that God does not stand face to face with the human person in the manner of a supreme object, but in the manner of a You, and therefore that we speak *about* God while presuming that we can speak *to* God. The theological assertion therefore cannot close full circle on itself, and its final coherence only emerges in the links that unite it to the doxology. Since this is so, it is not enough that God should be the universal object of successful semantic transactions: it is also necessary that the community of those who give a common meaning to "God" should also exist as a liturgical community of praise* and thanksgiving. It is certainly a sign of our historiality that we can speak about God, and moreover that we must do so. But amid the tasks (kerygmatic, reflexive, etc.) that history imposes on theology, it is also possible to set the whole historiality aside in order to anticipate liturgically a transcending of objectifying language. Theology certainly could not absorb itself without remainder in the doxological, for the empire of praise would then be bought at a high price—that is, at the price of a closure on itself of the liturgical community and a ban on its telling the reasons for the praise. But neither can theology reduce itself to the dimensions of a theory of the divine, for it would cause the subtraction from this theory of the sphere of existential verification which only the experience of the liturgy, and of any prayer*, gives it. Such an oscillation is essential for the proper use of God's name. Theory refers to liturgical practice as to the best use we can make of our words, while liturgical practice bases itself in turn on theoretical language as the condition of a universal communication of the reasons for believing in God and for speaking to God.

JEAN-YVES LACOSTE

See also **Language, Theological; Praise; Philosophy; Theology**

B. Philosophical Problematics

1. An Impossible Definition

Metaphysics seeks an unconditioned first principle, an absolute that goes beyond the rationality that is proper to the class of the conditioned; through this transcendence, metaphysics finds open the possibility of encountering the one who is beyond all finite names and that philosophical tradition itself has called, from the time of its Greek origins, *ho theos,* "God." But what this name covers is essentially problematic, because philosophy, forbidding itself to accept as truths historical data received through a tradition, can only know of God—if indeed it can know anything about God—that which comes from rational investigation (Thomas Aquinas, *ST* Ia, q.1, a.1). The fact that God is a subject for rational thought is itself a problem. Philosophy does not propose a unanimous doctrine about God, but only questions. What is this God, who can neither be found in experience, since he is the supersensible foundation of all empirical reality, nor be known in a sacred doctrine, since reason rejects the historicity of revelation, nor be met in a personal face-to-face encounter, since first principles are universal? Is it not simply a name given for convenience to the abstraction of a transcendental X? Could one not, in that case, challenge the legitimacy of this denomination and identification? Why "God"? Why not the Absolute, the First, the Supreme being? Rather than speaking of "God," should we not speak of the "Divine," the anonymous principle of the supersensible? Is it not the nearness, importunate but insistent, of the religions that call for a revelation, and in particular of Christianity, that, despite the methodological resolutions, causes a contamination of the God of metaphysics by the personal God, and that leads the philosopher, a Christian, to cross the threshold separating a principle of establishment and order from personal existence, and *eternity* of essences from eternal *life**? But if metaphysics is suspected of being nothing more than a theology in disguise, a surreptitious introduction to obedience in faith, should not a philosophy freed of all authority challenge fundamentally the claim to speak about God, and apply itself to a radical critique of the practices of power that, in God's name, and in the name of a supposed knowledge of the supersensible, hold consciences in ideological dependency? Philosophy's task would then be a deconstruction of the God-idol of metaphysics. And by doing this, would all thinking about God be invalidated, or reduced to the status of a historically obsolete tradition?

Swinging between the two extremes of methodological atheism and rational theism, philosophical discourse unfurls the whole range of human attitudes when faced with God. There is nothing that philosophy can say about God that does not also refer to man, or tell about one of man's ways; for it starts from man, uncertain about the end of its quest. Philosophy does not and could not claim to say everything about God, but at least to stay attentive to what every man can say about God. The question is to find out whether the God of the philosophers represents only a way of stating the essence of man, or if it is possible for reason to reach that which exceeds itself.

2. God and the Divine

a) The Divine as Image of Ideas.   While it is a human discourse on God, philosophy is not for that reason anthropology, for its methodological demands imply a setting aside of those cultural and religious data from which man derives an initial definition of his relation with the divine. The first Greek philosophy, challenging the divinity of the natural elements, broke with the universe of polytheistic mythology; Anaxagoras, Protagoras, then Socrates were condemned for impiety. Plato went on to set subtly at a distance what he called "theology" (*Republic* II, 379 *a*), meaning by that, not the philosophical discourse on the gods but the poets' well-regulated mythology. If the philosophical norm corrected the traditional, Homeric representations, it was by founding itself not on a knowledge of the gods' true nature, but on the idea of justice*, of which the gods must be, for human beings, satisfactory images. The psycho-cosmic theology of Plato's *Laws* (l. X) does not claim to state a final truth about the gods, but only to produce, through a persuasive, incantatory discourse (903d), belief in an order of retributive justice, a belief that, gently and without constraint, ultimately favors obedience to the Laws.

Thus the gods are useful images, pointing out to the soul the care it should take of itself—that is, of its original rooting in truth, as is shown by the myth of the winged steeds in *Phaedrus* (26 et seq.). The gods are immortal. The soul therefore is immortal in what brings it closer to the divine (*see Republic.* X, 611c). "The divine is what is beautiful, learned, good, and everything of that nature" (246*d*). The gods are the blessed (247*a; see Banquet* 202 *c*), whose lives, moving about among the numerous "blessed contemplations," are devoted to "thought, nourished by intellect and unadulterated knowledge" (*Phaedrus* 247 *d*); they possess the necessary knowledge (*Parmenides* 134 *e*). The divine therefore makes it possible to imagine the philosophical life. "Only the philosopher's thought is winged" (Phaedrus 249 *c*) because the philosopher, "always open through his reasonings to the idea of the being...turns his eyes to the divine" (*Sophist* 254 *a-b*); but if the philosopher alone can be called divine, it is not that in reality he has become a God, nor even that he finds in the gods models to imitate: it is because he attained the very reality that makes the gods (ibid.), a reality of which they themselves are only the images. The divine, blessed life is an image *ad usum populi* of the philosophical life: "he is possessed by a God, but the masses do not suspect it" (*Phaedrus* 249 *c*).

Plato therefore is not developing a theology for its own sake. He is not seeking the essence of the gods, nor that of the divine. His recourse to a mythical discourse is a way of evoking the Ideas, of translating philosophical concepts, into the language of Greek culture.

b) The First of the Beings.   What Ideas have in common with the Olympians is separation; the God, or the divine, on whom the philosopher (to protect him from any specificity) does not confer any mythological name, is the transcendent—the one who, in contrast to the *daimôn,* "does not mix with man" (*Banquet* 203a; see also *Parmenides* 134e). Aristotle retains this essential characteristic of the God, while criticizing the Platonic theory of the separation of Ideas. Consequently, the divine ceases to be identified with the world of Ideas, and theology as an autonomous science becomes possible, constituted by its proper object, and no longer as an ideological expression. The immanence of the intelligible consecrates the transcendence of the intelligence: it is the real registration of the birth of God in philosophical thought. "There is no doubt that, if the divine exists somewhere, he exists in that 'immobile and separated' nature..." (*Metaphysics* E, 1, 1026 *a,* 18 et seq.). In addition, this being is, with regard to every being, "the sovereign and first principle" (*Metaphysics,* K, 7, 1064 *b*1). Knowledge of the being as a being thus has with theology, or first philosophy, a favored relationship, even though—an arguable point—it might not blend with it. One cannot imagine what causes a being to be what it is, without imagining every being's first cause, which is the same thing as their end.

Aristotle initiated this theology in his *Metaphysics* L, 6–10. First, he proposed (L, 6) the existence of an immobile, separated, eternal being who is the cause, the end, the impetus of movement in nature (*see Physics* VII and VIII). But it is not enough to have discovered a first principle in order to talk about God; one must also assure oneself of the excellence of the life that the principle leads; because what God possesses in his own right is a perfect and eternal life (*Metaphysics*

1071 *b* 28). The perfection, the happiness that is felt in joy, in pure pleasure, belongs to the pure action, which has no other end beside itself; now, only contemplation 9*b* 24), or thought in conformity with itself (*b* 18), realizes in man already this coincidence of the act and the end. It is therefore as an "act of intelligence"—that is, "life in conformity with itself of the intellect, excellent and eternal" (*b* 27)—that the pure act can be described as divine. Chapter 9 specifies that "the sameness of the intelligence and the intelligible" (*b* 21), which characterizes the very act of thought in general, implies not only that God's life must be an intelligent life, but, much more, that God is thought itself, in conformity with itself—that is, "the thought of the thought" (*b* 34).

Theology is not reduced to thought about the principle, it is linked to a thought about the life of excellence. God's happiness surpasses everything that mortals will ever experience in their most perfect moments; but it is also the norm of the happiness of man, who is only man insofar as he is not only man (*Eth to Nic.* X, 7, 1178 *a* 5–7). This man par excellence, the most divine of all, is the philosopher; for Aristotle, as for Plato, to speak about God is to speak about knowledge of the divine, which is also divine knowledge, philosophy.

3. The Philosophical Contribution to the Theological Construction

a) The One and the Unique. For Greek thought, the superiority, the very transcendence of the divine, does not imply a commensurability of man and God; the divine is thought of as an extreme possibility of man. Paradoxically, God does not become radically other except in the greatest proximity with man. By making himself a man, God stops being divine and becomes foreign to man: madness for the wise, wisdom for the mad. God does not manifest himself as man imagined him. That is, Christianity had to appear before God became the infinite that no human understanding could understand, before the relation between God and man became that of the Creator to the *ens creatum.*

When Christianity wanted to find a philosophical model on which to build a theology, it did not therefore turn either to Aristotle or to Plato, but toward a late interpretation of Platonism, based on the fundamental dissociation between the primordial One and the Aristotelian order of the intelligence, which is homologous to that of being. The definition Plato applied to the Idea of Good (*epekeina tès ousias, Republic* VI, 509 *b*) is the keyword in a theology that affirms in its most radical consequences the transcendence of the One (*see* Plotinus, *Enneads;* Proclus, *Platonic Theology;*

Pseudo-Dionysius, *Divine Names*). This encounter between the monotheistic revelation and philosophical mysticism is a crucial event, not only for Christian theology, but also for the philosophical naming of God. The name "god" is not, in a theology of the polytheistic hierarchy, the proper name of the transcendent One, since it extends to the divinity of all other gods, among whom beings also participate (Proclus). If the One is "the cause of all deity," and if "the gods owe everything for their being gods to the first God" (Proclus), is the name "God" for this reason univocal, when it is a question of first among others? Strictly speaking no name, not even the name "God" is suited to the first one. Revelation, however, brings about, in the sphere of philosophy itself, a reversal in terms: on the basis of Holy Scripture, God can be named; but at the same time he is the one who is called unknowable and transcendent.

The analogy no longer consists of sharing out divinity among the first and the others, but in sharing out names (Being, One, Good, whichever might be the one granted preeminence) between God and creatures; on the other hand, God's mode of being cannot be shared by any other being (see *ST* Ia, q. 4, a 3; 1, q. 13, a 11, resp.). Henceforth, the Christian adoption of Neoplatonic theology makes it take on a quite different meaning: it is definitely God who is spoken of, in giving him a name that cannot be given to any other being (*ST* Ia, q. 13, a. 9).

b) God as Being. It remains to be discovered by what right philosophy can talk about God. If the decisive passage from thought about the supersensible to thought about God presupposes revelation; if God is not *per se notus*, knowable through himself alone, that is, by the sole aid of reason; then metaphysics may well be *sermo de divinis* (Thomas Aquinas, *In metaphysicorum,* L, VI, I, 1168), *scientia divina ST* Ia, q. 1, a.1), but not, strictly speaking, *theologia.*

According to Thomas Aquinas, the common use of reason is not only insufficient for obtaining knowledge about God's essence (*ST* Ia, q. 12, a 4 and a.12), but does not even manage to understand the meaning of the name "God," since certain individuals (the Stoics), using their reason alone, did not flinch at the conception of God as corporeal (*ST* Ia, q. 2, a. 1). It is therefore not possible to be certain of the univocity of the meanings of the name "God" according to whether it is used by philosophers, apart from revelation, and by theologians or the faithful. Furthermore, even if one were to admit, with Anselm of Canterbury, that every human being can be convinced *sola ratione,* according to the simple necessity of reason, of the necessary reason for a *summum omnium quae sunt* (*Monologion* I), and can deduce its essence from this concept to the point that *huic soli summae essentiae proprie nomen dei assignatur* (ibid.), the fact remains that rational investigation has its limits, for God is not only, as *quo maius cogitari nequit,* the necessary subject of thought, he is also *quiddam maius quam cogitari,* going beyond all thought, all finite understanding (*Proslogion*).

For God to become the subject not only of revealed theology, but of a philosophy based on natural light, he must be reduced to a common denominator. Although he restricts knowledge of God to the *doctrina sacra,* Thomas Aquinas opens the way for a secularization by finding, beyond Neoplatonism, the equivalence between God and being. 1) Among the names of God, "who is" is for him, in preference to the others, the proper one (*ST* Ia, q.13, a. 11). 2) God is identified with his own nature (deity*) or essence (*ST* Ia, q. 3, a.3); "God is not only his own essence... but he is his own being (existence)" (*CG* I, 21; *ST* Ia, q. 3, a.4). 3) On the purely metaphysical level the difference between the *ens primum* and the *ens commune* is abolished (*In Metaphysicorum, Prooemium*). The confusion between the being of creatures and God's being is only avoided by means of a theory of analogy, which retains the preeminence of the *esse divinum.* However, to raise oneself to this level, one must abandon the resolutions that belong to finiteness, and therefore experience the *esse commune,* which is not the *esse divinum,* but its closest term in the order of being. Even if theology is not reduced to ontology, it becomes inseparable from it.

4. God and Nature

a) God as the Basis of Scientific Knowledge. Modernity's inaugural event is the reduction of nature to what is mathematically knowable. The philosophical problem of God is consequently asked in new terms, independently of all revealed theology when, after Descartes, metaphysics is defined as the foundation of physics.

In fact this methodological overturning has the following consequences for the God of the philosophers. 1) Natural knowledge of God is based directly on the idea of God, which is neither received from tradition nor derived from the experience of creatures, since this knowledge has the same rationality as mathematical ideas. 2) This methodological identity between the knowledge of God and the knowledge of nature makes it possible to base the certainty of the latter on the former, because the creative act establishes a dependency, acting as a guarantee, between God and the ideas of things. 3) This dependency implies the immeasurable-

ness of the infinite from the finite, of God from nature as of God from the finite mind. Therefore, the properly Cartesian proof of God's existence (*Méditation* III) takes its starting point not so much from the idea of God, "infinite, eternal, immutable, independent, all-knowing, all-powerful substance and through which myself, and all the other things which are... have been created and produced" (ibid., A-T, IX, 36), but from the fact that finite understanding can have an idea of him. If the idea of the infinite is the clearest and most distinct of all ideas (ibid.), that is the sign of the divine registration in human thought: it is precisely because the infinite is incommensurable with the finite that the mind must propose the Other, that which it is not, as the cause of the idea of God. The foundation of natural science is therefore not the "I think," because thought's turning back in itself does not reach the otherness of an object to be discovered, but God, for it is only his veracity*, linked to his perfection, that guarantees the idea's relation to an object, to an essence (*Méditation* V), as it does to an existence (*Méditation* VI).

However, this dependency on the physical with regard to God, which is characteristic of the 17th-century philosophers, and which Pascal attacked specifically when he spoke of the "God of the philosophers [i.e., first of all the physicists] *and of the scholars*" (our emphasis), inversely reduces God's role to its epistemological dimension, disregarding the living God. Modern vanity consists of wanting nature to be founded on the idea of a rational God. The God of the modern (meta)physicians opens the way to atheism. In fact, God's metaphysical condition is ambiguous: rational knowledge of God is certainly indispensable with regard to primary philosophy, but it comes to its end in what it founds, which is secondary philosophy. This secondary philosophy, considered in its proper class, can also just as easily do without God.

b) The Need for God causa sui. Either physico-mathematical rationality develops its potentialities independently of any foundation; or, on the contrary, rational theology extends its sphere from the foundation up to the whole of the real and becomes an exclusively rational and totally ontotheological system (Spinoza). Understanding has freed itself from authority in the knowledge of nature by introducing into nature the principle of necessity; it should obtain the same result in its knowledge of God. The fundamental prejudice of theologians and of the majority of philosophers is the identification of power with indifference. Nature would thus be contingent with regard to God, although necessary with regard to us, as physics shows. Yet it is opposite that is true: our imaginations introduce contingency into nature, while the things that depend on the immutable power of God cannot be other than what they are because "God's will cannot be other" (*Ethics* I, prop. 33, note 2). The only thought in conformity with reason is that "God does not produce his effects through free will" (*Ethics*, I, 32, cor. 1) but through the necessity of his nature (*Ethics* I, 16, 17). God's causality is not the relation to an exteriority: he is the cause of finite beings by being the cause of himself; he does not relate to nature as if to something other than himself (*Ethics* I, 18). In short, it is impossible to associate the idea of God with the idea of transcendence. The relationship between cause and effect is internal to God's necessity (as with the relation of naturizing nature to natured nature: *Ethics* I, 29), and it is only from this viewpoint that he can be said to be a free cause (*Ethics* I, 17, cor. 2). The radical equivocity between the God of reason and the God of the theologians leads to this conclusion: if one admits the latter, then the system founded on the former is undeniably atheism. If God is not a separate being, situated outside the being of nature, he has no being of his own. But one can just as well say that it is the traditional theological system that constitutes an atheism, because it does not know what it is talking about when using the name "God": "Men professing openly to having no idea of God and not to know him except through created things (whose causes they are ignorant of), do not blush to accuse philosophers of atheism" (Gebhardt).

The Spinozist system considers in all its rigor what one cannot not think of God. The necessity of rationality unites with the very necessity of God. It follows that Spinoza has exhausted all that reason can say about God and that, as a result, any rational system ends necessarily with Spinozism, and thus with atheism. That is the conclusion which Jacobi draws from his examination of Lessing's Spinozism, leading the problem of God into a dilemma—either rational atheism, or fideist theism—which also tolls the death knell of all theology, both rational and revealed, leaving to feeling and belief the privilege of a relation to the true and living God.

5. The End of the Metaphysical Concept of God

a) God as Idea. Kantian criticism of metaphysics confirms Jacobi's analysis up to a point. On the one hand transcendental philosophy, which shows how the object is constituted a priori in the subject's faculties for knowing, founds the science of nature without recourse to God. On the other hand transcendental dialectics throws light on the logical defect that undermines any rational attempt to pass from the concept of God to his reality (*Critique of Pure Reason*).

Kant does not deny the necessity of thinking about God as *summum ens, ens realissimum, ens necessarium*; but he challenges the transition from this necessity in the realm of thought to the affirmation of a thing outside the realm of thought, which would correspond to necessity. God is not a concept describing a real being such as one might experience. It is an idea, a rule that reason makes for itself in order to thematize its own tendency toward the unconditioned, "a true abyss of human reason" (*Critique of Pure Reason*, AA III). Nothing in the order of being—that is, in nature constituted by understanding—corresponds to God. The ideal of pure reason, the regulator in the theoretic domain, corresponds in the practical domain to a God called up by the rational demands of the should-be (*Critique of Pure Reason*, AA V). But this moral God, moral author of the world (*Critique of Judgment*, §86–88), universal *imperans* of the categorical imperative (*Opus posthumum*, AA XXII) is only within ourselves, a product of practical reason, "the ideal of a substance that we create for ourselves" (*Opus posthumum*, AA XXII). However, reason constituted as desire demands not only transcendence but also the representation of God, thanks to an analogical path that makes it possible not only to reach it, but to think about the relation between the supersensible term and our reason (*Prolegomena to any Future Metaphysics*, §5–59; *Critique of Judgment*, §90).

b) The Crisis of Metaphysics and the Death of God. The rift between philosophy and life, between reason and belief, between speculation and revelation, is the symptom of a crisis. How can reason be deprived of the absolute? How can the revealed God remain hidden to the faculty in human beings that understands? This crisis has its origins in the confrontation between modern rationality springing from the natural sciences, and traditional metaphysics. To the extent that the physico-mathematical, as the norm of all scientificity, defines the sphere of the knowable in terms of what is quantifiable, empirically verifiable, God cannot be the subject of knowledge. However, the extenuation of the concept of God—one of the aspects of what Nietzsche calls the death of God—is not due only to the epistemological hegemony of measurable nature or to man's emancipation with regard to all transcendent authority, it is the result of a confusion proper to metaphysics itself. In fact metaphysics has constituted itself in such a way that the name of "God" has reached the point of covering what Aristotle called "being as being"; in other words, this name has been changed from the truth of being in its totality. As such, he is ruled by necessity: necessity of thought—he is the one that one cannot not think about—and necessity of being—he is the one who is necessarily such as he is, eternal and immutable (see *Metaphysics*, L.7, 1070*b* 10). The 19th century gives this subject of necessity another name: humanity (A. Comte), the Great Being, the being par excellence, for whom the whole of being is knowable through science, transformable through technique, and that manifests itself to itself in the process of history. The death of God is the moment of transition during which man discovers that the founder's position is vacant, but has not yet understood that he must occupy it himself, by becoming the subject in God's place.

c) God, the System, and Reaching Beyond Metaphysics. The equivocity that has undermined the concept of God since the encounter between Greek philosophy and monotheistic revelation derives from the fact that the same name is used to refer to the absolute subject and the Holy One of the Scriptures. The point of divergence of the two traditions is creation, which assumes the radical inequality of the created and the Creator; for reason, the break in the continuity of causality is a contradiction. That is why the article of faith encompasses the essential of revelation; revelation thus remains, in the main, incomprehensible, and therefore hidden. But does not the admission of a hidden God amount to a refusal to welcome the fullness of revelation? God as such is not thinkable unless the rational absolute and the revealed mystery are not reconciled in a dualist juxtaposition, but totally identified. The high point of metaphysics is where the concept of God is blended with God. Such is Hegel's speculative logic: the creative contradiction is the movement of the concept.

God not only manifested himself, he is the manifestation itself; in the act of creation, he moves out of himself in order to manifest himself. He is therefore, as Creator, what he is as God. Creation is consubstantial with him as both act and result *(Lectures on the Philosophy of Religion)*. Similarly, the logical concept is the gesture of placing oneself in finitude and, by this self-differentiation, of maintaining an infinite relation with oneself. Creating is identically the act of God and the act of the absolute Idea (*Enc.* §163). Contrary to the logic of understanding, which determines spiritual contents as external objects identified with their predicates, speculation understands God's determinations internally, as its own. By identifying itself with the God of revelation, the God of philosophy is no longer the being abstractly opposed to the void, he is the movement by which being finds its meaning, finds itself—by denying itself; in short, he is the Spirit (*Enc.* §384).

Comprehension of God can be interpreted indiscriminately as the sanctification of philosophy (making it a form of divine service), or as the dissolution of the divine in the human. This time it is not only reason but revelation itself that seems to lead back to man: God has delivered himself entirely, and in his manifestation there is no remainder. It follows, after Hegel, that God cannot return in philosophy except in the background (*see* Heidegger, *Beiträge*). If all God's names have been exhausted in the history of metaphysics, the end of metaphysics, and therefore of its theology, opens up the possibility of thinking—but is it still a question of thinking?—about the one that Schelling, the first thinker of this goal, evokes as the *Unvordenklich,* the one who can only be thought about in advance.

- É. Gilson (1941), *God and Philosophy,* New Haven and London.
  W. Schulz (1957), *Der Gott der neuzeitlichen Metaphysik,* Pfullingen.
  D. Henrich (1960), *Der ontologische Gottesbeweis,* Tübingen.
  C. Bruaire (1964), *L'affirmation de Dieu,* Paris.
  J. Moreau (1969), *Le Dieu des philosophes,* Paris.
  Col. (1970), *Dieu et l'être,* Paris.
  W. Weischedel (1972), *Der Gott der Philosophen,* 2nd Ed., Darmstadt.
  B. Welte (1973), "Versuch zur Frage nach Gott", in J. Ratzinger (Ed.), *Die Frage nach Gott,* QD 56, 13–26.
  W. Brugger (1979), *Summe einer philosophischen Gotteslehre,* Munich.
  É. Gilson (1979), *L'athéisme difficile,* Paris.
  A. Kenny (1979), *The God of Philosophers,* Oxford.
  R. Kearney and J.S. O'Leary (Eds.) (1980), *Heidegger et la question de Dieu,* Paris.
  J.-L. Marion (1982), *Dieu sans l'être,* Paris.
  J. Greisch (Ed.) (1985), *Dieu,* Paris.
  D. Dubarle (1986), *Dieu avec l'être,* Paris.
  W. Röd (1992), *Der Gott der reinen Vernunft,* Munich.

YVES-JEAN HARDER

See also **Being; Heidegger, Martin; Love; Nothingness; Philosophy; Reason; Schelling, Friedrich Wilhelm Joseph von**

Good

Theological reflection on the nature of good represents the confluence of two distinguishable streams of thought, one deriving from the Bible*, the other from philosophical traditions. By far the greatest philosophical influence has come from Greek speculation, particularly that of Plato, Aristotle, the Stoics, and the Neoplatonists. From the patristic period until the Reformation, Greek philosophy* formed a generally recognized frame of reference and was used in thinking about the idea of good contained in revelation* and dogma*. The Greek framework remains influential, owing in part to the importance for Catholicism* of Thomas* Aquinas's synthesis, and in part to the continued and, today, particularly strong interest in ancient and medieval philosophy.

The predominant features of the Greek framework are its metaphysical account of good in general (bonum in commune), and the idea of the importance of the metaphysical and psychological foundations of specifically human or moral goodness. The latter feature explains the eudemonistic structure of the ethical theories associated with this tradition, and the centrality of the concepts of virtue* and right reason*. Within this broad theoretical framework, Christian thinkers debated the nature of divine goodness, divine law*, evil*, sin*, grace*, and the beatific vision*. Modern philosophical accounts of good have been less amenable to broad systematic development and adaptation to theological purposes. For that reason, none has achieved the sort of hegemony in theological discussion of good that Greek speculation has.

1. Good in General

Classical thought provides two models for understanding the nature of good, both of which postulate a necessary connection between good (agathon, bonum) and fundamental reality or being* (einai/to on, esse/ens). Each model is found in Christian thinkers.

a) Participation. In the first model, Plato and others pointed to a dependence of being on good. In The Republic (508 b–509 b), Plato asserts that the form of Good, that which is good in itself (agathon kath'auton), is the source not only of everything that is good, but also of all the other Forms, and hence of all being. All other realities have their being and their goodness by virtue of participating in that Form. In the Timaeus (29 e–30 b), Plato suggests that this account of the metaphysical priority of goodness could be developed into a theory explaining the origin of the universe. The Neoplatonists developed this idea into a full-fledged cosmology involving the emanation of all things from the Good and their return to it.

Many early Christian thinkers found this cosmological view congenial. They found it natural to identify the Christian God* with the Good and, while recognizing the incompatibility of the doctrine of creation* with Neoplatonist emanationism, they were able nevertheless to accommodate the notion of participation within the doctrine of creation. For Christian Platonists such as Augustine* and Boethius*, this idea meant that the created being necessarily depends on God, who is the Good; as for the goodness of created things, that arose from their participation in—their being derived from—that which is good in itself. In the third of his theological treatises (Quomodo substantiae, c. 140–50), Boethius uses the language of emanationism: created things are good in virtue of their having "flowed from" (fluxit ab) God, the Substantial Good. In De divinis nominibus (IV, 693 b–700 c, 705 c–708 b), Dionysius* the Pseudo-Areopagite characterizes Good as essentially diffusive of itself, by its very nature pouring itself out into creation. This outpouring of the divine nature results in a hierarchy of created beings that participate in the divine goodness to various extents.

These ideas about participation led in the direction of an explicitly theological and relational conception of good: God is the first and highest good, and all created good is good in virtue of a certain relation—participation—to good in itself.

b) Natural Teleology. The second model links the notion of good with the notion of an end. A natural substance is constituted by a substantial form or nature, by virtue of which the substance possesses a capacity for performing the activity or function characteristic of substances belonging to that species. The end, completion, or perfection of a natural substance is its having fully actualized its capacity, its performing the activity for which its form or nature provides the capacity. Since the state or activity that constitutes a substance's full actuality is that substance's end, and since the end is good, that state or activity constitutes the substance's good. On this account, good for a substance of a given nature is the end determined by its nature, the fact of its being fully actual as a thing of that nature. One does not arrive, in this case, at an essentially theological or relational conception of good: the goodness of a thing consists in the actualization of a nature, and the state that results from it is intrinsic to the thing itself.

The natural-teleology account has extremely influential proponents in Augustine and Thomas Aquinas. Aquinas in particular developed its Aristotelian underpinnings in elaborate detail. The rational soul*, for example, is a human being's substantial form (its first actuality or *actus primus*) and gives to that human being the complex set of faculties and capacities (powers, *potentiae*) grouped together under the heading "reason" (ST Ia, q. 95, a. 1). These "powers" are disposed for the relevant activity *(operatio)* or final activity *(actus ultimus)* by certain settled dispositions *(habitus),* which are the intellectual and moral virtues. The activity characteristic of human beings as such is living in accordance with reason. Aquinas, then, identifies good with actuality or being, claiming that good for a given substance is that substance's actualization of its specifying potentialities. A thing is good to the extent that it has actualized the potentialities specific to its species.

Despite their differences, the participation and natural-teleology approaches are not necessarily incompatible, and philosophical theologians such as Augustine and Aquinas have held them together. They thought of natural teleology as specifying or explaining what it is for a created thing to participate in the divine goodness. Each created thing's nature is a limited and partial representation of God, and a created thing participates more fully in the divine nature to the extent to which it realizes or actualizes its constitutive potentialities.

c) The Hierarchy of Goods and the Highest Good. Both these accounts of good imply a hierarchy among the constituents of reality. On the participation account, a thing is more or less good to the extent to which it participates in, or in some way represents, good. In accordance with the metaphor of "emanation," things that participate to a greater degree in good are "nearer" to it and things that participate less are "farther" from it. The highest good *(summum bonum),* the reality at the top of the hierarchy of goods, is that that possesses in its own unified nature all the perfections represented in fragmented and diminished ways in the variety of particular goods. According to

Anselm*, we can identify pure perfections by finding those attributes that it is unqualifiedly better to possess than not to possess. The supreme nature must possess every pure perfection (*Monologion,* 15).

The natural-teleology account defines a hierarchy of goods in terms of degrees of actuality. Different substances belonging to the same species possess more or less actuality depending on the extent to which they have actualized their specifying potentialities. Moreover, substantial forms (the first actualities, in virtue of which things are the kinds of things they are) vary in their degrees of actuality insofar as they constitute kinds whose activities are more or less rich, full, and complex. It is from this perspective that one can understand Augustine's famous hierarchy, which rises from inanimate beings by way of living beings to beings endowed with reason. The activity characterizing each level of being includes the activity of lower levels of being: human beings exist (as stones do) and live (as plants and animals* do), but they also understand (as neither stones nor animals do). The highest good in the hierarchy is God, who not only exists, lives, and understands, but is Truth* itself, the eternal and immutable measure and source of all understanding. Augustine's hierarchy, therefore, is a ranking of things both according to their goodness and according to their degree of being. The supreme good, Augustine argues, is also the Supreme Being, the God whose name is "He who is" (*Lib. arb.* II, 3–16). In similar fashion, Aquinas describes the *summon bonum* as pure and complete actuality *(actus purus)* and as being itself *(ipsum esse)* (Ia, q. 3, q. 4, a. 2).

d) The Universality and Transcendentality of Goodness, and the Nonreality of Evil. It is a consequence of both the participation account and the natural-teleology account that everything that has being is good. A thing is good either in virtue of participating in that which is good in itself—that is, in God—and everything that exists participates in him; or it is good in virtue of actualizing its nature, and everything that exists is in actuality to some extent. Christian philosophers and theologians were intrigued by the universality thesis not only because of the support that it received from respected authorities, but also because it was confirmed by the Bible, for example in Genesis 1:31—"And God saw everything that he had made, and behold, it was very good"—or 1 Timothy 4:4— "For everything created by God is good."

The medieval doctrine of the transcendentals is closely related to the universality thesis. Beginning in the early 13th century (see Philippe le Chancelier, †1236, Alexandre de Halès c. 1186–1245, Albert* the Great, Bonaventure*, and Aquinas), this idea was discussed as part of a larger doctrine that holds that being *(ens)*, the one *(unum)*, and the true *(verum)*, in addition to good *(bonum)*, transcend the Aristotelian categories. While the ten categories identify ten irreducible ways of being, being transcends the categorical structure of the world. Anything that is ontologically classifiable is a being, and to say of anything that it is a being is not to identify it as a member of some kind distinct from other kinds of things. According to the classical doctrine, being is the primary transcendental, and other properties are transcendental because the ontological ground of their application to a given thing is the same as the ontological ground in virtue of which that thing can be called a being. In the case of good, for example, the actualities in virtue of which a thing is good are precisely those in virtue of which it has being. Transcendental terms are convertible, or the same in reality *(idem secundum rem)*. They are not synonymous, however, since they are conceptually distinct *(differunt secundum rationem)*.

If goodness is a transcendental, and therefore universal, feature of reality, evil cannot be a reality. In Book Seven of the *Confessions*, Augustine explains how this idea was the cornerstone of his intellectual reconciliation to Christianity. Augustine had returned to Manichean dualism because it offered a clear explanation of the existence of evil: just as good things have flowed from that which is good in itself, evils have flowed from that which is evil in itself—a highest evil opposed to the highest good. His reading of the Platonists, however, convinced him that evil is not a nature or substance, but a corruption or privation. If evil is corruption, it must be corruption of something that is good in some way and to some extent: what has no good cannot be corrupted. Moreover, there cannot be anything that is pure corruption or privation, and so there can be no pure or highest evil opposed to the highest good, as the Manicheans supposed. All substances are good to some extent and, as goods, all flow from God, the highest good.

2. Human Good

a) Happiness.

The metaphysics of good inherited from classical Greece provided grounds for a eudemonistic account of the human good: the human good is the state or activity in which complete actuality as a human being consists. Following the ancient tradition, thinkers in the Middle Ages called this state "happiness" *(felicitas)* or, with a theological nuance, beatitude* *(beatitudo)*. Aristotle's *Nicomachean Ethics,* which, after its full recovery in the early 13th century, exercised enormous influence over reflection on good, presents two apparently conflicting accounts of the activity constitutive of happiness. The account in the early books of the *Ethics* suggests that *eudaimonia* consists in an active life lived in accordance with practical wisdom*, whereas the account in Book Ten suggests that it is to be found in the activity of contemplation*, which is characteristic of the gods. Each of these accounts has attracted Christian thinkers, the former providing a model for the active life of service to others, the latter providing a model for the life of prayer* and contemplation.

However, from the Christian perspective, Aristotle provides at most an account of imperfect or merely human happiness. For Christianity, the ultimate end of human life is supernatural union with God, a state unattainable in this life. The ultimate good for human beings—perfect happiness—is therefore beyond this world, and beyond the natural capabilities of human beings. According to some theologians, special revelation is necessary in order for human beings to come to know what their supernatural ultimate end is, and special divine aid (grace) is necessary for attaining it.

b) Virtue, Right Action, Right Reason.

According to the Greek tradition, the specifically human capacities (those possessed by virtue of having a rational soul, in particular, intellect and will) require certain habits *(habitus)* that dispose them toward their complete actuality. These habits are the intellectual and moral virtues, and they dispose a human being toward the performance of the activities in which human perfection consists. The acquisition and exercise of the virtues, then, is an integral part of attaining happiness. In addition to the traditional cardinal virtues that dispose human beings with respect to purely natural, imperfect beatitude, Christianity has held that there are certain theological virtues—faith*, hope*, and charity (love*)—that dispose human beings toward their supernatural end. Moreover, the notion of grace gives rise to the notion of infused virtues: these are not only theological virtues, but also moral virtues, which are needed to incline human beings toward their supernatural end, and which are infused by grace rather than acquired through moral effort.

Later medieval philosophers applied their metaphysics of goodness not only to agents but also to human actions*. Actions can be viewed as realities or beings, and they can be judged good to the extent to which they possess all the attributes (actualities) that they ought to possess. Since any human action is an entity—a reality—just in virtue of being an action, it possesses goodness to some extent (natural goodness), but it may also possess generic moral goodness, specific moral goodness, or gratuitous goodness, provided that certain other conditions are satisfied. Provided the act (for example, the giving of alms) has an appropriate object (a person in need), the act has generic moral goodness: that is, it satisfies the most basic of several conditions necessary for the action's being purely and simply good. It has specific moral goodness if it is done for an appropriate end, in an appropriate way, and in appropriate circumstances. Finally, an action possesses gratuitous or meritorious goodness if it is performed out of charity.

Since the determination of the conditions of a good action is a matter for reason, these conditions were often summarized by saying that a good action must be in accordance with right reason. On the model of Aristotelian deduction, practical reasoning came to be viewed as starting from self-evident principles and progressing deductively to more determinate principles, and to applications of those principles in particular circumstances. The body of practical principles, whether self-evident (either to all people or only to the learned) or derived from such principles, is the body of natural law*.

c) Law and Divine Commands. For Augustine and Aquinas, the notion of law is closely connected with that of reason. Augustine identifies what he calls the eternal law as the source of all that is just and right in the laws that human beings develop to govern their temporal affairs, and he calls the eternal laws "the highest reason" (*Lib. arb.* I, 6–8). Developing these ideas of Augustine's, Aquinas holds that law is essentially an expression of reason. The eternal law, to which we have partial access through reason and revelation, is an expression of divine reason. The part of the eternal law to which we have access through reason is the natural law (Ia IIae, q. 90–94). Kant* falls squarely within this tradition that connects law with reason. For Kant, pure practical reason is the giver of the moral law. The rational will's dignity and autonomy consists in its being subject only to its own legislation (*Grundlegung* 1).

All Christian thinkers have recognized the existence of divinely revealed laws and precepts*, paradigms of which are found in the Decalogue*. However, contrary to some caricatures, very few have unequivocally endorsed a "divine command" theory of rightness and wrongness. Such a theory holds that the moral value of any act consists solely in its being approved or disapproved, commanded or forbidden, by God. Aquinas claims that only commands that issue from reason can have the force of law. Some thinkers, however, such as John Duns* Scotus or William Ockham (c. 1285–1347), clearly distinguish between positive and natural moral law. They claim that, in the case of divine positive moral law, the rightness of the acts com-

manded consists solely in their being commanded by God, and they take the prohibition of adultery and theft, for example, as falling within this category. Accordingly, these acts are morally wrong because God has prohibited them, and would be right if God enjoined them. Scotus and Ockham maintain, by contrast, that natural moral laws command or forbid actions the rightness of which is independent of the divine will. According to Ockham, not even God can alter the moral value of acts that depend on these laws, because that would involve a contradiction.

The view that God's commands or God's will fundamentally determine what is good or right represents a kind of theological subjectivism. This position *prima facie* appears to preserve God's independence and sovereignty by making God the creator of value, but the greater part of the Christian tradition has joined Augustine and Aquinas in eschewing it, preferring to think of the divine reason rather than the divine will as the ground of value.

3. The Philosophy of Good after the Reformation

In the modern period, philosophical reflection on the nature of good has generally led away from the idea that goodness supervenes on being. The most radical alternative is that presented by subjectivism. David Hume (1711–76), for example, argues that value is not an objective property: a thing's having value consists solely in its being valued by some agent. Value is something that agents impose on the world, not something they discover in the world. Christian thinkers have for the most part found subjectivist accounts unattractive.

The deontological tradition deriving from Kant leads away from the traditional idea of good in a different direction. Kant argues that the only thing that is unconditionally good is the good will, the will that is manifest in acting for the sake of duty. Kant conceives of duty as an imperative that is imposed on us by the universal moral law. His account therefore places the notions of duty and law at the center of moral philosophy, and philosophers who follow Kant in this respect begin not from an account of good, but from an account of justice*.

Finally, modern consequentialism is similar in structure to the tradition stemming from Greek thought: both provide what we might call a metaphysical account of good, and hold that morality has to do with promoting, maximizing, or bringing about good. The hedonistic utilitarianism* of John Stuart Mill (1806–73) exemplifies this view. According to Mill, the only thing intrinsically good is pleasure. All other goods are good, and actions are morally right, only insofar as they promote pleasure. Mill's utilitarianism is a monistic account of good insofar as it holds that only a single thing—pleasure—is intrinsically good. Many consequentialist accounts, however, are pluralistic, identifying more than one intrinsic good. G. E. Moore (1873–1958), for example, held that personal affection, aesthetic enjoyment, and knowledge are among the things that have intrinsic value (1903).

● Anselm, *Monologion*, in M. Corbin (Ed.), *L'œuvre de S. Anselme de Cantorbéry*, vol. I, 1986.
Augustine, *Confessions*, BAug 13–14; *De libero arbitrio*, BAug 6, 155–529; *De natura boni*, BAug 1, 437–509.
Boethius, *Tractatus* and *De consolatione philosophiae*, LCL no. 74, 1973.
D. Hume, *A Treatise of Human Nature*, l. II., 1740, London.
E. Kant, *Grundlegung zur Metaphysik der Sitten*, A.A. 4, Berlin, 1910.
J. S. Mill, *Utilitarianism*, London, 1863.
G. E. Moore, *Principia Ethica*, Cambridge, 1903.
Pseudo-Dionysius, *De divinis nominibus*, PG 3, 585–996, ch. 4.
Thomas Aquinas, *ST* Ia, q. 5, 6, 49; Ia IIae, q. 18–21; *De veritate*, q. 21.
● W. D. Ross (1930), *The Right and the Good*, Oxford.
O. Lottin (1942, new edition 1960), *Psychologie et morale aux XIIe et XIIIe siècles*, Gembloux.
G. H. von Wright (1963), *The Varieties of Goodness*, London.
S. MacDonald (1991), *Being and Goodness: The Concept of the Good in Metaphysics and Philosophical Theology*, Ithaca, NY.
L. Becker (1992), *A History of Western Ethics*, New York.
R. M. Chisholm (1996), "Bien et mal," *DEPhM*, 150–154.

Scott MacDonald

See also **Aristotelianism; Conscience; Ethics; Manicheanism; Platonism; Stoicism**

Gospels

Following contemporary usage, the word "gospel," derived from the Greek *eu-aggelion* in the singular, means the declaration or the message of the "good news" of salvation* in Jesus Christ. In the plural form, it is generally used to refer to the four Gospels regarded as canonical—that is, accepted by the churches* according to the rule (Greek *kanon*, anglicized as "canon*") of faith*. These four Gospels are arranged in the order Matthew, Mark, Luke, John, but this has no chronological significance, and the order has changed from time to time and from place to place. John's Gospel, for example, has sometimes been put at the head of the list; the sequence Matthew, John, Luke, Mark is also found. Other gospels, referred to as *apocryphal*, are known in addition: they include the Gospel of Peter, of which no more than a fragment has been preserved, and several sections of the Gospel of the Hebrews, which was used by some Jewish Christians. Finally, still other gospels, originating at later dates, were circulated in gnostic circles, including the Gospel of Thomas and the Gospel of Philip, which were recently rediscovered at Nag Hammadi in Egypt.

The canonical Gospels, gradually designated as such over the course of the second and third centuries, were circulated initially in the form of anonymous writings before they acquired titles and were ascribed to authors. The Gospels "according to Matthew" and "according to John" were given the names of two of the apostles*; then the other two evangelists were named in the titles of the Gospels "according to Mark" and "according to Luke." These attributions were made at a very early stage, during the lifetime of Papias, who was Bishop of Hierapolis in the early second century. They have every appearance of being historically authentic, even though it remains necessary to keep a distance between the Greek scripture of the Gospel known as Matthew, and the Semitic tradition* related to this Galilean apostle. It is also very likely that there was a considerable lapse of time between the earliest oral traditions gathered from among the followers of the apostle John and the definitive compilation of the Gospel that bears his name. With that said, it is difficult to date any of the Gospels with certainty. However, in line with the earliest approximations, and following the mainstream exegetical consensus—while not denying that discussions continue on this subject—we can specify that: 1) Mark's Gospel was written in Greek around the year 70, and, according to Irenaeus*, probably in Rome* after the death of Peter* (*Adversus Haereses* III, 1. 2); 2) Matthew's was written around 80–85 in Antioch; 3) Luke's was written around the same time, perhaps in Greece; and

4) John's was written around 95, probably in Ephesus in Asia Minor. All four gospels, like the rest of the New Testament, were written in Greek, though some of them may have been partly based on now-lost sources in Aramaic.

It should be mentioned that one of the oldest-known fragments of any of the Gospels, known as Rylands Papyrus 52, is from John's Gospel, and was written during the first half of the second century, barely a few decades after the text was probably first written down. In fact, we no longer possess the original forms of any New Testament texts. But numerous items of evidence in manuscript form allow us to work out the first states of these lost originals with some certainty, as is the case with some 108 fragments on papyrus, ranging from the second century to the fourth, and around 274 manuscripts in uncial (majuscule) Greek text from the fourth to ninth centuries, not to mention the very old versions in Latin and Syriac (eastern Aramaic). Of course, there is a relatively large number of variant readings among these manuscripts, but they are often of secondary importance. The main variations are indicated in critical editions of the New Testament—such as K. Aland and Bruce M. Metzger's *The Greek New Testament* (1983)—and are also mentioned in the notes attached to many of the various translations of the Gospels. Nevertheless, specialists in textual criticism have achieved some reliable reconstructions of the various states of the Gospel texts as they were transmitted in the churches in the second century and after, and have demonstrated the faithfulness of the tradition and transmission of the four Gospels.

It was somewhat later that Irenaeus (martyred in around 202) compared the Gospels to the four rivers of Paradise (Gn 2:10–14) and the four living beings who support God's throne (Ez 1:5–14 and Rev 4:6ff.). The iconographic symbols associated with each evangelist, and hence with each Gospel, are derived from this assimilation, by way of Jerome (the man for Matthew, the lion for Mark, the ox for Luke, and the eagle for John).

I. The Earliest Christian Discourse

The gospel—the proclamation of the Good News—was initially expressed in the register of speech, and therefore of orality, before it found written expression in the four Gospels, which were composed in the broad context of the destruction of the Temple* in Jerusalem* and its aftermath, between the year 70 and the end of the first century. The gospel tradition remained an oral one in Paul's time (between around 51 and 58). Various words are used to refer to this initial spreading of the word, notably *proclaim* and *proclamation*, *witness* and *evidence*, *evangelize* and *gospel*.

1. Three Modalities of the Word

The terms "to proclaim" *(kerussein)*, "to witness" *(marturein)*, "to evangelize" *(euaggelizomai)* evoke the idea of a word* of salvation, proclaimed with sovereign authority by one who does not himself claim to be its author, for its principle is God*, Jesus*, or his Spirit. Such words of revelation* are spoken in the name* of God, in the manner of the ancient prophets* of Israel*. In this way, they are to be distinguished from simple speech (*lalein* or *legein*), and even from the giving of instruction about God or Christ* (*didaskein*). Later, however, the ministers established within the churches as successors to the apostles and the first Christian prophets preferred to use the vocabulary of instruction, or tended to assimilate to one another the verbs just cited. Even so, each of these verbs retained its own nuances within the framework of classical rhetoric, the "deliberative" or "persuasive" type being related to proclamation *(kerugma)*, the "judicial" type to witness *(marturion)*, and the "demonstrative" or scholarly type to instruction *(didache)*, in which the speaker is located objectively, as if at a distance from the words being spoken. We shall examine each of these three modalities in turn.

a) To Proclaim. A kerygma, or proclamation, is a speech delivered in a loud voice, in public, and in the name of an authority* to which it refers. Through the mouth of a herald *(kerux)*, a proclamation announced the holding of games and religious festivals. In aretalogies (collections of narratives* about miracles* and other claims to glory), or within the framework of mystery cults*, proclamations were concerned with the powerful workings of various divine beings. This pagan context probably led the compilers of the Septuagint to limit their use of the word (it appears there only 33 times, including in Genesis 41:43; see ancient translations* of the Bible). However, the verb *kerussein* ("to proclaim") was adopted in translating several prophetic texts that were to play major roles in Christian reinterpretation—notably Isaiah 61:1, Zephaniah 3:14, and Zechariah 9:9, where the word is related to themes of liberation and salvation.

The verb is used frequently in the New Testament (nearly 61 times), other than in the Johannine* tradition, to mean not simply preaching*, but also a performative speech that effects salvation by proclaiming it. Like prophetic speech, it is already an act of God. Thus, Jesus proclaims the coming of the kingdom, and brings it about (Mt 4:17; Mk 1:38–39). The disciples proclaim it in their turn (Mk 3:14 and 13:10). In the

Pauline* writings in particular, such proclamations are directly related to the theme of the cross of the Risen One (1 Cor 1:23: "We preach Christ crucified"); and the Apostle proclaims "the word of faith" (Rom 10:8). However, just as, according to Greek custom, a herald was to be honored by all, so the *kerux* of such a proclamation appeared as his image inverted.

b) To Evangelize. Evangelizing, in the sense of announcing the "good news," was also a matter of using the register of performative speech, but in this case the content of the speech is more directly in consideration. The gospel is the Good News of a salvation that affects both the present, in all its novelty, and the future last days. It is the performative speech of a confession of faith (Rom 1:16); it has to do with a mission, and tends toward fulfillment (Mk 13:10). Here, too, there is a significant difference from the way the same verb was used in the Hellenistic world, where it connoted only the idea of destiny or good fortune, while the noun *euaggelion* simply evoked the idea of a reward or victory. In the later context of the worship of emperors, it was sometimes adopted to refer to the "good news" of the birth or enthronement of an emperor.

In the Hebrew Scriptures, the verb *basar,* meaning to announce the joyful news of a victory (2 Sm 4:10), had already become important. It is sometimes linked to the theme of salvation (Ps 96:2 and Is 40:2, 52:7, and 61:1). However, the Greek equivalent of this verb was rarely used by the compilers of the Septuagint, while the noun *euaggelion* was little known, or unknown, in Hebrew as in Greek. Nevertheless, the following version of a passage from Isaiah has been found at Qumran: "so that [the Master of Justice] announces the good news in the time of your goodness, evangelizing the humble according to the abundance of your mercy" (1QHXVIII, 14; cf. Lk 4:18).

Verb and noun alike then became very important in the Pauline writings (where they are used 60 times) and in the churches that were influenced by them, as well as in the writings ascribed to Luke (Luke's Gospel and the Acts of the Apostles). The Johannine tradition does not use either word, although the theme of witness plays a major role in it.

c) To Witness. Witness was understood as an aspect of the "judicial" type of rhetoric, within a situation of conflict in which the discourse of salvation is given confirmation by authentic testimony. In this case, both the verb *(marturein)* and the noun were used widely across the Hellenistic world. They both appear in the Septuagint (Is 43:9–12), and both John and Luke use them frequently. This insistence on the notion of reliable testimony, evident in the statements of those who witnessed the events of salvation (Acts 1:8 and 1:22), may be explained by reference to the need to stand the test of time and the challenge of the persecutions, during which some went so far as to give their lives to support their testimony (Rev 2:13)—hence the current meaning of the word "martyr*."

2. Paul's Gospel and Mark's Writings

In the Pauline writings, which were composed between around A.D. 51 and 58, *euaggelion* is not used to refer to any written text, but evokes all the force of a speech that effects salvation: "The Gospel is the power of God for salvation to everyone who has faith.... For in it is the righteousness of God" (Rom 1:16–17). In the Pauline writings, "righteousness" refers to the salvific action* of God, who pervades this speech, and acts through his very proclamation. Henceforth, Christ—and, therefore, the speech that proclaims him—is the only power of salvation, replacing the law* of Moses. Every part of that law retains the whole of its value as revelation, but it is now to be taken in relation to the new gospel as the promise* that points to its own fulfillment in Christ.

The earliest groups of Christians displayed a variety of opinions on this very question of the Mosaic Law. Some Jews who had become Christians sought to maintain the Law in its integrity, while the apostle to the nations insisted on the radically new nature of faith in Jesus Christ, which is offered to all believers, whether Jewish or not, and is effectively transmitted by *his* gospel (Rom 2:16 and Gal 1:7). This gospel openly confesses the cross of the Risen One as the principle of salvation. Paul proclaims it without even making use of the narratives or discourses that would later become the basis for the texts of the canonical Gospels. He was undoubtedly aware of these evangelical traditions, but he makes practically no reference to them, other than the narrative of the Last Supper (1 Cor 11:23ff.). Rather than reciting the words and acts of Jesus, Paul recreates their internal meaning—in his own terms, he "imitates" the Lord. Paul's gospel, then, is the proclamation of salvation through the cross of the Lord of Sacrifice. Occasionally, Paul even seems to minimize the importance of one of the other ways of gaining knowledge* of Jesus, "from a human point of view" (2 Cor 5:16).

The Apostle, of course, gives all his attention to the cross of the Lord who lives forever, but the prolonged existence of the church, and the political upheavals that accompanied the Jewish uprising in the years 66–73, posed a direct threat to the memory of Jesus' acts—it was no longer sufficient merely to allude to them, as in the Pauline corpus. It therefore became necessary to gather together in written form the various traditions of the churches in Jerusalem, Antioch, and elsewhere, in order to safeguard the tradition as a whole. It was probably in the wake of various earlier attempts (evoked in Lk 1:1–4), that the first of the narrative ensembles now known as "Gospels" (Mk 1:1) was written down, and it was probably Mark's. It stands midway between a proclamation of faith, in the Pauline manner, and a new type of presentation of the story of Jesus, transmitting his life and his words into the present within a didactic framework. Next, Matthew placed greater emphasis on Jesus' words, while Luke, an historian, brought to his compilation a style of presentation that made it more like a biography. As for John, he adopted an entirely different style of presentation, which is both precise and symbolic, being centered on the interior life of Jesus and of the one whom the Gospel calls the "disciple whom Jesus loved" (Jn 21:7).

II. Forms and Functions of Evangelical Writings

Mark's narrative was innovative in its comprehensive representation of Jesus, but its richness was drawn from a variety of sources. A critical reading of the four Gospels allows us to distinguish, even now, the specific features of these elements of the tradition, as Martin Dibelius and Rudolf Bultmann*, in particular, demonstrated in the first half of the 20th century. Here, we may cite only a few of the main elements, which were initially transmitted orally within the Christian communities before they were partially put into written form. Each of the evangelists made his own use of this heritage, in line with his own christological and missionary purposes.

1. Main Literary Forms
To begin with, the gospel was a confession of faith, a brief formulation of the kerygma (proclamation) of a Christian community, and presented in response to its needs. Traces of such confessions of faith are particularly evident in the Pauline writings (1 Cor 15:1–8), but they also appear in the Gospels (*see* Mk 15:39, Jn 20:28, etc.). Similarly, one also finds elements of blessings* (Mk 11:9–10) and even of ancient Judeo-Christian hymns, applied to Mary* or Zechariah (Lk 1:46–55 and 1:68–79), as well as elements of doxologies (Lk 2:14). However, the main materials of the Gospels may be classified as narratives or discourses.

a) Narratives. The Gospels contain several types of narrative. The narrative of Christ's passion* is the only one that follows a sustained chronological sequence

(such as laid out in Mk 14:1–16:8). Other narratives, initially transmitted in isolation from each other in the oral traditions of the Christian communities, include: apothegms in which a statement (Greek, *logion*) made by Jesus is inserted into a small-scale narrative framework (Mk 10:13–16); accounts of controversies or polemics (Mk 3:1–6); tales of miracles (Mk 1:29ff.) or exorcism* (Mk 5:1–20), in which the emphasis is placed on Jesus' salvific action and his struggle against the forces of evil*, and that are aimed at the active proclamation of the coming of God's kingdom; narratives with a biographical or christological focus (Mk 1:9ff and 9:2–10); popular legends (Mk 6:17–28); and, finally, accounts of the appearance of the Risen One (Mt 28 and Lk 24). There are also accounts of Christ's childhood, which were written at a later period (Mt 1–2 and Lk 1–2).

b) Discourses. The discourses are assemblages of the Lord's remarks *(logia)* put together according to the theme that they share. As examples are five discourses found in Matthew's Gospel: the Sermon on the Mount, which is a program for the evangelical life (Mt 5–7); the discourse on the mission*, which provides rules for the apostles whom Jesus has sent out (Mt 10); the discourse, in the form of parables*, on the kingdom of God (Mt 13); the discourse on communal life (Mt 18); and the eschatological discourse on the destruction of the Temple and the last days (Mt 24–25). These discourses are paralleled in Mark and Luke, although on a smaller scale.

2. Early Narrative Assemblages
It has also been recognized that, in addition to the groups of *logia* just discussed, the Gospels contain narrative assemblages, such as, in Mark's Gospel, a group of controversies (Mk 2:1–3:6), a group of miracles (Mk 4:35–5:43), and a group of apothegms or "nested remarks" within a narrative (Mk 10:1–31). Some of these assemblages, which made things easier for those Christians who first preached on given subjects, must have been put into writing at a very early stage, and the literary style of each of the evangelists remains recognizable. Such a procedure would not have been at all astonishing in the culture of that time. The historians of the ancient Greek world, for example, arranged their materials topic by topic, depending on the subject, without any great concern for the chronology of events. In other words, writers and readers alike knew in advance that the placing of an evangelical statement or narrative within a work of literature did not in itself say or imply anything conclusive about its precise historical placing within the ministry* of Jesus.

3. The Four Gospel Narratives

Mark was the first to organize these isolated traditions, these blocks of narratives and discourses collected in the various communities, into a narrative ensemble that progresses from Christ's baptism* to his passion. Thus, he drew from the tradition the large-scale biographical portrait that is glimpsed in Acts 1:22 and in Peter's speech at Joppa (Acts 10:37–43). Matthew and Luke then worked from Mark's text, correcting it, reorganizing it, and manipulating it with the aid of new materials. The Johannine tradition is much more independent. In every sense, each of the evangelists provides a synthesis of everything that goes to make a life, within the framework of his own particular Gospel. Each of them gathered memories of the Lord from those who survived him, and summarized the confession of faith of his own community, as well as the rules that should be observed in dealing with the faithful or their enemies, without overlooking the rituals of baptism and communal dining that structured his community. We shall now say a little about the way in which each book* is structured.

a) Mark. The evangelist known as Mark presents a discourse that has a proclamatory or confessional finality, within the framework of a sequential narrative that takes us from the baptism to the cross. Mark's introduction describes the baptism of Jesus by John the Baptist (Mk 1:1–13). The figure of Jesus, who is presented as the Son of the God in the strongest sense of the term, and his acts of salvation are continually emphasized throughout the three specific stages of the narrative: Jesus' ministry in Galilee and up to its frontiers (Mk 1:14–8:26); his journey to Jerusalem (8:27–13:37), which is punctuated by three announcements of the passion (8:31ff., 9:30ff., and 10:32ff.); and, finally, the account of the passion itself (14:1–16:8). Mark 16:9–20 is an addition, dating from the second century. The whole narrative is also structured around three pivotal moments at which God himself reveals his son: the baptism, the transfiguration (Mk 1:9ff. and 9:2–10), and the Roman centurion's confession of faith at the foot of the cross, "Truly, this man was the son of God!" (Mk 15:39). At the end, God, through the intermediation of his angel*, declares that Jesus has risen. This is the core of the Easter message (Mk 16:6).

Around the year 70, probably in Rome, and as a member of a church that admitted many different nationalities, Mark reworked an old Judeo-Christian catechism*, known in Peter's circle, placing greater emphasis on the theme of salvation through the cross. This brought him closer to Paul, whose companion he had once been (Acts 12:25). In this way, Mark, who

was described by Papias, in the early second century, as "Peter's interpreter," stood at the meeting point of two traditions.

b) Matthew. The Greek-speaking evangelist known as Matthew is traditionally situated within the sphere of influence of the Galilean apostle Matthew. He reworked and completed Mark's narrative. As a member of a church that was still largely Judeo-Christian, Matthew presents his Gospel in the form of a catechism, constructed chiefly on the basis of the five discourses mentioned above. The plan of his Gospel generally follows that of Mark's, but he added an account of Jesus' childhood (Mt 1–2) and some reports of the appearance of the Risen One (Mt 28:9–20). Matthew also reorganized the tales of miracles taken from Mark (Mt 8–9) and made use of numerous elements, unknown to Mark, that were collected from a second source, now known as "Q" (from the German *Quelle, or* "source"). This Judeo-Christian evangelist places a strong emphasis on the messianic figure of Jesus, who is Christ (that is, Messiah*), "son of David," and Lord.

c) Luke. The Greek-speaking evangelist known as Luke set to work as an historian (Lk 1:1–4) on a large-scale text arranged in two main sections. The first, Luke's Gospel, relates the life of Jesus; the second, the Acts of the Apostles, is the history of the first churches, gathered around Peter and Paul. As a member of a church of former pagans, which owed part of its heritage to Paul's apostolic activity, Luke reworked Mark's materials in his own way. His Gospel also contains an account of Christ's childhood (Lk 1–2) that is very different from Matthew's, as well as accounts of the appearance of the Risen One (Lk 24:13–53). Luke omitted certain elements from Mark (Mk 6:45–7:37) that a Greek readership would barely have understood; and, above all, Luke added a whole new set of the sayings of Jesus, most of them taken from "Q" (Lk 9:51–18:14). From the outset, Luke refers to Jesus as Lord (Lk 2:11), just as Paul had applied this title to Jesus. *Lord* evokes the idea of transcendence, and in the Septuagint the Greek word used refers to God.

d) John. The framework of John's Gospel, which starts with the testimony of John the Baptist and ends with the resurrection*, is very different from that of the three synoptic gospels. Here, the sayings and deeds of Jesus are depicted as much in relation to Judea as to Galilee, following a sequence of selected events generally accompanied by speeches (Jn 5:1–18 and 5:19–47). Ten of the narratives in John's Gospel have parallels in Mark's (for example, Jn 6:1–15); otherwise, John restricts himself to highlighting certain particularly significant events, starting with the miracle at Cana, the first of the signs presented by Jesus (Jn 2:1–12). John's main concern is not to pile up the *logia* or the actions of Jesus in the style of the synoptics, but to insert his own profound understanding of the sayings and deeds of the Lord. On more than one occasion, John gives the impression that he is addressing the material from a more mystical or symbolic perspective. In addition, he gives us a more precise and exact view of the chronology of Christ's ministry than Mark does. His allusions to the building of the Temple at Jerusalem (Jn 2:20) and to Jesus' three pilgrimages* to that city at the time of the Jewish Passover (Jn 2:23, 6:4, 12:1) allow us to establish that Christ's ministry lasted for more than two years, beginning around the year 27. These major differences between John's Gospel and the synoptics suggest that his was written in a very specific communal milieu, which was of a Judeo-Christian type but was also probably influenced by the Essenes and, still more, by an elaborate conception of Christ as the Word* of God preexisting in the world* (Jn 1:1, 8:58, and 20:28).

III. Brief History of the Exegesis of the Gospels

Since the early second century *(I Apologia 67)*, the time of Justin, if not earlier, the texts of the Gospels have been interpreted in the context of the liturgy* and with reference to the Lord's Supper. The Gospels have functioned, in a sense, in line with their original purposes—to confess the faith, and to help the community to live. Of course, from the first centuries of Christianity onward, there have been attempts to reduce, if not eliminate, the differences among the four narratives, but as early as the late second century Irenaeus called for the unity of their message to be respected, whatever the diversity in their statements of it.

Much later, starting in the 18th century, and notably with Reimarus in Germany, and with Voltaire and the Encyclopedists in France, the language of the Gospels, which is shot through with images and symbols in the Semitic manner, increasingly came to seem hermetic, and to be used in ways that contradicted modern views of history*. Little or nothing of Jesus' life seemed capable of surviving the historicism and positivism of the early modern era. Ernest Renan's novelistic biography of the Galilean, *La vie de Jesus* (1863; *The Life of Jesus*) represents something of an attempt to escape from this positivist straitjacket, but its literary success does not compensate for its methodological defects. A better understanding of the language of the New Testament has been promoted by major literary and archeological discoveries in the Middle East—notably at Qumran

from 1947—and these have at last allowed us to make some more pertinent assessments of the literary methods used by the writers of antiquity.

Critical study of the Gospels has been undergoing vigorous development for more than 100 years, starting with the work of J. Weiss and J. Wellhausen, and passing through several stages in succession. 1) First, critical discussion of the sources of the synoptic gospels has shed more light on the literary connections among them. Two conflicting theories have been elaborated. One theory postulates the existence of two sources underlying Matthew and Luke—Marks' Gospel and the source known as "Q"—inferred from the presence of common elements in both Matthew and Luke despite the fact that these two evangelists had no known contact with each other. This theory is upheld today by F. Neirynck of Louvain, among others. The other theory, associated with L. Vaganay, M.-E. Boismard, and X. Léon-Dufour, postulates one or several texts in Aramaic and Greek underlying all three synoptic Gospels. 2) From around 1920, however, Dibelius and Bultmann drew attention to the ancient literary forms that evolved from the oral tradition, launching a far-reaching reinterpretation of the Gospels known as *Formgeschichte* (form criticism). Bultmann was also the originator of a new hermeneutics* of the Gospels, adopting an existential interpretation inspired by his reading of Heidegger*. 3) From 1950 onward, a greater interest developed, in the *Redaktionsgeschichte* of the Gospels, and in the theology* or Christology* of each of the evangelists, as in Hans Conzelmann's study of Luke. Since then, what is known as historico-critical exegesis has become better equipped to understand the literary genesis of each Gospel and to trace the *Traditionsgeschichte* associated with it from the first oral traditions to the stage of composition in written form, which came with varying lapses of time in each case. 4) Since 1970 there has been a reaction against these earlier interpretations, which are reconstructions of the literary history of the texts rather than readings of the Gospels as they now are. Some new literary approaches have gradually received recognition, including the semiotic method inspired by A. J. Greimas, and the exploration of the structural or rhetorical procedures of antiquity. 5) Today, the study of the Gospel texts exploits, without bringing into conflict, both *synchronic* procedures—reading the texts in terms of their present literary state and internal mechanisms—and *diachronic* procedures—interpreting them by reconstructing the stages of their development. In particular, attention is being paid, within the framework of the sociology of religion, to the different milieus of the Judeo-Christian and Helleno-Christian communities from which the earliest elements of the Christian "memory" of Jesus were drawn. Such varied studies allow us to discuss the story of Jesus while taking account of the social and communal contexts of these elements. Reacting against some of Bultmann's conclusions, E. Käsemann has laid the foundations for a historical methodology that could underpin evaluations of the authenticity of the reported sayings and deeds of Jesus, including his miracles. Located at a distance from novelistic biographies of Jesus, and refraining from any interference with internalized religious interpretations, critical research on the Gospels remains open to an improved understanding of the Gospels and, through them, to an approach to the figure of Jesus, who nonetheless remains mysterious.

• General Introduction

X. Léon-Dufour (1963), *Les évangiles et l'histoire de Jésus,* Paris; (1976), "Les évangiles synoptiques," in A. George and P. Grelot (Ed.), *Introduction à la Bible: L'annonce de l'Évangile* III/2, 11–237.

R. Brown, J. A. Fitzmyer, and R. E. Murphy (Ed.) (1990), *The New Jerome Biblical Commentary,* Avon.

Apocryphal Gospels

E. Hennecke (1959), *Neutestamentliche Apokryphen* I-II, Tübingen.

J. Jeremias (1963), *Unbekannte Jesusworte,* Gütersloh.

Criticism (study of manuscripts)

B. M. Metzger (1968), *The Text of the New Testament,* 2nd Ed., Oxford.

L. Vaganay, C. B. Amphoux (1986), *Initiation à la critique textuelle,* Paris.

Some Critical Commentaries

M.-J. Lagrange wrote a series of commentaries on the Gospels, published in the Etudes bibliques, 1927–1929.

V. Taylor (1952, 1969), *The Gospel according to St Mark,* London.

P. Benoit, M.-E. Boismard (1965, 1972), *Synopse des quatre évangiles* I-II, Paris.

P. Bonnard (1966, 1970), *L'Évangile selon saint Matthieu,* Neuchâtel.

R. Brown (1966, 1970), *The Gospel according to John* I-II, Anchor Bible, New York.

R. Pesch (1976, 1977), *Das Markusevangelium* I-II, Friburg.

M.-E. Boismard, A. Lamouille (1977), *L'évangile de Jean* III, Paris.

J. A. Fitzmyer (1981, 1985), *The Gospel according to Luke* I-II, New York.

F. Bovon (1991), *L'évangile selon saint Luc* I, Geneva.

Synoptic Question and Some Studies on the History of the Tradition

M. Dibelius (1933), *Die Formgeschichte des Evangeliums,* 2nd Ed., Tübingen.

L. Vaganay (1954), *Le problème synoptique,* Paris.

W. Marxsen (1956), *Der Evangelist Markus: Studium zur Redaktionsgeschichte des Evangeliums,* Göttingen.

J. Dupont (1958, 1969, 1973), *Les Béatitudes* I–III, EtB.

H. Conzelmann (1960), *Die Mitte der Zeit: Studien zur Theologie des Lukas,* 3rd Ed., Tübingen.

E. Trocmé (1963), *La formation de l'évangile selon Marc,* Paris.

R. Bultmann (1971), *Die Geschichte der synoptischen Tradition,* 3rd Ed., Göttingen.

M. Didier (Ed.) (1971), *L'évangile selon Matthieu: Rédaction et théologie,* Gembloux.

M. Sabbe (Ed.) (1974), *L'évangile selon Marc: Tradition et rédaction,* Louvain.

J. Dupont (1985), *Études sur les évangiles synoptiques* I–II, Louvain.

On Historical Jesus

A. Schweitzer (1913), *Geschichte der Leben-Jesu Forschung,* Tübingen, gives precious indications on the ancient authors: Reimarus, Paulus, D. Strauss, J. Weiss, and J. Wellhausen (2nd Ed. 1951).

E. Käsemann (1954), "Zur Frage des historischen Jesus," *ZThK* 51, 125–53.

C. Perrot (1979), *Jésus et l'histoire,* Paris (2nd Ed. 1993).

J. P. Meier (1991 and 1994), *A Marginal Jew* I-II, New York.

CHARLES PERROT

See also **Bible; Book; Canon; Christ/Christology; Literary Genres in Scripture; Intertestament; Jesus, Historical; Messianism/Messiah; Miracle; Myth; Narrative; Parable; Passion**

Gottschalk of Orbais. *See* Augustinianism

Government. *See* Authority

Government, Church

The government of the Church encompasses all the duties and powers assigned to the Church of Jesus* Christ to enable it to fulfill its mission in history*. This mission, in accordance with the Church's fundamental mandate, is to proclaim the gospel, to administer the sacraments*, and to guide communities in a pastoral spirit, while respecting different sociocultural contexts. The Church cannot achieve this aim in practice without the function of internal government involving an institutional dimension. The various denominations, according to their respective ecclesiological principles, have established different forms of government. They are, however, united insofar as they maintain the essentials of all the structural elements prescribed by the New Testament, though each organizes these in its own way. This is why, for all the frequently unilateral exercise of government within each Church, dialogue is an important element, and vital to the success of the Church's work. Throughout history the question of what form Church government should take has often been linked to the problem of relations between Church* and State, initially from the standpoint of their external form (Caesaropapism/Papocaesarism, State Church/Church-State or city* of God*), then from the standpoint of the integration into the Church of political forms of government (the Church as monarchy, the debate over democracy*).

a) The Catholic Church. Its fundamental organization is not laid down by a constitutional charter, but is codified along with other regulations, chiefly in the *Code of Canon Law (CIC)* of 1983. It is underpinned by the conviction that the visible institution of the Church is the incarnation of the religious reality of grace*. As the people* of God, the Church is composed of believers among whom "there exists, as far as their dignity and activity is concerned, a real equality in accordance with which all work together at con-structing the Body of Christ, each according to his own station and function" (can. 208, *CIC*). They are guided in this by a number of duties and rights, among which are freedom* of opinion, apostolic activity, spiritual* direction, and freedom of association (can. 209–31).

The Church is structured vertically into universal Church, local* Church, and community (parish). In it, authority is exercised by an ecclesial power *(sacra potestas),* hierarchically organized and having divine right, within which should be distinguished the power of order *(potestas ordinis)* and the power of jurisdiction *(potestas iurisdictionis).* The former is conferred by the sacrament of order, is absolutely inalienable, and is composed of prerogatives linked to episcopal, priestly, or diaconal ordination*. The latter may be temporally restricted; it is subdivided into legislative, executive, and judicial powers. The Pope* holds supreme jurisdiction over the universal Church, over all the particular churches, and over every believer. His authority is unlimited and not dependent upon any other organ of government. He is elected by the members of the College of Cardinals who have not passed the age of eighty, and he assumes his dignity (provided he is already a bishop*) by the simple act of accepting his election. He loses it only on dying, unless he abdicates, commits heresy*, or becomes insane. To exercise his universal ministry* he has at his disposal the Synod of Bishops, the College of Cardinals, the Roman Curia, legates, and nuncios. A bishop receives his ministry by delegation from the Pope, and is in charge of a local Church of which he is the legislator, administrator, and supreme judge. In these functions he calls on a diocesan curia that comprises the holders of various offices: vicar general, vicar episcopal, official, chancellor, notaries, trustees of the episcopal estate, and treasurer. The cathedral chapter is often replaced by a council of diocesan priests or a college of advisers. Bishops belong to the episcopal college, whose members are hierarchically joined *(communio hierarchica)* to their head, the Pope. Except in the context of this union, they do not hold the supreme power of the Church, either in ecumenical councils or in the joint official decisions that they make across the world. The bishops, in addition, are generally assembled into an episcopal conference. At the community level it is the parish priest who fulfills the responsibilities of government, by delegation from the bishop.

This rigorously hierarchical structure is counterbalanced by a synodal principle of co-responsibility, in other words the working together of all the members of the Church according to their status. This principle expresses itself, on the level of the *universal Church,* in the ecumenical council and the Synod of Bishops (which since 1965 has been an assembly of bishops from different regions acting as a consultative body to the Pope). At the level of the *regional or national church* it can be seen in the episcopal conference (a permanent assembly of the bishops of a region or country, who exercise their pastoral responsibilities in it as a college; it is appointed by the Pope and constitutes a distinct legal entity), as well as in the regional councils (the plenary council for the territory under the authority of an episcopal conference, the provincial council for an ecclesiastical province). At the level of the *particular church* it appears in the diocesan synod, the presbyteral council, the pastoral diocesan council, and the board of trustees of the diocesan estate. At *parish* level it is to be seen in the pastoral council and the board of trustees of the parish estate. All these synodal bodies—with the exception of the ecumenical council and the authorities administering the estates of particular churches—have a merely consultative role and do not challenge the hierarchical principle.

b) The Orthodox Churches. While the different regional or national churches of the Orthodox community are governed by a common law, the principle of autocephaly and the lack, during the second millennium, of ecumenical councils with authority over the Church as a whole have made it impossible to codify the countless distinctive practices. Dispensations, and the principle of "economy" (which adapts legislation to different practical situations), serve moreover to give legal validity to departures from the regulations enacted by the first seven universally recognized councils. The basic church structure* is the local church, which administers the Eucharist* and is governed by a bishop. It is joined by the catholicity of the Church (in the *koinonia*—the *communio*) to all the other local churches, through their own bishops. In concrete terms, local communities joined together at an early date into regional unions, from which arose the patriar-

chates* and the autocephalous churches. The Orthodox Church has no central government as Catholicism* does. An autocephalous church is a particular church whose leader, usually a patriarch, is not appointed by a superior authority (patriarch, metropolitan, or archbishop), but rather elected and enthroned by a synod of bishops. He thus holds the entire power of jurisdiction, with the proviso that the rights of each particular bishop are preserved. The priest and real head of a local church is the bishop, on whom devolves the power of order *(exousia hieratikè),* of teaching *(exousia didaktikè),* and of jurisdiction *(exousia dioitikè).* His autonomy cannot be questioned by any other member of the hierarchy* (unless he is accused of neglecting the duties of his ministry).

The real constitutional principle of the Orthodox Church is the synodal structure, which has its theological basis in the equality of all the local Churches (and thus of their bishops). This principle is embodied in the following manner: the regional synod *(sunodos topikè)* is the supreme doctrinal, legislative, and judicial body of an autocephalous church, and has the right to elect its leader (a patriarch or other hierarch). The regional synod is either episcopal (composed only of bishops) or eparchial (also open to priests, monks, and lay* members). The *sunodos endèmousa,* a typically Byzantine structure, gathered together on an almost daily basis the bishops who were present at the patriarchal see. It has equivalents (the holy synod) in most of the autocephalous churches (for the *ecumenical synod,* see council*). The primatial principle also plays a part in the Orthodox Church, however, more or less pronounced in accordance with the bishop's authority over his diocese, of the metropolitan over his province, of the patriarch over the autocephalous church, and of the ecumenical patriarch over the autocephalous churches as a whole. The power of this last is admittedly contested, but there is a tendency nowadays to accept that the unity of the Church requires the existence of a superior authority.

The laity—the community at the mercy of the hierarchy—has a relatively strong position within the Church structure, which is expressed through the interpenetration of Church and State, on the model of the *sumphonia* between the Patriarch (the Church) and the Emperor (the State), which has allowed the apparatus of the State to have a great influence on the Church. The principle of catholicity aroused an interest on the part of 19th-century Slavophile Russian theology* (A. S. Khomiakov, 1804–1860) in the involvement of all Christians in the destiny of the Church. According to this approach, the responsibility for administrative and doctrinal government extends to all the faithful through the reception* of hierarchical rules, as well as by teaching in the faculties of theology (generally entrusted to lay-people) and by preaching* (which may also be entrusted to them). Furthermore, the Church as a whole is infallible.

c) The Churches Originating in the Reformation. On account of their origins, these churches are clearly differentiated from the hierarchical structure of the Catholic Church. They emphasize instead the common priesthood* of all the faithful and the unity of the spiritual ministry, whose different expressions are in their view a matter for human law *(ius humanum).* All ecclesiastical offices are temporally limited on principle. The freedom that the Protestant churches have thus granted themselves, but also historical circumstances (since not one German bishop adopted Lutheranism* in the course of the 16th century, the bishop's role in government was transferred to the prince as *summus episcopus in externis*), have brought about a proliferation of forms of government, which are codified in the key regulations of the various churches. We will consider only a few elements that they all have more or less in common.

In *Lutheranism,* a ternary structure is often encountered: within the parish community the tasks of government and administration are the responsibility of one or more pastors*, as well as a collegiate body (presbyteral council) consisting of the latter along with members elected from among the community. The parishes are grouped into associations on an intermediate level ("inspectorates," ecclesiastical districts, deaneries, or consistories), generally under a minister, council, or synodal body. The highest authority is the provincial or regional church *(Landeskirche),* whose system of government varies greatly from one region to another. Generally speaking, authority is held by the synod, the bishop (or president of the regional church), or a directory: these are responsible for maintaining the unity* of the regional church, coordinating its activities, and supporting the communities in their church work. In addition, there is an administrative structure and a judicial authority. There are also denominational federations on a national level (such as that Alliance nationale des Églises luthériennes de France) or the international level (the Lutheran World Federation). In the *Reformed Churches,* the "presbyteral" form of government was established from the outset, with a ministerial structure on four levels: pastor, reader, elder, and deacon*. In 1559 the French national synod incorporated this form of government within a synodal structure (the *moderamina*). Authority is never vested in an individual ministry. The *Anglican Communion,* by contrast, has retained the episcopate and accords a large measure of authority by divine right to the bishop, who takes his or her place in the apostolic* succession. The Church of England is a state church, which grants an important role to the episcopal and, to a lesser extent, the synodal authorities. It is subject to the Crown, and Parliament and the Government also have a right of intervention. The government of the Church is organized hierarchically around the ministries of the bishop, priest, and deacon. The parish councils, cathedral chapters, diocesan assemblies, and General Synod of the Church all have their own specific rights. The latter has the power to adopt laws, which must however be ratified by Parliament.

● E. Wolf (1961), *Ordnung der Kirche,* Frankfurt.
H. Dombois (1961–74), *Das Recht der Gnade,* 3 vols., Witten and Bielefeld.
A. Boussé, A. Mandouze (1963), *L'évêque dans l'Église du Christ,* Paris-Tournai.
G. Caprile (1968–78), *Il sinodo dei vescovi,* 5 vols., Rome.
W. Aymans (1970), *Das synodale Element in der Kirchenverfassung,* Munich.
H. Frost (1972), *Strukturprobleme evangelischer Kirchenverfassungen,* Göttingen.
W. Maurer (1976), *Die Kirche und ihr Recht,* Tübingen.
J. Listl, H. Müller, H. Schmitz (1983), *Handbuch des katholischen Kirchenrechts,* Regensburg.
K. Walf (1984), *Einführung in das neue katholische Kirchenrecht,* Zurich.
G. Ghirlanda (1985), "De natura, origine et exercitio potestatis regiminis iuxta novum codicem," *PRMCL* 74, 109–164.
E. G. Moore, T. Briden (1985), *Moore's Introduction to English Canon Law,* 2nd Ed., London and Oxford.
A. Jensen (1986), *Die Zukunft der Orthodoxie,* Zurich.
H. Frost, E. Wolf, W. Aymans (1987), "Kirchenverfassung," *EStL*3 I, 1711–71.
A. Anton (1989), *Conferencias episcopales – instancias intermedias,* Salamanca.
W. Aymans (1991), *Beiträge zum Verfassungsrecht der Kirche,* Amsterdam.
M. Kaiser, "Potestas iurisdictionis?", in W. Aymans (Ed.) (1991), *Fides et ius,* Regensburg, 81–107.
R. Puza (1993), *Katholisches Kirchenrecht,* 2nd Ed., Heidelberg.

WOLFGANG BEINERT

See also **Collegiality; Communion; Indefectibility of the Church; Infallibility; Jurisdiction; Orthodoxy; Protestantism**

Grace

Grace is the very essence of God's solicitude for mankind, as it is incarnated in Jesus* Christ and is communicated to the depths of human nature* as a gift from the Holy* Spirit. It also sums up the relationship that, based on this gift, is established between God* and a human being who will still need grace to answer to grace.

I. Biblical Theology

1. The Old Testament

The whole Bible* is a testimony of the act of God's grace. This purpose crystallizes in different concepts of the Old Testament, which are combined in many ways by formulas of reverence (for example, in Ex 34:6). At the same time, it points to the central importance of the confrontation of man with a God of grace in the veterotestamentary faith.

The Hebrew *chnn*, which, in human relationships, designates an attitude of kindness—most often from a superior to a subordinate—is the theological expression of God's boundless love* (Gn 6:8). The divine *chèsèd* founds a certain relationship with mankind, one that is marked by fidelity (Jer 31:3) and takes shape in the favors given by God (Gn 32:11); *rchm* represents the parental tenderness (Is 49:15 and Ps 103:13) and *çdq* an action dictated by fidelity to the community (Ps 36:7–9).

The veterotestamentary conception of grace is characterized by the consciousness of the free and unconditional solicitude of a God (Ex 33:19 and Dt 7:7f.) that exists for his people* (Ex 3:14). God's grace is shown in the Covenant* with Israel*, to which he binds himself as to a fiancée (Hos 2:21f.). His solicitude is seen in forgiveness and mercy*, YHWH answering to infidelity with more love (Is 54:7–10). Divine grace is also expressed in historical events (Is 63:7–14 and Ps 136), especially the Exodus. It is grace that prevents extreme peril or unjust persecution, that forgives a fault and favors prosperity on earth (by granting descendents or a country). The act of God's grace is first shown to a people, but as belief in his choice* falters, grace tends to be experienced by individuals. Post-biblical rabbinical Judaism* includes the events of Salvation*, in particular the Covenant and the Torah, as proofs of grace.

2. The New Testament

In the New Testament the act of God's grace finds its eschatological figure in Jesus Christ, in whom "the kingdom* of God is at hand" (Mk 1:15 par) and eternal life is granted (Jn 3:16). It is only in Pauline* theology that the term *kharis* itself becomes a central concept of the Christian message. Grace, here, is carried out above all in the justification* of sinners by Jesus Christ, who gave himself for them (Rom 3:23f.; 5). In Christ*, grace is offered to all men without consideration of merit (Gal 2:21). It is the power that triumphs over sin* and death*, and thus, that brings liberty* (2 Cor 3:17). A person participates in grace by proclaiming the Gospel*, faith (Rom 1:16), and baptism* (Rom 6). The act of God's grace unfurls in the charisma that forms the body of Christendom (Rom 12:3–21 and 1 Cor 1:4–9). The Deutero-Pauline emphasize the present existence in grace (Eph 1:3–14) which is granted in Jesus Christ (2 Tm 1:9f.), who is grace itself (Ti 2:11).

II. History of Theology

1. The Ancient Church

a) The Apostolic Fathers. Just as the neotestamentary epistles were already relating the consolation of grace offered in Jesus Christ to the exhortation of living in accordance with it, several texts by the Apostolic* Fathers stressed the ethical demands that the gift of grace entails. More specifically, it was in monasticism*, throughout the history of Christianity, that interest in the ethical consequences of grace was perpetuated.

b) Greek Patristics. The Greek patristics developed a doctrine of grace integrated into the universal perspective of the history of Salvation. Irenaeus* of Lyons thus understood grace as a salvific event *(oikonomia)* through which God, in a pedagogical process *(paideia),* brings man to participate in divine life, in accordance to an end assigned to him since his creation*. This concept holds the seed of the distinction between an original grace (resemblance to God) and a salvific grace (deification). The central event of this process of fulfillment of grace is the Incarnation*, through which the degraded image of God is restored and completed in man.

The conception of grace elaborated by Clement of Alexandria (140/150–c. 216/217) and Origen* is also from the perspective of the final deification of man. Influenced by Platonism* and stressing the free cooperation of man in the gift of grace, they opened the way to a mysticism* inspired by Neoplatonism (Evagrius Ponticus, 345–99, and Dionysius* the Pseudo-Areopagite) that interprets grace as purification, enlightenment, and union.

In the fourth and fifth centuries, christological and pneumatologic doctrine developed under the influence of the idea of deification, insofar as it presupposed the divinity of the Son and the Spirit. This allowed theologians to specify the tie between deifying grace with the Man-God Jesus Christ and the regenerate act of the Spirit, as well as the Trinitarian dimension of grace, as the dwelling of the three divine persons in man.

c) About Orthodoxy. The Eastern doctrine of grace perpetuates the notion of the Greek Fathers. Jesus Christ's grace, divine life bestowed upon man through the abundance of Christ's life, is closely linked to the operation of the Spirit. Grace makes man similar to God and includes him in the communion* of intratrinitary life. It is above all in liturgy* that this deification is carried out. Gregory* Palamas's theology played an important role in the Orthodox doctrine of grace.

d) Western Patristics. The West integrated this doctrine on grace, which the Eastern Church saw on a universal and cosmic plan, in an entirely different context. Christianity here was understood as the institution and materialization of a new legal relationship between God and man. It involved understanding how the individual, a prisoner of his sin, might find the path to salvation through his personal liberty*. Grace, in this perspective, is considered a divine force that helps man reach salvation. This thought, which has roots in Tertullian* and Cyprian*, found its shape in Augustine*'s theology. For Augustine, the powerlessness of the sinner to do good*, and also his non-liberty, must be abolished, healed, and transformed from the inside by God's grace before the sinner can make progress toward his salvation by himself. Through this strict definition of the respective powers of liberty and grace, Augustine established a competing relationship between the two that would considerably concern theology*.

Pelagius and his disciples opposed the Augustinian concept of grace. They wanted to include what they thought to be latitudinarian tendencies by relating man to an immanent grace, already manifested in his own natural aptitudes, as well as to external forms of grace *(gratia externa)*—the Law*, Jesus Christ, the Scriptures, and the Church*. Because God does not demand anything that man cannot accomplish, it is fundamentally possible for man to live without sin after his baptism, and he must endeavor to do so. And it is precisely this possibility that Augustine, in an in-depth analysis of the vicious circle of sin, excludes. Beyond instructions and external models, man needs grace like he needs an internal force *(gratia interna)*, the initiative of which radically and fully determines the salvific process.

In 418, against Pelagianism*, the regional Council of Carthage, influenced by Augustine—though not agreeing with him on every point—declared that man absolutely needs the specific help of grace *(DS 225–30)*. In response to Augustine, John Cassian (c. 360–435) and the monastic theologians of Provence championed a theology that left more room to the liberty of man. Named "semi-Pelagianism" sometime after, this theology was to be rejected in 529 at the Council of Orange *(DS 370–97)*.

2. The Middle Ages

a) The Scholastic Development. The Augustinian problematics (grace as a particular force through which God determines man from the inside, and the relationship between grace and liberty) thrived until medieval times. In accordance with the anthropological perspective that led the West to favor the practical and ethical aspect of faith, grace was then often integrated into the doctrine of virtues*. Peter Lombard (c. 1095–c. 1160), like any Augustinian, resolved the question of the relationship between grace and liberty in terms of the precedence of the former. Grace precedes the movement of the free will: it is an "infused" quality *(habitus infusus)* and not "acquired."

The essential elements of Thomas* Aquinas's conception of grace were developed in the *Summa Theologica* Ia, IIae, q. 109–14. According to Thomas, man, from the beginning, is destined to communion with God, which he would never be able to accomplish without grace (in any case and even independently from sin he could not accomplish it—even though, in fact, his sin makes grace a necessity). Grace being thus situated relatively to the external principles of action, it seems that man does not possess grace on his own, but receives it from God as sanctifying grace *(gratia sanctificans)*, in such a way, however, that it becomes truly internal (habitual grace, or *gratia habitualis*). The distinction between uncreated grace *(gratia increata)*, which is nothing else than God himself in his love for man, and created grace *(gratia creata)*, which is the effect of the act of divine grace in man, corresponds to this double aspect of grace.

b) Later Scholasticism. This internal connection between the divine aspect and the human aspect of grace waned in later Scholasticism*, which explains how, for example, champions of nominalism* could have wondered if the adoption of man by God depended on the internalization of grace. To preserve the liberty of God, it was thought that there was only a necessity of fact, which did not prevent a very optimistic view of man's natural capacity to prepare himself for grace through his own merits. The Reformers would object first and foremost.

3. Modern Era

a) The Reformation. It was first as an act of justification* of man that Luther* understood divine grace. The sinner, who seeks in vain to justify himself by his works* against the accusation of the Law, cannot find grace in God's eyes outside of the justification brought by Jesus Christ and which he only receives in faith. The union with Christ produces a real justice* that regenerates man from the inside. It cannot be, however, attributed to him by merit; it does not require any ontological roots—no created grace residing in man—but rather appears as the fruit of a new relationship with God, which gives man the liberating certainty of being saved. In the Lutheran tradition, the interest in grace as the bearer of salvation (sanctifying grace) was developed by Melanchthon (1497–1560). Pietism* would make the connection between justification and sanctification even clearer. Calvin* saw grace more as a link between the justifying and redeeming work of Christ, on one hand, and its assimilation in the life of Christians as influenced by the Holy Spirit, on the other. The federal theology stemming from Zwingli* saw grace from a theocentric point of view, highlighting God's global covenant with his creatures.

b) The Council of Trent. The Council of Trent* rejected the position of the Reformers, but answered it with key explanations: it thus stressed the necessity of grace and subordinated the doctrine of grace to that of justification, without reducing it to that (*DS* 1520–83). The grace of God, which awakens and rescues the creature (*DS* 1525), has absolute priority over all human action; however, man's liberty (*DS* 1521 and 1554–55), and the possibility he has to cooperate in a commendable way with grace (*DS* 1545–49 and 1582), are not abolished. Although the Council, in the debate that put it at odds with the Protestants, had to set itself apart from the reforming theses on faith and the certainty of Salvation (*DS* 1531f, 1562, 1533f, and 1563–66), it is the basic agreement between their respective positions that is more striking to us today. Suspecting that, for the Reformers, justification did not truly transform man, the Council specified the action

of created grace in terms of effects *in* man and *on* man: the distinction was to be referred to often. With regard to this foundation, the theology of the Counter-Reformation would mainly focus on the anthropological aspect of grace—on created grace and on the ethical consequences of justification.

c) Post-Tridentine Theology. The relationship between grace and liberty, and the idea that this involves a competition, gave rise, between 1597 and 1607, to the "grace dispute." The Thomist theologian Domingo Báñez (1528–1604) characterized grace as infallibly efficacious *(gratia efficax),* man's liberty therefore being preserved only by the basic concept of a sufficient grace *(gratia sufficiens)* that, as a result, does not reach its goal. Conversely, the Jesuit Luis de Molina (1535–1600) stressed man's liberty, the sovereignty of God thus only being preserved by "middle knowledge" *(scientia media),* which allows him to foresee the result of human actions. In 1607 Pope Paul V forbade the defenders of these two systems of grace to condemn each other (*DS* 1997).

Behind this dispute, two divergent images of man opposed each other, and the difference came to the forefront when Baius (1513–89), Jansen (1585–1638), and Quesnel (1634–1719) adopted Augustine's thought on the real corruption of nature by sin in order to apply it to the abstract concept of nature (to nature in its essence). Thus nature remains incomplete in man without grace and is destroyed in the fall. Grace is needed to complete the essential aspect of nature, but it is, by this fact, naturalized—that is, understood as an integral part of nature. This notion was to be officially condemned (*DS* 1901–80 [1567], 2001–07 [1653], 2301–32 [1690], and 2400–2502 [1713]).

It then became necessary to specify that the theological concept of nature did not include grace, and this terminological clarification gave rise to Baroque Scholastic and Neoscholastic speculations on "pure nature" *(natura pura),* a closed-in nature, geared toward its own end, to which an extrinsic grace is added, like a supplementary stage. It is against this background that the optimism of the Enlightenment (and the overestimation of nature's powers) developed, as did the processes of secularization* (concerned with ridding the secular world of a grace stripped of significance for the natural existence of man). It was to these tendencies, which sought to separate grace and nature, that apologetic thought on immanence (Blondel*) attempted to respond.

4. Contemporary Theology
In Protestant theology, which was more receptive to Enlightenment thought, it was Karl Barth* (1886–1968)

who protested more than anyone against reducing grace to a simple ethical force, and did so in the name of the immeasurable character of grace. In the Catholic camp, theological historians were charged with unearthing the patristic concepts of the history of Salvation and opening the way for the true intentions of Scholastic thought. Furthermore, dialogical personalism played a strong role in reviving the perception of a reality that had almost ended up being reduced to its ontic and natural dimension (E. Brunner and R. Guardini). Some theologians developed theories on the inhabitation of the Holy Spirit in man (Matthias Joseph Scheeben*) or the initial act of communication of God's self (Karl Rahner*). Thus, the unilateral interest in created grace waned, and it was henceforth more clearly connected to the initiative of a God of grace. In this way, they were given the means to avoid seeing the relationship between nature and grace in terms of juxtaposition and superposition—recognizing that the former came metaphysically after the latter (Eschweiler and Schmaus) and crediting man as having a natural desire for supernatural communion with God (Maréchal).

Contemporary theology is no longer based on an abstract nature with its own end, but on real man. It is man, in his historical and concrete being, who, from the moment he is created, calls to grace ("new theology"—Lubac*). He immediately moves, in fact, in the horizon of the act of grace through which God wanted to communicate with him and which determines him in an existential manner (Rahner's "supernatural existential man"). Moreover, this in no way diminishes the unmotivated character of grace, as emphasized in the encyclical *Humani Generis* (1950). The idea that God freely introduced the supernatural end of human nature, prior to all work, is, on the contrary, the most certain guarantee. From these theoretical specifications, the theology of grace finally evolved into a larger field than the one belonging to the Christian institution; its effects can also be extended all the way to the entire cosmic process (P. Teilhard de Chardin).

A tighter connection between nature and grace was also expressed in Vatican II (see, for example, *LG* 36 and 40). The Council fathers referred to the communion dimension of grace and focused on the signs of grace outside of the Church (*LG* 13 and 16).

The most recent works deal with the meaning of grace in the realization of the humanity of man (Schillebeeckx, Küng), the intelligence of grace as the advent of liberty (Rahner, Greshake, Pröpper), its communional and ecclesial dimension (Greshake), the worldly character of its experience, and its extension into ethical and political action (political* theology and liberation* theology).

III. Systematic Theology

1. The History of Salvation Perspective

Above all, grace is God himself, the triune and gracious God who offers his love. In his universal wish for salvation, he destined man from the beginning to be in communion with him, not so as to offer him *something,* but to share *himself* and his divine life. Even though this participation is meant to lead to a dialogical relationship, the eternal wish for salvation does not only have to be considered as an immaterial horizon; on the contrary, it materializes in history* and is there to be chosen freely by man. Sin, through which man hides from the call of grace, introduces a new accent in this divine act. Grace is now seen as signifying the forgiving pardon and the redeeming act through which the sinner finds himself justified, as well as the help that allows him to return to and continue down the path of God.

The history of the Covenant, through which God, for the first time, showed favor to the Israelites, culminated in the Incarnation of the Logos, which extended the Covenant to all of humanity. Jesus Christ is not only the outside mediator of God's grace; he is grace itself, which has been incarnated into human life to bear its responsibility and to deify it irrevocably. The life of Jesus materializes God's proximity and love* for the sinner. By acting as man in suffering and dying on the cross, he assumes sin, through which man closes himself off from God and grace, and in this very act, he establishes a new relationship between God and man and becomes, in his own being, the place of their reconciliation. Ascended to heaven, he sends the Holy Spirit, who is God's gift of himself, occupying man's heart (*see* soul*-heart-body). It is the Holy Spirit, which, for the Church as for the individual, transforms the external figure of Jesus into an internal reality through which they both participate in the life of God. The goal of the act of divine grace is the perfect communion of God's kingdom.

2. (Free) Grace and Nature

God, in his act of grace, is entirely free and sovereign. He is interested in man only out of pure choice of grace. Grace is therefore not primarily a reaction to man or his merits, but an original love that alone gives rise to the qualities of man, making him worthy of love. Therefore, the sinner is justified outside of all his prior merit, through a pure act of grace. His conversion* and his faith presuppose that God turned toward him with prevenience (*gratia praeveniens*). The priority of grace as God's free initiative does not, however, relate to the fact that it is offered, without reason, to man living fully in sin. It already appears in the Creation itself, through which God made man into a being looking outside himself. In this respect, it is not nature that asks to be carried out by grace, but grace that gives itself a nature that is able to receive grace, able to find its fulfillment in it.

Tradition* strove to define this relationship by acknowledging that man had either passive anchorage (obeiential potency or *potentia oboedientialis*) or an active desire to commune with God (natural desire for the Beatific Vision*, or *desiderium naturale visionis beatificae*). The axiom that says, "grace does not destroy but supports and completes nature," falls in line with the theme of unity as a result of grace and nature. Grace presupposes nature and leads it to its fulfillment. It therefore does not establish a "supernature," but rather introduces a complementary, and nevertheless new, dimension of grace in natural reality. However, nature and grace exist as distinct realities. Here, nature represents a basic concept (pure nature or *natura pura*), in which is expressed the fact that the relationship of grace between God and man is neither deducible from human essence, nor divine essence. It rather stems from a behavior that God freely chooses to adopt with regard to man. Paradoxically, grace—exactly inasmuch as it is free, unmotivated, and asks to be freely accepted—constitutes the gift of this love, which man needs in order to find the final fulfillment.

3. Grace and Freedom

God calls man to a personal communion with him, so that the free divine solicitude with regard to man only really takes effect if man freely agrees. This is why there is not a competitive relationship between grace and free will. Grace, does indeed work with sovereign power, but is not violent against man. Man, for his part, is not a static power before God, but a creature endowed with freedom in relation to God, a freedom that allows him to choose whether or not to respond to the call of grace, and so commit himself to the dynamic that fills him.

The freedom offered by God and directed toward him as it is toward its end, is nevertheless still an open freedom; it can, therefore, just as well reject grace—but, in this case, it rejects God's solicitude, without which it loses meaning. Before man in crisis, grace presents itself as an initiative force that starts by emancipating enchained freedom from its shackles. Man is not, as a result, able to rise to God through his own strength, but, from this, he recovers at least one freedom capable of being sought.

As a last resort, it is impossible to define the respective parts of grace and of freedom in faith. It is also impossible to say how the possibility of resistance of human free will before the sovereign efficaciousness of grace is reconciled with the power that the latter has

to conquer human resistance. There is a double mystery* here, in which the paradigm of predestination* takes root.

In the interactive play between grace and free will, God and man, therefore, do not represent two competing causalities. On the contrary, grace confronts the human will and sets it free (operating or prevenient grace or *gratia operans* or *praeveniens*) in order to act in conjunction with it (cooperating or concomitant grace—*gratia cooperans* or *concomitans*). It is in this cooperation between divine grace and human free will that each finds—in accordance with the Council of Chalcedon*'s christological model—its whole and specific efficaciousness without, all the while, canceling that of the opposite pole. Grace is revealed as the force that initiates, makes possible, and supports man's attempts to reach God, and free will is revealed as the force that God wants to engage in these attempts.

4. Uncreated and Created Grace

Because grace seeks to establish a relationship, the concept does not only designate God himself (uncreated grace), but also the different ways in which God transforms worldly reality and man himself (created grace). The incarnation of grace, God made man in Jesus Christ, moves through the Church and is mediated in several ways, notably through the Word* and the Sacraments*. Grace specifically deals with man as an individual, in his plural and corporeal reality, in the different stages of his life. It must, therefore, adapt itself both to situations and to the being* of man himself, bringing about a new form and a new idea of meaning *(habitus, gratia habitualis)*. These two things do not result from any kind of human learning, but are, rather, integrally assimilated by man. For the movement of grace aims to establish a dialogical relationship, and, for this reason, sustains man in a state in which he becomes capable of responding to love from his own reality. Therefore, even though the relationship between God and man is a goal of created grace, a person cannot, without losing its essential substance, consider it an experience that can be separated from the act of grace. The gifts of the Holy Spirit, in particular, are there to remind us that man cannot assimilate grace that is offered to him if he is not supported again by divine efficaciousness.

5. The Communion Character of Grace

The dynamic of Salvation granted to a being-in-communion, God's triune grace does not only establish a new communion with God, it also heals and transforms the relationship between men. This is why, by sharing himself, Jesus Christ founds the Church as his body. In order to establish this communion and to fulfill the

Church's mission, grace is given in the charisma *(gratia gratis data)* that include man in the movement of love of God. Among the obligations that grace makes known to man, there is commitment, with the force that it fills him with, to the work to eradicate sin.

6. The Experience of Grace

Inasmuch as grace allies itself with nature and articulates itself on the categoric level, it is also part of the concrete existence of man. Yet, we must not forget that in experience we only grasp the mediated forms of grace, while their original form, that is to say God himself, escape all experience. Also, the experience of grace is essentially ambivalent and grace itself remains hidden: it can only be seized as grace through faith, and can just as well be concealed in hardship and the cross—that is, in its opposite, *sub contrario.*

• J. Van der Meersch (1925), "Grâce," *DThC* 7/2, 1554–1687.
H. Bouillard (1944), *Conversion et grâce chez saint Thomas d'Aquin,* Paris.
H. de Lubac (1946), *Surnaturel,* Paris (new edition 1991).
A. M. Landgraf (1952), *Dogmengeschichte der Frühscholastik* 1/1, Regensburg.
K. Rahner (1954–1960), *Schr. zur Th.* 1, 323–45 . 347–75; 3, 105–109; 4, 209–236, Einsiedeln.
U. Kühn (1961), *Natur und Gnade,* Berlin.
J. de Baciocchi (1963), "Grâce," *Cath.* 5, 135–72.
M. Flick and Z. Alszeghy (1964), *Il Vangelo della grazia,* Florence.
H. Rondet (1964), *Essais sur la théologie de la grâce,* Paris.
H. de Lubac (1965), *Le mystère du surnaturel,* Paris.

K. Rahner (1968), *Gnade als Freiheit,* Friburg.
H. J. Stoebe (1971), "äm gnädig sein," *THAT* 1, 587–97.
G. Greshake (1972), *Gnade als konkrete Freiheit: Eine Untersuchung zur Gnadenlehre des Pelagius,* Mainz.
H. Conzelmann and W. Zimmerli (1973), "kharis, etc.," *ThWNT* 9, 363–93.
Gross *et al.* (1974), "Gottes Gnadenhandeln," *Mysal* IV/2, 595–984.
K. Koch (1976), "ödq gemeinschaftstreu/heilvoll sein", *THAT* 2, 507–530.
G. Liedke (1976), "shpt richten", ibid., 999–1009.
L. Boff (1977), *A graça libertadora no mundo,* 2nd Ed., Petrópolis.
G. Greshake (1977), *Geschenkte Freiheit,* Friburg (new edition 1992).
Y. M.-J. Congar (1979), *Je crois en l'Esprit Saint,* vol. II: "Il est Seigneur et Il donne la vie," Paris.
J. Martin-Palma (1980), *Gnadenlehre: Von der Reformation bis zur Gegenwart, HDG* III/5 b, Friburg.
O. H. Pesch, A. Peters (1981), *Einführung in die Lehre von Gnade und Rechtfertigung,* Darmstadt.
M. Theobald (1982), *Die überströmende Gnade,* Regensburg.
O. H. Pesch (1983), *Frei sein aus Gnade,* Friburg.
H. Reventlow et al. (1984), "Gnade", *TRE* 13, 459–511.
Th. Pröpper (1988), *Erlösungsglaube und Freiheitsgeschichte,* Munich (3rd Ed. 1991).
A. Ganoczy (1989), *Aus seiner Fülle haben wir alle empfangen,* Düsseldorf.

EVA-MARIA FABER

See also **Anthropology; Augustinianism; Bañezianism-Molinism-Baianism; Covenant; Jansenism; Nature; Pelagianism; Sin, Original; Supernatural**

Gratian (Francisco Gratiaziano)

c. 1090–1159

Francisco Gratiaziano, known as Gratian, was a Camaldulensian monk who drew up what became the single most influential codification of the legal decisions that together came to constitute canon* law. His great compilation, usually known as the *Decretum,* although more properly entitled the *Concordia discordantium canonum,* attempted to resolve the discrepancies and contradictions in the legal promulgations and decisions emanating from the supreme source of ecclesiastical jurisdiction.

The compilation was made from the papalist point of view, emphasizing papal authority in the investiture controversy of 1076 between Pope Gregory VII and the Emperor Henry IV, in which the conflicting claims of sacred and secular sovereignties confronted one another. Gratian's compilation implicitly defended papal claims to the right of investing prelates with their sees against the emperor's desire to retain a lucrative feudal suzerainty over ecclesiastical benefices, which in fact thrived on concubinage and simony. Its principal importance was to serve as a handbook of legal principles and decisions, and consequently to become almost a constitutional handbook for the jurisdictional and other papalist claims of the Roman church.

However, it was also important on account of the quotations from the Fathers* that it contained, and that played a disproportionate part in subsequent medieval theological debate. It was often the only, and even more frequently the most easily available source for the views of the Fathers. It also attracted a very large number of glosses, and became a principal source for the development of doctrine in the later Middle Ages, a counterpart to Peter Lombard's four books of *Sententiae,* also of the mid-12th century. Both north and south of the Alps, faculties of canon law were quickly established in the universities. Alongside theology*, medicine, and civil law, canon law, anchored in Gratian's *Decretum,* became one of the four graduate faculties when the universities north of the Alps came to be founded around 1200.

Ancient Roman legislative constitutions had been gathered together on the orders of Justinian into what was intended to be a definitive *codex,* in which form it was promulgated in A.D. 529. It later needed substantial modification and expansion, and was then repromulgated in 534, lapsing in Europe under barbarian rule and a weakening papacy in the tenth century. It lingered on in Constantinople's fluctuating sphere of influence; and also, in part, in Spain, where the early-seventh century *Collectio canonum Isidoriana* was attributed to Isidore of Seville (570–636), as was an enlarged ninth-century version, now known as the *Pseudo-Isidorian Decretals.* Most local* churches had their own legislative codes, collecting, organizing, and unifying imported legal norms. Scales of penances for sins began to circulate from the sixth century.

The revival of interest in Roman law started in the late 11th century in Bologna, where Irnerius (1055–c. 1125) was the most important master teaching in the law school. He systematically collated and compared the texts of Lombard and Roman law, and himself wrote glosses, summaries, treatises, and interpretations. By the end of the 12th century, Ivo of Chartres (c. 1040–1116), relying on a compendium compiled by Burchard of Worms († c. 1023), was able to produce his *Tripartita,* with 655 fragments of decretals, 789 conciliar canons or patristic texts, and 861 fragments of his own *Decretum,* altogether a compilation of 3,760 ordered, brief, and concise chapters in 17 parts, which constituted a compendium of canon law.

Inspired by Ivo and Irnerius, and relying on Isidore, Gratian undertook his huge task, codifying some 4,000 earlier legal enactments according to the categories of Roman law, without regard either to the dates of the decretals he included or to the clashes of legal principle between them, and only occasionally offering his own view of disputed matters. His collection of decrees and decisions formed the first section of the *Corpus iuris canonici* when it was eventually printed privately under that title (1499–1502), and later, under the same title, with its text authenticated by Gregory XIII, in the official Roman edition of 1580. That was the only authoritative compilation of the whole of canon law until the *Codex* of 1917. Gratian is also the chief source influencing the acceptance by the Middle Ages of the privileged status of the decrees of the councils of Nicaea, Constantinople, Ephesus, and Chalcedon, which he regarded as normative and as containing all the essentials of Christian belief. (Dict. Grat. before Pars 1a, dist. 5).

Gratian was concerned to reconcile the traditions and categories of Roman law with the Frankish codes of the barbarian tribes, which had obtained over most of Europe during the early Middle Ages, and to this purpose could draw on the work of other 11th and early-12th century predecessors, including Bernold of Constance, Ivo of Chartres, and Alger of Liège, all of whom had sought to distinguish particular cases from general principles in their works on church law. Gratian was also influenced by Abelard*'s attempt to show the contradiction between different Christian beliefs in his book of theological contradictions, *Sic et non* of about 1115.

Gratian followed the usual practice of prefacing the consideration of canonical practice with a theoretical section on the nature of law*. Since Europe's later secular legal systems, whether claiming to be based on customary law, on common law, on statutory law, or on Roman law, all derived more or less directly from ecclesiastical legal practice and the semi-theological jurisprudence set out by Gratian and his commentators, it is important to notice the ambiguities in Gratian's view. He makes natural law not only identical with the revealed provisions of divine law—which makes canon law a theological discipline—but he also makes it identical with the law ordained by human reason, which puts it in the realm we know as philosophy*.

Gratian follows Isidore in holding that natural law is that which is contained "in the law and the gospel" (Dist 1a, dict. Grat. *See also* Pars 1a, dist.v, dict. Grat.), and makes natural law identical with divine law, "everything which is legitimate is ascribed to divine and natural law" (Pars 1a, dist.1, c.i, dict. Post. *See* dist. 9, c.xi, dict. Post). But he also makes natural law the pure product of human reason, originating from the constitution of rational creatures, not varying in time, but remaining immutable (Dict. Grat. Before Pars 1a, dist.5). Both sides in the great theological debate of the later Middle Ages—whether holding on the one hand that divine law was the product of the divine reason*, of which human reason was a derivative reflection or, on the other, that divine law was decreed by God* without reference to human intellectual powers—could therefore claim inspiration from Gratian himself.

Gratian's compendium was adopted in the schools and by the Roman curia, even though it was not endorsed by the Church* as such until 1580. In the mid-12th century, supplements, commentaries, and glosses started to appear almost immediately, raising questions that the popes were asked to resolve. A further systematic collection of decretals or legal decisions from 1127 to 1170 was compiled by Bernard of Pavia in about 1179, who himself produced a collection of 900 decretals from 1140 to 1191, arranged in five books, which also became the subject of a dozen commentaries.

This was the first of five *Compilationes antiquae,* the most important decretal collections between Gratian's *Decretum* and 1234. It chiefly contained decretals subsequent to Gratian's *Decretum,* including those of the Third Lateran* Council in 1179. The second compilation of the five was so numbered because it contained decretals from the immediately subsequent quinquennium, but earlier than those of the third compilation, which included the decretals from the first twelve years, 1198–1210, of the reign of Innocent III, and was the first legal compilation to be officially promulgated to the whole Church.

The fourth of the *Compilationes antiquae* contained the later decretals of Innocent's reign, which ended in 1216, including the canons of the Fourth Lateran* Council in 1215. It may have been promulgated, as the fifth of the *compilationes* certainly was, by Honorius III in 1226, containing as it did the decretals of his pontificate. Glosses were written on all five of the books, and taken into account when the *Decretals* of Gregory IX were compiled following the general plan of the *Compilatio prima,* and incorporating 1,771 chapters of the 1,971 contained in the complete set of *Compilationes antiquae.* The most important of the glosses was the 1216 *glossa ordinaria* of Johannes Teutonicus, particularly important for its view that popes lost their jurisdiction *ipso facto* if they fell into heresy. It followed from this view that the ultimate criterion of orthodoxy* could not simply be the pope*'s view, but only the *sensus fidelium,* normally apparent only through a council of the universal Church.

The *Decretals* of Gregory IX, drawn up by Raymond of Pennafort, was the first authentic general collection of legal principles and decisions to be issued. Known also as the *Liber extravagantium,* it was promulgated in 1234, and unleashed a new wave of glosses and commentaries. The Teutonicus *glossa ordinaria* was brought into line with it between 1240 and 1245, leaving a single-volume compendium of canon law, which made possible the promotion of a centralized and unified ecclesiastical society. Supplements with later decisions and further glosses and commentaries continued to be drawn up until 1317, when John XXII promulgated the *Constitutiones Clementinae,* the final document in the *Corpus iuris canonici,* which consisted of Gratian's *Decretum,* the *Decretals* of Gregory IX, and four further books, the *Liber sextus,* the *Clementinae,* the *Extravagantes Joannmis XXII,* and the *Extravagantes communes.* By 1338 the whole flood of glosses and commentaries had been reduced to coherence, and there was a recognized canon law that, although it continued to grow, governed, at least in principle and in outline, the constitution and procedures of the Church.

It is to the principles of canon law, themselves often transmitting the more ancient principles of Greek and Roman law, that European legal systems ultimately owe the foundations of international law and the notion of a public law flowing from the exercise of sovereignty*. Modern concepts of personal property, the concepts of equity and good faith*, and the regulation of matrimonial relations were developed from ecclesiastical law, and until very recently the English concept of "contempt of court" remained a clear secularization of the canonical procedures governing excommunication. In many of its most important principles, medieval canon law was also adopted in the reformed communions of the 16th century. Modern US law owes to canon law many of the principles underpinning matrimonial law, criminal law, the laws of succession, property, human rights, and the principles of proof and evidence.

● (1879) *Corpus Iuris Canonici, I.* A. Friedberg (Ed.), Leipzig.

ANTHONY LEVI

See also **Canon Law**

Gregory of Nazianzus

c. 330–390

a) Life. In Eastern Orthodox Tradition, Gregory of Nazianzus is known as "the theologian." A doctor, like Athanasius*, of the Eastern Church, Gregory of Nazianzus stands together with his intimates Basil* of Caesarea and Gregory* of Nyssa among the Cappadocian Fathers. (The fourth century would come to be considered the "golden age" of patristics.) Born the son of the bishop of Nazianzen, a small town in Cappadocia, Gregory supplemented his Christian education with studies in rhetoric and philosophy, first in Constantinople and then in Athens. These studies were undertaken at the same time as Basil. His desire to reconcile Greek culture and Christian faith* provoked his great virulence against the religious policies of Emperor Julian, who in 362 had banned Christians from the teaching profession (*Discourses* 4 and 5, no doubt composed after Julian's death). Ordained a priest, then appointed a bishop (apparently much against his will, since he himself had chosen the monastic life), Gregory was to play an important role in the Church of Constantinople, where, after Archbishop Meletius's death, he was to preside over the Council of 381 (the Council of Constantinople* I), before resigning from his position to be replaced by Nectarius. His autobiographical work (*Carmina de se ipso,* PG 37), together with his correspondence, reveals the anxieties and the mystical aspirations of a Christian poet. Contrary to a tradition accepted until the 16th century, strong doubts exist today as to his authorship of the *Christus patiens* (SC 149), a pastiche of lines from Euripides, which form a Christian tragedy, probably dating from the Byzantine era.

b) Theological Contributions. As a preacher and theologian, along with Basil and Gregory of Nyssa, Gregory of Nazianzus contributed at Constantinople to the victory of Nicaean orthodoxy over the supporters of Arianism* (*Discourse* 27, "Against the Eunomians"). His *Theological Discourses* 27 to 31, speeches delivered in 380 (which are the chief source of Gregory's influence and posthumous fame) present his trinitarian theology* in a style that combines dogmatic rigor and lyricism. At the same time, he underlines the theologian's task: the theologian is one of those who "walked in the recesses of the deep" (Jb 38:16; *Dis-*

course 28:12) and in the theologian's works an apophatic language should counterbalance the elaboration of theological concepts. Gregory himself conforms to this prescription.

It was the idea of relationship *(skhèsis)* that made it possible for Gregory to define the differences between the three persons* encompassed in the Trinity*: "The Father* is neither the name of a substance nor the name of an action; it is the name of a relationship, a name showing the Father's position with regard to the Son or the Son's with regard to the Father" (*Disc.* 29:16). As for Gregory's theology of the Holy* Spirit, it daringly develops the themes of Basil's *Treatise on the Holy Spirit,* and it would be a deciding factor at the Council of 381. Against the Pneumatomachians, whom he accused of ditheism (*Discourse* 31:13), Gregory insisted that the scriptural argument gave legitimate grounds for asserting the divinity of the Holy Spirit. Neither did he hesitate to apply to the Holy Spirit the term *homoousios,* a point on which the Council of 381 would not follow him. Gregory deserves the credit of having coined the term "ekporesis" (*ekporeusis,* "procession," *Discourse* 31:8), which allowed him to distinguish the relationship of the Holy Spirit to the Father from the generation of the Son (Filioque*). Pointing out that each of the persons of the Trinity had been the object of a gradual revelation*, Gregory concluded his speech devoted to the Holy Spirit by showing that the Spirit's divinity had not been clearly manifest until after the coming of Christ* (*Discourse* 31:26).

Gregory's Christology* preceded the answers that the councils of Ephesus* and Chalcedon* would give to the Nestorians, and it affirmed the unity of the person of Christ. All the same, his presentation of the Son's humanity stumbles over the dilemma of Christ's will and of his ignorance. Maximus* the Confessor, in his *Ambiguorum liber,* was therefore to come up against several points in Gregory's Christology that he was obliged to develop before he could assert their complete orthodoxy (*see* A. Ceresa-Gastaldo, in C. Moreschini 1992).

c) Posthumous Fame. The acuity of Gregory's trinitarian theology, and his role in the first Council of Constantinople, assured his fame. His joint composition with Basil of the *Philocalia,* drawn from Origen's works, which was widely circulated and has preserved for us fragments of other works lost today, attests to Gregory's loyalty to Alexandrian exegesis*. Evagrius Ponticus, the propagator of Origenism in the era of early monasticism*, acknowledged Gregory as his master, a master whom he had served as a deacon in Constantinople. Until the Middle Ages, Gregory's dogmatic works, especially the *Theological Discourses,* translated into Latin by Rufinus of Aquileia as early as the beginning of the fourth century, inspired many commentaries in both East and West.

● PG 35–38

Discourses, SC 247, 250, 270, 284, 309, 318, 358

Letters, Ed. and translated into French by P. Gallay, 2 vol, CUFr, 1964–67, Paris; *Lettres théologiques,* SC 208.

(1997), *Le Dit de sa vie,* text and French trans., Geneva.

♦ P. Gallay (1943), *La vie de saint Grégoire de Nazianze,* Paris.

F. Lefherz (1958), *Studien zu Gregor von Nazianz,* Bonn.

J.-M. Szymusiak (1963), *Eléments de théologie de l'homme selon saint Grégoire de Nazianze,* Rome.

J. Rousse (1967), "Grégoire de Nazianze", *DSp* 6, 932–71, Paris.

J. Bernardi (1968), *La prédication des Pères cappadociens,* Paris.

T. Spidlik (1971), *Grégoire de Nazianze,* Rome.

F. Trisoglio (1974), *S. Gregorio di Nazianzo in un quarantennio di studi (1925–1965),* Turin.

C. Moreschini and G. Menestrina (Ed.) (1992), *Gregorio Nazianzeno: teologo e scrittore,* Bologna.

J. Bernardi (1995), *Grégoire de Nazianze: Le théologien et son temps (330–390),* Paris.

FRANÇOISE VINEL

See also **Constantinople I; Hellenization of Christianity; Negative Theology; Spiritual Theology**

Gregory of Nyssa

c. 331–394

1. Life and Works

a) Life. Gregory of Nyssa and his brother Basil* of Caesarea were children of an aristocratic family from Cappadocia. Born about 331 in Pontus, Gregory belonged to the third generation of Christians in his family. He seems to have turned toward a rhetorical and philosophical education after having held the office of lector in the church. A married man, he was called to the episcopacy and appointed to the see of Nyssa, near Caesarea, c. 372. He would assert himself as the representative of the Nicaean faith, especially after Basil's death. A victim of Arian opponents, Gregory was deposed as bishop, probably in 375–76, and forced into exile until the end of 377, when Emperor Valens abolished sentences of exile. Gregory was then restored to the see of Nyssa (see Basil, *Ep,* 225). In an attempt to bring to an end the doctrinal divisions linked to the Arian crisis (see *Ep.* 2, 3, 5), he traveled as far as Jerusalem*, visiting several episcopal sees in Asia Minor. He made a strong impression during the first council of Constantinople* in 381.

Under Basil's influence, monasticism* enjoyed considerable success in Cappadocia. Gregory too supported this movement and encouraged the development of the small monastery founded on the family property of his sister Macrina and their mother *(De virginitate; Vita Macrinae).*

b) Works. The chronology of Gregory's works is uncertain. Just like the more prolific correspondences of Basil and of Gregory* of Nazianzus, his *Letters* give us some insight into the way in which he performed his duties as bishop during troubled times. The three parts of *Contra Eunomium,* the short trinitarian treatises *(Adversus Arium et Sabellium de Patre et Filio, De deitate Filii et Spiritus Sancti, De differentia essentiae et hyspostaseos),* as well as the *Catechetical Oration,* revealed the broad lines of his theology*. Gregory presents himself explicitly as the continuator of Basil's work and also gives a role to his sister Macrina: thus, in a setting reminiscent of the *Phaedo,* or as Diotima inspiring Socrates, Macrina answers Gregory's anxieties about death* and the beyond *(De Anima et Resur-*

rectione). Lastly, the scriptural commentaries—and chiefly the *Homilies on Christ* and the *Life of Moses,* written in the last years of his life—showed how much the different senses of Scripture* render exegesis*, theology, and mysticism* inseparable. Gregory of Nyssa's hermeneutics* owes a great deal to Origen*, and therefore to Alexandrian exegesis, which was initially derived from Philo. Moreover, Gregory acknowledged his "close and fervent reading" of Origen (Hom. I On Christ). The idea of *akolouthia,* of the logical "linking" of the verses of Scripture, served to show revelation* at work in the biblical text, and so all the more enabled Gregory to bring human reason into harmony with the logic of the divine plan.

2. Doctrine and Spirituality

a) Theology of Creation and Anthropology. Like Basil, Gregory commented on the *Hexameron,* which he extended with a treatise on the Creation* of man *(De hominis opificio).* Gregory borrowed, not without a certain eclecticism, the concepts of Greek ontology (*see* Stead 1985). But in his case, by a decisive evolution, he placed little stress on the distinction between the sensory and the intelligible in order to accentuate the differences between the created and the uncreated. The concepts of limit and moderation therefore defined the *diastèma* (spacing out, temporal interval) of the Creation. Gregory made a close connection between cosmology and anthropology* in his meditation on nature* *(phusis).* He linked together ethics* and "physics"—Qo, on which Gregory wrote a commentary *(In Ecclesiasten Homiliae)* is, in patristic tradition*, the book of "physics," of knowledge of the created universe and of its limits—thanks to the idea of moderation. Man himself stands on the boundaries *(methorios),* on the borderline between the sensory and the intelligible; and in conformity with an anthropocentric viewpoint, man is the apex of creation (*see De hominis opificio,* chap. 2–4). The concept of the pleroma (*see Ep.* I, 23)—applied just as readily to the cosmos* as to the qualities shared by all humanity, and by the Church in search of its unity*—means in Gregory's work an accomplishment to which all creation aspires.

The verse from Genesis 1:26: "Let us make man in our image, after our likeness," is a key reference for Nyssean anthropology. The affinity *(suggeneia)* of nature that links man to the divine is shown, according to Gregory, by the existence of his fundamental liberty*, of a capacity for wanting and doing good, which is in fact its definition. The finality of human life is an "assimilation with God*," a Platonic expression *(Theaetetus* 176 b) adopted by Gregory. Taking the path of

righteousness (*see In Inscriptiones Psalmorum,* on Psalm 1) "results from freedom of choice *[prohairesis]* and we are thus, in a sense, our own parents" *(Life of Moses* II, 3)—an audacious statement, often repeated by Gregory. Since they are created by God, realities can only be good; consequently, evil* is nothing more than "what is not" *(to mè on),* and it only occurs as a result of using freedom* badly.

In Gregory's works the definition of man as the image of God takes clear precedence over the Stoic thesis of man as microcosm, which he also borrowed; but he expressed this idea in dualistic terms. Gregory thus made a distinction between the soul* and the body that owed a great deal to Platonism, and he located sin* in the realm of sensual and irrational urges, which mar the "resemblance" to God without however totally erasing the seal of "the image." Sexual differentiation (*see* Gn 1:27) was neither the cause nor the result of sin, and it was through a stroke of divine foresight (*De hominis opificio* 16–17) that it assured the continuity of the created in its finiteness. To define the soul and its "localization," Gregory was first inclined to refute the theory (defended by Origen in particular) of the pre-existence of souls and, through this very opposition, to reject the idea of metempsychosis (*De hominis opificio* 28–29; *De Anima et Resurrectione* 88s). Quite the contrary, the creation of both the soul and the body were concomitant—and Gregory's interest in the medical conceptions of his time gave him a concrete approach to man's constitution (*De hominis opificio* 30). It was the intellective part of the soul that, in the case of man, authorized the free choice of his actions. Conversely, "thoughtlessness" *(aboulia)* is what led to sin. To describe man's fallen nature (Daniélou 1944; *Hom. on Christ),* Gregory spoke of the "garments of skins" (*see* Gn 3:21), and interpreted them in a metaphorical sense. Finally, Gregory devoted the last part of his treatise *De Anima et Resurrectione* to the doctrine of the Resurrection*: this was a "restoration of our nature to its original state" *(apokatastasis, see* apocatastasis*), everything that caused this original nature's dissolution—passions*, sin, death*—being annihilated, in the end, by divine omnipotence*.

b) Christological and Trinitarian Doctrine. In his *Contra Eunomium,* which is much more developed than Basil's work on the same subject, Gregory answered the logical arguments of his adversary by stressing first of all the limits of the knowledge man can have of God—and therefore the limits of human language as applied to God (*see* Canévet 1983). In various ways the divine names* showed the energies of an unknowable divinity *(theotès),* offered only for contemplation* *(thea;* a word play on the two terms in *To Ablabius:* that there are not three Gods, *GNO* III, 1, 44). The treatise provided a classification of these names, of the scriptural terms that refer to God by means of the most material realities to the very names of Father*, Son, and Spirit. Gregory stressed their analogical status: the essence of the divinity was "above every name" (Phil 2:9). The three persons* worked together within the Trinity* and manifested themselves in an order that revealed the differences between the names. To make a clear distinction between *ousia* and hypostasis, Gregory resorted to analogy*, based on the distinction common to nature and the individual. Refuting thus the accusation of tritheism*, he confessed "a single God in three persons *[prosôpa]* or hypostases" (Epistle to the Greeks, based on commonly held ideas, *GNO* III, 1, 33)—*prosôpon* and hypostasis therefore both referred to the person, which statement notably clarified the trinitarian debate.

The Incarnation*, in the Nyssean view of divine economy, was first of all an answer to the great swarm of evil, to its maximal unfolding in the world (*Disc. cat.* 29, 4). Opposed to Apollinarianism*, Gregory was preoccupied with reconciling the twofold affirmation of divine impassibility and the complete humanity of Christ. Through incarnation, the Son shared in the "nature common" to all men, which included growth and "passions," *pathè* (that is, the ability to change from birth to death, *Orat. cat.*, 16, 6): this "yet without sin" (Heb 4:15). In order to connote the union of both natures in Christ, Gregory continually gave priority to a vocabulary signifying mixture, and he could affirm that the double union of the divinity with both the soul and the body of Jesus* subsisted until death (*Ep.* 3, 22; *De tridui spatio*, GNO IX, 273–306, *The Pascal Christ,* hom. 2, p. 45–71), as a guarantee of the total resurrection of the human composite. It was also because this human composite was a mixture of the immaterial soul and of the body, even after death, that a resurrection of the flesh was possible; and every soul also possessed the ability to recognize the body to which it was joined (*De Anima et Resurrectione,* 97; *see* Le Boulluec 1995). Finally, Gregory's *Catechetical Oration* stresses the cosmic dimension of the cross on which Christ "binds the universe tightly into a union and adjusts it to himself, by bringing the diverse natures of the world into one accord and one harmony" (32, 6).

c) *Mystical Theology.* "For from the greatness and beauty of created things comes a corresponding perception of their creator" (Wis 13:5). On several occasions Gregory relied on this verse (*CE* 2, 13.154; *in Eccl.* 1 and 8; *De hom. op.* 2) to define simultaneously and paradoxically man's ability to know and name God,

and the limits of his knowledge faced with divine infinity*. Gregory made of Moses the model of our access to the inaccessible; and, in order to recount this spiritual experience, favored the metaphors of darkness and the luminous cloud (*Life of Moses, Hom. on Christ*).

Although his treatise, *De Anima et Resurrectione* did not go beyond a conception of desire as a passion destined to disappear, the *Life of Moses* and the *Homily on Christ* provided the doctrine of another desire, the "epektasis" (*see* Phil 3:13 "Forgetting what lies behind and straining forward *[epekteinomenos]*to what lies ahead"; *see* Daniélou 1944); and in the logic of that desire, the man who turned towards God was led into an endless ascent. Moses (*Life of Moses* II, 224s) and the bride of Christ provided Gregory with the models of this never-ending ascent: "He who ascends never stops, rising from one beginning to another, and the beginning of the ever-increasing good has no end" (*Hom.* VIII *the Christ*). The concept of epektasis also gave a full range of meanings to a dynamic view of the eschaton; and in the image of the mystery* of the union of the two natures in Christ, the movement that led the created "from one degree of glory* to another" (2 Cor 3:18) in no way affected the permanence of the divinity: "The soul…never stops growing, but the good in which it shares remains the same, always revealing itself as just as transcendent to the soul which shares ever more in it" (*Hom.* VII *on Christ*).

3. Legacy

The first sign of Gregory's enduring influence was the circulation of his work, particularly of the treatise *De hominis opificio* and the *Homily on Christ,* of which translations existed in the various Eastern churches. A second sign was the extracts from his commentaries to be found in the works on the Scriptures composed from the start of the sixth century and in the anthologies of patristic texts. Latin translations gave his commentary on Christ, and also the one on Origen, a wide circulation in medieval monastic circles.

Cappadocian theology contributed to bringing the Arian crisis to an end by assuring a balance between the Christologies of Antiochian inspiration and those of Alexandrian inspiration. Through his philosophical range, Gregory assimilated and metamorphosed fundamental traits of Platonism* and of Neoplatonism*, which were integrated into the common expression of the faith* (see Ivánka 1964). His mystical theology, propagated particularly by Maximus* the Confessor and Pseudo-Dionysius*, has had a wide inspirational influence on Eastern Christian spirituality.

● PG 44–46; *Gregorii Nysseni Opera (GNO),* Ed. W. Jaeger, H. Langerbeck et al., 10 vols., Berlin then Leyden, 1921–.

SC 1 *bis (Life of Moses)*, 6 *(On the Creation of Man)*, 119 *(On Virginity)*, 178 *(Life of Macrina)*, 363 *(Letters)*, 416 *(Hom. On Ecclesiastes)*.

(1908) *Discours catéchétique*, French trans. L. Méridier, Paris.

(1992) *Le Cantique des Cantiques (Homélies)*, Paris.

(1995) *Gregory of Nyssa's Treatise on the Inscriptions of the Psalms, Introduction, Translation and Notes*, R.E. Heine, Oxford.

(1995) *Traité de l'âme et de la résurrection*, trans. J. Terrieux, Paris.

H. Urs von Balthasar (1942), *Présence et pensée: Essai sur la philosophie religieuse de Gr. de Nysse*, Paris (2nd Ed. 1988).

J. Daniélou (1944), *Platonisme et théologie mystique: Doctrine spirituelle de Gr. de Nysse*, 2nd Ed., Paris.

H. Merki (1952), Homoiôsis Theô: *Von der platonischen Angleichung an Gott zur Göttähnlichkeit bei Gr.*, Friburg.

J. Gaïth (1953), *La conception de la liberté chez Grégoire de Nysse*, Paris.

J. Lebourlier (1962–1963), "A propos de l'état du Christ dans la mort," *RSPhTh* 46, 629–49; and 47, 161–80.

E. von Ivánka (1964), Plato christianus: *Übernahme und Umgestaltung des Platonismus durch die Väter*, chap. IV, Einsiedeln.

D.L. Balàs (1966), Metousia Theou: *Man's Participation in God's Perfections According to Saint Gregory of Nyssa*, Rome.

W. Jaeger (1966), *Gregor von Nyssa's Lehre vom Heiligen Geist*, Leyden.

M. Canévet (1967), "Grégoire de Nysse," *DSp* 6, 471–1011.

J.R. Bouchet (1968), "Le vocabulaire de l'union et du rapport des natures chez saint Gr.," *RThom* 68, 533–82.

M. Harl (1971) (Ed.), *Écriture et culture philosophique dans la pensée de Gr. De Nysse Actes du Colloque de Chèvetogne*, Leyden.

J. Fontaine and Ch. Kannengiesser (Eds.) (1972), Epektasis: *Mélanges patristiques offerts au cardinal J. Daniélou*, Paris.

R. Hübner (1974), *Die Einheit des Leibes Christi bei Gregor von Nyssa*, Leyden.

H. Dörrie et al. (1976), *Gregor von Nyssa und die Philosophie. Zweites Internationales Kolloquium über Gregor von Nyssa*, Leyden.

M. Alexandre (1981), "Protologie et eschatologie chez Gr. De Nysse," in U. Bianchi (Ed.) *L'antropologia di Origene e di Gregorio di Nissa*, 122–59, Milan.

M. Canévet (1983), *Grégoire et l'herméneutique biblique: Étude des rapports entre le langage et la connaissance de Dieu*, Paris.

D.L. Balàs (1985), "Gregor von Nyssa," *TRE* 14, 173–81.

C.G. Stead (1985), *Substance and Illusion in the Christian Fathers*, London.

Th. Ziegler (1987), "Les petits traités trinitaires de Grégoire de Nysse, témoins d'un itinéraire théologique (379–383)," thesis, University of Strasbourg.

♦ M. Altenburger, F. Mann (1988), *Bibliographie zu Gregor von Nyssa: Editionen, Übersetzungen, Literatur*, Leyden.

H.R. Drobner and Ch. Klock (Eds.) (1990), *Studien zu Gr. und der christlichen Spätantike*, Leyden.

G. Castelluccio (1992), *L'antropologia di Gr.*, Bari.

B. Pottier (1994), *Dieu et le Christ selon Grégoire de Nysse*, Brussels.

A. Le Boulluec (1995), "Corporéité ou individualité? La condition finale des ressuscités selon Grégoire de Nysse," *Aug.* 35, 307–326.

Françoise Vinel

See also **Alexandria, School of; Apollinarianism; Arianism; Platonism, Christian; Stoicism, Christian**

Gregory of Rimini. *See* Nominalism

Gregory Palamas

1296–1359

The theology of Gregory Palamas is a major phenomenon of late-medieval Byzantine culture. A part of doctrine in the Eastern Orthodox Church, as well as a polemical crux between the Christian East and West, this theology* constitutes a dogmatic statement of Hesychastic* spirituality and represents one of the stakes in the ecumenical dialogue, as much by the soteriology that it encourages as by the closely connected notions that it implies regarding tradition*, pneumatology, and eschatology*.

a) *Historic Landmarks.* A monk of Mount Athos, archbishop of Thessalonica, and canonized in 1368, Gregory Palamas is commemorated as "Doctor of grace*." His teaching, expounded in the *Hagioritic Tome* or "The Book of Holiness" of 1340, then approved by the synods* of Constantinople of June and August 1341, was solemnly confirmed by the Council of Blachernissa in 1351. He also features in the *Synodikon,* the dogmatic anthology proclaimed liturgically on the Sunday called "On the Victory of Orthodoxy." His most systematic accounts can be found in the *Triad* or "Apology for the Holy Hesychasts" (1341) and the *CL Chapters* (1349).

"Palamitism" arose from a dispute over the relativism preached about the Filioque* by the philosopher Barlaam during the negotiations with Rome*. Barlaam's virulent attacks against Hesychastic circles spread the controversy. Complicated by the civil war of 1341–47, this dispute irremediably divided Byzantine intellectuals. This quasi-gnosticological controversy, hinging on such recurrent themes as the quality of prayer practices, the value of profane wisdom*, or the authority* of patristic sources, bore essentially on the nature of mystical experience as a way of attaining a knowledge* of God. The opposition to Gregory Palamas brought together two currents of anti-monastic humanism that had been regularly marginalized from the time of the iconoclastic period in the eighth and ninth centuries. The first movement, largely of Neoplatonic inspiration (Barlaam, Gregoras), aimed at the emancipation of philosophy*. The second, of conservative (Akyndinos) or pre-Scholastic slant (Kypariossitès), took up a position in favor of a rational theology, and would end by acknowledging itself as Thomist* (P. and D. Kydonès). Animated by the same preoccupation with a return to Hellenism and by a common interest in the new thinking coming from the West (among which was Scotism), the thinkers of both the above movements rejected the Palamite theses, holding them to be heretical. They themselves were anathematized for "atheism*." A century later, the representatives of the first movement (Bessarion, Plethon), as well as those of the second (Kalekas, Chrysobergès), would become the promoters of the Union of Florence, while the strict Palamites (Marcus of Ephesus), or the moderate ones (G. Scolarios), would reject it.

From that time onwards, the "Palamite error" would become a *leitmotiv* of the Catholic polemicists, a polemic sustained in the 16th century by the Latinized Greeks (Allatius, Arcadius, etc.); taken up again in the 17th century by the Jesuit "missionaries" (F. Richard) and the Dominicans (Le Quien), as well as by the systematicians (Petau); and lastly, perpetuated by the Greco-Catholics until the beginning of the 20th century. In the period between the two world wars, Gregory Palamas was still represented as an obscurantist pietist, the author of irrational dogmatics*, with neither precedents nor posterity (Jugie 1936). At the same time, the Neopatristic school, the chief expression of the theological renewal of modern Orthodoxy*, confirmed Palamitism as a doctrinal reference and a synthetic axis of the whole eastern tradition. Heralded by the methodical restructuring of V. L. Lossky and G. Florovsky, as well as by the work of B. Krivoshein, D. Staniloae, and C. Kern, J. Meyendorff's thesis (1959) revived research. Since that time, Palamitism's irreducibility to an ideological consequence of imperial Romanism (Meyendorff), its formative role in the neo-Hesychastic proselytism of the 14th and 15th centuries (Obolensky 1971), and its permanence and its dogmatic function in modern Orthodoxy (Podskalsky 1988) have been established. The debate is therefore no longer about the historic validity of Palamitism but its theoretical coherence.

b) *Doctrinal Aspects.* Gregory Palamas's first aims, the normativity of the context of his thought, and the topicality of certain major points of his spirituality, has also all been demonstrated. An organic whole thus emerges, centered on a concept of true participation in God which implies a realization in the present of the eschatological mystery, a whole that includes both the conceptual schemas of Greek patristics and those of Byzantine thought (Gregory of Cyprus), the ascetico-mystical postulations of early Hesychasm (Evagrius, Macarius) and those of later Hesychasm (Symeon the New Theologian, Gregory the Sinaite). From the polemical essay of the *Triad* to their summary exposition in the *CL* Chapters, several synthetic axes thus emerge, which are classics of Orthodox thought. There is a christological conception of the history of salvation* (*Tr.* III, 1, 16) in which, from the Creation* to the Parousia, the Incarnation* determines a cosmic dynamic of transfiguration (*Ch.* 2); a theocentric and monist definition of anthropology*, in which the ideas of continuous prayer*, of spiritual meaning, of the joint illumination of both the intellect and the heart (*see* soul*-heart-body; *Tr.* II, 2, 12–13) enter a theory of corporeal existence that aims to prove the superiority of human beings over the angels* (*Ch.* 39); and a charismatic ecclesiology in which the primacy of contemplation* has as corollary the prophetic ministry* of monasticism* (*Tr.* II, 1, 36), without its being, however, disassociated from the sacramental order (*Ch.* 57).

Once this whole was agreed upon (Kern, Meyendorff,

Mantzarides, etc.), the cardinal sign of Palamitism still remains its dogmatics. How can transcendence and communion* be reconciled? While the anti-Palamites insisted on interpreting it as "ditheism," the simultaneous distinction and unity of the *ousia* and the *energeia* in God helped Gregory Palamas to found a theory of deification. The final aim of the Christian experience*, the vision of God ("immediate, supra-intellectual, transfiguring"), implies that "grace*, which comes from the eternal Father*," is "uncreated" (*T. Hag.*, PG 150, 1225 s). The distinction between essence and energy corresponds to this implication. In fact it describes how, "without abandoning its non-manifestation," essence manifests itself as an energy—Gregory Palamas also speaks of *the* "energies," using a plural which does not connote any division—which is inseparable from it, "radiance," divine glory*, and splendor, which reveals and imparts trinitarian life through the power of the Holy* Spirit (*see* omnipotence*; *T. de 1341,* PG 150, 680 B). Palamitism thus portrays itself as a development of the ecumenical councils: there must be added to the communion *kat' ousian* of the Trinity* (one nature, three hypostases) and to the communion *kath' hupostasin* of the Word* incarnate (one hypostasis, two natures), the communion *kat' energeian,* which makes it possible for "myriads" of human hypostases to become participants, through grace, in the unique divinity (*T de 1351,* PG 151, 448B). The distinction, therefore, uncovers a mystery* that its antinomic structure reveals as such; it does not depend on our intellectual grasp of this mystery but is "real" (Vl. Lossky).

c) Theological Views. In outline, the construction is opposed to the Latin and Scholastic* theory of the Beatific Vision* of the divine essence, which is based on divine simplicity and on a mediate, deliberate conception of participation. Its contradictory canonization by Orthodoxy* and Catholicism* explains the contemporary debate. For J. Meyendorff, Gregory Palamas has perfected the patristic and conciliar heritage, against the secularizing tide that heralds the Renaissance and the Reformation, by correcting its Platonizing excesses along biblical and personalist lines. Palamitism, which is impossible to compress into a system, is then viewed as the apophatic expression of a mystical existentialism. Accepted by the Orthodox world (with the exception of Romanides), this thesis justifies the Palamite character of contemporary research devoted to ontotheological criticism (Yannaras), to the metaphysics of the person* (Clément), and to the phenomenology of ecclesiality (Zizioulas) or of the Holy Spirit (Bobrinskoy). It has received a mixed reception in the Catholic world. There have been, on the one hand, widespread refutations: it was the opposite of his intention that

Palamitism, which arose from a purely Byzantine dispute (Beck), should crystallize a mistaken reading of Greek tradition to the point of freeing from it its latent Neoplatonism, with the result of diluting its christological gain in knowledge into an essentialism that leaves place only for a degraded participation to divinity (Ivánka 1964). In this case it therefore becomes necessary to differentiate genuine Palamitism from Neopalamitism, the latter representing a disguised return to Maximus* the Confessor, nonetheless cut off at its roots from its evolution toward Thomist intentionality (Le Guillou 1974). Elsewhere one meets attempts at reconciliation: recognition of the interpretive legitimacy of Gregory Palamas would make possible the acceptance of a "theological pluriformity at the center of a unity of faith* and beyond all dogmatic exclusivism," and Palamitism could contribute to the solution of certain problems within the Latin Tradition (de Halleux 1973). In fact, the debate on sources—"Palamitism before Gregory Palamas"—seems to have run its course, and the most impartial commentators agree that there can be identified in the structure of thought and the conceptual elaborations of the Cappadocian Fathers (de Halleux 1975), of Pseudo-Dionysius* (Kühlmann), and of Maximus (Thunberg), prefigurations or models inherent in the Palamite distinction. Another fact: the reform of the Augustino-Thomist inheritance proposed by K. Rahner*, and at its heart the revision of the debate on nature* and grace, seems to be in harmony with Palamite preoccupations and feelings. A more realistic and optimistic understanding of salvation would imply the notion of uncreated grace. Is that sufficient to permit the passing over of the fundamental opposition of both the eastern and western hermeneutic circles?

From this viewpoint, the Palamite pneumatology of *Eros* (Lison 1994) seems essential. How is the eternal existence of the Holy Spirit with the manifestation of its gifts articulated within the divine plan? For Gregory Palamas, divinization is the coming of the Kingdom*, already received here below by adoption. Now, the Church is not the Kingdom but its icon: the personal dimension of sainthood (*see* cult* of saints) thus remains irreducible. Thus there would be, according to a theory sketched by Vl. Lossky but subsequently neglected by Orthodox theology, a "double divine plan," one but distinct, for the Son and the Spirit. There, it seems, lies the key to future research.

● G. Palamas (1959), *Défense des saints Hésychastes,* Ed. and Trans. J. Meyendorff, SSL 30–31.
(1962–88), *Suggràmmata,* Ed. P. Krèstou, Thessalonica, 4 vols.
N. Gregoras (1976), *Antirrhetika* I, edited and translated by H. V. Beyer, WBS 12, Vienna.
G. Akyndinos (1983), *Letters,* edited and translated by A. C. Hero, Washington.

(1988), *The One Hundred and Fifty Chapters*, edited and translated by R. E. Sinkewicz, STPIMS, Toronto.

(1995), *Traités apodictiques sur la procession du Saint-Esprit*, French trans. E. Ponsoye, Paris.

♦ M. Jugie (1936), *Theologia Dogmatica*, II, Paris, 68–183.

B. Krivochéine (1938), "The Ascetic and Theological Teaching of Gr.P.," *ECQ* 3, 26–33.

Vl. Lossky (1944), *Essai sur la théologie mystique de l'Église d'Orient*, Paris.

C. Kern (1950), *Antropologiia S. Grigoriia Palamy*, Paris.

J. Meyendorff (1959), *Introduction à l'étude de Gr.P.*, Paris.

J. Romanidès (1960–61), "Notes on the Palamite Controversy," *GOTR* 6, 186–205.

H. G. Beck (1963), "Die Byzantinische Kirche: Das Zeitalter des Palamismus," in *HKG(J)* III, 2, 588–624.

E. von Ivánka (1964), *Plato Christianus*, Einsiedeln.

J. Kühlmann (1968), *Die Taten des Einfachen Gottes*, Würzburg, 43–104.

D. Obolensky (1971), *The Byzantine Commonwealth*, London, 377–479.

A. de Halleux (1973), "P. et scolastique," *RTL* 5, 409–442.

G. Mantzaridès (1973), *Palamika*, Thessalonica.

M. J. Le Guillou (Ed.) (1974), "Jugements sur les Églises d'Orient au XVIIe s.," *Ist* 19, 301–320.

A. de Halleux (1975), "P. et tradition," *Irén* 48, 479–93.

L. Thunberg (1985; 2nd Ed. 1995, augmented Ed., Chicago and La Salle), *Man and the Cosmos*, New York, 131–56.

G. Podskalsky (1988), *Griechische Theologie in der Zeit der Türkenherrschaft*, Munich.

J. Lison (1994), *L'Esprit répandu*, Paris.

JEAN-FRANÇOIS COLOSIMO

See also **Ecumenicism; Fathers of the Church; Hesychasm; Spiritual Theology; Thomism; Vision, Beatific**

Gregory the Great

c. 540–604

1. Life

Gregory I was born into the senatorial class and was Prefect of Rome in 573. He became a monk in 574, and the pope's legate (*apocrisarius*) in Constantinople around 578. On his return to Rome, around 585, he became an abbot, and then pope* in 590. He concentrated as pope both upon the pastoral duties of his mission and upon the development of a theology of episcopal ministry*.

(a) Gregory was a significant figure in the process by which the Bishop of Rome came to claim and establish a hegemony among the ancient patriarchates*. By Gregory's time, the papacy, which had always been more autonomous, had largely taken over the running of Rome*; this gave it a temporal authority that was to be important to its subsequent development in the long-running struggle between church* and state during the Middle Ages.

(b) As an abbot, Gregory seems to have preached on the First Book of Kings, the Prophets, Proverbs, and the Song of Songs. In around 591, he completed the *Moralia in Job*, probably the most widely read of his works in the Middle Ages. In the same period, he worked on the *Regula Pastoralis*. In 591, ill and unable to preach, he composed sermons on the Gospels*. While the Lombards were besieging Rome, he gave his *Homilies on Ezekiel*, which he later published in two books (601). Some have doubted the authenticity of his *Dialogues* (593–94), which contain, most notably, a life of St. Benedict and accounts of miracles*, and they seem rather to represent Gregory's attempt at a different literary genre, akin to the lives of the desert fathers. A substantial body of letters survives.

2. Theology

Gregory was not an original thinker. His achievement was to present much of the body of Augustine*'s thought for a popular audience and to integrate something of the spirituality of the eastern tradition in a balanced presentation of Christian life. He worked for the most part through the exposition of scripture, tracing imagery and drawing out meanings whose vividness gave them wide currency throughout the Middle Ages.

(a) For Gregory, preaching* was the means by which a bishop* properly fulfills his function of guardianship and maintenance of the faith*. He was largely responsible for the model of the four senses of scripture* that

scholars used in the West until the 16th century: a literal or historical sense, an allegorical sense, an anagogic sense (prophesying eternal life*), and a tropological or moral sense.

(b) Gregory saw the Eucharist* as a manifestation of a harmony in the universe. It is a mediation between the human and the divine, a healing of all divisions. In the Eucharist, the saints are already united with God in this life. Christ* is offered as victim *(hostia)* and sacrifice* (a thesis stressed by Gregory, and an important contribution) in a humility and obedience that is the pattern for all Christians. The Eucharist's effectiveness depends upon participation in Christ's body, which means that Christians must not only practice contemplation*, but also seek to serve their neighbors. Finally, the Eucharist is able to benefit souls after death*.

Gregory himself constantly felt the existence of a tension between contemplation and action, and linked it to the bipolarity of the "inward" (the spiritual) and the "outward" (the bodily). Outwardly, all is distress, change, and decay. Inwardly, there is peace and tranquility, the foretaste of a Heaven that Platonists as well as Christians could long for. The late antique preoccupation with the dichotomy of body and soul* is developed by Gregory with a new richness of imagery. His emphasis on illumination is also typically Platonist in style, but for Gregory it is the divine light of grace* that shows us what we could not otherwise see in our sinful blindness.

(c) Gregory's use of biblical imagery in speaking of Christ has exerted a major influence on Christian language. Christ, the Church's Bridegroom, is the model for the intimacy that ought to exist between Christ and the soul. Christ is the gateway by which Christians come into the presence of God. Preachers imitate Christ in this. The church itself is the gateway between this world and the next. Christ's headship of the church is a paradigm for the bishop's authority*. Christ is also the Judge who weighs men's merits with both justice* and loving kindness.

3. Posterity

The *Regula Pastoralis* was to influence the medieval conception of the role of a bishop. Bernard* of Clairvaux used it in writing the *De Consideratione* for Eugenius III, and it thus affected theories of papal supremacy in the later Middle Ages.

The *Dialogues* were important in the success of Benedictine monasticism*, which provided the Rule by which western monks were to live at least until the 12th century. Gregory also advised Augustine of Canterbury, whom he had sent as his missionary to Great Britain, to make a sensible selection from all the existing rites so as to construct an appropriate rite for the new Christians of the island. A number of practices in the liturgy of the West, for example the use of the Lord's Prayer at the end of the Eucharistic prayer, seem to be indebted to Gregory's guidance. The *Gregorian Sacramentary* that was sent by Pope Hadrian I to Charlemagne around 790, and was thereafter circulated widely in the Frankish empire, goes back to Gregory's pontificate.

- PL 66 and 75–79; CChr.SL 140–44; *Homilies on Ezekiel,* SC 327 and 360; *Commentary on the first Book of Kings,* SC 351 and 391; *Moral Exposition on the Book of Job,* SC 32 *bis,* 212 and 221; *Dialogues,* SC 260 and 265; *Letters* SC 370–371; *Regula Pastoralis,* SC 381–82.
- R. Wasselinck (1965), "L'influence de l'exégèse de saint Grégoire le Grand," *MSR* 22, 205–219.

C. Dagens (1977), *Saint Grégoire le Grand, culture et expérience chrétienne,* Paris.

J. Richards (1980), *Consul of God: The Life and Times of Gregory the Great,* London.

W. D. McCready (1981), *Signs of Sanctity: Miracles in the Thought of Gregory the Great,* Toronto.

D. Norberg (1982), *Critical and Exegetical Notes on the Letters of St. Gregory the Great,* Stockholm.

J. M. Petersen (1984), *The Dialogues of Gregory the Great in their Late Antique Cultural Background,* Toronto.

G. R. Evans (1986), *The Thought of Gregory the Great,* Oxford.

L. La Piana (1987), *Teologia e ministerio della parola in San Gregorio Magno,* Palermo.

C. Straw (1988), *Gregory the Great: Perfection in Imperfection,* Berkeley.

R. Godding (1990), *Bibliografia di Gregorio Magno (1890–1989),* Rome.

GILLIAN R. EVANS

See also **Holiness; Mass, Sacrifice of the; Platonism**

Groote, Gerard. *See Devotio Moderna*

H

Hadewijch of Antwerp. *See* **Rhineland-Flemish Mysticism**

Happiness. *See* **Beatitude; Supernatural**

Hardening

a) Old Testament and Judaism. The terminology is very rich: hardness, rigidity (*châzaq, qâshâh;* Gr. *sklèrunô, sklèros; pôroô, pôrôsis,* sometimes synonymous with "blindness"); heaviness (*kâbéd,* Gr. *barunô, bareô*); stoutness, impermeability (*shâmén,* Gr. *pachunô*); deafness, blindness (often paired: Dt 29:3; Is 6:10, 42:18ff.; Jer 5:21); giddiness (Dt 28:28), vertigo (Is 19:14); torpor (Is 29:10); drunkenness (Ps 60:5); delirium (Dt 28:28; Zec 12:4); and so on. The eyes and ears are affected, but above all the heart, in the Semitic sense, as the center of conscious life. It is the most serious consequence to which sin* can lead: a spiritual condition in which an individual not only does not want to convert himself or herself, but is no longer able to do so (Jer 13:23). The good*, the path of salvation*, the voice of God* is not merely refused: it is no longer perceived.

The agent of this hardening is occasionally specified. Sometimes it is man himself, as in the case of Pharaoh (Ex 7:13, 14, 8:15, 9:35; Dt 29:18; Ps 95:8; Jer 7:24, 9:13, 11:8; Zec 7:11f.). However, the originator is often YHWH, who may bring it about for the purpose of punishment (1 Sm 2:25; 1 Kgs 12:15), but also of salvation (Ex 4:1, 7:3, 22, 9:12, 10:1, 20, 27; 14:4, 8, 17).

In later writings there appears a tendency on the one hand to eliminate this mode of expression (for example, the modifications of the Septuagint in Is 6:9f.) and, on the other hand, to accentuate it by coming close to a dualist and predestinarian vocabulary. What is involved, however, is more than an imperfection of thought and language, a sensibility less attuned to distinguishing between consequence and finality, between "permitting" and "wishing," or between the "first cause" and the "second cause." Beyond all these psychological or linguistic considerations, necessary as they may be, remains a more strictly theological content, indispensable and linked to the deepest core of the faith* of Israel*, to the biblical understanding of God and humanity.

By underlining the seriousness of the situation brought about by sin and the impossibility of curing or remedying it by human agency, the concept of hardening opened the way to a deeper understanding of salvation as grace*, as a gift of God (Ps 51:12; Is 63:17; Jer 31:18) and an eschatological event. One day, the incurable obstinacy of the human heart will be vanquished, in Israel as in the nations (Jer 3:17): God will remove the heart of stone and provide a new heart (Ez 11:19, 36:26f., 39:29; Jer 24:7, 31:33, 32:39; Dt 30:6), and eyes and ears capable of hearing (Is 32:3; Bar 2:31).

b) *New Testament.* More than to pagans or to unbelievers and sinners in general (Eph 4:18; 2 Cor 4:3f.; Heb 3:8, 15; 4:7), the theme of hardening is applied to Israel's unbelief. By linking it above all with Isaiah 6:9ff., this most mysterious and shocking fact is explained, at least in part. We are faced both with an apologetic argument (even in the fact of being rejected, Jesus* fulfilled the Scriptures*!) and, perhaps more important, with a theological interpretation. The situation in question had already been permitted by God himself in the past. If it comes to pass both now in the face of Christian preaching* (Rom 9:18, 11:7; 2 Cor 3:14f.; Acts 28:26f.), and already in Jesus' time in response to his own person (Mk 4:11f.; Jn 12:40), then it heightens God's mystery*.

Blindness, however, is in no way equivalent to a curse or a definitive rejection. Far from expressing an "anti-Judaic" attitude, this theological theme presupposes Israel's irreversible choice* as an actual race* and the certainty of its full participation in eschatological salvation (Rom 11:25–32; also 2 Cor 3:14ff.; and probably also Mk 4:21–25; Mt 23:39; Lk 13:35; 21:24).

● K. L. Schmidt, M. A. Schmidt (1954), "*pakhunô* ktl.," *ThWNT* 5, 1024–32.

J. Gnilka (1961), *Die Verstockung Israels, Isaias 6, 9–10 in der Theologie der Synoptiker,* StANT 3.

H. Räisänen (1972), *The Idea of Divine Hardening: A Comparative Study of the Notion of Divine Hardening, Leading Astray, and Inciting to Evil in the Bible and in the Qur'an,* SESJ 25.

V. Fusco (1980), *Parola e Regno: La sezione delle parabole (Mc 4, 1–34) nella prospettiva marciana,* Aloi, 13, 221–304.

J. Delorme (1982), "Savoir, croire et communication parabolique," in *Actes sémiotiques-Documents* IV/38, CNRS, Paris.

J. Delorme (1987), "La communication parabolique d'après Marc 4," *Sémiotique et Bible* 48, 1–17.

C. A. Evans (1989), *To See and Not Perceive: Isaiah 6, 9–10 in Early Jewish and Christian Interpretation,* JSOT.S 64.

R. Küschelm (1990), *Verstockung, Gericht und Heil: Exegetische und bibeltheologische Untersuchung zum sogenannten "Dualismus" und "Determinismus" in Joh 12, 35–50,* BBB 76.

L. Perrone (Ed.) (1992), *Il cuore indurito del Faraone: Origene e il problema del libero arbitrio,* Genoa.

VITTORIO FUSCO

See also **Conversion; Heart of Christ; Mercy; Wrath of God**

Harnack, Adolf von. *See* **Hellenization of Christianity; Liberalism**

Healing

The Hebrew *râfâ'* ("to heal") is linked to *rôfé'* ("doctor"). The Greek *Rhaphaèl,* in Tobit, directly transcribes the Hebrew: "God* heals." To heal is also very simply "to live" or "make live" (Gn 20:7 and 2 Kgs 8:8). The Greek books use *therapeuô* or *iaomai* for "to heal," and only *iatros* for doctor. The neuter *iama* (1 Cor 12) is reserved for the charisma of healing.

Healing, in literal sense, designates deliverance from physical evil*; in the figurative sense, it means deliverance from moral evil, relief from pain. While a contemporary Westerner is used to making the distinction between the two, the Scriptures* tell stories in which the literal and figurative senses intertwine. Sickness and sin* intersect, for the human body can be adequately treated only at the crossing of the two planes. The concept of healing cannot be separated from the notion of salvation*, nor from the notion of purification. The request for salvation from a patient can just as well be a request for organic remedies as a call for the words of the therapist.

The Old Testament records healings obtained through a man of God's prayer* or by his actions. To be noted are (1) the talking presence of an intermediary; (2) the sick person's effort to revisit in words his or her suffering (Ps; Is 38:10—"I said"); and (3) the insertion within the symbols of communal living. In the New Testament, healing becomes a privileged place in which the figure of Jesus is revealed as Christ* and Savior. The narratives of healing and discourses of teaching are so closely related that teaching-healing can be considered a key pair in interpreting them.

1. Doctors, Remedies, the Sick

a) Medicine. Job links doctors and charlatans (Jb 13:4). Tobit says that the physicians could not help his blindness (Tb 2:10), but that the angel would recommend a remedy. As opposed to the major literary works of ancient Egypt or Mesopotamia, the Old Testament attaches little importance to medicine. Ben Sirach judges it with moderation (Sir 38:1–14). A few remedies are mentioned (Is 1:6): the gall of the fish for Tobit's eyes (Tb 6:4f., 11:8, 11:12), a cake of figs for boils (2 Kgs 20:7), the leech, the use of healing herbs (Sir 38:4 and Wis 7:20). Wisdom of Solomon knows and uses the medical notions from the Greek world.

The New Testament mentions wine and oil (Lk 10:34), and Jesus uses his spit (Mk 7:33, 8:23; Jn 9:6) and touch (Mt 8:15; Lk 22:51). Most often, healing occurs during a verbal exchange with patients.

b) Places to Be Healed. Sickness, often contagious or considered as such, is considered a social plague, such as leprosy. It leads to exclusion, therefore healing requires control: the sick person presumed to be healed has to go and be examined by competent authorities—priests and Levites. The descriptions of procedures and prescriptions play an important role in the Torah (Lv 13f.). In the Gospels*, when Jesus heals the lepers, he subjects his patients to this law and sends them to priests (Lk 17:14).

c) Healers. Healing comes from God alone. The prophets* obtain it from him. Thus Elijah (1 Kgs 17:17–24), Elisha (2 Kgs 5), and—a typical case—Isaiah (2 Kgs 20:1–11; Is 38). The narratives focus on what the sick person and the one from whom he requests help have in common: there is no healing without true words. Jesus places healing within the creative work that gathered all people in a single, unique humanity. Upon YHWH's order (Gn 20:7), the pagan king Abimelech receives Abraham's intercession (he is then called "prophet") and is healed.

This request for the fulfillment of the creative work is carried out in prayer (mediators: Ps 35:13f.). The psalms*, in which most hardships are expressed through repercussions in the body, address the complaints of the suffering to God, who saves the innocent and sinners alike. The wounded man who exposed himself before God discovers cultural and social proximity in praise*.

2. Christological Dimension of Healing

In the desert, the people were healed from snake bites (punishment for revolt) by looking at a bronze snake that Moses placed on a pole (Nm 21:6–9). The typology of John 3:14f. sees Jesus' cross in the episode. Healing is henceforth perceived in unique connection to Jesus' body. The journey includes the presentation of the Lord as "I am the Lord, your healer" (Ex 15:26); it includes the vision of the Savior as both "lifted up" (Is 52:13; Jn 8:8, 12:40) and "healing" (53:6) blind eyes (Is 6:10 and Mt 13:15). The sick are healed by Jesus through his body and toward his body. They enter the world of the living, of the talking and seeing. After Pentecost, the lame man at the Beautiful Gate (Acts 3:1–16), after being taken "by the right hand" by Peter*, "clung to Peter and John." The place given in this story to the "name*" of Jesus (Acts 3:6, 16) suggests that we should understand healing as transplants onto the body of those named by Jesus Christ.

From the perspective of the healing stories, the body seems to be the manifestation of the intangible and problematic encounter between word and flesh*, thus suggesting the work to be done and the risks to overcome when it involves taking care of what is and continues to be the suffering in every man.

● H. W. Wolff (1974), *Anthropologie de l'Ancien Testament,* Geneva.

C. J. Groesbeck (1975), "The Archetypal Image of the Wounded Healer," *Journal of Analytical Psychology* 20, 122–45.

E. de Rosny (1984), "Les nouveaux guérisseurs africains," *Études* 361, 661–79.

F. Laplantine (1986), *Anthropologie de la maladie,* Paris.

L. Perrin (1987), *Guérir et sauver,* Paris.

D. Le Breton (1990), *Anthropologie du corps et modernité,* Paris.

J. Delorme (1991), *Au risque de la parole: Lire les Évangiles,* Paris, 17–92.

G. Kowalski (1991), "Santé et salut à l'interface entre biologie et société," *BICP* 40, 197–224.

M. McGuive (1991), "Religion, santé, maladie," *Con.* 324, 109–21.

P. Gisel (1992), *Corps et Esprit, les mystères de l'incarnation et de la résurrection,* Geneva.

X. Lacroix (1992), *Le corps de chair,* Paris.

T. Nathan (1994), *L'influence qui guérit,* Paris.

H. Avalos (1995), *Illness and Health Care in the Ancient Near East: The Role of the Temple in Greece, Mesopotamia, and Israel,* Atlanta.

CÉCILE TURIOT

See also **Anthropology; Faith; Flesh; Jesus, Historical; Miracle; Name; Psalms; Purity/Impurity; Sacrament; Salvation; Sin; Soul-Heart-Body**

Heart. *See* **Soul-Heart-Body**

Heart of Christ

The heart was long considered the origin or seat of the feelings, in particular, of love*, before it became its permanent symbol. This metonymy and later this metaphor, which have exploited a great number of phrases from Scripture, have been used in extremely variable ways, which range from the most dolorous sentimentalism to the most decided voluntarism*, and from the most rhetorical piety to the most precise conceptuality. The ancient veneration of the wound in Christ's side (Jn 19:34) was very quickly reinterpreted as a prehistory of the devotion to the heart of Christ* or the heart of Jesus* via medieval meditation on the Song of Songs and on John 13:23–25 (John leaning against the bosom and the breast of Jesus) and John 19:37 (the piercing by the lance exhibits the "inner" Jesus, his "bowels of mercy*," according to Bernard* of Clairvaux), and the veneration of the crucifix in the *devotio* moderna. In the 17th century, the devotion to the five wounds of Christ (Father Joseph de la Tremblaye, 1577–1638) and the devotion to his heart took separate paths. The common reference to the heart acquired a mass of voluntarist and affective meanings, being used first to refer to Mary* and then also to Jesus; these meanings communicated a renewed piety, in which the classical theology* of redemption was mixed with the idea of a duty of reparation. From that time onward, the devotion to the Sacred Heart, the carnal heart of Jesus wounded for our sins*, would consist in giving special honor to the love of Jesus Christ for mankind.

a) Heart and the States of Jesus. For the most part we owe the theology of the heart of Jesus to John Eudes (1601–80), an Oratorian (1623–43) very close to Father de Condren and later a founder of the Congregation of Jesus and Mary (the Eudists). In his *Le Coeur admirable de la très sainte Mère de Dieu* of 1681, John Eudes recognized eight principal meanings in the "heart": 1) the "corporeal and material heart," which 2) symbolizes memory or 3) "means the understanding by which holy meditation occurs"; 4) in the soul*, free will, and particularly 5) "the point in the spirit where contemplation* occurs"; 6) "the whole inner part of man"; 7) the Holy Spirit, "which is the heart of the Father* and of the Son"; and 8) the Son of God*, "called the heart of the eternal Father," but also "the soul of our soul, the heart of our heart." John Eudes does not suggest choosing between these meanings but rather their organization into a sequence that continually proceeds to an ever greater interiority, toward "the interior of Jesus." H. Bremond saw in this taxonomy an oscillation between the heart-as-person*—inherited from Bérulle*, and which would be found again in Pascal*—and the heart-as-love, preached by Bernardine of Siena, and which would reveal itself to Margaret Mary Alacoque. However, the two meanings merge in the connotation of a hypostasized love. In the Man-God himself there are three hearts: the divine one, the spiritual one, and the corporeal one. The first is the indissoluble expression of the Son's love for the Father, of the Word*'s love for humankind. The second is Christ's will to love what is lovable, to hate what is hateful (the identification of the heart and the will is characteristic of 17th-century voluntarism). The third is that "muscle" that the Jansenists (Jansenism*) scoffed at as the center of a spirituality. In fact, the whole of the Eudist typology is governed by his re-adoption of one of Bérulle's theories: that of the "states" (feelings or states of mind of Jesus) as it appears in the 1623 treatise *De l'état et des grandeurs de Jésus,* in which the proper role of the Word is always *referred back* to the Father (whence its theocentrism). The heart, synonym of the *interior* in John Eudes as in Jean-Jacques Olier (1608–57; *Catéchisme chrétien pour la vie intérieure* [1656]), transposes Bérulle's "state" into a less metaphysical piety, but one where we can still find all of Bérulle's most characteristic theses, such as that of the incarnate Word's fatherhood toward Christians—Jesus "father of hearts," or again, "a supplement for our duties" (Olier)—ideas that make it

possible to conceptualize Christ's mediating function (*La vie et le royaume de Jésus dans les âmes chrétiennes,* Caen, 1637). That is why the mysteries* of the faith*, in particular those that Bérulle examined—the Incarnation* and the Redemption, but also and above all the Trinity*—can be meditated on through the heart of Jesus. In this way, while creating an original work, John Eudes provided solid doctrinal foundations for devotion to the heart of Jesus.

b) Cult of the Sacred Heart and Its Doctrinal Acknowledgment. With Margaret Mary Alacoque (1648–90) the Trinitarian meditation dissipated to make way for a meditation on Jesus' love of humankind. Especially associated with this was the idea of a misunderstanding of, or contempt for, Jesus' love, which no longer required from the faithful a supportive solidarity, but an act of reparatory love—theocentrism thus became a preoccupation with reciprocity. In June 1675, this Visitandine sister from Paray-le-Monial received a vision of Jesus, who, "uncovering his heart" to her (that Jesus should *show* himself is an essential component of this spirituality), said: "Here is this heart which has loved mankind so much that it spared itself nothing, Even to the point of exhausting itself and pining away in order to show them this love, and by way of gratitude in return I receive from most of them only ingratitude."

Supported by her confessor, the Jesuit priest Claude de la Colombière, Margaret Mary circulated images abroad, asking for holy hours of reparation, and that people dedicate themselves to the heart of Jesus.

There is, however, an undeniable doctrinal continuity between the Feast of Jesus instituted by Bérulle in the Oratory in 1625 (or that of the "Vie intérieure de Notre-Seigneur" instituted at Saint-Sulpice by M. Olier) and that of the Sacred Heart inaugurated at Caen in 1678 by John Eudes (after the first celebration of the liturgy* of the heart of Mary in Autun in 1648); and still later, with that of the hearts of Jesus and Mary (John Eudes spoke "of the heart of Jesus and Mary," in this way reinstituting for Mary the Pauline ideal of life in Christ), which was authorized by a certain number of bishops* from 1672 onward; and with the Mass and Office of the heart of Jesus (in the litanies of which are found the multiplicity of meanings of "heart" and its Trinitarian core), which were conceded by the Congregation of Rites in 1765 after some reticence, refusals, and all kinds of pressure. Particular mention must be made here of the 18th-century Jansenists' opposition to this cult* of the "muscle," subscribed to by the "Cordicolae" (Scipion de Ricci, 1741–1809), an opposition that contrasted with the opinion of their elders at Port-Royal. And so the cult became public. The pastoral importance in the 19th century of a devotion to the heart of Jesus in which the aspect of redress or of reparation continued to grow should not be underestimated. Its voluntarist affectivity was a corrective to sentimentalism.

On 25 May 1899, Leo XIII's encyclical, *Annum sacrum,* dedicated the human race to the heart of Jesus, in this way inviting the unbaptized to baptism*, that is, to a recognition of what the heart of Jesus had won for them. By the bull *Miserentissimus Redemptor* (8 May 1928) Pius XI emphasized the obligation of adding man's subjective reparation to Christ to Christ's objective reparation of humanity. Finally, in *Haurietis aquas* (15 May 1956) Pius XII gave a specific definition of the nature of the cult: the heart of Jesus, pierced by the transfixion of the side, "so that through the visible wound we may behold the invisible wound of love" (a phrase attributed to Bonaventure*), is the "natural sign and symbol of his boundless love for the human race." Moreover, this encyclical settled a disputed question—can uncreated love form part of the proper objective of the heart of Jesus?—by specifying that this cult can elevate us to "the adoration of the *divine* love of the Word incarnate." The encyclical also uses the expression "eucharistic heart." Among the rare contemporary attempts that have been made to plumb the mystery of the heart of Jesus must be mentioned that of H. U. von Balthasar*, who gives it a cosmological dimension in *Das Herz der Welt* (Zürich, 1945).

● *Œuvres complètes du vénérable Jean Eudes,* Ed. J. Dauphin and C. Lebrun, 12 vols., Vannes and Paris, 1905–11.

J. de Galliffet (1726), *De cultu SS: Cordis Dei et Domini Nostri Jesu Christi,* Rome.

Vie et œuvres de sainte Marguerite-Marie Alacoque, Ed. L. Gauthey, 3 vols., Paray-le-Monial, 1915.

Le Sacré-Cœur: Textes pontificaux, Ed., Trans., and Comm. P. Galtier, Paris, 1936.

Cor Jesu, Ed. A. Béa, 2 vols., Rome, 1959.

◆ J. V. Bainvel (1921), *La dévotion au Sacré-Cœur de Jésus,* Paris.

H. Bremond (1923), *Histoire littéraire du sentiment religieux en France...,* vol. III, Paris.

A. Hamon (1924–40), *Histoire de la dévotion au Sacré Cœur,* 5 vols., Paris.

C. Lebrun (1933), *La spiritualité de saint Jean Eudes,* Paris.

Coll. (1950), *Le cœur, EtCarm.*

J. Chatillon et al. (1953), "Cor et cordis affectus," *DSp* 2, 2278–307.

A. Hamon (1953), "Sacré-Cœur," ibid., 1023–46.

J. Arragain (Ed.) (1955), *Le cœur du Seigneur: Études sur les écrits et l'influence de saint Jean Eudes dans sa dévotion au cœur de Jésus,* Paris.

H. Rahner (1956), "Les fondements scripturaires de la dévotion au Sacré-Cœur," in J. Stierli (Ed.), *Le cœur du Sauveur,* Mulhouse, 29–52.

P. Blanchard (1961), *Sainte Marguerite-Marie,* Paris.

K. Rahner (1966), "Der theologische Sinn der Verehrung des Herzens Jesu," *Schr. zur Th.* 7, Einsieldeln-Zürich-Köln, 481–90; "Einheit-Liebe-Geheimnis," ibid., 491–508.

F. degli Esposti (1967), *La teologia del Sacro Cuore di Gesu, da Leone XIII a Pio XII,* Rome.

B. de Margerie (1971), *Le Christ pour le monde,* Paris.

P. Milcent (1974), "Jean Eudes," *DSp* 8, 488–501.

M. Walsh (1977), *The Heart of Christ in the Writings of K. Rahner,* Rome.

J. Solano (1979), *Teología y vivencia del culto al corazón de Jesús,* 4 vols., Madrid.

J. Le Brun (1980), "Marguerite-Marie Alacoque," *DSp* 10, 349–55.

Coll. (1982), *Le cœur de Jésus cœur du monde,* Paris.

B. de Margerie (1992 and 1995), *Histoire doctrinale du culte au (envers le) cœur de Jésus,* 2 vols., Paris.

VINCENT CARRAUD

See also **Bérulle, Pierre de; Love; Mercy; Passion; Penance; Quietism; Soul-Heart-Body; Voluntarism**

Heaven. *See* **Kingdom of God; Life, Eternal; Vision, Beatific**

Hegel, Georg Wilhelm Friedrich

1770–1831

a) Life and Work. George Wilhelm Friedrich Hegel was born in Stuttgart on 27 August 1770. After studying philosophy* and theology* at the Stift in Tübingen (1788–93), where his friends included F. Hölderlin (1770–1843) and Schelling*, he became interested, among other things, in Kant* and the ideals of the French Revolution. He gave up his intention of becoming a pastor and became a tutor in Bern and Frankfurt (1793–1800). At the time he wrote a number of minor works on religious problems. While he was a teacher in Jena (1801–07) he published *The Difference between the Systems of Fichte and Schelling* (1801) and also collaborated with Schelling on the *Critical Journal of Philosophy,* but broke with him at the time of publication of the *Phenomenology of Mind* (1807). While he was director of the gymnasium at Nuremburg, he published *The Science of Logic* (1812–16). After a short stay in Heidelberg (1816–18), where he refined his philosophical system (*Encyclopedia of the Philosophical Sciences,* 1817), he finally became a professor at the University of Berlin. In 1821 *The Principles of the Philosophy of the Law* was published, and in 1822 he wrote a preface for a book on religion and science by H. F. Hinrichs. The book opposed Schleiermacher*. He died on 14 November 1831. His courses on the philosophy of religion*, on the philosophy of history*, on aesthetics and the history of philosophy would be the subject of a posthumous publication (Rosenkranz 1844).

b) Early Theological Writings. In his early work notes, Hegel envisaged the idea of a subjective, not positive, religion, which would reply to the demands of practical reason* yet would nourish sensibility (*GW* 1, 75–164), and to him it seemed essential for humanity to transform "fetish-faith" in order to bring it closer to rational religion. Rational religion opposed itself to an objective religion that was expressed more through a theological knowledge than through moral action. Hegel then asked himself about the possibility of creating a people's religion that, through its art and its festivals, would encourage the spontaneous display of fine moral sentiments and privilege the spirit over the letter. Indeed, the French Revolution already represented for him the victory of the living spirit of a people over its dead institutions (Legros 1980). *The Life of Jesus,* written in Bern and inspired by Kant, saw in Jesus* only the preacher of a religion that was purely moral and that issued entirely from practical reason (*GW* 1, 205–78). This book understood the birth of Christianity as resulting from a re-Judaization of the Gospel (Peperzak 1969). As for the *Positivity of the Christian Religion* (*GW* 1, 281–378), the text saw in Jesus' own religion a tendency, accentuated by the sectarian spirit of the apostles*, toward a religion of external authority* (Legros 1987).

After the so-called Bern period, with its exegesis* strongly inspired by Kant, there followed a more "mystical" perspective (Bourgeois 1970) during Hegel's stay in Frankfurt. And so we find *The Spirit of Christianity and Its Fate* dominated by notions of life and of love* (Nohl 1907). Life, as an originary unity, tears itself apart and grows hostile toward itself, but it overcomes this split through a reconciliation with itself. Love is then conceived as the feeling of life being rediscovered; destiny is reconciled (Haering 1929). Faith in Jesus, who reconciled everything in love, presupposes a unity of spirit, that is, a presence of the divine in the believers themselves (Nohl; Leonard 1970). But such a presence remained imperfect in the first disciples. They clung to the Risen One rather than recognizing the Spirit that was calling them from within (Nohl). An understanding of this type of Christian religion in terms of life and spirit prefigured the notion of dialectics as a unity that embraces all splits by suppressing them (Marsch 1965; Brito 1983).

c) Writings from Jena. In *Faith and Knowledge* (1802), Hegel considers the phrase "God is dead" to be the expression of the culture of his era, as "the feeling on which the religion of the new era is based" (*GW* 4, 315–414; Link 1974). Hegel's point is not to justify atheism* but to go beyond it by conceiving this death* as the event of God*'s self-negation: God does not want to remain "in himself," or abandon the world* to its finitude (Brunkhorst and Hasenclever 1976; Brito 1986).

The Phenomenology of Spirit is a treatise on the progress of consciousness from its first immediate opposition between it and the object to absolute knowledge. The seemingly chaotic wealth of phenomena of the spirit was laid out here according to a necessary order. In this order, imperfect phenomena dissolve progressively and turn into superior phenomena that constitute their closest truth* (Heinrich 1974). They eventually find their closest truth in religion (*GW* 9, 363–421) and finally in the knowledge of the absolute, which is the result of full comprehension of all these phenomena. Until consciousness arrives at an adequation with the system of "essences" it does not correspond exactly to its concept, and it is precisely this discrepancy between what it is in itself and what it is for itself that drives it forward. At the end of this process, religion reveals the absolute concept, but only in its relation to consciousness, that is, as a phenomenon.

Three stages scan this phenomenological development. In natural religion, the spirit perceives itself in an immediate manner (*GW* 9, 369–75); in the Greek religion of art, it knows itself in the figure of suppressed naturality or of the self (*GW* 9, 376–99); while in the context of a Christianity perceived as a revealed religion, the spirit takes the form of the unity of consciousness with self-awareness (*GW* 9, 400–421). The subjective for-itself of the unhappy consciousness and the substantial in-itself of faith are united and accomplished in a double Christian alienation-projection *(Entaüsserung)*. Substance, or God, removes itself from its abstraction by taking incarnation in the consciousness of a self, while the consciousness of self externalizes itself in a universal essence (*GW* 9, 403). *Phenomenology* articulates the stages of Christian spiritual content: the pure Trinitarian essence, the evolution of essence (creation*, fall, reconciliation), and community (Guibal 1975).

d) Encyclopedic System. The *Encyclopedia* laid out Hegel's system in its definitive structure: logic, philosophy of nature, philosophy of spirit. Taking up again the essential points of logic, the first stage establishes an identity between the laws of thought and those of being*, in the sense where the movement of being leads to the realization of the concept. Dialectics takes a ternary course here: being (immediacy), essence (reflection), concept (liberty*). Following a certain neo-Platonic and Christian tradition, Hegel compares the Idea-Logos (Word*) with the eternal essence of God before the creation of nature and of a finite mind (Bruaire 1965; Lakebrink 1968). But logic already contains the seeds of the two other stages of philosophy. Indeed, since it is identical to itself, thought is a return to itself from a being other than oneself. It is the negation of its own differentiation. The distance from self to self implied by this identification *with* oneself constitutes the idea as nature, and in this way founds

the philosophy of nature as a science of the idea in its particularity (*GW* 20, 235–375). As for the act of identification with oneself, it constitutes the idea as spirit and founds the philosophy of spirit as a science of the idea in its singularity (*GW* 20, 379–572).

The different moments of the subjective spirit (soul*, consciousness, consciousness of self, and reason, theoretical and practical spirit) are like a series of way stations along the path through which the spirit rids itself of the contradiction of its natural immediacy and manages to become aware of its own concept, freedom. In the second stage of its liberation, that of the objective spirit (law, morality, family*, society*, state, history), spirit appears bearing the features of a world it produces as such. Liberated from any dependency with regard to the nature from which it emerged as a subjective spirit and of which it was a part as an objective spirit, the concept of the spirit finally has, as an absolute spirit, its reality in the Spirit. Art, religion, and philosophy represent the moments when the identity of absolute spirit with its concept is affirmed. As philosophy progressively frees itself from the formal unilaterality of art and religion, it raises them to the absolute form of the thinking idea. Since it is for itself a relation of self to self, absolute spirit is, globally, religion (Theunissien 1970), but its perfect form does not appear until the end, in philosophy. Philosophy, placing itself above the figure of faith, thus dominates religion understood in a restricted sense (*GW* 20, 555–69).

e) Philosophy of Religion. The *Lectures on the Philosophy of Religion* (*GW* 17) have justly been considered Hegel's "theological *summum*" (Küng 1970). It is true that they do take up the principal points of Christian dogmatics*; focusing on the intelligence of faith, they concur with theological perspectives and are able to connect with a conception of theology as a science subordinate to the knowledge* of God by God. However, far from limiting itself to considering God as essence, Hegel's philosophy of religion knows only the God-Spirit that is only for the spirit and thus distinguishes itself from traditional natural* theology.

Hegel articulates the concept of religion, and thus the structure of his *Lectures,* in three stages: objective determination, the subjective dimension of consciousness, and the reconciliation of these two aspects in the Christian cult* (*GW* 17, 33ff.). Thus the givens of representation are closely akin to the speculative definition of religion as a knowledge of self peculiar to absolute spirit (Jaeschke 1986). Hegel points out that the content of religion and that of philosophy are "the same," that is, "God and his explanation." But the absolute content that religion seeks to represent must be elevated by philosophy to the form of thought by seizing its ideality.

In the first of its three parts this work details "the concept of religion," the logical germ that virtually exhausts the religious possibilities of humanity. Going on in the second part to describe the different stages of religion (being, essence, concept) in its objective being, Hegel follows the development of "determined" or finite religion, a religion that has not yet attained the fullness of the idea (religions of nature, of spiritual individuality, of finality). Finally, he presents absolute religion (Christianity) in which the concept of religion, completely objectified for itself, is revealed as spirit.

Expounding on each of these religions according to the same rhythm (metaphysical concept, concrete representation, cult), Hegel sees the concept of absolute religion in the God who gives himself objectivity and who is thus the absolute idea. The Christian God can thus determine himself metaphysically by means of the ontological proof that, although inadequate in language, leads from the concept of God to his being (proofs of the existence* of God; Ogiermann 1948). The concrete representation of the Christian religion is deployed in three spheres. The first, in the element of thought, considers the Trinitarian God in his eternal essence within himself, in the form of universality. The second, in the element of representation in the strict sense of the term, considers creation, the conservation of the finite world, and the natural particularity as a phenomenon of the Idea. The third, in the element of intuitive effectivity, presents the Christian history of salvation* (original sin*, the Incarnation*, and the Redemption) as the accomplished objectivity of the divine history of the spirit in its absolute singularity. The transition to the Christian cult indicates not only the passage from the one to the many, but also that of the objective representation of God in a human form to the region of the subjective immanence of the spiritual community. After the general determination (the Spirit of Christ*) and the objective reality of the community (faith and worship, the Eucharist*) the *Lectures* describe its spiritual disappearance: the church* finds its fulfillment beyond itself, in the eternal presence of philosophy (Fackenheim 1967; Schlitt 1990).

f) Structure of Theology. According to Hegel one can only conceptualize Christian revelation* by making use of the plurality of intentionalities of religious consciousness: to the varying dimensions of religious conscience correspond different levels of theological language* (Bodamer 1969).

1) To the level of representative consciousness corresponds the point of view of "dogmatics" from the *Lectures on the Philosophy of Religion.* This dogmatics begins with the logical concept of the Christian God, then goes on to discuss the naturally objectifying representation of the history of salvation, and concludes with the passage to the spiritual realm (Kingdom* of God) of the community and of the cult. This "positive* theology" is articulated according to a successive order of traditional representation and grants a large place to the language of historical effectivity.

2) The level of consciousness of self determines the theological perspective peculiar to the *Phenomenology.* In accordance with the global movement by means of which the phenomenological procedure detaches itself from immediate consciousness in order to arrive in the logical element, this "ascetic theology" (asceticism*) discerns, in the representation of the consciousness of self, the spiritual location where revealed religion relinquishes naturality and accedes to the rationality of absolute knowledge.

3) Reason finds itself within its own mode in the theology of the *Encyclopedia.* The universality of the truth appears there neither in an archeology of the concept of the Christian religion (*see* the *Lectures*), nor as a finalizing eschatology* of science *(Phenomenology),* but as the very element of the discourse (Chapelle 1971). Revealed truth is then seen to be the absolute mediation of the Spirit, which, by assuming the natural objectivity of historical representation and by reflecting the subjective demands of consciousness, systematically articulates therein its eternal life* (*GW* 20, 549ff.).

g) Dogmatic Content of Hegel's Thought. Hegel does not reduce divine attributes* to representations of abstract reflection, and he refutes all agnosticism* that thrusts the infinite* into a beyond that cannot be approached by speech (Brito 1991). Instead of dissociating metaphysical predication from concrete truth, as nominalism* does, Hegel conceives of the doctrine of divine names* as the speculative apprehension of the free deployment of the historical revelation of God. The Trinity*, the Creation, and biblical history are thus understood as correlative moments of the same process of revelation.

Hegel means to speak of the Trinity itself (Splett 1965), in its pure eternity*, but he thinks of it dialectically, that is, in terms of its historical involvement in the missions of the Son and of the Spirit. Hegel's Trinitarian speculation was elaborated as the deployment of lack with which the primary penury of the abstract universal and the native poverty of determined difference efface each other, in the final assent of the Spirit to its necessary division and its free reconciliation (Chapelle 1967).

As for the representation of the ex nihilo, it is not, according to Hegel, indispensable to Christian theology: the absolute Idea in fact posits everything on the basis of itself (Brito 1987). While acknowledging the originary unity of the creative Idea and created nature, Hegel absolutely distinguishes the eternal Son from the temporal world. Creation is the work of liberty, for it is the display of the Spirit; but this liberty excludes free will and implies that the Creator has exhausted his creative possibilities. Hegel also upholds the difference between possible and finite reality, but he challenges the possibility of another reality and therefore the contingency of the creative choice. In this way, pure contingency and the only possible possible [sic] are posited by creative freedom only to be denied.

Hegel reduces the representation of the Fall to the concept of natural man, torn by the contradiction between his natural immediacy and his spiritual potentiality (Ringleben 1977; Pottier 1990). In the wake of the Lutheran version of the communication of idioms* the Hegelian concept of the Incarnation dialectically articulates virtual unity and the effective union of divine and human natures. Far from preserving its own properties, each nature must deny itself in its other. Hegel does not deny that the Logos became flesh in the singularity of *one* man. But, if divinity must place itself outside of itself in renounced individual finitude, humanity reveals itself definitively absorbed in the divinity of the Logos (Brito 1983). Hegel consequently appears as a thinker of the cross: he places it at the center of his system, where all negativity and all contradictions are concentrated (Schultz 1964).

The scission of the Idea can be apprehended in the death of Christ. There, God achieves the transposition of his Trinitarian being in the effectivity of human history, in such a way that the appearance of the Kingdom in effective reality makes history the place of all reconciliations. With the "death of the death" of Christ, the immediate individual presence disappears and the intimacy of the infinite spirit bursts forth as the negative of the negative (Tilliette 1992). In such a scenario the Resurrection* is no more than the return already contained within death. As the ascent to the Father is speculatively excluded, Hegel knows no other exaltation than the elevation on the cross, which leaves the disciples in infinite sorrow. And so it is that in the renunciation of everything visible, the community discovers the life that is immanent to it. With unequaled power, Hegel envisions the Calvary of the Absolute, though without excluding from his speculative discourse the positive fullness of Easter (Brito 1983; Stähler 1928).

- *Sämtliche Werke* (1927–1939), so called "Jubilee Edition," Ed. H. Glockner, 20 vols., Stuttgart.

Gesammelte Werke (1968–), Hambourg.

Hegels theologische Jugendschriften (1907), Ed. H. Nohl, Tübingen.

K. Steinhauer (1980), *Hegel-Bibliographie,* Munich.

Vorlesungen über die Philosophie der Religion (1983–85), 4 vols., Ed. W. Jaeschke, Hamburg.

♦ K. Rosenkranz (1844), *G. W. F. Hegels Leben,* Berlin.

W. Stälher (1928), *Zur Unsterblichkeitsproblematik in Hegels Nachfolge,* Münster.

Th. Haering (1929), *Hegel: Sein Wollen und sein Werk* I, Leipzig (2nd Ed. 1963).

H. Ogiermann (1948), *Hegels Gottesbeweise,* Rome.

A. Chapelle (1964), *Hegel et la religion,* vol. 1 *(La problématique),* Paris.

W. Schultz (1964), "Die Transformierung der *Theologia crucis* bei Hegel und Schleiermacher," *NZSTh* 6, 290–317.

Cl. Bruaire (1965), *Logique et religion chrétienne dans la philosophie de Hegel,* Paris.

W.-D. Marsch (1965), *Gegenwart Christi in der Gesellschaft: Eine Studie zu Hegels Dialektik,* Munich.

J. Splett (1965), *Die Trinitätslehre G. W. F. Hegels,* Freiburg-Munich.

A. Chapelle (1967), *Hegel et la religion,* vol. 2 *(Dieu et la Création),* Paris.

E. Fackenheim (1967), *The Religious Dimension in Hegel's Thought,* Bloomington.

B. Lakebrink (1968), *Die europäische Idee der Freiheit,* I. *Hegels Logik und die Tradition der Selbstbestimmung,* Leyden.

Th. Bodammer (1969), *Hegels Deutung der Sprache,* Hamburg.

A. Peperzak (1969), *Le jeune Hegel et la vision morale du monde,* The Hague.

B. Bourgeois (1970), *Hegel à Francfort,* Paris.

H. Küng (1970), *Menschwerdung Gottes: Eine Einführung in Hegels theologisches Denken als Prolegomena zu einer künftigen Christologie,* Freiburg-Basel-Vienna.

A. Léonard (1970), *La foi chez Hegel,* Paris.

M. Theunissen (1970), *Hegels Lehre vom absoluten Geist als theologisch-politischer Traktat,* Berlin.

A. Chapelle (1971), *Hegel et la religion,* vol. 3 *(La théologie et l'Église),* Paris.

R. Heede (1972), *Die göttliche Idee und ihre Erscheinung in der Religion: Untersuchungen zum Verhältnis von Logik und Religionsphilosophie bei Hegel,* Münster.

J. Heinrichs (1974), *Die Logik der "Phänomenologie des Geistes,"* Bonn.

C. Link (1974), *Hegels Wort "Gott selbst ist tot,"* Zürich.

E. Schmidt (1974), *Hegels System der Theologie,* Berlin-New York.

F. Guibal (1975), *Dieu selon Hegel: Essai sur la problématique de la "Phénoménologie de l'Esprit,"* Paris.

A. Brunkhorst and Hasenclever (1976), *Die Transformierung der theologischen Deutung des Todes bei Hegel,* Bern-Frankfurt.

E. Jüngel (1977), *Gott als Geheimnis der Welt,* Tübingen, 83–131.

J. Ringleben (1977), *Hegels Theorie der Sünde,* Berlin-New York.

R. Legros (1980), *Le jeune Hegel et la naissance de la pensée romantique.* Appendix: *Le Fragment de Tübingen,* Brussels.

E. Brito (1983), *La christologie de Hegel,* Paris.

W. Jaeschke (1983), *Die Religionsphilosophie Hegels,* Darmstadt.

E. Brito (1986), "La mort de Dieu selon Hegel: L'interprétation d'Eberhard Jüngel," *RTL* 17, 209–308.

W. Jaeschke (1986), *Die Vernunft in der Religion: Studien zur Grundlegung der Religionsphilosophie Hegels,* Stuttgart–Bad Cannstatt.

X. Tilliette (1986), *La christologie idéaliste,* Paris.

E. Brito (1987), "La création chez Hegel et Schelling," *RThom* 87, 260–79.

R. Legros (1987), "Introduction" to Hegel, *Fragments de la période de Berne,* Paris.

B. Pottier (1990), *Le péché originel selon Hegel,* Namur.

G. Fessard (1990), *Hegel, le christianisme et l'histoire,* Paris.

D. M. Schlitt (1990), *Divine Subjectivity: Understanding Hegel's Philosophy of Religion,* London-Toronto.

E. Brito (1991), *Dieu et l'être d'après Thomas d'Aquin et Hegel,* Paris.

X. Tilliette (1992), *La Semaine sainte des philosophes,* Paris.

Ph. Soual (1998), "Amour et Croix chez Hegel," *RPFE* 188, 71–96.

EMILIO BRITO

See also **Hegelianism; Kant, Immanuel; Kenosis; Kierkegaard, Soren Aabye; Marx, Karl; Nietzsche, Friedrich Wilhelm; Passion; Schelling, Friedrich Wilhelm Joseph von; Sin, Original**

Hegelianism

a) Division of Hegelian School. The split of the Hegelian school into a "right" of "old Hegelians" and a "left" of "young Hegelians" was produced by differences that were more political and religious than philosophical (Moog 1930; Gebhardt 1963; Serreau 1971). The distinction, which is still employed today, was first made by D. F. Strauss and then by K. L. Michelet. Among the old Hegelians (the term designated at the outset the school founded by Hegel* himself) were H. F. Hinrichs, K. F. Göschel, G. A. Gabler, and K. Daub, as well as most of those involved in the publication of Hegel's works (von Henning, Hotho, Förster, Marheineke). Also known as old Hegelians were those who, after the revolutionary period, were the true preservers of Hegelian philosophy* (Rosenkranz, Haym, Erdmann, and Fischer). K. L. Michelet occupied an intermediate position between young and old Hegelians; his long life (1801–93) made it possible for him to establish connections between original Hegelianism and the beginnings of modern neo-Hegelianism (Löwith 1941).

At first the expression "young Hegelians" merely designated the younger generation of Hegel's students. It later took on the meaning of "left Hegelians" (Löwith 1962) and encompassed the handful of revolutionary thinkers claiming inspiration from Hegel: L. Feuerbach, A. Ruge, M. Hess, M. Stirner, B. Bauer, and Marx*. For these philosophers, attracted as they were by the Hegelian principle of dialectical negation, the argument of the *Philosophy of Law* that the real is rational (interpreted in a conservative sense by the right) turned into its opposite: the rational is real.

The left Hegelians directed their efforts toward a methodical reversal of Hegel's philosophy, desiring, as it were, to liberate their teacher from himself. These efforts dealt first with his philosophical theology. D. F. Strauss (1808–74), for example, attributed to Hegel the idea of a critique of evangelical history*, a critique already contained in Hegel's philosophy insofar as it assimilated historical events to forms of representation. But the methods were different: Hegel transposed religious representation into concepts, whereas Strauss related it to myth* (Brito 1979). And this mythical interpretation led to the conclusion that humanity was the true and absolute content of Christology* (Strauss 1835–36).

Independently of "theist" objections (deism*/theism) relating to the personality of God* (*see* Weiße and Fichte), Hegel's philosophical theology was historically subjected to three critiques. Focusing on the problems of the immortality of the soul* and the humanity of God, all these critiques—those of L. Feuerbach, B. Bauer, and K. Marx—reduced the essence of religion to man. Beginning like Strauss from Protestant theology, Feuerbach (1804–72) set the theme of personal immortality in a Hegelian perspective: individual subjectivity, destined to surpass itself in the objectivity of reason*, implied death* (Feuerbach 1830). Indeed, this theme occupied a preponderant place in the debate over the religious content of Hegel's philosophy. For example, in the wake of Feuerbach, F. Richter stressed that personal immortality was incompatible with the Hegelian concept of absolute reason

(Richter 1833; Cornehl 1971); whereas right-wing Hegelians would attempt to demonstrate the opposite. Feuerbach himself saw Hegel's philosophy as the last refuge of theology: refusing to transform "images" into "thoughts," as Hegel had done, he wished to strip from religion its "theological essence" in order to bring it back to its anthropological truth* (anthropology*) (Feuerbach 1841). He thereby returned to the "feeling" that had been scoffed at by Hegel. By considering God as a reflection of man, Feuerbach reversed the Hegelian identification of God and man: for Hegel, in fact, the argument that the absolute was the essence of man did not mean the divinization of man, but on the contrary his relativization.

In his religious critique, A. Ruge (1802–80), for his part, started from the Hegelian "spiritualization" of Christian representations and adopted an attitude close to that of Feuerbach: at the conclusion of religious evolution, humanism was to replace Christianity. B. Bauer simulated an orthodox pietism* in order to unmask the atheism* that he claimed Hegel concealed under the exterior of a philosophical rehabilitation of dogma* (Bauer 1841). In the final analysis, according to Bauer, Hegel had set self-consciousness in the place of God.

Finally, seeing in religion nothing but the "inverted world*" engendered by real poverty, Marx recognized in the process of objectification only the absolute negativity of mind acceding to itself. Consequently, he made no distinction between *Entäusserung* (alienation) and *Entfremdung* (estrangement) of consciousness.

b) Hegelianism and Protestant Theology. K. Daub and Ph. Marheineke are typical representatives of a speculative dogmatics* of a Hegelian persuasion. Influenced first by Kant* and later by Schelling*, Daub (1765–1836), beginning in 1818, rethought his entire theology in the spirit of Hegel's philosophy. Based less on biblical evidence and confessions of faith* than on a speculative understanding of the idea of God, and centered around the Trinitarian doctrine that Daub sought to elevate from faith to knowledge by deducing its necessity, his dogmatics was unable to resist the Hegelian subordination of history to the concept (Daub 1833).

At least in its second edition, the *Dogmatik* of Marheineke is the work of an orthodox Hegelian and was recognized as such by Hegel himself. Despite its strong points (the importance it grants to the concept of revelation* and to the Trinitarian pattern), because of the identity that it posits between thought and being* it tends to abolish the difference between the divine Spirit and the human spirit. Marheineke paid more attention to Luther* than Daub, and the affinity

of his theology with Lutheran Christology has frequently been noted, particularly by Barth* (1969).

Hegel's system led F. C. Baur (1792–1860)—the founder of the new Protestant school of Tübingen—to comprehend history as the manifestation of the self-movement of the idea. Resistant to any mixture of the human and the divine, the exegete and systematizer W. Vatke (1806–82) tended to go back from Hegel to Kant. Concerned with ascending from representation to speculative concept, the *Dogmatik* of his disciple A. E. Biedermann (1819–85), however, shows Hegel's persistent influence: Biedermann, for example, does set himself apart from Hegel by denying that the infinite spirit can have a personal existence. Not wishing to restrict himself to speculation on either the objective or the subjective, the dogmatist I. A. Dorner (1809–84) attempted to associate Hegel and Schleiermacher* and thereby distinguished himself from both (Barth 1969).

c) Neo-Hegelianism. Against all expectations, Hegelianism seemed to revive in the early 20th century, particularly through the works of W. Dilthey (1833–1911) on the young Hegel (Dilthey 1925) and the publication of the early theological writings by H. Nohl (1907). In 1905 Pastor G. Lasson undertook a critical edition of Hegel's complete works. In his famous lecture of 1910, W. Windelband officially proclaimed the "renewal of Hegelianism." Hegel was first considered from the point of view of orthodox Hegelianism, even that of an affirmation of Prussian-Protestant superiority (Kroner, Glockner, Haering), then along Marxist or *marxisant* lines (Lukács, Bloch, the Frankfurt School, Marcuse).

In France, J. Hyppolite (translation of *The Phenomenology of Mind,* 1941) and A. Kojève had a strong influence on the existentialists and brought about a revival of Hegel studies (Kojève 1947). The Jesuit G. Fessard (1897–1978) was one of the groups of thinkers who participated in Kojève's famous seminar from 1934 to 1939. A philosopher of liberty* and of history, Fessard drew theologically fruitful inspiration from Hegel's dialectic. But far from advocating a "Hegelian Christianity," he demonstrated its limits, particularly by criticizing the Hegelian primacy of sign over symbol (Fessard 1990). Following Fessard, and engaging first in a debate with Hegel's logic—whose dialectical challenges and syllogistic forms he accepted—the work of the Catholic thinker C. Bruaire (1932–87) showed with increasing clarity that the Hegelian enterprise had failed to grasp the theme of superabundance, the foundation of Christian pneumatology (Bruaire 1980).

Among the theologies of the death of God that flourished in the 1960s, that of Th. Alitzer (b. 1928) used

Hegel to interpret the self-negation by which God becomes Emmanuel. The attempt by J. Moltmann (b. 1926) to transcend by means of dialectics the theist concept of an impassive God would appear more relevant if it did not, in an almost Hegelian way, link the Trinity* to the history of earthly passion*.

● H. F. Hinrichs (1822), *Die Religion im innern Verhältnisse zur Wissenschaft*, Heidelberg.

Ph. Marheineke (1827), *Die Grundlehren der christlichen Dogmatik als Wissenschaft*, Berlin.

K. F. Göschel (1829), *Aphorismen über Nichtwissen und absolutes Wissen*, Berlin.

L. Feuerbach (1830), *Gedanken über Tod und Unsterblichkeit*, Nuremberg.

K. Daub (1833), *Die Dogmatische Theologie jetziger Zeit*, Heidelberg.

F. Richter (1833), *Die Lehre von den letzten Dingen*, Breslau.

D. F. Strauss (1835–36), *Das Leben Jesu kritisch bearbeitet*, Tübingen.

B. Bauer (1841), *Die Posaune des jüngsten Gerichts über Hegel den Atheisten und Antichristen*, Leipzig.

L. Feuerbach (1841), *Das Wesen des Christentums*.

M. Stirner (1845), *Der Einzige und sein Eigentum*, Leipzig.

G. Lasson (1916), *Was heißt Hegelianismus?* Berlin.

R. Kroner (1921–24), *Von Kant bis Hegel*, Tübingen.

W. Dilthey (1925), *Die Jugendgeschichte Hegels, Gesammelte Schriften* IV, 1–187, Leipzig-Berlin.

A. Kojève (1947), *Introduction à la lecture de Hegel*, Paris.

C. Bruaire (1980), *Pour la métaphysique*, Paris.

G. Fessard (1990), *Hegel, le christianisme et l'histoire*, Paris.

♦ W. Moog (1930), *Hegel und die Hegelsche Schule*, Munich.

K. Löwith (1941), *Von Hegel zu Nietzsche*, Zürich.

H. Arvon (1954), *Aux sources de l'existentialisme: Max Stirner*, Paris.

K. Löwith (1962), *Die Hegelsche Linke: Einleitung*, Stuttgart–Bad Cannstatt.

H.-M. Saß (1963), *Untersuchungen zur Religionsphilosophie in der Hegelschule 1830–1850*, Münster.

J. Gebhardt (1963), *Politik und Eschatologie: Studien zur Geschichte der Hegelschen Schule um den Jahren 1830–1840*, Munich.

K. Barth (1969), *La théologie protestante au XIXe siècle*, Geneva.

P. Cornehl (1971), *Die Zukunft der Versöhnung: Eschatologie und Emanzipation in der Aufklärung, bei Hegel in der Hegelschen Schule*, Göttingen.

R. Serreau (1971), *Hegel et l'hégélianisme*, Paris.

E. Brito (1979), *Hegel et la tâche actuelle de la christologie*, Paris-Namur.

J. Simon (1985), "Hegelianismus," *TRE* 14, 550–60.

EMILIO BRITO

See also **Kierkegaard, Soren Aabye; Lutheranism; Religion, Philosophy of; Schelling, Friedrich Wilhelm Joseph von; Schleiermacher, Friedrich Daniel Ernst; Tübingen, Schools of**

Heidegger, Martin

1889–1976

Heidegger's relationship to Christianity and its theology* is in the first place biographical. A brief attempt at joining the Society of Jesus, two years of theological studies at Freiburg (also interrupted for health reasons), the rapid acquisition of a reputation as the great philosophical hope of German Catholicism*, the recognition of his debts to Neoscholasticism, and his lectures on Paul and Augustine* constituted a first period. A second was marked by his refusal to have his first son baptized into the Catholic Church, his declared sympathy for Lutheran theology, his association with theologians at Marburg (in particular Bultmann*) during his years as a lecturer at the university there, and his insistence on philosophy*'s right to a methodological atheism. After his return to Freiburg, a third period was characterized by a cautious but undeniable anti-Christian polemic, on the basis that the Christian faith* denied the believer any philosophical experience. The fourth and longest period began with the *Kehre*, the "turnaround" in which he aimed to consider being* on its own terms and no longer on those of mankind: the "divine" and the gods made an appearance in his work, he developed a true phenomenology of the pagan experience (starting with the *Beiträge* of 1936, and then in "The Thing"), reopened a dialogue with theologians, and acknowledged theological "origins" that might retain some future importance ("Herkunft aber bleibt stets Zukunft," in *Unterwegs zur Sprache, GA* 12, 92). Heidegger's funeral took place in the Catholic church in his village of Messkirch, but did not follow the Catholic rite. The philosopher B. Welte (himself a Catholic priest) gave a short address. The burial followed the Catholic rite. However, Heidegger's tomb bears no Christian symbol.

a) Theology and Existence: Reception of Being and Time.   In a letter of 19 August 1921 to his pupil K. Löwith, Heidegger still defined himself as a "Christian theologian." By 1927, on the other hand, he presented *Being and Time* as a philosophical treatise entirely free from theology. It speaks of man—*Dasein*—as having "fallen" into the world*, but this "fall" makes no reference to a protology or to a lost *status pristinus*. The experience of transgression is presented, but culpability is linked neither to a lost innocence nor to a pardon received or hoped for. *Dasein* exists incontestably in the world in the absence of God*: it can attain what is most proper to it there—an "authentic" existence—without needing to invoke an Absolute. Though it may seem surprising that such a work received a theological reception, this surprise soon fades. The atheism of *Dasein* does not in fact tax God with nonexistence. It announces the reality of a structure of experience (being-in-the-world) in which no place is left to know God or to speak of him. Heidegger's world consequently lends itself to an interpretation that sees it as equivalent to the Pauline *kosmos* in which, precisely, man lives atheistically without God (Eph 2:12). So the basis of a possible theological reading appears. Man has no right to God's proximity by simple birthright. A hermeneutics* of "facticity," of the simple fact of being in the world, must therefore speak of man's wretchedness. God is he who appears; and to conceive of his arrival demands agreement too on mankind's distress after the fall. In other words, the sinner's condition is understood to be what reduces mankind to an existence on the model of *Dasein*. In this light, it can be understood how easily Hans Jonas could exploit Heideggerian concepts in an interpretation of the Gnostic experience (*Gnosis und spätantiker Geist* I, Göttingen, 1934) as an exacerbation of certain fundamental Christian experiences. There was another possible theological interpretation of the book, more readily adopted moreover, which took the form of reading *Being and Time* by way of a focus provided by the hermeneutic theory of comprehension. What was at issue—being and its meaning—was what *Dasein* had in any case already understood in advance. A shift in meaning was then possible: according to Bultmann, who incidentally coined the term "precomprehension," *Vorverständnis,* comprehension also involved God himself. To exist on the model of comprehension was in fact to ponder God; theological discourse was thus essentially one of response, and its first task was to take as its theme the theological questions implicit in the logic of existence. Then, on the assumption that the man to whom the Christian kerygma was addressed was indeed the one to whom the Heideggerian analytics of *Dasein* referred, a final step became possible in which the approach to faith could be interpreted as an exemplary passage from "inauthenticity" to "authenticity."

Notwithstanding these conflicting readings, the work's theological significance remains incontestable. In the conference "Phenomenology and Theology" (1927–28), Heidegger stated axiomatically that "theology is a positive science and, for this reason, is absolutely distinct from philosophy" (Frankfurt, 1970), and specified further that "theology, as a positive science, is fundamentally closer to chemistry and mathematics than to philosophy" (ibid.). This was undoubtedly a verdict some theologies could strongly relate to: Barth* had recourse to an equally strict separation between the theological and the philosophical in order to deny all validity to Bultmann's program. But this verdict too could doubtless be contested by way of the resources that *Being and Time* offers to any consideration of the intended beneficiary of theology and the "revelation*" that it proposes.

b) Theology and Ontology: God and Being.   Regarding the relationship between ontology and theology, Heidegger expressed himself in the most forthright way possible on the occasion of a meeting with students from Zürich: "Being and God are not identical, and I would never attempt to consider the essence of God in terms of being . . . . If I was again obliged to set down a theology in writing—something to which I sometimes feel myself prompted—the term *being* would in no circumstances have any part in it. Faith has no need of the 'thought' of being. When it has recourse to it, it is no longer faith" (in *Poetry* 13, 60–61). The theological implications are clear: these sentences confirm the death of the God of the philosophers; and, by denying the existence of a "point of connection,", *Anknüpfungspunkt,* between the discourse of philosophy and that of theology, they call for a theologically pure reconstruction of theology. Whether in picturing a God "uncontaminated by being" (E. Levinas), or in considering "God without being" (J.-L. Marion) as a love* that had no need of being in order to love and to give, the lesson was learned. Heidegger intensified his warnings, moreover. By bringing God into philosophy and obliging him to serve as the pinnacle of the edifice of "metaphysics," of an "onto-theological" structure, the way was in fact being prepared for the death of God. Those who introduced God into conceptual systems were forgetting that man's relationship with him was primarily one of worship and liturgy, and that God had less need of being considered than of being worshipped. The task of theology, then, was twofold: on the one hand it must free itself of all involvement with metaphysics, and on the other hand it must dissociate its destiny from that "school of thought" that, after metaphysics, seeks to welcome the truth of being. Of course, the mere fact of being assigned a task does not provide the means of accomplishing it. But if Heidegger's view of the question of being is correct, then theology must either face up to this task or strip God of his divinity.

c) Speech, Event, Hermeneutics. No part of Heidegger's oeuvre lent itself better to theological interpretation than the texts devoted to language. From 1934, commentary on poetic texts—Hölderlin, Trakl, Rilke, George—and consideration of the essence of utterance were among Heidegger's main preoccupations. These preoccupations were strictly ontological: speech was considered as the abode of being, so what was in question was merely the advent of the sense of being and its associated meanings (the diction of the sacred, of earth and heaven, etc.). But by refusing to link his investigation of speech to an investigation of the speaker, by denying that the production of utterances was the paramount and essential task of speech, and by considering speech on its own basis ("speech speaks"; *die Sprache spricht*), Heidegger replicated in the secular sphere the discourse that theology maintains concerning another speech—the speech of God. The themes of speech as event and as expression did not have to be unduly stretched for them to give rise, even before the publication of *Approaches to Speech,* to attempts at an interpretation that would allow the Word to speak in the very act in which it was produced—in the theological hermeneutics of E. Fuchs (*Hermeneutik,* 1954) and G. Ebeling ("Hermeneutik," *RGG3* 3, 1959, 243–63; "Wort Gottes und Hermeneutik," *Wort und Glaube* I, 1960, 319–48) and in the whole movement known as "new hermeneutics." The concepts of "speech event," *Sprachereignis* and *Wortgeschehen,* do not imply that Heidegger attributed to the words of the poet or the philosopher a vital force that belongs by right to God's word alone—but they do at least show that not every philosophy of language can be placed in the service of a theology of the Word, and they suggest that there can be no theology of the Word that is not based on a philosophy of language. Heidegger's influence was also to be felt, in a mediated form, through that of H.-G. Gadamer.

d) Sacred and Divine Beings: Reverse of the Theological. God might be "dead" as a result of entering into the constitution of metaphysics, while perhaps remaining theologically conceivable to anyone who freed him from any relationship with being; nonetheless it re-

mained possible for Heidegger to speak philosophically of the divine, and even of God. The *Letter on Humanism* (1947) stipulated precisely the conditions for this possibility: "It is only on the basis of the truth of being that the essence of the sacred can be conceived. It is only on the basis of the essence of the sacred that the essence of divinity is to be conceived. It is only in the light of the essence of divinity that we can conceive and utter that which the word 'God' must designate" (*GA* 9, 351). This divine subordinated to being takes its place, in Heidegger's late works, within the structure of the "Quadripartite," the *Geviert,* in which "earth" and "heaven," "mortals" and "divine beings" answer and correspond to one another. God's transcendence therefore gives way to the transcendence of being and to its direction; and the theology that is thereby established from the time of the *Beiträge* is in consequence supremely atheological. Is Heidegger's "theological" secret, then, the search for a substitute for the Christian experience and the Christian formulation of the conceivable? Characteristics such as the central role he accords to "serenity" *(Gelassenheit)* in the absence of any hope*, the subordination of God to a faceless sense of the sacred, and an account of the history of philosophy from which all reference to Christianity has been erased, among others, should enable us to conclude that theology has nothing to learn here, except that which it is absolutely not—which is, however, a most useful lesson.

● *Gesamtausgabe,* Frankfurt, 1976–, 102 vols. Works published during Heidegger's lifetime and not yet in the *GA: Vorträge und Aufsätze,* Pfullingen, 1954; *Was heisst Denken?* Tübingen, 1954; *Was ist das—die Philosophie?* Pfullingen, 1956; *Identität und Differenz,* Pfullingen, 1957; *Zur Sache des Denkens,* Tübingen, 1969; *Phänomenologie und Theologie,* Frankfurt, 1970; *Schellings Abhandlung über das Wesen der menschlichen Freiheit,* Tübingen, 1971.

◆ G. Siewerth (1959), *Das Schicksal der Metaphysik von Thomas zu Heidegger,* Einsiedeln.

J. M. Robinson and J. B. Cobb (Ed.) (1963), *The Later Heidegger and Theology,* New York.

J. Macquarrie (1965), *An Existentialist Theology: A Comparison of Heidegger and Bultmann,* New York–London.

B. Welte (1965), "Die Gottesfrage im Denken Heideggers," in *Auf der Spur des Ewigen,* Freiburg-Basel-Vienna, 262–76.

G. Nöller (Ed.) (1967), *Heidegger und die Theologie,* ThB 38 (articles and texts by K. Heim, R. Bultmann, K. Löwith, E. Brunner, E. Fuchs, K. Barth, H. Jonas, etc.).

J. Macquarrie (1968), *Martin Heidegger,* London.

J. Möller (1968), "Zum Thema 'Der spätere Heidegger und die Theologie,' " *TThQ* 147, 386–431.

K. Lehmann (1969), "Christliche Geschichtserfahrung und ontologische Frage beim jungen Heidegger," in O. Pöggeler (Ed.), *Heidegger: Perspektiven zur Deutung seines Werkes,* Köln, 140–68.

A. Gethmann-Siefert (1974), *Das Verhältnis von Philosophie und Theologie im Denken Martin Heideggers,* Freiburg.

A. Jäger (1978), *Gott: Nochmal Martin Heidegger,* Tübingen.

R. Schaeffler (1978), *Frömmigkeit des Denkens? Martin Heidegger und die katholische Theologie,* Darmstadt.

R. Kearney and J.S. O'Leary (Ed.) (1980), *Heidegger et la question de Dieu,* Paris.

A.C. Thiselton (1980), *The Two Horizons: New Testament Hermeneutics and Philosophical Description with Special Reference to Heidegger, Bultmann, Gadamer, and Wittgenstein,* Exeter.

L. Weber (1980), *Heidegger und die Theologie,* Königstein (Taunus).

J.-L. Marion (1982), *Dieu sans l'être,* Paris.

H.G. Gadamer (1987), "Die Marburger Theologie," *GW* 3, Tübingen, 197–208.

H.J. Braun (Ed.) (1990), *Martin Heidegger und der christliche Glaube,* Zürich.

F. Dastur (1994), "Heidegger et la théologie," *RPL* 92, 226–45.

P.L. Coriando (Ed.) (1995), "*Herkunft aber bleibt stets Zukunft*": Martin Heidegger und die Gottesfrage, Frankfurt.

E. Brito (1996), "Les théologies de Heidegger," *RTL,* 27, 432–61 (bibl.).

Ph. Capelle (1998), *Philosophie et théologie dans la pensée de Martin Heidegger,* Paris.

JEAN-YVES LACOSTE

See also **Being; Experience; God; Hermeneutics; Philosophy**

Hell

A. Biblical Theology

"I have set before you life and death" (Dt 30:19): by the time of Jesus*, a considerable section of Judaism* had already come to understand this ancient choice in the sense of an eternal bliss contrasted with utter destruction or even eternal woe. But it had not always been so.

a) Old Testament. Until the Hellenistic period, when the apocalyptic* genre of literature appeared, *sheol** was merely the abode of shadows. The sinner's punishment remained a miserable life, then death. It was extremely rare for the hand of God to strike an individual sinner (Nm 16:30–34: the earth opens up; *see* 2 Kgs 1:9–12). Concerning the hereafter, Isaiah (66:24) ("their worm shall not die" and "their fire shall not be quenched"—the conclusion of the whole book!) undoubtedly develops on Jeremiah 19:2–15: unburied corpses beside the ruins of Jerusalem*, in the valley *(géy)* of Ben-Hinnôm, which would become "Gehenna," from *geenna* (New Testament Gr.) < Aram. *gehinnam* < Heb. *géy hinnom.* Daniel 12:2 offers few words ("everlasting contempt") whose meaning is clear if one understands the eschatology* of the period (c. 160 B.C.) (*see* 1 Hen 10:7–16, 27:2f., 63:6). Jubilees 36:7–11 even declares that whoever harms his brother is liable for the eternal fire. Wisdom of Solomon, dating from the beginning of the Roman period, offers in veiled terms an eschatological transposition of the Exodus: the destruction of the sinner by his own sin* (Wis 11:16, 12:23, 17:21), and the intervention of the cosmos* (5:20, 16:17; *see* Lv 18:27f.) concerned at that sin. Wisdom 4:19 is a commentary on Daniel 12:2.

b) New Testament. According to Matthew 3:10–12, the unquenchable fire is uppermost in John the Baptist's message. Jesus puts the emphasis elsewhere, though his meaning is no less plain—indeed he is more explicit than anybody else in the Bible*. What he says of the final punishment takes on its full depth in the parables*: the chaff, the fish thrown back, the guest not wearing the nuptial robe, the unfaithful steward, the servant hoarding his talent, the wicked rich man. In view of all these, less vivid expressions such as "I will also deny before my Father who is in heaven" (Mt 10:33) or "I do not know you" (Mt 25:12) probably foretell a no better fate for the person rebuked. Jesus is the only person to speak of Gehenna (11 times). The most common image is that of fire (Mt 13:40, 13:50, 18:8 *Sq;* Lk 16:24), and the suffering is physical (Mk 9:43–47: hands, feet, eyes). Even the pain of separation is expressed in physical terms: "weeping and gnashing of teeth" (Mt 13:42, 13:50, 22:13, 24:51; Lk 13:28). "You will never enter the kingdom of heaven" (Mt 5:20, 18:3, 23:13) probably hints at an equally serious punishment. To be "outside" is also a way of expressing hell (Mt 8:12, 22:13, 25:30). What is unexpected is the contrast between the offence and this punishment*, which is visited only on those who fail to perform simple acts of compassion (Mt 25:24–28, 25:45). This must be seen as a key for interpretation: the accounts are brushed aside and humanity is confronted with two irreconcilable options, as vital in small matters as in great ones. What is at stake in each case is made unequivocally clear.

Hades (the *sheol* of the Greeks; four times in the synoptic Gospels), like the "abyss" (Lk 8:31), is a portion of the cosmos destined to be banished to the depths (Lk 10:15), with or without torments. It is not the "eternal fire prepared for the devil and his angels" (Mt 25:41). Although they mostly relate to the body, Jesus' images remain similar to those of the apocalypses, which are mainly cosmic: "the lake of fire" (Rev 20:14f.), "the lake of fire and sulphur" (Rev 20:10, 21:8). Death destroys itself endlessly, since this is where it is thrown (20:14). Sinners are those who are in league with it.

Paul (Pauline* theology) expresses himself altogether differently. Admittedly, he does describe the final punishment in an apocalyptic manner in 2 Thessalonians 1:9: "eternal destruction *[olethros]* away from the presence of the Lord and the glory of his might." Elsewhere, though, he confines himself to "perdition" (*apollumi, apolluiô, apoleia*: Rom 9:22; 1 Cor 1:18; 2 Cor 2:15, 4:3; Phil 3:19). To eternal life for some he opposes "wrath* *[thumos]* and indignation" for the rest, in the context of the "day of wrath" (*orgè*: Rom 2:5–8). It is "the wrath to come" (1 Thes 1:10). It is noteworthy that *katargein* (1 Cor 2:6, 15:24ff.; 2 Thes 2:8) is closer in meaning to an annihilation of the spirits of evil* than to their punishment. Hebrews 10:26–31 does not describe an eternal hell but suggests a punishment worse than death.

John uses few images (only Jn 15:6). He leaves it to the reader to interpret the words "resurrection of judgment" (5:29: resurrection of life) or "you will die in your sin" (Jn 8:21–24), "perish" rather than having "eternal life" (Jn 3:16). There is a sin that differs from other sins in that it "leads to death" (1 Jn 5:16f.): then it is a matter of "the second death" (Rev 2:11, 20:6, 20:14, 21:8).

● J. Jeremias (1933), "*Hadès*," *ThWNT* 1, 146–50; "*Geenna*," ibid., 655–56.
F. Lang (1959), "*Pur*," *ThWNT* 6, 927–48.
X. Léon-Dufour (1979), *Face à la mort: Jésus et Paul*, Paris, 47–61.

PAUL BEAUCHAMP

See also **Apocalyptic Literature; Cosmos; Demons; Eschatology; Evil; Hardening; Judgment; Limbo; Purgatory; Resurrection of the Dead; Sheol; Soul-Heart-Body; Vengeance of God; Wrath of God**

B. Historical and Systematic Theology

A theologian approaching the words of Scripture* on the subject of hell must first accept the meaning that the authorized teaching of the church bestows upon them and the explanation that it offers us for them.

a) Dogmatic Statements. Over the centuries this teaching, without ever being elaborated, has never varied. Since the so-called faith of Damasus of the fifth century (*DS* 72), it has been declared that "at the general resurrection, eternal life* will reward the good* that is deserved and eternal torture will be applied to sins*." The creed *Quicumque* (*DS* 76), also from the fifth century, together with the Fourth Lateran* Council at the beginning of the 13th century (*DS* 852), and the councils of Florence in the mid-15th (*DS* 1351) and Trent* in 1547 (*DS* 1575), all repeat the same doctrine. In 1992 the *CEC* adopted it in turn: "The teaching of the Church affirms the existence of hell, and its eternity. Immediately after death the souls of those who die in a state of mortal sin descend into hell, where they suffer the punishment of hell's 'eternal fire'" (no. 1035). What links the church's language to that of Scripture is that it does not prevaricate and avoids understatement. The two differ, however, insofar as Scripture generally talks in images that the church, when dealing with hell, reduces to a single image, terrible nonetheless in its uniqueness: that of an "eternal fire." While not emphasizing the metaphorical nature of this "fire," for fear of neutralizing the spiritual consumption that it symbolizes, the magisterium* forbids itself all the flights of imagination in which popular preaching* has long, and in vain, delighted. Nowadays historians (Delumeau 1983; Minois 1991 and 1994) readily condemn such excesses. "Infernalism," in all its forms, has discredited the faith* more than it has shaped truly Christian hearts (heart of Christ*). It has helped bring about a cultural world devoid of God* by disfiguring his true face. Harmful as these excesses may be, the teaching of the magisterium has never been based on them, but rather on Scripture alone and on what it reveals to us about judgment*.

b) Hell and Judgment. Among the well-known passages (including Mt 25), the Second Epistle of Peter (3:7), which echoes the text of Malachi on the day of YHWH, deserves special mention here. It speaks explicitly: "Judgment and destruction of the ungodly" (2 Pt 3:7). Malachi, meanwhile, which offers a synthesis of prophetic doctrine on the "day of YHWH," declares frankly to the faithful that the historical success of the wicked is misleading: "Then once more you shall see the distinction between the righteous and the wicked, between one who serves God and one who does not serve him. For behold, the day is coming, burning like an oven, when all the arrogant and all evildoers will be stubble. The day that is coming shall set them ablaze, says the LORD of hosts" (Mal 3:18–4). While awaiting judgment on the conduct of mankind, Scripture is categorical: there is for God, and thus also for us, no historically or eschatologically possible confusion between good and evil*. It was this obvious fact that John Paul II took as the inspiration for his encyclical *Veritatis Splendor* (no. 35, 41, 54 with a reference to *GS* 16). So hell signifies first and foremost that the difference between good and evil will never be revoked. It is this difference that opens or shuts the doors of the Kingdom*, depending on whether one respects or violates it, so giving us the right and the duty to distinguish the "accursed" from the "blessed" (Mt 25:41, 34). To question the status of hell as an unequivocal sign of this distinction between good and evil would be to shake the eternal foundations of the world. There is thus no question of doing so.

It is understandable that the Gospels* were obliged to use the most violent expressions that alone would be capable of denouncing, across the whole course of history*, the error from which we must be delivered at any cost. So they speak of the day of judgment in terms of "a fire which is never extinguished," of "Gehenna," of the "gnawing worm," of "outer darkness," and of "weeping and gnashing of teeth." The church interprets this by saying that for a free agent having the power to choose mortal sin "for ever, with no turning back" (*CEC,* no. 1861) to yield to this "possibility" is to expose oneself to "[that] state of definitive self-exclusion from communion* with God and the blessed [that] is called 'hell' " (*CEC,* no. 1033). Hell represents a choice of unequaled gravity, and some have sought to soften the horror of this choice by seeing hell as an "annihilation" of the damned rather than an eternal punishment (Lassiat 1974, 1979; Schillebeeckx 1989). This position, in spite of the attempts made to justify it

by referring to second-century writers (*see* Lassiat on Irenaeus* especially), is alien to tradition*. In traditional terms, no creature can annihilate itself, even by its own sin, any more than God can think of annihilating it.

c) Unanswered Questions. Nevertheless, the way in which Augustine* (e.g., *De civitate Dei* XXI, 12), followed by Thomas* Aquinas (*ST* Ia, q. 20–25; Ia IIae, q. 87; *De malo,* q. 5), saw judgment merely as a work of justice* gives such a merciless image of God as to be unworthy of the one whose revealed essence is love* (1 Jn 4, 16). The excesses of popular preaching have found a regrettable justification in Augustine's rationalization of hell in accordance with his own view of predestination*. It is possible, however, without in any way doing away with the distinction between good and evil, and while remaining faithful to the Gospels, to conceive of hell not as an inescapable reality for the free agent who believes or wishes himself to be devoted to evil, but as an avoidable contingency, which points us back to the innate greatness and crucial importance of a freedom that is given to itself so as to be able to respond to the love that is its foundation (Fessard 1967).

Scripture makes plain, however, that this sense of contingency does not eliminate the reality of hell, at least in one particular case: that of the "Devil" (demons*) and "his angels*" (Mt 25:41)—in other words that of the "prince of this world*," an emblematic figure who is primarily responsible (Jn 8:44) for the evil driven out by Christ* (Jn 12:31). Once again, without denying the difference between good and evil, nor the punishment that their incompatibility justly demands (represented in Scripture by the "wrath of the Lamb*" before which no one "can stand" [Rev 6:16–17]), should not a further distinction be made between the *criterion* for the judgment, in itself unmerciful, and the act of judgment? Surely this act must involve a rigorous execution of justice, or else how could it be a judgment? But should this judgment be, indeed can it be anything other than justice, when it is the judgment reserved to the One who "saves the upright in the heart" (Ps 7:10), and that John tells us is "greater than our heart" (1 Jn 3:20)? Surely God has the power, even while dealing with sin as it deserves, not to identify the sinner with it, however culpable he may be?

When indeed we glimpse the terrifying possibility of an "upside-down eternity" (Durrwell 1994), we are forced to confront "the darkness of all darknesses" (Ratzinger 1960) and the scandal of all scandals: how can this infernal reality exist, even for a single being? Faced with an infinity of joy transformed into misfortune, "incurable and sterile" (Elluin 1994), the church fathers* (led by Origen*) as well as other mystics and theologians did their utmost to find an emergency exit from this aberration in our freedom and from the non-meaning that it presupposes on the part of the damned person himself. There is a temptation finally to reduce God's mystery* to that of a justice that it is hard in this case not to see as purely vindictive. We are also faced with a double anomaly: on the one hand, we accord a finite being, who is rightly denied the power to save himself on his own, the power to damn himself, which is in a sense infinite; on the other hand, we establish for ever, until the end of history, an anti-God whose existence is rightly called into question from the outset. It is at this point that there arises in counterpoint a spiritually inevitable hope*, which cannot be silenced. Here, as much as or even more than elsewhere, the abyss calls for the abyss; the abyss of horror and the abyss of hope. Balthasar* (1986, 1987) (and Elluin before him) set himself up toward the end of his life as the courageous defender of such a hope, which is generally overlooked in this context, except by Orthodox theology (Evdokimov 1959). Perhaps it remains to be stated more clearly that its foundations lie deep within the Trinity.

d) Unfathomable Openness of the Trinity in Christ. Our creation* in Christ has made us, by vocation, into beings to whom the Father* is as essential as he is, by paternity, to the Son himself. But we should not forget the other face of this mystery, whereby we appear, in Christ, as eternally irreplaceable to the Father as the Son is to him. Confronted with the suicidal decision to reverse into hatred the love for which we have all been created, and which makes us, in the Father's eyes, inseparable from the person* of his Son, could God, even out of respect for our freedom, abandon forever the person who destroys himself in the self-torture of his aberration? How could he do so, this God who, in Christ, wishes to raise us by pure grace* to his likeness, and promises to share with us the life of his uncreated Son? Such in the choice is the unfathomable depth of his love for us. Henceforth there is no human rule, no safeguard of morality that can prohibit God from loving madly the madman who believes that in order to exist he must refrain from loving him who is love itself! God's remedy for madness consists then in bringing into play all the resources of his love to help the rebel overcome his insane refusal to love. For what kind of God would he be who, despite being declared all-powerful, was forever incapable of releasing from his mortal spell a freedom that was received without being requested, and that could become a snare of pain and hatred to its recipient, for all eternity?

Faced with the lights of the Kingdom of heaven in the night (in itself hopeless) of hell, we are therefore empowered by faith to throw ourselves naked into the love of God. As worthy descendants of Abraham—"In hope he believed against hope" (Rom 4:18)—we hope that the bottomless depths of God's fatherhood, of Christ's Passion*, and of the resources of the Holy Spirit* will allow us to escape from the fiery prison that is hell. We can say nothing of how this might be; but we must trust absolutely in the reserves of love, grace, and glory*, whose only measure is God's love for the Son in the Holy Spirit, a love in which we are forever included. Moreover, since God has revealed to us in his Son that we are saved and savable by pure grace, and never by our works* (Rom 1–4), how could it be otherwise when the eschatology* of every creature is decided, at the crowning moment when the mystery of grace, in which we have been established for all time by God himself, will be fulfilled?

In this light, hell becomes, with regard to a boundless faith, the locate of choice for God's victory over the most incomprehensible rejection—victory that could be called humanly unexpected and that is for the prayer of the spiritual and for the thought of the theologian "able to be hoped for."

● M. Richard (1924), "Enfer," *DThC* 5/1, 28–120.
S. Merkle (1930), "Augustin über die Unterbrechung der Höllestrafen," in *Aurelius Augustinus*, Köln, 197–201.
K. Adam (1951), "Zum Problem der *Apokatastasis*," *ThQ* 131, 129–38.
G. Jacquemet (1956), "Enfer," *Cath* 4, 168–86.
J. de Mahuet (1956), "Iconographie," "Enfer" V, ibid., 186–87.
P. Evdokimov (1959), *L'Orthodoxie*, Neuchâtel, 324–34.
J. Ratzinger (1960), "Hölle," *LThK*2 5, 446–49.
A. Turincev (1966), "Une approche de l'eschatologie orthodoxe," *Contacts* 18, no 54.
G. Fessard (1967), "Enfer éternel ou salut éternel?" *AF*, 223–64.
K. Rahner (1967), "Theologische Prinzipien der Hermeneutik eschatologischer Aussagen," *Schr. zur Th.* 4, Einsiedeln-Zürich-Köln, 401–28 (*Écrits théologiques* 9, 1968, 141–70).
H. Lassiat (1974), *Promotion de l'homme en Jésus-Christ d'après Irénée de Lyon, témoin de la tradition des Apôtres*, Paris, 393–434.
G. Martelet (1975), *L'au-delà retrouvé*, Paris, 1995, New Ed.
O. Rousseau (1977), "L'éternité des peines de l'enfer et l'immortalité naturelle de l'âme selon saint Irénée," *NRTh*, 834–64 (about and against Henri Lassiat).
H. Lassiat (1978), "L'anthropologie d'Irénée," *NRTh*, 399–417 (response to Olivier Rousseau); (1979), *Jeunesse de l'Église, la foi au IIe siècle*, vol. II, Paris, 77–93.
J. Delumeau (1983), *Le péché et la peur: La culpabilisation en Occident, XIIIe-XVIIIe siècles*, Paris.
H. U. von Balthasar (1986), *Was dürfen wir hoffen?* Einsiedeln.
H. U. von Balthasar (1987), *Kleiner Diskurs über die Hölle*, Ostfildern.
E. Schillebeeckx (1989), *Mensen als verhaal van God*, Baarn.
G. Minois (1991), *Histoire des enfers*, Paris.
G. Martelet (1992), "Malédiction, damnation, enfer...," *VS* 147, 59–75 (about Balthasar's thought on hell).

E. Guerriero (1993), *Hans Urs von Balthasar,* preface by J. Guitton, Paris, 316–21.

F.-X. Durrwell (1994), *Regards chrétiens sur l'au-delà,* Paris.

J. Elluin (1994), *Quel enfer?* foreword by Y.-M. Congar, preface by G. Martelet, Paris.

G. Minois (1994), *Histoire de l'enfer,* Paris.

G. Martelet (1996), "Sur l'ultime violence," *LV(L)* 226, 53–62.

GUSTAVE MARTELET

See also **Demons; Eschatology; Evil; Judgment; Life, Eternal; Limbo; Predestination; Purgatory; Vision, Beatific**

Hellenization of Christianity

a) Judaism and Hellenism. The principality of Judaea, governed by the Ptolemies from 301 to 198 B.C., then by the Seleucidae until 63 B.C., was not exempt from the general movement of Hellenization that touched all the territories of the ancient Persian empire that had been conquered by Alexander. This movement saw the introduction of "common" Greek *(koinè)* as both an official and a vernacular language, as well as the creation of new towns and the establishing of a Hellenic style of life in the ancient cities (thus the construction in Jerusalem* of a gymnasium and a palestra). In spite of resistance, which was at times frenzied and fanatical, Hellenism penetrated deeply into the daily lives of the Judaeans, even among those groups that were most attached to the Law* (for example, the sectarians of Qumran). It was Hellenism's religious ambitions—primarily the desire to reinterpret the cult* of YHWH and make it a local form of the cult of worshiping Zeus Ouranios—that were globally opposed, at least as early as the Maccabean revolt.

On the other hand, because of the harsh fiscal policy in effect in Palestine, the Hellenistic period saw a substantial Jewish emigration into the neighboring countries. Surrounded by a Hellenophone population, the Jewish Diaspora adopted a Hellenic lifestyle (*see* Hengel 1969) and Greek became a commonly spoken language in its midst (the "Hellenists" of the Acts 6:1 and 9:29). It was for these Hellenophone Jews that the Bible* was translated into Greek in Alexandria, in a version—the Septuagint (LXX)—permeated with the Greek genius. It was the milieu of this Judaism* that made possible the philosophical and theological activity of Philo of Alexandria, a contemporary of Jesus*. His apologetic project was to rekindle traditional beliefs that had been given up in favor of Hellenic doctrines, by showing that biblical thought and these doctrines (Platonism above all) were in fact complementary.

b) Christian Origins. The Hellenization of Christianity, therefore, was not born from the late encounter of two entities already in existence and independent from one another in their respective contexts; nor did it occur in a world where only Greek culture and civilization deserved to be described as "Hellenic." On the contrary, what we call the "Jesus-Christ event" may descend directly from the Jewish tradition*, but it is also inscribed within this extended Hellenic framework. Moreover, it was documents written in Hellenistic Greek and characterized by Hellenistic realia that bore primary witness to the event.

The very fact that the apostle* Paul belongs to three different groups—religious (Jewish Pharisee), cultural (Greek), and political (Roman citizen)—illustrates quite well the complexity of the Jewish milieus that provided Christianity's mission* with its starting point. Paul uses Greek literary sources (Acts 17:28): he is sufficiently familiar with popular philosophy* to be able to practice the genre of the *diatribe,* in imitation of the Stoic preachers, or to handle the skeptical paradox of the "liar" (Ti 1:12), at the service of a discourse that always finds its sources in the LXX version of the Jewish Scriptures. When he sets Jews and Greeks in opposition to each other (1 Cor 1:21f.), or Jews and pagans, this does not represent the opposition of two cultures: it is rather the clash of two spiritual destinies, both of which he understands as finding their realization in the Christian faith*.

Thus the first communities founded in the Diaspora and in pagan milieus spontaneously gave birth to a Christianity that had been explicitly Hellenized, using Greek as a liturgical language (Latin had to wait till the fourth century to become the liturgical language of the Western Church*). This Hellenized Christianity took on a preponderant importance for the whole of the Christian world, while, on the other hand, the Jewish Christianity of Palestine and Syria disappeared between the Jewish revolt of A.D. 66 and the final excommunication of the Judeo-Christians by the Sanhedrin at Jamnia (addition of the *birkat ha-minim* to the "Eighteen blessings," under Gamaliel II, v. 90).

c) Patristic Age. Rhetorically and conceptually the discourse of the Greek and Latin Fathers* was bound to be a Hellenic discourse. But even if their culture was indeed Greek, for many other Christian authors, Christianity constitutes a kind of parallel culture or counterculture, at least up to a point. This is evidenced in the way they use the Greek of the LXX or the Latin of the *Itala* (the first Latin translation* of the Bible), or even in their use of the very first Christian texts, which were devoid of any kind of literary pretense. Since Christian apologias were intended in the early centuries for a civilization that was simultaneously pagan and Greek, a global evaluation of Hellenism was required. Three distinct positions emerged: 1) the total rejection of any Hellenic philosophical doctrine, considered to be untruthful and immoral (Tatian, *Ad Graecos*): "What is common to Athens and Jerusalem? What is common to the Academy and the Church*?" (Tertullian*, *De praesc.* 7, 9); 2) a moderate overture that bases its argumentation on a supposed dependence of the Greek philosophers on the Hebrew books and insists on the monotheistic tendencies of Greek thought: "To look upon God*, for this is the end of Plato's philosophy" (Justin, *Dial.* 2, 6; *see* Athenagoras, *Pro christ.* 6); and 3) a positive evaluation that goes as far as a passionate defense of Hellenism: for example, the beneficent "showers" of truth* sown by the Logos of the Greek philosophers (Clement of Alexandria, *Strom.* 1, 7, 2), and the necessity of an extensive knowledge of Greece (Origen*, *Against Celsus*).

d) Middle Ages. The influence of Hellenism was preserved in Byzantine and Latin theologies. These retained the patristic heritage, and remained in debt for a long time to Platonism*, whether through the guarantee given by Augustine* to the *libri platonici* or through the reorganization of the neo-Platonic cosmos* by the Pseudo-Dionysius*. On the other hand, the Middle Ages saw a noteworthy intellectual crisis, sanctioned by the Parisian condemnations of 1277. Aristotelianism*, in its Averroistic version, had been introduced into the newly created universities of the Christian world by Arabic translators and commentators. It had not merely supplied theologians with new

conceptual instruments, but had also presided (e.g., in the cases of Siger of Brabant [1240–84] or Boethius of Dacia [?–c. 1270]) over a movement for the freeing of philosophical work and for the revival of the ideals of *vita philosophica*. These two aspects of its influence appeared to threaten Christian doctrine (for instance, that of the Creation* of the world and that of freedom*), as well as the very style of Christianity (as, e.g., when the enthusiastic use of the concept of magnanimity, the key to Aristotle's ethics, led to a refusal to call humility a virtue). By condemning 219 theses of Aristotelian and Averroistic origin on 7 March 1277, the bishop of Paris, É. Tempier, and his theologians were, in a way, only emphasizing an old methodological rule, the necessity of a critical reception of Hellenism, and we may consider that the faculties of theology did in fact hear the reminder. However, the condemnations did not prevent the survival, in university circles (in the faculties of philosophy), of a nonchristianized Hellenism, which was present in philosophies that aimed to be free of any theological interference. Through these philosophies, Christian intellectuals were assuming the task of cultivating Greek thought devoid of any Christian inflection.

e) Renaissance and Humanism. The Renaissance is the age of the *De transitu Hellenismi ad Christianismum* by G. Budé (Paris, 1535), a text in which the problem of Christian Hellenism is raised with real urgency. It is the age during which another new censorship was imposed (by the Fifth Lateran* Council, in 1515) against Averroistic Aristotelianism (in this particular instance, that of P. Pomponazzi). It is also the age of a revival of classical antiquity, over and above what the Middle Ages had managed to retain of it, a revival that sometimes seemed intent on introducing a lifestyle that owed more to paganism* than to Christianity. It is the age when Luther* developed a "theology of the cross," a theology that refused the Christian acceptance of external intellectual elements. On the contrary, it claimed that it could discern in the past alliances of Christianity and Hellenism a ferment that could corrupt the church. Since then, the hypothesis of a falsification of the Christian reality by the Greek spirit has always retained a sort of topicality, while any interest in Greece tended to represent more and more a kind of protest in favor of paganism (Veillard-Baron 1979).

f) Modern Developments, Metaphysics, and the Problem of Inculturation.* Thus, when A. von Harnack (1851–1930) speaks of the Christian dogma*, in a famous definition, as if it were a "creation of the Greek mind on the gospel's land" (*Lehrbuch,* 1909, 4th Ed.), the historiography of dogmas appears to have been an attempt at emancipation, aimed at retrieving an essence of Christianity that had been misrepresented. The attempt was, however, bound to fail, just as any juxtaposition of a pure Hellenism and a Palestinian Judeo*-Christianity that was itself allegedly intact and free from outside influence is bound to produce misinterpretation (*see* Meijering, BZRGG 20, 1978). And against Harnack, recent research has been able to bring into play the principles of a more refined analysis of the relations between Christianity and Hellenism: 1) To the myth that opposed a "Greek way of thinking," substantialist and ahistorical, and a "Hebrew way of thinking," purely descriptive and historical (e.g., Boman 1954), it has been possible to reply that the myth was supported above all by semantic and logical confusion (Barr 1961): the structures of a language do not constitute the theoretical a priori of the people who use that language. 2) To the hypothesis of a distortion of the Christian kerygma through the recourse to concepts that are Greek in origin, recent patristics has been able to respond by underscoring the inflections given by patristic theology to the Hellenic schemata it uses (e.g., Ivánka 1964). Much more than simply making concessions to Greece, theology is in fact abounding in Greek-looking concepts, all of which constitute conceptual monsters in Greek terms: connection of the *logos* and the "flesh*" in Johannine* theology, accidents deprived of their substance in the speculations on Eucharistic transubstantiation, and so forth. 3) To the idea of cultures so closed that translation of their contents into the language of other cultures is impossible, recent treatments of inculturation have countered with the idea of a Christianity that is essentially translatable and capable of using the linguistic and conceptual resources of any culture. The encounter of Hellenism and Christianity, from the time the latter came in existence, may indeed serve as a model for any evangelization that aims to transmit its good news in an intelligible form, and for any pastoral activity concerned with enriching the church with the universal values present in any cultural milieu (Neuner 1995).

The debate is not over. Recent discussion has still seen J. B. Metz and J. Habermas criticizing the fundamental concepts of a metaphysics supposedly too rigid "to be able to restore rationally, without mutilation, without any loss in the multitude of specific meanings, these experiences of redemption, of universal covenant, and of irreplaceable individuality that were expressed in Judeo-Christian terms in the history of salvation*" (Habermas 1992). And by interpreting "metaphysics," a Greek creation, as a closed figure of thinking, governed by the unthought that determines this enclosure—and therefore as something that one would need to escape in order to really be able to "think"—Heidegger* renewed the problematics and asked some questions to which answers (other than naive ones) remain to be found. No theological reason can oblige us to believe in the existence of a perennial reality of Hellenism as such; and neither can any theological reason oblige us to want to protect Christian discourse against "metaphysical" contamination. And if the history of metaphysics, in its Heideggerian sense, still remains to be written, the history of Christian doctrine is itself sufficiently well known to be able to appear as that of a fundamental loyalty to the words of its origin.

● R. Cohen (1939), *La Grèce et l'hellénisation du monde antique,* Paris.

H. R. Niebuhr (1951), *Christ and Culture,* New York.

Th. Boman (1954), *Das hebräische Denken im Vergleich mit dem Griechischen,* 2nd Ed., Göttingen.

J. Barr (1961), *The Semantics of Biblical Language,* Oxford, London (7th Ed. 1983).

P. H. Camelot (1962), "Hellénisme," *Cath.* 5, 588–92.

E. von Ivánka (1964), *Plato christianus,* Einsiedeln.

A. D. Nock (1964), *Early Gentile Christianity and Its Hellenistic Background,* New York.

H. Chadwick (1966), *Early Christian Thought and the Christian Tradition,* Oxford.

B. F. J. Lonergan (1967), "The Dehellenization of Dogma," in *A Second Collection,* Toronto, 11–32 (2nd Ed. 1996).

P. Stockmeier (1968), "Hellenismus und Christentum," *SM(D)* 665–76.

P. H. Camelot (1969), "Hellénisme," *DSp* 7, 145–64.

M. Hengel (1969), *Judentum und Hellenismus,* Tübingen (2nd Ed. 1973).

J.-C. Fredouille (1972), *Tertullien et la conversion de la culture antique,* Paris.

D. M. Mackinnon (1972), " 'Substance' in Christology: A Cross-Bench View," in S. W. Sykes and J. P. Clayton (Ed.), *Christ, Faith, and History,* Cambridge, 279–300.

C. Andresen (1978), "Antike und Christentum," *TRE* 3, 50–99.

J.-L. Vieillard-Baron (1979), "Platonisme et paganisme au XVIIIe s.," *ArPh* 42, 439–56.

M. Hengel and H. Lichtenberger (1981), "Die Hellenisierung des antiken Judentums als *praeparatio evangelica,*" in *Humanistische Bildung,* Ostfildern-Stuttgart, 1–30.

E. S. Gruen (1984), *The Hellenistic World and the Coming of Rome,* 2 vols., Berkeley, Calif.

H. D. Betz (1986), "Hellenismus," *TRE* 15, 19–35.

E. Arens (Ed.) (1989), *Habermas und die Theologie,* Düsseldorf.

J. Habermas (1992), "Exkurs: Transzendenz von innen, Transzendenz ins Diesseits," in *Texte und Kontexte,* 2nd Ed., Frankfurt, 127–56.

C. Stead (1994), *Philosophy in Christian Antiquity,* Cambridge, 79–244.

P. Neuner (1995), "Die Hellenisierung des Christentums als Modell von Inkulturation," *StZ,* no 213, 363–76.

J. Pelikan (1997), *What Has Athens to Do with Jerusalem? Timaeus and Genesis in Counterpoint,* Ann Arbor.

Michel Gitton

See also **Aristotelianism, Christian; Being; Inculturation; Judeo-Christianity; Philosophy; Platonism, Christian; Stoicism, Christian**

Henoch. *See* **Apocalyptic Literature**

Heresy

---

a) Concept. The *Theologische Realenzyklopädie* (Protestant) recommends (t. 15, 320; *see* 325) the use of the concept of "heresy" in the traditional sense as defined in Catholic canon law* (*Code of Canon Law* 1983, c. 751): heresy is a baptized person's obstinate denial (or doubting) of any truth* of faith*. It is to be distinguished from schism*, in which the believer refuses communion* with the pope* or other members of the Catholic Church*, and apostasy, which is total rejection of the Christian faith.

b) History of Heresy and Heresiology. In the New Testament (Acts) the religious parties of the Sadducees (5:17) and the Pharisees (15:5, 26:5) are designated as *haireseis;* Christian sects were similarly designated by Jews (24:5, 24:14, 28:22). Paul called the internal tensions and splits within the Christian communities "heresies" and "schisms" (Gal 5:20; 1 Cor 11:18f.). Pernicious teachings are clearly stigmatized as heresies in Titus 3:10 and 2 Peter 2:1. The pastoral Epistles mention present and future false doctrines (1 Tm 1:3–11, 4:1–5; 2 Tm 2:14, 4:2ff.; Ti 1:10–16, 3:9ff.). Ignatius of Antioch (†117) denounced as "heterodoxy" the heresy of Docetism* (*Magn* 8, 1), which denied the reality of the suffering and death* of the Son of God; for Ignatius, heresy meant "separation" (*Eph.* 6, 2; *Trall* 6, 1). Around 150 the philosopher and martyr Justin (†165) (who passed on to us the words of Jesus*: "There shall be schisms and heresies" [*Dialogue with Trypho* 35, 5]) wrote a *Syntagma* against all heresies. This work, which later disappeared, marked all subsequent catalogues of heresies. Justin argued that heresy is almost always a false doctrine of God; it is the work of demons*, and the arch-heresiarch is Simon Magus (*Apol. I* 20, 4; *see* Acts 8:9–24). Irenaeus* of Lyon († c. 202) is the author of an *Adversus haereses* against the Gnostics, which remains our major source of information on a heresy that posed a mortal threat to second-century Christianity. According to the jurist Tertullian* († c. 220), the Gnostics disqualified themselves from the start by their disagreement with the tradition* of the faith. *Heresiology* reached a—strictly quantitative—height with the *Panarion* of Epiphanus of Salamine (†402), a "universal history" that established an uncritical inventory of the 80 heresies dating from before and after Christ*. The fight against Arianism*, which was triumphant for some time, continued throughout the fourth century. In the following century, Augustine*, in his relentless battle against Manichaeism*, Pelagianism*, and Anabaptist Donatism*, finally had to call in the civil authorities. In 385—undoubtedly for the first time—a "heretic," the Spanish Priscillian, was executed in Trier. In the 12th and 13th centuries the Cathars* (from the Greek *katharos* meaning pure) were accused of heresy, as were the Waldensians*, a sect that still exists today, and the Albigenses; later, Hus* and Wycliff were denounced as heretics. The 16th-century Reformers were accused of heresy by the Catholics, who were themselves labeled "papists" by the Reformers; but both of these great churches agreed in condemning the anti-Trinitarians (Socinians) and "fanatics" (Anabaptists*, etc.) as heretics. Under the influence of humanism, pietism*, and the Enlightenment, judgments were sometimes reversed: Sebastian Franck (1499–1542) stigmatized all established orthodoxy as heresy, whereas Gottfried Arnold, in *An Impartial History of the Church and All Heresies,* reserved his sympathy for the latter.

c) "There must be heresies *among you."* It is said in 1 Corinthians 11:19 that factions are necessary to put Christians to the test. Christian revelation* establishes "the radicality of an altogether particular ethics* of the truth*" (Rahner 1962) on which the eternal salvation* of humanity depends. Paul declares that (Gal 1:8f.)

even if an angel from heaven announced something different, "let him be accursed!" We might assume that the attempt to develop a theological system on the basis of a single idea inevitably entails a tendency to produce heretics. In fact the great synods* of the early church drew christological and Trinitarian dogmas* from the opposition between different heresies (e.g., monophysitism* and Nestorianism*, modalism* and tritheism*). Even today, error and contradiction can help the church to progress in knowledge and truth (just as they must bring Israel* out of its blindness; *see* Rom 9–11) to the extent that some essential features of Christianity, that the church possesses virtually, have not yet been fully realized (*see* K. Rahner, *LThK2* 5, 8–10).

d) Where Does Heresy Lie Today?   The Second Vatican* Council does not use the term "heresy." Since the council does not exclude from salvation any person of goodwill (*Nostra Aetate* 2; *Lumen Gentium* 16; *Gaudium et Spes* 22) and designates non-Catholic Christians as "separated brethren" (*Unitatis Redintegratio* passim), the question is posed for Catholics

themselves. Their heretical tendencies seem to be primarily expressed within the church (*see* Rahner 1970), and perhaps this contributes to preserving them from the "obstinacy" that distinguishes "formal" heresy from simple material heresy.

● G. Welter (1950), *Histoire des sectes chrétiennes des origines à nos jours,* Paris.
J. Brosch (1956), *Das Wesen der Häresie,* Bonn.
K. Rahner (1962), "Was ist Häresie?" *Schr. zur Th.* 5, 527–76.
E. Droz (1970–76), *Chemins de l'hérésie,* 4 vols., Geneva.
K. Rahner (1970), "Häresien in der Kirche heute," *Schr. zur Th.* 9, 453–78.
Y. Congar (1972), "Die Häresie," *MySal* IV/1, 426–39.
M. D. Lambert (1977), *Medieval Heresy,* London.
A. Séguenny (Ed.) (1980–), *Bidi,* Baden-Baden.
H. D. Betz, A. Schindler, W. Huber (1985), "Häresie I-III," *TRE* 14, 313–48.
K. Lehmann, W. Pannenberg (Ed.) (1986–90), *Lehrverurteilungen-kirchentrennend?* 3 vols., Freiburg-Göttingen.
L. Gerosa (1993), "Schisma und Häresie," *ThGl* 2, 195–212.
B. Neveu (1995), *L'erreur et son juge,* Naples.

WALTER KERN

See also **Authority; Ecclesiastical Discipline; Jurisdiction; Notes, Theological; Schism**

Hermas. *See* **Apostolic Fathers**

Hermeneutics

An art or science of interpretation, hermeneutics is a product of the cultural or chronological distances that interfere with the understanding of texts. Confronted with the problem posed by meaningful objects whose meaning escapes us, or about which we believe that they hold a deep meaning to which we do not or no longer have access, hermeneutics proposes to determine what those objects really intend to say and to test whether what they say is relevant here and now. Theology* attains to its "thing"—God* and all realities subject to

consideration *sub ratione Dei*—only through the mediation of textual objects stamped by a culture and by a "world" that no one any longer inhabits as a birthright. It is therefore necessary that theology include a hermeneutic moment. The Latin term *hermeneutica* appeared in the 17th century as a designation for the *ars interpretandi,* at a time when this was becoming an independent discipline, an auxiliary to theology (*hermeneutica sacra*), philosophy*, philology (*hermeneutica profana*), and law* (*hermeneutica juris*).

1. Prehistory

a) Classical Antiquity. Without sacred texts, it was in reading the classics, more precisely the Homeric corpus, that the Greeks felt the need to postulate the existence of a deep meaning hidden behind the letter of the text (Pépin 1988). In its earliest stages hermeneutics came into existence in the form of allegoresis, as a way of making readable once again a language that had become shocking, either because it attributed to gods behavior unworthy of their divinity or because of the philosophical demand placed on myth* that it justify its existence by disclosing its rational content. Appearing cautiously in Plato, allegoresis was to be used more systematically in Stoicism. Philo of Alexandria was an heir of this philosophical tradition and put it to use in a broad allegorical reading of the Jewish Bible*. This had a decisive effect on patristic allegoresis, from Clement of Alexandria to Ambrose*.

b) Patristic and Medieval Theology. In Christianity the need to interpret arose from one of the first doctrinal decisions taken by the early church*, the decision to give canonical status to the Jewish Scriptures*. If the God of Jesus Christ was the God of Israel*, and if it was therefore necessary to reject the "anti-Semitic" tendencies of Gnosticism* and Marcionism*, then it was necessary to think of the relationship between Jewish and Christian experience* in terms of fulfillment. The problem was thus to provide a Christian reading of what thereby became the "Old Testament." The questions raised were many: Did Jewish legal texts still have meaning for a community that claimed to be authorized to no longer observe the commandments of the Torah? Did the warlike and violent history of the people of Israel still carry lessons for a community that intended to live in anticipation of eschatological peace* and harmony? Patristic exegesis* responded to such challenges by a proliferation of meaning; a spontaneous practice of *typology* and of *allegory* made it possible to theorize the plural meanings of the Scripture. The hermeneutics that was thereby established, and that governed the Christian reading of the Bible until the Reformation, was a "regional" hermeneutics, created to fit a text that faith* declared to be unparalleled and that it asked to determine everything: what had happened (the letter, *littera gesta docet*); what must be believed (allegory, *quid credas allegoria*); what must be done (tropology, *moralis quid agas*); and what must be hoped for (anagogy, *quo tendas anagogia*). But in dealing with a text, hermeneutics encountered the problems of interpretation raised by any text recognized to have authority*.

c) From the Reformation to the Enlightenment. Two rejections and an affirmation made up the core of Lutheran hermeneutics. On the one hand, the theory of the fourfold meanings of Scripture was discarded in favor of the literal meaning alone, which was deemed sufficient for the word* of God as expressed through the Scriptures. On the other hand, church statements outside the Scriptures were no longer valid as the norm for a proper reading of the Scriptures. Finally, Scripture was the Word insofar as it spoke of Christ*, the center and the heart of divine revelation*. And if we agree with Luther* that the literal meaning of the Scriptures is generally clear, then the problem of interpretation does not arise. If obscurity exists, a better knowledge of the language and reliance on parallel passages are enough to dissipate it (Matthias Flacius Illyricus, *Clavis scripturae sacrae,* 1567). The real need for hermeneutics arose less from the century of the Reformation and humanism—a time that in fact held the total readability of ancient texts as one of its articles of faith—than from the later appearance of a consciousness of history*.

The development of historiography and the appearance of the philosophy of history, together with the birth of modern science and of an epistemology organized around the concept of "fact," and the challenge to the processes of tradition*, these were all factors that led to the Christian Scriptures seeming to become partially obscure. In a world without miracles*, did miracle stories still have meaning (Hume, Lessing)? In a world that wondered about the true "aim" of Jesus* and his disciples (Reimarus), what veracity* could be attributed to the New Testament interpretation of what had in fact happened? More general questions were raised concerning the status of any work containing signification. In a world whose frontiers had expanded beyond those of the Western *oikoumenè,* cultural distances were objects of intense scrutiny; opacity was something that the monuments of primitive Christianity shared with those of China. In a world moving toward secularization*, any religious text began to take on the strangeness that I. T. Ramsey recognized as essential to religious language. In a world in which reality began to be identified with the observable, what knowability could be attributed to the past? What value should be given to a past process of meaning? To respond to these challenges, neither philology nor biblical exegesis could be of much help.

2. History

a) Schleiermacher. We owe to Friedrich Schleiermacher* (1768–1834) the first project for a general hermeneutics that might be capable of interpreting any object carrying meaning. A theologian and philologist, Schleiermacher was enough of an heir of the Enlightenment to know the value of criticism. Thus, the first task of hermeneutics was "grammatical" (or "objective," or "negative"): only someone who knew the culture in which a writer lived and the language that he spoke could, in a second stage, perceive the contributions to meaning that the writer made in an original manner. But Schleiermacher was also a romantic thinker, and the second task of hermeneutics (called "technical," or "psychological") consisted—in order "to understand a writer as well as, and even better than, he had understood himself" (*Herm.*, Ed. Kimmerle)—of carrying out a sympathetic introspection close to divination. Taking from romantic philosophy "its deepest conviction, that the spirit is the creative unconscious at work in individuals of genius" (Ricœur 1975, 82), Schleiermacher thus based the possibility of interpretation on an idea, "connaturalism." Through the mediation of the work, spirit spoke to spirit.

b) Dilthey. Between Schleiermacher and W. Dilthey (1833–1911) a century elapsed that saw the science of history reach its peak. Writing after Ranke and Droysen, and in an intellectual climate in which the dominant influence was neo-Kantianism, Dilthey had a single project, that of constructing a critique of historical reason. And because Dilthey also lived in a period that witnessed a certain triumph of positivism (the reign of objectivity considered as the measure of all reality), his ambition was to establish a kind of knowledge as valid as scientific knowledge, but served by entirely different cognitive instruments. The proper task of the objective sciences was to "explain" *(erklären),* while that of the sciences of the mind *(Geisteswissenschaften)* was to "understand" *(verstehen).* And since what was to be understood was the *life* of others, as that was expressed in structured and meaningful forms, Dilthey was led to adopt the psychological hermeneutics of Schleiermacher. With Dilthey, too, hermeneutics had a philological component; and here also, the interpreter was able to grasp meaning by transporting himself into others. It is of the author of the work that we ask for the revelation of the work's secrets, and we presuppose that the question can receive a satisfactory response.

c) Heidegger. While Dilthey is concerned with interpreting "life" as it takes on objective form, Heidegger* gives a new meaning to hermeneutics. At the core of *Being and Time* lies a reversal. Hermeneutics presupposed that one interpreted with the aim of understanding. But according to Heidegger, it is in fact the understanding that provides the object of interpreta-

tion. Understanding is what man—the *Dasein*—has always already done. When we raise the question of meaning (and for Heidegger this is an arch-meaning, the "meaning of being"), this is a question that we have already answered by anticipation, by the simple fact that we exist. "Existence," by which must be understood a mode of being that belongs to us and only to us, is in any event an act of understanding. Hermeneutics is thus an interpretation of "facticity," the interpretation of an existence located in a world, the interpretation of a finitude that is experienced in the dual mode of *Befindlichkeit* ("affection," "the meaning of the situation") and *Verstehen.* The theoretical reorganization is complete in several steps: recognition of the circular structure of hermeneutics (the "hermeneutic circle"); substitution of an ontological problem for the epistemological problem that troubled Schleiermacher and Dilthey; abandonment of a theory of understanding by means of sympathetic introspection in favor of a relationship between the self and the world; and the generalization of hermeneutic concerns that bear on the totality of the knowable and not merely on the products of human speech and art.

d) Gadamer. It fell to one of Heidegger's students, H. G. Gadamer (1900–), who heard the lectures on hermeneutics given before the publication of *Being and Time,* to resume a dialogue with the sciences of the mind, or human sciences, for which the fundamental ontology of his teacher left no room. Gadamer retains from Heidegger the idea of an anticipatory structure of knowing, which allows him to challenge the "prejudice against prejudice." It is an essential mark of human finitude, on the contrary, that we know only within traditions that provide us with a stock of preinterpretations. It is essential to the work of art, moreover, to have a "history of its effects" *(Wirkungsgeschichte),* the influence of which affects every consciousness that confronts the work (and that is thus defined as *wirkungsgeschichtliches Bewußtsein).* The task of hermeneutics, consequently, does not require the adoption of a scientific "method," something that Gadamer suspects of establishing an alienating distance *(Verfremdung)* between "subject" and "object." Rather, it requires the existence of a relationship of belonging *(Zugehörigkeit)* within which the perspectives inherent in the work may blend with those specific to the reader. The "fusion of perspectives" *(Horizontverschmelzung)* thus makes it possible for the relationship between the reader and the work to bear fruit in a dialogue. This dialogue will never produce the last word in interpretation, nor indeed a better interpretation. It will produce *another* interpretation, in which the text will speak directly to the reader and to the world he inhabits.

e) Ricœur. Between Gadamer and P. Ricœur (1913–) came an event that marked the latter's hermeneutics, the growth of the "sciences of the text" derived from linguistic structuralism and structural semantics. In response to the appearance of analytical and objectifying disciplines that he generally found fruitful, Ricœur's ambition was to do away with Dilthey's distinction between "explaining" and "understanding" in order to make explanation the necessary basis for understanding. Objectifying distancing no longer functions as an obstacle to interpretation, and the fascination exercised by critique and method probably comes together with the older influence of Husserl's phenomenology so that we may establish as a principle that the primary effort of hermeneutics is to allow the text to be itself, so that it must be *read* before it can be interpreted. Thereafter, phenomenology also provides material for understanding and a concept capable of articulating it. Around a text that is well read, says Ricœur, a "world" unfolds, which is offered for the reader to inhabit. That the "world of the text" can become "my world" proves both the classic character of the text and the exactness of the interpretation. And when I understand a classic text, I am in fact invited to understand myself through its mediation: "We understand ourselves only through the great detour of the signs of humanity deposited in the works of culture" (1975). We also need to note that in Ricœur's hermeneutics, as in the "sciences of the text" with which it is concerned, the author of the work has disappeared; the aim of interpretation is not the "pathetic search for buried subjectivities" (ibid.) but the search for a meaning of the work available in the work.

3. Theological Receptions

a) From Bultmann to the "New Hermeneutics." Incomplete and published posthumously, Schleiermacher's *Hermeneutics* became a point of reference only in the 20th century, and it was in fact the influence of Heidegger on Bultmann*, his colleague in Marburg, that determined the hermeneutic interests of recent theology. From Heidegger, Bultmann had learned that understanding is always preceded by "preunderstandings" *(Vorverständnisse),* the function of which is "to make possible an orientation for thought, not to dictate what must be thought" (Greisch 1985). From his own critical practice of exegesis, on the other hand, he had additionally learned that the biblical text is perhaps the most difficult of all texts. Finally, he had retained from the Enlightenment the very vivid sense of a modernity that had rendered obsolete the vision of the world accepted in biblical texts *(see* Thistleton 1980). Two tasks then seemed necessary: to identify the human

questions to which the text offers a response; and to deliver the text from all the ("mythic") elements that are unable to contribute to the creation of a theological understanding of the self. The historical character of existence and the anticipatory structure of understanding are borrowed from a *general* hermeneutics that takes an interest in anything interpretable, and for which, besides, everything must be interpreted. Demythologization and the establishment of a relationship between the true "thing" *(Sache)* of the text and the ultimate human questions are, on the other hand, procedures of a specifically theological hermeneutics. It is the goal of this particular hermeneutics to make it possible for the text to speak in the name of God.

The specifically theological contributions of Bultmann, together with a renewal of Lutheran studies, explain why the *word* was the center of the hermeneutic concerns of two of Bultmann's principle disciples, E. Fuchs (1903–83) and G. Ebeling (1912–). Reference to Luther, especially in Ebeling, makes it possible to name precisely the (strictly theological) problem of hermeneutics: through a text, interpretation should make it possible for the word of God to be heard. This theological necessity, reinforced by Heideggerian influences, led to the attribution of the status of key hermeneutic concepts to what Fuchs and Ebeling called "speech process" *(Wortegeschehen)* or "speech event" *(Sprachereignis).* The critical-exegetical process is not disavowed, but it is marginalized. Hermeneutic circularity is still presupposed, but the urgent hermeneutic work is to allow the Word to speak its own language (for Fuchs, the language of love*) and to prevail over any other language by virtue of its eschatological dimension. In the final analysis it is in preaching* that the Word comes in exemplary fashion. The desire to construct a theology that can be preached thus makes it possible for the "new hermeneutics" to coincide with a central concern of the young Barth*.

b) Theological Reception of Gadamer. The philosophical discussion of the arguments proposed in *Truth and Method* has been constant since the publication of the book. Objections are not lacking. For Popperian "critical rationalism," represented in Germany by H. Albert (1971), Gadamer's hermeneutics has as its principal characteristic the rejection of the Enlightenment's legacy of rationality. To this critique, Habermas (1970) added that the rehabilitation of "prejudice" makes impossible any critique of ideologies, and hence any social praxis. For Betti (1967), a defense and illustration of "method," as well as the use of objective canons of interpretation stand in opposition to Gadamer. But in the end the most radical objections have come out of the critique of the word developed since 1962 by J. Derrida: for a thought that asserts the priority of writing ("grammatology"), understood as "trace," as principle of "differance" and "dissemination," hermeneutics obviously falls victim to all the condemnations of "metaphysics," "logocentrism," "white mythology," and the like.

For obvious reasons, Gadamer's rehabilitation of prejudice was received with the greatest attention first of all in Catholic theology. What was in fact found in it, at first sight, was the controlling idea of a fundamental* theology of tradition. However, it soon became clear (*see* Hilberath 1978; Stobbe 1981) that while theology certainly conceives its work as that of an interpretive reading of the founding testimonies of faith within the very community that established those founding testimonies, it also understands interpretation as a critical procedure (e.g., Schillebeeckx 1971; Geffré 1983). It is then the principle of an open multiplicity of readings, all different and none definitive, that is learned from Gadamer. Although not resting on a choice between one or the other, what is involved here is the respective weight given to general hermeneutics and the (special) hermeneutics of the theologians. A theological hermeneutics can be developed on the basis of Gadamer's arguments, and can have as its aim the bringing to light of a principle of continuity, and of the existence of a place—the church—in which the "fusion of perspectives" and the dwelling in the "world of the Scriptures" come about without friction. We thus that see extremist theories know the ecclesiastical conditions of interpretive success so well that they can rely on a paradigm supplied by Eucharistic ecclesiology* (the bishop* concentrating in himself all theological competence when he comments on the Scriptures in the liturgy) to quickly resolve any hermeneutic question (e.g., Marion 1982). The debate is, however, dominated by more prudent voices, united by the rejection of any theological discourse that claims to hold an absolute point of view, and united in the recognition of a fruitful tension between tradition and critique; but carrying diverse emphases, according to whether they agree with Ricœur that the "thing" of the biblical text, "the new being" that it unfolds, has the reality of an inhabitable "world" (*see also* Tracy 1981), or whether they share with Bultmann the fear of past worlds believed to have been abolished by history. (e.g., Jeanrond 1991)

c) Perspectives. The finitude of existence and the finitude of knowledge: these two axioms of philosophical hermeneutics have been accepted by almost all recent theologies. Pannenberg (1967), for instance, has managed to recognize the truth of the hermeneutic problem, and to reformulate it in the framework of historical reference that he takes largely from Hegel*. The establish-

ment of a general hermeneutics authorized to impose its problems on theology and in part to dictate solutions to theology has also been widely accepted. There is, however, room for dissension based on the uniqueness that faith recognizes in the biblical text. For example, on the basis of structural semiotics, it has been argued that the Bible "is not a text" (Costantini 1976). Others have relied on the work of H. de Lubac* (*Exégèse médiévale,* Paris 1959–64; *see* van Esbrook 1968) to propose an alliance between contemporary hermeneutics and the older theory of spiritual meaning, or else (Chapelle 1973) to sketch out a systematic organization of theological language*. The questions that occupied the prehistory of hermeneutics are still genuine and live ones, and they make it impossible to believe too quickly in the existence of a general hermeneutics that one need merely apply to Christian texts: whether it is a question of seeing the Old Testament fulfilled in the New (*see* Beauchamp 1977 and 1990) or of reading the Scriptures in the communion of a tradition that lays claim to the right to provide a normative interpretation of those Scriptures. The theory of dogma* (e.g., Rahner* 1960), the theology of magisterial discourse, the theory of theology, the theory of *loci* *theologici*—services are expected from hermeneutics that it has yet to render in a satisfying manner.

- F. D. E. Schleiermacher (1805–33), *Hermeneutik, nach den Handschriften neu herausgegeben und eingeleitet von Heinz Kimmerle,* Heidelberg (2nd Ed. 1974).
- W. Dilthey (1883 a), *Einleitung in die Geisteswissenschaften, GS* 1–2, Stuttgart-Göttingen (2nd Ed. 1959); (1883 b), *Vorlesung zur Einleitung in die Geisteswissenschaften, GS* 20, Göttingen, 1990, 127–64; (1910), *Der Aufbau der geschichtlichen Welt in den Geisteswissenschaften, GS* 7, Stuttgart-Göttingen (2nd Ed. 1958).
- M. Heidegger (1927), *Sein und Zeit* (*GA* 2, Frankfurt, 1976).
- R. Bultmann (1952), "Das Problem der Hermeneutik," *GuV* 2, 211–35.
- E. Fuchs (1954), *Hermeneutik,* Bad Cannstadt (2nd Ed. 1958 with supplement).
- G. Ebeling (1959 a), "Hermeneutik," *RGG*3 3, 243–62; (1959 b), "Wort Gottes und Hermeneutik," *Wort und Glaube* I, Tübingen, 1960, 319–48 (3rd Ed. 1967).
- M. Heidegger (1959), *Unterwegs zur Sprache* (*GA* 12, Frankfurt, 1985).
- E. Fuchs (1960), *Zum hermeneutischen Problem in der Theologie,* Tübingen.
- H. G. Gadamer (1960), *Wahrheit und Methode,* Tübingen.
- J. Derrida (1962), *La voix et le phénomène,* Paris.
- E. Betti (1967), *Allgemeine Auslegungslehre als Methodik der Geisteswissenschaften,* Tübingen (abr. and rev. version by the author of the *Teoria generale della interpretazione,* Milan, 1990, 2 vols.).
- E. Fuchs (1968), *Marburger Hermeneutik,* Tübingen.
- J. Habermas (1970), "Die Universalitätsanspruch der Hermeneutik," in R. Bubner, K. Cramer, and R. Wiehl (Ed.), *Hermeneutik und Dialektik: Festschrift für Hans-Georg Gadamer,* Tübingen, 73–104.

H. Albert (1971), *Plädoyer für den kritischen Rationalismus,* Munich.

P. Ricœur (1975), "La tâche de l'herm." and other essays, in F. Bovon and G. Rouiller (Ed.), *Exegesis,* Neuchâtel, 179–228.

♦ K. Rahner (1960), "Überlegungen zur Dogmenentwicklung," *Schr. zur Th.* 4, 11–50.

E. Castelli (Ed.) (1963), *Ermeneutica e tradizione,* Rome.

J.M. Robinson and J.B. Cobb (Ed.) (1964), *The New Hermeneutic,* New York.

W. Pannenberg (1967), "Hermeneutik und Universalgeschichte" and "Über historische und theologische Hermeneutik," *Grundfr. syst. Th.,* 91–122 and 123–58.

C.E. Braaten (1968), *History and Hermeneutics,* New Directions in Theology Today 2, London.

B. Casper (1968), "Die Bedeutung der philosophischen Hermeneutik für die Theologie," *ThQ* 148, 283–302.

M. van Esbroeck (1968), *Herm., structuralisme et exégèse: Essai de logique kérygmatique,* Paris.

R.E. Palmer (1969), *Hermeneutics: Interpretation Theory in Schleiermacher, Dilthey, Heidegger and Gadamer,* Evanston, Northwestern University Press.

E. Biser (1970), *Theologische Sprachtheorie und Hermeneutik,* Munich.

E. Schillebeeckx (1971), *Glaubensinterpretation: Beiträge zu einer hermeneutischen und kritischen Theologie,* Mainz.

A. Chapelle (1973), *Herm.,* photocopied lecture, Institut d'études théol., Brussels.

H.W. Frei (1974), *The Eclipse of Biblical Narrative: A Study in Eighteenth and Nineteenth Century Hermeneutics,* New Haven–London.

R. Marlé (1975), *Parler de Dieu aujourd'hui: La th. herm. de G. Ebeling,* CFi 82.

J.-P. Resweber (1975), *La th. face au défi herm.,* Louvain-Paris.

M. Costantini (1976), "La Bible n'est pas un texte," *Com(F)* I/7, 40–54.

F. Mußner (1976), *HDG* I . 3 . c (2).

P. Beauchamp (1977), *L'Un et l'Autre Testament* I; (1990), II, Paris.

J. Greisch (1977), *Herm. et grammatologie,* Paris.

B.J. Hilberath (1978), *Theologie zwischen Tradition und Kritik: Die philosophische Hermeneutik H.-G. Gadamers als Herausforderung des theologischen Selbstverständnisses,* Düsseldorf.

S. Breton (1979), *Écriture et révélation,* CFi 97.

A.C. Thiselton (1980), *The Two Horizons: New Testament Hermeneutics and Philosophical Description with Special Reference to Heidegger, Bultmann, Gadamer, and Wittgenstein,* Exeter.

G. Stobbe (1981), *Hermeneutik—ein ökumenisches Problem: Eine Kritik der katholischen Gadamer-Rezeption,* ÖTh 8.

D. Tracy (1981), *The Analogical Imagination: Christian Theology and the Culture of Pluralism,* London, esp. 99–153.

J.-L. Marion (1982), "Du site eucharistique de la th.," in *Dieu sans l'être,* Paris, 197–222.

C. Geffré (1983), *Le christianisme au risque de l'interprétation,* CFi 120, 19–104.

J. Greisch (1985), *L'âge herm. de la raison,* CFi 133, esp. 15–121.

J. Pépin and K. Hoheisel (1988), "Hermeneutik," *RAC* 14, 722–72.

W.G. Jeanrond (1991), *Theological Hermeneutics,* London.

W. Alexander (1993), Hermeneutica generalis. *Zur Konzeption und Entwicklung der allgemeinen Verstehenslehre im 17. und 18. Jahrhundert,* Stuttgart.

J. Grondin (1993), *L'universalité de l'herm.,* Paris (*Einführung in die philosophische Hermeneutik,* Darmstadt, 1991).

J. Ladrière (1993), "Interprétation et vérité," *LTP* 49, 189–99.

J. Grondin (1994), *Der Sinn für Hermeneutik,* Darmstadt.

J.-Y. Lacoste (1994), "Urgences kérygmatiques et délais herm. Sur les contraintes élémentaires du discours théol.," *RPL* 92, 254–80.

Jean-Yves Lacoste

See also **Exegesis; Scripture, Fulfillment of; Scripture, Senses of**

Hermeticism. *See* Theosophy

Hesychasm

The semantic complex formed by *hèsukhia* and its derivatives represents a key concept in the ascetico-mystical literature of the Christian East, attested from the dawn of monasticism* to the present day. Of uncertain etymology (*hèsthai:* to be seated?) and difficult to translate (tranquility, vacuity?), it has undergone a variety of historical developments. It may denote a state of soul* (consisting of withdrawal, peace*, and silence), a way of life (the eremitical state), a method of prayer* (known as *monologistos* or "Jesus* prayer"), a theory of contemplation* (linked to the soteriology of the Greek Fathers*), a theological system (developed by Gregory* Palamas in the 14th century), or a cultural referent shared by different religious movements (including, from the 18th century, that of the *Philocalia*). Taken as a whole, these layers and meanings constitute for the Orthodox Church a methodical spirituality, organized according to dogmatic* theology.

a) Primitive Hesychasm. From the fourth century onward, *hèsukhia* summarized the two fundamental obligations of monastic life: outward anchoritism (seclusion from the outer world) and inward asceticism*. The writings attributed to Anthony (†356) and his disciples, the *Apophtegmata Patrum,* and the narratives of the chroniclers of the church (from Palladius's *Lausiac History* [c. 420] to the *Spiritual Meadow* [c. 610] by John Moschus), all restrict the title of hesychast to hermits alone. There is no *hèsukhia* without *monôsis,* solitude, or at the very least isolation. However, the organization into *lavrae,* the apostolic dimension of spiritual* direction (recognized in Ammonas's first *Letter on hèsukhia*), the equally contemplative vocation of cenobitism (intrinsic to the *Rule* of Pachomius, †346), and the model of reclusion in a community (promoted by Barsanuphius of Gaza, †540), underline the rapid rise to dominance of the inward sense of the term. As well as being a way of life, *hèsukhia* was also "an art and a grace" (Evagrius Ponticus [†399], *Treatise,* PG 40, 1260–62 *a*). It required *apatheia,* mastery of the passions*; *amerimnia,* absolute indifference to worry; *katharsis,* the discernment and eradication of thoughts *(logismoi);* and *nèpsis,* vigilance over the intellect and heart. The means and the end of these states was the *mnèmè tou theou,* the suppression of the world of the senses, imagination, and intellect, a suppression that made possible the recollection of God*—or more precisely of Jesus—in prayer. Based on a typological exegesis* of mystical preeminence (with the figures of Moses, Elijah, Mary of Bethany, and John the "beloved disciple") and a literal interpretation of the New Testament commandment to pray continually (Lk 18:1; Eph 6:18; 1 Thes 5:17), *meletè* or meditative prayer consisted of the oral repetition or mental contemplation of a formula of contrition, usually taken from the Psalms (Ps 6:3, 25:16, 51:3, etc.) or the Gospels* (the tax collector, the

blind man, the Canaanite woman). A method of constant epiclesis* (which according to Cassian [†432] constituted the "original secret" of the desert tradition [*Conferences,* X, 10]), *hèsukhia* opened the way to the anticipation of the Kingdom* and the vision of God (Pseudo-Macarius, 5th century, *Hom.* I, 12).

b) Prayer of Jesus and the Sinaitic School. The doctrinal formulation of hesychasm was faced from the outset with two major accounts of monastic life, each of which incurred a suspicion of heterodoxy. On the one hand, there was the Evagrian corpus. Rooted in an extreme intellectualism* inspired by the school of Origen, and notable as much for its psychological as for its lexical architecture, this body of work was later disseminated pseudonymously. On the other hand, there was the pseudepigraphical corpus of the *Macarian Homilies,* with its powerful biblical realism characterized by the concepts of experience*, of the heart, and of felt grace*, but open to question as to its possible Messalianism*. In the *Gnostic Chapters,* Diadochus of Photike (fifth century) achieved a christocentric and sacramental synthesis of these two currents that would be given its classic form by the Sinaitic school. The practice known as "prayer to/of Jesus" probably became associated with it by a process of gradual evolution, in the context of a continuous transmission. John Climacus (†649), who defined *hèsukhia* as "an uninterrupted service of God," stipulated that "the recollection of Jesus should be as one with breathing" (*Ladder* 27). Hesychius of Batos (eighth century) insisted on perpetual prayer and frequently employed the theme of respiration (*Centuries* I, 5, PG 93, 1481 *d*). Thus numerous parallels link the name* of Jesus and/or the activity of breathing with monological prayer. Their precise value and meaning (e.g., Nilus of Ancyra [*ODCC* calls him Nilus the Ascetic] [† c. 430] *Letters* III, 33, PG 79, 392 *b*), or their exact dating (e.g., Philemon, seventh century?, *Very Useful Discourse, Philocalia* II, 241–52), remain subjects of debate. Nevertheless, after the eighth century all metaphorical interpretation was ruled out, and the invocation assumed the now-familiar form: "Lord Jesus Christ*, Son of God, Saviour, have pity upon me, a sinner."

c) Method of Prayer. The hesychastic renaissance that occurred at Mount Athos between the 13th and 15th centuries coincided with the revelation of a psychosomatic technique—no doubt of earlier date and originating from within the tradition—that complemented the prayer of Jesus. Its classic statements are *The Method of Holy Prayer* by Pseudo-Symeon (perhaps attributable to Nicephorus [† c. 1280], himself the author of a short work, *Nepsis and the Care of the*

Heart), as well as two treatises by Gregory the Sinaite (†1346) titled *Of the Modes of Prayer* and *Precepts for Hesychasts*. The method, stated simply, consisted of withdrawing into a dark cell, sitting down with the head bent, controlling one's breathing, looking into "the place of the heart," and rhythmically repeating the prayer. Although some physiological explanations and descriptions of its effects appear to cast doubt on the purely instrumental character of the method, its only goal remained receptiveness to grace (*Of the Modes*, PG 150, 1329 *b*–1332 *a*). Theoleptus of Philadelphia (†1326), a disciple of Nicephorus, does not mention it (*On Secret Activity*, PG 143, 388 *ab*), and Gregory Palamas (†1359), associated with Gregory the Sinaite, plays down its importance in order to exclude any mechanical conception of *hèsukhia* (*Tr.* I, 2, 3–9). For all that, it became the pretext for the "hesychastic controversy" and shed light on far more decisive theological issues.

d) Byzantine Neo-Hesychasm. "To contain the incorporeal in a corporeal dwelling" (Climacus, *Ladder* 27): a doctrine as much as a form of spirituality, hesychasm contained something of the Greek Fathers' gnosiology. It verified it experimentally and gave it concrete expression by confirming the reality of divinization: full personal communion* with God realized the eschatological promise here on earth; participation in the mystery* was real and in no way diminished it. In parallel with the establishment of christological dogma*, the main current of patristic thought, from the Cappadocian Fathers (fourth century) to John Damascene (†749), incorporated the vocabulary of *hèsukhia*, its use of apophasis (negative formulations) and antinomy (contradictory constructions), and its discursive reduction to soteriological principles alone. The theory of divine indwelling adopted the anthropology* of the desert and its principal expressions—the transfiguration of the body, the spiritual senses, the heart as a projection of the *noûs* (the intellect or "transcendent I") and of the human totality. Hesychasm likewise helped to form a representation of deification (by way of the themes of light, glory*, and gifts) while at the same time prohibiting its conceptualization: the passage—the Passover—which made "man God by grace" implemented a radical disjunction with the whole of creation (Maximus* the Confessor [†662], *Theol. and Ec. Chap.* I, 51–60, PG 90, 1101–05). From the ninth century onward, Byzantine theology* would formalize this dialectic of divine incommunicability and communication by applying it to pneumatology. Symeon the New Theologian (†1022), a defender of the charismatic nature of the church, placed the vision of God in the perspective of a baptism* experienced consciously

(Cat. XIV, 68–164). According to Gregory the Sinaite, an analysis of the intellect and its manifestations tended to affirm an absolute transcendence of pure prayer, under the sole influence of the Holy Spirit* (*On hèsukhia*, PG 150, 1303–12): beyond the minor phenomenon of ecstasy, the state of divinization was seen to be both stable and dynamic. Finally, Gregory Palamas, reacting against the violent attacks of the philosophers and humanists of his time, endowed hesychasm with a dogmatic expression by defining the unity and distinctness of the essence and the uncreated energies. Sustained by a desire for liturgical reform, a return to the sources of iconography, and an intense activity of translation, and supported by the patriarchate of Constantinople, which had been won over to Palamism, neo-hesychasm spread across the whole Byzantine world. It was disseminated by Theodosius of Tarnovo (†1363) in Bulgaria, Romil of Vidin (†1375) in Serbia, Nicodemus of Tismana (†1409) in Wallachia, and Sergius of Radonezh (†1392) and Metropolitan Cyprian († c. 1420) in Russia. This inheritance was to play a decisive part in the development of modern Orthodoxy*.

e) Revival of the Philocalia. Hesychasm continued to fulfill the function of a theological benchmark in the general crisis that affected the Orthodox Church from the 16th to the 18th century: although marginalized, the "nonpossessors"—whose *Rule,* promulgated by Nil Sorsky (†1508), advocated this method of prayer—brought to completion its reception in Russia. And limited as they were, the efforts at publishing that accompanied the internal mission undertaken by the patriarchate of Jerusalem* under the pontificates of Nectarius, Dositheus, and Chrysantus (1661–1743) resulted in better access to the texts. As a result of the importance accorded to the monasteries, and to the institution of spiritual father (the *gerôn* or *starets*) in the preservation of the faith*, the Jesus prayer was taught to a wide circle of the laity*. It was, however, with the publication of the *Philocalia* in 1782 that the theoretical resurgence came to completion. This anthology of texts from the fourth to the 15th century, compiled by Macarius of Corinth (†1805) and Nicodemus the Hagiorite (†1809), was expressly intended to confront Enlightenment rationalism* with an encyclopedia of hesychasm, Palamite in its ambitions and linking dogma with spirituality. This revival was initially apparent in Greek- and Arabic-speaking circles. Thanks to the *Dobrotolubije,* a Slavonic version of the Greek text published in Moldavia by Paisy Velichkovsky (†1794) and simultaneously in Moscow in 1793, it then spread to central Europe, the Balkans, and Russia. The latter saw a flourishing of the Philocalian spirit during the 19th century. The translation of the original collection (St. Petersburg, 1857) by Bishop Ignatius Briantchaninov (†1867) was followed by a new, more extensive compilation by Theophan the Recluse (†1894), which, however, betrayed a pietistic bias in its cuts and additions (Moscow, 1877). Made famous by major figures of sanctity such as Seraphim of Sarov (†1833) or the *startsi* of Optino (especially Ambrose [†1891]), popularized by the anonymous work *The Sincere Narratives of a Pilgrim to His Spiritual Father* (Kazan, c. 1870), hallowed by art and literature (Dostoyevsky's *The Brothers Karamazov* being but one example), hesychasm regained all its cultural value. In 1912–13, however, the condemnation of the "onomatolaters" ("name-worshippers"), Russian monks of Athos who worshipped the divinity of the name of Jesus itself, revealed the difficulties inherent in this expansion.

f) Prospects. In the 20th century the monumental Romanian *Philocalia* of Dumitru Staniloae (†1994) significantly accorded pride of place to theoretical writings and in particular to Maximus the Confessor and Gregory Palamas. In contemporary Orthodox theology the neopatristic school regards hesychasm as a summary mapping of the Christian experience*, and indispensable as a prism through which to interpret that experience. At the same time, a movement toward the revival of monasticism has laid claim to its entire heritage; and as the writings of Joseph the Hesychast (†1954) and Paissios of Cappadocia (†1995) make clear, Mount Athos is still its epicenter. This air of completion and unchangingness are entirely characteristic. Hesychasm cannot be reduced to a matter of sub-religious technique, and comparisons with *prânâymâ yoga*, the Indian *Japa*, or the *nembûtsû* of Zen Buddhism (with the exception of the Sufi *dhikr*, which may have a related ancestry) fall within the province of fundamental anthropology or syncretistic sociology. Neither can it be classed as an Eastern variant of ejaculatory prayer, such as the Benedictine *quies* or the Ignatian *Exercises*, since the superficial similarities are canceled out by the difference in systematic and historical scope. In the consciousness of Orthodoxy, *hèsukhia* holds together spirituality and theology, prophecy* and tradition, truth and the Holy Spirit. The closest equivalent one might suggest would be "the logic of grace"—provided that it is understood as an experience incapable of being conveyed in words.

● Athanasius of Alexandria, *Vie et conduite de notre père saint Antoine*, PG 26, 837–976; SC 400; SpOr 28.

Apophtegmes des Pères, "série alphabétique," PG 65, 71–440 (French trans. SpOr 1, 1966), "série systématique," PL 73, 851–1222 (French trans. Solesmes, 1970; 2nd Ed. 1976); SC 387.

Evagrius Ponticus, *Practicos*, PG 40, 1220–76; SC 170–71.

Macaire, *Homélies spirituelles*, PG 34, 449–822; SpOr 40; *Die 50 geistlichen Homilien des Makarios*, Ed. H. Dörries, PTS 4.

Diadochus of Photike, *Œuvres spirituelles*, SC 5 ter.

Jean Climaque, *L'Échelle sainte*, PG 88, 631–1164; SpOr 24.

Simeon, The New Theologian, *Catecheses*, SC 96, 104, 113; *Hymns*, SC 156, 174, 196.

Grégoire le Sinaïte, *Œuvres*, PG 150, 1237–1330.

Gregory Palamas, *De la déification de l'être humain*, trans. J.-M. Monsaingeon and J. Paramelle, Lausanne, 1990.

Nicodème l'Hagiorite and Macaire de Corinthe, *Philokalia*, Venice, 1787 (repr. Athens, 5 vols., 1957–63); SpOr, 11 vols. (2nd Ed. 1994–95, 2 vols.).

Paissy Velichkovsky, *Autobiographie d'un starets* (French trans. SpOr 53).

Ignace Brianchaninov, *Approches de la prière de Jésus* (1867), Saint Petersburg (French trans. SpOr 35).

Théophane le reclus, *Dobrotoloubije*, Moscow, 1877–1905, 5 vols. (New Ed. New York, 5 vols., 1963–66).

Dimitru Staniloae, *Filocalia*, Sibiu-Bucarest, 1949–90, 12 vols.

Joseph the Hesychasm, *Grammata*, Mount Athos, 1982 (French trans. "Letters," *Contacts*, 1990, 42, 168–73).

♦ K. Holl (1898), *Enthusiasmus und Bußgewalt beim griechischen Mönchtum*, Leipzig.

J. Bois (1901), "Grégoire le Sinaïte et l'hésychasme à l'Athos au XIVe s.," *EOr* 5, 65–73.

I. V. Popov (1906), "Ideia obozhenia v drevne—Vostochnoi tserkvi," *Voprosi Filosofij i Psixologij* 97, 165–213.

S.L. Epifanovich (1915), *Propodobnyi Maksim Ispovednik i vizantiiskoe bogoslovie*, Kiev.

J. Gross (1938), *La divinisation du chrétien d'après les Pères grecs*, Paris.

H. Dörries (1941), *Symeon von Mesopotamien: Die Überlieferung der messalianischen "Makarios" Schriften*, TU 55, 1, Leipzig.

P. Galtier (1946), *Le Saint-Esprit en nous d'après les Pères grecs*, AnGr 37, Rome.

L. Gardet (1952–53), "La mention du nom divin dans la mystique musulmane," *RThom* 52, 662–79; 53, 197–216.

S. Boulgakov (1953), *Filosofia Imeni*, Paris (trad. fr. Lausanne, 1991, *Philosophie du verbe et du nom*, 171–207).

W. Nölle (1954), "Hesychasmus und yoga," *Byz* 47, 95–103.

A. Scrima (1958), "L'avènement philocalique en Roumanie," *Ist* 3, 295–328, 443–74.

I. Haussher (1960), *Noms du Christ et voies d'oraison*, OCA 157, Rome.

A. Guillaumont (1962), Les *"Kephalaia gnostica" d'Évagre le Pontique et l'histoire de l'origénisme chez les Grecs et les Syriens*, Paris.

Vl. Lossky (1962), *Vision de Dieu*, Neuchâtel.

J. Leclercq (1963), "A propos de l'hésychasme en Occident," *Le millénaire du Mont-Athos* I, 253–64, Chèvetogne.

L. Thunberg (1965), *Microcosm and Mediator*, Lund.

W. Völker (1965), *Maximus Confessor als Meister des geistlichen Lebens*, Wiesbaden.

D.J. Chitty (1966), *The Desert a City*, Oxford.

I. Haussher (1966), *Hésychasme et Prière*, OCA 176, Rome.

M. Lot-Borodine (1969), *La déification de l'homme*, Paris.

A. Scrima (1969), "L'apophase et ses connotations selon la tradition spirituelle de l'Orient chrétien," *Hermès* 6, 157–69.

K. Ware (1970), "Tradition and personal experience in late byzantine theology," *ECR* 3, 131–41.

G. Maloney (1973), *Russian Hesychasm: The Spirituality of Nil Sorskij*, The Hague.

J. Meyendorff (1974), *Byzantine hesychasm*, London.

H. Dörries (1978), *Die Theologie des Makarios/Symeon*, Göttingen.

J. B. Dunlop (1978), *Starets Amurosy*, Oxford.

I. Gorainoff (1979), *Seraphim de Sarov*, Paris.

A. Guillaumont (1979), *Aux origines du monachisme chrétien*, SpOr 30, 67–212.

B. Krivochéine (1980), *Dans la lumière du Christ: Saint Syméon le Nouveau Théologien*, Chèvetogne.

J. Gouillard (1981), *La vie religieuse à Byzance*, London.

D. Staniloaë (1981), *Prière de Jésus et expérience du Saint-Esprit*, Paris.

J. Meyendorff (1983), *Byzantine Theology*, 2nd Ed., New York.

B. Fraigneau-Julien (1985), *Les sens spirituels et la vision de Dieu selon Syméon le Nouveau Théologien*, ThH 67, Paris.

P. Deseille (1986), *L'Évangile au désert*, Paris.

T. Spidlik (1988), *La spiritualité de l'Orient chrétien*, OCA 206 and 230, Rome.

O. Clément, J. Serr (1989), *La Prière du cœur*, 2nd Ed., SpOr 6 b.

P. Miquel (1989), *Le vocabulaire de l'expérience spirituelle dans la patristique grecque*, ThH 86, Paris.

B. Bobrinskoy (1992), *Communion du Saint-Esprit*, SpOr 56.

K. Papoulidès (1993), *Hagioreitika*, Mount Athos.

JEAN-FRANÇOIS COLOSIMO

See also **Experience; Gregory of Palamas; Knowledge, Divine; Monasticism; Negative Theology**

Hexapla. *See* **Translations of the Bible, Ancient**

Hierarchy

In canon law* the word "hierarchy" (from the Greek *hieros*, "sacred," and *arkhè*, "origin," "domination") designates a religious structure characterized and determined by a power of transcendent origin. This kind of structure comes about only in a context in which essential theological decisions are constantly needing to be made. In a religion of the Law* or of the Book*, for example, where the principal concern is to interpret established principles, there can be no hierarchy. This is why hierarchy is a typically Christian phenomenon.

a) Development of Hierarchy in Christianity. The concept of hierarchy is not found in the New Testament, although it does present distinctions of rank among the associates of Jesus* (the primacy of "the Twelve," the special role of Peter*) and among the post-Easter communities (the authority of Paul, the gradation of ministries [1 Cor 12:28], emphasis on the role of the *episkopos*). It was out of these distinctions that there arose in the second century the ministerial triad (bishop*-presbyter*-deacon*). Pseudo-Dionysius* was probably the first to apply the term "hierarchy" to church structures*, by establishing an analogy between the threefold heavenly order and the ternary organization of the church* on earth. In this instance, hierarchy was a speculative category making it possible to interpret the order of salvation* (*see Cael. Hier.* 3. 1). With the development of canonical ecclesiology* in the 12th century, the church was characterized as a society* *(societas perfecta)* comparable to a political community, made up of unequal classes—clergy and laity*—the various functions of which determined in turn further differences in rank. For this reason, and also because of the importance of the clergy for the church as a whole, hierarchy became a central canonical concept. However, it presupposes a sacramental order (ministry*), so that it is encountered (in theory and in practice) only in Christian confessions that have such an order (the Catholic Church, the Orthodox churches, the Anglican Communion). While the churches that came out of the Reformation do also ordain their ministers, because of their doctrine of universal priesthood* the ministry has only a functional role.

b) Catholic Position up to the Second Vatican Council. Early on, bishops (as true holders of the ministry) received upon ordination* full power (potestas sacra) over a particular local* church (relative ordination). In the 12th century the idea emerged that ecclesial power contains two elements, one resulting from ordination (potestas ordinis) and the other from jurisdiction* over a particular church (potestas iurisdictionis). The power of ordination is gradually conferred by the sacrament* of ordination (deacon, priest*, bishop) and determines the hierarchy of the clerical order. The power of jurisdiction is attached to the ministries of the pope* and the bishop, falling to the former by the acceptance of his position and to the latter by his appointment. All other responsibilities are derived from one of these two hierarchical degrees. The pope thereby possesses primacy in matters of jurisdiction, but not in matters of ordination. Strictly speaking, the two elements should be linked in such a way that only an ordained minister would also have the power of jurisdiction. But in practice this principle is not respected at the present time (CIC of 1983, can. 129, following which the potestas regiminis falls to ordained ministers, while the laity* have the right to participate in the exercitum potestatis). Even today the fundamental solidarity of these two elements is evident in the fact that the hierarchical order is attributed to "divine right" (can. 330–31, 375, 1008). But because the church understands itself essentially on the basis of the idea that the community of believers makes up the people* of God, and also because relative ordination still defines hierarchy in relation to a particular community, hierarchical absolutism has never taken root. This is clearly highlighted in the doctrine of the sensus* fidei and the sensus fidelium, in the place of scientific theology*, and in reflections on reception*.

c) Vatican II and Current Law of the Catholic Church. Vatican* II attempted to combine the medieval model of the church as "society" with the concept of communio developed in the early church. This led to a reevaluation of the functions of the bishop, the local churches, and the laity. The concept of communio hierarchica made it possible to link the two approaches (LG 21). Particular emphasis was placed on the absolute bond between the church and the Pope (LG 22; nota praevia 3). The distinction between sacramental ordination and canonical mission was maintained by emphasizing the latter. In the CIC (Codex Iuris Canonici) the hierarchical structure is presented in the following manner: The pope holds supreme power—plenary, direct, regular, and universal power, that he may exercise freely at any time—in the legislative, executive, judicial, and doctrinal domains; and doctrinally he possesses infallibility when he speaks ex cathedra. The episcopal college, led by the pope, shares this full and supreme power in the official acts of its members, whether they are scattered around the world or meeting in an ecumenical council*. In addition there are certain organs common to the church as a whole: the synod* of bishops, the college of cardinals, the Roman curia, papal legates, and apostolic nuncios. The CIC of 1983 does not contain the noun hierarchia, but only the adjective hierarchicus, associated with the terms "structure," "constitution," "community," "recourse," and "superiors."

● Canon Law Texts.
R. F. Hathaway (1969), Hierarchy and the Definition of Order in the Letters of Ps.-Dionysius, The Hague.
H. Dombois (1971), Hierarchie, Freiburg-Basel-Vienna.
P. Krämer (1973), Dienst und Vollmacht in der Kirche, Trier.
H. Patee (1973), Hierarchy Theory, New York.
E. Schillebeeckx (1988), Das geistliche Amt, Düsseldorf.
G. O. Daly (1989), "Hiérarchie," RAC 15, 42–74.
P. Eicher, "Hiérarchie," NHThG2 2, 330–49.
G. Muselli (1992), Storia del diritto canonico, Turin.

WOLFGANG BEINERT

See also **Authority; Church and State; Communion; Government, Church; Indefectibility of the Church; Infallibility**

Hilary of Poitiers

?–died c. 366–368

Between the years 350 and 360, Hilary, Bishop* of Poitiers, was one of the most skilled spokesmen for the pro-Nicaean West. Except for his relations with Martin of Tours, whose monastic plans he favored, our knowledge of his life, based on the documentation at our disposal today, is contained in his works, almost all of which were inspired by his stance in favor of the Nicaean Creed. Although Hilary did not have the gift for speculative virtuosity of his exact contemporary Marius Victorinus, nonetheless, his works established him as an exegetist of absolutely first-rate abilities, well qualified to develop a biblical* theology of rare scope.

a) Brilliant Exegetist. The earliest of Hilary's works to have come down to us, a commentary on Matthew, already shows signs of his great hermeneutic agility in allegorical interpretation of the Gospels*. Because the allegorical method was rare in Western Christendom, Hilary's use of it proves the independent circulation of Origen's principles of exegesis*—apart from Hilary's personal knowledge of that master of Alexandria's treatises. Hilary's scrupulous regard for method, his careful implementation of the most coherent system possible for deciphering the Scriptures, was allied to his very uncommon purpose at this time, to propound a unitarian reading of the texts of the Gospels.

By means of a very Irenaean grasp of the whole plan of the history of salvation*, Hilary was intent on interpreting all the deeds and sayings concerning the life of Christ*, while preserving throughout their literal meaning, as forecasts of their later consequences—such as the incredulity of the Jews, the communication of the Good News to the Gentiles, and the growth of the church*. The annotations of doctrinal character that punctuate his work clearly reveal Hilary's debt to Tertullian* and Novatian—and, whenever the commentary touches on ecclesiology*, to Cyprian*, too. The first hints of an anti-Arian polemic can also be discerned in this work.

b) A Nicaean Astride East and West. A victim of the policy of bringing the Western episcopacy into line, a policy directed by Constantius II (an emperor concerned with safeguarding the empire's religious unity, founded on an expression of faith* hostile to the Nicaean Creed), and a policy enforced in the Gauls by Saturninus, Bishop of Arles, Hilary was exiled to Asia Minor in 356. His four-year-long stay in the East not only enabled him to discover the wealth of Eastern spiritual and theological exegetical tradition*—his works, *Tractatus super Psalmas* and a *Tractatus Mysteriorum,* no doubt composed when he returned from exile, show Origen*'s renewed influence on him. But his exile also allowed him to get to know at first hand the main documents in the Arian controversy, such as the *Epistle from Arius to Alexander of Alexandria* and certain confessions of faith from the anti-Nicaean synods, while he admitted to having discovered the Nicaean Creed only a short time before his banishment (*De synodis* 91).

More than any other Westerner, Hilary concerned himself with evaluating the complexity of the Eastern theologico-political field at a point in time when this domain, with the explosion of the anti-Nicaean front, was undergoing profound evolutions and reconstructions. Through this interest, he made close contacts with the chief representatives of the Homoiousian Movement. Members of this movement balked at the concept of *homoousios* (consubstantiation*) and claimed that the Son was not of the same substance as the Father, but merely of a similar substance (*homoiousios*). At the same time, these homoiousians remained just as vigorously opposed to both the radical Arianism of an Aetius or an Eudoxus as to the homoiousianism promoted by Valens of Mursa and Ursacius of Singidunum at the Council of Sirmium in 357.

In this context, Hilary saw the necessity of considerably modifying the schematic and oversimplistic view, largely derived from that of Athanasius of Alexandria, that the badly informed Westerners held of the Arian crisis and the theological positions of its various protagonists. In Hilary's eyes, all the adversaries of *homoousios* were not necessarily Arians, and the Nicaeans ought to try to seek agreement with these anti-Nicaean anti-Arians at a crucial moment in the Arian crisis (the meetings of the two Councils* of Rimini and of Seleucia had just been announced). He thus proposed himself as a sort of mediator (*De synodis* 7) between the two circles of influence, and it was to this purpose that at the end of 358 or the beginning of 359 he addressed to the bishops of Gaul and of Brittany, some of whom had consulted him, a treatise-epistle, the *De synodis,* in which he tried to demonstrate the significant conformity concealed beneath the terminological disagreement between the *Homoiousian* and *Homoousian* theses.

In the first part (*De synodis* §1–65), Hilary stressed the Homoiousian rejection of the "Blasphemy of Sirmium" of 357 (a commentary on the anathemas of the Synod that Basil of Ancyra had convened in 358 for this purpose) in order to bring about an examination of the confessions of faith to which this group subscribed: Antioch—351, Sardis—343, Sirmium—351. No doubt Hilary had already begun to apply such a method for the collation of a dossier of historico-dogmatic *testimonia* in a work of which only fragments are extant today, published under the title *Collectanea antariana parisina,* whose stages of composition are obscure. He deliberately exploited the lack of mention or imprecision with regard to the key points of the controversy, which these different creeds contained, as well as their repeated condemnations of radical Arianism, and he claimed to extract from them a Trinitary theology* in conformity with the Nicaean canons. Hilary's acuity deserves a passing mention: he was one of the first of only a few Westerners to perceive (*De synodis* §32) that the Latin term *substantia* can be translated just as well by *ousia* as by *hupostasis,* the Greek terms understood respectively as the unity of substance and the distinction of the Persons*.

In a second section (*De synodis* §66–92), he compared *homoousios* and *homoiousios* in order to show the equivalence of the two terms. Although he was under no illusions about the difficulties of the enterprise and the resistance it aroused in both parties to the dispute—the work included an address to the Homoiousian bishops—he attempted nonetheless to provide an Homoousian exegesis of *homoiousios,* in the framework of a homology between *similitudo* (similarity) and *aequalitas* (equivalence).

In the short run, Hilary's efforts were fruitless, or almost so. The Homoiousian positions were victorious finally at the Councils of Rimini and Seleucia (359). Moreover, Hilary's negotiations with Constantius II, thanks to his coming to Constantinople in 360, ended in failure, as seen in *Ad Constantium* and *In Constantium.* Lucifer of Cagliari and other radical Nicaeans accused Hilary of betrayal. As for Athanasius, in the *Peri sunodôn,* which he composed between 359 and 361, he cast the confessions of faith dear to the Homoiousians into the abyss of Arianism. Although

Athanasius might have borrowed the title of his work from Hilary, he never mentioned him in any of his writings. Hilary's success was therefore confined to Gaul above all. His influence on the synodal decree of the Council of Paris of 360–61, addressed to some Eastern bishops, is patent.

In 364–65, together with Eusebius of Verceil, Hilary failed in an attempt to oust the Homoiousian Auxentius from the See of Milan *(see Contra Auxentium).* Deeply conscious of his duties as a pastor*, Hilary was one of the first in the West to compose anti-Arian hymns, of which only fragments survive. His most lasting contribution is a great work, probably elaborated in its entirety in the East, the *De Trinitate,* to borrow the title given to this work since the sixth century, which demonstrates clearly the fruits of his Eastern exile.

c) Doctrinal Modifications and a New Style of Nicaean Theology. *De Trinitate,* an imposing treatise in 12 books written in an often difficult language, is not a general survey of theology drawn up according to a prearranged plan from its beginnings (*see* M. Simonetti's *Note sul commento a Matteo de Ilario di Poitiers,* 1964). It is a work of exceptional scope for the Nicaean West, and it leads progressively to the refutation of the Arianizing theses and their defenses, not without recapitulations, digressions, or anticipations, and it presents a very specific defense and demonstration of the Nicaean position. The rejection of technical argumentation, which was largely indebted to the philosophical field, in favor of a lavish biblical theology is coupled to very meaningful lexical choices. The Nicaean term *homoousios* is hardly mentioned, consistent with the reticence that is clearly evident in his other work of this period, *De synodis.* Contrary to Athanasius, Marius Victorinus, and Gregory of Elvira, Hilary thought that without a gloss, this term, just like *homoiousios,* was open to a "heretical" as well as an "orthodox" interpretation (*De synodis* 70–71). That is because his contact with the Homoiousians had given him a "strong anti-Sabellian outlook" (Simonetti) that made him condemn not only Photinus but also Marcel of Ancyra (*De Trinitate* VII:3).

Henceforth, Hilary constantly avoided all traditional analogies* that sought to explain the relations of the Father* and the Son, such as root/plant, source/stream, or fire/flame (*De Trinitate* IX:37). Moreover, he was keenly aware of the inadequacy of human language when speaking of God* (*De Trinitate* IV:14 and X:67), and his arguments spring above all from exegesis, especially of the Johannine writings. All the same, he did not abandon the theological tradition inaugurated by Tertullian and Novation. Rather, he used this tradition copiously to demonstrate, at one and the same time, the unity and the plurality of God (natura/persona), as well as the copresence of two centers of distinct characteristics in Jesus Christ*. However, he was not its slave; he abandoned the Tertullian doctrine of the corporeity of the soul*; he also developed an original doctrine (but one not exempt from Docetic traits) of the celestial body of Christ (De Trinitate X:14f.).

Despite the title under which his work is known, Hilary gave very limited space to the Holy* Spirit, which he considered to be a gift and which he never described as a persona. His whole effort was bent on showing, in the Father and the Son, that total copenetration of being, of action, and of will that their origin clearly distinguished, since the Father had engendered and the Son was engendered.

Augustine* would later recall this first attempt, which was created as a global confrontation of the most profound doctrinal issues of the Arian crisis, an attempt of which his commentary on Psalm 138 gives a synthesis.

● E. Dekkers (1995), Clavis Patrum Latinorum, 3rd Ed., Turnhout, no. 427–72.
Tractatus mysteriorum (SC 19 bis); Tractatus super Psalmos (CSEL 22), incl. Tract. sup. Ps CXVIII (SC 354 and 357); In Matthaeum (SC 254 and 258); De Trinitate (CChr.SL 62–62A); De synodis (PL X, 479–546, and TU 133, 539–47); Collectanea antiariana parisina (CSEL 65, 43–193); Liber II ad Constantium (CSEL 65, 193–205); Liber in Constantium (SC 334); Contra Auxentium (PL X, 609–18); Hymni III e cod. Aretino (CSEL 65, 209–16).
♦ P. Smulders (1944), La doctrine trinitaire de saint Hilaire de Poitiers, Rome.
A. Fierro (1964), Sobre la gloria en San Hilario, Rome.
M. Simonetti (1964), "Note sul commento a Matteo di Ilario di Poitiers," VetChr 1, 35–64; (1965), "Note sulla struttura e la cronologia del 'De Trinitate' di Ilario di Poitiers," Studi Urbinati 39/1, 274–300.
C. F. A. Borchardt (1966), Hilary of Poitiers' Role in the Arian Struggle, The Hague.
Ch. Kannengiesser (1968), "L'héritage d'Hilaire de Poitiers," RSR 56, 435–56.
Coll. (1969), Hilaire et son temps: Actes du Colloque de Poitiers à l'occasion du XVIe centenaire de la mort de saint Hilaire, Paris.
Ch. Kannengiesser (1969), "Hilaire de Poitiers," DSp 7/1, 466–99.
J. Doignon (1971), Hilaire de Poitiers avant l'exil, Paris.
C. Moreschini (1975), "Il linguaggio teologico di Ilario di Poitiers," La Scuola Cattolica 103, 339–75.
M. Simonetti (1975), La crisi ariana nel IV secolo, Rome.
L. F. Ladaria (1977), El Espíritu Santo en San Hilario de Poitiers, Madrid.
G. M. Newlands (1978), Hilary of Poitiers: A Study in Theological Method, Bern.
A. Grillmeier (1979), Jesus der Christus im Glauben der Kirche, I: Von der apostolischen Zeit bis zum Konzil von Chalkedon, Freiburg-Basel-Vienna, 451, (2nd Ed. 1990).
P. C. Burns (1981), The Christology in Hilary of Poitiers' Commentary on Matthew, Rome.
E. P. Meijering (1982), Hilary of Poitiers on the Trinity, De Trinitate, 1, 1–19, 2, 3, Leyden.
M. Figura (1984), Das Kirchenverständnis des Hilarius von Poitiers, Freiburg.
M. Simonetti (1985), Lettera e/o allegoria: Un contributo alla storia dell'esegesi patristica, Rome.
M. Simonetti (1986), "Hilaire de Poitiers," Initiation aux Pères de l'Église, IV: Les Pères latins, Ed. A. Di Berardino.
M. Durst (1987), Die Eschatologie des Hilarius von Poitiers: Ein Beitrag zur Dogmengeschichte des IV. Jhdts, Bonn.
R. C. P. Hanson (1988), The Search for the Christian Doctrine of God: The Arian Controversy, Edinburgh, 318–81.
J. Doignon (1993), "Hilaire de Poitiers," in Nouvelle histoire de la littérature latine, Ed. R. Herzog and P. Lebrecht Schmidt, vol. 5, Turnhout, §582, 503–37.
Coll. (1995), Biblia Patristica, vol. 6, Strasbourg.
P. Smulders (1995), Hilary of Poitiers' Preface to His Opus historicum: Translation and Commentary, Leyden.

MICHEL-YVES PERRIN

See also **Arianism; Athanasius of Alexandria; Trinity**

Hirscher, Johann Baptist von. *See* **Tübingen, Schools of**

History

Two things are to be understood by history: a scientific discipline (the "investigation," Greek *historia* [references in Winkelmann 1991] of mankind's past) and the overall object of this discipline ("that which has taken place," "that which has happened," insofar as it has involved people). The quality of being "historical" is consequently attributed both to texts—to "history books"—and to facts or events—"historical events": a double meaning that inevitably gives rise to ambiguities and calls for lexical clarifications. It might be added that the proper object of historical research (*see* A below) is the past, but that the philosophy and theology of history (*see* B below) generally permit themselves to consider history as a totality encompassing past, present, and future. Lastly, for the historical method and its employment in the interpretation of the New Testament corpus, see in the first instance Hengel 1979.

A. Historical Knowledge

Although prefigured elsewhere in the form of *annals* or *chronicles,* history originated in Greece, where it acquired the dual vocation of literary work (there could be no historian without the art of writing) and strict cognitive process. It was nonetheless in the modern period that it assumed its canonical form; and once the 16th century had made possible the advent of modern science and endowed it with statutes (Bacon), it took the greatest possible share of those enviable statutes. The subject matter of history, whether "fact" or "event," certainly has the capacity to perplex the historian (and especially the philosopher!). It is evident, simply by definition, that the past no longer exists, that it no longer has being other than in the traces, monuments, archives, and memories that it has left. The significance of a paradox advanced by Wittgenstein* may be understood in this light: all our archives and all our memories together do not prove that the world, and we ourselves, have existed for more than a day or two, since a perverse creator could well have made everything two days ago, including in his creation* everything that we take as proof that there has been a past. How then are we to speak of the past, when any interaction with it is forbidden, when experience (in the scientific sense) is only ever possible in the element of the present, when we always require a kind of "core of belief," in the Husserlian sense, in order to ascribe to a text, building, and so forth the status of a vestige or monument? The answer, which enables us to offer a solution to Wittgenstein's paradox and at the same time to specify the method that should be used in history, consists of an appeal to the idea of *witness.* Just as "exact" science, according to Bacon, is a matter of "making nature* talk" in the same way that in the process of law a suspect is made to talk, so texts and archives, insofar as they are accorded the status of witnesses (and common sense leads us to acknowledge that among all the objects of the present there are some that are the remains of the past), may be forced to tell the truth*. This insistence has a name: criticism. The aim of criticism is to understand the evidence (to speak the language that the witness speaks, to know what literary genre he or she is employing, and first of all to establish the exact text of the evidence, etc.) and to assign it a truth value without naïveté. Only facts or events that the historian acknowledges to be knowable to him through the mediation of trustworthy witnesses can have the status of "historical."

There remains one problem, however, that appears with growing insistence throughout the development of the historico-critical project: a witness is only trustworthy (a necessary though not a sufficient condition) if he or she gives evidence of a historical object that is accepted a priori to be possible. The existence of tales of miracles, as Hume remarked and Lessing reiterated, does not prove the existence of miracles. The critical standard for the past is revealed to the historian by the present—for where else could one be found? What is real at the present time reveals to him what may have been. The axiom upon which history is founded, as formulated by Troeltsch (1913), thus has every appearance of being indisputable: only things that could equally well happen today can aspire to the status of historical reality (event, speech, etc.). The past (and the future too, by the by) is expected to maintain a relationship of *analogy* with the present—a relationship in which similarity outweighs any dissimilarity. If, however, the question is asked what the present contains, man's modern, "scientific" ambitions lead necessarily (and tritely) to the conclusion that it contains *facts,* which we can try to deal with just as the "hard" sciences deal with the physical realities that fall within their domain. History does not claim to lay down the law on the level of existence proper to social, economic, or religious "facts," for example, but is content merely to record their existence. In so doing, however, it defines and establishes its subject matter: it is not the reality of the past, but that of the present, that dictates the meaning of "historical."

The consequences of such a problem need give no cause for alarm, provided that one is prepared to confront them head on. It is straightforwardly true, after all, that Troeltsch's axiom provides the starting point for any coherent ontology of the past, that "that which is" provides the most reliable criterion we have to interpret "that which is no longer." It is besides quite obvious that as far as what is concerned, the historian's starting point, because "scientific," is *secularized.* That which is—that which is in the factual order—includes neither the miracles, nor the wonders, nor the battles with giants, which are often the favorite ingredients of precritical ("premodern") narrative. That which is is defined as such in the context of a "vision of the world," our own, and within this framework some things exist and others do not. There are fairy stories; but a critical history of fairies would be no more than the history of a belief or superstition—it being understood that beliefs are historical objects just like any other.

One or two initial truths can thus be recognized: 1) The rules of what constitutes historical objects, to begin with, since they belong to science, to a "new science" (Vico) that appeared in the wake of the natural sciences*, are rules just as strictly atheistic as those of physics or chemistry, and displaying an atheism* just as strictly *methodological.* There is thus no unjust accusation to be leveled at what the critical historian has to say: he will never vouch for the reality of a miracle (whether worked by Jesus or by the spurious miracle worker Alexander of Abonuteichos, and whether recounted by the evangelist Mark or by Lucian of Samosata), for the good reason that his heuristic and hermeneutic principles deny that there can have been one; but the rationality of these principles prevents them from setting themselves up as absolutely right to the exclusion of any other correct statement. The critical historian can no more regard his statements as absolute than the physicist can make his theories absolute. Both would in fact jeopardize the scientific nature of their projects were they to lose sight of the axiomatic decisions that define their territory and their way of occupying that territory. 2) While history is competent only concerning historical matters, we should not be tempted to see it as devoted to a rather banal kind of positivism. Even that most spectacularly positivist of philosophers, Carnap (the architect of "logical positivism"), concluded his resolution of all philosophical *problems* by admitting the existence of *enigmas* (death*, evil*, etc.), which do not correspond to any scientific *question,* and which therefore do not call for a scientific *response,* but which must all the same be recognized to exist. The same goes for the historian. If he is naive, he will believe that nothing has existed that is not, ipso facto, a historical object—that "being historical" and "having been" are interchangeable. If he is less naive, he will say that the historical is merely historical, that "contingent historical truths" cannot be "proofs of the Spirit and strength" (Lessing, then Kierkegaard*; also Fichte, followed by Bultmann*, etc.), and that the important things—spiritual life, faith—begin by way of the leap that gives access to another territory. But why leap at all, if not because the past, even glimpsed within the limits of historicity pure and simple, also possesses a genuine and mysterious force—if not because the historical may also conceal more meaning, or more being, than its critical constitution assigns it a priori?

Epistemological common sense leads us here to a lexical distinction that has marked all the debates that have focused on the "historical Jesus*" and the "Christ* of faith," from M. Kähler (1896) to the *New Quest of the Historical Jesus* (Robinson 1959) and beyond: that between (in German) the *historisches* and the *geschichtliches*—one might say between the *historical* (as it has been defined on the basis of the historico-critical practice that constitutes it) and the *historial* (which may be defined, as generally as possible, as the flux of that which passes, that which has passed, and that which will pass, insofar as this flux is an object of human experience). Understood in terms of its more or less obvious meaning, the distinction expresses a refusal to authorize critical history to have the last word as to what has taken place. Taken positively, furthermore, it expresses a fruitful resolve to subject critical history to criticism. Such criticism, of course, must not end by stretching the links between the historical and the historical in such a way that the historical, in the eyes of the believer (and the theologian), ceases to appear as anything but a "factuality" immaterial to the logic of belief (Bultmann). Neither God* nor the miracles of Jesus nor his resurrection* are potential historical objects. Once it has done its round of the facts, history remains history; and if it encounters, for example, the mystery of an empty tomb, it cannot legitimately draw theological conclusions from it. Nevertheless, this distinction between the historial and the historical does not aim to support a gnosiological dualism, but rather to point out that the reality of the past goes beyond what history, as a science, can consider as absolutely certain. Because theology consists in the first instance of an act of *memory*, historical knowledge and theological knowledge are two ways of apprehending and interpreting the *same* reality. And while it is clear, in historical terms, that the past is accessible to whomever has eyes to see (and intelligence enough to assess the credibility* of the evidence), it is also clear, in theological terms, that the "eyes of faith" (Rousselot) see their object—the "image" or "face" of revelation* (Balthasar*)—only by being *passionate* for it (Kierkegaard) in a way that is either not truly "scientific" or else represents a scientific nature entirely of its own kind (e.g., T. F. Torrance).

Three codicils may be added. 1) History *(Historie)* itself has its history *(Geschichte)*, within which objects have at times lost their historical status, but within which the nonhistorical may also become historical. The extreme theoretical illustration of this is to be found in the fundamental* theology of Pannenberg, according to whom any historial reality and any theological object are candidates for inclusion in the class of historical realities. 2) A scrupulous definition of critical work, moreover, would also demand that one consider the use, within the writing of history, of a well-known epistemological principle, the "principle of charity" (in which any evidence is assumed to be innocent as long as its guilt has not been proved), and the tacit use of an opposite principle that could be called the "principle of suspicion" (any evidence is assumed to be guilty as long as its innocence has not been proved). 3) Finally, however much critical history is motivated by a desire for neutrality, the narratives it presents are still only theories, correct or incorrect, which reveal the theorist's viewpoint—his "tendencies"—as much and sometimes more than they reveal their subject. Some viewpoints are better than others; but in history just as in theology and indeed everywhere else, there is no "divine viewpoint" (H. Putnam).

● M. Kähler (1896), *Der sogennante historische Jesus und der geschichtliche, biblische Christus,* Leipzig (Rev. Ed. Munich, 1956).

E. Troeltsch (1913), "über historische und dogmatische Methode in der Theologie," *GS* 2, Tübingen, 729–53.

R. Carnap (1928), *Der logische Aufbau der Welt,* Vienna, 183 (Rev. Ed. Hamburg, 1998).

J. M. Robinson (1959), *A New Quest of the Historical Jesus,* London (Rev. Ed. Philadelphia, 1983).

A. C. Danto (1965), *Analytical Philosophy of History,* Cambridge.

F. P. Hager et al. (1974), "Geschichte, Historie," *HWP* 3, 344–98, "Geschichte/Historie," ibid., 398–99, "Geshichtlichkeit," ibid., 404–08, "Historik, ars historica," ibid., 1132–37.

M. Hengel (1979), "Historical Method and the Theological Interpretation of the New Testament," in *Acts and the History of Earliest Christianity,* London, 129–36 (*Zur urchristlichen Geschichtschreibung,* Stuttgart, 1979).

G. Lanczkowski et al. (1984), "Geschichte, Geschichtschreibung, Geschichtsphilosophie," *TRE* 12, 569–698 (bibl.).

J. Pelikan (1989), *The Christian Tradition,* 5: *Christian Doctrine and Modern Culture,* Chicago, 60–117 and 230–81.

S. Auroux (1990), "Histoire (épistémologie de l')," *LNPh* 1, 1151–52 (bibl.).

F. Winkelman (1991), "Historiographie," *RAC* 15, 724–65.

B. Theology of History

a) Biblical Theology. The theology* of history begins with the experience* of Israel*. It is the experience of a past perceived as the gift of order and finality: man lives in a creation*, within which a logic of choice* and salvation* governs the destiny of the people. It is the experience of a present structured by divine law* and the Covenant*, and in which the liturgy* serves as a perpetual reminder of God*'s great deeds *(ma'asey elohim)*. Finally, it is an experience directed toward an absolute future: the Covenant is sustained by divine promises* compelling a hope* of which prophecy*, messianism*, and apocalyptic* literature serve as reminders. Onto a cyclical experience of time*, marked out in religious terms by agrarian rituals, a linear temporality is superimposed whose divine origin ensures its intelligibility and continuity. A transcendent scheme of definitive peace* and salvation remain at work within the violent contingencies of human action, or simply in the succession of the generations *(toldoth)*.

In the New Testament, a language of fulfillment—of imminent fulfillment, moreover—takes the place of the language of promise. Not only does Jesus*' preaching* announce the extreme proximity of the Kingdom of God (Mt 3:17, etc.), not only is Jesus presented as him in whom Israel's expectations and Scriptures* are fulfilled (Mt 1:22, Mk 14:49, Lk 4:21, Jn 12:38, etc.), but his recognition as the Messiah* obliges us to accord his mission a strictly eschatological sense. Israel's history has reached its conclusion; and since this history is biblically inseparable from the history of all nations, the "fullness of time" (Gal 4:4) may be regarded as the end of history itself. Primitive Christianity was aware that it had arisen from a history, and that a new era was beginning with it; and it neither knew nor believed itself to be charged with any other mission than to call people to conversion* while awaiting the imminent return (the Parousia*) of the risen Messiah. The idea that the church* could have a history was not absent from the primitive Christian consciousness, whether the sense of this history resided in the mission* to the pagans (Paul, Luke) or was based on the "patience" of God, who allowed an extended time for this conversion (2 Pt 3:8f.). The first church appears furthermore to have been a structured community, not an enthusiastic sect incapable of surviving a delay in the Parousia. At any event, there was one key feature: the reality of this continuing history was only temporary. Whether the history of the world would continue after the world's salvation had been accomplished undoubtedly represented a major theological problem. At the end of the apostolic age, the problem was resolved in practical terms. But the New Testament clearly offers no more than the first rudiments of a theology of history for the use of believers for whom the future is no longer charged with any promise of salvation or revelation*.

b) History of the Church and the City of God. A radical refusal of the world and of history is one of the essential characteristics of gnosis*, and the Christian refusal of gnosticism reveals among other things an alliance between Christianity and history—retrospectively in Israel's experience, and prospectively in that of the church, history is subject to the benevolent government of divine providence*. There is admittedly an "eschatological impatience" (which would recur periodically) to be seen in numerous patristic texts. The deadline allotted to history was a short one—Lactantius still expected the world to end in 500. Millenarianism*, moreover, expressed dissatisfaction with the present conditions of historical existence by hoping for a history to come (a "millennium") in which Christ* would reign visibly in the world. The future belonged to other lines of thought, however. For Irenaeus* (despite his millenarian sympathies) a theology of tradition* and eschatological recapitulation *(anakephalaiôsis)* made it possible to ensure the conditions both of the church's perpetual fidelity to its mission and of a fruitful historical development. Eusebius of Caesarea, for his part, considered the new position the church occupied in the Roman world after the conversion of Constantine. The Christianization of the empire, in this earliest of all Christian political* theologies, appears as the fulfillment of history. The triumph of the imperial monarchy and the triumph of monotheism* are two events linked by providence; and the concept of "evangelical preparation" makes possible a broad account of universal history in which everything culminates in the dual, and unique, offer to mankind of the *pax romana* and the *pax christiana*.

Byzantine theology would retain Eusebius's overall scheme, and it reappeared without fail in Latin theology every time a secular power claimed to be the church's providential protector. The most confusing theological critique, however, arose as early as the fifth century. In 410, the sack of Rome* by Alaric marked the end of the *pax romana*. For Orosius, a disciple of Augustine*, this conclusion played out without any great drama marked a transition: the empire's civilizing mission was now inherited by the church. For Augustine, who wrote his *City of God* between 412 and 426, the death of the western empire was the occasion for an all-encompassing interpretation of history, which recognized that civilizations were mortal, and drew the appropriate lessons from this. History, in fact, was twofold: the history of the "City* of God," beginning with Abel, and the history of the "earthly city" beginning with Cain. Since Christ's coming, humanity had been living out the world's last age (the sixth), whose duration was unimportant. During this age, as during the previous ones, the City of God existed in the world in the form of the "pilgrimage*" *(peregrinatio)*, without undergoing any progress, always endowed with the same love* of God, visible in the church without being identified with the visible church, the two cities never ceasing all the while to be "interlinked" and "intimately mingled" (*Civ. Dei* I, 35). The details of universal history therefore ceased to be important. History was no longer any more than the arena in which "the two loves who have built the two cities" confronted one another. The theological significance of universal history was merely to accommodate that confrontation, which therefore manifested itself in every locus of experience. Providence could place a civilization at the service of the City of God—but civilizations themselves, and their histories, were mere secular realities.

While still accorded lip service, Augustine's theology of history was gradually overshadowed during the Middle Ages as attention came to be seized by the church's visible successes: so Otto of Freising concluded his *Historia de duabus civitatibus* (1147) with the observation that the two cities now formed just one, which was the church. The Middle Ages, moreover, witnessed the rise of the unprecedented theories (Lubac* 1978) of Joachim* of Fiore: the idea of an imminent Age of the Spirit, which would follow the Age of the Father* (the Old Testament) and the age of the Son; the idea of a monastic and ascetic church taking over from a church of the clergy (from the *ordo clericorum*); and the idea of an "eternal Gospel" of which the present time was still unaware—later taken up by the "Spiritual Franciscans" and destined to have a considerable following. Joachim was refuted by Thomas* Aquinas, and his historical preoccupations (and those of the Spiritual Franciscans) received an even more trenchant response from Bonaventure*. Leaving aside this major debate, however, the interest of the Middle Ages in history was slight, and their interest in a theological theory of history almost nonexistent. Authors such as Gehroh of Reichersberg, Honorius "of Autun" (c. 1080–c. 1156), Hugh of Saint-Victor (†1141), Rupert of Deutz (c. 1070–1129), Anselm of Havelberg (†1158), or Hildegard of Bingen (1098–1179) produced a symbolist and typological interpretation of history (both biblical and universal) that deserves attention—but Scholasticism* would follow other paths.

Augustinian nuances were to return with insistence in the theological polemics of the Reformation, whether it was a matter of rejecting the visible church's pretensions actually to be the Kingdom* of God or of maintaining, as in the radical theology of S. Franck (1499–1542), that the true church had never existed except as an "invisible diaspora." From Augustine to Luther*, or Catholicism*'s apologies against the Reformation (e.g., in the writings of C. Baronius [1538–1607]), one fact in any event remains constant: when history does appear, it appears first and foremost as a theological object; secular history only deserves mention by virtue of the theological services it renders or does not render to the church.

c) *History, Secularism, Philosophy.* It may be said that one and the same period, the 16th century, witnessed the birth of a scientific history of the church and saw history lose its status as a uniquely theological subject. Modernity arose, crucially, by secularizing history. According to J. Bodin (1529–96) the *historia divina* coexisted in principle with a *historia naturalis* and a *historia humana,* but it was the latter, stripped of any theological impulse, that would henceforth attract all the attention. Christological and soteriological meanings were not denied; nonetheless the emphasis passed to a future, which they did not really determine, and which, it was accepted, had been committed into man's hands. Conversely, I. de la Peyrère's (1594–1676) speculations concerning the "Preadamites" extended history to encompass a prebiblical past. In 1681 Bossuet was still able to propose a biblical interpretation of history as governed by providence and leading to the triumph of the church. But the view expressed by Lord Bolingbroke (1678–1751) when he stated "man is the subject of all history" would come to dominate.

In 1735 G. B. Vico (1668–1744) published the first edition of his *Scienza nuova;* in 1765 Voltaire coined the expression "philosophy of history." Vico was a Christian and Voltaire a deist; nonetheless their affinities are stronger than their dissimilarities. Seeking an unshakable foundation on which to base his "new science," Vico had in effect concluded that truth and fact (what man does) were interchangeable; and while he spoke of a divine providence that had given mankind history, and controlled it in a purely immanent manner, in practice nothing distinguished this immanent government from the merely initial responsibility exercised over humanity by Voltaire's God. In the ascents and descents *(corsi e ricorsi)* that according to Vico constituted the original rhythm of history, biblical events did not enjoy any privileged position—and from here it is easy to progress to Voltaire's idea of a history of civilizations in which biblical experience, compared, for example, to the wisdom of the Chinese, is seen as no more than a case of sheer barbarism.

During the Enlightenment theological motifs did not altogether disappear from the newly constituted philosophy of history. G. E. Lessing (1729–81) established a positive connection between reason* and revelation in the "education of the human race"; J. G. Herder (1744–1803) spoke of man producing history because he had received the "divine gift of reason." These motifs tended nonetheless to fade into the background in a process in which the idea of progress secularized the concepts of providence and salvation. Rousseau (who was not a proponent of progress) was certainly the first to offer an entirely secular interpretation of history. The Voltairean undertones, meanwhile, became more pronounced in the progressive visions of Turgot (1727–81) and Condorcet (1743–94): "The triumph of Christianity," wrote the latter, "was the signal for the complete decay both of the sciences and of philosophy" (*Esquisse d'un tableau historique des progrès de l'esprit humain,* Paris, 1795). And while

Lessing played an important part in the history of theology, this was largely because he believed and stated that eternal beatitude* could not be based on "contingent historical truths."

The theology of history was however to be revived within philosophy itself. In 1799 Novalis (1722–1801), in the context of a romantic rehabilitation of the Middle Ages, declared that "all history is Gospel"—an approach continued by F. Schlegel (1772–1829). As early as 1800, Schelling* put forward the concept of a history impelled by the manifestation of the Absolute: Hegel*, too, was to view history in these terms. Catholic traditionalism* and the Catholic school of Tübingen* echoed these reassessments, each in its own way. According to J.S. von Drey (1777–1853), at the root of universal history there was an innate revelation, which ensured its theological coherence; history appeared less as a human artifact than as a place of disclosure, and the condition by which that disclosure could reach all people. Schleiermacher*, though he employed a quite different theological axiomatics, also pondered the theological meaning of history, and saw the Spirit as "the ultimate force which constructs the world"; this appeal to the Spirit recurs in the work of J.T. Beck (1804–78) and F.A.G. Tholuck (1799–1877). Finally, the theologians of the school of Erlangen (G.C.A. von Harleß [1806–79], J.C.K. von Hofmann [1810–77], and F.H.R. von Frank [1827–94]), with their concept of the "history of salvation," *Heilsgeschichte,* provided the rallying-cry for all future theology of history.

The developments of historical criticism and its application to the sources of theology soon proved, however, that dogmatic assertions, even supported by the best philosophies of the time, were inadequate as a response to secularizing currents of thought. And while it is true that the Hegelian right was unquestionably more faithful to Hegel's intentions, the 19th century nevertheless saw the victory of left-wing followers (most notably D.F. Strauss) whose historiography undermined the foundations of all theology of history. Marx* consolidated this victory by proposing a radical secularization* of history, along with an equally secularized eschatology*. Henceforth only the earthly city existed; and at the end of history (at its conclusion and at its goal) the only conceivable salvation was offered by the intervention of a messianic class, the proletariat, anointed not by God but by dialectical laws inherent in the world. It is ironic that atheism* thus seized control of theology's most distinctive possessions at a time that also witnessed the appearance, under the guise of liberal Protestantism* ("cultural" Protestantism), of a theology notable for being purged of any eschatological reference.

d) History of Salvation and Eschatological Meaning of the Christian Experience. The most substantial critic of Christianity was not Marx, however, but Nietzsche*. The difficulty of atheistic historicism resides in the production of theodicies without God (Löwith 1949; Marquard 1973); Nietzsche's assertion of the "eternal return of the same" leads the negation of the Christian God to its only totally coherent conclusion: if this God is dead, then history too must be dead. Perhaps it was no coincidence, then, that the period of most radical negation coincided theologically, more or less, with the reopening of a subject that had long been closed, but whose reexamination made possible a theological reconceptualization of history—biblical eschatology. The reconsideration of this topic, at the turn of the 20th century, led to a new awareness of the real theological problem of historical time. In 1892 and 1893, J. Weiss (1863–1914) and R. Kabisch (1868–1914) put Jesus' preaching back in the apocalyptic* context of an expectation of the end. In 1906 A. Schweitzer (1875–1965) maintained that the idea of a history that would survive Jesus was alien to Jesus' own "thoroughgoing" eschatology. In opposition to thoroughgoing [*see* above] eschatology, Heidegger*'s influence led Bultmann* to develop an "existential" eschatology, in which the "authentic" existence that faith* attained was ipso facto the end of history. In parallel to Bultmann (though without much systematic interest), C.H. Dodd (1884–1973) suggested an interpretation of Johannine* theology under the banner of "realized eschatology." These interpretations were counterbalanced by O. Cullmann's work on the proper theological basis of church time. The scientific conflict between these interpretations of eschatology ultimately led, moreover, to the observation that the New Testament does not offer a unified theology of the last days and of church time, but rather a multiplicity of tendencies (Conzelmann, Kümmel, Käsemann, etc.). Leaving aside a debate that cannot be regarded as finished, and leaving aside the denominational choices that often underlie it, it may at least be suggested that the main benefit of this debate is the fact that it draws attention incontestably to one fact: for a theology that is faithful to its *logos,* eschatology always comes first, and the historical is always meaningful by virtue of its relationship with it.

The restoration of eschatological meanings and the collapse of systematic philosophies of history have together led recent theology to structure itself basically as a new Augustinianism*. The original outline of the problem has certainly not disappeared. J. Moltmann's (1926–) theology of hope, for example, is presented as a revival of Joachimism provoked by a confrontation with Marx and the utopian Marxism of E. Bloch, in which the future ends by offering "a new paradigm of transcendence." Hegel's theological impact, within both Protestant (Pannenberg, 1928–) and Catholic (Fessard) theology, led to a conception of history as hardly more than the arena for the "peregrinations" of the City of God. However, the choice between a theology of "existence" that was ignorant of history and a theology of history, which obliged Christianity to await a City of God embodied in the earthly city, would be misleading. The Christian experience has its place, which is the church; and while no Christian denomination—Catholicism included—is (or could be) tempted any longer to write a history of the world culminating explicitly in the church's present successes, nevertheless the church's *missionary* relationship with the world imposes a conception of history (e.g., Danielou 1953) just as much as does its *ecumenical* relationship with itself in the context of a divided Christianity. While moreover contemporary Catholic theology likes to speak of the church as a "sacrament* of salvation" among the nations (e.g., Vatican* II, *LG* 48), these terms do not betray a religious introversion, but rather signal a revival of Irenaeus's theology of recapitulation—for example, in the work of Balthasar*—in what may be seen as a process of christological deduction and reduction of history.

e) An Extraordinary Work. Twentieth-century Catholicism owes to G. Fessard S.J. (1897–1978) a powerful and original contribution to the philosophy and theology of history. From 1934 to 1939 Fessard took part in the seminars on Hegel's *Phenomenology of the Spirit* conducted by A. Kojève at the *École Pratique des Hautes Études,* whose other participants included G. Bataille, J. Lacan, M. Merleau-Ponty, and R. Aron. He was one of the greatest French thinkers of his period to devote himself to political philosophy, which he did not separate from active political resistance to Nazi and Marxist totalitarianism. In his theoretical works, Fessard establishes a philosophy of history in which he distinguishes three levels—natural, human, and supernatural. In his analysis of historical processes, he accords preeminence to dialectics such as those between man and woman*, between Jew and pagan, and between master and servant (*see De l'actualité historique,* vol. 1, Paris, 1960). The existence of these dialectics does not deny Paul's assertion that in Christ "you, brothers, like Isaac, are children of promise" (Gal 3:28): rather it reveals that we are living at present in history and not in a fulfilled eschatology. The *eschaton* can thus be considered as an abolition of these dialectics, although it remains possible to use them in a Christian (pre-eschatological) way that attempts to free each one from its potential content of vi-

olence*. One of Fessard's original touches is the choice of a commentary on the *Spiritual Exercises* of Ignatius de Loyola (3 vols., Paris, 1956, 1966, Paris and Namur, 1984) as a framework for his greatest systematic work: by pointing out how all reality is structured around the spiritual choice, and by showing to what extent Ignatius's choice is modern, he offers a genealogy of the whole of modernity in outline. Fessard's followers included important thinkers such as A. Chapelle S.J. and C. Bruaire, and his influence was felt throughout a whole school of Hegelian studies (Leonard, Brito S.J.)—see the bibliography in G. Fessard, *Hegel, le christianisme et l'histoire,* Paris, 1990; see also *Le mystère de la société, recherches sur le sens de l'histoire,* Ed. M. Sales, Brussels, 1997.

f) Outlook. The *eschaton,* then, is *not* realized wherever man grasps that which defines him in theological terms: on the one hand because Christian hope is not primarily concerned with the absolute future of the individual, but with that of a people (e.g., Lubac 1938), and on the other hand because the believer is a sinner and a mortal, and because the present of his experience is always a *judged* present, lived out in the certainty of a pardon but never restored to complete innocence. Nonetheless the *eschaton* is not history's abstract hereafter, but its present theological secret. The *eschaton* is not only that to which history cannot give rise, it is not only the critical authority of history—it has a hold upon it already. And it is impossible to speak of that hold without appealing to practical reason.

History, taken in its most neutral modern sense, is the indefinite arena of human action. Theology may define this arena, assign it limits and a teleology—but only on condition that it no longer interprets history naively as a clear and distinct manifestation of divine benevolence (on condition that it refuses the possibility of a theodicy conceived in Leibniz*'s terms), but instead searches it for "signs" offered by a hidden God. Man, Luther said, is "God's disguise" (*WA* 15, 373). The spectacle of the world would nonetheless be a theologically unwholesome game if man were to forget that his primary role in history is that of an agent. The precise locus of the Christian experience is in the interval that separates the "world*" from the "Kingdom." Within this interval, the words of Barth are completely true: "God's judgment is the end of history; one drop of eternity* has more weight than the whole sea of things subject to time" (*Römerbrief,* 1922). But nobody can give himself over to the contemplation of this if he does not also refuse to leave the "earthly city" as the sole mistress of history. The eschatological meaning of the Christian experience would lose itself in an eschatological dream if the theology of history did not link Christianity's oldest requests ("Thy kingdom come," "May thy grace come, and the world pass"—*Didachè* X, 6) to the concrete demands of theological ethics* and political* theology.

• H. Thielicke (1935), *Geschichte und Existenz,* Gütersloh (2nd Ed. 1964).
C. H. Dodd (1936), *The Apostolic Preaching and Its Developments,* London.
H. de Lubac (1938), *Catholicisme: Les aspects sociaux du dogme,* Paris.
O. Cullmann (1946), *Christus und die Zeit: Die urchristliche Zeit- und Geschichtsauffassung,* Zürich (3rd Ed. 1962).
J. Taubes (1947), *Abendländische Eschatologie,* Bern.
K. Löwith (1949), *Meaning in History,* Chicago (*Weltgeschichte und Heilsgeschehen,* Stuttgart, 1953).
R. Niebuhr (1949), *Faith and History,* New York.
H. Conzelmann (1953), *Die Mitte der Zeit,* Tübingen.
J. Daniélou (1953), *Essai sur le mystère de l'h.,* Paris (2nd Ed. 1982).
R. Bultmann (1957), *History and Eschatology,* Edinburgh.
H. U. von Balthasar (1959), *Theologie der Geschichte, neue Fassung,* Einsiedeln.
J. Ratzinger (1959), *Die Geschichtstheologie des heiligen Bonaventura,* Munich-Zürich.
G. Fessard (1960), *De l'Actualité historique,* Paris, 2 vols.
E. Käsemann (1960, 1964), *Exegetische Versuche und Besinnungen,* Göttingen, 2 vols., New Ed. in 1 vol., 1970.
H. U. von Balthasar (1963), *Das Ganze im Fragment,* Einsiedeln.
J. Moltmann (1964), *Theologie der Hoffnung,* Munich (8th Ed. 1969).

M. Seckler (1964), *Das Heil in der Geschichte: Geschichtstheologisches Denken bei Thomas von Aquin,* Munich.
O. Cullmann (1965), *Heil als Geschichte,* Tübingen.
G. Jossa (1965), *La teologia della Storia nel Pensiere cristiano del secondo secolo,* Naples.
W. G. Kümmel (1965, 1978), *Heilsgeschehen und Geschichte,* Marbourg, 2 vols.
J. V. Langmead Casserley (1965), *Toward a Theology of History,* Oxford.
G. Sauter (1965), *Zukunft und Verheissung,* Zürich.
E. Heimann (1966), *Theologie der Geschichte,* Berlin.
W. Pannenberg (1967), "Heilsgeschehen und Geschichte," *Grundfr. syst. Th.,* Göttingen, 22–78.
H.-I. Marrou (1968), *Théologie de l'h.,* Paris.
F. Flückiger (1970), *Theologie der Geschichte,* Wuppertal.
R. A. Markus (1970), *Saeculum: History and Society in the Theology of St. Augustine,* Cambridge.
O. Marquard (1973), *Schwierigkeiten mit der Geschichtsphilosophie,* Frankfurt (2nd Ed. 1982).
F. P. Hager and G. Scholtz (1974), "Geschichte," *HWP* 3, 344–98.
H. de Lubac (1978, 1980), *La postérité spirituelle de Joachim de Flore,* Paris-Namur, 2 vols.
J. I. Saranyana (1979), *Joachin de Fiore y Tomas de Aquino,* Pamplona.
J.-Y. Lacoste (1990), *Note sur le temps,* Paris.
B. Forte (1991), *Teologia della storia,* Milan.
R. Schaeffler et al. (1995), "Geschichte," *LThK*3 4, 553–63.

JEAN-YVES LACOSTE

See also **Eschatology; History of the Church; Time**

History of the Church

For Christian theology*, the history* of the church* forms the focal point for ecclesiological questions, about the nature of the church; dogmatic questions, about the theology of the Incarnation*; and a discourse, often couched as a narrative and with an apologetic dimension, whereby its credibility in relation to the culture in which it is immersed is put at stake.

1. Chronological Landmarks

a) Antiquity. The expression "history of the church" acquires its meaning from the attempts of members of the Christian church to interpret their own religious destiny in the light of historical events. The Acts of the Apostles may be taken to be the first such attempt, although other New Testament texts are also marked by reflection on the meaning of human history and the impact of Christ's advent upon it.

In his *Historia ecclesiastica,* Eusebius of Caesarea (265–340) ranges from the birth of Jesus* to the year 323, presenting both a cosmological explanation—the church's struggle against the world* reproduces the struggle led by God* against Satan—and an apologetic justification: the church remains faithful despite persecutions and heresies. This vision of history became a model, which was adapted and expanded by Socrates the Scholastic (c. 380–c. 450), Sozomen (c. 400–43), and Theodoret of Cyrrhus (393–c. 460) in support of orthodoxy, while Philostorgius (368–c. 425) upheld the Arian point of view. Theodore the Lector (c.

525–?) and Evagrius Scholasticus (536–600) adopted the same perspective. In the 14th century, Nicephorus Callistus (†1350) wrote an ecclesiastical history that takes the narrative up to the early 10th century.

Within the Roman Church, Rufinus of Aquileia (c. 340–410) made an abridged translation of Eusebius's history, taking it up to the late fourth century. In his *Chronicle,* Jerome (c. 347–420) repeats the work of Eusebius and Rufinus; his book on the great men of the church was expanded by Gennadius (?–495) and Isidore of Seville (c. 570–636). In his *Historia sacra* (Sacred History), the Gallic priest Sulpicius Severus (c. 360–c. 420) reprises the history of the world from the Creation* and takes the history of the church up to the late fourth century. Cassiodorus (c. 480–c. 575) used the works of Socrates, Sozomen, and Theodoret as sources when composing his *Historia Ecclesiastica Tripartita*, which became a standard reference, alongside Eusebius's history, throughout the Middle Ages.

b) Middle Ages. These large-scale syntheses then gave way to local and national histories, which were often written by monks: for example, the *Historia Francorum,* in which Gregory of Tours (c. 538–c. 594) gives the principal dates in the history of the world, followed by the ecclesiastical history of the Gauls; or the *Historia Ecclesiastica Gentis Anglorum* (731) by Bede "The Venerable" (637–735), which begins with the conquest of Britain by Julius Caesar.

c) Humanism and the Reformation. The 16th century witnessed an extensive revival of Christian consciousness of history. On the one hand, humanism* promoted an awareness of the age of the documents on which historians worked, as demonstrated by Lorenzo Valla (1407–57) in relation to the forged "Donation of Constantine." On the other hand, the Reformation reopened the question of heresy*, and both Protestants and Catholics used the history of the church to establish their doctrinal legitimacy.

The approach adopted in the *Centuriators of Magdeburg,* published in Basel from 1559 to 1574 under the editorship of the Lutheran Flacius Illyricus (1520–75), resembles the apologetics of the historians of antiquity, but the struggle between the church and the world is presented differently: Satan has introduced himself into the church, engendering superstition and error, and the papacy is presented as the work of the Antichrist. Drawing on the papal archives, Cardinal Baronius (1538–1607) opposed the *Centuriators* with his *Annales ecclesiastici,* published in Rome* from 1588 to 1607. In both these cases, the history of the church was used as a weapon in confessional controversy.

Catholic authors followed the example set by Florimond de Raemond (†1602) and assimilated Protestantism* to the heresies of the past. Bossuet (1627–1704) and others claimed the dogmatic heritage of the Fathers* and the councils*, drawing a contrast between them and the variety of doctrines among Protestants. In the Protestant camp, authors such as Flacius or S. Goulart (1543–1628) sought to establish that authentic Christianity had always been professed by a minority that had been opposed to Rome ever since the time of the apostles. Other Protestants, such as J. Daillé (1594–1670), sought to prove that Protestant doctrine was in accordance with the teachings of the church fathers. In opposition to the Catholic affirmation of the unchanging persistence of the faith*, Protestants undertook critical interpretations of the origins of medieval Christianity.

d) From the 17th Century to the Enlightenment. Nevertheless, during the 17th century the history of the church was not entirely held captive by controversy, as witness the labors of the Maurists, who edited patristic texts, J. Hardouin (1646–1729), who edited the documents of the councils, and the Bollandists, who researched the lives of the saints; as well as the birth of diplomatics (Jean Mabillon [1632–1707]), and the emergence of a critical historical consciousness (Pierre Bayle [1647–1706]). The increase in the number of historiographic tools, which continued in the 18th century (S. Le Nain de Tillemont [1637–1698], J.-D. Mansi [1692–1769]), and the development of rigorous methodologies gradually led to the appearance of a history of dogmas*. The defense of orthodoxy was also called into question. Gottfried Arnold (1666–1714) devalued the importance of dogmatic disputes and displayed sympathy for heretics. J.L. von Mosheim (1694–1755) sought to analyze the church as if it was the same as any other society*, with a maximum degree of objectivity. Johann Salomo Semler (1725–91) placed a clear distance between himself and any dogmatic or confessional presuppositions, asserting that dogma, far from being immutable, is impermanent and fluid. This idea that the truth of dogmas is relative, depending on the epoch, was taken up again by A. Loisy (1857–1940) and within modernism*.

2. History of the Church and Theology Today

a) History as the Church's Understanding of Itself. The history of the church is conceived and practiced in terms of a tension—which sometimes becomes a contradiction—between the requirements of historical method and the expectations of theology. From the theological point of view, the history of the church is generally conceived as a part of Christian thought, a "theological locus" (Congar), an activity of ecclesiastical consciousness. Thus, the possessive form in the expression "history *of* the church" is not only objective but also subjective, since it is conceived as an effort at "self-understanding *[Selbstverständnis]* by the church" (H. Jedin), an effort that is legitimate and indispensable within a systematic framework fundamentally structured around the advent of God himself within human history.

However, this traditional conception creates certain problems. First, the history of the church also turns out to be its *lack* of self-understanding, given that any form of self-awareness can be illusory or misleading (É. Poulat). Second, to the extent that Christianity is characterized by conflicts over interpretation, whether they are exegetical, ecclesiological, dogmatic, or historiographic, it is preferable to speak of a *plurality* of forms of self-understanding. Finally, the scientific nature of historical inquiry depends, at least in part, on the capacity of historians to detach themselves from the object that they are studying.

b) History and Theology of History.   The history of the church appears, therefore, to be epistemologically ambiguous. On the one hand, it is heir to the discipline of theology, whose task is to conceive ecclesiology* as an expression of God's revelation* within history. On the other hand, however, it tends to be aligned with general methodologies of history, that is, with the view that it should be practiced independently of any presuppositions of belief. We may, of course, make a typological distinction between a history of the church, developed within the church, and forming part of its reflection on its identity and its role in the world, and a "history of Christianity," which addresses the question of the phenomenon of Christianity in history from an external position. Such a distinction is pertinent to the extent that it underlines the specific position of those church historians whose discourse, from the beginning of their research to the end, is related to theological reflection. It hardly affects the question of methodology, however, for in both cases history is constructed through the elaboration of hypotheses, and the ordering, handling, and cross-referencing of sources whose language historians refrain from reproducing (e.g., by repeating anathemas against heretics).

Moreover, the history of the church is no longer limited to the gathering of conciliar texts, heresiological or hagiographic catalogs, or dogmatic syntheses. It has been profoundly influenced by the renewal of approaches, methods, and topics within the discipline of history as a whole. It now seeks to diversify its domains of investigation and its sources; and it also seeks to integrate the domain of theological ideas and religious mentalities within the larger domain of a history of representations and practices. In addition, the history of the church is conceived rather as a history of *churches*. The impossible goal of synthesizing and honoring the epistemological assumptions of both history and theology has been abandoned, and there is a tendency to leave reflection on the findings of historians to systematic theologians, working within a "theology of history."

On any hypothesis, the church, as an institution and as a population of believers, remains a crux of religious history that cannot be ignored. Moreover, the history of the church in particular and history in general are still obligatory ports of call for theological reflection. On the one hand, theology accounts for the history of a world in which God wished Jesus Christ to dwell. On the other hand, the community of faith finds in its own history one of the criteria by which it can measure its loyalty to the Gospel that it has a duty to preach.

● F. Bonifas (1879), "Histoire de l'Église," in F. Lichtenberger (Ed.), *Encyclopédie des sciences religieuses* 6, Paris, 279–96.

A. Fliche, V. Martin (Ed.) (1934–64), *Histoire de l'Église depuis les origines jusqu'à nos jours,* 21 vols., Paris.

H. Jedin (1961), "Kirchengeschichte," *LThK*2 6, 209–18.

R. Aubert, A. Weiler (Ed.) (1970), "L'histoire de l'Église au tournant," *Conc(F)* 57.

A. Weiler (Ed.) (1971), "L'histoire de l'Église comme autocompréhension de l'Église," *Conc(F)* 67.

E. Stöve (1988), "Kirchengeschichtsschreibung," *TRE* 18, 535–62.

F. Lebrun (Ed.) (1989), *Les grandes dates du christianisme,* Paris.

G. Bedouelle (1992), *L'histoire de l'Église, science humaine ou théologie?* Milan.

K. Ganzer et al. (1997), "Kirchengeschichte," *LThK*3 6, 2–10.

J.-M. Mayeur et al. (Ed.), *Histoire du christianisme,* 14 vols. Paris.

HUBERT BOST

See also **Apologists; Catholicism**

Holiness

A. Biblical Theology

Holiness belongs to God* alone. The term refers to the radiance of his power, the perfection of his being. He alone has the capacity to make those whom he calls to live in his presence participate in his holiness.

a) Vocabulary of the Sacred and the Holy. The root form *qadash,* used within the religious register, covers the notions of both the sacred and the holy. In ancient religions, it expressed the majesty and activating power of the divinity. Used in Semitic languages with the meaning of "consecration and purification," it has a primary positive sense of consecration and belonging, and a secondary sense of separation: thus, the statal verb *qadosh* may be translated as "to be holy," "to be consecrated," "to be set apart." In the intensive (76 times), it has the sense of "to consecrate," "to set apart," "to consider as holy." In the causative (45 times), it means "to consecrate," "to declare holy." Other forms of the verb indicate that God "manifests his holiness" and "is recognized as holy," or again, that human beings "are sanctified" for the purposes of a ritual act. The adjective *qadosh* (116 times) is used of God himself (Is 6:3), but also describes those persons and things that have a relation with him. The abstract noun *qodesh,* which is by far the most common form of this root (469 times), refers to holiness and what it affects. It can also have the meaning of "sanctuary," and in this sense comes close to another derivative, *miqdash.*

The "sacred" circumscribes the domain of divinity and of all that is related to it, whether persons, objects, times, or places. It is contrasted with the "profane" *(chol),* which derives from *pro fanum,* "in front of the temple*," a term applied to whatever was located outside the temple. The couplet "sacred" and "profane" has parallels with the couplet "purity*"/"impurity" (Lv 10:10; Ez 44:23). This refers primarily, and in most cases, to a ritual purity that defines one's capacity to take part in worship; rituals of purification are required if one is impure. Another Hebrew root, *nazar,* also expresses the idea of consecration to the divinity.

In the Septuagint, in the vast majority of cases, *qadash* is translated as *hagios* or one of its derivatives, all related to a verb, *hazomai,* that means "to feel a respectful fear," often with a religious nuance. These terms facilitated the transition from the notion of the sacred to that of moral holiness; *hagios* was preferred to *hieros,* which is oriented more toward the sacred. In the Septuagint, *hieron* is restricted to the temple.

b) The Sacred and the Holy in the Old Testament. The majority of the 842 examples of the root *qadash* are to be found in the priestly texts of the Pentateuch (Ex 102 times; Lv 152 times; Nm 80 times); in the book of the prophet and priest Ezekiel (105 times); and in the Levitical and priestly redactions of the Chronicles (120 times). Its usage remains fairly frequent in Isaiah (73 times) and the Psalms* (65 times), but is little documented in the wisdom* literature.

Moses experiences the place where the Lord presents himself as holy ground (Ex 3:5; *see* Jos 5:15). In Exodus, God, the liberator of his people, reveals himself "majestic in holiness" (Ex 15:11). The people* must be sanctified in order to go to their encounter on Mount Sinai (Ex 19:10). Deuteronomy, and the texts compiled under its influence, emphasize that Israel is a "holy nation" (Ex 19:6), a people consecrated to the Lord their God, chosen to become his personal portion among all the peoples on the surface of the Earth (Dt 7:6). The paragraphs of the Law* of Holiness (Lv 17–26) proclaim the affirmation both that the Lord is holy and that it is he who sanctifies. He calls his people to holiness—"You shall be holy, for I the Lord your God am holy" (Lv 19:2)—a holiness that, over and above rituals, demands a moral comportment that extends to loving one's neighbor as oneself (Lv 19:18). The priestly code contains an elevated notion of the holiness of a God whom one does not approach without impunity unless one has met the required conditions, which are particularly demanding for the priests consecrated to the service of the holiness of the people of God. The priestly texts tend to give greater weight to separation from the profane (Ex 19:12f., 19:20–25). The construction of the sanctuary and the installation of priests both draw attention to the degrees of participation in the holiness of God.

Ezekiel denounces the moral failings and disloyalties of the people and their rulers. Drawing on both liturgical and legal traditions, he envisages a new temple at the center of a purified land in which the people, sanctified and renewed by the Spirit, live in the presence of their God. Isaiah encounters the thrice-holy God in the temple at Jerusalem* (Is 6:3); he and his successors celebrate the greatness of the God of Israel (Is 57:15), and announce that Jerusalem will be called the "the Zion of the Holy One of Israel" (Is 60:14). The people are condemned, but the stock that survives will be "the holy seed" (Is 6:13). The prayer* of Israel echoes these statements of Isaiah's: the Lord is great in Zion, he is holy (Ps 99:2f.).

God is a holy and transcendent deity whom it is possible to approach. The prophets developed an understanding of holiness in a more moral sense: to consecrate oneself to God requires a faithful and resolute commitment, and an awareness of the necessary ruptures.

c) Holiness in the New Testament. In the New Testament, following the usage adopted in the Septuagint, the root *qadash* is translated as *hagios* or one of its derivatives: *hagiazo,* "to sanctify," "to consecrate" (28 times); *hagiasmos,* "sanctification," "consecration" (10 times); *hagiotes,* "holiness" (two times); or *hagiosune,* also "holiness" (three times). These last three terms are found only in the Gospels. Ninety of the 230 examples of *hagios* in the New Testament refer to the Holy Spirit*. *Hieron* refers to the temple, yet the adjective *hieros* appears only three times.

Jesus* addresses his prayer to the "Holy Father" (Jn 17:11) and calls his disciples to pray so that the name* of the Father* will be sanctified (Mt 6:9; Lk 11:2). Jesus is the one whom the Father has consecrated and sent into the world* (Jn 10:36); he is the "Holy One of God" (Mk 1:24), the "holy servant" of God (Acts 4:27). The Holy Spirit has been at work since his conception (Lk 1:35). Invested by the Holy Spirit at his baptism* (Lk 3:22), Jesus walks in the fullness of the Spirit (Lk 4:1). Jesus offers participation in the holiness of God to all believers: he who sanctifies and they who are sanctified have the same origin (Heb 2:11). Through a unique sacrifice, Jesus leads those whom he sanctifies to perfection (Heb 10:14). From this time forward, the church* is the holy nation, the people that God has redeemed (1 Pt 2:9; *see* Ex 19:5f.). Saints—holy ones—by vocation (Rom 1:7), Christians may receive this title now, even if their lives are not yet perfect. God's will is that they be sanctified; and this implies ruptures (1 Thes 4:3–8). The Holy Spirit has been active in the church since the Pentecost (Acts 2:1–13), and the way of holiness consists in allowing oneself to be guided by the Spirit, who dwells in each person and intercedes for the saints (Rom 8:1–17).

The sense of the greatness and holiness of God, and the assurance that he wants his people to participate in his holiness, form part of the heritage that Christians have received from Israel. By giving his life, Jesus has offered participation in the holiness of God to all, without any distinction, going beyond the cleavages and separations in the old covenant.

● F.J. Leenhardt (1929), *La notion de sainteté dans l'Ancien Testament: Étude de la racine,* QDSh, Paris.
O. Procksch, K. G. Kuhn (1932), *ThWNT* 1, 87–116.
H. P. Müller (1976), *ThWAT* 2, col. 589–609.
M. Gilbert (1978), "Le sacré dans l'Ancien Testament," in J. Ries et al., *L'expression du sacré dans les grandes religions,* Louvain-la-Neuve.
H. Cazelles, C. B. Costecalde, P. Grelot (1985), "Sacré (et Sainteté)," *DBS* 10, 1342–1483, Paris.
J. Ries (1985), *Les chemins du sacré dans l'histoire,* 2nd Ed., Paris.
W. Kornfeld, H. Ringgren (1989), *ThWAT* 6, 1179–1204.
Ph. P. Jenson (1992), *Graded Holiness,* Sheffield.

JOSEPH AUNEAU

See also **Cult; Expiation; Glory of God; Holy Spirit; Justice; Name; Priesthood; Purity/Impurity; Sabbath; Sacrifice; Temple**

B. Historical and Systematic Theology

Only God* is holy. For created human beings, holiness consists in sharing God's life. On this subject, John says: "we shall be like him because we shall see him as he is" (1 Jn 3:2). The two halves of this statement have given rise to the two traditions* of divinization in the East (*theosis* or *theopoiesis; see* Maximus* the Confessor, PG 90, 1193 D) and the vision of God in the West (beatific vision*; *see* Augustine*, PL 35, 1656 and 1895). The fact that these two traditions spring from the same text emphasizes that they belong together, as complementary accounts of holiness.

1. Eucharist and Church

Holiness is not an abstract concept. Concretely, holiness will consist in membership of the eschatological community in "the holy city, the new Jerusalem" (Rev

21:2), where, according to another typical Johannine vision, the assembly will wear radiant robes washed white in the blood of the Lamb* (7:14) and gaze upon God (7:9f.). In the heavenly Jerusalem, "the dwelling place of God is with man" (21:3), and human beings are *persons**, in the image of the God in three persons, in everlasting communion* with Christ*, as the Son and the Spirit* are in eternal communion with the Father*. Holiness is identical with being a person, and it is essentially in the celebration of the Eucharist*, where we are one with the church* on high (*see* Heb 12:22ff.), that we are made holy, consecrated, as persons in anticipation. In the eucharistic setting of the Last Supper in John's gospel*, Jesus* prays to the Father: "for their sake I consecrate myself, so that they also may be sanctified in truth" (Jn 17:19).

2. Augustine and the West

In his *Confessions,* Augustine describes the call to holiness, the call to belong no longer to himself but to God, that he heard before his baptism*. He saw with the soul's eye the immutable, transcendent light of God, and trembled as he felt a mixture of love*, awe, and a feeling of "dissimilarity" (*see* PL 32, 813)—the characteristic combination of attraction and rejection, familiarity and strangeness, that an encounter with the holy engenders (Otto 1917). The Word* of God spoke to him, saying: "I am the food of the fully grown; grow and you will feed upon me. And you will not change me into you, as food for your flesh; but you will be changed into me" (*Conf.* VII, 10, PL 32, 742). Henri Sonier de Lubac* interprets this as an anticipation of eucharistic participation in the communion of the church. Those who heard these words of Christ, he says, understood "that through the reception of the Eucharist they would be more deeply incorporated into the church" (1938, 7th Ed. 1983). Augustine emphasizes that holiness is ecclesial by likening the process of making the eucharistic bread to that of initiation into the church. Commenting on Paul's doctrine of "one bread...one body" (1 Cor 10:17), he urges: "Therefore be that which you see, and receive that which you are" (PL 38, 1247–48). To receive Christ is, in fact, to be received by him into the church: "He is himself the body of which those who eat it become the nourishment" (Lubac 1944, 2nd Ed. 1949).

At the start of the *Confessions,* Augustine diagnoses the condition of every human being: "You have made us, Lord, for yourself, and our heart is restless until it rests in you" (PL 32, 661). Each heart has a natural élan toward God, which is the vocation to holiness. This diagnosis echoes that of Irenaeus* and foreshadows the teaching of Thomas* Aquinas. According to Irenaeus, "the glory of God is man who lives; and the life of man is the vision of God" (*Adv. Haer.* IV, 20, 7). God and man are here set in a dynamic relationship, with the vision of God clearly identified as the end for which man was made. Over a thousand years later, Aquinas voiced the same coherent Western tradition when he taught that there is a natural desire for the (supernatural*) vision of God: "the end of a reasonable creature is to attain to beatitude," which is "the vision of God" (*CG* 4, 50, 5). More precisely, "every intellect naturally desires the vision of the divine substance" (3, 57, 3).

3. Gregory Palamas and the East

a) Hesychasm.   According to hesychasm*, the Eastern tradition of inner prayer* that goes back to the earliest centuries and was defended by Gregory* Palamas, the object of the beatific vision is not God's *essence,* as in the West, but the uncreated *energies* of God. The divine energies constitute the light that shone from Christ at the moment of his Transfiguration, a light that can be seen, according to this teaching, by the purified eyes of the holy while praying in this life. Using a specific posture to channel the mind into "the prayer of the heart," the monks believed that this method could yield direct experience* of God.

When Barlaam claimed that this practice violated the apophatic sense of God's unknowability (negative* theology), Palamas defended the reality of communion with God. Relying fundamentally on the distinction between the essence and the energies of God (PG 150, 1169 C), his doctrine preserves both the real transcendence of God and the real divinization of man, but although it is only in God's energies that we participate, these energies are uncreated and truly divine.

b) Complementarity of West and East.   Barlaam alleged that the distinction of essence and energy in God undermines the divine simplicity* (Jugie 1932; Williams 1977). By contrast, Meyendorff, a neo-Palamite theologian, alleges that the *human* simplicity, so to speak, of Byzantine anthropology* is undermined by the static, Western scholastic categories of nature* and grace*. In fact, both West and East can be seen to have adopted different, and incompatible, strategies in pursuit of the same goal that deeply unites them, namely that of preserving the crucial distinction between the creator and creation. The simplicity either of God or of man must be apparently disrupted in order to provide a "buffer" between God and man, preventing them from being thought of as equal partners, with man literally becoming God or God sharing all of his being* with man. The creator is essentially holy, and the creature is only called to be holy.

It was the foundational insight of Athanasius* that "the Son of God made himself man in order to make us God" (PG 25, 192 B; *see* Irenaeus, PG 7, 1109 A); but Aquinas likewise said that "the only Son of God...assumed our nature in order that he, being made man, might make men God" (*Opusc.* 57, *Office of Corpus Christi, see ST* Ia IIae, q. 3, a. 1, ad 1). These two affirmations are rightly found together in the *Cathecism of the Catholic Church* (§460). The *Catechism* readily invokes the Eastern Fathers* to emphasize the mystery* of divinization (*see* §1589, 1988), which Catholic and Orthodox have affirmed together in describing the destiny of man as "his deification through victory over death" (Catholic-Orthodox Commission 1987, n. 31; *see* 1982, I, 4 a and 4 b). It is simply aspects of the one mystery of the call to holiness that East and West vary in explaining, with varying degrees of success.

c) Deification. If the West is concerned with sin* and the fall from grace, the anthropological "simplicity" of the East focuses upon its stark consequence, death. Athanasius, for example, teaches that "man is mortal by nature, since he has issued from nothingness" (PG 25, 104 C). Sin cuts us off from God and renews the menace of death. The soul* is not intrinsically immortal, but equally threatened by the return to nothingness, for it too is created. The Western tendency to distinguish mortal body and immortal soul is thus overcome: it is body and soul, "both together," that have been created in the image of God (PG 150, 1361 C).

The image tends toward likeness, which is deification: "the image predestines man to *theosis*" (Evdokimov 1979). Gregory* of Nazianzus echoes Basil*'s words, that man is a creature who has "received the order to become a god" (PG 36, 560 A), although the distinction of essence and energies is found more clearly in Basil (PG 32, 869 A–B) than in Gregory (PG 36, 317 B–C). The Eucharist particularly accomplishes this deification (PG 35, 1200 B). Gregory* of Nyssa corrects the impression that the journey into God has an end in a static "vision" when he teaches that, even in the world to come, we shall ascend "from beginning to beginning, through a series of beginnings that never ends" (PG 44, 941 C). He adds that "Christianity is the imitation of the divine nature" (PG 46, 244 C), thereby clarifying that growth in likeness to God (for which free cooperation, *synergy,* with his grace is needed) is growth toward being a person who embodies the fullness of human nature, just as, in God, each person bears the totality of the divine nature.

Thus, deification consists in acquiring, not the divine nature, which is impossible, but the divine *way of being,* as persons in communion. Because God's way of being has been introduced into humanity by Jesus Christ, deification is found by sacramental union with him, reinforced by the Jesus Prayer in hesychasm. Zizioulas (1975) thinks that, because of the priority it traditionally gives to nature over person in its Trinitarian theology, the West has never really accepted *theosis,* because man can never acquire God's nature. However, restoring priority to the person enables the concept to be embraced fully.

4. Nature and Person

a) Protestant Reaction. Western reluctance regarding the notion of deification is particularly found in the Reformed tradition. Barth* rejects it firmly, actually in reaction to the Lutheran doctrine (Lutheranism*) that "the Son of God communicated his divine majesty to his assumed flesh" *(Formula of Concord).* It is notable that Barth's argument is conducted in terms of natures rather than persons (*KD* IV/2). The *Formula* explains the divinization of Christ's humanity by the interpretation of his divine nature, which Barth rejects as compromising both the true divinity and the true humanity of Jesus Christ. Moreover, since Christ's humanity is that of all men, its deification implies that all are able to be deified, or perhaps even have been deified, by his coming, and can therefore abandon him as the one hope for salvation* and look to their own potential. The doctrine destroys Christology*.

However, this implication only follows when the discussion is purely of impersonal natures rather than of living persons. Christ's humanity is divinized by being assumed by the person of the Son, and human beings are divinized by entering into personal relationship with Christ. Pannenberg (1966) thinks that the dispute between Lutherans and Reformed arises because both start from the Incarnation*, and understand Christ to be fully God and fully man already at his birth, instead of examining the utterly unique course of his life and concluding that he is the incarnate Son. The latter approach, we may note, is focused dynamically upon Christ's person rather than statically upon his natures, and allows for growth. Gregory of Nyssa believed that the divinization of Christ's human nature was a process accomplished only at the Resurrection* (PG 45, 1261 C–1265 B).

b) Sanctifying Grace. The Council of Trent* likewise taught that Christians grow in the life of grace (*DS* 1535). With Luther*, it affirmed that grace is necessary for all stages of justification*, but against him it taught that the human will must cooperate, and that justification brings not only forgiveness but also sanctification (*DS* 1521–29). The grace of charity inheres in the just; they do not simply have Christ's justice* imputed to them (*DS* 1530, 1561). These texts ground the Catholic doctrine of sanctifying grace, the transformation wrought in the just by the gift of the Holy Spirit (Rom 5:5). Because the transformation occurs in a creature, it is called "created grace"—hence the distinction of nature and grace disliked by the Orthodox (*see* above and, e.g., Zizioulas 1984), as well as by the Reformed—but the gift itself is "uncreated grace."

However, created grace is not a commodity separable from God. "It is not at all a question of conceiving a sort of entity separated from its source, a sort of cooled lava, that man appropriates to himself" (Lubac 1980). Lubac thinks that justification brings Christ to dwell in the faithful and that the mystical life begins with the welcome that he is given (1984). Created grace can then be seen as the Christian's bond with the Christ who indwells, and, since Christ is now actually enthroned with the Father, the effect of created grace is in fact to draw us out of ourselves, to live in the heavenly church that shares his glory (Col 3:1–4). "The fruit of the sacramental life is that the Spirit by adoption deifies the faithful, uniting them in life with the only Son, the Savior" (*Catechism of the Catholic Church* §1129). Barth's misgivings about the apparently excessive inwardness of mysticism (*KD* I/2, 839–40) and the apparent independence of created grace as "product" (*KD* IV/1, 89) can thus be overcome in personal terms.

5. Vatican II

It is strictly in relation to the church that Vatican* II defines holiness as "perfect union with Christ" (*LG* 50). Significantly treating "the call to holiness" within its Dogmatic Constitution on the Church (Ch. 5), the Council first acknowledges that it is only the Trinity* that is truly holy. From this source, holiness is communicated to the church by Christ, who gave himself up to it precisely to make it holy (Eph 5:25f.). All Christians are called to holiness by their very membership in the church. It is by participating in her holiness that they will find holiness, and, in turn, will sanctify others (*LG* 39). It follows that, although "the forms and tasks of life are many," nevertheless "holiness is one" (*LG* 41), always being prompted by the same Spirit (*LG* 39).

Moreover, since the Spirit is "the guarantee of our inheritance" (Eph 1:14), holiness is not only ecclesial but also eschatological. Like the church in which it is acquired, holiness "will attain its full perfection only in the glory of heaven" (*LG* 48). Meanwhile, the call to holiness involves participation in the tension between the present and the future that marks the life of the church itself. Our communion with the saints, who already contemplate "in full light, God himself triune and one, exactly as he is" (*DS* 1305), inspires us.

We "cleave together" with them in Christ, and they "establish the whole church more firmly in holiness" (*LG* 49).

6. Canonization of Saints

During the early Christian centuries, the saints inserted into the "canon" of those to be venerated in the liturgy were martyrs. Antony (†356) and Martin of Tours (†397) were among the first "confessors," martyrs *in voto* ("in desire"), heroic in spiritual struggle (*see* PG 26, 909 C–912 B; PL 20, 179). The saints were proclaimed either by public acclamation or by episcopal decree, and canonization, the inauguration of an official cult*, consisted in the "translation" of the saint's body into a tomb with an altar, which became the center of the cult. The spread of such cults brought papal intervention, and the first canonization by a pope* occurred in the late 10th century. Gregory IX restricted all canonization to the papacy (1234) and Sixtus V established the Sacred Congregation of Rites to deal with the scrutiny of candidates (1588). In 1969, the Sacred Congregation for the Causes of Saints took over this rigorous task, and the process of canonization was most recently revised by John Paul II in the Apostolic Constitution *Divinus perfectionis magister* (1983). Evidence of the heroic virtues and local cult of a candidate is required, together with a miracle* for beatification and a further miracle for canonization. Proclamations of a new "Blessed" or "Saint" are made by the pope in the context of the Eucharist.

In the Orthodox churches, canonizations are usually made by the synod* of bishops* of an autocephalous church and are then proclaimed by the patriarch (patriarchate*). The traditional term is not "canonization" but "glorification." God is glorified when the disciples of Christ do his work and bear fruit (Jn 15–17), and the saints are those whom the faithful have found to be great intercessors with God. By officially recognizing their status, the church glorifies God and glorifies the saint. A formal, evening, noneucharistic ceremony marks the new saint's transition from being someone prayed *for* to being someone prayed *to:* a final service of commemoration for the departed person is immediately followed by the first service of prayer to them. Next morning, the liturgy* is celebrated, with the new saint honored eucharistically for the first time.

● R. Otto (1917), *Das Heilige,* Stuttgart.

M. Jugie (1932), "Palamisme," *DThC* 11/2, 1735–76.

M. Lot-Borodine (1932), "La doctrine de la 'déification' dans l'Église grecque jusqu'au XIe s.," *RHR* 105/106, 5–43.

K. Barth (1938, 1953, 1955), *KD* I/2, IV/1, IV/2 (*Dogmatique,* Geneva, 1954–55, 1966–67, 1968–71).

H. de Lubac (1938), *Catholicisme* (7th Ed., Paris, 1983).

A. Michel (1939), "S.," *DThC* 14, 1841–70.

H. de Lubac (1944), *Corpus mysticum* (2nd Ed., Paris, 1949).

Vl. Lossky (1944), *Essai sur la théologie mystique de l'Église d'Orient,* Paris.

H. de Lubac (1946), *Surnaturel* (2nd Ed., Paris, 1991).

H. Rondet (1948), *Gratia Christi,* Paris.

P. Blanchard (1953), *Sainteté aujourd'hui,* Paris.

L. Hertling (1953), "Canonisation," *DSp* 2, 77–85.

J. Meyendorff (1959 *a*) (Ed.), *Grégoire Palamas: Défense des saints hésychastes,* Louvain.

J. Meyendorff (1959 *b*), *Introduction à l'étude de Grégoire Palamas,* Paris.

J. Meyendorff (1959 *c*), *Saint Grégoire Palamas et la mystique orthodoxe,* Paris.

G. Thils (1961), *Sainteté chrétienne,* Paris.

M. Labourdette (1965), "La sainteté, vocation de tous les membres de l'Église," in G. Baraúna (Ed.), *L'Église de Vatican II,* III, 1105–17, Paris.

I. Iparraguire (1965), "Nature de la sainteté et moyens pour l'obtenir," ibid., 1119–35.

W. Pannenberg (1966), *Grundzüge der Christologie,* Gütersloh.

Y. Congar (1972), "Die heilige Kirche," *MySal* IV/1, 458–77.

G. Philips (1972), "La grâce chez les Orientaux," *EThL* 48, 37–50.

G. Habra (1973), *La transfiguration selon les Pères grecs,* Paris.

J.-P. Houdret (1974), "Palamas et les Cappadociens," *Ist* 19, 260–71.

J. Meyendorff (1974), *Initiation à la théologie byzantine,* Paris.

A. de Halleux (1975), "Palamisme et tradition," *Irén* 48, 479–93.

J. D. Zizioulas (1975), "Human Capacity and Human Incapacity: A Theological Exploration of Personhood," *SJTh* 28, 401–48.

R. D. Williams (1977), "The Philosophical Structure of Palamism," *ECR* 9, 27–44.

P. Evdokimov (1979), *L'Orthodoxie,* Paris.

Y. Congar (1980), *Je crois en l'Esprit Saint* III, Paris.

H. de Lubac (1980), *Petite catéchèse sur nature et grâce,* Paris.

G. Thils (1982), *Existence et sainteté en Jésus-Christ,* Paris.

Commission mixte internationale de dialogue théologique entre l'Église catholique romaine et l'Église orthodoxe (1982), "Le mystère de l'Église et de l'Eucharistie à la lumière du mystère de la Sainte Trinité," *Irén* 55, 350–62.

J. D. Zizioulas (1984), "Christologie et existence: La dialectique créé-incréé et le dogme de Chalcédoine," *Contacts* 36, 154–72 (*see also* ibid., 37, 60–72).

H. de Lubac (1984), "Mystique et mystère," in *Théologies d'occasion,* Paris, 37–76.

D. Staniloae (1986), "Image, Likeness, and Deification in the Human Person," *Com(US)* 13, 64–83.

Commission catholique-orthodoxe (1987), "Foi, sacrements et unité de l'Église," *Irén* 60, 336–49.

P. Nellas (1987), *Deification in Christ: Orthodox Perspectives on the Nature of the Human Person,* New York.

J. Meyendorff (1989), "Theosis in the Eastern Christian Tradition," in L. Dupré and D. E. Saliers (Ed.), *Christian Spirituality,* III: *Post-Reformation and Modern,* New York.

T. Spidlik et al. (1990), "Saints," *DSp* 14, 196–230.

P. McPartlan (1993), *The Eucharist Makes the Church: Henri de Lubac and John Zizioulas in Dialogue,* Edinburgh.

PAUL MCPARTLAN

See also **Asceticism; Beatitude; Cult of Saints; Faith; Hope; Imitation of Christ; Person; Sin; Spiritual Theology**

Holy Oils

Oil, an unctuous liquid that has soothing absorptive qualities, has always been a preferred substance in religious rituals. In the Old Testament it is used for the anointing of kings (1 Sm 10:1), and after the subsequent exile of the high priest (Ex 29:7). However, the anointing of prophets* was metaphorical (Is 61:1). According to the New Testament, Christ*, whose title means "the Anointed One," "the one anointed with oil," receives the prophetic anointing at his baptism* (Acts 10:38; *see* Lk 4:18–21). Hebrew 1:9 also grants Christ the royal anointing of Psalm 44:7f. The imagery of anointing (2 Cor 1:21ff., 2:15f.; 1 Jn 2:20, 2:27) is also employed in speaking of his disciples.

As early as antiquity oils were commonly used in ritual celebrations of the Christian sacraments*. In the *Apostolic Tradition* (Rome, v. 215) the bishop* blesses an oil that will be used to comfort the sick (# 5). During baptism the bishop blesses an oil of exorcism* (oil of the catechumen) and an oil of thanksgiving with which the priest*, and then the bishop, will perform the postbaptismal anointings (# 21). In the West this perfumed oil received the name "holy chrism," and in the East the name *muron.*

After the fifth century, Maundy Thursday would become the day, in the West, for blessing the oils to be used during the baptisms at the Easter vigil. The 1955 reforms of Holy Week revived the Mass of Chrism, to be celebrated on Maundy Thursday (or on one of the days close to Easter). In the *Rituel* of 1970 the bishop, surrounded by his priests, blesses the "the sacred chrism" (*see* a recipe in Ex 30:22–25) that is to be used in baptism and confirmation*, as well as in the ordination* of priests and bishops. He can also bless the oil of catechumen and the oil for the sick, but in the *Rite* (# 7) the former can be blessed by the priest when it involves adults (*Rite of Christian Initiation of Adults* 131). The same is true, when necessary, for the oil used in the anointing* of the sick (70).

● *Ordo benedicendi oleum catechumenorum et infirmorum et conficiendi chrisma*, Rome, 1970 (*Bénédiction de l'huile des catéchumènes, de l'huile des malades, et confection du saint-chrême*, Paris, 1990).

◆ P. Jounel (1972), "La consécration du chrême et la bénédiction des saintes huiles," *MD* 112, 70–83.
E. Cothenet, J. Wolinski (1982), "Onction," *DSp* 11, 788–819.
B. Varghese (1989), *Les onctions baptismales dans la tradition syrienne*, CSCO 512.
W. Klein et al. (1999), "Salbung," *TRE* 29, 707–17.

PAUL DE CLERCK

See also **Anointing of the Sick; Baptism; Confirmation; Initiation, Christian; Ordination/Order**

Holy Saturday. *See* **Balthasar, Hans Urs von; Descent into Hell**

Holy Scripture

---

1. Origin of the Term

In 2 Chronicles 30:5, it is recorded that under Hezekiah the Mosaic prescriptions concerning the celebration of the Passover* had not been observed "as prescribed" *(kakkâtoûb)*, a phrase translated in the Septuagint as *kata tèn graphèn*, "according to the Scripture." Furthermore, the books* of the Old Testament were sometimes known as "the (holy) books" (Dn 9:2; 1 Macc 12:9; 2 Macc 8:23; 2 *Clement* 14, 2; perhaps 2 Tm 4:13; Flavius Josephus, *Antiquities of the Jews, Proem.*). No doubt under the influence of the expressions "for it is written" and "as it is written," the books of the Old Testament came to be referred to in the New Testament as "the Scriptures" (Mt 21:42; Lk 24:45; Rom 15:4; 2 Pt 3:16) or "the holy Scriptures" (Rom 1:2). Their unity was emphasized by the singular "Scripture" (Jn 10:35). These Scriptures were referred to as holy inasmuch as they were inspired by God* and transmitted wisdom* promoting salvation* in Jesus* Christ (2 Tm 3:15ff.). Certainly from the second century, if not earlier (*see* 1 Tm 5:18, which cites as Scripture a sentence from Lk 10:7 alongside Dt 25:4), the books of the New Testament were also considered an integral part of the Holy Scriptures. The expression "the holy books" may have tended to denote the books themselves as material objects, with the term "the Scriptures" referring more to their content.

2. Respective Positions of Tradition and Scripture within Their Common Relationship to the Word of God

By focusing attention on Scripture and its authors, the question of inspiration may encourage an unduly absolute and exclusive identification between Scripture and the word* of God. In fact tradition* has played an important part in the gradual development of the Scriptures.

a) In the Old Testament. Revelation* occurs by means of an experience undergone by the people* of God and interpreted in an utterance. These two linked elements were initially preserved and transmitted not in written form but in the continuity of community observances, such as the Passover celebration, which involved the recollection of divine acts (Ex 12: 25ff.). It was gradually, and much later, that the events and words of the past were put into writing. It may consequently be said that, on the one hand, the living tradition developed the potentialities of the message and adapted it to new circumstances; and, on the other, progressive recording in written form allowed the message to escape the vagaries of oral and observational transmission.

b) In the New Testament. The mission of introducing the gospel to the world was entrusted to the group of apostles*. The apostolic tradition, the fundamental and permanent basis of the faith* and practice of the churches*, consists of the memory of the acts and words of Jesus, recollected and understood profoundly in the light of his Resurrection* and of his entire mystery*. The apostolic churches would gradually set down a diverse and many-sided apostolic tradition, developed in response to the various needs of ecclesial life. This written recording was neither systematic nor complete. While the New Testament is an authentic representation of the apostolic tradition, it does not explicitly convey its full riches. It is for this reason that the Catholic faith refuses the Lutheran principle of the *Scriptura sola*, which is seen as giving a truncated picture of the apostolic tradition. Incidentally, some modern Protestant theologians (E. Käsemann, G. Ebeling, P. Gisel), while remaining true to this principle, emphasize the extent to which the Scriptures do not merely present a uniform word of God offered for our reinterpretation, but represent in themselves acts of interpretation that have their own history* and bear witness to the word of God.

3. Inspiration of Scriptures

In what is a continuation of the Jewish tradition, all Christian denominations make special reference to a collection of texts (canon*) that are regarded as establishing conventions for the faith and life of the community, since they are assumed to be inspired by God or the word of God. This profession of faith is linked to the conviction that God and his plan for humanity have been revealed through the covenant* with Israel* and the New Covenant in Jesus Christ. Faith in the divine inspiration of the Scriptures is thus an expression of faith in the privileged status of the Jewish and Christian traditions as regards divine revelation.

A number of indications of this faith are already to be found in the Bible* itself. God speaks through the voices of the prophets (Is 1:2, 6:6–9; Jer 1:9; Ez 3:10f.; Heb 1:1f.); he writes the Law* (Ex 24:12; Dt 4:13, 10:4) or dictates it to Moses (Ex 24:4; Dt 31:9); he commands that his divine acts be recorded in writing so that their memory should not be lost (Ex 17:14; Nm 33:2). In the same way, primitive Christianity accepted

the Jewish Scriptures of the Old Testament as the word of God (Mt 15:6). Quoting Jeremiah 31:33ff., the author of Hebrews introduces it with the words "And the Holy Spirit also bears witness to us" (Heb 10:15ff.); and in Acts 28:25 the quotation of Isaiah 6:9f. begins with these words of Paul: "The Holy Spirit was right in saying to your fathers" (Acts 28:25). Even more clearly, 2 Tm 3:15 talks of the "sacred writings" (2 Tm 3:15f.) and refers to all Scripture as "breathed out by God" (*theopneustos;* 2 Tm 3:16). Finally, regarding scriptural prophecies, 2 Peter 1:21 states that "No prophecy was ever produced by the will of man, but men spoke from God as they were carried along by the Holy Spirit." This last quotation shows well the insistence characteristic of biblical tradition. The personal contribution of the prophets or writers is not emphasized. Since it is not immediately evident, however, there is an insistence on the fact that in this Scripture God's word and intentions are expressed. The theandric process, that is to say the connection and cooperation between the divine author and the human author, is not considered important in this context and receives no explanation.

The same convictions and the same lack of theoretical development on the theandric process are found in the patristic period. The church fathers*, who scarcely distinguished between the theology of inspiration and the theology of revelation, made a twofold contribution. Firstly, since Jesus had fulfilled the Scriptures, they regarded as equally inspired the texts about him that originated in apostolic circles. For the Fathers, God was the author of both Testaments, each of which was to be preserved in its entirety (against Marcionism* and Manicheanism*). Secondly, in talking of inspiration, they had recourse to a variety of images.

They spoke readily of "Scripture dictated by the Holy Spirit" (Eusebius, *HE* 5, 28, 18; PG 20, 517; SC 41, 78), or even of "the Holy Spirit who dictated these things through the Apostle" (Jerome, *Letter* 120; PL 22, 997; CSEL 55, 500). In the same tradition, if more subtly, Augustine* writes: "Through the human nature which he assumed, Christ is the head of all the disciples, who are as the limbs of his body. For this reason, when these disciples wrote what Christ had shown and said, it may be said that it was Christ himself who wrote, since the limbs expressed what they knew under dictation from the head" (*De consensu evangelistarum* 1, 35; PL 34, 1070; CSEL 43, 60).

The other image employed, that of the musical instrument, allows for a subtler exposition. According to Athenagoras, "the spirit of God moves the mouths of the prophets like instruments . . . . The Spirit used them like a flute-player blowing on his flute" (*Petition concerning the Christians* 7, 9; PG 6, 904, 908). In the *Co-*

hortatio ad Graecos (PG 6, 256 *Sq;* a pseudo-Justinian work of the second or third century) it is also said that, in order to receive divine revelation, "it was enough for them to offer themselves sincerely to the action of the Holy Spirit, for that divine plectrum to come down from heaven, using men just like musical instruments, and to reveal to us celestial and divine realities."

Within the field of inspiration, it was above all prophetic inspiration that interested medieval theologians. The inspiration of all Scripture was taken for granted, and barely figured in teaching, to the extent that no mention of it is to be found, for example, in the *Sentences* of Peter Lombard. Scholastic theologians, for their part, attempted to develop a theory of inspiration with the help of philosophical categories. To express the respective roles of God and the human author, Albert* the Great talks of the "primary efficient cause" and the "next efficient cause" (*Institutiones biblicae* 20); while Thomas* Aquinas calls the Holy Spirit the "principal author" and man the "instrumental author" (*Quodlibet* 7, art. 14, ad 5); and Henry of Ghent refers to the former as the "principal author and one true author" and to the latter as the "secondary author, acting as minister," or alternatively as the "true author, albeit of the second degree" (*Summa Theologica*, a. 9, q. 2).

Luther*'s Reformation gave especial prominence to the authority* of Holy Scripture, considered as the unique source and sole norm for Christian faith and preaching* *(Scriptura sola).* Thereafter considerable efforts were made to develop a real knowledge of the Bible. The individual relationship of every Christian to Scripture was deemed essential, even if, in practice, it was through worship and catechetical* teaching that knowledge of the Bible was disseminated. The Catholic Counter-Reformation (Bellarmine*) responded by highlighting the Christian's relationship to the church, and maintained that access to Scripture was legitimate only through the intermediary of the latter. In order to protect the authority of Scripture, later Protestant theology was based on a strict teaching of the verbal inspiration of the Holy Scriptures. This conception, widely shared by Catholics at the time, led to a partial or complete questioning of inspiration following the development of biblical criticism from the 17th century onward (R. Simon). The customary, sometimes maximalist representations of the divine origins of Scripture, particularly when conceived in terms of an almost word-for-word dictation, were in fact badly shaken by the rediscovery of the role of human authors and of the culturally dated nature of their vision of the world. While the Eastern church remains focused on patristic exegesis* and seems hardly to have been touched by such debates, in the Western churches confrontation with the natural sciences and the human sciences, especially in a historical context, sparked a particularly serious crisis in the 19th century with the development of historico-critical exegesis.

On the Protestant side, the advent of liberal criticism tended to bring about the disappearance from theology of the doctrine of Scriptural inspiration, in favor of a more general doctrine of revelation. Nevertheless, Schleiermacher*, for example, accepted the personal inspiration of the apostles. He did not however believe that the books of the Bible called for a hermeneutical* and critical treatment that was distinct from usual procedures and would be based on divine inspiration. More recently, dialectical theology (Barth*) has brought the affirmation of a qualified Scriptural inspiration strongly back into favor, while strict verbal inspiration is still defended by fundamentalism*.

On the Catholic side, various reductive views of inspiration have been offered with the aim of resolving the crisis. These theories have been judged inadequate to convey steadfast faith in the divine origin of the whole of the Scriptures.

J. Jahn (1802) proposed a theory by which inspiration consisted of a negative divine assistance allowing the writer to avoid errors, while according to D.F. Haneberg (1850) it was a text's subsequent approval by the church that made it sacred (theories rejected by the constitution *Dei Filius* of Vatican* I; *see* EB 77). Then again, A. Rohling (1872) proposed that inspiration be materially restricted to those passages that constituted the essential basis of a dogmatic* or moral proposition (a theory rejected by Leo XIII's encyclical *Providentissimus Deus* in 1893) (*see* Burtchaell 1969).

Returning to the Thomist synthesis, M.-J. Lagrange presented scriptural inspiration as a special instance of the collaboration between Creator and creature: God causes the activity of the hagiographer and at the same time makes it truly free. God is the principal cause and the writer is the instrumental cause, although free. Inspiration is a charism by which God enters into, and makes his own, the free human activity of the sacred author, in such a way that the latter may be called an instrument of God. Pius XII's encyclical *Divino afflante Spiritu* (1943) speaks of a "living instrument endowed with reason*...who, acting under divine impetus, employs his faculties and talents in such a way that everyone may easily discern, from the work that has left his pen, 'his own personality and the marks and characteristics which distinguish him.'"

The constitution *Dei verbum* of Vatican* II is even more explicit on this point: "In order to compose these sacred books, God chose men to whom he had recourse in the full employment of their faculties and abilities, so that, as he worked in them and through them, they might put into writing, as true authors, everything which accorded with his desire, and that alone" (*DV* §11). Starting from these assumptions, later theology significantly rescues scriptural inspiration from the isolation in which it had been confined, by developing analogies of inspiration (P. Benoit). Divine inspiration is split into three types: dramatic or pastoral inspiration, which animated the shepherds of the chosen race and thereby sacred history; oratorical inspiration, which accompanied and complemented the pastoral inspiration; and scriptural inspiration, which brought about the setting down in writing of the things done and said. This division makes it possible to reconcile with a theory of scriptural inspiration the fact that the biblical text is the outcome of a long and sometimes turbulent history*, animated in its totality by the Holy Spirit. The writer's charism is but one of the charisms associated with the Word of God—the one that allows this word to become Scripture.

Moreover, the analogy between the mysteries of inspiration and the Incarnation*, highlighted by *DV* §13, is readily explained: "The words of God, passing by way of human tongues, assumed the character of human language, in the same way that, once, the Word* of the eternal Father*, having assumed the weakness of our flesh*, became like men." It is along these lines that theology nowadays attempts to conceive the collaboration between God the true author and the real human authors (*DV* §11), taking care not to formulate it on the model of competition which has proved so harmful in the past, as was also the case in Christology*. The Bible is the work of both man and God because it is the result of their meeting and communion, the perfect example of which is Jesus Christ, the incarnate Word.

4. Truth of Scriptures

The Fathers developed no theory on this subject. The truth* of Scripture as regards salvation was acknowledged and formed a background to theological thinking. At most, in response to the objections of Jewish or pagan opponents such as Celsus, Porphyry, or Julian the Apostate, a few simple explanations were developed for the supposed contradictions between the two Testaments or the four Gospels*.

It was above all the progress of science that, from the Renaissance onward, caused the truth of the Bible to be called into question. The natural sciences were the first to arouse conflict, as illustrated by the affair of Galileo (1564–1642). In the field of astronomy, Galileo professed the heliocentric system proposed by Copernicus (1473–1543). This questioning of the geocentric system ended in Galileo's being tried for

heresy* by the Inquisition and forced to recant. His new system did not, indeed, correspond to the biblical authors' representation of the world, and contradicted passages such as Joshua 10:12f., in which Joshua stops the sun. The questions had barely begun, however, and were to multiply. They ran from the smallest (it is incorrect to class the hare among the ruminants, as do Lv 11:6 and Dt 14:7) to the greatest: what remains of the truth of the stories of the Creation and original sin when they are put face to face with the theories of evolution* and polygenism. The church's first reactions were of two kinds: either it concluded that science must bend before the truth of Scripture (the affair of Galileo), or it sought to demonstrate at all costs the marvelous concord between the Bible's scientific teachings and those of contemporary science. However, both these approaches would soon end in deadlock. Concordism misunderstood the nature of science and was too ready to take as definitively proven matters that scientists considered as mere hypotheses within a given system of interpretation. Moreover, both approaches misunderstood the nature of the Bible and the teaching it offers.

On this subject, it was prudent to go back to the great principle already set out by Augustine*: "The Holy Spirit, which spoke through them [the sacred writers] did not wish to teach men things which were of no use for salvation [*ista...nulli saluti profutura*]" (*De Genesi ad litteram* 2, 9, 20; PL 34, 270). This was the principle that Leo XIII took up in the encyclical *Providentissimus Deus*, specifying the things that are of no use for salvation with the words: "in other words, the intimate composition of perceptible things." Augustine also wrote: "We do not read in the gospel that the Lord said 'I will send you a Paraclete to teach you the courses of the sun and moon'; he wished to make Christians, not mathematicians" (*Contra Felicem* 1, 10; CSEL 25, 812). Galileo's friend Cardinal Baronius was inspired by this to remark: "The Holy Spirit does not aim to teach us how the heavens work, but how to get there."

The conflict was revived in the 19th century with the development of a positivist historical science modeled on the natural sciences* and a fastidious quest for perfect objectivity. On this basis the documentary value of the books of the Bible was soon contested. This was one of the hotly contested issues of the Modernist crisis. The deadlock lasted as long as traditional apologetics questioned the value of historical research for the Christian faith instead of criticizing the assumptions of a rationalist view of history. Indeed it was only ended by criticizing these assumptions, and by reaching a deeper and at the same time more flexible understanding of history.

Faced with these objections, the first attempts at a solution at the end of the 19th century were not very successful. The theories of the material limitation of inspiration or of inerrancy (absence of error) were explicitly rejected by the encyclical *Providentissimus Deus.* Otherwise, while this encyclical already offered an important principle for the resolution of the relationship between the Bible and the natural sciences, it was only in 1943 with the encyclical *Divino afflante Spiritu* that the Catholic Church fully opened the way for literary and historical criticism of the Bible. Pius XII recommended the application "to the related sciences, in particular to history" of the Augustinian principle that Leo XIII had applied to the natural sciences. Furthermore he makes it the duty of Catholic exegetes to research "what literary genres the writers of those distant times sought to employ and did in fact employ."

Indeed, "in the sacred writers as in all the ancients, we encounter certain methods of exposition and narration, certain idioms, particular especially to the Semitic languages, and known as approximations, and certain hyperbolic or sometimes even paradoxical expressions, which impress the thought more strongly upon the intellect. None of these ways of speaking which were habitually employed in human language among the ancients, especially the Eastern peoples, is excluded from the Holy Books, always provided that the language used does not in any way offend against God's sanctity or his veracity*."

The constitution *Dei Verbum,* the most controversial of Vatican II, confirms these essential points. The narrow apologetic vocabulary of "inerrancy" is decisively abandoned in favor of the positive vocabulary of "truth," in the singular. The intellectual conception of revelation is left behind—the need is no longer to defend truths or religious doctrines, but to promote the search for the truth that leads to salvation and that is revealed by words and actions in Scripture. There is no longer any question of materially limiting the truth of the Scriptures, but it is made clear that the Bible expresses its truth from the particular formal standpoint of the order of salvation: "The books of Scripture teach firmly, faithfully, and without error the truth which God, for the sake of our salvation *[veritatem quam Deus nostrae salutis causa],* wished to see recorded in holy Letters" (no. 11). This fundamental theological principle met with a great deal of opposition at the Council before finally being adopted, even though it was entirely traditional. Not only had Augustine already expressed it, but 2 Timothy 3:15 stated that "the sacred writings ... are able to make you wise for salvation through faith in Christ Jesus"; and Thomas Aquinas, quoting John 16:13, added two words to the original: "When the Spirit of truth comes, he will guide you into all the truth necessary for salvation *[saluti necessariam]*" (*De veritate,* q. 12, a. 2).

Among the elements that helped to overcome the deadlock of traditional apologetics, without calling rationalist assumptions into question, was the rediscovery of the biblical understanding of truth.

The Greek concept of truth (*a-lètheia*) was linked to the idea of a revealing of reality or of an illumination of what was previously hidden. In these terms, truth was the true nature of things, the reality finally unveiled by intelligence. In this view the intellect is dominant. For the Bible, knowledge of the truth (*'èmèt*) is knowledge of the plan to which God remains faithful through his covenant (Old Testament), a plan that is fully revealed and fulfilled by and in Christ (New Testament). Consequently, truth is revealed first and foremost not through teaching but through people and actions expressing a fundamental faithfulness. God's truth denotes in the first place his loyalty (the root *'mn*) to his promise* concerning humanity's salvation. One can speak of dynamic truth in the sense of making the truth live in human beings, which also implies saving them.

By using the concept of truth as employed in the Bible itself, many spurious difficulties arising from a misconception of the type of truth that it offers can be avoided. This rediscovery opens the way to a calm and productive dialogue with the other orders of truth, once the salvation-centered truth of the Bible is no longer seen as being in competition with them. Biblical truth is a matter of the confession of faith, of trust in a God who is faithful to his promises. Far from being confused with the truth of experimental science, it should be appreciated in terms of its poetic dimension, in the sense in which Ricœur developed the concept of poetic truth.

What is more, exegetical research is emphasizing ever more clearly the plurality and diversity that exist within the Bible, which is understood as a library whose composition was spread over a number of centuries and associated with many quite different historical and geographical situations. Truth, of course, carries within it the desire for unity. There has been no lack of temptation through Christian history to wish to bring about this unity at all costs, even by force. Modern theology is conscious of the need for "eschatological caution": the unity of truth will never be fully achieved except through eschatology. The dynamic truth of Scripture—the word of many ages and many voices—can be grasped only by taking account of the whole, without singling out one part or another in order to create the illusion of a complete and simple truth. However, readers of Scripture tend to view this multiplicity hierarchically, the better to discern the word of God that is given and hidden behind the words of the Scriptures. In their search for truth, Jews find the unifying principle of the Bible in the Law, while Christians find it in a New Testament that refers to the person* of Christ. Even more precisely, Protestant theologians locate it in the Pauline epistles (Romans and Galatians according to Luther), while Catholics look more to the Gospels.

5. Authority and Role of Holy Scriptures in Christian Communities

In order for its sanctifying power to come into play, it is not enough for Scripture to be inspired. It must also be inspiring, and must therefore be received by the communities of the faithful, "read and interpreted by the light of the same Spirit which caused it to be written" (*DV* §12). Listened to, enacted, invoked, and shaped in the communities of Israel and the early churches, the word of God has been transmitted in inspired Scriptures that in turn inspire the life, prayer*, and activity of present-day communities. Never changing, yet always in need of translation, the Bible challenges each age and generation for whom it is the source of faith and life. Its authority is not tyrannical: it is at the service of the liberty* of the children of God. While Scripture is sacred as a witness to God's otherness, to his transcendence and his promise of love* for his people, it is also sanctifying inasmuch as reading it sustains the life of a people in covenant with God. It might therefore be expected that all Christians would be encouraged to study Scripture assiduously, since it is the source of life and faith for the people of God. But this has not always been the case.

a) In Catholic Church. *Lectio divina* has of course been promoted since antiquity. This protracted and patient reading, developed through meditation, contemplation*, and prayer, and especially cultivated in the monastic life (*Rule of Saint Benedict*, c. 48), was recommended to all clerics* by Pope* Pius XII in 1950 (*De scriptura sacra; EnchB* 592). As far as Christian people were concerned, however, contact with the Bible, at least in the Catholic Church, was provided indirectly by means of the liturgy*. The same church long displayed an explicit reluctance for the Bible to be read directly by nonclerics.

So, the famous fourth rule of the *Index of Trent* * (1564) "made the reading of Scripture in the vernacular subject to written permission granted by the bishop* on the advice of the parish priest or confessor" (Savart 1985, 22). It was not until long after it was abandoned in practical terms that this rule was tacitly abolished, when Leo XIII did not reiterate it in his con-

stitution *Officiorum ac munerum* (1897), whose wording nonetheless remains negative: "All versions in indigenous languages, even those published by Catholics, are absolutely forbidden unless they have been approved by the Apostolic See, or edited under the supervision of the bishops with annotations drawn from the church fathers* and from learned Catholic writers."

The approach adopted in the Catholic Church appears in a better light with *Dei Verbum*'s recognition of the need "for access to the Holy Scripture to be widely available to Christians" and its envisaging the possibility of translations that "would be the fruit of a collaboration with our separated brethren" so that they may be "used by all Christians" (*DV* §22).

Certainly it is the clerics* who are the first to be called on to read the Scriptures assiduously and study them in depth, but the faithful are also exhorted to this. For, as the council says, taking up a sentence of Jerome, "ignorance of the Scriptures is ignorance of Christ" (*DV* §25). The bishops have a responsibility not to teach the content of the book while exempting their flock from the necessity of reading it, but "to teach the faithful in their charge, in a suitable manner, to make the correct use of the divine Books" (ibid.). Finally, there is a recommendation judiciously to disseminate the Holy Scriptures "even for the use of non-Christians" (ibid.). On this basis it seems legitimate to suggest "that a proposal of biblical reading made according to the unfolding of God's mystery must be addressed, not exclusively to the man who acknowledges the Christian faith in himself, but to whomever might open his whole being to another truth besides the one he may already have mastered" (Beauchamp 1987).

Another important change introduced by Vatican II concerns the use of Scripture in the liturgy. The employment of vernacular languages in the liturgy has diminished the sacred distance that was maintained before the holy texts, and has developed their role of communicating meaning, a tendency further accentuated by an insistence on the homily (a sermon based on the text). Moreover, until Vatican II, the Roman liturgy drew only sparingly on scriptural sources. Thus the regular Sunday and feastday worshipper heard scarcely any Old Testament text, and only 4 percent of Maccabees or 2 percent of Revelation, the most frequently used book being Matthew (32 percent); and the same texts were repeated every year (Savart 1985). Following the council's recommendation to "read to the people over a set number of years a more significant proportion of the Holy Scriptures" (*De sacra liturgia* II, 51), liturgical reform has allowed the continuous reading, on a three-year cycle, of the Gospels and the Pauline epistles, and substantial portions of the

Old Testament retained on account of their thematic coherence with the Gospel.

On another level, returning to ancient tradition, *DV* §24 recommends that the study of Holy Scripture should be the very soul of theology and expresses the hope that it will give rise to a ceaseless rejuvenation of theology. By way of these efforts the council looks forward to a growth in the life of the church resulting from the reading of the Scriptures: "Just as the Church receives an increase in its life through regular participation in the mystery of the Eucharist, so it may be hoped that a renewal of spiritual* life will flow from a growing veneration for the word of God" (*DV* §26).

It remains to be said that for the Catholic Church it is not Scripture alone that brings knowledge* of God and salvation. "Somebody has read Scripture before us, and offers us a key to it, declaring this key to be fully in accordance with Scripture. If you accept this key, you will be entering the Book on his word: this process corresponds to what we mean by tradition" (Beauchamp 1987). The magisterium* ensures this transmission of evangelical truth within the church, while being subject to the word of God, which it is responsible for protecting and interpreting. And while there is a plurality of legitimate interpretations, as indeed the Pontifical Biblical Commission's recent document on "The interpretation of the Bible in the Church" (1993) made clear, "in the last resort it is the Magisterium which has the responsibility of ensuring the authenticity of interpretation, and of indicating when necessary that a particular interpretation is incompatible with the authentic gospel." This responsibility is presented as a service of the communion of the body of Christ (III, B, 3). The multiplicity of interpretations presented in a favorable light by the Biblical Commission is in itself an indication of the contemporary interest in the Bible and the many ways in which the Christian people approaches its sacred Scriptures.

b) In Protestant Churches. The authority of Scripture and the general recommendation to read it individually and collectively are fundamental characteristics of these churches. In order to facilitate general access to this reading, the need to translate the Bible into the vernacular was emphasized from very early on. Its dissemination, moreover, was taken in hand by numerous highly effective Bible societies. Following in this tradition, the Universal Bible Alliance, founded in 1946, set itself the task of translating the Bible into the greatest possible number of world languages and dialects (2,092 complete or partial translations by 1995) and of distributing it in cheap editions. In this way it has enabled a majority of the world's people to read the Bible privately.

In addition, the purely moralistic interpretation and use of the Bible by Kant* exerted a strong influence in Protestant intellectual circles in the 19th century. Catechetical teaching reacted by attempting to oppose what was perceived as a drift, in order to give more prominence to the dialogue between the Trinitarian God and the reader. Henceforth, far from neutrally imparting Biblical knowledge, the teacher had the task of announcing the word of God and conveying it in terms of the language and prior understanding of its readers.

In the second half of the 20th century, interest in the Bible and the role accorded to it underwent a considerable development due to the importance attached to the hermeneutic dimension. On the one hand, the debate over the interpretation of Scripture was boldly revived by E. Käsemann, according to whom the New Testament canon was not the basis of church unity*. Suddenly there arose the question of a canon within the canon, or indeed of deciding whether and in what way an interpretive canon was inevitable in the reading of a diverse Scripture. On the other hand, as early as the Second World War, Bonhoeffer* was emphasizing the extent to which the Bible does not by itself offer an answer to all our questions. While previously the Bible had enjoyed an almost indisputable authority in all areas of life, from the mid-1960s onward it was subjected to critical questioning by an ever-growing number of Christians. The solutions to many personal and collective problems were less and less sought directly in Scripture, but rather in scientific and ethical knowledge. This led to a partial loss of motivation with regard to reading the Bible and undertaking Bible study, but also to a refocusing on its essential role of calling, questioning, and offering a critical authority regarding the meaning of life.

Even though the 20th-century biblical renewal initially overshadowed to some extent a similar development among Catholics, it is nonetheless very real among them too. Among Christian people as a whole, the elements of prior understanding associated with a secularized mode of thought transcend denominational differences. Moreover, the approach to the Scriptures is undergoing a more or less parallel development in both Western traditions. This is undoubtedly due in part to the joint work of exegetes of various denominations, not forgetting the willingness of pastors to embrace ecumenism. The Traduction œcuménique de la Bible (TOB) completed in 1972 (New Testament) and 1975 (Old Testament) marked an important step in this progress.

● M.-J. Lagrange (1896), "Inspiration des livres saints," *RB* 5, 199–220.
R. Bultmann (1933), "*Alètheia*," *ThWNT* 1, 233–48.
K. Rahner (1958), *Über die Schriftinspiration*, Freiburg.
P. Grelot (1965), *La Bible, Parole de Dieu*, Paris.

P. Lengsfeld, H. Haag, G. Hasenhüttl (1965), *MySal* I/2 (*Mysterium Salutis: Dogmatique de l'histoire du salut*, vol. 2, 1969).

B.-D. Dupuy (Ed.) (1968), *Vatican II: La révélation divine*, 2 vols., Paris.

P. Benoit (1968), "Inspiration scripturaire et herméneutique," in id., *Exégèse et théologie*, vol. III, Paris, 17–156.

J. T. Burtchaell (1969), *Catholic Theories of Biblical Inspiration since 1810: A Review and Critique*, Cambridge.

E. Käsemann (1970), "Begründet der neutestamentliche Kanon die Einheit der Kirche?" *Exegetische Versuche und Besinnungen*, vol. 1, 6th Ed., Göttingen, 214–23.

L. Alonso Schökel (1971), *La Palabra inspirada*, Barcelona.

J. Beumer (1972), *L'inspiration de la Sainte Écriture* (Histoire des dogmes 5), Paris.

E. Oikonomos (1976), *Bibel und Bibelwissenschaft in der orthodoxen Kirche*, SBS 81.

P. Ricœur (1977), "Herméneutique de l'idée de révélation," in coll., *La révélation*, Brussels, 15–54.

P. Gisel (1977), *Vérité et histoire: La théologie dans la modernité: Ernst Käsemann*, Paris-Geneva.

H. Wildberger, "'mn, fest, sicher," *THAT* 1, 177–209.

H. Graf Reventlow (1980), *Bibelautorität und Geist der Moderne*, Göttingen.

G. Wanke, E. Plümacher, W. Schneemelcher, H. Karpp, K. Wegenhast (1980), "Bibel," *TRE* 6, 1–109.

C. Savart, J.-N. Aletti (Ed.) (1985), *Le monde contemporain et la Bible* (BTT 8).

K. R. Trembath (1987), *Evangelical Theories of Biblical Inspiration: A Review and Proposal*, New York-Oxford.

P. Beauchamp (1987), *Parler d'Écritures saintes*, Paris.

R. E. Brown, J. A. Fitzmeyer, R. E. Murphy (Ed.) (1989), *The New Jerome Biblical Commentary*, Englewood Cliffs, Part 2 (Topical Articles): R. F. Collins, "Inspiration," 1023–33; R. E. Brown and R. F. Collins, "Canonicity," 1034–54.

H. Bourgeois, P. Gibert, M. Jourjon (1989), *La cause des Écritures: L'autorité des Écritures en christianisme*, Lyon.

Commission biblique pontificale (1993), *L'interprétation de la Bible dans l'Église*, Paris.

J. A. Fitzmeyer (1995), *The Biblical Commission's Document "The Interpretation of the Bible in the Church"* (Subsidia Biblica, 18), Rome.

F. Martin (1996), *Pour une théologie de la lettre: L'inspiration des Écritures* (CFi 196), Paris.

CAMILLE FOCANT

See also **Bible; Biblical Theology; Book; Canon of Scriptures; Ecumenism; Exegesis; Hermeneutics; History; Liturgy; Magisterium; Modernism; Protestantism; Scripture, Fulfillment of; Scripture, Senses of; Theology; Tradition; Truth; Veracity; Word of God**

Holy Spirit

A. Biblical Theology

I. Old Testament

1. Terminology

In a little more than half of its occurrences in the Old Testament, the word *roûach* (fem., 378 times) is used in the physical sense of wind or breath. It also designates (approximately 80 times) the human spirit in the psychological sense of the term. The divine connection of the Spirit is noted in expressions such as "Spirit of YHWH," "Spirit of God," and, in context, "my Spirit" (13 times), "his Spirit" (10 times), "your Spirit" (eight times). In Genesis 1:2b "the *roûach* of God" circulates on the water. "Holy Spirit" is rare: Isaiah 63:10f.; Psalms 51:13; Wisdom 9:17.

2. Actions of the Spirit

The theme and its theological content appear in three main areas: 1) Archaic traditions related to the sudden intervention of an individual seized by the Spirit—saviors in the period of Judges, King Saul, Elijah, and Elisha. In these cases the Spirit is "on" or comes "over" someone. It may be "evil" (1 Sm 16:23) and yet come from God (Jgs 9:23; 1 Sm: four occurrences; 1 Kgs 22:2f.). 2) In Hosea 9:7 the prophet* is called "Man of *roûach*." In Numbers 11:16f., 11:24–30, and Joel 3:1, the exercise of prophecy is called a gift of the Spirit (*see* Nm 11: 25, 24:2; Neh 9:30; and, by contrast, 1 Kgs 22:24). 3) The Spirit can pass from one inspired person to a successor (case of Moses: Dt 34:9, laying on of hands, and Elijah, 2 Kgs 2:15) or even to a people (Is 59:21).

3. Properties of the Spirit

The immaterial, personal nature of *roûach* makes it appropriate to signify circulation, intimacy, and communication of intimacy. The Spirit spreads out (Is 32:15,

44:3), fills, and vivifies (Ez 37). Holy, it sanctifies. It approaches wisdom* when it becomes a permanent presence attached to a chosen one or to the people (Is 11:1f.; Prv 1:23; Ps 51:8, 51:13; Wis 1:6, 7:7, 7:22ff.; 9:17).

4. Promised Spirit

In the late writings of the Old Testament the concept of Spirit is associated with eschatological times (Jl 3:3f.; *see* Is 63:19: the "separator of the heavens" carried over in Mk 1:10) and the promise*. Insofar as it is inscribed within a new understanding of the covenant* (Is 59:21; Ez 11:19f.; 36:25ff. after Jer 31:33), it is seen as the principal object of the promise (*see* Lk 24:49). The concept of creation* is conceived by way of this novelty (Ps 51:12f.).

PAUL BEAUCHAMP

II. New Testament

1. Terminology

The Greek substantive *pneuma* (379 times) has four meanings in the New Testament: 1) the literal sense of breath or wind (three times); 2) the anthropological (approximately 47 times) sense of "Spirit" as breath, the spirit of life (Mt 27:50 etc.), but also of the human person in his or her totality or inwardness; 3) the demonological sense that goes back to impure or evil spirits (especially in the Gospels* and Acts (approximately 38 times); and 4) the theological sense, which is dominant (the transcendent Spirit of God or Christ* (approximately 275 times). The Spirit in the theological sense is used 149 times in the absolute sense; 93 times as Holy Spirit or holiness* (*pneuma hagion* or *hagiosunès*), 18 times as Spirit of God, once as Spirit of the Father, five times qualified christologically. It should be noted that with the exception of the Lucan corpus, the expression "Holy Spirit" is not dominant in the New Testament.

2. Pre-Pauline Usage

a) Historical Jesus. All the earthly Jesus*' *logia* on the Holy Spirit are probably post-paschal (*see*, e.g., Mk 3:29 parallel passage, 13:11 parallel passage; Mt 12:28, 28:19; Lk 4:18, 11:13). However, it would seem that the historical Jesus presented himself as invested with the Spirit (prophetic). The authority* he claims in his preaching* and actions is the demonstration of it— his proclamation of the imminent coming of the Kingdom* of God, his sovereign interpretation of the Law* (Mt 5:21ff.), his sending of the disciples on mission*, (Mk 6:7 par.), and his eschatological interpretation of exorcisms (Lk 11:20).

b) Easter. The oldest pre-Pauline formulas discern in Jesus' Resurrection* an act of God, sometimes described as the expression of the activity of the Spirit of God (Rom 1:3f., 8:11, etc.).

c) Hellenists and Hellenistic Communities. The Hellenists (*see* Acts 6–7) would seem to be the first group that claimed possession of the eschatological Spirit. In support of this thesis should be noted their characteristic thaumaturgic activity and their critiques of the Temple* and the Law. This vivid awareness of their possession of the Spirit was probably the profound reason for the rupture with the primitive community of Jerusalem*. It was subsequently perpetuated in the Hellenistic community of Antioch and was at the origin of the mission to the pagans (paganism*) (*see* the example of Paul, heir to Antiochian theology and apostle* to the Gentiles). However, it cannot be affirmed with certainty that Palestinian Judeo*-Christianity (especially the community of Jerusalem) shared this pneumatological consciousness.

3. Paul

To grasp the Pauline notion of the Holy Spirit we must be attentive to the circumstantial quality of his letters and the theological development of his thought (from the rudimentary affirmations in 1 Thessalonians, to the Corinthian controversy on pneumatic phenomena, concluding with the fully developed pneumatology of Romans 8). The dynamics of Christian existence is the privileged site where Paul's understanding of the Spirit appears in all its clarity.

a) Foundation and Fulfillment of Christian Existence according to the Spirit.

1) CHRISTOLOGY*. The proclamation of the gospel of Christ* is the work of the Spirit (1 Thes 1:5; 1 Cor 2:4; Kgs 15:18f.). The Spirit inspires faith* (1 Cor 12:3). Only the Spirit makes it possible to confess Jesus as Lord.

2) SOTERIOLOGY. The Spirit creates life. By the Spirit, man is torn away from the power of sin* and death* and placed in the space of life and liberty* inaugurated by Christ (*see* Rom 8; Gal 5; 2 Cor 3:17). Baptism* is the sacramental sign of this change of allegiance.

3) ECCLESIOLOGY*. The Spirit unites people in the visible communion* of the body of Christ (*see* 1 Cor 12). In the controversy with the Corinthian enthusiasm (1 Cor 12–14), Paul uses the notion of body to support his argument that all manifestations of the Spirit must be subordinated to the edification of the community.

The greatest charism is love* (1 Cor 13), which thus becomes the critical standard of all gifts of the Spirit. The theological perspective that supports this notion is the theology* of the cross.

4) ETHICS*. The Spirit is the agent of all action corresponding to the will of God (*see* the metaphor of the "fruit of the Spirit" in Gal 5:22), which can only be an action accomplished with love. The concrete expression of Christian freedom is love.

b) Eschatology. The Spirit's action is central to the *fulfillment* of the Christian existence. Though Paul, true to the tradition*, understands the Spirit as an eschatological gift, he makes a clear distinction between the Spirit and the eschaton; the gift of the Spirit is but the premise of the glory to come (1 Cor 1:22, 5:5; Rom 8:23). In this respect, it is the foundation of hope* (Rom 8).

4. Work of Luke

a) History of Salvation. This history is determinant for the notion of the Spirit in Luke. The promise of the Spirit dominates the Old Testament period. During Jesus' lifetime the activity of the Spirit is almost exclusively concentrated on his person, making him an almost exclusive depository. His birth manifests the creative activity of the Spirit of God (Lk 1:35) and his baptism makes him its messianic bearer (3:22). The narrative of the temptation* shows that Satan must retreat in the face of the bearer of the Spirit (the time of Jesus is a time when Satan is absent, until the Passion* (4:13, 22:3). The inaugural preaching in Nazareth connects the gift of the Spirit and the proclamation of the gospel (4:18f.). Only after he was raised to the Father*'s side did Jesus transmit the Spirit to believers (Lk 24:29; Acts 1:8, 2:33). The time of the church* is the time of the gift of the Spirit to all believers; Pentecost (Acts 2) is the act of foundation of the first Christian Church and the beginning of the time of the church. In becoming a constituent part of the third period of the history of salvation*, the Spirit no longer has eschatological grandeur, strictly speaking; it is an element of the penultimate time.

b) Reception of the Spirit during Time of the Church. Baptism and reception of the Spirit are also closely connected in Luke, but their articulation may take different forms. For one, baptism in the name* of Jesus is none other than the expression of the conversion* of a person to God and to Jesus; in view of this, it precedes the gift of the Spirit (*see* Acts 2:38). Prayer* also can prepare for reception of the gift of the Spirit (Acts 4:31). Second, reception of the Spirit may also precede baptism (*see* Acts 10:45–48). In this respect, the role played by the laying* on of hands should be noted (Acts 8:14–17, 19:2–6).

c) Functions and Effects of the Spirit. During the time of the church, four functions are enumerated: 1) The Spirit is given to all members of the church, and this gift is lasting. 2) The Spirit can manifest itself in a perceptible way: extraordinary physical and psychic phenomena are irrefutable exterior signs of the presence of the Spirit (Acts 2:3f., 4:8, 4:31, 10:45, 19:6). 3) The Spirit's most important function is prophetic-kerygmatic. The Spirit makes it possible to decipher the future (Acts 11:28, 20:23) and discern the hidden will of God (Acts 8:29, 10:19f.); above all it constitutes the foundation of the church's preaching (Acts 1:8, 4:8, 4:31, 6:10, 18:25, etc.). However, neither miraculous acts nor faith, prayer, and love are explicitly presented as fruits of the Spirit. 4) Luke's concentration on the ecclesiological dimension of the history of salvation should be noted. The Spirit determines the church's path in the world and guides it. Thus it ensures the continuity of the last phase of the history of salvation.

5. John

a) Points in Common. Aside from the farewell discourses (Jn 13–17), and despite noteworthy differences in emphasis, John's conception of the Spirit is close to that of classical primitive Christianity (especially Paul and Luke). The Spirit is conceived as a divine and transcendent grandeur (Jn 3:6, 6:63). It is the eschatological gift par excellence, proper to post-paschal times (7:38f., 20:22). Communicated at the moment of baptism (3:35), it is a vivifying force (6:63). Only the Spirit leads one into authentic prayer (4:23f.) and obtains the forgiveness of sins (2:22f.).

b) Farewell Discourses. This is where the specifically Johannine reflection on the Spirit appears, with the introduction of the "Paraclete," a new concept closely related to that of the Holy Spirit (14:26) or the Spirit of truth* (14:17, 15:26, 16:13). The five passages on the Paraclete are found in John 14:16f., 14:26, 15:26, 16:7–11, and 16:13ff.: 1) It is almost impossible to give a good translation of the concept of the Paraclete; each of the classical translations (helper, comforter, advocate, etc.) gives only one aspect. 2) The Paraclete and the Johannine Christ are related by an identity of function; what the earthly Jesus said and accomplished not long ago, the Paraclete says and accomplishes today in the church. In this sense the

Paraclete is none other than the authentic representative of the earthly Jesus during the post-paschal period. 3) As a consequence of this subordination of pneumatology to Christology the central function of the Paraclete is bound to the message. Essentially, the Paraclete is the post-paschal agent of Jesus' eschatological preaching (this concentration of the Spirit on the word is unique within budding Christianity). 4) The first role of the Paraclete is that of *bringing to mind* the words of Jesus (Jn 14:26). He enables a retrospective understanding of the person and history of Jesus. This makes him the central agent of the new interpretation of the story of Jesus, of which the Fourth Gospel is the figure. Subsequent reflection on the Paraclete, initiated in John 16, shows that he not only actualizes the past of the revelation* but interprets post-paschal time in its present and future dimension (judicial function: 16:8–11; hermeneutic: 16:13). 5) In agreement with the whole of budding Christianity, John sees the Paraclete as *a gift of the last times*. But he radicalizes this notion; the Paraclete is not a transitional figure between the time of the Incarnation* and the time of the final fulfillment. In the coming of the Paraclete it is the coming of the risen Christ that is fulfilled—Easter, Pentecost, and Parousia* become one and the same event. The Parousia always happens anew in the coming of the Paraclete.

• E. Käsemann (1958), "Geist. IV. Geist und Geistesgaben im NT," *RGG*3 2, 1272–79.
E. Schweizer (1959), "*pneuma, pneumatikos:* Das Neue Testament," *ThWNT* 6, 394–449.
D. Lys (1962), "Rûach," in *Le souffle dans l'Ancien Testament*, Paris.
F. Hahn (1974), "Das biblische Verständnis des heiligen Geistes," in *Erfahrung und Theologie des heiligen Geistes*, Ed. C. von Heitman and H. Mühlen, Munich, 131–47.
H. Schlier (1974), ibid., "Herkunft, Ankunft und Wirkungen des Heiligen Geistes im Neuen Testament," 118–30.
J. Kremer (1983), "*pneuma,*" *EWNT* 3, 279–91.
J. Guillet et al. (1991), "Saint-Esprit. II. Nouveau Testament," *DBS* 11, 172–398.
F. W. Horn (1992), "Holy Spirit," *AncBD* 3, 180–260.

JEAN ZUMSTEIN AND ANDREAS DETTWILER

See also **Church; Communion; Eschatology; Flesh; Holiness; Johannine Theology; Love; Pauline Theology; Promise; Scripture, Fulfillment of; Trinity; Word of God**

B. Historical and Systematic Theology

The Holy Spirit is the third Person* of the Trinity*. It is unique, equal to the Father* (Paraclete) and the Son, of the same substance and the same nature (Toledo synod XI, 675, *DS* 527). The Spirit is distinguished from the Father and the Son as a "Person" but is not of the same caliber with them as "God*" (*Catechism of the Catholic Church,* 1992, §253–56). The Holy Spirit is distinguished from the two other persons by a relation of origin, which is understood differently in the Catholic and the Orthodox traditions (tradition*). The Father sends the Son and, through the Son, the Holy Spirit for a history of salvation* that begins in the Old Testament (interventions of the Spirit in prophecy) and culminates in the New Testament with the Incarnation* of the Son (gift of the filial Spirit), but is still actualized in time by the Spirit. In this context the Spirit is given many different names (name*): Paraclete, Gift, Sanctification, Energy, Image of the Son, Unction and Seal, Love*, and Charity. Still other names are mentioned in the *CEC* (§691–702).

1. The Holy Spirit in the Tradition up to Council of Florence (1439–1445)

The theology of the Holy Spirit is elaborated between two extremes. The first, the *illuminist* tendency, already mentioned by Paul (the enthusiasts of 1 Cor 6:12–19), dreams of living a universal Pentecost and a palpable experience of the Spirit. This tendency includes Montanism* (second century), Messalianism* (fourth century), Macarius-Symeon (†430?), Joachim of Fiore (†1202) (millenarianism*), medieval mendicant orders, and post-Reformation pietist movements. At the other extreme, a rationalizing movement (Arianism*) made the Holy Spirit a superior vital principle in man, which is not God but an intermediary between God and man. A theology that gave value to the divinity of the Spirit and its personal existence gradually developed between these two extremes.

a) Beginnings. Primitive Christianity is characterized by the fundamental experience* of the presence of

God in human beings through the Spirit (*TRE* 12, 194), which is the overflowing onto them of Christ's Resurrection* (Acts 2; Jl 3:1–5; Eph 1:18ff.), bringing them peace*, joy, inner freedom, freedom before God *(parrèsia)*, fraternal love for each other, and filial love for God. The paschal mystery inaugurates a new era, and the Spirit is its guarantor.

Faith* in the Holy Spirit is rooted in the paschal kerygma (Acts 2:7, 2:32f.), the baptismal formula (Mt 28:19), and the Eucharistic celebration (Justin, *Apologies* I, 65 and 67; *Martyrdom of Polycarp* 14, 2–3). The Spirit inspires the bishop* (Ignatius, *To the Philippians* 7, 1–2) and the "prophets*." The prophetic spirit abandoned the Jewish people and was concentrated in Christ; from Christ it is given to all believers (Justin, *Dialogue with Trypho;* Origen, *De principiis*). Montanus presented himself (c.155–60) in Phrygia (Asia Minor) as the prophet who is the embodiment of the Holy Spirit–Paraclete (Jn 14:26) chosen to inaugurate, on the fringes of the church*, the time of the Spirit. After 200 Montanism reached the West, where it was adopted by Tertullian, who gave it his own style. The individuality of the Spirit was not always gainsaid (e.g., Athenagoras). Certain texts where the Holy Spirit is not mentioned are sometimes considered binitarian (Tertullien non montaniste, Hermas, *Le Pasteur* 59: *see* R. Joly, *SC* 53, p.32).

Irenaeus* of Lyons was the first to give an extensive description of the work of the Spirit (*Adversus haereses.* III, 1; *Epidexis tou apostolikou kerygmatos* 5–7). He clearly distinguished the Son and the Spirit, which are like the two hands of the Father (*Haer.* V, 20, 1; II, 7, 5). The activity of the Spirit is in the service of the Son who is himself subject to the Father (*Epid.* 6–7). His argument for the connection between the Holy Spirit and the church countered the Montanists, (*Haer.* III, 1, 1; 4, 1–2; 24, 1), while his emphasis on the economy of salvation (*Haer.* IV, 20, 6–7) was an answer to the Gnostics.

Tertullian*, in his reaction to the monarchianism of Praxeas, who denied the individuality proper to the Spirit, took the Montanist binitarian images and added a third term, the Spirit: "They are three. Third is in fact the Spirit out of God and the Son, just as third out from the root is the fruit that comes from the branch, and third coming out from the spring the brook that goes out of the river, and third coming out of the sun the point that comes from the ray" (*Against Praxeas* 8). The relationship of origin is envisaged but kept in the background; the perspective is primarily economic. "The Spirit of God" designates the Holy Spirit as it designates the Son or the being* *(substantia)* of God the Father who unfolds in the Son and the Holy Spirit.

The last is a "portion" of the total substance of the Father. It is numbered with him from the beginning (meaning forever) because it is "in the Son" who is numbered with the Father (Moingt). The Son is born of the Father and returns to him (Novatian, *De Trinitate* 31). Zeno of Verona makes the point that the Spirit comes from him, exultation of the one in the other (*Tractatus* II, 3; *see* I, 2, 9; II, 5, 1: Patrologia Latina 11). His unifying role in the church flows from the Trinitarian unity (Cyprian*, *On the Unity of the Catholic Church; Letter* 74, 4). Marius Victorinus (*v. 360: Hymns,* SC 68, 620 and 650), and even more so Augustine, believe that the Spirit is the connection *(copula, complexio)* between the Father and the Son. Ambrose* focuses on the unity of name and substance in God, to the point that what is proper to the Spirit in the common activity is blurred (*De Spir.* I, 13; *De sacram.* VI, 2, 5: Patrologia Latina 16 and SC 25 *bis*). It is not always possible to see what distinguishes the Spirit within the Trinity (Rufinus, *Commentarius in symbolum apostolorum*).

Origen*, on the basis of baptism*, associates the Spirit with the Father and the Son (*De principiis* I, 3, 2 and 5) and wonders about its origin, which is not mentioned in Scripture (ibid., Pref. 1; I, 3, 1). Arguing against the monarchians, he applies to the Spirit these words from John 1:3: "All things came to be *[egeneto]* through him [the Son]" giving *egeneto* the broad sense of a simple derivation in being. Thus the Spirit receives "from the Son," and that is why it is distinguished from him (*Comm. John* II, §75–76). In the following century the derivation of the Spirit with regard to the Son is evident for the Arians and the Macedonians concerned by the First Council of Constantinople* (381). Origen argues that the Spirit that receives from the Son "provides so to speak the matter of the charismas/gifts of God *[hulled tôn kharismatôn]* which, produced out of the Father by the Son subsist according to the Spirit" (*Comm. John* II, §77: *see De principiis* II, 7). The gifts subsist in him insofar as he actualizes them in us (*On Prayer* II, 6; *Commentary on John* VI, §225; *Fr. 8 on Ephesians* 1, 13; *Ser. Commentary on Matthew* 134). This theme is developed in *De principiis* I, 3, 5–8 and II, 7.

b) Fourth Century. Absent at Nicaea (325), the question of the Spirit did not come up for discussion until 359–60. Christians in Lower Egypt who accepted the equality of the Son with the Father made the Holy Spirit a "serving spirit," different only in degree from the angels* (Athanasius*, *To Serapion* I, 1: SC 15). In 374 the "Macedonians" (named after Macedonius, patriarch of Constantinople, deposed in 360) took a position close to that of Nicaea *(Homeousians),* but they too refused to confess the Holy Spirit as God, though never claiming he was a creature (Socrates, *Ecclesiastical Hierarchy* II, 45; Ps.-Dionysus, *Of Trinity* II, 7, 3, and II, 8; Ps.-Athanasius, *Dial. Maced.* I, 4; I, 15). An anonymous Macedonian provided the key to their attitude: " 'No one can say that Jesus* is Lord except by the Holy Spirit' (1 Corinthians 12:3). Therefore, the introduction to God must necessarily be made by another—the Holy Spirit. It follows that if I adore the Holy Spirit, by whom and in whom will I have access to him [the Holy Spirit] to adore [him]?" (*Dial. Maced.* I, 4: Patrologia Graeca 28, 1293 *CD*).

Since the Son is not there any more to make an imaginary bridge between God and man, the Holy Spirit does it in his place. This is what Athanasius and Basil* of Caesarea refused to admit. If the Holy Spirit makes divine, then its nature can no doubt be that of God (Athanasius, *To Serapion* I, 23; I, 25). It works by coming into man as a transforming power *(energeia)* and donation *(dôrea)* (ibid., I, 20; *see* Basil, *Of the Holy Spirit* 16, 47: SC 17 *bis*). But in the Spirit that comes there is the Son who gives it, and in the Son the Father (*To Serapion* I, 30).

The Cappadocian Fathers* (Basil, Gregory of Nyssa, and Gregory of Nazianzus) defended the divinity of the Holy Spirit against the Arian Eunomius. For the latter, the being *(ousia)* of God can be known because it was revealed, but it cannot be communicated, not even to the Son. Gregory* of Nyssa affirms conversely that the being of God is absolutely unknowable to the creature but is communicated to the Son in eternal generation, and may be participated in by creatures by virtue of "energies" *(energeiai)* that God distributes to them, and which are identified with the Holy Spirit insofar as the latter gives himself to believers. Basil insists on the fact that the Spirit reveals the Son without any intermediary, "in himself" (*in heautô: Of the Holy Spirit* 16, 47). Basil also defends the liturgical expression attacked by the Homeousians: "The Father is glorified with *[meta]* the Son and with *[sun]* the Spirit." Reserving the title of God for the Father, he thus expresses the divinity of the Holy Spirit by giving value to its *homotimie* (equality of honor) with the Father and the Son. Elsewhere, specifying what is proper to each of the Three in the Triad, he advances the properties of *paternity, filiation*, and *sanctification* (*Letter* 236, 6; *see Letter* 214, 4). Gregory of Nazianzus substitutes for *sanctification* the word *procession* (*ekporeusis: Discourse* 31, 8). The connection with the creature, still felt in the word *sanctification* (Basil), disappears with the use of the word *procession*, which takes a fully intra-Trinitarian sense (Gregory). This emphasizes the perfect independence of God with regard to the creature, but may lead to forgetting the bond that God freely made with the creature, and which is testified in Scripture.

c) Augustine. It is with Augustine* that the doctrine of the Holy Spirit as love or charity comes to impose itself in the West (*De Quant. animae 34; De fide et symbolo* 9, 19–20; *Trin.* VI, 5, 7; XV, 19, 37). The Spirit is the love of the Father and the Son "hypostasized" in a third "Person," but also the love of God spread in our hearts (Rom 5:5 cited more than 200 times by Augustine). This theme of the Spirit-as-love is one of the themes that structures Augustine's thought (Congar, *Bibliothèque augustinienne*).

In the anagogical context of the neoplatonic emanatist scheme, the Spirit constitutes, at the term of the *exitus-reditus,* the stabilization *(monè)* in love that unifies and brings happiness (*Soliloquies* I, 1, 3; *De ver. rel.* 55, 113). The psychological analogy* puts it parallel to human will and love. The link between Holy Spirit and love finds one of its justifications here (O. du Roy, *L'intel. de la foi en la Trinité selon saint Augustin,* 1966).

Augustine's distinction between absolute and relative divine names (Trinity*) raised a problem because in the "relative" double name Holy Spirit the two words are equally appropriate for the Father and the Son, but this is proper to "absolute" names. Augustine sees this as an indication that the Holy Spirit belongs to both of them (*Filioque*). The name Gift of God (Acts 8:20) does have a "relative" character, but *ad extra.* So Augustine calls on two other names, *donabile* and *donatum.* The Holy Spirit is in all eternity susceptible of being given *(donabile)* and this is why, within time, he is effectively given *(donatum).* The work of salvation thus finds a certain foundation in God himself.

d) Middle Ages. Augustine did not dare to apply the triad "lover, loved, love" to God (*Trin.* VIII, 10, 14). It can be found in operation in Richard of Saint-Victor (†1141; *Of the Trinity* III, 2; III, 18). Love implies openness and alterity (*condilectio, consocialis amor*) and thus "Trinity," a theme taken up by Bonaventure* (*I Sent.,* d. 13, q. 1). It survived in its Augustinian form, as illustrated notably by Anselm* of Canterbury (†1109), who underscores the extraordinary coincidence of intra-Trinitarian love (*Monologion* 53) with its overflow *ad extra* (*De la procession du Saint Esprit.* 9, Ed. M. Corbin, 1990, *Œuvres*).

Like Augustine, Paschasius Radbert (†860), William of Saint Thierry († c. 1149), and Peter Lombard (†1160) identify the Spirit and love *(caritas),* the Spirit being one with grace*, the Giver identified with the gift (*I Sent.*, d. 14 and 17; III, d. 22, q. 13 and d. 23, q. 30). Alexander of Hales (†1245) unites created grace (in man) and uncreated grace (the Holy Spirit present) on the basis of the hypostatic* union. The whole body communes in the grace of the head (*Summa Theologica* III, inquis. I, tract. I, q. 2, no. 609 resp.; tract. III, q. 1, no. 99 resp. and no. 112 resp.). Contrary to this, Thomas of Aquinas distinguishes grace—created gift—and the person of the Spirit—uncreated gift—truly given (*Summa Theologica* Ia IIae, q. 110; *Of Truth*, q. 27, a. 2; *Summa Theologica* IIa IIae, q. 23, a. 2 resp. where Thomas argues against *I Sent.*, d. 17 by Paraclete Lombard).

Thomas* Aquinas systematized the ideas of Augustine; the procession of the Spirit is made by way of will. It proceeds from the Father and the Son "as from a single principle" by a unique *spiration* (Trinity). In *Commentary on the Sentences by Peter Lombard*, Thomas presents the Trinitarian mystery* as the site where a theology of grace is rooted. An entire spiritual edifice is founded on the gift of the Spirit, personal intra-Trinitarian love, which makes itself temporal gift, principle of the gifts granted to human beings so that they might be adopted and made divine in the Son. The *Summa Theologica* carries over these ideas, but blurs the link between the Trinity and the *deification* of man. The Trinity is envisaged in itself and the divine Persons as such are isolated from the work of salvation. This can be seen as a "retreat" of the master under the hold of an Augustinianism* that dissociates the Trinity from its works (Bouyer 1980). In line with the *inseparabiliter operari* (Augustine, *Trinity* I, 5, 8), he treats filial adoption on the same footing as the Creation*, as a work *ad extra*. Consequently, in the rigor of terms we are not the sons of the Father but of the Trinity (*Summa Theologica* IIIa, q. 23, a. 2 resp. and ad 2; *see* Gregory* Palamas, Patrologia Graeca 110, 1213 AC). This trend of overly speculative theology gave rise finally to a reaction of opposition in medieval spiritual movements and, at the dawn of the modern era, Luther's Reformation.

e) The Spirit and the Mystics. Meister Eckhart (†1327), heir to Thomas and Augustine but also to Origen, takes up the theme of the believer endlessly engendered by the Father "in the Holy Spirit" (*Deutsche Werke* I; *see Livre consol. divine, éd. Libera*, 1993; *see* M. Vannini, "La justice et la génération du Logos," in *Voici Maître Eckhart*, 1994). John of the Cross declares that the soul* loves God as much as it is loved by him, "because it loves him with the will of God himself, in the same love with which he loves it, which is the Holy Spirit" (*Cant. Sp.* 38, 2). The Spirit informs it "so that it will aspire to God with the same aspiration of love that the Paraclete aspires for the Son and the Son for the Paraclete, which is the Holy Spirit itself." (ibid., 39, 3).

2. Conciliar Definitions

A major reference for the Christian creed, the Nicaea Council (325) mentions the Holy Spirit in a brief but significant formula at the end of its "Symbol," referring to it as a trace of the rite of baptism in the creed: "And [I believe] in the Holy Spirit" (*DS* 125). Constantinople I (381) mentions the Spirit in two places: "We believe... in Jesus Christ, made flesh of *[ek]* the Holy Spirit and [of] the Virgin Mary*." And, further on: "And we believe in the Holy Spirit, Lord and vivifier, who proceeds *[to ekporeuomenon]* from the Father *[ek tou patros]*, who with the father receives like adoration and like glory, who spoke through the prophets" (*DS* 150). This second development defends the divinity of the Spirit against the Macedonians. The substitution of *ek* for the *para* of John 15:26 must refer to the Nicaean *ek,* which has the strong sense of the origin "coming from the substance" (of the Father). But the technical vocabulary of Nicaea was not carried over. The origin from the Father is the principal sign testifying to the "divinity" of the Spirit, equally suggested by the divine title of Lord (*to kurion*) and the divine action of vivifying (*kai zôopoion*). The adoration and glorification of the Spirit with the father and with the Son signifies that it has the same rank (*connumeration:* Basil, *Of the Holy Spirit* 17, 42–3), but also that it is a divine "Person," receiving as and with them the same worship. By its liturgical and soteriological reference the symbol recovers the "economic" perspective of Scripture. Other councils mentioned the Holy Spirit. Toledo (several synods: *DS* 188, 470, 485, 490, 527); Lyons* II (1274), where it was specified that the Holy Spirit proceeds from the Father and the Son "not as from two principles, but as from a single principle..., by a unique *spiration*" (*DS* 850); and Florence (1439–45), where the question of the *Filioque* was answered at length (*Enchiridion Symbolorum* 1300–1302) and it was recalled that "in God all is one where an opposition of relation is no obstacle" (*DS* 1330).

3. Turning Point of the Reformation

a) Luther* broke with the traditional reading of Scripture and excluded the church's mediation in interpretation of the sacred text, leaving all the room for the Holy Spirit. His notion of justification* further increased the importance of the Spirit: human beings are justified insofar as, by the presence of the Spirit, Christ with his justice* covers the injustice of the sinner (*WA* 56, 280). The gift of grace must be received on a base of a sin* that endures. This is why the Holy Spirit is both the Illuminator who elucidates by "inner testimony" the word* of God and the Comforter who rescues from despair. The church remains the place where the gospel is announced. Salvation is accomplished within it but does not come from it. It directly reaches individuals, who constitute the invisible church, whose unity* is ensured by the Spirit (J. L. Witte, *DSp* 4, 1961, 1318–33; F. Refoulé, *RSPhTh* 1964, 428–70).

Calvin* adopted and organized Luther's thought. He emphasized the bond between the Spirit and the visible church. The presumption plays in favor of the church when it comes to interpreting Scripture, but in the last resort the decision is up to the believer who receives the immediate testimony of the Spirit (*De Inst.* IV, 9, 12; *see DSp* 4).

On the fringes of traditional Protestantism*, the pietist movements (pietism*) also emphasized the personal action of the Spirit, in a way that could make the "external testimony" of the church unintelligible. They could not surmount the 18th-century wave of rationalism, which dissociated the activity of Christ from that of the Spirit. Christ becomes a simple moral example and the Spirit a "divine force" identified with human intelligence. Nineteenth-century idealism, notably with Hegel*, developed a notion of the Spirit *(Allgeist)* in which it is very difficult to find the third Person of the Trinity. Schleiermacher*'s (1768–1834) attempt to reconcile Christian discourse with the exigencies of the new rationality worked to the detriment of the divine personality of the Spirit. A. Ritschl (1822–89) abandoned, in the name of reason*, the doctrine of the Trinity as dogma* of the faith. A. von Harnack in Germany and A. Sabatier in France reduced the dogmatic formulations to simple transitory expressions of Christian thought that can be explained by the historical conditions of their elaboration, consequently void of any constraining value in the present day. In the early 20th century Barth opposed the tendencies of what was known as "liberal" theology with his "dialectical theology."

b) Karl Barth* developed at an early stage a pneumatology based on the lordship of the Holy Spirit (*see* "The Lord, is that Spirit" [2 Cor 3:17]). This lordship is exercised over the destiny of man, who must recognize himself as radically a sinner, placed under the judgment* of God so that a new man will be born in him by the work of the Spirit. This is presented as the "subjective revelation*" of God coming to man by the Son. The Incarnation of the Son does not make the Spirit's mission useless; it postulates it. For man is in

fact incapable all alone of opening himself to the Son as God and to the Father. The opening of man to God, on the one hand, and the freedom of God to come into man, on the other hand, are identified with the given Holy Spirit. The Spirit actualizes *in us* that which is revealed, that is, our redemption. This thought shares the perspective of the church fathers, especially the Greek Fathers rediscovered in the 19th century.

4. Current Questions

a) Indwelling of the Holy Spirit in the Human Person. At the end of the 19th century, Scheeben* and Th. de Régnon (†1893), using D. Petau's (†1652) works on the church fathers, sought to give restored value to the personal role of the Holy Spirit in the work of salvation. A brief on the question was assembled by P. Galtier (*Le Saint-Esprit en nous d'après les Pères grecs,* Rome, 1946). His critique of Régnon is limited to the refutation of a thesis that supposedly makes the Holy Spirit's activity so personal ("hypostatic") that it would exclude the roles of the other two Persons. But this argument deforms Régnon's thesis and fails to consider the patristic texts and the true weight of the "becoming-son" that places man within and not outside the Trinity. "Those are not . . . pure relations with the outside, because just as well grace makes us really penetrate *ad intra Dei*" (G. Philips, *EThL,* 1948, 134). More recently, Bouyer (1980), Rahner* (*Theological Writings* 1, 110–11; 3, 65–69), and Congar (1979, vol. 2; *see Chrétiens en dial.,* 1964) have demonstrated that the patristic approach is in accord with Scripture.

b) Discernment of Spirits. In the primitive perspective, man is surrounded by various spirits, some of them working for the good spirit and others for the evil one. He must recognize what comes from which one, it being understood that the evil spirit tries to fool him by trying to pass for the good one (*see* Gn 3). This theme is already found in the second-century works of Hermas (*Le Pasteur,* 33–49: SC 53). It reaches a peak with Origen, who had a lasting influence on Eastern and then Western monasticism* *(DSp).* A significant resurgence (ibid.) is found in the teaching and practice of Ignatius of Loyola (†1556) (Ignatian spirituality).

c) The Holy Spirit and the Church. Russian Orthodox theology (modern and contemporary Orthodoxy*) was stimulated in the late 19th century by the thinking of Khomiakov, who claimed that the church is not first a visible institution but an invisible reality animated by the Spirit. What constitutes it "is neither the numerical figures of believers nor their visible assembly; it is the very bond that unites them. The church is the revelation of the Holy Spirit to the mutual love of Christians, and the very love that leads them to the Father by his incarnate Word" (*L'Église latine et le protestantisme, Lausanne*, 1872).

This pneumatological ecclesiology* was balanced by contributions of other Orthodox authors (Soloviyov*, Boulgakov, Florovsky, Afanassieff, and recently J. Zizioulas). But the restoration of the Spirit's value remains an accepted fact. It is also found in Germany (J. A. Moehler, 1796–1838) and England (Newman*).

In the Catholic Church some importance was given to the theme of the Spirit as soul of the church. It was rare in the earliest centuries. With Origen this role is played by the Word (*Contra Celsum* VI, 48). Augustine refers to it twice (*Sermons* 267, 4 and 268, 2; beginnings in *Commentary on John* XXVI, 6, 13 and XXVII, 6, 6). Thomas Aquinas takes it up and refines it (*De veritate* 29, 4 c). It is found in Leo XIII and Pius XII (*Mystici Corporis,* 1943: *Tromp, Litt. encycl.,* 3rd Ed., 1958). The comparison is not useful unless the difference from hypostatic union is noted. The Spirit in the church intervenes only on the level of freedoms (Vl. Lossky, *Essay on the Mystic Theology of the Eastern Church,* 1944, and already Origen, *De principiis* 3, 5: the Spirit acts only on the saints, who adhere freely to Christ). It is from the heart of believers that it establishes with Christ—and through them—a particular type of unity.

Mühlen (1964), going on the ancient notion of persona (Tertullian; Augustine and the only "persona" of "the complete Christ," both Head and Body of the church), takes from Thomas Aquinas the expression "mystical person" to say that the Holy Spirit is "a person in multiple persons." "Person" designates here the Spirit as engaged in a complex play of relations within the church, the "body of Christ" in the sense of *collective body,* in line with the Old Testament *basar* (flesh), but transposed to designate a "corporate personality" (J. A. T. Robinson*, The Body,* London, 1952; J. de Fraine*, Adam et son lignage,* Paris, 1959; R. H. Gundry*, Sôma,* Cambridge, 1976). This "body" of Christ, the new community of believers, is constituted in relation with the risen Christ. Christ unfolds in a "grand ego" (Mühlen) that is not the prolongation of the Incarnation but a distinct reality, constituted under the influence of the Spirit: "Just as the Logos really made itself man in the unique human nature [*see* Jn 1:14], so the Spirit of Jesus really 'made' itself Church in the social organism of the Church" (ibid.).

Y. Congar also noted the importance of the Holy Spirit in theology after Vatican* II, in counterbalancing a legitimate but sometimes overly unilateral emphasis on Christology*. The role of Christ is not limited to putting visible structures in place. Within the framework of a "pneumatological Christology," his role must be understood in relation to the action of the Spirit, which is necessarily invisible. But the Spirit in turn cannot be isolated from Christ. The church is the (mystical) body of Christ, not of the Holy Spirit (Congar 1979; *see* id., Mélanges G. Philips, Gembloux, 1970).

d) From Sects to Charismatic Movements. The sects (taken in the sociological meaning of the term) give great importance to the Spirit, which is generally accepted as the third Person of the Trinity, even if the mystery is often obscured. Its function is to realize "the inner illumination" in believers that unites them with the Spirit itself or with God. The emphasis is placed on the felt experience of a personal intervention of the Spirit in the individual, with particular attention to certain charismas (special gifts: 1 Cor 12), connected to the event of Pentecost. The "charismatic movements" or "movements of renewal" are a special case, distinguished from the sects, because they are officially recognized by the Catholic hierarchy* and have recently come to play a significant role in the life of the churches (Congar 1979; *see* Pentecostalism*).

e) The "Theology/Economy" Relation and the Filioque. Orthodox theology, insofar as it maintains a radical monopatrism (the Spirit proceeds from the Father alone), not as a *theologoumenon* but as a dogma of faith, cannot accept transposition from the level of economy, where the Son intervenes in the gift of the Spirit, to the level of theology, where he does not intervene (*see* the declaration of S. Verkhovsky at the Colloquia of Saulchoir [1950], *Russia and Christianity*). However, for Catholic theology, the correspondence from one level to another is evident (ibid.). Everything that the Old Testament reveals of God is done in an economic context. Rahner advances the axiom according to which "the Trinity manifest in the economy of salvation is the immanent Trinity and, reciprocally" (*Theological Writings,* 1967, *MySal* II/1, 328). In the economy God is revealed as he is in himself because his plan is to make us participate in his intra-Trinitarian life such as it is in itself, by making us "sons in the Son" by the gift of the Spirit.

Equally for Barth (1932), there is no other reality behind that of the revelation that would be God: "It is because of the intra-divine reciprocal communion* of the Holy Spirit that proceeds from the Father and the Son that there is, in the revelation, a communion of God and man, in which God is not only there for man but—and that is the *donum Spiritus sancti*—where man is also really there for God." The inconceivable possibility of communion with God already exists in the Trinity: it is the Holy Spirit, eternal foundation in God of what is given to humanity within time.

f) Among other subjects that could still be envisaged one might mention: 1) the question of the *eucharistic epiclesis** (does the conversion of the bread and wine into the body and blood of Christ in the eucharistic consecration depend on the words pronounced by the priest in the name of Christ, or on the invocation of the Holy Spirit?), with the more general question of the role of the Holy Spirit in the liturgy*; and 2) the question of the Spirit in the ecumenical movement. Another subject has hardly been studied though clearly suggested in Scripture (Acts 2; Rom 1:4)—the connection between the Holy Spirit and the paschal mystery. This is the theme of a resurrection that has already begun (2 Tm 2:18; Phil 3:1), of that resurrection as the overflow upon all humanity of the Resurrection of Christ. It is a theme that runs through the whole of patristic literature, but as evidence that one does not seek to demonstrate. It is concealed within a vocabulary where the Holy Spirit has an important place, but the word "resurrection" does not appear. Seeking deeper into this theme in Scripture and the church fathers might provide the occasion for developing a theology that interrogates the mystery of God through the extraordinary gift he made of himself to himself through man . . . in the Spirit.

• Th. de Régnon (1892 and 1898), *Études de Theologie positive sur la Sainte Trinité,* 4 vols., Paris.
K. Barth (1932), *Die Kirchliche dogmatik* I/1, §12 (*Dogmatique,* Geneva, vol. 2, 1953, 140–78).

Coll. (1950), "Le Filioque," *Russie et chrétienté.*
J. Guillet et al. (1961), "Esprit Saint," *Dictionnaire de spirtualité ascetique et mystique* 4, 1246–1333.
Coll. (1963), *Le Saint-Esprit,* Geneva.
H. Mühlen (1964), *Una mystica persona: Eine Person in vielen Personen,* Paderborn.
G. Kretschmar (1968), "Le développement de la doctrine du Saint: Esprit, du Nouveau Testament à Nicée," *Verbum Caro: Revue théologique et ecclésiastique oecuménique* 88, 5–55.
P. Evdokimov (1969), *L'E.S. dans la tradition orthodoxe,* Paris.
Coll. (1972), "La Procession du Saint Esprit," *Ist* 17, 261–456.
Rahner (1975), *Schr. zur Th.* 12, Zürich-Einsiedeln-Köln.
Coll. (1978), *L'Esprit Saint,* Brussels.
F. Bolgiani (1979), "La th. de l'Esprit Saint, de la fin du Ier s. au concile de Constantinople (381)," *Les quatre fleuves,* no. 9, 33–72.
Y. Congar (1979–80), *Je crois en l'Esprit Saint,* 3 vols., Paris; New Ed. in 1 vol., 1995.
L. Bouyer (1980), *Le Consolateur,* Paris.
J. Lison (1980), *L'Esprit répandu: La pneumatologie de Grégoire Palamas,* Paris.
Coll. (1983), *Credo in Spiritum Sanctum,* Atti del Congresso . . . di Pneumatologia, 2 vols., Rome.
J.-Y. Lacoste (1987), "La th. et l'E.," *NRTh* 109, 660–71.
H. U. von Balthasar (1987), *Theologik. 3. Der Geist der Wahrheit,* Einsiedeln.
A. de Halleux (1990), *Patrologie et œcuménisme,* 303–442 (repr. of six pneumatology studies).
W. Pannenberg (1993), *Systematische Theologie* 3, Göttingen, 13–114.
B. J. Hilberath (1994), *Pneumatologie,* Düsseldorf.
O. González de Cardedal (1997), "El Espíritu, la Iglesia y el Mundo," in *La entraña del cristianismo,* Salamanca, 683–870.

JOSEPH WOLINSKI

See also **Christ and Christology; Filioque; God, Father; Trinity; Word**

Hope

a) Biblical Theology. "The undoubted expectation of beatitude to come" (Thomas* Aquinas, *ST* IIa IIae, q. 18, a. 4) linked in Pauline* theology to faith* and to charity (1 Cor 13:13), hope is only theologically intelligible in a framework of biblical references in which the category of promise* plays a special role. The experience of Israel* does indeed replace the cyclical notion of time* that predominated in paganism* with the linear notion of a time arranged into a history*. In this history God* manifests himself as the master of the future, and destines human beings to a future—the very name* of YHWH, as it is revealed in Exodus 3:14, is perhaps already the guarantee of a future. Open by promises, the hope of Israel itself had to know a history. After the promise of a land there followed the promises made to the monarchy of David (2 Sm 7:12–17) or the prophetic announcement of eschatological salvation* (e.g., Ez 8:23b–9:6). The

Deuteronomist tradition* retains the hope of renewal and a universalization of the covenant* (Ez 34:25, 37:26), of a revivification of man (Ez 11:19f., 18:31, 36:26) and a new presence of YHWH amidst his people* (Ez 40–47). In the Psalms*, hope is expressed as trust in God in the midst of suffering (13:6, 22:5, etc.), or else it is a source of praise* (33:18–22). The various messianic representations orient history toward the people's absolute future; and in the face of death*, apocalyptic theology looks to the absolute future of the individual (Is 26; Dn 12:1ff.), while trust in the closeness of God is encountered even at the very heart of death (Ps 73:26ff.).

To an experience placed under the sign of unfulfillment, the New Testament first of all opposes an experience of fulfillment, such that hope cannot play a primary role and that, paradoxically, the fullness of theological realities is first offered to an act of memory. The event on which the Christian understanding of man and God is based—the "Jesus Christ event"—happened when "the time had fully come" (Gal 4:4); in Jesus* of Nazareth, it is equally the "fullness of God" that lived among men (Col 1:19, 2:9); and again, on Good Friday, it is a word of accomplishment that the Gospel* of John puts in the mouth of the Crucified (Jn 19:30). After the imprecise wait for the messiah that characterizes the time of the pre-paschal ministry*, there comes the time of the messianic confession; and if Jesus is indeed the Messiah* of Israel and the savior of nations, it must be said that, in him, the time of promise has come to an end. The first word of Jesus' preaching announces the proximity of the Kingdom* (Mk 3:2; Mt 10:7; Lk 10:9) and gives rise to an expectation—on Easter Day, it does seem that the time of waiting has passed.

The new classification of future promises is nevertheless essential to the Christian experience, even if it only happens subsequently. Since the founding events remembered in the liturgy*, the permanent—the *eschaton*—has its hold on the temporary—history—and the canon* of the New Testament refracts this hold in a plurality of eschatological notions that in different ways link the eschatological and the christological. Beyond this irreducible plurality (in Matthew, the eschatology* of the fulfillment of promises made to Israel; in John, a theology of the glory* of God manifested in the world; in Luke, the elucidation of the meaning of the time of the church*; etc.; *see* Woschiz, 1979), it remains true that in Jesus new promises were made to human beings, and that, in the time of the world, they must remain unfulfilled. Understood as promise (e.g., Rom 8:29), the resurrection* of Jesus teaches hope. Even for communities who expected the imminent return of Christ, it was quite necessary to

name hope at the same time as faith and charity (1 Cor 13:13); and the symbols of faith were to express the meaning of the fundamental Christian hope in speaking of awaiting "the resurrection* of the dead" ("of flesh") and "the life of the world to come" ("eternal life*").

b) Patristic and Medieval Theology. For classical antiquity, the concern for the present through the future, through both hope and fear, belonged only to the logic of affects, and the Stoic ethic concluded that access to virtue—to *ataraxia*—entailed the command of all hope. Except for Zenon of Verona († c. 375), author of the first treatise *De Spe, Fide, et Caritate* (PL 11, 269–80), Thomas Aquinas, and also Ambrose* of Milan (*In Ps. 118 Sermo Tertius,* PL 15, 1223–40) and Augustine* (*Enchiridion de Fide, Spe et Caritate,* PL 40, 230–90), the theology of hope would integrate the *pathos* of waiting within the framework of a doctrine of the virtues*.

The present of Christian experience cannot, in fact, really harbor the blessed life. And even if man does experience peace*—*hèsukhia, quies*—this is never the possession of definitive goods, but rather the pleasure of their "guarantee" (*see* 2 Cor 1:22; Eph 1:14). The ancient vision of an uncertain future that disturbs the present is then replaced by a present concerned with a promised beatitude that is not comparable to any bliss that can be experienced in the time of the world, a beatitude that is nothing man can give to himself, and cannot be hoped for without a divine initiative (grace*) that makes of man someone who hopes. The order of hope is that of the theology: like faith and charity, hope is therefore *totaliter ab extrinseco* (Thomas, *ST* Ia IIae, q. 63, a. 1).

But, just as theological faith and charity are not the only human experiences signifying love and having faith (just as there is also a "natural" experience of believing and love*), the supernatural logic of hope can be interpreted against the background of a "natural" capacity of hoping that can itself take place in a theory of virtue. Augustine had already interpreted the basic modes of temporality as preunderstandings of the fundamental logic of the Christian experience. Thomas went further. He considered that there exists a virtuous relationship between natural man and the future, and identifies *magnanimity* as the virtue that holds its (in proper Aristotelian terms) between the two vices of presumption and despair in order to wisely welcome what is not yet.

One can therefore offer an analysis of hope that pertains to the natural element as well as the theological one (*In Sent.* III, d. 16, q. 1–5). It is hope's distinctive feature to reach out toward a *good,* toward a good that is difficult to get to (*arduum*), to a *future* good, finally to a *possible* good. The present of all hope is therefore marked with insufficiency: just as one cannot "see" what one does not "believe," one does not possess what one hopes, both in the natural order and in the theological order. But because nonpossession is theologically linked to a certitude, it does not engender any misery. Thomas does of course acknowledge that a certain insecurity (*anxietas, angustia*) affects the hoping conscience (*ST* Ia IIae, q. 40, a. 8). The absolute future to which theological hope is related is nevertheless promised with enough strength for hope to hope "certainly": the reasons for hoping are rooted in the reasons for believing; thus, hope is as reasonable as it is virtuous.

c) Secularized Hope.   Hope hopes for the *eschaton*, under the formality of an eschatological beatitude that the time of the world cannot harbor. Its content is therefore that of the last item of the creeds of faith, and is especially *only* this; and if historic goods can also be hoped for, it would exclusively be "spiritual or temporal possession that are valuable as means for obtaining eternal life" (Billot 1905). Henceforth, history is only history. And if this history has its theological secret, which is to shelter the "city* of God" in its temporal peregrinations, hope in no way ceases to give believers a manner of referring to definitive realities. The classical theology of hope (theology for which nothing that happens before death can be the object of a theological hope, except for that in the world that brings a person to their eternal beatitude) is not, however, the first word of theology, nor the last possible figure of a hope.

In the church's beginnings, the millenarian temptation (that of waiting for a time before the end of time in which Christ visibly reigns amidst his people) was not that of a possible abolition of hope within a historical experience, but did lead to a new messianic dynamic of history. And although Joachim of Fiore's new millenarianism* did not hope either that the *eschaton* would happen fully in the "age of the Spirit" that he foresaw, his hope did postulate that there were still divine promises that would be realized in a coming history (or even an imminent one). The former millenarianism was eventually considered incompatible with an orthodox Christian eschatology, and Joachimism emerged as early as the 13th century as a heterodox version of Christian hope. Nevertheless, the "spiritual posterity" (Lubac* 1979–80, already Löwith 1949) of a vision of history that greatly influenced the modern reorientations of Christian hope was more considerable than the critiques of Joachism by Bonaventure (Ratzinger 1959) or Thomas Aquinas (Saranyana 1979). Is it possible to imagine a history

that leaves nothing to hope for? Modern thought suggests this by acting as substitute for traditional theological discourse on history. Outlining an approach to the idea of universal history, Kant* observed that "philosophy* too has its millenarianism" (Weischedel VI, 45). For Hegel*, philosophy is written at the end of history; and if this end is not an end of time, it at least opens a new aeon in which no eschatological tension seems to be able to animate human beings anymore. For Schelling*, the pneumatological wealth of the present and the mysticism* of the "Johannic" church also loses interest in hope. This immediately implies a God that no longer imposes the duty to hope on man has died, favoring immanent processes that govern the world; it also implies that man can also understand and master, in a way that he gives himself reasons to hope. There was also a theological debate during the classical age, with the quietism* controversy, in which the defense and illustration of hope had significance for the decisions of the Roman magisterium* (*DS* 2201–69, 2351–74). When they pleaded for a spiritual experience influenced by "quietude," the quietists or semiquietists seemed to disassociate man from his absolute future: pure love is given to God for the love of God, and not out of hope that God will fulfill promises; the "children" of God "love the Father* selflessly, not out of hope or fear*" (Fénelon, *Explication des Maximes des Saints...*, Ed. Chérel, Paris, 1911). The sustained language is in fact the language of eschatological anticipation, and therefore must be sustained with caution. Fénelon was right to recall the rights of mystical experience. These rights, however, can only be defended by simultaneously recalling that no kind of anticipation gives the mystic possession of his absolute future; the most "disinterested" hope continues to be a hope and proves that the praying figure today lives in the element of provisionality; all sound logic of spiritual life* must include a logic of eschatological desire.

The modern secularization* of hope was moreover accompanied by the disappearance of the idea of beatitude. With Fichte and also Hegel, it was possible for them to sustain the language of beatitude to express a philosophical experience that questioned the Absolute. But, when it involved giving a hope to human beings that divine promise no longer expresses, philosophy will promise them a bliss experienced in the shadow of death. Atheist and secularized eschatologies can certainly call on hope (*see* Bloch 1954–55). They can use the entire system of biblical images and symbols for their messianism. They can sustain the language of *salvation* (the world as *laboratorium possibilis salutis*). They can criticize the present in the name of an "ontology of being* that is not yet," for which the basic formula is not about a subject receiving a predication (the sky is blue), but about the predication being not yet possible (the world is not yet man's happy home). Nevertheless, they come up against death as against what is unthinkable, which they can only silence or trivialize; and the hope to which they give rise is in fact the unhoped for.

d) Contemporary Trends. Theology responded to the secularization of eschatology by spectacularly reaffirming its own *logos* and by affirming the eschatological weight of all its discourse. However, this response is not unified, and clear tendencies emerge. 1) Confronting Heidegger*'s existential analytics on the one hand, and inheriting on the other hand a project of demythologization that goes back to the Enlightenment, Bultmann* considers the *eschaton* in the present: the existence that seizes what is most its own—that reaches its authenticity—is eschatological existence. The meaning of its present cannot only (Heidegger's lesson) unfold in this single present: eschatological existence must have its own relationship to the future. But just as traditional representations of the absolute future were rejected as mythological products, a theology in which the conceptual pairing "available" and "unavailable" *(verfügbar/unverfügbar)* replaced "natural" and "supernatural*" had nothing better to categorize, in terms of hope, than an opening to the future understood as an opening to the God who is coming. It is postulated that it dissipates fears of death (1961)—a hope that is weak enough to be manipulated by F. Buri, whose "dekerygmatized" eschatology once again entrusted human beings with their own forces and offered a hope that was comparable to "new liberal Protestantism" (*Dogmatik*... III, 277–576). 2) In answer to theories for which the *eschaton* is a predicate of existence (Moltmann 1964; Metz 1968), there are theories for which the *eschaton* is the prolific instance of a historical practice. A concern for the "last things" comes first, because the first word belongs to the resurrection of Jesus. Hope, however, does not only hope for the last things. The time before the end of time— the time of the "second-to-last things"—should also be understood in light of theological hope: divine promises are not yet fulfilled. In theologies where "being itself must be considered from the future" (Pannenberg 1967), God and Christ therefore keep a "future," and it is by being at the service of God's future (ibid.) that the Christian experiences hope. According to Bloch, man will, in the end, give himself a "homeland" (Bloch 1955). Theology has a twofold answer to the offer of a secularized Kingdom. It concedes, on the one hand, that the present realm of Christian experience is not the eschatological homeland, but affirms

that Christian eschatological hope nevertheless has the status of a "historical force generating creative utopias" in world history (Moltmann 1969). On the other hand, it recalls that promises that allow for hope come from beyond death, in such a way that it would not be possible to experience the fulfillment of all these promises on this side of death.

The possibility of holding together this concession, this affirmation, and this reminder is without a doubt the *articulus stantis et cadentis* of such a theology. 3) Relearning to hope in the plural is not the smallest achievement of recent theology. The place of hope is the church, and being-in-the-church is being-in-communion. The idea of hoping to the end of one's eschatological destiny, and this idea only, is then clearly inconsistent. Formulated in 1689 by the Jesuit Th. Muniessa, then rediscovered and championed by P. Charles (1889–1954) (*NRTh* 1934, 1009–21 and 1937, 1057–75), the idea of a hope of Christ contradicts the Augustinian axiom according to which one hopes only for oneself (*see Enchiridion* ...PL 40, 235). And if Christ hoped (during his life on earth) and continues to hope (until the predestined have come into possession of celestial glory), it therefore means that the object of hope is not the eternal beatitude of the one who hopes, but the beatitude of all those who are capable of it. Hope, therefore, is found in the communion* of saints. In an almost purely philosophical analysis, G. Marcel also notes: " 'I hope in you for us'; this is perhaps the most adequate and developed expression of the act that the verb to hope still translates in a confused and general way" (1944). Balthasar* (1986) would also insist that the absolute future of others is not the object of eschatological speculations, but the object of a hope that applies to all. J. Daniélou (1905–74) had said it already: "Hope concerns the salvation of all men—and it is only in so far as I am included among them that it has any relevance for me" (*Essai sur le mystère de l'histoire,* Paris, 1953). 4) Continuing in the line of the theses of Muniessa and Charles, the classic theory that sees in hope a virtuous way to live in the element of the provisional had to be contested. Balthasar's christological interpretation of hope is mirrored by a threefold interpretation: the real secret of hope is the secret of a logic of giving, surrendering, and trusting in others in which one must see an image of divine life (1984). Rahner* had a similar suggestion. Considered as "a fundamental mode of the relationship to the definitive" (1967), Rahnerian hope is not understood in the light of an eschatological "possession" that is meant to abolish it, but is incorporated into a spiritual topology of that which is called to "abide" (1 Cor 13, 13): because God cannot be "possessed" and because he will eternally be "unavailable," *unverfügbar,* hope belongs both to the temporary structure as it does to the definitive one. 5) Lastly, the concept of hope was not ignored by philosophers of the first half of the 20th century. In a Bergsonian perspective, E. Minkowski categorized the conversion of our "becoming" into a "future" (*Lived Time,* 1970). O.F. Bollnow (1941) sought to bring to light a hope lodged at the root of our emotional life. Pieper (1935) "gave new clothes" to a theory of "natural" hope that could be harmoniously joined to a theology of "supernatural" hope. B. Welte reflected on hope and despair as two original ways of being, and saw in it a need for and an appeal to salvation in a way that the philosophical description leads to the "threshold" of faith (1982), in any case, Lain-Entralgo's conclusion echoes: "Man hopes, naturally, for something that transcends his nature; what is natural, in man, is to be open to the supernatural" (1956). A similar pathos also fills the writings of J. Monchanin: "Hope is consubstantial with the very movement that goes from matter to consciousness through life and ends with man going beyond himself, accepting to be polarized by the Absolute" (1949).

e) Questions. Philosophies of hope cannot, however, hide an important fact, and one that triggers a new hermeneutic situation. Do human beings hope a priori, in accordance with a transcendental determination of what they are? And does the kerygmatic work of theology consist in answering a vague hope, or in awakening hopes that are foreign to each other, by giving *reasons* to hope? This was the case, in the highly modern framework of a *conflict of hopes* in which it seemed absolutely established that man is a hopeful animal, and in which the only thing that mattered was proving that Christianity gives at least as much to hope for as secularized eschatologies and all historical progressivism (Moltmann, Metz, Lash, etc.). However, in the last years of the 20th century there emerged a questioning of all hope. After the time of the "principle of hope," there came the time of the "principle of responsibility" (H. Jones); after the time of utopias, there came a time in which the highest human expectations were simply the expectations of successful communication (J. Habermas, K.O. Apel). Henceforth, it was only right to debate the possibility of hope *as is:* it was no longer appropriate to question *what* we could hope for (Kant), even supposing that we want to hope. Rather, it involved radically knowing *if* we are still able to hope, and who will give us reasons to do so. Theology classically sustained the language of hope by presupposing its intelligibility and was able in this way to give itself the sole task of manifesting the truth of its discourse. But as soon as precomprehensions and intuitions are lacking, a new endeavor emerges that

dictates a new program for the fundamental* theology of hope: that of proving that the language of hope is a *sensible* language. Relying on one of the most venerable of Christian concepts, classical theological interpretation, with regard to hope, retained the language of fulfillment: the promises transmitted by Christianity came to satisfy a desire—for eternity, for beatitude—that is present in all human expectations. But if the time of the "death of God" is also the time when this desire is most denied, a new practical theology of hope becomes necessary, the first job of which is precisely that of learning how to hope.

However, the reasons of Christian hope are not commensurate with our present and are only revealed through an act of memory (e.g., H. Thielicke, *Der ev. Glaube,* v. III, Tübingen, 1978). And although the world no longer offers any prenotion of a possible hope, the wisest words are words of resignation (or of serenity: Heideggerian *Gelassenheit*), and although no theism any longer really has the means of offering a corresponding hope, it is before, in the "absolute past" of the "Jesus Christ event," that a logic of hope can be formed again. To those who live in a time that leads them to death, the words of promise pronounced and proleptically fulfilled in the story of Jesus say that it is really a question of a pre-paschal time, of a being *towards* death that is not a being *for* death. Those who remember the Risen One remain mortal. But through memory they learn that their destiny is linked to his. Their faith, in a certain way, *compels* them to hope. (Lacoste 1990).

Perhaps such a epochal situation reveals, slightly better than others, the factual condition of man called to believe and hope in the time of the world. There is prestigious support for those who suggest that hope is essentially Christian. Pagan existence is defined in Ephesians 2:12 by atheism and lack of hope. In *The Sickness unto Death,* Kierkegaard* has only one thing to say: that despair is the secret of the pagan experience, including a paganism experienced at the heart of visible Christianity. And when (as Heidegger has it) man only exists within the limits of the world, while the concrete reality of all his hopes is measured by the single eschatology that henceforth remains, death and the whole idea of absolute future is integrated again in the notion of an "authentic" present for which death, understood as a final possibility, is the only master of meaning. The idea of a human nature that is essentially open to a supernatural destiny, from which stems the idea of a certain natural ability to hope, is not thereby invalidated: it is not the supposed omnipresence of a mental fact that is called upon to prove the existence and the topics of the *desiderium naturale.* But a shift is necessary. The one who speaks of being-in-the-world speaks of despair, or rather, unhope (G. Marcel). But the world (understood in both a New Testament and a phenomenological way) is what theological life partly allows to subvert the experience, in a subversion that returns man to the most profound determinations of his being—"authentic" existence is theological experience. The protologic a priori ("natural desire for the beatific* vision," and therefore transcendental hope) is an altered a priori that can be restored through an act of faith. The theological virtues come to man from outside himself—to awaken in him the fundamental acts of existence experienced before God and in the memory of the mystery* of Easter. In the experience of these virtues, man passes *Dasein* as he passes the "mortal."

● L. Billot (1905), *De virtutibus infusis commentarius...*, vol. 1, 2nd Ed., Rome, 355–85.
J. Pieper (1935), *Über die Hoffnung*, Leipzig (*Werke*, vol. 4, Hamburg, 1996, 256–94).
O. F. Bollnow (1941), *Das Wesen der Stimmungen*, Frankfurt (8th Ed. 1995).
G. Marcel (1944), "Esquisse d'une phénoménologie et d'une métaphysique de l'espérance," in *Homo Viator*, Paris, 37–86 (2nd Ed. 1963).
K. Löwith (1949), *Meaning in History*, Chicago.
J. Monchanin (1949), "La crise de l'espérance," *Église vivante* 1, Louvain, 18–35.
E. Bloch (1954–55), *Das Prinzip Hoffnung*, 2 vols., Frankfurt.
R. Le Senne (1955), *La découverte de Dieu*, Paris, 249–78.
P. Lain-Entralgo (1956), *La Espera y la Esperanza*, Madrid.
J. Ratzinger (1959), *Die Geschichtstheologie des heiligen Bonaventura*, Munich-Zürich.
R. Bultmann (1961), "Die christliche Hoffnung und das Problem der Entmythologisierung," *GuV* 3, 81–90.
J. Moltmann (1964), *Theologie der Hoffnung*, Munich (8th Ed. 1969).
G. Sauter (1965), *Verheißung und Erfüllung: Das Problem der Zukunft in der gegenwärtigen theologischen und philosophischen Diskussion*, Zürich.
W. Pannenberg (1967), "Der Gott der Hoffnung," *Grundfr. Syst. Th.*, 387–98.
K. Rahner (1967), "Zur Theologie der Hoffnung," *Schr. zur Th.* 8, 561–79.
J. B. Metz (1968), *Zur Theologie der Welt*, Mainz (CFi 57).
F. Kerstiens (1969), *Die Hoffnungsstruktur des Glaubens*, Mainz.
J. I. Saranyana (1979), *Joachin de Fiore y Tomas de Aquino: Historia doctrinal de una polemica*, Pamplona.
R. Schaeffler (1979), *Was dürfen wir hoffen? Die katholische Theologie der Hoffnung zwischen Blochs utopischem Denken und der reformatorischen Rechtsfertigungslehre*, Darmstadt.
K. M. Woschitz (1979), *Elpis-Hoffnung: Geschichte, Philosophie, Exegese, Theologie eines Schlüsselbegriffs*, Freiburg-Basel-Vienna.
H. de Lubac (1979–80), *La postérité spirituelle de Joachim de Flore*, Paris-Namur, 2 vols.
B. Welte (1982), "Dasein als Hoffnung und Angst," in *Zwischen Zeit und Ewigkeit*, Freiburg-Basel-Vienna, 72–95.
J. Ratzinger (1983), "Über die Hoffnung," *IKaZ* 13, 293–305 (*Com[F]* IX/4, 32–46).
H. U. von Balthasar (1983), *Theodramatik IV, Das Endspiel*, Einsiedeln, 122–67, "Die Gestalt der christlichen Hoffnung."
H. U. von Balthasar (1984), "Die Einheit der theologischen Tugenden," *IKaZ* 13, 306–14.
N. Lash (1986), "All Shall Be Well: Christian and Marxist Hope," in *Theology on the Way to Emmaus*, London, 202–15.
H. U. von Balthasar (1986), *Was dürfen wir hoffen?* Einsiedeln.
J.-Y. Lacoste (1990), *Note sur le temps: Essai sur les raisons de la mémoire et de l'espérance*, Paris.
O. González de Cardedal (1995), *Raíz de la esperanza*, Salamanca.

JEAN-YVES LACOSTE

See also **Beatitude; Eschatology; Faith; History; Love**

Hugh of Saint-Victor. *See* Saint-Victor, School of

Humanism, Christian

According to classic historiography, an educational revolution started in western Europe during the second half of the 15th century and continued throughout the 16th century. Due, above all, to the rediscovery of ancient languages, advocated and taught by teachers of the *studia humanitatis*—the humanists—it then flourished as the movement of thought that historians have labeled "humanism." In fact, the noun was coined in Germany during the Enlightenment, while "humanist" entered into general use during the Renaissance. However, it should not be forgotten that during this period the advocates of Christian humanism, who were not all professional teachers, although they were concerned to teach and to communicate, shared a number of convictions that formed a coherent vision, a type of theological anthropology*, and believed that they could rediscover within it the major intuitions of the Bible* and the church fathers*. Whether in terms of method or of content, the Christian humanism of the Renaissance meant a return to the sources.

Humanism was often grounded in an opposition to medieval Scholasticism*, which it displayed with varying degrees of discretion, and defined its method as a return to the sources of pagan and Christian antiquity. This meant, first of all, a return to the Bible, or, more precisely, to its original texts, which the supremacy of the Vulgate had supplanted. The point of departure for this enterprise was provided by Lorenzo Valla's comparison of the text of Jerome's Latin translation of the New Testament with the Greek manuscripts, and his discovery of inaccuracies in the former. In 1504, the discovery of the versions of Valla's work led Erasmus* to translate the New Testament, annotate and paraphrase it, and make it the center of his theology. Biblical studies developed from this point on, thanks to innumerable new translations* into Latin, which were more accurate or more classical than the older ones, and then, soon after, into vernacular languages. Humanist "workshops" were set in motion, compiling multilingual Bibles, as at Alcala and then at Anvers. At the Dominican friary of San Marco in Florence, Sante Pagnini completed translations that had an influence throughout the 16th century.

Numerous Greek scholars who fled from the Turkish conquest of Constantinople (1453) arrived in western Europe and taught their language there, making a significant contribution to the fashion for Greek that accompanied the rediscovery, not only of the Greek Fathers, but also of the philosophers of antiquity, and of a more precise approach to texts and manuscripts. Marsilio Ficino reinterpreted Plato and the neo-Platonists; Lefèvre d'Étaples provided a pedagogic presentation of Aristotle; Johann Reuchlin rediscovered Pythagoras. This German humanist also took an interest in Hebrew, and in the texts of the Talmud and the Cabala.

This general curiosity was in danger of spreading itself too thinly, yet it was an indication of a positive attitude to learning. Christian humanists wanted to find "prefigurings of the Gospel" in the pagan authors, but in the course of comparing them, dating them, and seeking to understand the meanings intended by all these authors, whatever they might be, they also tended to adopt a more historical approach. The period of the Renaissance was the age of perspective, which had arisen within Italian painting, and which inevitably signified distanciation, the involvement of the spectator, and a certain relativization of the object. From the second half of the 15th century onward, the invention of printing increasingly allowed an unprecedented diffusion of these texts and ideas. All these means, methods, and multipliers were based on a theological vision that, beginning with meditation upon the Incarnation*, recognized the dignity and liberty* of created human beings and sought to lead human beings to charity, the founding principle of authentic peace*.

a) Dignity and Liberty of Human Beings. The theme of human dignity was frequently addressed in the Italian Renaissance of the 15th century. For example, Bartolomeo Fazio (1442) and Gianozzo Manetti (1452) both exalted "the excellence of man." However, it was Giovanni Pico della Mirandola above all who developed this theme, in his *Oratio de dignitate hominis* (1486; Oration on the Dignity of Man). Pico, who was a friend of Ficino's, but not one of his disciples, since he preferred to be a disciple of Savonarola, asserts that dignity is not simply a quality of humanity, but is part of its very being*. Human beings have been created by God* to love and admire creation*; they are themselves microcosms of creation because of their noble intelligence. Their intellects have their origin in God, one and triune, who has created humanity "in his image."

Human dignity in turn forms the basis for human liberty, a liberty that in reality is an existence characterized by metamorphosis and oscillation, for human beings partake of two different worlds, and are halfway between God and the animals. In their liberty, human beings choose between becoming like animals and being transfigured. Their greatness lies precisely in the fact that, being their own masters, they choose for themselves the forms that they prefer. In this way, Pico expresses both the open-ended nature of humanity and its divine vocation.

The Christian humanists coupled their affirmation of liberty with a more technical defense of free will. Valla had already written on this subject in his *De libertate arbitrii* (On Free Will), in which he asserted that God's foreknowledge does not impose any constraints on our will. In his polemic with Luther*, who accused him of Pelagianism*, Erasmus defended, with a seriousness that was unusual for him, the idea that the humanists regarded as the very core of Christian anthropology and the logic of creation: that God himself saves and renews the liberty of the creature that reflects his image, with a mercy* that is so generous as to make human beings collaborators in their own salvation*. Even so, contrary to what Luther thought, the cross of Christ* is not eliminated. If God indeed crowns Christ's own merits by crowning the merits of human beings, then those merits have some substance after all. The Council of Trent* reaffirmed this conviction of the Christian humanists who had preceded it, although in more scholastic terms, by specifying the notions of merit and works*, which come together in charity (love*).

b) From Philautia *to Charity.* Christian humanists took a dynamic, plenary, theological view of charity, rejecting the egotism and self-love that the Renaissance, following the Greek fathers, called *philautia.* In the *Tiers Livre* (Third Book) of Rabelais's *Gargantua and Pantagruel,* Panurge embodies this bad choice: "*Philautia* and self-love deceive you" (ch. XIX). Trapped between marriage* and celibacy, in an egocentric perplexity, Panurge is possessed by his love for himself. Like Erasmus, Rabelais recommends what seems to human beings to be folly: "Forget yourself, go outside yourself... That which vulgarly is imputed to folly" (ch. XXXVII). Thus, charity is taught by the poor in spirit, in the Sermon on the Mount, the foundation of "Christ's philosophy." The Kingdom* of God is made for pure and charitable hearts that liberate themselves from *philautia* by fulfilling God's will. Entry into the abbey of Thelema, whose name means "will,"

is forbidden to "hypocrites," who had already been rejected in the Gospel. The abbey's motto, "Do what thou wilt," should be understood as choosing God's will, that is, charity.

Just as Thomas More's *Utopia* is a subtle humanist construction, intended to show the community of believers that part of the righteousness of the Kingdom that natural reason* already permits us to prefigure and to realize, so Rabelais's utopia affirms its grounding in human nature solely in order to provide a broader vision of the Gospel ideal. Rabelais's comedy, with its sexual and scatological jokes, should be seen as a continual reminder of the animal nature of humanity united with the spirit. For Rabelais as for Pico, humanity is truly *copula mundi.* This human comedy, which is both humanist and Christian (Screech 1979), suggests that it is only through Christian wisdom* that human beings can recall their place in creation and in God's plan.

c) Harmony, Concord, and Utopia. Christian humanism was stamped with the seal of an optimism that one could characterize as theological, and sought harmony. Pico della Mirandola was obsessed with reconciling Plato and Aristotle, yet this young philosopher, writing to Aldus Manutius, shows that he was aware that revelation* alone provides the key to the unity of human thought: "philosophy seeks truth, theology finds it, religion possesses it." This truth is Christ, principle of synthesis and Prince of Peace. Indeed, in Pico's writings the quest for unity is combined with a desire for religious concord, and he places himself in the tradition that runs from Nicholas* of Cusa to Jean Bodin.

Lefèvre d'Étaples, the first person to edit Nicholas of Cusa's writings, had a similar aim. His hermeneutic ideal (hermeneutics*) was to reconcile literal exegesis* with spiritual meaning. He raised "concordance of the scriptures" to the level of a principle of interpretation in order to combine the Old and New Testaments in a single view of Christ. In addition, Lefèvre sought to avoid opposition between faith* and works when commenting on the Epistle of James. Luther's disciple Philipp Melanchthon also tried to avoid sacrificing free will for the sake of justification* by faith.

This aspiration to reconciliation and unity, which was an aspiration to the coming of the Kingdom of God, is reflected in the architectural and social reveries of utopias, whether carved in stone or written on paper, from Pope Pius II's (unfinished) city of Pienza to the works of More (1516) and Campanella (1602). Erasmus was a pacifist and a precursor of toleration, as was logical for one who gave primacy to charity, even though it led to accusations of relativism*.

It is a paradox that the 16th century was precisely

the age of the great religious rift in western Europe. By the end of the century, the enthusiasm that had given rise to predictions of the return of the golden age had disappeared. The age of another type of genius had arrived—the age of Montaigne, Cervantes, and Shakespeare, in whose works it is more difficult to pinpoint Christian ideas. The mystic* and pastor* François de Sales (Salesian spirituality*) retained the dynamism of early humanism with a balance that was both a maturation and a transcendence of the humanist movement. Touched by the grace of the imitation* of Christ, he taught humility and also stood witness to it. In the last months of his life, he wanted to write a sequel to his *Traité de l'amour de Dieu,* an *Histoire théandrique* in four volumes, but did not have the time to achieve what would have been a summary of devout humanism, giving shape to the intuitions of nearly 200 years of Christian humanism.

● C. Vasoli (1968), *La dialettica e la retorica dell'Umanesimo,* Turin.

H. de Lubac (1974), *Pic de la Mirandole,* Paris.
A. Prévost (1978), *L'Utopie de Thomas More,* Paris.
M. A. Screech (1979), *Rabelais,* London.
J.-C. Margolin (1981), *L'humanisme en Europe au temps de la Réforme,* Paris.
C. B. Schmitt (1983), *Aristotle and the Renaissance,* Cambridge, Mass., London.
L. W. Spitz (1986), "Humanismus/Humanismusforschung," *TRE* 15, 639–61 (bibl.).
G. Bedouelle and B. Roussel (Ed.) (1989), *Le temps des Réformes et la Bible,* Paris.
J. Pic de La Mirandole (1993), *Œuvres philosophiques* (Ed. O. Boulnois and G. Tognon), Paris.
B. Pinchard and S. Ricci (Ed..) (1993), *Rationalisme analogique et humanisme théologique: La culture de Thomas de Vio "Il Gaetano,"* Naples.
G. Fraccadori (Ed.) (1994), *Bessarione e l'umanesimo,* Naples.
E. Rummel (1995), *The Humanist-Scholastic Debate in the Renaissance and Reformation,* Cambridge, Mass.

GUY BEDOUELLE

See also **Aristotelianism, Christian; Erasmus, Desiderius; Platonism, Christian; Skepticism, Christian; Stoicism, Christian**

Humility. *See* **Bernard of Clairvaux**

Hus, Jan

c. 1369–1415

The Czech theologian Jan Hus (from Husinec in Bohemia) was condemned by the Council of Constance* and burned alive. His death and that of his friend Jerome of Prague, burned in Constance a year later, were one of the causes of the Hussite rising of 1419. Hus's supporters joined forces with the advocates of Wycliffism to create a Hussite movement that broke with the papacy. This led to the organization under the Emperor Sigismund of Luxembourg of a series of crusades against Bohemia. As a result Czechs consider Hus a martyr for truth*, for the national cause, and for reform.

Hus studied under the direction of Stanislav of Znojmo, the first important Wycliffite at Prague. John Wycliffe (1328–84), the English reformer, had become master of arts in 1361 and doctor of theology in 1372. Entering the service of the Crown as ambassador to Gregory XI, he opposed the policies of France and of the papacy. Against nominalism* he championed an extreme realism. Universals were of two kinds, uncreated and created: the first were identical to the divine Ideas, the second had real existence in the form of singular beings, from which they were strictly distinct.

Between the two extended the analogical being*, created instantaneously, in which resided the types of the genera and species according to which God* created singular beings.

Wycliffe argued for a return to Augustine* and to the Bible*, and in his *De benedicta incarnatione* (1370) undertook a Platonist synthesis of philosophy* and theology.* His work had strong political implications, as the titles *De dominio divino* (1375), *De civili dominio* (1376), *De officio regis* (1378), and *De potestate papae* (1379) clearly show. Wycliffe's God exercised his power directly over all earthly possessions, without the pope*'s mediation. Kings were therefore accountable only to God, and the church had no right to own property. Wycliffe's (Ghibelline) position was close to that of Marsilius of Padua. The true church was the sum of the faithful in a state of grace, the "assembly of the predestined"; and since God alone was the cause of predestination*, human beings could not hope to join the community of the elect other than by attempting to imitate Christ*. The holding of church office should be the simple consequence of a life of grace*, and so was annulled by mortal sin*. Because clerical abuses and the scandal of the Schism* were making church reform a matter of urgency, Wycliffe proposed a return to the ancient church, that of the time before the Donation of Constantine, which implied an abandonment of the hierarchical structure. Since the forgiveness of sins issued directly from God without human mediation, there was no reason for indulgences*. And since none other than God could rightly designate the pope, it would be better if he were chosen by lot. Already critical of the papacy, which he saw as an "addition" to the evangelical truths, Wycliffe's attitude developed markedly at the time of the Schism. Henceforth the pope himself, rather than the antipope, was the Antichrist.

Wycliffe seems to have acknowledged the sacraments*, on condition that the priest* be in a state of grace, without which they had a merely moral value. He confessed the real presence of Christ in the Eucharist* but criticized theories of transubstantiation. He understood the body of Christ to be really present in the nature of the bread, but present by its power *(virtualiter)* and not in substance—since by reason of its magnitude the nature of Christ was to be found only in heaven. He acknowledged the sacrament of confession, but recommended that it take place in public. He coordinated the propagation of his ideas by sending out his disciples, the "Lollards," to preach in the countryside. But their preaching* turned into social revolt (the Peasants' Revolt of 1381). Condemned by the archbishop of Canterbury in 1382, and struck by paralysis, he died in 1384. The Council of Constance (1415) repeated the condemnation of his writings. But his teachings were spread by clandestine circles in Oxford. There his works were incessantly copied—at just the time when Anne of Bohemia, wife of Richard II, was drawing the Czech elite to her court in England. They were subsequently circulated in central Europe and inspired the Hussite movement.

Hus became master of arts at Prague in 1396, and was appointed dean of the faculty in 1401 and rector of the university in 1409. He was ordained priest in 1400 and studied theology, though events prevented him from attaining the level of doctor. In 1402 he was appointed rector and preacher of the Bethlehem Chapel, founded to "offer the Czech population religious instruction in its native language" (De Vooght). This activity gave rise to a series of conflicts with the clergy, exacerbated by a crisis in the church* that was then reaching its peak (the rivalry between the three popes), by the weakening of the royal power, and by divisions within the university. Hus then became the leader of the reformists, mostly followers of Wycliffe, who gathered around him in his role of professor. He broke with Archbishop Zbynek, whose most valued collaborator he had been for the previous five years. In Prague, where several reformers before him had announced the imminent arrival of the Antichrist, Hus identified Zbynek's cause with that of the Antichrist. His open opposition to the archbishop, as well as his public criticism of John XXII's pseudo-Crusade against the King of Naples and of the selling of indulgences that was intended to underwrite it, earned him three excommunications, including a major one in 1412. At this point he exiled himself from Prague. Two years later he attended the Council of Constance, where he was imprisoned, tried, condemned to death, and executed on 6 July 1415. This sequence of conflicts shows that for Hus there was always an authority* higher than the one that judged and punished him at each stage. Thus he appealed against his bishop* to the pope, and against the pope to the forthcoming general council, ending at Constance with a solemn appeal to Jesus Christ.

Hus was completely bilingual, writing in Latin and Czech and translating into the latter. His academic works comprise occasional speeches, sermons, polemical texts, and questions, a *Quodlibet* (1411) debated in the Faculty of Arts, a commentary on the *Sentences* (1407–8), and a treatise, *De ecclesia* (1413), that was censured at Prague, Paris, and Constance. Apart from the sermons his Czech works include spiritual writings and works of exegesis*. His doctrines, as much philosophical as theological, are influenced by Wycliffe, although the nature and extent of this influence are disputed.

His commentary on the *Sentences* is conventional, however. For example, he makes no mention of Wycliffe's doctrine of the two stages of the Creation (in any case of Augustinian origin), or that of a created world that cannot be annihilated by God, while accepting their philosophical consequences—the concept of analogical being (not to be confused with the analogy* of being) and the realism of the genera and species. This same prudence can be observed in Hus's reformist activities: while a formidable critic of the clergy, the practice of simony, indulgences, and excommunications (at that time numerous and improperly applied), he was also a timid traditionalist who acknowledged the priestly function and the authority of the hierarchy*.

Before and after the Council of Constance Hus's opponents criticized him for his realist conception of the universals, accusing him of considering them as eternal and uncreated beings, existing independently of God*. He is usually spoken of as displaying an "extreme realism," without going into more detail. In fact in Hus's terms, just as in Wycliffe's, genera and species exist either in the analogical being ("the first created thing," according to the *Book of Causes*), or in singular things. In the first case they are the models for the singular things; in the second they have real, but formal, existence. The formal distinction (*see* Duns* Scotus), accepted by the whole Wycliffite school, is thus of primary importance. Pierre d'Ailly attempted to draw a connection between Hus's realism and the doctrine according to which the actual substances of the bread and wine remain after the eucharistic consecration—but in fact Hus constantly and clearly rejected this view, and this despite the opinion of several Prague theologians.

Hus defined the universal Church as the totality of the predestined living in the past, present, and future. To this concept he contrasted that of the local* church, in either a geographical or a moral sense; as in, for example, a gathering of several of the predestined (*De ecclesia*, c. 1). In absolute terms the unity of the former "consists of the unity of predestination*...and the unity of beatitude*." In temporal terms, "it consists of the unity of faith* and virtues*, and of the unity of charity" (c. 2). "Gathered and united by the bond of predestination," the members of the church constituted the mystical body of which Christ alone was the head (c. 3). Analysis of the concepts of the universal Church, faith, foundation, and ecclesiastical power led Hus to rule out any identification of the Roman Catholic Church with the church of the predestined (c. 7–11).

Hus's ecclesiology* poses numerous problems of interpretation, however, and its analysis often depends on the personal convictions of the historian. The non-Catholic tradition points to the place occupied in Hus's thought by the concept of predestination, the importance of his distinction between the state of grace and that of mortal sin* as a means of legitimizing (or not) ecclesiastical and civil power, the resemblances to Wycliffe's doctrines, the interpretation of simony as a heresy*, the possibility of an appeal to Christ, and so on. The Catholic interpretation of Hus, on the other hand, seeks to put his ecclesiology back in a traditional* context, and makes an effort to distinguish his actual assertions from the implications of his text—and from the accusations of his opponents. It attaches great importance to the precise analysis of Hus's language and of the limits of Wycliffe's influence. On occasion it even replaces historical analysis with a reference to the current state of theological knowledge. In short, the non-Catholic tradition emphasizes the factors that distance Hus from the Catholic Church, while the Catholic reading points out those that bring him close to it.

● P. Spunar (1996), *Repertorium auctorum Bohemorum provectum idearum post Universitatem Pragensem conditam illustrans*, I, Wroclaw, Polish Academy of Science, 211–13.
Hus, *Opera omnia*, unfinished work by W. Flajshans and M. Komínková, 8 vols., Prague, 1903–7.
Hus, *Opera omnia*, Académie des sciences, vol. 1 and 4, 7–9 (*Sermones de tempore, Passio Christi, Lectionum pars prima*), 13 (*Postilla adumbrata*), and 22 (*Polemica*), Prague, 1959–.
Hus, *Tractatus responsivus*, Ed. S. Harrison Thomson, Prague, 1927.
Hus, *Quodlibet*, Ed. B. Ryba, Prague, 1948.
Hus, *Tractatus de ecclesia*, Ed. S. Harrison Thomson, Cambridge, Mass., 1956 (same text in the Prague edition, 1958).
Wyclif, *The Latin Works*, 35 vols., London, 1883–1922, repr. Frankfurt, 1964.
Hus, *Tractatus de Universalibus*, Ed. I. J. Mueler, Oxford, 1985.
◆ M. Vischer (1955), *J. Hus, Aufruhr wider Papst und Reich*, Frankfurt.
P. De Vooght (1960), *L'hérésie de Jean Huss*, Louvain (2nd Ed. 1975).
P. De Vooght (1960), *Hussiana*, Louvain (2nd Ed. 1975).
M. Spinka (1966), *John Hus' Concept of the Church*, Princeton, N.J.
P. De Vooght (1969), "Huss (Jean)," *DSp* 7/1, 1194–1200.
J. Macek (1973), *Jean Hus et les traditions hussites*, Paris.
W. R. Thomson (1983), *The Latin Writings of John Wyclif: An Annotated Catalog*, Toronto.
E. Werner (1991), "Jan Hus im Spiegel moderner Historiographie," *Heresis: Revue d'hérésiologie médiévale* 16, 37–54.
Fr. Machilek (1986), "Hus/Hussiten," *TRE* 15, 710–35.
O. Chaline (1998), *La reconquête catholique de l'Europe centrale (XVIe-XVIIIe s.)*, Paris.

ZÉNON KALUZA

See also **Constance, Council of; Ecclesiology; Predestination; Protestantism**

Hutterians. *See* Anabaptists

Hypostasis. *See* Person

Hypostatic Union

---

a) In Cyril of Alexandria and until Ephesus. Hypostatic union is the expression used since the Council of Ephesus* to designate the union of the divine and the human in one single entity, Christ* (*DS* 250). It translates in technical terms the statement of John's gospel*, "And the Word* became flesh" (1, 14), as well as the confession (creeds*) of the Council of Nicaea*, "One Lord Jesus Christ, Son of God*, the only-begotten of the Father*,...who for us men and for our salvation* came down from Heaven, became incarnate, and was made a man" (*DS* 125). This formula answers the question: under what condition was born of Mary, in time, the very one and the same who is begotten by the Father from all eternity? How can one and the same being be true God and true man?

The hypostatic union, as understood by Cyril* and the Council of Ephesus, implies a number of givens that are closely linked: 1) Christ was not made of two concrete coexisting beings, as if the Son of God and Christ were "one and another"; or as if the Word, instead of becoming man, had merged with one particular man. 2) The union is so intimate that it occurs at the level of the very act of subsisting, where the Word "claims temporal birth as its own," and not at the level of natures, divinity and humanity remaining intact and distinct. 3) The act of subsisting can only be that of the Word, the eternal Son, who imprints on humanity his very own act of existing. 4) The humanity of Jesus has no existence prior to the Incarnation*, nor independently of the fact that the Word assumes it as his own. 5) The properties of the two natures communicate between themselves indirectly, through the intermediary of the subject, "the one who exists"—for example, the temporal birth of the Word is said to be of the *Word* or of *God,* not of *divinity,* as attested by Mary's title of "Mother of God" *(theotokos)* recognized by the church*.

b) Etymology of the Term "hypostasis." The notion of hypostasis had traveled a long road before Christ; it was first introduced into christology*, according to M. Richard (1945), to designate the principle of existence or reality as opposed to *phusis* or the essence of a thing. The term, borrowed from Greek natural science, was first synonymous with "precipitation," with obvious implications of solidification and manifestation. Subsequently, it meant for the Stoics the last stage of the individualization of an essence. With Origen* (*Contra Celsum* 8, 12: SC 150, 201), and then the Cappadocians, Christian theology* used the term to characterize the entities Persons of the Trinity* as against the essence *(ousia)* of divinity. The teaching of Christ, initially proposing itself perhaps rather more in a category of intuition than of definition, later constituted a decisive contribution that subsequent councils—from Chalcedon* to Constantinople* III—only revived and deepened.

c) Modern Difficulties.   The hypostatic union, with the hegemony of the divine element that it entails, has seemed in our own time to endanger the authenticity of Christ's humanity or deprive it of the solidity that the personality gives it. Besides the fact that the old, purely ontological meaning of *person* does not agree with the modern psychological understanding, it has been argued that "affirming the transcendence of the divine subject to include hypostatic union is both a warrant of the independence of man and the alterity of God" (R. Virgoulay, *RSR* 28, 1980). On the other hand, the humanity that the Word assumes, far from being depersonalized, in fact endows the entity with the personality that gives it existence.

d) Recent Reformulation.   Relying on the fundamental identity of being* and consciousness, and deriving from that, as the principal model of being, not the opaque thing itself but the cognizant and free subject, K. Rahner* has attempted an "ontological" transposition of the doctrine of the hypostatic union. Expressed until then in terms of an "ontic" mode, for Rahner the hypostatic union is like the union of a question with its absolute answer. The question is human nature, whose entire pursuit of knowledge* and love* is polarized and animated by the quest for God. Human nature in itself is a fundamental act of transcendence, received from God and turned toward him. The answer lies in God's self-communication to the opening that he creates, in this case, to be welcomed as an *absolute gift*.

Since the question is an intrinsic part of the answer, it is simultaneously the distinctive reality of God and a reality governed by him from the very beginning.

For Donald Baillie, who has considerably influenced the Anglo-Saxon world, the "paradox of grace*" is supremely at play in the Incarnation. While God in his grace creates in man that for which he himself is fully responsible (1 Cor 15:10), God is fully present in the particular man Jesus, who "*always* does that which is pleasing to God" (1948). But others have wondered why the *constancy* of the action would introduce anything else but a degree of difference between the condition of Christ and that of Christians (Robinson 1966).

● A. Michel (1922), "Hypostatique (Union)," *DThC* 7/1, 437–568.
M. Richard (1945), "L'introduction du mot 'hypostase' dans la théologie de l'incarnation," *MSR* 2, 5–32, 243–70.
D. M. Baillie (1948), *God Was in Christ,* London.
M. Nédoncelle (1948), "*Prosopon* et *persona* dans l'Antiquité classique," *RevSR* 22, 277–99.
H. N. G. Robinson (1966), *Theologians of Our Time,* Edinburgh.
J. Meyendorff (1969), *Le Christ dans la théologie byzantine,* Paris.
K. Rahner (1977), *Grundkurs des Glaubens,* Freiburg-Basel-Vienna.
A. de Halleux (1992), "Les douze chapitres cyrilliens au concile d'Éphèse (430–33)," *EThL* 23, 425–58.

GILLES LANGEVIN

See also **Anhypostasy; Christ and Christology; Constantinople II, Council of; Cyril of Alexandria; Ephesus, Council of; Trinity**

I

Icons. *See* **Images; Nicaea II, Council of**

Idealism. *See* **Realism**

Idioms, Communication of

This phrase explains one of the classical practices used to express the conviction that Jesus* is a single person* who is at once both fully divine and fully human: attributes predicated of him as a man are associated with titles denoting him as God* and reciprocally. Based on an understanding of Jesus's ontological status that is at the center of Christianity, it is essentially a rule of language* that allows the use of deliberately paradoxical phrases, such as referring to Mary as "Mother of God" or affirming that "one of the Trinity died on the cross."

(a) New Testament. The beginning of this practice can be discerned in the New Testament, where such paradoxical phrases are used to underscore the true identity of Jesus, the crucified Messiah (messianism/Messiah*): for example, Acts 3:15 ("You asked for a murderer to be granted to you, and you killed the Author of life"), 1 Corinthians 2:8 ("They would not have crucified the Lord of glory"), and Romans 9:5, as it was usually understood by early Christianity ("From their Jewish race, according to the flesh, is the Christ who is God over all"). The presupposition behind such phrases is that Jesus has his origin in, and is identified with, the mystery* of God (*see* Lk 1: 35, Jn 1:14, Phil 2:5–11, Ti 2:13).

(b) Patristic Usage. The first to notice this practice explicitly, and to formulate the reason for it, was Ori-

747

gen* (*De principiis* II, 6, 3). To emphasize the degree to which the Son of God has become identified with the soul (soul*-heart-body) of Jesus and with "the flesh that it has taken," one can actually say that "the Son of God has died" and that the Son* of man "will come in the glory of God the Father"; "for this reason," says Origen, "throughout the whole of scripture* we see the divine nature spoken of in human terms, and the human nature in its turn adorned with marks that belong to the divine."

During the age of christological controversies in the fifth century, in which the school of Antioch* opposed the school of Alexandria*, this paradoxical exchange of attributes played a major role in the intensification of the debate. The school of Antioch displayed great reluctance about the idea that God had truly taken part in human history, particularly in physical submission and suffering; against this position, Cyril* of Alexandria insisted on the importance of the description of Mary as "mother of God," which Nestorius had called into question, and also insisted that "the flesh of the Lord gives life," and that "the Word of God suffered in the flesh and was crucified in the flesh," because the Word* forms only a hypostasis or concrete individual with its "flesh" or humanity (ep. 3, to Nestorius, anath. 1, 2, 11, 12). This principle was accepted, not without hesitation, by the theologians of Antioch Theodore of Mopsuestia (hom. cat. 6, 7) and Theodoret of Cyrrhus (*Eranistes*, dial. 3).

It was only in the sixth century that the vocabulary of Porphyry and of Neoplatonism (Christian Platonism*) began to be used to indicate the ontological basis of this phraseology, under the name of "communication of idioms." In Neoplatonic terms, an individual (*atomon, hupostasis*) is defined and even constituted by the "specific traits" (*idia, idiomata*) that permit him to be recognized (Porphyry, *Isagoge*, CAG IV, 3, 90, 6f.). According to Leontius of Byzantium, because the unique hypostasis of Christ concretely unites divine nature with human nature "their characteristic traits *idiomata* are common to both of them," while each nature remains unchanged in respect of its own traits (*Epil.*, PG 86, 1941 A; *Contra Nest. et Eut.*, PG 86, 1289 C6–8). For the Greek Scholasticism* of the sixth century, as for later theological tradition, to speak of mutual "communication" (*antidosis*) or "exchange" (*perikhoresis*) of "idioms" between the two natures of Christ did not mean that there was any change in these natures, nor did it mean attributing traits that were foreign to them. It was simply a way of showing that the unique person of Christ, who could legitimately receive both human titles and divine titles, possesses in himself all the qualities of both natures.

(c) Later Usage. Since the sixth century, this theological principle, reaffirmed at the Second Council of Constantinople* (553), has been one of the touchstones of christological orthodoxy* for the Orthodox, Catholics, and Protestants alike. It also lies behind the paradoxes that poets and preachers have been happy to evoke in respect of Christ, above all at Christmas (e.g., Gregory* of Nazianzus, *De oratione* 38, 13; Augustine*, *Sermons* 184, 3; 187, 1; 191, 1), and it explains the practices of piety in which certain aspects of the humanity of Jesus are adored, such as the sacred heart (heart* of Jesus) or the Precious Blood.

● Gregory of Nyssa, *Contra Eunomium* III, 4, 64, *GNO* II, 158 *Sq*; *A Théophile*, *GNO* III/1, 137 *Sq*.

John of Damascus, *Expositio fidei*, 47 s., in *Die Schriften des Johannes von Damaskos* (B. Kotter, Ed.), Berlin, 1973, II, 115–18; *Contra Jacobitas* 81, Kotter IV, Berlin, 1981, 138 *Sq*.

Leo the Great, *Tomus ad Flavianum* 5, *ACO* II/2, 1, 29.

Leontius of Byzantium, *Contra Nestorianos et Eutychianos*, PG 86, 1289 B2–D3; *Epiluseis*, PG 86, 1940 C11–1941 A14, 1945 B4–D6.

Leontius of Jerusalem, *Contra monophysitas* 25, PG 86, 1785 B14–D1.

Maximus the Confessor, *Opuscula*, PG 91, 189 C8–192 A15; 237 D8–240 A9; *Dialogue with Pyrrhus*, PG 91, 296 D4–297 A6.

Origen, *De principiis* II, 6, 3, SC 252, 314 *Sq*.

Pseudo-Cyrille (VIIth c.), *De Trinitate* 27, PG 77, 1172 A7–D14.

Theodoret, *Eranistès*, Dial. III, Ed. G. Ettlinger, Oxford, 1975, 226 *Sq*.

Theodotus of Ancyra, *Expositio symboli nicaeni* 16, PG 77, 1336 D4–11.

Thomas Aquinas, *Summa Theologica* IIIa, q. 16 (especially a. 4).

♦ A. Michel (1922), "Idiomes (communication des)," *DThC* 7/1, 595–602.

K. Barth (1955), *KD* IV/2, 79–91 (*Dogmatique*, Geneva, 1968).

A. Grillmeier (1979, 1989), *Jesus der Christus im Glauben der Kirche* I, II/2, Freiberg-Basel-Vienna.

BRIAN E. DALEY SJ

See also **Anhypostasy; Chalcedon, Council of; Christ and Christology; Constantinople II, Council of; Ephesus, Council of; Hypostatic Union; Nestorianism**

Idolatry

a) Vocabulary Is Varied—It May Be Either Concrete or Metaphorical. To describe an idol in material terms the MT speaks of *çèlèm,* sculpture or engraving (Nm 33:52); of *'açabbîm,* sculptures (2 Sm 5:21); and more rarely (five times) of *sèmèl,* image (Dt 4:16); but above all of *massékâh,* cast metalwork (Ex 32:4, 8) and *pèsèl,* sculpture in stone (Is 21:9) or wood (40:20). A value judgment is implied by the terms *gilloûlîm,* filth (Lv 26:30), *'èlîlîm,* worthless objects (Lv 19, 4), *shiqqouç,* horror (Ez 20:7s.), *to'ebâh,* abomination (Is 44:19), *hèbèl,* vanity (Jer 10:14–15), or by the expression *ma-aséy yâdèykâ,* work of your hands (Dt 31:29; Mi 5:12; Is 2:8; Jer 25:6). People make (*'asâh*) an idol (1 Kgs 14:9), follow it (Jer 2:5, 23, 25), prostrate themselves before it (Is 44:17), and serve it (*'âbad:* Ez 20:39). To do so is to prostitute oneself (*zânâh:* Ez 20:30), to commit adultery (*nâ'af:* Jer 3:9), and to provoke the jealousy of YHWH (*qn'hifil:* Ps 78:58).

The Septuagint employs the classical terms *agalma,* statue (Is 21:9) and *eikon,* image (Dt 4:16) but introduces the term *eidolon* in the sense of idol (image in classical Greek). The New Testament, meanwhile, gives us the words *idolater* (seven, including Eph 5:5) and *idolatry* (four, including Col 3:5).

b) History. In ancient times there was some use of representations in the worship of YHWH. The golden calf (Ex 32) was not seen by Aaron as a case of religious infidelity, since the animal (animals*) symbolized the pedestal of the unrepresented deity. The same may have been true of the two golden calves erected at Bethel and Dan by Jeroboam after the schism* of 931 (1 Kgs 12:28f.). At the time of the Judges, Micah (Jgs 17–18) had at home a representation of YHWH (or of his bovine pedestal) in carved wood covered in silver. He also had an *'éfôd* and some *terâfîm* (Jgs 17:3ff.): the *l''éfôd* (*see* Jgs 8:27) may have been the covering of a statue, and the *terâfîm,* mentioned as early as the time of Jacob (Rachel's theft: Gn 31:19, 34), may have been household idols. These objects would have been used for divination (1 Sm 15:23). Tolerated initially (Hos 3:4; 1 Sm 19:13–16; 21:10), in time they were proscribed (1 Sm 15:23; 2 Kgs 23:24). The same went for the bronze serpent destroyed by Hezekiah (2 Kgs 18:4). On the other hand, the cherubim (Ex 25:18; Ez 10:18) placed on the ark of the covenant*, and later interpreted as angels*, were accepted. The disappearance of any other representation from the worship of YHWH is a result of their prohibition by the Ten Commandments (Decalogue*) (Ex 20:4; Dt 5:8, of disputed date). In any case the prophets (prophet and prophecy*) of the eighth century attacked such representations (Hos 8:5; 10:5f., 13:2; Am 8:14). They were derisively regarded as idols for which the glory* of YHWH had been bartered (Hos 4:7; Jer 2:11; Ps 106:20; *see* Rom 1:23).

The Hebrews' neighbors, and the peoples whose territories they conquered, did make representations of their own gods, most often in human form: the statue of Dagon (1 Sm 5:1–4) is one of the earliest examples. Throughout the whole royal period a religious struggle was waged against pagan cults. The Canaanite influence, with Baal, Astarte, and Asherah, remained strong for a long time, and latterly (Am 5:26, quoted in Acts 7:43) Assyrian deities were introduced. Elijah fought against the cult of Baal in defense of the one religion* of YHWH, but it was apparently only after his time, in the eighth century, that attempts were made to stamp out idols. The kings had introduced these idolatrous practices: Solomon (1 Kgs 11:5–8; 2 Kgs 23:13), Athaliah (idol of Baal: 2 Kgs 11:18), Ahaz (idol of Baal: 2 Chr 28:2), and Manasseh (idol of Asherah: 2 Kgs 21:7) were those principally accused. Asa (late 10th century: 1 Kgs 15:12f.) was supposed to have reacted against idolatry, but it was Hezekiah (2 Chr 29:5, 16) and Josiah (2 Kgs 23:13) who, influenced by the prophets, reacted strongly with their Deuteronomistic reforms. Idolatry became one of the most serious accusations made by the prophets, who foretold the punishment of the guilty (Am 5:26; Jer 16:18) and the destruction of idols (Mi 1:7; Is 2:18; Jer 10:11, 15; Ez 7:20; Zec 13:2). They foretold the exile as one of the punishments for this infidelity (Jer 13:24–27, 16:16f.; 25:6f.; Ez 22:3ff.), and the conversion of the people was also prophesied (Is 30:22; Ez 11:18, 20:39–44). Even the pagans' idols would disappear (Is 21:9; Jer 51:18, 52; Ez 30:13; Na 1:14). During the period of exile deutero-Isaiah marked an important stage in the clarification of the worthlessness of idols.

After the exile the Canaanite temptation disappeared, but in the second century, in the face of Hellenistic influence, the fight against pagan idols resumed. The oppressiveness of the Seleucids, in particular of Antiochus IV, ignited the Maccabean revolt (1 Macc 1:43; 2 Macc 12:40; Dn 3). The satirizing of idolatry became more widespread (Dn 14:1–22; Lt-Jr). At the dawn of the Christian era Songs 13–15 developed this current of thought, taking up the usual themes of anti-idolatrous criticism and adding that of the mysteries and the cult of rulers.

Among the Jewish community addressed by Jesus, idolatry no longer had a place—or at least there appears to be no allusion to it among his words. On the other hand, Christianity's contact with the Hellenistic world inevitably led to a revival of the subject.

It is Paul above all who finds himself confronted with idols (at Athens, Acts 17:16, 29; at Ephesus, Acts 19:26). He appeals to the pagans to renounce them and turn to the living creator God (Acts 14:15), as the Thessalonians (1 Thes 1:9) and Corinthians (1 Cor 12:2) had done. While Acts of the Apostles 15:20, 29 forbids the eating of idolothytes (food offered to idols), Paul imposes conditions on their consumption (1 Cor 8, 10:14–30). In any event he calls for idolatry to be abandoned (1 Cor 10:14). In his view the immorality of paganism derives from idolatry (Rom 1:23; see Sg 14:11–31). It is included among catalogues of vices (1 Cor 5:10, 6:9). In Ephesians 5:5 and Colossians 3:5 cupidity is itself considered as idolatry (see Mt 6:24). 1 Corinthians 10:20 and Revelation 9:20 follow Deuteronomy 32:17 in classing idols as demons*. Finally, Revelation 14:9ff. proclaims the punishment for worshippers of the idol of the beast. It is in the metaphorical sense of the erroneous doctrines of false prophets that 1 John 5:21, like the Qumranians (1QH4, 15f.), urges its readers to beware of idols.

c) Biblical Discussion. At Horeb-Sinai YHWH had not revealed himself: only his voice was heard. This, according to Deuteronomy 4:12 (a Deuteronomistic text), justifies the refusal of any representation of YHWH. Idolatry is first and foremost an act of infidelity to YHWH, as suggested by the Ten Commandments and maintained by the prophets (Hos 14:4; Is 57:11; Jer 2:26–29) and Deuteronomistic history (2 Kgs 17:7–17,

21:22). Idols are worthless (1 Sm 12:21), "vanity" (Ps 97:7: hbl, emptiness), and their followers too are reduced to vanity (Hos 9:10; Jer 2:5; Ps 115:8). In contrast with YHWH the creator (Jer 10:8ff.) they cannot bring salvation (Hos 14:4; Jer 2:28), since, being the work of human hands (Is 2:8), they are mute (Hb 2:18s.) and incapable of movement (Jer 10:5; Ps 115:4–7). Their manufacture is a butt of irony (Jer 10:3ff., 9). Deutero-Isaiah deepens the criticism with its insistence on Yahwist monotheism*: YHWH is the one God, the pagan deities do not exist, and so idols are nothing. The prophet enacts trials that oppose YHWH to the pagan deities and their idols (41:1ff., 21ff., 43:9ff.; 44:6ff.): the one creator, the one master of history, the one foreteller of the future, YHWH is the one and only God. It is he who has made Israel* and will set her free, while the nations make powerless deities (40:19f., 41:6f., 44:9–20, 46, 6s.). Following the examples of the Ten Commandments (Ex 20:3ff.–Dt 5:7ff.) and of biblical tradition (Dt 4:16–19; Jer 7:1–8, 3; Ez 8; Dn gr. 14)—also followed by Philo (Decalogue, 52–81) and the Letter of Aristeas (134–139)—Wisdom 13–15 places its criticism of idolatry in a wider context, attacking as well the pagans' other erroneous forms of worship. Idolatry is nonsense: made by God in his image, man makes for himself an idol that resembles him but is lifeless. This inversion of roles (Wis 15:11, 15:16f.) is sterile. Furthermore, as a repudiation of the true God idolatry leads to immorality (14, 11–31; see Hos 4:1), a theme that Paul (Rom 1:18–32) will develop in turn, showing also the extent to which paganism* stands in need of redemption (3:21ff.).

• A. Gelin (1949), "Idoles, idolâtrie," *DBS* 4, 169–87.

M. Gilbert (1973), *La critique des dieux dans le Livre de la Sagesse (Sg 13–15),* Rome.

W. M. W. Roth (1975), "For Life, He Appeals to Death (Wis 13:18). A Study of Old Testament Idol Parodies," *CBQ* 37, 21–47.

E. M. Curtis (1992), "Idol, Idolatry," *AncBD* 2, 376–81.

Maurice Gilbert

See also **Decalogue; Images; Monotheism; Paganism; Sabbath; Work**

Ignatius of Antioch. *See* Apostolic Fathers

Ignatius of Loyola. *See* Spirituality, Ignatian

Illative Sense. *See* Newman, John Henry

Image of God. *See* Anthropology; Trace (Vestige)

Images

1. Definition and Preliminary Remarks

a) "Image" is a notion whose semantic richness leads to ambiguity. We will examine here the theological reflection on the history of the Christian usage (abstention, refusal, destruction; fabrication, possession, exhibition, veneration, devotion, and piety) of the plastic image. We understand this as a fragment of matter, in two or three dimensions, defined as such (by its edges, its frame, or its surface) and composed according to a certain order, with greater or lesser degrees of art, sensitivity, style, science, or eloquence, to be recognizable and draw attention, and yet also lead that attention on to something further. We shall therefore leave aside the theology of the image in any sense of the term that is christological (Christ*, "image of the Father*"), anthropological (man created "in the image of God"), literary (metaphors, symbols, analogies used by the Bible* and then spirituality, and, to a lesser degree, theology and preaching), or psycho-sociocultural (for example, the "image" of the father, or of woman, or of God*, as reconstructed by the history of religious mentalities). While a connection between these issues and the notion of image is conceivable, it could only be tenuous.

b) In Latin (*icona* or *vera icona, imago, simulacrum, idola, statua, effigies,* etc.), in Hebrew (*çèlèm, pèsèl, massékât,* etc.), and especially in Greek (*agalma, eidôlon, eikôn,* etc.), the terms that serve to designate images of worship were far more numerous than they are in living European languages, which is further proof of the wealth of religious uses of the image in antiquity. *Imago* and *eikôn* are the most general terms for designating these two realms, which overlap significantly.

c) More than a mere vocabulary, emerging Christianity inherited a context and a problematic linked to the proscription in the Ten Commandments (Decalogue*): "You shall not make for yourself a carved image, or any likeness of anything that is in heaven above, or that is in the earth beneath, or that is in the water under the earth. You shall not bow down to them or serve them" (Ex 20:4–5), together with its initial interpretation, which was literal and restrictive during the entire era of persecutions. Aimed at preventing all forms of idolatry*, the commandment did not stop the Jews from decorating some of their synagogues with frescoes, such as that of the Doura Europos, which was decisive in the birth of Christian art (middle of the third century; Weitzmann-Kessler 1990); and very early on it was confronted with other arguments by Christians, in apparent contradiction, on the existence of images from the first covenant (the bronze serpent, Nm 21:9; the cherubs of the ark, Ex 25:18–22; the decor of Solomon's temple*, 1 Kgs 6:18, 35, 7:23–26).

2. Historical Overview

a) Jesus seems to have been unfamiliar with the problem of religious art. He did not have recourse to plastic images in preaching the Kingdom and revealing the Father. He did not encourage his disciples to make images of himself or of his mother, and still less, images of his Father in heaven. Nor is there any trace of a preoccupation with images in the preaching of the apostles (apostle*). And yet sculpted images, both small and large, abounded in towns around the Mediterranean. Thus the proclamation of the gospel took place without images, and there is every reason to believe that it still can. Orthodox Christians do of course remain very attached to the traditional belief according to which the preaching of the gospel was achieved from the beginning as much through the image as through the word (Ouspensky, 1980). Historical evidence does not, however, support the historicity of the *acheiropoietes* images (the legends of Abgar, Mandylion, or Veronica, Saint-Suaire: Celier 1992) or "apostolic" images (the image of the Virgin supposedly painted by Saint Luke), not to mention the statues of Christ alleged to be sculpted on the orders of the haemorrhois (according to Eusebius of Caesarea) and Nicodemus (Belting 1990).

b) During the first three centuries, to dissociate themselves from the pagans, who used images extensively, and also because of the persecutions that deprived them of the means to produce and exhibit images, the early Christians created or copied very few images (for example, those of orants, sinners, the Good Shepherd; *see* Prigent 1995), and only did so on small objects (seals, chalices) and in their catacombs (from the second century on). They were inclined, rather, to mistrust images and were opposed to their use for worship (Council* of Elvira; Minucius Felix,

Octavius). The advent of Constantine (313), to whose sister Eusebius of Caesarea wrote (between 313 and 324) that Christ could not be represented (Dumeige 1978), was not a turning point in favor of images: instead, the turning point would come when, under Theodosius in 386, Christianity was recognized as a religion of the empire. It was then that a specifically Christian art was developed (reliefs on sarcophagi, the sculpted door of St. Sabinus in Rome, mosaics, the use of gold, etc.; sculpture in the round remained rare or even forbidden). This Christian art marked the initial overcoming of theological hesitation regarding the interpretation of the second commandment [AuQ8] (Decalogue*), a hesitation that would be finally overcome only by the Council of Nicaea II.

c) From Nicaea I* (325) to Nicaea II* (787), in the light of the christological elaboration itself and through periods of crisis, a theological justification for the use of images slowly emerged, concerning itself first of all with images of Christ. Those who were opposed to the making of such images ("iconophobes," from Eusebius to Constantine V) claimed that they were unlawful because they represented a paradox: it is impossible to portray the God in Jesus Christ, and to portray the man in him is to deny one's faith (Council of Hieria, 754). The only tolerable "icons," if the leaders of the "iconophobic" party (such as Constantine V) were to be believed, were the cross and the Eucharist*. All the efforts of iconodulist ("image-worshipping") theology (John Damascene, Nicephorus of Constantinople) would consist in moving beyond this aporia by explaining that the icon of Christ represents neither human nature, nor divine nature, but the union of both of them, "without mixture or confusion" (*see* Chalcedon*) in a "theandric hypostasis" (the human-divine person) of Jesus Christ (Schönborn 1976). Crowning the christological work of the first six ecumenical councils, this doctrine would triumph at Nicaea II, after Byzantium had experienced "the quarrel of [the] images" (Dumeige 1978). It held iconodulism to be a consequence of christocentric nature of revelation. Regarding the icon as a tradition handed down from the apostles, and not an innovation, it declared that the image had a justification insofar as it confirmed, in its own particular way, what the kerygma announced: "the real, and not illusory, incarnation* of the Word of God." Henceforth, the icon (and after it religious images in general, though with certain reservations) could be perceived as a second voice supporting but not replacing the first voice of the kerygma, that of the witness in body proper prepared to become a martyr (martyrdom*) (Bœspflug 1993). The conciliar decree enumerated four subjects of the

icon: Christ, the Virgin, angels, and saints (the Trinity*
and God the Father were passed over in silence, the silence of deliberate exclusion, not omission). The decree recommended producing and exhibiting images
everywhere, in such a way that Christ's belonging to
the *oekoumenè* would be confirmed. Moreover, by applying Basil* the Great's christological affirmation
(*Treatise of the Holy Spirit*) the council emphasized
that although *adoration* was for God alone, the image-
icon, like the sign of the cross, was an object for legitimate *veneration* (prostration, kisses, lighted candles,
etc.) insofar as the honor that was paid to it did not stop
with the image's material nature but "goes as far as the
prototype" (doctrine of *transitus,* that is, of the holy
person that it represents).

In the East, after its reaffirmation at the Fourth
Council of Constantinople in 870, the conciliar decree would remain until our own time an effective reference point and a source of inspiration, providing an
ongoing and uninterrupted proof, if not of the artistic
fertility of religious art (icons were often repetitive),
then at least of its own regulating influence over the
icon, the art of the Church*. In fact churches in the
East hardly knew of any other art than that that was a
call to veneration. There was no purely ornamental art,
nor was there any purely didactic art, even in the private sphere.

In the West, on the other hand, in spite of pontifical
declarations that, at the height of past and present debates, from Gregory II (PL 89,511) to John Paul II
(apostolic letter *Duodecimum saeculum* in 1987),
marked their unremitting iconophilic position and their
sympathy with the decree of Nicaea II (*see* Lanne in
Bœspflug-Lossky 1987), the reception of this conciliar
decree by the Holy See did not always have an effect in
religious art. In the last centuries of the first millennium the West did indeed have a perception of the image that was already influenced by the strictly didactic
point of view formulated around the year 600 by
Pope* Gregory the Great, on the occasion of a bout of
iconoclastic fever in Marseilles. According to Gregory,
images were not to be adored, but they had established
themselves as a kind of alternative to the Bible for
those who were unable to read. Soon convinced, on the
basis of a faulty translation of the decree and quite
contrary to its genuine content, that the Eastern Fathers
were encouraging the adoration of icons, the Carolingian theologians took it upon themselves to dispute
Nicaea II on this point (*Livres carolins,* Council of
Frankfurt), believing that they must remind people that
"God cannot be painted." As for the rest, the theological question of images did not precipitate in the West
the same passionate confrontations as in the East. A.
Chastel had no fear of sustaining his view that, strictly

speaking, the West had never had a theology of the image. But that lack did not preclude Latin religious art
from producing, notably from the 12th century on, all
kinds of figurative art of an indisputably theological
density, such as the *Majestas Domini* and the Madonna
and Child.

d) West and the Icon. From the Middle Ages until the
present day the theoretical position stated by the West
on the subject of the veneration of images has sought
to be identical, or in accordance with, that of Nicaea II:
witness Thomas* Aquinas, in his ST IIIa, q. 25, on the
subject of the veneration due the images of Christ.
Against the Reformation and its sometimes violent
questioning of the veneration of religious images
(Zwingli* and Calvin* would encourage waves of
iconoclasm), the Council of Trent, in its turn, referred
to the decree of Nicaea II during the 25th session
(1563), something that the principal Treatises of Holy
Images written by Catholics (Molanus, 1570 and 1594;
cardinal Paleotti, 1594, *see* Prodi 1962) also did. In the
same manner Vatican II referred to it on two occasions
(*see* Bouchet in Bœspflug-Lossky 1987). The fact remains that this common reference to the seventh ecumenical council led, in both the East and the West, to
the development of two forms of art whose differences—not only in style and iconography but also in
status—would be increasingly accentuated. Furthermore, any influence of one upon the other would be
generally deplored by the influenced party, even up to
our own time.

It was not that the icon was ignored in the West or
was on the point of losing any of its prestige. On the
contrary, it was actually "imported" into the West—albeit on a more restricted basis than has sometimes
been estimated—following the Crusades and the sack
of Constantinople (1204). But even though a good
number of themes (in particular those of the cycles of
the Incarnation and Passion*: the Annunciation, the
Nativity, and the Baptism* of Christ; *Ecce Homo,* the
descent from the cross, "images of pity") were borrowed from the icon, Western art was taking an increasingly autonomous course. Its language was being
emancipated from the magisterial Church, from theologians, and, to a certain degree, from the liturgy.
While hesychasm* in the East was perfecting the doctrine of uncreated light (Gregory Palamas), which
would lead to the concept of the icon as an anticipation
of eschatological glory and as signifying the mysterious presence of the sanctified-transfigured—the icon
being, in this sense, a "window onto the absolute"—
the religious image of the Western Middle Ages was
becoming exploratory and exoteric, decorative and
playful. It proposed itself as the visual translation of

Scripture and of doctrine and of narratives of the lives of saints, the virtuoso presentation of the cross-references between the Old and New Testaments. The medieval "typology" that blossomed in the 12th century informed scholarly stock of images as represented by, among other things, the new basilica of Saint Denis inspired by Suger, the moralized Bible, the *Speculum humanae salvationis,* the *Biblia pauperum,* not to mention the frescoes, stained-glass windows, capitals, and tympanums of the Romanesque or Gothic churches. These were like so many books to be deciphered, inventing a multitude of formulations while giving voice to the feelings that arose from worship. In a way that with hindsight seems spectacular, through the intermediary of "speaking reliquaries" Western Christianity reconciled itself to statuary in the round, something that was almost totally absent throughout the first millennium in the West and remains so to this day in the East.

e) Theology's hold over medieval art has been greatly exaggerated. During the latter half of the Middle Ages Latin artists, who until the 12th century had been closely linked to the monastic *scriptoria,* would work in increasing numbers within the context of studios belonging to urban guilds and/or for the pleasure of those who gave them commissions, such as princes and merchants. The requirements of these patrons had only the most random, or even strained, relation to the theology and liturgy of the Church. The result was a courtly art that could be moving and carefully executed but that was not always in perfect harmony with the Christian theology of revelation. The movement to found communes and universities led to the rise of a new sort of artist: lay artists, often much sought after and extremely well paid, who would set up their own autonomous workshops as masters. Giotto, Masaccio, and Piero della Francesca would open new paths and create a new pictorial space. By the end of the Middle Ages, with the reappearance of the portrait, the discovery of perspective, and the interest in anatomy and landscape, the work of religious art became above all a work of art: the period of art, *das Zeitalter der Kunst* (Belting 1990), had begun. The artist was glorified for his imagination, for his genius. This also led to a multitude of "abuses" due to the growing popularity of the religious image: deviant representations, too numerous or too luxurious; superstitious devotional practices. From time to time certain theologians (Bernard* of Clairvaux, Savonarola) would raise their voices in protest against the invasive prestige of images, against their cost, their "worldliness," and the risk of "distraction" they represented. Protests were also heard against certain types of iconography that were considered aberrant or dangerous (Antonin de Florence, Gerson), or against superstitious uses (Erasmus*). In short, the idea that reform was necessary to control excesses in religious art was in the air well before the Reformation. The Council of Trent would attempt to find a remedy. But there was something lasting, if not irreversible, about this evolution. For a long time in Western art, and often, the religious subject would remain an opportunity, if not a pretext. The searing—but not always unjust—criticism that iconophile Christians (of East or West) voiced with regard to this art could be condensed into a few grievances: naturalism, sensualism, worldliness, or religiosity. The links between this art and the veneration of the mystery were loosening: a semblance of restraint and ecclesiastical regulation, of a theologically informed distance able to use symbolism, was being lost. Thus by the dawn of the 18th century, as Hegel* would point out, the image reputed to be holy no longer caused one to genuflect.

3. A Touchstone: The Question of "Images of God"

Proof of this evolution is provided by the rise (between the ninth and the 12th century) and dissemination (from the 13th century onward) of the figure of God the Father as an old man and, by way of consequence, of an entire collection of anthropomorphic representations of the Trinity that departed definitively from the outline traced by Nicaea II, a departure that would never take hold in the East (Bœspflug-Zaluska 1994). One could take the measure of the theological rift that had opened between the two art forms by comparing two works—Rublev's *Trinity* and that of Masaccio at the church of Santa Maria Novella in Florence—that differ in every aspect except their subject and their era (c. 1420–30). The former illustrates the Hospitality of Abraham (Gn 18), interpreted as prefiguring the Trinity. The latter makes use of a specifically Western iconographic type (the throne of grace) that could not claim to belong to any scriptural theophany. Furthermore, it presupposes an assemblage of motifs, portrays God the Father as a Jovian graybeard—anticipating Michelangelo's depiction of him as Creator in the Sistine Chapel—and takes the opportunity to demonstrate for the first time Brunelleschi's discoveries in linear perspective. Over two centuries later the Grand Council of Moscow (1666) once again condemned the figurative depiction of God the Father, while in the West on the other hand, in 1690, Pope Alexander VIII sided against the Jansenists and their opposition to images (Bœspflug 1984). The status of these Western images of God and of the Trinity remained problematic. The Council of Trent declared them to be "symbolic," that is, having no resemblance to the "prototype," which was equivalent to excluding them from the list of objects to be venerated. But it is doubtful whether this distinction between representative images and symbolic images was clear to the faithful.

The Catholic Church continued to teach that religious images were to be venerated; and yet those images, when they were recent, and whatever their other merits, were hardly venerable any more and hardly sought to be venerable. The images of God the Father as an old man with a crown (like a king, an emperor, or a pope) or as a Christianized Jupiter (Michelangelo) no longer succeeded in conveying his mystery in a credible fashion: the humanization of God was taken to its summit, like the confusion between the "economic Trinity" and the "immanent Trinity." And although these subjects have rarely been portrayed by artists for over a century, a critical summing-up should be made of this era of figurative representation. We might indeed suspect this figure of a "human, too human" God of having something to do with the rise in religious indifference and even of atheism. But theological reflection on what is at stake in this remarkable evolution has only just begun.

4. A Few Theological Tasks

The theological questions raised by the Christian images of the past or present cannot be dissociated from a reinterpretation of the decree of Nicaea II.

a) Images and Truth. In a world where images abound, and where their relation to reality is increasingly tenuous, one might wonder whether the theory of the *transitus* can be maintained without ambiguity. The religious image is indeed in danger at present of being stripped of the purpose assigned it by the Fathers of Nicaea II: to bear witness to a historical and "not illusory" reality of the Incarnation. The daily accumulation of images that are glimpsed but not contemplated shunts those images toward fiction and strips them of reality. How can they continue, after that, to bear witness to a historical truth? The answer requires a new Christian practice where the image is concerned, one that will be frugal, attentive, and selective. This practice would in turn imply some form of Christian instruction in the use of the religious image and a critical reappropriation of the traditional heritage.

b) Images and Style. Dissociated, or at least dissociable, from a theoretical approach to art, beauty, or language, Christian theology has as yet paid little attention to what, in an image, actually constitutes the image. It is difficult, however, to accept that an image might be reduced to lines and color, that the transmission of the gospel through the image is equally compatible with all styles, and that its "message," or its

"presence," is independent of its specific language. Although the principle of acculturation reiterated by Vatican II ("The Church has considered no artistic style as its own [...], but has accepted the styles of each era": *SC* VII, 122–23) remains the best guarantor of the freedom of local churches (church*) and their artists, its reaffirmation must not evade the problem of the image's legibility, its theological content, and its ecclesial function.

c) Images and Ecumenism. The controversial nature of the Christian use of images was for a long time the main aspect under which theologians encountered this issue. Nowadays, however, there is no longer a live controversy among Christians regarding this subject. The last "quarrel of sacred art" occurred in the 1950s and was primarily among Catholics. Since that time, a complex of historical factors has affected the issue: the failure of pious art; increasingly distant relations between the art world and the churches; the dubious nature and rarity of commissions; latent aniconism and chronic lack of concern with the liturgy of the recent tendencies in cutting-edge art; the movement to purify the churches; and the spread of icons in successive waves, most of which were related to Russian emigration during the 1920s and the Renewal shortly after 1970. As a result, there has been a slow convergence of the ways in which images are used, while official doctrines have not shifted from their positions. The two major signs of this are the reevaluation of images in some reformed circles in the West (Ramseyer 1963; Cottin 1994) and the reconciliation of the icon and Catholicism*, an event that, in the space of two decades, has seen Rublev's icon of the Trinity become the most widespread of the images of God, with all the ambiguities implied by this unpredictable transplantation.

d) Images and the Proclamation of the Gospel. All the Christian churches are now faced with the growing need for a traditional religious set of images. They are also faced with the challenge offered by the new techniques of communication, be it in the classical media or in the more recent multimedia contexts. However, either through a lack of interest or education, inclined as they are by tradition to view it as a mere *adia-phoron,* a question without importance, Catholic theologians are largely uninterested in the matter, favoring other questions deemed to be more urgent and considering the religious image to be, at best, a hobby. If need be they will apply themselves to thinking about the cinema, television, advertising images, or even virtual images and multimedia—in short, those forms of the image that have the most obvious relation to power. This has given rise to a considerable gap between the wealth of the artistic heritage of Christian art, in Europe and in those parts of the world touched by missionary work, and the relative poverty of contemporary creation in the domain of sacred art of biblical and Christian inspiration. Theological reflection on this gap is in itself all too rare, which also explains the improvised, to say the least, or perhaps chancy nature of the decisions adopted with regard to the media (televised broadcast of the Mass, for example). There is no doubt that this debate must be intensified in the decades to come: the theology of images, in view of the concrete situation facing the witnessing of the faith in the third millennium of the Christian era, is suffering at present from a certain shortfall in terms of elaboration and realization.

● H. Hennephof (1969), *Textus byzantini ad iconomachiam pertinentes,* Leyden.

Nicephorus, the Patriarch (1990), *Discours contre les iconoclastes,* translation of the *Antirerhetici* (PG 100) by M.-J. Mondzain, Paris.

D. Menozzi (1991), *Les images. L'Église et les arts visuels,* coll. "Textes en mains," Paris.

Saint John Damascene (1992), *La foi orthodoxe,* suivi de *Défense des icônes,* Trans. and notes E. Ponsoye, Suresnes.

H. G. Thümmel (1992), *Die Frühgeschichte der Ostkirchlichen Bilderlehre. Texte und Untersuchungen zur Zeit vor dem Bilderstreit,* TU 139.

F. Bœspflug, O. Christin, B. Tassel (1996), *Molanus, Traité des Saintes Images (1570, 1594),* Paris.

Theodore Abu Qurrah (1997), *A Treatise on the Veneration of the Holy Icons,* English trans. S. H. Griffith, Louvain.

♦ M. Denis (1890), *La peinture religieuse,* Paris.

V. Grumel (1927), "Images (culte des)," *DThC* VII/1, 766–844.

H. Jedin (1935), "Entstehung und Tragweite des Trienter Dekrets über die Bildverehrung," *ThQ* 116, 143–88, and 404–29.

V. Lossky, L. Ouspensky (1952), *The Meaning of Icons,* Berne; New York (2nd Ed. 1982).

A. Grabar (1957), *L'iconoclasme byzantin. Le dossier archéologique,* Paris (4th Ed. 1984); id. (1968), *Early Christian Art: From the Rise of Christianity to the Death of Theodosius,* New York; id. (1979), *Les voies de la création en iconographie chrétienne: Antiquité et Moyen Age,* Paris.

P. Prodi (1962), "Richerche sulla teoria delle arti figurativa nella riforma cattolica," *AISP* 4, 121–212.

J.-P. Ramseyer (1963), *La Parole et l'image,* Neuchâtel.

R. W. Lee (1967), "Ut Pictura Poesis," *The Humanistic Theory of Painting: XV–XVIII c.,* New York.

G. Lange (1968), *Bild und Wort: Die katechistischen Funktionen des Bildes in der griechischen Theologie,* Würzburg.

C. von Schönborn (1976), *L'Icône du Christ: Fondements théologiques élaborés entre le Ier et le IIe c. de Nicée (325–787),* Fribourg (2nd Ed. 1986, Paris).

C. Murray (1977), "Art and the Early Church," *JThS* 28, 303–45.

P. Dumeige (1978), *Nicée II,* Paris.

L. Ouspensky (1980), *La théologie de l'icône dans l'Église orthodoxe,* Paris.

H. Belting (1981), *Das Bild und sein Publikum im Mittelalter: Form und Funktion früher Bildtafeln der Passion,* Berlin; id. (1990), *Bild und Kult: Eine Geschichte des Bildes vor dem Zeitalter der Kunst,* Munich.

F. Bœspflug (1984), *Dieu dans l'art,* Paris; id. (1993), "La Seconde voix. Valeur et limites du service rendu par l'image à la predication," in F. Bœspflug, D. Menozzi, "Predicazione della Parola e immagini," *CrSt* XIV/3, 647–72.

P. Brown (1985), "Une crise des siècles sombres: aspects de la controverse iconoclaste," dans *La Société et le sacré dans l'Antiquité tardive,* Paris, 199–244.

F. Bœspflug, N. Lossky (sous la dir. de) (1987), *Nicée II, 787–1987: Douze siècles d'images religieuses,* Paris.

J. Wirth (1989), *L'image médiévale: Naissance et développements (Vie–XVe siècle),* Paris.

K. Weitzmann, H. Kessler (1990), *The Frescoes of the Dura Synagogue and Christian Art,* Washington.

G. Thümmel (1990), *Bilderlehre und Bilderstreit: Arbeiten zur Auseinandersetzung über die Ikone und ihre Begründung vornehmlich im 8. und 9. Jahrhundert,* Würzburg.

J. E. Ziegler (1990), *Sculpture of Compassion: The Pietà and the Beguines in the Southern Low Countries,* Bruxelles-Rome.

N. Duval (Ed.) (1991), *Naissance des arts chrétiens: Atlas des monuments paléochrétiens de la France,* Paris.

O. Celier (1992), *Le signe du linceul: le Saint Suaire de Turin, de la relique à l'image,* Paris.

F. Bœspflug, Y. Zaluska (1994), "Le dogme de la Trinité et l'essor de son iconographie, de l'époque carolingienne au IVe c. du Latran (1215)," *CCMéd* XXXVII, 181–240.

J. Cottin (1994), *Le regard et la parole: Une théologie protestante de l'image,* Geneva.

S. Michalski (1994), *The Reformation and the Visual Arts,* New York.

P. Prigent (1995), *L'art des premiers chrétiens: L'héritage culturel et la foi nouvelle,* Paris.

FRANÇOIS BŒSPFLUG

See also **Anthropomorphism; Architecture; Catechesis; Liturgy; Music; Nicaea II, Council of; Scripture, Senses of**

Imitation of Christ

The three major Christian confessions tend to view the imitation of Christ in different yet complementary ways. For Catholics, it signifies the acquisition, through actual *mimesis,* of virtues* exemplified by Jesus, and leads to a certain moral asceticism*. For Protestants, it suggests rather a conformity to Christ manifested by the discipline by "following" *(akolouthein)* Jesus in acts of love toward one's neighbor. Here, the stress is less on the acquisition of virtues than on salvation* by grace* received through faith. As for the Orthodox, they regard "imitation" as a "participation" in divine life through *sunergeia* or "cooperation" with God, through sacramental communion*, with a view to reaching *theosis* or "deification."

(a) Biblical Foundations. The Synoptics hardly explore the theme of the imitation of Christ, although it remains implicit. Jesus is the Son, and he teaches his disciples to have toward God the attitude of a son (filiation*), in prayer and in the call to be perfect "as your heavenly Father" (Mt 5:48; *see* Lv 19:2). He calls them to have attitudes that he himself assumes, as expressed by the Beatitudes (Mk 5; Lk 6). Jesus sends his disciples out to continue his own ministry* of proclaiming the Kingdom* and casting out demons. A common fate is promised to Jesus and to them: to be rejected (Mt 10:25). The necessity of *following* Jesus is more explicit: he summons that his cross be carried and that he be followed (Mk 8:34ff., 10:39). As the Suffering Servant and Son of man, Christ calls his disciples to follow the path of obedience to the Father's will and purpose, which inevitably involves the stations of the cross that he himself experienced.

The Johannine tradition turns the imitation of Christ into a formal precept. The episode of the washing of the feet highlights the example to follow (Jn 13:15f.). In John 15:12, the commandment of fraternal love is grounded in the expression "as I have loved you," which emanates from "as the Father has loved me" in John 15:9. Thus, Peter, summoned to feed Christ's sheep, will "follow" his master to martyrdom (Jn 21:15ff.). The imitation of Christ involves both behavior (to *do* as Jesus did) and participation in him who *is* the Way, the Truth*, and the Life (Jn 14:6). In 1 John, being "like" Jesus is presented as an object of hope* (3:2), but it is in this world (4:17) and "like" Jesus that the Christian is "in the light" (1:7), "pure" (3:3), and "righteous" (3:7), when he "walks in the same way in which he walked."

In Paul's epistles, Christ is the "image of God" (2 Cor 4:4; Col 1:15), the archetype of agape* or self-giving love (1 Cor 13). The Christian is predestined to be "conformed" to the image of the Son of God (Rom 8:29). For Paul, the imitation of Christ is first and foremost a conformity to the death and resurrection of Jesus (Rom 6). Imitation cannot be separated from sacramental "participation" through baptism* but also through eucharistic communion (1 Cor 10:16ff.).

Paul can also speak of himself as an "imitator of Christ" ("Be imitators of me as I am of Christ," 1 Cor 11:1; *see* 1 Cor 4:16; 1 Thess. 1:6; Thes 2:14; and the unique occurrence of *summimetes,* "imitator with," in Phil 3:17). As elsewhere in the New Testament, the verb used with *mimetes,* imitator, is *ginomai,* "be" or "become." It implies spiritual warfare against sin* that dwells within us (Rom 7:7–25), a continual struggle in and through the Holy* Spirit, which leads to life "in accord with Christ Jesus" (Rom 15:5), conformed to "the mind of Christ" (Phil 2:5). Paul's imitation of Christ, however, does not mean an exact reproduction of Jesus's specific acts or types of behaviors. It involves rather an absolute obedience to the will of God for the upbuilding and sanctification of the church: "Be imitators of God, as beloved children, and walk in love, as Christ loved us and gave himself on behalf of us, a fragrant offering and sacrifice to God" (Eph 5:1f.).

Elsewhere, the New Testament speaks of imitating examples other than Christ, such as the Israelite ancestors (Heb 11). Yet here as well Jesus, as "founder and perfecter of our faith" (Heb 12:2), serves as the prime model for Christian conduct. The supreme expression of this model remains his Passion and redeeming death. "Christ also suffered for you, leaving you an example that you should follow in his steps" (1 Pt 2:21).

(b) From the Testimony of the Fathers to the Reformation. During the first centuries of Christianity, the imitation of Christ occupied a central place in the definition of a specific way of life, but the interpretations that it received varied according to the historical contexts and the actual situation of Christians in the Ro-

man Empire. Up to the early fourth century and the official recognition of Christianity, and above all during periods of persecution, to imitate Christ was first of all to accept martyrdom, if not seek it out. Early in the second century, Ignatius of Antioch begged the Christians of Rome* not to prevent his martyrdom, so that he might, as he said, "imitate the passion of his God" (*Ep. Ad Romanos* 6, 3). The dissemination of accounts of the acts and passions of martyrs and the establishment of liturgical celebration in their honor show how Christian perfection was defined first and foremost through this imitation of Christ's suffering and death. In the third century, this theology* of martyrdom played a prominent role in the letters that Cyprian* of Carthage addressed to confessors of the faith before he himself was martyred. Origen and Tertullian* wrote treatises exhorting martyrdom (*see* the texts collected in *Le martyre dans l'Église ancienne,* Paris, 1990). Paul's texts on baptism had made the imitation of Christ's Passion and death the crux of the definition of this sacrament*, and in the first centuries baptismal catechisms and treatises on baptism frequently reiterated it. Basil* of Caesarea emphasizes that such imitation is unavoidably an imitation of the perfections of Christ and, through baptism, an imitation of his interment *(De Spiritu Sancto)*. The entire Christian life must therefore be in conformity with Christ, the imitation of Christ being the foundation of Christian morality; homilies thus give a great deal of attention to this theme. The prominent place given to the monastic life underlines this ideal of the full accomplishment of the virtues. However, the emphasis in the Epistle to the Hebrews on Christ as high priest also led to the development of a theology of priesthood* centered on the imitation of Christ: "the pontifical dignity...implies the imitation of the high pontiff Jesus" (*Apostolic Constitutions,* VIII, 46, 4).

By emphasizing the sinful condition of man, in the course of his polemic against Pelagianism*, Augustine created conditions in which the imitation of Christ could be called into question. His conception, developed within a largely Pauline* theology, had a broad resonance among the Lutheran Reformers. The imitation of Christ (*Nachahmung Christi*) was largely interpreted as succeeding Christ (*Nachfolge Christi*), in light of the emphasis on justification* by faith or grace* alone. The concept of moral and spiritual transformation through ascetic discipline gave way to that of the obedience of the disciple, a distinction that Augustine had explicitly rejected (*Quid est enim sequi, nisi imitare?*- *De sancta virginitate* 27). For Calvin and the Genevese Reformers, however, active imitation—taking up one's cross in self-denial, to enable true participation in Christ's holiness*—remained the

central tenet of a biblically based ethics. The most radical denial of any concept of imitation perhaps came from the Quietists of the 17th century, and especially Miguel de Molinos (†1697). For the Quietists, perfection consists not in imitation of Christ but in an experience in which one rejects all effort and, consequently, all responsibility, resulting in a complete passivity that gives free rein for divine action.

(c) The Imitation of Christ *by Thomas à Kempis.* The attribution of *The Imitation* to Thomas Hemerken à Kempis (c. 1380–1471) is no longer disputed (Delaissé 1956). The most widely circulated Christian work after the Bible, its title was supplied by his publisher in the late 15th century, at a time when the vogue for Plutarch compelled people to think of all pedagogy in terms of the imitation of illustrious individuals. *The Imitation* is a collection (or *rapiarium*) of rhythmic sentences that can easily be memorized, for use by the young canons regular of the abbey of Mont Sainte-Agnès (Netherlands) in their orations. This abbey, which was affiliated to the congregation at Windesheim, stood at the confluence of Ruusbroecian mysticism*, the erudition of Saint* Victor of Paris, and the interiority of the *devotio* moderna of the Brothers of the Common Life. Thomas à Kempis studied with the brothers at Deventer in the days of Gert Groote and Florent Radewijns, who initiated the pre-Jesuit educational tradition. They provided the basic content of *The Imitation*, Thomas's contribution being more its form, which he developed along with his own monastic *ruminatio*.

Modern spirituality grew out of *The Imitation,* a spirituality more psychological than intellectual or moral, concerned with pinpointing and discerning the motions of the soul (soul*-heart-body) that has resolved to follow Christ. Spiritual life then became inner life. Biblical expressions are favored to report this spirituality: 1,500 quotations, most of which are implicit, notably from the Psalms*, the books of wisdom, and Paul. There are also numerous borrowings from Augustine, Bernard of Clairvaux, Bonaventure*, David of Augsburg, and from Suso, who gives the text its melancholy tenderness overtone, if not a certain pessimism. Misled by the title and a certain kind of Stoicism*—Seneca's—that looms over modern spirituality, some read *The Imitation* as a work of asceticism. However, the moral aspect of the text as a whole is much less important than its resolutely mystical purpose, which is to invite the young monk to undertake an internal dialogue with Jesus, to bring him back, unceasingly, to the source hidden within himself and from which divine life springs. This religious pedagogy places personal *pietas* above observance of rules, and thus provides a spiritual basis for all the forms of the religious life that were to flourish during the Renaissance.

This absolute Christocentrism is grounded in consideration of the humanity of Jesus, the Friend (in the chivalrous sense that was to be shared by Ignatius of Loyola) rather than the Spouse, up to the mystic union. Among the four books that comprise *The Imitation,* the second and the third, the author's true spiritual journal, make this doctrine of friendship as a form of "pure love"; the first book is an initiation to the monastic life according to the Windesheim ideal; and the fourth is a collection of meditations on the Eucharist*.

(d) Imitation of Christ and the Christian Life Today. Nowadays, thanks to the ecumenical movement (ecumenism*), much has been accomplished in terms of the recognition of attitudes that are at least comparable among Christians of different traditions, and this also involves the imitation of Christ. A large majority of Christians have rediscovered patristic theology and its refusal to separate theology from spirituality. In addition to the collection of the *Sources Chrétiennes,* we should also mention the rapprochement—and the observation of a frequently common experience— among the religious in the various churches. While the forms of the imitation of Christ are not always the same, its deep meaning is felt by all as a growth in life in Christ.

In the early 20th century, a time of conflict between East and West, some Orthodox theologians stated that the East did not know of the imitation of Christ (in relation to a "naturalistic" imitation of Christ). One can no longer say this. Indeed, if only during the Holy Week, the Byzantine tradition possesses numerous texts such as the following: "Initiating your disciples, Lord, you instructed them with these words: 'O my friends, awaken! Let not any fear separate you from me. What I suffer is for the sake of the world. Do not be troubled on my account, for I have not come to be served, but to serve, and to give my life as ransom for the world. *If you are my friends, do as I do:* so that he who would be first shall be last, so that the master becomes the servant. Dwell in me and you shall bear fruit, for I am the vine of life.'"

On the other hand, contemporary Protestant theology owes to Bonhoeffer*, and then to Barth*, the vigorous rehabilitation of the *sequela Christi* through a resumption of intuitions found earlier in Kierkegaard*.

The vision of the imitation of Christ unites most Christians in a tension around the teaching of Christ (Lk 22:24–27): "I am among you as the one who serves" and in the memory of Galatians 3:27 "For as many of you as were baptized into Christ have put on Christ."

● D. Bonhoeffer (1937), *Nachfolge,* Munich (*DBW* 4, Munich, 1994).
I. Hausherr (1948), "L'imitation de Jésus-Christ dans la spiritualité byzantine," *Mélanges offerts au R.P.F. Cavallera,* 231–59, Toulouse.
L.M.J. Delaissé (1956), *Le manuscrit autographe de Thomas à Kempis* and *L'Imitation de Jésus-Christ.: examen archéologique et édition diplomatique du Bruxellensis 5855–61* (2 vols.), London.
E.J. Tinsley (1960), *The Imitation of God in Christ: An Essay on the Biblical Basis of Christian Spirituality,* London.
A. Schulz (1962), *Nachfolgen und Nachahmen: Studien über das Verhältnis der neutestamentlichen Jüngerschaft zur urchristlichen Vorbildethik,* Munich.
K. Barth (1964), *KD* IV/2, *Die Lehre von der Versöhnung,* 603–26.
H.D. Betz (1967), *Nachfolge und Nachahmung im Neuen Testament,* Tübingen.
M. Hengel (1968), *Nachfolge und Charisma,* BZNW 34, Berlin.
R. Lovatt (1968), "The *Imitation of Christ* in Late Medieval England," *Transactions of the Royal Historical Society,* 5th series, 18, 97–121.
A. Ampe, B. Spaapen (1970), "*Imitatio Christi,*" *DSp* VII/2, 2338–68.
E. Cothenet et al. (1970), "l'imitation du Christ," *DSp* VII/2, 1536–601.
W.C. Creasey (1989), *The* Imitation of Christ *by Thomas a Kempis,* Macon, Ga.
U. Luz et al. (1994), "Nachfolge Jesu," *TRE* 24, 678–713.

JOHN BRECK

See also **Conversion; Experience; Heart of Christ; Holiness; Kenosis; Monasticism**

Immaculate Conception. *See* Mary

Immensity of God. *See* Infinite

Immutability/Impassibility, Divine

I. Philosophy and Scripture

At the beginning of the Christian era, it was already traditional to contrast reason, a stable and relatively self-moved force, with the emotions, the domain of "passion," in the sense of "submission to an alien force" (Frohnhofen, 1987). However, only the Stoics espoused *apatheia,* an ideal state of impassibility in which the mind is undisturbed by any sort of movement. As for transcendental realities, they were conceived, following Plato and Aristotle, to be without change or passion.

Several passages in the Bible seemed to conflict with this notion by describing God as moved to regret, pity, or anger (Gn 6:6, etc.). However, other passages (e.g., Mal 3:6, "For I the Lord do not change"; *see* Ps 102 [101], 27, Jas 1:17) appeared to suggest that the former passages should be interpreted either figuratively or as implying an emotion in God that was constant and depended only on himself. The same duality was repeated and intensified in the christological context. Ignatius of Antioch affirms, more explicitly than the New Testament, "the passion of my God" (*Ad Romanos* 6, 3), but on the other hand speaks of him "who cannot suffer, who for our sakes endured suffering" (*Ad Polyc.* 3, 2).

II. Patristic and Scholastic Discussions

1. Passion and Emotion

Of all the fathers of the church, only Clement of Alexandria, who assimilated love* to a state of true knowledge (gnosis), espoused the Stoic position on *apatheia.* Most of the fathers were rather partisans, as with Augustine (*Civ. Dei* VIII, 17), of the good use of the passions and an incorporation of the Platonic *eros* (e.g., the Cappadocians, Augustine, Pseudo-Dionysius*). However, beyond the legacy of philosophy, the fathers and the Scholastics (Scholasticism) insisted on constant emotions, such as love or compassion, as attributes of the Godhead and thereby started to separate emotion from passion (John Damascene, *Expositiones de fide* iii, 18; Thomas Aquinas, ST Ia, q. 20, a. 1).

2. Apatheia *and Orthodoxy*

Since the 19th century, there has been a tendency to suppose that the question of God's *apatheia* arose within Christian thought because it was caught between a need to relate to a God who is not impassible and the logical requirements of metaphysics. There is some truth in this view, and one finds Anselm, for example, wondering how God could be both "pitiful" and "impassible" (*Proslogion* 8). However, more crucially, it can be argued that it was part of the inner logic of Christian orthodoxy to think more and more clearly about the absolute as unchangeable and impassible, to the extent that the concepts inherited from philosophy were modified through the teaching of the Bible. This resulted in new distinctions, not just between passion and emotion, but also between passivity and receptivity. The argument concerns especially the areas of creation, the theory of the Logos (Word), and Christology (Christ and Christology).

(a) Creation. In the first two centuries of the Christian era, the idea of ontological mediation between creator and created had priority over any doctrine of an absolute distinction between the two. In consequence, the Logos, taken to be not fully divine, could be passible, such that the sufferings of Christ raised relatively few problems (Mozley 1926; *see* Rowan Williams, *Arius*). Sometimes, this was conjoined with the view that while, by nature, God was impassible, he had freely chosen to become subject to suffering. Even those authors who accepted the full divinity of the Logos dealt in this way with the question of the sufferings of the Logos in the flesh* (Mozley).

In this context, the cosmological debates of the third century, and especially the work of Methodius of Olympus († c. 311), are of crucial significance. For Methodius, there is a radical ontological distinction between creator and created, such that there can be absolutely no sense (as with Origen) that in creation some aspect of God proceeds outward from him and so is passively affected by God himself: the passionless God is not changed through the creation of the world (*De creatis,* PG 18, 331–44). Nor can the Incarnation* involve any change in the Logos. God does not subject himself to suffering in Christ's sufferings, which are therefore pure paradox: he suffered while remaining impassible (*De cruce et passione Christi,* PG 18, 398–403).

A further crucial aspect of Methodius's position is the denial, against Origen, of the eternity of the world and of any sort of subsistence or permanence of matter as a principle of things. Otherwise, the creating God must have been engaged with some reality outside himself and so been, to this degree, "passive." For this reason, Gnostics such as Valentinus denied that the supreme God is also the creator God. Dionysius of Alexandria († c. 264) had remarked that, if matter was unoriginate, it was strange that it was not, like God himself, impassible and immutable (*Epistolae,* Ed. C.L. Feltoe, Cambridge).

The insistence on creation *ex nihilo* by Methodius and others was required to get rid of this inconsistency and ensure God's full activity in creating. Basil and Gregory of Nyssa (*Contra Eunomium* VI, 3) added that, if the creation is "of itself" *nothing,* then even within the creation there is no ontological passivity, but only degrees of participation in divine activity. The world is composed of bundles of active qualities, not of compounds of form and matter. Such a position meshes very well with their view, also found in Athanasius (*De Incarnatione,* SC 199, 7), that human beings were originally created incorruptible and that the Incarnation restores this incorruptibility.

Hence, the implication of the strict thinking through of creation *ex nihilo* was not that God was entirely active, whereas finite things were essentially passive, but rather that created things also, when not impaired by sin, were entirely active yet never received the infinite measure of divine action. This indicates a kind of paradox: to *participate* in divine activity is not fully to *receive* it in its infinite plenitude. This paradox could only be spelled out in terms of the theology of the Trinity.

(b) The Logos. One of the grounds for the opposition of Arius and Eunomius to the divinity of the Son was that this contaminated divine impassibility: first, because a generation in God implied passion; second, because the emanation of the Logos was intrinsically linked to the work of creation, and that implied passionate involvement (Mozley). Arianism* avoided a solution of the Valentinian type through a voluntaristic theology that claimed that a God absolutely one and simple in essence had nonetheless willed to descend into creation and incarnation. Its exaltation of divine sovereignty, and its preference for a negative theology, left it with hardly any possibility of ascribing *feelings* to God. Hence, even though the Arians accepted the sufferings of the Logos, they recognized no natural grounds for involvement with finitude and passibility within the Godhead. For more orthodox thinkers, such as Tertullian, certain divine attitudes, for example, those of love and mercy, were permanent and unalterable. Hence, a biblically derived emotive characterization of the absolute demanded an "essentialist" characterization of God as unchanging and impassible.

Athanasius, in opposition to Arius, and Gregory of Nyssa, in opposition to Eunomius, insisted that generation in God does not necessarily imply passivity. Even natural generation does not necessarily divide the essence of a thing, and in divine generation there is only the action of the Father and the Son, as fire gives out light. It was possible to conceive of a reception so intrinsic to the being that receives it that it is not strictly speaking passive in relation to that reception, it *is* that reception (Gregory of Nyssa, *Contra Eunomium* 1, 13). In consequence, the finite creation does not fully share in the plenitude of the divine act, *not* because it is essentially passive, but because, unlike the Logos, it does not fully receive.

Hence, action itself is redefined to mean "to give, to effect, to influence," and, at the same time, "to receive, to be effected, to be influenced by." Just as it had been realized that emotions might be active, and that creation does not impair autonomy, so also it was now realized that action could be relational and even receptive. By these means, the idea of impassibility was in a *new* sense reinforced. The more the emanation or utterance of the Logos was recognized as fully divine, the less could the divine nature be subject to suffering, and no act of will could alter anything.

(c) Christology. Trinitarian orthodoxy therefore rendered impossible the voluntaristic solution of the problem of God's suffering, a solution that was in any case subject to the suspicion of attributing Christ's sufferings to the Father (patripassionism). The legatees of the Cappadocians and the school of Alexandria insisted that no change or passivity was involved for the Logos in the Incarnation. At the same time, the primacy of salvation* in Athanasius and Cyril led them

to insist that we are healed by the divine initiative, and that we can only escape from passion and suffering if God has first assumed them by taking on our mortal condition (Athanasius, *De Incarnatione* SC 199, 7). Hence, Cyril insists strongly on the Logos as subject to the passion and repeats Methodius's paradoxical formulations (*Epistola dogmatica* 3).

However, a ground for this paradox gradually emerged as the doctrine of the hypostatic* union was formulated. Since what holds together divinity and humanity in Christ is not a substantial reality, the same divine hypostasis that of its essence does not suffer can express itself *both* in the eternal impassibility proper to the divine, *and* in the suffering proper to human nature. This is nonetheless an entirely active suffering because it is freely chosen, in a manner impossible for a sinful creature, for whom involuntary suffering is an inevitable consequence of sin. Since entirely active suffering is immediately transfigured into pure activity, the notion of *apatheia* is used to grasp the specificity of *redemptive* suffering: an entirely nonreactive and unresented suffering that is imposed from without and yet consists of a gift offered freely from within and that reveals the constancy of love.

III. Modernity

Luther* went beyond Cyril in his version of the communication of idioms, declaring that God himself has suffered and died for us. However, the exact import of this claim remained unclear, and it was rejected by several Lutheran Scholastics, as well as by Calvinists (Mozley). Only in the 19th century did divine impassibility become subject to widespread rejection, partly among Lutheran kenoticists but more drastically with a group of English and Scottish theologians.

In their view, only a God who is capable of sorrow and compassion is a God whom we can recognize as truly God. At first sight, one might think that theologies of a compassionate or essentially historical God, and christologies of kenosis*, in which the Logos loses its character as God, free the biblical vision from the shackles of metaphysics. What one sees instead is surrender to secular categories, for all these constructions assume the prime reality of evolution and the idea of progress through struggle and sacrifice. The ideas of an original perfection of creation and of the Fall (original sin) recede into the background, and a human experience is idolatrously projected upon God and made absolute. Mozley cites the Anglican Storr, for example: "He God enters into creation, experiences the struggle, feels the pain of the whole of His creation. He does so *because* it is love's nature to

go out of itself in self-sacrifice." God comes to be regarded as worthy of love and worship simply because he is involved in the same struggle as human beings and has played a supremely heroic part in it. These theories have had two consequences. First, the idea that redemption involves a transformation of our mortal condition is lost sight of; instead, purely human goals—the struggle of mankind for the future and the quest for the perfect city—are made absolute. Second, the nature of redemptive suffering is misconstrued, for where suffering is eternally inevitable (as in the common 19th-century idea of "a cross always in the heart of God") and sacrifice is held to be the essence of virtue (virtues), the evil occasion of suffering is secretly celebrated as the occasion for heroism (Mozley). The truth is that suffering is only redemptive when embraced (if necessary) in order to manifest a free self-bestowing gift prior to all evil, such that to suffer is to continue to give in dire circumstances, rather than to prove oneself "virtuous."

The reaction against the idea of impassibility therefore risked distorting Christianity into a sickly celebration of sacrifice and weakness. Given this development, Nietzsche*'s reaction was salutary; and yet his lesson has scarcely been learned by much 20th-century theology.

In more recent debates, one can contrast the position of Eberhard Jüngel with that of Hans Urs von Balthasar* on this subject. For the former (1978), God is only "established" through the encounter with meaninglessness, suffering, and death. This view is subject to the same suspicions that have been voiced. For Balthasar, by contrast (1993), the *passionless generations* of the life of the Trinity are nonetheless the ground for divine involvement in the world and in suffering. Such a view recaptures the best patristic intentions.

● J. K. Mozley (1926), *The Impassibility of God*, Cambridge.
B. R. Brasnet (1928), *The Suffering of the Impassible God*, London.
G. Koch (1968), *Die Zukunft des toten Gottes*, Hamburg.
K. Kitamori (1972), *Theologie des Schmerzes Gottes*, Göttingen (1st Japanese Ed. 1946).
J. Maritain (1973), "Quelques réflexions sur le savoir théologique," in *Approches sans entraves*, Paris, 292–326.
W. Maas (1974), *Veränderlichkeit Gottes*, Paderborn.
F. Varillon (1975), *La souffrance de Dieu*, Paris.
J. Galot (1976), *Dieu souffre-t-il?*, Paris.
E. Jüngel (1978), *Gott als Geheimnis der Welt*, Tübingen.
H. U. von Balthasar (1983), *Theodramatik* IV, Einsiedeln, 191–222.
H. Frohnhofen (1987), *Apatheia tou Theou*, Frankfurt.

JOHN MILBANK

See also **Aseitas; Attributes, Divine; Eternity of God; Justice, Divine; Knowledge, Divine; Omnipresence, Divine; Simplicity, Divine**

Impurity. *See* **Purity/Impurity**

Incarnation

The term goes back to the prologue of the Gospel of Saint John where it is said that "the Word became flesh." Here we offer a brief interpretation of this prologue, a summary of the treatment of the topic in ancient and then medieval theology, and finally, indicate several issues raised in recent theology by the use of the concept of incarnation.

1. Theology According to John

To understand the perspective adopted by John we must first show how the prologue to the Fourth Gospel (Gospels*) establishes a connection, through the concept of the "flesh," between the two titles it gives Christ: "Word" and "Son."

a) John clearly gave the term *Word (logos)* the broadest possible meaning. From a biblical point of view, "Word" evokes the prophecies (prophet and prophecy) marking God's intervention in human history and revealing his purpose (*see* Heb 1:1). It also evokes (especially with regard to literary form) the wisdom that accompanies God in his creation of the world and even, according to more recent texts (Sir 24; Bar 3:37f.; Wis 7:17, 10, etc.,), in the history of Israel. This is a wisdom to which later biblical speculation would attribute a still uncertain hypostatic character, while Paul would see it as effectively actualized in Christ. Wisdom 9:1f. associates "Word" and "Wisdom" with God to an equal extent. The Word is treated as mystery, that is to say, as the plan of salvation hidden in God since eternity*.

Yet all of these biblical associations between the two testaments are contained in the Greek word *logos,* which in Stoicism denotes the immanent and eternal "reason*" for the world's cohesion, the living principle of its intelligibility. In Middle Platonism it also points to the first emanation of the unknown God, the emanation through which he manifests himself. A complex interaction between the Greek and Hebrew concepts was bound to occur.

All these meanings relate to the world and to humans as well as to God considered in his economy. But the opening formula of John's prologue (v. 1) uses a preposition ("the Word was with God") and a verb ("the Word was God") and so introduces a paradoxical relationship of simultaneous difference and identity between God and his Logos.

b) "And the Word became flesh" (v. 14). This phrase, which stands at the origin of the term *incarnation,* suggests more than the mere unification of the Word with human nature. "Flesh*"connotes the precarious condition of human beings who are subject to death. Thus the term also alludes to a communication with human beings that shows them the way through the history of salvation.

c) At first glance the title of Son complements that of Word. With its accompanying epithet of monogenic, "only", "Son" expresses the relationship between the unique Word and God's own uniqueness and, at the same time, what distinguishes Christ from the other "children" of God (v. 12). Glory* is the very sign of God and it is through it that the Father communicates with his Son. This "only" Son is "at the Father's side" (v. 18) and the one who "has made him known" (ibid.), the one who externalizes him.

All his action in the world thus appears as a manifestation of God, an externalization for the people and for their benefit of "the glory that I [the Son] had with you before the world existed" (Jn 17:5). In other words, "things [that] were made through him" (1:3)— that is, creation and salvation—find their meaning in a precise historical event: "without him was not any thing made that was made" (1:3). Hence, this event and its meaning, as well as all the other events with their meaning, have an existence in God that the Logos expresses. Reciprocally, the Logos is externalized in the events of creation and history until the decisive moment of the Incarnation—by means of which, as well as by means of the events themselves, the Logos reveals God to those who believe.

Christ thus reveals the Father's glory in and through an authentic human history. The incarnation of the Word and "all things . . . made through him" are truly of this earth but they also express a mystery that is interior to God, and they lead to him by communicating the divine reality that fills them. Furthermore, this flesh is not isolated in history: it fulfills what happened in Israel and recapitulates the entire work of creation. So we see that there is a definite continuity here between a series of distinct levels: the theological level (that which is in God), the level of creation, the level of "Israel" (what happened before the Incarnation, represented by Moses and John the Baptist), the ecclesial level, and, finally, the level of the Incarnation.

Thus, in John's prologue, Christology (Christ and Christology) is primarily a theology: it draws its unity from "at God's side" or alternatively, "in the bosom of the Father." The two aspects, theological and historical, while each retains its own specificity, are indivisible.

2. Patristic Developments

In the patristic era the historical dimension of John's global perspective was to a certain extent overshadowed. What mattered most of all to the church fathers was salvation through knowledge. In order for such a doctrine of salvation to be possible it was necessary that the Word had really contemplated that which was in God in order to reveal it; therefore, the Word needed to be truly God since only God could know God completely. This presupposed, on the other hand, that the Word had become truly human. In this way there was no separation between the one who revealed and those to whom he was revealed, neither from the ultimate perspective of knowledge, nor from the intermediate perspective of the stages by which human beings (especially as sinners) were rendered capable of knowing God's glory. Finally, it was necessary that Christ, "consubstantial* with God in divinity, consubstantial with men in humanity" (Chalcedon), remained *one*. Thus, a systematic theory of the Incarnation developed in which focusing on Christ's being* eclipsed certain meanings (creation, history of salvation) that were essential to Johannine theology.

The historical stages of this discussion are well known. The cultural world of Alexandria focused on the Logos. This favored a christological perspective inspired by John 1:14, dominated by the distinction word/body (soul*-heart-body), *logos/sarx,* and in which some difficulty was experienced in attributing to Christ a created human soul (soul*-heart-body). Sometimes this is even explicitly rejected and the Word is substituted for the soul, whether it is considered as something created (Arianism) or as something uncreated and consubstantial (Apollinarianism*). We may even observe a prudent silence over this difficult issue (Athanasius*). When, in reaction to the above, it becomes necessary to highlight Christ's total humanity *(logos/anthropos),* the discussion shifts to the mode of union. It is from this necessity that we should begin to understand the emphasis placed in Ephesus* on the unity of Christ proclaimed as truly God; then, to try to understand the efforts made at Chalcedon to establish a distinction between the two "natures" and the unity of "the person*"; and finally, to comprehend the statements on Christ's will and human action that were made during the final two centuries of the patristic era. Throughout these various stages a fundamental hermeneutic (hermeneutics*) principle was at work: affirming the perfection of what was divine and what human in the unity of Christ ensured human salvation through true knowledge.

Such an endeavor, pursued over the course of centuries, gave theology the opportunity to elaborate on the philosophical categories it had borrowed from Greek authors with whom they dialogued or disputed. The concepts of "substance," "relation," "essence," "nature," "faculty," and furthermore, the analysis of knowledge and will, as well as the refinements required by the theme of the communication of idioms*—all this represented a conceptual benefit for Western thought as a whole. The noun "incarnation," *ensarkosis,* appears in Irenaeus (*Adv. Haer.* III, 18, 3.) *Incarnatio* came into usage in Latin in the third century.

3. Scholastic Theology

Partly through a rereading of ancient conciliar texts, Scholastic (Scholasticism) theology inherited from tradition a developed concept of the Incarnation. The christological dogma was fixed and the concept of the Incarnation did not seem to call for further refinement. It will suffice here to outline two persistent themes: that of the mode of union and that of the motive of the Incarnation.

a) If we consider the problem of maintaining the humanity of Christ in his divinity, we find several possible solutions, all of which come down to the issue of the hypostatic union. These ideas or "opinions" were summarized in a famous text by Peter Lombard (adoptionism*) that opened the way for Thomas Aquinas's classical speculations on "the union in the person" and his analysis of the characteristics of each of Christ's natures, especially his human nature.

b) As to the "motive for the Incarnation," we can formulate the question as follows: "Had there been no sin to expiate, would the Word have become incarnate?" There are in fact two types of theology to be discerned behind this supposition. One is centered on the theme of creation considered as a sufficient manifestation of the being, the power (omnipotence*), and the eternity of a God whose unity is perhaps more crucial than his Trinitarian nature. From this point of view the Incarnation is not required in order to demonstrate God's being per se, but it testifies to his infinite mercy* (see Thomas Aquinas, ST IIIa, q. 1, a. 3, ad 2.) The other theology, on the contrary, sees the Incarnation as fulfilling God's design for the world. Here the history of salvation and God's Trinitarian being become central. The Incarnation is the most important moment of God's manifestation by the Word who is the Creator of the world, the inspiration of the Scriptures, the savior of the human race, and the fulfillment of all things and all events (see Bonaventure, Coll. in Hexaemeron, Prol. and I, 10–26.)

4. Contemporary Problems

"The Word became flesh": this was the basis of the treatises of Verbo incarnato—but the Christologies of the 20th century, which have replaced the Scholastic and Neoscholastic treatises of former times, make it appear more as the conclusion. A brief account of the most notable christological works offered since the 1960s will suffice to show this important shift. In Pannenberg's Grundzüge der Christologie (1964), the point of departure is a paschal recognition of the divinity of Jesus, which permits a retrospective interpretation of the pre-Easter events; it is only the last theorems that give a thought to such cruces interpretum as the anhypostasy* and the communication of idioms. The Incarnation is very much the last word. In Moltmann's Der Gekreugzire Gott (1972) a theologia crucis absorbs everything and reduces the theme of the Resurrection to a congruent portion; and the passion for the future (including "the future of Jesus Christ") regards with indifference all "non-historical" questions on the Incarnation. Schillebeeckx's Jesus (1975), undoubtedly the most articulate of contemporary endeavors, uses a combination of an exegetical critical method and a hermeneutic (hermeneutics) procedure, which allows the author to follow Jesus from his preaching to his death in order to reinterpret the theologoumena of the Resurrection and determine the very meaning of Christology as the idea that "in Jesus

a definitive salvation has come to us from God." O. Gonzalez de Cardedál, in his no less complex book of 1978, organizes first an anthropology of man's meeting with God before adopting three perspectives aimed at defining Christ's "newness": a metaphysical horizon, an anthropological horizon, and a secular ethical (ethics*) horizon. Since the emphasis is now placed on Christ as living and encountered, the Incarnation is as much presupposed as passed over in silence. Finally, another example is B. Forte's Jesus of Nazareth (1981), which makes a convincing effort to answer a good question: "How can a divine subject be the agent of a human history?" It tries to link the pre-Easter events to the post-Easter events by means of a very flexible hermeneutics—which, however, certainly does not draw from the Christology of John's prologue.

We can see, therefore, that the Christology of the Incarnation is to a certain extent put in parenthesis. We may cite, for example, J. Galot's neoclassical essay (1980), L. Bouyer's more eclectic one (1974), both explicating the Incarnation with the help of the patristic traditions, together with M.-J Le Guillou's unclassifiable work of spiritual theology, L'Innocent (1973), an unfashionable meditation on John's Christ and his consciousness (Christ's consciousness). We can also cite G. Lafont's outline (1969) of a Christology that is interested in the Word as invested with human consciousness, a Christology consequently designed "to enlarge, if not [...] transform the metaphysical method used in post-Nicaean theology." In addition we might note that a kind of classical Lutheranism—Jüngel 1976–in trying to open a way between theism (deism*/theism) and atheism at the time of the "dead God," is fully capable of developing a theologia crucis that attain to the secrets of Trinitarian love* by linking "the word of the cross" and "the Word made flesh" under the theme of "the humanity of God." But, faced with these defenses of a theology that is little practiced today, we need only mention a few of the criticisms made of it. Starting from the very idea of the Incarnation, J. Hick and various Anglo-Saxon authors loudly proclaimed that it was perhaps not the best theory for explaining the divine aspect of Christ (Hick 1977; Lampe 1977) and that Christianity could happily dispense with such a myth. On the other hand, a certain vague criticism of "metaphysical" language among those who have read a bit of Heidegger* invariably leads them to note that terms such as person, nature, hypostasis, and Logos are all related to one and the same episteme and that no episteme has words of eternal life*—this is how J.-M. Pohier proposed to bring an end to the "metaphysics" of the Incarnation in order to start talking about God's presence in Jesus as "a

Shekinah mode." Finally, a new—political—aspect of *theologia crucis* leads us, quite logically, to suspect that both a post-cross (Resurrection) and a pre-cross (Incarnation) discourse would be totally deaf to the cries of the poor (Sobrino 1978).

Some responses do indeed exist or have been in the process of formulation. T. F. Torrance, a theologian and amateur physicist (to the point of authoring a critical edition of the Scottish physicist J. C. Maxwell), devoted two works to situating the Incarnation in time and space (1969 and 1976), which are considered important enough to be cited as opening the cosmological dimension of Christology. There is some awareness of the problem of metaphysical statements. We cannot be certain that J. Moingt's treatise (1993) has succeeded in its ambitious mission: to attach consistently some simple "rumors" about Jesus to the paschal faith of the disciples, to a pre-Easter Christology, and finally, to the reemerging Nicaean idea of the consubstantial, all of which use the fluid and historical categories largely borrowed from Hegel—but it is important that the author tries to achieve it. D. M. MacKinnon (1972) also expressed some doubts about the supposedly "metaphysical" character of christological statements.

Perhaps what all of these attempts were seeking was simply an integral Christology. Having been plagued for a long time by an opposition between "Christologies from above" and "Christologies from below," which, according to N. Lash (1980), only obscured rather than enlightened the subject, current research can at least guard itself against the dangers of a one-dimensional Christology. The object of such inquiry is something temporally defined—the "event of Jesus Christ"—which must be interpreted in all its logic by precisely following the traces it has left. It does not then matter if Christology chooses to have John's prologue as a beginning or as an end. What matters is constructing a rich theology of the Incarnation, drawing on all the perspectives offered by other major concepts and capable of accomplishing an inquiry first into the "earthly Jesus," then into "Christ risen and glorified," through a contemplation of "the mystery of Jesus Christ" (for example, Kasper 1974). It can thus be said, for example, that: "at the basis of the movement through which Jesus, just as any of us, achieves the truth of what we are and reveals himself as the Other, divine and filial, there is another movement, an unthinkable initiative by which the Other freely enters destiny or allows destiny to enter him" (Sesboüé, 1982).

● *See also* the general bibliography for "Christ/Christology."

P. Lamarche (1964), "Le Prologue de Jean," *RSR* 497–537.

W. Pannenberg (1964), *Grundzüge der Christologie*, Gütersloh.

R. E. Brown (1966), *The Gospel According to John* I, Garden City, NY.

G. Lafont (1969), *Peut-on connaître Dieu en Jésus-Christ?*, CFi 44; id. (1986), *Dieu, le temps et l'être*, Paris.

T. F. Torrance (1969), *Space, Time and Incarnation*, London; id. (1976), *Space, Time and Resurrection*, Edinburgh.

D. M. MacKinnon (1972), "Substance in Christology," in S. W. Sykes, J. P. Kleyton (Ed.), *Christ, Faith and History*, Cambridge, 279–300.

J. Moltmann (1972), *Der gekreuzigte Gott*, Munich.

M.-J. Le Guillou (1973), *L'innocent*, Paris.

L. Bouyer (1974), *Le Fils éternel*, Paris.

W. Kasper (1974), *Jesus der Christus*, Mayence.

E. Schillebeeckx (1975), *Jesus: Die Geschichte von einem Lebenden*, Freiberg-Basel-Vienna.

E. Jüngel (1976), *Gott als Geheimnis der Welt*, Tübingen.

J. Hick (Ed.) (1977), *The Myth of God Incarnate*, London.

G. Lampe (1977), *God as Spirit*, Oxford.

O. Gonzalez de Cardedál (1978), *Jesus de Nazaret. Aproximación a la Cristologia*, Madrid.

J. Sobrino (1978), *Christology at the Crossroads*, New York.

M. Goulder (Ed.) (1979), *Incarnation and Myth*, London.

J. Galot (1980), *Who Is Christ? A Theology of the Incarnation*, Rome-Chicago.

N. Lash (1980), "Up and Down in Christology," in *New Studies in Theology*, vol. 1, London, 31–46.

B. Forte (1981), *Gesù di Nazaret, storia di Dio, Dio della storia*, Rome.

A. E. Harvey et al. (1981), *God Incarnate, Story and Belief*, London.

B. Sesboüé (1982), *J.-C. dans la tradition de l'Église*, Paris.

J. Moingt (1993), *L'homme qui venait de Dieu*, CFi 176.

THE EDITORS

See also **Chalcedon, Council of; Christ and Christology; Ephesus, Council of; Hypostatic Union; Kenosis; Word**

Incomprehensibility, Divine. *See* **Knowledge of God; Negative Theology**

Inculturation

Theologically, pastorally, and liturgically, inculturation is one of the most striking elements of the late 20th century. Defined as an adequate relationship between faith and any human person (or community) in a particular social and cultural situation, inculturation is doubtless a reality as old as the history of salvation. One might even assert that all acts of faith and all understanding and experience of faith are, in the end, a question of inculturation. However, the missionary encounter of the "old Christendom" of Europe with peoples of different cultures and beliefs, and the option of Vatican II* for an evangelization (mission*/evangelization) and a Church that would be in close touch with the "world of today," have led to a renewed understanding of the importance and urgency of the cultural grounding of the message of salvation. The neologism "inculturation" thus corresponds to a new state of awareness.

1. Inculturation, a New Concept

To designate the encounter of the biblical message and various cultures, use has been made of a plethora of terms each one as unsatisfactory as the others: stepping stones, adaptation, accommodation, indigenization, implantation, contextualization, incarnation, and so on. It required progress both in theology and in the social sciences to put at our disposal the concept of inculturation. North American anthropologists, who invented the term, spoke of *acculturation* as early as 1880 to designate the phenomena of contact and interaction between different cultures. In the same anthropological circles in the 1930s, "acculturation" was linked to "inculturation" to define the mechanism of ongoing integration of any individual into the culture of the group to which he or she belongs.

It was no doubt under the conceptual influence of this research in cultural anthropology that missionary theology, followed by the official discourse of the Church, began to use the terms *acculturation* and *inculturation* indiscriminately. From 1953 the Belgian missionary theorist, P. Charles, followed by other theologians, used "acculturation" in this sense. Pope John Paul II also used it as a synonym of "inculturation," explaining that this "neologism perfectly expresses one of the elements of the great mystery of the Incarnation."

"Inculturation" has gradually achieved dominance over "acculturation," since it underlines that the encounter between the gospel and a particular culture is not reducible to a simple relationship between cultures. Rather, it sees the Good News as a factor of conversion and enrichment of culture while simultaneously making culture the location of a deepening of the message of salvation. It was used in this sense in Louvain in 1959, at the *19th Week of Missiology,* to designate the existence of a Catholicism that was open to the major human cultural groups. In 1975 Y. Congar asserted that the word *inculturation* had been used in Japan as a modification of the term *acculturation,* in the sense of "planting the seed of faith in a culture and causing it to develop there, to express itself according to the resources and the spirit of that culture." But it was not until 1977 that an official Roman document, the message to the people of God from the synod* on catechesis*, used the word for the first time.

Since then, the concept of inculturation has been both a frequent subject of theological investigation and a term used in declarations of the magisterium*. In more than one local church, of all denominations and in every country, inculturation has taken the form of liturgical, catechetical, and pastoral praxis, a set of concrete activities intended to associate faith closely with life, so that it might be understood, celebrated, proclaimed, and lived in relation to the aspirations and concerns of the particular milieu.

As a result, the notion of culture implied by inculturation cannot be defined by using a sketchy analysis of "archaic societies" trapped in the myths, rites, and symbols of primeval times. Vatican II used a fortunate expression when it affirmed that the human person attains true and full humanity only through culture, and when it defined culture as "everything through which man affirms and develops the many capabilities of his mind and body (soul-heart-body), transforms the world, humanizes social life, and preserves the great spiritual experiences and the major aspirations of mankind" (*GS* §53–1). Hence, all cultures from antiquity to the present contain three characteristics. First, every society is an object and subject of culture; that is, it produces and fosters normative representations, a project of a collective identity. There is no society without a specific cultural heritage and a specific cultural identity. In other words, culture represents both the reason for being and the way of being of any given society. It is thereby easy to understand—and this is the second characteristic—that there is a plurality of cultures and cultural particularities, because every human society has its own heritage, a source of particular and universal values. Finally, the third characteristic is that culture has no goal but to bring the individual and society to fulfill themselves by internalizing in the logic of the system the available endogenous and exogenous forms.

These considerations, sketchy as they are, confirm the fact that inculturation is not only a process necessary for any life of faith and hence for every local church, but that it is also a reality as old as the history of salvation.

2. Inculturation, a Permanent Reality

The process of inculturation has never been absent throughout the history of salvation. We know "the debts of the Old Testament to the surrounding cultures" (Cazelles 1981). For example, circumcision, one of the oldest and most sacred of Jewish practices (Jesus was circumcised), was originally a rite of initiation into marriage, specific to totemic cultures. The sacrifice of Passover* is a spring sacrifice for nomads engaged in transhumance. The Sabbath*, the name given at a certain period to the rest of the seventh day, was already known among the Semites (Ugarit). Of course, in assimilating these cultural elements, the Bible subjected them to profound transformations. But in preserving them it maintained something of the aspirations of the peoples to which they belonged. This is the case with the respect for God and for one's neighbor recommended by the Ten Commandments"(Ex 34:20; Dt 4:13, 10:4): these are found in Egypt and Babylon, in different but stereotypical formulations. Similarly, the God of Abraham, honored under the name of El, was the supreme deity of the Caananite-Phoenician pantheon (Ugarit), worshiped in the Caananite sanctuaries frequented by the patriarchs (Gn 14:19, 16:13, 21:33). In the early monarchy, Israel honored its God under the name of "Baal," "the master" (Eshbaal, son of Saul, 1 Chr 8:33), a name that the Bible later rejected (Hos 2:18). Hellenism also posed problems of inculturation to Judaism*, a term that appeared in 2 Maccabees to express the way of life of the peoples of the Torah. Under the influence of Greek art and rationality, the groups springing from the breakup of Judaism did not have the same interpretation of the Torah, but a continuous reference to revelation caused them to respect fully the divine value of the Torah and allowed them to traverse the centuries in osmosis with various civilizations. The Bible is thus not tied to any particular culture but rather uses cultures to express and stabilize a unique religious experience that is fulfilled in the gospel of Jesus Christ.

The process of inculturation continued in the New Testament. The four versions of the single gospel (Gospels*), written according to the cultural and contextual particularities of local communities; the specific language of Paul's letters, a teaching closely connected to the religious and existential questions of the time; and similar phenomena were all practices of inculturation of the Word of God made flesh into the history of humankind. The relationship of Christianity to Judaism, and thereafter to paganism, was a source of tension and conflict. Jesus's debates with the scribes and pharisees, and dissensions within the Christian community of Jerusalem* (Acts 6:1–6) and between Jewish Christians and converted Gentiles (Acts 15: Council of Jerusalem), posed the thorny problem of the movement of faith from one culture to another, the problem of faithfulness to the elements of the faith in the face of the requirements of conversion and of the fostering of diverse cultures.

The Church has always been confronted with this problem, since, as Vatican II declared, "from the beginning of its history, it has learned to express the message of Christ by using the concepts and the languages of diverse peoples" (GS 44–2; UR 14–3). For example, the question of the various rites and customs of local churches was long a subject of vigorous debate between the papacy and the bishoprics (Congar 1982). In the late second century Irenaeus* attempted to prevent Pope Victor from excommunicating the churches of Asia that, because they broke their fast on the 14th day of Nisan, celebrated Easter on different days of the week. "This diversity of observances," he wrote, "has not come about now, in our time, but came about long ago, under our predecessors.... All of them nevertheless kept peace with one another; the difference in the fast confirms the agreement in the faith." In April 591 it was the turn of Pope Gregory the Great to write to Bishop* Leander of Seville concerning the rite of baptism* by immersion: "If there is unity of faith, a difference in custom causes no harm to the Holy Church." Unity* in diversity thus became a basic principle of various local churches confronted with the challenge of inculturation. To be sure, Pope Damasus, in contrast, argued that unity of faith called for unity of discipline, and Gregory the Great said the same. Gregory VII went so far as to order that the Spanish-Visigoth liturgy be replaced by that of Rome. The expansion of the gospel into other cultural traditions, however, almost always led the Church to reassert the imperative of inculturation. For example, in 1659 an instruction of the Sacred

Congregation of Propaganda (now the Congregation for the Evangelization of Peoples) addressed to the apostolic vicars of Annam, China, Korea, and Tartary recommended respect for the customs of the country. Leo XIII (Apostolic Letter *Ad extremas,* 1893) and Benedict XV (encyclical *Maximum Illud,* 1919), not to mention Pius XI (encyclical *Rerum Ecclesiae*) and Pius XII (encyclicals *Summi Pontificatus,* 1939, and *Evangelii Praecones,* 1951) each in turn insisted that the particular values of the peoples being evangelized be taken into consideration. But it was not until Vatican II, and in its wake Paul VI and John Paul II, that there was talk of cultural exchange as a source of mutual enrichment within a single Church, and that the new churches were exhorted to borrow from the customs and traditions of their people everything that might help to bring Christian life within them to fruition.

It is in this tradition, as old as the history of salvation, that is rooted the question of inculturation in Africa, Latin America, and Asia. As the bishops of Africa asserted, meeting for the first time in Rome as a continental synod in 1994, inculturation is a priority and a matter of urgency for particular churches, a major stage on the road toward full evangelization. This is not merely a pastoral strategy, and therefore optional and secondary, but a condition for the relevance and credibility of evangelization. And as a consequence inculturation appears not only as an essential element in the manner of evangelizing but also and primarily as a specific characteristic of the gospel itself. In Santo Domingo in October 1992 the Fourth General Conference of Latin American Bishops declared: "The analogy between the Incarnation and Christian presence in the social, cultural, and historical context of peoples leads us to the theological perspective of inculturation. Inculturation is a dynamic process that moves from the gospel to what is the heart of each people and community, through the mediation of language and symbols that are accessible and that are accepted by the Church."

3. Inculturation, a Requirement of Faith

Christian faith bears on what Jesus Christ, the fullness of revelation, showed about God and about man, and it thereby bears on the relationship between God and man, between man and man, and between man and his cosmic environment. The Good News of the Word made flesh is thus the basis of faith's own relationship to the believing person; and it consequently provides the decisive criterion for the content, as well as for the hermeneutical, methodological, and practical norms of inculturation. The theological question of inculturation thereby has three aspects, relating to Trinitarian theology, to creation, and to redemptive incarnation.

a) *Unity in Diversity within the Trinitarian God.* The mystery of the Trinitarian God, the primordial and total object of faith, is that of the communion of three genuinely distinct persons and of a communion in which the specificity of each is as essential as their unity. The Father is God only as Father, the Son is God only as Son, the Holy Spirit is God only as Spirit (Holy Spirit). God is God and one God only in the unity of nature and the distinction of persons, in a relation of perfect love (1 Jn 4:16) that can be characterized as a "communion of differences." In God, difference is not an obstacle to communion but a demand for perfect communion. The theology of inculturation can find a model here. By agreeing to establish itself analogically in God, the enterprise of inculturation derives its true benefits not primarily from the particularity of a given culture but above all from the inexhaustible mystery of love of the Trinitarian God, the creator of all things.

b) *Unity in Diversity at the Heart of Creation.* By making human beings in his image and likeness, God created them both similar to and different from himself, on the one hand; on the other hand he made them both similar to (of the same nature) and different from one another (man and woman) (Gn 1:26f.). He thus intended to establish with human beings and among human beings a relation of love—both identity and otherness—the secret of which is Trinitarian. The Trinitarian theology of creation thus confirms that the problematics of inculturation are indeed those of a relationship of unity in diversity, of a communion of differences. Since each person and each people are a unique and irreducible image of the infinite riches of the Creator, it seems that this image, constitutive of his personal dignity, is the necessary location for his understanding and experience as a believer. This leads to two implications. Firstly, and because he or she is created in the image and likeness of God, every human being is a "sacred history," the bearer of specific values useful for the human race. And inculturation specifically takes into account this dimension of human person, helping individuals to be aware of it and to enrich it so that they may be ever more faithful to their dignity. As a consequence, and this is the second implication, interpersonal and intercultural relations cannot be defined a priori in terms of antagonistic opposition but in terms of an encounter among equals and of complementary exchanges. Because its goal is the communion of differences, inculturation is thereby opposed to any form of discrimination or exclusion.

c) *The Mystery of the Redemptive Incarnation, an Enterprise of Inculturation.* Perceived as a real entry of the eternal Son, Word of God and God himself, into the human and carnal world, the event of Jesus Christ is the unfolding of the love of the Trinitarian God in the history of human beings and of the world. The Word of God truly dwelt among us; he established his tabernacle there (Rev 21:3). He was recognized as a man like all men, says Paul (Phil 2:7f.); and the Epistle to the Hebrews emphasizes that Jesus made himself like his brothers in every way (2:17). The incarnate Word is thus the first to inculturate himself (*see* Sales 1980–81). He does this first by "taking on flesh"—the Gospel of John speaks of the Word "becoming flesh" (Jn 1:14) rather than "becoming man" and thereby emphasizes the realism of his humanity and his total insertion in the history of humanity. He does it also by his death, for in dying crucified like a common criminal, Jesus goes to the limit of man condemned to death, and that in the most ignominious conditions. He does it finally by his resurrection*-glorification, because he thereby reaches and fully achieves the desire for eschatological beatitude* inherent in every human person. It must be added that the inculturation of Jesus Christ is not a conformist solidarity with the human race; it is aimed rather at removing human beings from everything that might undermine their dignity as creatures of God. One might speak here of "desolidarizing solidarity." Christ thus appears as the unique incultured and inculturing model, as the decisive and ultimate norm of any enterprise of inculturation. The problematics of inculturation thus turn out to be essentially christocentric. As the image of the invisible God, the first born of all creation, and the first born from among the dead (Col 1:15, 18), only Christ establishes and reveals the origin and the aim of every relationship between the Creator and his creation. He alone brings to perfect realization, in and by his person, the relation of love of God with human beings in which is accomplished the definitive fulfillment of every person. And this is indeed the object and the aim of inculturation, which is in fact directed toward the embodiment of Christ's message of salvation in all sectors of life, so that any experience of faith may be expressed in particular cultural forms, and especially so that that experience may become a principle of inspiration, of interpretation, and of conversion of those cultural forms themselves. Inculturation thus raises the two related problems of the evangelization of cultures and the cultural understanding of the gospel. It was indeed a back and forth movement of this kind between faith and culture that led John Paul II to say in 1982: "The synthesis between culture and faith is not only a requirement of culture but also a requirement of faith. A faith that does not become a culture is a faith that is not fully re-

ceived, entirely thought through, and faithfully lived" (*DC* 1832, 1982. 604–6).

● M. J. Herskovits (1936), *Man and His Work,* New York.
R. Redfield, R. Linton, M. J. Herskovits (1938), "Outline for the Study of Acculturation," *AmA* 38, 149–52.
P. Charles (1956), *Études missiologiques,* Louvain.
Coll. (1959), *Missions et cultures non chrétiennes.* Rapport et compte rendu de la XXIXe Semaine de missiologie, Louvain.
J. Masson (1962), "L'Église ouverte sur le monde," *NRTh* 84, 1032–43.
T. Tshibangu (1974), *Le propos d'une théologie africaine,* Kinshasa.
M. Hebga (1976), *Émancipation d'Églises sous tutelle. Essai sur l'ère postmissionnaire,* Paris.
Coll. (1979), *Libération ou adaptation? La théologie africaine s'interroge,* Colloque d'Accra.
B. Adoukonou (1980), *Jalons pour une théologie africaine: Essai d'une herméneutique chrétienne du "vodun" dahoméen,* 2 vols., Paris-Namur.
J.-M. Ela (1980), *Le cri de l'homme africain: Questions aux chrétiens et aux Églises d'Afrique,* Paris; id. (1985), *Ma foi d'Africain,* Paris.
P. de Meester (1980), *Où va l'Afrique?,* Paris.
M. Sales (1980–81), "Le christianisme, la culture et les cultures," *Axes,* October 1980–January 1981, 3–40 (repr. in *Le Corps de l'Église,* Paris, 1989, 145–79).
A. Shorter (1980), *Théologie chrétienne africaine,* Paris.
O. Bimwenyi-Kweshi (1981), *Discours théologique négro-africain. Problème des fondements,* Paris.
H. Cazelles (1981), "Quelques dettes de l'Ancien Testament envers les cultures ambiantes," *in* coll., *Foi et culture à la lumière de la Bible,* Turin, 17–27.
F. Eboussi-Boulaga (1981), *Christianisme sans fétiche: Révélation et domination,* Paris.
J.-M. Ela, R. Luneau (1981), *Voici le temps des héritiers: Églises d'Afrique et voies nouvelles,* Paris.
Y. Congar (1982), *Diversités et communion,* Paris.
A. T. Sanon, R. Luneau (1982), *Enraciner l'Évangile: Initiations africaines et pédagogies de la foi,* Paris.
C. Geffré (1983), *Le christianisme au risque de l'interprétation,* Paris; id. (1987), "Mission et inculturation," *Spiritus* 109, 406–27.
Coll. (1984), *Théologie et choc des cultures,* Paris.
E.-J. Pénoukou (1984), *Églises d'Afrique: propositions pour l'avenir,* Paris.
F. Lapointe (1985), *Une expérience pastorale en Afrique australe pour les communautés enracinées et responsables,* Paris.
E. Messi Metogo (1985), *Théologie africaine et ethnophilosophie: Problèmes de méthode en théologie africaine,* Paris.
E. Mveng (1985), *L'Afrique dans l'Église: paroles d'un croyant,* Paris.
J. Doré (Ed.) (1986), *Chemins de christologie africaine,* Paris.
M. J. Agossou (1987), *Christianisme africain: Une fraternité au-delà de l'ethnie,* Paris.
H. Carrier (1987), *Évangiles et cultures: De Léon XIII à Jean-Paul II,* Paris.
R. Luneau (1987), *Laissez aller mon Peuple: Églises africaines au-delà des modèles,* Paris.
A. Mbembe (1988), *Afriques indociles: Christianisme, pouvoir et État en société postcoloniale,* Paris.
A. Peelman (1988), *L'inculturation: L'Église et les cultures,* Paris.

P. Poupard (1989), *L'Église au défi des cultures: inculturation et évangélisation,* Paris.

F. Eboussi-Boulaga (1991), *A contretemps: l'enjeu de Dieu en Afrique,* Paris.

F. Kabasele-Lumbala (1993), *Le christianisme en Afrique: une chance réciproque,* Paris.

K. Ä. Mana (1993), *Théologie africaine pour temps de crise: christianisme et reconstruction de l'Afrique,* Paris.

EFOÉ-JULIEN PÉNOUKOU

See also **Hellenization of Christianity; Religions, Theology of; Rites, Chinese**

Indefectibility of the Church

According to the Nicene Creed the Church is "holy." But theologians have also described it, in its concrete reality, as a *corpus permixtum,* made up of sinful members who are to some extent unworthy, a body in constant need of reformation. Although sanctity (holiness*) and sin are not directly opposed, we may ask to what extent such judgments are compatible with the idea of a "holy Church." In its constitution on the Church (*LG* 8), the Second Vatican* Council says that the Church "is holy, but [that] it also always needs to be purified." The decree on ecumenism (*UR* 3) reduces the scope of this declaration by establishing that the people of God, during its pilgrimage, remain "subject to sin in its members."

Protestant theology, for its part, has not hesitated to speak of a Church entirely delivered into sin. Luther's formulations sometimes led to making the "sinful Church" (*peccatrix,* WA 34/I. 276. 7ff.) into a confessional "criterion" (Jüngel 1983) characterizing the manner in which the Church views its relationship with God. But despite divergent formulations, it is legitimate to ask whether there is in this regard a basic difference between Catholics and Protestants, for "the belief in the indestructibility, in the continuity, and in the permanence of the one and holy Church also constitutes for the Lutheran Reformation an essential characteristic of its conception of the Church" (Meyer 1989). Turning to the patristic tradition, we are struck by the abundance of images through which this question is treated (Balthasar 1960). For the fathers of the church, it was especially the prostitute Rahab, impious and impure (Jos 6:25; Heb 11:31; Jas 2:25), who became the paradigm of pagan Christianity, and hence of the Church of Christ. They also attributed to the Church the words of the bride of the Song of Solomon (1:5): "Let the Church say: 'I am very dark, but

lovely,' dark according to your judgment, but lovely according to the radiance of grace" (Gregory the Great, PL 79. 486). Thomas Aquinas wrote: "The Church, 'glorious, with no stain or wrinkle' (Eph 5:27) is the ultimate end to which we are led by the Passion of Christ. It will therefore be realized only in the heavenly kingdom, and not in this life in which 'if we say we have no sin, we deceive ourselves' (1 Jn 1:8)" (ST IIIa. q.8. a. 3. ad 2).

In current ecumenical discussions *Church and Justification,* a document realized by Lutherans and Catholics, attempts to find common formulations. For example, the text confirms the doctrine of *Lumen Gentium (LG),* according to which the Church is "indefectibly holy" (150; *LG* 39). From this point of view it is possible to say "there is no difference between the two parties with respect to the fact that the Church is at the same time 'holy' and 'sinful'" (156).

What precise meaning should be given to the term *indefectibilitas* in *LG* 39? There is no doubt that all Christians, as members of the Church, must pray: "Forgive us our sins" (Mt 6:12). We may also observe that the council document does not attribute the predicate of sanctity to the eternal Church alone but also to the earthly Church, indicating thereby the "subjective" holiness of its members and not the "objective" holiness of institutions and doctrines. But, whereas particular members of the Church may be, for Catholics as for Protestants, "simultaneously justified and sinners," Catholics do not extend this characteristic to the Church itself. The Church is not simply *simul iusta et peccatrix,* for its sanctity prevails over its sin. Holiness is an essential mark of the Church, determinative in relation to sin (Rahner 1965). In the same context (*LG* 41) the ministerial grace *(gratia muneris)* of bishops (bishop*) and priests is presented as a source of their exemplary sanctity. Although the concept of indefectibility does not appear here, the close link between the sanctity of the Church and that of its ministers may pose ecumenical problems, in particular because *UR* (3. 32) points to "defects" *(defectus, defectus sacramenti ordinis)* in other Christian Churches. Although Protestant Churches often use the expression "sinful Church" without reservation, it goes without saying that a local* church cannot purely and simply accept the obvious sins of a sister church. Ecumenical discussions on what is called the *status confessionis* illustrate the attitude of Protestant Churches in this kind of case. The exclusion from the ecumenical community of the South African churches that practiced apartheid was thus referred to the *status confessionis,* in the absence of which it would be impossible to identify and judge a "sinful church." The discussions were not able to establish whether apartheid, in this case, was to be considered a heresy* or a moral fault (or both at once).

● *LG,* AAS 57, 1965, 5–64.
UR, AAS 57, 1965, 90–99.
Kirche und Rechtfertigung, Paderborn, 1994.
♦ H. U. von Balthasar (1960), *Sponsa Verbi,* Einsiedeln.
K. Rahner (1965), "Sündige Kirche nach den Dekreten des Zweiten Vatikanischen Konzils," *Schr.zur Th.* 6, Einsiedeln, 321–47.
E. Jüngel (1983), "Die Kirche als Sakrament?," *ZThK* 80, 432–57.
A. Birmelé (1987), "La peccabilité de l'Église comme enjeu œcuménique," *RHPhR* 67, 399–419.
H. Meyer (1989), "Sündige Kirche? Zur katholisch/evangelischen 'Grunddifferenz,'" *ÖR* 38, 1989, 397–410.
F. Herzog (1991), "Status confessionis," *Dictionary of the Ecumenical Movement,* Geneva, 956–57.

RISTO SAARINEN

See also **Church; Infallibility; Sin**

Indulgences

An indulgence is the remission before God of the temporal punishment* for sins (sin) whose error has already been absolved. The faithful who are well disposed to receive remission can obtain it with the Church's help under certain well-defined conditions. As minister of redemption, the Church distributes and applies with authority the treasure of the satisfactions of Christ and of the saints (Paul VI in 1965, definition used again in *CIC* of 1983, can. 992). The conditions are defined as a spiritual work (a pilgrimage* or a visit to a church, prayer, almsgiving, etc.). An indulgence can be partial or plenary (can. 993) and can be applied both to the living and the dead (can. 994).

a) The Birth of a Practice. The first evidence of indulgences can be traced back to the 11th century and is linked to the changing nature of penitential discipline. In ancient public discipline the conversion of a sinner could not be accomplished without him or her devoting to penance a certain amount of time proportional to the seriousness of the sin. During this time the repentant sinner was refused the Eucharist and had to undertake various ascetic practices. Reconciliation was not granted until the end of this process. It was accompanied by the prayers of the Church, and such prayers were judged as being indispensable for obtaining pardon. These two aspects of this practice are combined in an indulgence: sin engenders "temporal punishment"; the execution of this punishment is inseparable from the prayers of the Church.

From the moment absolution is given, immediately after confession and before the accomplishment of an often rigorous and long "satisfaction" (determined in penitential *"tarifs"* and expressed in weeks, months, or years), the sacramental absolution of the sin must be distinguished from the liberation from the "temporal punishment" due to sin, which is the purpose of the indulgence. In addition, the faithful ask that a long punishment be commuted to a shorter, if the shorter punishment comprises an onerous act, such as a pilgrimage. For its part, the Church is conscious of its duty to help the sinner through intercession and to contribute to the lightening of the "temporal punishment" by invoking ecclesial solidarity—which is nothing less that the communion* of saints—and by drawing on the "spiritual treasure" of Christ's merits (all redemption comes from Christ) and of the saints justified by his grace. This is the origin of the indulgences through which bishops (bishop*) or the pope* propose to Christians certain satisfiable brief practices in place of temporal punishment for their sins.

Indulgences multiplied in the 12th century. The most famous indulgence was that of Portioncula in Assisi and involved a pilgrimage. The idea of a plenary indulgence came about when the popes remitted of all their temporal punishments Christians who took part in the Crusades. In 1300 Pope Boniface VIII announced the first Jubilee with a plenary indulgence for those Christians who visited the four Roman basilicas.

b) Classical Theology of Indulgences. Abelard* had vigorously opposed the principle of indulgences. The first Scholastic (Scholasticism*) theologians were hesitant. Thomas Aquinas formulated a doctrine of indulgences that would remain a classic (ST, Suppl. 25–27). He regarded them as being derived from the "power of the keys" given by Christ to his Church (Mt 16:19). This power is just as effective in heaven before God as it is on earth in the Church, where the pope is its guardian. In such circumstances the Church uses its "key to jurisdictional," which is not sacramental. An indulgence relies on the superabundance of the Church's treasure and has no value if it is not accomplished in charity and piety.

Catholic theology has always remained circumspect on two points. On the one hand, the success of the practice of indulgences has led to abuse on the part of those with authority to bestow them, and the multiplication of indulgences has often reduced them to insignificance. The faithful have sometimes too easily seen them as works that were automatically effective, as a sort of assurance of salvation. This mentality has engendered a banklike conception of the Church's treasure and a commercial perception of an exchange of merits to profit the dead. On the other hand, the actual way indulgences work poses a problem. An action "through absolution" for the living has been distinguished from an action "through intercession" for the dead, who do not fall under the Church's jurisdiction. Nonetheless, "even in the case of a plenary indulgence, [...] assurance cannot be given that it has been completely remitted at God's tribunal" (Didier, 1963).

c) Reformation's Contestation of Indulgences. Despite some intervention by the Fourth Lateran Council (1215) and severe criticism by J. Wyclif (1378) and J. Hus (1420), the proliferation of the practice of indulgences in the 14th century and 15th century (during which time they were applied to the dead) led to financial malversation in the course of "quests for indulgences." Indulgences became the object of organized trade. Various collective bodies, and even bankers, were charged with their distribution. Preaching on the subject of indulgences gave way to a dangerous simplism. The indulgence preached by the Dominican Tetzel, the profits of which went to the construction of Saint Peter's in Rome, was accompanied, according to Luther, by the following formula: "The money has barely clinked into the offertory plate and already the soul has leaped out of Purgatory*." The question of indulgences would become central to the conflict of the Reformation. Luther rejected them in his 95 theses of Wittenberg in 1517. He considered them contradictory to the doctrine of justification by faith alone, independently of all works, and held them as an example of the abuse of spiritual power within the Roman Church.

In response to this situation the Council of Trent* formulated a reminder of the doctrinal principle of indulgences. The power to bestow them had been given to the Church by Christ; their use, approved by the council, must be preserved due to their salutary nature for Christian people. Those who claim that indulgences are useless, or who deny that the Church has power to grant them, are anathema (session 25). The council also recognized the abuse to which indulgences were subject and prohibited any monetary trafficking in respect of them.

d) Renewing the Doctrine. In 1948 B. Poschmann proposed a "new" theological conception of indulgences with which K. Rahner agreed. They combined the old "absolution" of temporal punishment for sin— efficient absolution as the Church's prayer—with a jurisdictional remission of ecclesiastical penance. The same held for plenary indulgences: the Church could only attempt to gain temporal remission of all punishment for a sin, but it could not guarantee with any certainty that the punishment had been entirely remitted by God (K. Radner 1955, trad. Fr. 123). Taken in this sense, an indulgence always works through intercession, whether for the living or for the dead. But it is an official intercession, undertaken by the Church under the authority of the apostolic ministry, which relies on the merits of Christ and the saints. This position was defended at Vatican II by the Patriarch Maximos IV.

In 1967 Pope Paul VI reexamined the doctrine and formulated new norms. He rejected the banking concept of the treasure of the Church: there is not a totality of goods but a whole that is Christ Himself. The doctrine of "treasure" is none other than that of the communion of saints. With indulgences, however, the Church, as the dispenser of the redemption of Christ, not only prays but in its authority distributes the treasure of the satisfactions of Christ and the saints to the well-disposed faithful for the remission of temporal punishment (*DC* 62, 210). Conversion is nonetheless always necessary, or else the indulgence is illusory. Finally, the practical norms that accompany the Constitution of Paul VI prohibit all quantification of partial indulgences. Rahner believed that prayer and authority should not be opposed and that indulgences were at once a form of prayer and an act of authority and that they carried all the efficacy of the Church's intercession. Rightly understood, the theology of indulgences is then an aspect of the theology of grace and of the communion of saints, and its practice is of the order of works of faith. This theology does not put justification into question. The teachings of the Catholic Church would nonetheless gain much from using language that avoids all ideas of mechanical efficacy ("to gain" an indulgence) and by underlining the value of indulgences as intercession.

● F. Beringer (1925), *Les indulgences: Leur nature et leur usage*, 4th Ed., Paris.

B. Poschmann (1948), *Der Ablaß im Licht der Bußgeschichte*, Bonn; id. (1951), *Buße und letzte Ölung*, Freiberg.
K. Rahner (1955), "Bemerkungen zur Theologie des Ablaßes," *Schr.zur Th.* 2, 185–210 (*Écr. th.* 5, 1966, 111–40).
J.-C. Didier (1963), "Indulgences", *Cath.* 5, 1520–28.
Paul VI (1967), Const. apost. *Indulgentiarum doctrina*, DC 64, 198–218.
K. Rahner (1967), "Kleiner theologischer Traktat über den Ablaß," *Schr.zur Th.* 8, 472–87; id. (1967) "Zur heutigen kirchenamtlichen Ablaßlehre," ibid., 488–518.G. A. Benrath (1976), "Ablass," *TRE* 1, 347–64.
H. Vorgrimler (1978), *Buße und Krankensalbung*, HDG IV/3, 203–14.
B. Sesboüé (1983), "Les indulgences. Problème œcuménique à nouveau posé?," *Études* 359, 115–21.

BERNARD SESBOÜÉ

See also **Communion; Expiation; Justification; Luther, Martin; Penance; Purgatory; Solidarity; Works**

Inerrancy

Inerrancy is a concept used in ecclesiology* and in theological epistemology in conjunction with the concepts of infallibility* and indefectibility*. A negative concept (like the other two), inerrancy means first that Holy* Scripture, both as the Word* of God and as words about God, cannot lead to error (corresponding to the negative concept of inerrancy in this context is the positive concept of inspiration). Inerrancy also means that the Church cannot "err" in its doctrine (corresponding to the negative concept of inerrancy in this context is the concept of assistance given by the Holy Spirit to the Church). In recent discussions about the exercise of the magisterium in the Catholic Church, there has been a tendency to consider inerrancy as an inclusive concept—the Church cannot deceive through its teaching—often linked to a theory of doctrines that accepts that Catholic dogma* is inalterable but that there is a constant possibility that it may be reformulated. Inerrancy also means the continuity of a true word through the diachronic multiplicity of words and concepts serving to affirm that doctrine. A teaching of the Church, finally, might possess the charisma of inerrancy without involving infallibility as that has been defined by the two Vatican councils.

JEAN-YVES LACOSTE

See also **Holy Scripture; Indefectibility of the Church; Infallibility**

Inerrancy of Scriptures. *See* Holy Scripture

Infallibility

a) Use of the Concept. According to Roman Catholic doctrine, the charism of infallibility is granted to the Church* and is also bestowed on the episcopal body when that body exercises the supreme magisterium* in conjunction with Peter*'s successor (*LG* 12, 25).

The Catholic doctrine of infallibility emphasizes that the revealed truths have remained unaltered in the Church's proclamations. All the same, this characteristic is subject to the given historic conditions and to the analogical nature of all theological statements. That is why even infallible doctrinal decisions cannot express the whole truth* of the supernatural* object of the faith* (Lang 1965).

The Protestant Churches do not teach infallibility. However, most of the Christian confessions have defined the conditions that the teaching within the Church must satisfy, founded on the principle that the continuity of the Christian faith is guaranteed by the Holy Spirit. Thus Luther's Reformist thought teaches that the Church as a whole cannot err, because, according to John 10:28, Christ* promised that no one could snatch it out of his hand (Pannenberg 1993). The infallibility of the Holy Scriptures, which is both the consequence and the proof of their true inspiration, is stressed by many Churches.

b) History of the Concept. In the New Testament, the idea of infallibility is founded mainly on the passages in which Jesus gave his disciples or the apostles (apostle*) the authority* to teach (for example, Lk 10:16) or on the definition of the Church as "a pillar and buttress of truth" (1 Tm 3:15). In the early Fathers, in Irenaeus for instance, there are statements that describe the Church as the guardian of the whole of Christian truth. Although such passages indeed show that, from the beginnings of Christianity, the Church exercised control over the doctrinal opinions of its members, nonetheless, historical criticism cannot find any actual doctrine of infallibility in them. As Hans Küng puts it: "With regard to infallibility, in the sense of the impossibility of falling into error, as little mention is made of it in the texts of the Scriptures as in the rare quotations from the Fathers" (Küng 1970).

Even though, during the whole of the Middle Ages, the Church's supervision often manifested itself in rigorous disciplinary forms, it has to be admitted that as far as concepts are concerned, *infallibilis* remained primarily—for instance in Thomas Aquinas and Luther—a characteristic of God, a consequence of his prescience and of his providence*. In the Middle Ages the question of infallibility was discussed from the most diverse angles (Tierney 1972). From the end of the Middle Ages, the partisans of papal infallibility (for example, Pierre Olivi and Guido Terreni) did however single out the broad theological aspects of this issue.

The concept of infallibility took on particular importance from the time of the decision made at Vatican I* (1870). The dogmatic constitution *Pastor aeternus* attributed infallibility to the pope when he spoke *ex cathedra*—that is, when he made a decision, in the discharge of his pastoral (pastor*) duties and as a teacher of all Christian people, that a doctrine regarding faith or "morals" *(mores)* should be held by the universal Church (*DH* 3074). From 1870 onward, the question of papal infallibility has dominated public theological debate. Vatican I had already planned to expound a general doctrine about the infallibility of the Church, but circumstances prevented its dealing with these questions. A detailed development of this notion had to wait for the texts that resulted from Vatican* II, and especially for the constitution concerning the Church *(LG)*. The latter document stresses that the community of the faithful cannot err and that the laity (lay*/laity) shares in the "supernatural appreciation of the faith *(sensus* fidei)* of the whole people"—that is, in the instinctive sensitivity and discrimination that the members of the Church possess in matters of faith (*LG* 12; *see also DH* 4852). Within this community, the pope is endowed with infallibility "by virtue of his office." But the infallibility held in common by the bishops (bishop*) is also emphasized. When the bishops teach points of faith or of morals unanimously and authentically, they infallibly proclaim the doctrine of Christ (*LG* 25).

Since Vatican II this extension of the Catholic doctrine of infallibility has often been criticized. That was the central theme of the polemic provoked by Küng's theses (1970). In its 1973 declaration *Mysterium Ecclesiae (see DH* 4530–41), the Congregation for the Doctrine of the Faith confirmed the decisions resulting from the two Vatican Councils.

c) Infallibility in Interconfessional Discussion. Among the various Christian confessions, the Eastern Orthodox and the Anglican faiths are relatively open to the idea of the Church's infallibility, although they reject the primacy of the pope. In the joint text drawn up in 1984 under the title "Declaration of Dublin," they sum up as follows their conception of infallibility (29–30): "The Eastern Orthodox and the Anglican believers consider that infallibility is not the privilege of a particular person in the Church.... We believe that, by virtue of their ministry, all the bishops hold the power to attest to the truth; but if the doctrine of infallibility means that it is possible, by means of external criteria, to guarantee the absence of error in such and such a declaration by a particular bishop, then we cannot accept this doctrine. What is more, such a guarantee cannot be given regarding the declarations of a council of bishops, since the ecumenicity of a council can only be demonstrated by the fact of its recognition by the whole Church."

Despite all these reservations, the declaration did not deny the principle of infallibility. And specifically, ecumenical councils recognized by the universal Church might be infallible. The first seven councils fulfilled the set conditions and are therefore infallible. The "Declaration of Dublin" (29) quotes, in addition, the agreement of the 1982 Anglican–Roman-Catholic International Commission (*The Final Report,* 32), according to which infallibility "in an absolute sense is applicable only to God." This obvious postulate translates the fact, important to many confessions, that in the history of dogma infallibility is seen, above all, as a divine characteristic, and for this reason it cannot be extended directly to the earthly Church.

As early as 1972 the Lutheran-Catholic dialogue stated that: "Despite the historic vicissitudes of preaching, Lutherans and Catholics are convinced that the Church is constantly guided to the truth by the Holy Spirit and, through this Spirit, it is kept within the truth. It is in this context that the notions of indefectibility* and infallibility, current in Catholic Tradition*, must be understood... . Infallibility should be recognized above all as a gift bestowed on the universal Church, which constitutes the people of God."

Although infallibility continued to pose an ecumenical problem, the Lutherans and the Catholics made another joint statement, published in a document of 1985: "There thus exists in both Churches a supralocal responsibility as regards doctrine: It is exercised in different ways, but with a certain concordance. In both Churches, as far as doctrinal affairs are concerned, this responsibility is included within their testimony to the faith of the universal Church. In this matter, both Churches recognize their subjection to the authority of the Gospels."

Aside from the question of the magisterium, the current discussion about infallibility is engaged with the fundamental question of whether the idea of theses a priori infallible can have any theological legitimacy, inasmuch as the truth of these declarations would not then need to be recognized by the faithful. According to Vatican I, the exercise of an infallible magisterium was the privilege of the pope who does not depend on the ecclesial reception of his teaching (*DS* 3074). Now, as W. Pannenberg has stated, it is "a known fact from the earliest days of Christianity" that no doctrine can be authoritative if it is not accepted by those to whom it is communicated (Pannenberg 1993; an opinion that is shared by all engaged in the dialogue with Catholicism).

● *LG,* AAS 57, 1965, 5–64.
ARCIC, *The Final Report,* London, 1982, 79–98.
H. Meyer et al. (Ed.), *Dokumente wachsender Übereinstimmung* 1–2, Paderborn, 1983–92.
The Dublin Agreed Statement, London, 1984.
Commission internationale catholique-luthérienne, *Face à l'Unité,* Paris, 1986.
♦ A. Lang (1965), "Unfehlbarkeit," *LThK2* 10, 482–87.
E. Castelli (Ed.) (1970), *L'infaillibilité,* Paris.
H. Küng (1970), *Unfehlbar? Eine Anfrage,* Zurich.
K. Rahner (Ed.) (1971), *Zum Problem Unfehlbarkeit,* Freiberg.
B. Tierney (1972), *Origins of Papal Infallibility,* Leyden.
P. Chirico (1977), *Infallibility: The Crossroads of Doctrine,* London.
H. Fries (1985), *Fundamentaltheologie,* Graz, §58, 480–95.
W. Pannenberg (1993), *Systematische Theologie* 3, Göttingen, 458–72.

RISTO SAARINEN

See also **Church; Magisterium; Word of God**

Infinite

In theology the attribute of infinity designates that absence of intrinsic limits that is proper to the divine essence. In the absolute sense, infinity signifies divine perfection, simplicity, and uniqueness; it can only apply to God. A being whose essence is limitless possesses all possible perfection to the sovereign degree. Such a being cannot enter into composition with anything and no other being could share this attribute (attributes*, divine). Therefore, this being is unique. Moreover, absolute infinity excludes all indeterminacy, insofar as God is a distinct, singular being. The divine essence remains unknowable to a finite intelligence. The infinity of the essence of God thus founds his unknowability.

Theology* has always conceived God's power (omnipotence*) as infinite, but the application of the concept of infinity to the divine essence has not always seemed legitimate. The Bible does speak of divine perfection (Mt 5:48 and Is 40:17), eternity* (Dt 32:40), and so forth, but there is no passage where it is said that God is infinite. The one that comes closest is Psalm 145:3, which reads: "Great is the Lord, and greatly to be praised, and his greatness is unsearchable" (the Vulgate translated the last two words as "non est finis" or "without end"). Though the affirmation did not seem to create any problem for certain Neoplatonists and Fathers of the Church, it was achieved at the cost of many battles in the Latin Occident. The infinity of the divine essence was not explicitly proclaimed until a 19th-century synodal text (Vatican* I, DS 3001).

A. Greek Antiquity

a) *From the Pre-Socratics to Plato.* Anaximander was the first to use the word *infinite* for the first principle. He reasoned that because the origin cannot be identified with any of the elements at its source, the principle can only be indeterminate or infinite. Infinity maintained its importance for the Pythagorists, but *apeiron* was conjugated in the finite in the production of things. The infinite is a material principle, the finite a structuring, determinant principle. There is no place for infinity in the thought of Parmenides: the One is immutable, simple, but finite. Melissos, another Eleatic, stood against his master on this point. He argues that the uniqueness of the One presupposes its infinity: the One would not be unique if it were finite; by its infinity it is the positive principle of real. Anaxagoras, Leucippus, Democritus, and Epicurius also conceived the infinite as a perfection, as opposed to both Parmenides and Pythagoras and also to Plato and Aristotle.

In Plato's *Philebus,* the infinite and the finite are, as for the Pythagorists, the two constituent principles of reality. The infinite of indetermination connotes the excessive and imperfect; for the constitution of things it requires a limit *(peras).* However, in the second part of *Parmenides* (137 d.) there is a brief allusion to the infinity of the One that hardly accords with the doctrine of *Philebus.* Plato hypothesizes that "If it is true that it has no beginning and no end, then it is true that the One is infinite." And since *Parmenides* was the subject of a large number of commentaries by the Neoplatonists, who took its hypotheses as descriptions of reality rather than logical exercises, the text is a source of the Plotinian (and even the Dionysian) doctrine of the infinity of the One.

b) *Aristotle.* Even if Aristotle did not know the ontological infinite, the long analyses in *Physics, l. III* were a major influence on the history of this concept in the sciences and theology. Aristotle conceived infinity as an exclusive attribute of quantity (numerical or dimensional); therefore it can never be encountered in the form of a finished whole. The infinite is always in potential, which led to the idea that "the infinite as infinite is unknowable," cited by medieval thinkers in support of divine unknowability, and the principle that "nothing is greater than the infinite," invoked in favor of the absolute, inexhaustible nature of the divine essence.

c) Plotinus. Plotinus was the first thinker to attach importance to the divine infinity. The One is infinite, he declared, in that it is not contained by any form and escapes all specific or material determination. All that exists has an essential determination; by its infinity the One is radically distinguished from the intellect, the soul (soul*-heart-body), and being*. This is by no means a negative or extrinsic characterization of the infinite and cannot be reduced to saying that the One has a limitation individually different from that which affects beings; on the contrary it implies that the One is, by essence, free of all limitation.

B. Christian Era

1. Patristic

Many Latin church fathers and to an even greater extent the Greek Fathers conceived of God as infinite. Marius Victorinus saw God as pure *esse* ("to be"), or infinitive being, which was distinct from and prior to participial "being." If every being is a particular thing, that is, a form partially participating in being, pure being is infinite, limitless *(infinitum, interminatum)*. If the determination of participial-being implies limitation (because this being is not that other one), God is determined only by the infinity of the being that he fully is. Victorinus's doctrine, by attaching infinity to the being of God, announces the doctrine of Thomas Aquinas. However, Marius differs from the latter by conceiving the infinity of being as incompatible with God's simplicity or uniqueness. He argues that pure being is so totally non-participial that it must be conceived par excellence as before the one and beyond simplicity. But Victorinus did not feel the need to imagine a sur-infinity—as Pierre de Candie would do in the 14th century—which shows that the concept of infinity was in itself sufficient to express absolute transcendence.

Augustine did not have much to say about infinity as attribute of the divine essence. The infinite figures in his thought as a synonym for eternity, almightiness (omnipotence*), or incomprehensibility, depending on the context; in God it signifies the absence of spatial and temporal boundaries. Generally speaking, Augustine thought of infinity in its mathematical sense; but toward the end of his life he also evoked the possibility that God is infinite *(aliter)*.

In his *Life of Moses,* Gregory* of Nyssa described the divine as infinite according to its nature, that is, as non-circumscribed by a limit. And in *Against Eunomius,* he gave the first definition of the infinite as positive attribute: "The infinite *(to aoriston)* is not such with regard to a relation to something else, but thought according to itself it escapes from all limits." Basil*, similarly, made God an *aoristos* and *apeiros* with no boundaries. Analogous thoughts are expressed in the works of Clement of Alexandria and Gregory* of Nazianzus.

Though infinity is relatively absent from Latin speculation from the fifth to the 12th century, the contrary is true in the Byzantine tradition, starting with Pseudo-Dionysius*. The Dionysian reflection reveals two influences that nourish two antinomic doctrines of infinity. One group of texts subordinates the *peras* and *apeiron* of the One, following the Neoplatonic tradition (Proclus and Damascius) but, in another group of texts, the Pseudo-Dionysius attributes the infinite directly to God. In *Divine Names,* c. 5, he states that "God does not exist in this or that way, but possesses all being ever since the origin, simply and without limits *(aperioristôs)*." The Dionysian reflections were made available in a 13th-century Latin *Corpus dionysien* with glosses attributed to Maximus* the Confessor. One of these glosses (written in fact by Jean of Scythopolis) describes God as infinite *(aoristos)* "because he does not fall within any limit." Albert* the Great comments on this assertion, applying it directly to the essence of God. Jean of Damas explains that "Who is" is the name that best suits the essence of God, which explains his incomprehensibility for a finite intelligence.

2. Latin Middle Ages

a) Before the 13th Century. The 11th- and 12th-century Latin authors hardly attached any importance to divine infinity. Anselm*, for example, never writes that "God is infinite." A century later, Peter Lombard would say that God is infinitely powerful, without thinking of applying infinity to the essence. Pierre de Poitiers, in the last third of the 12th century, did not use the word, nor did Robert de Melun. Stephen Langton saw it as nothing more than a synonym for indetermination; Hugh of St. Cher took it as a synonym for divine incomprehensibility. And yet *Liber de causis,* an Arabic work of Neoplatonic inspiration that explicitly named the *Primus* "infinite being," was translated in the 12th century. The *Primus,* being nothing but its being, is pure being bereft of all other formal *(hilyah)* determination. Its determination lies in its very infinity. This is constitutive of God's ipseity.

b) Doctrinal Condemnation of 1241. The question of infinity rebounded with a controversy over the possibility of seeing the essence of God *in patria* (beatific [beatitude*] vision). Some early 13th-century authors, influenced by Pseudo-Dionysius and John the Scot Eriugena, accentuated the distance between God and creatures, with particular emphasis on the unknowability of the divine essence. They were able to draw on a rich tradition, and yet they brought Aristotle into the argument: in *De caelo* it is declared that "between the finite and the infinite there is no proportion." Invoking this lemma was recognizing that God is infinite and is distinguished from the creature by that attribute. But this notion was condemned in 1241, and certain authors later contested the right to preach for the divine essence, an attribute that Aristotle said was applicable only to quantitative magnitude. Guerric of Saint-Quentin, for example, considered the question "Is God finite or infinite?" meaningless. The divine essence, by definition immaterial, is not one of the things about which one can ask if they are finite or infinite, so speaking of an infinite essence is committing an error of category. Bonaventure* argued that the contemporaries of Guerric would have even said that God is finite with regard to essence. In fact, the real problem at that period was to reconcile divine simplicity (which excludes composition) with infinity (which supposes it), and this reconciliation would rapidly occur. Richard Fishacre, Albert the Great, Alexander of Hales, and John Pagus were the first authors to maintain that God is both knowable by the beatified intellect and simple and infinite in his essence. Bonaventure and Thomas Aquinas were inspired by their solution.

c) Propositions of the Great Scholastic. The absence of biblical texts that clearly state the infinity of God posed a problem for medieval thinkers who sought to legitimize this controversial concept. The silence of Scripture was interpreted by some as a guarantee. The author of *Summa halensis* explains that God must be infinite in his essence because the Bible does not state the contrary! For lack of biblical references, there were attempts to rely on synodal authorities but they offered little more than (pseudo-) symbol of Athanasius, who speaks of immensity. That was enough for Bonaventure, who identified immensity and infinity, followed later by John of Ripa; this provided him with an adequate point of contact between the authority and the new doctrine. In order to put this idea in accord with Aristotle's claim that infinity can only apply to quantitative substances, a different acceptance of the term had to be found for theological purposes. Three distinctions were introduced. Two different kinds of quantity were posited: "dimensional" quantity (that of Aristotle) and "virtual" quantity (which designates the degree of perfection of a being that one may consider infinite without betraying Aristotle). Two types of infinity, privative and negative, were distinguished. A being to whom it pertains to have an end but who does not have one is privatively infinite. A being to whom it does not pertain to have an end and who has none is negatively infinite (it is in this sense that God is infinite). And a distinction between the absolute infinite *(simpliciter)* and the relative infinite *(secundum quid)* parries all danger of confusion between God and the creature, because an infinity realized in matter—supposing that such a thing were possible—could never be but a relative infinity. An infinitely large body would be limited by the matter in which it is found. Therefore, only God is infinite in the full sense.

These distinctions were widespread in the Middle Ages, but each author used them in his own way. In Thomism*, the privative-negative notion was articulated on the distinction between material infinity and formal infinity. Matter is determined *(finitur)* by form, and form is determined by matter. However, the lack of (formal) determination in matter is synonymous with imperfection, the absence of (material) determination allowing form to reach its fullness. Here matter is a hindrance; there it is the necessary condition for access to substantiality.

In the thought of Alexander of Hales, Albert the Great, Thomas Aquinas, and Bonaventure, the infinite qualifies in its own right the divine essence, but always in terms of the negative attribute. Infinity means absence of limits, which certainly connotes perfection, but it does so in denying that the essence has a term; therefore it designates in God nothing positive that would correspond to our idea of infinity. Another conception, sketched out by Bonaventure, came to light at the end of the 13th century in the thought of Henry of Gand and Richard Middleton, culminating with Duns* Scotus. The latter argued that infinity is both the most adequate concept of God and his distinctive modality, prior to all propriety. I can think God without thinking of him as perfect or good, but I cannot think him without thinking of him as infinite. Infinity becomes a positive attribute that adds something to God. Duns Scotus founded the ontological primacy of infinity on an authentic demonstration of the "thinkable" nature of this concept. In the fifth *Quodlibet,* he shows that going from the infinite in potential of Aristotle one can arrive at an intensive infinity that encloses all perfection of the entity. His disciple Francis of Mayronnes established an even closer connection between the infinite and God in affirming the priority of infinity over existence.

d) Late Middle Ages. Nicholas* of Cusa conceived God as an infinity in which are dissolved the oppositions of the finite. The infinity of God is not simply opposed to a universe that contains infinities in potential, but to a universe that constitutes an infinity in act, in the quantitative order. The closed world* of antiquity burst open to leave room for an infinite universe whose very existence testifies to the infinite power of its creator. In the thought of Giordano Bruno, the infinity of space, conjugated with that of God and his power, brings along the existence of a limitless number of worlds. The difference between the infinity of God and that of the created universe tends to fade (pantheism*).

3. Modern Era

Descartes* reversed the classic conception of the negative infinite. Duns Scotus had already seen the infinite as designating a pure positivity, but Descartes went one step further in posing primacy of the infinite with regard to the finite in the very order of the ideal genesis. The infinite, adequate attribute of God, has par excellence the status of clear and distinct idea because it is the idea of absolute perfection, with regard to which the thinking substance grasps itself as limited and blemished with imperfection. It is in fact the absoluteness of that perfection that gives the thinking ego to understand that it cannot have for cause a being other than one who has in formal reality the same degree of perfection it has in objective (thinkable) reality. The idea of infinity—which Descartes distinguishes from the indefinite, characteristic of numbers and geometrical or physical magnitudes—is ontologically anterior to the idea of the finite. Descartes denies "that we conceive the infinite by negation of the finite, seeing that, on the contrary, all limitation includes the negation of the infinite." For Spinoza the last step would be: The existence of the infinite substance makes impossible its coexistence with all other substance. One could not go any further in the affirmation of the primacy of the infinite.

Other noteworthy 17th-century authors are Charron, Malebranche, Pascal*, and Leibniz*. Leibniz, inspired by the results of infinitesimal calculation, confounded the Aristotelian axiom related to the impossibility of an infinity-in-act in nature. He admits the existence of actual infinites, whether in a continuum or in simple or composed substances. However, this does not affect the notion of divine infinity: "God is absolutely perfect; perfection being none other than the grandeur of positive reality taken precisely, setting apart the limits or boundaries in these perfect things."

The empirical tradition was an exception to the unanimous medieval belief in the necessity of conceiving God as infinity. Hobbes, for example, was impenitently agnostic in the matter. He argued that because all knowledge comes from the senses, the infinite is never given to us in experience and so cannot be the subject of knowledge. This skepticism was a prelude to the generalized mistrust of natural* theology that prevailed in the 18th century. D'Alembert declared that asking oneself about the infinity of God is a simple case of "abusive metaphysics." Kant* went so far in this direction that his thought could be described as a "philosophy* of finitude." He raises the problem in the context of the insoluble antinomies of pure reason; infinity falls out of the field of categories of application of pure reason. Kant described the divine nature as "almighty" or "perfect" rather than infinite.

Hegel*, on the contrary, saw the finite and the infinite as interpenetrating. He introduced a new distinction between poor infinity (*schlechte Unendlichkeit),* which is but the negation of the finite, and an authentic infinity (*wahrhaft Unendliche),* which he saw as the negation of the negation, the conquest of self by the mediation of the other. Authentic infinity is, first, that of the Spirit conceived as negativity, and the Spirit does not reach full infinity but as absolute Spirit, at the term of a process of self-realization during which it actively frees itself of all finitude. The reciprocal admission of the finite and the infinite leads to elimination of the distinction between absolute Spirit and created being. Furthermore, this conception of infinity, which is both dynamic and negative, prevents seeing in infinity an attribute referring to immutability, the autarchy of the divine being.

4. Contemporary Period

Speculation on the infinite was not neglected in the 19th and 20th centuries, but the most original reflections are situated in the field of science (physics and mathematics) and ethics.

a) Ethics and Infinity. The doctrine of infinity in its traditional theological form found its most original expression in the 20th century in the thought of E. Levinas, rooted in a reflection on alterity. The Western conscience, in its epistemological function, has always tended to bring the Other down to the same. However, the Cartesian analysis of the infinite, in *Méditation III,* permits a reversal of this logic of assimilation. What Levinas found remarkable in the Cartesian idea of infinity is that its *ideatum* surpasses its idea: Thinking infinity I think more than what I think. Nonetheless Levinas believes that the infinite takes all its sense in the field of ethics, not theology. The infinite is an experience of irreducible alterity; its paradigm is revealed to me in the face of the Other and the Other's resistance to my desire to assimilate. The logical structure of the Cartesian analysis is thus retained in preference to the divine referent it was destined to manifest. The concept of infinity that medieval thinkers sought to attach to the divine essence is thereafter considered usable in other contexts.

Many original contributions mark the history of the infinite, but it can be said that the essential was already glimpsed by Marius Victorinus, and even Plotinus, and clearly stated by 13th-century Scholastics. They all expressed the existence of an infinite being, unique and distinct in virtue of this very infinity. It is, again, that fundamental intuition that Descartes adopted and modulated and Cantor did not disavow.

● Aristotle, *Physics* III, chap. 4–8.
Augustine, *The City of God* XII, chap. 2, 4, 8–9.

Bonaventure, *Sentences* I, d. 43, art. *unicus,* q. 2 (Quaracchi, vol. I).
Jean Damascene, *De fide orthodoxa* I, chap. 9; II, chap. 3 (Kotter I, II).
Descartes, *Méditations métaphysiques* (A–T, vol. IX–1).
Duns Scotus, *Quodlibet* V (Vivès, vol. 5).
E. Levinas, "La philosophie et l'idée de l'i," *RMM* 62 (1957), 241–53.
Thomas Aquinas, ST I, q. 7, a. 1.
♦ H. Guyot (1906), *L'infinité divine depuis Philon le juif jusqu'à Plotin,* Paris.
A. Edel (1934), *Aristotle's Theory of the Infinite,* New York.
É. Gilson (1954), "L'infinité divine chez saint Augustin," *AugM,* I, 569–74.
C. de Vogel (1959), "La théorie de l'*apeiron* chez Platon et dans la tradition platonicienne," *RPL* 49, 21–39.
P. Vignaux (1976), "Être et infini selon Duns Scot et Jean de Ripa," in *De saint Anselme à Luther,* 352–66.
J. W. Dauben (1977), "Cantor and Pope Leon XIII: Mathematics, Theology and the Infinite," *JHI* 38, 85–108.
L. Sweeney (1992), *Divine Infinity in Greek and Medieval Thought,* Berne-New York.
A. Côté (1995 *a*), "L'infinité divine dans l'Antiquité et au Moyen Age," *Dialogue (Revue canadienne de philosophie)* 34, 119–37; id. (1995 *b*) "Guerric de Saint-Quentin et le problème de l'infinité divine," in *Les philosophies morales et politiques au Moyen Age: Actes du IXe Congrès international de philosophie médiévale* III, Ottawa, 1132–48.

ANTOINE CÔTÉ

See also **Attributes, Divine; Duns Scotus, John; Negative Theology; Omnipotence, Divine; Omnipresence, Divine**

Initiation, Christian

Initiation can be understood to have three meanings. For the fathers of the church, who adopted the notion from the religions with holy mystery, it designated the sacraments (sacrament*) through which one is made a Christian. Today is added the idea of a progressiveness, of entering upon a journey (initiation *to*). Finally, the ethnological sense designates the process by which individuals reach a new membership status to a tribe or specific group.

The fathers recognized the notion of initiation as early as the second century but hardly used it before the end of the fourth century. From then on they used it to indicate the sacraments that determine Christian identity: baptism, together with its related rites that would later receive the name confirmation*, as well as the first Eucharist. According to Kretschmar (1977), baptism "is the original name for initiation in its entirety."

The concept was unknown during the Middle Ages except in the vocabulary of the religious novitiate (the shift is significant). It would be revived by scholars from the Renaissance onward, but especially, at the end of the 19th century, by L. Duchesne, who devoted a chapter to it in his *Origines du Culte Chrétien* (1889). It was adopted by the Vatican* II Council: *AG* 14 (which also included the catechumenate) and *PO* 2 speak of the *sacramenta initiationis christianae; SC* 71 affirms "the close connection between this sacrament [confirmation] and the entire Christian initiation," and the apostolic constitution that introduces the 1971 Rite of Confirmation speaks—for the first time in an official document—about the "unity of Christian initiation." Henceforth, the mention of *Christian initiation* acted as a title for the Rites of Baptism and Confirmation, and for the presentation of the three sacraments in the *CEC.*

The theological notion signifies the restoration of an encompassing vision of the three sacraments, beyond their medieval independence. The *Notes Doctrinales et Pastorales* in *Rituel de l'Initiation Chrétienne des Adultes* express it with vigor: "According to the oldest usage, [...] an adult will not be baptized without receiving confirmation immediately after the baptism, unless there are serious reasons presented. This connection expresses the unity of the paschal mystery, the close relationship between the mission of the Son and the gift of the Holy* Spirit, and the conjunction of these sacraments through which Christ* and the Holy Spirit communicate with the Father to the baptized" (n. 34, *see CIC,* can. 866). The unity of the three sacraments is therefore not only circumstantial: its stems from Trinitarian theology. This theological unity, however, is realized differently in the respective cases of adults and children. At the paschal vigil the former usually receive the three sacraments at the hands of the bishop, though the priest (priesthood*) is lawfully permitted to administer them in the bishop's absence (*Rituel,* 228). In the case of children, the Western Church spreads these three celebrations over a period of time, while the notion of initiation means that they are nonetheless understood in terms of a dynamic unity rather than as isolated celebrations. These perspectives were accepted, with some variation, by the Orthodox and Catholics (document by Bari 1987).

Another question concerns the relationships between the structures of initiation of a specific society and Christian initiation. This question certainly influenced the history of the West (question of spiritual relationship, *see* Lynch 1986), while today it is crucial in several African countries (Sanon-Luneau 1982) where the debate concerns its pertinence for the future of a continent that is more and more influenced by Western lifestyles.

● P.-M. Gy (1977), "La notion chrétienne d'initiation Jalons pour une enquête," *MD* 132, 33–54.
G. Kretschmar (1977), "Nouvelles recherches sur l'initiation chrétienne," *MD* 132, 7–32.
A. T. Sanon, R. Luneau (1982), *Enraciner l'Évangile: Initiations africaines et pédagogie de la foi,* Paris.
J. Lynch (1986), *Godparents and Kinship in Early Medieval Europe,* Princeton.
J. Ries, H. Limet (1986), *Les rites d'initiation,* Louvain-la-Neuve.
Commission mixte internationale catholique-orthodoxe (1987), "Foi, sacrements et unité de l'Église" (doc. by Bari), *DC* 85, 1988, 122–26.
A. de Halleux (1988), "Foi, baptême et unite: A propos du document de Bari," *Irén.* 61, 155–87.
E. Lanne (1988), "Réflexion complémentaire sur le document de Bari," ibid., 189–205.
A. Fayol-Fricout, A. Pasquier, O. Sarda (1991), *L'initiation chrétienne, démarche catéchuménale,* Paris.

PAUL DE CLERCK

See also **Baptism; Confirmation; Eucharist; Inculturation; Sacrament**

Inspiration of Scripture. *See* Holy Scripture

Integrism

Integrism (from the French, *intégrisme*) is a term that appears in sociology and religious history and that is almost totally lacking in theological (or philosophical) development. *Intégrisme* is commonly understood in the Catholic world as the conjunction of fundamentalism*, ultramontanism*, an erroneous concept of tradition*, and the fear inspired by modernity. *Intégrisme* wishes to preserve the integrity and the entirety of the doctrines and institutions of the Church*, but at the cost of a strict prohibition of any change in doctrines and any legitimate reform of institutions. The opposite of *intégrisme* is "progressivism," another phenomenon that has not been given adequate theological analysis.

● Y. Marchasson (1993), "Intégrisme," in P. Poupard (Ed.), *Dictionnaire des religions,* Paris, 3rd Ed. I, 963–68.

THE EDITORS

See also **Fundamentalism; Liberalism; Traditionalism**

Intellectualism

1. Definition

"Intellectualism" made its appearance toward the end of the 19th century, in the historiography of the Latin Middle Ages, as an antonym of "voluntarism*." It is important to keep in mind that it is a concept developed by commentators and is absent from the original sources. It is used to designate several different arguments, all of which arise from the same impulse: an affirmation of the primacy of the intellect over the will. It is also sometimes used in a less precise sense to designate confidence in the intellect's capacity to attain to the divine, a confidence that rests on an affirmation of the divine nature of the intellect itself.

2. History

The privileged domain to which the concept, in its strict sense, is applied is Scholastic (Scholasticism*) thought of the 13th and 14th centuries. The controversies that arose in this period, in particular those between Franciscans and Dominicans, clearly set forth the alternative that until then had been latent between the primacy of the intellect and the primacy of the will. Dominican thought was at the time predominantly intellectualistic and was opposed to what has been called "Franciscan voluntarism." During the same period another movement with an intellectualistic tendency appeared, based on the adoption by Albert* the Great of the Aristotelian notion of "conjunction" (Christian Aristotelianism*). This movement developed in two directions: on the one hand, Latin Averroism, notably in Jean de Jandun (naturalism*); on the other, the German Dominican school, notably in Meister Eckhart and Dietrich of Freiburg (Rhineland-Flemish mysticism*). We will leave it to one side: in fact, it chiefly emphasizes philosophical happiness without implying an intellectualistic theory of beatitude*, whereas the debate between intellectualism and voluntarism in the 13th and 14th centuries grew primarily out of theological questions.

If intellectualism experienced a rapid expansion in the 13th century, this was by virtue of its privileged relation to Aristotle, whose works were then being rediscovered in the West, particularly the theories of choice (*Nicomachean Ethics* III. 5; VII. 5), happiness (*Nicomachean Ethics* X. 7), and knowledge (*De Anima* III. 5). However, it is not in the 13th century that the birth of intellectualism should be situated, nor can it be thought of solely with reference to Aristotle. The first appearance of intellectualism in the strict sense can be traced back to Greek patristics with the intellectualism (in the broad sense) of Platonic thought and its adoption in a Christian context.

3. Theological Issues

The affirmation of the primacy of the intellect over the will in created beings raises two principal questions: the basis of liberty in higher beings and the nature of the movement toward beatitude.

a) Liberty. A theory of liberty is intellectualistic if it bases free will on the intellect and not the will. The will is directed toward absolute good. But nothing in this life fully realizes the good, because all good is mixed with evil. This gives rise to two consequences: on the one hand, a finite thing can never be desired except as a means to the end, and it thereby escapes the necessity that binds the will to its end; on the other hand, no finite thing provides the will with the means necessary for it to reach its end. Free will therefore functions in the determination of means to the end. But for intellectualism, this choice of means does not derive from the will; it is the intellect that convinces the will to will a certain object, and it does so according to the way in which it conceives that object, presenting it to the will as something that is good or evil. The apprehension of the object therefore determines the desire or repulsion that the will experiences with respect to that object, for the will does not have the power to reject what the intellect perceives to be good or to desire what the intellect perceives to be evil. Intellectual knowledge thus plays the role of determining cause in the specification of the acts of the will. The will, according to the intellectualistic conception of free will, is not free to choose what it wills, neither its end nor the means leading to that end. It is the object, insofar as it is known, that causes the determination of voluntary acts; free will is thus based on the indeterminacy of judgment and not on an indeterminacy of the will itself. Historically, it was Boethius*'s commentaries on Aristotle that provided the Latin tradition with an intellectualistic conception of liberty as *liberum de voluntate judicium* (PL 64. 492–93). This conception, for which free will resides in reason, was adopted and developed by Abelard* and Prevotinus of Cremona, and then by William of Auxerre, before flowering in Thomas Aquinas and Godefroid of Fontaines. Some Averroists adopted it for their own, notably Siger of Brabant. In the list of theses condemned by Étienne Tempier in 1277, propositions 151 and 162 to 166 correspond to this position (naturalism).

b) Nature of the Movement toward Beatitude. In the treatment of this question, the intellectualistic theory asserts that the essence of beatitude resides principally in the action of the intellect and not the action of the will. Many arguments can support this affirmation of the intellectual character of ultimate happiness. One can rely first on the superiority of the intellect as a faculty. It will then be said that the intellect is a nobler faculty than the will because the will is an appetite and because every existent is endowed with appetite, whereas intellect belongs only to higher beings; it is therefore more fitting that the process by which those beings attain their particular end be produced by the intellect. It also happens that the intellectualistic conception is based on the comparison of acts of intellection and volition in relation to the end sought, namely, union with God. By reason of the unifying capacity of those acts, a hierarchy is established between the faculties. The matter at issue is important. Does the most perfect access to divinity derive from knowledge or from love? Any answer to this question requires a determination of which of the two acts most fully unites us with its object and a decision as to whether or not love may be conceived as that which makes it possible to go beyond the limits of knowledge. According to the intellectualistic answer, the act through which we are most intimately united with God is an act of intellection, and love does not go beyond knowledge. Like any act of will, love proceeds from knowledge and receives from it its limits; since its object is external to it, it falls short of the kind of union with the object that can be produced by intellection. The Aristotelian theory of an intellect that becomes everything makes it possible in this context to describe union with God in terms that ensure the superiority of intellection.

It should be noted that this argument does not necessarily apply to intellectual knowledge *in via* (intellectualism is not necessarily a naturalism, although naturalism is its constant temptation). The question of the primacy of intellectual knowledge over love is indeed complicated when a distinction is established between the historical reality—*in via*—and the eschatological reality—*in patria*—of both of these acts. Thus, an intellectualistic understanding of beatitude is perfectly compatible with the argument according to which the ecstasy of love in this life goes beyond any intellectual knowledge of God (Gregory* of Nazianzus, Pseudo-Dionysius*), or even with the affirmation of a primacy of the will within the limits of this life (Thomas Aquinas).

The intellectualistic understanding of beatitude often relies on John 17:3, and it appeared as early as the Greek Fathers, particularly Justin (apologists*), Clement of Alexandria, and Origen*. It was later developed in the Latin tradition, particularly by Abelard*. And in the 13th and 14th centuries it was under the influence of the theme of theoretical happiness in Aristotle's *Nicomachean Ethics* that the intellectualistic understanding of beatitude achieved prominence both in the faculty of arts (philosophy) and in that of theology. Whether happiness and beatitude were identified with one another (as for Pseudo-Peckham and Arnoul de Provence), or philosophical happiness was conceived of as an imperfect beatitude (according to Thomas Aquinas, Boethius of Dacia, and Gilles d'Orléans), the Aristotelian description of theoretical happiness provided the model in both cases according to which beatitude was conceived, and it was principally concerned with the intellect. It was particularly on this point that the Franciscan Guillaume de la Mare attacked Thomas Aquinas in his *Correctoire,* and the Franciscan order officially gave him its support in 1282, prohibiting any reading of the *Summa Theologica* that was not supplemented by the reading of the correction. Godefroid de Fontaines and the literature of the "corrections of the corrupter" came to the defense of Thomas and strengthened intellectualism. And the question was again at the heart of the debate that, in the early years of the 14th century, would oppose Meister Eckhart and Gonzalvo of Spain, both directly and indirectly (a debate in which "Eckhart's reasons" were clearly intellectualistic). Points of opposition were nevertheless not always as clear-cut as it may seem, as evidenced precisely by Eckhart's conception of beatitude (which involved love as well as knowledge) or, in the Dominican John of Paris (Quidort), a conception of reflexive vision that attempted to combine intellectualism and voluntarism.

4. Intellectualistic Theory Applied to God

A certain manner of understanding divine liberty and power (omnipotence*) also deserves to be called intellectualistic. But intellectualism in this context can no longer signify a primacy of the intellect over the will, which moreover are not really distinct in God. It offers an answer to the question of the relation between divine will and the good or the relation of divine intellect and the possible. On the one hand, does the good impose itself on God or does God determine the good? On the other hand, does the possible impose itself on God or does the power of God go so far as to determine the possible? These are the questions.

In one discussion, it seems that only Hugh of Saint-Cher and Descartes* asserted that God determines the possible. Thomas Aquinas, Duns* Scotus, William of Ockham (nominalism*), and later Leibniz* all asserted in one way or another that the possible does not depend on God.

The other discussion has patristic origins, and Augustine already provided an understanding of divine action according to which God does not determine the good and cannot do evil. This notion recurs in Abelard, directing God's action toward the best so that God cannot do evil, but above all can do only what he does. This extreme argument, which limited God's liberty in the name of his wisdom, was condemned by the Council of Sens. The principal writers of the 13th century, notably Thomas Aquinas, belonged to this tradition. It was only in the 14th century, with speculations on divine power, that the contrary argument was developed, particularly in the nominalist movement. For this argument, divine will does not have to submit to the good, because that will on the contrary determines the good (voluntarism*). Leibniz returned to the "intellectualistic" tradition by allowing the principle of the best to provide a norm for divine action.

- Abelard, *Epitome theologiae christianae*, c. 20, PL 178, 1724–28; *Introductio ad theologiam*, l. III, c. V, ibid., 1093–103.

Boethius, *In librum Aristotelis de interpretatione libri sex.*, PL 64, 492–93.

Boethius of Dacia, *Opuscula*, Copenhagen, 1976. *Chartularium Universitatis Parisiensis*, Ed. Denifle-Chatelain, Paris, 1889–91.

Clement of Alexandria, *Stromata* V, SC 278, ch. X–XIII, p. 124–72, and XIV, 94-3, 96-3, p. 180–82.

Pseudo-Dionysius, *De divinis nominibus*, Ed. B.R. Suchla, PTS 33, 1990; *De mystica theologia*, Ed. G. Heil and A.M. Ritter, PTS 36, 1991.

P. Glorieux, *Les premières polémiques thomistes*, vol. 1: *Le correctorium corruptorii "quare,"* n. 24, 54, 58, Kain, 1927; vol. 2: *Le correctorium corruptorii "sciendum,"* Paris, 1956.

Godefroid de Fontaines, *Quodlibeta*, in *Les philosophes belges*, vol. 2, 3, 4, 5, and 14, Louvain, 1904, 1914, 1931, 1935, 1938, especially II, q. 9; III, q. 15–16; VI, q. 7–10; VIII, q. 16.

Jean Quidort (Ed. J.-P. Muller), *Le Correctorium Corruptorii "circa" de Jean Quidort de Paris*, Rome, 1941.

Justin, *Dialogus cum Tryphone judaeo*, Text and French trans. by G. Archambault, 2 vols., Paris, 1909, chap. 2–6.

Origen, *Contra Celsum*, SC 132, 136, 147, 150, and 227 passim, *see* index s.v. *gnôsis, noûs, pisteuein, pistis*.

Siger de Brabant, *Quaestiones in Metaphysicam*, l. V, q. 8; l. VI, q. 9, Louvain, 1981 and 1983; *Quaestiones super Librum de causis*, q. 25, Louvain-Paris, 1972.

Thomas Aquinas, ST Ia, q. 82, a. 1, 2, 3; q. 83, a. 1, 3, 4; Ia IIae, q. 3, a. 4; q. 8, q. 9, a. 1, 3, 4; q. 10, a. 1, 2; *De Veritate*, q. 22 and 24; *Quaestiones disputatae de Malo*, q. 6.

William of Auxerre, *Summa aurea*, l. II, vol. X, c. II, Paris-Rome, 1980–87.

♦ P. Rousselot (1924), *L'intellectualisme de saint Thomas*, Paris.

O. Lottin (1925), "L'intellectualisme de la morale thomiste," *Xenia thomistica* I, Rome, 411–27.

M. Grabmann (1940), "Das Studium der aristotelischen Ethik an der Artistenfakultät der Universität Paris in der ersten Hälfte des 13. Jhs," *PhJ* 53, 339–54.

O. Lottin (1942), *Psychologie et morale aux XIIe et XIIIe siècles*, Louvain.

J.-P. Muller (1947), "La thèse de Jean Quidort sur la béatitude formelle," *Mélanges A. Pelzer*, Louvain, 493–511.

N. Wicki (1954), *Die Lehre von der himmlischen Seligkeit in der mittelalterichen Scholastik von Petrus Lombardus bis Thomas von Aquin,* Freiberg.

R.-A. Gauthier (1964), "Les *questiones supra librum Ethicorum* de Pierre d'Auvergne," *RMAL* 20, 233–60; id. (1975), "Le cours sur l'*Ethica nova* d'un maître ès arts de Paris (1235–1240)," *AHDL* 42, 71–141.

R. Hissette (1977), *Enquête sur les 219 articles condamnés à Paris le 7 mars 1277,* Paris-Louvain.

E. zum Brunn, Z. Kaluza, A. de Libera (1984), *Maître Eckhart à Paris, une critique médiévale de l'ontothéologie,* Paris.

A. de Libera (1984), *Introduction à la mystique rhénane,* Paris.

A.J. Celano (1986), "The *'finis hominis'* in the thirteenth cen-

tury commentaries on Aristotles's Nicomachean Ethics," *AHDL* 53, 23–53.

O. Boulnois (Ed.) (1994), *La puissance et son ombre, de Pierre Lombard à Luther,* Paris.

F.-X. Putallaz (1995), *Insolente liberté: Controverses et condamnations au XIIIe siècle,* Fribourg-Paris.

C. Trottmann (1995), *La vision béatifique, Des disputes scolastiques à sa définition par Benoît XII,* Rome.

LAURENCE RENAULT

See also **Beatitude; Liberty; Love; Vision, Beatific; Voluntarism**

Intention

(a) Definition. Intention is the goal that one hopes to achieve through an action. Since aims may be immediate or long term, and since an action may serve multiple purposes, intention refers to the entire structure of meaning that informs the action. Intention is one of the crucial aspects of the morality of an action.

(b) Thomas Aquinas's Analysis. In the summary of the process of action (ST Ia IIae, q. 12), intention comes first, since all action begins with the desire to reach some end. This ending may be general and true for all people, such as health, or it may be particular to the individual, such as an ambition to become an architect. In the latter case, a genuine intention results in preparations in order to make the goal a reality. Intentions are not vague wishes.

Both an end and the means (or series of means) leading to it are included in intention. The end can be realized only through particular means, and the means need to be chosen in relation to the desired end in order to initiate the execution of the action. Thus, intention includes both the overall purpose or "ultimate" end, such as health, and the object of the act or its "nearing" end, such as the preparation of a remedy (ST Ia IIae, q. 12, a. 3). Desire for an end is properly a matter of the attraction of the will to what appears good (Ia IIae, q. 8, a. 1), but the intellect also plays a part, since there is no intention without knowledge of its end (Ia IIae, q. 12, a. 1, ad 1).

(c) Modern Viewpoints. Modern moral ideas tend to take the goodness of the end as a sufficient condition

for the goodness of the act, forgetting that intention includes the means toward this end. With utilitarianism* especially, one can easily justify actions from which good results are expected. Another tendency has been to make the end subjective (Pinckaers 1961). This results in the substitution of vague sentiments, such as benevolence, rather than actual goods (good*) as objects of intention.

(d) "Double Effect." The nature of intention can be better understood when considering the problem of an action with two effects—one good and one bad—and distinguishing between the intended good effect and the evil result as a side effect. Thomas* Aquinas evokes this possibility while discussing legitimate* defense (ST IIa IIae, q. 64, a. 7): a person has the right to defend him- or herself against unjust attack by using force, perhaps even killing the assailant, but the prime intention must be to save one-s own life and not to harm the attacker, plus the use of force must be proportionate to the situation.

Further treatment of this idea, especially by Vitoria (c. 1485–1546), Suarez*, and Jean de Saint-Thomas (1589–1644), resulted in the formulation of the following criteria: 1) the act itself must be good, or indifferent; 2) the good effect must be what the agent intends; 3) the good effect must not be produced by the evil effect; and 4) a proportionately grave reason is required for allowing the evil effect. Some think that this is in continuity with the doctrine of Aquinas (Mangan 1949), others that it is a significant departure from his thought, especially on the part of Jean de Saint-Thomas (Ghoos 1951).

Critics of double effect argue that if the evil consequences are foreseen, then they are intended, because the agent knows that the act, freely performed, will have these results (e.g., that attacking a group of terrorists will result in the death of some civilians). The negative effects are part of the action and must certainly be considered part of the agent's responsibility. The objection fails to realize, however, that intention involves more than awareness, since it is a matter of the will, and that it is not the results of an action that determine its moral value.

The distinction between formal and material cooperation in sin also illuminates the role of intention: material cooperation consists in coming to the aid of a criminal or a sinner, without condoning the sin, while formal cooperation involves sharing the intention and agreeing with the purpose of the sinner.

Despite the risks of self-deception or rationalizing (in particular, in time of war), the importance of intention must be acknowledged to judge the value of an act. The double effect doctrine may seem artificial or casuistic in a bad way, but the idea of providence must imply a similar analysis. The presence of evil in the world is explained by making a distinction between God's intention of creation, which is that the universe should be good, and the foreseeable yet unintended results that are sin and evil.

● H. D. Simonin (1930), "La notion d'*intentio* dans l'œuvre de saint Thomas d'Aquin," *RSPhTh* 19, 445–63.
J. T. Mangan (1949), "An Historical Analysis of the Principle of Double Effect," *TS* 10, 41–61.
J. Ghoos (1951), "L'acte à double effet: étude de théologie positive," *EThL* 27, 30–52.
S. Pinckaers (1961), "Le rôle de la fin dans l'action morale selon saint Thomas," *RSPhTh* 45, 393–421.
E. Anscombe (1963), *Intention,* Oxford.
J. Finnis (1991), "Object and Intention in Moral Judgments According to Aquinas," *Thom* 55, 1–27.

DANIEL WESTBERG

See also **Conscience; Legitimate Defense: Ethics**

Intercession. *See* **Indulgences; Prayer**

Intercommunion

(a) Definition. Intercommunion means, most generally, Eucharistic fellowship between distinct churches, but its meaning has become more restricted in the course of the 20th century. At the First World Conference on Faith and Order (1927), the term *complete intercommunion* was synonymous with "full communion" or "complete collaboration" (*Acts* 453, 462). Already, however, the term "intercommunion" was criticized as "ambiguous" (462).

Spurred by the lack of mutual admission to the Eucharist* by the Churches, the Faith and Order Commission conducted a major study of intercommunion in preparation for the Third World Conference in Lund (1952). In its definitions, the conference distinguished "intercommunion" from "full communion." Intercommunion exists where two churches that are not in the same confessional family agree to permit their communicant members to take part in the holy supper or to participate in the Eucharist freely in one or the other church. In most cases, intercommunion involves intercelebration, that is, that "the ministers can celebrate the sacrament…freely in one or the other church"

(*Rapport* 1952). At the request of the World Council of Churches, in 1968, the commission again took up the question of intercommunion and (redefined it) simply as "reciprocal admission" to the (Eucharist) by two or more churches (1971).

This definition corresponds to the present use of the term *intercommunion*. Intercommunion exists between two churches that officially and reciprocally admit members of the other to partake of the Eucharist. It may be strengthened when the churches not only admit but reciprocally invite members of the other churches to participate or when the churches urge their members to accept such an invitation.

(b) History and Present Situation. In the patristic church, intercommunion without full communion was understood as fellowship with schism* or heresy* and, therefore, was rejected (Elert 1954). Lutherans and Calvinists maintained a similar policy following the Reformation; intercommunion was a sign of unity* in the faith, which it presupposed (Baillie-March 1952). The Orthodox churches, the Catholic Church, and some conservative Protestant churches still maintain such a policy.

In the first half of the 20th century, the question of intercommunion was central to certain bilateral agreements that stopped short of full communion, such as those between the Church of England and the Scandinavian Lutheran churches. In the middle of the century, restricting communion to members of one's own church or of churches in full communion with it was increasingly questioned in many Protestant churches (*see,* e.g., the studies of *Koinonia* [1957] by the Lutheran churches in Germany and *Intercommunion Today* [1968] by the Church of England). In 1954, the World Alliance of Reformed Churches recommended the admission of all baptized Christians to the Eucharist, regardless of their church of origin. Many Lutheran and Anglican churches adopted similar policies. Explicit declarations of intercommunion among these churches thus lost much of their significance, since intercommunion is implicitly practiced between all churches, in the sense that their members are admitted to communion. Declarations of intercommunion have remained significant as elements within more comprehensive declarations of communion (e.g., the Leuenberg Agreement [1973] among Lutheran, Reformed, and United churches in Europe).

(c) Theological Problems. Intercommunion raises the question of the relation between the eucharistic fellowship realized by reciprocal admission to the Eucharist and the unity that exists or is sought in the church. Churches that admit all baptized Christians to the Eucharist sometimes argue that such general intercommunion is demanded by the unity given in baptism. Such general intercommunion expresses the unity of all Christians more than the unity of any specific churches.

Official declarations of intercommunion, especially when accompanied by joint celebrations of the Eucharist, are sometimes seen as foretastes of a fuller communion that the churches are seeking (see the Meissen Agreement [1991] between the Church of England and the Evangelical Church in Germany).

For the Orthodox churches, the Eucharist, as the sacrament of the unity of the church, is incompatible with division. *Inter-communion* is a contradiction in terms, for *communion* points to the unity of the church while *inter-* indicates a plurality of churches. The Eucharist thus can be rightly celebrated and received only by those within the unity of the church.

The Catholic Church also insists that "eucharistic communion" is "inseparably linked to full ecclesial communion" (*Ecumenical Directory*). Intercommunion is therefore rejected in principle. Nevertheless, because a real but imperfect communion is acknowledged with all baptized Christians, with other "ecclesial communities," and especially with the Orthodox churches, the Catholic Church is open to "a certain communion *in sacris,* and therefore within the Eucharist," with the Orthodox churches (*CEC,* 1399), and accepts to administer the sacraments in case of emergency to "Christians who do not have full communion with the Catholic Church…provided they manifest Catholic faith in these sacraments and are properly disposed" (ibid. 1401). Since it does not recognize the validity of the sacrament of ordination (priesthood*) in the Protestant churches, "eucharistic intercommunion with other communities is not possible for the Catholic church" (ibid. 1400).

● Foi et Constitution (1927), *Actes officiels de la Conférence mondiale de Lausanne,* Paris.
D. Baillie and J. March (1952), *Intercommunion,* London.
Foi et Constitution (1952), *Rapport de la Conférence œcuménique de Lund,* Paris.
W. Elert (1954), *Abendmahl und Kirchengemeinschaft in der Alten Kirche, hauptsächlich des Ostens,* Berlin.
Oekumenischer Ausschuß der Vereinigten evangelisch-lutherischen Kirche Deutschlands (1957), *Koinonia.*
Archbishops' Commission on Intercommunion (1968), *Intercommunion Today.*
Foi et Constitution (1971), "Au-delà de l'intercommunion," in *Ist* 16 (1971), 352–75.
G. Limouris (1986), "The Eucharist as the Sacrament of Sharing: An Orthodox Point of View," *ER* 38, 410–15.
Catéchisme de l'Église catholique (1992), Paris, par. 1398–402.

MICHAEL ROOT

See also **Church; Communion; Eucharist; Unity of the Church**

Interpretation. *See* **Hermeneutics**

Intertestament

1. Terminology

The term *intertestament* covers both a period, from the second century B.C. to the second century A.D., and a literary production. But, with the discovery of the manuscripts of the *Astronomical Book* of Enoch found in Qumran, the period has been extended back to the late third century B.C. From the literary point of view, the intertestament brings together, over the course of these centuries, heterogeneous Jewish writings representing the interpretation of the biblical revelation in different circles. Some reject the term *intertestament* as being too ambiguous and prefer to speak of "ancient Jewish literature." For: 1) Chronologically, the intertestament is not located "between" the Old Testament and the New Testament but encompasses the two eras. 2) The idea of the two testaments is Christian. Judaism prefers to speak of "Jewish literature between the Bible and the Mishnah" (Nickelsburg 1981). 3) This title itself is equivocal, because the concept of Bible as a completed book presupposes a canon* of Scripture, a definition that, for Jews as for Christians, took place only at the turn of the second century, precisely when the intertestament came to an end.

However, Mosaic law* was very early considered the quintessential book (Sir 24:23) and the focal point of divine revelation, seconded by the writings of the prophets (prophet* and prophecy) (*see* the Greek prologue to Sirach; Mt 5:17). Different Jewish circles supplemented this central axis with various writings that made it possible for them to specify their particular orientations. Following the model of the ambient Hellenistic culture, Jewish culture of the period tended to fix its history and traditions (tradition*) in writing, in order to identify itself in relation to other groups and nations. Some of these books entered into the canon of Hellenistic Judaism (Tobit, Judith, the additions to Daniel and to Esther). Others were excluded from the Jewish canon but accepted by certain churches (church*): for example, the *Syriac Apocalypse of Baruch* (Chaldean Church) and the *Ethiopian Enoch.* As a consequence the border between "biblical" and "intertestamentary" writings has become porous. It is difficult to specify further here the fruitful concept of intertestament and to retrace "the social space of the book" (A. Paul, *EU* 15. p. 996), everything through which, in its diversity, the ancient Jewish world evidenced its manner of receiving and interpreting the divine revelation to which it lay claim.

2. Stakes

Christian exegesis* long paid special attention to the influences that inserted the ancient Church into the currents of the Roman Empire: Hellenistic-Oriental religions, Gnosticism, Mandeanism. Christianity was given a privileged status as the child liberated from its Jewish matrix, and the literature of the intertestament served as a foil demonstrating the superiority of Christian ideas over Judaism. For its part, Jewish scholarship removed from the intertestament, as heterodox, everything that rabbinic Judaism had later excluded (Urbach 1979), namely the apocalypses and pseudepigrapha (or apocrypha*) of the Old Testament. By the beginning of this century Christian writers had the intuition that the roots of Christianity were better explained in terms of its Jewish origin than by Hellenistic or Mandean influences. From this came the literary monument of *Pfarrer* P. Billerbeck, sponsored by H. L. Strack: *Kommentar zum neuen Testament aus Talmud und Midrash* (1926). But the documentation assembled by Billerbeck was often from a period too late to shed valid light on the New Testament. Similarly, later popularized works, which were based on Talmudic documentation from the fourth and fifth centuries, tended to make Jesus into a rabbi (*see* Tassin 1986).

Current interest in the intertestament has its sources in a methodological reorientation. Whereas rabbinic

Judaism subsequent to the destruction of the temple in A.D. 70 appears as a unified world, earlier Judaism, by contrast, was polymorphous and scattered. Its diversity is shown both in ancient translations of the Bible and in pseudepigrapha. This Judaism was a mosaic that included the pharisees, the sadducees, the Essenes, the Baptists, and the movement of Jesus, not to forget the Jewish diaspora that set out to translate the biblical message in the Hellenistic environment.

The Jews of the first century did not read the Bible as a bare text but spontaneously supplemented it with interpretive traditions that were ramified in the profusion of the intertestament. For example, the exultation of Abraham in John 8:56 is understood in the context of a Judaism that, in Genesis 17:17, changes the incredulous laughter of the patriarch into joy; hence the translation of the Targum of Onqelos: "He rejoiced." But this theme had already been emphasized in the second century B.C. in the book of Jubilees (14:21, 15:17, 16:19; Grelot 1988 *RdQ* 49–52, 621–28). The intertestament thus requires critical work that attempts to date the development of traditions (Vermes 1961) in order to distinguish those that are capable of restoring the Jewish background to the New Testament. *La nuit pascale* (Le Déaut 1963) represents a model of this method.

3. Works

It is impossible to enumerate and classify here all those works that have in common their Jewish origin and thereby are to be distinguished from the New Testament apocrypha. They include the apocalyptic* literature and the pseudepigrapha of the Old Testament. This latter category includes books that "rewrite" the Bible, such as the *Apocryphal Genesis* (in Aramaic) found in Qumran, and texts providing elaborations on biblical characters, such as *Joseph and Aseneth,* a religious romance of love and knighthood. But other works do not fit into these categories. Based on the narrative of the martyrs in 2 Maccabees 6–7, the Fourth Book of the Maccabees (first century A.D.) sets out an argument, influenced by Stoicism, on the value of "pious reason*" in ordeals. Some religious narratives are not directly rooted in biblical texts. The *Letter of Aristeus to Philocrates* (second century B.C.) recounts the legendary origin of the Septuagint. The Third Book of the Maccabees is a novel, frequently confirmed by the hazards of history, about a persecution suffered by the Jews of Egypt. An entirely different category is represented by the works of Philo of Alexandria (born c. 15 B.C.) and Flavius Josephus (born 37 A.D.).

The study of the intertestament must deal with three problems:

a) Dating. Works are often anonymous or conceal their author behind a pseudonym; for example, the *Sentences* of Phocylides (first century A.D.), a gnomic poem that "transposes into Greek form elements of Jewish wisdom*" (Grelot 1994). As for the apocalypses, they mask events by the use of hermetic images. In short, the attempt to date documents as earlier or later than the beginning of our era is sometimes impossible.

b) Revisions. By the end of the first century A.D., Judaism's interest in this abundant literature had been superseded by its interest in wisdom literature. Christians, on the other hand, preserved these texts in which they saw, according to the title of Eusebius of Caesarea, a providential *praeparatio evangelica.* The documents were thus transmitted with Christian interpolations, like the Trinitarian doxology that concludes the *Testament of Abraham.* But the identification of Christian additions is often a matter of debate, with respect to the *Testament of the Twelve Patriarchs* (Levi, 18:6–8; Judah, 24:2), for example.

c) Language of Transmission. Many of these writings, particularly in Alexandria, were composed in Greek, a language that assured them a wide audience, even if there is some question as to whether this literature was read outside Jewish circles (Tcherikover 1956, Eos 48, 169–93). Because of their transmission by Christians, some books from Palestine have survived only in the languages of the early Churches: Latin *(Biblical Antiquities of Pseudo-Philo, Testament of Moses),* Syriac *(2 Baruch),* Ethiopian *(1 Enoch, Jubilees),* or Slavonic *(2 Enoch).* But fragments discovered in Qumran have restored the antiquity and the original language of several of these works—Aramaic for *1 Enoch* and Hebrew for *Jubilees.*

4. Elements of Classification

With no claim to establishing a precise classification, we can distinguish five groups:

a) Works of Philo and Josephus. They are precisely situated in time, and if they did not exist we would know almost nothing of Jewish history from the end of the Persian era to the end of the Jewish war* against Rome (Philo: *In Flaccum. Legatio ad Gaium;* Josephus: *The Jewish War, Autobiography).* In addition, Josephus sets forth his understanding of Mosaic institutions and biblical history *(Antiquities of the Jews, Against Apion).* In doing so he echoes interpretive readings and, through cross-references, confirms the antiquity of documents that are less definitely dated. Similarly, beneath the allegorical surface of Philo's commentaries ancient Palestinian traditions emerge.

For example, in Exodus 28, Philo, Josephus, and the Targum agree in giving an allegorical interpretation of the high priest's costume.

b) Qumran Writings. They present not only an outline of a particular sect. The biblical manuscripts of the caves now clarify certain discrepancies in ancient translations. The biblical commentaries of Qumran *(pesharim)* and other anthologies and *Testimonia* confirm the convergence of biblical interpretations known from other documents with respect to eschatological expectations: the prophets Elijah, Moses, and the Messiah (messianism/Messiah*), and even the use of the figure of Melchizedek in the Epistle to the Hebrews (replaced by Elijah in the rabbinical tradition).

c) Pseudepigrapha of the Old Testament. They include the apocalypses, legendary histories *(3 Maccabees),* instructions in narrative form *(Jubilees),* and poetic works: in Alexandria, for example, Ezekiel the tragedian presented the Exodus of the Hebrews in the form of a tragedy in verse. There is also a large number of "Testaments": The fiction is that a biblical hero on his deathbed brings his heirs together and gives them his spiritual testament. This genre influenced the New Testament (Lk 22; Jn 13–17; 2 Tm; 2 Pt). It is still difficult to evaluate the size and identity of the public reached by the pseudepigrapha.

d) Targums. Targums, on the other hand, reached the broad audience of the synagogues. These are versions of the Bible in Aramaic, at first oral, in the framework of the liturgy, for listeners who no longer understood Hebrew. The Targum often uses paraphrase. Even though the versions from synagogues that we have are late and require critical analysis, this type of writing is ancient, since a Targum of Job has been found in Qumran (4QtgJob). The traditions transmitted by Targums were addressed to the popular audience of the synagogues, who spontaneously rejected interpretations that were too sectarian or too innovative. They thereby reflected a kind of consensus that flourished in rabbinic literature.

e) Midrashim, the Mishnah, the Talmud. In ancient synagogues and in schools, explicit interpretation of the law was often entrusted to "wise men" or "scribes" (Mt 23:2). Between the beginning of our era and the early third century, they made up the generation of *Tannaïm* ("tutors"). Their scholarship was nourished by the intertestament and enriched it in return. It took concrete form in *midrashim* (commentaries) of the Pentateuch, of which only later recensions survive. It led to the publication of the Mishnah (*see* Strack-Stemberger 1986). With the Mishnah began a sifting

and a codification of the proliferating traditions of the intertestament. What had been merely "the traditions of the elders" (Mt 15:2) became the oral law, supposed to have come from Moses himself, endowed with an authority equal to that of the written law, and later to be set out precisely in the Talmud.

A new history begins at that point. On the one hand, Christians collected the writings of the intertestament. In the framework of their mission to the Gentiles they appreciated the pseudepigrapha that attempted a "Greek explanation" of biblical revelation to the Jewish diaspora. As for the Palestinian traditions of interpretation of Scripture, Christians placed them at the service of faith in Jesus the Messiah. On the other hand, in the wake of the destruction of the temple, Judaism abandoned Jewish-Hellenistic writings, considered too dispersed and thereby dangerous for an identity that had to be reconstructed, and it selected in the intertestament legacy everything that might focus believers on the Torah and the Torah alone. In short the intertestament was a breeding ground that made it possible for the disciples of Jesus to identify themselves as a "Church" and for ancient Judaism to become rabbinic Judaism.

● T. Reinach (Ed.) (1900–1932), *Flavius Josèphe, Œuvres complètes,* Paris.
Flavius Josèphe, *Contre Apion* (1930), Text by Th. Reinach; Trans. L. Blum, Paris.
R. Arnaldez, J. Pouilloux, C. Mondésert (Ed.) (1961–88), *Les œuvres de Philon d'Alexandrie* (Text and trans.), 36 vols., Paris.
A. Pelletier (1962), *Lettre d'Aristée à Philocrate* (Text and trans.), Paris; id. (Ed.) (1975–84), *La Guerre des Juifs* (Text and trans.), 5 vols., Paris.
M. Schuhl (Ed.) (1974, 3rd Ed. 1983), *Les Maximes des Pères* (Text and trans.), Paris.
J. H. Charlesworth (Ed.) (1983–85), *The Old Testament Pseudepigrapha* (2 vols.), London.
A. Dupont-Sommer, M. Philonenko (Ed.) (1987), *La Bible: Écrits intertestamentaires,* Paris.
♦ P. Dalbert (1954), *Die Theologie der hellenistisch-jüdischen Missionsliteratur,* Hamburg.
G. Vermes (1961), *Scripture and Tradition in Judaism,* Leyden.
R. Le Déaut (1963), *La nuit pascale: Essai sur la signification de la Pâque juive,* AnBi 22; id. (1984), "La Septante, un Targum?," in R. Kuntzmann, J. Schlosser (Ed.), *Études sur le judaïsme hellénistique,* Paris.
A.-M. Denis (1970), *Introduction aux pseudépigraphes d'Ancien Testament,* Leyden.
A. Paul (1972–), "Bulletin critique" bisannuel sur l'Intertestament, *RSR*; id. (1975), *Intertestament* (CEv 14), Paris.
E. E. Urbach (1979), *The Sages* (2 vols.), Jerusalem.
A. Dupont-Sommer (1980, 1996), *Les écrits esséniens découverts près de la mer Morte,* Paris.
J. H. Charlesworth (1981), *The Pseudepigrapha and Modern Research,* Missoula.
G. W. E. Nickelsburg (1981), *Jewish Literature between the Bible and the Mishna,* London.
A. Diez Macho (1982), *El Targum,* Madrid.
J. Cazeaux (1983), *Philon d'Alexandrie* (Supplement to CEv 44), Paris.

M. E. Stone (1984), *Jewish Writings of the Second Temple Period,* Assen-Philadelphia.

H. L. Strack, G. Stemberger (1986), *Introduction au Talmud et au Midrash,* Paris.

C. Tassin (1986), *Le judaïsme* (CEv 55), Paris.

A. Paul (1987), *Le judaïsme ancien et la Bible,* Paris.

S. Safrai (1987), *The Literature of the Sages,* Assen/Maastricht-Philadelphia.

M. Hadas-Lebel (1989), *Flavius Josèphe,* Paris.

See also in *New Jerome Biblical Commentary* (1989), p. 1054–82; R. E. Brown, "Jewish Apocrypha," §1–52; "Dead Sea Scrolls," §79–123; A. J. Saldarini, "Philo, Josephus, Rabbinic Literature," §124–143 (bibl.).

P. Grelot (1994), *L'espérance juive à l'heure de Jésus,* new Ed., Paris.

CLAUDE TASSIN

See also **Apocalyptic Literature; Apocrypha; Bible; Book; Canon of Scriptures; Gospels; Holy Scripture; Israel; Judaism; Law and Christianity; Translations of the Bible, Ancient**

Investiture Dispute. *See* Lateran I, Council

Irenaeus of Lyon

c. 140–200

1. Biography

a) Life. We have little information on the life of Irenaeus. Everything we know derives from his still extant works or from lost works of which a few extracts were preserved by Eusebius of Caesarea in his *Ecclesiastical History.* Irenaeus came originally from Asia, perhaps from Smyrna. In any event, it was there, while still a youth, that he listened to the teachings of Bishop* Polycarp, who was already an old man (*HE* 5, 20, 5–8). The difference in age between Irenaeus and Polycarp and the date of the latter's martyrdom* (155/156 or 167) make it possible to place Irenaeus's birth about the year 140.

Without our really knowing the reasons why, except that there were very strong links between the Christian communities of Lyons and Asia, Irenaeus came to Lyons. He was already there at the time of the persecutions of 177, in the course of which Pothinus, the first bishop of this town, met his death. Irenaeus succeeded him before his journey to Rome as the community's representative in order to bear a letter to Pope Eleutherius (*HE* 5, 4, 1). Irenaeus also interceded with Pope Victor (189–98) about the currently disputed question of the date of Easter. We know nothing more about Irenaeus, not even the date of his death. The traditional story that Irenaeus was a martyr dates from the beginning of the 6th century.

b) Works. Irenaeus wrote several works in Greek, the list of which figures in Eusebius (*HE* 5, 26; 5, 24; 5, 20, 1). Only two among them are extant. Composed of five books, the *Elucidation and Refutation of Pseudo-Gnosticism* exists in its entirety only in a Latin translation from the fourth century. Apart from fragments in Armenian and in Syriac, we also own the Armenian translation of books IV and V. Only fragments of the Greek text remain, especially for book I. This work is better known under the title of *Against Heresies (Adversus Haereses),* given by certain manuscripts and by its first editors. The second work, entitled *Demonstration of the Apostolic Preaching,* is extant in a sixth-century Armenian translation only.

Can these two works be dated? In the conclusion of the *Demonstration,* Irenaeus referred to his *Against Heresies.* That might indicate that the two works were written at the same time, or, more probably, that the *Demonstration* followed closely on Irenaeus's first treatise. Moreover, in *Against Heresies* (3, 3, 3), Irenaeus mentioned Victor's predecessor Eleutherius as bishop of Rome*. It can therefore be confirmed that at least the first three books of *Against Heresies* were written before 189, the first year of Victor's reign as bishop.

The *Demonstration* is a catechesis that interprets the sacred history of Israel as a prophecy (prophet* and prophecy) of Christ Jesus. On the other hand, his *Against Heresies* is a theological treatise in which Irenaeus refutes three main types of heresies: Ebionite, Marcionite, and Gnostic. In reality Irenaeus himself had only met with Gnosticism. But the systematic nature of the treatise encompasses in fact the whole theological domain and uses the heresies as counter-proofs in order to expound the Catholic doctrine.

2. Irenaeus's Theology

a) Sources and Theological Method. Irenaeus had read his predecessors. But he worked above all on the Scriptures, and it was in the biblical domain that he was most influenced by these predecessors. From them he got the *Testimonia,* those collections of more or less enlarged scriptural quotations. Also from that source, particularly from Papias, Polycarp, and Justin, he inherited a method of interpreting the Scriptures. And he borrowed Justin's way of understanding the Old Testament as a prophecy of the New Testament. The Old Testament tells of God's deeds undertaken in favor of the men of that time and of the words that He transmitted to them, and these deeds and words prefigure and herald Christ Jesus. The Scriptures form a whole: the New Testament is the realization of the Old Testament (*Adv. Haer.* 4, 26,1).

The Scriptures and their interpretation by the Church are the nucleus of the doctrine preached, particularly during baptismal instruction; they are summed up by the rule of faith and the rule of truth (*Adv. Haer.* 1, 9, 4). Scriptures and doctrine belong to the tradition of the Church, a tradition that is inseparable from the apostolic* succession of the bishops. According to Irenaeus, the Church cannot in fact exist except when grouped around the bishop, who transmits the tradition and guarantees the apostolic origins of the Church by reason of his belonging to a line going back to the apostles (apostle*) (*Adv. Haer.* 3, 3, 1). Of course the episcopal structure (structures*, ecclesial) of the Church was established only in the second

century and contrasts with other more ancient forms of organization. But, having become acquainted with this structure only through Polycarp, Irenaeus had no doubt that it went back to the apostles.

Meditation about faith takes place in the Churches governed by bishops by means of the tradition that they transmit and the control that they ensure. For Irenaeus, those who do not recognize the episcopal organization are therefore outside the communion of the Church: those are the heretics whom he refutes.

Citing no Marcionite documents, Irenaeus likely borrowed from Justin his presentation of Marcionism* and arguments to refute it. As for Gnosticism, Irenaeus had read several Gnostic texts, especially those by the Valentinians. Here too he completed his information with the help of Justin's works.

In the state in which it has come down to us, the documentation collected by Irenaeus did not always allow him to make an exact and thorough interpretation of Gnosticism. Despite that, he was capable of perceiving the theological issues, which set the Church against Gnosticism. It was primarily a question of man's salvation, in his soul and in his body (soul*-heart-body), and consequently of the salvation of the material world. The controversy bore correlatively on the status of the Son and the Holy* Spirit in relation to the Father*; they depend solely on him and have no share in the divine plan. In this context, Irenaeus used in a personal way several ideas found in the Scriptures and in his predecessors' works, in which moreover they played only a restricted role. He used them to explain the Church's teaching on salvation and on God. Theology then becomes a meditation on the divine plan of salvation that leads to the mystery of God.

b) Plan of Salvation. God had a plan and he realized it: that is what Irenaeus calls the "economy," or plan of salvation, a central idea in his theology. God created man in order to have him share in his life (*Adv. Haer.* 4, 14, 1). Creation was undertaken for man's sake in order to bring about the meeting of God and man (*Adv. Haer.* 4, 7, 4; 4, 20, 4; 5, 29, 1). Irenaeus took from the Scriptures different ways of presenting salvation.

A prime notion is that of the adoptive filiation (Gal 4:4–6) that Christ Jesus brings to men through the gift of the Holy Spirit (*Adv. Haer.* 3, 6, 1; 3, 19, 1). Another derives from the theme of man created in the image of God and in the likeness of God (Gn 1:26). Body and soul, man is naturally the image of God by reason of his corporeity (*Dem.* 11). To put it more precisely, man is the image of the Word made man Christ Jesus, the prototype of humanity brought to full perfection by the gift of the Spirit, and therein lies the resemblance (*Adv.*

Haer. 5, 6, 1). The presence of the Spirit thus perfects the modeling of man, who increasingly comes to resemble Christ.

These examples show that the plan is divided into two phases. The first phase starts with the beginning of the world and prepares the incarnation of the Word of God; during the second phase, humanity is brought to its perfection. The transition from the first phase to the second is accomplished by the Word of God made man, Christ Jesus. That is what is called the recapitulation, *anakephalaiósis*. It carries out the transformation of the whole human race, not only of the future generations until the end of time, when creation itself will be transfigured (*Adv. Haer.* 5, 36, 1.3), but also of preceding generations as far back as Adam* himself (*Adv. Haer.* 3, 23, 1; *Dem.* 78).

Through this recapitulation Christ Jesus gathers all men together. He also conquers the devil, sin, and death, and frees men from them (*Adv. Haer.* 3, 18, 7). Finally he brings man to perfection by giving him the Holy Spirit (*Adv. Haer.* 4, 33, 8; 5, 20, 2). During the second phase Irenaeus no longer links the plan to the Son but to the Spirit. After the ascension and the gift of the Spirit, Christ in fact works through the Holy Spirit that lives in man. The Spirit prolongs Christ's work. It makes men new by freeing them, by gathering them together, and by perfecting them (*Dem.* 6). Irenaeus thus perceives two characteristics of the effusion of the Spirit. On the one hand, Christ spread the Spirit throughout the whole human race (*Adv. Haer.* 3, 17, 1–2; *Dem.* 6 and 89). On the other hand, this Spirit is transmitted to believers by means of baptism (*Dem.* 42) and the Eucharist (*Adv. Haer.* 4, 18, 4–5 and 5, 2, 3) in order to create the Church as its visible abode (*Adv. Haer.* 3, 24, 1).

c) Christ's Recapitulation of Adam: Creation and Salvation. Adam was the first man. But he is also a collective figure, for all men have their origins in him through succeeding generations, and for this reason they compose a single humankind (*Adv. Haer.* 4, 33, 15).

Similarly, Christ Jesus is the origin of this new humanity, that is, of this spiritual humanity. In his work of recapitulation, Christ is in the same situation as was Adam with regard to the human race, for he was modeled from virgin clay as Adam had been. "Just as the first man to be modeled, Adam, received his substance from a still virgin and intact clay . . . so, recapitulating Adam in himself, the Word's generation, which is the recapitulation of Adam, very fittingly came about by means of the still virgin Mary*" (*Adv. Haer.* 3, 21, 10).

But, placed in an identical situation, Christ Jesus succeeded where Adam had failed. Indeed, the disobedience of the first model—which subjected man to sin, death, and Satan—corresponds to the obedience of the second one, who freed man from those powers (*Adv. Haer.* 3, 18, 6–7; 3, 19, 3; 5, 21, 3). All the same, Christ also confers divine life, which Adam could not impart. Insofar as Christ is man and Word, he could on the one hand be tested and obey the Father, and on the other hand be glorified for thus transmitting divine life to the other men (*Adv. Haer.* 4, 20, 2).

Lastly, just as Adam transmitted to man his nature and his state of sin, so Jesus gave to man the Spirit, which perfected that nature and corrected that state by destroying sin. The relations between Adam and Christ thus express the link between creation and salvation. Adam gives his humanity to the Son by means of Mary, but it was for the sake of Christ's advent that Adam had been created. Salvation is the completion of creation.

d) Christ Jesus, the Origin and the Purpose of the Divine Plan. The plan for salvation presupposed the existence of a Savior and the existence of men to be saved. But for Irenaeus, the Savior does not exist because there are men to be saved—on the contrary, there are men to be saved because the Savior pre-exists. "It is for this reason therefore that Paul calls Adam himself the 'pattern of the one to come'" (Rom 5:14); because the Word, the artisan of the universe, had sketched out in advance, in order to prepare the ground for himself, the future plan of the human race in its relation to the Son of God, with God first of all establishing natural man in order, quite obviously, that he might be saved by spiritual man. Indeed, since he who would be the Savior pre-existed, it was necessary that what would be saved should also come into existence, for this Savior had to have a *raison d'être*" (*Adv. Haer.* 3, 22, 3).

In this text (*see* Fantino 1994), Irenaeus established that the relation between Adam and Christ is the same as the one between natural man and spiritual man (1 Cor 15:45s.), the one between the pattern and the perfected reality. Thus Adam is the pattern of Christ Jesus, who came in order to realize in himself perfect humanity (Rom 5:14). But, as Paul teaches (1 Cor 15:42–48; quoted in *Adv. Haer.* 5, 12, 2), what existed first was the pattern, Adam, the natural man, transformed later into the perfect man, a spiritual man. Therein lie the two phases of the plan. The creation of humanity comes first, secondly comes its perfection through the incarnation of the Son, Christ Jesus, who transmits the Spirit to the whole human race. But it is only at the end of time that the full gift of the Spirit will come, an event linked to the Resurrection and to the advent of the Kingdom of the Father. The key to the whole plan manifested in creation is not the existence of evil or of sin but of the person of the Savior. Sin is incorporated into the realization of the plan, which in effect includes the freeing from sin (*Adv. Haer.* 3, 19, 3; 3, 23, 1).

Irenaeus does not identify evil with sin. In fact he recognizes two types of evil. Physical evil arises from the nature of the creature, for it is due to the opposition of contrary forces or to the sequence of events that obey natural laws: what seems to be an evil in the short run is a good on the cosmic (cosmos*) scale (*Adv. Haer.* 2, 25, 2). The second type of evil, moral evil, is sin. It arises from the jealousy of Satan and of certain angels* who lured Adam into transgression (*Adv. Haer.* 3, 23; *Dem.* 16). Following Johannine writings, Irenaeus considers sin to be a condition of human existence rather than a collection of individual actions.

In his prescience, God had foreseen the angel's sin as well as that of man, including the consequences, and he had sanctioned it (*Adv. Haer.* 3, 20, 1; 3, 23, 1; 4, 38, 4; 5, 36, 1). But putting man to the test is part of God's original design (*Adv. Haer.* 5, 24, 3; *Dem.* 15). For it is through experience that man acquires knowledge and therefore knowledge of good and evil (*Adv. Haer.* 4, 37, 6–7; 4, 38, 4).

e) Plan Reveals the Mystery of the Father, the Son, and the Holy Spirit. Basing himself on the plan, Irenaeus reflects on the salvation that God bestows on man and on the means by which he grants it to him. Since the Son and the Spirit indeed transmit God's life to us, it is because they themselves possess this life. They are therefore not created, their existence is not "part of the divine plan."

In this way Irenaeus makes a clear distinction between the uncreated, which is God, and the created. The created consists of the temporal world, both visible and invisible. The Father, the Son, and the Spirit, co-eternal, belong to the uncreated. For Irenaeus, the divine nature of the Son and the Spirit is revealed by the Scriptures. But, although the Son and the Spirit are uncreated, nonetheless they have their origin in the Father.

Irenaeus states precisely the difference in origins of the Son and of the Spirit on the one hand and of creation on the other. The created arises out of the divine will. The Son and the Spirit themselves sprang from the substance of the Father. The act of generation established the unity of the Father and the Son as well as their difference. Insofar as the Spirit is concerned, Irenaeus is more reserved. He follows the Scriptures. The Spirit is co-eternal with the Father and the Son, not a creature but sprung from God, and remains forever with the Father and the Son.

The unity of the three lies not only in the realm of action but also in the realm of being. Irenaeus recognizes God as a single substance. But he expresses this unity through recourse to images, for example, God's hands, the Son and the Spirit, are always attached to him (*Adv. Haer.* 5, 28, 4). This procedure stresses the constant presence, and indeed, the eternal one, of the Son and the Spirit alongside the Father.

However, Irenaeus acknowledges a difference among the three with regard to the plan and attributes a specific role to each. Here again he follows the tradition of the Scriptures. The Father decides, the Son acts, and the Spirit orders and makes grow, but there is only one divine action (*Adv. Haer.* 4, 20, 1; 4, 38, 3). That interpretation is in harmony with the fact that Irenaeus's theology is founded on the plan. Indeed, it is through this plan that men accede to the Father, to the Son, and to the Spirit, who realize the plan by creating man and by leading him to his destiny: that of meeting and loving God, that is to say, the three. In theology, the transition from the plan to the mystery of God is therefore quite natural for Irenaeus, because it corresponds to the progress of the plan, which is a road to God.

● *Demonstration of the Apostolic Preaching,* Ed. K. Ter-Mekerttschian (1919).

A. Houssiau (1955), *La christologie de saint I.,* Louvain-Gembloux.

A. Benoît (1960), *Saint I., Introduction à l'étude de sa théologie,* Paris.

Against Heresies, Ed. and trans. in French by A. Rousseau (1965–82), SC 100, 152–53, 210–11, 263–64, 293–94.

A. Orbe (1969), *Antropología de san Ireneo,* Madrid; id. (1985–88), *Teología de san Ireneo, comentario al libro V del Adversus Haereses,* Madrid.

L. Doutreleau, L. Regnault (1971), "I. de Lyon," *DSp* 7, 1923–69.

H.J. Jaschke (1976), *Der Heilige Geist im Bekenntnis der Kirche,* Münster; id. (1987), "Irenäus von Lyon," *TRE* 16, 258–68.

New Arminian Fragments from Adversus Haereses *and* Epideixis, Ed. and trans. in French by C. Renoux (1978), PO 39.

R. Berthouzoz (1980), *Liberté et grâce suivant la théologie d'I. de Lyon,* Paris-Fribourg.

Y. de Andía (1986), Homo vivens, *incorruptibilité et divinisation de l'homme selon I. de Lyon,* Paris.

J. Fantino (1986), *L'homme image de Dieu chez saint I. de Lyon,* Paris; id. (1994), *La théologie d'I.,* Paris.

R. Aubert (1995), "I. (saint)," *DHGE* 25, 1477–79.

JACQUES FANTINO

See also **Apologists; Creeds; Gnosis; History; Salvation**

Israel

1. Old Testament and Judaism

a) *Terminology.* "*Yiserâ'él*" is among the proper names most frequently used in the Masoretic text (2,514 times). In Genesis it is essentially applied to the patriarch Jacob after his change of name, interpreted in Genesis 32:29 (*see* Hos 12:4) as "to fight with God*" (however, in theophoric names, God is subject: "God combat," " God reign"). Thereafter, "Israel" almost always designates the people* ("sons of Israel" 637 times, "House of Israel" 146 times, "land of Israel" 17 times). They are designated in other ways such as "my people," "Jacob," "Jerusalem," "Zion," "you," and so forth.

From the beginning the ethnic and religious aspects are inseparable: "Israel" designates a league of tribes united not only by political ties but also by the covenant with the Lord, who in turn is defined by the relationship with his people: "God of Israel" (201 times; a total of 231, with other analogous syntagms: "the Holy One of Israel," etc.).

This remains constant down through the vicissitudes of history. After the schism of the ten tribes (1 Kgs 12:20–33), "Israel" designates the northern kingdom and "Juda" the southern kingdom (1–2 Kgs, passim, particularly in political contexts). This may be a return to an older terminology (1 Sm 17:52, 18:16; 2 Sm 2:8–11, 5:1–12, 19:41–44, etc.). Nevertheless, in more explicitly religious contexts the name Israel still indicates the people as a whole, particularly in Prophets (prophets* and prophecy) (Is 1:3, 8:18; Am 3:1, 9:7...) and Deuteronomy.

After the period of exile, the people is practically reduced to the tribe of Juda, and the name "Jew" (Hebrew *yehoûdî*, Aramaic *yehoûdây,* Greek *ioudaios*) becomes current. The term is used by foreigners (Ezr 5:1; 1 Macc 11:30), and also by Jews themselves, in an ethnico-political context (1 Macc 12:3). But the name Israel does remain, taking on an even more decisive religious value (Is 44:5; Ezr 2:2; Neh 9:1s.; Sir 36:11; Jdt 4:1, 4:8; 1 Macc 13:26).

b) *Theological Dimension.* Despite an ever-increasing emphasis on individual responsibility (*see* Ez 3:16–21, 18:1–32), the collective aspect maintained its place within the development of the theological reflection with its new reading of the past from the angle of the history of salvation* (choice*, promise*, covenant*), and the projection toward an eschatological future. The promises are not delivered to a group of individuals but to the people as such. Sometimes, in the perspective of judgment, the people is limited to a faithful "remnant" (Is 1:9, 4:2–6, 10:20–23; Jer 21:7; Am 3:12, 5:15, 9:8f.; Mi 4:7, 5:6f.; Sg 3:12f., etc.); and sometimes it is also globally included in salvation, which will be the gratuitous work of God's power (omnipotence*) (Jer 31:31ff.; Ez 36:26f.).

The reconstitution of the twelve tribes becomes an object of prayer*, an eschatological hope* (Ez 47:13–48, 35; Sir 48:10; Ps Sal 17). With the image of the pilgrimage* to Zion, the nations are brought within the perspective of final salvation without loss of their respective identities (Is 2:1–5, 25:6–9, 45:14–25, 60:1–22, 66:18f.; Zec 14:16).

2. New Testament

a) *Jesus and Israel.* In announcing the kingdom of God, Jesus* did not proclaim a general ethico-religious message but rather the eschatological fulfillment awaited by Israel. His constitution of a group of Twelve shows he knew that he was sent to constitute the eschatological Israel (Mt 19:28 par.; Lk 22:28ff.). He spoke of the salvation of pagans using Old Testament images of the pilgrimage and the banquet (Mt 8:11; Lk 13:29). Jesus came "born under the law*" (Gal 4:4), to interpret it "as one who has authority*" (Mt 7:29), but he definitely did not abolish it or abrogate any part of it. He accomplishes his service in favor of the circumcised (Rom 15:8), limiting his activity and that of his disciples to the "lost sheep of the house of Israel" (Mt 10:6; though these expressions may be post-paschal they are inspired by the historical reality). His encounters with pagans (Mk 5:1–20 par., 7:24–30 par.; Mt 15:31; Jn 12:20ff.) or Samaritans (Lk 17:11–19; Jn 4:1–42) were never more than occasional.

Jesus interpreted his own mission within the horizon of the faith of Israel and at the same time gave the definitive interpretation of Israel. This is what he did when he connected the Kingdom to the mystery of his own person and demanded an adherence of unconditional faith, beyond all other criteria and every other authority, from those he called to "follow" him. In this sense, even if the movement he initiated might on a purely sociological level seem to be one among many "reform movements" that arose within Judaism at that time, it cannot be reduced to that. Subsequent developments, no matter how gradual and tortuous—conflicts with the Jewish authority, constitution of the Church as a distinct religious community, evangelization of pagans, going beyond the law—originated not only in the paschal event but also in the pre-paschal teachings and practices of Jesus.

b) New Testament Reflection on Israel.

b) New Testament Reflection on Israel. The lexical framework is formed by the more solemn and religious term *Israel* but includes others such as *Jews, the people, this generation,* and so forth. As for the historical framework, New Testament writings reflect the experiences of Christian preaching to Jews and to pagans. Never more than partially successful with the Jews, it ended in failure and rupture, whereas it was increasingly successful with the pagans and ended up making them (at least in tendency) the majority and giving them a dominant position. These writings also reflect the attempt at theological interpretation of such experiences in order to situate them within God's plan. This reflection, which was never fully systematic (and is not so in Rom 9–11), puts multiple categories into operation and leads to various perspectives.

The author who undertook the most profound approach to the question was Paul, precisely the one who placed the greatest emphasis on the newness of Christianity. His path led him from a more conflictual vision (1 Thes 2:14ff.; Gal 3–4) to a more positive, serene position in Romans 9–11. Without denying his whole theological vision of the law and the cross, or (better) in giving to gratuity the statute of fundamental instance, he crowns these chapters with the announcement of the final salvation of all Israel.

Some writings—Mark and even more so John—bear hints of a polemical vein against the unbelief of Judaism (always meaning, concretely, the Judaism contemporary with Jesus and the first communities). Coexisting with these positions are others that recognize the special role of Judaism in the history of salvation (Jn 4:22, 11:51f.), though there is no attempt at synthesis. Matthew is more systematic, being dominated by the polemical schema of "substitution": "the kingdom of God will be taken away from you, and given to a people producing his fruits" (Mt 21:43). Once the priority of Israel has been respected by the earthly Jesus (even if the end result is negative), the Crucified immediately sends his disciples to the nations (Mt 28:16–20) with no further mention of Israel.

He simply refers in passing to the future salvation of this people (Mt 23:29).

In Luke-Acts, on the contrary, the Crucified asks the disciples not to go far from Jerusalem, to bear witness to him above all in that city (Lk 24:46–49; Acts 1, 5). Evangelization (mission*/evangelization) will gradually embrace the gentiles as well (Acts 11:18): "a light for revelation to the Gentiles, and for glory to your people Israel " (Lk 2:32). These pagans will be received, not to take a place that has been left vacant but to fulfill the universalist prophecies (prophet* and prophecy) of the Old Testament. The unbelief of the Jews is not considered final (Lk 13:34f.; Acts 1:6ff.). Its historical consequence will be that, after a certain point, preaching can only be addressed to the pagans (Acts 13:46, 18:6, 28:125). This is how the historical reconstruction of Luke is turned into a legitimation of the missionary Church.

Apocalypse also distinguishes between the chosen people of the tribes of Israel and the chosen people of the nations (Rev 7:1–10; *see also* 21:12, 24). However, in other writings the distinction seems to pertain only to the past (Eph 2:11–18); it is never mentioned in Hebrews.

Nonetheless, the role of Israel in the history of salvation is not denied, as it would be later, for example with Marcion (Marcionism*). There is no affirmation of an absolute rejection of the Jewish people as such, nor of its pure and simple replacement by the Church. The term always keeps its originary meaning, the idea of the Church as "the true Israel" being basically foreign to the New Testament, even if some texts seem to move in that direction. Galatians 6:16, *Israèl tou Theou,* remains controversial. 1 Corinthians 10:18 *Israèl kata sarka* is not the opposite of a "spiritual Israel." If the salvific prerogatives of certain Jews are sometimes denied (Rom 9:6f.; Jn 8:31–58; Rev 2:9, 3:9), those of the people in general are never denied. They are sometimes extended to Christians, called the descendants of Abraham (Gal 4:21–31), people of God (Acts 15:14), chosen lineage, holy people (1 Pt 2:9), people of the diaspora (Jas 1:1). These expressions do not yet have the meaning that they would subsequently acquire, that of an exclusion of the historical Israel.

● E. Peterson (1933), *Die Kirche aus Juden und Heiden,* Salzburg.

G. von Rad, K. G. Kuhn, W. Gutbrod (1938), "Israël," *ThWNT* 3, 356–94.

G. A. Danell (1946), *Studies in the Name Israel in the Old Testament,* Uppsala.

M. Simon (1948), Verus Israel. *Étude sur les relations entre chrétiens et juifs dans l'Empire romain,* Paris, 135–425.

J. Jeremias (1956), *Jésus et les païens,* Neuchâtel-Paris.

W. Trilling (1964), *Das wahre Israel: Studien zur Theologie des Matthäus-Evangeliums,* StANT 10.

A. George (1968), "Israël dans l'œuvre de Luc," *RB* 75,

481–525, repris in *Études sur l'œuvre de Luc,* Paris, 1978, 87–125.

R. de Vaux (1971), *Histoire ancienne d'Israël des origines à l'installation en Canaan,* EtB.

J. Jervell (1972), *Luke and the People of God,* Minneapolis.

L. De Lorenzi (Ed.) (1977), *Die Israelfrage nach Röm 9–11,* Rome.

F. Mußner (1979), *Traktat über die Juden,* Munich.

V. Fusco (1980), *Parola e Regno. La sezione delle parabole (Mc 4, 1–34) nella prospettiva marciana,* Aloi 13; id. (1986), "Progetto storiografico e progetto teologico nell'opera lucana," in coll., *La storiografia nella Bibbia,* Bologna, 123–52; id. (1989), "Rivelazione di Gesù—rivelazione di Dio. Il problema del 'Dio di Gesù Cristo' nella prospettiva marciana," *ScC* 117, 149–66; id. (1993 *a*), "Gesù e le Scritture di Israele," in E Norelli (Ed.), *La Bibbia nell'antichità cristiana, I. Da Gesù a Origene* (La Bibbia nella storia, 15/a), Bologna, 35–63; id. (1993 *b*) *Le Scritture nella tradizione sinottica e negli Atti,* ibid., 105–49.

H. J. Zobel (1982), "Jisrâ'el," *ThWAT* 3, 986–1012.

M. Remaud (1983), *Chrétiens devant Israël serviteur de Dieu,* Paris.

E. P. Sanders (1983), *Paul, the Law and the Jewish People,* Philadelphia.

F. Refoulé (1984), "*… et ainsi tout Israël sera sauvé*": *Romains 11, 25–32,* LeDiv 117.

R. Albertz et al. (1987), "Israel," *TRE* 16, 368–93.

J. D. G. Dunn (Ed.) (1992), *Jews and Christians. The Parting of the Ways. A.D. 70–135,* WUNT 66.

G. M. Smiga (1992), *Pain and Polemic. Anti-Judaism in the Gospels,* Mahwah, NJ.

D. Sänger (1994), *Die Verkündigung des Gekreuzigten und Israel. Studien zum Verhältnis von Kirche und Israel bei Paulus und im frühen Christentum,* WUNT 75.

D. Marguerat (Ed.) (1996), *Le déchirement. Juifs et chrétiens au Ier s.,* Geneva.

G. Caron (1997), *Qui sont les juifs dans l'Évangile de Jean?,* Québec.

A. Marchadour (Ed.) (1998), *Procès de Jésus, procès des Juifs,* Paris.

VITTORIO FUSCO

See also **Apostle; Choice; Church; Eschatology; Jerusalem; Jesus, Historical; Judaism; Messianism/Messiah; Paganism; Pauline Theology; People of God; Promise; Scripture, Fulfillment of; Universalism**

J

Jansenism

Strictly speaking, Jansenism is a heresy* defined by several condemnations of the post-Tridentine magisterium*. More generally it designates a movement within Catholicism* that denies the need for these condemnations, limits their impact, and especially seeks to present an image of Christianity that is faithful and loyal to its origins and its objectives.

1. Jansenist Heresy

In the beginning there was *Augustinus* (1640), the book by Cornelius Jansen (1585–1638), professor of Holy Scripture at the University of Louvain, then bishop of Ypres. The elaboration of this Augustinian synthesis on salvation and grace was a counter-offensive intended to weaken the impact of the Molinist opinions (Bañezianism*-Molinism-Baianism) that were being taught by the Jesuits. Its publication contravened the pontifical decisions that forbade disputing these themes after the closing of the *De Auxiliis* assemblies. This was the cause of an initial wave of condemnations, the principle one being the bull *In Eminenti* (1642, published 1643). This censure was explicitly presented as something that did not call into question the privileged status of Augustinianism* with regard to these discussions.

This matter had reverberations in France, where it took on the politico-religious complexion that would mark it to the end. A friend of Jansen, Jean du Vergier de Hauranne, the abbot of Saint-Cyran (1581–1643), had a major influence, advocating Catholic reform based on the model of the early Church* (in writings under the name of *Petrus Aurelius*) and a spirituality of inner renewal. He turned a monastery of Cistercian nuns, Port-Royal, into an influential center for these views. Disagreeing with Richelieu's Protestant covenants, he also opposed the cardinal on the subject of penance* (notably the question of attrition, or imperfect sorrow for sin). He charged Antoine Arnauld (1612–94), one of his disciples as well as a Sorbonne doctor, with researching the Church's ancient tradition with regard to penance and the Eucharist*. The essay met with some difficulties in Rome* (*La Fréquente Communion*, 1643). Arnauld also came to the defense of *Augustinus,* which had been publicly attacked by Isaac Habert, the canon of Paris.

It was through the upholding of theses at the Faculty of Theology of Paris that Jansenism found its first expression. By asking the Faculty to take a stand (1649), the syndic Nicolas Cornet sought to impede the reinforcing of a strict Augustinianism among the younger generation. The Faculty doctors were too divided to act and five propositions out of the seven noted in *Augustinus* were subjected to the judgment of the Holy See by several French bishops. They were judged heretical and were condemned by the apostolic constitution *Cum Occasione* (May 31, 1653, *DS* 2001–7).

The five propositions were as follows:

1) Some of God's commandments (Decalogue*) are impossible for the righteous who want and

strive to follow the forces they currently have; they also lack the grace that would make them possible.

2) In the state of fallen nature, one can never resist internal grace.

3) In order to fall or not in the state of fallen nature, the liberty that excludes the need is not required; the liberty that excludes the constraint is enough.

4) The semi-Pelagians acknowledged the need for a prevenient interior grace for each specific act (action*), even for the act of initial faith, and they were heretical in that they wanted this grace to be such that the will could either resist it or obey it.

5) It is semi-Pelagian to say that Jesus Christ is dead or that he shed his blood generally for all men.

The Roman consultors had proceeded, as they usually did, by focusing on the meaning contained in the examined propositions. They situated their condemnation in the continuation of the teaching of Trent* but added necessary clarifications. Only "the first of the propositions can be found textually in the *Augustinus*, the four others correctly express doctrine that it does contain, extensively elaborated upon and developed in many forms" in the book (the *Brière* 1916). Could this condemnation fall on Augustinianism? Innocent X had explicitly dismissed it. Moreover, it was Jansenius's book, mentioned twice, that provided the context for the condemnation. And it was the connection between the propositions and the book that reignited the debate, provoking new interventions. Against Arnauld and his friends, who acknowledged the abstract condemnation (the *right*) but denied the *fact*, that is to say the *verbatim* presence of the propositions in the book, Pope Alexander VII followed the French clergy and asserted that they were found here and that they had been condemned in the sense of the author (*Ad Sanctam,* 1656, *DS* 2010–12); he later imposed a decree in this line (*Regiminis Apostolici,* 1665, *DS* 2020). The decision was important since it affirmed the Church's authority to establish "dogmatic facts" and in this way demanded the consent of faith. Arnauld was censured by the Paris Faculty of Theology* for his *Seconde Lettre à un Duc et Pair* (1655), in which he was held to have revived the error condemned in the first proposition and also to have shown disrespect by denying the fact. He was dismissed along with a great number of doctors (1656). This decision was due more to political than to religious considerations, and it gave rise to the successful counter-offensive of Pascal*'s *Lettres Provinciales.*

Pascal was able to shift the debate to the domain of moral theology and with some success since both the Paris Faculty and the Roman Inquisition then published severe condemnation of latitudinarian propositions (1665–66; *DS* 2021–65, 1679, *DS* 2101–67).

Negotiated in 1669 to resolve Gallican tensions that resulted from various Roman condemnations, the "Peace of the Church" should have marked the end of the dispute, because it implicitly acknowledged the distinction by authorizing a "respectful silence." This was a fruitful period for the Port-Royal circle, which devoted itself to biblical, patristic, and liturgical renewal in an anti-Protestant perspective (*Perpétuité de la Foi,* Bible de Sacy). However, the tensions endured and even grew as a result of underground initiatives on both sides. They were given a particular boost in 1704 with the publication of a "matter of conscience" that was submitted to the Paris Faculty of Theology and that concerned inner submission to the pontifical condemnations. As a result of this, previous judgments were reiterated (*Vineam Domini,* 1704, *DS* 2309), and especially the censure expressed in the constitution *Unigenitus* (1713) of 101 propositions extracted from the *Réflexions Morales* by Pasquier Quesnel, one of Arnaud's disciples (*DS* 2400–502). This last condemnation showed that Jansenism had, by that stage, taken on a new meaning, since in terms of grace (prop. 1–43) it added an extreme conception of the role of theological charity (prop. 44–93) as well as of the origin and character of the powers within the Church (prop. 94–101). The Roman text nevertheless lacked clarity, and qualifications applied *in globo* were susceptible to varying interpretation. Sizable and highly vocal, resistance to *Unigenitus* exposed real differences within French Catholicism (call to council, 1717). It gave rise to a new condemnation, *Pastoralis officii* (1717), as well as to vigorous intervention on behalf of the political powers. This resistance gave its specific identity to a certain "Catholic Enlightenment"*(katholische Aufklärung),* which won sympathy during the 18th century in most Catholic countries. In the Netherlands it triggered the schism of the Old Catholics (1724). The acts of the synod* of Pistoie (1783), censured by the bull *Auctorem Fidei* (1794), provided the most complete example of this Jansenism, elements of which could also be found in the Church that issued from the Civil Constitution of the Clergy (1790). *Auctorem fidei* thus condemned (*DS* 2600–700) errors concerning the constitution and the authority of the Church (prop. 1–15), the natural and supernatural condition of man (prop. 16–26), the sacraments (sacrament*) (prop. 27–60), cult* (prop. 61–79), religious figures (prop. 80–84), and the convocation of a national council (prop. 85).

2. A Reformed Catholicism

Recent historiography has tended to highlight the nuances and differences that prevent us from considering Jansenism as a coherent whole. On the dogmatic level it is most certainly true that Jansenius's intransigent Augustinianism can hardly be detected in his later disciples. A. Arnauld himself, in his successive explanations, eventually criticized Thomist thought. There are, however, common elements, beyond political components, that express a particular vision of Catholicism, and of precisely the kind that the Roman condemnations sought to prohibit, directly or indirectly, with measures that had serious repercussions on the evolution of faith and Christian practice in general.

a) An Austere and Demanding Christianity. This is the popular image of Jansenism, according to which it is seen as contradicting the kind of easygoing, extroverted Catholicism associated with the Society of Jesus. But the real opposition was less clear since the rigorous quality of Jansenism was in fact characteristic of the Catholic reform in general. But it remains true that wherever the Jansenists had influence, a distinctly severe notion of salvation was subscribed to. This notion was linked to a rejection of the Molinist concept of grace and, especially, to the accent placed on the primacy of love of God and on the efficacy of divine help. It is this rejection of "sufficient grace," noted as early as the publication of *Augustinus*, that justifies the anti-Jansenist accusations summarized in the five propositions.

b) The insistent demand for "truly" sacramental practice—mainly penance and the Eucharist—but also a liturgical one, with a request for active participation that was at the origin of several translations (Scriptures, missal, breviary) and a revision of the liturgy* (neo-Gallican liturgy).

c) An ecclesiology of participation, and therefore a profound and active resistance to an authoritarian type of Church. This perspective, already expressed by Saint Cyran, was only amplified in reaction to magisterial decisions. Corresponding to a particular form of Gallicanism*, it was abused in a millenarian, convulsionary, figurist way. These somewhat reactionary tendencies, reminiscent of the early church, were nevertheless combined with progressive elements, which explains the transformation of Enlightenment thinkers.

d) Individualism. By opposing their meaning to the judgment of the pope, the champions of *Augustinus,* and then of *Réflexions Morales,* expressed the rights of conscience and Christian liberty.

e) Rationalism.* By stressing the rational character of their process, they set in motion an important discursive process, distinguished by logic (*Logique de Port-Royal,* 1662) and Cartesian philosophy.

f) Political Theology. By finally justifying their disregard of the laws of the state, they developed a new and influential theology of authority.

Jansenism disappeared with the turmoil of the Revolution, even if the term was widely used by the 19th century Ultramontanes to disqualify their austere, Gallican adversaries.

● Y. de la Brière (1916), "Le jansénisme de Jansenius," *RSR* 6, 270–301.
A. Gits (1940), *La foi ecclésiastique aux faits dogmatiques dans la théologie moderne,* Louvain.
L. Ceyssens (1957), "L'origine romaine de la bulle *In Eminenti*," in *Jansenistica: Études relatives à l'histoire du j.,* Malines, 9–110.
L. Cognet (1961), *Le jansénisme,* Paris.
B. Plongeron (1969), "Recherches sur l'*Aufklärung* catholique en Europe occidentale (1770–1830)," *RHMC* 16, 555–605.
L. Ceyssens (1971), "Les Cinq propositions de Jansenius à Rome," *RHE* 66, 449–501, 821–86; id. (1980), "L'authenticité des Cinq propositions condamnées de Jansenius," *Anton.* 50, 368–424.
B. Plongeron (1973), *Théologie et politique au siècle des Lumières (1770–1820),* Geneva.
M. Rosa (Ed.) (1981), *Cattolicesimo e lumi nel settecento italiano,* Rome.
L. Ceyssens, J. A. Tans (1987), *Autour de l'*Unigenitus, Louvain.
J. M. Gres-Gayer (1988), "The *Unigenitus* of Clement XI: A Fresh Look at the Issues," *TS* 49, 259–82.
J. Orcibal (1989), *Jansenius d'Ypres (1585–1638),* Paris.
P. Blet (1993–94), "Louis XIV et les papes aux prises avec le jansénisme," *AHP* 31, 109–92; 32, 65–148.
L. Ceyssens (1993), "Que penser finalement de l'histoire du jansénisme et de l'anti- jansénisme?" *RHE* 88, 108–30.
B. Neveu (1993), *L'erreur et son juge: Remarques sur les censures doctrinales à l'époque moderne,* Naples.
P. Stella (1994), *Il Giansenismo in Italia: La Bolla* Auctorem Fidei *nella storia dell'ultramontanismo: Saggio introdutivo e documenti,* Rome.
J. M. Gres-Gayer (1995), *Le jansénisme en Sorbonne, 1643–1656,* Paris.
L. Kolakowski (1995), *God Owes Us Nothing. A Brief Remark on Pascal's Religion and on the Spirit of Jansenism,* Oxford.

JACQUES M. GRES-GAYER

See also **Augustinianism; Bañezianism-Molinism-Baianism; Gallicanism; Grace; Pascal, Blaise; Ultramontanism**

Jealousy, Divine

"[T]he Lord, whose name is Jealous, is a jealous God" (Ex 34:14). This title for YHWH, used in texts of major theological significance (such as the Ten Commandments: Ex 20:5 and Dt 5:9) is one of the most peculiar descriptions of the God of Israel*.

In Hebrew the concept of jealousy is expressed by the root *qn'* (83 times); the noun *qin'â* is very frequent (43 times), the adjective "jealous" is rarer and used exclusively of YHWH (*qannâ'*: Ex 20:5, 34:14; Dt 4:24, 5:9, 6:15; *qannô'*: Jos 24:19; Na 1:2). The Septuagint usually translates this as *zèloô* (or derived verbs), with nouns and adjectives from the same root; whence our terms *jealousy* and *zeal*. The NT has substantially adopted the terminology of the Septuagint, but the concept of "divine jealousy" is infrequently used (2 Cor 11:2; Heb 10:27).

The term *jealousy* designates a powerful passion (Sg 8:6), where love and hatred seem to be united and inseparable (Eccl 9:6). Its various manifestations are neither all morally acceptable nor all applicable to divine behavior.

Among human beings jealousy is often the equivalent of *envy*: the desire to possess that which belongs to others, something that causes hatred and violence (Gn 26:14, 30:1, 37:11; Prv 27:4; Sir 30:24, etc.). As such, the Scriptures (Scripture*) condemn this emotion (with particular emphasis in the NT: Mt 27:18; Rom 1:29; 1 Cor 13:4; 2 Cor 12:20; Gal 5:20f, 26, etc.) and obviously do not ascribe it to God.

In marriage jealousy is displayed as possessive love, with the connotation of suspicion with regard to the beloved (Nm 5:14–30) and vindictive anger against the rival (Prv 6:34). There are very few biblical passages in which such a meaning of the term is applied metaphorically to God (Ez 16:38, 16:42, 23:25) Those that do so are to be found within the context of parables, where the history of the covenant* is described in terms of a conjugal relation. There, jealousy is identified with the punitive wrath that punishes adultery.

Finally, words with the root *qn'* describe the feeling of passionate and exclusive love for a given object. In modern languages this nuance of meaning is conveyed by the word *zeal*. However, this does not adequately express the character of all-encompassing passion, with a touch of extremism, that belongs to the biblical concept. Human beings can feel this kind of exclusive jealousy for God (Ps 119:139; Jdt 9:4; Rom 10:2), for the temple (Ps 69:10; Jn 2:17), for the law (1 Macc 2:27, 50; 2 Macc 4:2; Acts 21:20, 22:3; Gal 1:14), and for the good (Ti 2:4; 1 Pt 3:13).The Scriptures praise those who uncompromisingly choose the cause of God by giving themselves utterly to it—individuals such as Phinehas (Nm 25:11ff.; 1 Macc 2:54; Si 45:23), Elijah (1 Kgs 19:10, 14; 1 Macc 2:8; Si 48:2), Jehu (2 Kgs 10:1), Mattathias (1 Macc 2:2ff.).

It is this last aspect that will enable us to understand the meaning of "divine jealousy," God's exclusive and irrevocable attachment to Israel as his partner in the covenant (Renaud); and it is through this concept that the Bible* expresses the unique and absolute nature of YHWH as the God of Israel. Indeed the concept of a "jealous God" appears to be the foundation of the law of monotheism* and provides the justification for the absolute prohibition of other gods or the worship of idols (idolatry*) (Ex 20:5; Dt 4:24, 5:9, 6:15, 32:16, 32: 21; Jos 4:14, etc.).

Divine jealousy implies two apparently contradictory aspects. The first is the most obvious and the most widely attested: "I the Lord your God am a jealous God, visiting the iniquity of the fathers on the children to the third and the fourth generation of those who hate me" (Ex 20:5). This is a punitive expression in which jealousy and anger appear as closely related (Dt 29:19; Ez 5:13, 35:11, 36:5f.; Na 1:2; Sg 1:18, 3:8, etc.). This aspect shows how serious the choice of adhering to a "holy" God is (Jos 23:16, 24:19) and how the betrayal (or "hatred") of his love is the equivalent of death (Dt 6:15, 29:19).

The other aspect of the jealousy of God must not, however, be neglected: "but showing steadfast love to thousands of those who love me and keep my commandments" (Ex 20:6). In this case jealousy signifies election (choice*), an overwhelming and eternally faithful love. The term is applied above all when Israel finds itself in conditions of extreme need, and then the jealous love of the Lord of armies will come down upon the enemy (Is 26:11; Zec 1:14f., 8:2), while revealing itself as mercy and salvation to God's own people (Is 9:6, 37:32, 42:13, 59:17, 63:15, etc.).

- H. A. Brongers (1963), "Der Eifer des Herrn Zebaoth," *VT* 13, 269–84.
- B. Renaud (1963), *Je suis un Dieu jaloux: Évolution sémantique et signification théologique de* qine'ah, LeDiv 36.
- W. Berg (1979), "Die Eifersucht Gottes—ein problematischer Zug des alttestamentlichen Gottesbildes?" *BZ* 23, 197–211.
- C. Dohmen (1990), " 'Eifersüchtiger ist sein Name' (Ex 34, 14):

Ursprung und Bedeutung der alttestamentlichen Rede von Gottes Eifersucht," *ThZ* 46, 289–304.
- E. Reuter (1993), "*qn'*," *ThWAT* 7, 51–62.

PIETRO BOVATI

See also **Anthropomorphism; Choice; Love; Universalism; Wrath of God**

Jerome. *See* **Scripture, Senses of; Translations of the Bible, Ancient**

Jerusalem

The name *Urusalim* is attested from the time of the pharoah Amenophis IV (1377–58). It appears in the Old Testament as *Yeroûshâlaim,* in the Septuagint in the Semitic form *Ierousalèm,* carried over into the New Testament where the Hellenistic form *Hierosoluma* is also used.

a) Old Testament. Jerusalem is not named in the Pentateuch but simply suggested by anticipation as "the place that he will choose, to make his name dwell there" (Dt 14:23). Genesis 14 probably connects Jerusalem to that "Salem" whose king Melchisedek collected the tithe of Abraham (Ps 110:4; Heb 7:4). David made Jerusalem his city (2 Sm 5:9; Is 22:9, 29:1)—until then it had been in the hands of Jebusite Canaanites (Jos 10:1; 15:63). He installed the ark there and acquired the land where Solomon would build the temple (1 Kgs 6–8). Jerusalem then became the religious center of the whole of Israel, though competing sanctuaries were built in the northern kingdom. The old Canaanite name "Zion" designated the Temple Mount. Jerusalem was besieged by the Assyrians in 701 (2 Kgs 18:17–19, 35), captured by the Babylonians in 597, and reconquered and sacked in 587 (2 Kgs 24:10–25, 21).

The city was reconstructed when the Israelites came back from exile during the Persian era (Ezr 3–6; Neh 3–6) and remained the great center of attraction for the Jews of the Diaspora and those of Palestine (Is 60; Ps 122, 126).

"Daughter of Zion" had been a collective name for exiles welcomed (Is 1:8) into a neighborhood of Jerusalem after the destruction of the northern kingdom, but from the time of the exile it came to denote the population of the entire city (Is 52:2, 62:11; Zec 9:9).

Dominated by the successors of Alexander the Great and in the grips of internecine conflicts, the city was liberated by the Maccabees (reconsecration of the temple that had been profaned by Antiochus IV: 1 Macc 4:36–59). Then, under the Romans, Herod restored the former splendor of the city and the temple.

The major testimony of the extraordinary symbolic and theological charge with which the city became invested is found in the Books of Isaiah and Psalms (Ps 46, 48, 84, 87 and within the "psalms of ascent," 122, 125–129, 132–134). The prophets (prophet* and prophecy) reproach the personified city (Is 5:3, 40:2, 9...) for its crimes (Is 1:21, 5:3, 28:14; Jer 2:1–3, 5), predict its ruin (Is 29:1–7; Jer 7:1–8, 3, 11:11, 26), and weep for it (Lam). But, in the name of an irrevocable promise (Is 28:16, 54:6), Jerusalem will see the eschatological paroxysm of triumph and rejoicing (Is 51–54, 60–62; *see* oracles of salvation added to the Old Testament after the misfortunes of Israel: Is 1:25ff., 4:4ff., 6:13; Jer 3:14–18). The wife that YHWH cannot repudiate, and mother of every man and of all other pardoned cities (Ez 16:53–63), Jerusalem, washed and purified, will become once more the permanent abode of God* (Ez 48:35) and of justice, the meeting place of the surviving remnant of the nation (Ez 4:2f; 1 Jn 3:1–5), the chosen focal point of a vision of salvation for all nations (Is 2:2ff., 65:18–21; Mi 4:1ff.; Hg 2:6–9; Zec 14:16; Tb 13). The fate of Jerusalem is bound to the fate of the Davidic dynasty (Ps 132; Is 22:9; Jer 33:15f.) or detached from it (Ez 45:7–46, 18).

b) New Testament. In the Gospels Jerusalem is first and foremost the site of the Passion* and Resurrection* of Jesus Christ. Jesus* fulfills the prophecy of Zechariah 9:9 by his final entry into Jerusalem (Mt 21:5; Jn 12:15), and here the symbolic, prophetic name "Daughter of Zion" is used. John differs from the synoptics by punctuating his whole narrative with various passages that see Jesus in Jerusalem, from 2, 13–25.

In the Gospel of Mark, Jesus' entry into Jerusalem frightens the disciples who are following him. Jerusalem becomes the place of suffering and death (Mk 10, 32 *Sq*). By contrast, Galilee becomes the place of resurrection and revelation (14:28, 16:7). Matthew modifies Mark: at the death of Jesus the rebellious city becomes the "holy city" (Mt 27:53 prepared by 4:5), where the chosen are for a time raised from the dead and appear to a great number of people.

Jerusalem is highly significant in the book of Luke. He brings together all the apparitions of the risen Jesus (Lk 24) in one single day in Jerusalem or nearby, making that place the unique center of the redemptive drama, the city of the Risen One, the site of the Pente-cost and the beginnings of the Church (Acts 1–7), where God's plan is fulfilled, where Jesus realizes salvation in history. The community of Jerusalem (Acts 15; Gal 1:18–2, 10) is the starting point of the mission* (Lk 24:47; Acts 1:8) and the center of the new faith* (Acts 2:14, 5:28, 9:21).

It seems on several occasions that Luke deliberately uses the Hellenistic form *Hierosoluma* to designate the unfaithful city; the form is used in Acts 21–23 when Paul is arrested and held in Jerusalem before being transferred to Caesarea (La Potterie 1981 and 1982, Sylva 1983). The fourth gospel (Gospels*), written after the destruction of Jerusalem, uses this form. In Galatians Paul uses the Semitic form for a positive or negative *symbolic* meaning (4, 25f.) and the Greek form for a *geographical* meaning (1:17, 2:1).

In Hebrews 12:22, Christians approach Mount Zion and the city of the living God, the celestial Jerusalem (Semitic form). Greater than the city of David and prefigured by it, Jerusalem is the "celestial Jerusalem" called "new Jerusalem" in Revelation 21:2, permanently, indestructibly founded by God (Heb 11:16, 12:22); Jerusalem comes down from heaven next to God (Rev 21:2, 10–27). It reveals the true nature of the Church as the people* of God, both body and city.

● J. Jeremias (1962), *Jerusalem zur Zeit Jesu,* 3rd Ed., Göttingen.

W. D. Davies (1975), "Jérusalem et la terre dans la tradition chrétienne," *RHPhR,* 491–533.

E. Otto (1980), *Jerusalem, die Geschichte der Heiligen Stadt: Von den Anfängen bis zur Kreuzfahrerzeit,* UB 308.

I. de La Potterie (1981), "Les deux noms de Jérusalem dans l'Évangile de Luc," *RSR* 69, 57–80; id. (1982), "Les deux noms de Jérusalem dans les Actes des Apôtres," *Bib* 63, 153–87.

Dennis D. Sylva (1983), "Ierousalem and Hierosoluma in Luke-Acts," *ZNW* 74, 207–22.

MAURICE CARREZ

See also **Apocalyptic Literature; City; Eschatology; Israel; Jesus, Historical; Kingdom of God; Parousia; Rome; Temple; Universalism**

Jesus Christ. *See* Christ and Christology; Jesus, Historical

Jesus, Historical

The term *Jesus of history,* or *historical Jesus,* designates the Jesus whose life can be reconstructed on the basis of "scientifically neutral" historical data. Neutrality is understood here as either in opposition to the intervention of faith—which transforms historical (history*) data—or in opposition to the distortions of time—which alter the memories of witnesses.

I. How Can the Historical Jesus Be Reconstructed?

Due to the scarcity and particularities of available information, methodological problems inevitably arise in any attempt to reconstruct the life and the words of a personage from antiquity. In the case of the historical Jesus the enterprise is both facilitated by the multiplicity of sources and complicated by the nonhistoriographical approach of testimonials.

1. *Documentary Sources*

We do not have direct access to Jesus' thought, as no document written by him has been handed down to us. We do have indirect access in the form of five different types of documentary sources (*see* Meier 1991) from various historical witnesses.

a) Sources from Christian Canon (in Chronological Order).   The most ancient of these is the Pauline correspondence (from the years 50–58). In addition to discussing the Crucifixion and Resurrection* of Jesus, Paul reports four pronouncements of the Lord (1 Cor 7:10 and 9:14, 1 Thes 4:16, and Rom 14:14). The apostle seems to be acquainted with some early collections of Jesus' sayings, which he uses (sometimes without quoting them) in his argumentation. There, the fundamental structure Jesus' ethics—an ethics of love (as stated in Gal 5:14)—can be found, along with the idea of an essential coherence between his life and death (2 Cor 8:9, Gal 1:3–4, and Rom 3:24–25).

The second source is the so-called *Q* source, sayings pronounced by Jesus as a master of wisdom within the horizon of the eschatological kingdom. Collected in Palestine in the years 50–60, and subsequently lost, these sayings are postulated by the majority of exegetes as underlying the Gospels of Matthew and Luke. The third source is the Gospel of Mark (written about the year 65), which is the first document that integrates the teachings of Jesus into the narrative of his life. Mark draws on the collections of miracles (miracle*), parables (parable*), and sayings presented by tradition, combing them with a narrative cycle of the Passion that had been established in the 40s within the Church of Jerusalem*. The Gospels of Matthew and Luke, which integrate materials from *Q,* constitute the fourth source. The fifth source is the Gospel of John, which includes fragmentary historical information.

b) Christian Apocrypha Sources.   The dating and the historical accuracy of the Christian apocrypha, which consists of various extracanonical early writings, are intensely debated. The oldest texts are dated from the middle of the second century, but the traditions they represent may have been taken from archaic forms close to the historical Jesus. This might be true of the Egerton 2 papyrus and the papyrus of Fayoum; the Fathers handed down to us fragments of Judeo-Christian gospels (from the Nazarenes, *Ebionites,* and Hebrews). The Coptic Gospel of Thomas (from about 170) includes 114 sayings, some showing a late Gnostic influence while others are a more sober (therefore archaic?) version Jesus' word attested by the synoptic Gospels. Certain of these sayings might emanate from teachings of Jesus that were not preserved elsewhere. For example, the Gospel of Thomas 82 reads: "Jesus said, 'He who is near me is near the fire, and he who is far from me is far from the Kingdom.' " A fragment of the Gospel of Peter (from about 150) narrates the Passion and Resurrection of Jesus with motifs close to those of Matthew's Gospel. The *Protoevangelium Jacobi* (150–200) relates the childhoods of Mary* and of Jesus, in which the theological fictions recounted may indeed contain hints of historical truths. In general, it is preferable to avoid sweeping judgments and evaluate case by case the credibility of material contained in apocryphal sources.

c) Jewish Sources.   Jewish sources are extremely rare. This quasi-silence can be explained by rivalry between Jews and Christians and hostility toward the founding hero of the Christian movement. There are about 15 allusions to *Yeshua* in the Talmud; they mention his activity as a healer and his execution (*Baraïtha Sanhedrin* 43 a *Abodah Zara* 16 b-17 a). A popular fifth-century text, the *Toledoth Yeshua,* is ironical about Jesus' impurity (purity*/impurity) and contradicts his virgin birth, making him the illegitimate son of the soldier Pentera, who supposedly suborned Mary.

Events are related on an entirely different level in a fragment of the Jewish historian Flavius Josephus's *Testimonium Flavianum,* dating from 93–94: "Now there was about this time, Jesus, a wise man, if it be lawful to call him a man, for he was a doer of wonderful works,—a teacher of such men who receive the truth with pleasure. He drew over to him both many of the Jews and many of the Gentiles.... And when Pilate...had condemned him to the cross, those that loved him at the first did not forsake him" (*Antiquities of the Jews* Book 18, 3:3; *see also* Book 20, 9:1). Although Flavius Josephus's actual text was glossed over by a Christian scribe, but with a primitive core still possible to attribute to the author, it stands as the sole attestation of Jesus independent of Christianity.

d) Latin Sources. Latin historians had more to say about the faith of the first Christians than about their master. The oldest document is a letter from Pliny the Younger to Trajan (about 111–12). This was followed by Tacitus (*Annals* 15:44) and Suetonius (*Life of the Emperor Claudius* 25:4).

2. Problems

Nevertheless, historians have no other documentation so readily abundant or close to historical events on any other figure of antiquity other than the life of Jesus. Although the Gospels were written between 65 and 90 and are based on an oral tradition and collections of sayings or narratives subsequently lost, some of which go back to the 40s, this chronological gap is minimal for ancient historiography.

But major difficulties are encountered in attempts to exploit these sources, which are not firsthand documents or neutral accounts and which do not seek the documentary exactitude demanded of a modern historian. On that count, they are no different from other biographies and histories of Jewish and Greco-Roman antiquity. Ancient historians were, of course, bound by an ethic of precision and verification of facts (*see How to Write History,* written by Lucian of Samosata in about 160). But their writings were also meant to defend a position or a point of view, which led them to select, interpret, and distort the data they collected. Neutrality was not of concern to ancient historiographers, whether Greek, Jewish, or Roman.

Furthermore, the Gospels create an additional problem for historians. Not only is their understanding of history governed by a confession of faith, but this faith in the glorified Lord is also their very reason for telling the story of Jesus and his disciples. Consequently, the modern historian in search of the historical Jesus studies the Gospels with a documentary perspective that does not coincide with the theological edification that motivated them. It is erroneous to claim that the ancient Church was not interested in setting down the words and deeds of the earthly Jesus. On the contrary, the Church believed that the glorified Lord could not be known outside of the life of the man from Nazareth. But this interest in the story of Jesus was not archeological; words and deeds were recorded in order to express their meaning for the community at hand. The miracles of healing* were told because they attested to the power (omnipotence*) of God acting through Jesus and because this power reverberated within the community. The words of Jesus were preserved but, because they were recognized as authority, they had to be modified to adapt to the situation of those who received them.

Therefore, scholars looking for the historical Jesus view the narrative framework attributed to the words and deeds of Jesus with suspicion. For example, the *Formgeschichte,* the school of literary genre or form, has demonstrated that this framework is largely a product of the literary activity of the Evangelists. Scholars search for information on the social, cultural, economic, and religious context of the land where Jesus lived, which is missing from the Gospels. This requires knowledge of intertestamentary Jewish writings, Jewish historiography (Flavius Josephus), rabbinical literature (the *Mishnah*), and Roman law. Cultural anthropology* gives an idea of the social fabric of an agrarian society in antiquity (*see* Crossan 1991).

3. Criteria of Authenticity

Oscar Cullmann is basically correct when he asserts that everything in the tradition of Jesus is secondary because it is all filtered by the faith of the post-Pascal community, and at the same time everything is authentic because whatever changes are made by the community, they are made in order to transmit the message of Jesus (Cullman, 1925). Nonetheless, four primary criteria and three secondary criteria of authenticity are applied in research aimed at going back to the most ancient strata of the tradition of Jesus (*see* Meier 1991; Fusco in Marguerat 1997).

Primary criteria: 1) Multiple attestation: The words and deeds of Jesus are reputed authentic if they are attested by at least two literary sources independent of each other (*Q*, Mark, Paul, John, Gospel of Thomas, etc.) or in more than one literary form (parable, controversy, miracle, *logion,* etc.). 2) Ecclesiastical difficulty: The words and deeds of Jesus that have created difficulties (historical or theological) in their application within the first Christian communities are retained. 3) Discontinuity: Any tradition is considered authentic if it "cannot be deduced from Judaism* or attributed to primitive Christianity, particularly where Judeo-Christianity tempered the received tradition as audacious or rearranged it" (Käsemann 1954). This criterion should be balanced by the following: 4) Sufficient explanation (or historical continuity): Anything may be attributed to the historical Jesus that helps explain certain incontestable facts about his destiny (e.g., the conflict with the authorities in Jerusalem and his physical elimination) and who helps us understand the diversity of movements derived from him in primitive Christianity (e.g., differing positions on the question of the Torah). The secondary criteria include 5) Coherence: It is postulated that the various characteristics attributed to the historical Jesus should not contradict each other. 6) Language: Words attributed to Jesus must allow for retroversion in Aramaic and have characteristics of Semitic rhetoric (antithetical parallelism, alliteration, divine passive, etc.). 7) Conformity with the Palestinian environment: Words and deeds are accepted if they mention customs, beliefs, legal procedures, commercial and agricultural practices, or socio-political conditions historically attested in first-century Palestine.

The presumption of authenticity demands the joint use of several of these primary or secondary criteria.

4. Framework for the Biography of Jesus

Reconstruction of the life of the historical Jesus operates within a chronological and geographical framework marked out by the testimony of sources and data from Jewish historiography. Researchers agree on the following information:

Birth: the year 4 B.C. (the year of Herod the Great's death).

Death: April 7 A.D. 30, which on the Jewish calendar is Friday, 14 *Nizan.* (Another possible date is April 3 A.D. 33.)

Public activity: three years, mainly in Galilee (miracles, preaching to the humble, infractions against the code of purity); then journey to Jerusalem, where he came into conflict with religious authorities, precipitating the decision to have him put to death.

II. The Historians' Quest

Up to the Enlightenment period, the question "Who is Jesus?" was answered in dogmatic* terms. Precursors of the late 17th-century English school of Deism* (John Locke et al.) had already expressed doubts on the relevance of this response.

1. Initiator

Hermann Samuel Reimarus's work *Von dem Zwecke Jesu und seiner Jünger,* which was published posthumously by Lessing in 1778, caused an uproar. The author maintained that the teachings of Jesus had been falsified by his disciples, who were disappointed by the failure of their master's pretensions to political messianism. Reimarus founded a new literary genre, the "Life of Jesus," which was marked by three major characteristics: 1) The biography of the historical Jesus was reconstructed above and beyond evangelical information, and often opposed to it. 2) The alternative between the Jewishness of Jesus and his quality as founder of a new movement was posed, and if one of these was affirmed the other tended to be denied. 3) The works created controversy within the Church; they were reproved as subversive and even blasphemous.

2. The Rationalist Quest

In a first current, the Life of Jesus imposed upon the Evangelical tradition a rationalist critique mistrustful of everything supernatural. H. E. G. Paulus (1828) and Friedrich Daniel Schleiermacher* (1832) accepted the miraculous only when it conformed to a rational explanation. A mythological current—including D. F. Strauss (1835–36), L. Couchoud (1924), and the Tübingen* school (F. C. Baur) saw the Gospels as a symbolic expression of spiritual truths; the historical reality of the life of Jesus dissolves into nothing more than a mythological concretion derived from the religious imagination of the first Christians.

3. The Liberal Quest

The middle of the 19th century is marked by the strong return to the humanity of Jesus. The Gospels are taken as biographical-type documents created out of followers' spontaneous interest. Jesus is seen as a fascinating religious personality whose psychological development needed to be reconstructed. There was a plethora of liberal "Lives of Jesus," including works by E. Renan (1863), A. Sabatier (1880), B. Weiss (1882), and A. Reville (1897). Renan's study was a brilliant success, which cannot be explained exclusively by its excellent literary quality. Renan succeeded in making an audacious synthesis of the positivist heritage ("everything in the story has a human explanation") and the imagination and sensitivity of the romantic tradition.

4. The Apocalyptic Quest

In 1906 Albert Schweitzer, summing up two centuries of "Lives of Jesus," came to a devastating conclusion on their methodological fragility—every period dressed "its" Jesus in the ideological outfit that suited it. But his combat against the recuperation by modernity of the historical Jesus did not stop there. Inspired by the works of J. Weiss (1901), Schweitzer affirmed that the reign of God, which represents the heart of Jesus' preaching, should be understood in the Jewish apocalyptic* sense. Jesus was aware of living the imminence of the end of the world and precipitating its coming by his prophetic activity; his ethics is radical because it holds for that short intermediary period remaining before the great upheaval.

The double traumatism provoked by the publication of Schweitzer's book stopped the flow of liberal biographies by declaring the failure of the attempt to give to modernity a "non-dogmatic" Jesus bearing universal values. But the reestablishment of the image of the historical Jesus in his times was so powerful that it brutally cut him off from the movement derived from him. That position was summed up in the slogan formulated by A. Loisy (1902): "Jesus announced the Kingdom and it is the Church that came."

5. The Existential Quest

The school of literary form, which followed immediately after Schweitzer, saw the primitive Church as the author of the tradition of Jesus, thus destroying every possibility of reconstructing the biography of Jesus. Rudolf Bultmann*'s *Jesus* (1926) illustrates this program, which created an unbridgeable gap between Jesus and the kerygma. Nevertheless, under the impetus of E. Käsemann, a "new quest" took shape in 1953 around the determination to articulate the historical Jesus and the kerygma. This was the line followed by Joachim Jeremias (1947), E. Fuchs (1956), Hans Conzelmann (1959), J.-M. Robinson (1960), Norman Perrin (1967), and particularly Gunther Bornkamm (1956). While recognizing the post-Pascal origin of christological formulations, these disciples of Bultmann gave value to the salvational dimension of the words and deeds of Jesus in which the present offer of the Kingdom is concretized. At the most a mediating function is recognized for the historical action of Jesus, though its christological reach is "implicit."

6. Return to the Jewishness of Jesus

The quest for the historical Jesus is currently split into three currents, whose common denominator is a revalorization of his Jewishness.

One trend is fed by the rediscovery of the Judaism of Palestine beyond the caricatures left to us by history. It underscores Jesus' participation in the apocalyptic effervescence of his times and his proximity to messianic ideals of the restoration of Israel. From this viewpoint,

integration of Jesus into the Jewish faith is admitted without reserves (Vermès 1973; Sanders 1985).

Conversely, a neoliberal current purges the tradition of Jesus of all apocalyptic elements (which are considered post-Pascal). It recenters the preaching of Jesus on a sapient-type moral message of direct communion with God, material egalitarianism, and spiritual fraternity. On the basis of strong exploitation of extra-canonical traditions (Crossan 1991), the provocative preaching of Jesus is assimilated with the teaching of the cynical philosophers (*see* Chilton-Evans 1994).

Proponents of a sociopolitical trend detect a state of social and cultural crisis in first-century Israel. The successive messianic eruptions that marked the period are understood as attempts to reform Palestinian society, and Jesus is placed within this series of protest reformers (Horsley 1985, Theissen 1986).

III. Jesus: A Unique Figure?

Palestinian Judaism at the time of Jesus was not monolithic; the sociocultural fabric was varied and multicolored. A profusion of groups, parties, and subversive cells rubbed together, sometimes actively proselytizing. Can Jesus' group be assimilated with one of them?

1. Comparable Figures

Jesus had little in common with the Saducees, the priestly aristocracy, and members of the sect of Qumran, who practiced retreat from the world. The closest comparable figures would have been the rabbi, the zealot, and the messianic prophet (*see* Schubert 1973).

Jesus shared several features with Pharisaic rabbis, including interest in commentary of the Torah (*see* Lk 6:20–49 and accounts of controversies), concern for educating the people, and formation of a circle of students who shared the life of their master. The miracle-making rabbi was also a familiar figure in Judaism (*Honi le Traceur de cercles, Onias le Juste et Hanina ben Dosa* in the first century B.C.; *see* Vermès 1973). It has been shown that most of the sayings in the Sermon on the Mount are closely analogous to the rabbinical teaching preserved in the *Mishnah* (*see* Klausner 1933). But the historical Jesus partially escaped from the model in several ways. His teaching does not enter into the casuistic (casuistry*) game of the rabbis (Mt 5:21–48). The state of disciple was neither voluntary nor transitory but permanent and on call from the master. Jesus was nomadic, unmarried, and expressly committed to breaking away from the family (Lk 14:26) in contradiction with the family ethic and sedentarization of the rabbis.

Jesus is radically separated from the Zealot movement by his ethic of non-resistance to others (Lk

6:27–35). Nevertheless, Jesus' awareness of a crisis brought about by the imminence of the Kingdom, and the active reaction it demanded, explains a rapprochement with the Zealot project, apparently with the consent of Pilate (Mk 15:2–9 and 15:17–20 and Jn 19:19).

There is greater proximity between Jesus and the numerous first-century messianic prophets (prophet and prophecy) (see Grelot 1978). John the Baptist animated a popular movement of awakening and baptized people in the Jordan for remission of sins (sin*) (Mk 1:4–5). Shortly after Jesus' death, a Samaritan prophet led a crowd of followers to Mount Garizim, with the promise of letting them see the sacred bowls that Moses had buried there; Pilate's repression was so murderous that it cost him his appointment (Josephus' *Antiquities* Book 18, 4:1–2).

The entire period of the procurators was marked by these charismatic figures who announced the advent of a "sign" that would typologically repeat the story of salvation. These miracles, which were connected with the Exodus or the entry into Canaan, brought back Israel's sacred past. Before he succumbed to Roman repression, Theudas had rallied hundreds to the messianic cause by promising them to part the waters of the Jordan in order to give them an easy passage across it (*Antiquities* Book 20, 5:1). Another prophet of the new times, the Egyptian referred to in Acts 21:38, stirred up the crowd at the Mount of Olives, predicting that they would see the walls of Jerusalem come crumbling down as in the days of Jericho (*Antiquities* Book 20, 8:6).

Jesus—who assembled disciples, preached to the crowds, announced the Kingdom, and worked signs and miracles—can be more easily compared with the messianic prophets than with the rabbis and Zealots. And it would seem that this was his contemporaries' opinion because the Gospels say that the crowd took Jesus for a prophet (Lk 7:16 and 7:39 and Mk 14:65 and 16, 4) or compared him to prophets of old (Mk 6:15 and 8:28). The people asked him for a "sign" (Lk 11:29). The loaves shared in the desert (Mk 6:34–44) are certainly a substitute for manna. Furthermore, the discourse of Jesus included typical elements of prophetic discourse, such as announcements of salvation, threats, predictions, and visions (Lk 10:18).

But what accounts for this profusion of messianic prophets in first-century Israel?

2. Messianic Protest Movements
Close study of sociocultural components of first-century Palestinian society reveals a situation of social and religious crisis (see Theissen in Marguerat 1997). Though the country enjoyed the exceptional political stability prevailing in the Roman Empire during the *Principat (pax romana),* this facilitated the forceful strategy of cultural assimilation practiced in the provinces under the Roman yoke. The Pilate government (A.D. 26–36) consistently strove to acculturate Palestine to the values of the empire. Coins were minted with pagan symbols, military insignia with the effigy of the emperor were introduced in Jerusalem, and the treasure of the temple was spoliated to finance public works (see *Antiquities* Book 18, 3:1).

The greatest resistance in the entire empire against this policy of assimilation was in Palestine. On the death of Herod the Great (4 B.C.), a "war of brigands" brought forth numerous messianic pretenders to the throne; the shepherd Athronges crowned himself with the royal diadem before a crowd of enthusiastic followers. When Archelaus was deposed (6 A.D.), Judas the Galilean led a campaign of refusal to pay taxes based on the theology that the land belongs to YHWH. His partisans, fired by this theocratic ideal, were crushed by the Roman legions. Josephus highlighted John the Baptist's strong criticism of Herod Antipas on the grounds of morality and respect for the law (*Antiquities* Book 18, 5:2). It is no surprise that in this tense atmosphere Jesus was interrogated on the emblematic question of taxes due to Caesar (Mk 12:13–17).

The growth of messianism* in first-century Palestine should be understood against a background of resistance against cultural assimilation. This resistance came from the common people because the aristocracy of Judea and Galilee (including the Saducees) were affiliated with the values of the ruling power. The survival of Israel's religious traditions was endangered under pressure from Roman modernism. This caused an effervescence of messianic piety focused on the imperative need to restore the purity of a land sullied by the presence of sinners and the impious. It led to the emergence of charismatic prophets, spiritual adventurers who exacerbated Jewish nationalism under the theocratic ideal of the Kingdom of God.

The activity of the historical Jesus should be situated in a context of the rise of protest messianism. This helps us understand how Jesus aroused the interest of the humble, but it also explains why some were disappointed and rejected him because he did not support rising Jewish nationalism.

3. Jesus, Disciple of the Baptist
The Gospels let us imagine a close affinity with one of those prophets, John the Baptist, whose role was changed by the Christian tradition after the facts. Jesus, like John, proclaimed a message of conversion. The first Christians reversed their roles, making John a precursor of Jesus when in fact he was the master and Jesus the pupil.

The comparisons are obvious. Jesus presented himself to the baptism* of John; this episode is related to the manifestation of the divine filiation* of Jesus (Mk 1:9–11). The public activity of Jesus in Galilee followed that of John (Mk 1:14). The two are often associated, either by Herod (Mk 6:16), by the multitudes (Mk 6:14 and 8:28), or by Jesus himself, who associates his rejection with that of John the Baptist (Mk 11:27–33 and Mt 11:18–19). Jesus honored John and raised him above the Old Testament prophets (Mt 11:9 and Lk 7:26).

The first Christians did not invent these parallels. On the contrary, the proximity of these two prophets of the Kingdom soon became troublesome for the primitive Church, which was in rivalry with Baptist circles. The criterion of ecclesiastical difficulties applies here. Christianity strove to subordinate John the Baptist to Jesus; the fourth gospel is the clearest testimony to this reversal of hierarchy (Jn 1:19–36 and 3:22–4:3).

It is most likely that when John was executed in the year 28, Jesus took over for his master (Mk 1:14). Like his master, he called for conversion and founded the urgency on the proximity of the Kingdom (Mt 3:8 and 4:17). Like John, he destroyed all spiritual security based on belonging to the holy people (Mt 3:7, 12:41, and 8:11–12). His first disciples came from John's circle (Jn 1, 29–42). Jesus did not found a separate community like the Pharisees or members of the sect of Qumran. Jesus addressed himself to all the people and particularly to the outcasts of the official religion as did John (Lk 3:10–14 , 7:28–29, and Mt 21:32).

But these close affinities also enlighten Jesus' originality. The very fact that the Baptist movement and the Jesus movement became competitive early in their development indicates that these two theologies, which arose in the same place, were not identical. The first difference is that Jesus was not an ascetic; he did not live in retreat in the desert but favored public places. In fact, he was reprimanded for not fasting (Mk 2:18) and called a glutton (Lk 7:33–34). The second difference, judging from the scattered remnants of John's preaching available to us, is that John's announcement of the conversion seemed to function against a background of the wrath of God. Jesus transformed the Baptist's preaching of judgment and restructured it around a God of grace, breaking the crime-punishment correlation. Jesus' God is a God of limitless love, a God who loves bad people as much as good people (Mt 5:45). The announcement of judgment persists in Jesus' teaching but the primacy of salvation, backed by miracles, is patent; divine wrath is no longer the reason for action. On this major point, the Galilean reversed his master's message (see Becker 1972 and 1996).

A third difference touches on Jesus' statute. Jesus

does not announce, he accomplishes. By acts of exorcism*, he makes the royalty of God intervene as a present rather than a future reality. "But if it is by the finger of God that I cast out demons, then the kingdom of God has come upon you" (Lk 11:20). John threatened the imminent advent of the God of wrath; Jesus was aware that he accomplished, by his words and deeds, the turn of events called for in the incantations of the messianic prophets. The future of God is so pressing that it has already invaded the present; the Kingdom is "in the midst of you" (Lk 17:21). The man from Nazareth was aware of causing an upheaval in the history of God and men.

IV. The Horizon of the Reign of God

Initiatives taken by Jesus concretize a strong conviction: Jesus was aware of living and, by his words and deeds, hastening the coming of the reign of God. His activity was thoroughly invested in the face of the *basileia tou theou,* a concept that is both spatial (Kingdom of God) and temporal (reign of God), open to the immediacy of an "already there" and the imminence of a "not yet."

1. Insuppressible Urgency

The words and deeds of Jesus were dominated by a sense of urgency. The call to follow him upset the most untouchable solidarities. To follow Jesus was to take leave of his kind (Lk 9:61–62), ignore burial duties for his own father (Lk 9:59–60), and even "hate his own father and mother and wife and children and brothers and sisters" (Lk 14, 26). This disregard for funeral rites and familial responsibilities was a radical departure that was unknown in antiquity, except among the Greek cynical philosophers.

There were other signs of the urgent need to announce the Kingdom. Disciples were ordered to bring neither purse nor sandals and not to greet anyone on the way (Lk 10:4). Pressed by the imperative necessity of saving lives, Jesus healed on the Sabbath* (Mk 3:4 and Lk 13:15). In Jesus' commentary on the Torah, the imperative of loving others outweighed all other rules; even the sacrificial rite at the Temple of Jerusalem had to be interrupted, if necessary, to reconcile with others (Mt 5:23–24). The parables of judgment induced a rapid, decisive reaction in the face of the coming event (Mk 13:34–36, Mt 25:1–13, and Lk 12:42–48 and 16:1–8).

In short, the state of emergency dictated by the imminence of the Kingdom precipitated everything, including the call of Jesus to walk in his footsteps *(sequela Christi),* the healing, the reading of the Law, and the discourse in parables. "Truly I say to you, there are some standing here who will not taste death before they see the kingdom of God has come with power" (Mk 9:1). Jesus had the conviction that he was living in the immediate proximity of the coming of God who, by his judgment, would eliminate all causes of suffering and assemble his own around him. Nothing else mattered but the call to convert before the coming of the great day of liberation (Mk 1:15).

2. Signs

The conviction of the approaching reign was concretized in acts that have the power of signs—healing and speaking in parables.

There are many traces in the Gospels of Jesus' miraculous activity. Five different types of miracles are attributed to him: healing (to the point of raising the dead), exorcism (where a man is liberated from the evil spirit that dispossessed him of himself), miracles justifying a rule (for example, forgiving sins), feats of generosity (the abundance of the loaves), and lifesaving on the lake (vanquishing the disciples' fear).

As a matter of fact, miracles of this sort were known in Jewish writings and Greco-Roman literature. The Romans had healers such as Apollonios of Thyane, the Jews had miracle-making rabbis and messianic prophets who performed feats. The miraculous activity of Jesus was not an exception. Jesus had the same skills as other first-century miracle-makers, and the way he cured a deaf mute (putting a finger in the ears, spitting, and touching the tongue; Mk 7:33) corresponds to common therapeutic practices in antiquity.

Nonetheless, it cannot be concluded that the healing activity of Jesus blended in with commonplace popular medicine of his times. Jesus gave an uncommon sense to his miracles. He made them signs of the reign already there (Lk 7:20–22 and Mt 11:2–5). The distinction between Jesus and other healers in his times lies in his assigning the miracles to the royalty of God. His cures and exorcisms were indications that God's titanic battle against evil was under way then and there in the combat of Jesus against illness, which disfigures humanity. Sending out 72 disciples charged with the power to exorcise, he exclaimed: "I saw Satan fall like lightning from heaven. Behold, I have given you authority to tread upon serpents and scorpions, and over all the power of the enemy; and nothing shall hurt you" (Lk 10:18–19). By his healing acts Jesus restored the dignity of the human in the order of creation, contesting a religious culture in which evil was taken as a fatality and a divine sanction and the ailing were considered responsible for their suffering (Jn 9:2–3).

Jesus did not invent parables as a form of communication but he made much greater use of them than did the rabbis from whom he borrowed the form. Jesus did not eschew the charm of tales. The Gospels attribute some 40 parables to him. Why was that so? Parables, by their indirect veiled discourse, are the language suited to the Kingdom; they make it known that an event has taken place in the present, which changes the face of things. But this mystery must be sought out. The parables of growth give to understand that the grandeur of the reign is to be paradoxically discovered in the humble environment of the activity of Jesus (Mk 4:3–9 and Lk 13:18–21). The relation between history and the reign is reversed. History is not hurtling to a brutal end as described by the Apocalypticians; the reign invests the present. The parable gives word to the hidden presence of a God whose surprising initiatives upset the everyday order (Lk 15:11–32 and Mt 20, 1–16).

There is a correspondence between the parables and the activity of Jesus, which can be seen in their biographical dimension. The meals Jesus shared with the sinners emerge in the parable of the Prodigal Son (Lk 15, 11–32) and the invitation to the banquet (Lk 14:15–24). His offer of forgiveness (Mk 2:5) appears in the story of the merciless debtor (Mt 18:23–35). His openness to marginal religions comes through in the parable of the Good Samaritan (Lk 10:30–37) and the one about the Pharisee and the Publican (Lk 18:9–14). The patron of the Workers in the Vineyard justifies his apparent disdain for the law (Lk 20:1–16). Thus the narrative material of the parables, fruit of the free imagination of Jesus, was also steeped in his life, encounters, and conflicts. It verbalizes his experiences and includes a clearly autobiographical dimension.

3. The Choice of Social Solidarity

The Gospels and the Talmud agree in noting the shocking liberty taken by Jesus in his associations. He espoused all social categories marginalized by Jewish society of the times, whether by social or political distrust or religious discrimination.

Jesus did not accept the ostracism of tax collectors for political reasons (Lk 19:1–10 and Mt 11:19) or the Samaritans for religious reasons (Lk 17:11–19). He chose children as the model of openness toward God (Mk 10:13–16). He refused the religious disqualification of women (woman*) by accepting them in his entourage (Lk 8:2–3). He allowed the ailing to approach and touch him and used his healing powers to reintegrate them into the holy people. He spoke out to country people, those people of the land (ham-ha-aretz) decried by the Pharisees because they could not respect the code of purity and pay the three tithes levied on every product.

The meal partaken with the reprobates and women of easy virtue was the most stinging sign of Jesus' rejection of all particularism (Mk 2:15–16 and Lk 15:2). These meals, which indicate an option for social and religious tolerance, are set against a background of the much-awaited messianic banquet of the end of times (Mt 8:11–12). They anticipate the banquet of salvation while already embracing those who would be taken into the Kingdom of God to come. We should note that community meals at Qumran were also considered as anticipation of the messianic banquet that would be presided by the Messiah-priest (1Qsa II:17–21 and 4Q 521). Thus it appears that the meals of which Jesus partook are "expressions of the mission and the message of Jesus (Mk 2:17); these are the eschatological banquets, first manifestations of the banquet of Salvation at the end of time (Mk 2:19)" (Jeremias 1971). Table companionship with the outcast displays Jesus' hope for a reign that invests the entire society of his times, contradicting the structure of Jewish society as partitioned by the religious order founded on the Torah and the temple.

4. Disciples and Adherents

The Gospels clearly stress the group of twelve disciples gathered around their master; the entourage of the historical Jesus, however, was organized in three concentric circles. First, the circle of the Twelve, all Galileans; then, men and women who followed Jesus (Lk 8:1–3 and Mk 15:40–41); and a larger circle of sympathizers, such as Joseph of Arimathea, Nicodemus, and Martha and Mary.

This large range was the opposite of a sect. Unlike the Master of Justice of Qumran, Jesus did not found a cell and did not retire to the desert in order to preserve the purity of his followers. The composition of the group of the Twelve confirms the option of openness; there was a tax collector, a Zealot, and men with Greek and Hebrew names (Mk 3:16–19). All or most came from the "people of the land" marginalized by the law. This anti-elite composition was all the more striking in that the number 12, based on the 12 tribes of Israel, is indicative of a symbolic reconstitution of the people of God (Lk 22:30). The circle of the Twelve prefigures the Israel of the Kingdom, the family of God. The God of Jesus does not select or classify when he reassembles in his reign; he welcomes all those who recognize themselves as seeking forgiveness (Mk 2:17).

Jesus' strategy of integration was the opposite of that practiced by the Pharisees, John the Baptist, and the messianic prophets who sought by exclusion to constitute a pure Israel. Jesus did not found the Nazarene sect, or a remnant of Israel, nor a separate synagogue that would become the Church. His ambition was to reform the faith of Israel by breaking up the internal fundamentalist strains that nourished the hope

of the Kingdom. The Twelve symbolized and at the same time realized a salvation that excluded no one. This prepared a theology of a universal God, the God of each and every one, which would later be spread by the first Christians (Acts 10:34–35 and Rom 1:16).

5. Recomposition of the Torah

Within the extraordinary diversity of first-century Judaism the Torah represents the seat of identity par excellence. Thus, it is not surprising that representatives of Jewish factions who wished to evaluate Jesus questioned him on his interpretation of the law.

The Gospels point out Jesus' infractions against the Law of the Sabbath, based on the axiom: "The Sabbath was made for man, not man for the Sabbath" (Mk 2:27). This position, which corresponds to the most liberal currents of Judaism, did not invalidate the principle of Sabbath rules. The novelty of Jesus is that, unlike the rabbis, he placed the preservation of life as an absolute instead of regulating the particular cases for exemption. The individual is free to manage this as he sees fit, but the rule must bend before this absolute.

The posture adopted with respect to the Sabbath exemplifies the position of Jesus with regard to the law. Jesus placed himself within the practice of the Torah, which he ratified like any other observant Jew. But his assent to the divine imperative went with a recomposition of the law around the call to love. The will of God is entirely recapitulated in the double call to love God and love one's fellow man (Mk 12:28–34). Jesus was not the first to opt for the priority of the ethical law over the ritual law; Hellenistic Judaism had already done this. The focus on love, and notably placing love of one's neighbor over love of God, was not foreign to the great liberal rabbi Hillel, who lived one generation before Jesus. But these rapprochements, though they confirm the integration of Jesus in the debate of Judaism on the Torah, should not obscure the originality of his interpretation of the law, which can be particularly grasped in his new reading of the Decalogue (Mt 5:21–48).

First, the decision to give predominance to love was portentous because it placed in the heart of the Torah an instance that must govern its reading and can authorize the validation or invalidation of such any given rule. Thus, the prohibition against murder must be broadened to wrath (Mt 5:21–22), whereas the Talion Law is abrogated (Mt 5:38–42). This means that the law is no longer to be respected because it is the law; it should be followed because it serves love, and only when it serves love.

Second, when Jesus recomposed the Torah around the imperative of love, he ignored the rabbinical rule that requires exegesis* to be based on the tradition of the elders. Jesus opposed to the elders an "I" that was at the same time sovereign, impertinent, and liberating (*see* Marguerat 1991). The "but I say to you" of the antitheses (Mt 5:21–48) indicates that Jesus takes his authority from God without deriving it from Moses. The thrust of God's unconditional love is so strong that it leads him to collide with the dogma* that Judaism holds most dear—the infallibility of the law. Jesus declared that only obedience guided by love could claim to be infallible. But what was the image of God that authorized him to overturn the law?

6. The God of Jesus

Side by side with the reference to the God of the Kingdom who will give welcome to the eschatological banquet, along with the reference to the God-judge who will reward each according to his works, the ethical discourse of Jesus was open to tonalities close to the literature of the wise men of Israel.

Jesus' call to take no heed for the morrow is based on the example of the birds in the sky and the lilies of the fields, whose needs are magnificently satisfied by God (Mt 6, 25–34). The exhortation to the disciples to testify without fear refers back to the God-providence* who watches over every single creature (Mt 10:29–31). The moral exhortation is governed here by a theology of the Creation* that does modify the eschatological register.

The same holds true when Jesus calls on the experience of God: "Love your enemies, and pray for those who persecute you, so that you may be sons of your Father who is in heaven; for he makes his sun rise on the evil and on the good, and sends rain on the just and on the unjust" (Mt 5:44–45). Several parables work on this precedence of God's gracious offer over the response of the believer—the invitation to the banquet (Mt 22:1–10 and Lk 14:16–24), the Unmerciful Servant (Mt 18:23–35), the fig tree (Lk 13, 6–9), the treasure in the field and the pearl (Mt 13:44–46). These parables confirm the preponderant place occupied by the precedence of God's bounty over the call to act. The God of Jesus is a God of unconditional love. On this conviction he establishes his practice of welcome (partaking of meals with reprobates) as well as the invitation to call God by the familiar name *abba,* that is, "daddy" (Mk 14:36), and the call to unbounded love for others (Mt 5:43–48).

Here we confront a sapiential dimension of Jesus' preaching that led some scholars to ask if he is not closer to the wise men than the messianic prophets (*see* Chilton-Evans 1994). However, the factor that clearly distinguishes Jesus from the wise men is the absence, in his thought, of reflection on the possibility of acting according to the required obedience. The ethic of the Sermon on the Mount, with its immoderate demands (to love one's enemies, not to have concern for the morrow), contradicts the concern of sages and rabbis to limit obedience, keeping it within the measure of the reasonable. Jesus did not follow this policy of the acceptable. The conscience of God that inhabited him was so imperious that the shadow of the reign totally invaded the present. Excess and absolutism were the only fitting tones (Marguerat 1997).

V. The Crisis

According to the scenario retained by the synoptic Gospels, the conflict between Jesus and the religious leaders of Jerusalem culminated during Jesus' visit to the holy city at the end of his life.

1. The Attack against the Temple

We do not know what led the historical Jesus to leave Galilee, where he had been practicing his activity and recruiting disciples, and go to Jerusalem for the Passover* pilgrimage in the year 30. Up until then he had been a local prophet. Did he now want to give national scope to his message? Did his disciples push him? Was the spectacular Cleansing of the Temple his sole objective?

As it happens, his entry into the holy city fired a latent, explosive messianic effervescence (Mk 11:1–10). The celebration of a Last Supper with his companions does denote that Jesus was aware of the gravity of the conflict engaged with the priestly authorities. Even if we do not project into this event the salvational dimension of his death, as would the first Christians, the way that Jesus integrated the eventuality of his death as a manifestation of his theological conviction can be noted. (Schürmann, 1975, speaks of "pro-existence.")

Basically what the sources report on his life in Jerusalem is the cleansing of the temple (Mk 11:15–17). This act is, of course, related to the prophetic protest against the moral perversion of cultural rites (Jer 7:11). Moreover, its destructive symbolism fits into the messianic perspective of the disappearance of the old temple in favor of the new temple that would mark the era of salvation (*see* Sanders 1985). The first Christians interpreted this act as an abolition of the institution of the temple in favor of mediation with God within the framework of the community, the body of Christ* (1 Cor 3:16–17 and 6:19, Mk 14:58, Acts 6:14, and Jn 2:19–22). Might this interpretation be postulated on the commentary Jesus made on this act in the circle of his followers? Whatever the case may be, the sympathy of the crowd that Jesus had acquired was lost by the attack against the temple. The crowd turned against the prophet from

Nazareth, facilitating the manipulation by the religious authorities that resulted in the withdrawal of all popular support from Jesus.

2. The Crucifixion

Jesus was sentenced to death by crucifixion for the crime of high treason against the state, in application of the *Lex Juliae majestatis.* It is common knowledge that the procurators, and especially Pontius Pilate, made extensive use of this jurisdiction. But the denunciation, according to all evidence, was Jewish. The Sanhedrin, dominated by the Sadduceen aristocracy, gave Pilate the motive for capital punishment.

Execution on the cross was a long, drawn-out torture, a slow process of tantalization that ended in death by asphyxiation. The agony of the Nazarene was abnormally brief, indicating a weak constitution, which surprised Pilate (Mk 15:44). Jesus died in the afternoon on the eve of Passover (Mk 15:34). Already the lambs were slaughtered at the temple and families were preparing to partake of the Passover supper. Joseph of Arimathea, a follower, got permission to bury Jesus in a sepulcher instead of letting his corpse be thrown to the dogs.

3. Why Was Jesus Condemned?

The crime of messianic insurrection sufficed to set in motion the repressive apparatus of Pontius Pilate, who was described by King Agrippa I in the year 40 as a merciless, cruel governor (*see* Lk 13:1). But what was the real motive for the physical elimination of the Galilean?

The scene of the trial before the Sanhedrin is a Christian recomposition (Mk 14:53–65). Judaism did not generally denounce men to the Romans for messianic pretension. However, the attack against the temple was infinitely serious, considering the symbolic role of the temple in the national conscience. Josephus reports the case of Jesus ben Ananias, an oracular prophet who, four years before the Jewish War, went around Jerusalem announcing the destruction of the city and its temple. The priestly aristocracy handed him over to the Romans, who took him for a madman and released him (*The War of the Jews* Book 6, 5:3). This parallel accredits the idea that Jesus was rejected for false prophecy (prophet* and prophecy) (messianic) and sacrilege against the holy place.

J. Klausner, a Jewish scholar, explains that Judaism had to get rid of Jesus because he was an extremist whose radical, extravagant interpretation of the Torah and critique of religious practices imperiled national cohesion. By his outrages, Jesus gave the "kiss of death" to Judaism (Klausner 1933). We will also note that Klausner includes liberties taken by Jesus in interpreting the law among the causes for this incrimination. It is likely that this was an additional motive, though it was not reason enough for accusing Jesus. The absence of any mention of participation of Pharisees during the proceedings might well indicate that the sympathy awakened by Jesus in their ranks was not extinguished and, further, that the dispute was not primarily centered on the Torah. Several years later, Stephen was accused of crime against the temple and the law and stoned to death in Jerusalem (Acts 6:8–7:60).

VI. Jesus the Messiah

What awareness did the historical Jesus have of himself, his role, and his mission? Documentary sources situate us before a paradox: On the one hand, Jesus kept silent about his identity; on the other hand a clear claim to authority transpired in his preaching on the reign.

1. Jesus and the Son of Man

Almost all the declarations Jesus made about his identity (*see* the Johannine pronouncements beginning *"I am"*) emanated from the Christian community. The synoptics respected the Nazarene's discretion about his identity. None of the titles such as Son of God, Son of David, Messiah, Christ (except in Mark 12:35–37) is pronounced by him. However "Son of man" often comes up in his statements.

Since the parables of Enoch (1 Enoch 37–71) the expression *Son of man* had designated a celestial figure connected to the eschatological judgment. On several occasions Jesus associated his person with the Son of man (Mk 2:10, Mt 19:28, and Lk 7:34, 9:58, 12:8–10, and 17:26–30,). However, the Aramaic expression he used, *bar nasha,* can also be understood as the common equivalent of "I." Jesus drew on the title Son of man to claim the power to forgive sins (Mk 2:10), consequently rendering obsolete the mediation of the sacrificial cult. He ruled that the attitude adopted toward him would be sanctioned in the Kingdom by the Son of man (Lk 12:8–10). He contrasted the dignity of the Son of man with the fragility of his own nomadic existence (Lk 9:58).

Exegetes are divided on this point; some deny all authenticity to the sayings on the Son of man, others think that Jesus did declare himself to be the Son of man. But it is observed that: 1) Jesus never identified himself explicitly with the Son of man; and 2) the profusion of sayings on the Son of man prohibit a priori their attribution to the primitive Church. To sum up, the historical Jesus understood himself to be the person who by his words and deeds introduces the reign of

God into history. He saw himself as the one who initiated the ending, but without confusing himself with the principal agent of that end. Nevertheless, he was convinced that the position adopted with respect to him would be a decisive criterion at the time of judgment by the Son of man (Lk 12:8–10; *see also* the Gospel of Thomas 82).

2. Implicit Christology

Did Jesus call himself the Messiah (messianism*/Messiah)? Except for the Christian recomposition in Mark 14:62, the Gospels attribute a deferred reply when the question is put to him (Mt 11:2–5). This vagueness about his identity is the signature of a man who effaces himself behind the event he brings to fruition. The Galilean does not say he is the Messiah but the "finger of God" (Lk 11:20). Jesus was certainly aware that he surpassed the prophets. He categorically affirmed that here there was more than Jonas and more than Solomon (Lk 11:31–32), but it is clear that this statement avoids any clear fixation of identity. The announcement of the coming of the reign predominates over any form of messianic pretension. Jesus' preaching was millenarian; it was not the harangue of a pretender to the title. This subtle game can be labeled "implicit Christology [Christ* and Christology]."

The refusal to assume any messianic title could well express a withdrawal from the underlying nationalistic ideology associated with all the Jewish messianisms, whether prophetic, royal, or priestly. But in upsetting the game of messianic aspirations, in claiming the prerogatives of the Son of man without confusing himself with him (Mk 2:10), in referring back to messianic signs without declaring himself (Mt 11:2–5), Jesus announced and prepared for the surpassing of the messianic categories on which the faith of the first Christians worked (*see* Grappe in Marguerat 1997).

Nonetheless, the Romans condemned Jesus as a messianic pretender (Mk 15:18 and 26 and Jn 19:19). This confirms to what extent the words and deeds of Jesus, despite his reserve, offered a hold to popular messianic aspirations (Mk 6:30–44, 8:27–30, and 11:1–10).

3. Easter: Blossoming of the Faith

The events of Easter are inscribed in history as a strong spiritual experience for the companions of Jesus. Even if the outlines of this revelation remain historically out of reach (irreconcilable divergence among the Evangelists), its effects in history are obvious. The disciples in flight reassembled, their fear turned into courage, and the death of Jesus was no longer considered as a failure but as the solidarity of God with the impotence of the reprobate. The memory of the Master's words begins.

Overwhelmed witnesses, the disciples, bring a decisive testimony—the identity of the Crucified/Resuscitated is not to be detached from that of the Galilean.

Easter would function as focal point of new reading or rather new readings of the history of Jesus. The question of the identity of the Galilean became primordial as the spread of Christologies made explicit that which the Master had deliberately left in suspense. The varying Christologies should be understood as so many attempts to respond to the mystery of the one who had always been a question for those who encountered him. The first formulations of faith in Jesus found their cultural matrix in the Jewish apocalyptic tradition, reservoir of messianic hopes.

VII. The Jesus of History and Theology

By preserving and canonizing four Gospels, which are four new Pascal readings of the history of the earthly Jesus, the primitive Church sanctioned a theological choice. The identity of Christ cannot be grasped outside of a narrative reconstruction of the Galilean's life. All Christological discourse, then, finds its standard and limit in the exposition of the words and deeds of Jesus of Nazareth. Forever after, the scripture of the Gospels refers the knowledge of the Lord that the Christians confess to the field of a past history. Whoever claims to approach the Christ of faith must verify his knowledge by attachment, by the narrative mediation, to the words and deeds of the Jesus of history.

This choice is theological. By posing the irreducibility of the history of the Galilean as criterion of all christological words, the gospel assigns to theology a responsibility of conformity with the Incarnation*. A theology attached to the vicissitudes of the life of the Galilean, his encounters and conflicts, his wrath and his compassion, will not be inclined to turn into an escapist spirituality. In the Christian regime, reference to the earthly Jesus constitutes the site of obligatory verification of all words on salvation.

It has already been said that the memory of the earthly Jesus that structures the theology of Paul, Mark, and John is not to be confused with the reconstruction of the historical Jesus undertaken in modern research. The first Christian theologians assuredly did not subscribe to the canons of historical exactitude, though in his way Luke was not a stranger to the concerns of a historian. Yet the Evangelists and the scholars who search for the historical Jesus participate in the same movement back to the Jesus of history. In canonizing the four Gospels, the primitive Church ratified both the plurality of access to the worldly Jesus and the impossibility of claiming a unique reading of the Galilean's life. The quest for the historical Jesus confirms this verdict by its very incompletion because, like all historical undertakings, it remains constantly open to new reconstructions. But this incompletion in research makes sense theologically, for the outstanding uncertainty about the biography of the Galilean impedes closure of the dogmatic debate on Christ.

- H. S. Reimarus (1778), *Von dem Zwecke Jesu und seiner Jünger,* Ed. G. E. Lessing, Braunschweig.
- E. Renan (1863), *Vie de Jésus,* Paris.
- A. Loisy (1902), *L'Évangile et l'Église,* Paris.
- A. Schweitzer (1906), *Von Reimarus zu Wrede: Eine Geschichte der Leben-Jesu-Forschung,* Tübingen.
- O. Cullmann (1925), "Les récentes études sur la formation de la tradition évangélique," *RHPhR* 5, 459–77, 582–94.
- R. Bultmann (1926), *Jesus,* Berlin.
- J. Klausner (1933), *Jésus de Nazareth: Son temps—sa vie—sa doctrine* (original in Hebrew), Paris.
- E. Käsemann (1954), "Das Problem des historischen Jesus," *ZThK* 51, 125–53.
- G. Bornkamm (1956), *Jesus von Nazareth,* Stuttgart.
- H. Conzelmann (1959), "Jesus Christus," *RGG* 3 3, 619–53.
- E. Fuchs (1960), *Gesammelte Aufsätze,* II: *Zur Frage nach dem historischen Jesus,* Tübingen.
- J. M. Robinson (1960), *Kerygma und historischer Jesus,* Zurich.
- X. Léon-Dufour (1963), *Les Évangiles et l'histoire de Jésus,* Paris.
- D. Flusser (1968), *Jesus,* Reinbek.
- J. Jeremias (1971), *Neutestamentliche Theologie,* I: *Die Verkündigung Jesu,* Gütersloh.
- E. Trocmé (1971), *Jésus de Nazareth vu par les témoins de sa vie,* Neuchâtel.
- J. Becker (1972), *Johannes der Täufer und Jesus von Nazareth,* BSt 63; id. (1996), *Jesus von Nazareth,* Berlin-New York.
- K. Schubert (1973), *Jesus im Lichte der Religionsgeschichte des Judentums,* Vienna.
- G. Vermès (1973), *Jesus the Jew,* Glasgow.
- J. Dupont (1975) (Ed.), *Jésus aux origines de la christologie,* BEThL 40.
- H. Schürmann (1975), *Jesus ureigener Tod,* Leipzig.
- P. Grelot (1978), *L'espérance juive à l'heure de Jésus,* Paris.
- Ch. Perrot (1979), *Jésus et l'histoire,* Paris.
- R. A. Horsley (1985), *Bandits, Prophets and Messiahs: Popular Movements at the Time of Jesus,* San Francisco.
- W. G. Kümmel (1985), *Dreissig Jahre Jesusforschung (1950–1980),* BBB 60.
- E. Sanders (1985), *Jesus and Judaism,* London.
- G. Theissen (1986), *Der Schatten des Galiläers,* Munich.
- J. Schlosser (1987), *Le Dieu de Jésus,* LeDiv 129.
- C. A. Evans (1989), *Life of Jesus Research: An Annotated Bibliography,* NTTS 13.
- D. Marguerat (1990), *L'homme qui venait de Nazareth: Ce qu'on peut aujourd'hui savoir de Jésus,* Aubonne; id. (1991), "Jésus et la Loi dans la mémoire des premiers chrétiens," in *La mémoire et le temps: Mélanges P. Bonnard,* Geneva, 55–74; id. (1997) (Ed.), *Jésus de Nazareth: Nouvelles approches d'une énigme,* Genève.
- J. D. Crossan (1991), *The Historical Jesus: The Life of a Mediterranean Jewish Peasant,* San Francisco.
- J. P. Meier (1991 and 1994), *A Marginal Jew: Rethinking the Historical Jesus,* 2 vols., New York.
- B. Chilton, C. A. Evans (1994) (sous la dir. de), *Studying the Historical Jesus: Evaluation of the State of Current Research,* NTTS 19.
- Ch. Perrot (1998), *Jésus,* Paris.

DANIEL MARGUERAT

See also **Apocalyptic Literature; Apostle; Bultmann, Rudolf; Christ and Christology; Conscience; Gospels; History; Kingdom of God; Law and Christianity; Mary; Messianism/Messiah; Miracle; Mysticism; Narrative; Parable; Passion; Resurrection of Christ; Son of Man; Temple; Theology**

Joachim of Fiore

1135–1202

The work of the Calabrian abbot Joachim of Fiore (1135–1202) represents the first attempt at apocalyptic* millenarianism during the Middle Ages. It was, however, an orthodox millenarianism, compared with the literal chiliasm refuted by Augustine*. Joachim was a monastic reformer who in 1187 abandoned the Cistercians to found a new order in Fiore. Like Bernard of Clairvaux, he disputed Scholastic (Scholasticism*) Trinitarian theology* and accused Pierre Lombard of *quaternitas*—that is, of introducing too clear a disjunction between substance and Person* (*Psalt,* 229 r-v, e 277, *De vita s. Benedicti,* 76–77, *Liber Figurarum,* ms. Dresden, f. 89r).

Joachim could conceive of neither a unity separate from Persons and anterior to them nor of Persons cut off from substance. And in order to preserve the prerogatives of a God who was "triune *but* not composed," a *but* which was not singular (*De articulus* *fidei* 8), he went from the "trinum" to the "unum." The fundamental question, therefore, was how can three Persons be one? The answer was based upon the notion of *inesse* (to exist within). Each of the three Persons exists within the two others; the dynamism of the reciprocal relations constitutes the substance of divine life. Considering intra-Trinitary relations, Joachim mentioned two *diffinitiones* of the Trinity. The first was symbolized by the triangular letter *alpha (missio):* the Father* was at the summit, and he sent the Son and the Spirit. The second was symbolized by the lowercase letter omega *(processio),* of which the *virgula* in the center represented the Spirit (Holy* Spirit) that emerged from the Father and the Son. And these two figures referred back to two different representations of history, according to a ternary model (three states, three orders) and a binary model (two Persons [person*], two testaments).

Joachim was convinced that the two models were not mutually exclusive, and he endeavored, therefore, to integrate them reciprocally. As a result, his name and his doctrinal legacy remain tied to this ternary, which represents the most innovative aspect of his doctrine. Joachim believed that all through history, therefore, there came three stages, in succession and partially superimposed—that of the Father (the time before the law and under the law, *ordo conjugalis*), the Son (the time of grace*, *ordo clericalis*), and of the Holy Spirit (the time of an even greater grace, *ordo spiritualis*). The third state, which had been gestating since the time of Benedict, marked a significant progress in comparison with the two preceding ones. It was indeed through the Holy Spirit that the full manifestation of the Spirit would allow "spiritual men" to decipher in its entirety the divine mystery still sealed in the letter of the Old and New Testament. The third state was, therefore, an era where history would grow younger. The meek and humble would be its protagonists, and during this time the promise of the *Magnificat* would be fulfilled, and the mystery of the divine election (choice*) of the youngest—Jacob—instead of the eldest—Esau—would be fully revealed (*see Dial. de praesc.* I). Issues such as the future existence of an ecclesiastical hierarchy, of the permanence of the sacraments (sacrament*), and of the role and the aims of the monastic elite remained open for historiography to debate.

In Joachimism, the principle of concord, fundamental for a precise understanding of history, was no longer applied simply to the relations between Old and New Testaments, as in the earlier exegetic tradition. The Joachite concord was more complex and allowed one to establish a perfect, or almost perfect, rule of correspondence among various generations situated at the same level in the historical development of the three orders and the two nations. Even for the concord there were, therefore, two models (Joachim speaks of the *duplex assignatio concordiae*) and a double calculation, with a gap of 10 generations between one and the other (*Conc.* II, 44).

While Trinitary theology had led him to the vision of the second state, the exegesis of the Book of Revelation would lead Joachim to draw the same conclusions (*Exp. in Ap.,* 1184–200). The dominant method of interpretation at that time was to proceed "vision by vision," a method perfected by Bede and shared, among others, by Richard of Saint Victor. In this perspective, the text was divided into seven visions, viewed in turn as so many autonomous thematic blocks. Each vision contains a complete knowledge of the history of the Church (divided in turn into seven states). After one vision mysteriously described the entire history of the Church, that which followed started again at the beginning, recapitulating the entire story from another angle.

Joachim shared this disposition of the visions, while affirming, however, that there were eight of them and not seven; but he endeavored first of all to read Revelation as a text tracing the entire course of the history of the Church, progressively, vision upon vision, from the origins until the final expected outcome. And from this perspective, he perceived Revelation 20 as the annunciation of a future era that would be fully intramundane, in which he recognized the features of a third state. Joachim agreed with Augustine, therefore, on the criticism of literal millenarianism, but, unlike Augustine, he remained convinced (*non tam opinio, quam serenissiumus intellectus, Exp.* 211r) that a sabbatical period, a brief interlude of peace and freedom within history, would occur between the coming of the Antichrist and the final attack of Gog and Magog. Joachim's millenarianism resided in just such a concept.

The Fourth Council of Lateran* (1215) condemned Joachim's Trinitary theology (*DS* 803–7) without attacking his person or his historico-eschatalogical vision. That vision would be disseminated over the coming decades, thanks not so much to the monachism* of Fiore as to certain Franciscans, who saw a prefiguration of their experience in the prediction of an order of "spiritual men." The first pseudo-Joachite writings appeared in the atmosphere of prophetism that arose both around and against the figure of Frederick II. The most famous of these, the commentary *Super Hieremiam,* was transmitted in at least two different versions, the first of which seems to have originated in the circles of the order of Fiore, while the second (about 1243) was the fruit of a new elaboration by Franciscan circles.

The spread of Joachim's ideas encountered difficulties from the middle of the 13th century on. Convinced that the work of the Calabrian abbot constituted "the eternal Gospel" that he himself advocated, the Franciscan Gerard de Borgo San Donnino provoked a reaction among the secular masters in Paris, bringing about his own condemnation and the censure of excerpts from Joachim's work by a cardinalatial commission (Protocols of Anagni, 1255). Also criticized in more assertive theological contexts (Thomas Aquinas, *ST* Ia IIae, q. 106, a 4 ad 2: against the idea of a third state of the Spirit), Joachite theses nevertheless did endure, with changes, in the minority circles of the spiritual Franciscans. In his *Lectura super Apocalipsim* (1297–98), Peter Olivi advanced the doctrine of the three comings of Christ: between the first coming, in the flesh, and the last, in the glory of the last judgment, Olivi posited an intermediary coming, through the Spirit, to work an evangelical reform of the Church. And this second coming had already taken place through St. Francis of Assisi at the beginning of the third age of the world. The schema of the three comings imposed a thorough revision of the Joachite point of view, since it sought to place the period of the Spirit within a Christocentric sphere and give it a historical significance of a Franciscan nature. But as far as the millennium itself was concerned, Olivi took a decisive step in the direction of a literal millenarianism, for he seemed convinced that the third age was destined to last for 70 years. In his wake, in 1349, the Franciscan Jean de Roquetaille dared to maintain that the duration of the world between the death of the great Antichrist and the last judgment would be exactly 1,000 years by the solar calendar.

In the 14th and 15th centuries the wave of Joachite prophetism expanded remarkably, all the more so in that with the flow of authentic works was mixed an even greater influx of works of dubious origin (attributed progressively to the Calabrian abbot in order to invest them with authority). Prophetic literature of a Joachite mold, in claiming to foresee and to calculate, represented either an instrument for political and ecclesiastical propaganda or a motive for erudite accumulation—and sometimes both at once—which accompanied the ever-increasing occurrences of visions, vaticinations, sibylline oracles, and cabalistic calculations. The deepest layer of Joachite apocalypse, in turn, fueled the representations and expectations of popular religious movements, thus working to radicalize its revolutionary social impetus. At the threshold of the modern era, the frail profile of the third reign was finally projected into a situation that differed significantly from the one originally envisaged by the Calabrian abbot.

● *Expositio super Apocalypsim,* Venice, 1527, 1–224 (reissued in Frankfurt, 1964); *Psalterium decem chordarum,* Venice, 1527, 226–81; *Concordia Novi ac Veteris Testamenti,* Venice, 1519 (reissued Frankfurt, 1964); *TAPhS* 73, 8th part (1983) (critical edition of books I–IV); *Dialogi de praescientia Dei et de predestinatione electorum,* Rome, 1995.

GIAN-LUCA POTESTA

See also **Apocalyptic Literature; Church; Exegesis; History; Kingdom of God; Spirituality, Franciscan**

Johannine Theology

More than any other text of the New Testament, the Gospel (Gospels*) of John is the product of a long and complex composition spread over several generations, with two major stages: 1) in Palestine before 70; 2) in the pagan world, once the break between the synagogue and the Johannine community had been completed. It is therefore not surprising to encounter in the fourth gospel distinct and even contradictory points of view. However, its completed version as a single book makes it possible to speak of a unified Johannine theology, even if the many internal tensions between the views expressed cannot be ignored. In addition, in order to account for the particularity of the fourth gospel in relation to the synoptics, various sources have been mentioned: Gnostic (R. Bultmann*) or hermetic (C. H. Dodd) movements, Samaritan religion, heterodox Jewish movements like the Qumran sect. Nevertheless, the fact that it belongs to the genre (literary* genres in Scripture) "gospel" is not in any doubt: the first conclusion (Jn 20:30f.) is explicit about the purpose of the book. Finally, the fourth gospel belongs to a corpus that includes the three epistles of John and Revelation. There is near unanimity in treating Revelation separately, in view of its important stylistic and theological differences from the fourth gospel. On the other hand, the three epistles seem to be indissociable from the gospel; for example, for R. Brown, the first constitutes a rereading of Johannine theology in reaction against certain deviations that had appeared in the community in the late first or very early second century.

1. The Son Sent by the Father

As the conclusion of John 20:30f. asserts, the purpose of the fourth gospel is to inspire faith in "Jesus Christ the Son of God*." The central axis is radically christological, but the intention to illustrate the mystery of the Son inevitably raises the question of his relation to the Father.

a) Reinterpretation of Messianic Titles. In the final stage of composition, the titles "Christ" and "Son of God," applied to Jesus (20:31), whose actions are reported by the book (20:30), take on a fullness of meaning that is favorable for later theological developments. But the fourth gospel nonetheless sets out the Old Testament roots of these designations. The first scene of the gospel (1:19–51), devoted to the witness of John the Baptist (v. 19), is set against the background of a many-sided messianic hope, associating with the royal Davidic Messiah* (vv. 20, 25), translated by "Christ" (v. 41), the figures of Elijah restored to life and the Mosaic prophet* (vv. 21, 25), following the lines of Deuteronomy 18:15. In fact the protagonists of the narrative recite a series of titles, all of which may refer back to messianic expectation, something that was intense in Baptist circles: for example, the Lamb of God (Jn 1:29, 36); the Son of God (vv. 34, 49) (variant "God's chosen one": v. 34), the king of Israel (v. 49). Added to this are characteristic traits such as the presence of the Holy Spirit (vv. 32f.), the unknown character (vv. 31, 33) fitting for the Messiah (*see* Justin, *Dialogue with Trypho* 8. 4; 49. 1; 110. 1); the recapitulation of the Scriptures (Scripture*) (v. 45); and, in light of the Messiah's link to Bethlehem (7: 40ff., 52), Nathanael's surprise about Nazareth (v. 46). In this sense, Johannine Christology does not derive from belated speculations but originates in the earliest Christian memory, applying to Jesus of Nazareth all the titles and characteristics supposed to characterize the divine envoy who is the inaugurator of the salvific age.

b) Exposition of "High" Categories. Rooted in apostolic preaching, Johannine Christology emphasizes the heavenly character of the divine envoy. More than a providential man, for whom the traditional titles might be fitting, the figure of the Son of man, which is of apocalyptic origin (Dn 7:13), forms the basis for understanding the initial pericope (Jn 1:19–51). Assimilated to Jacob's ladder (1:51), Christ occupies a mediating position between God and humanity, and the future ("you shall see": vv. 50f.) invites the reader to interpret the gospel narrative as a whole as illustrating the quasi-divine condition of the one whom the Baptist and the first disciples recognized as the Christ-Messiah. In these circumstances the ancient titles take on added meaning. This is particularly the case for filiation, intended to express not only divine election but the community of destiny with God. Similarly, in what follows in the gospel, various debates illustrate the equality of Jesus with God, for example in reference to the Sabbath rest, which is judged to contradict the permanence of divine activity (5:17–21). And again, urged to locate himself in relation to Abraham (8:53), Jesus asserts his absolute antecedence (8:56) and places his existence under the sign of an eternal present that assimilates him to God himself: "Before Abraham was, I am" (8:58). In the eyes of the Jews, such a claim to divinity is blasphemous (10:33). Although Jesus does escape from stoning at that point (10:31), the close link between the resurrection of Lazarus and the final plot reveals, beyond strictly political arguments (11:48f.), the Jewish rejection of a "high" Christology. This Christology comes after the experience of Easter, but the fourth gospel proposes an explicit formulation of it even before the event of the cross.

c) The Impact of the Prologue. The prologue (Jn 1:1–18) opens the gospel narrative by attaching it to categories of thought familiar to the reader (theology* of the Word*) and also to the liturgical experience of the community (the hypothesis of an original hymn reworked by the writer of the prologue). It also determines the conditions for interpreting the text, as well as its grammar. The heart of the prologue consists of the identification between the historical Jesus, the subject of the Baptist's witness (vv. 6ff.) and founder of a community of believers (vv. 12f.), and the divine Word that preexists creation (vv. 1f.) and that is both distinct from God (v. 1b) and identified with him (v. 1c). The source of life and principle of creation (vv. 3ff.), the Word is addressed to humanity as a whole (the "world," v. 9). Responses are diverse (vv. 10ff.), but the universality of his mission is nonetheless strongly asserted. In these circumstances, the concrete being of Jesus (the "flesh," v. 14) is an instance of particularization on the basis of the broadest universal, existing before the universe and encompassing history.

Whatever the origin of the prologue and the time at which it was set at the beginning of the gospel, its proleptic function invites us to read the succeeding narrative as a whole not only in the binary thematic context of the two covenants (covenant*) (v. 17) but as the decisive manifestation of God, through the mediation of his only Son, himself God in a relation of perfect proximity to the Father (v. 18). This perspective authorizes a consideration of christological statements at the deepest level of their meaning.

d) The Relation to the Father. The divine origin of Jesus is his true legitimation (see the image of the royal "seal," the basis for the authority* of a duly appointed minister: 6:27). The Son of man descended from heaven (3:12), Jesus presents himself as the only Son of God (the "monogenic": 1:18, 3:16 and 18); He defines his mission as that of an envoy (3:31f.) from the Father (6:46) entrusted with speaking the words that have been entrusted to him (3:34, 12:49f.) and as one armed with full authority (3:35). This is why the attitude adopted toward him adequately expresses the acceptance or rejection of God (3:33, 36). The participation of human beings in the work of God is nothing other than the faith in Jesus as an envoy of God (6:30, 12:44, 13:20). The attachment of Jesus to the divine plan is such that even adherence to his person comes from the initiative of the Father (6:37, 38, 44). Between the Father and the Son there exists a perfect communion of wills (6:37–40), on the ground of a love that, although reciprocal, nevertheless proceeds first from the Father (3:35), for whom the gospel recognizes a perfect priority of initiative.

Hence, whereas the existence and the mission of Jesus derive from the Father, his Passion and death are themselves a return to the Father (13:1, 16:28). Anguish and suffering seem to be overshadowed by the certainty of accomplishing a mission in full conformity with the will of the Father and carried to its conclusion in perfect order (the motif of the "hour": 12:23, 13:1, 17:1). The intimate union of Father and Son then reaches its perfection and, although the superiority of the Father is not denied (14:28), shared love turns out to be fully reciprocal: the mutual indwelling of Father and Son (14:10f.) establishes Jesus' claim to accomplish the work of the Father, in complete fidelity to the mission he has been given (14:31).

2. The Son Revealing the Father

a) The Motif of Glory. Already in the prologue, the intimate relation that characterizes Jesus as Son (1:14) is a matter for communication to believers, themselves born of a divine will (v. 13) to the point of sharing the condition of children of God (v. 12). This manifestation of Jesus as Son, which makes up the body of the gospel (v. 18), is called "glory" (twice in v. 14), a term which has to be given its full relational value. Present from the opening sign of Cana (2:11), the motif of glory comes to the fore principally at the time of the Passion, constituting a veritable leitmotif throughout the speeches before the cross (ch. 14–17) (noun *doxa*: 17:5, 22, 24; verb "to glorify" *[doxazein]*: 14:13, 15:8, 16:14, and 17:1, 4f., and 10). It is the Father's initiative that remains predominant: he alone has the power to manifest his Son in Jesus, thereby revealing his own paternity, through the nonviolence of the crucified one (8:54, 12:28, 13:31f., 16:14, 17:1–5 and 10). However, Jesus is not simply passive: his own obedience, freely given, represents in itself a manifestation of the Father and contributes to the revelation of Jesus as Son (13:31f., 14:13, 15:8, 17:6ff.). In short, from the perspective of the fourth gospel, glory is not a static attribute of God but resides in the reciprocal revelation of the Father and the Son (17:1–5), from the first days of public life (in Cana: 2:11) up to the fulfillment of the cross.

Above all, the disciples are fully associated with this manifestation of glory, not only as spectators (1:14, 17:24) but insofar as they themselves contribute to this revelation, by means of a mission (15:15ff.) that qualifies them as witnesses in the heart of the world (17:18). Centered on the motif of community unity (17:21f.), the "priestly" prayer of chapter 17 assigns to the disciples the task (14:21f.) of pursuing the revelation of the Father and the Son in their mutual relation (17:10f., 23, 26).

b) The Mention of the Paraclete. Witnesses to and actors in the mutual revelation of Father and Son, believers benefit from the support of the Holy Spirit, called "Paraclete" (14:16 and 26, 15:26, 16:7), a social term designating an advocate "called to" (verb *parakalein*) an accused to assist him in his defense. Identified with the Spirit of truth* (14:7, 15:26, 16:13), the Paraclete is presented as a personal being, the subject of a certain number of actions having principally to do with the realm of knowledge: teaching, remembering, testifying (14:26, 15:26), or speaking, proclaiming, glorifying (16:13f.), always with reference to the Son and on the basis of the Son's teaching.

The mission of the Paraclete is in some sense to make up for the absence of Christ (14:16). Its arrival among human beings is dependent on the departure of Jesus (7:39, 16:7). A substitute for the Son, the Paraclete comes from the Father (15:26); we can say that it is sent or given by the Father (14:16, 26), but it is sent by the prayer of the Son (14:16) or in his name (14:26), when not simply by the Son himself (15:26); but the Holy Spirit is sent from the Father. Thus the relations of the Holy Spirit with the Father and with the Son turn out to be intimately connected; later theological difficulties were to arise on this point.

Developed in the section of speeches (ch. 14–17), the Johannine theology of the Holy Spirit sheds light on the entire gospel narrative. From the baptism* (1:32ff.) to the cross (19:30), the gift of the Holy Spirit accompanies the designation of Jesus as Son and marks the advent of the Church (represented in 20:22 by the disciples), itself pointed toward the universal, according to the principle of a new cult* "in spirit and truth" (4:23f.). Similarly, it falls to the Holy Spirit to ensure the "spiritual" understanding of the teachings of Jesus, so that they may be received as a revelation of his divine mission (3:5–8, 6:63).

c) The Ambiguity of Signs. While the disciples who came after the Resurrection, assisted by the Holy Spirit, had the ability to bring out the deep sense of the words and actions of Jesus (2:22, 12:16), the witnesses to his public life were confronted with actions whose spectacular or unprecedented character should have been enough to reveal the singular personality of Jesus. We might also speak of a series of signs (*see* miracles [miracle*]), coextensive with the earthly existence of Jesus (2:11, 4:54, 20:20f.) and supposed to be able to lead directly to faith (2:11 and 23, 6:2 and 14, 12:18), since signs form a part of the process of revelation or "glory" (2:11).

But the great misunderstanding of the multiplication of the loaves reveals the partial failure of signs, that is the lack of recognition of their role as signs and the excessive attachment to apparent material reality (6:26). In this sense the reiterated demand for signs (2:18, 6:30) is less the mark of an attachment to Jesus than the refusal to follow him on his own territory. Similarly, actions following signs remain vague and imprecise (3:2, 6:14, 7:31, 9:16), sometimes even hostile (11:47). It is easy to understand the impatience of Jesus in the face of a reception of a sign that reduces him to the status of a vulgar miracle worker (4:48). Finally, the fourth gospel emphasizes the inability of signs to give rise to faith (12:37). Conversely, the nakedness of the cross and the emptiness of the tomb call for an act of faith (19:35, 20:8), beyond any tangible appearances, in an absence of signs that is in harmony with the very excess of the mystery. Only then does perfect coincidence of "seeing" and "believing" occur (20:8). A similar experience is offered to the post-Resurrection disciples (20:29) who, like Thomas, are asked to find their happiness in bare faith, with no support other than the gaping wounds of the Crucified One

(20:27), a reminder of the cross and the tomb. Thus, the Easter experience of the first day of the week (20:1, 19), repeated a week later (20:26), informs the time of the Church, a time of faith in "Jesus Christ the Son of God" (20:31) and a time of missionary proclamation (20:17, 21), in continuity with a witnessing (21:24) whose source is located precisely at the place of the cross (19:35). This is the place of the "lifting up" (3:14, 8:28, 12:32) of Jesus.

d) The Debate on Works. If the actions of Jesus are truly signs only in the framework of a church-based rereading of his entire career (20:30f., 21:24f.), the motif of works, also frequent in the fourth gospel, expresses a complementary point of view with respect to the revelatory function of the Son and the circumstances in which human beings receive revelation.

In the speech to Nicodemus, Jesus refuses to be constrained by the problematic of signs, as urged by the Pharisee rabbi (3:2), who is effectively a spokesman of the Jewish world (2:23). The call to be born "from above" (3:3) or "from water and the spirit" (3:5–8) is an introduction into a spiritual understanding of the teachings of Jesus (3:8). Their subject is not only "earthly realities," related to the condition of disciple (3:12), but also "heavenly realities": the divine origin of the Son (3:13) and his salvific mission (3:15, 17), manifested in the event of the cross (13:14). In this context, mention is made of good and bad works (3:19f.), which themselves have the effect of revealing the deep nature of the man who has accomplished them.

Applied to the activity of Jesus, the motif of works has a revelatory function: it throws light on the close connection between the action of the Son and the will of the Father who has sent him (5:19f., 14:10ff., 15:24, 17:4). Thus, the works of Jesus are included in the category of authorized witnesses (5:36), on the same basis as the word of the Father (5:37f.) and the letter of the Scriptures (5:39f.). Similarly, a symbolic action like the healing* of the man born blind is a manifestation of the works of God (9:3) and attests to the unity between the activity of Jesus and the will of the Father who has sent him (9:4). Finally, the great controversies of chapters 8 and 10 demonstrate the opposition between the works of Jesus, accomplished in the name of the Father (10:25f., 32, 38), and the persistence in unbelief displayed by the Jewish authorities of Jerusalem (8:39–47, 10:33). Far from automatically bringing about an acceptance of faith, the works of Jesus strengthen the hostility of his opponents (15:24f.) and accelerate the judicial process that has been unleashed against him (8:59, 10:3, 11:53).

As for believers, who receive the works of Jesus as the sign of his close communion with the Father

(14:10), they enter into a movement of love that gives them the capacity in turn to carry out similar works or even "greater" ones than those of Jesus (14:12). Thus, to fulfill their function as revelation, works call for the commitment of the disciple in an act of faith (20:30f.). Without this act of faith the actions of Jesus are meaningless.

3. The Son as Mediator of Salvation

From the outset (1:51) the identification of Jesus with Jacob's ladder designates the Son of man as the mediator, instituting perfect communication between heaven and earth: the definitive opening (past participle: v. 51) of heaven makes the tearing of the veil of the temple related by the synoptics unnecessary.

a) The Images of Salvation. On two occasions (3:17, 12:47), the verb "to save" *(sôzein)* explicitly designates Jesus' activity with respect to the world. But rather than describing the content of this action, the fourth gospel contrasts it to its opposite, "judgment," understood in terms of condemnation, given the malignity of men, more inclined to "love the darkness" than "the light" (3:19). The mission of the Son sent by the Father consists of "saving" the world, by protecting it from the "judgment" and the death that would ensue if human beings, left to themselves, were to bring forth only their own works (3:20). Conversely, from their very faith in Christ (3:16), believers open themselves to the light, which reveals to them their own truth (3:21a) and enables their works to find their fulfillment in God (3:21b).

The metaphors of life (6:33, 35, 48, 51, 53, 57), often characterized as eternal (4:14 and 6:27, 47, 54, and 58), and of light (8:12) are associated with one another from the prologue onward (1:4) and are the privileged expressions of a salvation expressly linked to the person of Jesus. Repeating the miracles of the desert, he also presents himself as food (6:33, 41, 48, 51) and source of living water (4:10, 14). The victories over hunger (6:35) and thirst (4:14, 6:35) are metaphors for a salvation born of faith (6:35), itself understood as the work of God (6:29), as a free gift (6:44, 65). This salvation brings about more than intellectual acceptance. It enables believers to enter into the communion of divine life, permitting them to be engendered in filial status (1:12f.) through a birth from above (3:5) and finally brought to an everlasting resurrection (6:39f.). Thus, believing in "Jesus Christ the Son of God" and "having life in his name" (20:31) are the two inseparable aspects of salvation.

However, the fourth gospel manifests a certain reserve with regard to physical healing, whereas the synoptics emphasize its continuity with the overall experience of salvation, particularly through the forgiveness of sins (sin*). Only one passage evokes physical healing as a form of salvation (11:12), but the remark is placed in the mouths of the disciples and rather expresses a lack of understanding of Jesus' purpose: only victory over death adequately expresses the radical nature of salvation.

Finally, the universality of the divine plan of salvation (3:16f., 12:47) does not exclude the historical mediation of Israel (4:22), even as Jesus reveals to the Samaritan the overcoming of ethnic and religious divisions (4:21, 23).

b) The Time of Salvation. Coinciding with the act of faith in Jesus Christ the Son of God (20:31), salvation is rooted in the current situation of the believer (17:3). Access to eternal life (life*, eternal) implies not so much projection onto a distant horizon as grasping the present as the location of a possible judgment (3:18ff., 5:24). According to the perspectives of an eschatology* known as "realized" or "anticipated," the gift of life is often expressed in the present (6:27, 32f., 50, 53f., 56), but we also find the future (6:35, 51, 17), including the evocation of a last judgment opening onto a final resurrection (5:28f., 6:39f., 44, 54).

The tension between the "already there" of salvation and the "not yet" of its fulfillment finds expression in the motif of the "hour." Identified with the moment of the cross (7:30, 8:20, 12:27, 13:1, 19:27), the Johannine hour is presented as already having "come," not only with respect to the historical fate of Jesus (12:23, 13:1) but in its later manifestations: the universal assembly of believers (4:23), the resurrection of the dead (5:25), the unleashing of persecutions (16:32). However, the anticipation of the hour ("And it has come"; "And it is now") is inseparable from the striving toward an expected fullness ("The hour is coming": 4:21ff., 5:25–28, 16:2 and 25). Only the first epistle, in an outburst related to persecution, goes so far as to identify purely and simply the "now" of the church crisis and the "final hour" of the Antichrist preceding the final revelation (1 Jn 2:18–25). The emphasis placed on realized eschatology derives from the christological presentation of the fourth gospel. The cross is indeed the specific place of revelation (Jn 17:1–5), but Jesus' public life anticipates his full manifestation as the Son. This is true of the "glory" of Cana (2:11), following directly from the prologue (1:14) and in conformity with the promise made to Nathanael (1:51). It would, however, be erroneous to think that the "already there" of glory can overshadow the reference to the cross as the central event of salvation. At Cana the manifestation of Jesus and the belief of the disciples represent glory (2:11), but there is no confusion with the hour of the cross (2:4).

c) The Place of the Church. The Johannine preference for existential metaphors, like life (10:10), light (8:12), and knowledge (8:19), brings in its wake a relative thinness in collective or historical expressions of salvation. For example, the notion of the Kingdom* of God appears in a single passage (3:3, 5), and we do not know whether this was an early element, preceding specifically Johannine perspectives, or a late compositional addition with a harmonizing aim. Similarly, the traditional metaphors of the people of God (flock, vineyard) are modified in a personal sense. Emphasis is placed on the relationship between Christ the vine and each of his branches (15:1–10) or on the close knowledge linking each of his sheep to the shepherd (10:1–5, 27f.); the image of the door (10:8f.) makes of salvation a personal passage into Christ.

The reality of the church does not escape unscathed from this individualization of salvation. Not only are the Twelve marked by their inadequacy to accomplish the plan of Jesus (hence the clumsiness of their interventions: 13:22, 14:5, 8, and 22, and 16:17f.—including Peter*: 13:6, 8f., 36), but their very existence as a symbolic community of the Church (6:70) proceeds from a rigorous selection carried out through the discourse on the bread of life (the crowd: 6:22, 24; the Jews: 6:41, 52; the disciples: 6:60, 66; finally the Twelve: 6:67, 70f.). Constituting the final remainder who have gone through the ordeal of faith (6:67ff.), the Twelve nevertheless remain open to division, symbolized by Judas, called a "devil" or "divider" (6:70f.)

On the other hand, the privileged reference to the beloved disciple, recognized interpreter of Jesus' sayings (13:23–26), eyewitness of the crucifixion (19:25ff., 35), and initiator of the Easter act of faith (20:8, 21:7), evidences the particular character of a community jealously protective of its singularity. The authority of the "disciple" (21:24) takes the place of the referential function of the Twelve, but the last stage of composition (ch. 21) proceeds to a redistribution of roles (21:10), around the symbolic figure of Peter, recognized as pastor (21:15ff.) on the grounds of his martyrdom* (21:18f.).

d) The Role of the Sacraments. Since John proposes to lead one to a faith that is first of all a "life" in Christ (20:31), it is not surprising that, since the Fathers of the Church, commentators have recognized many allusions to the bread and wine of the Eucharist (speech at Capernaum: 6:22–71; the wedding of Cana: 2:1–12), as well as to the celebration of baptism (birth of water and the spirit: 3:3–8; a spring providing eternal life: 4:14; restoration of sight to the blind man sent to the pool of Siloam: 9:6f.; the washing of feet as participation in the Easter mystery of Christ the servant*: 13:7f.).

However, deeper study of the documents shows that the sacramental motif is neither primary nor unique. For example, the discourse on the bread of life is first of all a homily on faith in the divine envoy (6:27ff.), whose coming to earth repeats the miracle of manna (6:31f.) and constitutes the true food for believers (6:35, 48, 51a). The practice of the Eucharist appears only in second place, with the explicit allusion to the sacramental reality (chewing the bread: 6:54, 56ff; the two species: 6:53–56), which is performed as a memorial of the cross (6:51b).

Similarly, the narrative of the washing of the feet brings together two aspects. It represents a symbolic act carried out as a prefiguration of the cross (13:7f.), within a perspective that is close to that of baptism. It also contributes a teaching of Jesus with respect to community behavior (13:12–16), lived in the form of service, in imitation of the exemplary gesture made by Jesus (13:14f.).

Thus, sacramental practices do not constitute the principal object of John's narrative but are rooted in the logic of a discourse centered on the person of Christ and communion with his life (20:31). The effusion of both water and blood at the moment of death (19:34), before explicitly designating baptism and the Eucharist, evidences the continuity between the concrete being of Jesus and the communication of the Holy Spirit (19:30; *see* 1 Jn 5:6–9), according to the promise made to the disciples (7:39, 14:17, 15:26, and 16:13, 20, 22).

Conclusion

Marginal in many respects, the Johannine community nevertheless had its theology canonized by the great councils (council*) of the fourth and fifth centuries. For example, the motif of the "Incarnation*," inaugurated by the prologue (1:14) in the framework of a "high" Christology implying the preexistence of the Word (1:1), became the authorized expression of Christian faith in Jesus Christ, the son of God and Savior. One can therefore understand the interest in shedding historical light on chapter 21, in relation to the integration of the Johannine community and the audacious theology of John's book into the Great Church as a whole.

● R. Bultmann (1941), *Das Evangelium des Johannes*, Göttingen.
C.H. Dodd (1953), *The Interpretation of the Fourth Gospel*, Cambridge; id. (1963), *Historical Tradition in the Fourth Gospel*, Cambridge.
R. Schnackenburg (1965, 1971, 1975), *Das Joannesevangelium*, ThK IV, 1–3.
R.E. Brown (1966, 1970), *The Gospel According to John*, 2 vols., New York; id. (1979), *The Community of the Beloved Disciple*, New York.
O. Cullmann (1976), *Le milieu johannique: Étude sur l'origine de l'Évangile de Jean*, Neuchâtel-Paris.

D. Mollat (1979), *Études johanniques,* Paris.

R. A. Culpepper (1983), *Anatomy of the Fourth Gospel, a Study in Literary Design,* Philadelphia.

X. Léon-Dufour (1987, 1990, 1993, 1997), *Lecture de l'Évangile selon Jean,* 4 vols., Paris.

Coll. ACFEB, A. Marchadour (Ed.) (1990), *Origine et postérité de l'Évangile de Jean,* Paris.

J.-D. Kaestli, J.-M. Poffet, J. Zumstein (Ed.) (1990), *La Communauté johannique et son histoire (La trajectoire de l'évangile de Jean aux deux premiers siècles),* Geneva.

Y.-M. Blanchard (1995), *Des signes pour croire? Une lecture de l'Évangile de Jean,* Paris.

YVES-MARIE BLANCHARD

See also **Bultmann, Rudolf; Eschatology; Father; Filiation; Flesh; Glory of God; Holy Spirit; Incarnation; Judgment; Lamb of God/Paschal Lamb; Love; Sacrament; Truth; Word; Works; World**

John Duns Scotus. *See* **Duns Scotus, John**

John of Ripa. *See* **Duns Scotus, John**

John of Salisbury. *See* **Chartres, School of**

John of the Cross

1542–1591

a) Humanist and Mystic at the Heart of the Spanish Golden Age. Juan de Yepes was born in Fontiveros (Avila), the third son of a family of weavers. Left fatherless from his first months, his mother had to send him to an orphanage for the poor in Medina del Campo, where his first education was oriented toward craftwork. Very early on he acquired an exceptional artistic and religious sensibility. Noticed by a benefactor, he was able to receive a solid classical education from the Jesuits in the town before entering the local Carmel in 1563. From 1564 to 1568 he worked his way through the university of Salamanca, an institution that was still basking in the glory of Vitoria and Melchior Cano and was under the present influence of Luis de Léon. All the theological schools were represented here and could debate freely. Besides a solid biblical and patristic training, the university gave him all that he would later need in order to link the realities of the mystical life to a technically flawless theology.

Spain was experiencing a spiritual explosion at that time and despite censorship directed against the Illuminism of the Alumbrados (a censorship that was not actually effective), the works of the northern mystics, as well as the interiority of the *Devotio* * *moderna* introduced by Montserrat around 1500, became widespread. John was ordained to the priesthood* in 1567, which was also the year he met Teresa of Jesus. She made him abandon his idea of complete withdrawal into a Carthusian monastery, recruiting him instead to help her in the reform of Carmel, which she had just begun. In 1568 he returned to Medina and then began to reform the male branch of Carmel by founding the small monastery of Duruelo. Here he adopted the name John of the Cross. Henceforth he divided his time between the spiritual formation of the reformed Carmels and management of the reform.

Internal and external frictions, which resulted in his nine-month incarceration in the dungeon at the monastery of Toledo between 1577 and 1578, would lead to him being marginalized within his own religious family. He preferred not to impose himself on the institution that he reformed. He died of osteitis on 14 December 1591 in the monastery of Ubeda.

b) Works and Influence. It was after his release from the Toledo dungeon that John of the Cross began to put in order a poetical work that showed perfect mastery of the new style—it was employed in Italy by Garcilaso de la Vega—and to write down the commentaries that he had given orally in the parlors of Carmelite convents. The *Spiritual Canticle,* which traces the mystical (mysticism*) journey with reference to the games of the couple in the Song of Songs, achieved its first completed form in 1584. It was dedicated to Anne of Jesus, Teresa's companion. Anne took it to northern Europe, where she launched the reform of the French and Belgian Carmels after 1604. The development of this essential text, reworked until John's death, was later lost. The *Vive Flamme,* written in the last few weeks of 1585, would be a dazzling account of the final developments of mystical perfection. At the same time he carefully began writing *The Ascent of Mount Carmel* and *The Dark Night of the Soul.* Both represent a clearer explanation of his spiritual doctrine.

Because the second generation of Spanish reformers did not favor him, because his manuscripts were destroyed and not made available, and because obvious doctrinal changes introduced obscure circumstances, a genuinely critical edition of John's work has still not appeared today even though his writing was published in stages from 1618 onward. His gradual return to favor would only lead to his beatification in 1675 (Teresa was already canonized in 1622). It was in France that he had the earliest and deepest influence (thanks to the magnificent French translation of the Complete Works by Cyprian of the Nativity of the Virgin [1605–80], 1641), even though his works were also translated into Italian, Latin, Dutch, and German, less than a hundred years after his death. When, on 24 August 1926, John of the Cross was declared a Doctor of the Church, he became a main reference for mystical doctrine in the modern West.

Much more proficient in theological discourse than some others writers, and therefore more open to attacks in this terrain, John was to pay a high price for the divorce between theology and mysticism. The permanent disputes over his work, the quasi-universal moralism of some of his best-intentioned translators and commentators, as well as the intense opposition that he and his disciples faced show to what point mysticism has become unintelligible to modern theology. It is when John describes a journey that entails man's acquiescence, a journey of which God is nonetheless the sole driving force, that rational and apologetic theory has relentlessly chosen to find the difficult rise of a mandatory asceticism*. He does warn us, however, that he is speaking of a theology "in which we know by love, and in which we do not only know, but simultaneously taste" (*CT,* prologue).

c) The Ascent of Mount Carmel. My main intention is not to address everyone, but only some of the persons of our holy Order of the Primitive Observance of Mount Carmel, both friars and nuns, whom God favors by putting them on the path leading up this mount" (S, prologue). All of John of the Cross's doctrine presupposes this vocation, which involves nothing more than letting it be carried out by marking the way to the summit "where only the honor and the glory of God can be found" (diagram of Mount Carmel). However, the honor and glory of God come together to join man through love: "The summit of the mount is the high state of perfection that we call the union of the soul with God." (S, argument). John of the Cross's entire work does nothing but develop this theme of union. On the path leading to this union, man does not belong to any system: he allows God to act and eliminates any pretext for not allowing him to act, always leading the soul (soul*-heart-body) back to the passivity of unconditional faith.

Entrance into contemplation, strictly speaking, corresponds to this transition to passivity. In order to identify it, John of the Cross offers three signs, which have become classic in spiritual guidance (spiritual* direction): it is authentic if 1) the soul has become incapable of meditation; 2) if it feels detached from what is not God; and 3) it feels established in "simple and loving attention to God" (S. II, 13).

On this path of enlightenment, phases of bedazzlement, of hyper-lucidity, will be perceived painfully. This is precisely the theme of the nights, which denotes the process of the soul's accommodation to the divine light. John distinguishes two principle nights, corresponding to the two regions of the soul, the sensitive and the spiritual. These must be gathered and returned from the outside to the inside. Once these nights are completed the soul is reestablished to its original state in the image of God; henceforth, "in this state, the soul cannot perform acts (action*). It is the Holy Spirit that makes them all, moving the soul—which is the reason that all these acts are divine, because it is moved and activated by God" (Ll. 1–4). This state of union is called "spiritual marriage," in that it presupposes a reciprocal and free commitment between the soul and God, to which all pedagogy of nights led, and which initiates a stable and continuous delight between the two partners. Even death will be received in this state as abundant love, a complete assumption of the person in God: "Here, all the wealth of the soul comes together, and the soul's rivers of love start to flow into the sea... , all their treasures uniting to accompany the righteous one who is leaving to go to [God's] kingdom" (Ll. 1, 30).

d) The Fundamental Spiritual Attitude. The necessary passivity of the soul takes the shape of both solitude and poverty, the two vectors of all spiritual progress. Solitude is necessary in that love is secret, impossible to identify from the outside. This is the theme of the hiding place, of the soul in disguise, needing to pass unnoticed by the world, or by the tempter, or even by itself, so as to go forward in the total security of one who is allowing himself to be guided by another who sees better: "In an obscure night,/ in the anxiety and blaze of love,/ Oh happy adventure!/ I left without being seen,/ my house now at rest.—In darkness and safety,/ by the secret ladder, in disguise,/ Oh happy adventure!/ in darkness and in hiding" (poem of the night). Poverty is liberation, enabling a greater joy in true wealth: this is the spirit of the celebrated *todo y nada* (S. I, 13), which is the spirit of contemplation and not asceticism. It is because the soul already has all—that "all" that was at the starting point of its vocation—that the soul can consider all the rest as nothing. At both the beginning and the end of his famous litany on how it is necessary to be completely dispossessed before advancing toward the summit of Carmel ("to be inclined always to the most difficult, the most insipid, the most exhausting, etc."), John designates the only motive that should suffice to satisfy us: "For the sole honor and the sole glory of God... through the love of Jesus Christ" (ibid.).

In this solitude and poverty the soul knows that the union has in fact already been carried out since Good Friday (*see* Ct. 28), although hidden in its eyes, and it knows that its unveiling only presupposes entrusting oneself to God who, from the beginning, does all the work. It is from this, then, that comes the fundamental optimism that runs through John of the Cross's work. In the deepest darkness of the night, his words are filled with encouragement, and if he can be forthright when it is a question of what is essential, he reserves his harshest words for those nervous spiritual directors who, alarmed by the night's obscurity, discourage souls who are called to make this leap into the light.

- Silverio de Santa Teresa (1929), *Obras de San Juan de la Cruz,* Burgos.
- R. Garrigou-Lagrange (1923), *Perfection chrétienne et contemplation,* Saint-Maximin.

J. Baruzi (1924), *Saint Jean de la Croix et le problème de l'expérience mystique,* Paris.

Crisógono de Jesús (1929), *San Juan de la Cruz, su obra científica y su obra literaria,* Avila.

J. Maritain (1932), *Distinguer pour unir ou les degrés du savoir,* Paris, 615–765.

Crisógono de Jesús (1946), *Vida de san Juan de la Cruz,* Madrid.

H. Sanson (1953), *L'esprit humain selon saint Jean de la Croix,* Paris.

G. Morel (1960), *Le sens de l'existence selon saint Jean de la Croix,* 3 vols., Paris.

J. Orcibal (1966), *Saint Jean de la Croix et les mystiques rhéno-flamands,* Paris.

F. Ruiz Salvador (1968), *Introducción a San Juan de la Cruz,* Madrid.

M. Andrés (1976), *La teología española en el siglo XVI,* Madrid.

A. Cugno (1979), *Saint Jean de la Croix,* Paris.

M. Huot de Longchamp (1981), *Lectures de Jean de la Croix,* Paris; id. (1991), *Saint Jean de la Croix,* Paris.

Coll. (1991), *Juan de la Cruz: espíritu de llama,* Rome-Kampen.

O. Steggink, E. de la Madre de Dios (1992), *Tiempo y vida de san Juan de la Cruz,* Madrid.

Max Huot De Longchamp

See also Carmel; Contemplation; Mysticism; Rhineland-Flemish Mysticism

John the Evangelist. *See* **Johannine Theology**

Judaism

---

a) Historical and Social Context. Relations between Judaism and Christianity take place in a concrete context, notably the presence of Jewish communities in Christian lands. Even though the life of these communities, with its economic and social aspects, does not concern us here, it does dictate the nature of the strictly theological question. First, because this places the confrontation of ideas against a background that necessarily falsifies it, in that the Jews live under the domination of Christian rulers. Second, this very situation becomes part of the argument: the fact that the Jews are dominated is taken as proof of withdrawal of the divine favor promised to Israel.

Legally prohibited from owning land in many parts of medieval Europe, the Jews had to turn to financial professions: commerce and lending money against interest (the latter being forbidden to Christians). By institutionalizing their position, in a certain sense, these laws encouraged a residual anti-Jewish resentment that existed prior to Christianity (*see* Juvenal, Tacitus). This was further complicated by various phantasms such as the accusation of "ritual crime." Forced conversions (conversion*) were outlawed by the Council of Toledo (633) and again by the bull of Calixtus II *Sicut judeis* (1122 or 1123), which defined the legal status of Jews in Christian lands. The Fourth Lateran* Council (1215) imposed the wearing of a distinctive garment, later replaced by a round yellow badge.

Intellectual controversy was lively and reciprocal. Sometimes it was institutionalized. Jews were forced to take part in debates *(wikkuah),* often at the insistence of Christian converts. Treatises by Christians against Jews were usually addressed to fellow Christians. And there was no lack of Jewish treatises against Christianity during the whole medieval period, before the expulsion of Jews from Spain in 1492 (Lasker 1977). The first treatises were written in Arabic in the Islamic East, then in Hebrew in Christian lands, and even in Catalan; for example, the *Refutation of the principles of Christians of Crescas* (1412 manuscript). The controversy continues in modern times, in a more moderate tone, but also in that wider public space that is opened up by publication in modern languages.

Jewish philosophers sketch out a theology of Christianity, sometimes reversing categories forged by Christian theologians. This has been the case in Germany (Hirsch, Formstecher), and Italy (Benamozegh) (Fleischmann 1970).

However, the controversy is not to be confused with the question of relations with Judaism and does not prevent intellectual exchange (Dahan 1990). This is true even in the theological domain: with Rachi, Jewish exegesis came to have an important influence on the exegesis of the Victorines and Nicholas of Lyre, and, by way of the latter, on Luther*. The philosophy and theology of Maimonides influenced Thomas Aquinas (Wohlman 1988) and Meister Eckhart. Reciprocally, late Scholasticism is present, without explicit citation, perhaps in Gersonide, certainly in Crescas (Pines) and Joseph Albo, and explicitly in Hillel of Verona. The Kabala influenced the Renaissance and humanism. Present-day Catholic and Protestant theologians read Martin Buber, Franz Rosenzweig, and Emmanuel Levinas.

b) Conceptualizing Continuity. Christianity's relation with Judaism is not on the same level as its relations with other religions that are either foreign to the Abrahamic tradition (religions of India and China) or claim to be connected but reject the preceding sacred books (Islam). Christianity and Judaism are not simply exterior to each other. Christianity "came out of" Judaism in the two senses of the word: it constituted itself in distinguishing itself from Judaism as such. Therefore, in conceptualizing Judaism, Christianity is indirectly conceptualizing itself.

Christianity arose and developed in a Jewish environment. Jesus and the apostles were Jewish, as were all the authors of the New Testament except for Luke. The Christian Church appeared at first as nothing more than a tendency within first-century Judaism. The separation occurred gradually, beginning when Paul prevailed over James and imposed his solution, that of requiring of pagan converts only a minimal respect for the law (Acts 15). Judeo-Christian communities persisted for centuries. Within the second-century Church there was a strong temptation to push Paulinism to the extreme and reject the Old Testament. Marcion's rejection of this claimed a justification in attributing it to the evil creator posited by Gnosticism. Under the influence of Tertullian* and Irenaeus*, the Church rejected this temptation.

It remained to be demonstrated that the Old Testament announced the coming of Christ and a new law. On the first point, passages such as Psalms 2 and 110 were invoked and above all Isaiah's prophecy of the "suffering servant" (Is 53), and on the second, Jeremiah's prophecy of the new covenant inscribed in the heart (soul*-heart-body) (Jer 31:31–34). Various solutions were offered to the problem raised by the abandonment of certain legislative provisions. First, a distinction was made between those provisions that were permanent and those that had only pedagogical and therefore transitory value. This was simple in principle but difficult to apply. Laws labeled "ceremonial" were no longer in effect; but moral laws were deemed permanent and sometimes labeled with the Stoicist term "natural" (Justin, *Dialogue with Trypho*). Later, the commandments (Decalogue*) were interpreted allegorically (*Gospel of Barnabas* 9, 7; SC 172, 146 *Sq*). Prophecies (prophet* and prophecy) of messianic times were interpreted not as referring to the first coming of Jesus but his glorious second coming.

It also had to be shown that Christianity did not go back on the affirmation of monotheism. The theology of the Trinity* strove to distinguish itself from any kind of triplicity. Indications of the Trinity were sought in the Old Testament, as in the plural "Let us make man" (Gn 1:26) or in the passage where Abraham receives three supernatural visitors (Gn 18). Similarly, it had to be shown that the cult of images and of the cross did not amount to the worship of idols (idolatry).

However, the relation to the ancient covenant and the texts that tell its story (the Old Testament) is just one aspect of the relationship with Judaism. Post-Christian Judaism crystallized after the destruction of the temple and the loss of the land. Jewish elements that had been centered on the temple and the land—such as the Sadducees—disappeared, leaving only the Pharisees, whose focus was the study of the Torah.

c) Conceptualizing the Persistence of Judaism. The question for Christianity was that of knowing what role remained for the unconverted people of Israel. This problem already tormented Paul, himself born and raised as a strictly observant Jew, and he entertained in coexistence themes that were hard to reconcile. On the one hand, by adhering to the law, the Jews refuse grace (Gal 5:4). The *Epistle to the Hebrews,* basing its argument on Jeremiah 31:31–34, notes with the same sense: "In speaking of a new covenant, he [God, through the mouth of Jeremiah] makes the first one obsolete. And what is becoming obsolete and growing old is ready to vanish away" (Heb 8:13). On the other hand, "the gifts and the calling of God are irrevocable" (Rom 11:29) so it follows that "all Israel will be saved" (Rom 11:26). The same ambiguity is expressed in the Johannine writings: in the fourth gospel (gospels*) Jesus' enemies are plainly named "the Jews," but it is also affirmed that "salvation is from the Jews" (Jn 4:22).

The church fathers introduced a new theme: the Church is *verus Israel,* "the real Israelite race" (Justin, *Dialogue with Trypho*). The promises (promise*) made to ancient Israel are understood to be valid for the Church, that is, for all of Christianity. The fact that the scepter has left Jacob proves that "the one to whom it must return"—if the word *šîloh* is interpreted this way—has come (Gn 49:10). So it should be no surprise that the Jews are deprived of their land and all political power and dispersed throughout the world. Nor, conversely, that Christians should appropriate cultural features taken from the Old Testament and abandoned by Judaism, such as the anointing of kings and the Aaronic imagery of the priesthood. The universalist prophecies are interpreted as referring to the conversion of the nations to the Church.

The Church's claim to being the true Israel is interpreted as an exclusive one: the Jewish communities are no longer Israel (Augustine, *En. Ps.* 75, 2; CChr.SL 39, 1038), and this means that they are situated outside of themselves. An explanation must be found for their persistence. The effective cause is the hardening* of hearts and blindness, as expressed in the image of the blindfolded synagogue. The final cause is the testimony they give, in spite of themselves, of the validity of the gospel. As Augustine has it, the Jews are kept in their dispersion in order to bear witness (Augustine, *City of God* XVIII, 46; BAug 36, 653).

A change in themes can be observed from the 12th century onward (Funkenstein 1968). From around 1240 the procedure of allegorization of the Bible was extended to the Talmud, until then unfamiliar to Christians, and then to the Kabala, both of which understood as announcing a messiah (messianism*/Messiah) who resembled Jesus.

d) Recent Developments. The favorable context created by the religious neutrality of modern states does not explain everything but does facilitate matters. On the other hand there was an upsurge of a modern, social, pseudo-biological anti-Semitism dissociated from Christian anti-Judaism even if it shared certain themes (Hadas-Lebel 1993). The Shoah, ultimate consequence of this anti-Semitism, led to the concretization of the Zionist project and the creation of the State of Israel.

But intellectual factors are also at work. Emancipation allows Jews to participate in modern intellectual life and Christians have a more positive attitude, which had been developing for centuries. Some called Bernard of Clairvaux a "saint" for his action against the pogroms connected with the Second Crusade (Joseph ha-Cohen, *Vale of tears …1881*). Abelard*, at the same period, provides an example of irenic dialogue sensitive to the sufferings of Israel *(Dialogue between a philosopher, a Jew, and a Christian).* From the 15th century onward, knowledge of Hebrew spread. Progress in biblical studies produced a better awareness of the implications of Jesus' Jewish origins. At the Council of Trent the Catholic Church explicitly condemned the idea of a "deicide people." In *Le salut par les Juifs* [Salvation by the Jews] (1892), the writer Léon Bloy (1846–1917) opposed anti-Semitism. He was followed by Jacques Maritain (1882–1979), Erik Peterson (1932), Charles Journet (1945), and the Jesuit Gaston Fessard (1960), who deepened an irenic meditation on the mystery* of Israel. At the same time, Jews rediscovered the person of Jesus.

Vatican II* represents an important stage, but not an entirely new departure. The declaration *Nostra Aetate,* §4, extended by *Orientations and suggestions for the application of the conciliar declaration Nostra Aetate* (1975), and then *Notes for a proper presentation of Jews and Judaism in the Preaching and Catechism of the Catholic Church* (1985), sought to reorient Christian teaching as a whole. The work of Franz Mußner (1979) is important, if only for the symbolic impact of its title: it marks the transition from a discourse against the Jews to a discourse about the Jews.

However, the theological problem of the status of non-converted Israel is not specified in any official document and continues to be disputed. It is further complicated by the division of the Jewish people into different congregations (Reform, Conservative, Orthodox) and by the foundation of the State of Israel. It is in itself a mysterious question, one reserved for God alone. Among the questions that can be dealt with, some are concerned with the very status of Israel, others with its relation to the Church.

Paul called for immediate conversion (Rom 12:31), while suggesting that a conversion will eventually occur (Rom 11:25). For what period, era, or epoch does the Church have the right to hope for this conversion? Within the time of human history? Will it be gradual or en masse? Or is it an eschatological event, reserved for Christ's second coming?

Are there two peoples of God? Will the Church only be fully the true people of God after the conversion of Israel? Is there a separate path of salvation for Israel that could forego belief in Christ? Of course, "there is one mediator between God and men, the man Christ Jesus" (1 Tm 2:5). But acceptance of this, which is an article of faith for Christians, might, for the Jews, be a vision, the eschatological vision of "him whom they have pierced" (Jn 19:37 citing Zec 12:10).

● E. Peterson (1933), "Die Kirche aus Juden und Heiden," *Theologische Traktate,* Munich, 1951, 241–92.

C. Journet (1945), *Les destinées d'Israël,* Paris.

M. Simon (1948), Verus Israel. *Étude sur les relations entre Chrétiens et Juifs dans l'Empire romain (135–425),* Paris.

G. Fessard (1960), *De l'actualité historique,* I. *A la recherche d'une méthode,* Paris.

S. Pines (1967), *Scholasticism after Thomas Aquinas and the Teaching of Hasdai Crescas and His Predecessors,* Jerusalem.

A. Funkenstein (1968), "Changes in the Patterns of Christian Anti-Jewish Polemics in the 12th Century" (hebr.), *Sion* 23, 126–44.

E. Fleischmann (1970), *Le christianisme "mis à nu": La critique juive du christianisme,* Paris.

D.J. Lasker (1977), *Jewish Philosophical Polemics Against Christianity in the Middle Ages,* New York.

C. Thoma (1978), *Christliche Theologie des Judentums,* Aschaffenburg.

F. Mußner (1979), *Traktat über die Juden.*

P. van Buren (1980–87), *A Theology of the Jewish-Christian Reality,* San Francisco.

J.-M. Garrigues (Ed.) (1987), *L'unique Israël de Dieu,* Paris.

A. Wohlman (1988), *Thomas d'Aquin et Maïmonide: Un dialogue exemplaire,* Paris.

M. Sales (1989), *Le corps de l'Église,* Paris.

C. Thoma (1989), *Theologische Beziehungen zwischen Christentum und Judentum,* Darmstadt.

G. Dahan (1990), *Les intellectuels chrétiens et les Juifs au Moyen Age,* Paris.

M. Hadas-Lebel (1993), "Renan et le judaïsme," *Commentaire* 62, 369–79.

H.U. von Balthasar (1995), "Le problème Église-Israël depuis le Concile" (posth.), *Com(F)* XX/3, 23–36.

RÉMI BRAGUE

See also **Church; Choice; Ecclesiology; Israel; Judeo-Christianity; Pauline Theology**

Judeo-Christianity

a) Various Notions. The notion of Judeo-Christianity employed in the history of ancient Christianity, as in the history of Christian doctrines, expresses the connection between nascent Christianity and Judaism. The content varies from one author to another, but three major concepts can be brought out.

In its first meaning Judeo-Christianity represents Christians who were born Jewish and confess the messianism of Jesus, his resurrection from the dead, and the new life he begins according to the announcement made to the prophets (prophet* and prophecy). Those Christians who continued to observe Jewish law became the minority by the end of the first century as a result of the development of Christian communities made up of a majority of formerly pagan (pagans*) believers.

This concords with the definition of "Judeo-Christians" given in his time by L. Marchal (*DThC* 8, 1925, col. 1681): Christians of Jewish origin who kept the Mosaic observances while confessing the Christian faith. According to this hypothesis, confession of Christ's divinity would mark the limit between orthodox and heterodox Judeo-Christians. To one side of this line there would be the Nazarenes and on the other the *ebionites* and the *elchasaites,* a group of marginal Christian communities mentioned or described by some church fathers from the middle of the second century to the forth century.

From another viewpoint, Judeo-Christianity would include communities that came from Judaism and recognized Jesus as the Messiah (messianism*/Messiah) but not as God. The Judeo-Christians would constitute heterodox primitive Christian communities, on the fringes of other Christian communities, at the end of the first or beginning of the second century.

Another line of research starts with the observations that the Christian communities express and celebrate their faith with the use of Jewish theological and liturgical notions taken from the environment in which they were born. From this viewpoint Judeo-Christianity designates a Christian theology and practice of Jewish origin.

These varied notions in fact all use a similar approach. They all seek to bring out Judaizing intellectual fashions or practices within a number of more or less important of Christian communities developed notably after the year 70. In so doing, all of these notions place the Judeo-Christian problematic in a period after the first Jewish war (66–73) and identify the Judaism of that time with the rabbinical Judaism derived from the Pharisaic tradition. And from this viewpoint, the majority of the Christian communities of that period were characterized by their abandonment of traditional, that is, Pharisaic Jewish observances.

However, by revealing first-century Judaism in its diversity and not as a uniform entity, recent studies invite reconsideration of the question.

b) First-Century Christianity and Judaism. Judaism at that time was composed of various groups that shared an ensemble of practices and beliefs: faith in the unique God who revealed himself to the Fathers, covenant established by God with Israel, law that engages observances, in particular the cult celebrated in a unique temple. On this common basis, each group was characterized by particular practices and doctrinal interpretations; the Christians appeared then as a new group among other older ones, Sadducees, Pharisees, Essenes, Zealots...They were all designated by the same term, *hairèsis* (sect or group), in literature of that time, whether Jewish (for example, Flavius Josephus, *Antiquities of the Jews* 13, 5, 9; 18, 1, 2) or Christian (Acts 5:17, 15:5, 24:5; etc.). Thus, the Church and rabbinical Judaism do not derive from a uniform clearly defined Judaism but from two different traditions of first-century Judaism (*see* Neusner 1991; Dunn 1991).

Early Christianity went through a phase where it elaborated its own practices while still belonging to Judaism. This phase lasted up to the separation from Judaism, which took place after the first Jewish war* in the opening decades of the second century. After this war, in fact, certain groups constituting Judaism would more or less rapidly be jeopardized, mainly the Essenes, Sadducees, and Zealots. However, there is no indication of their total disappearance. Though most Jewish traditions other than the Pharisaic and Christian lost importance, the Judaism from which Christianity separated cannot be identified exclusively with the Pharisaic group.

The fact is that the Roman authorities considered the Christians as belonging to Judaism up to the early second century. Up to that period, the same accusations were made against Jews and Christians, which shows that they were not distinguished (Flavius Josephus, *Against Apion* 79; Suetonius, Nero 16, 3; Tacitus, *Annales* 15, 44).

The Christians were still subject to harassment down through the second century but it became occasional. They were prosecuted by judges who used their police power to restore order, and their attitude shows the beginnings of a distinction between Christians and Jews. The prosecution of Christians around 111–12 by Pliny the Young, governor of the *Pont* and *Bithynie,* shows that the Christians were no longer considered as Jews. Letters exchanged on that occasion between Pliny and the Emperor Trajan are the first documents attesting the separation, at least in that site. This is far from the date usually given, which is the reign of Nero (54–68) or Domitian (81–96).

c) New Perspective on Judeo-Christianity. The question of Judeo-Christianity should be posed from the question of what was first-century Judaism. Christianity at that time was a new group within Judaism and can legitimately be called Judeo-Christianity during the period in which it was part of Judaism (*see* Dunn, 234). The duration of that period varied according to different communities, because the characteristic diversity of first-century Judaism also marked all the groups that constituted it. Christianity did not escape from this situation. In fact it shared with the other groups constituting the Judaism of the Second Temple a common stock of practices and beliefs that also included Scripture (the Old Testament), an ensemble of prayers (prayer*) and liturgical practices, and a way of organizing communities. But this common stock was interpreted and valorized in different ways according to the communities. This led to tensions and conflicts, not only between Christians and other groups within Judaism, notably the Pharisees, but also within Christianity, to such an extent that when Christianity and Judaism separated in the second century, some Christian communities did not find a place within Christianity as it was defined. Those are the communities that the church fathers in the second century perceived as Judaizing.

The notion of Judeo-Christianity, thus redefined, takes into account the characteristic diversity of the first Christian communities and the Jewish nature of their practices. From this perspective, the classical interpretations of Judeo-Christianity reflect, in their divergence, the situation of Christianity during the initial, Judeo-Christian phase of its history.

- M. Simon (1948), Verus Israel. *Étude sur les relations entre chrétiens et juifs dans l'Empire romain (135–425),* Paris (2nd Ed. 1964).
  H. Schoeps (1949), *Theologie und Geschichte des Judenchristentums,* Tübingen.
  J. Daniélou (1958), *Théologie du judéo-christianisme,* Tournai-Paris (2nd Ed. 1991).
  M. Simon, A. Benoît (1968), *Le judaïsme et le christianisme antique,* Paris (4th Ed. 1994).
  G. Strecker (1988), "Judenchristentum," *TRE* 17, 310–25.
  J. H. Charlesworth (Ed.) (1990), *Jews and Christians. Exploring the Past, Present and Future,* New York.
  J. E. Taylor (1990), "The Phenomenon of Early Jewish-Christianity: Reality or Scholarly Invention?" *VigChr* 44, 313–34.
  J. D. G. Dunn (1991), *The Partings of the Ways between Christianity and Judaism and Their Significance for the Character of Christianity,* London-Philadelphia.
  J. Neusner (1991), *Jews and Christians: The Myth of a Common Tradition,* London-Philadelphia.
  S. Mimouni (1992), "Pour une définition nouvelle du judéo-christianisme ancien," *NTS* 38, 169–82; repr. in *Le judéo-christianisme ancien,* Paris, 1998.
  L. L. Grabbe (1994), *Judaism from Cyrus to Hadrian,* London.

JACQUES FANTINO

See also **History of the Church; Judaism**

Judgment

1. Preliminary Philosophical Remark

Man perceives reality both as *being* and as an *obligation to be;* he experiences himself as existing in the present but at the same time his relationship to the external world allows him to take a detached look at his own behavior. Western philosophy* bears witness to this irreducible duality: metaphysics and practical philosophy (in the classical tradition), or the critique of pure reason and the critique of practical reason (for Kant*), are fundamental forms of philosophical activity. It follows that history is neither mere contingency nor an immediate realization of morality. It is of a mixed nature and asks to be evaluated. It is therefore inevitable that, from within faith, with the living and revealed God as starting point, there should be postulated an evaluating and judging act of God. God can have no other relation to history. The idea of divine judgment is thus not merely an allegory derived from human judicial practice and transposed to God by analogy*. We perceive that reality and history call for judgment through a transcendental experience, implicitly contained in everything that we live through. The widespread opinion that sees in theological discourse about the judgment of God a mythological survival to be abandoned, or merely a symbol (see, e.g., Tillich*, *Systematic Theology* Chicago, 1963, vol. 3), does not take this point of departure into account. If it is also true that the relation of God to history is determined by grace, then judgment and the fulfillment of history constitute two indissociable notions.

2. Old Testament

The categories of judicial procedure are amply employed in biblical literature, in both the Old and New Testaments, because the exercise of human and divine justice is represented there in an elevated form. The concept of justice in particular has a specific range of meaning insofar as it condenses a whole series of operations carried out to "do justice" in circumstances in which justice is threatened or flouted.

a) Judicial Procedure in Israel. Conflicts break out between individuals, who, often provoked by wrongs suffered or presumed, feel that their rights have been infringed, and who institute proceedings (*rîb*) against the responsible party to bring a complaint before a competent judicial body so that justice may be done. The law regulates this procedure (Dt 19:1f.; 2 Sm 15:2), which contains organically structured stages that assure the lawfulness of the judgment.

The starting point of any judicial consideration is a criminal deed, that is, the violation of a law. It is also necessary that the offense be brought to the knowledge of the legal authority, who is attributed the title and the competence of *judge (shôfét)* and who will then assume the action of punishment.

At an evolved stage in the history of Israel, judicial bodies seem to have been divided into specific jurisdictions: "elders" probably presided over local tribunals "at the gates" of the city (Dt 21:19, 22:15, 25:7; Jos 20:4; Proverbs 31:23); "priests" decided questions concerning sacred norms (Nm 5:15–28; Dt 17:8ff.,

19:17ff.; 2 Chr 19:8–11); and the most difficult cases were reserved for the king and his officials (1 Kgs 3:16–28), who may have also dealt with cases on appeal (2 Sm 14:4–8; 2 Kgs 8:1–6). The judicial body usually had a collegial form in order to guarantee greater impartiality; this model was also followed in imagining the heavenly tribunal in which God administers justice, assisted by a counselor (1 Kgs 22:19; Ps 82:1; Jb 1:6).

The judge was responsible for all actions necessary for a judgment to be lawful *(shèfèt)*. Simplifying greatly, the procedure provided that the magistrate would examine the validity of relevant legal matters: by means of careful investigation (Dt 13:15, 17:4 and 9, 19:18) he would make certain of the facts and circumstances, and by questioning witnesses and the accused, he would develop a conviction leading to the pronouncing of a sentence (1 Sm 22:7–16; 2 Sm 14:5ff.; 1 Kgs 3:16–27; 2 Kgs 6:28, 8:6; Greek Dn 13:50–59). The public aspect of the entire procedure, as well as the involvement of the people, would be emphasized in the various stages of the process (Jer 26).

The totality of the acts decided or verified by the judge was called "judgment" (*mishepat*). Each moment of the procedure might, by metonymy, signify its end; for example, "accusing," arresting a guilty person, or turning him over to the authorities might each be enough to designate the entire procedure. This is particularly true for poetic texts, which prefer allusive language to the technical terminology of the law. The term *judgment* was applied particularly to the concluding stage of the process, becoming a synonym with *verdict,* a sentence of condemnation or absolution, as well as the articulation of motives, all making up the end and the summit of the judicial action as a whole.

The purpose of punitive judgment was threefold: repression of evil (Dt 13:6, 17:7 and 12, 19:19, 21:21, etc.), social deterrence (Dt 13:12, 17:13, 19:20, 21:20; 1 Kgs 3:28, etc.), and reformation of the guilty (2 Kgs 19:4; Jer 2:19; Ps 6:2, etc.).

b) Judgment in the Prophetic Tradition. The entire judicial proceeding revolved around the figure of the judge; it was incumbent on him to see that justice was done, because the actions of any other legal subject were rendered futile if not ended in a decision by the competent body and made in a speech authoritatively defining the judicial truth that was imposed on everyone. With that purpose in mind, the law prescribed that the choice of magistrates take into account the level of wisdom and moral uprightness indispensable for the office; judges indeed had to be *"men of value who fear God, men of truth who hate venality."* (Ex 18:21; *see also* Dt 1:15). Impartiality and incorruptibility were in a sense the bedrock of the tribunal (Ex 23:6; Lv 19:15f.; Dt 1:16f., 16:18f.).

The history of Israel did not conform to that ideal. Prophets (prophet* and prophecy) repeatedly denounced the perversion of judicial acts, subjected to venality (1 Sm 8:3; Is 1:23; Jer 5:28, 22:17; Ez 22:27; Mi 3:11) and used by the powerful against whom an innocent man was unable to defend himself. Given that improper administration of justice was the hallmark of an iniquitous government (shâfat meant both to judge and to govern), the prophets proclaimed that God himself would establish a higher tribunal to pronounce a judgment against both judges and rulers. Thus, once the mighty had been brought lower and the poor saved, justice would reappear on Earth. Many exegetes have therefore identified the message of the prophets with the proclamation of judgment.

The literary genre (literary* genres in Scripture) characteristic of prophecy (prophet* and prophecy) may be called "judicial discourse" (Gerichtsrede). It should, however, be noted that in order to be able to speak of judgment, a legal structure consisting of three elements is necessary; that is, that two opposing parties must be present. These take on the figures of the accuser (accompanied by his witnesses) and that of the accused (who may have a defender but is often alone). The judge, the third element, stands above the parties; he listens (holds "audience") and decides (separates good* from evil). But not all legal proceedings in the Bible have this structure. For example, the prophets frequently evoke the procedure of the trial (rîb), which was essentially bilateral and thus did not provide for mediation between the accused and the accuser. This process typically took place within the family and was metaphorically applied in circumstances in which covenant relationships were in force. The accuser tried to convince the accused to recognize his wrongs and to recover the conditions of an understanding based on reciprocal respect; but if his words turned out to be futile, he could also turn to punitive means to the extent necessary—always, however, with the intent of reaching a reconciliation. Whereas in the dynamic play of judgment the accuser tended to seek the condemnation of the opposing party, in the logic of the bilateral trial the one who accused, even if he threatened in anger, wished only for the other to confess his wrong so that he might be forgiven.

c) *Judgment of God.*   In the Bible the power of judgment rests heavily on those who also hold another form of authority (political and religious). It is therefore clear that, since sovereignty over the entire world is recognized as belonging to YHWH, the character of

a judge is also attributed to him (Gn 18:25; Ex 5:21; 1 Sm 24:13–16; Is 2:4; Jer 11:20; Ps 7:12, 9:5, 82:1).

Of course, the judgment of God does not only apply to the rather limited number of cases of ordeals, where individuals, unable to decide, leave it to chance or to prescribed rituals to decide between guilt and innocence (Ex 22:6ff.; Nm 5:16–28; Jos 7:16–19; 1 Kgs 8:31f.). But Scripture sees the entire history of the human race subordinated to the constant judgment of the God of heaven, who knows all and intervenes wherever people fail to render justice.

The stories of Cain and Abel (Gn 4:9–12), of Sodom (Gn 18:16–33), of the liberation from the Egyptian yoke (Ex 3:20), and the like are examples of the price God attaches to an equitable judgment, to punishing the guilty and to rehabilitating and saving innocent victims. Thus, not only is God's absolute and impartial justice revealed but also his sovereign concern for the poor. Indeed, he listens to the lament of the weak, and his judgment is equivalent to saving intervention. This explains why the judgment of God and his justice are so often signs of salvation (1 Sm 26:23f.; Is 19:20; Ez 34:22; Ps 7:9, 26:1, 43:1, 54:3). It should also be noted that God's judgment is often accomplished through warlike actions; a defeat in war is in fact seen as a verdict of condemnation issued by God against the guilty party.

This vision of things, which governs the biblical narration (and not only the Deuteronomist strand) and largely inspires prophetic and omniscient literature, corresponds to the axiom in which "God rewards everyone according to their deeds" (Ps 62:13; Prv 24:12; Jbb 34:11; Eccl 12:14; Rom 2:6). Negative events of individual and collective history are interpreted as the manifestation of the just judgment of God, who punishes faults with rigor. The exile of the people of Israel is to be read as the tragic outcome of a history subordinated to divine judgment, the emblem of an analogous condemnation of all nations (Jer 25).

The metaphor of the judgment of YHWH claimed to explain the meaning of history. However, the doctrine was criticized by various prophetic and intellectual currents, which objected that the wicked prospered in the world while the poor continued to suffer injustice and abuse. The protest of the prophets (Jer 12:1f.; Hb 1:2–4:13; Mal 3:15) and of the suppliants of Israel (Ps 10:13, 73:3–12, 94:3–7 and 20f.) was echoed by the denunciation of the wise (Jb 21:7–33; Eccl 7:15, 8:14, 9:2). Thus, history does not provide an adequate revelation of the divine government of the world. In order to maintain complete faith in a supreme justice that was inherent in human events, the metaphor of the tribunal was displaced to a concluding act of history: judgment became the "last judgment," or final judgment, the quintessentially eschatological act, which would definitively separate the just from the wicked (Is 26:20f.; Jl 4:1–17; Mal 3:19–21; Dn 7:9–14). The Wisdom of Solomon (5) adopts this line of interpretation. New Testament passages proclaim that the final event of God's judgment is "imminent" (Mt 3:7–12, 24, 25, and parallel passages).

3. New Testament and Historical Theology

a) The background in the Old Testament, the *mishepat* of YHWH, is indispensable for any understanding of the preaching of John the Baptist. He too establishes an immediate relationship between the condemnation and the favor of God; no one may feel safe in the face of the coming judgment. Only conversion and repentance, sealed by baptism, give promise of salvation (Mt 3:7–12). If we were to reduce the judgment announced by Jesus to formulas, parables (parable*), and the like, we would lose sight of the fact that the proclamation of the Kingdom of God, like the message of John the Baptist, brings together the idea of unreserved concern for sinners and the idea of their condemnation (*see* in particular the Sermon on the Mount [Mt 5:22, 26 passim] or the images used in Mt 13:24–30, 47–50 and 24:50f. passim). The measure of this twofold divine justice is the commandment (Decalogue*) of love, which is valid for Jews as well as for Gentiles (Mt 25:32).

Human beings can be saved from divine condemnation by divine forgiveness, which is granted to the sinner without restriction (Lk 15), whatever the gravity of his sin (*see* Lk 7:36–50; Mt 18:21–35). But man will be saved only if he can also pardon himself with that same unconditional intention to forgive (*see* Mt 6:14, 18:22 and 35 passim). The Kingdom of God, in which divine judgment is situated, is the future that is being prepared on the threshold of the present, a future that takes form in the words and deeds of Jesus. Although only some exegetes argue that Jesus designated himself as the Son* of man through whom judgment is fulfilled (Mk 14:62), there is on the other hand no doubt that the post-Easter Church* expected that the Christ who had ascended to heaven would return to judge humanity (for the synoptics, *see* Mt 13:41, 24:31, 24:35–51, 25:31 passim; Acts 10:42, 17:31; 2 Thes 1:5–10; 1 Cor 4:5; 1 Pt 4:5). The one who returns to judge humanity is the savior and the establisher of law* insomuch as he condemns evil.

This fundamental structure of Jesus' proclamation, and of the Easter faith in relation to the judgment of God in and through Jesus Christ, is found in various forms in the different corpuses of New Testament. The Pauline writings, through the doctrine of the justification of the sinner, develop the present aspect of judgment and forgiveness worked by God in Jesus Christ. They define justification in relation to the future judgment of God (Rom 2:6) or of Christ (2 Thes 1:7). In the proclamation of the last judgment, Paul calls on many apocalyptic elements, and a comparison of 1 Thessalonians 4:13–5:11 with 1 Corinthians 15:20–58 exhibits the freedom with which he varies these images. The proclamation of salvation and judgment in this context are based on the death and resurrection of the Lord, both harbingers to the resurrection of the dead (*see* 1 Cor 15:17, 20). The imminence of final events is thus attenuated to some degree. Deutero-Pauline writings (*see* Eph 2:1f.; Col 3:1–4) more strongly emphasize the present character, already at work, of the mystery of Jesus Christ, although they do not exclude the future dimension. This aspect of judgment is even more strongly emphasized in the Johannine corpus. *"He who believes in God is not judged, he who does not believe is already judged"* (Jn 3:18). In John 5:24–30 we can see how apocalyptic* language is used to proclaim the present event of judgment, the already given reality of resurrection to eternal life (life*, eternal) and of condemnation. H. Conzelmann comments: "The future dimension is not dismissed but rather made present... John is of course acquainted with the expectation of the Parousia* (as of the resurrection and judgment). He does not eliminate it, but integrates it into the present understanding of salvation" (*Grundriß der Theologie des NT* [Munich, 2nd Ed. 1967]).

The future dimension of judgment certainly appears in John (John 5:28ff., 6:39f.). Entirely similar pronouncements can be found in Acts. Christ brings together the present and future realities of judgment and fulfillment; he is the Lord, and he comes as the Lord. In the Johannine corpus, judgment is understood as condemnation. The believer is not subject to judgment, which affects only "this world" (John 12:31). According to the synoptic Gospels, although those who believed or loved are nevertheless subject to judgment (Mt 25:31), as disciples of Jesus they are also those who exercise judgment with him (*see* Mt 19:28; Lk 22:30). In the Gospel (Gospels*) of John, in accordance with his interest in the present aspect of judgment, the Church is created by the Holy* Spirit to confound and judge the world (*see* Jn 16:8, 11).

b) The first formularies of faith in the early Church—like the great majority of Western and Eastern confessions of faith, including the creeds of Nicaea* and Constantinople* (*see* DH 10–76)—attest to a belief in the judgment of God or in the return of Jesus Christ to judge the living and the dead. Debates about Marcionism*, Gnosis*, millenarianism*, and the doctrine of apocatastasis* (*see* Constantinople II*, *DH* 433) gave rise to deeper theoretical developments, in the areas of both ethics and theology. In part, these developments went back to Plato (*Apology* 40c ff.; *Gorgias* 523a–527a; *Republic* X. 614–615d) and were also not distant from the ideas about judgment as held by Plutarch, the neo-Pythagoreans, and the Neoplatonists. The three Cappadocians, especially Basil*, (*see Com. in Isaiah* I. 43, PG 30. 201), understood divine judgment strictly as the end point of human liberty, so that even one condemned by God acquiesces to the divine sentence. Judgment is thus the advent of liberty to truth. In that way, the freedom of the created being is implicitly conceived not only as the capacity to choose but also as the ability to do good and evil, a thought that in the modern era finds full theoretical expression in Kant and Schelling*.

Latin theology of judgment was later essentially governed by the profound Augustinian synthesis of the *eschata* or last things (*see Civ. Dei* XX–XXII) and the more parenetic discussions of Gregory the Great. Both were weighty authorities whom medieval theologians invoked to defend the idea of individual judgment after death, a doctrine that appeared only implicitly in Eastern and early Latin theology, for example in the cult of martyrs and saints. Art and religious practices show how belief in a universal judgment deeply marked spirituality and piety. There is abundant evidence of this in Romanesque and particularly in Gothic churches, as well as in the illuminations produced by monks. At the same time, judgment was one of the principal themes of preaching up to and beyond the Reformation and the Counter Reformation; it also played a central role in literature and plastic art.

The theology of the early Middle Ages up to the 12th century did not undertake a systematic discussion of divine judgment in the framework of the *eschata*. Such discussion was made possible only in the 13th century, with the development of an anthropology* endowed with a structured conceptual apparatus. Death now represented the threshold through which the soul, after undergoing an individual judgment, acceded to its fulfillment. As a rational principle, the soul found its supreme perfection in the beatific (vision*, beatific) vision: that is, in the immediate vision of divine essence, granted by God without the mediation of any created being. Conversely, damnation was characterized by eternal privation of that vision. The souls in purgatory*, for their part, acceded to the beatific vision only at the end of a period of purification. As for the body, the material principle of the human person, it was inextricably tied to the physical world, but its reality continued beyond the death of the individual (*see*

Thomas* Aquinas, *ST* IIIa. q. 59. a. 5); this is why it was included in the universal judgment. It would be resurrected for that judgment and then receive its sentence. In this way the theologians of the great medieval period emphasized that a close bond united individual and universal judgment. According to Thomas and Benedict XII, for example, the resurrection and exaltation of the body would bring to the human soul both a quantitative and a qualitative increase in happiness.

This systematization of eschatology brought about a tension between Latin and Eastern theology, because the latter had not undertaken the same conceptual development of anthropology. Whereas the Latin formularies of the early Middle Ages were still content with emphasizing the judgment of Christ "according to works" (*see DH* 574, 681 passim), the creed of the Second Council of Lyons* already reflected the systematization of Latin eschatology (*see DH* 856–59). The constitution *Benedictus Deus* (*DH* 1000–02) of Benedict XII, intended to correct the sermons of his predecessor John XXII, adopted the doctrine of divine evaluation of individual souls after death, although without using the term *judgment,* which Thomas was the first theologian to do.

The attribution of judicial power to Jesus Christ was frequently debated in medieval theology. According to Thomas Aquinas, the *judiciaria potestas* of Christ is based on the fact that, as Son, he is the truth and the work of the Father (*ST* IIIa. q. 59. a. 1). This power falls to him as a man, as leader of humanity and as author of salvation. For Thomas, judgment was essentially a part of the salvific unveiling of the truth, the truth of man and the truth of history. The three possible sentences of the judgment of God or of Jesus Christ— eternal beatitude, eternal damnation, and purification—are justified in a strictly argumentative mode.

c) Martin Luther argued against this idea of a twofold judgment; he spoke of a sleeping of the soul until the last judgment, rejected the doctrine of purgatory, and understood the judgment of Christ as a condemnation, the antithesis of grace. In Calvin*, with the notion of positive predestination* (*see Inst.* III. 20–22), these two elements, condemnation and grace, were again placed in an immediate relation to one another, although in a way different from that of the medieval tradition. Moreover, the Protestant polemic against the piety of works denounced with some reason an understanding of indulgences that, in preaching, in popular faith, and even in the theology of the period, often manifested magical characteristics that tended to place restrictions on the sovereign judgment of God and Jesus Christ. In its decree on justification (*DH* 1545–49, 1582) the Council of Trent characterized Jesus Christ as the "equitable judge" who grants eternal life *tamquam gratia...et tamquam merces*. That council rejected the principal characteristics of "justice by deeds" and maintained purgatory as the moment of judgment (*DH* 1580, 1820).

Although Catholic Scholasticism of the baroque period and Protestant orthodoxy presented many common points in relation to the doctrine of universal judgment, Enlightenment thought led theology to concentrate almost exclusively on morality. In this perspective, divine judgment served to strengthen the moral motivation of human beings. The doctrine of judgment disappeared entirely from the dogmas (dogma*) of certain liberal Protestant currents. Despite the reaction of the dialectical theology of Barth*, H. Merkel is able to take note of the uselessness of the concept of judgment in current Protestant theology: "Whoever proclaims the absolutely gratuitous character of grace can no longer grant decisive importance to judgment according to works" (*TRE* 12, 492). The development of Catholic theology followed other paths. Under the influence of the confrontation with Schleiermacher, German idealism, and romanticism, the school of Tübingen again granted a particular place to eschatology. In his *Encyclopedia of Theological Sciences* (1834–40), A. Staudenmaier treated universal judgment as an essential moment in the fulfillment of revelation and of the kingdom of God. Conversely, neoscholastic theologians, who did not generally demonstrate a very developed sense of history, saw the traditional doctrine of judgment as a strict calling to judgment of humanity and the world, some of them distinguishing clearly between a period of divine mercy lasting until the death of the individual and a period of rigorous justice beginning after death. This idea was carried to an extreme in the work of J. Bautz, *Weltgericht und Weltenende. Im Anschluß an die Scholastik und die neuere Theologie dargestellt* (Mainz, 1886). Some Anglican writers, as well as some neoscholastics, had a view of modernity that expressed the expectation, not devoid of apocalyptic tones, of an imminent judgment (*see* P. Toulemont, "La question de la fin du monde et du règne de Dieu sur la terre," *Études*, 1868).

Hermeneutic (hermeneutics*) reflection on eschatological pronouncements (Rahner*), a better articulation of individual judgment and individual *eschata* with what is said about a universal resurrection and judgment (Y. Congar, M. Schmaus, R. Guardini, P. Teilhard de Chardin), and the attachment of judgment to the domain of soteriology and Christology (Balthasar*, Blondel*), have all given new impetus to recent theological analysis. The Second Vatican* Council, for its part, integrated its articles on judgment into the universal eschatological perspectives of the Christian experience of faith (*see LG* 48, *GS* 45).

● M. Blondel (1946), *La philosophie et l'esprit chrétien*, Paris.
D. Mollat (1949), "Jugement II. Dans le NT," *DBS* 4, 1344–94.
L. Scheffczyk (1957), "Das besondere Gericht im Lichte der gegenwärtigen Diskussion," *Schol.* 32, 526–41.
K. Rahner (1960), "Gericht," V, "Systematisch," *LThK* (new Ed.) 4, 734–36.
M. Blondel (1961), *Carnets intimes,* Paris.
J.-P. Martin (1963), *The Last Judgment in Protestant Theology from Orthodoxy to Ritschl,* Edinburgh-London.
K. Rahner (1965), "Schuld—Verantwortung—Strafe in der Sicht der katholischen Theologie," *Schr.zur Th.* 4, Einsiedeln, 238–61.
J.N.D. Kelly (1968), *Early Christian Doctrines,* 4th Ed., London, in particular 459–85.
G. Augustin (1969), "Das Gericht Gottes: Interpretationsversuch zu einem eschatologischen Thema," *Conc(D)* 5, 3–9.
P. Grelot (1971), *De la mort à la vie éternelle: Études de théologie biblique,* Paris; id. (1974), *Le monde à venir,* Paris.
H.U. von Balthasar (1983), *Theodramatik IV: Das Endspiel,* Einsiedeln, especially 223–337.
K. Seybold et al. (1984), "Gericht Gottes," *TRE* 12, 459–97.
M. Schmaus et al. (Ed.) (1986 f), *HDG* IV 7 a–d.
R. Schaeffler (1987), "Vollendung der Welt oder Weltgericht. Zwei Vorstellungen vom Ziel der Geschichte in Religion und Philosophie," in H. Althaus (Ed.), *Apokalyptik und Eschatologie. Sinn und Ziel der Geschichte,* Freiburg-Basel-Vienna.
W. Pannenberg (1993), *Systematische Theologie* 3, Göttingen, 656–77.

PETER HÜNERMANN

See also **Eschatology; Hell; Kingdom of God; Limbo; Mercy; Parousia; Purgatory**

Jurisdiction

The term *jurisdiction* is of Roman origin. It concerns the exercise of a power or *potestas*. In canon* law, commentators gave it a more precise definition beginning in the 12th century, a period of a certain renaissance of Roman law. Certain concrete questions arose, and although these questions were admittedly old, commentators used them to articulate tools for legal analysis. Two major problems presented themselves: the validity* of celebrations of the Eucharist and ordinations (ordination*/order) carried out by excommunicated, heretical, or schismatic (schism*) ministers; and the origin of the power exercised by the pope* and the bishops (bishop*) before their consecration. Doctrine relied more and more systematically on the distinction between two powers, one of order, *potestas ordinis,* the other of jurisdiction, *potestas iurisdictionis.* The former, which could not be lost, was acquired by ordination and granted the authority to carry out sacramental acts. The latter was given in a canonic mission and authorized the exercise of the power of governing and teaching. In particular it authorized the carrying out of magisterial acts, understood in their jurisdictional sense, which made it possible to impose on the faithful a doctrine that was to be believed or followed. The distinction between the two powers is reiterated in the Code of Canon Law of 1917.

The Second Vatican* Council* made little use of the term *jurisdiction.* It sought rather to go beyond the duality between order and jurisdiction by endorsing a mode of presentation of the functions of the Church on the basis of a distribution that Catholic theology had used since the 19th century and that had been adapted from Calvin. As priest (priesthood*), prophet, and king, Christ has given a mission to the Church to carry out duties of teaching, sanctification, and government. After Vatican II, Catholic canon law was influenced by this way of presenting the activity of the Church, although it did not abandon the distinction between the power of order and the power of jurisdiction. New theories on the origin of the power of the pope and the bishops have taken shape, because the council was unable to set out with clarity the elements of an acceptable position. The council clearly set forth the sacramentality of the office of bishop and introduced the notion of *potestas sacra* received in ordination but failed to clarify the efficient role played by the canonic

mission. If ordination is the source of the power of the bishops, does the canonic mission simply determine the place in which power is exercised, or does it confer a portion of a power that can be fully acquired only with a canonic mission? A *nota praevia* attached to the dogmatic constitution *Lumen gentium* did not answer the questions left unresolved by doctrine.

In the *CIC* of 1983, the power of jurisdiction is also called "power of government" *(potestas regiminis).* It may be exercised personally or in the name of another. In this case, power is called personal or vicarious. It may be delegated. The legal categories organizing the power of jurisdiction are described for themselves or on the occasion of the definition of competencies attached to various canonic offices or duties. However, even if the organization of the Church is presented as a structure of duties that may be entrusted to the faithful clergy (cleric*) or laity (lay*/laity), some of these duties are restricted to ordained ministers, and when a competency including jurisdictional power is involved, they are reserved for those who have received holy orders, bishops or priests. Canon 129 of the Latin Code of Canon Law makes an innovation by declaring that faithful laymen may cooperate in the exercise of the power of government. But the use of such cautious terms shows that the principle of a link established between ordination and jurisdiction remains an essential principle of the Church's organization.

Elements of reflection on the exercise of government in the Catholic Church are to be sought more in relation to the question of pastoral responsibility *(cura pastoralis)* within communities. In fact this is organized in such a way that the faithful participate in the power that is conferred on the bishop set at the head of a diocese or a priest set at the head of a parish. The canon law that came out of the revision that took place after Vatican II has considerably furthered the implementation of participation in the power of government in the Church. We should also mention the place taken by the movement to increase the prestige of synods (synod*) in the Church, synods in which participation in legislative power is institutionalized. This is true for diocesan synods, ancient institutions of the Church, that have often met in dioceses following Vatican II. With respect to participation in executive power, the law sets out principles to be implemented within the participatory institutions whose competency may be expanded. Through the exercise of this power, the holder of an office is given the possibility of making decisions, but he may also be given the obligation in particular cases of making known the decisions he intends to make in order to solicit advice and consent.

Finally, canon law has set in place mechanisms for the control of the exercise of the power of jurisdiction, the constituent elements of which come from canonic tradition* and from the experience of major state systems. Legislative power is under the control of the Pontifical Council for the interpretation of legislative texts, an organ that has jurisdiction over the entire Church and may receive complaints about the nonconformity of particular laws to universal laws. This recourse to an institution is not possible in the case of universal laws, which remain subject to the principle of discretionary appeal. Executive power may also be subject to control in case of an appeal made against particular decisions considered to be illegal or requiring reparation for a violation of subjective rights. Canon law provides a system of administrative appeals, followed by appeal to an administrative jurisdiction that was established in 1967 and that needs further development in canonic doctrine. Lastly, the exercise of judicial power is itself carried out in a hierarchy of jurisdictions allowing persons who are seeking reparation for rights violated by another member of the Church to present their complaint to a judge or to have a legal fact recognized, as in cases of marriage annulment. This hierarchy of tribunals is ancient and includes diocesan, regional, or interdiocesan tribunals and a tribunal in Rome, the *Rota Romana,* which judges in the name of the pope and largely functions as a court of appeal.

● J. Gaudemet (1985), "Pouvoir d'ordre et pouvoir de juridiction. Quelques repères historiques," *ACan* 29, 83–89.
P. Valdrini (1994) (Ed.), "Charge pastorale et communautés hiérarchiques: Réflexions doctrinales pour l'application du can. 517, §2," *ACan,* 37, 25–36.

PATRICK VALDRINI

See also **Canon Law; Ecclesiastical Discipline; Law and Legislation; Hierarchy**

Justice

In our time, *justice* refers to an ideal of fairness in the distribution of the goods and burdens of society. It is primarily a virtue (virtues*) of institutions and social arrangements; indeed, it is the fundamental moral quality of a society. By contrast, in classical and medieval writings, more emphasis was given to justice as a personal virtue, defined as "a constant and perpetual will to render to each person his due" (*Digest* I, 1 tit. 1, leg. 10). Of course, justice, so understood, has a social dimension: it is preeminently (although not exclusively) a virtue of rulers and judges.

1. Antiquity

(a) Old Testament. In the Bible, the term that is generally translated as "justice," *mishpat,* has various meanings. Sometimes, it refers to one of the legal ordinances in the Pentateuch. In other passages, it refers to a custom or ordinary practice and does not necessarily carry a positive moral connotation. Most importantly from our perspective, *mishpat* can also refer to the right order of society, which may be violated in practice but respect for which is morally obligatory. Used in this sense, it is often paired with *çedaqah,* "righteousness," and the two together are characteristics of God (e.g., Am 5:24). Both the Pentateuch and the prophetic writings stress that justice includes a special concern for children, widows, orphans, aliens, laborers, and the poor (e.g. Am 5:7–13 and 8:4–8; Mi 6:9–14).

(b) Greece. In Greece during the Homeric era, the word usually translated by "justice," *dike,* referred to an eternal order of right relations that structured the natural and social worlds. In human society, this order was expressed in a hierarchy of roles, within which each individual found his or her place; the individual's role, in turn, determined either his or her obligations to others and the claims that he or she could make on others and on the wider society. Both gods and human

judges were thought to be bound by this order, and the justice of a particular law or judgment was evaluated in terms of its conformity to *dike*. As Greek society became more urbanized, this model of justice was increasingly called into question; this provides the context for understanding the work of Plato and Aristotle.

In both the *Republic* and the *Laws,* Plato identifies justice as one of four qualities that comprise moral goodness; this led to the traditional identification of justice as one of four cardinal virtues (*Rep.* 4, 433 *b–c; Laws* 1, 631 *d*). Plato also internalizes justice, interpreting it as a quality of the soul (soul*-heart-body) in virtue of which the individual's passions* are brought under the control of reason (*Rep.* 4, 434 *d*–445 *c*). Justice is thus presupposed by the other virtues.

Aristotle identifies two senses of justice and injustice. In the wider sense, justice comprises the practice of any virtue insofar as the act in question affects another person. Correlatively, any vicious action that harms another can be considered as a form of injustice (*NE* 5, 1129 *b* 1–1130 *a* 15). In a more limited sense, justice is a specific virtue: it consists in a commitment to render to each person what is due to him in accordance with fairness (*NE* 5, 1129 *a* 1–20; 1130 *b* 30–1131 *a* 30). That is, neither party to a transaction should benefit more than the other or at the expense of the other (*NE* 1132 *a* 10–1132 *b* 20). In Aristotle's view, this conception of justice as fairness was compatible with a strict social hierarchy because, according to him, persons are naturally unequal (*Pol.* 1, 1260 *a* 9–15).

Finally, the Stoic idea of a natural law—the idea of a moral order set by nature and discerned by reason—set the context for reflection on justice well into the modern period. Although this natural law never had one definite, fixed content, for the Stoics it always implied the idea that all persons are equal as moral agents, and therefore that the institutions of society are conventional rather than natural. The idea of natural law, with its corollary notion of natural justice, served as a vehicle for the classical notion of a moral order that is more basic than particular social arrangements and can serve as a basis for criticizing them.

2. Christian Conceptions

(a) New Testament. In the New Testament, God's justice is held up as the standard by which all human conceptions of justice are evaluated. In the synoptic Gospels, this ideal is taken as the basis for a radical critique of human relations, as set forth in the Sermon on the Mount (Mt 5:1–6:29; *see* Lk 6:14–29), in accordance with the injunction, "You must therefore be per-

fect just as your Heavenly Father is perfect" (Mt 5:48). However, Paul's contrast between the justice of God, manifested in Christ, and human unworthiness has been even more influential for subsequent theology. In Paul's view, the human person is incapable of attaining justice through his or her own efforts, even through obedience to the law (Rom 2:12–29). Justification (*dikaiosune),* that is, finding grace before God, can only come through faith in Christ (Rom 5:1–11).

(b) Augustine. Augustine expounds his views on justice in the *Civitas Dei (City of God).* Taking as his starting point the definition of a republic offered by Cicero (106–43 B.C.), as a community organized around a common good, Augustine argues that neither the Roman Empire nor any other community has ever attained true justice (*Civ. Dei* 19.21). In order to do so, it would be necessary to acknowledge the true God and to place all other relationships and goods in their proper relationship to God (ibid., 19.21, 23). There cannot be even a true idea of justice apart from God's revelation in Christ. At the same time, Augustine acknowledges that human societies can attain a kind of justice that is not without value, since life would be impossible without it. Accordingly, the Christian can and should give allegiance to earthly societies, so long as he or she recognizes their imperfect and transient character (ibid., 19.5, 6, 17, 26).

(c) Thomas Aquinas. Aquinas (Thomas* Aquinas) accepts the view, shared by civilian jurists and canon lawyers in his day, that there is a natural justice, the demands of which can be known, at least in their broad outlines, by all persons (*ST* Ia IIae, q. 94, a. 6; IIa IIae, q. 57, a. 2). Thus, in contrast to Augustine, Aquinas believes that a genuine justice can exist even in non-Christian communities, and he argues that Christians are bound by natural justice to respect the legitimate claims of non-Christians (*ST* IIa IIae, q. 10, a. 12). For Aquinas, too, justice is one of the four cardinal virtues, more specifically, the virtue of the will (*ST* Ia IIae, q. 56, a. 6; q. 61, a. 2; IIa IIae, q. 58, a. 4). He accepts the traditional definition of justice as the will to render to each his due, in accordance with the norm of equality (*ST* IIa IIae, q. 58, a. 1, 2, 11). On this basis, he distinguishes between "commutative" and "distributive" justice (*ST* IIa IIae, q. 61, a. 1, 2). Distributive justice comprises the norms by which society distributes rewards and punishments (punishment*) and imposes obligations on its members. Commutative justice comprises the norms that govern relations among individuals, including norms of non-maleficence; for example, the prohibition against murder, adultery, or theft. Aquinas also incorporates the traditional virtue of

epieikeia*, or equity, into his account of justice: through this virtue, one acts outside the letter of the law if that is necessary to preserve the intention* of the legislator (*ST* IIa IIae, q. 120, a. 1). The significance of equity for Aquinas can only be appreciated once we realize that, in his view, no moral rule can be applied with absolute certainty in every possible situation (*ST* Ia IIae, q. 94, a. 4; IIa IIae, q. 47, a. 2, ad 3).

3. Modern and Contemporary Conceptions

In the late Middle Ages and during the Reformation, preoccupation with the notion of justification displaced reflection on justice from the center of theological attention. However, the school of Salamanca (e.g., Suarez* and Vitoria [c. 1485–1546]) offered an exception to this trend, anticipating later doctrines of the rights of man. At the beginning of the modern period, the Stoic-Christian conception of natural law was reformulated into a doctrine of natural rights, and the idea of the rights of man offered a basis for moral claims across social boundaries; it was then a revolutionary element in the political transformation of societies. In the late 18th century and, above all, in the 19th century, it was replaced by utilitarianism* in English-speaking countries.

(a) Contemporary Theories of Justice. In Anglophone political philosophy, *A Theory of Justice,* by John Rawls (1921–), has the greatest influence. Rawls criticizes the utilitarian conception of social order in the name of a constructivist account that attempts to establish the norms of justice by asking what social rules would be accepted by rational legislators who know nothing about their own particular situation and interests. Rawls argues that, in these circumstances, rational persons would agree to create a social order characterized by respect for fundamental liberties (liberty*); furthermore, social and material inequalities would be justified only to the extent that they generate a higher standard of living for those who are worse off than would be possible in a more nearly equal society.

On the European continent, reflection on justice has been most deeply influenced by the Frankfurt School. Its most influential representative is probably Jörgen Habermas (1929–), whose account of justice is based on his theory of communicative action. Like Rawls, Habermas argues that social norms can only be justified through a process of reasoned discussion, leading to consensus among those subject to these norms. He further insists that this process must take place through public dialogue in which all participants try actively to place themselves in the position of their interlocutors. Unlike Rawls, Habermas believes that a conception of justice can be grounded in something more universal than the particular tradition of liberal universalism, namely, in the universal features of social and linguistic interaction.

Theological reflection on justice has not been wholly detached from philosophical thought on the subject, but it has different priorities. As a result, some issues that are central to political philosophy today have scarcely surfaced in theological discussions, such as the distinction between substantive and procedural conceptions of justice, whereas others are almost exclusively theological, for example, the question of the limits of human societies from the perspective of God's justice.

(b) Problem of Social Justice. Trenchant theological critiques of government policies were a feature of life in both Europe and the United States throughout the early modern period. In the late 19th century, the focus of this criticism shifted to society itself. Within Protestantism*, this new emphasis on society gave rise to "social Christianity" in Europe (e.g., Charles Gide [1847–1932]) and the "Social Gospel" in the United States (W. Rauschenbusch [1861–1918], *A Theology for the Social Gospel* [1917]). Within Catholicism*, the encyclical *Rerum novarum* (1891) laid the foundations for what was to become the "social teaching of the church." The Protestant movements attempted to take Jesus's moral sayings as a basis for a social order characterized by social and economic equality. The encyclical of 1891 was not so radical, but it also attempted to develop a Christian response to social injustice. It was a response to Marxism: it acknowledged the force of Marx*'s critique and offered an alternative model of society in which laborers and owners of capital would work together for the common good.

Protestant theologians were responsive to the social ideas of the movements that we have just mentioned. While the two world wars (war*) disillusioned them, they continued nonetheless to draw inspiration from these ideas well into the middle of the 20th century. Perhaps the most influential Protestant theory of justice is the "Christian realism" of Reinhold Niebuhr (1892–1971), who argued that Christians are morally obliged to work with others to attain the best possible social order, even while acknowledging that any society will necessarily fall short of the ideal of Christian love. The debate between Karl Barth and Emil Brunner (1889–1966) on the possibility of natural justice has also exercised a profound influence on Protestant thought.

Catholic thought drew inspiration from *Rerum novarum,* expanding Aquinas's categories of justice with a third, social justice, which is concerned with the obligations of society to its members. The most notable figure in the revival of Thomistic political thought (Thomism*) was Jacques Maritain (1882–1973), whose defense of human rights has had a great deal of influence. Maritain should be linked with the German Jesuit O. von Nell-Breuning, who has inspired numerous pontifical documents. More recently, the combination of Marxist elements with Catholic social teaching that constitutes the theology of liberation, with its insistence on reaffirming God's love for the poor, has sought to mount a radical critique of the global economic order. It has been widely criticized, but some of its ideas have been incorporated into official Catholic teaching, notably the claim that God has a "preferential option for the poor." This idea certainly has enduring value as a critique of uncontrolled liberalism.

● O. Lottin (1931), *Le droit naturel chez saint Thomas d'Aquin et ses prédécesseurs*, 2nd Ed., Bruges.

J. Rawls (1971), *A Theory of Justice,* Cambridge, Mass.
C. Bruaire (1974), *La raison politique,* Paris.
R. Tuck (1979), *Natural Rights Theories,* 2nd Ed., Cambridge.
J. R. Lucas (1980), *On Justice,* Oxford.
O. von Nell-Breuning (1980), *Gerechtigkeit und Freiheit: Grundzüge katholischer Soziallehre,* Vienna.
J. Habermas (1983), *Moralbewußtsein und kommunikatives Handeln,* Frankfurt.
G. Grant (1985), *English-Speaking Justice,* 2nd Ed., Toronto and Notre Dame, Ind.
K. Lebacz (1986), *Six Theories of Justice,* Minneapolis.
A. MacIntyre (1988), *Whose Justice? Which Rationality?,* Notre Dame, Ind.
M. Colish (1990), *The Stoic Tradition from Antiquity to the Early Middle Ages,* Leyden.
T. Nagel (1991), *Equality and Partiality,* Oxford.
C. Audard (1996), "Justice," *DEPhM,* 781–89.

JEAN PORTER

See also **Authority; Epieikeia; Justice, Divine; Justification; Law and Christianity; Political Theology; Society**

Justice, Divine

The definition of justice *(çedâkâh, dikaiosunè)* cannot be used as the starting point for an understanding of divine justice because in this case the term is polysemic. In fact, before justice was thematized as a property of the divine essence it was understood or experienced as an action or manifestation of God with respect to human beings (Descamps 1949; Quell-Schrenk 1935). Justice, then, is clearly an attribute related to God (divine attributes*, III). Now the question is to say exactly how they are related.

1. Scripture

a) Old Testament. "The Lord is righteous in all his ways and kind in all his works" (Ps 145:17). This divine justice confessed throughout the Old Testament has, as this verse implies, a double aspect: a legal or judicial aspect of conformity to standards by which the judge rewards or punishes, and an aspect of intervention to deliver and save (Johnson 1987). The latter corresponds to the function of the judge in the ancient Near East, the essential function of the king responsible for establishing peace and prosperity for his people. These two senses mutually imply each other

because it is in judging human beings, individually and collectively, that God communicates his salvation* to them.

Firstly then, God is the just judge who does not favor one person over another (carried over in the New Testament, Rom 2:11; Eph 6:9; Gal 2:6; Col 3:25; 1 Pt 1:17; Acts 10:34; Jas 2:1), meaning that he cannot be corrupted (Dt 1:17; 2 Chr 19:7; Jb 34:19). It follows that he does not favor the rich and powerful. On the contrary (Wis 6:1–8), he does justice for the poor, the abandoned, the widow, the orphan, the stranger (Dt 10:18). Consequently, he is called upon in the Psalms*, when one is sure of being in the right: sure, that is, of one's own "justice" (for example. 7:9–12, 34:18–21, 35:24). But he is also the judge of sin, before whom one admits transgression (Ps 130:3, 51:5f.), and imploring his pardon.

In liberating the oppressed and pardoning the sinner God manifests the fullness of his justice, which is more concerned with salvation than chastisement. This is shown, for example, in the episode where Abraham intercedes on behalf of Sodom (Scharbert 1984). Far from being exclusively punitive (of the oppressor or sinner), divine justice is essentially faithful to the promise and the covenant, gift of salvation, the "communication of grace and glory" (Descamps 1949) within a universalist (ibid.; Aubert 1974) and even a cosmic perspective (ibid.; Pidoux 1954).

b) New Testament. The theme of divine justice is rarely carried over into the non-Pauline texts (Descamps; Aubert), unless from an eschatological viewpoint (Rev 15:3f, 16:5, 16:7, 19:2, 19:11, e.g.). Though Paul also preaches about the last judgment* (Acts 17:31), when one will reap what one has sown (Gal 6:7ff.) and God will "render to each one according to his works" (Rom 2:6), he usually employs the expression "justice of God" in a new sense that it is not always easy to harmonize with the earlier meaning. Here, justice is no longer proper to God, it is the justice he communicates to man "justified by faith" (justification*, Pauline* theology). The theme of redemption by the death* of Christ*, who acquits the debt to divine justice owed by sinful humanity, runs through the whole of the New Testament (Mt 20:28, 26:28; Mk 10:45; Gal 3:13; Eph 1:7; 1 Tm 2:6; 1 Pt 1:18f.; Rev 1:5, 5:9 par. ex., *see* 1 Cor 6:20, 7:23).

2. Theology

a) The Fathers. Within the Greco-Roman context in which Christianity developed it became increasingly difficult to resolve the latent tension between the two different aspects of divine justice. In that context the Bible was read first in Greek. In the Septuagint (older translations* of the Bible) *çedâqâh* was usually translated by *dikaiosunè* (*ThWAT* 6, 922–23), a term that does not (any more than *justitia* in Latin) convey the idea of a merciful salvific justice (ibid., 923; *see ThWNT* 2, 197) but rather the Aristotelian concept of distributive justice (*see EN* 5) (Aubert). If God's justice consists in rendering to each his due, if one should "only have what one deserves," how can one hope for salvation and divine life? The *massa peccati,* to use the words of Augustine, owes an unpaid debt to divine justice (*Quaestiones ad Simplicianum,* BAug 10, 480; *De diversis quaestionibus,* BAug 10, 274). How then can God's love and mercy be reconciled with his justice? Almost all the Fathers responded to these questions using a soteriological language: if salvation consists in the fact that Christ paid this debt, then justice and love are profoundly united. Irenaeus, for example, argued against the Gnostic (gnosis*) distinction between a good god and a just god (*Adv. Haer.* III, 25, 2–5). Divine justice and bounty shine in the redemption that the Word of God gives to humanity by his blood (*Adv. Haer.* V, 1, 1); God "recovers his own good in all justice and goodness") (V, 2, 1). In all justice because he

pays for us the ransom due, instead of using violence, be it against the demon (demons*) (same idea in Augustine, *Trin* XIII, 14–15, BAug 16, 314–19; in Gregory* of Nyssa, *Oratio catechetica* 20–26, PG 45, 55–70). Augustine understands divine justice in the same sense as Paul: "The justice of God does not signify that by which God is just, but that justice which God gives to man so that he will be just by the grace of God" (*Homilies on the Gospel of St. John* 26, BAug 72, 482; *see* Council of Trent*, session 6, ch. 7).

b) Middle Ages. For Anselm*, "God is justice" (*existit justitia*—Monologion 16) and justice is the very example (ibid.) of those divine attributes that belong by essence to the supreme nature *(summa natura).* But mercy is also one of those attributes, because we know for sure that God pardons and saves. Highly aware of the problem raised by attributing to God seemingly contradictory properties (as that of justice itself: "can he do an injustice" in sparing evildoers?; *Proslogion* 9), Anselm resolves the antinomy with recourse to the unity of the divine essence in which all the attributes of the sovereign good* mysteriously coincide. God is just, not in that he treats us according to our merits, but in that he treats us in a manner fitting to what he is: "You are just, not because you render us our due, but because you do that which is worthy of you, Sovereign good" (ibid., 10. Note the same idea in Barth*, *KD* II/1).

This shift in sense with respect to the ordinary notion of the virtue (virtues*) of justice is found also in Thomas, for whom God, by being just, renders to himself that which he owes himself (*ST* Ia, q. 21, a. 1, ad 3). This justice is indeed distributive (*CG* 1, 93), but above all it is fundamental because it consists in "given to each that which is fitting in virtue of his nature." And it has a cosmic dimension, to the extent that it also constitutes an order of the universe (q. 21, a. 1). There is no opposition between justice and mercy (which are treated in the same question) because mercy is the fullness (ibid., a. 3) of justice. Even more deeply, it is its "root" and "foundation," because nothing is due to the creature but by the will of his Creator, but everything is given superabundantly, "more than the measure of things demands" (a. 4).

c) Modernity. Apparently the message of Thomas did not persist. Divine justice was reduced to retributive or vindictive justice, with all the problems that entailed for considering justification. When Luther set forth the justice of God in the Pauline and Augustinian sense—the justice that God bestows on us, which he named " passive justice"—it was in opposition to an "active justice" that he regarded as solely a justice of condemnation (e.g., *WA* 40/1, 45, 25–26; 40/2, 331). This explains why he understood justice as an action of salvation by God, not a divine attribute (Hauser 1974).

K. Barth should be credited with rethinking the unity of mercy and justice, retaining for the latter its proper sense of "distributive justice" (countering modern interpretations, *KD* II/1). This justice is manifest in the death of Christ as both the chastisement of sin and of the sinner (ibid.): justice is therefore a mercy that saves. Barth is one of the rare theologians of modern times who still posit a justice in God and consequently affirm the seriousness of redemption (§30, 2, 3, e.g.). By being absorbed in mercy, which in fact changes its nature, justice, divine justice is dissolved in it and, without being explicitly denied, today often disappears from the list of divine attributes (Pesch 1995). Perhaps modern thinkers find it difficult to discern the justice of God in creation and in history. After all, as one of them has said, "the vision of justice is the pleasure of God alone."

● Anselm, *Monologion* 16.
Anselm, *Proslogion* 9–11.
Thomas Aquinas, *ST* Ia, q. 21; *CG* 1, 93.

Luther, *Commentary on Galatians* (1531), *WA* 40/1, *Commentary on the Psalm 51*, *WA* 40/2.
K. Barth, *KD* II/1, §30, 2.
◆ G. Quell, G. Schrenk (1935), "Dikaiosunè," *ThWNT* 2, 194–214.
A. Descamps, L. Cerfaux (1949), "J. et justification," *DBS* 4, 1417–1510 (bibl.).
G. Pidoux (1954), "Un aspect négligé de la j. dans l'Ancien Testament: Son aspect cosmique," *RThPh* 4, 283–88.
J.-M. Aubert (1974), "J. (de Dieu et de l'homme, Justification)," *DSp* 8, 1621–40 (bibl.).
R. Hauser (1974), in "Gerechtigkeit," *HWP* 3, 330–34 (bibl.).
J. Auer (1978), "Die Rede der Gerechtigkeit Gottes," *KKD* 2, §43, 523–32.
B. Hägglund (1984), "Gerechtigkeit" I, *TRE* 12, 432–40.
H. Merkel (1984), "Gerechtigkeit" V, *TRE* 12, 420–24.
J. Scharbert (1984), "Gerechtigkeit" I, 3, *TRE* 12, 408–11.
B. Johnson (1987), "Çadaq," *ThWAT* 6, 898–924.
K. Kertelge, O. H. Pesch (1995), "Gerechtigkeit Gottes," *LThK* (new Ed.) 4, 504–7.

IRÈNE FERNANDEZ

See also **Attributes, Divine; Cosmos; Eternity of God; Immutability/Impassibility, Divine; Judgment; Justice; Justification; Knowledge, Divine; Omnipresence, Divine; Providence; Simplicity, Divine**

Justification

a) New Testament. How are people to please God? Or, more specifically, how are they to enter into communion with him? According to Christian theology, this question can only be answered by bearing in mind the following two points. On the one hand, the situation of sin in which human beings are immersed makes them incapable of this communion—they are unable to free themselves from the distorted vision, or from the weakness and the corruption of the will, that the situation imposes on them. On the other hand, God's liberty is total: he cannot be compelled or even persuaded to act in one way or another. So, if human beings are to find grace in his eyes, it can only be on his account.

As early as the Dead Sea Scrolls, there is reference to God's acting to enable human beings to enter into communion with him by virtue of his justice *(tsedâqâh)*. Divine justice does not condemn but rather liberates: "Thanks to God's justice, my justification will endure for ever" (1QS11, 12): "Your justice has brought me into the service of your Covenant*" (1QH7, 19). It is true that the primary sense of the Hebrew words formed from the root *ts-d-q* is "to acquit," "to declare innocent"; but it should also be noted that, in the case of a number of the texts from Qumran, God's action brings about a change in the sinful man and makes him capable of bearing genuine witness to the covenant. So we see arise the complications that would characterize later Christian thinking: was the divine action above all an acquittal (a simple declaration), or was it above all a transformation?

The New Testament usage of *dikaioun* (to justify) and *dikaiosunè* (justice) does not resolve the problem. In the parable of the Pharisee and the tax collector (Lk 18:14), we see that the tax collector goes home "justified," in other words innocent in the eyes of God, because he has laid claim to no innocence or virtue (virtues*) of his own; but no conclusion can be drawn as to the effect that this has had upon him. Paul discusses this question at length, particularly in the Epistle to the Romans; he is chiefly concerned with the reasons why God treats us as if we were not culpable, a decision based only on his free choice. Thus we are "justified" by God's grace manifested in Jesus Christ (Rom 3:24ff.), or by the blood of Jesus stretched upon the cross (Rom 5:9). When we fully acknowledge the divine action, we receive its fruits; it is for this reason that it can be said that we are justified by faith (Rom 3:28, 5:1; Gal 2:16, 3:24). Whoever has confidence in what was accomplished by the death of Jesus is therefore innocent in the eyes of God (Rom 3:26). The later and disputed formula of "justification by faith *alone*," the *sola fide* of some Protestants, is not to be found in these terms in Paul's writings; and the very expression "justification by faith" must be understood in the context of the whole dramatic scheme set out in Romans and Galatians, in which God, in the person of Jesus, redeems and remits sins. Failing this, there is a risk of forgetting that it is *God* who has taken this unparalleled initiative.

According to Paul the divine acquittal is the beginning, in history, of a process of transfiguration of humankind, which nonetheless has its origin in God's eternal foreknowledge (Rom 8:29f.). But this is not his only observation concerning salvation, and it would be wrong to detach this point from his whole conception of it: salvation also includes "glorification" and is achieved in union with the glorified Christ, by participation in his death and resurrection, and by incorporation into his body, the Church. It very soon became clear, however, that the intensity, the excessiveness even, of Paul's language in Romans and Galatians when he speaks of a "justice" entirely distinct from obedience to the law, could be interpreted in an antinomian or quietist sense; consequently the Epistle of St James strongly opposes the idea that one can be "justified" by faith alone, without avoiding sin and without practicing justice and generosity in human relations (2:14–26).

b) Before Augustine. The question was hardly discussed in Christian literature before Augustine, although Origen* is very close to Pauline* thinking in his commentary on Romans (4:1): "It cannot be said that justice derives from works*; rather it is the fruit of good works which derives from justice"; and this "justice" comes from faith, since it is with respect to those who show proof of their faith that God exercises his power of granting it. Origen also employs *dikaioun* in its less technical but significant sense of "to rectify"

(*Against Celsus* 4, 7): from this point of view, "justifying" human beings is a matter of making them live in accordance with the rational principle that is within them, and thus with God's will. Origen aside, few of the Greek Fathers* really dealt with the question. Later Greek catechesis* (in the work of Cyril of Jerusalem or John Chrysostom, for example) generally recognized that human liberty* played a part in the observance of the commandments (Decalogue*) but did not consider that this was the means by which our relationship with God might find its full expression. An excellent summary of the Eastern attitude to the subject is to be found in a work attributed to Mark the Hermit (certainly from the fifth century), *On those who consider that they are justified by works: Two hundred and twenty-six texts*. Good works act to counterbalance sin and are essentially defined negatively. They make it possible to "retain the purity*" of baptism. But perfection ("justice" or "sanctification") is a matter of living fully as adoptive sons of God, free from all passion (passions*). It is an inner state resulting from God's grace alone but which may be prepared for by way of asceticism and attentive prayer. The problem of justification is located here in the typically monastic context of the relationship between *praktikè*, the active practice of the virtues, and *theologia*, the gift of inner purity and stability. This is certainly not a very Pauline point of view, but it would be a mistake to see it as mere Pelagianism*.

c) Augustine. Augustine was the first to take the Pauline doctrine seriously in the sense in which Paul himself had conceived it; and despite what is often alleged, the Pelagian controversy was not the sole reason for his absolute conviction of the supreme priority of God's grace. From his works of the 390s, indeed, he increasingly emphasizes God's initiative in everything concerning salvation: our will is corrupt and has no freedom, and even when we fleetingly glimpse the good we are incapable of fulfilling it (this point lies at the heart of his theology, as can be seen from the *Confessions*). It is certain, nonetheless, that the Pelagian controversy led him to formulate more and more energetically the central idea that God, "when he crowns our merits, is merely crowning his own gifts" (*Ep.* 194:19). Left to its own devices, our will can do nothing to deserve God's gifts, since it is incapable of turning itself toward him. It must, however, be recognized that for Augustine divine justification is precisely what makes us *righteous*. To be a righteous person is to fulfill the law; but the fulfillment of the law, according to Paul, is love (Rom 13:10), and this love is the gift made us by the Holy Spirit (Rom 5:5), so that in the last analysis, to be righteous is to participate in the divine life (*Treatise* 26, 1). For Augustine, *justitia* is in effect equivalent to *caritas:* justice thus consists of our incorporation into the body of Christ, and the indwelling of the Trinity within us, by the operation of the Spirit (*De Trinitate* 15, 18, for example). From a slightly different standpoint, it can also be said that to be *righteous* is to be in one's place in the universe, since *justitia* may also denote the balance and interconnection of all things in their proper order and hierarchy (*City of God* 19, e.g.): to be "justified," then, is to have this just relationship with the rest of creation and with the Creator. Our love must be properly ordered, so that we may take created things for what they are and not for God; the divine life present in the baptized will thus find expression in a measured love of the world. If God is truly present to us, it is impossible to confuse his beauty with the beauty of the world. The inner justice of the divine life is expressed in the outward justice of ordered relations, which demands the exercise of a will that has been redeemed and healed: "He created you without your help, but he will not justify you without your help; he created you without your knowing, he justifies you with the assent of your will" (*Fecit nescientem, justificat volentem,* sermon 169, 3). It is not that our acts of will bring about our justification, but rather that the process of justification brings about a willed activity on our part. Justification would not be real if it was not expressed in a transformation of the will.

d) Latin Middle Ages. For Augustine, justification was inseparable from a whole series of processes, including our adoption as children of God, our sanctification, and even our "deification." Until the 13th century the Latin West accepted this model, on the one hand attaching great importance to the quasi-identity between the Holy Spirit and justifying and sanctifying grace, and on the other hand approaching the question from the standpoint of the divine presence in the soul (soul*-heart-body). Scholasticism, however, was more interested in the effect produced by that presence. On the basis of observations that Augustine had made in passing on the necessity of expressing our justice through the will to good, it erected the theory of what came to be known as "created grace" (this expression, doubtless derived from the 13th-century *Summa Alexandri,* is uncharacteristic of Thomas* Aquinas). The "formal" cause of our justification was the sum of the created aptitudes produced in us by divine action and presence. There was not the slightest doubt as to the author of the real initiative: it was God who brought about justification. In concrete terms, however, justification was a transformation—the acquisition of new aptitudes, and the formation of a particular

moral and spiritual state. God's grace worked to make us ready to receive his gifts to the full and to ensure that those gifts took root in us. As in Augustine's conception, we can do absolutely nothing by ourselves to deserve divine favor, but grace does not come upon us unawares. There is in fact a preparation for grace, which makes us worthy to receive it. This "merit" that prepares us for supernatural life is itself the work of God within us and is in no way binding on God. At every stage God's action remains free. There is thus a distinction between merit *de condigno,* in which there is an exact parity between an act and its consequences, and merit *de congruo,* which is an openness to or a general fitness for God's gifts. In the view of some authors, the second type of merit left mankind with a limited degree of initiative (though it never existed without divine help). Generally speaking, Thomas and the Dominicans limited the role of merit *de congruo,* while the first Franciscans (Alexander of Hales and Bonaventure* among them) allowed it more scope and considered that there was a predictable relationship between human activity (assisted by grace) and the culmination of God's gift in justification: he who endeavored to do what God inspired him to do had no *right* to justification but could reasonably hope that God's mercy would not fail him.

In the 14th century, above all among the Franciscans influenced by Duns* Scotus, a much stronger emphasis began to be placed upon the absolute gratuitousness of the divine initiative, to the point that the formal cause of justification was increasingly defined as God's declaration of our state of justice. The habitus created by grace ensued from it, admittedly, and could even be considered as a second formal cause; but, above all, it was never to be seen as the reason for the decision that God took to look upon us with favor. God decided from all eternity that some sinners would be treated as righteous, and that they would be distinguished from other sinners by the fact of receiving the grace to live in supernatural love; but this last decision was not a condition of the first one. God could have decided that the distinction would be quite different. So at the end of the Middle Ages the problem of justification was discussed with the help of the idea of God's "two powers," *potestas absoluta* and *potestas ordinata,* the absolute power to do what pleases him, and a power in which he restricts himself and decides that he will "react" in a given way to a given situation. The same emphasis was placed on the priority and liberty of the divine will by William of Ockham, Gabriel Biel, and other supporters of the *via moderna* in the 14th and 15th centuries and is also found at the same period in the work of numerous theologians of the Augustinian order, for example Gregory of Rimini. All agreed that there was nothing in the life of grace of a created being, with all its resulting faith, love, and so on, to oblige God to accept it. Such a life could, in the abstract, be meritorious on a moral level, but this moral quality had nothing to do with salvation. However, God had decided that he would accept this life. If therefore we lived according to God's law, we could presume that our salvation was probable—with reservations, however, since we never know for certain whether we have observed the law as well as we could have done.

e) Reformation.   It is a characteristic trait of late medieval thought to make a complete separation between justification and participation in divine life. For Augustine and for many other older authors, to be acceptable to God entailed living a life that reflected the nature of God; but for the theologians of the *via moderna,* there was in the life of grace nothing intrinsically connected to the divine nature. It is paradoxical that the two main currents in the Reformation returned to the earlier model, albeit in fundamentally different ways. Luther is faithful to some aspects of the *via moderna,* in particular to the principle that God alone can be the cause of what God does or decides, but concludes that the principle of our justice must be God *in Christ**. Faith grasps the essential and decisive fact that God chooses to regard us as though Christ's justice were our own. This justice remains "foreign" to us—we can never own, cultivate or develop it—and so there can be no question of there being a model of grace inherent to us. It is a mistake, as is generally recognized today, to say that Luther makes justification dependent upon *our* faith; rather he sees faith as a consequence of justification, which is simply God's decision to ascribe Christ's justice and faith to us. Luther's lectures on the Epistle to the Galatians (early 1530s) offer a powerful conception of the unity of the believer and Christ (by *conglutinatio* and *inhaesio*); and this unity is seen as initially dependent upon God's decision, and only later taken up by faith. Christ's justice thus remains forever external to us; however, as faith grasps the reality of the divine decision, we begin to act in a way appropriate to our new status. So our lives reflect the fact that we are accepted by God and also the basis of this acceptance—Christ's justice.

For Augustine and earlier writers in general, justification implied a participation in Christ's justice, and thus in the life of God. For Luther, on the other hand, there is certainly an identity between Christ and ourselves, but it is still dependent upon God's pleasure and never upon anything that might become innate to us. Nonetheless, the Christocentric nature of his theology in this field, and the force of the language* he employs to talk of the effective identity that exists in God's eyes between Christ and ourselves, mean that he is still very close to the patristic tradition. Among the Lutherans of the following generation (Lutheranism*), however, it is the purely *juridical* character of justification that is highlighted: justification is considered as the remission of a debt without (human) payment. The Latin technical term *acceptilatio* was often used to convey this (Erasmus* had pointed out that it could denote the decision to consider an unpaid debt as paid, and Melanchthon [1497–1560] seems to have taken this as his starting point in order to understand the meaning of the "imputation" of justice); it was distinguished from *acceptatio,* which presumed that one had actually been paid. So theologians concerned themselves more and more with the way in which Christ pays our debts for us and less and less with what interested Luther, namely the union between Christ and the believer. The latter point was treated in more depth, indeed, within Calvinist theology (Calvinism*). Calvin shared with Luther the conviction that Christ's justice and obedience could be attributed to the believer by virtue of his union with him, which brought with it the gift of sanctification. Christ had "consecrated" or sanctified himself for us, according to the Fourth Gospel (Gospels*) (Jn 17:19; in the Vulgate [translations* of the Bible] *pro eis ego sanctifico meipsum*), and God considered his justice, his perfect obedience, and his sanctity (holiness*) to be ours, as well as the sacrifice* that he offered for us as our high priest. Other Calvinist theologians put a greater emphasis on the eternal and unconditional acquittal pronounced by God. It was Calvin and John Knox (1505 or 1513–72) who situated both justification and sanctification most firmly in our adoption by God in Christ. Seventeenth-century Protestant thought was almost completely dominated by the idea of the covenant between God and humanity in general (the covenant of obedience to the law promising grace under the old dispensation, and the new covenant in which salvation is promised in exchange for faith in Christ). It offers many echoes of the late medieval speculation on the decisions in which God limits his power, though this theology is increasingly remote from Calvin himself.

f) Counter Reformation.   The Catholic reaction to the Reformation was extremely complex, but the Council of Trent's decree on justification (COD 671.681) is actually much closer to Luther and Calvin than to the medieval debate, in particular because it largely abandons the technical vocabulary of Scholasticism in favor of an Augustinian or even Pauline language. Justification is seen as entailing the gift of a new status as adoptive children of God, a gift that remits sins by virtue of incorporation into the second Adam*. Even though baptism is defined as the instrumental cause of justification, it is very clearly stated that it has one and only one formal cause, God's justice, understood as the justice by which he makes us righteous. By linking justification so clearly to the nature of God in actuality, the council was therefore clearly asserting that there could be no created cause of justification. Certainly one could speak of merit *de congruo* to describe gifts granted before justification properly speaking, but this would be to take the words in their Dominican sense, according to which merit was never effective before the grace of justification. The brevity and the general nature of the Trent decree nonetheless opened the way to many further debates on the relative priority of created and uncreated grace.

The Catholic controversies of the late 16th century show that disagreements concerning justification do not follow denominational lines—some Catholic authors of the period are closer to some Protestant theologians than to their own coreligionists, and more than one of the various theological opinions presented at the Calvinist synod of Dordrecht in 1619 would have met with the complete approval of some Catholics. The pope's condemnation of Baianism (Bañezianism*-Molinism-Baianism) in 1567 was directed against the idea of a grace that would be necessary even to perform actions related to the natural order of things—a much more pessimistic vision of the human condition than Calvin's. But no papal decision came to put an end to the debate *de auxiliis* that began in Spain at the close of the century between the Jesuits and the Dominicans. The Jesuit position, represented by Molina, gave a major role to liberty in justification: God created conditions that he knew (by his perfect foreknowledge) would be sufficient for a human will to turn to him. The Dominicans, whose most formidable representative was Domingo Bañez (confessor to Teresa of Ávila) (Bañezianism-Molinism-Baianism) maintained that the soul always turned to God as a result of a "physical premotion" of divine grace. The final Roman document on the subject (in 1607) was careful not to take sides; but the later condemnation of Jansenism* was to incline Catholic theology somewhat toward Molinism.

The Anglican theology of this period (Anglicanism*) also underwent a debate on the problem of justification. At that time in England there were supporters of an extreme position that categorically refused any idea of a grace "internal" to the justified soul—a position more extreme than Calvin's and one that led to the conclusion that Catholics were absolutely outside the true Church and excluded from salvation. Richard Hooker (c. 1554–1600) spoke out against these views

during the 1580s, which caused him to be regarded by some as a traitor to Protestantism*. But his understanding of the relationship among justification, adoption, and sanctification would to a large extent have met with Luther's agreement as much as Calvin's. He summarizes it in his first sermon on the subject: in this life, the justice that justifies us (that of Christ) is "perfect but not inherent," while the justice that sanctifies us, and that depends entirely upon the first, is "inherent, but not perfect"—it expresses, but neither causes nor influences in any way, the justice by which we are adopted and incorporated into Christ. Anglican theology subsequently evolved at best toward a kind of Molinism, at worst toward what was effectively Pelagianism. The teaching of Newman* (while still an Anglican, 1837) on the subject belongs broadly to this tradition, although it accords great importance to the priority of the divine presence.

g) Modern Times. The religious thinking of the Enlightenment made a fundamental break with Protestantism's central concern and rejected the idea of an absolute priority of divine action in our reconciliation with God, which appeared particularly arbitrary. In *Religion Within the Limits of Simple Reason,* Kant* ingeniously transposes the idea of justification by a justice not our own onto a moral and individualistic plane: the virtues of a man new born from a free conversion* to moral virtue may be ascribed to the man he used to be before he turned toward the good—a fact that ensures the forgiveness of his sins, since God considers the former man as though he were new and converted. In the same way, once the will has turned toward the good, God regards the newly (even if imperfectly) virtuous person as though he had already attained perfect virtue: he looks on such a person with approval and compensates for his deficiencies. (This is already far removed, however, from the kind of thinking to be found elsewhere at the time, which maintained a strict parity between virtue and reward.) Schleiermacher*'s position resembles Kant's, though it is much more Christocentric: we need a salvation that does not come from ourselves, and this need is fulfilled through the gift of participation or communion in Christ, in whom there is a perfect correlation between moral goodness and divine favor.

The most important contribution to the study of the issue, at the close of the 19th century, was undoubtedly that of A. Ritschl (1888–89), by virtue of the balance he was able to achieve between the objective and subjective aspects of justification. For Ritschl, justification is the pardon granted by God to the sinner, as revealed by Christ, and the purpose of this pardon is to establish a perfectly just society, the Kingdom of

God. The goal of justification is thus a moral situation, the existence in the world of a just and peaceful (peace*) community; and in order for this to come about, the freedom and action of the believer are necessary to make manifest God's plan as revealed by the absolution of our sins. Ritschl says little about the way in which the event of Jesus Christ reveals to us the (eternal) fact that God is a forgiving God, and he was criticized for not clarifying the specific nature of God's action in Christ.

Barth approaches the problem of justification in various ways. In his earliest works, particularly the second *Commentary on the Epistle to the Romans* (1921), he insists that no human virtue, knowledge, or achievement is commensurable with God's justice; on the contrary, the incommensurability is so complete that without grace we would not even know that it existed—without grace, indeed, we would have no criterion of comparison. Moreover, we discover God's justice at the same time as his judgment on all our works, good or bad. It is at the very moment when we hear the devastating "No" pronounced by God upon all that we are, that we also hear the divine "Yes," since it is at this point that we learn what God is, and who he is—a God who does not hide but who manifests himself. "God's justice is the place where we remain in uncertainty, in other words where it is impossible to remain...the place in which we are entirely in his hands, so that he may treat us as he pleases" (*Der Römerbrief* [1922], new corr. Ed. 1967).

For God, to reveal himself as just is to reveal his desire for reconciliation. Barth was to say the same in the first parts of the *Dogmatics,* leading to criticism of the notion of a salvation apparently based exclusively upon a progression in knowledge. In the fourth part, however (*see* above all §13), the theory is complemented by a reference to the deed of Christ who allowed himself to be judged in our place. By accepting condemnation and even "annihilation" in our place, he in fact showed that there could no longer be any condemnation for anybody and so established a truly new humanity, an objectively new status of communion with the God who has chosen us all in him. The tendency to emphasize knowledge is still apparent but is more clearly linked to the traditional themes of incorporation and adoption.

We owe one of the most important ecumenical contributions on the subject to Hans Küng (1957), in whose view there is no fundamental difference between Barth's theory of justification (or those of the great reformers) and the teaching of the Catholic Church. The pronouncements of Barth and the reformers on faith in justification would be more meaningful, in general, if they were interpreted in the context of the Catholic doctrine of hope: we put our trust in God to look upon us in the light of his eschatological plan. This concern for eschatology is evident in the declaration on "justification by faith" that emerged from the Lutheran-Catholic dialogue of 1983 (in the United States) and in the document *Salvation and the Church* produced by ARCIC II (1987). These texts prove that Catholics and non-Catholics are able to agree on key aspects of the doctrine and to recognize in particular that the community of believers, while it exists *in via,* is nonetheless able to proclaim and realize sacramentally the sanctity of Christ on which it is based. Contemporary Protestantism increasingly recognizes that the idea of sanctification within the Church, or even through the community and sacramental life of the Church, does not put God under any "obligation" toward it. Contemporary Catholicism, moreover, is increasingly prepared to incorporate into its theology a consideration of the sins of the Church throughout history and to accept that Christ's justice, celebrated and made present and effective in the sacraments (sacrament*), is nonetheless given in an entirely gratuitous and unconditional way.

● A. Ritschl (1888–89,), *Die christliche Lehre von der Rechtfertigung und Versöhnung,* 3rd Ed., Bonn.

K. Barth (1922), *Der Römerbrief,* Munich (new corr. ed., Zurich, 1967).

K. Barth (1953), *KD* IV/1 (*Dogmatique,* Geneva, 1966–67).

F. J. Taylor (1954), *The Doctrine of Justification by Faith,* London.

H. Küng (1957), *Rechtfertigung: Die Lehre Karl Barths und eine katholische Besinnung,* Einsiedeln.

J. Chéné (1961), *La théologie de saint Augustin: Grâce et prédestination,* Le Puy-Lyon.

W. Joest (1963), "Die tridentinische Rechtfertigungslehre," *KuD* 9, 41–59.

T. F. Torrance (1965), *Theology in Reconstruction,* London.

O. H. Pesch (1967), *Theologie der Rechtfertigung bei Martin Luther und Thomas v. Aquin,* Mayence (3rd Ed. 1985).

O. Loyer (1979), *L'anglicanisme de Richard Hooker,* Lille.

O. H. Pesch, A. Peters (1981), *Einführung in die Lehre von Gnade und Rechtfertigung,* Darmstadt (2nd Ed. 1989).

J. Reumann (1982), *Righteousness in the New Testament: Justification in the United States Lutheran-Roman Catholic Dialogue,* Philadelphia.

E. P. Sanders (1983), *Paul, the Law and the Jewish People,* Philadelphia.

G. H. Tavard (1983), *Justification: An Ecumenical Study,* New York.

H. Anderson et al. (1985), *Justification by Faith (Lutherans and Catholics in Dialogue,* vol. 7), Minneapolis.

A. McGrath (1986), Iustitia Dei. *A History of the Christian Doctrine of Justification,* 2 vols., Cambridge.

K. Lehmann, W. Pannenberg (Ed.) (1987), *Lehrverurteilungen-Kirchentrennend?,* vol. 1: *Rechtfertigung, Sakramente und Amt im Zeitalter der Reformation und heute,* Freiberg-Göttingen.

K. Lehmann (Ed.) (1989), *Lehrverurteilungen-Kirchentrennend?,* vol. 2: *Materialen zu der Lehrverurteilungen und zu Theologie der Rechtfertigung,* Freiberg-Göttingen.

U. Kühn, O. H. Pesch (1991), *Rechtfertigung im Disput,* Tübingen.

M. Beintker et al. (1995), *Rechtfertigung und Erfahrung,* Gütersloh.

ROWAN WILLIAMS

See also **Augustinianism; Choice; Indulgences; Judgment; Knowledge, Divine; Mercy; Nature; Predestination; Puritanism; Wrath of God**

Justin. *See* Apologists

K

Kant, Immanuel

1724–1804

To begin with, one must examine the concept of religion as it is presented in Kant's work. This will serve to reveal that which may be of interest to theology* in Kant's thought and also to understand the significance of his actual influence upon Christian theology.

a) The Kantian Notion of Religion. "Religion is the recognition of all our duties and of divine commandments." The first appearance of this definition can be found in the *Critique of Practical Reason* (1788, AA V, 129). It would continue to be valid, above all in the two major works devoted to religion: *Religion Within the Limits of Reason Alone* (1793) and *The Conflict of the Faculties* (1798). It hinged upon that which the *Critique of Practical Reason* called the "primacy of practical reason*" (AA V, 119), which referred on the one hand to the theological attitudes adopted in the *Critique of Pure Reason* (1781–86) and on the other to the major features of the theology contained in the *Critique of Practical Reason.*

This primacy comes at the expense of theoretical reason, whose aim to *know,* supported by proof, fails when the idea of God* is in question. Such knowledge is indeed restricted to the phenomenal object, given to sensibility, and of which we can henceforth dispose, a last feature that suffices to make one understand why a proof (existence* of God, proofs of) of God's existence is out of the question. Moreover, one must be able to *think* of God, something that can only be done on the basis of our knowledge, which is still linked to sensibility. Kant would develop an analogous use of the idea of God, which he did not hesitate to describe as anthropomorphism* (AA III, 457–59). The main thing was in fact to not remain limited to deism (deism*/theism) (the "Supreme Being") and to move on to theism, to the affirmation of the personal God, which implies an analogy* with the human person*. The theology of the *Critique of Practical Reason* is double. On the one hand, the moral obligation present in the conscience* of moral law* (the "categorical imperative") does not need a theological foundation, as moral law is henceforth autonomy (that in which reason recognizes itself). But if one's relation with God does not precede duty and its fulfillment, it is nevertheless called upon an exigency contained in the moral imperative itself, that of the possibility of an achievement, the "sovereign good*", where accomplished virtue (virtues*) and happiness are joined. (*Critique of Practical Reason,* AA V, 110–13). This amounts to "postulating" the immortality of the soul (soul*-heart-body) and the existence of God, object of a "faith* of reason" (*Critique of Practical Reason,* AA V, 142–46).

Religion Within the Limits of Reason Alone, in a first stage, expounds upon a religion of reason, transcribing original sin* into a radical evil* and setting forth in Christ* "the idea of a man who is pleasing to God" (AA VI, 62–63). In a second stage, moral law, taken from the violence* of history*, demands to become, as a law of liberty*, the law not only of individuals but also of the group. This is equivalent to setting up a legislator of inner law, one who "scrutinizes hearts," as the link of "people* of God under ethical laws" (AA VI, 98–100). One must read it as an interpretation of the *Church**.

b) Christian Theology. The problem stated is that of a *rationalization of religion reduced to morality* (a reduction with no trace of the Pietism* in which Kant was raised). It would be found again all through the theological reception of Kant, with some notable differences, however, between Protestant theology (Protestantism*) and Catholic theology (Catholicism*).

Protestant reception began during Kant's lifetime, and the debate was centered upon the "religion of reason." Its moral interpretation, which placed the value of the act (action*) first of all in respect for the law, and not in "works*," refusing any "merits," was an explicit acknowledgment of the Gospels* (*Critique of Practical Reason,* AA V, 81–83) and was consonant with the ideas of Martin Luther*. But it would be too easy to view it as a departure from biblical revelation*. One might be reminded of Schleiermacher*, who initially leaned toward Kant but later moved away from his ideas when he turned toward a hermeneutic (hermeneutics*) theology. Of note, in the era of neo-Kantism, are the works of Albrecht Ritschl (1822–89), who insisted in particular on the socio-political dimension of Kant's religious writings. With Karl Barth*, dialectical theology would be opposed to such a position and would firmly refuse any reduction of the Word* of God to a moral or political attitude.

It is remarkable that on the Catholic side the debate moved from the notion of religion toward its foundations, the critique of the proofs of God's existence, and the morality of autonomy. During Kant's lifetime, it was in southern Germany that supporters and adversaries confronted each other. In the 19th century, Georg Hermes (1775–1831) would firmly uphold a dogmatic* theology that preserved, from Kant's work, the dignity of the person and his analyses of faith. Rome* banned the teaching of Hermes's ideas in 1835. The negative image of Kant would characterize the beginnings of Neoscholasticism at the end of the century. A change of great significance occurred in the first half of the 20th century, when the Belgian Jesuit Joseph Maréchal (1878–1944) published *Le point de départ de la métaphysique,* notebook 5, *Le thomisme devant la philosophie critique* (Brussels-Paris, 1949). This work introduced Kant in order to accomplish the initial aims of Neoscholasticism: a return to Thomas* Aquinas, but taking modernity into account—something that could not be done if Kant were merely an adversary. Kant's a priori was reexamined within the

framework of the Thomist "formal object"; access to the being* was maintained, however. Development within a German context was enriched by the contact with Heidegger*, as with J.-B. Lotz. It was in this fertile ground of "transcendental Thomism" that Rahner* was educated, and this fact alone is proof of the movement's fertility.

c) Theology in a Plural World. The above remarks, both from a Protestant and a Catholic point of view, show that Kant can still provide "food for thought" to the theologian. It is no accident that Catholic reception, undoubtedly more hesitant than the Protestant one, found its most fertile development when, with Joseph Maréchal, it discovered in Kant one of the most radical interrogations of Christian thought, that of the possibility of being human, in the understanding and accomplishment of the moral imperative, without first making the relation to God explicit.

Kant's *Critique of Judgment* is exemplary: There Kant acknowledges the full moral sense of the atheist and concludes that in order not to lessen the transformative power of moral law, he will become a "believer from a practical point of view" (§91, AA V, 469–70). This is the radical proposal that a plural world* is possible, one that will form a whole despite the radical differences in religious options. The "practical point of view" means that no confession* of faith can be separated from an exchange among freedoms. No idea about God can be anything other than the act of free thought, which does not exclude the fact that it is committed to ties of solidarity* that may be those of a Church.

Kant did not find his inspiration from theologians: his reexamination of incarnation* is poor and is in strong contrast to the treatment given by Hegel*. It was rather to Scripture that Kant returned. He knew how to give it the status of a reading, as in the appendix to the first section of the *Conflict of Faculties.* In this capacity, Paul Ricoeur belongs to the best Kantian tradition in his programmatic aims: "Symbols make us think," a long path to follow, where Kant is merely a starting point.

● (1922), *Kant's gesammelte Schriften* herausgegeben von der königlich preussischen Akademie der Wissenschaften, Berlin-Leipzig (AA).
Kant-Bibliographie 1945–1990, Ed. M. Ruffing, Frankfurt.
♦ K. Jaspers (1952), "Le mal radical chez Kant," *Deucalion* 4, 224–52.
P. Ricoeur (1960), *La symbolique du mal,* Paris.
J.-L. Bruch (1968), *La philosophie religieuse de Kant,* Paris; id. (1969), *Kant. Lettres sur la morale et la religion,* Paris.
O. Reboul (1971), *Kant et le problème du mal,* Montréal.
R. Malter (1980), *Das Reformatorische Denken und die Philosophie, Luthers Entwurf einer transzendental-praktischen Metaphysik,* Bonn.

F. Marty (1980), *La naissance de la métaphysique chez Kant: Une étude sur la notion kantienne d'analogie*, Paris.

H. d'Aviau de Ternay (1986), *Traces bibliques dans la loi morale chez Kant*, Paris.

FRANÇOIS MARTY

See also **Agnosticism; Ethics; Ethics, Autonomy of; Hegel, Georg Wilhelm Friedrich; Kierkegaard, Soren Aabye; Knowledge of God; Rationalism; Reason; Schleiermacher, Friedrich Daniel Ernst**

Kenosis

1. Scriptural Basis

The term *kenosis,* coined by the Greek Fathers of the Church* from the verb *kénoô,* "to empty" (hence, used reflexively, "to empty oneself of oneself"), derives from an expression in the hymn of Philippians 2:7. The naming of Jesus* as Lord (2:9) is preceded by a sequence describing the humbling of the man who was "of divine condition" (2:6). His elevation comes at the end of a descent and an annihilation *(heauton ekenôsen)* that takes him, because of his obedience, to his death* on the cross. The entire event of Jesus is the outcome of the free initiative of the man *"who was not considered as a victim, but as equal to God*"* (2:6), who chose the "condition of servitude." Whether this text refers to the Son before his incarnation* (following the ancient tradition*) or in Jesus as incarnate (following the majority of modern exegetes), preexistence is understood. Jesus comes from God and returns into the glory* of God, after having divested himself in a human existence. In the Gospel of John, Christ*'s journey is also represented as a dramatic descent and ascension. The path he follows begins in heaven (1:1f.) and leads him to earth (1:11f.) and eventually to the cross (19:17f.); there follows the reascension of the Risen One in his earlier glory. According to the prologue of John, the divine Word has become flesh (1:14); however divine the Word may be in God, its presence in the "flesh" is nonetheless absolutely real. The originality of the Johannine contribution lies in the sharpness of this contrast. In Greek thought, indeed, there can be no stronger contrast than that between *logos* and *sarx.*

2. Revival of the Theme in the Fathers of the Church

The problem of kenosis remained misunderstood in gnosis*, which attributed to the Word as only an apparent body; in Arianism*, which denied the equality of being* between Son and Father; and in Nestorianism*, which emphasized the "promotion" of a man to the dignity of man-God. In its struggle on these three fronts, orthodoxy had to tread a fine line: it had to avoid defending divine immutability* in such a way as would have implied a sheltering of the Word from a real event, and on the other hand it had to avoid falling into an immediate affirmation of a change in God. A first fundamental idea was used by Athanasius* against Arius and Apollinarius, by Cyril* against Nestorius, and by Leo against Eutyches: the divine decision that the Word should become man indicated a genuine humbling. For God, the Incarnation is not an "increase" but an emptying, an exhaustion. Hilary* went a step further. He sees everything as taking place by virtue of the sovereign liberty* of God, who, while dwelling in himself, has the power to lay his glory aside (*De Trin.* VIII. 45; PL 10. 270). If the two forms were simply compatible (as the three Doctors of the Church* previously mentioned thought), nothing would occur in God. For Hilary, the subject no doubt remains the same; but between the form of slave and the form of glory there is the "disposition to annihilation" (ibid. IX. 41; PL 10. 314 B), which does not change the Son of God but signifies the action* of "internally ridding himself of power" (ibid. XI. 48; PL 10. 432 A). The only thing lacking in these arguments is the Trinitarian dimension. The eternal condition for the possibility of the kenosis of the Incarnation indeed lies in the tri-personal gift. For divine "power" (omnipotence*, divine) is so constituted that it can contain within itself the possibility of an emptying of self, such as is represented by the Incarnation and the cross.

3. Modern Theological Essays on Kenosis

There is a common distinction between 1) a theory improperly called a theory of kenosis, and 2) kenotism properly speaking.

a) In the 16th and 17th Centuries. Lutheran kenotism of the period had as its basis the concept of the "communication of idioms*" adopted by Luther*. According to him, certain attributes* of the divine nature of Christ become attributes of human nature. Later there was discussion of an "attenuation" or kenosis of these "divine" attributes in humanity, so as not to alter their divine character. The school of Giessen, under the influence of M. Chemnitz (1522–86), taught that Christ possessed divine majesty in his humanity and during his earthly life but customarily refrained from using it. It was only upon his glorification that he would make full use of that majesty. The theologians of Tübingen*, on the other hand, following J. Brentz (1499–1570), contended that Christ had never renounced the use of his divine attributes, but that he had only hidden them for a time, "according to the economy." They criticized their opponents for abandoning Lutheran principles in favor of the Calvinist doctrine known as the *extra,* according to which, throughout the time of the Incarnation, the government of the world was to be entrusted to the Word considered separate from its flesh. Whatever the divergences among these theories, for them, kenosis has a direct effect on humanity. They consider the exaltation and the humbling of Christ with respect to his human nature alone and not a humbling of the Son of God himself. Hence, they do not touch on the central point of kenosis.

b) In the 19th and 20th Centuries. The 19th-century German theorists of kenosis wrote under the influence of Hegel*, for whom the absolute subject, in order to become concrete and for-itself, becomes finite in nature and in the history* of the world. Unlike the schools of Tübingen and Giessen two centuries earlier, the subject of kenosis is no longer he who became man, but he who becomes man, the divine Word himself. This represents a "self-limitation" of the divine (G. Thomasius, 1802–75). The Word abandons the attributes related to divinity, which concern the Trinity* considered in its relations with the world* (omnipotence, omniscience, omnipresence*) but not the absolute attributes of the immanent Trinity (truth*, sanctity [holiness*], love*), which, far from being emptied out, are revealed in the Incarnation. F. Frank (1827–94) spoke more radically of a self-degradation of the consciousness of the eternal Son into a finite consciousness of self; the Son made man, however, has the consciousness of being the Son of God. For the Calvinist W. F. Geß (1819–91), an incomprehensible lacuna even interrupts the course of divine life: the Word made man gives up the immanent properties of God and his eternal consciousness of self. He recovers the latter only gradually, through his human experi-

ence (notably through a reflection on the prophecies [prophet* and prophecy] concerning himself); once glorified, he recovers his divine attributes and divine functions.

The "kenotic torrent" found in Anglican theology between 1890 and 1910, no doubt stimulated, under the influence of T. H. Green, by Hegel, constitutes an independent, more cautious, and less speculative attempt to reconcile patristic theology* with the earthly realism of the man Jesus, as highlighted by scholarship on the Gospels*. Ch. Gore (1853–1932) accepts a mitigated kenosis, refusing to divide divine attributes and to posit a metamorphosis in God. According to him, the Word does not abandon his attributes but limits their use; in the act of his Incarnation, he restrains his omnipotence and refuses omniscience; he limits himself only in relation to the sphere of his individual humanity. But as Creator he retains the full use of all his attributes. Gore is thereby forced to posit two vital centers of consciousness in the Word according to his divine nature. The duality for which Scholasticism* had been criticized is here not distributed according to the two natures but conceived as a psychological division in the divine nature and hence in the divine person* himself. F. Weston (1871–1924) tries to harmonize the conception of the councils (council*) with a psychological idea of the person. Arguing against Gore, he asserts that there is in Christ only a single consciousness of self; he accepts, however, two volitional and intellectual faculties, one dependent on the other. Through the Incarnation the Word limits the use of his divine attributes so that they are always conditioned by the status of his humanity.

Kenotism also made its way into Russian Orthodoxy. V. Tareev (1866–1934) develops the idea that creation* itself is a kenotic action. But his most original ideas bear on the temptations (temptation*) over which Christ triumphs by ratifying his kenotic status; this very ratification brought about a deeper ordeal for his "faith*." According to S. Bulgakov (1871–1944), there is a divine kenosis in the Incarnation only because there is a kenosis in the Trinity as a whole and a divine kenosis in creation. The kenosis in the Trinity consists of the mutual love of the divine persons, which goes beyond any individuation. The creation situates God in time* and involves for him a certain risk of failure. The kenosis of the Incarnation is located principally in God, in the Word's will to love (it is the infinite* who limits himself). The Word ceases to be subjectively a divine hypostasis, while remaining such in his objective being. As incarnate Word, he becomes conscious of his divine filiation* only in accordance with his human and gradually developed consciousness of self. The Father and the Holy* Spirit participate in the eternal kenosis of the Incarnation, as well as in the historically accomplished kenosis that takes Christ to his death. It seems possible to strip Bulgakov's basic conception of its sophiological presuppositions and of the Gnostic temptation that leads him to think that the historical cross is merely the phenomenal translation of a metaphysical Golgotha.

4. Presence of the Theme in Philosophy

Nineteenth-century kenotism would probably not have existed without the impulse of Hegelian philosophy*. Hegel thereby returned to theology what he had borrowed from it. An intense kenotic schematism is at the heart of his system: the absolute Idea empties itself like the Word. It was Hegel who gave philosophical credentials to the term *Entäußerung*, the translation of kenosis in Luther's Bible*. In *The Phenomenology of Mind* the term reveals all its spiritual scope only in the representation of the Absolute Spirit, religion*. It evokes the dual movement of substance becoming self-consciousness and self-consciousness becoming universal being. The redemptive incarnation of the Word appears as the *Entäußerung* of absolute essence, which emptying itself of itself, leaves nothing unrelated to the accomplishment of its kenosis. The *Entäußerung* of Absolute Spirit implies a disappropriation of finite consciousnesses; but this abnegation does not estrange consciousness from itself. By stripping itself of itself, consciousness accedes in truth, according to Hegel, to its most authentic essence. One might, however, fear that Hegel reduces religious representation of kenosis to a sort of speculative allegory. Schelling* more fully preserves the positive content of Christianity. He offers an original conception of kenosis. The Incarnation reveals true divinity, and kenosis, as a divestment of the divine glory acquired in the course of the mythological process, removes from the Word only a fallacious glory. Unlike Schelling, Kierkegaard* does not identify incarnation and kenosis. His kenotic theory touches on the mode of the Incarnation, an incessant self-emptying of the Word as he places himself within the reach of created beings. It does not bring about an eclipse of divinity.

On the other hand, the Christ of Baron F. von Hügel (1852–1925) is immersed body (soul*-heart-body) and soul in human obscurity: kenosis obliterates his consciousness of his own divinity. Blondel* protests that his divine consciousness could at no point have deserted Jesus Christ and that exinanition is purely mercy and charity. It resides in the "stigmatizing sympathy" through which Christ experiences human suffering. Christ does not know himself as God otherwise than by identifying himself with human beings through love. Humanity, the humanity of all of us, serves as "a

screen for his," which would otherwise be set ablaze and consumed by the flame of divinity. The divine union of the man Jesus is also a deadly embrace. But "the vessel of his humanity" is "dilated by divinity." For S. Weil (1909–43), the divine attitude that dictates his conduct to the created being is thoroughly kenotic. The Creator has withdrawn in order to allow us to be. God has gone to an infinite distance. "This infinite distance between God and God, supreme rift…marvel of love, is the crucifixion" (Weil 1950).

5. General Assessment

Christology (Christ* and Christology) must take seriously the fact that God himself, in the Son, abased himself while remaining entirely God. In his total powerlessness, in the mortal distress of the Crucified One, is found undiminished the full divinity of God. God's humiliation shows the superabundance of his power; grandeur "allows itself to be perceived in baseness without being impaired in its exalted condition" (Gregory* of Nyssa, PG 45. 64 D). As God's renunciation of self, kenosis depends on sovereign divine liberty* (Hilary), which excludes any conception according to which the process is natural and Gnostic or logical and Hegelian. The problem of the true humanity of Jesus only arises when his true divinity is maintained; one cannot therefore deduce from kenosis that Jesus was ever in a really sinful condition. To link the extremes, reference may be made to the theme of "The sacrificial lamb since the creation of the world" (Rev 5:6–9 and 12, 13:8), which must not in any way be conceived as a heavenly sacrifice* independent of Golgotha but as the historical sacrifice offered on the cross considered from the point of view of eternity. The heavenly sacrifice of the Lamb binds together the world and God; in him, creation and redemption intersect. The cross "reveals a mystery* of divine life itself" (Temple 1924, 262). God alone goes to the very end of the abandonment of God. It is therefore appropriate to consider kenosis in three perspectives. Its ultimate presupposition is the "disinterestedness" of the persons (as pure relations) in the intra-Trinitarian life of love. Then, with the creation, a fundamental kenosis takes place because God, from all eternity, assumes responsibility for the success of creation and, in anticipation of sin*, takes into account the cross. Finally, in the sinful world, the redemptive Passion of Christ begins at the moment of his Incarnation. And since the will to redemptive kenosis is an indivisibly Trinitarian will (Bulgakov), God the Father and the Holy Spirit are deeply engaged in it (Balthasar* 1969).

● G. Thomasius (1853, 1857, 1861), *Christi Person und Werk*, 3 vols., Erlangen.

F. Frank (1878–80), *System der christlichen Wahrheit,* Erlangen.

W. Geß (1887), *Das Dogma von Christi Person und Werk,* Basel.

Ch. Gore (1891), *The Incarnation of the Son of God,* London.

F. Weston (1907), *The One Christ,* London.

P. T. Forsyth (1909), *The Person and Place of Christ,* London.

W. Temple (1924), *Christus Veritas,* London.

S. Boulgakof (1943), *Du Verbe incarné,* Paris.

S. Weil (1950), *Attente de Dieu,* Paris.

♦ F. J. Hall (1898), *The Kenotic Theory,* New York.

O. Bensow (1903), *Die Lehre von der Kenose,* Leipzig.

N. Gorodetsky (1938), *The Humiliated Christ in Modern Russian Thought,* London.

J. St. Lawton (1947), *Conflict in Christologies,* London.

P. Henry (1957), "Kénose," *DBS* 5, 7–161, especially 136–58.

P. Althaus (1959), "Kenosis," *RGG3* 3, 1244–46.

A. M. Ramsey (1960), *From Gore to Temple,* London.

D. G. Dawe (1962), "A Fresh Look at the Kenotic Christologies," *SJTh* 15, 337–49.

P. Lamarche, Y. Congar (1967), "Kénose," *Cath* 6, 1399–403.

R. P. Martin (1967), *Carmen Christi: Philippians II 5–11 in Recent Interpretation and in the Setting of Early Christian Worship,* Cambridge (bibl.).

H. Urs von Balthasar (1969), "Mysterium Paschale," *MySal* III/2, 133–326.

M. Lienhard (1973), *Luther témoin de Jésus-Christ,* Paris.

X. Tilliette (1975), "L'exinanition du Christ: théologies de la kénose," *Les Quatre fleuves* 4, 48–60; id. (1986), *La christologie idéaliste,* Paris; id. (1990), *Le Christ des philosophes,* Paris.

E. Brito (1983), *La christologie de Hegel,* Paris.

EMILIO BRITO

See also **Anglicanism; Calvinism; Christ's Consciousness; Hegelianism; Hypostatic Union; Johannine Theology; Lutheranism; Modernism; Orthodoxy, Modern and Contemporary; Pauline Theology**

Kerygma. *See* Creeds

Kierkegaard, Søren Aabye

1813–1855

---

1. Life

In Kierkegaard's lifetime, Denmark began a process of modernization and liberalization that brought into question the traditional sources of authority in church (church* and state) and state. The period of his youth also coincided with the "golden age" of Danish literature, a time of high idealism that was followed by a more materialistic and even cynical reaction. Kierkegaard himself defended the values of the older generation on many occasions. His critique of Hegel* has extensive affinities with the critiques developed by older Danish philosophers, such as P. M. Møller or F. C. Sibbern. A common theme is the absence from Hegel's system of a distinctive sense of individual personality (human and divine) and an incorrect understanding of the relationship between logic and life. Yet Kierkegaard also flirted with Danish Hegelians (Hegelianism*), such as J. L. Heiberg, whose influence was particularly marked in Kierkegaard's formalistic view of art. His own writings also reflected the doubts of the 1830s and 1840s and were themselves to culminate in an attack on the church/state establishment.

Kierkegaard's father bequeathed him a melancholy but deeply religious outlook. A brief engagement (1840–41) to Regine Olsen seemed to promise him a normal life, but a combination of his sense of guilt and something on the order of a religious vocation led him to break the engagement and commit himself entirely to his writing. After completing the pseudonymous books that made his reputation, he became involved in a bitter controversy with a satirical journal, *The Corsair* (1846), and this led to his increasing isolation. In the last year of his life (1854–55), he published a series of tracts bitterly attacking the established church for its compromise with worldly values.

2. Thought

Kierkegaard's works can be divided into four: the pseudonymous works, the religious discourses, the literary and other works published under his own name, and the extensive journals, published posthumously. Kierkegaard's influence is directly associated with the pseudonymous works. However, he both distanced himself from the views expressed in these works and asserted the distinctiveness of each pseudonym: it is therefore an open question as to how far his thought can be understood as offering a systematic view of things. Even the threefold schema of the aesthetic, the ethical, and the religious is only one way of organizing the complexity of his work. It should also be acknowledged that much of the impact of Kierkegaard's work is due to the parables, stories, and aphorisms that it contains and to its elements of satire, irony, and humor, all of which are used to disrupt the reader from a simple intellectual approach of its fundamental themes. Nonetheless, it is possible to group much of his work around two such themes: the problematic nature of human liberty*, and the qualitative transcendence of God*. The elliptical path of his writing around these two points makes it possible for us to see him as the forerunner of both Bultmann* and Barth*. It remains an open question as to which is decisive or whether they are both held in a tensile balance.

a) Anthropology. *The Concept of Anxiety* is a psychological exploration of original sin*. Seeing the prelapsarian state of human beings (Adam*) as one of innocence, he draws attention to the curious phenomenon of nothingness*, the correlate of the subject's potential freedom that has as yet no object. In anxiety at its own freedom—the openness of its future—the subject "grasps at finitude" and submits itself to all the sexual and other compulsions. Thus, although "subjectivity is truth," as "Johannes Climacus" (one of Kierkegaard's pseudonyms) states, the subject exists in untruth, as a failed project. This failure, called "despair," is analyzed in *Either/Or* as it appears in various forms of aesthetic existence, building on his dissertation *On the Concept of Irony,* where he had unmasked romantic idealism as a solipsistic flight from the claims of ethical reality. In *Two Ages,* the focus is on collective forms of failure: idle chatter, envy, association, cowardice, leveling—all the characteristics of an "age

of reflection." Later, in *The Sickness unto Death,* the emphasis is on the inability of the self to synthesize its constitutive polarities: possibility and necessity, finitude and infinity (infinite*), time* and eternity.

Is there any way out of despair? In *Either/Or,* assessor William, proponent of the ethical viewpoint, argues for a transcendental act of self-choice in which the subject chooses himself "from the hand of God" in the entirety of his existence. Is such a choice possible? In *Philosophical Fragments,* it is argued that the recollection of a truth immanent in human existence—such as William's position seems to imply—is essentially Socratic and ignores Christianity's revelation of the incorrigibility of human error. In *Fear and Trembling,* a distinction is drawn, using the story of Abraham and Isaac*, between infinite resignation, in which the world is surrendered for the sake of eternity, and authentic faith, in which, by the power of the absurd, the "knight of faith" believes he will receive again what he has surrendered. Thus, the faith of Abraham is not that he consented to offer Isaac but that he continued to believe that God would restore Isaac to him *in this life.* Kierkegaard asks whether we can understand Abraham. In *Repetition,* a poetic youth who has left his fiancée reflects on Job as offering hope that a "repetition" might be possible, and that God might transform him, making him capable of marriage. Repetition is thus the idea that the subject's self-choice can never be a given, a constitutive datum of the self, but must be affirmed repeatedly—but can the subject himself ground such an act?

In the *Edifying Discourses* that accompany all these books and represent an immanent form of religiousness, the ultimate possibility of the human subject is seen as a voluntary act of annihilation that removes the obstacles to God's transfiguration of human finitude. Yet this psychological anthropology* requires a theological and dogmatic grounding.

b) Theology. Kierkegaard's theological sources are chiefly Lutheranism*, and, especially, Pietism*. In works such as *Philosophical Fragments* or their *Concluding Unscientific Postscript,* he stresses that a true relationship with God is dependent on the redeeming activity of God himself, incarnate in human form. Indeed, it is only the revelation of the uniquely individual incarnation* of God that absolutely demonstrates our incapacity and our need of redemption. In faith, each believer becomes a contemporary of that event, historical knowledge and philosophical speculation being irrelevant to such contemporaneity. Faith also demands a qualitative leap by the individual, leading Kierkegaard to acknowledge his kinship with Gotthold Ephraim Lessing (1729–81) and David Hume

(1711–76) against Hegel. This leap cancels out all intrahistorical differences, so that the contemporary disciple of Jesus* (who literally saw and heard him) is no more privileged than the 19th-century believer is.

However, even faith—as a merely external religious confession or a merely passive state of inwardness (quietism*)—can itself be a way of evading the task of acceding to authentic selfhood. In his later works, Kierkegaard therefore increasingly emphasizes the importance of what he calls "reduplication," that is, supplementing faith with works*, above all the active suffering witness of the authentic imitation* of Christ. Although respectful of Luther*, he is critical of how Luther's teaching on faith undermines the ideal of discipleship. Kierkegaard also stresses the irreducibility of apostolic and kerygmatic preaching*, warning against the dangers of judging apostolic authority on the basis of such human criteria as poetic artistry or intellectual depth.

In his religious discourses, Kierkegaard offers sensitive studies of prayer*, spiritual trial, and the practice of Christian love. He counsels submission to God in patience, silence, and obedience. Those who aspire to this life must accept that they will become as nothing and give thanks for all things, even sufferings, willing the "one thing" only of God's will for us in repentance. Although God is separated from humanity by an "infinite qualitative difference," he cares for the believer as a father for his children, having a special providential care for each individual. The divine image in humanity is to be renewed through self-abandonment in worship. The lilies in the field and the birds in the sky (Mt 6:25–30) are repeatedly cited as "teachers" of faith. Among Kierkegaard's religious writings, the short meditations for the Friday Communion* should also be mentioned: they provide a singularly powerful exploration of the Lutheran understanding of the Eucharist* as the offering of forgiveness by the present Christ*.

The Bible* is central to Kierkegaard's spirituality. His treatment of Scripture is highly original, and he reworks or develops biblical themes in an imaginative and idiosyncratic fashion, as he tells the story of the Incarnation as the fairy-tale love of a king for a humble maiden, or has David criticizing Nathan's parable on aesthetic grounds. Apart from the Sermon on the Mount, his most used text is the Epistle of James (despite Luther's criticism of it), with its stress on works. He is critical of the scholarly approach to Scripture, both orthodox and revisionist (exegesis*), not only because of its tendency to reduce scripture to a merely human text but also because it lacks the passion that must fire an authentic engagement with the Word* of God. Scripture is a mirror in which we are to read our own destiny, and we should read it as urgently as a lover reads a letter from the beloved.

Despite Kierkegaard's statement of the absolute authority of faith, he was no mere dogmatist, and his work has a strongly apologetic element. He is committed to meeting his readers where they are and therefore, necessarily, to communicating the truth in forms that belong to untruth. His critique of the aesthetic attitude, for instance, is presented in a highly aesthetic form—so much so that these works are important documents in literature. Johannes the Seducer is a leading representative of this aesthetic attitude, and Kierkegaard could see his own literary activity as a kind of seduction, deceiving the reader in the cause of truth. Another model for such "indirect communication" was that of Socrates, the Socrates who compared himself to a midwife, assisting others to see the truth that was in them. In Kierkegaard's case, however, such maieutic practice aims to show readers that, apart from faith, they are not in possession of the truth. He was himself insistent that his literary activity had been religious from the beginning, adducing as proof the publication of his religious discourses alongside the pseudonymous aesthetic works.

The importance of "indirect communication" to Kierkegaard cannot be overestimated. To present his teachings, as objective results, would be to falsify his fundamental project, for it is only in the process of appropriating the truth that the subjective passion that is a necessary precondition of faith can be fully aroused. The unique form of his served the awakening of such subjective self-concern and, in the later works, to call the subject from the concealment of hidden inwardness onto the stage of public witness. Kierkegaard had two reasons for using such indirect communication: the exigencies of an apologetic approach and the requirements of faithfulness to the principles of the incarnation. The God-man, as Kierkegaard argues in *Training in Christianity,* exists as a sign of contradiction: his humble and suffering human form is entirely incommensurable with the reality of his divinity. His truth can therefore never be directly assimilated into any human system, not even one that is theologically "correct."

c) *Philosophy.* Kierkegaard's main influence on modern philosophy* has doubtless been through Heidegger*'s adoption of his anthropological description in *Being and Time:* the "existentialist" themes of anxiety, guilt, repetition, nothingness, subjectivity, and the absurd are all anticipated in Kierkegaard. So too are the critique of totalizing systems of truth and the depersonalizing effects of mass culture.

At the same time, Kierkegaard made important contributions to the critique of idealism, arguing in the *Concluding Unscientific Postscript* that all idealism is essentially skeptical. No philosophy can completely guarantee its own presuppositions but must accept the givenness of being. Idealism can therefore serve only to clarify the concept, not to determine the concept in its existence. Whereas a logical and a priori system may be possible, an existential system is altogether impossible, except from the standpoint of God.

Kierkegaard's most interesting contribution to philosophy probably comes from his interest in the boundaries between kinds of discourses: psychology, logic, faith, and so on. In this respect, we should read him not so much as seeking to demonstrate the falsity of Hegel's position as showing the inappropriateness of Hegel's method for dealing with religious issues. Wittgenstein's admiration for Kierkegaard is known and it is possible to see in Kierkegaard an early philosophical grammarian, when, for example, he points out the differing rules that govern some of the diversity of language games, especially those that concern God.

- (1901–6), *Samlede Værker,* Copenhagen, 15 vols. (3rd Ed. 1962, 20 vols.)
(1909–48), *Papirer,* Copenhagen, 24 vols.

♦ Georg Brandes (1877), *Søren Kierkegaard,* Copenhagen.
E. Hirsch (1933), *Kierkegaard Studien,* Gütersloh.
Jean Wahl (1938), *Études kierkegaardiennes,* Paris.
G. Malantschuk (1968), *Dialektik og Eksistens hos S. Kierkegaard,* Copenhagen.
L. Mackey (1971), *Kierkegaard: A Kind of Poet,* Philadelphia.
J. Colette (1972), *Histoire et absolu, Essai sur Kierkegaard,* Paris.
N. Thulstrup, M.M. Thulstrup (1978–88), *Bibliotheca kirkegaardiana,* 16 vols., Copenhagen.
M. Theunissen, W. Greve (Eds) (1979), *Materialen zur Philosophie S. Kierkegaards,* Frankfurt.
N. Viallaneix (1979), *Écoute, Kierkegaard: Essai sur la communication de la parole,* 2 vols., Paris.
H.-B. Vergote (1982), *Sens et repetition: Essai sur l'ironie kierkegaardienne,* 2 vols., Paris.
R.L. Perkins (Ed.) (1984–), *International Kierkegaard Commentary* (24 vols.), Macon, Ga.
G. Pattison (1992), *Kierkegaard: The Aesthetic and the Religious,* Basingstocke.
J. Colette (1994), *Kierkegaard et la non-philosophie,* Paris.

GEORGE PATTISON

See also **Beauty; Fideism; Hegel, Georg Wilhelm Friedrich; Kant, Immanuel; Language, Theological; Marx, Karl; Nietzsche, Friedrich Wilhelm; Rationalism; Schelling, Friedrich Wilhelm Joseph von; Schleiermacher, Friedrich Daniel Ernst**

Kingdom of God

A. Terminology: *Reign* and *Kingdom*

While Hebrew or Aramaic *(malekoût)* treat it as a single term, as does Greek *(basileia)* in certain contexts, the term *kingdom* encompasses various nuances through which English expresses different words: *royalty, kingdom,* and *reign* (the nuance expressed by *royalty* is of little importance in New Testament texts and may be ignored here). *Kingdom* is to be used for texts where the spatial connotation is predominant; for example, the phrase "in the *basileia*" (Mt 18:1, 4), or where a movement is implied of which the *basileia* is the goal—*to enter into* (for example Mt 7:21). *Reign* expresses the act of ruling, the exercise of royal power. This dynamic meaning, which appears fundamental, emerges quite clearly from a number of observations:

1) the verb *to reign* in the Hebrew text is more than once rendered by the noun in the Aramaic versions (e.g., Is 52:7 and the targum to this verse) (translations* of the Bible, ancient); 2) the Semitic noun is used in parallel with a synonymous *nomen actionis* such as domination (e.g., Dn 4:33); 3) the same phenomenon is borne out in corresponding terms in Greek (e.g., Rev 12:10); 4) there is a parallelism between the noun *basileia* and the corresponding verb (e.g., Lk 1:33).

Important as it is, the distinction between reign and kingdom cannot account for every usage: where the vocabulary concerns a gift, inheritance, or property, the term *basileia* is effectively used as an all-embracing term for the totality of salvific good* that God intends for his own people. Two forms appear in the New Testament: *reign of God* (the usual expression) and *reign of the heavens* (an expression typical of Matthew, who is not, however, unaware of the other). This distinction does not affect the meaning, since *heavens* has here, as in some other texts (e.g., Lk 15:18), the status of a divine epithet. The expression *reign of God* seems to be original. As was his habit, Matthew appears to have shifted the accepted vocabulary in the direction of the developing rabbinical phraseology.

I. Old Testament

The expression *reign of God* is practically absent from the Old Testament. It is found as such only once (Wis 10:10—but *see* 1 Chr 28:5; 2 Chr 13:8) and rarely in equivalent forms (e.g., Ps 103:19; Dn 3:33; Tb 13:2). The thematic unity appears more substantial, however, when one considers the royal title (God is referred to as "king" around 30 times, the oldest text being without doubt Is 6:5), the affirmations in verb form (various verbs: *mâlak, mâshal,* etc.), and the various royal symbols or attributes (throne, etc.).

It appears that the perception of God as king cannot have begun earlier than the royal period: it owes its admission into the faith* of Israel* to the influence of the prevailing milieu, chiefly "Hierosolymitan," perhaps in association with the building of the temple* where God henceforth "sat over the cherubs" (2 Sm 6:2). Despite the tradition of hostility to the monarchy in Israel, the human king was not generally considered to be in competition with the divine king. In keeping with the royal ideology common to the ancient East, the king was seen as God's lieutenant, but there was no question in Israel of his being of divine descent; while he is sometimes referred to as "son of God" (e.g., Ps 2:7) (filiation*), this is solely in terms of the judicial reality of adoption. God's reign is initially shown as being beneficial for the people of Israel, whose attentive shepherd he is; but it also encompasses creation* and other peoples, as appears particularly in the psalms* of the reign (Ps 47:93, 96–99). The eschatological dimension of divine royalty, which certainly cannot be ruled out from these psalms, is more clearly expressed in the great texts of Deutero-Isaiah (52:7, etc.), by which Jesus* was in all probability strongly inspired. After the exile, the former conviction of the actual and permanent reign was adopted and reinforced in the theocratic tradition represented by the "Chronist." The tradition established by Deutero-Isaiah was consolidated in the texts that bear witness to the birth of apocalyptic* literature, above all in Isaiah 24–27.

II. Ancient Judaism

As in the Old Testament, the theme of the reign is expressed in ancient Judaism* by way of the predicates attributed to God and the verbs that express his actions. However, the noun *reign* now appears more frequently, albeit by no means as frequently as would be the case in the New Testament. The theme is presented above all in apocalyptic and related literature (Dn, *The Testament* [or *Assumption*] *of Moses,* etc.), as well as in ancient prayers (prayer*) (the Kaddish). At Qumran, the theme assumes some prominence in the *Scroll of War* (1QM) and in the fragments of 4Q on the *Songs for the Sabbath Holocaust* (or *Sacrifice*). As for the documents deriving from rabbinism, their dominant idea is that obedience to the law* is a matter of taking upon oneself the yoke of the reign and of recognizing this reign. These documents, however, are hard to date.

There is nothing uniform about the ideas of the reign: alongside a reign already in force, which one recognizes by submitting to it and in which one may participate through the liturgy*, there is recognition of a reign that has yet to appear and that will crown the history* of God with his people, with humanity, and with the cosmos*. At times the transformation by comparison with the present world* is emphasized to a point at which the reign to come is seen as a reality situated in a heavenly hereafter (particularly in *Testament of Moses* 10). More often, however, the perspective remains that of the earth—a renewed earth, of course. God's sovereignty is emphatically established over all people, but the centrality of Israel is strongly accentuated.

III. New Testament

1. Jesus' Preaching

The critics are almost unanimous in judging that the theme of the reign forms the heart of the historical Jesus' preaching*. Jesus gives it an emphasis that goes well beyond that which it had in the Old Testament and in ancient Judaism, and which it was to have in the post-Easter Christian tradition*. Explicitly or implicitly present in the majority of the parables (parable*), the reign is the object of many maxims attested in all currents of the synoptic tradition (notably in the source of the *logia*) (Gospels*) and belongs to a large extent to the earliest layers of this tradition. The principal characteristics of this preaching are as follows:

a) Reign as Activity. The dynamic sense is fundamental; this is linked to a conception firmly centered on God himself. An eschatological reference—presented in this instance through an insistence on new-ness—seems very probable, even if this point is freshly disputed today by some of the most recent (in particular American) research (B. B. Scott 1981; M. J. Borg 1984 and 1994).

b) Salvation. Contrasting with the theme of judgment* and in tension with it, reign is the supreme category tending to salvation, employed by Jesus much more emphatically than, for example, the vocabulary of salvation* or of eternal life (life*, eternal). God assumes power in order to succor and reward the poor (Mt 5:3; *see* Mk 10:25) and the young, along with those who resemble them (Mk 10:14), as well as the little flock of disciples (Lk 12:32).

c) Bipolarity. It is generally accepted nowadays that, in its temporal aspect, Jesus' message regarding the reign is characterized by a polarity between the future and the present. The reign is an eschatological reality, a fulfillment (Scripture*, fulfillment of) of divine promises, and belongs fundamentally to the future; on this point Jesus does not reject the apocalyptic tradition. The future dimension of the reign is proclaimed in the Lord's Prayer* (Lk 11:2), for example, or in the *logia* of the "entry into the kingdom" (Mk 9:47,;10:25), or again in the Beatitudes (Lk 6:20f.). However—and this characteristic is almost unparalleled in ancient Judaism—Jesus also maintains that God is in the process of invading the world, that his eschatological work is under way and may be verified: Luke 11:20; Matthew 11:12; Luke 17:21; *see* Luke 7:18–23, 10:18, 10:23f.; Mark 3:27. It was perhaps because he was anxious to affirm both aspects that Jesus did not have recourse to the dualist vocabulary of ages ("this world"/"the world to come"), which implies a radical opposition between the two temporal spheres. The language of reign, with its dynamic overtones, allowed him, on the basis of the fundamental continuity of divine action, to express the idea that the future had already burst in upon the present and affected it with its eschatological character. The experience of the present reign, meanwhile, would doubtless have intensified the expectation of fulfillment. Several parables (e.g., Mk 4:26–29) appear to have as their message the paradox of the temporal bipolarity of the reign.

d) Christ and the Reign. The resolutely theocentric conception of the reign does not prevent there being a connection between it and the person of Jesus*. As far as the reign in its present dimension is concerned, the impact of God's coming may be seen in Jesus' words (word*) and salutary actions (especially in his exorcisms [exorcism*] and healing*). The role of God's

lieutenant or representative in his actions should undoubtedly be seen in the context of Jesus' close proximity to him whom he calls, with emphasis, his Father*. Did Jesus assign himself a similar role concerning fulfillment? The christological title of Son* of man seems at first sight to suggest as much. It may be remembered that in Daniel 7, he who rises up "like a son of man" receives investiture, and that the "Reign" of God is entrusted to him. However, criticism has thrown up almost insurmountable difficulties—at any rate, not surmounted yet—on this point. In actual fact, the connection between the maxims of the reign and the *logia* of the Son of man is never explicitly stated. Moreover, it is not clear that Jesus ever spoke of the Son of man; and even if one accepts that he did speak of him, one should not be too ready to assume that he identified himself with this figure. Besides, in the one speech in which Jesus speaks of his own person in connection with the reign to come (Mk 14:25), he offers no information that would enable one to conclude that he was expecting to play a defining role: he simply expresses the conviction that he will not remain in the thrall of death*, and that he will be a guest at the banquet of the reign. The very pronounced theocentrism of Jesus' teaching means that only for general reasons, namely the very reality of the Christology (Christ* and Christology) implicit in his message and the continuity between the present reign and the future reign, can one assume for Jesus a particular role in the coming and the life of the future reign.

2. Post-Easter Resumptions of the Theme

Even if it was not its sole focus, the "kerygma" of the post-Easter communities was centered on Christ, and in particular on the salvific events of his death and resurrection*. The announcement of God's reign was no longer foremost, but it did not disappear.

a) Gospels and Acts. The theme remains prominent over the whole course of synoptic tradition, even as far as its compilation is concerned. It is taken up differently by each of the evangelists, though it is very hard to attribute an absolutely coherent and precise position to each of them. However, it is at least possible to recognize characteristic emphases. In Matthew, for example, one may note the prominence afforded to ethics*: the entry into the Kingdom, which remains a strictly eschatological reality and should not be confused with the Church*, is linked to a respect for certain ethical demands (*see* Mt 5:20, 7:21, 18:3; *see* 5:3–12, 21:43). In the case of Luke and Acts, a dominant characteristic is the presentation of the reign as an object of preaching or teaching, with a tendency—as can be seen especially in some phrases from Acts (19:8, 2:31, etc.)—to endow the term with a wide, vague meaning: the phenomenon of Christianity or the Christian religion (*see* Col 4:11). The relationship between the expressions concerning the reign in the two parts of Luke's work suggests that it may be one of the symbols by which the author emphasizes the continuity between Jesus' time and that of the Church. In John, only two statements concerning the reign (Jn 3:3, 5) are to be found. But the semantic connotations of the theme are quite widely present in the vocabulary of "eternal life," with which John makes clear connections (*see* 3:3 and 3:36), as indeed the synoptic tradition had already done (Mk 9:43–47, 10:17–31).

b) Pauline Corpus. The first impression here is that the theme of reign is ephemeral and merges into that of justification* or justice* (with which, moreover, a connection is made in Rom 14:17): the instances are relatively infrequent and above all seem largely stereotypical. By analogy with the *logia* of the entry into the Kingdom preserved in the synoptic tradition and in the compiling of Matthew, most of Pauline (in the broad sense) uses the theme present in the Kingdom as the eschatological dwelling of the righteous (1 Cor 6:9f.; Gal 5:21; 1 Thes 2:12; 2 Thes 1:5; Eph 5:5). Nonetheless, the presence of reign, linked to justification (Rom 4:17) and to the active power (omnipotence*, divine) (of the Holy* Spirit) (1 Cor 4:20) is not neglected, so that one finds again in Paul's writings the fundamental tension to be seen in Jesus. In spite of the lack of emphasis in his explicit references to it, the gospel theme of reign undoubtedly played a more important part in Pauline* theology than appears at first sight.

c) Specific Character of the Reign. Two distinctive characteristics recur within various theological currents of developing Christianity and deserve special mention: the christological application of the theme and its transcendental interpretation.

The christological application is revealed in the fact that the vocabulary of reign or kingdom is used in various ways concerning Jesus. The variety of epithets employed in the texts and the late character of most of the latter encourage us not to overemphasize the strictly messianic strand (though *see* Lk 1:33) but to accord full importance to the exaltation of Easter and the perspective of the Second Coming (Mt 13:41, 16:28, 20:21; Lk 22:30, 23:42; 1 Cor 15:24; Col 1:13; 2 Tm 4:1, 18; 2 Pt 1:11). Understood in the vast majority of texts as being God's prerogative, once reign is attributed to Christ there arises the problem of the relationship between the two forms of reign. Only Paul, however, considers this point explicitly (1 Cor 15:20–28). Christ's reign is temporary: at the "end" the

"Son" will submit to the Father and God will be "all in all"—it being understood that the emphasis is on God's universal sovereignty and not on the transitoriness of the Son's reign. It is generally considered enough to associate God and the Son in various ways (*see* Eph 5:5; Rev 3:21, 11:15, 12:10, 22:1)—in fact this is a distinctive aspect in the connection between Christology and theology*. The group of texts relating to the Son's reign present several assertions that call for speculation as to the relationship between reign and the Church (*see* especially Mt 13:41; Col 1:13; Eph 5:5). Generally speaking, it is not possible to identify the Church with the Kingdom of God, but it is legitimate to consider the Church as the community over which Christ's rule is exercised and which has received a call to participate in the fullness of God's reign.

As far as the oldest layers of the tradition are concerned, it is very hard to characterize the nature of the reign. Is it a matter of an eschatology* of restoration, the reign being exercised over an Israel that is renewed but that remains centered on the earth and thus retains its institutions? Or, does it rather belong to a transcendental, celestial, and strictly indescribable universe? The indications seem rather to argue for the *totaliter aliter*. In any event, the post-Easter resumption of the theme and its reinterpretation on the basis of Christ's exaltation at Easter were to favor a transcendental conception that is clearly to be seen in a number of texts, especially in the connection or even identification with what later Christian tradition would call "heaven." The second century saw a highlighting of Jesus' pronouncements on the entry or on inheritance; of the identification of reign with eternal life; and of its being set in opposition to punishment. Above all, it is overwhelmingly referred to as "heavenly." But these descriptions are already to be found in some New Testament texts. According to 2 Timothy 4:18, salvation is equivalent to entry into the "heavenly kingdom" of Christ, and "the eternal kingdom of our Lord and Savior Jesus Christ" of 2 Peter 1:11, which can be identified with a heavenly hereafter that the elect will attain, in a kind of triumph, on the day of judgment. It is not impossible that a similar idea is expressed in Acts 14:22. Certainly the traditional image of the entry is to be found there—an image that does not in itself point to a transcendental conception. However, if one takes account of the beginnings of an individual eschatology to be found in the writings of Luke (especially Lk 16:19–31, 23:39–43), and if one brings into play the resemblance between Acts 14:22 and Luke 24:26, there is some reason to think of the entry into heavenly glory as taking effect from the very moment of death.

● R. Schnackenburg (1959), *Gottes Herrschaft und Reich,* Freiburg-Basel-Vienna (4th Ed. 1965).

J. Schlosser (1980), *Le Règne de Dieu dans les dits de Jésus,* Paris.

J. Coppens, J. Carmignac, A. Feuillet, E. Cothenet, P. Prigent (1981), "Règne (ou Royaume) de Dieu," *DBS* 10, 2–199.

H. Merklein (1983), *Jesu Botschaft von der Gottesherrschaft: Eine Skizze,* Stuttgart (3rd Ed. 1989).

H. Schürmann (1983), *Gottes Reich – Jesu Geschick,* Freiburg-Basel-Vienna.

O. Camponovo (1984), *Königtum, Königsherrschaft und Reich Gottes in den frühjüdischen Schriften,* Freiberg-Göttingen.

E.P. Sanders (1985), *Jesus and Judaism,* London.

G.R. Beasley-Murray (1986), *Jesus and the Kingdom of God,* Grand Rapids-Exeter.

E. Zenger, A. Lindemann (1986), "Herrschaft Gottes/Reich Gottes," *TRE* 15, 176–89, 196–218.

W. Willis (Ed.) (1987), *The Kingdom of God in 20th-Century Interpretation,* Peabody, Mass.

D.C. Duling (1992), "Kingdom of God, Kingdom of Heaven," *AncBD* IV, 49–69.

B. Chilton (1994), "The Kingdom of God in Recent Discussion", in B. Chilton, C.A. Evans (Ed.), *Studying the Historical Jesus,* Leyden, 1994, 255–80.

J.P. Meier (1994), *A Marginal Jew,* II, New York, 237–506.

JACQUES SCHLOSSER

See also **Church; Cosmos; Creation; Eschatology; Gospels; Jesus, Historical; Judgment; Messianism/Messiah; Parousia; Preaching; Psalms; World**

B. Historical Theology

In Jesus*' announcement of the Kingdom* of God, and in the New Testament declarations that bear witness to the fact that Christ* crucified and raised to heaven truly inaugurates the perfect communion* of God* with human beings—the goal of creation* and of history*—the Christian tradition* has at all periods found a theme that it has been able to present with the help of the conceptual, cultural, and linguistic means at its disposal. Since these elements have themselves been modified in the course of this process, belief in the Kingdom also appears as a factor in historical change.

a) Pre-Nicene Theology of the Kingdom of God. The earliest Fathers* characterized the Kingdom of God by bringing together different elements provided by the New Testament declarations, including their purely narrative and allegorical aspects. Thus the announcement of the Kingdom of God, together with Jesus Christ's crucifixion and elevation, is seen as the axis of a history of salvation* that runs from the creation and original sin (sin,* original) to the judgment* and the fulfillment of creation in God (Irenaeus*, *Adv. Haer.*, PG 7, 431–1224). Jesus Christ, God's Word* made flesh, is the *"autobasilèia"* (Origen*, Tertullian*, *Adv. Marc.* 4, 33, PL 470–72(, the "Kingdom of God himself" (Cyprian*, *De orat. domin.*, PL 4, 535 *Sq*): in his life as in his death*, it is God who determines everything.

Christians attain the Kingdom of God through faith* and baptism*. They merge more closely within it by "becoming like" God through the practice of the virtues*. This sense of participation is expressed especially in the state of virginity (Tertullian, *De virg. velandis*, PG 2, 935–62), in the "angelic life" directed toward the Kingdom of God, and in martyrdom* (Cyprian, *Exhort. de mart.*, PL 4, 677 *Sq*). In this way Christians testify to the completely finite nature of all created reality and reject any mythical glorification of state authority* and of the Empire. They live among the nations, integrating themselves into social relationships as one people among others (*Epistle to Diognetus*, SC 33 *bis*).

The apocalyptic events announced in the New Testament were at this time interpreted as a process of purification, sanctification, and illumination. In opposition to the opinion of, for example, Dionysius of Alexandria (in Eusebius, *HE*, PG 20, 691–95), many Fathers then distinguished between a first and a second resurrection*, each heralded by a final period of calamity. These two resurrections framed the seventh week of the world*, during which Christ, after chaining Satan, would reign for a thousand years and prepare the saints for perfect communion with God (Victorinus of Pettau, Methodius of Olympus, etc.).

The idea of the Kingdom of God, so conceived from the standpoint of the history of salvation, takes its main conceptual framework from the Platonic doctrine of man's absorption into the divine mystery*, through a gradual succession of eschatological situations.

b) Post-Constantinian Theology of the Kingdom of God. The assertion of the essential identity of the Son and the Father*, and of the divinity of the Holy*

Spirit (Nicaea* [325] and Constantinople* [381]), brought about obvious changes in the theology* of the Kingdom of God. The eschatological significance of the Lord's first coming on earth was reinforced, so that the idea of an intermediate reign of a thousand years before the Last Judgment became less plausible (Jerome, *Comm. in Evang. sec. Matt.*, PL 26, 15–228; *Ep. CXX ad Hedibiam*, PL 22, 908–1006; Augustine, *De civ. Dei* 20, 7, PL 41, 666–69). Henceforward, a number of narrative elements, which the pre-Nicene Fathers had accorded the status of historical reality, were now understood as a stock of images and metaphors applicable to the present-day experience of the faithful (*see* Augustine, op. cit., on the subject of the chaining of Satan).

So Christ's first coming inaugurated the sixth age of the world (Augustine, *De civ. Dei* 22, 30, PL 41, 801–4), which was to be followed only by eternal fulfillment (the seventh age). Modifying the Neoplatonist theme of the "intelligible world," Augustine* here develops his doctrine of the heavenly city, consisting of disciples living in communion with God, who, loving only him and seeking only beatitude*, fight against the earthly city*. The Church* that has existed since Abel (*Ecclesia ab Abel*) thus becomes the sacramental representative of the Kingdom of God, in which nonetheless the chaff may mingle with the good grain. The history of the world and the history of salvation are inextricably linked, without, however, merging. The different theological positions were distinguished at this time by the way in which they conceived the actuality of a Kingdom of God whose advent remained fundamentally postponed until the fulfillment of time. Cassian, as a monastic theologian, considers that it is above all through purity (purity*/impurity) of heart (soul*-heart-body) that the Kingdom of God is announced in the present (*see Collatio nona, De oratione* XIX, PL 49, 791 *Sq*); other Fathers emphasize its official representation. In the "imperial theology" inaugurated by Eusebius, the Christian emperors act as Jesus Christ's vicars for the Empire, and the Empire itself is elevated to the status of a Christian reality (*see*, e.g., *Orat. Eusebii de laud: Constantini in eius tricennalibus habitae*, PG 20, 1315–456). Some writers, moreover, boldly identify the Church with the Kingdom of God. Gregory* the Great, for example, takes Jesus' parables (parable*) concerning the Kingdom (e.g., Mt 13:41) as direct allusions to the Church (*Homil. in Evang.*, II, Homil. 32, 6, PL 76, 1236) at the risk of abandoning all critical distance with regard to the latter.

c) Medieval Theology of the Kingdom of God.
While the patristic "imperial theology" found prolongment in the Eastern Church, the *sacrum imperium* was similarly understood in the Western Empire as an initial materialization of the Kingdom of God, whose propagation, internal organization, and defense were the responsibilities of the emperor, as a new David—while to the pope* and the bishops (bishop*) fell the role of Moses in prayer*. An opposite understanding was to develop in the context of the Cluniac reform, under the banner of "liberty* of the Church": the universal and cosmic order established under God's salvific counsel was represented in time* by the priesthood*. Thus it was the pope who held the fullness of power (*plenitudo potestatis*), and imperial or royal power played only a secondary role: it was necessitated by human sin, inasmuch as this threatened the temporal order (*see* Gregory VII, *Dictatus Papae*). Boniface VIII's bull *Unam Sanctam* (*DH* 870–75) is an intensified expression of this political and ecclesiological theology of the Kingdom of God. The medieval movement of return to evangelical poverty nonetheless reemphasized the difference between the Kingdom of God and all the forms of power exercised through history. One entered it by way of poverty, humility, and simplicity. In this regard the doctrine of Joachim of Fiore was spectacularly successful among the Franciscan "spirituals." According to this view it was necessary to distinguish three ages of the world: the reign of the Father, characterized by the Old Testament economy of salvation and the ascendancy of secular powers; the reign of the Son, subject to the New Testament economy of salvation and to priestly domination; and finally the reign of the Spirit, which was that of the monastic community inspired by the Paraclete. Francis of Assisi was considered to be the herald of this third age and sometimes represented as *alter Christus*. The ideas of Jan Hus* and the Czech friars (Moravian Brethren) and the theories of Thomas Münzer and the Anabaptists* of Münster would be steeped in this theology of the Kingdom of God.

In the face of these arguments, Thomas* Aquinas—like other theologians of his time, who marked the high point of the Middle Ages—did not accept the theme of the Kingdom of God but rather developed an overall vision of reality based on the scheme of emanation from and return to God (*egressus/regressus*). The world thus conceived is characterized by a perfect communication with God, within which it is at the same time judged.

d) Thematics of the Kingdom of God in Modern Times.
The tendencies of medieval theology survived until the modern period. Nicholas* of Cusa developed a speculative conception of the Kingdom of God: humankind and the world, in their history, were the ex-

pressions that God unfolded outside himself. Their relationship with God was inherent in the present moment but simultaneously encompassed all history: "There is only one heavenly reign, of which there is but one archetypal image [...] what Zeno says on the subject of truth* is the same as what Parmenides, Plato and all the others say of it; all had the same thing in mind, but expressed it in different ways" (*De filiatione Dei op.* IV, 83).

This assimilation of the Kingdom of God with the rule of the Spirit or of liberty* was to form an important theme in modern philosophy. For Leibniz* the existing world was the best of all possible worlds by virtue of a preestablished harmony based on divine rationality. In Kant*'s opinion the Kingdom of God represented the development of human society* according to ethical laws: this society—the Church—sprang from faith in revelation* but must raise itself to the level of a pure religious faith. In Hegel*'s view, finally, the doctrine of the reign of the Father, the Son, and the Spirit concluded the succession of forms that the Spirit assumed in its journey toward itself.

This conception of the Kingdom of God was also echoed in the utopias of Savonarola, Campanella, Thomas More, and Bucer*, whose tradition is in a sense continued in the ideas of the left-wing Hegelians, the Marxist theory of the communist society, and the utopian philosophy of E. Bloch. In this context the Kingdom of God is no longer the effect of God's unforeseeable grace* but rather a vision of what humanity can make of its own existence.

Luther* developed a doctrine of the two reigns that was distinct on the one hand from a Catholic and theocentric view of the Church and on the other hand from millenarian fanaticism. God's invisible spiritual government was based on justification* by faith, while secular government was based on the law*. Calvin* and Zwingli* developed a conception of Christian society that has bibliocratic and theocratic characteristics. The idea of the Kingdom of God also played a central role in Pietism*: biblical teaching, set out and put into practice in conventicles, allowed God's sovereignty to exercise itself over the world. Schleiermacher*, under the influence of Pietism, defined the Kingdom of God as "the free community, united in pious belief" (WW, III-2, 466), whose members developed their individuality as a living work of art. For A. Ritschl, finally, the Kingdom of God was the ethical (ethics*) community instituted by Jesus Christ, a conception that was used to glorify the bourgeois ideals of liberal Protestantism. Within Catholicism*, for its part, Ignatius Loyola and a number of Counter Reformation leaders identified the hierarchical Church with the reign of Christ, which was to be extended by throwing

all one's strength into planned missionary activity (*Spiritual Exercises,* no. 137–48, 365).

Within Catholic theology the doctrine of the Kingdom of God has been principally developed (following B. Gallura) by the school of Tübingen*. According to J. S. von Drey, the Kingdom of God is "that idea of Christianity which contains within it and draws from itself all others" (*Einleitung in das Studium der Theologie,* Tübingen 1819, 19). J.-B. von Hirscher envisages his "Christian morality" as a doctrine of the realization of the Kingdom. The rediscovery of the eschatological message of Jesus (J. Weiss), as well as the theologies of Barth* and Tillich*, helped to orient Catholic exegesis* (L. Cerfaux, J. Bonsirven, R. Schnackenburg, etc.) and ecclesiology* (M. Schmaus) toward the problematics of the Kingdom of God.

Building on this preparatory work, the Second Vatican* Council was able to define the Church as the Kingdom of God already present "in mystery" (*LG* 3) and also as the community that must at the same time, with (perhaps add "the cooperation of") all its members, serve the Kingdom of God by the proclaiming of the Word* (*LG* 35), the giving of mutual assistance, and daily observance (*LG* 36). It was right, moreover, to distinguish between the growth of the Kingdom and earthly progress (*GS* 39). The theology of hope* since the Council, along with political* theology, liberation* theology and feminist theology (woman*), all oppose one or other implication of the Kingdom of God—universal salvation, liberty, justice*—to the fixed certainties of Church and society or to the traditionalism* of theology. These movements, however, often expose themselves to the risk of dissociating the Kingdom of God and the Church, or even of moving away from Jesus Christ, as a result of their ideological commitment and their drift toward political messianism. There is an opposite danger, too: the making absolute—from an apparently orthodox standpoint—of the received forms of Christianity.

e) Systematic Perspectives. If man is a paradoxical being who achieves fulfillment only beyond humanity, and so beyond the historical scope of all human powers, then the same must go for history, inasmuch as it constitutes the space in which human existence, being together, and being in the world are enacted. In terms of faith, the fulfillment of the human is attested as divine salvation. This salvation allows itself to be conceived negatively, for as long as philosophy highlights the fragility and insufficiency of all the other ideas that human beings advance of their end and fulfillment. As an all-inclusive promise guaranteed by Jesus Christ's death and resurrection, the Kingdom of God thus plays a defining role in humankind's historical practice; and in philosophical terms it represents an asymptotic idea that can be approached only by way of successive negations. It follows that faith is alive in the Church only when, sustaining its hope and love* in the real expectation of the Kingdom of God, it rejects the limits and obstacles that history puts in the way of human salvation. This concrete action breaks the shell of certainties and established traditions, steering clear of fanaticism while it integrates the negative and critical dimension of the idea of the Kingdom of God, which emphasizes the relative nature of all the real progress achieved in this direction.

● E. Hirsch (1921), *Die Reich-Gottes Begriffe des neueren europäischen Denkens,* Göttingen.
R. Frick (1928), "Die Geschichte des Reich-Gottes Gedankens in der alten Kirche bis zu Origenes und Augustin," *ZNW,* suppl. no 6.
A. Dempf (1929), *Sacrum Imperium. Geschichts und Staatsphilosophie des Mittelalters und der politischen Renaissance,* Munich-Berlin.
E. Staehelin (1951–63), *Die Verkündigung des Reich Gottes in der Kirche Jesu Christi: Zeugnisse aus allen Jahrhunderten und allen Konfessionen,* vols. I–VI, Basel.
É. Gilson (1952), *Les métamorphoses de la cité de Dieu,* Louvain-Paris.
K. Löwith (1953), *Weltgeschichte und Heilsgeschehen: Die theologischen Voraussetzungen der Geschichtsphilosophie,* Stuttgart.
J. Bonsirven (1957), *Le règne de Dieu,* Paris.
Ch. Walther (1961), *Typen des Reich-Gottesverständnis: Studien zur Eschatologie und Ethik im 19. Jahrhundert,* Munich.
J. Pief (1965), *Reich Gottes und Gesellschaft nach J. S. Drey und J. B. Hirscher,* Paderborn.
E. Benz (1969), Ecclesia spiritualis. *Kirchenidee und Geschichtstheologie der franziskanischen Reformation,* Darmstadt.
W. Pannenberg (1971), *Theologie und Reich Gottes,* Gütersloh.
J. Moltmann (1980), *Trinität und Reich Gottes: Zur Gotteslehre,* Munich.
A. von Ström et al. (1986), "Herrschaft Gottes/Reich Gottes," *TRE* 15, 172–244.
M. Seckler (1988), "Das Reich-Gottes-Motiv in den Anfängen der katholischen Tübinger Schule (J.S. Drey and J.B. Hirscher)," in *ThQ* 168, 257–82.
M. Arndt (1992), "Reich Gottes," *HWP* 8, 510–30.

PETER HÜNERMANN

See also **Church; Eschatology; History; Life, Eternal; Millenarianism; Salvation**

Kleutgen, Josef Wilhelm Karl. *See* **Philosophy; Realism**

Knowledge of God

It is a commonplace that the first theological fact is that God* is known by human beings and known because he has made himself known to them. But what does "knowing" mean in the case of knowing God? Several themes come together here to clarify the topic of an experience* that is not without analogies, though certainly without equal.

1) Biblical language indicates that the knowledge of God expresses its meaning primarily in a logic of existence. Before being theoretical, meaning is practical, ethical (ethics*), and spiritual. Knowledge of God is a matter of conversion*, obedience, and recognition (Bultmann* 1933; Bergman-Botterweck 1982); it is articulated significantly in a symbolism of betrothal (Hos 2:22). Man is shown to us not as a rational animal but as a religious and moral subject. According to the Old Testament the one who knows God is the one who fulfills his law* and lives in the covenant* according to justice*. Knowledge is a way of being; it marks the existent in his

totality. And because it originates in a history*, its intelligibility is not articulated in a framework of metaphysical references but calls upon the construction of a logic of existence in history, a "metahistorical" perspective (Müller 1971).

2) The term *existence* refers to a general aptitude for experience, so that nothing fundamentally determines human beings that is absent from the conditions according to which they achieve knowledge of God. The logic of knowing brings liberty*, rationality, and emotion into play. Liberty, because the existence of God does not impose itself on human beings but solicits consent (*see* Thomas* Aquinas, *ST* IIa IIae. q. 2. a.1). Rationality, because that consent depends on the work of an "intellect in search of faith*," *intellectus quaerens fidem,* and is accomplished in the work of a faith seeking its greatest understanding, *fides quaerens intellectum* (Anselm*). Lastly, emotion, because it is also as the Lovable Sovereign that God confronts the human person; rationality is thus indissociable from an *ordo amoris* (M. Scheler) in which the person plays the role of *animal amans.*

3) The primacy of conversion requires that human beings should not have known God from time immemorial, or at least that the manner of being that is implied by conversion is born of a rupture, rather than relying on continuities. But are human beings born in a state of total ignorance with respect to God? Or do the prethematic structures of their experience already represent an implicit confrontation with the mystery* of God and, as it were, a certain pre-knowledge? "Transcendental Thomism" (Rahner* 1976; Lotz 1978) has followed the second path; it remains possible, however, to read the native condition of the human person in terms of atheism* and/or of paganism* (Lacoste 1994). It is in any event the major task of the theology of religions*, of the philosophy of religion*, and indeed of philosophy* itself, to say under what conditions the human person is a being to whom God is not foreign. This task has particular urgency in Catholic theology*, insofar as the latter grants to the secular experience of reason* the intrinsic possibility of acceding to a "certain" (*DS* 3004) knowledge of God. However, not only in Catholic theology but in all Christian traditions (tradition*), man appears in his deepest self as an animal (animals*) in whom God is in question, hence as an animal in a hermeneutic (hermeneutics*) situation who always "pre-understands" God in some way (Bultmann 1952).

4) From the fact that the question is first of all existential, it does not follow that it does not have a theoretical dimension. In the Bible, knowledge of God is related to what Bertrand Russell calls "knowledge by acquaintance," knowledge born of the familiarity between human beings and God within the space of the covenant. But it is also in terms of knowledge, of *gnôsis*, that God is spoken of from as early as the Pauline writings, so that knowledge also designates the right to use of God a language that can be called cognitive (knowledge of God thus also matching Russell's knowledge by description). Knowledge of God is first a spiritual fact, but it also plays a role in the work of theologies. Divine knowability has as a privileged consequence the possibility of articulating a true discourse. And while the act of faith relies on a divine act of speech, the very conditions under which that act of speech asks to be understood today commit the believer to speak in his turn, and to speak with rigor; theological experience is nothing but a *theologal* experience that is capable of being articulated with complete precision.

5) The production of a theology is not only possible but also necessary, because faith deals with an act of speech. However, the *logos* here comes up against divine incomprehensibility as a critical factor present at every level. It is possible to speak logically of God (God is of no genus but may enter into many classes), and he may be spoken of through speculative concepts, but only with the reservation of excess: that is, reason can confront the God who is "always greater" or "always more God" only by accepting the status of an intelligence that is not comprehensive. The last word always escapes human beings. And what is said in terms of being* (Przywara) must also be said in terms of knowledge: it is not possible to posit a knowledge of the Creator by the created being without also positing an even greater lack of knowledge (*see DS* 806).

6) Knowledge, moreover, enjoys no particular privilege. Theological theories and theorems articulate knowledge and the knowable, but knowledge needs to be appropriated in a living way, beyond the simple conceptual appropriation of theoretical knowledge; and this vital appropriation may very well take place in the absence of a formal appropriation of words and concepts. In opposition to logics of experience that culminate in the enjoyment of knowledge (Hegel*), and to intellectualist theologies that attribute to the experience of Christian "Gnostics" greater richness

than to the faith of the humble (of the "Pistics," e.g., in Clement of Alexandria and Origen*), the coherence of theological reasoning requires us to counter the insurmountable meaning of the faith of the simple or of children (spiritual childhood*). On the one hand, knowledge may exist when theoretical knowledge is weak, and it is also, on the other hand, called upon to raise up theoretical knowledge; if there is an expression of the theologal in theology, there is also an assumption of the theological in the theologal that imposes a bond between theology and sanctity (holiness*) (Balthasar* 1948). It is not a love of paradox that is the basis for attributing to Silouan or Theresa of Lisieux the status of Doctor of the Church.

7) Knowledge of God is the work of individuals, and the act of faith may even operate as a spiritual principle of individuation (Kierkegaard*). It is, however, not possible to account for it without recognizing its interpersonal and more specifically "communional" coordinates, hence without linking knowledge and "ecclesial being" (Lubac* 1938; Zizioulas). This link itself is both diachronic and synchronic. On the one hand, the act of knowledge is inserted into the history of a confessing, narrating, and interpretive community that guarantees the continuity of meanings through the discontinuities of time. On the other hand, the present community provides the living context for knowledge; in its word* and in its sacraments (sacrament*), it is primordially through the medium of the Church* that God gives himself to be known.

8) Knowledge of God is thus centrally attested in the liturgical action of the Church. In the liturgical celebration the sense of what it means to know God is played out in the most precise manner possible. On the one hand, God gives himself to be known by a people whom he assembles. On the other hand, the God who communicates himself gives himself sacramentally, while his proximity in no way undermines his transcendence but rather accentuates it. Finally, the gift of divine proximity finds its proper response in the language of memorial *(anamnesis)*, praise* *(Eucharist*)*, and invocation *(epiclesis*)*, and this language appears to be the most appropriate one in which to express knowledge.

9) The liturgy* anticipates the *eschaton* in history and thus cannot be mentioned without also noting the strictly inchoate character of all knowledge of God in the time* of the world. Eternal life*, beatific vision*, these key concepts tell us that, in the final analysis, the knowledge of God is an eschatological event, which in history can only be anticipated or sketched out. Between a lack of knowledge to which human beings are not abandoned and a full knowledge that cannot be experienced this side of death*, a mediating term is thus supplied: sacramental knowledge and its preeschatological order. Here and now, the knowledge of God bears the stamp of the time before the end.

- R. Bultmann (1933), "*Ginôskô, gnôsis…,*" *ThWNT* 1, 688–719; id. (1952), "Das Problem der Hermeneutik," *GuV* 2, 211–35.
- H. de Lubac (1938), *Catholicisme: Les aspects sociaux du dogme*, Paris, 4th Rev. Ed.1947, especially 51–55, 169–78, 283–305.
- H.U. von Balthasar (1948), "Theologie und Heiligkeit," *WuW* 3, 881–96, new Ed. in *Verbum Caro*, Einsiedeln, 1960, 195–225.
- Cl. Bruaire (1964), *L'affirmation de D.*, Paris, especially 113–34.
- C. Yannaras (1967), *Hè theologia tès apousias kai tès agnôsias tou Theou*, Athens.
- M. Müller (1971), *Erfahrung und Geschichte*, Freiburg-Basel-Vienna.
- J. Splett (1973), *Gotteserfahrung im Denken*, Freiberg.
- K. Rahner (1976), *Grundkurs des Glaubens*, Freiburg-Basel-Vienna, 35–96.
- P. Miquel (1977), *L'expérience de D.*, Paris.
- J.B. Lotz (1978), *Transzendentale Erfahrung*, Freiburg-Basel-Vienna.
- J.-L. Marion (1978), "De connaître à aimer: l'éblouissement," *Com(F)* III/4, 17–28.
- B. Welte (1978), *Religionsphilosophie*, Freiburg-Basel-Vienna.
- J. Bergman, G.J. Botterweck (1982), "Yadac," *ThWAT* 3, 479–512.
- R. Schaeffler (1982), *Fähigkeit zur Erfahrung*, Freiburg-Basel-Vienna.
- I.U. Dalferth (1984), *Existenz Gottes und christlicher Glaube*, Munich.
- J.-Y. Lacoste (1994), *Expérience et Absolu*, Paris.
- S.L. Frank (1995), *Das Unergründliche: Ontologische Einführung in die Philosophie der Religion*, Freiberg-Munich (original Russian edition published in Paris in 1939).
- T. Pröpper (1995), "Erkenntnis Gottes," *LThK3* 3, 781–86.

JEAN-YVES LACOSTE

See also **Experience; Faith; Mysticism; Theology**

Knowledge, Divine

Following the distinctions established by Pseudo-Dionysius* in the treatise *Divine Names*, divine knowledge classically designates an affirmative divine attribute (attributes*, divine); that is, an operation of God* that qualifies his intellective life. Its use therefore posits that there is an action in God for which intellect or intelligence—that is, what allows human beings to have knowledge—is the created analogue (*see*, e.g., Origen, *Periarchon*, I. 1. 6).

a) *Divine Knowledge in the Typologies of Divine Attributes.*   Two passages in Paul (Rom 11:33 and Col 2:3) couple wisdom* (*sophia, sapientia*) with Gnosis* (*gnôsis*), the latter translated by the Latin *scientia*, the French *science*, and English "knowledge," sanctioning a distinction reinforced by the division of gifts in 1 Corinthians 12:8. In Chapter VII of *Divine Names*, wisdom is not identified with intellect (the latter may exist without the former, even though it derives from it, as demonstrated by the intellect of devils (demons*), of which it is a "waste"). This distinction of wisdom from knowledge, thematized by book II of the *Sentences*, dist. 35, was of capital importance for the whole of medieval theology*. But divine knowledge was often also assimilated to the wisdom of God, since, according to Augustine* (*Trin* XIV. I. 3), wisdom is properly speaking the knowledge of divine things. Treatises on divine attributes assign a definition and a function to knowledge following a dual typology. On the one hand there is the tripartite division wisdom/knowledge/intelligence (*sunesis, intellectus*, or *intellegentia*), attested by Isaiah 11:2 (*Sentences*, book III, dist. 35 then adds the distinction mentioned above that intelligence is a speculation whereas wisdom is rather a contemplation* and a delectation); on the other hand there is the triad power (omnipotence*, divine)/knowledge (sapience)/will (goodness), often reduced from the 17th century onward to the duality of divine knowledge and divine power. But the latter notion, probably by reason of the importance of what was at stake (in particular the question of the existence of evil*), gave rise to more theoretical developments than that of knowledge, which appeared less problematical and was therefore less frequently denied (explicitly or not) and less frequently worked through. In addition, the affirmation in the creed, doxologies, and blessings (blessing*) of the omnipotence of the Father* clearly manifests an imbalance between power and knowledge. The oldest mention in *DS* of divine knowledge refers to the Council of Rome of 382, which said that God the Son can do all and knows all in the same way as God the Father (*DS* 164), and repeated the same thing of the Holy* Spirit (*DS* 169). But it is not until 15 centuries later, in Vatican* I, that we find an explicit dogmatic* formulation of the infinity of divine knowledge (*DS* 3009), irreducible to a worldy order (§1 of the *Syllabus* condemned those who deny a very wise [*sapientissimum*] divine Being [*Numen*] distinct from the universality of things, *DS* 2901). The Church* confesses a God infinite* in all perfection, hence in intellect (*intellectu ac voluntate omnique perfectione infinitum*, dogmatic constitution *Dei Filius, DS* 3001).

The divine attribute of knowledge contains within itself two difficulties. What does "knowledge" mean when the concept is applied to God? To what does the postulated totality of divine knowledge extend? A third question may also express the problems: is the analogy* between divine knowledge and human knowledge valid, with the proviso that the former is unlimited? Like all his other attributes, God's knowledge is marked by its infinity (Augustine, *De civitate Dei*, I. 12. 18–19). Divine knowledge is then characterized as omniscience or all-knowingness, understanding by these words (which appear to have been coined in the modern period, whereas "omnipotence" is much earlier) that divine knowledge or intelligence extends to everything and perhaps beyond (infinitely); that is, beyond what we ourselves can consider an object of thought: everything that is, everything that is not but is to come, the possible, indeed the impossible, God himself. But the development of the concept by the Greek and Latin Fathers very largely precedes the word, particularly with respect to prescience (Augustine). A. Michel (1941) recapitulated patristic treatment of the subject on the basis of the *Enchiridion patristicum*. The examination of various objects of divine knowledge is organized with varying degrees of difficulty depending on whether the theologies concerned borrow their concepts from Platonism* or Aristotelianism*.

b) *Biblical Treatment: From the Knowledge of Secrets to the Knowledge of Everything.*   The Old Testament frequently asserts that God knows what it is difficult to know: the secret thoughts of man (Ps 91:11), his sins and his offenses (Ps 69:6), the depths of the heart (soul*-heart-body) and the mind (Ps 7:10; Prv 15:11; 1 Kgs 8:39—repeated against indifferentism in the encyclical *Quanto conficiamur moerore* of 10 August 1863, *DS*, 2866), the person* even before he or she exists (Jer 1:5; *see also* Rom 8:29; 1 Cor 13:12), or events before they occur, which is known as prescience (Is 44:7; Dn 13:42). The knowledge that God has of human beings is always more than information: it expresses his interest in humankind (Ps 33:13), his tender love, or indeed his choice* (e.g., Gn 18:19). God sees what is hidden (Dn 13:42), the Father sees in darkness (Mt 6:4f.), the Son knows what is in man (Jn 2:25), and he knew in advance who would betray him (Jn 6:65). Nothing is invisible for God (Heb 4:13, which Vatican I relies on). But this lucidity on God's part is not enough to provide a conceptual foundation for omniscience. As for the pairing wisdom and knowledge, sometimes joined by intelligence, it is not infrequent in the Old Testament but is attributed to the one to whom God has given the gift of his spirit (e.g., Ex 35:31; 2 Chr 1:11f.; Eccl 2:26; Is 33:6; Dn 5:11), or to the spirit as given (Is 11:2), and is not predicated of God himself (commentators have not been unanimous in relating to God the counterexample, Jb 12:13). Unlike omnipotence, omniscience therefore does not seem as such to constitute a divine name* in the Old Testament, whereas Paul clearly mentions the "riches and wisdom and knowledge of God" (Rom 11:33 and Col 2:3).

1 Samuel 2:3 says of the Lord that he is the "God of knowledge" (*gnôseôn, scientiarum* [Bernard* of Clairvaux, *De consideratione* V. 4]). In Islam, omniscience is one of the 99 names of God. The three Old Testament passages that the treatises *De Deo uno* traditionally quote to confirm the omniscience of God are the following (the Vulgate each time translates *scientia*): Esther 14:15 (Vulg. = Greek Esther C, 25), "Lord, Thou hast knowledge of all things (gnôsis)" (*see also* 13:12 = C, 5); Ecclesiasticus 42:18 (Vulg. 19), "The Most High knows all that may be known (eidèsis)"; Job 21:22, "Will any teach God knowledge (sunesis kai epistèmè)?" (we might add Bar 3:32 and Jb 28:24). Except for the Pauline references already mentioned, the New Testament is rather preoccupied with the knowledge of Christ*, as in John 21:17. Similarly, in John 16:30 it is the omniscience of Jesus* that causes him to be recognized as Son of God (*see also* Jn 4:19, 25, 39); 1 Corinthians 2:10, for its part, confirms the omniscience of the Holy Spirit. However, it is not certain that the question of the knowledge of Christ finds a clear basis in the New Testament. Relying on Acts 2:23 ("this Jesus, delivered up according to the definite plan [*boulè, consilium*] and foreknowledge [*prognosis, praescientia*] of God"), one might propose the schema: there is prescience on the Father's part and obedience on the Son's part to what the Father knows. Acts also contains a single occurrence of *pronoia* in the sense of *providentia* (and not *cura*): in Acts 24:2 the pagan Tertullus speaks of the *pronoia* of the governor Felix. The "pre-thought" of Proclus was also translated by *providentia*.

c) Does God Know Himself? The argument according to which God knows himself is problematical in the framework of a Neoplatonic philosophy* that thinks of God as the One, and this for two reasons. On the one hand, since knowledge implies a distinction between the knower and the known, or the intelligence and the intelligible, and so produces a duality, it must be excluded that the One may know; it is the second hypostasis (*noûs*) that has the capacity to contemplate the One in itself and hence to know itself (*see*, e.g., *Enneads* V). There would thus be a contradiction between the transcendental predicate of unity and the operative attribute of knowledge; this is why Dionysius, although he holds that the wisdom of God knows itself, has no hesitation in saying that God has no intellectual activity (*Divine Names* VII. 2). Further, taking seriously the fact that God is infinite makes it impossible for his essence to be known, even by himself. For John the Scot Eriugena, the proposition "God does not know himself" is true if it is understood to mean "God does not know himself in his quiddity, for God is not an objectified *quid*," not being any of the knowable existents (nothingness*). In this sense alone is it possible to say that "God remains unknowable both for himself and for any intelligence" (*De divisione naturae*, Book II. 589 B–C); and the intelligence is forbidden to inquire about the substance of God even more than about his name (Jgs 13:18). Furthermore, if God knew himself in his substance, he could define himself: his infinity would then be relative, not absolute (587 B).

On the other hand, God's knowledge of himself causes no difficulty in an Aristotelian context, nor later for natural* theology. According to the *Metaphysics* 7 and 10 (which also joins together *sophia* and *epistèmè*) and *De Anima* III. 6 ("if there is anything that has no contrary, then it knows itself and is actually and possesses independent existence"), the God of Aristotle, an act of intelligence (*energeia noûs*), knows himself, he is *noèsis noèseôs* (*Metaphysics* 9, 1074$_b$ 35), thought of thought: "And thought thinks on itself because it shares the nature of the object of thought... so that thought and object of thought are the same" (*Metaphysics* 7, 1072$_b$ 20–22). Thus the *epistèmè* is *théologikè* (even though Aristotle does not use the word) because it is the knowledge that God has of God; here is posited the central thesis of theological knowledge of the Middle Ages. Thomas strictly repeated the argument in showing that in the case of God, as pure act, the intellect (operating) and the intelligible (object of the operation) are identical (*ST* Ia. q. 14. a. 2 resp.; *CG* I. 45); for if God were intelligent without being himself the object of his intelligence, a distinction would have to be made in him between power and act. God's intellect is thus his essence, and God knows his essence (1 Cor 2:10) through his essence itself, which is the intelligible species of his intellection (*CG* I. 46–47). To know, for God, is to know first his essence, hence to know himself (*CG* I. 48); that is, to know what is fundamentally incomprehensible to us, God himself. We must therefore posit a (for us) unknowable knowledge, a (for us) incomprehensible comprehension. It is therefore not paradoxical that omniscience and incomprehensibility have always been linked, from Pseudo-Dionysius (*Divine Names* VII. 2–3) to Descartes* (*Letters to Mersenne* of April and May 1630).

d) Does God Know What Is Not Himself? It is a disputed question in Scholastic (Scholasticism*) theology whether, on the basis of *Physics* 8 and *Metaphysics* 7, the God of Aristotle knows the world. It is obvious that he does know it, since the primum mobile is known; but because his intellect is what is best and must think what is best, it could only think of itself. His thought is nothing but the act of thinking his own act of thinking (*a fortiori* the idea of omniscience was radically foreign to Aristotle, and to Greek philosophy in general, despite the fragment [21 B24 DK] of Xenophon of Colophon, whose interpretation is open to question). Thomas* Aquinas, following Themistius (*In Metaphysicam* 28. 28f.), asserts that the God of Aristotle thinks the world. In this debate, Hebrews 4:13 again provides the necessary reference for a positive answer. Thomas demonstrates it as follows: God could not know himself perfectly without knowing his power. Knowing power implies knowing what that power governs; that is, the existing things of which it is the efficient cause. This demonstration of the knowledge of God is mediated, at least for created things, by recourse to his power. In addition, every effect, pre-existing in God as in its cause, is necessarily known in him according to its intelligibility (as the intelligible is in the intellect). In this way we see that the knowledge of things other than the self is for God still knowledge of himself (*ST,* ibid.; *CG* I. 49; *see also De veritate,* q. 2). For God knows or sees the things that are outside himself only in himself and not in themselves. Augus-

tine claimed that God sees nothing outside himself (q. 46 of the *Eighty-Three Questions*) and God, "in thinking himself, thinks all things" (*CG* I. 49): Thomas adopts from Dionysius (*Divine Names* VII. 3) a formulation first used by Plotinus about the *noûs* (IV. 4).

Neoplatonism indeed made it easy to think that God knows everything in himself, since intelligence reaches the intelligible without going outside itself (*Enneads* V. 2). For Dionysius, relying on Daniel 12:42, it is as cause of all things that divine intelligence contains in itself in advance the notion of all things and hence knows all things in their principles (*Divine Names* VII. 2). The divine intelligence therefore knows not on the basis of existing things but on the basis of itself: "God does not know existing things by knowing them, but by knowing himself"—it is by anticipating the knowledge of the thing that the divine intelligence confers on it its essence (ibid.). The concept of cause thus has a dual function: not only does God give being to all things as their cause, but it is in the same way that he knows all things. Similarly, Augustine says: "It is not because they are that God knows all created beings…but it is because he knows them that they are" (*De Trinitate* XV. 13, based on Ecclesiasticus 23:20). Thomas, quoting Dionysius in *CG* I. 49, reiterates the argument (ibid., a. 8; *see De veritate,* q.2, a. 14): "God is the cause of things by his intelligence" (*CG* I. 51). It is thus through the same modality that God knows himself and knows what is not himself: he sees himself in himself, he sees truths in himself, and he still sees things in himself and not in themselves, by means of his universal causality. This entire schema fell apart with Duns Scotus and was ignored as long as it was thought that God produced representations themselves.

e) Objects and Modalities of Divine Knowledge. The plurality of objects of knowledge imposes on divine knowledge—which itself remains single—conceptual determinations and specific denominations. Alexander of Hales distinguishes between divine knowledge considered in itself, considered relatively (prescience and disposition), and finally, considered in relation to divine government (providence*, fate, predestination*, reprobation, election, tender love). Thereafter, Bonaventure*, among others, soon prepared a list in the *Breviloquium* (Ia. c. 8), which he chose to subsume under the heading of wisdom: knowledge of possible things; vision of what happens in the universe; approbation of what is good; prescience or foresight with regard to what will happen; disposition for what God will do; predestination of what is worthy of recompense; reprobation of what deserves to be condemned.

We cannot fully examine here these various objects,

all of which pose particular problems: the singular, for the knowledge of God has the same extension as his causality (*CG* I. 50); matter, the principle of individuation; evil, which God knows as limitation (in accordance with its nature); and the infinite, for "all infinity is in some ineffable way made finite to God" (*De civitate Dei*, book 12. c. 18). We will mention here only the questions of the contingent as contingent and the prescience of God. Among the things that are not, some have been or will be: God knows them through a knowledge called "of vision" (*ST* Ia. q. 14. 1. 9), for the present gaze (*intuitus*) of God extends through all time* (*see* eternity* of God). As for things that have never been or will never be, God knows them through a knowledge called "of simple intelligence" (ibid.), for these things have no being distinct from the subject that conceives them.

In modern times the invention of combinatorial analysis gave Leibniz* the means of thinking about this knowledge of simple intelligence in order to rationalize the divine choice of bringing into being the best of all possible worlds. Indeed, God knows not only all things but all possible relations between possible things or phenomena (compossibility). God "looks at all the facets of the world in every possible manner, since there is no relationship that escapes from his omniscience" (*Discourse on Metaphysics*, §XIV). For Leibniz (*Letters to Arnauld*), the divine calculus even takes into account the possible decrees of his will. These arguments were adopted in a Scholastic vein by the *Theologia naturalis* (p. I/1 §§141–311) of Wolff, important for the history of the treatises and the teaching of *De Deo uno* until the middle of the 20th century. For Wolff as for Leibniz, it is God's intelligence, and not his power or his will, that is the source of the possibilities that power actualizes (he calls actualizable possibilities "existables," §221).

It can thus be understood that divine knowledge extends to contingent futures; the basic scriptural reference is Ecclesiasticus 23:20 (= Vulg. 29), and commentaries on it by Augustine (*De Trinitate* XV. xiii; *see also De Genesi ad litt.* book V. 18) and Origen (*Super epistulam ad Romanos* VII), quoted by Peter Lombard in Book 1 of the *Sentences* (d. 38. c. 1), which organizes the entire subject of prescience around the initial dilemma with which the Middle Ages and the modern period were to pose the question: are knowledge and prescience the cause of things, or are things the cause of knowledge and prescience? What is at stake is the status of human liberty*: does God's prescience not abolish it? It was intellectually necessary to maintain both that an action is free (hence contingent) and yet that God knows what man will freely choose. The Thomist solution refers again to the

eternity of divine knowledge (*ST* Ia. q. 14. a. 13). Later Scholasticism was divided between the hypothesis of physical pre-motion (that is, physically and not only psychologically determinative) and that of middle knowledge (*scientia media*), which works on the conditions required in order to maintain that the contingent is known in a way that is certain (God knows what a given free will would do in given circumstances); this kind of contingency (Mt 11:21) is called "futurible" (*see* Bañezianism*-Molinism-Baianism). Leibniz speaks of necessity *ex suppositione* and in this context distinguishes between a "necessitated" event (something that [an act of the] unconstrained human will is not) and a "determined" event (following the principle of sufficient reason). In every case the infallible knowledge that God has of free actions is characterized as "independent knowledge," for it takes place a priori.

In relation to the Aristotelian conceptual system and to a modern determination of science, divine knowledge appears more as concrete knowledge-of-content than as rational knowledge-as-way-of-knowing (*epistème*, despite a few occurrences in the Septuagint in Job), to the extent that it never proceeds by discursive reasoning: it accommodates neither compound nor division (*Divine Names* VII. 2; *CG* I. 57 and 58; *ST* Ia. q. 14. a. 7). Thought of as *visio* or *intuitus*, the knowledge of God is a simple and immediate act: "God sees everything at once" (Augustine, *De Trinitate* book 15. c. 14). Intelligence, knowledge, wisdom, counsel, or prudence (that is, practical knowledge) are thus identified in God who knows everything according to a single and simple knowledge (*ST* Ia. q. 14. a. 1. ad 2). Because of its amplitude as because of its modality (knowing in its essence), this is called "comprehensive knowledge."

The affirmation of the univocal character of knowledge continued to grow in strength during later Scholasticism to the point that in the modern period, comprehensive knowledge, reserved for God, became the conceptual model for all knowledge. Of course, for Descartes, "only God himself is perfectly wise, that is, only he has complete knowledge of the truth* of all things" (*Letter-Preface* to the *Principles*). In resistance to this dominant position, he asserts that "in God it is a single thing to will, to understand, and to create, with none preceding the others, *ne quidem ratione*" (*Letter to Mersenne* of 27 May 1630); this is why he firmly maintains the Augustinian distinction between conceiving ("touching with thought") God and understanding him ("embracing with thought"); we are capable of the former, not the latter (ibid.). Descartes tirelessly repeats that the power of God, creator of our rationality, is incomprehensible to us.

But his principal contemporaries and successors were not afraid to think of human knowledge following the model of the knowledge of vision or of the beatific vision*. This is true of Spinoza, for whom knowledge of the third type makes it possible to know as God knows (*Ethics* II, prop. 40, note 2 and props. 45–47); and for Malebranche, for whom we see all things in God and who totally subjects divine power to divine wisdom (*Treatise of Nature and Grace* I, a. 1, add.); and for Leibniz, who articulates the univocal character of knowledge by making finite and infinite understanding totally homogeneous, subject to the principles of contradiction, of sufficient reason, and of the best. Finally, the "absolute knowledge" of Hegel enables man to accede to knowledge of a comprehensive type. Schleiermacher*, for his part, proposes the interpretation adopted by the principal current of Protestantism* in the 19th century: what is to be understood by divine omniscience is the absolutely spiritual character of divine power.

VINCENT CARRAUD

f) Perspectives. Even though one major question, that of the divine knowledge of evil, has never ceased to be a subject of debate in Catholic theology (Nicolas 1960; Maritain 1963; Garrigues 1982; Sentis 1992), it seems that recent scholarship has undergone a displacement of the problem of divine knowledge. On the one hand, the theological repercussions of critical exegesis* of the New Testament have necessitated a renewed interest in the knowledge of Christ, itself interpreted most frequently, in a kenotic perspective omnipresent since the 19th century, as the "faith* of Christ" (J. Guillet, Balthasar*; *see* Christ*'s consciousness), implying a certain ignorance on Christ's part. On the other hand, the concept of divine intellect, already criticized by Spinoza and Hume, then by Fichte at the dawn of the *Atheismusstreit,* and finally shattered in the Hegelian logic of the absolute spirit (*see* Brito 1991), is an unquestionable subject of embarrassment in more than one contemporary theology (e.g., the critique of God conceived as *noûs* in Pannenberg 1988). The notion of divine subjectivity is not absent from contemporary dogmatic* discussion, and the theory of predestination is not dead (e.g., in Barth*); nevertheless, a reelaboration, governed in particular by the concept of divine love* or divine charity, has preoccupied contemporary theology in the most fruitful manner. And this reelaboration is no doubt still incomplete enough for us not yet to have at our disposal well-developed theories of the modes of knowledge appropriate to love. Anglo-American philosophy, however, has shown continued interest in the problem of divine omniscience, either in denying the consistency of the concept (A. N. Prior, *Philosophy* 37 [1962] 114–29; N. Kretzmann, *Journal of Philosophy* 63 [1966] 409–22; also Castañeda, 1989, and Hasker, 1989) or in maintaining the possible existence of a spiritual being who knows everything that it is logically possible to know while restraining his preknowledge of the future to preserve his own liberty and to leave human beings free (Swinburne 1977). Finally, omniscience cannot be attributed to the God of Process Theology, whose very being* is a "process" and one that he does not entirely govern.

JEAN-YVES LACOSTE

● Origen (v. 230), *Peri archôn, Super epistolam ad Romanos.*
Augustine (388–96), *De diversis quaestionibus* LXXXIII, q. 46 (BAug 10, Paris, 1952, 126–27); (v. 420), *De Trinitate* XV, 13 (BAug 16, 484–89); (v. 420), *De civitate Dei,* l. 12, c. 18–19 (BAug 35, 208–17).
Pseudo-Dionysius (v. 480–500), *Divine Names* VII.
John the Scot Eriugena (864–66), *De divisione naturae,* l. II.
P. Lombard (1152), *Sentences,* l. I, d. 35–41 (new Ed., Rome, 1971, vols. I/II, 254–91).
Alexander of Hales (1240–45), *ST,* tract. V (Ed. Quaracchi, vol. 1, 1924, 244–359).
Bonaventure (1254–56), *Questiones disputatae, De scientia Dei* (in *Opera omnia,* Ed. Quaracchi, vol. 5, 1891, 1–43); id. (1256), *Breviloquium* Ia, c. 8 (ibid., 216–17).
Thomas Aquinas (1259), *CG* I, 44–49; id. (1261), *In Dionysium De divinis nominibus;* id. (1266) *ST* Ia, q. 14; id. (1268–72), *In Metaphysicam,* l. XII.
Molina (1588), *Concordia liberi arbitrii cum gratiae donis, divina praescientia, providentia, praedestinatione et reprobatione ad nonullos partis divi Thomae articulos,* Lisbonne.
F. Suarez (1597), *Disputatio metaphysica* XXX, "De divina scientia naturaliter cognoscibili," in *Disputaniones metaphysicae,* Madrid (repris in *Opera omnia,* vol. 26, Paris, 1861, 170–83); id. (1599), *De scientia Dei futurorum contingentium,* in *Opuscula theologica sex,* Madrid (repr. ibid., vol. 11, 1858, 294–375); id. (1606), *De divina substantia ejusque attributis,* l. III, c. In–V, in *De Deo* (repr. in ibid., vol. 1, 1856, 194–214).
Lessius (1610), *De gratia efficaci, decretis divinis, libertate arbitrii et praescientia Dei conditionata,* Antwerp.
Salmenticenses, Cursus theologicus (1631–1712), tract. III, in q. 14, Iae p., Salamanca-Madrid (new Ed., Paris, 1870–83, vol. 1, 315–670).
Jean de Saint-Thomas (1637), *Cursus theologicus,* t. 2, in q. 14, Iae p., Alcala (new Ed., Paris, vol. 2, 1883, 417–684).
D. Petau (1644), *De Deo Deique proprietatibus,* l. IV, in *Opus de theologicis dogmatibus* (new Ed., Bar-le-Duc, vol. 1, 1864).
B. Spinoza (1677), *Ethica,* Amsterdam.
L. Thomassin (1680), *De Deo Deique proprietatibus,* l. VII, in *Dogmata theologica,* Paris (new Ed., Paris, 1865, vol. II).
N. Malebranche (1684), *Traité de la nature et de la grâce,* 4th Ed., Rotterdam.
G. W. Leibniz (1686), *Discours de métaphysique.*
C. Wolff (1736), *Theologia naturalis* I, §141–311, Frankfurt and Leipzig (repr. of the 1739 edition, Hildesheim, 1978).
D. Hume (publ. 1779), *Dialogues Concerning Natural Religion,* London (Ed. H. D. Aiken, London, 1977), parts 3 and 4.
J. G. Fichte (1798), "Über den Grund unseres Glaubens an eine göttliche Weltregierung," WW (Ed. I. H. Fichte), vol. 5, 177–89.

G. W. F. Hegel (1807), *Phänomenologie des Geistes,* Bamberg-Würzburg (Ed. Hoffmeister, 549–64); id. (1816), *Wissenschaft der Logik* II, Nuremberg (*Theorie Werkausgabe,* Frankfurt, 1969, vol. 6, 487–573).

D. F. Schleiermacher (1821), *Der christliche Glaube,* Berlin, §55 (Ed. Redeker, Berlin, 1960, vol. 1, 289–300).

♦ M.-J. Schebeen (1869–75), *Handbuch der katholischen Dogmatik* II, I, c. III (GS, Freiberg, 1948–54, 4).

D. Kaufmann (1877), *Geschichte der Attributenlehre in der jüdischen Religionsphilosophie des Mittelalters von Saadja bis Maimuni,* Gotha.

M. J. Rouët de Journel (1911), *EnchP* (25th Ed. 1981).

K. Barth (1932), *KD* II/I (French trans. *Dogmatique* II/1/2, 1957, Geneva).

A. Michel (1941), "Science de Dieu," *DThC* 14, 1598–620.

L. Gardet, M.-M. Anawati (1948), *Introduction à la théologie musulmane,* Paris.

J.-H. Nicolas (1960), "La permission du mal," *RThom* 60, 5–37, 185–206, 509–46.

J. Maritain (1963), *Dieu et la permission du mal,* Paris (3rd Ed. 1993).

C. Bérubé (1964), *La connaissance de l'individuel au MA,* Paris-Montréal.

A. Plantinga (1967), *God and Other Minds,* Ithaca, N.Y.

R. Imbach (1976), Deus est intelligere, *Das Verbältnis von Sein und Denken in seiner Bedeutung für des Gottesverständnis bei Thomas von Aquin und den Pariser Questionen Meister Eckharts,* Freiberg.

R. Swinburne (1977), *The Coherence of Theism,* Oxford, 162–78.

J.-M. Garrigues (1982), *Dieu sans idée du mal,* Limoges (new Ed., Paris, 1990).

A. de Libera et al. (Ed.) (1984), *Maître Eckart à Paris, une critique médiévale de l'ontothéologie,* Paris.

A. Funkenstein (1986), *Theology and Scientific Imagination,* Princeton, N.J.

R. Brague (1988), *Aristote et la question du monde,* Paris.

W. Pannenberg (1988), *Systematische Theologie,* vol. I, 401–16.

H. N. Castañeda (1989), "God and Knowledge: Omniscience and Indexical Reference," in *Thinking, Language, Experience,* Minneapolis, 143–59.

W. Hasker (1989), *God, Time and Knowledge,* Ithaca-London.

J.-F. Courtine (1990), *Suarez et le système de la métaphysique,* Paris.

R. Brague (1991), "Le destin de la "Pensée de la Pensée" des origines au début du MA," in T. de Koninck, G. Planty-Bonjour (Ed.), *La question de Dieu selon Aristote et Hegel,* Paris.

E. Brito (1991), *Dieu et l'être d'après Thomas d'Aquin et Hegel,* Paris, 211–51.

L. Sentis (1992), *Saint Thomas d'Aquin et le mal: Foi chrétienne et théodicée,* ThH 92.

S. T. Bonino (1996), *Introduction générale* à Thomas d'Aquin, *De la vérité,* Paris-Fribourg, 1–240.

V. C.

See also **Attributes, Divine; Bañezianism-Molinism-Baianism; Eternity of God; Immutability/Impassibility, Divine; Intellectualism; Justice, Divine; Negative Theology; Omnipotence, Divine; Omnipresence, Divine; Predestination; Providence; Simplicity, Divine; Theology; Truth; Vision, Beatific**

Kuhn, Johann Evangelist von. *See* **Tübingen, Schools of**

L

Laity. *See* **Lay/Laity**

Lamb of God/Paschal Lamb

Of all the books of the Bible*, the Gospel of John is the only one to use the phrase "Lamb of God." With the exception of the two passages concerned (Jn 1:29, 1:36), *amnos* for "lamb," only appears in Acts 8:32 and 1 Peter 1:19. The term used in Revelation is *arnion* (28 times). Interpretation will vary depending on what one considers to be the completed form of the figure of the book, thus granting the christological titles of John 1:19–51 their full meaning, or, depending on whether one refers to the origins, adhering to a more archeological approach.

a) Baptist Origins. Lamb of God appears to be a christological title and should not be disassociated from other titles in the litany that accompanies the story of the four inaugural days (Jn 1:19–51), which are themselves referred to John the Baptist's authority (1:19). He sees in Jesus* the one who "comes," "the Lamb of God, who takes away the sin of the world" (v. 19), then the "Lamb of God" (abbreviated form, v. 36). Then come the titles "Son of God" (v. 34, with variations "Chosen One," or "Chosen Son"), "Mes-

siah*," which means Christ* (v. 41), "Son of God" and "King of Israel*" (v. 49), and even the mysterious reference to the "Son of man," in relation to the image of Jacob's ladder (v. 51). Even the unknown Jesus (v. 31, 33) can be understood as a messianic feature, as can the insistence on the Holy* Spirit (v. 32 f.). Several authors (e.g., Brown and Schnackenburg) now share the view that this story contains an affirmation both of Jesus' own baptist roots, and those of the Johannine community itself, which seems particularly attached to the memory of John the Baptist (*see* Jn 3:22–30, 4:1 f., 5:33 f., 10:40).

b) The Paschal Lamb. The reading that is most influenced by the last stage of the book consists in interpreting it through the Paschal Lamb, starting from the founding story of Exodus 12. This figure appears in 1 Peter 1:19: "You know that you were ransomed...with the precious blood of Christ, like that of a lamb without blemish or spot"; and in 1 Corinthians 5:7: "For Christ, our Paschal Lamb, has been sacrificed." This theme is not neglected in the fourth

Gospel: the chronology of the Passion implies a coincidence with the sacrifice of lambs for the paschal dinner that very night (Jn 19:14), and the crucified Christ is identified with the Paschal Lamb, not one of whose bones would be broken (Jn 19:36; *see* Ex 12:46). Nevertheless, this interpretation does not fit well in the context of royal appointment in a baptist environment.

c) Servant of Isaiah. With 1 Peter 1:19, the catechism scene described in Acts 8:32 offers the second occurrence of *amnos*. Here, the "Servant" found in Isaiah 52:13–53:12 is presented "like a lamb that is led to the slaughter, and like a sheep that before its shearers is dumb," (Is 53:7). It is therefore tempting to relate the "Lamb of God" to the Servant. Jeremias suggested that "lamb" could be explained as a pun involving the Aramean *talya* (lamb) and the Hebrew *talèh* (servant). The latter term bears traits of archaic Christology (*pais:* Jesus, "child" or "servant"), still employed by the Apostolic* Fathers (Clement 59, 2. 3. 4; *Didache* 9, 2 f., 10, 2 f.). However, aside from the fact that the possibility of word play has not yet been definitively established (Dodd), the reference to Servant presents the same difficulty as the mention of the Paschal Lamb. Referring to the beginning of Jesus' ministry, it does not seem to match the pericopal context. Furthermore, the "Lamb of God" (Jn 1: 29) "takes away" (Greek *hairein*) sin, while the Servant of Isaiah 53:4 "carries" it (*pherein*), according to the perspective of the emissary victim (Is 53:5 f., 53:10).

d) The Victorious Lamb. Revelation gives the Lamb, called *arnion* (originally a diminutive of *arèn,* but as early as the Septuagint, the three terms—*amnos, arèn*

and *arnion*—seem equivalent), a certain number of characteristics related to royal power (Rev 7:17, 17:14). The same perspective can be found in apocalyptic* literature (Testament of Joseph 19:8; 1 En 90:6–19). Rather than the sacrificed lamb, we now encounter a young ram with budding horns, whose insolent spirit represents the vitality of the messiah-king. This suggestion, supported by Dodd, has not been unanimously accepted by exegetes. Nevertheless, given the current state of research, it at least seems the best suited to the context of the pericope devoted to the testimony of John the Baptist. Given that, through the theme of the Lamb, the apocalyptic aspect brings together royal symbolism and the tradition of sacrifice (*see* especially Jn 5:6, 5:9), exegesis* can take into account that process of reinterpreting Old Testament figures by means of which, as early as the New Testament, the first christological ideas were developed.

Thus, far from being incompatible, the various levels of meaning attest to the integration of the pericope of John 1:19–51 into the whole hermeneutic plan of the Gospel according to John.

● J. Jeremias (1933), *"Amnos-arèn-arnion," ThWNT* 1, 342–5.
C. H. Dodd (1963), *Historical Tradition in the Fourth Gospel,* Cambridge.
R. E. Brown (1966), *The Gospel according to John,* I-XII, New York.
A. Dupont-Sommer, M. Philonenko (Ed.) (1987), *La Bible: Écrits intertestamentaires,* Paris.
P. Grelot (1994), *L'espérance juive à l'heure de Jésus,* 2nd Ed., Paris.

YVES-MARIE BLANCHARD

See also **Animals; Apocalyptic Literature; Expiation; Messianism/Messiah; Passover; Sacrifice; Sin**

Language, Theological

The problem of theological language, and the criteria for its coherence and validity, is not new in theology*. But the most important debate on the subject in our times has doubtless taken place in England, where the validity of religious language has been questioned by linguistic philosophy*. The latter is based on the premise that the traditional metaphysical problems are

not real problems but only follow from linguistic misunderstandings. Many statements in reality have a very different function from the one they appear to have.

a) Logical Positivism. Post-1945 linguistic philosophy was a reaction against the logical positivism dominating English language philosophy and, specifically, the philosophy of religion* since the publication of *Language, Truth and Logic* (1936) by Alfred J. Ayer (1910–89). During the next five decades it was impossible to deal with these questions without including long introductions devoted to the nature of religious language. Logical positivism, which was born in Vienna in the 1920s, was in itself a reaction against metaphysical idealism. Its proponents maintained that all propositions were either analytical or synthetic and that all synthetic propositions were empirical—that is, based on tangible observation. A metaphilosophical problem thus ensues: are philosophical propositions empirical or tautological? What the Viennese were mostly interested in was giving an empirical content to the terms employed by the natural sciences*. If these did not come down directly to tangible observation, they had to be at least part of a theory consisting of propositions that could be verified or falsified through observation. This meant that scientific language had its basis in experience, while metaphysical language or a fortiori theological language did not. Therefore, the latter were languages devoid of meaning. As for the language of ethics or esthetics, it was a disguised way of expressing emotions: This language of values was meaningful without having any claims to truth*. Facts and values were strictly distinguished.

Theology was quickly called into question. In fact, its very existence became problematic: was it really a rational discourse whose statements were subject to verification or falsification? How was a discipline to be taken seriously if it did not state its solution to the problem of truth-value and the cognitive status of "religious language" to begin with? In reality, it was "religious language" and not "theological language" that was discussed—and this was misleading, since it was precisely the justification and truthfulness of theological statements that were at issue. It was only very late, for example, that interest in metaphor and symbol appeared. As for what constituted the essentials of religious language (such as rituals and gestures) for believers, as well as for liturgists, historians, and sociologists of religion, it was as if it did not exist.

As much as Ayer subsequently modified his version of logical positivism, he still denied the value of all claimed statements on the subject of God* (*see* his last important work of 1973). But in so doing, he based his reasoning much more on the distinction between fact and value, than on any contribution by the philosophy of language. In fact, all terminology in the debate on the cognitive status of religious language was, for the most part, prescribed by philosophers who had no subtle or innovative ideas with regard to language but who, carrying Hume's legacy, were obsessed by the distinction between value and fact. According to

Hume, what *ought* to be cannot be deduced from what *is;* there is such a "logical hiatus" between fact and value that we can principally separate all things respectively concerning them in any statement.

These philosophers were more interested in ethics* than in theology, and in the context of this debate they evolved in the direction of moral noncognitivism. Ayer, for example, classifies into four categories what had previously been considered in ethics to be statements endowed with a value of truth: 1) term definitions, 2) descriptions of moral phenomena, 3) exhortations to good conduct, and 4) ethical judgments. Only the first of these categories is philosophically respectable, since it is analytical in the Kantian sense. The second category refers to "soft" sciences such as sociology and psychology. Exhortations, in their turn, have no relation to reality, but are "exclamations or orders whose goal is to lead the reader [*sic*] to such and such an action." As for ethical judgments, they "express only sentiments." This is how Ayer formulated his version of moral theory known by the name of emotivism.

The same criterion of verifiability is then applied to assertions about a transcendental God. The affirmations of believers express only what they are feeling and can by no means depict or represent what is, or what could be, in reality. As Ayer observes, not without malice, this analysis goes very well with the idea of negative* theology. After all, theologians are very fond of saying that existence and divine nature are beyond language. We must make Pascal*'s wager or Kierkegaard's leap, but we must also stop thinking that theological statements speak of the reality of things. Ayer does not quote any theologian (it is unlikely that he never read a single one), but it is evident that a kind of radical fideism* would fit very well, at least on a superficial level, with the purely subjective theological statements. In fact, those theologians who wanted to keep up with the times felt obliged to adopt the perspective of logical positivism and to reject to a great extent the usual theological discourse. Instead of reaching into the heart of things and objecting to the reduction of all esthetic, ethical, and religious statements to a noncognitive status, many theologians between the 1940s and the 1980s instead tried to reformulate Christian theism in a way that would satisfy all of Ayer's principles.

b) Logical Empiricism in Theology. We must cite here David Cox's essay "The Significance of Christianity" (*Mind*, 1950), a remarkable document that is clearly symptomatic of theological reductionism. The word *God* is rightfully used only in phrases like "meeting God" but is considered improper any time it is meant to designate a reality independent of the speaker's subjective experience*. We should not take the proposition "God is love*" as some sort of information; in fact, it means that one cannot call "meeting God" the meeting with some person who does not love one. The statement that "God created the world from nothingness" (creation*) means that everything we can call "material" can serve to benefit humanity. According to the author, this kind of reinterpretation allows Christianity to avoid "the exile to which metaphysics are relegated, and rightfully so, by logical positivists." Cox's example is obviously an extreme case of submission to the criteria of logical positivism, but many other theologians admire the fact that theological language does not claim to convey truth and loses nothing from being considered purely an expression.

R. B. Braithwaite, for instance, supported the idea that Christianity provided a fund of "stories" to help us to behave well while the question of their truthfulness or falsity was not posed at all (*An Empiricist's View of the Nature of Religious Belief,* 1955). The essence of Christian stories is to inspire "a disposition to *agape.*" John Hick's theory of "eschatological verification" shows a bit more respect for the cognitive status of theological statements. For Hick, religious affirmations that are not susceptible to being verified experimentally will be so in the future world (*Faith and Knowledge,* 1957). Richard M. Hare, who had a great influence on the debate, maintained, for his part, that moral judgments as well as some religious judgments have a "prescriptive" meaning. To say that an act, for example, is good or bad, does not mean one attributes it a value of its own but that one recognizes that it is universally imperative to give it some standing or to avoid it in this or that case. For Hare, religious affirmations certainly do not represent reality; nevertheless, he suggests (*see* Flew and MacIntyre, 1955) that we regard them as quasi-metaphysical outlooks on the world (he even proposes a name for them, "blik").

It is understandable that the problem of religious language should arise in these terms. However, we shall see in retrospect that a dilemma of choice between factual usage and emotional usage of language cannot lead anywhere and dooms one to incomprehension, both in the area of religion and in the moral and esthetic area.

Some philosophers, such as Ian T. Ramsey (1915–72), while staying in the essentially positivist framework of linguistic analysis, made great efforts to explain the "strangeness" of religious expressions. Upon further scrutiny, theological propositions, even though lacking the realism that is usually attributed to them, are neither totally devoid of cognitive content

(as Ayer, Cox, Braithwaite, and Hare believed), nor do they offer direct information on the world (as traditional metaphysical realism was supposed to believe). As Ramsey rightly saw, to say that theological language is not concerned with reality is not the result of some extraordinary progress made by the philosophy of language, but it is a sign that the distinction between truth and value persists. Hence, the importance of some religious affirmations comes, for him, from what they can express or from their ability to create what he calls "revelation" situations. He attempts to show, by means of familiar expressions—such as "break the ice" and "it sticks out a mile"—that an everyday event can sometimes be a "revelation" and that ordinary relationships can suddenly become meetings that can change one's life. Ramsey supplies the perfect example of a fundamentally orthodox theologian who accepts the rules of logical empiricism and must, therefore, turn to everyday life to find cases of language escaping the distinction between truth and value. In any case his conclusions are perfectly valid: there is a kind of language usage that, although it expresses subjectivity, can reveal and transform a real situation.

c) Principle of Falsification. The volumes of essays coming out under the editorship of A. Flew and A. MacIntyre (1955) as well as Ramsey (1966), testify to an evolution of ideas leading, for example, from Flew's fierce antitheological position ("Theology and Falsification," 1949) to a more open agnosticism*, as demonstrated by R. W. Hepburn and Iris Murdoch ("Vision and Choice in Morality," 1956). According to the "principle of falsification," a proposition is devoid of meaning if it cannot be falsified, at least in principle, by an empirical observation. A proposition that cannot be falsified, cannot be verified either. Therefore, it has no cognitive status. If we apply this principle, as Flew does, to the theological propositions that speak of a loving God-Creator, we can say, still according to Flew, that the observable state of affairs—the order of nature—remains the same, whether we say that there is a Creator or not. We add nothing and take nothing out of this order by our affirmation or rejection. Therefore, the notion of a Creator is an empty one. The same is valid for the proposition "God is love," which is empty of meaning because it is obviously compatible with the most atrocious suffering. It is only by playing infinitely with the word *love* that we can avoid or circumvent the contradiction between God's love and suffering. In a famous formulation, Flew says that *suffering* is a word that has ended up a hundred times dead by virtue of its subtleties; it is a word that has gradually emptied itself of all empirical sense since it excludes no state of things observable, and no specific kind of suffering.

In Anglo-American culture it is generally assumed that only empirically verifiable propositions are cognitive and that all others are either analytical (tautological) or noncognitive (emotive). Plenty of theologians have adopted this view. Among them, Don Cupitt, for example, is the most eloquent representative of the noncognitive and nonrealist theology. He views religion as a great collective work of art, a profound expression of the human spirit, and a spontaneous burst of creative faith that "cannot, strictly speaking, be attributed either to God or to the ego, for it precedes any distinction between them" (*Life Lines*, 1986). Hence, religion can comply with the criteria of logical positivism while at the same time being what Cupitt calls an esthetic expression.

d) Philosophy of Anti-Empiricist Religion. Other philosophers, such as Hepburn and Murdoch, while being interested in ordinary language, and therefore recognizing linguistic analysis, pay equal attention to poetry and prose (Murdoch was also a novelist). As the latter says in her 1956 essay, which was the first sign of a moral philosophical evolution allowing her to abandon emotivism and regain a certain realism, we must distinguish between "the man who believes that moral values are a type of activity that can be observed empirically and of which he approves, from the man who believes that they are visions, inspiration, powerful forces coming from a transcendent source that he is called upon to discover, and about which he knows very little at the moment." But philosophers still had a long way to go before they realized that linguistic analysis was prisoner to the truth/value distinction and returned to metaphysics.

By the time Ayer arrived in Vienna, Wittgenstein (1889–1951) had already discovered that the members of the Viennese circle had not really understood his *Tractatus Logico-Philosophicus* and mistook him for a supporter of logical positivism. Indeed, in the beginning of his career Wittgenstein had been influenced a great deal by the works of Bertrand Russell (1872–1970) on the foundations of mathematics and logic. Russell was trying to restructure mathematics on a purely logical basis. To achieve this, he made use of a type of logic where the truth (or falsity) of a whole (e.g., "It is raining and it is Friday") was fully determined by the truth of each of its parts ("It is raining" and "it is Friday") considered *separately*. The truth of a whole is a function of the truths of its constituents. This inspired in Russell a concept of reality that he called "logical atomism": reality is essentially constituted of atoms of perceivable observation, each of which is certain and beyond doubt, all making up the basis for any knowledge. One can determine the truth or falsity of any statement by reducing the complex statement to its founding atoms and comparing them one by one, by means of observation, to "atomic" facts.

In the *Tractatus* Wittgenstein sought to demonstrate which type of propositions made sense within the limits of this logic and which didn't. It turned out there were very few that made sense. And in any case, it was no longer possible to talk about ethics, esthetics, metaphysics, or theology. However, this did not make Wittgenstein much of an ally to the Vienna Circle. He believed that reality was above what could be said about it and that the *in*expressible was far more important than the expressible. "The meaning of the world is to be found outside of the world" (§6, 41), but "whereof one cannot speak thereof one must be silent" (§7). This last remark from the *Tractatus* is far from being a warning to the positivists. On the contrary, "even if one has resolved all the scientific issues, one has not touched on the problems of life" (§6, 52).

Wittgenstein's thought, which had grown roots in Cambridge since 1930, helped English philosophy to rid itself of the tyrannical truth/value opposition. In his view, whenever philosophers speak of knowledge, being*, subject, object, and so on, they should always consider first whether these terms have the same meaning in ordinary language—"the point is to bring these terms of metaphysical use back to daily use" (1953, §116). This is clearly reminiscent of the antimetaphysical project of logical positivism, and it has usually been understood in that fashion. But the truth/value distinction is no less metaphysical than the propositions that logical positivism attacks, and according to Wittgenstein's principles, it does not resist being "transferred" to ordinary language. Instead of talking about language in the abstract, as he had reproached himself for doing in the *Tractatus,* it suffices to see how language is used in reality to define what can and what cannot be said, and to understand what is meant. Speaking is like playing a game or, rather, playing multiple games. Wittgenstein invented the expression "language games" (§23) in order to note that speaking is part of an activity, a "form of living." It is about giving orders, obeying, describing, making attempts, telling a story, singing, joking, congratulating, praying (1953, §23). Although he did not write much on the usage of religious language (*see,* however, *Lectures and Conversations on Aesthetics, Psychology and Religious Belief*), his insistence on the "multiple kinds of language games" was deeply liberating.

John Wisdom (1904–94), who had already published some important work in the area of logical atomism, wrote, under Wittgenstein's influence, several essays of philosophical theology. One of these, "Gods" (1944; in *Philosophy and Psychoanalysis*, 1953) is a fundamental text in the philosophy of religion. It basically discusses Hume's position and aims to show that Hume's concept of reason* is too narrow. Calling upon the authority of ordinary language, Wisdom draws his inspiration from Wittgenstein in criticizing a philosophical theory he finds inadequate. He shows very accurately that the kind of reasoning that is at work here does not correspond to the truth/value opposition. It is like in a trial (his favorite example): the facts may be known, but this does not necessarily mean that they will be reasonably interpreted; and it is not because one gets at this interpretation informally, instead of through deduction, that it will be arbitrary or entirely subjective. By this analysis of the real usage of language, Wisdom demonstrates to what extent our thoughts are richer and more complex than philosophical theories sometimes allow. His redemption of "informal reasoning" influenced some theologians (e.g., Renford Bambrough, who wrote *Reason, Truth and God*, 1969, and Basil Mitchell, author of *The Justification of Religious Belief*, 1973).

For Kai Nielsen, it was a "Wittgensteinian fideism" to try to avoid in this way working out the proof of the existence* of God by studying only the way of speaking about "God" in a religious context (*Philosophy*, 1967). However, there is one philosopher, D. Z. Phillips, who on first consideration might be considered an absolute fideist of Wittgenstein's type. Phillips is credited with the idea that religious language is such a different kind of play from all other forms of language play that it can only be understood by initiates; what makes sense in religious discourse can only be determined by believers; religious propositions cannot be criticized from the outside; and finally, religious beliefs cannot be affected by the evolution of the world. In this case, religion is a "language game" or a "form of living" that has its own rules of meaning and truth, and which the nonbeliever cannot enter. Nielsen did not accept this view in the name of an atheism* that sought to imply that he understood religious language too well to expose it as false.

It is not too certain, however, that Phillips was such a fideist in reality. He seems to be defending mostly the idea that since religion is necessarily related to birth, death*, and sexuality, the language of believers, at least in its fundamental forms (liturgy* and prayer*), is quite close to that of the common people. Once again the Wittgensteinian process lies in remembering how language is truly used in spite of what philosophical theories say. For Phillips, religious philosophy within the English academy has never really ceased to be logico-positivist, and he sees it as his task to combat theological rationalism*, which consists in applying to beliefs and religious practices criteria that are not appropriate to them. Theological language must be rooted in the language of piety and Christian life without forgetting the more general concerns of humanity.

The work of J. L. Austin (1911–60), independently of Wittgenstein's later research, owes a great deal to the Aristotelian tradition at Oxford and has had a considerable influence. From the perspective of "linguistic phenomenology," Austin created a distinction between performative and constative statements (1962). Constative or descriptive statements are true or false; performative statements are "felicitous" or "infelicitous," but they cannot be either true or false. For example, the statement "I christen this vessel *Queen Elizabeth*" cannot be false but it can be "infelicitous" if this is not my business or if it is not the right moment to do it. Inversely, "I have christened this vessel" is true or false.

Austin distinguished three kinds of linguistic acts: locutionary, in which one speaks to describe what is happening; illocutionary, in which one tells something to somebody with a certain "force"; and perlocutionary, which is the indirect effect of the statement upon the listeners. He ended up believing that all statements were simultaneously locutionary and illocutionary, and by the time of his premature death he had even abandoned these distinctions except in an approximate sort of way, for the sake of restoring to contemporary philosophy the meaning of language that we see in Aristotle's *Rhetoric*. In Austin's wake, John Searle (1969) examined the necessary logical conditions for accomplishing illocutionary acts, such as "to promise" or "to give an order." This allowed theologians to understand better that forgiveness, blessing*, and praise* have a different function from stories and descriptions (*see* A. C. Thiselton, *New Horizons in Hermeneutics*, 1992). But it is quite clear today that the theory of linguistic acts was only one more effort to evade the truth/value distinction.

By 1970, under the influence of Wittgenstein and Austin, English philosophers no longer treated the problem of religious language with their initial empirico-positivist aggressiveness; they were also open to Continental philosophy, particularly thanks to Paul Ricoeur. Well-acquainted with Anglo-American philosophy, Ricoeur expanded the deliberations on language by integrating Freud*'s contribution and the phenomenological tradition of Edmund Husserl and Maurice Merleau-Ponty. Although he may not have marked English-language philosophy in general, his influence is still quite clear in the sphere of theology and the philosophy of religion.

e) Beyond the Debate on Religious Language? Today, analytic philosophy is far more interested in the issues of meaning, truth, and reference (Quine, Dummett, and Davidson) than in the issue of language. Philosophers of religion—and therefore theologians—are wondering if it is not time to stop questioning themselves on the cognitive status of theological language and start treating the more general problem of metaphysical and ethical realism. Janet Martin Soskice's book (1985) and the collected essays of J. Runzo (1993) approach the question without allowing logical positivism to direct their process.

This trend is evident in textbooks. In 1967 the index of *God-Talk* by John Macquarrie had more references to "language" than to any other concept; in 1982 the word "language" did not even appear in the index of Brian Davies's book *Philosophy of Religion*. We can therefore consider the matter of religious language, which lasted in English language philosophy from 1936 to 1986, to be closed. It is now part of history. This does not mean that it did not leave a trace on people's minds. It is impossible to doubt metaphysics for years on end without losing all dogmatism. Today English-speaking philosophers and theologians are very careful whenever they need to affirm something—which has nothing but advantages. On the contrary, for a philosopher like Soskice, what needs to be done is to put aside the distorted theories of language (and the rejection of metaphysics supposedly authorized by these theories) and reexamine the cognitive possibilities of metaphors, analogies, and symbols. In her studies on the referential aspect of metaphor, Soskice maintains that theists can reasonably claim to be speaking of God, but that this affirmation is linked to a more general strategy seeking to speak in a valid way of that which cannot be fully defined in other areas as well. With the help of H. Putnam's work in particular, Soskice moves away from the empiricism that linguistic philosophy and the analysis of religious language never managed to get rid of, and moves closer to metaphysical realism.

● L. Wittgenstein (1922), *Tractatus Logico-Philosophicus*, London.
A. J. Ayer (1936), *Language, Truth and Logic*, London.
L. Wittgenstein (1953), *Philosophical Investigations*, Oxford.
L. Wittgenstein (n.d.), *Lectures and Conversations on Aesthetics, Psychology and Religious Belief*, Berkeley-Los Angeles, 53–72.
A. Flew, A. MacIntyre (Ed.) (1955), *New Essays in Philosophical Theology*, London.
I. T. Ramsey (1957), *Religious Language*, London.
J. L. Austin (1962), *How to Do Things with Words*, Oxford.
J. M. Bochénski (1965), *The Logic of Religion*, New York.
I. T. Ramsey (Ed.) (1966), *Christian Ethics and Contemporary Philosophy*, London.
J. Macquarrie (1967), *God-Talk*, London.
John Searle (1969), *Speech-Acts*, London.
D. Z. Phillips (1970), *Faith and Philosophical Enquiry*, London.
A. J. Ayer (1973), *The Central Questions of Philosophy*, London.
B. Casper (1975), *Sprache und Theologie: Eine philosophische Hinführung*, Freiburg-Basel-Vienna.
I. Murdoch (1975), *The Sovereignty of Good*, London.
I. U. Dalferth (1981), *Religiöse Rede von Gott*, Munich (bibl.).
J. M. Soskice (1985), *Metaphor and Religious Language*, Oxford.
M. Dummett (1991), *The Logical Basis of Metaphysics*, London, 322–51.
H. Putnam (1992), *Renewing Philosophy*, London.
J. Runzo (Ed.) (1993), *Is God Real?* London.
I. U. Dalferth (1995), "Sprache und Theologie," *EKL* 4, 425–34.

FERGUS KERR

See also **Credibility; Deism and Theism; Existence of God, Proofs of; Hermeneutics; Knowledge of God; Narrative Theology; Nominalism; Philosophy; Religion, Philosophy of; Truth**

Last Things. *See* Eschatology

Lateran I, Council

1123

The first three Lateran councils formed a continuity with the efforts of Pope Gregory VII (1073–85) to liberate the church* from any secular tutelage, especially from the German emperor, and with his active desire for reform, especially of the clergy. The "investiture controversy" had to be resolved during the pontificate of Calixtus II (1119–24). The antipope Gregory VIII was arrested and died in 1121. The Concordat of Worms was signed on 23 September 1122. According to the terms of this concordat, the emperor was to renounce the appointment of the prelates on the spiritual level (appointment "by the cross and ring"). He would respect the full freedom of election and consecration and would restore the goods of the Holy See and of other churches. The elected prelate would receive from the emperor, "by the scepter," his worldly possessions *(regalia),* and would observe the commitments made toward the ruler. The edict of Worms was ratified by the "general council" that met in the Lateran between 19 and 27 March 1123 in the presence of at least two hundred bishops* and priests. Canons 3, 4, 8, and 123 refer to this question.

On the jurisdictional and disciplinary level, Lateran I strengthened episcopal power in several ways, notably in relation to the absolution of the excommunicated (can. 2), and canonical institutional and pastoral responsibility in churches served by monks (can. 12). It prohibited simony—all practices that consist in giving or receiving a spiritual good (for example, the sacrament* of Holy Orders) in exchange for a worldly good, generally money (can. 1). It condemned the omission of any of the formal stages on the way to Holy Orders (can. 6), as well as the cohabitation of clerics with women other than their close relations (can. 7). It prohibited marriage* in the case of high-ranking clerics* and imposed separation to prevent this law from being violated (can. 21). It renewed previous prescriptions regarding the "peace*" and the "truce" of God*, the safety of travelers and pilgrims (cans. 14 and 15), the status of crusaders, and the protection of families and their property (can. 10). The council also condemned intermarriage (can. 9) and counterfeiters (can. 13).

Although previous councils (Clermont in 1095 and Toulouse in 1119) had inspired Lateran I, this council would serve as an example for numerous reforming synods* of Western Europe. Furthermore, canons 1, 4, 6, 9, 10, 15, 17, 18 and 20–22 were integrated into *Gratian's Decree* (c. 1140).

● Acts: Mansi 21, 277–304.
Decrees: *COD,* 187–94 (*DCO* II/1, 409–25).
R. Foreville (1965), *Latran I, II, III et IV, HCO,* 44–72 and 165–79.
G. Alberigo (Ed.) (1990), *Storia dei concili ecumenici,* Brescia.

JEAN LONGÈRE

See also **Church and State; Cleric; Ecclesiastical Discipline; Structures, Ecclesial**

Lateran II, Council

1139

The Second Lateran Council was, like the first, known for abolishing a schism*, in this case the schism of the antipope Anacletus II (reigned 1130–38). Convened by Pope Innocent II (reigned 1130–43), it brought together roughly a hundred participants, mainly from western Europe, between 2 and 9 April. Innocent II opened the assembly with a solemn speech on the unity* of the church; he dismissed Antecletus's supporters, including Peter of Pisa (can. 30), who was nevertheless supported for several months and defended by Bernard* of Clairvaux.

The 30 canons of Lateran II are more developed than those of Lateran I. They are often upheld by the Acts of the Councils of Clermont (1130) and Pisa (1135).

Ecclesiastical* discipline was greatly stressed and a number of practices were condemned, including: simony (cans. 1, 2, and 24), secular investiture (can. 25), and the holding of churches or tithes by laity*, giving ecclesiastic responsibilities to adolescents or clerics* who had not received the required orders (can. 10). Monks and canons were forbidden to be lawyers or doctors for payment (can. 9). Episcopal seats could not remain vacant for more than three months (can. 28). The decision made at the Council of Pisa (1135) that annulled the marriage* of a major cleric or monk was reiterated (cans. 6 and 7) and was applied to cloistered nuns (can. 8). Proclaiming the annulment of a major cleric's marriage was supremely important in the legislation concerning ecclesiastic celibacy. Moreover, the council defended the sacraments (the body and blood of Christ*, baptism* of children, priesthood*, and marriage*) against heretics—that is, the Cathars (can. 23). It warned against "false penance*" which consists of, for example, repenting for only one sin* (can. 22) and it renewed the prohibition of marriage between blood relations (can. 17).

In terms of social morality, the council aimed at limiting violence by encouraging truce and the peace* of God* (cans. 11–12). It also discouraged tournaments (can. 14) and issued condemnations of arson (cans. 18–19), brutality against clerics and violations of the right of sanctuary (can. 15), and the use of deadly weapons against other Christians (can. 29).

● Acts: Mansi 21, 423–546.
Decrees: *COD*, 195–203 (*DCO* II/1, 427–45).
R. Foreville (1965), *Latran I, II, III et IV, HCO*, 73–95 and 180–94.
G. Alberigo (Ed.) (1990), *Storia dei concili ecumenici*, Brescia.

JEAN LONGÈRE

See also **Catharism; Ecclesiastical Discipline; Heresy; Lateran I, Council; Schism; Unity of the Church**

Lateran III, Council

1179

On 7 March 1159, Orlando Bandinelli was appointed pope under the name Alexander III; a minority favored Octaviano of Monticello, whom Frederick Barbarossa would acknowledge at the Council of Pavia (1160) under the name Victor IV. This new chapter in the battle between church and empire was marked by the emperor's incursions into Italy, the exile of the pope*, and the support given to Alexander by most of Europe's rulers. The peace* brought about in Venice in July 1177 was a victory for the papacy; the agreement prepared for a general council* for ratification intended to guarantee the unity* of the church, which had been upset over the past decades by schisms* and a series of antipopes.

The Third Lateran Council opened with a speech given by Rufinus, the bishop* of Assisi, on universality and the unity of the church around Rome*. The council's three sessions were held between 5 March and 19 March and brought together about 300 members—predominantly the bishops of Italy, but also including eight Fathers of the Latin East and representatives of central Europe.

To avoid schisms resulting from contested papal elections, it was decided that from then on, a pope could be elected only by members of the College of Cardinals and by no less than a two-thirds majority (cans. 1 and 16), a principle that was thereafter respected. Moreover, the elections of the "heresiarchs" (antipopes) were declared null and void (can. 2).

On a doctrinal level, Lateran III examined certain christological opinions attributed to Peter Lombard, who had taught in Paris before becoming bishop (1158–60) (Scholasticism*). Peter was reproached for his notions concerning Christ's humanity—as a man,

Christ "was not something." Some concluded "that he was nothing," and the name *Christological nihilianism* was given to this odd position. Today it is thought to have been influenced more by Abelard*. Adversaries of Peter Lombard and Alexander III himself sometimes judged Peter's christological teachings severely. But there were several Fathers linked to him and his thought who did not want his memory to be tainted by any reprobation, and so the council did not make any dogmatic decisions against him.

Without accusations of specific errors, Lateran III condemned the Cathars, those who protected them, and also armed groups that "destroy and devastate everything." Bearing arms against them was authorized (can. 27). Two canons regulated and limited the relationships Christians had with Jews and Saracens (cans. 24 and 26). The council also wanted to broaden access to knowledge. Thus, each cathedral church was obligated to offer a benefice to a teacher so that he might teach for free; the council asked that the *licentia docendi*, or authorization to teach, be awarded free of charge (can. 18). Lateran III greatly helped to make the bishops' right to monitor the group of priests in charge

in his diocese indisputable. It sought to preserve the heritage of churches (cans. 4, 9, 14, 15, and 17); it forbade nonresidence and amassing benefices (cans. 13 and 14), and provided for a priest* and chapel for lepers (can. 23).

Books on moral theology* from the end of the century would partly make the teachings of Lateran III known. In particular, its 27 canons would appear in the collections of papal decrees (*Compilationes* 1–5) at the end of the 12th and beginning of the 13th centuries. They all appeared in *Decretals* by Gregory IX (1234).

● Acts: Mansi 22, 209–468.
Decrees: *COD*, 205–25 (*DCO* II/1, 447–85).
R. Foreville (1965), *Latran I, II, III and IV, HCO*, 116–58 and 210–23.
J. Longère (Ed.) (1982), "Le troisième concile du Latran (1179): Sa place dans l'histoire." Paper presented during a round table session of the CNRS, Paris, 26 April 1980.
G. Alberigo (Ed.) (1990), *Storia dei concili ecumenici*, Brescia.

JEAN LONGÈRE

See also **Christ and Christology; Church and State; Cleric; Ecclesiastical Discipline; Structures, Ecclesial**

Lateran IV, Council

1215

After the fall of Jerusalem* in 1187, the pope* was able to have the leaders of the West suspend their debates and focus on helping the East. The Third Crusade, a partial success, led to the seizure of Saint-Jean-d'Acre in 1189. The Fourth Crusade, called by Pope Innocent III (reigned 1198–1216) was, for political reasons and in spite of the pope's opposition, turned toward Constantinople. The pope thought, incorrectly, that the attacks on Constantinople might favor unification between the Greek and Latin Churches and lead to renewal of the crusade on better foundations.

In the West there continued to be conflict between France and Germany, and between the emperor of Germany and southern Italy. Cathar heresy* ravaged southwestern France. South of the Pyrenees the reconquest gained ground with the victory of Las Navas de

Tolosa (1212). In Paris, spurred by the construction of Notre Dame Cathedral, there was intense theological activity, mainly pastoral in nature. In the end, the seven sacraments* were emphasized and teachers on the faculty were obliged to preach. It was first in Paris, then in Bologna, that Innocent III had been trained. Around 1205, the bishop of Paris, Eudes de Sully, promulgated synod statutes. Many of their canons inspired Lateran IV. As a group, they would guide all synod legislation for European dioceses in the 13th century. Starting in 1206 Dominic de Guzman preached, alone or with others, in the countries won by Catharism*. That same year Francis of Assisi gave away all his possessions and left for Gubbio. The first friars joined him in 1208.

Innocent III's personality strongly marked the government* of the church. Despite defeats and deviations, he never abandoned the idea of a crusade. He thought that the development of Cathar heresy resulted from a general decline in morals and from the pastoral passivity of clerics* and passion for profit, especially among the prelates. On 19 April 1213 he launched one bull to convene the Fourth Lateran Council and another to announce the crusade for which he claimed responsibility so as to avoid any drift toward temporal ends.

Attendance at the November 1215 council was high and much greater, in number and representation, than at the three preceding councils. At least 400 Fathers were present, including many from the Latin East. Heads of orders, abbots, and representatives from cathedrals and collegiate churches came in throngs. The leaders from the West all sent delegates.

Lateran IV opened with a canon, *The Catholic Faith,* which is often called by its first word, *Firmiter.* Thus it raised the dogmatic concerns from the first ecumenical councils. The first of the canon's three parts is on the Trinity* and Creation*. The second part concerns the mysteries of the Incarnation* and Redemption, emphasizing judgment* and eschatological sanctions. The third part focuses on the church* and questions of sacramental theology—especially on the Eucharist*, baptism*, and penance*.

Without naming them, canon 1 designates the Cathars and the Waldensians*. It refers to the Cathars by affirming the goodness of all creatures, even demons*, who were created good but became evil through their errors and who bring down man with them (liberty*). The canon refers to the Waldensians when it declares the priest the only minister of the Eucharist and affirms that baptism is necessary for the salvation* of children and adults. Canon 3, on preachers without a mission, among other itinerant preachers, involves both the Cathars and the Waldensians.

During the council an accusation of Tritheism was made against Joachim de Flore (†1201) in connection with a lost work in which he attacked Peter Lombard. But the thought of Joachim de Flore, represented in his other texts, was always orthodox with regard to divine unity*. It was rather because he attacked Peter Lombard that Joachim de Flore was condemned by Lateran IV (can. 2), a sentence that would scar his memory, even though his loyalty to the church was recognized and even though Pope Honorius III spoke in favor of him and his order (December 1220).

Canon 2 "reproaches and condemns the extravagant beliefs of the ungodly Amaury." It does not, however, note any heresy in Amaury (Amalric) of Bène, undoubtedly to avoid a repeat of the notoriety that had surrounded the Council of Paris in 1210, which forbade teaching Aristotle's books on natural philosophy.

Lateran IV also focused on all the sacraments*, except for Confirmation*. In addition to favoring baptism for children (can. 1), it forbade rebaptism—a prohibition aimed at the Greeks, who had had "the temerity to do it" (can. 3).

The most famous decision (can. 21) concerns the obligation of every Christian to confess at least once a year to his or her parish priest and to receive the Eucharist at Easter. Many believers would respect these requirements until the 20th century. This same canon also invites the confessor to discernment, to pastoral prudence*, and to strict respect of the sacramental secret. Priests and believers must show reverence for the Eucharist (cans. 19–20). The council authenticated the word *transubstantiation* to denote the conversion of bread and wine into the body and blood of Christ*. This term was fairly new, having been used and discussed by theologians only since the middle of the 12th century. Coined independently from any Aristotelian influence, it would henceforth become part of dogmatic* vocabulary.

Because of pastoral concerns, marriage was forbidden only between blood relations (can. 50). In order to safeguard the liberty* of spouses and the unity of the couple, secret marriages were condemned (can. 51).

The council also took interest in church government* and the life of clerics. The diversity of rituals and languages in a single area was acknowledged to fall under the responsibility of a single bishop* (can. 9). The council instituted the practice of appointing preachers to help ordinaries (bishops and other officials) in their teaching work (can. 10) and establishing teachers in each cathedral to undertake the training of clerics (can. 11; *see also* Lateran III, can. 18). Monks were to have general chapters every three years (can. 12). Prohibition of new orders (can. 13) was to only slightly curb the development of new religious families, but the obligation to chose an existing rule was to bring the Order of Preachers (Dominicans) to adopt the *Rule of Saint Augustine* and to be considered canons.

Lateran IV sought to consolidate the dignity of the clergy. It condemned any disrespect of chastity and accompanied these condemnations with heavy sanctions. Clerics were prohibited from doing many things (cans. 14–18). Lateran IV once again denounced all forms of simony or greed for clerics (cans. 62–66). The council Fathers also made several positive recommendations. They called for simplicity of clothing and the worthy celebration of offices, and they insisted that close attention be paid to church cleanliness, the maintenance of holy oils and the Eucharist, and the choice and veneration of relics* (cans. 16, 17, 19, 20, and 62).

While the council acknowledged the patriarchates of the East and the eminence of Constantinople, after

Rome*, its centralized and pyramidal notion of the church was completely foreign to Orthodoxy* (can. 5).

Finally, the constitution "To liberate the Holy Land" (14 December 1215, can. 17) mobilized people and resources, set the times and place for meeting, specified protective measures concerning all crusades, and declared peace* for four years in order save all the forces for expedition. It renewed the indulgence* of crusades.

Innocent III had planned a trip to the East on 1 June 1217, but he died on 16 July 1216 at age 56. The Fifth Crusade would first capture Damietta (1218–19) and then lose it (1221). All the canons of Lateran IV, except for canon 71, were included in the *Decretals* (1234) of Pope Gregory IX.

● Acts: Mansi 22, 953–1086.
Decrees: *COD,* 227–71 (*DCO* II/1, 487–577).
R. Foreville (1965), *Latran I, II, III and IV, HCO,* 227–386.
G. Alberigo (Ed.) (1990), *Storia dei concili ecumenici,* Brescia.

JEAN LONGÈRE

See also **Cleric; Hierarchy; Marriage; Ministry; Penance; Scholasticism; Structures, Ecclesial**

Lateran V, Council

1512–17

The Fifth Lateran Council took place in Rome between 3 May 1512 and 6 March 1517 under Popes Julius II and Leon X. The context was essentially political—to oppose the activities of King Louis II of France, who, in order to secure his territories in Italy, had successfully assembled a small ecclesiastical gathering, first in Pisa and then in Rome. (Louis's gathering was called a *conciliabulum* by the pope*'s supporters). Even if the legitimacy of Lateran V was never questioned, historians have been harsh, referring to it as the "draft for the Council of Trent*" or even "the Council of the Indecisive." Erasmus* even wondered if it could really be considered a council at all.

Lateran V had three set goals: peace* in Europe, reform "of the head and of the parts," and the crusades in Turkey. But even though these issues were continually discussed during deliberations, it was unquestionably the church's plans for reform that most occupied the council, and had done so even during the period of its preparation. Nearly everything cleared the way for Trent, including the meeting at Burgos in November 1511, which was summoned by King Ferdinand of Aragon; the *Libellus* of the Venetian Camaldolese Paul Giustiniani and Pietro Quirini; the major speeches delivered at the council by Giles of Viterbo, Cajetan, Pucci, and others—*see* N. H. Minnich's *The Fifth Lateran Council (1512–1517),* 1993, IV—and, finally, shortly before the final session, the *De Reformandis Ecclesiæ Moribus* by Giovanni Francesco Pico della Mirandola. But it is true that even the council's theological contribution seems to have been more a matter of urgency or current events—for example, the legislation on the state-owned pawn shops—than a grand and needed vision.

a) Ecclesiology. The council first wanted to react against the almost conciliarist* or Gallican* tendencies of the Pisa-Milan meeting. Its victory over the schismatic meeting is in itself an assertion of pontifical ecclesiology*, determined in the 11th session (1516): "The pope has authority* over all councils; he therefore has full power to convene, adjourn, and dissolve them" (*see* J. D. Mansi's *Sacrorum Conciliorum nova et amplissima collectio* 32, 967). The ecclesiological doctrine of the council drew inspiration from the doctrine offered by the Dominican Cajetan (Thomism*) as early as 17 May 1513 (*Sacrorum Conciliorum* 32, 719–27). It could be called "curialist" (*see* O. de la Brosse's *Latran V et Trente,* 1975). The monarchical structure of the visible church* was clearly stated here—a monarchy modeled after that of the Lord Jesus Christ, who reigns over Jerusalem* from above.

From this perspective, the council did not specially legislate on the responsibilities of bishops*, and did not need more than to reaffirm their dignity and their necessary independence before secular powers. The council also discussed their relationship to members of religious orders, but the pastoral problems posed by the exemption of episcopal jurisdiction*, a privilege for regulars, was regulated in a much more practical than theoretical manner.

Although the Maronite Christians had actually been in contact with Rome since at least the 13th century, the union had never been officially acknowledged. Negotiations for acknowledgement began in 1514 and were ratified by the council, contributing to the pope's prestige. The concluding of a concordat with France was a similar success.

b) Doctrinal Work. Pope Leo X refused to have the council discuss the delicate question of the Immaculate Conception of the Virgin Mary*. He stuck to Pope Sixtus IV's constitutions of 1477 and 1483.

The Averroist school of Padua, represented by Pietro Pomponazzi (1462–1525), a teacher in Bologna at the time of the council, considered—contrary to Thomas* Aquinas—that the Christian doctrine on the immortality of the soul* could not be defended in philosophical terms (that is, in Aristotelian terms). In opposition to this, Lateran V referred to the decisions of the Council of Vienna* (1312) and reasserted the doctrine that the soul is the form of the human body, that it is immortal, and that it is individually infused in a multitude of bodies (*see* the 1513 bull *Apostolici Regiminis* and Mansi's *Sacrorum Conciliorum* 32, 842). In its pronouncement, the council was refuting the Averroist theory that purported the existence of a single intellective soul that was the same for all people (even Pomponazzi himself was against this theory). The council's text continues by asking "Christian philosophers" to fight against arguments that back the mortality of the soul or the idea of a single intellective soul for all men, and condemns the idea of "double truth*," stating: "Any assertion opposing the truth of faith is false," for "the truth cannot oppose truth."

The council decree required a retraction from Pomponazzi, which he gave in 1518, but this did not end the controversy that incited theologians like Spina, Javelli, Contarini, and Nifo to interpret the text. *Apostolici Regiminis* stated that clerics* could not study philosophy* or the liberal arts without having been trained beforehand in theology*. Lateran V, therefore, was wary of humanism*, whether it was Christian or not.

c) The Council and Humanism. Nevertheless, there were talented humanists like Giles of Viterbo, Alexis Celadoni from Greece, the astronomer Paul de Middelbourg, and Cajetan himself. Lateran V took place at the same time as the "Reuchlin affair," in which the German humanist Johannes Reuchlin was reproached for recommending the study of Jewish books to Christians. The 4 May 1515 *Inter Sollicitudines* constitution (*see* Mansi's *Sacrorum Conciliorum* 32, 912–13), while offering congratulations for the invention of printing, which was seen as a "gift from Providence*", foresaw the dangers involved for faith* and proper standards of behavior. It therefore organized censorship codes to be applied before books were printed.

In its final session, the council voted for a text on the need and importance of preaching* in the church, warning against scandalous sermons. Less than a year later, Luther* rose up against indulgences*, taking a first step toward a Protestantism* that would strive to base itself on preaching "the pure Word* of God."

● Acts: Mansi 32, 665–1002.
Decrees: *COD* 593–655 (*DCO* II/1, 1211–1338).
P. Pomponazzi (1516), *Tractatus de immortalitate animae*, Bologna.
O. de La Brosse, et al. (1975), *Latran V et Trente*, HCO 10, Paris.
É. Gilson (1986), *Humanisme et renaissance*, Paris.
N.H. Minnich (1993), *The Fifth Lateran Council (1512–1517)*, Aldershot.

GUY BEDOUELLE

See also **Conciliarism; Gallicanism; Humanism, Christian; Philosophy; Trent, Council of; Truth**

Law and Christianity

A. Biblical Theology

In principle, every interpretation of the law of God in Christian theology* should be based on the teachings of Jesus*. However, each New Testament text is understood as transmitting this teaching by way of an interpretation on behalf of a concrete community. Modern research hesitates when it comes to recovering the thinking of Jesus from such discordance (Marguerat 1991). If, as some have thought, Jesus clearly challenged the Law of Moses, then Matthew "judaized" his teaching. On the other hand, if Jesus never abrogated that law, then it was Paul who betrayed him. Perhaps the terms of the debate are poorly posed. Paul's teaching concerning "the law" is based on the cross, which opens up the messianic age. He emphasizes what is new, and the novelty is such that his position has nothing to do with whatever might shed light on the personal behavior of Jesus. Moreover, the disciples of Jesus may have been more ready to recommend a radical change in the system of the law because their master had encouraged them to do so by his own activity. On the other hand, during his trial no one accused Jesus of having transgressed "the law." We should point out that when the New Testament mentions "the law," the reference is generally to the Jewish Torah. Coherence is therefore to be found only through a study of the whole of the Torah.

I. Law in the Old Testament

1. Vocabulary

Originally, each of the different terms for "the law" related it to the specific authority* from which it emanated: to the priests, in the case of torah and 'edout; to the judges, in the case of mishepat; and to the king in the case of choq and miçewah. Later, the psalmist took pleasure in meditating lovingly upon all the names of the law in order to express its unity and to make it come alive for the whole people.

The primordial meaning of torah is an oracle given by a priest, after consultation, in order to settle a contested point (Hos 4:6; Is 8:20). In Deuteronomy, the word refers to a collection of statutes. In the Septuagint, this is translated as nomos, which is an equivalent rather than a direct translation.

'Edout is a response obtained from God* positioned above the ark (Ex 25:22); in the plural, it refers to the prescriptions of God in the Covenant* (Dt 4:45). In another context, the stipulations of treaties of covenant in the Middle East are called adey in Aramaic.

Mishepat originally meant a judgment by the elders aimed at reestablishing peace* within a clan. In Israel*, the prosperity of the state depended on the king having respect for mishepat, which was associated with Moses (Ex 21:1 ff.) and God on Sinai.

An choq is a royal decree. 1 Kings 3:3 mentions the chouqqot of David; Micah 6:16 refers to those of Omri. It is said of Moses, as of a king, that he has given an choq to Israel (Ex 13:10, 15:25). In Ex 18:16–20, the term means no more than written statutes.

A miçewah is a royal order. Abimelek (Gn 26:11), the Pharaoh (Gn 47:11), and David (1 Kgs 2:1–43) give such orders; God imposes his miçewot (Gn 2:16, 3:11; 1 Sm 13:13; 1 Kgs 13:21, etc.). In the Septuagint, this is generally translated as entole.

The devarim are the words of the code in Exodus 34 and the Ten Commandments, the Decalogue* (Ex 20:1 and Dt 5:22). In Deuteronomy, the singular form came to refer to the "Word of God."

Underlying all these terms, what predominates is the unity of the law, which has its source in God. By contrast to the law codes of the Middle East, the laws in the Bible* are not gathered together under the names of kings: law comes from God through Moses according to the faith* of Israel.

2. Sets of Statutes

According to recent research (Crüsemann 1990), the statutes gathered in the Pentateuch are those that were promulgated on the authority of the King of Persia as the law of Israel at the time of the return from exile. They were compiled from two major traditions*, Deuteronomy and priestly writings, which had previously been rivals. The coupling of law and narrative* that structures the Torah encouraged the contemporary practice of the commandments by illustrating them through the examples of the patriarchs. Alongside the codes applicable in Judea, the stories of the patriarchs also offered a Jewish way of life that was more practicable in the eastern diaspora.

The legal sections comprise, first of all, the statutes compiled in relation to Sinai (Ex 20:1 to Nm 10:10, and Nm 28:1–30:17). Aside from the Decalogue, one can also distinguish the code of the Covenant (Ex 20:22–23:19), the code in Deuteronomy (1–6), and the law of sanctity* (Lv. 17–26); then comes the testament of Moses (Dt 4:45–30:20).

The code of the Covenant is probably the oldest of these. It states the consequences of belief in the one God in terms of life in the real world.

The code in Deuteronomy sets out a demanding program—one God, one sanctuary, one people, one law—constructed by compiling prescriptions that, in many cases, are restatements of the code of the Covenant, although in new formulations and with a new spirit (e.g., Dt. 15:1–11 and Ex 23:10 ff.; Dt15:12–18 and Ex 21:2–11; Dt 15:19–23 and Ex 22:28 ff.). One of its characteristics is the concern for others, whether neighbors or strangers (Dt 15:12–18, 24:6 and 10–13, 17–22, etc.).

The law of sanctity is concerned with ritual and priesthood*, but also with marriage* and sexuality (ethics*, sexual). YHWH invites Israel to reveal its sanctity to the world* through its practice of the Torah. One should note its parallels with the code in Deuteronomy (e.g., Lv 19:26 and Dt 18:10; Lv 19:27 ff. and Dt 14:1; Lv 19:29 and Dt 23:18), as well as its attention to the poor and to immigrants.

3. Forms of Law

There are purely imperative, "apodictic" laws, given as short sentences, which sanction death* (Ex 21:12 and 21:15–17), subject certain crimes to curses (Dt. 27:15–26), and prohibit certain forms of sexuality (Lv 18:7–17). Deuteronomy 27:1–11 gives us the context for such laws: a solemn festival where everyone re-affirms the clauses of the Covenant. These formulas are specifically Israelite and ancient. There are also "casuistic" laws, based on the exposition of a case ("if..."): the law codes of the Middle East have been shown to contain laws very similar to these.

II. The Torah in the Jewish World

Until A.D. 70, the Jewish world was multiform. The Jews of Qumran (probably the Essenes) are well known to us because of the discovery of their library from 1947 onward, while the tradition of the Pharisees is known through its transmission in rabbinical literature. The Sadducees were also important, but we know little about them.

1. The Torah of the Pharisees

Following the reception of the Torah on Sinai, within the framework of the Covenant, every Israelite had to confess the sovereignty of God on earth, to take upon himself "the yoke of the kingdom of heaven," to enter into the concrete practice of the Torah, and to take upon himself "the yoke of the commandments."

a) Written and Oral Torah. The Torah gives no more than general principles: it must be summarized; it contains contradictions that need to be reconciled; and, while it is perfect, it cannot regulate life once for all, so there is a permanent need for actualization. The Pharisees did not hesitate to say that "Moses received two Torahs" on Sinai (TB *Shab.* 31 a; TJ *Péah* 2, 6, 17 a), one written and one oral, which continue to complement each other. In this way, the masters secured the responsibility for stating practice for Israel here and now, through debate and majority voting.

b) The Torah in the Days of the Messiah. The Messiah will be a new Moses, but the Jewish sources avoid the idea of a radical change in the Torah. The tradition gives two answers to the question of the status of the

Torah in the messianic age: 1) radicalization—understanding and observance of the Torah will be perfect; 2) mystical renewal, for a precept* can hardly be the same both when human beings struggle against evil* and when the Torah existing in their hearts is practiced in liberty*.

2. The Torah at Qumran

The Rule of the Community (1QS) affirms that every novice must swear "to return to the law of Moses" according to "all that has been revealed of it to the sons of Zadok" (5, 8–9; *see* CD 6, 18 f.). The law is to be rewritten, to become a more contemporary and coherent code. Thus, the Temple Scroll (11QT) promulgates new laws for Israel under the very authority of God. The Book of Jubilees is a rewriting of Genesis and Exodus that proclaims the "perpetual status" of the Torah. At Qumran, the law was also interpreted in the light of practice, as is shown, for example, in 4QMMT (*see DJD* X, 5): the Zadokites reproach the priests of Jerusalem* for abandoning the rules of purity at the Temple, in more than 20 detailed cases, under the influence of the Pharisees.

3. The Sadducees

This group venerated the Torah above all, although they did not reject the Prophets* or the Psalms*. Their exegesis* was literal: the Torah was clear in and of itself. As with the Pharisees, there were disputes about its content, but there were still more disputes about the authority and the obligatory nature of tradition.

III. Law in the New Testament

1. Paul and the Law

In Paul's writings, *nomos* generally means the law of Moses. However, the term is never defined, and moral laws are never distinguished from ritual laws. It follows that he assumed that those receiving his letters were capable of perceiving the variations in the meaning of the term.

a) Impotence and Necessity of Law. The law cannot save: for Paul, as for every other Jew, it is God alone who saves human beings. A Jew should practice "the whole of the law," but he knows that he can never succeed in this, and the days of penance* exist to remind him of it. Paul departs from this faith by radicalizing it (Gal 3:10; Rom 2:17–24, 3:19–23, 8:7 f.), passing from fact to the affirmation of principle. Through his experience* of Christ*, he understands the following paradox: in his effort to become righteous before God, he has made himself into an "enemy of God," rejecting the dependence that is the truth* of the created being and the glory* of the Creator. Paul reinterprets the whole of the history* of his people in this light, and understands the danger that threatens it. On the other hand, by displaying man's sin* to him (Rom 7:7–10), the law is man's "guardian" (Gal 3:23 ff.), revealing its truth to him and opening him up to the expectation of a savior (Rom 8:1–4).

b) "Christ is the end of the law" (Romans 10:4).   In the light of the relationship between the Old Testament and the New Testament (1 Cor 10:1–11), all the events in which the law is present must be understood as manifestations of Christ. According to Romans 10:5, it is necessary to come to the end of the process of reasoning: human beings live only through Christ, and therefore the justice* that comes from the law, of which Moses speaks, today comes from Christ. The commentary that Romans 10:6 ff. applies to Deuteronomy 30:12 ff. confirms this: only Christ, who has descended from heaven and risen from the abyss, provides the justice that the Old Testament proclaims.

c) Messianic Age of the Spirit.   Jesus inaugurates the messianic age. For Paul, the law has become internal and everyone practices the whole of the law in the Spirit: this is the "law of Christ." The "law of the Spirit" is to bring oneself into conformity with Christ: this is what Paul has done (1 Cor 9:21) and taught (Phil 2:5–8), and this is what baptism* gives (Rom 6:1–11). Paul sees the fulfillment of the law in love*, and can announce its commandment with every certainty from now on (Rom 13:8 ff.; Gal 5:14).

2. Matthew and the Law
Alone among the synoptics, Matthew makes the law into a central theme.

a) Jesus and Moses.   Moses on Sinai received the whole of the Torah (see Abot I, 1): that was the traditional belief of the Pharisees, but Christ transposed this into the statement: "All thing have been handed over to me by my Father" (Mt 11:27). According to Matthew, one must learn from Jesus, for the law of Moses finds its plenitude in him (11:28–31): this is God's plan (11:26). Jesus presents himself as having authority over the law (7:29), which is a radical innovation. Jesus, the new Moses, has received this authority from the Father*. He has the power to command his apostles* to make disciples (see Abot I, 2), but they are to be from every nation; he also commands them to transmit the Torah (see ibid.), but in the form that they have received from him; finally, he has the right to assure them that "All authority in heaven and earth has been given to me" (Mt 28:18 ff.).

b) Fulfillment.   Jesus came to fulfill the whole of the Torah (5:17), initially through his interpretation of it, but also through his life and his paschal sacrifice*, and, finally, through the inauguration of the messianic age. The Christian must invest the whole of his life in faithfulness to the Torah (6:33), in "perfect righteousness" (5:20). This is, first and foremost, a call to follow Christ; in this way, the happiness of the kingdom is assured (5:6–10). Its fulfillment goes so far as to radicalize the law: Jesus calls us to "do more" than the Pharisees (5:20) in these times, which are the times of the Messiah. The last two "antitheses" in the Sermon on the Mount (5:38–48) show that this "more" is love, which can even lead us to transgress the law (Mt 12:15–22, 15:1–20). Jesus invites us to pass beyond all hypocrisy (Mt 23) in order to achieve the conversion* of the heart. He restores the primary purpose of the law: righteousness and pity (Mt 9:13, 12:7). The imitation of God is the ultimate motif that he proposes.

3. James's Epistle and the Law
James polemicizes against justification* by faith separated from works* (2, 14–26). The law must be practiced as a whole (2:11); it is summarized in the Decalogue and completed in the "royal law" (2:8), which is the love of one's neighbor. The "law of liberty" (1:25, 2:12) dwells in the heart of the believer. According to James, it is "mercy" (eleos) that accomplishes the whole of the law and the triumph of judgment* (2:13).

4. Law in the Johannine Tradition
The law belongs to the Jews (Jn 8:17, 10:34, 15:25, 18:31), but John applies himself to demonstrating that Jesus fulfills it (5:16 f., 7:21–24), that he witnesses in its favor (1:45, 8:16–20), and that he interprets it better than his opponents (10:34–36), who are in fact violators of the law (7:17, 7:19, 7:24, 7: 51, 8:15).

a) "The Truth."   John asserts in principle that while the Torah remains a gift from God, the truth brought by Jesus represents a full understanding of the Torah (1:17). Two expressions summarize this principle: to do "what is true," which, for the Jews, is to act according to the Torah, is, for John (Jn 3:21; 1 Jn 1:6), to recognize Jesus as the revelation* of God; while to "walk in the truth," which, for the Jews, is to be faithful to the Torah, is, for John (2 Jn 4; 3 Jn 3 and 4), to walk in the footsteps of Christ.

b) Commandments.   Placed in relation to the will of the Father (Jn 4:34, 7:17), the commandments are concentrated in love (10:18, 12:25 f., 13:34). Jesus leaves his commandments to his disciples (14:15 and 15:10; see 1 Jn 2:3, 3:22, 3: 24; 2 Jn 6)—his new commandment of love (Jn 15:12; *see* 1 Jn 3:23). "Keeping" the commandments is "not burdensome" (1 Jn 5:3), for God, through his gift of faith, permits the Christian to vanquish evil and practice the commandments readily: this is a sign of the messianic age.

c) Jesus As the Norm for Christian Conduct. "I am the path" (Jn 14:6); "Whoever follows me will not walk in darkness" (8:12): the true disciple practices the *halakha* of the Master. It is through the law (*Abot* III, 19) that a Jew becomes a child of God, while for John it is through faith in his only Son (1:12).

d) Jesus Is the Perfect Law. In the Old Testament, the law is identified with Wisdom* (Bar 4:1; Sir 24:23) and with the Word (Ps 119:15–18): on this basis, John affirms that Jesus is Word and Wisdom incarnate. John attributes the Jewish teaching on the role of the law in the creation*, and on its preexistence, to the only Son (Jn 1:3, 14, 18). Accordingly, the diversity of interpretations of the New Testament should not lead us to overlook the point on which they agree: that the law finds its fulfillment in Jesus, the Messiah. This is why the christological reinterpretation that is presented to us in the New Testament—the Gospel understood as an oral and messianic Torah—has to be the foundation of all Christian action.

• A. Alt (1934), *Die Ursprünge des israelitischen Rechts,* Leipzig.
H. Cazelles (1946), *Études sur le Code de l'Alliance,* Paris.
W. D. Davies (1952), *Torah in the Messianic Age,* Philadelphia.
N. Lazure (1965), *Les valeurs morales de la théologie johannique,* EtB, Paris, 119–59.
H. Cazelles (1966), "Le sens religieux de la Loi," *Populus Dei,* CPIUI 10, 177–94.
G. G. Scholem (1971), *The Messianic Idea in Judaism,* New York.
S. Pancaro (1975), *The Law in the Fourth Gospel, New Testament, TS* 42.

Coll. (1977), "L'enracinement du droit canonique dans l'Écriture, XIIIe sess.- SIDC," *ACan* 21, 19–230.
U. Lutz (1978), "Die Erfüllung des Gesetzes bei Mt.," *ZThK* 75, 398–435.
D. Marguerat (1979), "Jesus et la Loi selon Matthieu," *CBFV* 18, 53–76; (1982), "L'avenir de la Loi: Matthieu à l'épreuve de Paul," *ETR* 57, 361–73.
E. P. Sanders (1982), *Jesus, Paul and Judaism,* in *ANRW* 25, 1, 390–450; (1983) *Paul, the Law, and the Jewish People,* Philadelphia, 3–167.
M.-J. Seux (Ed.) (1986), *Loi de l'Ancien Orient,* CEv.S 56.
H. Cazelles (1987), "Le Pentateuque comme Torah," in M. Tardieu (Ed.), *Les règles de l'interpretation,* Paris, 35–68.
R. Martin-Achard (1987), *La Loi don de God,* Aubonne.
B. Lindars (Ed.) (1988), *Law and Religion: Essays on the Place of the Law in Israel and Early Christianity,* Cambridge.
S. Amsler (1989), "Les documents de la Loi et la formation du Pentateuque," in A. de Pury, T. Römer (Ed.), *Le Pentateuque en question,* Genève, 235–57 (2nd Ed., 1990).
G. J. Brooke (Ed.) (1989), *Temple Scroll Studies,* JSPE.*S* 7.
E. P. Sanders (1989), *The Jewish Law from Jesus to Mishnah,* London.
D. Marguerat (1991), "Jesus et la Loi dans la mémoire des premiers chrétiens," in D. Marguerat, J. Zumstein (Ed.), *La mémoire et le temps,* Geneva, 55–74.
F. Crüsemann (1992), *Die Torah, Theologie und Sozialgeschichte des Old Testament Gesetzes,* Munich.
G. Lasserre (1993), "Quelques études récentes sur le Code de l'alliance," *RThPh* 125, 267–76.
D. Luciani (1993), "Paul et la Loi," *NRTh* 115, 40–68.
L. H. Schiffman (1993), *Law, Custom and Messianism in the Dead Sea Scrolls* (Hebrew), Jerusalem.
G. Lasserre (1994), *Synopse des laws du Pentateuque,* VT.S, Leyden.
E. Quimron (1994), "The Halakha," *DJD* X, 5, Oxford, 123–30.

MATTHIEU COLLIN

See also **Casuistry; Covenant; Decalogue; Ethics; Faith; Jesus, Historical; Judaism; Judeo-Christianity; Judgment; Justification; Liberty; Pauline Theology; Priesthood; Purity/Impurity; Sacrifice; Scripture, Fulfillment of; Spirit; Violence; Works**

B. Law As a Theological and Philosophical Problem

1. Moses and Jesus: Continuity or Categorical Reversal?

The problematic of the "law," and the meaning, whether constant or variable, that this notion takes on at different points in the Bible*, may be summarized in the following question: should the parallel drawn in John 1:17 be understood as a synthesis or as an antithesis? The writer of the *Letter of Barnabas* (Apostolic* Fathers), from around A.D. 130, clearly opts for the first solution when evoking "the new law of Our Lord Jesus Christ" (*Barn* 2, 6). With this interpretation of the gospel as the "new law," the writer lays the foundation on which the primitive church* was to develop a doctrine of the law that Catholicism* continues to be influenced by. Conversely, one can find in Paul's writings (Pauline* theology) a contrast between Christ (that is, the gospel) and the law of Moses (2 Cor. 3:6)—and this is the approach that Protestantism* has restored to a place of honor. Thus, ever since it began, Christianity has contained the seeds of questions that, even today, do not receive a unanimous response from within the *oikoumene*.

2. Conceptual Approach

a) Concept and Vision of the Law.   Following the fundamental biblical orientations we have just outlined, theology should first of all understand the law as the law of God*. It must determine what should be attributed to this divine law, with regard both to content and the tasks and functions that it once accomplished and still accomplishes today. There is also the question of the relationship between this divine law and the positive law expressed in the legislation of the societies* that history* has witnessed arising and disappearing. Do both types of law equally depend on particular situations and need to be brought up to date in line with the development of such situations? Or is it necessary to attribute to the divine law, or to part of it, a supratemporal validity?

b) Concept and Vision of Natural Law.   In every case, law requires a founding authority. God is the authority in Holy* Scripture, while Plato and the Stoics, for example, prefer to invoke a "natural law," a universal order inherent in the Ideas or the Logos that rule the world, and that human beings have knowledge of through their contemplation* of nature or in their own consciences* to the extent that they participate in this universal order. With the idea of creation, Christianity combines the two approaches, referring simultaneously to the divine authority of the biblical law and to natural law (*see* 4 a below). By contrast, Enlightenment critics sought evidence for what is best called a "rational law," which the individual can arrive at solely by the exercise of his own will and intelligence. In opposition to theorists of positive law and supporters of utilitarianism*, who reject all suprahistorical norms, there have been several attempts—most notably in response to experience of totalitarian political systems—to restore such ideas as justice (*see* 4 f below) or human dignity to their rightful places as ultimate norms.

3. Law in the Catholic Tradition

a) Beginnings.   The combination of the gospel, understood as the "new law," with the philosophical tradition of natural law was reinforced in the primitive church by a number of internal and external controversies. On the one hand, the combination provided a means of rejecting the Gnostics' hostility to law—the antinomianism of gnosis*—as well as the diastases of Marcionism*. On the other hand, this same combination formed part of the extended attempt by apologists* to demonstrate that Christianity represented the true philosophy*. Accordingly, some fundamental elements of tradition* were put in place during this early phase of Christianity. Tertullian*, for example, interpreted the double commandment of love* and the second table of the Decalogue* as the natural law previously given to Adam* and saw Jesus as the bearer of the "new law" that extends the law of Moses by spiritualizing its ceremonial precepts.

b) Augustine.   Augustine* assimilated the "eternal law"—a Stoic concept referring to God's ordering reason*—to natural law and the law of Moses, but, following Paul, he related this single law to grace*. The law accuses human beings and convicts them of sin in order to make them open to grace, just as, conversely, grace places human beings in a condition to satisfy the demands of the law. Augustine made this idea more profound in his dispute with the Pelagians (Pelagianism*). In their view, grace entails the attribution of free will, the gift of the law, the example of Christ, and the remission of sins; with these, human beings are able to fulfill the law. According to Augustine, however, original sin entails the loss of free will—the "power not to sin" (*see*, e.g., *De civitate Dei* 22, 30)—and thus produces a fundamental distortion of the will, which henceforth "can no longer avoid sinning," based on a real corruption of human nature. Such corruption cannot be healed by any human endeavor, but solely by grace (*gratia sanans*), that is, by the remission of sins and the infusion of the Spirit of love (Rom 5:5). Only grace, or the faith* that it produces, allows human beings to be just in the eyes of God, that is, to be sanctified: "Faith obtains what the law ordains" (e.g., *En.Ps. 118*, XVI, 2).

c) Thomas Aquinas.   In his treatment of the law (*ST* Ia IIae, q. 90–108), Thomas* Aquinas distinguishes among the eternal law, human law, and the divine law, and then divides the divine law into the old law (Old Testament) and the new law (New Testament). It is human law, above all, that it seems possible to define as "a command of reason aimed at the common good, promulgated by him who has responsibility for the community" (q. 90, a. 4). However, this definition also applies, on a higher plane, to the divine law, to the extent that, along with grace (*ST* Ia IIae, q. 109–14), it constitutes an "external" aid through which God assists human beings to gain beatitude* and to make progress on the way of love, which leads them on toward their creator: "The external principle that makes us act well is God, whether he instructs us by his law or sustains us by his grace" (q. 90, prol.). In the history of salvation*, the old law and the new law take the place of the natural law, which, in a broad sense, demands faith and, above all, love of God, but which can also be restricted to the commandments in the second table of the Decalogue, for they can be recognized by natural reason independently of divine revelation*. Just as human beings, because of the Fall, cannot attain beatitude through the natural law alone, so they are no more capable of attaining it within the framework of the Old Covenant, which, being incapable of bringing about grace, cannot be really satisfying; as a result, it fulfills the function of accusation, or death*. It is only through the new law, the New Covenant, that human beings can rediscover the grace (q. 106, a. 1) that they enjoyed in their primordial state, in order to fulfill the natural law. Grace is the new law as a conferred law *(lex indita),* a law of liberty* (Jas 1:25, 2:12), the law of the Spirit who gives life (Rom 8:2). Aquinas thus has a different vision than Augustine's of the relationship between law and grace. Christ, as the pivot of the history of salvation, perfectly fulfills the law and, through the salvific action of his life and death, abolishes the old law. Of course, Christ is also a law-giver, in a secondary sense; but the new law consists principally of grace, and it is in this regard that Aquinas writes of Christ as the "founder of the New Covenant" *(auctor novi testamenti;* q. 107, a. 1, ad 3). Grace, acting through the new law, allows human beings to love God, to offer themselves to him in a "singular mixture of liberty and dependence" (Pesch 1967), and thus to return to their Creator.

d) *Nominalism and Late Medieval Piety.* Aquinas uses the term "new law" only in a derivative sense and refers to Christ's law-giving function as a secondary matter. However, these references were sufficient to encourage later theologians once again to make the gospel, understood as the new law, into a way that human beings can and must take for themselves—with the assistance of grace, of course—in order to achieve salvation. As a result, there appeared within the theology of nominalism*, and in the forms of piety linked to it, some tendencies toward legalism that seem to have had little to do with either Augustine or Aquinas. Luther* could thus denounce the "Pelagianism" of Gabriel Biel (before 1410–95), who took up an idea that Aquinas had condemned in this form (*ST* Ia IIae, q. 112, a. 3) and taught that God does not refuse grace to those who do that which is in them (*see,* e.g., *Collectorium* II, d. 27, q. un. O). While the accusation of Pelagianism does not do justice to the whole of Biel's theological thought, Luther, for his part, did not remain content with reformulating the ideas of Augustine and Aquinas: taking Paul's teaching as his primary guide, he developed an authentic and profound understanding of the gospel and its justifying action, which is independent of any law (*see* 4 a–c below).

e) *Council of Trent.* Reformation theologians formulated their conception of law primarily within the framework of the doctrine of justification*. The Council of Trent*, in turn, brought about a dissociation from the tendencies of the late Middle Ages that we have referred to above. Its decree on justification (13 January 1547), the first dogmatic definition of this doctrine, relates salvation to grace as mediated by the sacraments*, and not to human merit. However, it also teaches that human merit can cooperate in the action of divine grace by virtue of created grace *(gratia creata),* although it does not state precisely what role human liberty plays in this cooperation. (This question later gave rise to the conflict between Bañezianism and Molinism; *see* Bañezianism*-Molinism-Baianism). The council also rejected certain opinions that were central to the Reformation. For example, chapter 11 deals with "the necessity and possibility of observing the commandments" (*DH* 1536–39), and canon 21 lays down that "Christ Jesus was given by God to humanity...also as a law-giver who is to be obeyed" (*DH* 1571). This proposition clearly expresses a refusal to confess Christ exclusively as Redeemer, and, along with canons 18–20 (*DH* 1568–70), constitutes an explicit rejection both of Luther's teaching on justification by faith alone, and of the distinction between law and gospel (*see* 4 b below, and Pesch 1995) that Jerome Seripando (1492–1563), the general of the Augustines, had sought in vain to have accepted at Trent.

f) *Present State of the Discussion.* The *Catechism of the Catholic Church* (1992, no. 1965) recognizes that "the new law, the law of the gospel" is stated "first and foremost in the Sermon on the Mount," even though there may also be a question of grace in this regard (nos. 1949–86). Ecumenical dialogue has more to expect from new research on Aquinas and from the concern for direct interrogation of the sources over and above what has been handed down within the Thomist tradition. It is not by chance that this work of exhumation, conducted along the major lines that we have set out (*see* 3 c above), appropriately constitutes one of the structural supports for ecumenism (Kühn 1965, Pesch 1967).

4. Understanding of the Law in Luther and in Protestant Teaching

a) *Universality of the Law: The Decalogue and Natural Law.* Reformation theologians also made an association between the Decalogue and natural law, thus affirming the universality of God's will. This universalism* is attested in Holy Scripture, for example in Matthew's Gospel, in which the "pagan" Golden Rule is placed on the same level as the double commandment of love: "This is the Law and the Prophets" (Mt 7:12; *see* 22:40). It is also attested in the intermingling of a morality of faithfulness to Christ (e.g., Lk 9:57–62) with a morality of family* (e.g., Eph 5:21–6:9), and in Paul's restatement of certain Stoic themes (e.g., Rom 2:14 f.). Luther cites this text, as well as Romans 1:19–21 and 3:29, to affirm that "the Ten Commandments . . . are nothing other than the law of nature, naturally inscribed upon our hearts" (*WA* 16, 431, 26–28).

The Decalogue had this universal validity in Luther's view because it tallies with the Word of the Creator, as may be seen by comparing Genesis 2:16 f. with Exodus 20:2 f. Both these words of God to humanity contain promises* of life (Gn 2:16 and Ex 20:2) reinforced with threats of death (Gn 2:17 and Ex 20:3): one must fear God if one does not entrust oneself to his love. In this sense, the first commandment is to be contrasted, as "Do not be anxious about your life" (Mt 6:25), to the existential anxiety of humanity: it recalls us to our finite nature, and discharges our anxiety about infinity*. This bond of correlation between the first commandment and the Word of the Creator may be formulated as follows: without the first commandment, concern for the world would be blind; without concern for the world, the first commandment would be null and void.

Furthermore, this thesis means that Luther's doctrine of the law is structurally related to his theory of the three "estates," which represent fundamental forms of life, irreducible modes of being that the creative Word of God has assigned to humanity: the church; the economy, which includes marriage* and the family; and political organization. The church, understood as an "estate," does not mean the Christian church in particular, but the fundamental condition, prior to any economic or political determination, of each human being before God, which is inherent in creation (Gn 2:16 f.). These "estates" precede the commandments. Thus, the fourth commandment, for example, presupposes marriage and the family, while the first presupposes the church, conceived as an order of the creation (Bayer 1994).

In this sense, the Decalogue is universally applicable to every individual. It is on the basis of these commandments that God has willed life in the universe, created it, desired it, and preserved it. However, the commandments have a positive content only on the level of immanence: they have value only in the do-

main of "civil justice" (*iustitia civilis*). By contrast, they play no role in the justification of human beings before God. According to Luther, the rupture marked by baptism*—a rupture that, according to the Catholic tradition, obliges us specially to observe the law (*DH* 1620–22)—must be understood as a renewal of the intellect (Rom 12:2) that brings human beings into relation with the commandments in this world. Nevertheless, the law has no effect on justification.

b) Law and Gospel.   Luther had learned from Paul and Augustine that respect for the law plays no role in our justification before God; but he had also had profound experience of this himself. He was thus capable of describing his reforming work as the discovery of the difference between the law and the gospel (*WA.TR* 5, no. 5518). The law confounds human beings, judges them, and even kills them. Within the law, God comes to human beings with harsh and ineluctable questions, saying to Adam, "Where are you?" (Gn 3:9), or to Cain, "Where is Abel your brother?" (Gn 4:9). Such questions confound human beings; they see what they had no awareness of appearing in the light of day (Ps 90:8). They are revealed, alone, as human beings destined to die: "You are the man" (2 Sm 12:7). Human beings cannot say these things to themselves: they must come to them from outside, from an Other. Nevertheless, they are so clearly confounded that they pronounce their own condemnation at the same time (2 Sm 12:5). The externality of the law does not mean that there is any heteronomy.

However, while God speaks against human beings in the law, he speaks for them in the gospel, the decisive and definitive Word of God that acquits them, promises them life, and makes them live. It is to this promise that faith responds within human beings: and "faith alone justifies" (*sola fides iustificat*). The gospel is therefore not a new law. Even in the form of grace, it is not to be confused with the law (*see* 3 c above), for it is "something other," a second Word of God. It cannot be related to the word of the law by reference to some third term, such as the unique self-manifestation of God (*see* 4 d–e below), any more than one of these two words can be made to lead to the other. One cannot play tricks with the distinction between the law and the gospel: to neglect this distinction is, in reality, to recognize only the law, which no human being can fulfill and which therefore brings death.

It is not enough, however, to grasp this distinction between the law and the gospel solely on the level of knowledge. It is not to be confused with the distinction between the Old Covenant and the New Covenant, as may be seen by comparing Genesis 2:16 f. and Exodus 20:2 f. (*see* 4 a) above). On the contrary, it must be realized again and again, at every instant, and particularly in cases of temptation*. Here, the techniques of homiletics or spiritual* direction are of no use, for what matters is the divine Word, through which God himself brings us either consolation or terror, death or life. The distinction between the law and the gospel thus evades the commands of our will: it takes effect and is a gift renewed on each occasion.

What can be said is that, if the gospel is a promise, then faith is power and permission. One must guard against the gospel becoming a law, to which faith responds as a positive act. It is this that Luther seeks to demonstrate when he distinguishes between the gift and the example in Christ. Christ must first be accepted as a gift, by which God freely accords all his goods to us, before he can provide a model for our actions. If we already possess all the divine gifts in Christ, our actions will no longer be aimed at justice before God, but will be entirely directed toward our neighbors.

c) Double Usage of the Law. In this perspective, Luther refers to a "double function of the law" *(duplex usus legis),* in accordance with the sacred terminology. The first function is the "political usage of the law," that is, its application within the domain of civil justice (*see* 4 a above); the second function is the "elenctic or theological usage of the law," which convicts us of our sins and thus recalls us to the distinct reality of the gospel (*see* 4 b above). In Luther's view, it is this second usage that constitutes the "principal" *(praecipuus)* usage of the law, in conformity with the preponderant role that the doctrine of justification plays in his theology. A comparison with the Catholic tradition will underline the meaning that this second usage has in this instance: Luther could still accept natural law within the domain of civil justice, but he could not give it any role in relation to justice before God. He reached this intuition, which was so decisive for the Reformation, by following Paul and Augustine: the gospel is not a new law, nor a demand, but an acquittal and a consolation that makes real what it promises: *promissio* (Bayer 1971).

d) Law and the Regenerate in Reformation Doctrine. While the Council of Trent (*see* 3 e above) finally refused to follow Luther down this road, the internal development of Protestantism shows that divergences could appear even among those who fundamentally adhered to the Reformation project. This is what happened in the disputes over "antinomianism" and the "third usage of the law." In these cases, what was at stake—depending on the position adopted with regard to the law—were different conceptions of the way in which Christian ethics* should be formatted and applied. Have those human beings whom the gospel proclaims to be just already fulfilled the will of God in themselves ("Every healthy tree bears good fruit," Mt 7:17 f.), or must they—can they—be exhorted and guided by the law to be made by this will? Conversely, can the law, through its exhortations and directives, guide human beings toward authentically Christian practice, or does it result in a pure legalism that no longer sees one's neighbor as the primary criterion of a free act, in accordance with the double commandment of love? To put the question more crudely: does Christian practice have need of a law, or will the law always be a hindrance to it?

In the history of the church, the term *antinomianism* is used with reference to two controversies that arose during the age of the Reformation. While they should not be confused with each other, both were centered on the question of the power and form of the gospel, which could be obscured in two different ways. On the one hand, too much might be expected from the gospel, if one assigned it the functions of the law and thus deprived it of its specificity. On the other hand, too little might be expected from it, if one sought in some sense, through fear of enthusiasm and abuse of the liberty that the gospel accords and guarantees us, to come to its aid in order to support its action.

The first of these two dangers was awakened by J. Agricola (1499?–1566), who maintained that the gospel was not only the declaration of grace, but also a message of penance* and judgment*. Agricola, and others, inevitably misconstrued the role of the law by failing to distinguish between the law and the gospel and by attributing to the gospel the functions proper to the law, which are to accuse human beings and convince them of their sins, and thus to lead them to repent. Not only did they then fall into antinomianism, but, above all, and as an unforeseen consequence, they misconstrued the specific character of the gospel, its form as pure promise. This promise does not contain any ambiguity and is thus the source of all certainty.

Philipp Melanchthon (1497–1560) and his followers, the Philippists, originated the second danger, within the framework of a discussion of sanctification and the role of the law with regard to those who are justified. The question was debated in the chapter on the "third usage of the law" *(tertius usus legis)* or the "usage of the law among the regenerated" *(usus legis in renatis).* These terms appear not only in Melanchthon's writings (e.g., *Loci,* 1559; *StA* II/1, 325 f.), but also, and most importantly, in those of Calvin*. Contrary to Luther (*see* 4 b above), Calvin does not make the distinction between the law, which condemns, and the gospel, which acquits—the center and principle of his theology. Instead, he subordinates this Pauline opposition to the unity of the divine Covenant. Thus, the gospel is reduced in practice to a new form of obedience to the law. It is no longer a pure message of consolation and acquittal: instead, consolation and acquittal are no more than aspects of the single Word of God, which also contains a requirement to fulfill the law by living in conformity with the divine will. The focus of interest is thus displaced away from justification and toward the sanctification of believers, which is understood as a distinct process, oriented toward the single Word of God, which in this case takes on the characteristics of law. Hence, the central function of the law is no longer to accuse human beings and convince them of their sins—even though Calvin still accepts this "elenctic usage," which, contrary to the order established by Luther, he makes into the "first usage" of the law (*Inst.*, 1560, II, 7, 6 f.). Instead, the central function of the law is to give shape to Christian morality: this is the "third usage," which constitutes the "principal usage of the law" (*praecipuus usus legis; Inst.*, 1560, II, 7, 12). The crucial question for theology is no longer how the human being condemned by the law can be regenerated, but how the regenerated human being can live in accordance with the will of God. Concrete ethical practice thus finds a distinguished theological legitimization.

By comparison, Luther's ethics, in which the event is never separated from justification, is remarkably free. This theological liberty leaves every latitude to the gospel to accomplish its work of giving life and regeneration to humanity, with all that is entailed on the ethical plane. However, to the extent that Christians continue to belong to the old world, they remain under the command of the double usage of the law until they die, as is emphasized in Article VI of the *Formula of Concord* (1577), which basically reprises Luther's position (*BSLK* 793–95 and 962–69, in particular 969, 16–37).

e) Monism and Dualism: The Dispute between Barth and Elert. The dispute over the Lutheran conception of the law found an echo in 20th-century Protestantism when the Calvinist theologian Karl Barth* reversed the order established by Luther as between the law and the gospel (Barth 1935). Like Calvin with his idea of the divine Covenant, Barth reduces the gospel and the law to the higher unity of the single Word of God, which he understands primarily from a christological perspective. Starting from the basic postulate that "God's speaking to us is already, in itself and in every way, a form of grace" (6), he arrives at the thesis that "the law is nothing other than the necessary *form* of the Gospel, and its content is grace" (13).

This monistic approach was met with lively criticism by some Lutherans. W. Elert (1885–1954), for example, opposed Barth and the very principle of a "third usage of the law," resolutely taking his stand with Luther in order to affirm, in a still more energetic manner, the validity of the conceptual coupling of law and gospel (Elert 1948).

f) Christological Revelation versus Natural Law. Emil Brunner (1889–1966), a Calvinist theologian who had been an ally of Barth's in the early stages of his "dialectic theology," opposed Barth's christological monism from a different perspective. He reproached Barth for neglecting the other task of theology, which is to bring to light the anthropological repercussions of the Word of God. Brunner's fundamental conception of humanity led him to take an interest in the justice that we are capable of realizing in this world. In order to apprehend this level of reality, notably in the face of Nazism (this was in 1943), he deliberately made use of the ideas of natural law and of order in creation.

5. Law and Gospel in Modern Times

According to Luther, what makes an authentic theologian is the capacity to distinguish between the law and the gospel (*see* 4 b above). Even Protestants have often lost sight of the precise content of this distinction, or have reduced it to a purely circumstantial preoccupation, related to the Reformation and Luther's theology. Nevertheless, the problem affects relations between reason and faith, and between faith and politics; it underlies the condemnation of evil* and violence*, as well as reflections on the possibility of bringing them to an end, and, therefore, reflections on the future of humanity. It thus touches upon fundamental questions of anthropology*, ethics, and eschatology*.

It may be possible to clarify this problematic with the aid of the following assertion: that the modern age, by giving the gospel a universal meaning, has been an antinomian age, but has also increasingly returned toward a conception that may be called "nomist." In its self-designation as "modern," the new age was already betraying an "evangelical" trait: it was understood as a rupture without any equivalent, placed under the sign of liberty. However, within this enthusiastic generalization, the concrete christological determination of the gospel took on an abstract character. The christological formula "It is finished" (Jn 19:30) was replaced by the idea of a liberation already and forever accomplished. All human beings are by nature "emancipated" and "mature" (*naturaliter maiorennes),* according to Kant* (*Antwort an der Frage: Was ist Aufklärung?* 1784). This presupposes that the law has, fundamentally, already been abolished: human beings in themselves are free, good, and spontaneous (Rousseau). It is in this sense that "modernity" is antinomian (*see* 4 d above).

However, what this new human being has been forever he still has to become. At the same time, the universal gospel of liberty obliges human beings to conform themselves to it and to give it a body. Not only are human beings liberated, as in the concrete promise of the gospel, but they are "condemned" to be liberated (Jean-Paul Sartre, *L'existentialisme est un humanisme*, 1946). One cannot be authorized to be free: one must liberate oneself. Here we see a form of "nomism" being outlined on the other side of antinomianism.

Antinomianism and nomism are two sides of the same process. In its secular or secularized forms, this process is understood as a rapport between law and liberty. With his concept of autonomy, Kant sought a position above and beyond antinomianism and nomism alike. Hegel* discussed liberty as "law and conviction," and thus, in his turn, came up against the question of secularized liberty, in which one can see the post-Christian version of the problem of the law and the Gospel. In this sense, the importance that Luther attached to this distinction is still as topical as ever (Bayer 1992).

• **a) Conciliar or Confessional Texts**
BSLK.
CEC.
DH 1520–83 (*COD* 671–8).

b) Works by Specific Theologians
Thomas Aquinas, *ST* Ia IIae, q. 90–114.
M. Luther, *Commentary on the Epistle to the Galatians*, *WA* 40/1, *Commentary of the Epistles to Romans*, *WA* 56.
P. Melanchthon (1559), *Loci praecipui theologici*, in *StA* II, 164–780, 1952 (II/1) and 1953 (II/2).
J. Calvin (1559), *Inst. de la religion chrestienne*, 1560, Ed. J.-D. Benoît, Paris, 1957–63.
K. Barth (1935), "Evangelium und Gesetz," *TEH* 32 (New Ed., *TEH* 50, 1956; *see also* E. Kinder, K. Haendler [1968] below).
W. Elert (1948), "Gesetz und Evangelium," *Zwischen Gnade und Ungnade: Abwandlungen des Themas Gesetz und Evangelium*, Munich.
E. Brunner (1943), *Gerechtigkeit: Eine Lehre von den Grundgesetzen der Gesellschaftsordnung*, Zurich (3rd Ed. 1981).
♦ U. Kühn (1965), *Via caritatis: Theologie des Gesetzes bei Thomas von Aquin*, KiKonf 9.
O. H. Pesch (1967), *Theologie der Rechtfertigung bei Martin Luther und Thomas von Aquin: Versuch eines systematisch-theologischen Dialogs*, WSAMA.T 4.
E. Kinder, K. Haendler (Ed.) (1968), *Gesetz und Evangelium*, WdF 142.
O. Bayer (1971), Promissio: *Geschichte der reformatorischen Wende in Luthers Theologie*, Göttingen (New Ed. 1989, Darmstadt).
K. Koch, et al. (1984), "Gesetz," *TRE* 13, 40–126 (bibl.).
A. Peters (1989), "Gesetz 3.," *EKL*3 2, 143–9 (bibl.).
O. Bayer (1992), *Leibliches Wort. Reformation und Neuzeit im Konflikt*, Tübingen; (1994), *Theologie, HST* 1.
S. Feldhaus, W. Korff (1995), "Gesetz V," *LThK*3 4, 586–8.
O. H. Pesch (1995), "Gesetz und Evangelium II-IV," *LThK*3 4, 591–4 (bibl.).
J.-F. Kervégan (1996), "Law," *DEPhM*, 855–62.

Oswald Bayer and Axel Wiemer

See also **Casuistry; Gospels; Justice; Justification**

Law and Legislation

The term *law* does not admit of easy definition. Viewed as the collection of norms that govern life within society*, law comprises everything that regulates human conduct, including, for example, moral precepts*, state statutes, church* canons, rules of family life, commercial habits, and customs. Viewed in narrower terms, law consists of norms formulated by political authority* and actualized by persons subject to its jurisdiction*. In the Western legal tradition, the principal responsibility for law has fallen to the state, but other institutions have played key roles in its development, notably the church, with its canon* law. The religious history of Western law had four key periods.

1. Rome before and after Christianity

a) Roman Law. Until the conversion* of Constantine, Roman law reigned supreme throughout the West. It defined the status of persons* and associations, established legal actions and procedures, proscribed delicts and crimes, protected the welfare of the state, and regulated commerce, private property*, inheritance, and the family*. Roman law established the imperial cult* and ordained its priests, architecture, rituals, and festivals. A refined jurisprudence emerged in the first century B.C. Cicero (106 B.C.–43 B.C.) and Seneca (A.D. 4–65), for example, cast in legal terms Aristotle's methods of reasoning, rhetoric, and interpretation, as well as concepts of natural, distributive, and commutative justice*. Gaius (110–80), Ulpinaus (†228), Pomponius (second century), and other Roman jurists drew classic distinctions between civil law *(ius civile)*, custom, or the law of nations *(ius gentium)*, and natural law *(ius naturale)*. Civil law is the set of statutes and procedures that deal with actions, persons, and things in a particular community. The law of nations is the set of principles, customs, and rights common to several communities, and is the basis for treaties and diplomatic relations. Natural law is a set of immutable principles perceived by reason*; their authority is sovereign and they must prevail in instances of legal or diplomatic dispute.

b) The Church and Roman Law. The church initially stood largely opposed to Roman society. Christians could not accept the imperial cult or participate in the pagan rituals required for military service, commercial relations or civil litigation. Their ideal of liberty* with *nomos*—a term that was related as much to the institutional aspect of law as to the moral aspect of statutes— and of faithfulness to evangelical love* compelled them to form communities largely withdrawn from society. Ecclesiastical constitutions such as the *Didache* (c. 120) or the *Didascalia Apostolorum* (c. 250), rooted in the Decalogue* and the teaching of Christ* and his apostles*, set forth rules for church government*, liturgy*, ecclesiastical* discipline, charity, the family, and property. Following Christ and Paul, the clergy taught obedience to political authority up to the limits of what was authorized by conscience*. However, following Tertullian* and Ambrose*, the clergy also urged their Roman rulers to make political and legal reforms consonant with Christianity. From the late first century onward, such attitudes provoked severe imperial edicts and waves of persecution.

The conversion of Constantine in 312 and the establishment of Christianity as the official religion of the Roman Empire in 381 blended Roman and Christian elements. The empire came to be understood as the universal Christian body *(corpus christianum)* on earth. The emperor, who reigned supreme throughout Christendom, was viewed as both pope and king. Roman law, particularly as codified in the *Corpus iuris civilis* (534), was viewed as the pristine expression of statute *(ius civile)* and custom *(ius gentium)*. However, according to Augustine*, Isidore of Seville (c. 560–636), and other writers, secular law derived its authority and core content from natural law, now understood as the expression of the commandments of God* written on the hearts and consciences of all, and rewritten in the Bible*, particularly the Decalogue and the Beatitudes*. The *ius civile* and *ius gentium* were thus viewed as vehicles for establishing the basic precepts of moral and natural law. Knowing precisely which precepts should be established by secular law, however, was a problem theologians kept discussing from the late fourth century onward.

This syncretism of Roman and Christian beliefs allowed the church to imbue Roman law with its teachings. The *Codex Theodosianus* (438), and Justinian's *Corpus iuris civilis* (482–565) and *Novellae* (565), incorporated Christian teachings on the Trinity*, the sacraments*, the liturgy*, the Sabbath*, sexual ethics*, charity, and education. Similarly, various heresies* were proscribed, especially Arianism*, Apollinarianism*, and Manicheanism*. However, the church was also subordinated to imperial rule. The emperors convoked councils* and synods*, appointed and removed clerics*, established and administered parishes, monasteries, and charitable foundations, and controlled ecclesiastical property. This "caesaropapism" was accepted with little resistance in the Orthodox churches of Byzantium until well into the 14th century. Eastern Bishops readily merged the Christian and the secular, leaving the legal affairs of the church to the emperor as Vicar of Christ and devoting themselves to Christian mystery* and liturgy. Caesaropapism met with more resistance in the West, where popes such as Gelasius I (492–96) and Gregory* the Great insisted on a sharper separation of the spiritual and the secular.

2. Papal Revolution

a) Autonomy of the Church. The second key period came with the papal revolution of the late 11th through 13th centuries, aimed at the emancipation of the church from the temporal power. The initiative was taken by Gregory VII (c. 1021–85) in the investiture dispute, and this resulted in legal and political autonomy for the church. The church now claimed to exercise jurisdiction over such persons as clerics, pilgrims, students, the poor, Jews, and Muslims, and over such subjects as doctrine and liturgy, ecclesiastical property and polity, patronage of benefices, marriage* and the family, education, charity, inheritance, oral promises, oaths, contracts, and all manner of moral or ideological crimes and delicts. The church predicated these claims in part on its traditional authority over the sacraments, in part on the power of the keys bequeathed by Christ to Peter* (a key of knowledge and a key of power). It used the extent of its jurisdiction to translate its dogma* into legal terms.

The oldest canon law provisions were synthesized in the famous *Decretium Gratiani* (c. 1140), and then heavily supplemented by papal and conciliar legislation, not to mention juridical glosses and commentaries. By the late 13th century, canon law was preeminent in the West. Many private parties litigated their claims in consistory courts, and civil law appropriated the substance of canon law. Canonists such as Hostiensis (Heinrich von Segusio, †1271) or Joannes Andreae (c. 1270–1348), and civilians under their influence, such as Gandinus (13th century), Bartolus of Saxoferrato (1314–57) or Baldus de Ubaldis (c. 1319–1400), developed new doctrines of public, private, and criminal law, comprehensive rules for the resolution of conflicts of laws, and elaborate hermeneutical methods for their equitable application. They also developed concepts of legislation, adjudication, and executive administration, and many other concepts that still form the core of Western constitutionalism. They developed a good deal of the Western law of corporations and associations, as well as refined doctrines of popular sovereignty, representation and consent, and individual and corporate rights and liberties.

b) Theories of Law. This legal transformation brought new theories of law and authority by such Scholastic writers as Anselm*, Abelard*, John of Salisbury (c. 1115–80), Albert* the Great, and Thomas* Aquinas. Aquinas's synthesis proved to be the most enduring. For Aquinas, all law and authority are rooted in the eternal law *(lex aeterna),* the divine reason that ordains and orders all creation*. All human beings participate in this eternal law through the natural law *(lex naturalis)* that is within them *(ST* Ia IIae, q. 91, a. 2, and q. 94), that is, through intuitive knowledge *(synderesis)* of the core principles of practical reason (Ia, q. 79, a. 12; conscience*). These principles—doing good*, avoiding evil*, preserving self, living in a couple, having children, seeking truth*, living in society, and avoiding harm to others (Ia IIae, q. 94, a. 2)—must be adapted to particular circumstances by human statutes *(leges humanae,* q. 91, a. 3) of canon, civil, criminal, and customary law. Aquinas's theory of law met with sharp criticism by John Duns* Scotus, then by William of Ockham (c. 1285–1347) and other proponents of nominalism*, but it was dominant within Catholicism by the time of the Council of Trent* and Iberian Neoscholasticism, led by Vitoria (c. 1485–1546) and Suarez*.

3. Reformation

a) Protestant Reformers. The third key period for law came with the Reformation. Protestant reformers such as Luther*, Bucer*, or Calvin* taught that canon law obscured a true understanding of the Bible* and denatured the church by making a community of saints into a political corporation. The jurisdiction of the bishops had obstructed the church's mission of preaching the Word*, administering the sacraments, educating the young, and caring for the needy; moreover, it had usurped the role of the state, perceived as the representative of divine authority. To be sure, the church must have internal rules of organization, teaching, and discipline. The church must also criticize legal injustice and combat political illegitimacy. Nevertheless, the law is primarily the province of the state, not the church.

b) Effects of the Reformation. European law was transformed by the Reformation and Christian humanism*. The international rule of the Catholic Church and canon law was permanently broken, and Western Christendom was fractured into competing nations and regions, each with its own religious and political system. State rulers now assumed jurisdiction over numerous subjects previously governed by the church. Particularly in Lutheran and Anglican polities, inspired by the writings of Philipp Melanchton (1497–1560) and Richard Hooker (c. 1554–1600) respectively, as well as by Roman prototypes, the state came to exercise considerable control over the clergy, organization, and property of the church.

These changes did not suddenly deprive western law of its religious dimension. Canon law remained an ineradicable part of European law and one of its principal legal sources. Moreover, in Catholic countries and their Latin American colonies, the papacy still held considerable sway over legislators and judges. In the Protestant countries and their North American colonies, a certain number of Protestant concepts shaped new law: new social statutes, new criminal law, new legislation on marriage and divorce, and new doctrines of rights and liberties. The idea that power corrupts helped to inspire such restraints as the separation of powers, limited terms, and the codification of statutes.

4. Enlightenment

a) Revolutionary Individualism. The fourth key period in the history of law was the Enlightenment. Hume (1711–76), Rousseau (1712–78), and Jefferson (1743–1826) offered a secular theology of individualism, rationalism*, and nationalism. The individual was no longer viewed primarily as a sinner who has need of salvation*. For the philosophes, every individual was created equal in dignity, vested with the same rights to life, liberty, and property, and the same capacity to choose his own conception of happiness. Reason was no longer the handmaid of revelation*, and rational disputation was a sufficient source of morality and law. The nation was no longer identified with a national church or a chosen people. The nation deserved to be glorified in its own right. Its constitution and laws were sacred texts, reflecting the morals and mores of the national culture. Its officials were like priests, representing the sovereignty and will of the people.

Such ideas were revolutionary in their time, and contributed to the American and French Revolutions*; they had already been present in the English Revolution of 1688–89. Then, too, Western law underwent sweeping changes: constitutional provisions for limited government and civil liberties, separation of church and state, new criminal and commercial law, new laws of property and inheritance, shifts toward a definition of criminal and civil responsibility, abolition of slavery, and the gradual removal of discrimination based on race*, religion, or gender.

b) Influence on the Philosophy of Law. One can see the influence of the Enlightenment in many theories of law. Numerous writers, from John Locke (1632–1704) to Thomas Paine (1737–1809), postulated a mythical state of nature that antedated and integrated human laws and natural rights. Nationalist myths were grafted onto this myth* of origins to unify and sanctify national legal traditions. Thus, Italian jurists appealed to a utopian Roman heritage, English jurists to their ancient constitution and Anglo-Saxon roots, French jurists to the Salic law, and German jurists to ancient constitutional liberties. No one placed much faith in all of this, and three legal philosophies came to prominence in the later 18th and 19th centuries. Positivists such as Jeremy Bentham or John Stuart Mill (utilitarianism*) contended that the ultimate source of law lies in the will of the legislator and its ultimate sanction in political force. Natural law theorists, notably Kant*, sought the ultimate source of law in pure reason and conscience, and its ultimate sanction in moral suasion. Jurists of the German historical school, such as Friedrich Karl von Savigny (1779–1861) or Otto von Gierke (1841–1921), contended that the ultimate source of law resides in the customs and character of the people, and that its ultimate sanction is the condemnation of crime by the community. These three philosophies have persisted to this day, although they are heavily supplemented by an array of realist, socialist, feminist, and other theories.

c) Influence on Legal Institutions. The ideas of the Enlightenment also led to the transformation and secularization* of legal institutions. Individualism was expressed in measures for the protection of privacy, and rationalism in the freedom of speech, press, and association; as for nationalism, it manifested itself in diverse ways in democracy*, fascism, and socialism. The clear separation of church and state in America and in certain European countries served to privatize religion, and to drive religious organizations from the political process. Increasingly, there are laws rather than law in the singular: each nation tends to have its own legal system, itself divided into several types of law according to domains of application. This tendency was offset somewhat, in the second half of the 20th century, by the growth of international law, and by the new social and political programs of liberation* theology, Catholicism after Vatican* II, and the ecumenical movement (ecumenism*). However, this has not prevented a number of writers from announcing a worldwide law crisis.

Today, there are still many links between law and religion, and many forms of mutual interaction, ranging from the domain of concepts to that of institutions. In recent years these interactions have attracted a considerable body of interdisciplinary studies. It can be hoped that these studies will contribute to a better understanding of law and justice, and to preparation for the emergence of a common law of all humanity in the new millennium.

● *Codex Theodosianus*, Ed. T. Mommsen, 2 vols., Hildesheim, 1890.

Corpus iuris canonici, Ed. E. Friedberg, 2 vols., Graz, 1955 (repr.).

Corpus iuris civilis, Ed. T. Mommsen, P. Krüger, Berlin, 1889.

O. von Gierke, *Das deutsche Genossenschaftsrecht*, 4 vols., Berlin, 1868–1913.

La Didachè, ou Doctrine des douze apôtres, SC 248.

La didascalie, ou Doctrine catholique des douze apôtres, in *Constitutions apostoliques*, SC 320.

♦ J. Ellul (1946), *Le fondement théologique du droit*, Neuchâtel.

B. Tierney (1981), *Religion, Law and the Growth of Constitutional Thought 1150–1650*, Cambridge.

L. Vallauri, G. Dilcher (Ed.) (1981), *Christentum, Säkularisation und modernes Recht*, 2 vols., Baden-Baden.

J. Gaudemet (1985), *Les sources du droit de l'Église en Occident du IIe au VIIe s.*, Paris.

J.M. Kelley (1992), *A Short History of Western Legal Theory*, Oxford.

H.J. Berman (1993), *Faith and Order: The Reconciliation of Law and Religion*, Atlanta.

J. Witte, Jr., J.D. van der Wyver (Ed.) (1995), *Religious Human Rights in Global Perspective*, 2 vols., The Hague.

JOHN WITTE

See also **Authority; Church and State**

Lay/Laity

From the lexicographic point of view, the word *lay* and its derivatives fall into two main semantic domains. On the one hand, *lay* means "independent from any specific religious belief" (Robert *sv*). This is a modern sense, used in speaking of the secular state or secular education in order to indicate the *absence* of any religious reference in the political or educational system. There is another meaning, specifically connected to the structuring of the church* as a religious society*: here a distinction is made between the *laity*, members of that society who perform only the activities deriving from a shared belonging to the church through baptism*, and the *clergy*, who receive a specific status in the same society, a status from which derive acts of government*, teaching, and presiding over ritual celebrations. This second sense (a member of the laity is someone who "does not belong to the clergy") has sometimes been transposed onto other religious societies, but it comes specifically from the Christian ecclesiastical tradition*.

Modern usage of the term in fact derives from this second meaning to the extent that it is rooted in the process by which the civil authorities of the Christian West attempted, from the late Middle Ages, to assert their independence in the conflict between the two powers, spiritual (the pope* and the church) and temporal (the power of princes conceived of as not clerical and therefore secular). From the 18th century on the conflict became increasingly violent. It conditioned the entire religious and political history of the 19th century and resulted in rather varied legal solutions, ranging from the legal separation of church and state to a series of concordats. The secular spirit, which claims absolute autonomy for temporal power and defines itself by rejecting any reference to the religious dimension of man (*see* Bedouelle and Costa 1998) is the latest manifestation of the conflict.

I. Historical Determination

The meaning of the term *lay* in the church was constructed in several main stages, which are themselves revealing of the theological and ecclesiastical problems underlying historical reality. It is not by chance that one of the major ecclesiologists of this century, Y. Congar, elaborated one aspect of his ecclesiological analysis on this theme in a classic work, *Jalons pour une théologie du laïcat* (1953).

1. A Term Absent from the Biblical Tradition?

Lay comes from the Greek *laïkos* (one who belongs to the people or comes from it: nonofficial, civil, or common, Liddell Scott *sv*). The absence of the term from the New Testament has often been noted. We must however remember that *laïkos* is an adjective derived from *laos* (people), a term that is omnipresent in both Old and New Testaments (*see*, e. g., the key passages of Exodus 19:5 [frequently repeated in the New Testament, in 1 Pt 2:5, 2:9; Rev 1:6; 5:10; 20:6], and Lv 26:12 and Jer 31:33 [repeated in 2 Cor 6:16; Heb 8:10; Rev 21:3]; *see* Grelot 1970). And since belonging to the people* of God formally constitutes the Christian experience* (by comparison, the disciples of Jesus* were very early given by pagans the name *christianus* [Acts 11:26], which is precisely an epithet of belonging [-*anus* = supporter of] to *Chrestos*), it is probable that when it appeared in the vocabulary of the church, *laïkos* carried this meaning. The *laïkos* is then the one who belongs to the people of God, established as the heir of the covenants* and the beneficiary of the promise* of salvation*: "You too, laymen, Church elect of God, listen to this: Church means first of all people; you are the very holy Catholic Church, the royal priesthood, the holy multitude, the adopted people, the great assembly, the bride adorned for the Lord God" (*Didascalios* II. 26. 1). Hence, "our word 'lay' is connected to a word that in Jewish and then in Christian usage precisely designated the consecrated people in opposition to the profane peoples" (Congar 1953).

The term does appear in certain texts like Clement, *Ep. to Cor.* 40.5 and Tertullian, *De Praescriptione Haereticorum* 41. 8, which enumerate series of distinct functions in the assembly (high priest, priests, levites, laity), but we should not use that fact to infer categories linked to a later ecclesiological approach make the opposition between clergy and laity into a principle of analysis. Congar points out that we are, at this stage, in a context where the institution of the church is not yet seen "as an order of means for the calling of salvation" (ibid., 21). Thus, even if the progressively greater emphasis on a hierarchy in both secular life and church membership became an element of Christian consciousness from the third century onward, and led in particular to seeing in the *ordines* the structuring elements of the society (Hippolytus, *In Danielem* I. 17; Tertullian, *Ad uxorem* I. 7; *De monogamia* 12; *De exhortatione castitatis* 7. 3 and 14. 1–4; Methodus of Olympus, *Symposium* VII. 3), something that further led to the distinction proposed by Pope Gregory the Great between *pastores, continentes,* and *conjugati* (see *Moralia* I. 14; V. 13 and 30), we cannot yet speak of a systematic division in which the laity were defined only negatively in terms of their distinction from clergy or pastors*. Ecclesiological reflection has always instinctively sensed the foundational character of a baptismal and sacramental belonging to the people of God, whatever the specific status of each individual.

2. Canonical Divergence about Laity in the Medieval Period

It is still difficult to evaluate the importance of the pastoral, canonical, and ecclesiological orientations of the Gregorian reform. In a Western Europe that was becoming self-aware through a renewal of the dual legacy of ancient political thought and the Augustinian theological tradition (the two cities), the mutual relations of church and princes took shape in terms of a conflict of powers (spiritual and temporal). Generally, the division took place as follows: the church exercised its power in the person of the clergy (pope and bishops*); and the princes, who were laymen not clergy, became holders of temporal power. The task was then to determine in legal terms the scope of the two powers; and a new schema took shape according to which the laity did not exercise power in the church, because the clergy alone had that responsibility. This new ecclesiological approach, heavily conditioned by political and social circumstances, produced three results. In the first place there was an attempt to clarify and distinguish the respective domains of natural (political) society and church society, with an inevitable logical hardening of the opposition between what fell under the temporal (power of lay princes)and what fell under the spiritual (power of the clergy). Second, there was an attempt to justify clergy's specific character in relation to the laity, including, as this did, the massive introduction of a legal problematics of power within the life and the mystery* of the church. This is the framework in which we can locate the axiom of the decree of Gratian, *Duo sunt genera christianorum...,* contrasting the "clergy given over to the divine office, devoted to contemplation* and prayer*, removed from the affairs of the world*," to the laity, who possessed temporal goods, could marry, cultivate the soil, administer human justice*, carry on business, and offer gifts at the altar (c. VII, c. XII. q. 1; *see* commentary in

Congar 1953 and GVEDL I, 678). Finally, there emerged an ecclesial power that claimed the right to operate even over the "natural" structure of society, the church believing that its role included helping to construct a present world whose institutions were influenced by the ethical, social, and cultural implications of revelation*.

At this point we can evaluate the differences in which the two understandings of the laity specific to the churches of the West and the East developed. Because it had always existed in a preestablished civil and political society, the Eastern church had always spontaneously understood itself in its sacramental essence. Political power (the Byzantine *Basileus*) was thus understood as one component of the gift of the church as sacrament, and the king was recognized as having a particular priestly identity and therefore the formal right to intervene (*see* Dagron 1996). This represented a perspective of *integration* of the prince and of natural society into the mystery of the church. The Western church, on the other hand, was very early defined by the *separation* between the *sacerdotium* and the *imperium* (the donation of Constantine symbolizing, by the "gift" of the Papal States, this radical autonomy of the *sacerdotium*). It was not long before there emerged a situation of conflict between the two powers, which saw spiritual power constantly attempting to assert its supremacy over temporal power.

3. Crisis of the Reformation and Contemporary Rediscovery of the Baptismal Priesthood

The coming of the Reformation was as deeply connected to the secular powers and their claims to autonomy as to a radical critique of the church as objective mediation for salvation. It is therefore against the background of a new situation that we must understand the positions adopted by Luther*, and his assertion of the absolute primacy of a common priesthood* of the faithful in radical opposition to the ministerial priesthood. This crisis situation provoked in the Catholic Church a hardening of the opposition between clergy and laity *within* the very life of the church, in a theology that accentuated contrasts like that between the teaching church (the clergy) and the taught church (the laity), and which saw in the clerical state the preeminent representation of Christian identity.

The appearance of societies based on a recognition of the free individual as the subject of rights and duties; a critical rereading of historical sources (biblical, patristic, medieval); a renewal of evangelization in societies with a Christian tradition (Catholic Action*)—these factors enabled contemporary theology to take up in new terms the major ecclesiological notions, and consequently also the notion of lay/laity. To the work of Y. Congar already mentioned, we should add that of M.-D. Chenu, H. de Lubac*, and H. and K. Rahner*, who have all had a profound influence on the *aggiornamento* of the church proposed by Pope John XXIII and formulated programmatically in the major documents of Vatican* II (particularly *LG*, chaps. II, IV, and V; *GS; AA; AG*, chap. VI; *IM; DH; GE;* as well as the *Messages of the Council,* of 20 October 1962 and 8 December 1965). The implementation of these major programmatic documents was continued in particular by the Roman synod* of October 1987 on "the vocation and the mission* of the laity in the Church and the world twenty years after Vatican II," and the publication by John Paul II of the post-synodal apostolic exhortation *Christifideles Laici (CL)* of 30 December 1988. Current theological thinking is not really unanimous, but the various tendencies are rooted in a few major shared convictions.

II. Dogmatic Approach

1. Difficulties of a "Positive" Approach to the Notion of Laity

As history shows, the difficulty encountered in defining the reality of the *laity* comes from the use of a negative concept: formally, a lay person is any member of the church who does not belong to the clergy, that is, who has not received the sacrament* of ordination*. For this reason the customary tripartite division of the members of the people of God into priests, monks and nuns, and laity is formally inaccurate, since monks may be members of the clergy (if they are ordained) or lay brothers (if they are not). Basically, the notion of laity is a pastoral-canonical notion that makes it possible conveniently to make rules concerning the members of the people of God according to the way of life or ministerial activities that are specific to them. This is clearly evident in the procedure of the *CCC* of 1983, which begins by defining the *christifideles,* those "who, insofar as they are incorporated into Christ* by baptism, are established as the people of God" (can. 204. 1), and later asserts that "by divine institution, there are in the Church, among the faithful, sacred ministers who are of right *(in jure)* called clergy, and others who are called laity" (can. 207. 1; *see LG* 31).

The principal problem is thus one of ecclesiological methodology. Is it possible to begin with a practical given of a pastoral and legal character and give it dogmatic value in ecclesiology* without committing a kind of paralogism? It is on the basis of this question that we should understand the attempts of the several theologies* that try to define the laity *positively:* those of the canonists (Corecco 1990); of theologians intent on promoting specific features of certain charisms pertaining to lay movements (G. Chantraine); of actual members of those movements (*Communione e Liberazione* and *Opus Dei* principally, as far as Europe is concerned); of the earlier theoreticians of *Catholic Action* who derived the apostleship of the laity from a mandate of the hierarchy*; and finally, of historians who, in a concern for "declericalization," criticize the "bipolar structure" of the church (e.g., A. Faivre, *Ordonner la fraternité,* Paris, 1992).

Behind the apparent diversity of approaches, the point of departure is in fact always the same: it is the life of the church, essentially seen from the perspective of *functionality, activity,* and *powers,* that legitimates the questioning. As a consequence, some theologies of the laity may take on a combative or challenging aspect and be organized essentially in order to ask what the laity may or may not do, in reference to the presbyteral or diaconal ministry. This aspect is no doubt exacerbated by the current situation of a church that is experiencing not only a deep crisis of vocations but also considerable uncertainty about the identity of the ministerial priesthood. Similarly, to make the distinction between charism and institution (Congar) a constituent element of ecclesiology creates the danger of assimilating institution to ministerial responsibility on the one hand, and on the other, lay life to the spontaneous diversity of charisms, which leads to the desire for a "promotion" of the laity in terms of charismatic diversification (Corecco 1990; Chantraine 1987). This would represent a modern extension of the theology of the founding charisms of religious institutes. Last, another tendency that can rightly call on tradition and certain conciliar documents (particularly *LG* 31: "the secular character [*indoles saecularis*] is the specific and particular character of the laity," repeated in *CL*), seems to wish to give a positive specificity to the Christian laity in entrusting it with a concern for the affairs of the world *(saeculum),* and in this way providing a contemporary version of the medieval division of powers, the clergy being concerned with affairs of the church and the laity with temporal affairs. This dichotomy, however, even very attenuated, does not seem capable of responding to the fundamental question of the *theological* determination of the status of the laity in the Church. The question, in fact, brings us back to that of the pairing baptismal priesthood/ministerial priesthood, and it is this pairing that structures the church in its very being.

2. Reconsideration of the Problem in Terms of the Sacramentality of the Church

To respond to contemporary ecclesiological requirements, a theology of the laity seems to be obliged to go beyond the canonical oppositions that define it negatively in relation to the ministerial priesthood and to call on a theology of the sacramentality of the Church as it is defined in *LG* 1: "The Church being, in Christ, in some sense the sacrament of—that is, both the sign and the means of—the intimate *union* with God and of the *unity* of the whole human race [*intimae cum Deo unionis totiusque humani generis unitatis*].... This assertion implies that the Church is inseparably what *signifies (sacramentum)* the communion* that it *is (unio or communio).*"

The fundamental and insurpassable form in which the Church signifies itself, in and by the acts of its members, is the common or royal priesthood of the baptized. Thus, all members (laity or clergy) receive through *baptism* the priestly existence defined in Scripture in Romans 12:1 ("I appeal to you therefore, brothers, by the mercies of God, to present your bodies as a living sacrifice, holy and acceptable to God, which is your *spiritual worship*"; *see* Rom 1:9, 15:15 f.). There is no more fundamental basis for a life of faith than this filial gift of one's life to the Father* in and through the single priesthood of Christ, "sole Mediator between God and man." Vatican II comments as follows: "Christ the Lord, high priest taken from among men (*see* Heb 5:1–5), has made of the new people 'a kingdom of priests for his God and Father' (*see* Rev 1:6, 5:9 f.)." The baptized, in fact, through the regeneration and the anointing of the Holy* Spirit, are consecrated to dwell in a spiritual home and a holy priesthood; to offer, through all the activities of the Christian, so many spiritual sacrifices and to proclaim the wonders of the one who has called them out of darkness into his own admirable light (*see* 1 Pt 2:4–10). This is why all the disciples of Christ, persevering in prayer and the praise* of God (*see* Acts 2:42–47), should offer themselves as holy victims, acceptable to God (*see* Rom 12:1), and should bear witness to Christ over the face of the earth, giving to all who ask an account of the hope that lies in them of eternal life (*see* 1 Pt 3:15)" (*LG* 10).

The problem is thus not to be a member of the *laity* (not the clergy), but to be *baptized* (*laïkos* as member of the people [*laos*] of God): no longer a canonical definition by negative differentiation, but a positive recognition of the sacramentality of all Christian existence, both in the world and within the Church, of the sacramentality of the royal baptismal priesthood based on the one priesthood of Christ. Because Christian existence is given by grace* in a sacramental mode, it is itself called on to be totally sacramental: "pastors should recognize and promote the ministries*, the offices, and the functions of the lay faithful *which have their sacramental basis in baptism, Confirmation*, and for many in marriage**" (*CL* 23).

At this point arises the question of the relationship between the two priesthoods (baptismal and ministerial). The major document of Vatican II formulates it in these terms: "The common priesthood of the faithful and the ministerial or hierarchical priesthood, although they differ in essence and not in degree *(licet essentia et non gradu tantum differant),* are nevertheless ordered together; in fact, each in its own way participates in the single priesthood of Christ *(suo peculiari modo de uno Christi sacerdotio participant)*" (*LG* 10).

Even though the document does not provide a formal solution with respect to the constituents of this essential difference, it appears to be a difference *in the order of meaning*: the two priesthoods (baptismal and ministerial) signify the same *res* (the one priesthood of Jesus Christ), but following two different registers of meaning (and that is enough to provide an *essential* difference, for two signs, as signs, do not differ in degree but in essence, even if they designate a single reality). Both signify the same Christ high priest but in two different aspects. The ministerial priesthood signifies Christ acting to save the world, the Lord taking the initiative to fulfill the purpose of the Father, founding and establishing the actions of salvation, the eternal Word* making himself the *means and bearer of salvation by grace.* Each time that the Church appears as the sacramental sign of Christ the Savior the ministerial priesthood signifies the gratuity of the grace given in this saving act. The baptismal priesthood, for its part, signifies Christ insofar as he realizes in us and recapitulates in himself his work of salvation, the Christ-Pleroma, the one who shapes us to himself as he offered himself to the Father "once and for all," the one who contains all and in whom all things are brought together.

Understanding baptismal existence as a sacrament of the priesthood of Christ then makes it possible to articulate the condition of the laity in the Church following the theology of the "triple function" (prophetic, royal, and ritual). One might schematize it as follows:

a) Prophetic Function. To the extent that any baptismal life relies on the confession of faith*, everything that derives from confession, witnessing, and the proclamation of faith belongs fully to all the baptized. Only the function of authentication of faith in all its forms belongs to the ministry as *charisma veritatis* (Irenaeus*).

b) Royal Function. The royal function of the baptismal priesthood consists of the exercise of a liberty* moved by the charity that is the Holy Spirit and pertains equally to all the baptized. It sounds the basic note of the sacramentality of their Christian existence, in the infinitely varied forms required by the diversity of human needs and human distress. Only the critical function of bringing these charisms together in the service of communion belongs formally to the ministerial priesthood.

c) Ritual Function. The ritual function is the work of the whole assembly: "This entirely redeemed city, that is, the assembly and the society of the saints, is offered to God as a universal sacrifice* by the high priest who, in the form of a slave, went so far as to offer himself for us in his Passion*." (Augustine*, *De civitate Dei* X. 6)

Thus, every liturgical action is the work of all, with the ministerial priesthood, through the sacramental sign of presidency, manifesting in it the transcendent initiative of Christ the Head, the source of grace. In this perspective it is clear that the reality of the ministerial priesthood is totally subordinated to that of the royal priesthood as a means to an end, since the ultimate reality of the Church is the participation of all (through adoptive filial life) in the Son's eternal gift of himself to the Father in the Holy Spirit. We can imagine no more fundamental recognition of the dignity of the estate of a baptized lay person in the Church.

● Y. M.-J. Congar (1953), *Jalons pour une théologie du laïcat*, Paris.

K. Rahner (1955), "Über das Laienapostolat," *Schr. zur Th.* 2, Einsiedeln, 339–73.
Y. M.-J. Congar (1959), "Conscience ecclésiologique en Orient et en Occident du VIe au XIe siècle," *Ist* 6, 187–236.
M. Jourjon (1963), "Les premiers emplois du mot l. dans la littérature patristique," *LV (L)* 65, 37–42.
B. D. Dupuy (1967), "L," (théologie et droit canon), *Cath* 6, 1627–43.
P. Grelot (1970–1981 [5th ed.]), "Peuple," *VThB*, 979–91.
P. F. Bradshaw (1983), "Modèles de ministères, le rôle des l. dans la liturgie," *MD* 154, 127–50.
G. Chantraine (1987), *Les l., chrétiens dans le monde*, Paris.
E. Poulat (1987), *Liberté, laïcité: La guerre des deux France et le principe de modernité*, Paris.
E. Corecco (1990), *Théologie et droit canon: Écrits pour une nouvelle théorie générale du droit canon*, Fribourg.
A. M. Ritter, et al. (1990), "Laie," *TRE* 20, 378–93.
M. Spinelli (1990), "L," *DECA* 2, 1399–1400.
D. Bourgeois (1991), *L'un et l'autre sacerdoce*, Paris.
G. Chantraine, et al. (1996), *Baptême et ordre: L'un et l'autre sacerdoce, Com(F)* XXI/6, 9–83.
G. Dagron (1996), *Empereur et prêtre: Étude sur le "césaropapisme" byzantin*, Paris.
G. Bedouelle, J.-P. Costa (1998), *Les laïcités à la française*, Paris.

DANIEL BOURGEOIS

See also **Baptism; Cleric; Church; Ministry; Priesthood; Sacrament**

Laying on of Hands

The laying on of hands (or of the hand: the usage is undecided) is a gesture used in several religions. The gesture has many meanings, however, so that its significance must be specified on each occasion by the context.

In the Old Testament the laying on of hands is used (under the name of *semikah*) in sacrifices* (Lv 4), blessings* (Gn 48:13–20), when bestowing a particular function on someone (Nb 27:15–23), or to exclude a troublemaker (Lv 24:14). Most authors acknowledge the existence of a *semikah* for the inauguration of rabbis: Ehrhardt (1954) considers that this usage can only date back to A.D. 70, but Hoffman (1979) disputes Erhardt's view.

As in the Judaism* of his time and in the pagan world, Jesus* laid on his hands in order to heal (Mk 6:5), or to bless children (Mk 10:16). The early church* understood the laying on of hands as a complement to Baptism* (Acts 8:17, 9:17 ff., 19:6; Heb 6:2), as a means of designating someone to a function (Acts 6:6, 13:1 ff.), as an ordination* rite (1 Tm 4:14, 5:22; 2 Tm 1:6), and as a gesture of healing* (Acts 9:12).

The laying on of hands was widely used in the early church. The *Apostolical Tradition* (Rome*, v. 215) saw it as a rite of exorcism* used during the catechumenate (no. 20; *see* 19), as a gesture for invoking the Spirit (epiclesis gesture), to be performed by the bishop* after the water rite of baptism (no. 21). The ordination of bishops, presbyters*, and deacons* also required the laying on of hands (nos. 2, 7, and 8). This last passage specifies: "During the ordination of the deacon, only the bishop lays on his hands, because the deacon is not ordained to the priesthood*, but to the service of the bishop"; and regarding the widow: "There will not be a laying of hands, because she does not offer the oblation and does not have liturgical service *(leitourgia)*" (no. 10). The presbyters and the bishop also perform a laying on of hands during the eucharistic prayer (no. 4).

Cyprian* also mentions that the Roman Church performed the laying on of hands to reconcile heretics (*Ep.* 74:2, 2–3; *see* baptism*).

These practices were taken into the future, to the extent that the laying on of hands plays a role today in the rites of all the sacraments*, though with various meanings (exorcism, healing, blessing). It most often has a pneumatological and ecclesiological value (Confirmation*, eucharistic epiclesis, ordination).

The laying on of hands is used by other Christian churches. Orthodoxy distinguishes between chirotony (laying on of hands for major functions) and chirothesy (for secondary functions).

● J. Coppens (1925), *L'imposition des mains et les rites connexes dans le NT et dans l'Église ancienne,* Wetteren-Paris.
A. Ehrhardt (1954), "Jewish and Christian Ordination," *JEH* 5, 125–38.
J. Coppens (1979), "L'imposition des mains dans les Actes des Apôtres," in J. Kremer (Ed.), *Les Actes des Apôtres: Traditions, rédaction, théologie,* BEThL 48, 405–38.
L. Hoffman (1979), "L'ordination juive à la veille du christianisme," *MD* 138, 7–47.

PAUL DE CLERCK

See also **Liturgy; Sacrament**

Legend. *See* Myth

Legitimate Defense

The question whether it is morally justified to kill in order to defend oneself is an important moral question in itself, and the answer that one gives is key in the ethics* of war*. Does justice alone warrant death, or does legitimate defense constitute a right that fundamentally justifies war? Christian notions of legitimate defense have shifted between Christianity's origins and the modern era.

The response of the Fathers* is typified by Tertullian*, following texts such as Matthew 5:39 and 26:52. He thought that Christians ought rather to be killed than kill, and that when harmed they should not seek revenge, even by means of a tribunal. No cause in the world, not even the protection of one's own life, could justify being tainted with the sin of killing.

Ambrose* and Augustine* agreed with this point, but differed from Tertullian about war. Ambrose did not think it legitimate for a wise man to save his life from a shipwreck at the expense of an ignorant sailor; analogously, it is no more legitimate to save one's life at the expense of an assailant's life *(De officiis)*. For Ambrose and for Augustine, who agreed with him on this point, the necessity of self-defense did not justify murder. Augustine wrote that he could not accept that people could be condemned to death to prevent them from killing others, unless the executioner were a soldier or a civil servant legally appointed to do so and not acting on his own behalf, but on the behalf of others (*Ep.* 47).

Tradition changed with Thomas* Aquinas, who found it legitimate to use force against an unjust assailant in order to save one's life (*ST* IIa IIae, q. 64, a. 7). Debating the issue led him to the doctrine of "double effect" or "twofold intention." Luther* would say on the other hand that "no Christian shall wield or invoke the sword for himself and his cause" (*WA* 11, 267). Maintaining order and waging war were matters for public authority* alone.

The Counter-Reformation refined and systemized Aquinas's authorization. Vitoria (c. 1485–1546), along with many others, considered legitimate defense as a kind of private war *(bellum privatum)* and referred to discussions by the Scholastics* on what might justify self-defense in case of an attack (*De iure belli* 1, 2). Some accepted legitimate defense only as an emergency measure, to save one's life, while others extended it to saving one's honor and property. Vitoria thought that an individual could legitimately declare a "private war," but only to defend himself and as the offense occurred. One could not wage a private war to seek revenge or to punish, although these are reasons a state can invoke to declare war, even if defense is its immediate object. Suarez* also thought that only the necessity to defend one's life and property allowed for legitimate defense, but would not extend this right to dueling. The deliberate defense of one's honor, with the possibility of killing one's opponent, is not to be compared with the necessity to defend oneself against an actual act of aggression, and a challenge to a duel is not an aggression (*De bello* diss. XIII, 9, in *De fide, spe et caritate*).

For Grotius (1583–1645), legitimate defense was permissible only when faced with an actual assailant. The danger had to be immediate and certain. The assailant himself might be blameless, as, "for instance, a soldier acting in good faith, or one who mistakes you for someone else," but this did not abrogate the right of legitimate defense. Grotius did not, however, go as far as to allow killing an innocent person who would hinder one's flight to safety. Certainly, "if we look to nature alone," this might be accepted, but the law* of the gospel did not permit the killing of the innocent (II, 1, 3–5).

When the doctrine of human rights replaced the classical tradition of natural law in the 17th century, legitimate defense replaced justice as the fundamental cause for war, as in Samuel von Pufendorf (1632–94) or Emmerich de Vattel (1714–67). All men and all states, according to Vattel, had the absolute right to do what was necessary for their preservation. This notion slowly gained importance and is understood in the teachings of John XXIII on war, which was no longer seen as a means to reestablish justice. Therefore, there could no longer be any war of recovery or punishment, but only defensive wars (*Pacem in terris* 127). Similarly, the United Nations Charter speaks of the inherent right of individual or collective legitimate defense in case of an armed attack (Art. 51). Moral thought thus has now moved away from Ambrose and Augustine's initial direction.

● H. Grotius, *De iure belli ac pacis*, Ed. W. Whewell, Cambridge, 1853.
John XXIII, *Pacem in terris*, AAS 55, 257–304.
M. Luther, *Von weltlicher Obrigkeit*, WA 11, 245–80.
E. de Vattel, *Le droit des gens; ou, Principes de la loi naturelle appliquée à la conduite et aux affaires des nations et des souverains*, London, 1758.
F. de Vitoria, *Relectio de iure belli*, Ed. L.G. Alonso Gatino, Madrid, 1933–36.
♦ G. Fletcher (1996), "Légitime défense," *DEPhM*, 815–18.

DAVID ATTWOOD

See also **Intention; Love; Violence; War**

Leibniz, Gottfried Wilhelm

1646–1716

During a long career as a jurist and counselor to the German princes (in Mainz and then Hanover), Leibniz wrote a great deal and published little. In addition to his administrative duties as a jurist, feudist, and historian, he devoted considerable time to science, especially mathematics, and to philosophical and theological reflection. In an era marked by changes in religion owing to the political adventures of the Germanic states, Leibniz, who was a Lutheran, entertained a lengthy and abundant correspondence with eminent

Catholics, Anglicans, and Calvinists. A German "patriot" above all (he invented the word), he refused any form of conversion* (even to become librarian to the Vatican), but played an active role in both the public and secret discussions regarding the union of the different churches*. The primacy of his religious concerns goes some way toward explaining his initial hostility toward Cartesianism, which he later compared to Spinozism. Nevertheless, it was in the midst of this hostility that he built his own system, renewing, by means of the concept of force, the notion of substance, reintroducing formality in method, responding with harmony to the issue of the union of soul* and body.

Moral responsibility was dependent upon the metaphysical basis of Leibniz's system. Every simple, or monadic, substance possesses an inner force, which is its principle of action; the plurality of what is possible maintains contingency; the finality of the mind makes it capable of deliberately choosing the best. But that does not eliminate individual responsibility: although there are an infinite number of possible worlds, all our personal shortcomings are contained in the world that is called into existence by virtue of its great goodness, and with a view to the highest perfection (*Letter to Arnauld*). God* is to creatures "what the inventor is to his machine," and to the mind "what a prince is to his subjects, or even a father to his children" (*Monadology* §84, 1714). The harmony of the "divine city of the mind" and its happiness are therefore ascertained through "the reign of final causes." Leibniz did not attempt to avoid the "labyrinth" created by the question of the origin of evil*, however, and he suggested that evil was determined by three sources—metaphysical, physical, and moral—in order to make the theses of God's omnipotence* compatible with his goodness and the existence of evil (*Essais de Theodice* and *Causa Dei,* 1710).

Leibniz asserted both the freedom of man, even if man is ignorant of the divine plan, and the confidence that will obtain through one's reasonable certainty of having made the best choice. To existing proofs of the existence* of God (those described as cosmological and ontological) he added his own proof of divine reason*, as an argument against atheists and as the source of possibilities that implicated a will capable of choice: "His understanding is the source of essences, and his will is the origin of existence" (*Theodice* I, §7). God is duty bound to "act in perfection, obeying his supreme reason" (*Discourse on Metaphysics* §3, 1686). Leibniz was a champion of the univocality both of being and of knowledge. Like Malebranche, Leibniz believes that the perfection of the work is achieved through the simplicity of means; but the world, which remains contin-

gent, necessarily refers to a Creator, to whom one returns as "the final reason of things" through the principle of sufficient reason. Leibniz was the first to formulate this idea in his *catholic demonstrations* (1668–9). It takes on a twofold canonical form: Nothing ever happens without a reason 1) for which this thing exists; 2) for which it exists in this way rather than in any other (*Theodice* I, §44).

However, it is difficult to determine to what degree, for Leibniz, God himself is subject to the principle that allows us to have access to him, in the way that Descartes*'s God was subjected *to a degree* to the principle of causality in the form of the *causa sui.* The rational and reasonable unity of Leibniz's thought emphasized the urgent nature of a meeting among the churches, something that had already been suggested for geopolitical reasons in Europe in the face of the Ottoman advance. Following in the path of Georg Calixt and the masters of the University of Helmstadt, and as a resident of a Catholic milieu, be it in Frankfurt or Mainz, in Paris or at court in Hanover, Leibniz encouraged exchanges in the form of meetings and correspondence: with Bossuet; with Nicholas Sténon, a Danish Protestant and anatomical scholar who had converted to Catholicism, become a priest*, bishop* and head of a mission* in Northern Europe; with Spinola, the bishop of Neustadt; with the Calixtine pastor Molanus, who was president of the Hanoverian consistory; and with Burnett, an Anglican. Leibniz's interest in missions, to China in particular, came from the same source (Chinese rites*); he found among the Jesuits and the monastic models similarities with his own academic and religious projects. The union of churches was, in fact, not only a matter of circumstances; for Leibniz, it represented the precise application of his system, narrowed down to three main issues: 1) grace*, for there is a preestablished harmony between the realm of nature and the moral realm of grace; 2) pure love*—an issue where Leibniz's definition and the use of classical distinctions (pleasure/interest, concupiscence/kindness/cupidity) were not favorable to Fénelon ("It is not possible to have a love of God above all things, separate from our own interest, since the pleasure which we find in the contemplation* of his perfection is essential to love" Leibniz wrote in his *Letter to Princess Sophia*); 3) the Eucharist*, for which he suggested in the 1670s a rational explanation, that of transubstantiation. As the extension is not primitive, the essence of the body consists of strength. It is not, therefore, unthinkable for a corporeal substance (the body of Christ*) to act in several places at once. Real presence, therefore, is a presence of force or virtue, at a distance, and transubstantiation amounts to a "real multi-presence" (*Letter to Arnauld,*

1671). It is the supernatural operation through which the bread and wine are converted into elements of the corporeal substance of Christ.

In his correspondence with the Jesuit Des Bosses, 30 years later, Leibniz would expound his theory of the "substantial link" to complete and complicate this first explanation, promoting the idea of the unity of the body without reducing the organism to the phenomenality of the *unum per accidens*. In transubstantiation, according to this new theory, God uses a supernatural application of a new substantial connection (that of the body of Christ) to the accidents of bread. Leibniz's death brought an end to the correspondence and left the complex hypothesis of the substantial link unresolved. It was the last great attempt to provide a physical explanation of the Eucharist. It provided Blondel* with the subject for an important thesis.

Leibniz's theories on human freedom, divine rationality, and the unity of substance allowed him to hope for a consensus on these debated issues. His system, or successive systems, have an ecumenical virtue. In the face of failure and incomprehension, Leibniz appealed to a universal Christianity: he offered to assemble—beyond the churches, which would retain their particular confessions of faith*—an elite body, an "order of charity" that would implement on a practical level the unification of Christians separated by dogma.

● *Leibniz-Bibliographie,* pub. K. Müller and supplemented by A. Heinekamp, et al., I: *Die Literatur über Leibniz bis 1980,* 1967 (2nd Ed., 1984); II: *1980–1990,* 1996, Frankfurt.

Sämtliche Schriften und Briefe, 31 vols., Darmstadt-Berlin, 1923.
C.J. Gerhardt (Ed.) (1879), *Die philosophischen Schriften,* 7 vols., Berlin (New Ed., Hildesheim-New York, 1978).
P. Schrecker (Ed.) (1934), *Lettres et fragments inédits sur les problèmes philosophiques, théologiques, politiques de la réconciliation des doctrines protestantes (1669–1704),* Paris.
G. Grua (Ed.), (1943), *Textes inédits,* Paris (2nd Ed. 1999).
Y. Belaval (Ed.) (1961), *La profession de foi du philosophe,* Paris.
C. Fremont (Ed.) (1981), *Lettres au P. des Bosses,* Paris.
C. Fremont (Ed.) (1987), *Discours sur la théologie naturelle des Chinois,* Paris.
M. Fichant (Ed.) (1991), *De l'horizon de la doctrine humaine: La restitution universelle,* Paris.
◆ M. Blondel (1893), *De vinculo substantiali et de substantia composita apud Leibnitium,* Paris.
J. Baruzi (1907), *L. et l'organisation religieuse de la terre,* Paris; (1909), *L.* (with many unpublished texts), Paris.
A. Boehm (1926), "L.," *DThC* 9, 173–95.
J. Baruzi (1927), "Le problème du salut dans la pensée religieuse de L.," repr. in *L'intelligence mystique,* Paris, 1985.
G. Grua (1953), *Jurisprudence universelle et théodicée selon L.,* Paris.
G. Preti (1953), *Il cristianesimo universale di G. G. Leibniz,* Milan-Rome.
E. Naert (1959), *L. et la querelle du pur amour,* Paris.
J. Jalabert (1960), *Le Dieu de L.,* Paris.
V. Mathieu (1960), *L. e des Bosses (1706–1716),* Turin.
Y. Belaval (1962), *L.: Initiation à sa philosophie,* Paris.
J. Le Brun (1976), "L.," *DSp* 9, 548–57.
E. Holze (1991), *Gott als Grund der Welt im Denken des Gottfried Wilhelm L.,* Stuttgart.

JEAN-ROBERT ARMOGATHE

See also **Descartes, René; Ecumenism; Eucharist; Lutheranism; Quietism; Rites, Chinese**

Leo the Great. *See* **Chalcedon, Council of**

Levinas, Emmanuel. *See* **Infinite**

Lex Orandi. *See* **Liturgy**

Liberalism

The terms *liberal* and *liberalism* commonly denote various currents of thought—political, economic, religious, and theological—that appeared at the time of the Reformation and solidified between the Enlightenment and the 19th century. They have in common an appeal to the concept of liberty*, but have never formed a homogeneous whole. In the history of theology, moreover, Protestant liberalism and Catholic liberalism represent two similar but distinct forms of a debate between Christianity and modernity, or between Christianity and the Enlightenment, in which liberty and authority* still to some extent maintain a relationship of fundamental antagonism.

a) Liberty and Liberties. Modern philosophy* did not invent the concept of liberty, but it did put it in the context of new structures of meaning. In its modern sense, the self asserts itself in the work of Descartes* by bracketing the authority of the philosophical tradition. Luther* affirmed the liberty of the Christian by curbing the pretensions of the Catholic Church's magisterium*. In Luther's century, scientific reason was also affirmed by Bacon, who did so by staking the authority of the real against that of the traditional discourses. Likewise during the same century, texts and testimonies—religious texts included—were subjected to the critical attention of philologists and historians (Christian humanism*, the appearance of a critical history* of the church* in the work of Valla, then Baronius, etc.). This period also witnessed the rebirth of the classical Greek ideal of the liberty of the citizen; and following the English political philosophers of the 17th century, absolute political power no longer appeared reasonable.

The ideas, as well as the ideals, of the Enlightenment hardly did more than radicalize (and popularize) the principles of a direction that had already been taken. Liberty of conscience, religious freedom, the hope of a rational reshaping of social and political ties—most of these themes were already in place. Nonetheless, an acute awareness of belonging to a new age was the source of the 18th century's intellectual unity: the consciousness of representing a humanity that had reached adulthood and finally dared to know (*see* the manifesto published by Kant* in 1784, *Was ist Aufklärung?* Weischedel IX, 53–61), and self-consciousness as the consciousness of a break and "progress."

Committed to the ideal of liberty and to various attainments of the French Revolution—the legacy of the Enlightenment—Catholics such as Chateaubriand set themselves up during the Restoration as defenders of freedom of the press and of opinion. When liberal revolutions* broke out all across Europe in 1830, Lamennais and his followers Lacordaire and Montalembert founded the newspaper *L'Avenir,* whose program called for six freedoms: 1) freedom of conscience or religion (and therefore a separation between church* and state); 2) freedom of teaching; 3) freedom of the press; 4) freedom of association; 5) freedom of suffrage (the extension of the electoral principle); 6) freedom of local administration (in the face of revolutionary and imperial centralization). This liberal Catholic school of thought enthusiastically advocated the freedom of nations (the Belgians, the Polish, the Irish). "Liberty as in Belgium"—a new state that enjoyed liberal institutions—became a watchword, and Pope Gregory XVI caused outrage when he urged the Poles who had revolted to submit to the czar.

b) Catholicism and Revolution. It is a remarkable peculiarity of Catholicism that its acceptance of the Enlightenment, or its refusal to accept it, has always been linked to an interpretation of the French Revolution. So liberal Catholicism initially found expression in a moderate interpretation of the Revolution, which distinguished the Constituent Assembly and its achievements (1789) from the Convention and the Terror (1793) (e.g., in the work of H. Maret and F. Ozanam), in the same way as conservative Catholicism (Maistre, Bonald) initially took the form of explicitly counterrevolutionary theories in terms of which the fall of the ancien régime was a theological event and the plain product of the forces of evil. Counterrevolutionary Catholicism was impelled by its own logic to develop traditionalist theological epistemologies (the heterodox parts of which would be determined by the church's magisterium). The logic of liberal Catholicism, on the other hand, led it to more limited theorizing: the search for a theological method that would link history and the "philosophy" of dogma* ("The dignity of human reason and the necessity of divine revelation," Maret, 1856), the defense of Christian democracy (Maret and Ozanam's *L'Ère nouvelle,* 1848), and the defense of the separation of church and state ("The free church in the free state"—Montalembert's speech at Malines, 1863).

The real theological problem was of course that of preaching the gospel* in a changed society* and a new culture. While in the *Aufklärung* (Enlightenment) these changes initially (though not exclusively) took the form of a critique of Christianity by non-Christians or sinful Christians, liberal Catholicism took as its main aim the critique of Christianity (or its traditions* and institutions) by Christianity itself (or its evangelical message). A theology renewed through contact with the dominant philosophies of the time (the School of Tübingen*); concern with identifying the *particula veri* of the objections raised against Christianity (e.g., Monsignor d'Hulst's stance concerning Renan); and concern with ensuring that the theologian's theoretical work enjoyed sufficient independence within the church—all this does not add up to a "liberal" school in 19th-century Catholicism, but the distinctive signs of a trend are certainly there.

c) Protestantism and Modernity. The French Revolution has never been the object of fear and censure on the Protestant side, and the history of "liberal" Protestantism is one of continuity—the continuity of successive currents, each bringing a plan for the modernization or "revision" of Christian theology. Liberal Protestantism takes it place in this sequence of ideas after physico-theology, neology, and rationalism*, and also after Kant and Schleiermacher*. Moreover, it arose in its pure form after the left-wing Hegelians (D. F. Strauss's *Life of Jesus,* Feuerbach, etc.) or the "free" theologians (A. I. Biedermann, E. Zeller, F. Overbeck, etc.) had shown how far the criticism of Christianity could go—that is, to the point of

anthropological reduction, or of a demythologization that allowed none of the affirmations of faith to survive. In the face of this impoverishment, liberal Protestantism aimed to be Christian while being supremely scientific. However, when Harnack gave liberal Protestantism its catechism (his lectures on *The Essence of Christ*) he illustrated perfectly how the movement of which he was the last and most glorious representative came to redefine Christianity: its distinctive characteristic ceased to be faith* *in* Christ* and became the faith *of* Christ, which reveals God as the Father*; and under the influence of numerous criticisms of the development of Christian dogma, the traditional affirmations of the Christian faith came to seem (even to Harnack) to be no more than "products of the Greek spirit in the soil of the gospel." With its refusal of "Hellenized" forms of Christ, its refusal of "metaphysics" due to the moral implications of the Christian faith (A. Ritschl) and to the "dogmatic* method" in theology (E. Troeltsch), and its refusal even of the Jewish origins of Christ (Harnack again, *Marcion: Das Evangelium vom fremden Gott* [repr. Darmstadt, 1996]), liberal (or "cultural") Protestantism was full of good intentions for bringing about an *aggiornamento* (updating) of Christian discourse that would make it audible and credible in the context of a new culture. Rather than enabling a new access to the "essential," however, the path that it took was one that reduced Christianity to a form of bourgeois humanism.

d) Refusals and Condemnations. Within Catholicism the history of liberal tendencies, from the end of the Napoleonic Wars until the middle of the 20th century, is in part one of failure. In 1832 Gregory XVI (in his encyclical *Mirari Vos*) condemned Lamennais's liberalism, in particular the idea of freedom of conscience, which the pope saw as a "madness" deriving from indifferentism and extending to the freedom of the press. In Pius IX's *Syllabus* (1864)—a compendium of "modern errors"—liberalism, when not targeted specifically, is targeted indirectly "in all its forms: rationalism, or the human intellect's tendency to free itself from the authority of revelation* and the doctrinal magisterium; moral and religious indifferentism, or the tendency to reject moral norms and the demands of truth* in the name of the rights of the individual; laicism, or the rejection of the church's influence on the life of societies; and Gallicanism*, which was increasingly seen in Rome* as encompassing a tendency to conceive church organization after the model of parliamentary governments and to reduce the pope*'s divine authority in favor of subordinate powers" (Aubert 1963). Prior to this, the repudiation of the conference of Catholic scholars who met under Döllinger in Munich (1863) had censured the theologians' demand for freedom from the magisterium in matters of research. Finally, Montalembert was reprimanded for maintaining in his speech at Malines (1863) that the extension of civil and political liberties was conducive to the freedom of the church.

Moreover, the same period saw the establishment of the theological and philosophical project of Neoscholasticism. With its manifesto provided by J. Kleutgen *(Die Theologie der Vorzeit vertheidigt, Die Philosophie der Vorzeit vertheidigt),* under the papacy of Leo XIII it became an official project of the church. Despite this setback, theological liberalism came back in force only to be condemned still more forcefully: this time, however, it bore the name of modernism*. (With all the irony of history, the modernist crisis exploded with the publication of Loisy's "little book," *L'Évangile et l'Église,* conceived by its author as a refutation of the ideas advanced by Harnack in *The Essence of Christ.*)

Within Protestant theology, Barth*'s commentary on the *Epistle to the Romans* aimed to sound the death knell of liberalism, in the name of everything the latter rejected, which was indisputably a great deal (the eschatological meaning of the Christian experience*, the church's responsibility for theological work, fidelity to confessions of faith, etc.); a celebrated exchange of letters between Barth and Harnack (in Barth, *Fragen und Antworten, Gesammelte Vorträge* 3, 1957) summarizes the theoretical disagreements with the utmost clarity and concision. To the idea of a Christianity comfortably rooted in the culture of its time, "dialectical" theology opposed that of a humanity perpetually plunged into crisis—along with its time, its culture, and its religious sense—by God's Word*. To a theology that Barth regarded as entirely derived from Schleiermacher, and in which God* was always in danger of being the variable while the religious man, the moral man, and the scientific man were the constants, it opposed the absolute primacy of a God whose "unavailability" Bultmann emphasized, borrowing a term from Heidegger*. (Moreover, in the face of a liberal Protestantism that was politically and economically short-sighted, dialectical theology offered sustained attention to sociopolitical questions and exhibited a pronounced sympathy with the social Christianity exemplified before Barth, in Switzerland, by H. Kutter and L. Ragaz.)

e) Rehabilitations. The history of theological liberalism did not end with the modernist crisis, nor with the bracing violence of the dialectical theologians. 1) Recalled by Barth (whose masterpiece was a work of "Church" dogmatics, *Kirchliche Dogmatik*) to the demands of ecclesiasticism, Protestant theology clearly could not however cut itself off from the demands of academia's scientific standards, the criticism of sources, and so forth—the strongest contemporary defense of the scientific nature of theology was, after all, the work of one of Barth's students, T. F. Torrance. For all Bultmann's continuing fidelity to the intuitions that guided the founders of dialectical theology, the same Bultmann was also the originator of a program—of "demythologization"—that one of his followers, F. Buri, could take with little addition as the basis for a "liberal neo-Protestantism." 2) Doubtless because liberalism had never assumed a violent form within it, contemporary Catholicism was able to break with a policy of blanket condemnation and do justice to the profoundly truthful aspects of the liberals' demands. Pius IX and even Leo XIII defended the freedom of conscien*ces* against totalitarianism—as distinct from the freedom of conscience, which they saw as making undue claims for the creature in relation to the Creator. In the political field the "coming together" that Leo demanded of French Catholics sanctioned the existence of forms of government derived from the Revolution, and Catholicism was ultimately able to accommodate many models of separation between church and state. In the economic sphere, the "social doctrine of the church" established under the influence of the encyclical *Rerum Novarum* (Leo XIII, 1891) enabled progressively more varied and less naïve stances to be adopted. In the field of biblical exegesis* a belated but effective liberation of critical work (in the encyclical *Divino Afflante Spiritu,* 1943) simultaneously brought a healthier atmosphere to theological circles and produced brilliant intellectual results. Despite the persecutions that followed the modernist crisis and continued until just after the Second World War, innovative thinkers who took no part in the Neoscholastic revival, from Newman* to Lubac and Congar by way of the young Blondel*, were attended to and frequently thanked. Finally, the Second Vatican* Council, in its texts and often in its decisions, had the distinction of putting an end to the Catholic fear of modernity and of designating as a perpetually urgent task an *aggiornamento* of ecclesiastical concepts and practices, something that had previously been regarded as a perverse temptation.

Some problems remain, while additional ones have emerged. There are voices in theology, particularly from the United States, that object that liberalism is the child of a situation that has passed: if we are now in the age of postmodernism* (J.-F. Lyotard, et al.), then theology should be striving toward a "postliberalism" (G. Lindbeck, et al.). The Hegelian criticism of the Enlightenment (that it presented only an impoverished aspect of thought, "understanding," *Verstand,* and that it lacked true "reason*," *Vernunft*) is more in evidence today than formerly. While the opposition between liberty and authority seems more and more to have been founded on misunderstanding with regard as much to the essence of liberty as to that of authority, tensions still remain to which no precise and satisfactory theological answer has been found. In Catholicism and Protestantism alike there is lacking a detailed theology of the Church's teaching; and in Catholicism the freedoms conceded to biblical scholars appear sometimes not to be extended to the exegetes of the magisterium's texts. In any event, one thing is clear: theology must go beyond liberalism and the Enlightenment, but it must also go as far as them.

● H. Stephan (1911), *Die heutigen Auffassungen von Neuprotestantismus,* Giessen.
R. Aubert (1963), *Le pontificat de Pie IX,* in A. Fliche, V. Martin (Ed.), *Histoire de l'Église depuis les origines jusqu'à nos jours,* New Ed., Paris.
M. Prelot, F. Gallouedec Genuys (1969), *Le libéralisme catholique,* Paris.
Coll. (1974), *Les catholiques libéraux au XIXe siècle,* foreword by J. Gadille, Grenoble.
G. Mathon (1975), "Libéralisme," *Cath* 7, 548–63 (bibl.).
M. Prelot (1975), "Libéralisme catholique," *Cath* 7, 563–77.
B. Reardon (1975), *Liberalism and Tradition,* Cambridge.
C. Bressolette (1978), *L'abbé Maret, le combat d'un théologien pour une démocratie chrétienne, 1830–1851,* Paris.
J. J. Sheehan (1978), *German Liberalism in the 19th Century,* Chicago (2nd Ed., Atlantic Highlands, N.J., 1995).
U. Dierse, et al. (1980), "Liberalismus," *HWPh* 5, 256–72.
R. S. Michaelsen, W. C. Roof (Ed.) (1986), *Liberal Protestantism: Realities and Possibilities,* New York.
J. Schmidt (Ed.) (1989), *Aufklärung und Gegenaufklärung in der europäischen Literatur, Philosophie und Politik von der Antike bis zur Gegenwart,* Darmstadt.
D. Langewiesche, H. Vorländer (1991), "Liberalismus," *TRE* 21, 78–83.
H. M. Müller (Ed.) (1992), *Kulturprotestantismus: Beiträge zu einer Gestalt des modernen Christentums,* Gütersloh.
W. Behr (1995), *Politischer Liberalismus und christliches Christentum.*
J.-Y. Guiomar (1996), "Romantisme politique," *DPhP,* 583–88.
M. Lilla (1996), "Anti-Lumières," *DPhP,* 16–19.
P. Raynaud (1996), "Libéralisme," *DPhP,* 338–44.
P. Colin (1997), *L'audace et le soupçon: La crise du modernisme dans le catholicisme français,* Paris.

CLAUDE BRESSOLETTE AND JEAN-YVES LACOSTE

See also **Gallicanism; Modernism; Rationalism; Ultramontanism**

Liberation Theology

a) Origins. Liberation theology arose in Latin America in the years immediately following Vatican* II. The council (and some texts that followed it, such as Paul VI's letter *Octogesima adveniens* of 14 May 1971 to Cardinal Roy) had accorded social and political change a greater meaning than official Catholic theology generally gave them, and had insisted upon the social dimension of salvation* (Sigmund 1990; earlier, Lubac*'s *Catholicisme* of 1938). At this time, moreover, the bourgeoisie and intelligentsia of Latin America had lost confidence in the concepts of "development" and "progress" on the European or North American model, which had led to the adoption of the market economy and liberal democracy* (and sometimes even of Protestantism*, Sigmund 1990). The conference of Latin American bishops met at Medellin in 1968 and adopted several elements of what was to become liberation theology—the most important being the idea of the church*'s "preferential option" for the poor. Finally, the political* theology inspired by J. B. Metz had considerable influence, as did discussions in Latin America on European (and North American) theology (*see* Hoffmann, *Glaubensbegründung,* FTS 36, 1988).

b) Concept of Liberation. In the sense in which it became common parlance, following a book by Gutierrez (1971) that was its first structured manifesto, *liberation* has a fourfold meaning. 1) The term alludes first of all to the Exodus, in other words, the idea of a salvation achieved within history, whose content may be expressed in terms of the disappearance of social evils and the construction of a just society* here on earth (Miranda 1974, Assmann 1976). Liberation theologians have taken great pains to prove that Jesus*' preaching* did not abandon this Old Testament theme in favor of a "faith*" whose "inwardness" might obscure social and political needs. 2) It assumes a theory of secularization*, borrowed in part from European and North American thinkers (F. Gogarten, H. Cox), that defines it as liberation, itself defined as the negation of all alienation. 3) Next, it assumes that this process of liberation will be multiplied by the destruction of capitalist society and the appearance of a classless—in other words, just—society. 4) Finally, it assumes an idea that derives from Rahner* (e.g., "Theologie der Freiheit," *Schr. zur Th.* 6, 215–37): in every person there exists, as a sign of his or her receptiveness to God*, an a priori tendency to free the self from all natural or societal constraints.

c) Relationship with Marxism. No liberation theologian is Marxist in the strict or orthodox sense of the word, and most owe to L. Althusser an (inexact) interpretation of Marx (*see* Marx* 4) that enables them to dissociate the supposedly "scientific" aspects of Marxism from its supposedly purely "metaphysical" aspects. At any rate, all are indebted to Marxism (and to Hegel* by way of Marx) for a dialectical vision of history in which no progress is conceivable without struggle (Segundo 1973–74; there are parallels in Dussel's liberation *philosophy,* 1985). They maintain, moreover, that it is possible to take the side of the oppressed, violently if need be, without compromising the Church's mission, insofar as the oppressors behave in a clearly "idolatrous" way. Finally, they take a central theme from Marxism: that of the "priority of praxis," making theology into either a reflection of Christian praxis or a Christian commentary on a theoretical consideration of political praxis (Gutierrez, Segundo; philosophical groundwork in C. Boff 1987).

The views of liberation theology on the question of revolutionary violence* are not unanimous. Most authors refuse to identify the peaceful revolution* preached by Jesus with the revolution demanded by Marxism. The latter is held to be justified in some cases, and the traditional theory of the just war* is often invoked to justify it. Sometimes, too, Jesus' opposition to violence is played down, on the basis that the historical conditions of proletarian revolution did not yet exist in his time (Segundo).

Once Marxism and socialist revolution ceased to be the paramount subjects of debate in Latin America, in particular after the failure of Nicaragua's experiment, in which liberation theology had been heavily involved (*see* Berryman 1984), the latter evolved so as to concern itself more with ecclesiological questions—the experience of the "base communities," of course, was not without ecclesiological lessons—and more concrete political, social, and economic programs (Sigmund 1990).

d) Reactions from Rome. During the 1980s liberation theology was several times on the receiving end of criticisms formulated by Pope John Paul II and Cardinal J. Ratzinger (prefect of the Sacred Congregation for the Doctrine of the Faith). It was rebuked for accepting the idea that violence was necessary for the progress of history, for reducing doctrine to the mere expression (historically and culturally limited) of a religious impulse, for transforming the history of the church into a simple by-product of relations of production, for accepting the concept of class struggle and taking sides in that struggle, for identifying the poor in the Bible* with the victims of capitalism, and finally, for making the theologian into an "organic intellectual." A work by L. Boff (1982) crystallized Rome's anxieties and led to his being disciplined. In it the author defended an ecclesiology* of a conciliarist character (conciliarism*) and called for a redefinition of papal supremacy (Sigmund 1990). Boff was reproached above all for offering a political reading of theology (as opposed to a theological reading of politics); for constantly opposing "charisma" and "power"; for seeing the present structure of the church as an obstacle to the proclamation of the gospel; and for applying Marxist categories to the relations between clergy* and laity, accusing the former of appropriating the means of spiritual production and depriving the latter of them. However, John Paul II did not discourage the Latin American bishops, who at Puebla (1979) reiterated and amplified the declarations they had made at Medellin. Then in 1988 the encyclical *Sollicitudo Rei Socialis* offered acceptance to themes originating in liberation theology: while defending the "right to economic initiative," it also defended a "preference for the poor."

Going beyond the use of Marxist theories, it may be noted that liberation theology is first of all astonishingly *modern* in its relativistic approach to the metaphysical, mythical, doctrinal, and mystical dimensions of Christian experience*, and often reveals the influence of liberal Protestantism* upon the Latin American intelligentsia. While liberation theology is frequently criticized for its collectivism and its utopian ideals, it is rarely remarked that it often still lacks a conception of religious and Christian acts which fully integrates their social meanings. The influence of Rahner means that the liberation theology is still somewhat tempted by the belief that the content of revelation* is external to history and indifferent to its concrete manifestations—and thus peculiarly insensitive to historical and dialectical processes that are held to be all powerful in a social order considered a priori as secular. An insufficiently perceptive approach to the links between sociohistorical exteriority and religious interiority explains why it took a long time for liberation theology to concern itself with ecclesiology and a specifically theological doctrine of social realities.

Nonetheless, it should be added that right from its first manifestos, usually misunderstood, liberation theology had the means to avoid the pitfalls into which critics saw it falling by the sheer force of theoretical gravity. So, for example, in the work of Gutierrez, to whom we will give the last word: "The growth of the kingdom is a process that is historically fulfilled *in* liberation, insofar as the latter signifies a better realization of mankind, which is the precondition of a new society. But it goes further than this: because it finds fulfillment in historical events that bring liberation, it exposes their limits and ambiguities, announces its full accomplishment and in effect impels it to total communion. We are not dealing with an identification. Without liberating historical events, there can be no growth of the Kingdom" (1971).

● J. Comblin (1970), *Théologie de la révolution*, Paris.
G. Gutierrez (1971) *Teologia de la Liberacion*, Lima.
J. L. Segundo (1973–74), *Theology for Artisans of a New Humanity*, 5 vols., New York.
J. Comblin (1974), *Théologie de la pratique révolutionnaire*, Paris.

J. P. Miranda (1974), *Marx and the Bible*, New York.
J. L. Segundo (1976), *The Liberation of Theology*, New York.
L. Boff (1978), *Jesus Christ Liberator*, New York; (1982), *Church, Charism and Power*, New York.
E. Dussel (1985), *A Philosophy of Liberation*, New York.
C. Boff (1987), *Theology and Praxis: Epistemological Foundations*, New York.
♦ D. E. Mutchler (1971), *The Church As a Political Factor in Latin America*, New York.
G. Fessard (1973), *La Théologie de la libération*, Paris.
H. Assmann (1976), *Theology for a Nomad Church*, New York.
Internazionale Theologenkommission (1977), *Theologie der Befreiung*, Einsiedeln (contributions by K. Lehmann, H. Schürmann, O. González de Cardedal, and H. U. von Balthasar).
G. Fessard (1978), *Chrétiens marxistes et Théologie de la libération*, Paris-Namur.
P. Berryman (1984), *The Religious Roots of Rebellion*, London.
J. Ratzinger (1984), *Libertatis Nuntius (Instruction sur certains aspects de la Théologie de la libération)*.
John Paul II (1988), *Sollicitudo Rei Socialis, AAS* 80, 513–86.
P. E. Sigmund (1990), *Liberation Theology at the Crossroads? Democracy or Revolution*, Oxford.
G. Collet, et al. (1994), "Befreiungstheologie," *LThK*3 130–7.

JOHN MILBANK

See also **Catholicism; Liberty; Market Economics, Morality of; Marx, Karl; Property**

Liberty

A. Systematic Theology

The Christian concept of liberty was essentially developed through a confrontational relationship with Greco-Roman antiquity, in particular with the ancient concepts of necessity *(anagke)* and destiny *(moira)*. Paul integrated liberty into the Christian message, as the perspective of salvation*.

1. Concepts
In linguistic terms, Greek initially had an adjective *eleutheros*, "free," which referred to a man who did not depend on any master; *eleutheria*, "liberty" in the philosophical sense, was eventually derived from this. The Latin term *libertas* was understood in the same sense, and in Rome* there was certainly never any notion of guaranteeing individual civil rights. The words *free, liberty,* and *liberate* were linked above all to the *polis* (city*) as an urban entity, and to the status of citizen.

Starting with the philosophical usage of the term, we may distinguish a series of concepts of differing content. First, the Greek word *ekon* (related to "autonomous"), referred to individual liberty and signified that a man is not subject to, or bound by, any external power. Second, Socratic liberty consisted in "doing what is best" (Xenophon) and found its most fitting characterization in the principle of autarky *(autarkeia)*, or self-sufficiency. Third, Aristotle understood man as a being capable of making choices, and therefore interpreted liberty as freedom of choice *(proairesis)*, by contrast with the will *(boulesis)*. Fourth, Augustine* distinguished *voluntas*, a fundamental faculty of human beings, from freedom of decision *(liberum arbi-*

trium). Finally, since Kant*, liberty, as a transcendental reality, has been linked with the faculty of acting spontaneously, outside any external determination (causality as liberty, liberty as autonomy).

As for the Christian concept of liberty, it has a double meaning, with reference to "divine liberty" and "human liberty." It is the task of every type of Christian theology* to determine exactly what relationship can bring these two meanings together.

2. Divine Liberty

a) The Bible. No detailed conception of liberty appears in the Bible. The Greek notion of *eleutheria* has no exact equivalent in the Old Testament, yet God's liberating action* is attested throughout its text. Liberty never appears independently of such divine action, and is therefore always to be understood as liberation. Since the departure out of Egypt constitutes the symbolic act of birth for the people of Israel*, the Exodus provides the central reference for the biblical idea of liberty: "I am the Lord your God, who brought you out of the land of Egypt, out of the house of slavery" (Ex 20:2). In Deuteronomy, God's liberating action appears for the first time by contrast with juridical or profane uses of the word (Ex 21:8, 21:30), and within the theological category of redemption (*pdh,* meaning "to set free" or "to liberate": Dt 7:8, 9:26, 13:6, 21:8, 24:18; Mi 6:4): "You shall remember that you were a slave in the land of Egypt, and the Lord your God redeemed you" (Dt 15:15). The decisive factor here is that Israel understands God's intervention as an act of power for which there can be no corresponding human compensation. Finally, the witness of the prophets* connects the salvation of the people, associated with the desired end of the exile, with the definitive liberation of the last day (Is 35:10 and 51:11; Jer 31:11).

Liberty also appears as God's liberating action in the New Testament. The coming of the kingdom*, in the life, death, and Resurrection* of Jesus*, may be interpreted entirely as a free decree and free gift from God. In Jesus Christ, God reveals the plan of universal salvation by which, through his unfathomable, free, and gracious will, he has destined human beings to enter into communion* with him (Eph 1:3–14). In this regard, the family of words *eleutheros, eleutheroo, eleutheria* are used in the New Testament to express no more than a part of the history* of God's liberating action toward humanity. Thus, we see in Paul's writings the development of an outline of a theology of liberty in which liberty appears as a gift from Christ* (Gal 5:1 and 2:4). Liberty is probably not a truly crucial concept in the Pauline corpus, yet it does have a concep-

tual function. Paul's idea of liberty, which he understands as a salvific universal good*, attests to the gratuitous character of salvation, which frees humanity from all powers, including the power of death* (Rom 8:2, 8:19, 8:21). Liberty thus acquires an eschatological dimension.

b) Early Church to Contemporary Theology. In the course of their debate with Greek philosophy* on the subject of liberty, the theologians of the patristic period based their arguments exclusively on the biblical conception. It was first and foremost from a theological perspective that they developed the theme of liberty. Irenaeus* took a decisive step in Christian thought when he established that God alone is absolutely free, that he has "by himself, freely, and on his own initiative, made and ordained all things, and that his will alone is the substance from which he has drawn everything" (*Adv. Haer.* II, 30, 9; *see* IV, 20, 2). In the writings of the Greek theologians, divine liberty is rooted in the omnipotence of God the Creator, who integrates reconciliation and redemption in a unique plan of salvation.

Augustine, by contrast, thought of liberty as the bestowal and power of God's grace*. This was followed in Western theology by speculations on God's will that were to shape conceptions of liberty. Thus, to begin with, Thomas* Aquinas related God's will to his intellect: God's will is his essence, which has total liberty to act effectively (*CG* I, 72; I, 73). Next, nominalism* provided the pure outline of a theory of God's unconditional liberty. Hence, in the writings of William of Ockham and others, while the determination of God's will depends entirely on *potentia absoluta,* a divine power that is limited to ordaining purposes *(potentia ordinata),* its absolute lack of any limitation is an authentic theological and metaphysical mystery.

Luther*, in his debate with late medieval theology and humanism, rediscovered the biblical theme of liberation and placed God's grace at the heart of his salvific action. The idea of liberty was thus entirely absorbed into the overriding theme of justification*. God alone has freedom of decision, which is exclusively "a divine name" (*De servo arbitrio, WA* 18, 636). This idea is expressed still more clearly by Calvin* (*Inst.* III, 19, 1).

Following on from German idealism, in particular as expounded by Hegel* and Schelling*, as well as from the philosophy of Kierkegaard*, it fell to Barth* to give God's liberty a central place in recent Protestant theology. Barth defines "the being of the living and loving God" as "his being in liberty," and thus repositions the question of liberty as an aspect of the definition of the divine essence; as a result, Barth is able to perceive the origin of God's liberty in his grace and love* (*KD* II/1, 340, 394). Eberhard Jüngel drew on Barth for his meditation on God's being in his coming into the world, from a Trinitarian perspective, and on the basis of his self-determination as love. Within Catholicism*, Karl Rahner* has discussed the subject of the essence of the transcendental God as an occasion in a "forgiving self-communication" of God that "must be understood as an act of supreme and personal liberty" (*Grundkurs des Glaubens*). Consequently, it has become possible to expound the classical doctrine of grace in the form of a doctrine of liberty. This approach has also been taken up within liberation* theology, which proposes a radical identification between God's action, in its history alongside humanity, and the abolition of the unjust structures that weigh down upon human communities.

3. Human Liberty

a) The Bible. Human liberty is not explicitly addressed in the Old Testament: humanity is subject to the power of God, who alone can deliver humanity from slavery and captivity. Emphasis is placed on the contrast between slave and free man, with the result that human liberty is hardly ever evoked except in the context of the freeing of slaves (Ex 21:2, 21:5; Lv 19:20, 25:10; Dt. 15:12 f.). It is also primarily in this juridical and social sense that liberty appears in the New Testament (1 Cor 7:21, 12:13; Gal 3:28, 4:22; Eph 6:8; Col 3:11).

Nevertheless, Paul is also capable of interpreting this contrast between slave and free man in a christological and eschatological sense, thus opening up a new and specifically Christian perspective that was to have a profound influence on the concept of liberty: "For he who was called in the Lord as a slave is a freedman of the Lord. Likewise he who was free when called is a slave of Christ" (1 Cor 7:22). Within the Christian community, those contrasts that prevail in the world* are abolished: the slave "called in the Lord enjoys the same rights as the free man. As an eschatological good, the gratuitous gift and bestowal of Jesus Christ (Gal, 5:1, 5:13, 2:4), liberty is universal. For the Christian called by Christ, liberty takes on a concrete form as liberty in relation to sin* and the power of death: "We know that our old self was crucified with him in order that the body of sin might be brought to nothing, so that we would no longer be enslaved to sin. For one who has died has been set free from sin" (Rom 6:6–7). It is, however, the work of Christ alone, and humanity plays no part in it at all: "having been set free from sin, you have become slaves of righteousness" (Rom 6:18). As a human being is freed from the power of sin, so liberty appears ultimately as liberation from the law* ands from any piety based on works* (Rom 7:5 f.). This does not, of course, imply arbitrary judgment or licentiousness, for love is the law of liberty (Rom 13:18; Gal 5:14). Liberated by Christ, Christians receives the Spirit in faith* and thus become free human beings (Gal 3:14), because they accomplish God's will.

b) Early Church. Early Christian thinkers attempted to establish a fitting relationship between divine grace and human liberty by finding a balance between the tradition of Greek philosophy, biblical texts, and the proclamations of the church. Clement of Rome linked human behavior to God's commands, thus making a connection between liberty and the love due to God. According to Irenaeus, human beings can participate in the perfect liberty of God provided that they opt freely for God and for self-integration into the order that he has created (*Adv. Haer.* IV, 34, 2). Clement of Alexandria and Origen* emphasized the free decision (*proairesis*) of human beings, to the point of accentuating the antinomian nature of liberty. Eastern patristics reached its final summit in the thought of Maximus* the Confessor, who associated human liberty, conceived as self-determination, with divine grace in the work of divinization (*theosis*) of humanity. Human beings, whose will tends toward salvation, attempt in their liberty to develop the seed of goodness that they carry within themselves (*Ambigua ad Iohannem* 7; PG 91, 1081–84). Liberty is thus presented as a process of assimilation (*homoiosis*), a realization pf God's image (*eikon*); and the principle of liberty has been inscribed within nature since the creation* (*Amb. Io* 42; PG 91, 1345). It is in their movement of love toward God that human beings are realized as human (*Amb. Io* 45; PG 91, 1353).

c) Late Antiquity and the Middle Ages. The question of the relationship between divine grace and human liberty was explicitly conceptualized for the first time in the dispute between Augustine and Pelagius (Pelagianism*). Augustine, drawing on his experience of an unmediated encounter with God, turned away from the Eastern vision, centered on the history of salvation, and put the emphasis on the primacy of the will (*voluntas*). For Augustine, the will is the fundamental faculty and active principle in the spiritual nature of humanity, and it exerts itself as free will in the act of deciding (*De spiritu et littera* V; *De libero arbitrio* I, 12, 26; II, 19, 51; III, 3, 7). Since, in the final instance, every will is turned toward God, liberty is fulfilled in decisions for or against what is demanded of the will. Consequently, evil* proceeds only from the free will of human beings, and to the extent that the will is consciously turned away from God (*CD* XII, 6). God gives the will its importance by inclining human beings to love him. Human liberty thus finds its fulfillment in the capacity given to the sinner to love God. Liberty is so fundamentally connected with divine grace that human beings appear to be incapable of winning this grace by themselves, and can do no more than receive it (*Retractationes* II, 1).

From Augustine onward, the theme of Christian liberty was always discussed in terms of an unbreakable dialectical relationship with grace. Within early Scholasticism*, Anselm* of Canterbury helped to elaborate a definition of liberty that went beyond Augustine's conception in a fundamental sense: for Anselm, the freedom of the will is defined on the basis of its end, designated by reason* and freely chosen by the will (*De libertate arbitrii* III). Finally, Thomas Aquinas investigated the metaphysical bases of liberty. Because the source of liberty is in God himself, human beings fulfill their liberty by attaching themselves to God; indeed, in each of their actions, liberty is implicitly related to God, and it thus takes on its material form in the concrete decisions of the will (*ST* Ia, q. 83). The voluntarism* that Aquinas thus laid the foundations for was developed later by John Duns* Scotus; William of Ockham reprised his approach without going beyond it.

d) Reformation.
The problem of liberty cropped up in the dispute over what free will is capable of in itself, in the face of the salvation that comes from God. The humanists saw Luther's doctrine of justification as a mortal threat to human liberty. Erasmus* understood free will as "the effective action of the human will that permits human beings either to attach themselves to that which leads them to eternal salvation, or to turn themselves away from it" *(Discourse of Free Will)*. Obscured by sin, yet not extinguished by it, the will is corrupted; but the grace that remits this sin makes the will free once again to open itself up to eternal life*, and sustains it constantly in its effort (ibid.). Luther, replying to Erasmus, declared that, on the contrary, he relied entirely on Christian revelation*. In the confrontation between God and human beings, it is absurd to speak of free will: "for if I can obtain grace through my own effort, what need is there for the grace of Christ?" (*De servo arbitrio, WA* 18, 777). It is certainly not the case that the human will does not exist; but it is so corrupted that it cannot do anything other than "those things that are contrary to the will of God" (*WA* 18, 709). Following Paul, Luther maintains accordingly that human beings are justified only by God's grace, independently of their works.

However, Luther occasionally speaks of human liberty in positive terms. In his view, it is the fruit of the liberation effected by Christ: it therefore arises from faith, and signifies that the Christian enjoys sovereign liberty and is subject to no other person. When faith is combined with charity, human beings discover the liberty of becoming slaves, bound by love to their neighbors: in this sense, Christians are servants zealously subject to all (*Von der Freiheit eines Christenmenschen, WA* 7, 21). Faith in justification gives Christian liberty the capacity of being exercising as spontaneity.

e) Modern Times.
A purely human conception of liberty, intended to be affirmed and delineated in contrast to Christian liberty, has emerged in modern times. This fundamental will to liberty expresses the ethical demand of the era, defined in an exemplary fashion by Kant. The idea of human liberty thus finds appropriate expression in the concept of autonomy: liberty is the capacity to determine oneself as a being endowed with reason. Against the idealist interpretation that Fichte and Hegel developed later, Kant shows that human beings can represent liberty to themselves only as the untraceable origin of their unconditioned self-realization (*Critique of Practical Reason* I, §6). In this sense, the principle of autonomy serves to bring to light a logic of absolute obligation inherent in human liberty, which for Kant also constitutes the foundation of human dignity (*Fundamentals of the Metaphysics of Morals*).

Since contemporary human rights ethics* is organized on this foundation, Christian thought, if it is to be topical, can be asserted only through a fertile dialogue with the modern concept of liberty that has been developed on the basis of such rights. Christian liberty must be capable of being expounded as the promise* contained in God's grace, and that grace as the advent of a meaning that does not annul human liberty, but fulfills it. For Christianity, the dignity of the human person, and therefore the liberty of that person, are grounded in the grace that calls us to supernatural communion with God.

● H. de Lubac (1965), *Le mystère du surnaturel,* Paris (1st Ed., 1946, *Surnaturel: Études historiques,* Paris).
E. Jüngel (1966), *Gottes Sein ist im Werden,* Tübingen (3rd Ed. 1976).
J. Schwartländer (1968), *Der Mensch ist Person: Kants Lehre vom Menschen,* Stuttgart, etc.
D. Nestle (1972), "Freiheit," *RAC* 8, 269–306.
W. Warnach, O.H. Pesch, R. Spaemann (1972), "Freiheit," *HWP* 2, 1064–98.
K. Rahner (1976), *Grundkurs des Glaubens,* Freiburg-Basel-Vienna.
J.J. Stamm (1976), "*Pdh,* auslösen, befreien," *THAT* 2, 389–406.
G. Ebeling (1979), *Dogmatik des christlichen Glaubens,* vol. III, Tübingen.
H. Krings (1980), *System und Freiheit,* Freiburg-Munich.

G. Greshake (1981), *Geschenkte Freiheit,* 2nd Ed., Freiburg-Basel-Vienna.

G. Chantraine (1982), *Érasme et Luther: Libre arbitre et serf-arbitre,* Paris-Namur.

W. Kasper (1982), *Der Gott Jesu Christi,* Mayence.

H.-W. Bartsch, et al. (1983), "Freiheit," *TRE* 11, 497–549.

W. Thönissen (1988), *Das Geschenk der Freiheit,* TTS 30.

G. Bausenhart (1992), *"In allem uns gleich, außer der Sünde": Studien zum Beitrag Maximos' des Bekenners zur altkirchlichen Christologie,* TSTP 5.

K. Niederwimmer (1992), *"Eleutheros,"* EWNT 1, 1052–58.

T. Pröpper (1995), "Freiheit Gottes," *LThK3* 4, 108–13.

F. Ricken, J. Eckert, T. Pröpper (1995), "Freiheit," *LThK3* 4, 95–105.

Wolfgang Thönissen

See also **Anthropology; Grace; Justification; Sin, Original**

B. Moral Theology

a) Christian Liberty. In the New Testament, it is chiefly through the Pauline epistles that the question of liberty is addressed (but note significant occurrences in James and John 8). The term appears in the synoptic Gospels hardly at all. Yet contemporary interpretations of Jesus*' message that relate it especially to expectations of Israel*'s renewal (e.g., E. P. Sanders) warn us against putting too much weight on this terminological divergence. The Old Testament has its own vocabulary for speaking of Israel's liberation, for example, *redemption* or *salvation* (*see* 1 Macc 4:9–11). The kingdom* of God was a social transformation that must loosen the hold of the powers, political, demonic, moral or natural, that held Israel in bondage. Thus, the "sons of the kingdom" are free from taxation (Mt 17:26); a "daughter of Abraham" is "loosed" from her infirmity (Lk 13:12). Political liberty ("salvation from our enemies") was included in the "putting away of sins" for which Israel looked (Lk 1:71 ff.). This gave Christian understandings of liberty psychological as well as political elements. Here, it found a certain affinity with the Stoic paradox that "every good man is free" (Philo), which made liberty into a moral reality, although Christian thought never discounted its social aspect, something Stoics tended to do.

A perennial observation of political philosophy* distinguishes two sorts of liberty: "negative" or "formal" liberty, and "positive" or "material" liberty. The first is the slave's dream of overcoming constraint, the second is the condition for self-realization, the ideal of the aristocrat. The one lacks any goal other than the removal of restraint upon choice; the other requires no act of negation to bring the goal of self-realization within view. Both these ideas have a theological value: the first, because the imprisoned cannot free themselves entirely on their own (*see* Lk 4:18), so that it would be false, from a Christian point of view, to admit no need of deliverance, in the name of positive liberty alone (Jn 8:32–36); and the second, because liberty is not only an escape from constraints but an entrance into a new life (Gal 5:1), a life of liberty that has its own law* (Rom 8:2; Jas 1:25 and 2:12). A purely negative liberty would afford no stability, but would open the way to reenslavement. A paradoxical dialectic thus aligns the liberty of the believer with a "slavery to righteousness" (Rom 6:18). The notion of freedom as untrammeled will (Aristotle, *Pol.* 1317 *b*: "to live as one likes") is rejected for something closer to the Roman republican ideal: "to be a slave of the laws…in order to be capable of being free" (*legum servi…ut liberi esse possimus,* Cicero, *Pro Cluentio* 146). That the service of Christ* is perfect liberty became a patristic commonplace (e.g., Ambrose* of Milan, *De Spiritu sancto* 44, 60). It could claim antecedents in Seneca (*De Beneficiis, Ad Lucilium Epistulae Morales*), as well as in Paul.

Life in liberty is a life available for others, even, paradoxically, "to serve" others (Gal 5:13). It is social, not solitary. Much of the polemic about liberty in Christian history has been concerned, therefore, with the "liberty of the church*" *(libertas ecclesiae),* the self-ordering of the Christian community in sole obedience to its Lord. In the modern period, theological ideas of liberty have clashed with contractarian ideas of a state of nature in which the individual could be considered as free from all social commitments. Rousseau's famous dictum in *The Social Contract* that "man is born free, but everywhere he is in chains" seems to be a direct echo of Ambrose's formula, *ut qui nascimur in libertate moriamur in servitute* ("in order to be born in liberty, we die in slavery," *Ep.* 7, 32), but the sense is opposite. For Ambrose, man was born into a state of liberty, but the Fall has deprived him of it. Yet within the social bonds of the Church, the individual is a free partner, the member of a brotherhood. The sign of individual liberty is baptism*, undertaken singly and voluntarily by each believer, the ambiguities surrounding infant baptism notwithstanding. Without the community, the believer could have no focus for this act of self-determination; without the believer's act, the community would not know itself as a community of liberty. In the Church, distinctions are abolished (Gal 3:28; Jas 2:1 ff.). The natural structures of social order remain in place, however, and this opens the way to the idea of a free obedience, of wife to husband, child to parent, and so on, which is rendered intelligible within the context of mutually serving love (Col 3:18 ff.; Eph 5:21–6:9; 1 Pt 2:12–3:7).

Obedience is key in monastic life (monasticism*), but it is not always free of danger. Losing its dialectical relation to liberty, obedience can be presented as abnegation of personal judgment, since one submits oneself to the judgment and authority of another (*ambulantes alieno judicio et imperio,* Reg. Mag. SC 105–7 7; *see* Reg. Ben. SC 181–86 5). By contrast, the idea of liberty in the Holy* Spirit (2 Cor 3:17) contributed to the formulation of the idea of democracy* in Europe. The Pentecost experience (Acts 2:18), interpreted in the light of Joel's oracle that men and women slaves would prophesy (Jl 2:28 ff.), was one of liberty of utterance for every believer, not confined to any order of ministry. The New Testament term *parrhesia* (Acts and John especially) refers to the liberty of speech born of confidence, especially in the proclamation of the gospel.

b) Slavery. The early Christian attitude to slavery has often been a matter of controversy, not because the facts are in doubt but because the interpretation of them is complicated. Ever since the great debate over the abolition of slavery in the 18th and 19th centuries, there has been a distinct idea of slavery as an institution that could be present in, or absent from, any given society, and that could be challenged on its own terms, apart from other economic or social practices. Such an idea was lacking in early Christianity. The dependence and subjection in which a slave was placed were seen as comparable to other forms of dependence and subjection, such as that of women, children or subjects. All of them reflected what early Christians took to be the core reality of subjection, namely the moral and psychological impotence of sin. Their talk about slavery was more wide ranging than ours and more fluid, passing easily from one manifestation of dependence to another. Their vocabulary lacked a clear distinction between "servitude" and "service," encouraging a tendency to paradox. Where moderns are tempted to accuse early Christians of evading the real point about slavery, they

could be imagined to reply that moderns take formal economic and legal structures too much at their face value, thereby falling into an unhistorical abstractness that is sometimes not free of self-righteousness, given the forms of dependence that persist in the modern social world.

Presented with the propositions that are supposed to have defined ancient slavery, such as that the slave was a property of his master (*Lex Aquila,* 286 B.C.), or that friendship was impossible between slave and free, early Christians never hesitated to deny them categorically (e.g., Gregory* of Nyssa, *In Eccl. Hom.* 4 SC 416). In this, however, they merely associated themselves with positions taken by the Stoics on this subject (Stoicism*, Christian). The Stoic paradox that every good man is free, and every bad man a slave, was intended as more than a psychological truth* metaphorically expressed; it was meant to expose a social reality underlying legal appearances. Common humanity bound slave and free together in equality; to refuse to respect human nature was to fall victim to delusion (Philo, Seneca). Sociolegal slavery was an unreal fiction that had no purchase except on the mind enslaved to passion*. The legal sphere of bodily slavery lay beneath serious philosophical notice.

Christians attached themselves to this approach, adding distinctive arguments. Slave and master alike were servants of Christ, or "freedmen" of Christ. As such, their relation to each other was determined by a higher obligation that each owed independently. It had to be reconceived, therefore, in terms of free mutual service. While the formal roles remained the same, the content was changed. The slave who saw his master as a brother recognized him as one to whom he was bound in trust and love (1 Tm 6:2); the master conscious of his own slave status recognized in his slave one who had a right to his "justice and equity" (Col 4:1). Slavery to Christ excluded slavery to human beings; this conviction could support an ambition on the slave's part for emancipation, but it at least demonstrated that one could heed Christ's call to liberty in any condition of life (1 Cor 7: 20–23). The major difference between Stoic and Christian approaches was that liberty took a concrete form in the church, where social barriers were broken down. Within that context, Paul refused to acknowledge any legal obligation to return the fugitive slave Onesimus to his master, while claiming the authority to require Philemon to renounce the right of punishment that Roman law accorded him (Phlm 4–20).

The assertion that the church knew no distinction between slave and free was maintained in the patristic era (Lactance, *D.I.* 5, 16, SC 204 and 205; Ambrose, *Ev. Luc.* 9, 29, SC 45 and 52). The rite of manumission could be performed with legal effect before a bishop*, at least after Constantine's legislation of 321. Emancipation was praised as an act of mercy*. Yet the integral role of slaves in the agrarian economy made slaveowning inevitable, and in the fourth century churches as well as lay Christians owned slaves. Preachers urged humane treatment, including the protection of the sexual dignity of slaves and the integrity of their marriages*. Access to the monastic life was open to slaves without their masters' permission; the same principle, however, was not maintained in relation to ordination*. There was a deep reluctance to take any step that might result in someone's becoming a slave (Augustine, *Ep.* 24, BAug 46 B); yet it was recognized that there were worse plights into which one suffering from economic calamity or war* might fall. The conception of slavery as being, like all other forms of subjection, a providential discipline of God (providence*) for punishing sin formed the basis for a later denial that slave status could be inherited (Wyclif, *De dominio civili* I, 32–34).

The disappearance of slavery in Europe (effective in most regions by the end of the 12th century) has sometimes been credited to the influence of Christian criticism (e.g., Leo XIII). While Christian attitudes were a significant factor, an essential precondition was the evolution of alternative economic patterns. The re-

appearance of slavery in the colonial context was based on Roman law*, which permitted the enslavement of captives in war, reinforced in some humanist circles by Aristotle's doctrine of "natural slavery" (race*), which theologians denied.

- J. Maritain (1933), *Du régime temporel et de la liberté,* in J. and R. Maritain, OC 5, Paris-Fribourg, 1982.
- C. Verlinden (1955), *L'esclavage dans l'Europe médiévale,* Bruges.
- I. Berlin (1969), *Four Essays on Liberty,* Oxford.
- H. Gülzow (1969), *Christentum und Sklaverei in den ersten drei Jahrhunderten,* Bonn.
- J. Ellul (1973), *Éthique de la liberté,* Geneva.
- C. Taylor (1979), "What's Wrong with Negative Liberty," in A. Ryan (Ed.), *Idea of Freedom: Essays in Honour of Isaiah Berlin,* Oxford, 175–93.
- R. Minnerath (1982), *Le droit de l'Église à la liberté: Du Syllabus à Vatican II,* Paris.
- U. Faust (1983), Christo Servire Libertas Est: *Zum Freiheitsbegriff des Ambrosius von Mailand,* Salzburg-Munich-Pustet.
- J. Raz (1986), *The Morality of Freedom,* Oxford.
- R. Klein (1988), *Die Sklaverei in der Sicht der Bischöfe Ambrosius and Augustinus,* Stuttgart.
- H. Chadwick (1994), "Humanität," *RAC* 16, 663–711.

OLIVER O'DONOVAN

See also **Democracy; Religious Freedom; Society**

Lie. *See* Veracity

Life, Eternal

Belief in eternal life is a key element of the Christian faith*. In the Church*'s oldest documents, the Apostles' Creed ("I believe in...the resurrection of the body, and the life everlasting") and the Creed of Nicaea-Constantinople ("I await the resurrection* of the dead and the life to come"); indeed the expression "eternal life" seems to be associated with "Credo" and "amen," and appears as an epithet for God* himself. Indeed, knowledge* of God and sharing in eternal life nourish one another. From the standpoint of the eschatological realities (purgatory*, hell*, heaven), eternal life corresponds to heaven (or "paradise"). On a biblical as well as a theological level, statements of faith concerning the beatific* vision, the resurrection of the dead and the kingdom* of God demand a consideration of eternal life. This calls into play both the collective and individual dimensions of eschatology*.

1. Biblical Sources of the Theme of Eternal Life

a) Old Testament. In the Old Testament, God is the Living Being above all others and the source of life (Psalms 36, 10). If he withdraws his breath, creatures return to dust (Ps 104:29). Eternal life is thus an exclusive property of God (Dt 32:40; Dn 12:7). While not in direct opposition to time*, eternity* (*'olam*)—which, incidentally, is very rarely attributed to God—denotes a life that encompasses all time, from the furthest past to the most distant future. In the Garden of Eden man could have tasted immortality (the "tree of life" in Gn 2:9), but as a result of his disobedience he was subjected to death*, just like every other earthly creature. The idea of an eternal life following the sleep of death in Sheol* does not appear until late in the Old Testament. For that we have to wait until the "apocalypse" of Isaiah (Is 26:19) and especially Daniel: "Many of those who sleep in the dust will wake, some for eternal life, others for opprobrium, for eternal horror" (Dn 12:2).

b) New Testament. Even though the concept of eternal life may already denote a form of earthly life, the New Testament unquestionably proclaims it as a promise* for the hereafter. In other words, it interprets the mystery* of Christ*, who in his death and Resurrection* abolished the law of sin* and death, as a promise made to all humanity.

1) As for what lies beyond death, Jesus' clearest statements before he "returned to his Father*" are to be found in John's Gospel: "There where I am, you will be also." (Jn 14:3); "Eternal Life, it is for they who know you, you the only true God, and he whom you have sent, Jesus Christ" (Jn 17:3). According to Paul, faith* in Christ implies faith in an eternal life: we should be the most wretched of people if we put our faith in Christ only for the duration of this life (1 Cor 1:9). "For now we see through a glass, darkly, but then face to face" (1 Cor 13:12).

2) However, in many New Testament passages, eternal life is not only the object of a hope* for the hereafter, but is already anticipated for all those who have a share in God's reign. In the Gospels especially, the terms "eternal life" and "God's reign" are practically interchangeable. One enters the kingdom of God as one enters eternal life (*see* Mk 9:43 ff.; Mt 5:20, 19:29, 25:34). John establishes close connections be-tween eternal life and the Word* of life received in faith (3:15, 3:36), the Eucharist* (6:54), and brotherly love*: "We know that we have passed death in life, since we love our brothers" (1 Jn 3:14).

3) The New Testament concept of eternal life belongs essentially to a doctrine of salvation*. Because humanity is under the yoke of sin, there is no continuity between earthly life and eternal life. Paul interprets the existence of a human being saved by grace* and glorified (Rom 5:8, 5:21, 6:22) as a new creation*. By faith, the believer already shares in the life of the risen Christ, even if it is not yet clear what he really is. By way of baptism*, the believer's life is a death and a burial with Christ (Rom 6:3f; Gal 2:20; 2 Cor 6:9), as well as a complete participation in the life of the risen Christ: " I live but it is no longer me, it is Christ who lives in me" (Gal 2:20). This new life, which is a promise of eternity, remains nonetheless "Hidden in God with Christ" (Col 3:4).

4) Finally, the New Testament uses a variety of images to illustrate the hope of a joyful eternity. The image of heaven itself is the first, and as in the Old Testament denotes "the abode of God." The concrete images of the meal and the wedding feast (Lk 22:29 f.) deserve particular emphasis. In the New Testament the basic elements of human existence, bread (John 6), water (John 3) and wine (John 2), take on an anticipatory symbolic value. Eternal life is described in the Apocalypse as a celestial liturgy* in which the elect will take part in the eternal wedding of the Lamb* (19:6) in a new heaven and a new earth (19:6 ff.).

2. Historical Landmarks

Belief in eternal life has been unceasingly taught by the Fathers* and the church's dogmatic* tradition. And, since the latter cannot proclaim eternal life without using whatever cosmological images are current at the time, the progression which led "from the closed world to an infinite universe" (A. Koyré) is also reflected in the history of theological doctrines.

The Fathers and the doctors of the Middle Ages, who in their theory of final destinies employed a cosmology hardly different from that of the Bible*, acknowledged (as an inadequate creed and with constant reference to Augustine*'s formula *Ipse Deus post hanc vitam sit locus noster,* "It is God who will be our place after this life") the existence of "places" surrounding the world. Eternal life was thus associated with a "place," heaven, located above the sky, by contrast with hell, which was situated beneath the earth, and purgatory, which was considered as an intermediary. When man, who is composed of a soul* and a body whose union was the work of the Holy* Spirit, died, his soul was supposed to separate from his body. While the latter decayed in the earth, waiting to be brought back to life by the soul on the last day, the soul appeared before God. If the soul had believed and acted according to the principle of charity during this life, it entered heaven immediately to enjoy eternal beatitude*, which was the Love that repaid love. If it had not believed in this sharing to come, and had gone astray, it was cast into hell, there to undergo eternal punishment. At the end of time, when Christ returned and the world came to an end, the general resurrection would ensue and souls finally reunited with their own bodies would be able to love God without hesitation or anxiety, just as they were loved by him.

Having discovered the infinite nature of the universe and the difficulties that follow from it, the modern period has ceased to assign a location to the hereafter, even symbolically, since it can no longer recognize the existence of "places" beyond the world. Because of its biblical origin the vocabulary of places continues to be used, but the images of a "heaven" beyond the firmament and a "hell" have tended to disappear in favor of states or modes of being. So recent theologies* of the "history of salvation" (particularly in the work of Protestant thinkers such as O. Cullmann) define the hereafter in chronological terms. Three successive stages are distinguished, corresponding to earthly life, the sleep of death, and the resurrection:

1) From birth to death, the eternal life promised in Christ's Resurrection has already begun, but has not yet triumphed over death.

2) After death a second period begins: the believer has escaped the mortal state but is not yet alive with the definitive life of the kingdom; since immortality is not a property of human nature, the just await Christ's return, living with him in a kind of sleep (like the just of the Old Testament in Sheol or the "bosom of Abraham").

3) The third period corresponds, finally, to the coming of God's kingdom, where God will be "all in all." It coincides with the resurrection of the dead for an eternal life of blessed communion* with God.

Contemporary theology also has an existential current, which in eschatological terms tends to remove the hereafter from a cosmological and temporal framework. So, while the differences are respected, this world and the hereafter, the present and the future, must be considered as simultaneous. For R. Bult-

mann* eternal life is not linked to a place or a time to come, but is rather a quality of Christian existence. The person who lives by faith in Christ has already died and risen. ("You are resurrected with Christ himself and by him," Col 2:12). And without denying an eternal life after death, a writer such as Tillich* considers it an inexpressible reality: the immortality of the soul, the resurrection of the body, and the bold image of the "spiritual body" constitute a set of symbols that can evoke it, but nothing more.

3. Theological Consideration

a) Concept of Eternal Life. Whereas the Platonist tradition conceives access to eternity as a natural return to immortality beyond death, Christian thought sees eternal life as a free gift, a sharing of divine life. Thus it is not a return to a former life, but a new creation, a life totally renewed and received from God. It responds to spiritual death on a more profound level than freeing people from biological death; and between man's earthly life and his eternal life there exists the same distance as exists between the animal (psychic) body and the spiritual body of which Paul speaks (1 Cor 15:42 ff.). This is an imperfect comparison, however, inasmuch as the concept of human life denotes, as a single whole, both the carnal and the spiritual dimensions of existence. So, insofar as man defines himself in terms of spirit and liberty*, eternal life expresses the fulfillment of the moments of eternity that man already experiences in his earthly life; but insofar as he is spirit present in flesh, it conveys the fact that this fulfillment is inconceivable unless it is the whole man, body and soul, who receives an eschatological vocation from God.

b) Time and Eternity. Eternal life denotes something more than an endless duration, something that could be conceived entirely outside the context of salvation. On the contrary, the concept of eternal life is meaningful only in relation to the mystery of sanctity* and blessed life which is the very mystery of God—the mystery, that is, of a "living" God. Scripture, moreover, envisages the possibility of an "eternal death" (Jn 5:29) that is the opposite, not of earthly life, but of eternal life. And while it is a free gift offered to those whom Christ's death and Resurrection have justified, eternal life is not a reward that comes as it were from the outside, without respect to the spiritual destiny of the faithful. These axioms, then, make it impossible to define eternity in terms of the absence of time. On the contrary, the eternity promised to humanity "occurs in time as its proper fruit, come to maturity" (Rahner*). While immortality merely denotes the emancipation of temporality and the endless continuation of a spiritual existence, eternity is a part of the history of human destiny and brings it to perfection. It is the visitation of earthly time *(chronos)* by "vertical" time *(kairos*—that is, the irruption of God's grace*) that enables the former to give birth to eternity *(aiôn)*. In order to suggest that eternal life is not alien to our temporal destiny, Scripture and theological tradition frequently employ symbols of unending joy. The beatific vision*, for example, evokes the kind of rapture we experience when confronted with beauty*; and the metaphor of the wedding anticipates the bliss that humanity will enjoy in communion with the exchanges of the three divine Persons* in a Trinity* whose life is itself supremely joyful.

c) Eternal Life and Historical Responsibility. A remarkable feature of the modern period is the nominal Christian, who confesses the God of Jesus Christ without believing in the promise of a hereafter beyond death. This attitude is in part a reaction to a certain type of Christianity, historically dated, that linked the expectation of another world to a devaluing of life in this world (the "valley of tears") and to the refusal of historical responsibility. Thus Christian salvation, reduced to a matter of the individual sinner's reconciliation with God, was understood first and foremost as a remedy for the mortal finitude intrinsic to the human condition. Faced with this confusion between the condition of a sinner and that of a created being, however, Christian eschatology objects that the created state, far from being an evil to be overcome by obtaining eternal life, is on the contrary a promise of eternal life. Eternal life does not impose meaning on this present life from without. Far from being experienced as a means of escape, the hope of eternal life gives the history of human liberty, and the ethical choices that determine an eternal destiny, their whole value.

d) Communion with God and Personal Identity. By eternal life we mean the culmination of a communion with God that is begun in this life by participation in the risen Christ. "Your life is hidden with Christ in God. When Christ, your life, appears, then you will also appear with him in full glory" (Col 3:3 f.). And while it is a communion with God, eternal life cannot be properly conceived without an awareness also of the promise of a new communion between human beings in the image of the life of the Trinity, this latter being understood as a perfect communion of divine Persons as completely united as they are wholly distinct. The "heaven" of popular devotion and the "eternal life" of theology both refer to the perfect fulfillment of the Church in coincidence with the kingdom of God. As the concept of the resurrection of the dead expresses (better than others), the personal identity of each individual will be preserved for all eternity. Nonetheless, the relationship of communion between the elect, freed from the limits inherent in the spatiotemporal condition and the obstacles entailed by the sinner's withdrawal into himself, will attain the greatest possible transparency. Glorified alongside the Father, the blessed will take part in the celestial liturgy of the sacrificed Lamb*; and the faithful who pursue their earthly pilgrimage are already a party to their intercession (the communion of saints). In the same way that the communion between the elect does not do away with their personalities and therefore the relationships of otherness between them, of *I* and *Thou,* so the sight of God does not bring about the dissolution of the glorified subject like a drop of water in the ocean of divinity. The elect merely participate in God's eternity and in his knowledge of himself. They remain creatures "before God" in adoration and praise. The divinization of man coincides with the culmination of his personal destiny. There is certainly a knowledge of God "face to face" (1 Cor 13:12), but God does not cease to live in an "inaccessible light" (1 Tm 6:16). And it is precisely because the eternal life of the blessed is nothing more than a sharing in the eternity of God himself that it is not absurd to maintain, as does the Latin tradition, that there are levels of beatitude measured by the degree of charity shown in this life; and that there is a progression in the discovery of God's unfathomable mystery—a living eternity that therefore cannot turn into an eternal boredom.

e) Disparity between Eternal Life and Eternal Death. Eternal life is intimately connected to Christ's victory over sin and death—it is a promise of eternal bliss. It is not easy to see, therefore, what an eternity of woe might involve. However, some scriptural texts do envisage a kind of resurrection, or, more accurately, survival of woe (*see* Mt 25:31–46; Jn 5:29). The Book of Revelation, moreover, introduces the idea of a "second death" (2:11; 20:14), which in contrast to the first and temporal death is an eternal death, and thus the opposite of eternal beatitude. It is clear that the resurrection of the dead coincides with a judgment* that may lead to eternal damnation (Mt 25:46). This possibility has to be upheld, since without it, the free decisions made by human beings would lose their infinite seriousness. At the same time, however, care must be taken not to put the assertions of eternal life and eternal death on an equal footing. Certainly, the church's official theology has always refused to incorporate apocatastasis* into its official doctrines and foresees the possibility of eternal woe for some. It is advisable, therefore, to maintain the discretion that the subject of the "last things" demands, while preserving an asymmetrical approach. In other words, because of the victory of God's merciful grace manifested in Jesus Christ, the church proclaims ceaselessly that all the just who have died in Christ will obtain eternal life; but, as far as the eternal perdition of a specific number of sinners is concerned, the church does not consider itself qualified to make an equivalent pronouncement.

- R. Bultmann, G. von Rad, G. Bertram (1935), *"zaô, zôè, bios,"* ThWNT 2, 833–74.
- F. Mußner (1952), ZOE, *Anschauung von "Leben" in vierten Evangelium*, Munich.
- O. Cullmann (1956), *Immortalité de l'âme ou résurrection des corps?* Neuchâtel.
- P. Althaus (1958), "Ewiges Leben," RGG3 2, 806–9.
- K. Rahner (1960), "Theologische Prinzipien der Hermeneutik eschatologischer Aussagen," *Schr. zur Th.* 4, 401–28, Einsiedeln-Zurich-Köln (*Theological Writings* 9, 1968, 141–70).
- P. Tillich (1963), *Systematic Theology* 3, Chicago, 406–23.
- P. H. Menoud (1966), *Le Sort des trépassés*, Neuchâtel.
- C. Bruaire (1968), *Philosophie du corps*, Paris, 231–68.
- D. Z. Phillips (1970), *Death and Immortality*, London.
- G. Martelet (1975), *L'Au-delà retrouvé*, Paris (New Ed. 1995).
- J. Ratzinger (1977), *Eschatologie: Tod und ewiges Leben*, Regensburg, (6th Ed. 1990).
- H. Thielicke (1978), *Der Evangelische Glaube*, III: *Theologie des Geistes*, Tübingen, §32.
- C. Ebeling (1979), *Dogmatik des christlichen Glaubens*, III, Tübingen, §38–39.
- H. Küng (1982), *Ewiges Leben?* Munich.
- H. U. von Balthasar (1983), *Theodramatik*, IV: *Das Endspiel*, esp. 389–446.
- R. Marlé (1985), "Peut-on encore parler de la vie éternelle?" *Études*, 245–56.
- A. Gounelle, F. Vouga (1990), *Après la mort qu'y a-t-il? Le discours chrétien sur l'au-delà*, Paris.
- J. Hick (1990), *Death and Eternal Life*, London.
- C. Chalier (1993), *Pensées de l'éternité: Spinoza, Rosenzweig*, Paris.
- A. Gesché (1995), *La Destinée*, Paris.
- A. Gounelle (1995), "Mort et vie éternelle," *Encyclopédie du protestantisme*, Paris, 1045–56.

CLAUDE GEFFRE

See also **Beatitude; Death; Eschatology; Eternity of God; Kingdom of God; Resurrection of the Dead; Vision, Beatific**

Life, Spiritual

I. Definitions

The term *spiritual life* is relatively modern. Earlier ages seem to have used both words in a much more restrictive sense than in modern usage. Life, in the sense of "way of life" (Greek *bios* or *politeia*), could hardly be characterized so generally as to apply to all Christians, although the expression "way of life belonging to Christians" *(ho bios ho Khristianon)* is found (Clement, *Paedagogus* 1, 13). There was, however, a wealth of terminology used to characterize the pursuit of monasticism: "single [literally: monadic] life," "godlike life," "angelic life," "philosophical life." The term *spiritual,* if used at all, tended to refer to the clergy. In its modern use, the expression *spiritual life* shares many of the determinants of the expression *spiritual* theology:* a vagueness as to dogma* and the sacraments*, combined with a sense that what is important about religious profession is the manner of life. Such appeals to "spirituality" suggest disillusionment with the traditional categories of theology, and a

yearning for some deeper meaning to life, characterized by the "spiritual." It is legitimate to explore what resources Christian reflection can offer for such a quest, without yielding to its exclusions.

As with *spiritual theology, spiritual life* may be analyzed from two distinct points of departure, depending on the way in which one understands *spiritual.* This term can refer to the Holy* Spirit, or to the spiritual element *(pneuma)* in human beings. The latter point of departure leads down a path much trodden in the world in which Christianity first developed, for it is based on philosophical analysis of the person*. Since the text of the Bible* read by Christian circles (as by earlier Hellenistic Jewish circles) was that of the Septuagint (ancient translations* of the Bible), they regularly used *pneuma* to refer to spirit, instead of the more normal Greek *nous.* However, the equivalence remained: the spiritual life, the life proper to the *pneuma (bios pneumatikos),* was therefore the life that is proper to the *nous,* the contemplative life.

II. Scriptural Foundations

Both the word *pneuma* and the Hebrew world *rouach* that it translates have the original meaning of "breath" or "wind," and have the meaning of the life that God* breathed into the first human beings (Adam*). The spiritual is the life that is a gift of God: this life is not just a series of natural processes (although there is no suggestion that it does not include these), but something given by God, which will return to him after death* (Eccl 12:7). Spirit is something powerful, in contrast to the frailty of flesh: it is this contrast between the powerful and the frail that is implied in the well-known contrast between spirit and flesh, not the contrast between the immaterial and the material (Is 31:3).

The spiritual life in this sense is a life lived in dependence on God: a life exemplified by the prophets*, and also by the "poor," for whom in their poverty the only source of strength is God (*see* the use of the term *poor* in the Psalms*, esp. Ps 71 [72], 81 [82], 108 [109], and 131 [132]). The "poor in spirit" whom the Lord blesses are those who have no source of strength save God (Mt 5:3).

1. New Testament

This notion of spiritual life, a life lived in communion* with God, is developed in the New Testament as the life that grows out of faith* in Jesus Christ.

a) The Kingdom of God. In the synoptic Gospels, this life is spoken of in terms of the kingdom* of God, the coming or imminent presence of which Jesus* proclaims. Life in the kingdom is life in accordance with God's will, a life in which barriers among human beings, and between human beings and God, will have been broken. Several sayings of Jesus, and also his response to the repentant thief (Lk 23:42), suggest that the kingdom (and life within it) become reality as a result of the Crucifixion, in which these barriers are finally broken down (something symbolically suggested in the rending of the Temple* veil: *see* Mt 27:51 and par.). It is perhaps for this reason that in the main theological traditions of the New Testament, the notion of the kingdom of God is displaced by the notion of the life that Jesus has released: "eternal life" in the Johannine tradition, "life in Christ" in the Pauline tradition.

b) Eternal Life. For John, eternal life is a present reality in this world, in communion with Jesus; but it is a present reality that transcends death, because of the power of Jesus' Resurrection*. To enter into eternal life it is necessary to be "born again" (Jn 3:3), to be born of "water and the Spirit" (Jn 3:5), an evident reference to baptism*. Possession of eternal life is dependent on a eucharistic eating of the body and blood of Christ (Jn 6:56): "Whoever feeds on my flesh and drinks my blood abides in me, and I in him. As the living Father sent me, and I live because of the Father, so whoever feeds on me, he also will live because of me. This is the bread that came down from heaven.... Whoever feeds on this bread will live forever." Eternal life, for John, is synonymous with knowledge* of God: "And this is eternal life, that they know you the only true God, and Jesus Christ whom you have sent" (Jn 17:3)—eternal life is thus mostly contemplative.

c) Life in Christ. Paul's understanding of life in Christ is the same, but he expresses it in different language. Entry into life in Christ still takes place through baptism, but, whereas John sees baptism in terms of rebirth, Paul sees it primarily in terms of sharing in Christ's death and Resurrection (Rom 6:3 f.): "Do you not know that all of us who have been baptized into Christ Jesus were baptized into his death? We were buried therefore with him by baptism into death, in order that, just as Christ was raised from the dead by the glory of the Father, we too might walk in newness of life." This imagery of death and resurrection does not apply simply to our initiation into this life, but to our continuing in it: Paul speaks of "carrying in the body the death of Jesus, so that the life of Jesus may also be manifested in our bodies" (2 Cor 4:10). Participation in the Eucharist* is a means of sharing in this life (1 Cor 10:16 f.): "The cup of blessing that we bless, is it not a participation in the blood of Christ? The bread that we break, is it not a participation in the body of Christ? Because there is one bread, we who are many are one body, for we all partake of the one bread." Paul brings out how life in Christ is essentially life in the Church*, and that participation in the Eucharist constitutes belonging to the Church, which is the body of Christ. This sacramental life in the Church is also characterized in terms of the Spirit: within the Church, the Spirit dispenses his gifts, which are different for each member, but to all are forms of love (agape). However, the Spirit is still more intimately involved in the living of this new life in Christ. It is the Spirit who realizes our status as adopted sons and daughters of the Father, brothers and sisters of the Son. It is through the Spirit that we can make our own Jesus' way of addressing God as "Abba" (an intimate, though not familiar, form of address); it is the Spirit that overcomes our frailty and enables us to enter into a communion with God that transcends anything human (Rom 8:26 f.): "Likewise the Spirit helps us in our weakness. For we do not know what to pray for as we ought, but the Spirit himself intercedes for us with groanings too deep for words. And he who searches hearts knows what is the mind of the Spirit, because the Spirit intercedes for the saints according to the will of God." This Trinitarian (and cosmic: *see* Rom 8:19–23) understanding of life in Christ as a life of prayer* through the Spirit is a powerful illustration of the way in which reflection on the spiritual life can issue in dogmatic clarification.

d) Fruits of the Spirit.   One feature of the spiritual life as depicted in the New Testament is that it is not simply seen in terms of the perfection of human life. The Christian lives a life that is not his own. As Paul puts it, "I have been crucified with Christ. It is no longer I who live, but Christ who lives in me" (Gal 2:20). The virtues* of the Christian life are therefore not something that we can develop by ourselves, but something that blossoms within us. So Paul speaks, not of virtues, but of the "fruits of the Spirit": "love, joy, peace, patience, kindness, goodness, faithfulness, gentleness, self-control" (Gal 5:22 f.). Similarly, love, in which is summed up the essence of the Christian life according to the command of Christ (Mt 22:37 and par.), is presented by Paul as the greatest of the gifts of the Spirit (1 Cor 13).

2. Imitation of Christ

Imitation* of Christ, as modeling one's life on the features of Jesus' earthly life, is not such a prominent feature in the New Testament and the early church as would later become. Imitation of Christ *is* an ideal, but more as following Christ, or imitating what was involved in the Incarnation* of the Son of God. When Jesus speaks of giving his disciples an example (Jn 13:15), it is that they should "wash one another's feet": that they should love one another (Jn 13:35). When Paul speaks of the example of Christ that Christians are to imitate, it is the example of Christ in his becoming human and accepting the human lot—"though he was rich, yet for your sake he became poor, so that you by his poverty might become rich" (2 Cor 8:9)—or his humility in becoming man (Phil 2:5–11). The example of Christ to which Peter* appeals is that of innocent suffering in his passion* (1 Pt 2:21–25).

In all these cases, instead of a model against which one measures oneself, Christ is presented as an example, in the following of whom one shares in his grace*: "in order that you by his poverty might become rich"; "work out your own salvation with fear and trembling, for it is God who works in you" (Phil 2:12, immediately following the hymn to Christ's *kenosis*); "by his wounds you have been healed" (1 Pt 2:24). In following Christ, one is tracing the movement of God's coming down to the level of the human in order to raise the human to the level of the divine: Christ as an example is not that of an exemplary man, but of God living a human life. All these ideas are merged in the prayer of Ignatius of Antioch, when he begs the Christians of Rome* to let him, in his coming martyrdom*, be an "imitator of the passion in my God" (*Rom.* 6:3).

III. Martyrdom

This plea by Ignatius holds together two themes that have been powerful in shaping the Christian understanding of the spiritual life: martyrdom and deification. Although persecution was by no means systematic imperial policy during the first centuries of Christianity, it was a perennial threat, and most early Christian communities experienced persecution at some stage. Martyrdom thus became the ideal of Christian living: not that all Christians expected to become martyrs (and they were discouraged from courting martyrdom), but that all Christians were expected to live such a life that, if they were faced with the choice between apostasy or death, they would choose martyrdom. The martyr became the archetypal saint, that is, one who fulfilled what was potentially the vocation of every Christian, who in baptism had been called to be holy.

The accounts of martyrdom (the *acta martyrum*) became the earliest form of hagiography. A strong apocalyptic sense pervades them: the Christian martyr (like the Jewish martyr before him) is seen as fighting on the front line in the war between good* and evil*. The persecuting power of the Roman state is only the tool of cosmic powers of darkness, which are the real enemies of the martyrs. The martyrs are soldiers of Christ, on active service, and all Christians are seen as being in training for this struggle. The language of warfare and athletic contest is used to describe the Christian condition (*see,* notably, Eph 6:10–17; 2 Tm 4:7 f.; Heb 12:1 f.; 1 *Clement* 5, 1; Ignatius, *Polycarp* 1, 3 and 3, 1). Already in the second century, there developed alongside the challenge of actual ("simple") martyrdom, the ideal of spiritual (or "gnostic") martyrdom (*see* Clement of Alexandria, *Strom.* IV), which is manifest in "the perfect work of love" (ibid., IV, 4, 14, 3).

When, with the Peace of the Church, martyrdom ceased to be a threat, the ideal of martyrdom was fulfilled by the growing popularity of monasticism*. The monk stepped into the martyr's shoes: monasticism became a seedbed for holiness* and preserved the sense of living in the last days, on the brink of the final struggle between the forces of good and evil. Monasticism thus came to replace martyrdom as the ideal of the spiritual life.

IV. Monasticism

1. Monasticism As the Archetypal Form of Spiritual Life

Within monasticism, there developed a rich understanding of the spiritual life. The idea of struggle with evil powers, with demons*, was inherited from the concept of martyrdom, and is a prominent feature of the early monks, the "Desert Fathers." A great deal of reflection was devoted to understanding the nature of demonic warfare. Alongside this, however, there developed an understanding of the spiritual life as the development of the spiritual in the human, which drew on the resources provided by classical philosophy. The notion of the eight temptations—in its later Western form, the seven deadly sins* (asceticism*)—is part of this development. Although monasticism might seem a specialized and minority form of Christian life, from the fourth century onward it was held up as the exemplary form of Christian life, working out in a strikingly clear form ideals that applied to all Christians, whether monastic or not. According to John Chrysostom*, those who live in the world*, although they have wives, must live the same life as that of monks (*Hom.* 7 *on Hebrews*). The contemporary Orthodox Church still holds that there is no essential difference between the requirements of the monastic life and those of life in the world.

2. Stages of the Spiritual Life

Within monastic circles, there developed an understanding of the spiritual life as the fulfillment of the new life implanted in baptism, although monastic conversion—the turning from the world to join the monastic community—was seen as the practical starting point. It was a life with a beginning, a middle, and an end, and notions of development, or of stages, were readily applied to it.

a) Spiritual Growth. The analogy of human growth was widely used, with a progression to eventual spiritual maturity, although the idea of growing out of spiritual infancy was not readily entertained. Closely associated with the notion of growth was the theme of the spiritual senses (spiritual theology), their discovery, reawakening, and use. The idea of progression in the spiritual life as a journey was also common. This journey was often seen as making one's way back to paradise, or as an ascent: these two themes were often associated, since paradise was often thought of as a mountain. The spiritual life was also seen as a passage from earth to heaven (the monastic life was regularly called the "angelic life"), by a ladder, as dreamed of by Jacob (Gen 28:12) and alluded to by the Lord (Jn 1:51).

b) Pilgrimage. The one who embarked on this journey was a pilgrim, *peregrinus,* an alien who was no longer at home where he was sojourning. The radical dispossession that lies at the heart of the monastic life was readily evoked by the imagery of the pilgrim, who travels light and has no time for nonessentials. Sometimes the spiritual journey became a literal journey, as with the Celtic monks whose detachment from the world took the form of tireless traveling. Already by the sixth century, the heyday of the Celtic *peregrinatio,* others saw such wandering as a form of self-indulgence, and a way of escaping any discipline: Saint Benedict thought them the worst kind of monks and called them "gyrovagues."

c) Spiritual Ladders. Ladders became popular as images for the spiritual life in monastic circles. The longest chapter in the *Rule* of Saint Benedict (chap. 7) discusses the "ladder of humility." Unusually, the discussion concerns the construction of the ladder, and not just its ascent: the sides are our body and soul*, and the rungs the degrees of humility. These 12 rungs give a good idea of the essential qualities of the monastic life, as Benedict saw it. They are: fear of God, lack of self-will, subjection to the superior, patience with the difficulties and contradictions involved in obedience, confession of sins and thoughts to the abbot, being content with the meanest and worst of everything, sincere inward humility, strict adherence to the *Rule,* silence, abrogation of laughter, brief speech when necessary, and external humility in one's behavior. There is no progression, as such, in this list: they are all ways of establishing and preserving humility and obedience, the essential virtues of the monk. Having made this ladder, the monk will be able to ascend it and come to that "perfect love of God that casts out fear." Six centuries later, Bernard* of Clairvaux expounded Benedict's ladder in his treatise *De Gradibus Humilitatis et Superbiae* (On Degrees of Humility and Pride), making it much more a ladder that traces an ascent, from humility through love to contemplation*, and complementing it with a ladder of pride that leads from curiosity by various stages to contempt of God. In the East, the most influential monastic "ladder," *The Ladder of Divine Ascent,* which is read in Orthodox monasteries each year in the course of Lent, is that attributed to John of Sinai (seventh century), of whom we know nothing save his having written this work, for which he is usually named John Climacus, or John of the Ladder. This is very much more elaborate than Benedict's ladder, with 30 rungs to his 12, and is clearly arranged in a progression, leading from the break with the world (renunciation, detachment, exile), through the fundamental virtues needed for the monastic life (obedience, penance*, remembrance of death, sorrow), to a detailed analysis of ascetic struggle, with all its temptations, a struggle that bears fruit in the virtues of simplicity, humility, and discernment. Having reached this stage, the monk is able to engage in contemplation, and to progress from stillness *(hesukhia)* through prayer and dispassion *(apatheia)* to love.

d) The Three Ways. Rather simpler than the ladder is the division of the spiritual life according to the three ways. In the later Western terminology, these are the three ways of purgation, illumination, and union. Although similar ideas can be traced back at least as far as Origen*, they first clearly emerged as a triad in the writings of Dionysius* the Pseudo-Areopagite (early sixth century). For Dionysius, this triad of purification, illumination, and union (or sometimes perfection) is valuable in expounding the operation of the sacraments and the ministers of the sacraments. This remained the case in the Orthodox tradition, as can be seen from *The Life in Christ* by Nicolas Cabasilas (14th century). God, through the sacraments, overcomes the effects of the Fall by purifying and illuminating those human beings who respond to his call, and leading them to union. The sacraments are central to this process, as is the sacramental community, which itself imitates a process typified in the celestial hierarchy of angelic beings. In the Western tradition, the triad was interiorized and individualized: it is a threefold path leading from a state of sin and alienation from God to a state of union with him. The purgative way is concerned with the overcoming of vice and the fostering of virtue. It takes place in response to God's call, but consists of practices that are within human control. It is a matter of acquiring self-control and openness to God. The prayer characteristic of this way is vocal prayer, and meditation on Scripture and the truths* of the faith. On the illuminative way, there is growing experience of the grace of God. The soul is now settled in virtuous habits, and meditation yields to stillness as the mind is opened to the illuminating effect of divine grace (this stage is sometimes called "prayer of quietude"). This leads ultimately, for some at least (spiritual theology, III 2 b), to the way of union, where the soul comes to contemplation, that is, a simple openness to God in which the soul is filled by grace and united with God (prayer*, V 2 b). Unlike in Pseudo-Dionysius's use of the triad, where these three phases, even though they are progressive, allow for overlap, the Western "three ways" impose a more rigid progression. Instead of a continuous synergy between the soul and God, as in the Eastern conception, there is a movement from apparently purely human activity to purely divine activity that is theologically unsatisfactory. Despite these limitations, the definition of the three ways trodden by beginners (the purgative way), proficients (the illuminative way), and the perfect (the way of union), attained almost canonical authority in the West from the High Middle Ages until the 20th century.

e) Spiritual Direction. According to Father de Caussade (1675–1751), "God still speaks today as he spoke in earlier times to our fathers, when there were no directors and no methods" (*L'abandon à la providence divine* 25). Although Caussade envisaged a golden age when God revealed himself directly, without any need for spiritual* direction, the institution of spiritual fatherhood is in fact very ancient. Paul himself speaks of being a father to those whom he has brought to the faith (1 Cor 4:15). Spiritual fatherhood is perhaps first clearly glimpsed in the Christian tradition in the *gnostikoi* of Clement of Alexandria (*see Quis dives salvetur,* Which Rich Man Shall be Saved 31–34): it lies behind his characterization of Christians as *nepioi* ("little children") throughout his *Paedagogos,* and the qualities of a *gnostikos* are the subject of *Stromata* VII. However, the institution of spiritual fatherhood coincides with the growth of monasticism in the fourth century. The Desert Fathers were the pioneers of monasticism, but they also fulfilled an important role in relation to the society* that they had rejected, as sources of spiritual wisdom* and guidance. Many of the stories about them concern people who come to ask them for personal guidance: "Speak a word to me." Within the monasteries themselves, especially in the East, one of the basic relationships into which the monk entered was that which he had with his spiritual father or *geron* (elder). A monk would regularly visit his *geron,* not simply for confession but for the revealing of his thoughts, and strict obedience to his *geron* was required. The *geron* was a senior monk (or nun), and not necessarily a priest*. This institution continued and even underwent periods of revival, notably in 19th-century Russia, (where the *geron* was called a *staretz*), and in Byzantine and Slav monasticism. A similar role, although much more closely related to the sacrament of penance, was found in the West.

There are two fundamental documents about the nature of spiritual fatherhood: the letter called "The Shepherd" by John Climacus (often printed as chap. 31 of his *Ladder*); and the first *Letter* of Symeon the New Theologian (949–1022). From these closely related works there emerges a rounded picture of the *geron,* who is held to fulfill in relation to his spiritual children the role of physician, counselor, intercessor, mediator—which entails, especially for Symeon, personal experience of the grace of the Spirit—and sponsor, that is, one who assumes responsibility for, and bears the burdens of, his spiritual children (*see* Gal 6:2).

V. A Way of Affirmation?

The dominance of monasticism in reflection on the spiritual life has given the traditional account of this life in Christianity a markedly ascetic turn. It is a way of detachment, of dispossession: in short, a way of negation. There have, however, occasionally been attempts to construe the spiritual life affirmatively, to see it in terms of attachment and the enjoyment of created things. An example of this can be seen in the priest and poet Thomas Traherne (c. 1636–74), especially in his prose meditations *Centuries of Meditation* (first published in 1908). For Traherne, attachment and the fulfillment of desire are positive principles in which we reveal our likeness to God (*Centuries* I, 44 f.): "You must want like a God, that you may be satisfied like God. Were you not made in his image? He is most like God that is sensible of every thing. Did you not from all eternity want some one to give you a being? Did you not want one to give you a glorious being? Did you not from all eternity want someone to give you infinite treasures?" It is significant that such a way of affirmation develops its own ascesis, since selfishness deprives us of enjoyment. Such a way of affirmation, explicitly called such in contrast to the way of negation, is sketched out in the works of the Anglican lay theologian Charles Williams (1886–1945), who was probably influenced by Traherne, and is also explored by T. S. Eliot (1888–1965) in *Four Quartets,* especially "East Coker" and "Little Gidding."

● F. X. Funk, K. Bihlmeyer, W. Schneemelcher (Ed.), *Die apostolischen Väter,* 3rd Ed., Tübingen, 1970.

Apophtegmata Patrum, PG 65, 71–440 [*Les sentences des Pères du Désert,* Solesmes, 1981].

La Règle de saint Benoît, SC 181–6.

Bernard de Clairvaux, *De gradibus humilitatis et superbiae,* in *Sancti Bernardi Opera* 3, 13–59, Rome, 1963.

J.-P. de Caussade, *L'abandon à la providence divine,* Paris, 1966.

N. Cabasilas, *La vie en Christ,* SC 355, 361.

Clement of Alexandria GCS 12, 89–340 (*Le pédagogue,* SC 70, 108, 158).

Dionysius the Areopagite, *Corpus dionysiacum,* 2 vols., PTS 33, 36.

John Chrysostom, *In epistulam ad Hebraeos homiliae,* PG 63, 9–236.

John Climacus, *Le livre du Berger,* PG 88, 1165–1210; *Scala Paradisi,* PG 88, 628–1164 (*L'Échelle sainte,* Bégrolles-en-Mauges, 1978).

T. S. Eliot, *Four Quartets,* London, 1944.

Origen, *Exhortatio ad martyrium, Origenes Werke* 1, 3–47, GCS 2.

Simeon the New Theologian, *Letter 1,* in K. Holl, *Enthusiasmus und Bußgewalt beim griechischen Mönchtum. Eine Studie zu Symeon dem neuen Theologen,* 110–27, Leipzig, 1898.

T. Traherne, *Centuries, Poems and Thankgivings,* 2 vols., Oxford, 1958.

C. Williams, *The Image of the City,* Oxford, 1958.

◆ D. Bonhoeffer (1937), *Nachfolge,* Munich (*DBW* 4, 1994).

I. Hausherr, *Direction spirituelle en Orient autrefois,* OCA 144 (English trans. with a preface by K. Ware, repr. of StPatr XVIII/2, 299–316).

M. Lot-Borodine (1958), *Un maître de la spiritualité byzantine au XIVe s.: Nicolas Cabasilas,* Paris.

H. von Campenhausen (1960), "Die asketische Heimatlosigkeit im altkirchlichen und frühmittelalterlichen Mönchtum," in *Tradition und Leben. Kräfte der Kirchengeschichte,* Tübingen, 290-317.

E. J. Tinsley (1960), *The Imitation of God in Christ,* London.

M. Lot-Borodine (1970), *La déification de l'homme,* Paris.

Sophronius (Archimandrite) (1984), *Voir Dieu tel qu'Il est,* Geneva

Sophronius (Archimandrite) (1988), *La félicité de connaître la voie,* Geneva.

J.-Y. Lacoste (1994), *Expérience et Absolu,* Paris.

ANDREW LOUTH

See also **Asceticism; Contemplation; Mysticism; Prayer; Spiritual Theology**

Liguori, Alphonsus. *See* Alphonsus Liguori

Limbo

The classical Latin word *limbus,* meaning "border," has come to mean both the Old Testament Sheol* from which Christ delivered the just from the Old Covenant* and that part of hell* inhabited by children who have died unbaptized (baptism*).

a) Limbo of the Fathers. There is theological consensus about the eschatological destiny of the just who have died before the Resurrection* of Christ. "Paradise" and "hell" are christological realities that could not exist before the salvation* of the world has been realized. The eschatology* of Israel* was valid until Easter: the dead survived in Sheol; or again, they rested and were "carried by the angels to Abraham's bosom" (Lk 16:22). But since the salvation bestowed by Christ also applies to those who did not know him, the icon of Easter Saturday represents the Son of God* breaking down the gates of Sheol to open the kingdom* of God to the just of the Old Testament, to whom a verse from 1 Peter 3:19 says that he went to preach *(ekèruxen).* The "limbo of the Fathers" was therefore deeschatologized. It is now nothing more than a superseded reality. Bonaventure* specified that the limbo of the Fathers really was an infernal place, but that it was a hell in which, paradoxically, hope* lived *(Commentary on the Sentences,* IV, Dist. 45, Art.1, Q. 1).

b) Limbo of Children. Gregory* of Nyssa devoted a treatise to children who had died prematurely, Ephraim placed little children in his paradise, but it was not until the advent of Augustine's theology* of original sin* that the fate of children who had died unbaptized became a topic of urgent theological concern. In the terms chosen by Augustine*, the question had only one possible answer: children who had died without baptism were damned. In 418 the anti-Pelagian Council of Carthage formally ratified this theory. "If anyone says that the Lord said 'in my Father's house are many rooms,' (Jn 14:2) in order to make us understand that in the kingdom of heaven there will be an intermediary place—wherever it is situated—where will live as blessed the children who have left this life unbaptized, without which sacrament one cannot enter the kingdom of heaven, that is, life eternal, let him be anathema. For, since the Lord said 'unless one is reborn of water and the Spirit he cannot enter the kingdom of God' (Jn 3:5), what Catholic will doubt that whoever has not deserved to be the co-heir of Christ belongs to the Devil?" *(DS* 224).

Once this thesis was accepted, it became necessary to decide on the infernal punishments reserved for these children. They could have chosen an extremist position, which consisted of dooming these children to the "tortures of the fires of hell" as did the Pseudo-Augustine in *De Fide ad Petrum (PL* 40, 774). A middle position was also available, and—along with Augustine himself—that position prevailed. It entailed reserving for those children the gentlest punishment* possible: "The punishment of those who have added no sin to the one they contracted originally will indeed be the gentlest of all" *(PL* 40, 275). The chief movement in medieval Latin theology would thus endeavor to diminish the infernal tortures incurred by children who had died unbaptized. The accepted solution came from Peter Lombard's *Sentences* (II *Sent.,* Dist. 33, C. 2): the punishment they had to undergo was that of *damnus,* an everlasting banishment from the beatific vision*, and they did not undergo the punishment of the senses—that is, the physical tortures endured by the damned in their resurrected bodies.

In 1201 Pope Innocent II stated what became the accepted opinion. "The punishment undergone as a result of original sin is the deprivation of the vision of God. The punishment undergone as a consequence of actual sinning is the torture of everlasting Gehenna" *(DS* 780). Henceforth, since a new word, *limbo,* existed, the concept of an intermediary place, which had been condemned by the Council of Carthage, could in fact be traced. Thus, regarding the children in limbo, Bonaventure confirmed that "in some ways they hold the middle ground between the blessed and those who suffer eternal damnation" *(Commentary on the Sentences,* II, Dist. 33, Art. 3, Q.1). It would be only a step to conceive, as did Thomas* Aquinas, the notion of a limbo that was in fact a place of natural beatitude* *(Quaestiones Disputatae de malo* 5). That notion would be taken up again by Duns* Scotus *(Commentary on the Sentences* II, Dist. 33).

Faced with these theological elaborations, the magisterium*'s formal statements showed less zeal to know and to describe. The Council of Florence would define the disparity among the torments of Hell

(*DS* 1306). In opposition to the Jansenist Council of Pistoia, Pope Pius VI emphasized that the existence of limbo was not a "Pelagian fable" (*DS* 2626—the only formal document in which limbo is mentioned by its name). By the end of the Middle Ages, the question of the fate of the children who had died without baptism had ceased to center on the certainty of their damnation, and theology as a whole endeavored thenceforth to envisage the conditions for their salvation.

Durand de Saint-Pourcain (c. 1275–1334), J. Gerson (1363–1429), and then Cajetan (1469–1534) developed a theory destined to influence all future discussions: the intercession of the parents would in fact amount to a "desire for the sacrament*" (*votum sacramen*). Karl Rahner* would specify that the "Church's desire" (*votum Ecclesiae*) is allied with the "parents' desire" (*Schriften zur Theologie* 2:7–94). H. Schell would propose an interesting hypothesis: the death of unbaptized children would be the equivalent of a quasi-sacrament insofar as, like Christ, they do penance* for sinners (*Kath. Dogmatik* III:2, Paderborn, 1893, 478). One point at least seemed have been gained: even if it was still possible in 1972 for Jacques Maritain to propose an imperturbable readoption of the theory of Thomas Aquinas, today the limbo of the children hardly exists anymore outside the domain of historians of Latin theology.

• **a) Limbo of the Fathers**
I. Lans (1583), *De limbo patrum,* Köln.
L. A. Muratori (1755), *De Paradiso,* Venice.
T. M. Mamochi (1766), *De animabus iustorum in sinu Abrahae ante Christi mortem,* Rome.
C. Gschwindt (1911), *Die Niederfahrt in die Unterwelt,* Münster.

J. Kroll (1922), *Beiträge zum Descensus ad inferos,* Königsberg.
J. Kroll (1932), *Gott und Hölle: Der Mythos vom Descensus Kampfe,* Leipzig.
G. Philips (1932–33), "La descente du Christ aux enfers," *REcL* 24, 144–5; "L'œuvre du Christ aux enfers," ibid., 272–86.
I. Chaine (1934), "Descente aux enfers," *DBS* 2, 391–435.
A. Grillmeier (1975), "Der Gottessohn im Totenreich," *Mit ihm und in ihm: Christologische Forschungen und Perspektiven,* Freiburg-Basel-Vienna, 76–174.

b) Limbo of Children
V. Bolgeni (1787), *Stato dei bambini morti senza Battesimo,* Macerata.
J. Didiot (1896), *Morts sans baptême,* Lille.
D. Stockum (1923), *Das Los der ohne die Taufe sterbenden Kinder,* Freiberg.
I. Lelièvre (1948), "Sort des enfants morts sans baptême," *La pensée catholique* 2, 43–50.
A. Michel (1948), "Salut des enfants morts sans baptême," *L'ami du clergé* 58, 33–43.
A. Michel (1951), "Encore le sort des enfants morts sans baptême," *L'ami du clergé* 61, 97–101; (1954), *Enfants morts sans baptême,* Paris.
P. Gumpel (1954), "Unbaptized Infants: May They Be Saved?" *DR* 72, 342–58.
W. A. van Roo (1954), "Infants Dying Without Baptism: A Survey of Recent Literature and Determination of the State of the Question," *Gr* 35, 406–73.
P. J. Hill (1961), *The Existence of a Children's Limbo according to Post-Tridentine Theologians,* Shelby, Ohio.
V. Wilkin (1961), *From Limbo to Heaven,* New York.
G. J. Dyer (1964), *Limbo, Unsettled Question,* New York.
J. Maritain (1992), "Idées eschatologiques," in *Approches sans entraves,* 2nd Ed., *OC* 13, Paris-Fribourg, 455–64.

GALAHAD THREEPWOOD

See also **Descent into Hell; Life, Eternal; Salvation; Vision, Beatific**

Literary Genres in Scripture

Before belonging to the biblical field and to the history of exegesis*, the concept of literary genre derives from the field of universal literature and more precisely suggests the idea of comparative literature. By its very nature, any literary genre—any "category of literary or artistic work defined by a group of rules and common characteristics" (Larousse, 1987)—runs through literatures separated in time and space and is thus recognizable wherever it may be found. In this sense it derives from the principle of classification, with its requirements for signposts and relative stability in its conception. In its theoretical development, the notion of literary genre and its system of categorization or classification have their roots in Plato (*Republic* III) and Aristotle *(Poetics).* Closer to our time, in Goethe *(Notes and Remarks for the East-West Divan),* that is, in our cultural sphere, the universalism of the notion has been relativized. But whatever the theories, the definition of genres also belongs to spontaneous common practice: for example, in sorting the mail or reading the daily newspaper, where in one case we spontaneously recognize and distinguish a bill, a death announcement, and a love letter, and in the other, an editorial, a weather report, and a news item. Sometimes confused with literary form, literary genre has, however, been fairly clearly distinguished from form in the history* of the last two centuries and particularly in the history of biblical exegesis.

Marked by the school of the history of forms *(Formgeschichtliche Schule)* that emerged in Germany in the early 20th century, whose indebtedness to Hermann Gunkel (1862–1932) must be mentioned, the concept of form is more dynamic than that of genre *(Gattung)*. It is used to "designate the literary aspect of a particular Gospel element, but also, and even especially, the various transformations undergone by the materials that were transmitted in the early church* between the death* of Jesus* and the composition of the first written Gospel*—in this sense the term is almost synonymous with *formation* ("Formes, méthode de la critique des," *Encyclopedia Universalis, Thesaurus,* 1996, col. 1316). Two exegetes were influential in this development: Martin Dibelius, with *Die Formgeschichte des Evangeliums* (Tübingen, 1919), and Rudolf Bultmann*, with *Die Geschichte des synoptischen Tradition* (Göttingen, 1921).

There is, however, an organic link between the two concepts, even if it is sometimes difficult to specify, because the sense of each term varies depending on the literary critic or the biblical exegete.

In some ways, critical biblical exegesis, beginning in the second half of the 18th century and pursued most vigorously in the course of the 19th, considerably overloaded the concept of literary genre because of the truth* that was at stake, particularly the historical truth implicated in the reading of the Bible. The reliance on distinctions, and hence on the diversity and multiplicity of literary genres, is closely dependent on questions that the reading of the Bible raised for modern rational and critical consciousness. This explains the suspicion that such a reliance incurred on the part of ecclesiastical, and particularly Catholic, authorities* in the late 19th and early 20th centuries, until it was accepted and even recommended by Pius XII in his encyclical *Divino Afflante Spiritu* (1943).

In the biblical framework we can distinguish three possibilities for the determination of literary genres: by explicit designation in the biblical text, by implicit definition, and by the more or less extrinsic contribution of an exegesis, properly speaking, of the text. Explicitly designated are, for example, the parable*, when Jesus is said to "speak in parables" (Lk 6:39,

8:4–10); the song (Is 5:1) and the oracle in the prophets* (Am 3:10, 3:13); the psalms* (various as they are) in the collection that bears that name; the proverbs in the book of Proverbs, and so on. Implicitly defined are genres that arise from the context, such as the parable that the prophet Nathan recounts to King David whose unjust conduct he denounces (2 Sm 12:1–15); the prophecy when it is placed in the mouth of a person designated as a prophet or occasionally performing that function (Caiaphas in Jn 11:47–52); wisdom* in the books that fit into this genre. But in all these cases, subclassifications are often necessary.

It is more difficult to establish a literary genre by means of critical exegesis, an operation that can follow two methods or techniques: that of the "recognition" of a genre on the basis of other cultures in which that genre has been identified and recognized, and that of a genre peculiar to the biblical corpus, which is therefore established on the basis of the text. In both cases, even if rigorous analysis and precision are the rule, things are always relative, subject to verification or revision. It is easy enough, particularly because of the historical improbabilities and narrative exaggeration, to recognize, for example, the characteristics of the tale in the books of Jonah and Judith, following the laws of the genre in any literature, as long as we specify that it is an edifying genre appropriate to the biblical context. On the other hand, it is more difficult to speak of myth* or mythic narrative* with reference to the first four chapters of Genesis, for example, or to the gospel accounts of the infancy of Christ* (Matthew 1–2 and Luke 1–2), even if it is possible to recognize in them mythic elements characteristic of the ancient Near East. At this point the culture of the exegete enters into play. He has seen the concept of myth vary over the course of almost two centuries between the Hellenistic legacy, conceptions of ethnography, and the history of religions, psychoanalysis, and biblical studies themselves. This determination is also complicated by the fact that, in the Old Testament corpus (from Genesis to 2 Kings) and in the Gospels, literary genres designated as such are applied to elements of books taken from a historically synthesized whole that, in principle, abrogates all distinctions.

This is why literary genre cannot be reduced to the static condition of a classification, however universal and generally understood it may be. The study of the Bible, and not only the history of its exegesis, requires a constant refinement of concepts insofar as, in both Old and New Testaments, any literary element reveals a particular situation, a precise need, and a specific function. Hence, if any designation of a literary genre by the exegesis of the text always implies the possibility of a revision, it at least makes possible the discovery of the complexity of a text that is itself the product of a rich history.

- H. Gunkel (1910), *Genesis,* XI-LXXXIX, 2nd Ed., Göttingen.
- A. Robert (1957), "Littéraires (Genres)," *DBS* 5, 405–21.
- O. Eissfeldt (1966), *Einleitung in das Alte Testament,* 3rd Ed., Tübingen.
- H. Bausinger (1968), *Formen der "Volkspoesie,"* Berlin.
- C. Koch (1974), *Was ist Formgeschichte? Methoden der Bibelexegese,* 3rd Ed., Neukirchen.

P. Gibert (1979), *Une théorie de la légende: Gunkel et les légendes de la Bible,* Paris.
E. Kushner (Ed.) (1984), *Renouvellement dans la théorie de l'histoire littéraire,* Ottawa.
H. Dyserinck, M. S. Fischer (1985), *Internationale Bibliographie zur Geschichte und Theorie der Komparatistik,* Stuttgart.
Y. Chevrel (1995), *La littérature comparée,* 3rd Ed., Paris.

PIERRE GIBERT

See also **Bible; Book; Bultmann, Rudolf; Exegesis; Hermeneutics; History; Holy Scripture; Myth; Narrative; Parable; Truth**

Literature

There are two main reasons for considering "theology* and literature." On the one hand, the sources of theology belong to the history of literature, and theology itself belongs to the history of written language. On the other hand, literary creation can have theological relevance. This second reason has two aspects: first, a work of literature may have genuinely theological ambitions; and second, theology may attempt to interpret its concerns in the mirror of literary works.

a) The Bible As Literature. The Word* that Christianity claims to represent is set out in writings made up of many literary* genres: narrative claiming historical truth, saga, poem, proverb, and so on. Among these writings, some have literary value (Psalms, Song of Songs, etc.), some are written in awkward language (a large part of the New Testament matches this description) but possess a highly developed literary structure. Postbiblical Christian writings also fall into several categories: the language is often mediocre, but Augustine* is one of the greatest prose writers in Latin. The liturgy*, on the other hand, very early on produced numerous works, and Christian hymnography (like its Jewish counterpart, for that matter) includes some fine literary compositions. Old translations* of the Bible* are often of mediocre literary quality (e.g., the Greek of the Septuagint and the Latin of the Vetus latina), but the exercise has also produced great works: the German Bible of Luther*, the King James Version in English, the French Psalms of Clément Marot, and, more recently, the English Psalms of P. Levi. Among the most fruitful studies that

the biblical corpus has recently stimulated, the contributions of literary historians and theorists occupy a privileged place (e.g., Frye 1982).

b) Spiritual Literature. Spiritual, or mystical, literature abounds in fine writings in prose (*The Cloud of Unknowing,* the works of François de Sales) and verse (Jacopone de Todi, Hadewijch of Anverd, John of the Cross, the French translation of John of the Cross by Cyprien de la Nativité). We may add that major Christian thinkers (Montaigne, Pascal*) are also major writers, and that theology written in modern languages since the 16th century has included first-rate prose stylists (Newman*, the Calvin* of the *Institutes*). We should mention the apologetics of G. K. Chesterton and the theological writings of C. S. Lewis, two masters of the English language. Moreover, some theologians have chosen to use literary fiction (e.g., the novels of Newman, *Callista* and *Loss and Gain,* and the *Fragments of Tegel* by Bonhoeffer*). The literary history of religious feeling and religious thought is a very rich history, showing a large Christian contribution to the literatures of the world. Bremond's great virtue was to have demonstrated this fact persuasively.

c) Literature and Theological Intentions. Alongside works with an edifying purpose and great literary value, such as the sermons of Bossuet or the religious discourses of Kierkegaard*, there is a great deal of fiction that conveys theological themes. The purest example may be found in the fiction of C. S. Lewis or of his friend J. R. R. Tolkien. On occasion, the literary form of the fairy tale or the science fiction story is used either to rewrite biblical events or to "sub-create" (Tolkien 1947) worlds with a history rich in spiritual teachings. In some cases, a work is theological in an anonymous or pseudonymous way (see Lacoste 1990): in Lewis (*Chronicles of Narnia*), the Christ figure is a lion named Aslan; in Tolkien, elves and goblins embody the traditional figures, angels*, demons*, and others, of Christian narratives (see Lacoste *FZPhTh* 36 [1989]). In addition to these extreme examples, the literary appropriation (or the expression in literature) of Christian themes and episodes is very widespread: Racine's biblical tragedies, literary versions of the martyrdom of the Carmelites of Compiègne (in works by both von Le Fort and Bernanos), theatrical hagiography in Corneille's *Polyeucte*, embellishment of a biblical episode in Victor Hugo's "Booz endormi," Milton's eschatological epic; a substantial part of Western literature was written with reference to the Bible and to the history of the church*, and there is at least one major literary work that occupies an important place in theology: *The Divine Comedy* of Dante*. We might add that some works were written with this context in mind, although they had no Christian theological purpose: e.g. "Moïse" by Vigny or *Port-Royal* by Montherlant. Other works reflect a philosophy of religion*: for example, Lessing's *Nathan the Wise*. Some works refer to the Bible while violently challenging Christianity (e.g., Kazantzakis).

d) Literature, Images of Experience, and Creation of Languages. Other literary works lend themselves to a theological reading because of the realities that they mirror, as well as because of the manner in which they perform that function. Whether exploring the logic of spiritual experience with Christian novelists (Dostoyevsky, Bernanos, Pater, Graham Greene, Flannery O'Connor), the logic of a wholly atheist world with novelists unconcerned with Christianity (Stendhal, Flaubert), or the logic of evil* in Thomas Mann's *Doctor Faust*, the novel is often the best key to a theological hermeneutics of modernity. Poetry, which may take on the appearance of a confession of faith* (e.g., in Claudel and Péguy), or the expression of theological positions (e.g., the mixture of Scotism and nominalism found in Hopkins), is important in any event, because as Heidegger* says, it "makes being more present," presents reality better than reality shows itself to us outside the mediation of language: eucharistic meanings in Hölderlin and Trakl, the feeling of praise* in Pessoa, prayer* in Rilke, repentance in Apollinaire, or a sense of the cosmos in Hugo, are all reflected in poetry. It can also, as with Celan, express human distress in the face of horror, and attempt to do what Adorno said was unthinkable, to write poetry after Auschwitz (*see* Dupuy 1994). Everything can be made into poetry. Any poem, in a sense, can provoke a theological or philosophical commentary. And every poem can provide new words with which to speak of God.

e) "Literary Theology." Theology's interest in literature is recent but extensive. It has several sources and several aspects. 1) The existence of secular universities, in which biblical and Christian works are subjected to the same protocols of reading as any other work, has made it necessary to investigate the specifically literary character of the biblical sources of Christianity: the multiplicity of literary genres in the sources of Christianity has provoked, among others, structural readings and narratological analyses (e.g., Frye 1982). In the same context of secularization*, there have also been explorations of the strictly "religious" ways of reading a work (Griffiths 1999). 2) The influence of Henri Bremond (1865–1933) made possible a revision of the history of French literature, in which spiritual works receive the literary attention they deserve, and it has also made it possible to build bridges between literary and religious experience; to Bremond we may add Charles Du Bos (1882–1939), an exemplary reader of Claudel, Bérulle, Pater, and the English poets, as well as a commentator on Bremond's *Prière et Poésie*. 3) The influence of H.U. von Balthasar cannot be overestimated and has led to the recognition that the best modern theologians were often men of letters. It was often through the mediation of Balthasar, both his books and his translations, that Hopkins, Bernanos, Péguy, and others were admitted into the club of theologians. 4) The question of language has been subjected to profound reexamination in recent philosophy* and theology, and this has led to a reevaluation of the image, metaphor, narrative—of everything that cannot be reduced to expression in strictly propositional terms. The recognition that all religious language is metaphorical (*see* J.M. Soskice, *Metaphor and Religious Language,* Oxford, 1985) has led to a better understanding of the language of parables*, of biblical symbolism, and of the narrative formulation of theological ideas (narrative* theology). We might also note the defense and illustration of liturgical language by K. Pickstock (*After Writing,* Oxford, 1998), an original response to the critique of "phonocentrism" by Jacques Derrida. 5) The liturgical reform that came out of Vatican* II has given rise to literary and theological endeavors: the composition of new prefaces and the translation of biblical passages for liturgical use, among other things, have led to collaborations between men of letters and theologians: the poet Patrice de la Tour du Pin, for example, was involved in the French translation of Paul VI's missal. 6) At the same time, the interest taken by men of letters in theology has given rise to fruitful undertakings: the poetry of P. Levi (1931–2000), for example, attempts to speak of Christmas and Good Friday, and the poetry of C. Campo (1923–77) is saturated with Christian themes. More generally, the persistence of a poetry interested in the "religious" (Rilke, T. S. Eliot, Kathleen Raine, among others) has helped to make poetry a sui generis "theological locus." 7) Finally, by developing the concept of the "world of a text," the hermeneutics of Paul Ricoeur has given us the means to link reading and existence, text and world, in a manner that has as much resonance in theology as in philosophy. Biblical* theology now has more resources than ever before to draw attention to the "habitability" of biblical texts. A new discipline is in the process of development under the combined impetus of all these factors, "literary theology," which seeks "to demonstrate the possible opportunity for a renewal of the language of faith, not by using writers but by listening to them" (J.-P. Jossua).

- H. Bremond (1916–36), *Histoire littéraire du sentiment religieux en France,* 12 vols., Paris.
J. R. R. Tolkien (1947), "On Fairy-Stories," in *Essays presented to Charles Williams,* Oxford, 38–89.
H. U. von Balthasar (1962), *Herrlichkeit* II/1 and II/2, Einsiedeln.
N. Frye (1982), *The Great Code: Bible and Literature,* London.
J.-P. Jossua (1985), *Pour une histoire religieuse de l'expérience littéraire,* vol. 1, Paris (vol. 2, 1990; vol. 3, 1994; vol. 4, 1998).
J.-Y. Lacoste (1990), "Théologie anonyme et christologie pseudonyme: C. S. Lewis, *Les Chroniques de Narnia,*" *NRTh* 112, 381–93.
R. Faber, et al. (1991), "Literatur und Theologie," *NHThG* 3, 240–78.
P. Gerlitz, et al. (1991), "Literatur und Religion," *TRE* 21, 233–306 (bibl.).
B. Dupuy (1994) "Selon le mot d'Adorno—L'invocation par Paul Celan de la poésie de Mandelstam," *Istina* 39, 242–67.
O. González de Cardedal (1996), *Cuatro poetas desde la otra ladera,* Madrid.
K. J. Kuschel (1997), *Im Spiegel der Dichter: Mensch, Gott und Jesus in der Literatur,* Düsseldorf.
P. J. Griffiths (1999), *Religious Reading: The Place of Reading in the Practice of Religion,* Oxford.

JEAN-YVES LACOSTE

Liturgical Cycle. *See* Liturgical Year

Liturgical Year

This notion appeared in the 18th century, a period in which the West clearly distinguished secular time* from the time of religious practice. In this perspective the liturgical year designates the particular manner in which numerous Christian churches* live the time of the year and organize over its course the unfolding of their celebrations. It expresses theologically the specific style according to which Christians are aware of living within the time of salvation* unfolded by God*.

a) Liturgical Year until the Fourth Century. The New Testament clearly shows that, as early as the time of the apostles*, the church celebrated every Sunday*. Had it begun at this time to celebrate other days in addition to Sunday? Or did Christians first give up all the festivals customary among the Jews, and then after the apostolic age establish a Christian festival of Easter by strongly emphasizing the paschal character of the Sunday closest to the Jewish Passover? For lack of clear indications in the New Testament, past historians tended to incline toward the former hypothesis. Today, however, it is the latter that seems most probable, although it is still not certain. In fact, it makes it easier to understand the argument over Easter that first arose within the Church of Rome at the time of Pope Victor (c. 189–200), and then caused serious conflict between the Asian churches (in Asia Minor) and the Roman Church (joined by most other churches). The Asian churches celebrated the Christian Easter on the same day as the Jewish Passover, that is, the 14th day of the month of Nisan, whatever the day of the week: hence the name quartodecimans. The other churches, by contrast, celebrated Easter (or had come to celebrate it) on the Sunday following 14 Nisan, and thereby established a coherence between the weekly celebration of Sunday and the annual celebration of the Christian festival of Easter. On either side, as far as we know, these churches certainly had the same celebration of the death* and Resurrection* of Christ*, the same celebration of the paschal mystery*, even if their respective approaches to Christology* and to redemption, Pauline in the one case and Johannine in the other, had a different coloration. After a while, Easter was celebrated on Sunday everywhere, including in Asia Minor.

By the second century at the latest there was a paschal vigil, with preparatory fast, which celebrated both the death and the Resurrection of Christ. By the late second century, there was a celebration on the 50th (*pentekostè*) day after Easter, a festive time whose song is the alleluia and which brings eschatological joy into the time of the church. It was not until the fourth century that there developed the Liturgy* of the paschal triduum (from the night of Maundy Thursday through Easter), the 50th day of the paschal time was celebrated as the day of the descent of the Holy* Spirit, and the 40th as the day of Ascension.

By 240 the preaching* of Origen* in Jerusalem* indicates that there was a period of 40 days in preparation for Easter (Renoux 1993). It therefore does not seem (against Talley's hypothesis) that Lent derives its origin from a fast coming immediately after the Epiphany. In any event, this time became the exclusive (or privileged) time for patristic catecheses* and for the preparation of adult catechumens for the sacraments* of Christian initiation.

b) Christmas and Epiphany. Christmas was certainly celebrated in 336 in Rome, and the festival is probably earlier than the Peace of the Church (edict of Milan, 313). It is possible that its date was set during the winter solstice to oppose the pagan celebration on that day of the birth of the sun god (the invincible Sun, *sol in-*

victus). In another part of the Mediterranean world, in Egypt, the baptism of Christ was celebrated on 6 January. In the course of the fourth century the two festivals came to be celebrated in the East as well as the West, although the gospel events commemorated did not exactly correspond. The Roman liturgy celebrated the Nativity of Christ on 25 December, and on 6 January principally the adoration of the Magi and the revelation* of the Savior to the Gentiles (and secondarily the baptism of Christ). The Byzantine liturgy celebrates both the Nativity and the adoration of the Magi on 25 December, and the baptism of Christ on 6 January. The Roman liturgy of Christmas is strongly influenced by the dogma of the two natures of Christ, as it was defined at the Council of Chalcedon*, whereas the piety of the faithful, from the 13th century onward, was gradually colored by the devotion of Francis of Assisi to the Infant Jesus in the manger, which gave Christmas an importance comparable to that of Easter.

c) Complete Liturgical Year. The celebration of Easter, on the one hand, and those of Christmas and Epiphany on the other, have since Christian Antiquity been the two high points of the liturgical year. Times of preparation or prolongation were spread around those points. In addition, and independently of the two cycles, there was the ordinary time of the year, in the course of which each Sunday was celebrated in its own right, and throughout which the Holy* Scriptures were read in the liturgy in a continuous or semicontinuous manner. Several new elements appeared in the fourth and following centuries:

1) The importance in the year of baptismal and monastic declarations of intent: the former considerably influenced the development of the 40 days before Easter (Lent) as well as the Easter vigil, and the latter later took on great importance in the Byzantine year.

2) The passage (particularly for Easter) from a celebration of the mystery* taken in its unity to a celebration, that was in a sense historical, of the detail of the events lived through by Christ. This displacement appeared in Jerusalem in the late fourth century, according to the pilgrimage narrative of the Spanish woman Egeria (late fourth century), then in the following century in the unfolding of the liturgical year in the various sanctuaries of the Holy City, as we know it from the Armenian lectionary (the fifth century Jerusalem lectionary, which was adopted in its entirety in Armenia).

3) An eschatological element of varying importance depending on the times and the liturgies. In

Western liturgies this was prominent in Advent, placed as much at the end of the year as in preparation for Christmas, and perhaps even more so, in the broad patristic perspective of the two advents of Christ, the first in humility and the second in glory*, that formed the framework for the time of the church. From this point of view, the theme (proposed by Bernard* of Clairvaux) of an intermediate advent in hearts and the emphasis on Christmas might make less perceptible how the history* of salvation strove toward its final end.

4) The beginning of the year differed in East and West, depending on particular liturgies. In the Roman liturgy it began at Christmas, and subsequently on the first Sunday in Advent.

d) In the Churches from the Reformation there was sometimes preserved, in particular with respect to the organization of eucharistic readings, a liturgical year inherited from the Middle Ages. This was the case for Anglicans* and Lutherans*.

e) The liturgical movement, which began in the 19th century, showed the importance of the liturgical year for the Christian life. Among many writers, two Benedictines warrant particular mention: in France, Prosper Guéranger (1805–75), restorer of the monastic life at the abbey of Solesmes, with his *Année liturgique* (completed after his death by Dom Lucien Fromage); in Germany, Odo Casel (1886–1948), a monk of Maria Laach, whose numerous writings emphasize the presence of the mystery of salvation in the Divine Liturgy, particularly at Easter. Their work was bound up with the action undertaken by Pope Pius X to reform the liturgical year by restoring the primacy of Sunday over saints' days.

f) The liturgical reform of Vatican II gives a prominent place to the liturgical year, which is the subject of an entire chapter of the conciliar constitution on the liturgy. This chapter emphasizes the commemoration of the history of salvation, centered on Easter, the celebration of Easter and Sundays, the baptismal and penitential aspect of the liturgical year, and the subordinate position of the cult* of the saints in relation to the commemoration of the mysteries of Christ. The implementation of this program, which included the Roman missal and the lectionary of 1970, as well as the Liturgy of the Hours (formerly the breviary) of 1971, was particularly noteworthy for a very substantial increase in biblical readings in the Mass, as the council had demanded. From now on the biblical readings would be spread over a liturgical cycle of three years. This lectionary has been very warmly welcomed in English-language Protestant Churches.

● P. Guéranger, L. Fromage (1841–66, 1878–1901), *L'année liturgique,* Le Mans-Poitiers-Paris.
B. Botte (1932), *Les origines de la Noël et de l'Épiphanie,* Louvain.
O. Casel (1932), *Das christliche Kultmysterium,* Regensburg.
A. Baumstark (1940), *Liturgie comparée,* Chèvetogne.
B. Botte (Ed.) (1967), *Noël, Épiphanie, retour du Christ,* Paris.
C. Renoux (1969–70), *Le codex arménien Jérusalem 121,* 3 vols., Paris-Turnhout.
H. Auf der Maur (1983), *Feiern im Rhythmus der Zeit,* I: *Herrenfeste in Woche und Jahr,* Regensburg.
P. Jounel (1983), "L'année," in A.-G. Martimort (Ed.), *L'Église en prière,* IV: *La liturgie et le temps,* Paris, 43–166.
T. J. Talley (1986), *Origins of the Liturgical Year,* New York.
P. Bradshaw (1992), *The Search for the Origins of Christian Worship,* London.
C. Renoux (1993), "La quarantaine pré-pascale au IIIe siècle à Jérusalem," *MD* 196, 111–29.

PIERRE-MARIE GY

See also **Cult of Saints; Passover; Time**

Liturgy

Liturgy here denotes the Christian worship* considered as a whole, particularly in its historical forms and in relation to the tradition* of the church* and the rules of its discipline. Reference should be made to the article Cult for the theological interpretation of the acts through which human beings express their religious relationship to God*.

1. Meanings of the Word Liturgy in History; Equivalent Terms

a) The word *leitourgia,* in Christian Greek as earlier in the Greek translation of the Old Testament, had various uses, but it did not serve to designate Christian liturgy in its totality, as has become the case in the modern West. In the Byzantine tradition the term *Divine Liturgy* became the specific name for the celebration of the Eucharist. In the West the term began to be used after the Protestant Reformation, when there was an attempt to find a neutral term permitting the avoidance of the two denominational designations of *Mass* (Catholic) and *Communion* (Protestant). In the 17th and 18th centuries *liturgy* took on a general sense among Catholics, Anglicans, and then, more gradually, Protestants* as a whole. Once this general sense was established, a series of derivative terms appeared: *liturgist* (specialist in the liturgy), *liturgical* (liturgical* year; liturgical law; liturgical science—with different connotations in the German *Liturgiewissenschaft* and the English *liturgiology*). Thereafter, the scope of reference of the word *liturgy* was expanded by reference to its etymology, which made it possible to emphasize a dimension of public service, service of the people* *(laos)* of God in its religious practice.

b) The historical equivalents are many. In the Latin Middle Ages two general terms corresponded to the modern meaning of the word *liturgy*. The first was *ecclesiastical offices (officia ecclesiastica)*, already attested in the seventh century by Isidore of Seville, who received and transmitted the culture of late antiquity. The second term was *divine service* (corresponding to the German *Gottesdienst*). Theologians and jurists (the latter under the influence of Roman law) also used the expression *cultus Dei,* it being understood that the Latin word had, until the beginning of modern times, a very broad scope (like the French *cultiver* and the English *worship*), and that only the object (of God, divine) gave it a religious sense. The Renaissance borrowed from antiquity the expression *rites and ceremonies,* from which come expressions such as *religious ceremony, ceremonial, ritual,* and especially the use of the word *rite* to designate all the liturgical practices of a particular church, especially in the case of Eastern churches.

2. Liturgy and Various Aspects of Theology

a) Liturgy and the Theology of the Sacraments. Around the 12th century Western theologians distinguished within the liturgy an essential kernel made up of the seven sacraments*. In the course of the centuries that followed, this sometimes meant that the importance of the liturgy as a whole was lost sight of. Vatican* II, by contrast, attempted to restore a global vision.

b) Liturgy and Mystery of the Church. In New Testament Greek the word *ekklèsia* designates, depending on circumstances, the local* church community or the

universal Church, or even the liturgical assembly as such. The liturgy thus must be the action of the Church (Congar 1967; Pottie 1988), an action in which, of course, roles are sacramentally diversified.

c) Liturgy as Locus Theologicus. This is one of the fundamental reference points in Catholic and Orthodox theology*, and it holds for the faith* of all Christians as it does for the work of theologians. In this respect Catholic theology refers to a formulation sometimes attributed to Pope Celestine I (*DS* 246), according to which liturgical prayer (prayer* III 1) expresses what should be believed: *lex orandi, lex credendi.*

d) Liturgy and the Praying Life of the Christian in the Church. It seems clear that there are quite profound differences in this domain between Orthodoxy*, the approach of the Protestant Reformers, and the current expression of the Catholic vision.

In the Orthodox perspective liturgical practice is closely bound to the experience* of the Christian mystery* on the one hand, and on the other, to the identity of a concrete church community, from which it has never been dissociated.

Various 16th-century Protestant Reformers attempted to distinguish what came from the New Testament from later accretions. The latter were all considered as optional, even if the manner of experiencing them might strongly color the identity of various communities.

Over the last few centuries there have been tensions in Catholic liturgical theory and practice between law*, spirituality, and sacramental dogmatic* theology. Following the liturgical movement growing out of the work of Dom Prosper Guéranger (1805–75), Vatican II and its liturgical reform sought to restore unity between spiritual life* and liturgical practice, and to resituate the experience of the church so that it would be seen less in its institutional reality than in its mystery and its sacramental reality. This movement seems often to have encountered genuine interest on the part of Protestant churches.

3. Liturgical Books and Liturgical Law

According to their conceptions of the Church and tradition, different Christian perspectives have different positions of principle on the relationship of each celebration to traditional practices and to the books used in the celebration. At one extreme there is a feeling that the books or the rules provide merely a convenient outline for the celebration as it may be organized in any particular place, and at the other a concern for conformity in the greatest detail to what is provided by custom or the prescriptions of the liturgical books. In history* and practice, the liturgy has been performed from memory and by custom for centuries and, to a large extent, by using books, but it has gradually given an ever larger place to written material—to liturgical books and written rules—as well as to the desire to conform to the practice of the principal churches, especially those of Rome* and Constantinople. In the West liturgical books were divided first according to the role of each person (bishop*, priests*, deacons*, cantors) in the liturgy, and then, because of the growing importance of the private mass and the individual recitation of the divine office, according to complete liturgical actions (missal, breviary).

In the Catholicism* of the West the liturgical reform of Vatican II relaxed uniformity and attributed some degree of liturgical responsibility to the bishops of the various countries.

4. Liturgical Languages

In the early church the principal languages used in the liturgy were Greek, Syriac, and later also Latin. Latin replaced Greek in the Roman Church in the third and fourth centuries, and it remained for centuries the language of culture and the liturgy, even as it gradually ceased to be understood by the majority of worshippers. In the 16th century, the liturgical use of spoken languages was adopted by the Reformation churches, while the Council of Trent* maintained the nearly exclusive use of Latin in the liturgy of the Catholic Church. Vatican II left it to the bishops of the various countries to choose the languages to be used in the celebration, as has traditionally been the case in the Eastern churches.

● A.-G. Martimort (Ed.) (1984), L'Église en prière, vol. 1, New Ed., Paris.

1)
J. Oehler (1925), "Leiturgie," RECA 12/2, 1871–79.
O. Casel (1932), "Leiturgia-Munus," OrChr 3/7, 289–91.
H. Frank (1936), "Leiturgia-Munus," JLW 13, 181–3.
P.-M. Gy (1990), La liturgie dans l'histoire, Paris, 50–57, 177–194.

2)
Y. Congar (1967), "L'Ecclesia ou communauté chrétienne, sujet intégral de l'action liturgique," in J.-P. Jossua, Y. Congar (Ed.), La liturgie après Vatican II, Paris, 246–82.
I.-H. Dalmais (1984), "La liturgie et le dépôt de la foi,", in A.-G. Martimort (Ed.), L'Église en prière, vol. 1, New Ed., Paris, 282–9.
C. Pottie, D. Lebrun (1988), "La doctrine de l'Ecclesia: Sujet intégral de la célébration dans les livres liturgiques depuis Vatican II," MD 176, 117–32.

3)
P.-M. Gy (1990 a), "Typologie et ecclésiologie des livres liturgiques," in La liturgie dans l'histoire, Paris, 75–89; (1990 b), "Traits fondamentaux du droit liturgique," MD 183, 7–22.
T. Elich (1991), "Using Liturgical Texts in the Middle Ages," in G. Austin (Ed.), Fountain of Life, Washington D.C., 69–83.

4)
A.-G. Martimort (1966), "Essai historique sur les traductions liturgiques," MD 86, 75–105.

PIERRE-MARIE GY

See also **Architecture; Cult; Images; Music; Prayer**

Local Church

By *local church* is meant the Church present in a particular place. The definition, significance, and role of the local church have evolved in the course of history*, and differ from one Christian family to another. The universal Church is the communion* of local churches.

a) The New Testament uses *Church (ekklèsia)* in the singular as a name for the One Church of Christ* (Mt 16:17 f.; 1 Cor 12; Rom 12:4 ff.; Eph 4:4 ff.; 1 Pt 2:4–9, etc.), and in the singular or plural to denote the local churches: the church of God* at Corinth or Rome (1 Cor 1:2; 2 Cor 1:1, etc.), the churches of Asia, or the domestic churches (1 Cor 16:19; Rom 16:3–5; Col 4:15; Phlm 2). Diversity was not simply a matter of territory: it could also be theological (pagan-Christian or Judaeo-Christian communities), or based on differing church structures. The question of the unity* of the local churches within the One Church of Christ was raised from the outset, and resolved by means of visits, synods*, or joint assemblies (such as the "council of apostles" in Acts 15), and later by a common reference to the canon of Scriptures.

b) Within the triadic structure of ministry* instituted by the early church*, the bishop* was responsible for the local or territorial church. He was assisted by presbyters* and deacons*, to whom he could delegate some functions. In the empire under Constantine, when Christianity had become the state religion, the local church was an ecclesiastical district: there were eparchies (provinces) in the East and dioceses (from the Greek *dioikèsis,* which originally denoted an administrative region of the empire) in the West. The word *parish (paroikia),* at first synonymous with the local church governed by a bishop, was used to denote either the diocese or the various locations within the diocese where Christian communities lived. Alongside the diocesan local churches there began to appear the religious orders, which were not in any sense local churches, but which enjoyed an "exemption" under canon law removing them from episcopal jurisdiction*—an exemption destined to become an ecclesiological problem in the 13th century. The monasteries themselves would sometimes be regarded as *ecclesiolae in Ecclesia,* but this expression had no canonical authority.

c) Vatican* II confirmed that

> A diocese is a portion of the people of God which is entrusted to a bishop to be shepherded by him with the co-operation of the presbytery. Thus by adhering to its pastor and gathered together by him through the Gospel and the Eucharist in the Holy Spirit, it constitutes a particular church in which the one, holy, catholic, and apostolic Church of Christ is truly present and operative. (*Christus Dominus* 11).

The terminology is certainly "hesitant" (H. Legrand 1983), since dioceses are referred to either as local churches or "regional" churches. The ecclesiological vision is clear: the diocese or local church is the place in which the Church of Christ is actualized. However, it attains completeness only in communion* with the other local churches: together they comprise the Catholic Church. Unity is maintained by the college of bishops, the pastors of the local churches answerable to the bishop of Rome*, and finally, the pope*. He has power of jurisdiction and magisterium* over the local churches, collectively and individually.

d) The Orthodox churches have a similar approach, but insist on the autonomy of the local churches. In the celebration of the Eucharist *(sunaxis),* each local church is a full expression of the one Church of Christ. The bishops ensure the unity of the local churches. A centralized authority with power of jurisdiction exists at the level of the autocephalous churches (indeed this is what defines them), but not at the level of the Orthodox Church as a whole.

e) In Protestant* terms the local church is the parish. Wherever Christians celebrate the Word* and the sacraments* together there is a church: thus local churches are not defined in terms of the bishops, whose power was strongly contested by the Reformation. In some denominations (Anglicanism*, Lutheranism*, etc.) the overall direction of local churches is achieved by means, on the one hand, of a consensus between the direct representatives of the local churches gathered as a synod*, and by the bishops or presidents of the regional or national church structures on the other (the Episcopalian synodal system). In other traditions (for example the Calvinist tradition), such direction takes place on a synodal basis (the Presbyterian synodal system), while in yet others the autonomy of each local church or parish is central and it alone has authority (Congregationalism*).

f) The fragmentation and loss of identity of local structures in all areas of society* has not been without consequences for local churches. Alongside the geographical structure of parishes, there exist sectional communities (academic, hospital, and professional chaplaincies, Catholic Action, etc.). Shared spiritual choices give rise to new, sometimes interdenominational, incarnations of the Church. The unity of this multiplicity of incarnations of the Church is a question raised within each Christian family and between the different churches. It represents a new ecclesiological challenge, which calls for a new form of the ministry* of *épiskopè* to serve the communion of these different churches coexisting in the same place.

● W. Elert (1954), *Abendmahl und Kirchengemeinschaft in der alten Kirche, hauptsächlich des Ostens,* Berlin.
H. de Lubac (1971), *Les Églises particulières dans l'Église universelle,* Paris.
J. Neumann (1980), "Bistum," *TRE* 6, 697–709.
J. Hoffmann (1983), "La recomposition de l'unité," in B. Lauret and F. Refoulé (Ed.), *Initiation à la pratique de la théologie,* vol. 3, Paris, 347–84.
H. Legrand (1983), "La réalisation de l'Église en un lieu," ibid., 143–345.
C. Möller (1984), "Gemeinde I," *TRE* 12, 316–35.
A. Houssiau (1985), "Paroisse," *Cath* 10, 671–87.
J.-M.R. Tillard (1987), *Églises d'Églises: L'ecclésiologie de communion,* Paris.
G. Siegwalt (1992), *Dogmatique pour la catholicité évangélique* II/2, 11–82, Paris; (1993), "Confessionnalité et catholicité," *PosLuth* 41, 222–38.
M. Lienhard (1995), "La direction personnelle, collégiale et communautaire de l'Église," *PosLuth* 43, 177–202.

J.-M. R. Tillard (1995), *L'É. l.: Ecclésiologie de communion et catholicité,* Paris.

GÉRARD SIEGWALT

See also **Bishop; Communion; Pastor; Presbyter/Priest; Regional Church; Synod**

Loci Theologici

Catholic theology gives the name *loci theologici* to the various fields from which theological knowledge may develop its understanding, and to the various sources it uses: Scripture, tradition*, the Fathers* of the Church, the magisterium*, the liturgy*, and so on. The problematics developed around this expression are essentially the work of the Dominican theologian Melchior Cano (1509–60), whose treatise *De locis theologicis,* published in the historical context of the Council of Trent*, enjoyed a following for several centuries and exercised a decisive influence on the history and teaching of theology.

a) Melchior Cano and the Reform of Catholic Theology. The renewal of Catholic theology in the 16th century was the result of struggles between various tendencies—Thomism*, Scotism, nominalism*, Augustinianism*—and especially of the challenge represented by the radical work of Luther*. It was characterized by a renewal of the Scholastic method in the Spanish schools brought by the return of humanism* to Latinity and classical culture, and by the weight granted to arguments drawn from the authority* of the church* (*see* the Council of Sens, held in Paris in 1528). For example, Ignatius of Loyola composed "rules to follow in order that we never depart from the true feelings that we should have in the Church militant" (*Spiritual Exercises,* Rule 11, no. 363). Spain was experiencing at that time a revival of Thomism whose most brilliant representative was Thomas of Vio (Cajetan, 1470–1534), and for which the Dominican school of Salamanca was the standard-bearer before the creation of the Society of Jesus. There, the great theologian Francisco de Vitoria (1483–1546) taught Dominique de Soto (1494–1560) and Melchior Cano. In this school the treatment of each theological question required the successive exploration of the various fields that were later named *loci theologici.* These methods, transmitted to the early

Jesuits Laynes and Salmerón, were later used at the Council of Trent.

Cano was a professor at the University of Salamanca, bishop* of the Canary Islands, and an active architect of the decisions of the Council of Trent. A contemporary historian judges him harshly: "an intellectual wrapped up in doctrine and devoted to the power of scholarly language"; "major architect of the policy of repression and the closed mind" (A. Milhou, *Histoire du christianisme,* Paris, 1992). Along with the Grand Inquisitor Fernando de Valdès, he took an active part in the Inquisition: against illuminism, sometimes against the Jesuits, and even against the Dominican Bartolomeo Carranza (confessor of Charles V and Philip II, provincial of the Dominicans, theologian at the Council of Trent, and archbishop of Toledo).

Cano, whom Gardeil calls "the founder of theological method," bitterly criticized decadent Scholasticism*, primarily for its lack of rigor. For example, he stigmatized those who transformed the opinions of a school into indisputable dogmas* and the contrary opinions into heresies*. Vitoria had launched a movement, and Cano was to codify it. J. de Maldonat (1533–83) was the faithful propagator of the Salamanca method of Cano and defined the ideal of theology as the union of sacred letters with the Scholastic method.

b) Sources of the Notion of Locus Theologicus. Although Cano's work was without precedent, the key notion of *De locis theologicis* was not radically new. Cano obviously referred to the idea of *loci dialectici,* repertories of arguments for eristic controversies codified by Aristotle in the *Topics,* on the basis of the most general notions (logical predicates: genus, species, difference, particularity, and accident). But it was less from Aristotle himself than from the *De inventione dialectica* of Rodolphus Agricola (1527), and through him the *Topics* of Cicero, that Cano drew in importing the notion into theology. Because theology relied on particular propositions of diverse origins and because it made broad and precise use of the argument from authority, the topics of Cicero and Agricola were more applicable than those of Aristotle to a study of the principles of faith. Indeed, those principles had to be connected to one another in order to be able to reach more general conclusions.

The notion of *locus theologicus* was current at the time of *De locis theologicis,* but it designated the governing positions of theology or of a theologian, or else the commonplaces of theology, or the *loci* of the Protestant theologians (*see* Lang 1924, c. II, §2–3). Melanchthon, for example, had written a *Loci communes rerum theologicarum* (1521, revised in 1559, *Loci praecipui theologici*). This was an exposition of the principal themes found in the heart of Scripture: the fallen human condition, sin*, justification*, faith*. The way in which Cano understood it, on the other hand, and in accordance with the spirit of the *Topics,* the notion designated the repertory of fields from which the arguments *(loci arguandi)* of the discipline of theology could be drawn. He defined them as the "domiciles of all the theological arguments, where theologians will find support for all argumentations, either to prove or to refute" (*De locis theologicis* I. III). A sketch of Cano's doctrine had already appeared, curiously, in a speech delivered at the Council of Trent in 1547 by B. Carranza, although it is impossible to say which of the two "enemies" influenced the other. They both referred to a passage from Thomas* Aquinas (*ST* Ia. q.1. a. 8. ad 2) in which *locus* appears incidentally applied to theology, with the sketch of an enumeration. Vitoria had noted it. But it was less to this passage than to the theological practice of Thomas that Cano often referred, taking him as a model in the use (invention) of *loci theologici* (*De locis theologicis* XII. c. III). The originality claimed by Cano cannot, however, be questioned, because the systematization of theology that he proposes on the basis of the *loci theologici* is specific to him.

c) Organization of De locis Theologicis.   Published in 1563, one year after the close of the Council of Trent and three years after the death of Cano, the 12 books (out of 14 planned) of *De locis theologicis* are presented by the author as a systematic and original work. The enumeration of the ten *loci theologici,* however, should not be considered an exhaustive decalogue (I. III). He divides and subdivides them as follows (I. III and XII. III):

A)   The *loci proprii* are those that rely on *authority* and are divided into fundamental *loci,* which contain the entire revelation*: 1) the authority of Scripture; and 2) that of the (oral) traditions of Christ* and the apostles*, and *declarative loci,* concerning only the preservation, interpretation, and transmission of the revealed content, themselves distinguished according to whether they provide absolutely *certain* principles; 3) the authority of the Catholic Church; 4) the councils (especially the general councils), 5) the authority of the Roman Church (magisterium of the pope), or *probable* principles; 6) the ancient saints, that is, the Fathers of the Church; 7) Scholastic theologians and canonists.

B)   The *secondary loci* call upon reason* and might correspond to the use of the *social sciences* in theology; they are: 8) natural reason, 9) philosophers and jurists, 10) history*, documents, and oral traditions.

According to Cano the work of the theologian is to practice both *invention* (that is, the search for intelligible elements in revealed phenomena) and *judgment.* The art of theology lies in the combination of the two: neither in pure invention and discussion for the love of discussion (the academy), nor in the conclusion alone (the Stoics). *Invention* discovers its arguments in the ten *loci theologici.* Theological judgment, for its part, should train itself to use the *loci theologici* with relevance, by appreciating the nature and the probative force of each authority for each particular question. It may well be, for example, that human history, although an inferior *locus theologicus,* is a more certain authority (a more effective *locus theologicus*) than reference to a verse of Scripture with too vague a meaning. The "theological notes*" designed to qualify certain propositions from the point of view of their agreement or disagreement with Catholic faith function as a way of evaluating the theological questions and conclusions. When those conclusions are unanimous, whether they come from the church, a council, the pope, or saints, they belong to the faith with the same right as the content of Scripture and the apostolic traditions (XII. V).

The second part of the work, beginning with Book XII, would have set out the way of using *loci theologici* depending on interlocutors and contexts: Scholastic argument (XII), explanation of Scripture (XIII), controversies with heretics, Jews, Muslims, and pagans (XIV).

d) Aspects of the Theology of De locis Theologicis. The book is a fairly accurate representation of the Tridentine theology that Cano strongly helped to shape.

The systematization by means of *loci theologici* gave two distinctive characteristics to almost all Catholic theology of the succeeding centuries: a central reliance on authority *and* a necessary reliance on copious erudition (scriptural, patristic, magisterial).

As for Scripture, Cano deals with its inspiration, its inerrancy, and the church's determination of the canon (canonicity being distinguished from authenticity). He defends the value of the Vulgate. On tradition, formulations very close to those of Trent cannot conceal the fact that his theory says a bit more than the conciliar documents, which fundamentally remained rather cautious (*see* Ratzinger in Rahner and Ratzinger, *Offenbarung und Überlieferung,* Freiburg, 1965). Cano speaks most frequently of traditions in the plural, considering them in objective fashion as "transmitted things," and stressing that they constitute a *locus theologicus* independent of Scripture, since the Church is older than Scripture. Against the *sola scriptura* of Luther's disciples it seems that we can attribute to Cano the paternity of a theology of the two sources of revelation (*partim…partim,* an expression that was, however, withdrawn by Trent), which long remained a dominant model (*see* Holstein 1969).

It is probably with reference to the certain declarative *loci,* which specify the various forms of the authority of the church, that Cano presented his most influential arguments, once again more because of their systematic character than because of their content. The authority of the Catholic Church is that of the entirety of the body of the visible Church, which cannot be mistaken in its faith *(in credendo),* whatever the period of time. Inerrancy is also attributed to the pastors* and the doctors in their teaching *(in docendo).* Cano hierarchizes the authority of the councils according to their representativeness: the general councils, ecumenical and sufficient in size, represent in fact the entire church and thus have an authority equivalent to that of the church if they have been called and confirmed by the pope. A council's decision is infallible if it bears the character of a universal and definitive obligation, even if its subject does not belong to faith while being sufficiently linked to revelation for the church to guarantee its validity. Finally, the authority of the pope is linked to that of Peter*, and to his inerrancy as guaranteed by Christ. Pontifical inerrancy is thus a truth of faith limited to the public exercise of the authority of the pope; and against the supporters of absolute and universal inerrancy, Cano says that the pope "does not need our lies and does not need our adulation" (Lang, quoted by Sesboüé 1996).

e) Influence. De locis theologicis went through 30 editions up to 1890. The historical context of Cano's work and the gradual discrediting of the Scholastic method in philosophy* and theology justify its success. Together with the breadth and the composition of the book, this explains its influence. Without radically contrasting the style of medieval *Summas,* which gave a privileged place to speculative argumentation, to that of the treatises (and particularly of treatises *De locis* based on Cano's model) and manuals that flourished after the Council of Trent, the true birth of positive* theology can be dated from *De locis theologicis.* The place given by Cano to authority, and that reserved for Scripture and the ecclesiastical magisterium, followed by the argumentation of the Fathers of the Church and of theologians, as well as his appeal to history, shows in fact his concern to support dogmatic proof with positive data. Cano himself does not use the term (it was in use earlier, found in Jean Mair in 1509 and, in 1556, in Rule IX of the Constitutions of Ignatius Loyola), and, because of his attachment to the speculative method, he can only be considered as the initiator *per accidens* (Gardeil 1926, col. 740) of positive theology.

The expression became general by the end of the century as a means of characterizing a manner of teaching that emphasized more the affirmation of revealed phenomena than speculative questioning. It was only gradually that a distinction was established between positive theology, which was concerned with establishing the whole matter of the theologian's study, and speculative or Scholastic theology, which limited itself to rational argumentation on the basis of what positive theology had established. But the priority given to the positive establishment of doctrine, to the qualification of any given thesis by the theological note that specifies the degree of assent due to it, before showing the speculative reasons for it and drawing from it possible theological conclusions (contrary to the order followed by Thomas in the chapters of *CG,* as Cano notes, *De locis theologicis* XII. XI), presages the abandonment of the Scholastic method as the principal means of teaching.

Two independent, if not contradictory, consequences may be attributed to the influence of Cano's theology of *loci.* The first is the gradual narrowing of focus of theological science onto the problems of critical history, whether sacred history or the history of the church, which gave to the 10th and final *locus* a growing importance. In the 17th century Petau and Thomassin, by a return to the Fathers of the Church and a copious historical erudition, developed an important erudition that had started in the preceding century. The new importance granted to authority was strengthened by that which the Enlightenment gave to reason alone, and by the influence of Enlightenment thinkers on the theology of the Reformed Churches.

The 19th century, with the school of Tübingen* and Newman*, saw the apogee of the positive method (Hocedez 1949–52) and of a theology taught according to the order of its *loci* (*De locis theologicis* was modernized by J. Berthier in his own *De locis theologicis,* Turin, 1900). This occurred under the pressure of the nascent social sciences and of Protestant theologies, whose "scientific," exegetical, and patristic argumentation was often directed against the speculations of the Catholic tradition. The idea of a history of dogmas and the idea of a development of dogma certainly have an important source in Cano.

The other influence is to be sought in the evolution of the notion of the pontifical magisterium and in the increasing role that the pope was led to play after Trent, by means of bulls, briefs, and constitutions. Although the specific notion of magisterium was not developed until the 18th century, the political organization of the church along the lines of modern states, the universal regulation by means of different forms of censure (defined by Benedict XIV, 1740–58), and the debate on the indefectibility (before the infallibility* defined by Vatican* I) of the pope and the councils, as well as on the relative superiority of the former or the latter (Jansenist polemic), together form a bridge between Trent and Vatican I. The reestablishment of Catholic universities in the 19th century went along with the spread of Roman teaching by means of encyclicals (*Mirari Vos,* 1832), by the recall of the magisterial tradition (first edition of the Denzinger), and by the concern to attribute theological notes and dogmatic notes to old and contemporary teachings.

Although for historical and pedagogical reasons emphasis had been placed on the positive ground of theology and on the authority of the various sources of teaching, this change of perspective was not accompanied by a new conception of theological science. Cano remained an Aristotelian and could define science only by the deduction of conclusions. His successors did not take up the challenge. The development of a doctrine of science adapted to the new reality, such as Thomas Aquinas had accomplished in his time by his reception of Aristotle, did not take place. Cano and the succeeding centuries long maintained the coexistence of a "positive" theology of sources, derived from the new requirements of thought and a "scholastic" theology that had retained a medieval status (Tshibangu 1964, 330). This unstable balance, finally upset in the contemporary period, perhaps partly explains the now chaotic evolution of "theological science."

● M. Cano, *De locis theologicis* (1714), Ed. H. Serry, Padua. (1839), Ed. Migne, *Cursus completus,* vol. I; (1890), Ed. Cucchi, 3 vols., Rome; a new edition by the Navarre University is in the works.
M. Jacquin (1920), "Melchior Cano et la théologie moderne," *RSPhTh* 9, 121–41.
A. Lang (1924), *Die* loci theologici *des Melchior Cano und die Methode des dogmatischen Beweises,* Munich.
A. Gardeil (1926), "Lieux théologiques," *DThC* 9, 712–47.
A. Duval (1949), "Cano (Melchior)," *Cath* 2, 465–7.
E. Marcotte (1949), *La nature de la théologie d'après Melchior Cano,* Ottawa.
E. Hocedez (1949–52), *Histoire de la th. au XIXe s.,* 3 vols., Brussels.
V. Beltrám de Heredia (1953), "Cano (Melchior)," *DSp* 2/1, 73–76.
J. Beumer (1954), "Positive und Spekulative Theologie: Kritische Bemerkungen an Hand der *Loci theologici* des Melchior Cano," *Schol.* 29, 53–72.
C. Pozo (1962), *Fuentes para la historia del método teológico en la escuela de Salamanca,* vol. 1: *Francisco de Vitoria, Domingo de Soto, Melchior Cano y Ambrosio de Salazar,* Grenada.
T. Tshibangu (1964), "Melchior Cano et la théologie positive," *EThL* 40, 300–339; (1965), *Théologie positive et théologie spéculative: Position traditionnelle et nouvelle problématique,* Louvain- Léopoldville, esp. 169–210.
G. Holstein (1969), "Les deux sources de la Révélation," *RevSR* 57, 375–434.
J. Belda-Plans (1982), *Los lugares teológicos de Melchior Cano en los comentarios a la Suma,* Pamplona.
B. Körner (1994 *a*), "Cano Melchior,", *LThK*3 2, 924–5; (1994 *b*), *Melchior Cano*—De locis theologicis: *Ein Beitrag zur theologischen Erkenntnislehre,* Graz.
B. Sesboüé (1996), "Melchior Cano et les lieux théologiques," *Histoire des dogmes,* vol. 4: *La parole du salut,* 165–73.

CYRILLE MICHON AND GILBERT NARCISSE

See also **Hermeneutics; Notes, Theological; Revelation; Theology**

Logos. *See* Word

Lombard, Peter. *See* **Lateran III, Council**

Lonergan, Bernard John Francis

1904–84

Bernard Lonergan, Canadian Jesuit, philosopher, and theologian, taught at Montreal, Toronto, and the Gregorian University in Rome*. His work is dedicated to an ever more adequate understanding of both human intelligence and the mysteries of Christian faith*.

a) Writings on Thomas Aquinas. In *Grace and Freedom: Operative Grace in the Thought of St. Thomas Aquinas,* Lonergan traces the development of the theology* of grace* from Augustine* to Aquinas*, sets out the relations between operative grace and cooperative grace, and presents an analysis of Aquinas's theory of causation, operation, divine transcendence, and human liberty*. This work convinced Lonergan that what was needed to reach up to the mind of Aquinas was not simply historical, philosophical, or theological reconstructions of Aquinas's work. For any of these reconstructions to be accurate, profound changes are needed within those who work on them.

From Augustine, Lonergan learned that conversion* to Jesus Christ involves intellectual and moral dimensions, as well as the religious dimensions. The psychological and phenomenological narratives of Augustine's intellectual conversion to truth, his moral conversion to good*, and his religious conversion to God* revealed in Christ Jesus ground experientially the shift toward theory in Aquinas. This threefold conversion becomes in Aquinas the division of the virtues* into intellectual, moral, and theological virtues (*ST* Ia IIae, q. 55–67; IIa IIae, q. 1–170). To understand the systematic breakthrough in Aquinas's theology, Lonergan realized that he had to undergo what he later termed an "intellectual conversion."

Lonergan's *Verbum: Word and Idea in Aquinas* sets out the basic terms operative in Aquinas's cognitional theory, and also how these terms are derived from the human experiences of questioning, understanding, and judging. Insight into images generates understanding, and this understanding expresses itself in concepts. Human understanding is not content with thinking, however: we want to know what is true, so questions of truth emerge, and only when we grasp the sufficiency of the evidence do we reach judgment, and therefore truth or falsity. Lonergan shows that what Aquinas terms "the light of active intellect as a created participation in divine light" is in fact our human capacity to raise ever further questions.

b) Studies on Human Knowledge and Theological Method. In *Insight: A Study of Human Understanding,* Lonergan transposes the cognitional theory that he learned from Aquinas into contemporary contexts. The book is an invitation to the reader to appropriate his or her own acts of experiencing, understanding, and judging. The first part sets out *insight* as activity, showing how attention to acts of understanding enables the reader to correlate the methods of the sciences in such a way as to arrive at a coherent and open understanding of the world*, designated as "emergent probability." The second part builds on the reader's own self-appropriation as a knower, showing how developmental and dialectical methods operate in cognitionally grounded metaphysics, ethics*, and natural theology*. The work demonstrates how human understanding does in fact consist in related and recurrent operations, and that failure to attend to these operations has led to the dialectical contradictions in modern culture, philosophy*, and theology. The program of the book is succinctly stated by Lonergan (*Insight*, p. xxviii):

> Thoroughly understand what it is to understand, and not only will you understand the broad lines of all there is to

be understood, but also you will possess a fixed base, an invariant pattern, opening upon all further developments of understanding.

From his discoveries in *Insight,* Lonergan advanced to *Method in Theology,* where he shows that his notion of transcendental method can restructure how theology is done. Transcendental method is neither Cartesian (Descartes*) nor Kantian (Kant*), but is a set of related operations of understanding yielding cumulative and progressive results. After treating human good, meaning, and religion, the book develops the notion of functional specialties in theology. There are three types of specialties. 1) Field specialties continually divide and subdivide the fields of data to be investigated, as in the field of biblical studies. 2) Subject specialties classify the results of the investi-gations in order to teach those results, as when departments are separated into areas such as Hebrew history*, early Christian antiquities, and so on. 3) Functional specialties differentiate the successive stages in the process from the data to the results of the investigations.

● *The Collected Works of Bernard Lonergan (CW),* Toronto, 1988. (1957), *Insight*: *A Study of Human Understanding,* London (*CW* III, 1992).
(1967), *Collection,* London (*CW* IV, 1988).
(1967), *Verbum*: *Word and Idea in Aquinas,* Notre Dame, Ind.

(1971), *Grace and Freedom*: *Operative Grace in the Thought of St. Thomas Aquinas,* London.
(1972), *Method in Theology,* New York.
(1976), *The Way to Nicea*: *The Dialectical Development of Trinitarian Theology,* London.
(1980), *Understanding and Being*: *An Introduction and Companion to Insight* (*CW* V, 1990).
(1982), *Les voies d'une théologie méthodique,* Paris (collection of articles on theology by Lonergan).
(1991), *Pour une méthodologie philosophique,* Montréal (collection of articles on philosophy by Lonergan).
◆ H. Meynell (1976), *An Introduction to the Philosophy of Bernard Lonergan,* London.
Coll. (1978), *The Lonergan Workshop,* Atlanta.
M. O'Callaghan (1980), *Unity in Theology: Lonergan's Framework for Theology in Its New Context,* London.
M. Lamb (1981) (Ed.), *Creativity and Method: Essays in Honor of Bernard Lonergan,* Milwaukee.
L. Roy (1982), "La méthode théologique de Bernard Lonergan," *Com(F)* VII/1, 66–74.
Method: *A Journal of Lonergan Studies,* Los Angeles (1983–91), Boston (1992–).
M. Lamb (1984), *History, Method and Theology,* Atlanta.
V. Gregson (1988) (Ed.), *The Desires of the Human Heart: An Introduction to the Theology of Bernard Lonergan,* New York.
F. Crowe (1992), *Lonergan,* London.

MATTHEW L. LAMB

See also **Augustine of Hippo; Bible; Ethics; Knowledge of God; Mystery; Nature; Theological Method; Thomas Aquinas; Thomism**

Lord. *See* **Christ/Christology; Name**

Love

If God* reveals himself to humanity as love, or agape (1 Jn 4:8), it would follow that he makes himself known through love: we know God by loving him and by loving our fellow human beings. But we also knows a love that is independent of the love of God. Human beings love themselves in their search for happiness; they love others by inclination, desire, or passion. Are these two radically distinct and incompatible kinds of love? Or does love of God presuppose a strictly human love if it is to be understood by human beings? Is charity—the love inspired by grace*—a transformation of natural love or does it require a total rupture with that love? To answer these questions we must know what love itself is. Is it the search for self-satisfaction by possession of the other or, on the contrary, disposses-sion of oneself, ecstasy?

I. Metaphysics of Love

1. An Essential Trial for Human Beings

a) Unsuitable Love.   Amorous passion is not the only form of love. Compared to indefectible maternal love it is in fact the most fragile and vulnerable form. But passion is an event that, by its unpredictability, has the nature of a revelation. One discovers that the meaning of one's existence does not depend on oneself but on another who bursts into one's life without warning. The beloved object does not correspond to the expecta-tions, tastes, and interests—that is, to the constitu-tion—of the ego. On the contrary, the beloved exceeds the ideal image a person could make of his or her hap-piness. In this way, the beloved breaches all propriety. This disparity serves as the essential mechanism of tragedy, poetry, and the novel, in which love is most often connected with its forbidden forms: adultery, so-cial incompatibility, incest, misalliance (Tristan and Isolde, Romeo and Juliet, Phaedra and Hippolyte, Swann and Odette).

b) Ecstatic Quality of Love.   Passion works a trans-formation, an alienation of the subject. In that it arises from hope (Stendhal, De l'amour [On Love] chaps. 2 and 3) that is, from the subject's representation of the happiness the beloved object could bring him, passion would seem to be derived from self-love. But the ego-istic point of departure, which leads the subject to try to possess the other, functions like a lure to bring the subject out of himself or herself and make the very ex-istence of the ego depend on the other: without you I am nothing. The totality of meaning is gradually trans-ferred to the other ("crystallization"): the object is not lovable because of his/her value (qualities); on the contrary, love is the first cause on the basis of which the subject places value and meaning.

The lover sees the beloved with new eyes. Instead of being considered as a dangerous illusion, as blindness, this alteration should be recognized as deep wisdom*. In the trials of love, in the pure pathos of devouring fire, the subject acquires essential knowledge of sacrifice and the gift of self without discursive or logical media-tion. In the detachment from self, self-renunciation, putting one's destiny in the hands of the other, aban-doning one's self to the other, the subject can give meaning to his or her existence.

c) Oath of Fidelity.   If passion arises out of emotion, out of the contingency of a physical upheaval such as sexual desire, it prolongs itself in a willed act that en-gages the totality of being. The truth of love does not lie in the satisfaction extorted by possession but in the generosity of heart that gives emotion a value of essence. The oath of fidelity which love immediately calls forth is not a guarantee of inalterable emotion. Rather, it attests to the will's full assent to that gift of oneself that transports the subject beyond all self-interest and self-satisfaction.

Love acquires a value that not only exceeds the ego, but also the me-you relation. It tends to diffuse and transform the world*, regardless of the obstacles the world might place in its path.

2. Love and the Meaning of the World

a) Cosmic Principle.   Traditional forms of wisdom make love the unifying principle that presides over the formation of the world. The most ancient ritual prac-tices associate sexuality with the renewal of the sea-sons and the fertility of crops. Empedocles taught that love assembles the elements in such a way that they "constitute a unique order" (Fr. B. 17), whereas hatred separates them. Here love is participation in a univer-sal movement of nature rather than an individual senti-ment. In the cosmic myth* related by Aristophanes in Plato's Banquet (189 d-193 d) the love that moves a man to unite with a woman manifests the aspiration to return to an original unity, lost and forgotten since the occurrence of separation.

b) Ruse of the Life-Wish.   But if the meaning of love is extended to the dimension of the world, it no longer has meaning for the subject who feels it. It is as if love were the phenomenon of an obscure fundamental force that toys with the helpless individual in its power. The senti-ment that moves the individual to discover his or her ipseity through the choice of a singular, unique, irreplaceable object would be an illusion employed by the cosmic principle to achieve its own ends of self-realization. This "metaphysics of love" (Schopenhauer, The World As Will and Representation) leads to pes-simism. If love is an individualization of the sexual in-stinct by which the life-wish indefinitely repeats itself, then the individual has no other truth than dissolution in the species, death*. The sacrifice to which the individ-ual consents, believing it has meaning, is in reality a re-turn to nothingness*: that is, the affirmation of absence of sense. The only escape from this fatality is to re-nounce the illusion of meaning and so to renounce love.

Love has no meaning because it is not the source of any [real] fertility. The reproduction of the same ob-structs all future, all novelty, all possibility. It is not, strictly speaking, procreation. If the difference between the sexes, between lover and beloved, is reduced to an illusion and dissolved in cosmic unity, love is not the ecstatic élan toward the other, it is the indefinite return to an impersonal self. But this is not an explanation of love, it is simply its denial.

3. Eros and Transcendence (Plato)

a) Sons of Poros and Penia. Diotima, whose comments are related by Socrates, (*Banquet* 201 e-212 a) understands love (Eros) as an intermediary, (*metaxu* 202 a *Sq*) a demon *(daimôn)* born of the union between Penia (penury) and Poros (resource) (203 a-d). To love is to desire something one lacks (200 a), so love is deprived of beauty (201 b) and poor like its mother (203 c). But it is not enough to think of love in negative terms, as lack. Lack has its term in satisfaction. Need can be satisfied by fulfillment, but the same is not true of love, which does not seek possession. And yet this radical dissatisfaction is not any kind of impotence, because love is activated by its father's inventiveness (203 d-e).

b) Transcendence. The person who loves recognizes in the other all the beauty* or value that he himself does not have, and yet he does not seek by fusion to become that which he is not. His aim is not to be beautiful (or learned): it is to contemplate the beauty in the other, as that which in this other exceeds all communication. By uniting with the other he does not appropriate the other's beauty, but maintains it in its constitutive alterity. Love is made possible only by the transcendence of the Beautiful.

c) Fertility. This is why love is in itself operational and can only be thought in its works (ergo, 199 a, developed starting from 204 c). The object of love is not to obtain something from the beloved, because love is already in itself in relation with that which is beyond essence, the Good* (206 a, *see The Republic* 509 b). Its object is rather "to give birth in the Beautiful" (206 b), that is, to be made fertile by the transcendence that, in enlightening it, gives meaning to being. The interest of lovers' conversation is not their reciprocal satisfaction but the creativity by which they, mortals, give birth to the absolute novelty of the immortal (206 e *Sq*).

If love has a universal, divine sense (206 c) valid as well for physical love as for love of thought, it is because, born of the difference between same and other, it is creative—it produces the unpredictable, the new.

4. Friendship and Being (Aristotle)

a) Unity of the Community. Whereas the Platonic Eros is animated by a perpetual motion of going be-yond self, the Aristotelian *philia* (*Nicomachean Ethics* l. VIII and IX) is inscribed in the stability of a community of which it forms the bond and maintains the unity. Man is destined by nature to live in a city* (*Politics* I, 1253 a 2). This is not only because he is endowed with language and can discuss with other men what is just and unjust, but because he is united to others by a form of familiarity and friendship (*NE* 1155 a 22). Unlike Eros, *philia* is not the exclusive choice of another, it is the relation of mutual affection and benevolence (1155 b 32) that naturally unites those who live together (1157 b 7) and who, consequently, resemble each other (1159 b 2).

However, just as there are several forms of community, there are several kinds of friendship. When people unite out of self-interest or for pleasure, they do not seek out the presence of the other for its own sake. Friendship is perfect only between virtuous beings because they prefer loving to being loved, desire the Good for their friends without expecting anything in return (1156 b 9), and thus draw their pleasure from friendship alone (1159 a 27 *Sq*).

b) Ethics. Aristotle resolves the contradiction between self-love and love of one's fellow human being. True friendship presupposes that one be disinterested and renounce egoism (1168 a 32). Nonetheless it is founded on a proper understanding of self-love. Because he who prefers the Good over all things and consequently sacrifices his own interests to the welfare of his friend, in reality loves that which is best for himself; so he loves himself by attaching himself to the higher part of the soul* (1168 b 28–1169 a 35).

Friendship is "intimately connected with virtue" (1155 a 3) because it is beautiful in itself (1155 a 28) and because perfect friendship is necessarily accompanied by virtue (1156 b 7), but also because one cannot "live well" without having friends (1169 b 3–1170 b 19). For human beings, "living well" means "living well together," so friendship is "the greatest good for Cities" (*Politics* II, 4, 1262 b 9).

c) Friendship As Experience of Being. Friendship is not only an ethical and political value, it is an experience of an ontological nature. Aristotle repeatedly emphasizes the pleasure procured by association, intimacy, and presence of friends, particularly when they are virtuous (1157 b 7; 1157 b 17–18; 1158 a 4 *Sq;* 1171 a 1; 1171 b 14; 1172 a 7). The incapacity to live together spoils friendship, whatever the feelings of benevolence and inclination toward the other. Aristotle gives the justification for this physical proximity by explaining why a happy man needs friends. He develops the idea that a friend is an alter ego (1170 b 7). I need another who is at the same time me, not so I can withdraw into self-satisfaction and find myself in others, but in order to contemplate (1170 a 2) or rather feel (1170 a 31) in or with him that which I cannot fully feel in myself, for lack of distance and communion*. For a happy man, what is most worthy of being felt is the "good life" that is his—in other words, life-in-act, the fact that his life is not drudgery but an activity having its end in itself, a praxis. We enjoy being alive because we rejoice at our friends' being alive. Aristotle goes further: what we enjoy in the presence of friends is supremely desirable Being itself (1170 b 8) through the shared feeling of existence.

II. Revelation of Love

Though Aristotle thinks the perfection of the relation that can exist between free and equal human beings, he cannot conceive of the possibility of friendship between beings as dissimilar as human beings and gods (1158 b 35). But Thomas* Aquinas, defining charity as "a sort of friendship of man for God," (*ST* IIa IIae, q. 23, a. 1, resp.) speaks of a commerce or intimacy *(conversatio)* between man and God. That God could consider human beings as friends (Jn 15:15) is the revelation* that changes the meaning of love.

1. Old Testament

a) God's Love for Humanity.   Love of God for human beings is manifest in the creation* by the role given to them (Gn 1:26–29) and renewed in the covenants* concluded with his people (Noah, Gn 2:18; Abraham, Gn 12:3, Gn 15and 17; Moses, Ex 19). God loves his people by grace, without judging them on their merits. He helps them in times of affliction and delivers them from slavery in the land of Egypt (Dt 4:37; 8:17; 9:4–6; 10:15). God recalls his eternal love and unfailing fidelity to the Covenant (Dt 7:7–9) at times when he suffers the infidelity of his people (Jer 31:3; Sg 3:17; Mal 1:2). This is why the love of God (Hebrew *chesed*, Greek *eleos*) takes the form of mercy* (Is 54:8).

This fidelity resembles the love and tenderness (Ex 3:14; Ps 103 (102):4, 103:8, 103:13) of a father or mother for their children. They give birth to their children, cherish and nourish them, bring them up, and forgive their escapades and rebellion (Is 1:2, 49:15; Jer 31:20; Hos 11:1, 11:3 f.). But the violence* of love and the exclusivity of election place God in the position of a husband jealous or betrayed because his wife has prostituted herself (Is 54:5, 62:4–5; Jer 2:2, 31:22; Ez 16). The marriage* of Hosea with a harlot is the symbol of the marriage of God with Israel* (Hosea 1–3).

The Psalms* invoke the mercy of God in asking for his help or forgiveness (Ps 51 [50]:1; 89 [88], 89:2, 89:3, 89:25, 89:29, 98 [97]:3, 145 [144]:8). They express the desire and expectation of being loved by God (Ps 89 [88]:50, 119 [118]:41), as well as confidence in his eternal love (Ps 136 [135]).

b) Love of Human Beings for God.   As a counterpart of the love of God for his people should correspond, according to a commandment* that sums up the entire law*, the love of human beings for God (Dt 6:5; Hebrew *ahaba,* translated in the Septuagint by *agape,* quite rare in Greek), manifest not only by observance of precepts* but by the heart's disposition to receive the Word* (*see* Psalm 119 [118]). The fear that goes with the love of God is not slavish submission; to fear nothing but God means to have no object of fear on earth (Dt 7:18).

c) Love of One's Fellow Human Beings.   God also commands love of one's fellow human being, (Lv 19:18) who is not only the child of Israel, but the stranger, *"for you were sojourners in the land of Egypt"* (Ex 22:20, 23:9; Dt 10:18 f., 19:33; Prv 25:21 f.).

d) Love between Man and Woman.   The Old Testament grants an important place to love between man and woman*: it is as *"male and female"* that God created humanity in his image (Gn 1:27); the history of the people of Israel is traversed by couples* united in love: Adam* and Eve, Abraham and Sarah, Isaac and Rebecca, Jacob and Rachel, Samson and Dahlila, Boaz and Ruth, David and Bathsheba. The Song of Songs celebrates carnal union.

2. Synoptic Gospels

a) Love As Center of the Law.   The preaching* of Jesus* is inscribed in the Jewish tradition* that centers the precepts of the law around the two commandments of love (most often agape). The commandment to love God (Deuteronomy 6) is *"the greatest commandment";* but Jesus immediately associates it with its likeness, the commandment to love one's neighbor (Mt 22:36–40; Mk 12:28–31; Lk 10:25–28; Lv 19:18). Recalling that love is the essential of the law—in a context in which there is an attempt to test him—Jesus shows that his doctrine is not meant to be original. But he insists on the actualization, in the heart and in practice, of the already well-known sense of the "law."

b) Love of Neighbor.   This recentering of the law on love entails displacements in the order of ethical priorities. Love for God has no sense unless it is translated into love of one's neighbor, which is the touchstone of justice*. We do not honor God through respect for ceremonial and cultural precepts but by helping those who are in need (Mt 12:1–8; Mk 2:23–28; Lk 6:1–5, 13:10–17). Human beings will be judged by their love for their fellows, and particularly for the least of these (Mt 26:31–46).

Love and the works of mercy it brings forth are addressed to the poor and downtrodden, the prisoner, the sick, and the stranger. Forgiveness should also go out to those whose behavior is judged reprehensible: publicans and sinners (Mt 9:10–13; Mk 2:15 ff.; Lk 5:29–32). The great parables* of mercy (Lk 15:1–32) show the gratuitous nature of the gift of forgiveness and the joy that accompanies it.

c) Love for One's Enemy. The commandment to love is radicalized when it is extended to one's enemy (Mt 5:43–48; Lk 6:27–35). In the Gospel of Matthew Jesus underscores the opposition between his own teachings and the tradition as kept by the Jews. The new way comes not to *"abolish [them] but to fulfill [them]"* (Mt 5:17), to bring the precept back to its original meaning by pushing it to its most extreme case. It is incumbent upon the one enlightened by the law, the Jew, to be better than publicans and pagans. These last do not have the law and yet they love their friends. Jesus believes that the commandment to love as a simple movement of the heart would not be immediately universal. The Samaritan is not a pagan; he knows the law and, showing more love than the priest* or the Levite (Lk 10:29–37), accomplishes it better than those at whom it is directly aimed.

d) The Chosen One. The major revelation of the synoptic Gospels is the name* given to Jesus by God at his baptism (Mt 3:17) and transfiguration (Mt 17:5; Mk 9:7): "The Chosen One" (Lk 9:35). This citation from Isaiah 42:1 (repeated in Mt 12:18) makes Jesus the Servant who must face suffering (Isaiah 53) in order to liberate Israel (Isaiah 54). This parallel allows for the interpretation of his Passion (announced in a passage close to the account of the transfiguration in Mt 17:22–23; Mk 9:31; Lk 9:44) and Resurrection* as a manifestation of the love of God.

3. Letters of Paul

For Paul, *"the love of God in Christ Jesus our Lord"* (Rom 8:39) is not so much an object of teaching or preaching as a mystery* *"which surpasses knowledge"* (Eph 3:19). We do not participate in this love by conforming to precepts, no matter how legitimate and useful they may be, but by giving ourselves over to the Holy* Spirit, whose fruit is love (Gal 5:22).

a) The Event of Love in Christ. In fact it is in the very event of Christ's coming, his death and Resurrection that love radiates and gives itself to be seen by those whose eyes have been opened by the Spirit. It is no longer a matter of the *sign* of God's love but of its absolute *advent.* God not only sent the Liberator to save his people, he delivered (both gave to the world and abandoned into the hands of sinners) his own *Chosen One.* The Son offered by the Father* offers himself in turn. He abandons himself, renounces himself to the point of dying on the cross (Phil 2:7–8; Rom 5:8). Love is the condition, the meaning, and the fruit of this sacrifice*, which is the decisive event of the passage from the old to the new for the world, for the Jewish people, for all humanity (Eph 2:15, 4:22; 2 Cor 5:17; Col 3:9).

b) Theological Virtue. By the Spirit we participate in the death of Christ and so are introduced into the mystery of his life (Rom 6:8–11). We cannot think of our death in Christ without being incited by love (2 Cor 5:14), because sacrifice* inspires love. This spiritual life* in communion* with Christ rests on a bringing together so that now "faith*, hope*, and love abide" (1 Cor 13:13). These are known as the "theological virtues*" because in their diversity and complementarity they structure the constitution of human beings in their relation to God. It is as an element of that structure that love becomes charity: the Vulgate, which translates *agapè* as *dilectio*, uses the term *charitas* in the letters of Paul. However, the term *charity*, which came to mean compassionate beneficence in French *(charité)*, may be preferable to *love*, despite the theological usage. Love exists only in its relation to the other two virtues, and is often named together with them (1 Thes 1:3, 5:8; 2 Thes 1:3; 1 Cor 13:7; Gal 5:6; Rom 5:1–5, 12:6–12; Col 1:4 f.; Eph 1:15–18, 4:2–5; 1 Tm 6:11; Ti 2:2); faith brings us to discover love in God, which in turn is diffused in the heart of the believer and expands his or her faith to the dimension of hope, which is confidence in the love of God already manifest in its fullness (Rom 8:35–39).

c) Primacy of Love. But the greatest of the three virtues is love, (1 Cor 13:13; Col 3:14) not because faith represents an imperfect certainty, but because it is by love that we believe and hope (1 Cor 13:7; Rom 5:5). Love is the source of all values. Generosity, the gifts of the Spirit, liberty*, respect for the law, all of these have value only because they derive from love and produce love (1 Cor 13:1 ff.; Gal 5:14; Rom 13:8 ff.). Not only does love communicate life, it is life.

4. The Johannine Texts

The Gospel* of John is the gospel of love. Jesus came into this world to bear witness to the love of the Father for Jesus himself (3:35, 10:17) and for all human beings (3:16).

a) A New Commandment. Jesus gives his disciples a new commandment of love: *"that you love one another just as I have loved you"* (Jn 13:34). The measure of love that one must give to others is no longer the love one bears for oneself, as in Leviticus 19:18. The radical exigency of love consists of giving what one does not have, being for the other as Christ was for his disciples. This is possible only if the Spirit (Jn 14:16, Jn 26) creates new human potentialities. Moreover, the reciprocity of this love (each other) supposes a community of those who love in Christ (Jn 17:20).

b) Trinitarian Love. The love which human beings have for one another should be a reflection of the love of Christ for them because the source of this love is the Son's love for the Father (Jn 15:9) as expressed in the priestly prayer* (17:1–26). The Son offers himself out of love for his Father, but he knows that the sacrifice to which he consents demands in return the same love from his Father. At the time of the Passion it is love that unites the Father and Son (17:10, 17:21). Love manifests the Trinitarian dimension of God; it is, strictly speaking, the Spirit.

c) "God Is Love" (1 John 4:8). This statement, which decisively brings together the entire revelation, is not a deification of love (which would have a purely anthropological import), nor a simple evocation of a loving God. God is not a loving ego, he is the very event of love such as it is manifested in the Passion and the Resurrection. God did not keep the beloved for himself: he gave him, and thus included the world itself in his love. In loving Jesus all the way to the cross, he loved humanity like his Son and introduced humanity into his mystery, so that, abiding in his love, it pursues his works.

III. Developments

1. Love of Self and Love of God

a) Saint Augustine* (*De civitate dei* XIV, 28) radicalized the opposition between love of self and love of God, which are at the origin of the two cities, the earthly city (born of "love of self unto contempt for God") and the heavenly city (born of "love of God unto contempt for self"). In *The Confessions* he de-

scribes the spiritual journey of one who has renounced a vain love oriented toward pleasure (III, 1) for an ever greater love of God (XIII, 8).

b) This opposition is an essential theme of Protestant* doctrine, which perceives only one rupture between the order of grace* and the order of nature*. Luther* (thesis 28 of the Heidelberg dispute, April 1518, *WA* 1, 365) criticizes the love that consents to go out toward an object only to the extent that it recognizes a value, in other words, where it expects satisfaction in exchange. The love of God for man is totally gratuitous because it is not conditioned by the certainty of being accepted. It is pure gift.

c) Eros and Agape. Taking an even more severe position within this Protestant tradition, A. Nygren states the radical difference between love that comes from God (agape) and purely human love (Eros). The romantic exaltation of love is a form of self-complacency, a deification of the human that leads to self-destruction and death (Tristan and Isolde). Agape, on the other hand, is received as a grace in filial obedience.

But however relevant the opposition between *amor hominis* and *amor Dei,* it can hardly be validated by the terminological opposition between *eros* and *agape.* Eros cannot be reduced to the search for satisfaction; as Plato reminds us. True Eros consists in giving one's life for those one loves (*Banquet* 179 b *Sq*). And it is not out of the question that love for God can also take the form of Eros. Nonetheless, Nygren rendered service to contemporary theology in proving untenable the contradiction between *Eros* and *agape,* thus giving contradictors the opportunity to suggest more precise topologies and more subtle conceptualizations (D'Arcy 1945; Lotz 1971).

d) Eros More Divine. Dionysius* the Pseudo-Areopagite (*Divine Names* IV, 12) went so far as to assert that *"Eros* is a term more worthy of God than *agape."* Thomas Aquinas took the idea and made it his own (*ST* Ia IIae, q. 26, a. 3), arguing that the attraction exerted by God and passively endured by man in love (*amor = eros*) is stronger than the motives man draws from his own reason*. Love can indeed be motivated by concupiscence (when we seek satisfaction for ourselves) but this does not preclude the existence of a "love of friendship," where the object is loved for itself and the lover wishes its good (*ST* Ia IIae, q. 26, a. 4).

e) Self-Love out of Charity. While self-love that deflects the subject from alterity and keeps him from loving God and his fellow human being is the source of sin*, love of God, charity, commands a form of self-love (*ST* IIa IIae, q. 25, a. 4). After loving God for love of self, man "loves himself for God alone" (Bernard* of Clairvaux, *Traité de l'amour de Dieu,* chaps. VIII-X [Treatise on the love of God]). Sinners do not really love themselves, because they mistake what is truly for their own good; the good do love themselves because they want to conserve the inner person in its integrity (*ST* IIa IIae, q. 25, a. 7; *see* I 4 b above).

2. Mystical Love

a) Ecstasy. If the furthest extreme of love is the void it produces, the self-dispossession, then Eros is indeed its most divine manifestation. Eros is in itself a kenosis* in that the lover must abandon the images he has drawn over his personality, and reveal himself in his nakedness. If I am nothing without you I have to go through this nothing in order to reach you. The asceticism* of destitution, pushed in this way to the extreme of nothing, characterizes both mysticism and eroticism. The common error is that of thinking of mysticism, like eroticism, in terms of union and possession, whereas their common ecstasy is separation from self, dispossession. To intoxicate oneself with divine love is to "forget oneself," "hold oneself for nothing more than a discarded vase," "in a way, to lose oneself as if one did not exist any more, to lose the feeling of self and be emptied of oneself, almost canceled out" (Bernard of Clairvaux, *Traité de l'amour de Dieu* X, 27).

b) Indifference to One's Own Happiness. What is reduced to nothing in the ego is the will, inasmuch as it seeks satisfaction. To this end it must renounce all objects, renounce all desire. In the Song of Songs passion is put to the test of the night (Sg 3:1–3). One wanders without finding anything, the beloved escapes, the Lovable does not let itself be confused with phantoms. "Charity…makes a void of all things in the will, seeing that it makes us love God over all things?" (John of the Cross, *Ascent to Carmel II,* 6). The soul* "totally destitute, desiring nothing" (ibid. II, 7) is in imitation* of Christ, who at the moment of his death was "annihilated and reduced as to nothing" (ibid). This passage through death is the affirmation of life, because death was vanquished in death by love: "Oh death amorously vital, oh love vitally mortal!" (François de Sales, *Traité de l'amour de Dieu* VII, XIII). Fire is simultaneously the erotic and the spiritual metaphor of this vivification in annihilation (*see* the liturgy* of Pentecost: *Et tui amoris in eis ignem accende;* John of the Cross, *Vive flamme d'amour,* stanza II, verse 1).

Once the will is liberated of all self-interest, all expectation of personal happiness, the soul experiences "pure love," "without the mixture of any motive other than that of loving, solely in itself, the sovereign beauty of God" (Fénelon, *Explication des maximes des saints* [Explanation of the maxims of the saints], Art. II). God's love for us being both source and end of our love for him, our love is a reflection of its gratuitous origin. Consequently, love for God cannot be conditioned by the expectation of happiness, even that of salvation*. This is love experienced in a historical present where the individual simultaneously exists in the element of hope (major lesson to be drawn from the quietist crisis), and this is quite different.

To construe hope as primarily a logic of interest is a fundamental misunderstanding. Hope is that relation to the future in which the promises* of God are engaged, and these promises (and all they imply in terms of anticipated realization, centered on the Resurrection of Jesus) bring forth the action of graces and love on the part of the believer. "Pure love," correctly understood, is lived in the fullness of a theological experience. Perhaps it must be said that hope is lived in that experience as a truly "erotic" transcendence toward God. And perhaps that transcendence is the secret of all hope, a secret that would let hope be not just a way of being-in-time but also being eternally.

c) Absence As a Mode of Presence. Pure love accomplishes the precept of virtuous friendship: "love the friend for himself" (*see* I 4 a above). But Christianity introduced a radical difference: when the friend is God, the intimacy, the "living together" that is the act of love and source of pleasure, is a mode of presence characterized by infinite distance. The closer God comes to human beings in his love, the more he makes felt his inaccessible grandeur. "When he loves, all the actions of his love are infinite. He comes down from heaven to earth to look for the creature of clay that he loves, he makes himself man and clay with him, he gives his flesh to be eaten. Such are the prodigious feats of love by which the infinite* surpasses all affection of which men are capable. He loves in God, and nothing is incomprehensible in this love" (Fénelon, *Lettres et opuscules spirituels* XXXI). Claudel describes an "essential absence" that unites the lovers in presence itself (*Le soulier de satin, IVe journée,* sc. VIII).

3. Ethics of Love

a) Principles of Moral Virtues. Pure love has been criticized (by Bossuet) because the disinterestedness of love, the abandon, the state of prayer may plunge the will into indifference, leading it to forget good and evil* and enter into a state of passivity that could turn it away from action. The other extreme is a busy involvement in what is useful, to the extent that the quest for meaning is forgotten. Authentic love is in itself ethical because it is the rectitude of the heart, the virtue that commands man to the good. That is why it is "the principle of all good deeds," and all the moral virtues are enclosed in it.

b) Law of Love. A work cannot be said to be good if it is not accomplished by love. Conversely, all that is done by love accomplishes the law (Rom 13:8). There is no need to fear that love might be mistaken in its conduct or remain idle in the face of a suffering person. The Christian is liberated by love from all external prescription that does not flow from an internal movement of the will (Rom 7:1–7). *Ama et fac quod vis.* But this liberty is not license, precisely because it is conditioned by a love whose demands are superior to those of the ancient law. Love institutes a new law (*ST* Ia IIae, q. 107, a. 2, resp.), which is not written but rather introduced into the heart by grace (*ST* Ia IIae, q. 106, a. 3).

c) Love and Respect. It is common practice to oppose the rigorism of Kantian moral law to this ethic of love. Kant* does in fact warn against a morality derived from the love of men. Because this love cannot "be commanded," moral action would be abandoned to the arbitrariness of each individual's subjective dispositions, which ruins duty in its principle (*Critique of Practical Reason,* AA t. V, 83). But this love is definitely not the love of which Scripture speaks: it is a pathological love, a philanthropy that operates, or does not, according to passing moods. However, Kant admits a practical love (ibid.) that is "good will" put to the accomplishment of duty. It remains the case, however, that this love itself cannot be the principle of duty; it is simply an ideal that completes the duty. The discipline of the law then remains the only standard. Duty toward one's fellow man is not the consequence of love for him, but of respect, and is primarily addressed to the law. Nevertheless, morality is not confused with legalism, that is, a purely external conformity with prescriptions. The common point between respect and love is that neither is subordinate to the principle of personal happiness, and therefore they are not conditioned either by hope for advantages or fear of punishment. The law, like pure love, demands that the will void itself of all objects (or matter).

4. Conclusion

It is always possible to explain the ecstatic dimension of love as a ruse of self-love, to explain mystical love as a sublimation of the sexual instinct, and annihilation before the other as delectation in oneself, as if love were nothing but a cultural valorization of self-satisfaction, self-esteem, vanity (La Rochefoucauld). It is true that the flame that consumes is in itself a purely subjective mode of experience. For love to be truly distinct from egoism the other must exist and precede me by his love. There is no love without revelation of the other. But how can we be reassured without falling into the aporias of subjective confinement? Here, whatever form it takes, love demands that we resolve its ambiguity and make a decision: it is for the will to say what love is. Consequently, the general definition of love supposes a form of generosity: we have to give it credit and consent to absence as an essential mode of being*. This is the confidence of the lover who by oath gives infinite sense to the finitude of his emotions; the confidence of the Socratic philosopher who desires thought within the heart of nonknowledge; the confidence of the believer who accepts to be loved by someone he does not see.

● P. Rousselot (1908), *Pour l'histoire du problème de l'amour au Moyen Age,* Münster (repr. Paris, 1933; 3rd Ed. 1981).
H. Arendt (1929), *Der Liebesbegriff bei Augustin,* Berlin.
H. Scholz (1929), *Eros und Caritas,* Halle.
A. Nygren (1930, 1936), *Eros och Agape,* 2 vols., Stockholm.
G. Quell, E. Stauffer (1933), "Agapaô…," *ThWNT* 1, 20–55.
L. Robin (1933), *La théorie platonicienne de l'amour,* Paris.
É. Gilson (1934), *La théologie mystique de saint Bernard,* Paris.
D. de Rougemont (1938), *L'amour et l'Occident,* Paris (Rev. Ed. 1954).
M. C. D'Arcy (1945), *The Mind and Heart of Love—Lion and Unicorn: A Study of Eros and Agape,* London.
L.-B. Geiger (1952), *Le problème de l'amour chez saint Thomas d'Aquin,* Montréal-Paris.
G. Bataille (1957), *L'érotisme,* Paris.
C. Spicq (1958–59), *Agapè dans le Nouveau Testament,* 3 vols., Paris.
C. S. Lewis (1960), *The Four Loves,* London.
M. Lot-Borodine (1961), *De l'amour profane à l'amour sacré,* Paris.
H. U. von Balthasar (1963), *Glaubhaft ist nur Liebe,* Einsiedeln.
E. Levinas (1964), *Totalité et infini,* The Hague.
V. Jankélévitch (1970), *Traité des vertus,* vol. 2: *Les vertus et l'amour,* Paris.
I. Murdoch (1970), *The Sovereignty of Good,* London.
J. B. Lotz (1971), *Die drei Stufen der Liebe,* Frankfurt.
J. Pieper (1972), *Über die Liebe,* 3rd Ed., Munich.
G. Wallis, et al. (1973), "Ahab," *ThWAT* 1, 105–28.
B. Welte (1973), *Dialektik der Liebe,* Frankfurt.
H. Kuhn (1975), *"Liebe": Geschichte eines Begriffs,* Munich.
E. Jüngel (1977), *Gott als Geheimnis der Welt,* Tübingen, 430–70.
J. Leclercq (1979), *Monks and Love in Twelfth-Century France,* Oxford.
L. A. Blum (1980), *Friendship, Altruism and Morality,* London.
J. Macquarrie (1982), "Love," *In Search of Humanity,* London, 172–86.
C. Yannaras (1982), *Person und Eros,* FSÖTh 44.
J.-L. Marion (1986), *Prolégomènes à la charité,* Paris.

J.-L. Chrétien (1990), "Le regard de l'amitié," *La voix nue: Phénoménologie de la promesse*, Paris, 209–24.

P. Gerlitz, et al. (1991), "Liebe," *TRE* 21, 121–91.

J. Derrida (1994), *Politiques de l'amitié*, Paris.

T. De Koninck (1995), "L'amitié," *De la dignité humaine*, Paris, 203–22.

M. Adam (1996), "Amour de soi," *DEPhM*, 45–51.

M. Canto-Sperber (1996), "Amour," ibid., 33–45.

A. Petit (1996), "Amitié," ibid., 27–32.

J.-L. Marion (1997), *Étant donné: Essai d'une phénoménologie de la donation*, Paris.

P. Bartmann (1998), *Das Gebot und die Tugend der Liebe*, Stuttgart.

YVES-JEAN HARDER

See also **Communion; Faith; Hope; Trinity**

Lubac, Henri Sonier de

1896–1991

a) Life. Born in Cambrai on 20 February 1896, Henri de Lubac became a novice in the Society of Jesus in 1913. Between 1915 and 1917 his Jesuit training was interrupted by the First World War, in which he received head wounds. During the first half of 1920, while he was in Canterbury undergoing the six months of training known as the *juvenat,* he became "entranced" by Saint Augustine*'s *Confessions* and by the last three books of Irenaeus's *Adversus Haereses.* There he also read, "in a state of wonderment," the article "Jésus Christ" by L. de Grandmaison (1868–1927) and the thesis "L'Intellectualisme de Saint Thomas" by P. Rousselot (1878–1915). From 1920 to 1923 he completed his required philosophy* studies on the Island of Jersey where he formed firm friendships with C. Nicolet (1897–1961), G. Fessard (1897–1978), Y. de Montcheuil (1899–1944), A. Valensin (1879–1953), and P. Teilhard de Chardin (1881–1955). A dozen years after Pius X's condemnation of modernism* (1907), which affected the intellectual climate in theological colleges, Lubac and his companions were forced to endure P. Descoqs's highly Suarezian* instruction. On the other hand, they enjoyed the courses taught by J. Maréchal (1878–1944). In 1922, in Aix-en-Provence and in the company of Auguste Valensin, Lubac met M. Blondel*, whose *L'Action* he had read in its 1899 edition. In 1924 he began his theological studies in Hastings, continuing them after 1926 at Fourvière. After his ordination as a priest in 1927 he began to teach fundamental theology at the Institut Catholique in Lyons in 1929. From 1931 on he also taught a course there on the history of religion.

On friendly terms with J. Monchanin (1895–1957), a priest in the diocese of Lyons who read Sanskrit and was preparing for a journey to India, Lubac independently studied Buddhism by studying the volumes held in the Musée Guimet. In 1935 he began an extra course on Buddhism at the Jesuit Faculty at Fourvière. He renewed his contacts with Teilhard, made the acquaintance of P. Claudel (1868–1955), and befriended H. U. von Balthasar*, a Jesuit and a theology student at Fourvière with Daniélou. In 1938, at the request of Y. Congar (1904–95), Lubac published his first book, *Catholicisme.* In the early 1940s he stopped his courses at Fourvière and took a stand alongside P. Chaillet (1900–1972) and G. Fessard in a "spiritual war" against Nazism. In the Free Zone, the three of them created the *Cahiers du témoignage chrétien.*

Inspired by an idea of V. Fontoynont, he founded the collection Sources Chrétiennes (SC), for which J. Daniélou (1905–74) was the correspondent in the Occupied Zone. From 1924 on, at J. Huby's suggestion, Lubac began an investigation into the problem of the supernatural*, which was to challenge the then-current interpretation of Thomas* Aquinas's concept of "pure nature." E. Gilson (1884–1978) would confirm this topic's "centrality." Lubac's *Le Surnaturel* (The Supernatural) was published in 1946 and would soon become the subject of a polemic linked to the debate over the "new theology." In 1947 Lubac was appointed group leader of the periodical *Recherches de sciences religieuses* (Studies in religious sciences), but in 1950, in the wave of Roman suspicion that displaced several French theologians, he was relieved of this post as well as of his chair at the Institut Catholique.

Lubac took advantage of the health problems that followed his war wound to read in Migne's folio editions all the ancient and modern authors who interested him. He became a great expert on the medieval Latin writers and tried to elucidate the caesura of the Renaissance. Having already written a book in 1950 on Origen*'s understanding of the Scriptures, between 1959 and 1964 he published his *Exégèse médiévale,* whose importance for recent developments in hermeneutics* has been acknowledged by P. Ricoeur.

When it appeared in 1953 (although it was made up of texts written before 1950), Lubac's *Méditation sur l'Église* (Meditations on the Church) played somewhat the same role in his life as the *Apologia* had done in Newman's. In August 1960 John XXIII completed Lubac's rehabilitation by calling on him to become, together with Congar, a consultant to the theological commission that was doing preparatory work for Vatican* II. Although this labor initially caused him some unease, Lubac was to become one of the most respected experts at the council*. After it was over, it pained him to notice a certain breach of trust that only accentuated his own solitude, even within the Society of Jesus. He upheld the *Communio* enterprise and drew up several commentaries on the Vatican II documents *Dei Verbum, Gaudium et Spes,* and *Lumen Gentium.* But above all he pursued wide-ranging research, as witnessed by his publication in 1979 and 1981 of the two volumes of *La Postérité spirituelle de Joachim de Flore* (The Spiritual Heirs of Joachim de Flore), in which he criticized the eschatological utopia. Pope John Paul II elevated him to the rank of Cardinal in 1983. Lubac died on 4 September 1991.

b) Aspects of Lubac's Complete Works. Although several of Lubac's writings might be regarded as "occasional theologies," to use Lubac's own phrase, Balthasar was correct in saying that he is the author of an "organic body of work." Moreover, his early *Catholicism* supplied most of the themes he would later tackle. In the above work he shows the social, historical, and inner character of Christian dogma*. By means of a method that has become famous, his expositions are peppered with quotations drawn from the inexhaustible wealth of a tradition* in which the author felt at home. He has the style of a writer and his reflections respond to the needs of the time. In both tone and content he disconcerts those readers accustomed to textbook-style theses.

In his *Corpus Mysticum: Essai sur l'Eucharistie et L'Église au Moyen Age* (Corpus Mysticum: An Essay on the Eucharist and the Church in the Middle Ages) Lubac demonstrates that until the middle of the 12th century the expression *corpus mysticum* (mystical

body) was applied exclusively to the Eucharist*. Its later application to the Church makes the sacramental realism (sacrament*) of the Pauline doctrine of Christ*'s body all the more evident. This was the source of the famous definitions that Lubac's *Méditation sur l'Église* would expand: "The Church creates the Eucharist...the Eucharist *creates the Church.*" Behind the historian of dogma could already be glimpsed one of the forces inspiring Vatican II's ecclesiology*. All the same, it was thanks above all to his *Supernatural* (1946) that Lubac was to profoundly change the field of theology. Battling with the critics, he would supply, with his *Le mystère du surnaturel* (1965) his most polished synthesis on the subject.

Lubac had to rediscover the deep meaning of Thomas Aquinas's texts by going back through four centuries of Thomist commentaries, all of which had been based on a misinterpretation by Cajetan (1468–1533) that had subsequently been passed on by Suarez. According to these authors, Thomas Aquinas was supposed to have defended the idea of a finality proper to man according to nature*, and to which his supernatural finality had been appended. From this derived a theology that, by allowing a "separate philosophy" to deal with everything that had to do with the life and history of man, confined itself to speaking only about the *extrinsic* fringes of that reality.

Even if, as he confessed, other problems had caused him more toil (especially those involving the history of religions), it is indeed in the natural desire for God, innate in man created (creation*) in his image*, that the guiding thread to all Lubac's works should be sought. Such is the "paradox" of man, a spiritual but finite creature whose unique finality is supernatural. "Whence comes his sort of lurching gait, his mysterious limping, which is not only the lameness of sin*, but primarily and more radically that of a creature created out of nothing, who, strangely, approaches God" (*Mystère du surnaturel* 149). Lubac's truly humanist feelings are revealed in many works that find in that "paradox" the essential key to understanding. *Pic de La Mirandole* (1974) is a model of the type. Lubac's enterprise, in conjunction with works by Rahner*, Balthasar, M.-D. Chenu (1895–1990), Y. Congar, and others, allowed theology to return from an "exile" that had forbidden it all contact with living thought. He himself confronted that thought through the "Western atheism*" of P. J. Proudhon (1809–65), Marx*, and A. Comte (1798–1857) (*Le drame de l'humanisme athée,* first published in 1944, went through seven editions during Lubac's lifetime) as well as through "Eastern atheism," and particularly through Buddhism. Lubac's specific contributions to the Christian intellectual current of his own century can be summarized as a theology of the call that opens onto the mystery* of the Church as *convocatio* and as *congregatio*.

c) *"New Theology."* Under this term, used for the first time in the *Osservatore romano* by P. Parente, the representatives of neo-Thomist orthodoxy fustigated everything to do with efforts to change theology in postwar France. M. D. Chenu's little book, *Une École de théologie: Le Saulchoir* (1937) was the first to be put on the Index for having dared to make an appeal for theology's practical function as opposed to the hypertrophy of its speculative function. The controversy flared up again with an article by Daniélou in *Les Études* of April 1846, "Les orientations présentes de la pensée religieuse" (Current directions in religious thought). There Daniélou boldly advocated a return to the sources of Christian thought, scriptural, patristic, and liturgical (Fathers* of the Church, liturgy*), in order to enable it to make contact again with contemporary thought. M. Labourdette answered him in *La Revue thomiste*, an answer that in turn received an immediate response in *Le Bulletin de l'Angelicum* in R. Garrigou-Lagrange's (1877–1964) "La nouvelle théologie: Où va-t-elle?" (Where is the new theology going?). The latter attacked in particular a book by a young companion of L. H. Bouillard, *Conversion et grâce chez Thomas d'Aquin* (1944). Following in the footsteps of Garrigou-Lagrange, the Dominicans of Saint-Maximin claimed to be defending the Thomist notion of grace* and attacked the investigative methods of the Jesuits of Fourvière. B. de Solages, dean of the Institut Catholique of Toulouse, came to the defense of the latter for "the honor of theology."

Already suspect, Lubac was soon at the center of a polemic because of an article in *Recherches de science religieuse* (1948) devoted to the question of the development of dogma (Newman*). C. Boyer, dean of the Gregorian University, could not rest until he and Garrigou-Lagrange had obtained the condemnation of a mythical "School of Fourvière," of which Lubac was supposed to be the leader. As early as 19 September 1946 Lubac had managed to get the "new theology" mentioned negatively by Pius XII himself in a speech at the close of a General Congregation of the Jesuits. The encyclical *Humani Generis* (1951), although it attacked no one directly, was considered a victory by the conservative wing and brought a temporary halt to the renewal of theology.

Although the "new theology" can today be viewed as a "chimera from a fable," in line with Y. Congar's retrospective judgment, the debate of the years 1938–50 is perhaps not definitively over. During that period, the adversaries of renewal, moved by their antimodernist phobia, were wrong to scent doctrinal relativism* everywhere. By their recourse to the "symbolic theology" of the Fathers, the supporters of renewal were, on the contrary, right to refuse to restrict themselves to a "theology of conclusions" that paid no attention to the historical aspect of dogma. But according to Guardini's observation, dogma will always be like "an arc flashing between two poles." A rigorous effort must therefore be made so as to be able to distinguish an authentic development from its corruptions. Besides, scholarship cannot do without a sense of Christian mysticism* or personal contact with the great spiritual traditions. Lubac's works bequeath us an extraordinary testament to that fact.

- K.-H. Neufeld, M. Sales (1974), *Bibliographie Henri de Lubac, 1925–1974*, Einsiedeln.

For 1974–89, *see* H. de Lubac (1990), *Théologie dans l'histoire* II, 408–20, Paris, and *Com(F)* (1992), 17/5, 133–7.

H. U. von Balthasar (1976), *Henri de Lubac: Sein organisches Lebenswerk*, Einsiedeln.

H. de Lubac (1985), *Entretien autour de Vatican II*, Paris.

H. de Lubac (1989), *Mémoire sur l'occasion de mes écrits*, Namur.

E. Guerriero (Ed.) (1991–), *Henri de Lubac, Opera Omnia*, Milan.

OCC (1998–), Paris, 57 vols. planned.

- M. Figura (1979), *Der Anruf der Gnade: Über die Beziehung des Menschen zu Gott nach Henri de Lubac*, Einsiedeln.

E. Maier (1979), *Einigung der Welt in Gott: Das Katholische bei Henri de Lubac*, Einsiedeln.

H. U. von Balthasar, G. Chantraine (1983), *Le cardinal Henri de Lubac: L'homme et l'œuvre*, Paris.

A. Russo (1990), *Henri de Lubac: Teologia e dogma nella storia: L'influsso di Blondel*, Rome.

R. B. Martinez (1991), *La teologia del sobrenatural en los escritos de Henri de Lubac*, Burgos.

B. Sesboüé (1992), "Le surnaturel chez Henri de Lubac," *RSR* 80, 373–408.

O. de Berranger (1994), "Des paradoxes au Mystère chez J. H. Newman et H. de Lubac," *RSPhTh* 78, 45–79.

A. Russo (1994), *Henri de Lubac*, Paris.

R. Winling (1994), "Nouvelle théologie," *TRE* 24, 668–75.

Coll. (1995), *Henri de Lubac et la philosophie*, *EPh* 161–267.

A. Vanneste (1996), *Nature et grâce dans la théologie occidentale: Dialogue avec H. de Lubac*, Louvain.

F. Inciarte (1999), "Natur und Übernatur: Ihr Verhältnis nach Henri de Lubac," *ThPh* 74, 70–83.

OLIVIER DE BERRANGER

See also **Aristotelianism, Christian; Balthasar, Hans Urs von; Blondel, Maurice; Dogma; Fathers of the Church; History; Humanism, Christian; Newman, John Henry; Nietzsche, Friedrich Wilhelm; Philosophy; Spirituality, Ignatian; Supernatural; Thomism**

Lulle, Raymond. *See* **Positive Theology**

Luther, Martin

1483–1546

Martin Luther was the initiator of a vast religious movement known as the Reformation, the ecclesiastical, cultural, and political consequences of which can still be felt to this day.

a) Education. After studying at the faculty of arts at the University of Erfurt in 1505, Luther entered the convent of Augustinian hermits. There he experienced an inner crisis: he was haunted by a Christ* perceived above all as a judge and underwent the experience* of the permanence of sin* and the impossibility of producing proof of a perfect obedience to God* that might enable him to subsist before him.

During his studies at the faculty of arts and then of theology*, Luther was confronted with the *via moderna* and with nominalism* represented by Gabriel Biel (†1495), who had himself been inspired by the ideas of William Ockham (†1349), John Duns* Scotus, and the earlier Franciscan tradition (Bonaventure*). Through its conception of God not as a Supreme Being* but as will, through its insistence upon revelation* as the sole source of his knowledge*, through its criticism of the use of Aristotle in theology and, in form more than in content, through its concept of salvation*, this movement had a lasting influence on Luther. He was also influenced by Saint Augustine*, particularly by his anti-Pelagian treatises, and this would lead Luther to campaign vigorously against the idea that man can, through his own efforts, prepare to receive grace*. (According to Lortz, Luther's Augustinianism* enabled him, by criticizing nominalism, to overcome "a Catholicism* that was not Catholic" but neo-Pelagian. But Ockhamism was never condemned by the magisterium*, and Luther's attacks were such that they encompassed all of Scholasticism* in one reprobation.)

German mysticism* also played a role in Luther's intellectual development. Like Tauler, Luther located the root of sin in will and self-affirmation; and in his insistence upon humiliation he expanded upon Tauler's discourse on the *ad nihil* reduction—that is, on the annihilation of man. Luther's readings were always selective, not exempt from misunderstandings, and sensitive to convergences before they discovered differences. If, like Augustine, Luther spoke of sin as the true corruption of man, in fact he went even further. After conversion*, he contended, there subsists in man more than a "remnant" of weakness. Sin, according to Luther, is a reality that is permanently present in human will itself. As for grace, which Augustine considered to be an innate gift conferring upon man new strength and qualities, Luther saw it rather as an attitude of God. Moreover, Augustine's Neoplatonism is absent from Luther's ideas, with the exception of a few references in the first lecture on the Psalms*. As for German mysticism, Luther followed neither its speculative orientation nor its concept of man deemed capable "in the fine point of his soul*" of apprehending God.

Humanism* no doubt had a greater impact upon Luther than is generally admitted, given his confrontation with Erasmus*. Proof of this is to be found in the preference given to the Fathers* of the Church regarding the later tradition*, Luther's aversion for Scholastic theology, the importance given to the Bible*, the critical examination of the texts, the use of ancient authors, and the influence of humanist rhetoric.

b) At the Heart of Luther's Interpretation: Holy Scripture. In his first lecture on the Psalms (1513–15), Luther interprets the text according to the traditional schema of the four senses of Scripture, but new interpretations were developing. In opposition to the medieval exegete Nicolas de Lyre, who vouched only for a literal sense, Luther resorts to a literal-prophetic sense to explain the Psalms. Moreover, he refines the tropological sense by establishing a link between the biblical text and the existence of the believer—whatever is said of Christ is applied to Christians. The faithful therefore appropriate Christ—his life, his work, and his death. The schema of the four senses would be abandoned with the *Commentary on the Epistle to the Romans* (1515–16); allegory would never totally disappear, but Luther thereafter concentrated on the literal sense. Especially when controversy arose, only the literal sense carried authority in Luther's opinion. He would not limit himself, however, to a purely philological commentary, but always sought out the fundamental idea of the text, the "scopus" in relation to the actual situation of the faithful. The interpretation of Scripture is set within a broader perspective, as a function of the message of salvation clearly proclaimed in the Letter to the Romans. The love* of God is revealed through Jesus Christ; because of Christ, God awards grace to the sinner, independently of his works* and merits. From that moment, Jesus Christ becomes, as Savior, the key to a global interpretation of the books in the Bible. He is the center of Scripture, "its mathematical point" (*WA. TR* 2, no. 2383).

When the experience of "seeing the gospel" was challenged by the ecclesiastical authorities, Luther proclaimed that the primary authority* lay within Scripture, and denied that in its interpretation the last word should be granted to the magisterium. Scripture is sufficiently clear, in his opinion, to be understood by all Christians. It is not the book* as such that is the Word* of God. Scripture is, in fact, a "good shout" before being a text. It is a living message, first entrusted to the apostles*, then handed down through the ages, but it always refers back to the apostolic message. To be sure, when confronted with heretical distortions of preaching* one had to have recourse to what was written, and the written word also comprised a sort of counterweight to the ministers, allowing the faithful to maintain a critical distance toward those ministers. Luther affirms that "Scripture provides its own interpretation" (*WA* 10, III, 238, 10). This principle was in opposition both to Rome*, which granted too much power to the magisterium, and to various spiritualists, who sought to include the Spirit. The Spirit comes to readers through Scripture, and not from outside Scripture. Luther also emphasizes the clarity of Scripture: ordered in relation to the center that was Jesus Christ, it suffices to inform man of what needs to be known of God and of salvation. Traditional ecclesiastical customs can certainly be maintained if they do not contra-

vene the biblical message; and the doctrinal and dogmatic tradition of the ancient church will be useful, as a secondary authority, in helping one to read the Scripture.

c) God's Justice.   In his lecture on the Letter to the Romans and in various theses, Luther attacks the concept of man in which man sees himself as an autonomous subject called on to produce a certain number of acts in order to fulfill himself as a person*. When Luther speaks of sin, he does not mean a moral shortcoming, but more radically a human tendency to affirm oneself in the sight of God, to wish to live according to one's own justice* and not that which God wants to deliver; through his criticism, a vision of original man would be born, in which the founding instant was a relation to an exterior reality, Christ. (*See,* in particular, the commentaries on the *Magnificat* of 1521 and the theses on man from 1536.)

Scholastic theologians, according to Luther, did not really think through the idea of sin and man as sinner; they merely added the need to obtain help from a supernatural source—grace, that is, which insofar as it is innate has become an inherent quality of the soul, "like the whiteness of a wall," according to Luther's critical expression. However, in Luther's view the will of the sinner is strictly incapable of accomplishing acts that lead to the attribution of grace, and grace cannot become a quality of the soul. (Luther rejects the concept of "habitual" grace.) Only a new relation to God brought on by his Word of pardon can make man just in the sight of God and capable of accomplishing just deeds. The justification* of man by faith* does not depend on qualities or accomplishments peculiar to man, for one, nor is it acquired once and for all, by virtue of the permanence of sin. Christians, according to Luther, will be both sinners and penitents by virtue of what they are in themselves, and they will become just through the divine pardon imputed upon them through the justice of Christ.

But although Luther criticizes the Ockhamist idea that justification occurs when God extends his grace as a new quality to those who "do what is within their power," is this not nevertheless bound to another Ockhamist concept, which posits that man might be just because God, in his *potentia absoluta,* would accept him as such outside of any infusion of grace, through a simple imputation of justice? The objection is not exact, for the Lutheran concept of imputation does not base salvation on divine omnipotence* alone, but on the accomplishment of the law* through Jesus Christ and his merits. To the abstract sense of the Ockhamist imputation Luther opposes his principle of the *propter Christum,* "because of Christ." In later autobiographical texts, Luther evoked what was for him the liberating discovery of the exact meaning of Paul's characterization of the gospel as "the power of God for salvation to every one who has faith" (Rom 1:17). This is when he understood that the issue was not the punishing justice of the God, who aims at the works of man, but the (passive) justice by which the just live from the gift of God—that is, justice by faith (*see* in particular *WA* 54, 186, 8–9; the date of this liberating experience is debatable: either 1514–15 or the spring of 1518).

d) Conflict with Rome and the Question of Authority in the Church. The 95 theses against indulgences* that Luther wrote in October 1517 quickly made him known to the general public. For Luther, indulgences led to a deceptive sense of security: the faithful received them not only as a temporal penalty due for sin, imposed upon penitents after they had confessed their sins and received absolution, but also as a dispensation of authentic contrition and a guarantee of salvation. He also rejected the idea of a "treasure" constituted by the supererogatory merits of Christ and his saints, and which the church could dispose of as a sort of celestial bank account in order to give benefits to those faithful who were less well endowed in sanctity. The only treasure that the church can and must transmit is the Word of God. And as for indulgences, which Luther did not impugn as such, they encompassed only the canonical penalties imposed by the church on earth, and not the penalties of purgatory.

The question of indulgences led back to the pope*, evoked in over a third of Luther's theses. Was it not the pope who gave them authority? Luther did not set himself up as a revolutionary against traditional authority, but aimed to bring about a return to the standard of the Scripture. Referring to the 15th-century canonist Nicolas de Tudeschi, Luther affirmed as early as 1518 that "the pope, as well as the council*, can err" (*WA* 1, 656, 32)—and during the Leipzig Disputation, which would pit him against Johann Eck in 1519, Luther would say that the church had no need of a leader on earth, for Christ alone was its leader. When confronted by the pope's legate, Cardinal Cajetan, Luther refused to recant unless he were proven wrong by biblical arguments, and he affirmed that "truth* is master even over the pope" (*WA* 2, 18, 2). The debate with Cajetan also centered upon the certainty of salvation. According to Scholastic theology, it was only in the form of a *conjecture* that individual believers could affirm their salvation, when they managed to discern signs of Christian life in their existence: no one could know with *certainty* whether they were in a state of grace. However, according to Luther, salvation is granted to

man from without, through the promise* of God, and this is the basis for certainty. It is only if a believer has the benefit of a personal certainty of salvation that a justifying grace can be of use to him during the absolution of sins.

e) Sacraments and the Church, Faith, and Works. In 1517–18 Luther published numerous treatises. Some, in German, were addressed to laymen; others, more technical and written in Latin, were instead intended for theologians. The most important were published in 1520: *Von den guten Werken (Of Good Works), Von dem Bapstum zu Rome: Widder den hoch berumpten Romanisten zu Leiptzck (On the Papacy at Rome: Against the Most Celebrated Romanist in Leipzig), An den christlichen Adel deutscher Nation (Appeal to the Christian Nobility of the German Nation), De captivitatae Babylonica ecclesiae praeludium (A Prelude Concerning the Babylonish Captivity of the Church),* and *Von der Freiheit eines Christenmensche (Of the Liberty of a Christian Man).*

In dealing with the question of the sacraments*, Luther emphasized that only the believer can make a salutary use of them. Thus he challenged the Scholastic distinction between sacraments of the Old Covenant*, which had effect only *ex opere operantis*—that is, on the basis of the faith of those who made use of them—and the sacraments of the New Covenant, which had effect simply by virtue of their celebration, *ex opere operato*—provided the faithful did not raise any obstacles thereto by consciously opposing an *obex*. But Luther placed an emphasis on the inner attitude—the *opus operantis*—of those who made use of the sacraments, with the understanding of course that faith itself was a work of God. Luther also reacted against the medieval tendency that led people to increase the importance of sacraments in relation to the importance of the Word that was preached, for Luther regarded the Word as a means of salvation: grace was communicated not only through the sacraments, but also through preaching.

Luther further reduced the number of sacraments to two: baptism* and the Eucharist*, which he viewed as the visible form of God's promise and the only sacraments possessing a biblical legitimacy. It was for that reason that he would fight against what he considered to be the principal error of the Roman Church: the error was neither the Communion under one species (even though the practice diverged from the biblical account of the institution of the Eucharist), nor was it the doctrine of transubstantiation (a useless Scholastic hypothesis), but the doctrine of the Mass as sacrifice* and as a deed of man offered to God, which prevented one from perceiving that there was a promise of God, the gospel calling for faith. Several liturgical consequences resulted from this theological presupposition, including the spoken recitation of the story of the institution and the suppression of masses destined for particular purposes—private masses or low masses in which the faithful did not participate.

The question of the Church was then inevitable. Excommunication from the Church of Rome, affirmed Luther, does not deprive the believer of communion* with the Church of Jesus Christ. The gift of grace is not linked solely to the sacraments bestowed by the Church of Rome. The pope, and the council, were capable of error; between priests* and laymen there was only a difference of function. Assertions of this nature called to question the traditional tripartite power of the Church of Rome (sanctification, magisterium, and jurisdiction*) in favor of the unique and exclusive power of the Word of God. The Church, according to Luther, is a communion of faith that extends to the entire earth and is not identified with the organism of the Church of Rome. It is not the fact of belonging to a visible community which makes one a Christian. The two types of Christianity could certainly not be dissociated, for they are linked as body and soul are linked. But where spiritual communion is concerned, Christianity has only one leader, Christ, for Christ alone can infuse faith. To be sure, Christ can use messengers, but strictly speaking he has no representative or vicar on earth. He communicates with mankind through the Gospels and the sacraments. When preaching, baptism, and Holy Communion are in keeping with the Gospels, the true Church is present.

What, then, is a Christian? The major criterion is faith, which Luther describes as trust, a connection to Christ, an attachment to the Word, something he opposes to a purely intellectual belief, to moralism, and to sentimentalism. Faith exists because God speaks: "The soul can do without everything except the Word of God" (*WA* 7, 22, 9–11). God's Word reaches man in two forms, as a law and as the gospel. In Scripture there are texts whose purpose is to accuse man and make him aware of his sin (the Ten Commandments, e.g.); others, on the contrary, announce God's pardon (the Gospels, therefore). Only this distinction can keep faith from moralism, by revealing man's powerlessness on the one hand, and on the other, by emphasizing the miracle* of grace.

Attached by faith to God alone, Christians are supremely free, both with regard to the conditions in which they live and to the accusations brought by the law of God. They are free, too, to approach God directly, in trust. All believers, from this point of view, are priests. Sincere faith, however, must necessarily be proven by the good deeds that it will inform and direct.

These deeds are not addressed to God to obtain his grace, since salvation is granted freely to man; they are addressed to one's neighbor, in conformity with the vocation, or call, that God entrusts to each man.

In June 1521 Rome ordered Luther to recant within 60 days. He asked to be convinced of his "errors" by means of scriptural arguments. On 3 January 1521 he was excommunicated. Authorized to appear before the Diet of Worms in April, he made his famous reply: "Unless I can be convinced through the testimony of the Scripture and through evident reason—for I believe in neither the infallibility of the pope nor in that of the councils, since it has been established that they have often made mistakes and contradicted themselves—I am bound by the biblical texts that I have mentioned. For as long as my conscience is the captive of God's Word, I cannot and will not recant, for it is neither safe nor salutary to act against one's conscience" (*WA* 7, 838, 3–8).

f) Pastor and Inspirer of Evangelical Churches. Luther's influence began with his translation of the Bible. The New Testament was published in 1522, and the Old Testament was completed in 1534). The translations met with considerable success, continuing right up to the 20th century. Luther's commentaries and preachings (some two thousand sermons have been preserved) have also played an important role, as has his advice for the establishment of an "evangelical" worship. In these writings, Luther asked that the weak be taken into consideration, and that before changes were introduced there be a convincing argument, and above all that a distinction be made between the necessary, the articles of faith, and the relative, something that had the right to vary according to the different liturgical usages and ecclesiastical structures*. In comparison with others, the first liturgical formularies that Luther published in 1523 were fairly conservative, even though they had been purified of anything that might suggest a sacrificial concept of the Mass.

Luther contributed to the development of liturgical music by composing 36 hymns, including the famous "Ein fester Burg ist unser Gott" ("A Mighty Fortress is Our God"). He was also aware very early on of the necessity of educating the young, particularly in faith (1529, *Small* and *Larger Catechism*).

After 1525 Luther asked the prince elector to act in the capacity of a "provisional bishop" (*Notbischof*) by undertaking an inspection of the parishes by jurists and theologians in order to bring some order to the pastoral cure and to solve financial problems. In this way the territorial church was born, where political authority would exercise a greater power than Luther had originally envisaged. It has often been supposed that Luther wanted a total separation of the religious domain and the sociopolitical domain; in fact, even though it was not up to the preachers themselves to establish new institutions or elaborate a political program, Luther considered that they must be vigilant, must remind those who governed of their duty, must instruct all the states in Christianity of "that which is useful and salutary," and, when needed, must voice their criticism. The aim was to sharpen people's consciences*, thus to address individuals, and to take a stand on the various institutions of society—schools (which must be promoted), systems of trade, marriage*, law*, and political institutions—to ensure that they served the concrete needs of mankind and conformed to the will of God.

Through his correspondence (2,650 letters in his own hand) and numerous occasional writings, Luther also practiced the *cura animarum* (cure of the soul), and gave pastoral directives, providing enlightenment on the attitude to be adopted in times of plague, taking up the defense of baptism for children, giving indications on prayer*, consoling or reprimanding, and giving counsel to those authorities who wished to introduce the Reformation.

g) Doctrinal Conflicts. The controversy with the theologians of the traditional church was unrelenting (*see* in particular *Against Latomus, Reply to Ambrosius Catharinus,* and the *Articles of Schmalkalden*). The polemic was above all about justification by faith, about the church and the sacraments, and about the papacy. In 1518 a doubt was born in Luther's mind: since the pope established new articles of faith and did not want to conform to Scripture, perhaps he could—as an institution (not as a person)—be the Anti-Christ announced in 2 Thessalonians 2:3–4. Luther remained uncertain about this until 1521. Meanwhile, his struggle against the papacy grew increasingly bitter.

In 1522 controversies also arose opposing Luther to partners who had been close to him but who had become more radical, or more nuanced—Erasmus, for example. Thus, in the treatise *De servo arbitrio* (1525), Luther once again denied that the will of man could prepare him to receive grace and cooperate in his salvation. In everyday things man disposes of a certain amount of freedom of choice; but with regard to God or the realities that concern salvation or damnation, free will does not exist (*WA* 18, 638, 9–10).

Luther also set himself against those he qualified as "fanatics" (*Schwärmer),* and challenged the Old Testament justifications to which they resorted in order to remove images* from the churches (Karlstadt's point of view) or to implement a sort of theocracy where the impious would be excluded (Thomas Münzer). Luther also stigmatized these "fanatics" for conduct that, in

his opinion, led to an immediate experience of the Holy Spirit in a way that relativized the Bible and the Word preached. Finally, he reproached them for once again allowing themselves to be in thrall to the idea of justification through deeds, by making Christ an example to follow rather than the Savior proclaimed by the gospel of the justification by faith.

Between 1525 and 1529 Luther was in opposition to Zwingli* over the real presence of Christ in the Eucharist, in particular in *That These Words of Christ "This Is My Body" Still Stand Firm against the Fanatics* (1527) and the treatise, *Confession of the Lord's Supper* (1528). Since Christ, from the time of his ascension, can no longer be present on earth in his humanity, argued Zwingli, Holy Communion has only a symbolic meaning. Luther refuted this affirmation by vigorously upholding the idea of real presence: the bread *is* the body of Christ. The ascension, in fact, did not shut Christ away in a given place, but placed him "above and in all creatures." Luther referred to Ockhamist distinctions to assert that there exist several types of unity, and that there is one thinkable unity, a sacramental unity, between the bread and the wine of Holy Communion, on the one hand, and the body and blood of Christ on the other. Real presence, in his opinion, prolonged Incarnation*. It was Christ himself, in the way in which he brought about the work of redemption, who offered himself to the believer and thus founded his certainty. Along with the Word, this sacrament is one of the paths chosen by God to communicate salvation.

From 1527–28 on, Luther also entered into conflict with those who would be called the Antinomists. According to their spokesman, Johann Agricola, true penitence cannot be achieved through preaching of the law, as Luther had affirmed, but only through preaching of the gospel, and law no longer concerned the Christian. For Luther, however, to preach the gospel without the law is the same as losing the gospel as a form of "good news." The law, to be sure, does not justify, but it impels all humans, Christians included, for as long as they remain sinners, to receive the gospel— that is, forgiveness. To fail to distinguish the law of the gospel prohibits one in fact from acknowledging the redemptive role of Christ. Luther does concede, however, that penitence, in the full sense of the term, is compelled by faith, and that for those who simply remain under the law there is nothing left but despair.

h) God, Christ, and Man: History in Luther's Theology. The majority of Luther's writings—more than one hundred volumes, or roughly 60,000 pages, in the Weimar edition—were occasional works. He was more a commentator on the Bible than a systematician.

His ideas were not always presented in the form of a doctrinal body, but, using a theological process that was always centered upon Christ and the Bible, he placed his emphases differently according to the time and circumstances.

The existential implication of the theologian is primordial in this case. Indeed, only those who allow themselves to be judged and liberated by the Word of God can truly apprehend the mysteries* of faith. One receives the liberating gospel through an unceasing effort of reading and interpreting Scripture. The idea that reason* could, by analogy, trace a path from the Creation* to the Creator via a purely theoretical process is therefore excluded. Luther insists in his theses of the *Heidelberg Disputation* (1518) that the true God can be known only in the flesh of the Crucified. And to a theology that speaks of God without this reference (a "theology of glory") Luther opposes a "theology of the cross" in which the power of God is revealed in his weakness: God reveals himself by concealing himself, and it is through his death that man will live. Only those who renounce speculation and adopt the paradoxical revelation chosen by God, only those who renounce the glory of deeds to live in a faith experienced in the shadow of the cross, can obtain knowledge* of God.

Luther's God is a person who speaks and to whom one speaks. The unceasing activity of the Creator is emphasized (*WA* 7, 574, 29–31), and if Luther insists upon the sovereignty of God in relation to the world, he can also describe his transcendence in terms of a hidden presence within the very depths of the creature's being. God, above all, is love, the very nature of which is to create and to give to those who deserve nothing. But, given the sins of man, the biblical text also speaks of the wrath* of God, a wrath that must serve to remind the believer that God's love cannot be taken for granted, but that it is the victory of God through Jesus Christ over that which accuses man—wrath and the law. Wrath and law are, in their way, the "improper works" of God, and they cause man to flee toward the heart of God.

Despite certain reservations with regard to the vocabulary used, Luther adopted the Trinitarian and christological dogma of the early church. They were truly fundamental from his soteriological perspective: if Jesus Christ was not truly God, man would not be saved. And how could man attain faith, his only means of salvation, without the divine work of the Holy Spirit? In a very Western way, Luther also insists upon the unity between the three Persons of the Trinity*, in such a way that he might be accused of modalism*. But if faith is born when man discovers the face of the Father* in Jesus Christ, Luther also knew how to express, in various ways, the encounter between Father and Son. As a theologian of Incarnation he insisted, contrary to Zwingli in particular, upon the close union of Christ's two natures. To establish Christ's presence in the Eucharist, Luther sets himself up as a theoretician of the communication of idioms*; and the same theory enables him to say that divine nature also plays a part in the suffering of Jesus* the man.

As for redemption, the Lutheran position is also traditional, and has similarities in a number of ways to Anselm*'s in the *Cur Deus homo*. But although it was in our place that Christ satisfied the law and submitted to its accusations, his act of substitution did not elicit the love of God, for that love was primary and was made evident through the sending of the Son. The Christ of reconciliation was, moreover, the Christ who liberated man from the evil power, classically, of death* and the devil, to which Luther added the law and the wrath of God. Christ's work of "satisfaction" and redemption, finally, was not confined to the past. Christ did not extend grace, but stood "before the Father as a comfort [to man] and an intercessor" (*WA* 20, 634, 18) and gave himself to the believer as his justice.

"Justification by faith alone" is at the heart of the Lutheran message, affirming that only man's faith in Christ will render him just before God. What is more, faith for Luther took on a full meaning that the Scholastic tradition had not ascribed to it. Faith was in fact interpreted as the act of reason that acquiesces to revelation, and any process of this kind must be completed by the love for God. But, for Luther, faith immediately implies one's entire person. It is not only knowledge, it is also trust. This existential concept is one of the reasons why Luther reacted against everything that in theology and in the practice of the Catholic Church could turn grace into a sort of supernatural force transmitted by the sacraments to take root in the soul as a quality: one cannot speak of faith and grace without insisting upon the Word, that of Christ and of his witnesses. To insist upon mediation—of Christ, of the witnesses, of the Word, including its sacramental form—was also a way of forewarning against the numerous forms of mysticism and spiritualism. Luther's theology granted considerable importance to the immediacy of a relationship founded on belief, but it did not give rise to absolute individualism, and did not reduce Christianity to a pious interiority.

Luther did not speak only of faith or inner realities. He also often evoked the works of God in Creation and in history, and he called on believers to cooperate. In the face of an ascetic piety, Luther restored value to the human body and to everything that comprises life on earth, marriage in particular. Christians are not permanent in the world*, however good that world may be through the will of God the Creator. Aware of the reality of evil*, confronted with the incessant activity of Satan, man remains a stranger on earth and aspires to the sudden arrival of the "last day." Luther often evoked the devil, and this was more than a mere medieval legacy for him. He viewed history* as the uninterrupted struggle between God the Creator and Satan the destroyer. Satan attacks the worthy institutions willed by God, destroys civil society* through sedition (the peasant uprising), usury, and war*. But Satan also intervenes in the realm of faith, perverting the preaching of the gospel or attacking its witnesses. In accordance with the Lutheran distinction between the two reigns, the struggle against Satan is waged on two levels: on the one hand, through temporal institutions, law, and constraint; on the other hand, through the message of the gospel and the lives of Christians themselves. It is to his acute awareness of the permanence of evil that Luther owes his eschatological expectation, free of any millenarianism*. There will be no perfect state, either in the church or in secular society. Progress will never be anything more than relative. Only on the last day will one witness the appearance of Jesus Christ and the total destruction of the powers of the devil.

● The standard Weimar Edition (WA), Böhlau, 1883– , comprises four sections: (1) Writings (treatises, commentaries, preachings, etc.): Vols. 1–59, 61–63; (2) Correspondence, 18 vols. (WA.B); (3) Tischreden (Table Talks), 6 vols. (WA.TR); (4) Deutsche Bibel (German Bible) series, 12 vols. (15 vols.) (WA.DB).
Complementary collection: Archiv zur Weimarer Ausgabe.
♦ K. Holl (1927), Gesammelte Aufsätze zur Kirchengeschichte, vol. 1: L., Tübingen (7th Ed. 1948).
L. Febvre (1928), Un destin: Martin L., Paris (5th Ed. 1988).
P. Vignaux (1935), Luther, commentateur des "Sentences," Paris.
P. Althaus (1952), Die christliche Wahrheit, 3rd Ed., Gütersloh; (1952), Paulus und Luther über den Menschen, 2nd Ed., Gütersloh.
L. Grane (1962), Contra Gabrielem: Luthers Auseinandersetzung mit Gabriel Biel in der Disputatio Contra Scholasticam Theologiam 1517, Copenhagen.
H. Strohl (1962), Luther jusqu'en 1520, Paris.
P. Althaus (1963), Die Theologie Martin Luthers, Gütersloh (3rd Ed. 1983).

P. Althaus (1965), Die Ethik Martin Luthers, Gütersloh.
T. Süss (1969), Luther, Paris.
J. Lortz (1970), La Réforme de Luther, 2 vols., Paris.
M. Lienhard (1973), Luther, témoin de Jésus-Christ: Les étapes et les thèmes de la christologie du Réformateur, CFi 73.
L. Grane (1975), Modus loquendi theologicus: Luthers Kampf um die Erneuerung der Theologie 1515–1518, Leyden.
W. Joest (1975), Ontologie der Person bei Luther, Göttingen.
D. Olivier (1978), La foi de Luther: La cause de l'Évangile dans l'Église, Paris.
T. Beer (1980), Grundzüge der Theologie Martin Luthers, Einsiedeln.
M. Brecht (1982), Martin Luther, vol. 1: Sein Weg zur Reformation 1483–1521, Stuttgart.
O. H. Pesch (1982), Hinführung zu Luther, Mayence.
Y. Congar (1983), Martin Luther: Sa foi, sa Réforme: Études de théologie historique, Paris.
G. Ebeling (1983), Luther: Introduction à une réflexion théologique, Geneva.
H. Junghans (1983), Leben und Werk Martin Luthers von 1526 bis 1546, Berlin.
M. Lienhard (1983), Martin Luther: Un temps, une vie, un message, Paris-Geneva (3rd Ed. 1991).
M. Monteil (1983), Martin Luther, la vie, oui la vie, Paris.
H. Junghans (1984), Der junge Luther und die Humanisten, Weimar.
M. Brecht (1986), Martin Luther, vol. 2: Ordnung und Abgrenzung der Reformation 1521–1532; vol. 3: Die Erhaltung der Kirche 1532–1546, Stuttgart.
R. Schwarz (1986), Luther, Göttingen.
M. Lienhard (1989), L'Év. et l'Église chez Luther, Paris; (1991), Au cœur de la foi de Luther: Jésus-Christ, Paris.
H. Guicharrousse (1995), Les musiques de Luther, Geneva.
M. Arnold (1996), La correspondance de L.: Étude historique, littéraire et théologique, Mayence.
D. Crouzet (1996), La genèse de la Réforme française, Paris.
H. Flachmann (1996), M. L. und das Buch, Tübingen.
G. Ebeling (1997), Luthers Seelsorge, Tübingen.
M. Lienhard (1999), M. L.: La passion de Dieu, Paris.

MARC LIENHARD

See also **Baptism; Ecclesiology; Erasmus, Desiderius; Faith; Grace; Holy Scripture; Indulgences; Law and Christianity; Lutheranism; Mass, Sacrifice of the; Nominalism; Pope; Scripture, Senses of; Word of God; Works; Zwingli, Huldrych**

Lutheran Church. *See* Lutheranism

Lutheranism

1. Concept and Origin

The term Lutheranism denotes the totality of Christians, churches*, and Christian communities whose life and faith* are distinctly marked by a new understanding of the biblical message of salvation*, as formulated and defended by the 16th-century Reformation in Wittenberg and especially by Martin Luther*. This movement arose, of course, in the context of the social, cultural, and political upheavals of the time, and was influenced by them. Essentially, however, it was a spiritual phenomenon, which signaled the revival of the biblical message of salvation at a time when it appeared that this was no longer being preached in a satisfactory way. This reorientation was conducted through an appeal to apostolic testimony, as definitively preserved in Holy Scripture*, but at the same time it claimed a continuity with the teaching and doctrine of the early church. The adjective *Lutheran* was initially used by the opponents of the Reformation, while its supporters (especially Luther) accepted the term only with reluctance, since it seemed to accord a central importance to the person of the reformer. The term is nonetheless perfectly justified, on both a historical and a theological level.

2. Fundamental Beliefs

This new understanding of the biblical message of salvation is expressed in three fundamental beliefs, all closely interlinked.

a) God's Disinterested Condescension toward Mankind Is the One Path to Salvation. In Jesus Christ, God* himself approaches mankind and takes it back into communion with him. Therein is salvation. Mankind does not need to lift itself toward God. Through the virtue of the Incarnation* the meeting between God and man takes place in the finite sphere—that is to say, in the audible words of the preaching* of the gospel and in the material nature of the sacraments*.

b) Justification of the Sinner Is the Center of the Church's Message and Doctrine, and the Heart of the Christian Existence. In Christ*, God mercifully welcomes the sinner, in other words, the person stricken by judgment*. Whoever believes wholeheartedly in this event is justified by God and at the same time in-

troduced to another life. This is the "principal element" or "center" of the Christian message, to which all Christian proclamation and teaching must conform.

c) Law and Gospel Are to Be Distinguished and Put in Order. The Word* of God is on the one hand a word of command and judgment (law*), and on the other hand a word of absolution and regeneration (gospel). These two things should be clearly distinguished, but not dissociated. They must be distinguished in order to ensure the gratuitous nature of salvation; and they must be put in order or linked with one another in order to prevent the gospel of God's grace* being understood as the granting of a "just grace." These fundamental convictions are linked to a particular vision of the Church, which is seen as a "communion* of believers" and a "creature of the gospel" *(creatura evangelii)*. This means that the Church is born of and lives by the gospel, which leads people to God, and thereby also unites them by means of preaching and the sacraments (baptism* and the Eucharist). In these two ways, people receive the gospel, which gives rise to the Church. The ecclesial ministry* conferred by ordination* is not eliminated, however, since it is instituted by God. As a ministry of preaching and administering the sacraments it is the instrument of the proclamation of the gospel.

The Lutheran understanding of the world and society*, and Lutheranism's activity in the cultural, social, and political spheres are linked by three guiding principles: 1) a positive attitude toward the world, seen as the good work that God will not abandon, even in the face of the destructive power of sin* and evil*; 2) the idea that an earthly profession (work*) is the framework that God assigns the Christian within which to realize and bear witness to his "sanctity," in other words, the liberty* that is accorded him in faith to serve his neighbor; 3) the doctrine of the two rules (or of the two orders of sovereignty) by which God fights evil in the world: the spiritual rule, which God exercises through the Holy* Spirit, causing the gospel to be proclaimed through Word and sacrament, and, second, the worldly rule, which God assumes by way of civil authority. This doctrine should not be interpreted as implying a separation between the two kingdoms of God, as Lutheranism has done at certain periods and in certain situations.

3. Church Doctrine and the Confession of Faith

On the level of principles as much as in practice, church doctrine plays a more important role in Lutheranism than in the other Protestant churches. Lutheran confessions of faith appeared at a very early date, modeled on the *credo* of the early church. First came the *Augsburg Confession* (1530), which was followed by other confessional writings; all were finally collected in the *Book of Concord* (1580). This attachment to the creeds of the early church (the Creed of Nicaea-Constantinople, the Apostles' Creed, and even the apocryphal Athanasian Creed) and to the Lutheran confessional writings is proclaimed in the constitutions of all the Lutheran churches. The church's creed is clearly subordinate to the authority* of Holy Scripture, which is accepted as the "only rule and measure." For all that it is seen as historically determined, the confession of faith retains a sense of permanent obligation within the churches, serving above all to guarantee the authenticity of church teachings. The *Augsburg Confession* is the first and principal confessional writing, and is recognized in almost all Lutheran churches. The others, which have not been so widely accepted, can mostly be understood as interpretations of, and complementary to, the *Augsburg Confession*. Among these texts, Luther's *Little Catechism* (1537) has been particularly influential, especially in terms of religious teaching and parish activities. In fact, the Lutheran credo has not evolved since the completion of the *Book of Concord* (1580), a fact that today more than ever appears to pose a problem. When new developments arise in response to specific circumstances (e.g., in Indonesia) the church strives to preserve "substantial agreement" with the historical creed. The relationship between Luther's own theology* and Lutheran confessional writings is a complex one, and not without occasional tensions. Indeed, while Lutheranism is inconceivable without Luther, in practice the doctrine officially professed by the churches is most often given priority.

4. Institution of the Church

The Lutheran Reformation initially and for a long time saw itself as a movement of renewal within the Catholic Church. The reformers had no intention of founding their own church. But insofar as the existing church was not prepared to tolerate such a movement within itself, it was inevitable that this movement should form itself into a separate church. This development took place under the then-prevailing sociopolitical conditions in the various countries of Europe. It displayed two characteristic traits: on the one hand, the universal—one might say "ecumenical"—aim of the reforming movement, for which the new vision of the biblical message of salvation was a matter for the whole of Christendom; and on the other hand, the belief that the transformation of the movement into a church would be a merely provisional step. However, the end of the religious disputes and the conclusion of the Peace of Augsburg (1555) heralded another outcome—sealed by the Treaty of Westphalia (1648)—in which the Lutheran Reformation's universal, ecumenical project foundered. Breaking with the established church, Lutheranism set up its own churches. In Northern Europe whole countries went over to Lutheranism in this way. In Germany various regional churches arose and found a place within the established sociopolitical landscape. Elsewhere, Lutheran communities and churches developed in opposition to the established political power.

The Lutheran Reformation's reservations concerning this new church it was producing, and its own original intention rather to set up a movement of renewal within the one Church, have nevertheless remained strong features of Lutheranism. They find expression today in energetic ecumenical activity (*see* 8 below).

5. Spread of Lutheranism

In Germany, Lutheranism's period of growth ended, for all intents and purposes, as early as 1580—at the latest in 1648 (Treaty of Westphalia). The same may be said of the Scandinavian countries, where Lutheranism became the official or dominant religion, and of the countries of central and eastern Europe, where it remained a minority faith. Emigration from Germany and Scandinavia in the 18th and 19th centuries led to the founding of Lutheran churches, first in North and South America, and then in Australia. During the 19th and 20th centuries missionary activity gave rise to Lutheran churches in Asia and Africa. Today there are around 58 million Lutheran Christians in the world. In quantitative terms Lutheranism is undoubtedly strongest in the Scandinavian countries, with 21 million followers, and Germany, with 15 million. There are 8.7 million Lutherans in North America, 5.5 million in Africa, 4.5 million in Asia, 1.6 million in central and eastern Europe, and 1.2 million in Latin America.

6. Lutheranism's Internal Diversity

A fundamental unanimity in the understanding and confession of faith enables Lutheranism to assume the most varied forms: state churches, multitudinist churches, and free churches; episcopal, synodal, and congregationalist structures; an elaborate liturgy* derived from the classical mass, or a sparse liturgy chiefly focused on preaching. At present, however, there is a clear tendency toward frequent and regular celebration of the Eucharist, and toward a development of the episcopal ministry. This diversity of forms of worship and ecclesial structures is made possible and justified by the Lutheran conception of the Church and its unity*. For Lutherans the necessary and sufficient condition of this unity lies in a fundamental agreement on the understanding of the gospel and its proclamation by Word and sacrament. Thereafter, the particular form of worship and ecclesial organization is only a secondary question, to which different responses are permitted. Both this conviction and the practices that result from it are not without danger, however. They can lead to indifference and to an unrestrained pluralism in liturgical and organizational matters, which could endanger the ecclesial community. Both these attitudes were alien to the Lutheran Reformation: on these subjects, too, it was clearly aware of the limits within which diversity could be tolerated, and strove to maintain as much coherence as possible.

7. Church Union

During the second half of the 19th century rapprochements developed, at both a national and a regional level (in Europe and North America), between Lutheran churches and groups that previously had often been cut off from, or even in conflict with, one another. At the beginning of the 20th century these attempts at internal unification spread to Lutheranism as a whole, leading in 1947 to the creation of the Lutheran World Federation. Almost all Lutheran churches—with the exception of the Lutheran Church Missouri Synod in North America, and a few free churches—now belong to this organization, which encompasses some 55 million Christians. For a long time the Lutheran World Federation saw itself as a purely federative structure, whose constitution did not envisage the eucharistic Communion of the member churches. However, consciousness of the universal solidarity of Lutherans has recently grown to such an extent that the federation now officially regards itself as a "communion of churches," united in the communion of pulpit and altar.

8. Ecumenical Commitment

In its early period Lutheranism retained a strong ecumenical focus inherited from the Lutheran Reformation (which saw itself as a movement of renewal within the established church and did not aim to found a new church). At that time Lutherans were in regular discussion with representatives of the official church, and also with members of the Swiss wing of the Reformation and the Church of England; they even attempted to establish links with the Eastern Orthodox churches. By and large these ecumenical efforts lapsed over the following centuries. At the beginning of the 19th century, united Lutheran-Reformed churches were formed in Germany; these however were rejected by large sectors of Lutheranism. The churches, and a number of well-known Lutherans, have since played a part—sometimes a leading one (as in the case of Archbishop Söderblom, for example)—in the 20th century ecumenical movement, and the Lutheran World Federation has set itself in its constitution the objective of encouraging Christian unity*. The interdenominational dialogue that opened up in the wake of Vatican* II gave a new impetus to these ecumenical efforts. From the outset the Lutheran churches and the Lutheran World Federation have been among the chief promoters of this dialogue. Since then a huge network of national and international exchanges has arisen, in which the Lutheran churches take part. Some of these exchanges, as for example the discussions between Lutherans and the European Reformed churches, have already led to the creation of a communion of churches (Leuenberg Concord, 1973). Others, such as the dialogue with the Anglicans, have at least come close to this goal.

The nature of this ecumenical commitment is determined by the Lutheran conception of the Church (*see* 2 and 6 above): the communion of churches, and thus the unity of the Church, is essentially a communion in the profession of the one apostolic faith. Consequently the ecumenical efforts of the Lutheran churches are particularly focused on this communion in the apostolic faith. This means that Lutherans give priority to *doctrinal* dialogue with the other churches, and that they are more reserved about the ecumenical initiatives that have been developed in other directions. More so than in the past, it is nonetheless accepted today that this communion in the confession of the apostolic faith may be achieved even when the churches present and formulate their confessions of faith and their doctrines in different ways. In this sense the goal of the ecumenical movement, especially from the Lutheran perspective, is understood as "unity in a reconciled diversity."

● H. Stephan (1907), *L. in den Wandlungen seiner Kirche,* Berlin (2nd Ed. 1952).

W. Elert (1931–32), *Morphologie des Luthertums,* 2 vols., Munich (3rd Ed. 1965).

P. Althaus (1962), *Die Theologie Martin L.,* Gütersloh (5th Ed. 1980).

Coll. (1976), "L'identité luthérienne face aux défis de notre temps," *PosLuth* 24, 214–20.

T. Bachmann (1977), "Lutherische Kirchen in der Welt," *LR* 27, 163–500.

V. Vajta (1977) (Ed.), *Die evangelisch-lutherische Kirche, Vergangenheit und Gegenwart,* Stuttgart (2nd Ed. 1983).

Coll. (1980), *La Confession d'Augsbourg, 450e anniversaire: Autour d'un colloque œcuménique international,* PoTh 37.

A. Birmelé (1981), *La tradition luthérienne,* Chambray.

M. Lienhard (1983), *Martin Luther, un temps, une vie, un message,* Paris-Geneva (3rd Ed. 1991).

A. Birmelé, M. Lienhard (1991) (Ed), *La foi des Églises luthériennes, Confessions et catéchismes,* Geneva-Paris.

A. Birmelé (1993), "Responsabilité et engagement des Églises luthériennes dans le domaine de la théologie," *PosLuth* 41, 20–37.

P. Bühler (1993), "La responsabilité devant Dieu, fondement théologique de l'engagement éthique," ibid., 48–67.

A. Joly (1993), "Histoire de l'Église luthérienne à Paris: Affermissement et expansion, 1809–1872," ibid., 5–19.

G. Siegwalt (1993), "Les Églises luthériennes, responsabilité et engagement dans le domaine de la spiritualité," ibid., 38–47.

I. Dingen (1996), Concordia controversa: *Die öffentlichen Diskussionen um das lutherische Konkordienwerk am Ende des 16. Jahrhunderts,* Gütersloh.

HARDING MEYER

9. Intellectual History of Lutheranism

Toward the end of the 16th century Lutheranism crystallized into what has been called "Lutheran orthodoxy*": a theology meant to develop and consolidate (especially under the pressure of its polemics with Catholicism*) the ecclesial and doctrinal structure that issued from the Reformation. The emphasis was then placed both on the preservation of the Lutheran heritage and on its systematization, which was not possible without considerable modifications and reorientations, both in the field of theology and in that of spiritual doctrine. A theory of the literal inspiration of the Scriptures thus arose (also incidentally to be found in post-Tridentine Catholicism) which had a different emphasis to that of the Reformers. Further, the "doctrinal texts" came to be isolated from their historical context and regarded as immutable norms that were, moreover, in perfect agreement with one another. A systematic theology worthy to be called Scholastic was finally developed, under the influence of Melanchthon and within his circle. Associated with a learned metaphysics betraying Aristotelian origins and above all the considerable influence of Suarez* (Pedersen 1921, Wundt 1937, Courtine 1900), it was notable for abandoning (in the work of J. A. Quenstedt, J. Gerhard, and many others) the kerygmatic and homiletic style characteristic of Luther's great reformist writings.

The end of the 17th century, for Lutheranism as for all Christian denominations, was a period of crisis (*see* Pelikan 1989, 9–59, e.g.), which broke up what could have been seen as an untroubled marriage between Christianity and a kind of modernity (that of Luther's existential faith, or of the Cartesian metaphysics of the subject, etc.). Lutheran theology was to offer two concurrent (and not entirely antagonistic) responses to this crisis: Pietism* and theological rationalism*.

Pietism was a movement of spiritual regeneration that influenced every Christian denomination; within Lutheranism it was associated with various elements peculiar to the Reformation and which orthodoxy had in part obscured: a personal understanding of the Christian faith, a return to Scripture as a living source of faith, a refusal to reintroduce the metaphysics implemented by Melanchthon, a justification of universal priesthood* against any tendency to set up a church of ministers, and finally a vision of the Church as communion*. In other respects, however, its "modern" understanding of man and the world led Pietism astray from its reformed heritage: the devout man, the regenerate individual, assumed such importance that the objective elements on which Christian faith and life are based were largely obliterated. In this way the church found itself viewed above all as an assembly or gathering of the regenerate. Sacramental life was in danger of breaking down because the emphasis was placed on the dignity of the person receiving the sacrament and on the transformation to which his or her life bore witness; the significance of confessions of faith was played down, and denominational links were loosened. Even in the area of justification, there was less interest in the God who gives grace, and in the faith that receives that grace, than in the justified man and the effects of justification on his life. Zinzendorf produced a commentary on the *Augsburg Confession,* admittedly, and the majority of Lutheran Pietists remained orthodox, to judge by the beliefs they confessed. However, the "affective transposition of doctrines" (Pelikan 1989, 119–30) in which they all engaged, combining quietist influences (e.g., in the work of the great hymnographer G. Teerstegen [1697–1769], a disciple of the Huguenot P. Poiret), recollections of Rhineland*-Flemish mysticism, and a desire for a God "who can be felt in the heart," and so on, represented a genuine shift: in a Lutheran context, which was its environment of choice, Pietism was more pietist than Lutheran. Moreover, there arose a Pietist critique of Luther (by P. J. Spener and G. Arnold, e.g.), which accused him of carrying out a reformation in the doctrinal sphere, but not in that of piety.

The influence of modern thought was more strikingly present in the Enlightenment's effects on Lutheran theology. In the complex history of theological rationalism, in both the broad and the strict sense, any connection with the original inspiration of the Reformation seems to disappear among authors who nonetheless present themselves as its heirs and followers, but who are often impelled by the image of Luther the liberator to liberate themselves from Luther himself (*see TRE* 21, 571). In this way the Reformation came to be understood as an emancipating force, paving the way for the Enlightenment, and as a refusal of all the restraints (priestly, "supernaturalist," and institutional) that hampered the autonomy of the rational subject. Man's immediate relationship with God offered an argument against mediation through the church and against the constraints imposed upon faith by dogmas and confessions. As well as a decline in the liturgical and sacramental elements of the Christian faith, faith itself was now barely considered except on an ethical level, with the result that practical reason served as the yardstick for all religious life or discourse (Kant* would have the last word on behalf of this trend). Preaching consequently took on a strong moral and pedagogical focus. Everything supernatural* was expunged. Theological rationalism (like Pietism) was admittedly to bear fruit in the biblical field, where it made a great contribution to the development of historico-critical research (J. S. Semler, etc.); but in so doing it accorded its method power over any Christian document—including the confessional texts of the Reformation—and denied the church any authority in the matter.

In reaction against Enlightenment theology (and against the state's hold over the church), the 19th century witnessed a Lutheran revival (neo-Lutheranism) that took up the polemic begun during the previous century by supernaturalist theologians, and also attempted to find a middle way between Schleiermacher*'s theology (in which a kind of neo-Pietism may be discerned) and the demands of a confessional theology. Exemplified above all by the Erlangen School (A. von Harleß, G. C. K. von Hofmann, F. H. R. von Frank) and widely disseminated by the *Zeitschrift für Protestantismus und Kirche,* this current opposed the ruptures of rationalism with a system of thought based on a principle of organic development. Moreover, by bringing about a return to confessional dogmatic* theology, it attempted to give an important place to the Lutheran orthodoxy of the 17th century (*see* the *Dogmatik* by H. Schmid, the "Kirchenschmid" [1843], the most widely read German theology manual of the period). This movement was not limited to academic work, but formed part of a process of awakening felt throughout the Christian world, both in theology and in the daily life of the church (*see TRE* 10, 205–20), and linked in Germany to great evangelical preachers such as the Blumhardts, Johann Christoph (1805–80) and his son Christoph Friedrich (1842–1919). Lutheranism thus opened out to encompass new dimensions, thanks to the development of a lively and varied missionary project, as well as intense social and diaconal activity. Ecclesiology* aroused new interest, from a nonindividualist perspective: the rehabilitation of the ministry of the church, and the reestablishment of the divine service in its full sacramental dimension.

The 19th century, however, was also the century of Hegel* (who incidentally gave the annual commemorative speech for the *Augsburg Confession,* at the behest of Berlin University, in 1830) and his theological following (F. C. Baur and the Protestant school of Tübingen, etc.). It appears to have culminated, in the work of its greatest scholar, A. von Harnack, in the triumph of a "liberal" or "cultural" Protestantism/Lutheranism, which, of the sources of Christianity, kept only a portion of the New Testament texts, and retained virtually nothing of the content of the Christian faith but Jesus' revelation* of the fatherhood of God.

The tendencies of neo-Lutheranism and a return to Luther also ran through the 20th century in various ways. Studies of Luther; a theological response to Kierkegaard* (a Lutheran who died an apostate from Danish Lutheranism, famous among many other things for his polemic against Luther on the subject of the Epistle of Saint James, but with obvious Protestant loyalties); the resumption of some fundamental Reformation ideas in the shape of "dialectical theology" and its rejection of liberal Protestantism; the development, in the mature works of Barth* (a Calvinist who owed much to Luther), of a theological project with a neo-orthodox structure; denominational realignment necessitated by the demands of ecumenical dialogue; and often a liturgical realignment too: these are among the influences and impulses that have shaped contemporary Lutheranism and given it its living face, visible as much in the internal debates that trouble it as in its participation in the debates common to all Christian denominations.

●P. Petersen (1921), *Geschichte der aristotelischen Philosophie im protestantischen Deutschland,* Leipzig (2nd Ed., Stuttgart-Bad Cannstatt, 1964).
M. Wundt (1939), *Die deutsche Schulmetaphysik des 17. Jahrhunderts,* Tübingen.
K. Barth (1946), *Die protestantische Theologie im 19. Jahrhundert,* Zürich.
E. Hirsch (1960), *Geschichte der neuern evangelischen Theologie im Zusammenhang mit den allgemeinen Bewegungen des europäischen Denkens,* 5 vols., Gütersloh.
J. Pelikan (1989), *The Christian Tradition,* vol. 5: *Christian Doctrine and Modern Culture,* Chicago.
J.-F. Courtine (1990) *Suarez et le système de la métaphysique,* Paris.
W. Mostert (1991), "Luther III: Wirkungsgeschichte," *TRE* 21, 567–94 (bibl.).
K. Beyschlag (1993), *Die Erlanger Theologie,* Erlangen-Nüremberg.
M. Matthias (1995), "Orthodoxie I: Lutherische Orthodoxie," *TRE* 25, 464–85 (bibl.).
For further references, *see* bibliographies for **Hegelianiam; Liberalism; Pietism; Rationalism.**

HARDING MEYER AND JEAN-YVES LACOSTE

See also **Anglicanism; Calvinism; Congregationalism; Ecumenicism; Family, Confessional; Luther, Martin; Methodism; Protestantism; Puritanism**

Lyons I, Council of

1245

The First Council of Lyons belongs to the series of general or pontifical councils of the Middle Ages (*see* Lateran* I). Post-Tridentine canonical tradition regards it as the 13th ecumenical council.

Pope Innocent IV, having established himself at Lyons in 1244, convoked a council in the city with the aim of settling the problems of Christendom—the chief of these being the disagreement between the Roman Church and the emperor Frederick II, whose desire for hegemony was threatening the pope in Italy.

Around 150 bishops* and prelates came to Lyons, along with abbots, princes such as the Latin emperor of Constantinople, and ambassadors, including representatives of Frederick II. After a preparatory sitting on 26 June 1245, the council held its first session on 28 June. The pope asked the council to find solutions to the five woes or "wounds" of the church: the moral corruption of clerics* and laity*; the plight of the Holy Land; the weakening of the Latin empire in the east in the face of Greek reconquest; the threats of the Tartars (Mongols); and, last but most important, the persecution of the church by Frederick II. The second session (5 July) dealt largely with the imperial question. During the third and final session (17 July), despite the opposition of some bishops and ambassadors, the emperor was found guilty by the majority, and was excommunicated and deposed.

Frederick II's deposition was the principal achievement of the council. The theological dimension and the desire for reform were almost entirely lacking. The history of the council's decrees is confused: some texts that had not been composed in the context of the council were nonetheless associated with it by Innocent IV. Apart from the bull for Frederick II's deposition, two groups of documents are generally considered as official texts. The first comprises 22 canonical decrees or constitutions concerning ecclesiastical trials (1–3, 6, and 8–17), elections (4–5), the powers of legates (7),

the punishment of hired killers (18), and excommunication (19–22). The second consists of five constitutions, more extended, that address the first four wounds of the church mentioned by the pope at the opening of the council: measures were agreed against the corrupt management of church properties and against usury (1); assistance was promised to the Latin empire of Constantinople (2); the fight against the Tartars was encouraged (4); and steps were taken to restart the Crusade (taxes, measures against Jews, and a prohibition on the sale of strategic goods to the Saracens) (3 and 5). The 22 decrees were adopted almost wholesale into the *Sext*, Boniface VIII's canonical compendium (1298).

Lyons I is remembered chiefly as marking a new stage in the assertion of pontifical "theocracy," as well as for its acknowledgement of the sudden influx of Asian peoples into the church's domain, which initially gave rise to fear before being seen as a new opportunity for evangelization.

● Acts: Mansi 23, 605–86.

Decrees: *COD* 273–301 (*DCO* II/1, 581–633).

Brevis nota (contemporary account of the council.), Ed. L. Weiland, MGH.L, 1886, IV, 2, *Constitutiones* II, 513–6 (no. 401).

Matthieu Paris, *Chronica majora* (council told through witness accounts), Ed. H. R. Luard, Rolls Series 57, 4, London, 1877 (2nd Ed. 1964), vol. 4, 410–4, 430–78.

♦ J.-B. Martin (1905), *Conciles et bullaire du diocèse de Lyon*, Lyon.

H. Wolter, H. Holstein (1966), *Lyon I et Lyon II, HCO* 7 (bibl.).

M. Mollat, P. Tombeur (1974), *Les conciles Lyon I et Lyon II, Concordance, Index, Listes de fréquence, Tables comparatives*, Conciles œcuméniques médiévaux 2, Louvain.

G. Alberigo (1990) (Ed.), *Storia dei concili ecumenici*, Brescia (*Les conciles œcuméniques*, I: *L'histoire*, 189–201).

B. Roberg (1990), "Zur Überlieferung und Interpretation der Hauptquelle des Lugdunense I von 1245," *AHC* 22, 31–67; (1991) "Lyon I," *TRE* 21, 634–7 (bibl.).

JEAN COMBY

See also **Church and State, Political Theology**

Lyons II, Council of

1274

The Second Council of Lyons, like the first, belongs to the series of general or pontifical councils of the Middle Ages (see Lateran* I). Canonical tradition regards it as the 14th ecumenical council.

Pope Gregory X was elected in 1271 after the see of Rome had been vacant for three years, during which period he had witnessed at Saint-Jean d'Acre the death throes of the Christian settlements in the Holy Land and the intrigues of the Latin church against the Greek Empire, the latter having been reestablished in 1261. He immediately decided to convoke a council at Lyons. The council would have three aims: to relaunch the Crusade, to reunite the Greek and Latin churches, and to reform Christian morals.

With the ground prepared by reports sent to the pope*, in particular those of the Franciscan Guibert of Tournai, the Dominican Humbert of Romans, and the bishop* of Olomouc, Bruno of Holstein-Schauenberg, the council brought together an impressive number of prelates. Some sources speak of five hundred bishops and several hundred other prelates. Thomas* Aquinas died on the way there, but Bonaventure*, the minister general of the friar minors attended, as did Peter of Tarentaise, the former archbishop of Lyons, and cardinal and future Pope Innocent V. Besides the six official sessions (7 and 18 May, 4 June, 6, 16, and 17 July) the council witnessed some memorable events: the arrival of the representatives of the Greek Church and a first common celebration of the Eucharist (24 and 29 June); the welcoming of Tartar ambassadors and the baptism* of one of them (4 and 16 July); and the death and funeral of Bonaventure (15 July).

Gregory X was overoptimistic in thinking that the council had realized its proposed aims. The constitution Zelus fidei reorganized the Crusade, introducing a tithe spread over six years and offering indulgences* in return for unsolicited gifts. The highly unpopular decimations were not reintroduced; and the last settlement in the Holy Land, Saint-Jean d'Acre, fell in 1291.

The council made a large contribution to canonical legislation: its 31 decrees were almost all incorporated into the Sext (1298), and several saw some application. The constitution Ubi periculum (can. 2) regulated the election of popes by introducing the conclave. The traditional election procedure for appointments to offices and benefices, and the conditions of ordination* were more strictly defined (can. 3 and Sq). Clerics* were reminded of their duty of residence (can. 14) and the prohibition of the accumulation of benefices (can. 18). Religious orders created without the consent of the pope were to be disbanded (can. 23). There were measures concerning the safeguarding of the dignity of worship and the church, and devotion to the name* of Jesus* was encouraged (can. 25). The prohibition of usury (lending with interest) was repeated, and usurers were refused religious burial (cans. 26–27). Excommunication (cans. 29–31) was again discussed.

Lyons II is remembered as the council at which the Greek and Latin churches were briefly reunited. The desire for reunion which had existed prior to Gregory X's pontificate arose in the context of complicated political and religious circumstances. The emperor Michael VIII Paleologus, who had restored Constantinople to Byzantine rule (1261), judged that reconciliation with the Roman Church would preempt a reopening of hostilities by the Latin barons, and was prepared to make the necessary concessions, though these were refused by the Byzantine patriarch, the bishops*, priests*, and monks. The popes' reason for welcoming the reconciliation were of a more religious kind, but they wished to impose the Roman point of view without discussion. The union was proclaimed at the fourth session of the council on 6 July, when Michael Paleologus's representative read out the Byzantine emperor's profession of faith. This was not a text worked out jointly by Latin and Greek theologians, but a form of words imposed and revised several times by various popes, in particular Clement IV, who had died in 1268. The emperor professed the Filioque*, and recognized that "the holy Roman Church has sovereign and entire primacy and authority* over the whole Catholic Church." He furthermore accepted a number of points of doctrine and discipline contested by the Greeks, regarding eschatology* and sacramental theology: immediate retribution after death*; the fire of purgatory*; the seven sacraments (including Confirmation*, administered by a bishop, and extreme unction); the permissibility of unleavened bread for the Eucharist*; the concept of transubstantiation; the lawfulness of second and third marriages after the death of a spouse; and the condemnation of the repetition of baptism upon moving from one church to another. The emperor insisted, however, that the Greeks should not in any respect change their traditional liturgical formulae. The whole assembly sang the Credo in Latin, and then in Greek, inserting the words, *ex patre filioque procedit.*

The constitution *Fideli ac devota* on the Trinity* (can. 1) was the only official trace retained by the council of this reconciliation between the two churches. This was no more than a reminder of the Latin theology* of the *Filioque:* "The Holy* Spirit proceeds eternally from the Father* and the Son, not as from two principles, but as from a single principle, not by two spirations but by one single spiration."

The Greeks were then asked for a straightforward capitulation. The emperor Michael attempted to impose by force a union, which was universally refused in Constantinople. The patriarch Joseph was deposed and replaced by John Bekkos, who accepted the Latin theology before himself being disgraced. Michael died having been twice excommunicated: by Rome* for having failed to bring about the union, and by the Greek Church for having wished to impose it. The union was immediately denounced (1283). Lyons II had ultimately succeeded only in widening the chasm that separated the two churches. The issue would be taken up again under more favorable conditions at the Council of Florence (1439).

● Acts: Mansi 24, 37–136.
Decrees: *COD* 303–31 (*DCO* II/1, 637–89).
Brevis nota or *Ordinatio Concilii generalis Lugdunensis per Gregorium Papam X* (contemporary account of the council.), Ed. A. Franchi, Rome, 1965.
V. Laurent, J. Darrouzès, *Dossier grec de l'union de Lyon (1273–1277),* Paris, 1976.
♦ J.-B. Martin (1905), *Conciles et bullaire du diocèse de Lyon,* Lyons.
H. Wolter, H. Holstein (1966), *Lyon I et Lyon II, HCO* 7 (bibl.).
M. Mollat, P. Tombeur (1974), *Les conciles Lyon I et Lyon II, Concordance, Index, Listes de fréquence, Tables comparatives,* Conciles œcuméniques médiévaux 2, Louvain.
Coll. (1977), *1274, année charnière: Mutations et continuités,* Paris.
C. Capizzi (1985), "Il IIo Concilio de Lione e l'Unione del 1274: Saggio bibliografico," *OCP* 51, 87–122.
B. Roberg (1989), "Einige Quellenstücke zur Geschichte des II. Konzils von Lyon," *AHC* 21, 103–46.
G. Alberigo (Ed.) (1990), *Storia dei concili ecumenici,* Brescia.
B. Roberg (1990), *Das zweite Konzil von Lyon (1274),* Paderborn; (1991) "Lyon II," *TRE* 21, 637–42 (bibl.).

JEAN COMBY

See also **Ecumenicism;** *Filioque;* **Lyons I, Council of**

M

Magisterium

a) *Magisterium according to the Catholic Church.* Just as medieval universities had a body of masters authorized to teach and decide points of doctrine, similarly, the magisterium designates in the Catholic Church* a body authorized to speak in matters of theology* and church practice. According to the Catholic understanding, it was Christ* himself who conferred on the church the legacy of faith* by instituting an authentic magisterium (*DH* 3305). The church has the right and the duty to expound revealed doctrine, for it is its guardian and dispenser (*DH* 3012, 3020).

The magisterium adds nothing new to the legacy of faith; it explains what might beforehand have appeared obscure and reaffirms what has been called into question (*DH* 3683). The representatives of the magisterium, the pope* and the bishops*, do not receive a new revelation* (*DH* 4150–51). The magisterium does not prevail over the word* of God*, but serves it by teaching solely what has been preserved by tradition* (*DH* 4214). By nature the magisterium can only be exercised within the hierarchical community, which brings together the head and members of the episcopal college (*DH* 4145).

The pope is the supreme doctor* (or teacher) of the church. He has the right to define the articles of faith and to interpret the decisions of the councils (*DH* 3067). The bishops succeed to the college of apostles* in the exercise of the magisterium. They preserve the apostolic doctrine and lead, "in the place of God" (*loco Dei, LG* 20), the flock that is entrusted to them (*DH* 4144, 4146, 4233). The episcopal college holds supreme power over the church as a whole and solemnly exercises this power in the course of the ecumenical council* (*DH* 4146). The council, however, is not superior to the pope (*DH* 3063). The magisterium is exercised in an ordinary way (through the pope and the bishops' teaching and preaching) or in an extraordinary way (through the teaching of a council or the dogmatic decisions of a pope).

b) *Historical Development of the Magisterium.* Very early on, certain passages of the New Testament (e.g., Mt 16:16–19; Lk 10:16; Jn 21:15ff.) were understood as indicating that a magisterium had been conferred by Christ. Historical and critical exegesis*, however, cannot draw any precise conclusions from these passages. The idea and the practical realization of the monarchical episcopate in the second century (particularly attested in the letters of Ignatius of Antioch), as well as the organization of the ecclesiastical ministry* along the lines of imperial Roman administration, played a decisive role in the historical formation of the magisterium. As Congar's studies (1976) have shown, in church Latin, *magisterium* originally denoted a position of authority* or leadership.

In the Middle Ages discussion of the magisterium took place within the framework of the theory of the two powers—the "sacred authority" of bishops and the "royal power" of princes. Within the church itself the clergy occupied a position superior to that of the laity*. Thomas* Aquinas made a further distinction between the *magisterium cathedrae pastoralis* of bishops and the *magisterium cathedrae magistralis* of university theologians. Controversies between supporters of the pope and supporters of the councils further complicated the picture.

The current meaning of the term *magisterium* was principally introduced by German canonists in the early 19th century (*see* Congar 1976). But, strictly speaking, it was not until the First Vatican* Council (1870–71) that a normative and coherent doctrine of the magisterium was established, with the affirmation of the jurisdictional and doctrinal primacy of the pope over the entire church, not only in matters of faith and morals but also in the realm of ecclesiastical* discipline.

c) Magisterium outside Catholicism. At the time of the Reformation and in later Protestantism* the theology of ministries was often defined in opposition to Catholicism*. The more the Catholic Church gave to its magisterium a broad and detailed theological basis, the more Protestantism emphasized the liberty* of Christians. This general statement must, however, be qualified.

For example, depending on the context, there are already some variations in Luther*'s statements on the power of church leaders. From a terminological point of view, for Luther and often in Protestantism in general, the concept of "ministry" encompasses all the questions that Catholics treat under the term "magisterium." According to Lutheran confessional writings, God established the ministry of preaching* (*CA* 5). A minister of the church must be appointed according to the rules (*CA* 14). Episcopal power is understood as a divine order to preach the gospel, to remit sins*, and to administer the sacraments*. In their spiritual government, bishops do not have the right to introduce rules contrary to the gospel (*CA* 28). It follows from these principles that, even in Lutheranism*, ecclesiastical ministry is of divine right, although the power of the clergy is strictly limited. Holy* Scripture and it alone provides the criterion for the magisterium of the church.

In addition, in Protestantism the concept of "doctrine" *(Lehre)* is often used in a broad sense to mean proclamation, witness, or confession. Thus the formulation *pure docere* (*CA* 7) may mean "dispense pure teaching" or "preach the true word," with the task of the magisterium *(Lehramt)* consisting primarily in preaching and teaching rather than defining normative articles of faith. Nevertheless, Lutheran confessional writings do, for example, seek to expound the lineaments of doctrine (*forma doctrinae, BSLK* 833), some-

thing that also confers on their articles the status of a doctrinal norm in the strict sense. It is incumbent on ecclesiastical leaders, if need be on bishops, to ensure that the gospel is indeed proclaimed in accordance with the content of the confession of faith.

For Anglicans the episcopate is a ministry of divine right that may be traced back to an act of institution by the apostles* or by Christ himself. This high status conferred on the position of bishop brings the Anglican understanding close to the magisterium of conciliarist Catholicism. In the Orthodox Church as well, the bishop represents the central and supreme spiritual authority. It is through him that the Holy* Spirit implements the prophetic gift of teaching. In his own diocese the Orthodox bishop enjoys absolute and independent power, and indeed all bishops are absolutely equal in theological terms. Only an ecumenical synod* has authority over the whole body of Orthodox churches. Through its coherent episcopalianism, the Orthodox understanding of the magisterium presents both hierarchical characteristics and democratic elements.

d) Doctrinal Discipline. In spite of the different conceptions they have of the magisterium, all churches in fact have procedures for doctrinal discipline that make it possible for the magisterium to control the pronouncements of ministers. Catholic canon* law (*CIC*) specifies in detail the duties and rights of the clergy, as well as the sanctions and proceedings incurred in case of fault. A theologian who professes dissenting opinions, for example, may have his authorization to teach *(missio canonica)* withdrawn.

With respect to problematical theological theses, the Catholic magisterium, with the help of canonical scholarship, had established a series of censures that variously characterized these theses. A proposition might thus be judged heretical, next to heresy*, schismatic, false, rash, erroneous, scandalous, blasphemous, offensive to pious ears, or evil sounding. The use of these censures, or "theological notes*," became obsolete in the 20th century.

On the Protestant side the vows of ordination* of pastors* often contain doctrinal commitments. These vows and commitments are formally invoked in the case of disciplinary procedures. In such circumstances the ecclesiastical authorities examine the teaching of the accused minister, generally at the request of the parish, to determine whether it is in accord with the confession in question.

e) Magisterium in Ecumenical Discussion. The multilateral ecumenical movement has avoided discussion of the concrete jurisdictions* on which might be established a "visible unity*" of the churches. Models of unity often begin with the principle that local churches must preserve their specific structures within the one Church ("the unity of all in each place") or that confessional churches may survive as structural units while recognizing without reservations the teachings of sister churches ("unity in reconciled diversity").

In these complex discussions the relationship between pluralism and obligatory doctrine poses a fundamental problem, which can be formulated in the following way with respect to the magisterium: must a theological magisterium exercise complete and undivided jurisdiction in order to be really efficacious? Ecumenical discussions tend to answer in the negative, by relativizing the need for the jurisdictional component. The Catholic-Lutheran commission, for example, declared in 1972: "Greater awareness of the historicity of the Church...requires that in our day the concepts of *ius divinum* and *ius humanum* be thought through anew. In both concepts the word *ius* is employed in a merely analogical sense. *Ius divinum* can never be adequately distinguished from *ius humanum*" (31). This idea was extended in 1994: "Even where, in line with the traditional view and terminology, the character of "divine law," a *ius divinum,* is attributed to church legislation, it has a historical shape and form, and it is therefore both possible and necessary to renew and reshape it" (*Kirche und Rechtfertigung,* 227).

On the other hand, Protestants today to a certain extent accept the principle of a magisterium with a legal character: "Catholics and Lutherans together say that God, who establishes institutional entities in his grace* and his faithfulness, and who uses them to preserve the church in the truth of the gospel, also uses church law and legal ordinances for this purpose" (ibid., 224).

● *CIC,* 1983.
H. Meyer et al. (Ed.), *Dokumente wachsender Übereinstimmung 1–2,* Paderborn, 1983–92 (International Catholic-Lutheran Commission, *Face à l'Unité,* Paris,1986).
BSLK (FEL), DH, DS.
Kirche und Rechtfertigung, Paderborn, 1994.
♦ W. Bassett, P. Huizing (Ed.) (1976), *Conc.* 12, no. 8–9.
Y. Congar (1976), "Pour une histoire sémantique du terme *magisterium*" and "Bref historique des formes du 'magistère' et de ses relations avec les docteurs," *RSPhTh* 60, 85–98 and 99–112.
D. Michel et al. (1978), "Amt," *TRE* 2, 500–622.
J. Lécuyer (1980), "Magistère," *DSp* 10, 76–90.
A. Maffeis (1991), *Il Ministero della chiesa, uno studio del dialogo cattolico-luterano (1967–1984),* Rome.
J. Brosseder, W. Hüffmeier (1992), "Lehramt, Lehrbeanstandung," *EKL3* 3, 60–70.
R. R. Gaillardetz (1997), *Teaching with Authority: A Theology of the Magisterium of the Church,* Collegeville.

RISTO SAARINEN

See also **Authority; Bishop; Collegiality; Council; Ministry; Pope**

Malebranche, Nicholas. *See* Augustinianism

Man. *See* Adam; Anthropology

Manicheanism

Up to the early 20th century, Manicheanism was known only through the polemical writings of the church fathers*, principally Augustine*. He had been an adherent of Manicheanism for six years—although as a "hearer," not as one of the "elect"—and hence knew its teachings from the inside. Despite the refutation that he composed after his conversion* to Christianity, he remains a reliable source, quoting its scriptures accurately, as was demonstrated during the 20th century by discoveries in the Turfan (early 1900s) and at Tebessa (1918), Medinet Madi (1929), and Oxyrynchus (1979).

a) Manichean Sources. These three series of discoveries confirmed the new image of Manicheanism that was already being formulated by scholars. Up to the 18th century, Manicheanism appeared to be a Christian heresy* that the Fathers had struggled against. It was Isaac de Beausobre who, as recently as 1728, undertook the first critical studies of the Manichean sources. As a result, Mani ceased to be characterized as a heretic and came to be seen as the founder of a religion. During the 19th century, F. C. Baur demonstrated that the main source of the dualism in Manicheanism was to be found in Indian religion, and had parallels with Buddhism: ever since then, Manicheanism has been given its own place in the history of religions. In addition, materials uncovered by Assyriologists helped to show the Babylonian origins of some of Mani's ideas. However, the decisive change followed the discoveries of Manichean scriptures during the 20th century: they have shown that Manicheanism was in fact not a mere sect at all, but a major Eastern religion, which had its basis partly in such scriptures. Those that have survived into our own day include the texts gathered in the *Shabuhragan* (dedicated to King Shabuhr I); the *Kephalaia,* found at Medinet Madi, which recount the revelations* that Mani received; and part of the *Codex Mani,* found inside a tomb in Oxyrynchus, to the South of Cairo, which contains three fragments of Mani's "gospel." As well as its scriptures, the Manichean religion had a set liturgy and a communal organization, and its missionaries taught a catechism of which one example has been found in the Turfan.

b) Life of Mani. The life of Mani, the founder of Manicheanism, has been known ever since the *Codex Mani,* which itself draws on the "gospels" of his childhood, was deciphered. According to the *Shabuhragan,* Mani was born on 14 April 216 at Mardinu in northern Babylonia. It is known for certain that from 220 to 240 he lived with his father, Pattikios, in an Elchasaite community, where ritual played a dominant role. He experienced his first vision of an angel*, his "twin," in 228; the second took place in 240. It was on these occasions that, according to the first of the *Kephalaia,* "the mystery of light and darkness, their struggle, and the creation of the world, was revealed" to him. This revelation led Mani to break with the Elchasaite, to reject the Old Testament, and to set out on a mission* to proclaim his new religion. He founded communities, which received protection from King Shabuhr I, and by 270 his religion had been established throughout what is now Iran. In around 277, however, Mani was put to death on the orders of Shabuhr's son, Vahram. After his death, Mani's disciples spread his teachings to the East and the West, and his influence lasted into the Middle Ages, when his doctrines were revived, in part, by Catharism*. In Augustine's time, there were some particularly active Manichean communities in North Africa, where they brought together part of the intellectual elite of the region.

Mani's teachings are to be found mainly in two works: the *Shabuhragan,* which is an exposition of the bases of Manichean dualism, by way of the doctrine of the two principles; and the *Pragmateia,* an exposition of Mani's cosmogony, which is worked out in terms of three "ages." During the first age, according to Mani, there was nothing but the two principles of "good" and "evil." During the second age, there are various confrontations between the King of Darkness and the Father of Light, which give rise to several "emanations," including the Mother of the Living, the Primordial Man, the Living Spirit, the Archons, and Jesus in Splendor. The last age has yet to begin: Mani's eschatology foresees a last judgment* and the decisive triumph of his religion.

c) Augustine and Manicheanism. It is understandable that Augustine was drawn to this religion, which was of a new type, and which combined mysteries* that he hoped to be initiated into with an ethical rigor of the kind that he was seeking. However, his meeting with

Faustus of Milevis led him to question both of the principal doctrines in the Manichean system, the doctrine of the two principles and the doctrine of the three ages (first, second, and last). In the *De Gn. contra manichaeos,* he abandons the Manichean theme of an evil world, the result of the various "emanations," which are also stages in degeneration, in favor of the theme of a creation* that is basically good. Augustine was impelled to write this polemic against Manicheanism very soon after his return to Africa by his need to justify to himself, and to demonstrate to others, the process whereby he had ceased to be an adherent of Manicheanism, having been a Manichean when he left Africa. Later, he had to defend his community, as its pastor*, against the Manicheans, and this is why he wrote *De natura boni* (On the Nature of Good) and *De libero arbitrio* (On Free Will), in which he argues that evil* does not arise from an evil principle, but from a free choice of the will (*see also* BAug 17, *Six Anti-Manichean Treatises*).

● P. Alfaric (1918), *Les écritures manichéennes,* 2 vols., Paris.
H. C. Puech (1972), "Le manichéisme," *Histoire des religions* II, coll. "Pléiade," 637–41 (list of sources), Paris.
Der Kölner Mani-Kodex (1988), pub. by L. Koenen and C. Römer, Opladen.
♦ I. de Beausobre (1734–39), *Histoire critique de Manichée et du manichéisme,* 2 vols., Amsterdam.
F. C. Baur (1831), *Das manichäische Religionssystem nach den Quellen neu untersucht und entwickelt,* Göttingen.
H. C. Puech (1949), *Le manichéisme, son fondateur, sa doctrine,* Paris; (1979), *Sur le manichéisme,* Paris.
M. Tardieu (1981), *Le manichéisme,* Paris.
J. Ries (1988), *Les études manichéennes,* Louvain-la-Neuve.
A. Böhlig (1992), "Manichäismus," *TRE* 22, 25–45 (bibl.).

MARIE-ANNE VANNIER

See also **Creation; Eschatology; Evil; Religions, Theology of**

Manning, Henry Edward

1808–1892

a) Life.   Manning was the third and youngest son of a Tory member of Parliament and governor of the Bank of England. Undistinguished at school, except as a cricketer, he preceded Gladstone, his later theological opponent, as president of the Oxford Union. After a short spell in business he returned to Oxford, was ordained under evangelical influences into the Church of England, and became a fellow of Merton College. In 1833 he was presented to a Sussex rectory and married at a ceremony conducted by Samuel Wilberforce, brother-in-law of the bride and afterward bishop of Oxford and of Winchester. Grief on the death of his wife in 1837 was assuaged by a religious move toward the High Church, Newman*, and the Tractarians. He paid a first visit to Rome with Gladstone late in 1838, calling on Wiseman, and in 1842 published his treatise *On the Unity of the Church.* He was by now a noted preacher, and four volumes of his sermons were published between 1842 and 1850.

Newman's secession to Rome forced Manning into a higher profile as a High Church leader, but a serious illness in 1847 led him to recuperate in Rome, where he spent the following winter, getting to know Wiseman, the Catholic scholar whose erudite works on the early church had a profound influence on Newman and the Anglican dignitaries of the Oxford movement. Manning was twice received in audience by the pope, and became both increasingly aware of what appeared to him to be the defects in the Church of England and drawn to the religious qualities of the Roman communion. On his return to England he continued to devote himself to pastoral duties and an ascetic way of life, turning down a post normally leading to a bishopric. His own religious crisis came to a climax late in 1850, when he found himself unable to join in the protests against the insensitively aggressive ecclesiastical style of Wiseman, recently made a cardinal and charged with reestablishing the Roman hierarchy in England.

On Passion Sunday 1851 Manning became a Roman Catholic, a week later receiving communion and confirmation from Wiseman. Nine weeks thereafter Wiseman ordained Manning priest. Manning then studied theology in Rome, where he was frequently received by the pope. During brief returns to England he acted as Wiseman's assistant, contriving to remove the Catholic army chaplains from subordination to Anglican military superiors, and in 1857 was appointed head of the Westminster cathedral chapter and superior of the "Oblates of St Charles." These were similar to Newman's Oratorians, except that they placed themselves at the disposal of the local bishop.

Manning swiftly became the leader of the Romanizing Ultramontane party among English Catholics, distrusted by the older, more liberal Catholic families. On Wiseman's death in 1865 it was against considerable opposition that Pius IX imposed Manning as archbishop of Westminster. Manning's contribution to Catholic life was henceforward more social than theological. He furthered Catholic education, especially industrial and reform schools; opposed the attendance of Catholics at Oxford and Cambridge; failed in an attempt to found a Catholic university; and, to the detriment of all ecumenical endeavor, emphasized the exclusivity of Roman claims, strongly supporting the dogmatic definition of papal infallibility at the First Vatican* Council. On 15 March 1875 he was created cardinal, and in 1878 was considered a plausible candidate to succeed Pius IX. He himself supported Pecci, who became Leo XIII and whose famous encyclical on the claims of labor, *Rerum novarum,* was influenced by Manning. His later years were devoted chiefly to social questions and to the care of the Irish immigrants who formed the chief part of his flock. He sat on royal commissions on housing for the working classes (1884) and on primary education (1886), and played a leading part in the settlement of the dockers' strike in 1889.

b) Thought. Manning was not notable as a theologian, whether speculative or evangelical, although he much influenced the thinking of pastoral and moral theologians by his own pastoral attitudes and by his concern for the well-being and organization of labor. It was the religious style of everyday Catholicism rather than the erudition of Wiseman or the theological niceties of Newman that drove him to leave the Anglican communion for Rome, although the crux was the dogmatic impropriety implied by the controversial investiture of G. C. Gorham with the benefice of Brampford Speke in spite of Speke's declared disbelief in baptismal regeneration.

In 1860 Manning delivered a series of lectures defending the pope's temporal power, having already, while still an Anglican, denounced in an open letter to his bishop the appellate jurisdiction of the English crown in spiritual matters. He strongly believed in the divine institution of a hierarchical church, not only headed by an infallible pope, but also intolerant of such widespread exemptions from the normal chain of hierarchical authority as were enjoyed by the regulars, particularly the Jesuits.

● Lemire, *Le cardinal Manning et son action sociale,* Paris, 1893.
Edmund Sheridan Purcell, *Life of Cardinal Manning,* 2 vols., London, 1896.

ANTHONY LEVI

Marcionism

Marcion, the propagator of the most threatening Christian heresy* to face the "Great Church" in the latter half of the second century, is known only through what his adversaries said about him. Nonetheless, anti-Marcionite patristic literature provides a countertestimony from which we are able to reconstruct the original characteristics of the doctrine and the movement.

1. Doctrine

Marcion's major intuition was to theorize the opposition between the Old Testament and the New Testament. In order to declare the radical separation of the law and the gospel,* he erected a dualistic system governed by ditheism.

a) Theology. Two gods are placed in opposition, a just god* and a good god. The first, who has been known for the longest time, is revealed in the Old Testament. Demiurge or creator of the universe that he organized out of preexisting matter, a principle of evil*, he also created man, and is his despotic master. Though not essentially wicked, this god of the world and of the Jews is characterized by his exclusive concern for justice*, his vindictiveness, and his inconstancy and lack of foresight. Above him—and unknown to him—reigns the higher god, the god of pure goodness who neither judges nor punishes. This god remained foreign to our world until his revelation* in Jesus Christ*. And through his manifestation in the gospel, he came to liberate human beings from the power of the Creator and bring them salvation*.

b) Christology and Soteriology. They are essentially Docetist. In the 15th year of the reign of Tiberius, the son of a higher god—a spiritual being hardly distinct from the Father*—suddenly appeared in Jesus Christ, who came into the world without experiencing the humiliations of human birth. In a "flesh" of pure appearance, he manifested his divinity by his preaching and his miracles*, beginning in the synagogue of Capernaum. His work was to undo that of the Creator, and to substitute his own teachings and institutions for those of the Creator. He endured the Passion* and death* on the cross, a victim of the powers of the Creator and those faithful to him, and at this price he "bought man" from his master. Those who believe in Jesus Christ are "saved" by their faith*, but this salvation applies only to the soul*: the "flesh*" or "matter" is unworthy of salvation and is doomed to annihilation, as the Creator too will be annihilated once his function in the economy of the world and history* is accomplished.

c) Morality. Marcionite ethics* is based on the law of love* as articulated in the "beatitudes*," and opposed to Judaic prescriptions such as talion law. Its main aim is to detach the person from the grasp of a "flesh" that is essentially evil, and its principle is to refuse to perpetuate the world* of the Creator. Consequently, Marcionite ethics advocated the ascetic practices of "Encratism": strict abstention from marriage* and procreation*, vegetarianism, fasting, and a willing acceptance of ordeals, notably martyrdom.*

d) Scriptural instrumentum. The originality of Marcionism is that it justified its doctrine with the help of a historico-philological reconstruction based on the idea that the church* went astray from the original gospel, polluting it with Judaizing interpretations and interpolations. Marcion composed an *instrumentum* drawn from a revision of New Testament literature combined with an explanatory treatise that served as foundation. This treatise, entitled *Antitheses,* which included explanations of the role of Paul, seen as the sole possessor of the authentic gospel, placed both in parallel and in opposition the words and deeds of the Creator and those of Jesus Christ. As for the *instrumentum* strictly speaking, it was composed of a gospel without an author's name (the gospel of Luke, corrected and excluding the first chapters) and an *apostolicon* (10 letters of Paul, also revised, and placed in a particular order, giving the greatest importance to Galatians because of the incident at Antiochus). Aside from the notion of a scriptural "canon*," which he may have helped the church to establish, Marcion stimulated the reflection of the Fathers by refusing all christological and typological exegesis* of the Old Testament, notably the prophecies*: for these texts he followed the literalist interpretation of Judaism.

2. Organization and History of the Movement

As Hippolytus recounts, Marcion was born in Sinope, the son of a bishop. He went to Rome around 140 after being excommunicated by his father for immorality. In 144 he broke with the Christian community of Rome* and created his own church, which spread rapidly and widely throughout the empire. This success can be explained by Marcionism's radical attitude toward Judaism* and by a moral rigor that was in harmony with certain pagan intellectual trends at the time. Sacramental life and liturgical life followed the "Catholic" model, with some differences: baptism* was granted only at the price of a commitment to absolute continence; the Eucharist* was performed with bread and water; the hierarchy* was not as rigid, and women fulfilled certain ministries. Whereas in the West, and notably in Africa, the movement ceased troubling the church around the mid–third century, it retained its vitality much longer in the East, where it finally blended into Manichaenism.*

3. Modern Interpretations

Was Marcion, classified with the Gnostics by the heresiologues of the patristic period, really a Christian theologian overcome by a Pauline* conception (the opposition between the law and faith) that had been pushed to its extreme consequences by Marcion's ditheism? This is the position taken in a work—in other respects fundamental—by Harnack (1924). The position was recently repeated by Hoffmann (1984), who combined it with views taken from Knox (1942) and a questioning of the chronology, and who portrayed Marcion as a theologian who restored authentic Christianity, a legitimate interpreter of the Pauline gospel, ignorant of the apostolic tradition* that was employed to attack him. Critics have stressed the weaknesses of this thesis in its two successive forms; the point of view prevalent today accords with the interpretation of the Fathers: despite the particular feature of his refusal to speculate on the Pleroma, Marcion was indeed a Gnostic, marked by the philosophy* of his time, who put a Christian "veneer" on a dualist doctrine nourished by the basic preoccupations of gnosis* (systematic depreciation of the world and matter, belief in a higher, "separate" god).

● A. von Harnack (1924), *Marcion: Das Evangelium vom fremden Gott,* 2nd Ed., Leipzig (repr. 1960, Darmstadt; English trans. 1990, Durham).

J. Knox (1942), *Marcion and the New Testament,* Chicago.

E.C. Blackman (1949), *Marcion and His Influence,* London.

U. Bianchi (1958), *Il dualismo religioso,* Rome; (1967), "Marcion théologien biblique ou docteur gnostique," *VigChr* 21, 141–49.

B. Aland (1973), "Marcion: Versuch einer neuen Interpretation," *ZThK* 70, 420–47.

G. Quispel (1981), "Gnosis," *Die orientalischen Religionen im Römerreich,* EPRO 91, 425–26.

R.J. Hoffmann (1984), *Marcion: On the Restitution of Christianity,* Chico, Calif.

G. May (1986), "Ein neues Markionbild," *ThR* 51, 404–13.

E. Norelli (1987), "Una 'restituzione' di Marciano," *CrSt* 8, 609–31.

G. May (1988), "Marcion in Contemporary Views: Results and Open Questions," *SecCent* 6, 129–51; (1993), "Marcione nel suo tempo," *CrSt* 14, 205–20.

A. Orbe (1990), "En torno al modalismo de Marción," *Gr* 71, 43–65; (1991), "Marcionitica," *Aug.* 31, 195–244.

D.W. Deakle (1991), *The Fathers against Marcionism,* thesis, Saint Louis University.

RENÉ BRAUN

See also **Canon of Scriptures; Christ and Christology; Docetism; Gnosis; Tertullian**

Marechal, Joseph. *See* Thomism

Market Economics, Morality of

The church* has never found it easy to come to terms with market forces. It has tended to oscillate between an overdismissive criticism of commercial activity, often based on inadequate information or poor understanding, and an uncritical acceptance of the status quo. Some Christian thinkers, however, have combined empirical knowledge with a theological basis for understanding business, from which its operation can be constructively challenged.

1. Old Testament

The Old Testament contains a considerable amount of material on the conduct of economic life. The basic economic unit is land. In his gift of the Promised Land, God* gives Israel* a rich resource (Dt 8:7–10), which it is expected to make productive. There is freedom for buying and selling, and some movement in landholding is allowed, but effectively this is only a matter of lease holding for a limited time, because in the 50th

("Jubilee") year property* is expected to be returned to its original owner (Lv 25:8–17). A sabbatical year (sabbath*) for the land to lie fallow, to prevent its over-exploitation, is also ordained (Lv 25:1–7). The Torah's concern for the potential plight of the poor is illustrated by its insistence that the borders of fields should be left for "gleaning" (Lv 19:9–10); that the payment of a hired laborer's wages should not be delayed (Lv 19:13); and that interest should not be leveled on loans made to a fellow Israelite (Ex 22:24–26; Lv 25:35–37). By contrast, interest on loans to foreigners is allowed (Dt 23:20), allowing Israel to play its part in the commerce of the ancient Middle East. In the descriptions of trading activity under King Solomon, for example (1 Kgs 3–10), we see that substantial national wealth resulted, although it tended to be concentrated disproportionately at the royal court. The eighth-century prophets* condemn the exploitation of the poor by the rich (Am 5:21–24; Mi 3:9–12), while the wisdom* literature strikes a different note, seeing prosperity as the sequel to industrious endeavor, but also recommending trustworthiness and integrity (e.g., Prv 10:9 and 12:11).

2. New Testament

In the New Testament, the basic assumption that human beings should work remains (e.g., 2 Thes 3:6–13), but references to economic activity tend to be more incidental. Some claim that in parables* such as the laborers in the vineyard (Mt 20:1–16) or the talents (Mt 25:14–30), Jesus* was laying down principles for the payment of wages (the one seemingly very egalitarian, the other highly meritocratic). This is very doubtful, however: it is more likely that the parables were means for him to explain and teach God's relationship with humanity. On the other hand, Jesus repeatedly warned about the dangers of wealth and the worship of Mammon (Mt 6:19–34; Mk 10:17–31; Lk 12:15–21). Merchants are included along with rulers and mariners in the condemnation of Babylon in Revelation 18, in which they are seen as no more than traffickers at the service of ostentation.

3. From the Patristic Period to the Reformation

The difference in emphasis between Old Testament and New helps to explain why the function and occupation of trade were accepted more readily in Jewish communities than Christian ones in the patristic period and in the Middle Ages. However, while the church often sought to distance itself from such activities, it could not wholly avoid questions relating to it, not least because the church was an institution that depended on wealth-creating activity for its survival.

This is graphically illustrated in the case of the monastic orders, which were committed to vows of poverty. The Cistercian order, for example, eventually acquired considerable economic power. In the 13th and 14th centuries, issues of economic morality became associated with the Dominican and Franciscan chairs of theology in Paris. Three key issues dominated the debates.

a) *Compulsion* (ius necessitatis). Thomas* Aquinas affirms the right to private property, qualified by concern for the common good*. There is an obligation to minister to those in need and, if this is not met, the person in dire need may steal (*ST* IIa IIae, q. 66, a. 7). This latter was not a view that met with universal agreement, and other writers (particularly, later, the Puritans) would emphasize the rights of property holders.

b) *Just Price*. Aquinas, Duns* Scotus, and Peter Olivi (1248–98) developed the concept of a "just price," the one that rewards the seller and satisfies the customer. A seller may guard against loss, but should not take advantage of the buyer's need. This was also taught by Luther*, who criticized the avarice of contemporary merchants, but recognized that such considerations as the cost of labor, distance of transport, and level of risk serve to make precise calculation of a just price complex, and something that could be variously settled by local law, custom, or individual conscience*.

c) *Usury*. Basil* (*Hom. II in Ps. 14*, PG 29, 264D–80D), Ambrose* (*De Tobia*, PL 14, 591–622), and John Chrysostom* (*Hom. in Matt.* 56, 5–6, PG 58, 555–58) explicitly condemn the charging of interest, or usury, which they believed ran contrary to Christian obligations of love* and mercy*. (It is only much later that the word "usury" would acquire the meaning of *excessive* charging of interest.) This disapproval was embodied in church canons from the Council of Elvira (306) onward, and maintained for the next millennium, although enforcement of it was never complete. A variety of arguments were used in condemning usury, some being borrowed from the Bible* (e.g., Lk 6:35, cited alongside Old Testament references), others being based on natural law (e.g., Aristotle's argument that money is essentially barren, so that it is "unnatural" to make money out of it, *Politics* 1, 10, 1258 *b* 7). Aquinas argues that money has no value except in use, and that therefore lending represents double-charging and is unfair (*ST* IIa IIae, q. 78). However, he allows payment of compensation for the risk involved in lending, an exception formalized by other Scholastic theologians (Scholasticism*) in the phrase *damnum emergens* and a practice that came to be commonplace at the time loans were made. Hostiensis (†1271) and Antoninus (1389–1459) also permitted interest on the grounds of loss of gain *(lucrum cessans)*. Questioning of the ban on interest therefore predated the Reformation, but relaxation of it accelerated from that period. Calvin* did not regard the Israelite prohibition as universal (regarding it as an aspect of the Mosaic law particular to their "political constitution"); he therefore allows interest, in a limited way, so long as it does not infringe charity and equity (CR 24, 679–83). From the 16th century onward, there was a tendency, reflected in national legislation (e.g., the 1571 Act in England) to evaluate lending not so much in terms of the declared motive, but in terms of the level of interest charged.

4. Modern Times

Calvin's more tolerant attitude to trade is often linked to the expansion in economic activity that took place in the 16th century. In exploring why Protestant countries grew faster than Catholic ones, Max Weber (1864–1920) posited a link between the burgeoning spirit of capitalism and the Calvinist doctrine of predestination*, claiming that insecurity about salvation* led people to look for signs of God's blessing* in their material condition. Attitudes of thrift and industriousness, and an understanding of God's world as ripe for discovery and development, probably did encourage a "work ethic" that paved the way for the Industrial Revolution. However, this ethic has gradually become secularized, just as economics has come to be regarded as an autonomous discipline in which the laws of supply and demand wield ultimate authority when it comes to the setting of wages and prices. As the global economy has grown increasingly sophisticated, so the influence of the churches had been reduced, although they sometimes intervene in the economic domain. Christian individuals and organizations (e.g., in England, trade unions inspired by Methodism*) played a part in the struggle against inhuman conditions during the initial period of industrialization.

5. Contemporary Problems

The growth of the modern company has been accelerated, in many countries, by legislation that limits the liability of shareholders and reduces the risk in investment. Although limited liability has helped to provide industry with the capital it needs, it has not escaped moral criticism from some observers (Goyder 1987). First, it tends to separate stewardship from ownership, since shareholders, increasingly represented by intermediate institutions, such as pension funds, have little or no involvement in the running of the company. Share-ownership schemes among employees go a small way toward overcoming this separation. Second, limited liability fails to guarantee the exercise of corporate moral responsibility, because creditors of a failed company are often left with debts unpaid.

The large, anonymous nature of many modern organizations and the repetitive nature of work on assembly lines have also been challenged (e.g., Schumacher 1987) on the grounds that they fail to respect the person and allow no space for creativity and responsibility. Changes, however, are taking place, with companies being restructured into smaller units and semiautonomous work groups, while nonspecialized work is increasingly done by robots. This in turn creates a new problem, since it leads to the unemployment of unskilled workers.

Another practice that has been criticized is the way goods are marketed and advertised. Marketing has been blamed (Packard 1957) for high-pressure sales, misleading claims, the use of subliminal messages, and promoting materialism. Yet if goods are to be bought and sold in the marketplace, a process of communication between consumers and producers is inevitable. Nevertheless, the techniques used warrant careful attention.

Finally, some fundamental questions remain and are still being debated. Some Christians (e.g., Novak 1991) have embraced economic liberalism enthusiastically; others have criticized it strongly, on Marxist lines (theology of liberation*). The history of eastern Europe, however, demonstrates that a centralized economy is not viable. A more balanced view of capitalism recognizes that it is not simply an unjust system, and that there are many variants upon it, rather than a single entity of this name. One thinks of the difference between the social or "communitarian" concerns of Germany or Japan, on the one hand, and the individualism of the United States and Britain on the other—not to mention the French paradoxes in this respect.

Perhaps the main moral challenge facing affluent countries today is that of aid to the Third World, which is not just a matter of the provision of emergency aid, but of finding ways to help poorer countries to become true participants in the world's trading system. At present, producers in these countries struggle because of the high cost of loans from the West (which triggered a "debt crisis" in the 1980s) and the low level of prices for primary commodities. Their plight will be alleviated only by the emergence of a new type of self-denying "ethical" investors and consumers, and by employees from such countries reaching positions of seniority and influence in multinational corporations. At present, all this is somewhat unlikely to happen.

- M. Weber (1920), *Die protestantische Ethik und der Geist der Kapitalismus*, in *Gesammelte Aufsätze zur Religionssoziologie*, vol. 1, Tübingen.
- R. Tawney (1926), *Religion and the Rise of Capitalism*, London.
- W. Temple (1942), *Christianity and Social Order*, Harmondsworth.
- J. Ellul (1954), *L'homme et l'argent*, Neuchâtel.
- J. T. Noonan (1957), *The Scholastic Analysis of Usury*, Cambridge, Mass.
- V. Packard (1957), *The Hidden Persuaders*, New York.
- C. J. H. Wright (1983), *Living as People of God*, Leicester.
- B. Griffiths (1984), *The Creation of Wealth*, London.
- A. Storkey (1986), *Transforming Economy*, London.
- G. Goyder (1987), *The Just Enterprise*, London.
- C. Schumacher (1987), *To Live and Work*, Bromley.
- M. Tamari (1987), *With All Your Possessions*, London.

- D. Hay (1989), *Economics Today*, Leicester.
- John Paul II (1991), *Centesimus annus*, AAS 83, 793–867.
- M. Novak (1991), *The Spirit of Democratic Capitalism*, London.
- R. H. Preston (1991), *Religion and the Ambiguities of Capitalism*, London.
- O. Langholm (1992), *Economics in the Medieval Schools*, Leyden.
- R. Higginson (1993), *Called to Account*, Guildford.
- T. J. Gorringe (1994), *Capital and the Kingdom*, London.
- H. Puel (1995), *L'éthique au défi*, Paris.
- P. van Parijs (1996), "Économie," *DEPhM*, 459–65.

RICHARD HIGGINSON

See also **Ethics; Marx, Karl; Property; Society; Work**

Maritain, Jacques. *See* Thomism

Marriage

A. Sacramental Theology

1. Overview

From the beginning, Christian communities intervened, in certain circumstances or situations, in order to guide and celebrate the life of couples*, whose members received baptism* and had to take part in the Eucharist*. As the Eastern churches (Greco-Byzantine, Armenian, Syriac, Coptic, and others) developed over the course of the first millennium, the practice of having a bishop* or a priest* solemnly bless a couple became widespread. This mystery* in the form of liturgy* became the obligatory form for the entry of believers into the state of marriage. Its development took longer in the Latin West, where it was linked to the elaboration of the notion of sacrament*. Later, the Eastern churches adapted some aspects of this notion to their own dogmatic* theologies. According to this approach, a sacrament is a sacred sign instituted by God*, through Jesus Christ, so that the sanctification that this sign has received as its signifying function may be operative, by this means, among the believers in question. A definition of this type acquired its technical status around 1150. From then on, it was applied to seven sacred signs, including marriage (Peter Lombard, *Summa Sententiarum* IV, d. 2 and 26; PL 192, 842, and 908).

This did not put an end to debate, which was given new impetus when the Reformers expressed an extreme attachment to the idea that marriage between believers does not have the status of a sacrament of Christ in the strict sense. This was the view taken by Luther*, for example, from whose writings were derived the formulas suggested to pastors* in the "booklet on marriage" attached as an appendix to the *Lesser Catechism* of 1529 (*BSLK* 528–34, *FEL* 320–22).

Calvin* takes the same view in the final version of the *Institutio Christianae Religionis* (Institutes of the Christian Religion, 1560, Book IV, ch. XIX, §34–37). Nevertheless, the Reformers strongly emphasized the honor and duties of the conjugal bond, and of the family*, and the formation of couples among the faithful was normally accompanied by the giving of a blessing by a pastor.

Both in the East and in the West, such theological positions were based on a small group of fundamental texts, above all on the words of Jesus* that had established the Christian rule of the indissolubility of marriage. According to the Gospels*, Jesus interpreted the verse "they shall become one flesh" (Gn 2:24, quoted in the New Testament in Greek, from the Septuagint) as evidence for the primordial vocation of the sexes at the time of the Creation*, and provided the authentic and definitive interpretation of it: "What therefore God has joined together, let not man separate" (Mt 19:6; Mk 10:6–9). With his sovereign authority*, Jesus rejects the forms of divorce that the law* of Moses had provided for Jewish couples (Mt 5:31f. and 19:7–9; Mk 10:3–9; *see* Lk 16:18 and 1 Cor 7:10f.).

The same text, "one flesh," is repeated on other occasions in the New Testament, in teachings that became important to the theology of marriage. The union of a man and a woman* is an image for the participation of believers in Christ according to the body and the spirit (1 Cor 6:15–20); above all, it is an image of the relationship between Christ and the church, his spouse (Eph 5:29–32). The latter passage uses the term "mystery," and the Latin translation of this term as *sacramentum* helped to fix the image of marriage in medieval theology and in Catholicism*. However, there is a larger body of biblical texts at stake.

2. Biblical Sources

a) Ancient Israel. Marriage in Israel is not marked by any religious act and has nothing to do with priestly authority, but being united in marriage is defined as entering a holy covenant* (Ez 16:8; Prv 2:17; Mal 2:14) and is celebrated by a blessing, either in public (Gn 24:60; Ru 4:11f.) or in private, between the man and the woman (Tb 8:4–8; the formula given in this apocryphal work has had an influence on Christian liturgies). Violation of marriage (adultery) is generally regarded as an offense against the law of God, which is the basis of the collective existence of the holy people; it is subject to public punishment. Marriage to a foreigner is strictly forbidden (Dt 7:3f.) as an offense against the holiness* of the people. To turn away from the true God is, by analogy, to commit adultery (Hosea; Jer 3:1–10; Ez 16 and 23). Conversely, God's

faithfulness and tenderness are praised in images of marriage: these are reprised in the New Testament (Rom 9:25, quoting Hos 2:25, or 2:23 according to the Septuagint; 2 Cor 11:2; Rev 19:7f. and 21:1–11). These same images came to typify the spiritual theology* both of the relationship between humanity and Christ and the relationship between Christ's human soul* and the eternal divine nature of the Word*.

b) Christ's Disciples. The disciples of Christ form a holy community in their turn (Acts 9:13 and 9:31–41; 2 Cor 1:1 and 13:12; Col 1:2ff.; 1 Pt 2:9f.). Infidelity to the Son of God is compared to prostitution (Rev 2:18–23); it follows that the misconduct of one who has been baptized calls for a response from the assembled church (1 Cor 5, which concerns an incestuous relationship). It is not to his hearers in general but to his disciples that Jesus teaches the absolute rejection of divorce—at any rate, that is the narrative construction that Mark puts on the point (Mk 10:10ff.). Again, it is to his disciples alone that Jesus addresses the saying (Mt 19:10ff.) about those who are celibate for the sake of the Kingdom*, a condition of life that presupposes a special vocation or gift—what Paul calls a *charisma* (1 Cor 7:7).

In New Testament times, abstention from marriage could be presented as a duty for all the disciples. Two verses in Luke's Gospel (14:26 and 18:29), praising those who leave their wives, could be interpreted in this sense. Paul is aware of this view, but refuses to approve it as a rule of conduct valid for all (1 Cor 7:25ff.). Although his condemnation of marriage ("Encratism") was possible in the spiritual climate of the time, one letter in the Pauline corpus denounces it as a false doctrine (1 Tm 4:3) and presents motherhood as a good way of life (2:15 and 5:14).

Those Pauline texts that describe the life of a married couple situate it within the framework of the Hellenistic household as a whole, including children as well as servants or slaves. Christian husbands and wives form the focus of the household, being ordained for one another through relations of faithfulness and love* (Col 3:12ff.; Eph 5:18ff.). At the heart of the household, the Christian couple, living in mutual accord, open up a privileged space for prayer* (1 Cor 7:5; 1 Pt 3:7). Additionally, the household is quite frequently presented as the center of a local church, a specific community (1 Cor 16:15f. and 16:19; Rom 16:5; Col 4:15; Phlm 2; *see* Heb 13:1–6). This is not in every case a matter of couples in which both husband and wife are believers. According to Paul, a man or woman who is converted to Christianity is not required to end his or her marriage to a spouse who remains a non-Christian (1 Cor 7:14ff.; *see* 1 Pt 3:1f.). Nevertheless, a widow who wishes to remarry "is free to be married to whom she wishes, only in the Lord" (1 Cor 7:39).

These themes could be interpreted, as they frequently have been within Protestantism* (*see* Grimm 1984), in the context of family and social ethics*. The inspiration of Christianity could overhaul behavior, or provide it with clearer motives, but this did not mean the introduction of any new notion of marriage within the church, specifically related to the conditions of life shared by men and women. Nevertheless, the theology of the Eastern churches, as of the Catholic Church, has based the value of Christian marriage not on a simple ethical confirmation of the primordial status of the conjugal vocation but on the gift of participation, through the grace* of the Spirit of God, in the new creation* and in the body of Christ (2 Cor 5:17). Certain types of Protestant theology, interpreting Paul's ideas, have adopted a similar approach (*see* Schrage 1995). Within these churches, there has been a recognition of marriage as something truly *new*: the novelty of an intimately transforming grace that is not simply the grace of the aid that God might give on other occasions in order to support the maintenance of family virtues*.

In respect of the nature of family structures, the innovation in Christianity, by contrast to the first covenant, is based first and foremost on the figure of Christ himself. According to the faith* of the church, the Son of God is also the Son of David, and belongs to the house or lineage of David, which is the lineage of the kings appointed by God for his people. With Jesus, the genealogical principle that sustained the series of royal anointments and structured the history* of God's people ceases to be valid. Jesus does not prolong the line of descent, and the central group of disciples formed for the future does not include his brothers and sisters: the genealogical structure ends with Jesus (Mt 1:17f.), because the totality of the innovation is present in him, in the plenary action of God's Spirit (Mt 3:17 par.). The permanent celibacy of some of the baptized could then be understood within the church as a participation in Christ's innovation, as a *charisma.*

Paul's teaching suggests (1 Cor 7:7) that, nonetheless, the married life of the baptized might contain a complementary innovation, a specific grace that parallels such celibacy for the sake of the kingdom. Yet it also suggests—as in the statement that "it is better to marry than to be aflame with passion" (1 Cor 7:9)—that the innovation of Christ's graces in respect of married couples is merely that of protection against misuse of sexuality. The Western church spoke of marriage as a sacrament, a sacred sign of the relationship between Christ and the church, long before there was a recognition, during the 13th century, of the positive, sanctify-

ing efficacy of marriage, similar to that of the other sacraments of the New Covenant (Schillebeeckx 1963).

3. Traditions of the Churches

a) Churches in the First Centuries. During its first centuries, there was a tendency within Christianity to distrust marriage, as Encratism was taken up by certain forms of gnosis* and then by Manicheanism*. However, the churches recognized marriage as having a positive value in the life of Christian communities. Ignatius of Antioch suggests that the formation of a couple by two baptized people should be subject to the supervision of a bishop (*Ad Polycarpum* 5, SC 10 *bis*, 174–77); Tertullian* eulogizes the marriages that the church has fostered and blessed (*Ad Uxorem* II, 8, 6, SC 273, 148f.). Yet there was no systematic development of the liturgical aspect of marriage within the churches, if we are to believe the sources that are available to us. By contrast, we have evidence of numerous disciplinary decisions, in line with the spiritual and ethical guidance contained in the apostolic writings. The precise wording of these decisions varies from region to region and from period to period, but the issues that they address are fairly constant: whether a marriage is legitimate, whether it is to be prohibited as incestuous or degrading, or whether a separation is required in view of the reception of baptism by an adult or participation in the Eucharist.

The main problem in respect of marriage concerned the situation that may have been the intended topic of two passages in Matthew's Gospel that both include the clause "except on the ground of sexual immorality [*porneia*]" (5:32 and 19:9). The church fathers* usually interpreted this clause as referring to the situation that arises for a couple when one of them has committed the sin of adultery. Three questions then arose: whether the other spouse should separate from the one who has committed adultery and cease to cohabit with him or her; whether the other spouse could contract a new marriage; and whether the same rules applied for husbands as for wives. Such questions followed on from Paul's question (1 Cor 7:15) about a couple in which one spouse remains a nonbeliever, thus disrupting the marriage: how should the Christian spouse behave?

The problem of remarriage after being widowed was also the subject of varying responses; the prohibition on remarried men being ordained was particularly strict (ordination*). For the laity*, remarriage was merely tolerated, and it was not honored in the same way as first marriages were. This is one example of a moral question (*see* B below) being treated in the patristic period as if it were a legal question. Unlike the New Testament texts on marriage, these decisions could not be interpreted simply as exhortations or pieces of wisdom.

Among Jews and pagans, sterility, attributed to the woman, had often been regarded as a sufficient motive for allowing the husband to become free to contract a new marriage. According to the consensus among the churches, however, failure to produce children could not justify a couple separating. On this point, the Christian position was clearly a distinctive one: it is agreement between a man and a woman that constitutes the essence of marriage, not fertility as such. It was then asked whether a spiritual agreement of wills could in itself be an authentic marriage, or whether bodily union was necessary for a relationship that had been given as a sign of the union between the Word and humanity. Theology and law both accepted that a marriage that is valid according to the laws of the church—in the medieval Latin phrase, ratum—could exist between two baptized spouses without being consummated (consommatum) in sexual union. What was essential in order for a marriage to be valid was the free and responsible exchange of consent to be joined to one another indissolubly and irreversibly. However, according to the canonical statements issued during the Middle Ages—and still accepted in the canon law of the Catholic Church—a marriage that is merely ratum may be dissolved by a church tribunal. Hence, one could argue that, strictly speaking, only a marriage that is both ratum and consommatum is indissoluble. Nowadays, nonconsummation can be established on the basis of the apparent affective and psychological comportment of the couple, whether or not there have been physical sexual relations. Annulments are a different matter: they depend on the initial absence, recognized later, of a true agreement, conscious (fully informed) and free, between the two parties.

Despite the influence over the church fathers of the ancient popular philosophy* that saw the purpose of marriage as procreation*, it is clear that patristic theology made a fundamental connection between the holiness* of marriage and the union of two persons seeking mutual support and love. The union of their bodies, whether it produced descendants or remained infertile, was seen as the normal accompaniment to this spiritual agreement of two wills. This theology endowed the sexual act with spiritual meaning but did not regard it entirely without suspicion. According to Augustine* in particular, whose influence was enormous, the sexual act, while it is good in itself, is always accompanied by a culpable indulgence among the sons of Adam*. The act appears suspect even in the case of those who have been redeemed; and this reservation had an impact upon views of marriage itself as a way of life.

One more factor influenced the history of marriage as sacrament. Rabbinical Judaism* had developed a marriage ceremony that includes blessings in which God is praised for his gifts and his favor is sought on behalf of the young couple (according to the Talmud, Posner 1973, 1038f.; on contemporary practice, see French translation in Boudier 1978, 36f.). In particular, these texts celebrate the primordial fertility of the woman. Similar sentiments can be found in the formulas of blessing that gradually came into use in the Christian churches, yet these were not necessarily understood as being part and parcel of the formation of an indissoluble marriage as such.

b) The East. A crucial step was taken in the Christian East around 900, when the Byzantine Emperor Leo VI ordered the official codification of legal decisions on marriage among the subjects of the "New Rome*." The law required that for a marriage between two baptized people to be authentic, the couple had to receive a liturgical blessing administered by a bishop or a priest.

This imperial legislation, in the form of decrees, also confirmed an older Eastern practice by permitting remarriage for the husband of a woman who had been found guilty of adultery. This interpretation of the clauses in Matthew's Gospel* remains in force today, with variations, such as on the question of whether tolerance of remarriage extends to wives betrayed by their husbands. From time to time, remarriage was sometimes accepted in the Latin West, but it was definitively rejected by the Catholic Church. The seventh canon of the Council of Trent*, on the sacrament of marriage (DCO 1532–35), confirmed the rejection of tolerance of remarriage, but it is written in such a way as to exclude any formal or direct condemnation of practice among the Greeks.

Of course, the development of the theology of marriage in the East did not depend on imperial legislation alone: analogous theological positions are also to be found in several non-Byzantine Eastern churches. This may be explained by reference to the fundamental role of the liturgy in Christian life as interpreted in the traditions* of these churches. In its celebrations, presided over by a bishop or a priest, the liturgical gathering takes part in the new creation engendered by the Easter mystery, made present by the Holy Spirit. Within this gathering, the making of a marriage, the sign of the covenant between Christ and the church, is, in some sense, also called to take part in this holy act of new creation. It is this participation that is announced and effected by the liturgical blessing on the couple at the threshold of their shared life. The full and solemn form of this blessing cannot be renewed, and a simpler ritual is provided for a second marriage, which can take place only after one has been either widowed or separated as a result of one's spouse having committed adultery.

c) The West. The decree *Tametsi,* issued by the Council of Trent in 1566 (*DCO* 1534–39) has had an impact comparable to that of Leo VI's *Novellae.* The decree established a strict obligation to celebrate marriage in public, in the presence of a minister, being a priest endowed with a special power of jurisdiction* for this purpose: normally, this is the priest of the prospective wife's home parish, or a priest whom he has delegated. The council laid down that the absence of such a privileged witness was sufficient to render a couple incapable of giving a mutual consent that would be valid and therefore sacramental.

By adopting this complex formulation, the council avoided making the involvement of the priest into the basis of the matrimonial bond. While the priest's involvement was necessary, the council respected the doctrine that had become most widely accepted among Western canonists and theologians in earlier centuries: that the element that constitutes marriage is the valid exchange of consents—an exchange that was not required to be performed in public before the Council of Trent. The rules laid down by the council were gradually imposed throughout the Catholic Church. However, the rules that came into effect in the wake of Vatican* II have modified the decisions made at Trent by accepting that the privileged witness mentioned in *Tametsi* need not be a priest (or a bishop). In "ordinary" cases, a deacon* may also receive jurisdiction to exercise this ministry; and in cases where it is necessary, laypeople may also be given it, as what Catholic canon law calls an "extraordinary" measure. However, these two modifications are valid only for Catholics of the Latin Rite. The special code issued in 1990 for Catholics of the Eastern Rite, on the authority of the Holy See, does not contain these provisions; canon 828 of this code (*AAS* 1990, 1225–26) recognizes valid sacramental unions among such Catholics only on the basis of the liturgical rite of marriage, that is, on the basis of the blessing celebrated by a priestly minister, in line with the common tradition of the Eastern churches mentioned above. Thus, the 1990 code adopts the same position as the Eastern churches, which do not permit deacons to preside at the sacramental celebration of marriage.

In opposition to the Reformers, the Council of Trent also affirmed the sacramental nature of marriage between baptized persons: not only did Christ desire that marriage should signify the union of the Son of God with the church, his spouse, but he also conferred upon this sacrament the power to raise the union of the couple into the life of grace, giving this union a definitive sacred aspect. This view of marriage has been continually reiterated in the teaching of the Catholic Church. However, it has often been subject to both legal and theological questioning.

Questions have been raised on the interpretation of the respective roles, in the constitution of the sacramental and indissoluble bond, of the two main elements, the exchange of consents, which, in a sense, the couple themselves "administer," and the public celebration in a church, which a priest normally "administers," not only on the basis of his jurisdiction but also, and in correlation, on the basis of his status as a priest (priesthood). It seems that the Eastern theology on the role of the liturgy in the sacrament of marriage was not rejected at Trent (Duval 1985; Bourgeois and Sesboüé 1995). Other questions have been raised on the relationship between the authority of the church and that of the state and its tribunals. Following the Council of Trent, one of the commonest sources of conflict was the question of the need for children to have the consent of their parents in order to be married. States often supported parents against children, while Catholic canon law tended to do the opposite. In modern states, a doctrine has been developed that makes a distinction between, on the one hand, the establishing of a conjugal bond according to the rules and values of the existing social order—a "contract" that, of course, goes beyond the mere financial "contract" of marriage in the contemporary sense—and, on the other hand, the elevation of this contract to the rank of a holy sacrament within the life of the church. In opposition to the opinions of the jurists of the modern state, the Catholic Church has consistently affirmed that it is impossible to separate the "contract" from the "sacrament" among the baptized members of the church.

4. Contemporary Issues

Today, Catholic practice is characterized by a greater attention to the liturgical celebration of marriage, comparable not only to the traditional position of the Eastern churches, but also to recent practice among Protestants, who are also tending to strengthen the role of the blessing of marriage, although there are divergences as to the interpretation of this ceremony (on French Protestants, *see* Ansaldi 1995). This common tendency has been encouraged in many countries by the rise in the number of marriages between Christians from different churches.

There are shared difficulties too. Nowadays, baptized people who no longer clearly confess their agreement with the faith of the church, or even state plainly that they have distanced themselves from it, frequently request the liturgical celebration of their marriages. Catholic theologians in particular have discussed whether their requests should be granted, and how the nature of their conjugal bond should be defined (Millas 1990; Candelier 1991; Lawler 1991). The diversity of cultures and customs poses different problems: in Africa, in particular, the problem of ancestral heritage; in the East, changes in sexual socialization and marital morality. Some Christians influenced by such cultures live in family situations that have a certain stability and human value but, for Catholics in particular, do not meet the conditions required for them to be granted access to the sacrament. Should the canon law principle of the inseparable nature of the "contract" and the "sacrament"—a principle frequently reiterated and upheld (Baudot 1987)—go on being applied, or should the churches, in conditions to be determined, recognize a certain moral and social value in the "contract" that links such couples? Could a public status for such couples be combined with the duties of Christian life that they obviously have? Within the Catholic Church, which has seen such questions being urgently raised, some theologians have formulated responses compatible with the tradition that their church has inherited (e.g., Sequeira 1985; Örsy 1986; Deimel 1993; Puza 1993).

A spirituality of Christian marriage has frequently developed within the various churches since 1940, and numerous documents have been influenced by it. Vatican II defined the role of marriage in the structuring of God's people in the second chapter of the constitution *Lumen Gentium* (no. 11, §2). The constitution *Gaudium et Spes* (December 1965, nos. 47–52) combines spiritual perspectives with attention to contemporary problems concerning fertility (*see* B below). The decree on the apostolic tasks of laypeople (*AA*, November 1965) includes an important passage on the role of married couples in society and in the church (no. 11). Other terms, and other ideas, are used in other Christian traditions, but it appears that there is a common tendency among the churches to breathe new life into the liturgies that govern the celebration of the realities of married life, and give spiritual guidance to Christians so that they may cope with the sorrows and joys of this vocation.

- W. Kornfeld and R. Cazelles (1957), "Mariage... ," *DBS* 5, 906–35.
- E. Schillebeeckx (1963), *Het huwelijk,* vol. 1, Bilthoven (*Le mariage,* 1966).
- R. Posner (1973), "Marriage Ceremony," *EJ* 11, 1032–42.
- P. Vallin (1974), "La croissance de l'espèce humaine... ," *RSR* 62, 321–46.
- J. Meyendorff (1975), *Marriage: An Orthodox Perspective,* Crestwood, N.Y.
- P. Boudier (1978), *Mariages entre juifs et chrétiens,* Paris.
- C. H. Ratschow et al. (1982), "Ehe/Eherecht/Ehescheidung," *TRE* 9, 308–62.
- P. Rémy (1983), "Que l'homme ne sépare pas... ," *RDC* 33, 250–75.
- E. Schmitt (1983), *Le mariage chrétien dans l'œuvre de saint Augustin,* Paris.
- R. Grimm (1984), *L'institution du mariage,* Paris.
- A. Duval (1985), *Des sacrements au concile de Trente,* Paris.
- J.-B. Sequeira (1985), *Tout mariage entre baptisés est-il nécessairement sacramentel?* Paris.
- W. Günther et al. (1986), "Marriage... ," *Dictionary of New Testament Theology* 2, Exeter, 575–90.
- L. Örsy (1986), *Marriage in Canon Law,* Wilmington.
- D. Baudot (1987), *L'inséparabilité entre le contrat et le sacrement de mariage,* Rome.
- J. A. Brundage (1987), *Law, Sex, and Christian Society in Medieval Europe,* Chicago.
- J. Gaudemet (1987), *Le mariage en Occident,* Paris.
- C. Brooke (1989), *The Medieval Idea of Marriage,* Oxford.
- P. Brown (1989), *Body and Society,* New York.
- J. Vernay (1989), "Le droit canonique du mariage," in P. Valdrini (Ed.), *Droit canonique,* Paris, 370–437.
- J. M. Millas (1990), "Fe y sacramento del matrimonio," *Gr.* 71, 141–51.
- G. Candelier (1991), "Incroyance et validité du mariage sacramentel," *RDC* 41/42, 81–145.
- M. G. Lawler (1991), "Faith, Contract, and Sacrament," *TS* 52, 712–31.
- S. Demel (1993), "Standesamt, Ehe, Kirche," *StZ* 211, 131–40.
- G. Mathon (1993), *Le mariage des chrétiens,* vol. 1, Paris.
- R. Puza (1993), "Der Abschluss des Ehebundes," *ThQ* 173, 81–98.
- P. Vallin (1994), "Les traditions chrétiennes... ," in *Religions et démographies...,* Colloque du Saulchoir, Paris, 17–35.
- J. Ansaldi (1995), "Notes sur la bénédiction nuptiale," *ETR* 70, 99–103.
- H. Bourgeois and B. Sesboüé (1995), *Les signes du salut (Histoire des dogmes,* vol. 3), Paris, 110–42, 192–99, 214–17.
- W. Schrage (1995), *Der Erste Brief an die Korinther, 2 Teilband, 1 Kor 6–11* (Evangelisch-Katholischer Kommentar z. NT, VII/2), Göttingen.

PIERRE VALLIN

See also **Anointing of the Sick; Baptism; Church and State; Confirmation; Eucharist; Family; Ordination/Order; Penance; Sacrament**

B. Moral Theology

a) Scriptural Witness. In the Old Testament, marriage is envisaged first and foremost as a structure of patriarchal authority*, intended mainly to secure the perpetuation of the clan: the institutions of the levirate (Dt 25:5–10), concubinage (Gn 16), and provisional polygamy should be understood in this light. However, with the principle of exogamy, which makes its appearance in the prohibition of certain consanguinary marriages (Lv 18:6–18), marriage is also interpreted as an institution through which persons can recognize others: the other person becomes, through the very relationship of the couple*, a necessary "opposite," to whom a bond of obligation is formed.

Under the influence of the theology* of the covenant*, in particular, marriage was increasingly understood as a relationship involving the human person in all his or her integrity, an exclusive relationship placed under the protection of the law of YHWH (Ex 20:14). Hosea evokes the one and only God* who, out of his free will and love, turns to his one and only chosen people* and reaches a lasting covenant with them (1–3; Jer 2:2; Ez 16). This approach, taken up in other books of the Bible, reinforced the tendency toward monogamy and gave a positive value to the woman* as the personal partner of the man (Mal 2:14ff.). The legal regulation of divorce reflects this approach: while the decision to divorce is left in the hands of the husband, he is obliged to write a letter of repudiation that will allow the wife to remarry (Dt 24:1–4).

As for the idea of the shared life of husband and wife, based on a personal and reciprocal relationship, its origins were traced to the narratives of the Creation*, in which individuals of both sexes are created in the image of God (Gn 1:27) and their living together is established by God, who wants to remedy human solitude by creating sexual union (Gn 2:18). Of course, there is no question here of an explicit basis for marriage, but the Yahwist commentator does make a link between the two partners becoming "one flesh," having sexual relations, and conceiving children, on the one hand, and the legal act of "abandoning" one's clan of origin.

Finally, as a basic unit of shared life, marriage is directly involved in original sin* and its consequences, manifested in the loss of innocence (Gn 3:7), and in the establishment of a structure of male domination over women (Gn 3:16).

References to marriage in the New Testament take up the traditions of the Old Testament, in particular those that are linked to the theme of the covenant.

They are marked by a characteristic tension. On the one hand, Jesus*—who himself remained unmarried, even though it was normal for rabbis to have wives—reduces the importance of all the old, familial bonds (Lk 14:26) in view of the approach of the Kingdom* of God, and attributes to celibacy a specific evangelical value (Mt 19:12). On the other hand, however, Jesus radically alters the status of the reciprocal commitment that constitutes marriage. Adultery is no longer to be understood as harming the well-being of another person, but as a wrong directly inflicted on one's partner, and equally in the case of men as in the case of women (Mk 10:11f.). Just as Jesus does not limit his definition of adultery to the legally reprehensible act, but extends its meaning to the very moment that it is born "in his [the adulterer's] heart" (Mt 5:27), so, in his view, marriage is a matter, not of effective possession, but of feeling. This is why the prohibition of divorce (Mk 10:2–12; Mt 19:9, subject to cases of "sexual immorality") should lead the believer to repent his "hardness of heart." While Moses took this hardening* into account when he authorized divorce, Jesus recalls us to the primordial will of the Creator, and presents marriage as a created order, attributing to God himself the Yahwist's commentary on the union of a man and a woman who leave their parents in order to attach themselves to each other. Hence, he declares that those whom God has united may not be separated by human beings (Mt 19:4ff.). This rule should, however, be understood as being related not to the law* but to the gospel*: Jesus fulfils the prophecy* of the heart of flesh* that is to replace the "heart of stone" (Ez 36:26).

Jesus' sayings are characterized by a tension arising from the expectation of the coming of the Kingdom. Once it had come, marriage would be abolished as an institution, if not as a way in which human beings relate to each other (Mk 12:25); at the same time, the notion of the Kingdom is specially expressed precisely through the image of the wedding (Mt 22:1–14; Acts 19:7). This eschatological tension is maintained in the teachings and exhortations of the apostles*. On the one hand, marriage is presented as one of the domains of everyday life ordained "in Christ" (Col 3:18f.; Eph 5:22–33; 1 Pt 3:1–7). On the other hand, Paul recommends that, because "the appointed time has grown very short" (1 Cor 7:29), the faithful should either follow his example and remain unmarried, or live within their marriages "as though they had [no wives]" (*hos me,* 1 Cor 7:29). Paul generally elaborates his precepts* in opposition to three rival positions. Against those who tended toward Encratism, he emphasizes the value of marriage as a gift of the Creator, who permits human beings to enjoy it "with thanksgiving" (1 Tm 4:3ff.). Against those who upheld the ascetic ideal of unconsummated marriage, he upholds the sharing of the sexual life as an integral and reciprocal obligation (1 Cor 7:3ff.). Finally, against those who tended toward spiritualism or libertinism, he celebrates the body as the temple of the Holy* Spirit and recognizes sexuality as a factor in social cohesion (1 Cor 6:12–20). Paul's endorsement of the submission of wives in Ephesians 5:22–33—the *locus classicus* of the New Testament's theology of marriage—is tempered by the exhortation that precedes it: "submitting to one another" (Eph 5:21), and the duties of husbands are to be motivated by their devoted love of Christ*. Thus, the idea that marriage should be modeled on the relationship between Christ and his church* forms the link between the Christian ethics* of marriage and the church as a community within which one's first training is conducted.

b) Ancient and Medieval Church. There was a tendency within the ancient and medieval church to transpose the eschatological tension that pervades these New Testament texts into a system of values. The value of marriage certainly continued to be emphasized, in opposition both to Manicheanism* and to Montanism*, but marriage came to be definitively subordinated to the ideal of virginity (Thomas* Aquinas, *ST* IIa IIae, q. 152, a. 3), partly as a consequence of the general deprecation of the active life as compared to contemplation*. Separation by mutual consent, which was permitted in Roman law*, was strictly forbidden to Christians, with the sole exception of those cases in which both husband and wife entered the monastic life. The ideal of virginity was even introduced into the doctrine of marriage. Thus, Augustine* was able in his later works to emphasize the physical nature of marriage while postulating an ideal progression from sexuality without desire to "continent" marriage, and then from such marriage to celibacy.

By identifying what could be called concupiscence with sexual desire, Augustine reinforced a traditional attitude of anxiety about the passions*, which Christianity had inherited from Greek thought, and introduced an internal tension in the doctrine of the "three goods" of marriage: procreation* *(proles)*, control of sexuality *(fides)*, and indissolubility *(sacramentum)*. Of course, these goods presupposed physical union, but they were also celebrated as counterweights to carnal desire, which became a venial sin within marriage. In particular, the indissoluble sacramental bond of marriage could be envisaged, through a remarkable abstraction, as being independent of the actual conjugal union, so that, for example, the sacrament could be seen as in itself an obstacle to remarriage (*De nuptiis et concupiscentia* I, 11). In this way—and despite the fact that Augustine set his reflections on marriage within the framework of a way of life, considered more generally—he opened the way, despite himself, to an approach that saw these goods as "ends," to which the life shared within marriage could be subordinated. This attitude lasted from Augustine's day into modern times.

It fell to Aquinas to open up a new line of thought within this overall development. Adopting Aristotle's teleology of nature* and reason*, Aquinas makes the perpetuation of the human species through procreation the decisive criterion for sexual union. Accordingly, the conscious pursuit of this purpose determines whether specific actions "conform" (*ST* IIa IIae, q. 153). In this context, sexual pleasure itself is reevaluated to the extent that, despite the momentary extinction of individual reason, it nonetheless serves the superior purpose of nature and reason (perpetuation of the species). This logic still characterizes the Catholic Church's teaching on marriage today, including its answers to specific questions of moral theology, such as the question of contraception. The Western Christian tradition* has generally been characterized by a degree of rigor—notably in its prohibition of remarriage after civil divorce—and by the role that it gives to theological conceptions. The teaching and practice of the Eastern churches in this domain have been shaped above all by the liturgy* of marriage: the remarriage of divorced spouses gives rise to a specific ritual in which this act is presented as a penance* and a new beginning.

Marriage was initially regarded as a purely secular matter, to which the church did no more than give its blessing* (*missa pro sponsis*, c. 400). Eventually, however, it became an authentically ecclesiastical institution, both in the West (*Decretum Gratiani*, 1140) and in the East (Leo VI, 886–912). In German-speaking regions, the priest* even took the place of the provost who united the couple *in facie ecclesiae*: the legal act itself was performed in the nave of the church and integrated into the religious service.

c) Reformation and the Early Modern Period. Luther* defended liberty* in marriage on a number of grounds. As against the plethora of complications to which marriage was subjected in his day, both in secular law* and in canon law, he emphasized that no one could be excluded from marriage, which is a necessary aspect of the identity of every man and woman as created beings. As against the church's assertion of the superior status of the monastic life, he argued for the preeminence of the married state, which represented a "vocation" to faith* and love. It is a vocation to faith because, unlike the "clerical state" and the vows that commit the clergy to it, marriage does not give human beings the power to justify themselves by their characters or their works*. It is a vocation to love because, unlike monks, married men do not remove themselves from daily interaction with the distress of their neighbors, as represented by their wives and children. Finally, as against the sacramental conception of marriage as a way of salvation*, Luther emphasized the fact that sexual relations need to be purified and sanctified by the word* of God. Accordingly, while he regarded marriage as a "profane thing," subordinate to the earthly government of God, he never considered it to be a condition deprived of spirituality. On the contrary, the everyday temptations and miseries of marriage make it the "most spiritual condition of all" (*WA* 12, 105, 29), to the extent that "by nature, it teaches us to see the hand and the grace of God, and obliges us truly to believe" (*WA* 12, 106, and 126f.). This conviction pervades Luther's pamphlet on marriage, the *Traubüchlein* (1529), in which the consent of husband and wife is also conceived as a "witness of humility," an appeal to the "divine aid" provided in the blessing* of the wedding. On the question of divorce and remarriage, Luther adopts a pastoral approach, permitting them for injured parties in cases of adultery, voluntary abandonment of the marital home, and concealment of impotence. Zwingli* in Zurich (from 1522) and Calvin* in Geneva also took care to establish matrimonial courts; in Geneva, legitimate grounds for divorce remained decidedly more limited. (There were frequent appeals from these institutions to regional consistory courts.) Some groups of radical Reformers developed a libertine and functionalist ethics of marriage: for example, polygamy was permitted in the "Anabaptist kingdom" of Münster as a way of ensuring that the holy ones of the apocalypse could be born.

d) Contemporary Problems. The traditions of the Enlightenment and romanticism have formed an unstable compound in modern thinking on the couple and on marriage.

During the Enlightenment, marriage, like all other social relations, was conceived on the model of the contract. Marriage did not merely begin with a contract—as in the traditional formula, *consensus facit matrimonium* ("consent makes a marriage"), it was by its very nature a contract, by which two individuals consented, in the formula devised by Kant*, to "the reciprocal possession, throughout their lives, of their sexual attributes" (*Grundlegung zur Metaphysik der Sitten [Foundations of the Metaphysics of Morals]*, Doctrine of Law, §24). As a result, considerations of individual, social, and political utility came to be regarded as primary, as evidenced in the massive increase in the number of grounds for divorce, emancipation from the moral teachings of the churches, and the establishment of (compulsory or optional) civil marriage. The "rational" easing of restrictions on divorce was already implied in the logic of contractual thought: the principle of individual autonomy, which permitted the partners to conclude the contract, also allowed them to break their commitment whenever it ceased to bring them the benefits that they had anticipated.

This "reification" of the conjugal bond inevitably provoked a reaction, which arrived in the form of "romantic subjectivization." The formal element of marriage was reduced to a troublesome detail, and marriage was based entirely on affection. Love is marriage: such was the motto that Friedrich Schlegel (1772–1829) popularized through his novel *Lucinde,* and for which the young Schleiermacher* provided a theological foundation by exalting love and lovers into the celestial realm. Yet, while romanticism was a protest movement, it also had some obvious affinities with Enlightenment thought: for both movements, marriage had its roots in the resources of the individual. Whether it was interpreted as a "contract" or as a "relationship," marriage remained an artifact, a bond that could be made, and broken, by the exertion of the sovereign will.

It was on this basis that the two traditions became compounded, producing the contemporary state of mind, which is defined by the dubious attempt to combine the greatest possible degree of individual autonomy with the greatest possible degree of affective intensity in mutual relations. Enlightenment utilitarianism* is thus freighted with all the demands of romanticism, which have become the very purpose of marriage and are therefore no longer necessarily linked to the concrete reality of a shared life. The relationship need not be maintained if it does not bring the partners the happiness that they expected. However, happiness is not something that can be directly assigned as a purpose, and it is characteristic of modernity that it expects more from the relationship of couples than it is capable of providing. The tendency to favor nonmatrimonial forms of shared life does not resolve the problem, for such relationships are also structured on the assumption that the bond should last only as long as it fulfils its affective purpose.

Christian theology and ethics must undoubtedly oppose this new version of the purposes of marriage by reactivating the critical system that they have already used over the course of the 20th century against traditional notions of the purposes of marriage. Karl Barth*, for example, has emphasized that marriage, as a form of shared life established by God, carries its own purpose in itself and is not to be legitimized by the realization of other purposes: he therefore defines marriage as an "exemplary sharing of life" (*KD* III/4, 211f.). This idea has not failed to find a response, for the canon law of the Catholic Church, as overhauled in the *CIC* of 1983, has also placed an emphasis on the personal dimension of marriage—marriage as unity of personal life (canon 1,055)—as against an approach invoking contract and purpose. However, in opposition to modern thought, which reduces the traditional goods of marriage to the self-fulfillment of the partners conceived as its only purpose, it is worth recalling once again the role that liberty* plays in the institution of marriage, and the organic solidarity that unites marriage as a form of life with the "fruits" that it produces. It is true that children do not give meaning to marriage; nevertheless, they must not be excluded a priori from the shared life of the married couple. Like those who are "celibate" on principle, couples who remain childless are displaying not disobedience to the "commandment" to multiply the species, but rather a radical lack of confidence in the goodness of the world*, as creation, and in the promise* of God's blessing. Every marriage is also blessed in its children, through whom the world continues to be turned toward its eschatological goal. To claim a right to marriage and/or to the religious ceremony for homosexual couples is to neglect this organic link between marriage and its benefits, and to fail to understand that marriage is based on the physical and structural difference between the sexes, which are destined to experience their "unity" not on the basis of the same sex, but by finding their complement in the other sex.

● Augustine, *De Genesi ad litteram; De bono coniugali; De nuptiis et concupiscentia; De civitate Dei,* book XIV (BAug 18–19, 2, 23, 35).

K. Barth (1948–51), *KD* III/2, III/4, (*Dogmatique,* vol. 11–12, 15–16, Geneva, 1961–65).
J. Calvin (1559), *Institutio Christianae Religionis,* §34–37.
CIC (1983).
M. Luther, *Ein Sermon von dem ehelichen Stand,* WA 2, 166–71.
M. Luther, *Vom ehelichen Leben,* WA 10/2, 275–304.
M. Luther, *Ein Traubüchlein für die einfältigen Pfarrherrn,* WA 30, 3, 70–74.
M. Luther, *Das siebente Kapitel S. Pauli zu den Corinthern,* WA 12, 95–142.
F. D. E. Schleiermacher (1800), *Vertraute Briefe über Friedrich Schlegels "Lucinde,"* Lübeck-Leipzig; *Die christliche Sitte,* Berlin (2nd Ed. 1884).
Thomas Aquinas, *ST* Ia IIae, q. 30–31; IIa IIae, q. 151–55.
◆ Kenneth E. Kirk (1933), *Marriage and Divorce,* London (2nd Ed. 1948).
O. Lähteenmäki (1955), *Sexus und Ehe bei Luther,* Turuku.
R. Bainton (1962), *Sex, Love, and Marriage,* London.
H. Thielicke (1964), *Theologische Ethik* III, Tübingen.
John T. Noonan (1965), *Contraception,* Cambridge, Mass. (2nd Ed. 1986).
H. Ringeling (1968), *Theologie und Sexualität,* Gütersloh.
M. F. Berrouard (1971), *Saint Augustin et l'indissolubilité du mariage,* StPatr 11, 291–306.
J. Meyendorff (1975), *Marriage: An Orthodox Perspective,* New York.
P. Ramsey (1975), *One Flesh,* Bramcote, Great Britain.
M. Foucault (1976), *Histoire de la sexualité,* t. I: *La volonté de savoir,* Paris.
W. Kasper (1977), *Zur Theologie der christlichen Ehe,* Mainz.
William E. May (1981), *Sex, Marriage, and Chastity,* Chicago.
C. H. Ratschow et al. (1982), "Ehe, Eherecht, Ehescheidung," *TRE* 9, 311–62.
S. Hauerwas (1984), "Marriage and the Family," *QRT* 56, 20/2, 4–24.
L. Orsy (1986), *Marriage in Canon Law,* Wilmington, Del.
O. Bayer (Ed.) (1988), *Ehe: Zeit zur Antwort,* Neukirchen-Vluyn.
Ch. Brooke (1989), *The Medieval Idea of Marriage,* Oxford.
B. Wannenwetsch (1993), *Die Freiheit der Ehe,* Neukirchen-Vluyn.
P. L. Reynolds (1994), *Marriage in the Western Church,* Leyden.

BERND WANNENWETSCH

See also **Adam; Couple; Creation; Ethics, Sexual; Family; Procreation; Woman**

Marsilius of Inghen. *See* Nominalism

Martyrdom

1. Origin and Meaning of the Term

"Martyrdom" comes from the Greek *marturia* or *marturion,* meaning "witness," "testimony"; but in Christian usage it means, more narrowly, death undergone in witness to Christ*. (Those whose sufferings for Christ did not result in death are called "confessors.") This narrower meaning is not attested until the latter half of the second century, in the *Martyrdom of Polycarp,* and there are a number of theories as to how it developed. An obvious link between witness and suffering is provided by the Roman practice of verifying the testimony of legal witnesses (other than *honestiores,* those from "honorable" families) by torture: by his suffering and death*, the witness, *martus,* demonstrates the truth* of his witness to Christ and the gospel.

However, the idea that the martyr is rather a witness of the truth of the age to come finds support from the passion* narrative* in Luke, where we see Jesus* passing directly from the cross to Paradise, taking with him the repentant thief (Lk 23:43); from the account of the death of the first Christian martyr, Stephen, who, as he dies, sees "the heavens opened and the Son of Man standing at the right hand of God" (Acts 7:56); and from the vision of the Apocalypse, in which John, exiled on Patmos "on account of the word of God and the testimony of Jesus" (Rev 1:9), sees Heaven opened (Rev 4:1) and a throng of martyrs, worshipping God and the Lamb*, and bearing palms of victory (Rev 7:9–17). Such an understanding of martyrdom (but not the term) had already existed within Judaism*, where it had been developed especially in connection with the age of the Maccabeans. The martyr was seen to stand on the threshold of the age to come. His death was an atonement for the failings of those who lived in expectation of the coming age, and it brought that age nearer. His death was part of the final struggle between good* and evil* that would usher in the final age: the opponents of the martyrs were not so much the earthly authorities as the spiritual powers of darkness, who were later called demons* (Eph 6:12).

2. The Martyr as Saint

The death of Jesus was much more than a martyrdom: of the Evangelists, only Luke comes close to presenting Jesus as an archetypal martyr. Nevertheless, Jesus is occasionally called a martyr in the New Testament (1 Tm 6:13; Rev 1:5, 3:14), and the martyr was soon seen as the perfect disciple: indeed, the term *teleiosis,* "perfection," came to be used of the martyr's death. The martyr was very early assimilated to Christ, and his death to the paschal mystery* celebrated in the Eucharist*. Thus, Ignatius of Antioch begs the Christians of Rome* to do nothing that will prevent him from being an "imitator of the passion of my God" (*Rom.* 6, 3), and sees his martyred body as becoming the "pure bread of Christ" (ibid., 4, 1). Similarly, Polycarp's prayer* before his death is a paraphrase of the eucharistic prayer (*M. Pol.* 14).

Because the martyr is to pass to Paradise and there join the angels in the court of God, even in his lifetime his intercession was regarded as peculiarly efficacious, and his words as having prophetic power (*M. Pol.* 16, 2). Jesus himself had promised that the Spirit would speak through the mouths of those who bore him faithful witness (Mk 13:11 par.). After their deaths, the bodies of martyrs were treasured and preserved as relics*, and altars were built over their tombs (architecture*). The anniversaries of their martyrdom (their "heavenly birthdays") were honored by the celebration of the Eucharist on such altars. The image of the martyr thus became that of the saint, one who had fulfilled the common vocation of all Christians to holiness* (*see* Rom 1:17; 1 Cor 1:2; 1 Pt 2:9; and the common designation of Christians as *hagioi*—"holy"—in Acts and by Paul). The martyr, as saint, was not simply a model but also a friend in the heavenly courts, to whom one could turn for help. He was especially concerned for those who lived where he had lived during his earthly life or who showed special devotion to him. It is not surprising that the church* felt the need to discourage those who provoked martyrdom ("voluntary martyrdom") and presented martyrdom as a vocation not to be sought, but not to be refused.

3. Martyrdom and Persecution in the Roman Empire

This understanding of the martyr developed very rapidly: almost all its features can be found in the *Martyrdom of Polycarp,* a largely eyewitness account written around the middle of the second century. Three centuries of persecution by the Roman Empire made it an ineradicable part of Christian consciousness.

Henceforth, Christians looked back on these centuries as the "Age of Martyrdom," and they exaggerated the nature and extent of the persecutions. It is not in fact known for certain why they took place. The veneration of one who had died a criminal's death would hardly be regarded with much favor by the authorities, and they would have had little hesitation about oppressing a group that refused to conform to what were regarded as little more than acts of courtesy to the gods, on whose favor the prosperity of the empire depended, and to acts of loyalty to the deified emperor, whose cult* symbolized the fragile unity of the empire. It is clear from the "acts" of the martyrs that Christians were executed simply for being Christians ("for the Name"), but there was no systematic attempt to exterminate Christians (as there was with regard to the Druids, for instance). For the first two centuries, persecution seems to have been local and sporadic. Nevertheless, to become a Christian carried the risk of someday being faced with the alternative of apostasy or death. General persecution—throughout the Roman Empire, and by imperial decree—seems to have occurred first during the reign of Decius (c. 200–51), when, in what looks like an attempt to secure their failing support, everyone was required to sacrifice to the gods. This provoked mass apostasy and also many cases of martyrdom. It also provoked a crisis in the Christian community, for martyrs awaiting their death (called confessors in the West) claimed the power to forgive their frailer fellow Christians who had apostatized, thus overruling the power of the bishops*. Some bishops acknowledged the power of the martyrs, for example, Dionysius in Alexandria (Eusebius, *HE* VI, 42, 5f.), but others did not, notably Cyprian* in Carthage. Further general persecutions underlined the limits to the assimilation of Christianity into the pagan empire, culminating in the "Great Persecution" initiated by Diocletian in 303. Again, there was much apostasy, but there was also a long drawn-out attempt, by torture, imprisonment, and forced labor, to weaken the church fatally; and this resulted in many martyrdoms. The Great Persecution came to an abrupt end in 312 with the conversion* of Constantine and the toleration of Christianity established by the Edict of Milan.

4. The Ideal of Martyrdom after the Peace of the Church

During these persecutions, the combination of widespread apostasy, followed by a desire to return to the church, and, by contrast, the steadfastness of the few focused attention on the intercessory power of the martyrs, and also challenged the authority* of the bishops, whose control over admission to eucharistic communion* had developed as a way of preserving the

integrity and identity of the church. For both bishops and martyrs, baptism* and its opposite, apostasy, defined the boundaries of the church. With the acceptance of the church in the empire in the course of the fourth century, the boundaries became much less clear. The age of the martyrs now receded into the past, but the church of the martyrs did not. There was active promotion of the cult of the martyrs, notably in Rome under Pope* Damasus, who sought to make the city into a center of pilgrimage* on account of its wealth of martyrs. On the other hand, one of the main ideas that accompanied the development of monasticism* was that the monk was a successor of the martyr, his asceticism* matching the martyr's passion, so that monks inherited the role of intercessors with God. Monks now became saints.

5. Development of the Cult of Saints/Martyrs

With the Peace of the Church, the memory of the age of the martyrs was preserved by the cult of the martyr and the production of increasingly embroidered accounts of martyrs. These had a liturgical role, not just in the yearly celebrations of martyrs' relics, but also in the celebrations of the liturgical year, which became a roll call of martyrs. There were, increasingly, other saints, mainly monks and bishops, but the martyr remained the archetype of sainthood. The relics of martyrs and other saints did not lie undisturbed: their bodies were dismembered and their relics, with their miraculous powers, found their way throughout the Christian world. It soon became normal for altars to house relics, a practice that was made obligatory by the Seventh Ecumenical Council (Nicaea* II, canon 7).

6. Later Martyrs

a) Byzantine Martyrs. The Peace of the Church did not, however, bring martyrdom to an end. Christians persecuted Christians, and, when the emperor was a heretic, he made martyrs. Monothelitism*, for example, was responsible for the death of Martin I (the last martyr-pope) and the torture of Maximus* the Confessor during the seventh century. Iconoclasm yielded Stephen the Younger and several other martyrs. Theodore the Studite (759–826) presented compromise with iconoclasm as apostasy and thus sought to revive the spirit of the age of the martyrs. Confrontation with paganism* and Islam also produced martyrs in the Byzantine Empire.

b) Royal Martyrs. Although martyrs were regarded as spiritual fighters, death while fighting, even against the enemies of Christianity, was rarely regarded as martyrdom (by contrast to Islam). Most Christian soldier martyrs lost their lives because of a perceived conflict between the requirements of military practice and those of the Christian life. Despite the rhetoric that accompanied the Crusades, none of the Crusaders was canonized, with the exception of Saint Louis, who did not became a saint solely because he was a Crusader. Nevertheless, in the history of the Christianization of Europe there was a small number of royal martyrs, some of whom died fighting pagan foes. Anglo-Saxon England, where the struggle against paganism* was most prolonged, produced most of these: Oswald of Northumbria (641), Oswin of Deira (651), Ethelbert (794) and Edmund of East Anglia (839), and the Anglo-Saxon Edward (978). Other royal martyrs include Wenceslaus of Bohemia (929), Olaf of Norway (1030), Magnus of Orkney (1116), and, in Kievan Rus', Boris and Gleb (1015), the sons of the first Christian ruler, Vladimir. Their immediate significance was the dynastic validation that their cults provided. In several cases (Wencelaus, Magnus, Boris and Gleb), it is not at all clear that they died because of their faith.

The history of Christian martyrdom does not end there. The precarious cohabitation of Christians with Islam (despite the privileged status of *dhimmis* that Islam accorded to them as "people of the Book") included some persecutions and martyrdoms. The history of missions, from the 16th to the 19th centuries, was also distinguished by numerous martyrdoms. The 20th century has probably seen more extensive martyrdom than at any other time in the history of the church. The full story of the persecution of Christians under Nazism and Communism, as well as in various parts of Africa and Latin America, has yet to be written.

- F. X. Funk, K. Bihlmeyer, W. Shneemelcher (Ed.), *Die Apostolischen Väter,* Tübingen, 1903.
- H. Musurillo (Ed.), *The Acts of the Christian Martyrs,* Oxford, 1972.
- Ignatius of Antioch, Polycarp of Smyrna, *Letters: Martyrium Polycarpi,* SC 10 *bis.*
- Eusebius of Caesarea, *Ecclesiastical History,* SC 31, 41, 55, 73.
- ♦ E. E. Malone (1950), *The Monk and the Martyr,* SCA 12.
- Coll. (1953), *Limites de l'humain,* EtCarm 32.
- J. Moreau (1956), *La persécution du christianisme dans l'Empire romain,* Paris.
- H. von Campenhausen (1964), *Die Idee des Martyriums in der alten Kirche,* 2nd Ed., Göttingen.
- W. H. C. Frend (1965), *Martyrdom and Persecution in the Early Church,* Oxford.
- K. Rahner (1965), *Zur Theologie des Todes: Mit einem Exkurs über das Martyrium,* QD 2, 73–106.
- H. U. von Balthasar (1966), *Cordula oder der Ernstfall,* Einsiedeln (3rd Ed. 1967).
- T. Baumeister (1980), *Die Anfänge der Theologie des Martyriums,* Munich.
- W. Rordorf, A. Solignac (1980), "Martyre," *DSp* 10, 718–37.
- D. Balfour (1983), "Extended Notions of Martyrdom in the Byzantine Ascetical Tradition," *Sob.* 5/1, 20–35.
- G. Bonner (1983), "Martyrdom: Its Place in the Church," *Sob.* 5/2, 6–21.
- N. Russell (1983), "Neomartyrs of the Greek Calendar," *Sob.* 5/1, 36–62.
- Kallistos Ware (1983), "What Is a Martyr?" *Sob.* 5/1, 7–18.
- A. M. Allchin (1984), "Martyrdom," *Sob.* 6/1, 19–29.
- G. Klaniczay (1986), "From Sacral Kingship to Self-Representation: Hungarian and European Royal Saints in the 11th–13th Centuries," in E. Vestergaard (Ed.), *Continuity and Change: Political Institutions and Literary Monuments in the Middle Ages,* Odense (repr. in G. Klaniczay, *The Uses of Supernatural Power,* Princeton, 1990).
- P. Gerlitz, E. Kanarfogel, M. Slusser, E. Christen (1992), "Martyrium," *TRE* 22, 196–220.
- J. A. Coope (1995), *The Martyrs of Cordoba,* Lincoln and London.

ANDREW LOUTH

See also **Asceticism; Cult of Saints**

Marx, Karl

1818–1883

1. Introduction

Between the October Revolution and the demolition of the Berlin Wall, the hostility between Christianity and atheistic Communism has been a defining feature of the 20th century; it ranged from official denunciations of "Marxism" to the persecution of Christians by Marxist regimes. In contrast, theologians showed little interest in Marx's writings. Paradoxically, while most of what Marx has to say about religion in general and Christianity in particular is unoriginal, the themes he discussed, and the manner of their treatment, remain of central significance for Christian life and thought.

2. Life

Marx was born in Trier, of rabbinical lineage, although baptism was the price that his father had paid for retaining his position as a lawyer. At Bonn and, later, at Berlin, Marx studied law* and philosophy* (his doctoral thesis was on the philosophies of nature of Democritus and Epicurus) and spent much time in "Young Hegelian" company. Exiled to Paris in 1843, he moved to Brussels in 1845 and in 1849, to London, where he remained until his death. The "Economic and Philosophical Manuscripts" of 1844 were followed by the *Theses on Feuerbach* (1845), the first part of the *German Ideology* (1846), the *Communist Manifesto* (1848), and the *Grundrisse,* or notebooks preparatory to *Capital* (1857, 1858), while the first volume of *Capital* appeared in 1867. Devoted to his wife (who died in 1881) and to his children, he combined revolutionary politics with the lifestyle of a Victorian gentleman.

3. Themes

a) Religion.
Assuming that religious beliefs reflect social circumstances and self-understanding and, in particular, that images of God* are reflections of the state, Marx took it for granted that once human beings have taken their existence into their own hands, and external forms and structures of oppression have been abolished, then religious beliefs will fade away with the healing of the suffering that called them forth. From as early as 1843, he showed little interest in religion. The assumption that religion would simply disappear, whereas others forms of thought, literary or aesthetic, philosophical or political, would find ideal form in an ideal society, indicates Marx's indebtedness to the widespread early modern belief that the reality, autonomy, and liberty* of "god" and "man" are antithetical.

b) Truth.
For Marx, truth* is the coincidence between appearance and reality, fact and description, the way things are and the way they seem to be. It is a relationship in both theory and practice, and, in this sense, truth does not exist independently of knowledge and right action. A "true" human individual could only be "truly" such as a member of a "truly human" society. There is, accordingly, a utopian or eschatological element in Marx's account. For Christians, his account may illuminate the mutuality between Christology* and eschatology*: between the confession that a truly human individual has existed and the hope that, in him, all things in heaven and on earth will be united.

c) Materialism.
Marx's "historical materialism" (adapted by Engels [1820–95] into "dialectical materialism") emphasizes, as against Hegelian idealism, that it is people, rather than ideas, that make and change the world. It is also opposed to Feuerbach (1804–72): people make and change the world by their work* with hand and head, and not by thought alone. The link between Marx's materialism and his atheism* lies not in some metaphysics, reducing all reality to extension, but in the assumption that God is, and can only be, an idea, and that it is idealist to worship an idea. If Christians or Marxists speak of love* or liberty while acting otherwise, or if they act as if the redemptive transformation of the world occurs in consciousness alone, then one is confronted with the idealist sin par excellence, that of idealist practice, whether it arises from idealist theory or contradicts materialist theory.

d) Ideology.
Marx's metaphor of a socioeconomic "base" and an ideological "superstructure" (law, politics, religion, art, and philosophy) is easily and frequently misread as meaning that the latter exert no influence on the former; yet Marx constructed a theory of their interaction. However, despite this interaction, it remains the case that, in Marx's view, "structure" and "reflection" are initially unified through a relationship of contradiction, such that the distorting pressure of the former on the latter prevents reliance on the elements of the superstructure alone. Moreover, if one considers that the way of thinking of people in power becomes an element of this power, then it is understandable that the Marxist theory lends a pejorative connotation to the term "ideology."

e) Alienation.
To alienate a good is to give it to another: *ad alium.* Marx, unlike Hegel*, does not see objectification as the direct cause of alienation (that is, becoming estranged from oneself). We may give something of ourselves to our work, but that does not necessarily mean that we lose that something. It's only within the measure that our work, our relations, and our selves become commodities; the system they depend on becomes an alien power ruling an alienated world. Marx sees religion as the paradigm of alienation: the alien power of God renders humans aliens to themselves. However, since God's power is in fact a dispossession (of the self), so that, theologically, the cure of any alienation comes from a divine *kenosis*, there are fruitful analogies to be explored between Marx's account of the transcendence of alienation and Christian doctrines of redemption. Nevertheless, Marx omits one point: his critique can certainly help Christian theory not to deal with God (in word or deed) as

an alien omnipotence, and not to allow a theory of redemption to substitute for the work of its achievement. Christianity, however, takes seriously an aspect of alienation that Marxism virtually ignores, our dependence on the "alien power" of death*.

f) Poverty and Revolution. Under capitalism, wealth takes the form of private property* and poverty the form of dispossession. Consequently, the rich is defined as one who "needs" to have more; the poor as one who needs to be more. The need of the poor is closer to reality than the desire of the rich is (Marx was much influenced by Hegel's dialectic of master and slave). In a world in which all alienation has been superseded, "poverty" would then only refer to our need for each other, and "wealth" the relationships created by this need. The idea of the proletariat as the agent of the final revolution*, which would thus invert the fact and sense of wealth and poverty, is, in part, mythological, for no social class exists in pure negation nor acts without particular self-interest. The Marxist analysis of social transformation contains nonetheless rich materials for Christian soteriology.

g) Hope. Marx had no time for speculation: insofar as circumstances permit effective action to be undertaken, the utopian imagining of a better world must give way to its construction. By contrast, the eschatological dimension of Christian hope prevents its contraction to the realm of social action, and always contains (in Marx's sense) utopian elements. Hope is always for more than can be given in the transformation of the world. One could also point out that Marx's understanding of the future is irredeemably flawed by an abstract and ungrounded optimism, while Christianity retains a tragic element even within its optimism. "Alleluia" is always to be sung while remembering the tension that unites it with the silence of Gethsemane.

4. Marxisms and Christianity

Christianity had little to learn from the Marxist-Leninist "dialectical materialism" that became Communism's orthodoxy (except, perhaps, the ease with which an all-embracing faith*, inflexibly interpreted and ruthlessly applied, coagulates into an inhuman system). There were other Marxist currents with which more fruitful interaction was possible. Thus, with the shift in mood during the 1960s, and the transition from anathema to dialogue, theologians, especially in Germany, began to pay serious attention to the utopian humanism of Ernst Bloch (1885–1977) and the "critical theory" of the Frankfurt School. More generally, the awakening, at this period, of theological interest in public fact and social transformation (under such labels as "political theology," "theology of the world," "theology of revolution," "theology of work," "theology of earthly realities," and so on) was diffusely influenced by aspects of Marxism without, for the most part, close examination of Marx's texts. Theologies of liberation* are a special case, not only because they were linked to the flourishing of base communities in countries of the Third World (whereas most European and North American theology has remained a largely academic enterprise) and had a general indebtedness to the Marxist idea of the primacy of praxis, but also because of the brief use in Latin America of the thought of Louis Althusser. Althusser took an extreme position in Marxist debates concerning the continuity between Marx's "early" and "mature" thought and sought to save the appearances of Communism's claims for the finality of its theories by arguing for radical discontinuity between Marxism's final ("scientific") form and its idealist or ideological beginnings (a view rendered untenable with the publication of the *Grundrisse*). Because of their Althusserian interpretation of Marx, some Latin American theologians sought to endorse Marxist theories of social transformation as "scientific," while dismissing the atheism* associated with them as a discredited ideology.

- K. Marx and F. Engels, *Marx Engels Gesamtausgabe (MEGA)*, 11 vols., Moscow, 1927–35.
- K. Marx, *Grundrisse*, Berlin, 1953.
- K. Marx and F. Engels, *Marx Engels Werke (MEW)*, 39 vols., Berlin, 1957–72.
- ♦ E. Bloch (1959), *Das Prinzip Hoffnung*, 3 vols., Frankfurt.
- L. Althusser (1965), *Pour Marx*, Paris.
- J.-Y. Calvez (1970), *La pensée de Karl Marx*, Rev. Ed., Paris.
- L. Althusser (1972), *Lénine et la philosophie*, Paris.
- D. McLellan (1973), *Karl Marx: His Life and Thought*, London.
- L. Kolakowski (1978), *Main Currents of Marxism*, 3 vols., Oxford.
- E. P. Thompson (1978), *The Poverty of Theory and Other Essays*, London.
- N. L. A. Lash (1981), *A Matter of Hope: A Theologian's Reflections on the Thought of Karl Marx*, London.
- D. McLellan (1987), *Marxism and Religion*, London.
- H. Fleischer and H. Rolfes (1992), "Marx/Marxism," *TRE* 22, 220–58.

NICHOLAS LASH

See also **Deism and Theism; Hegelianism; Religion, Philosophy of**

Mary

A. Biblical Theology

Mary, the mother of Jesus*, occupies a relatively small place in the New Testament as a whole. Theology* and piety have given considerable weight to those texts that mention her, with major differences in appreciation from one Christian confession to another. For this reason the exegete must be careful to distinguish between the objective givens of the texts and later constructions, however legitimate the latter might be from a dogmatic* point of view (see *Mary in the New Testament* [1978], an exemplary work carried out by Catholic and Lutheran exegetes in the United States).

1. Paul, Synoptics, Acts

a) Paul. A theologian of the paschal mystery, Paul speaks little of the life of Jesus. He mentions his birth on only one occasion: "God sent forth his son, born of woman, born under the law" (Gal 4:4). The expression is surprising: one might have expected the name of the father. Paul is here emphasizing the solidarity of Christ* with mankind, the weakness of the Son of God*, born of woman among a people* subject to the law.

b) Mark. In the Gospel of Mark, where the birth of Christ is not narrated at all, the Judeo-Christian opposition becomes evident. Mary is to be found in only two episodes. In Mark 3:21, "his [Jesus'] family" are hostile, but Mary is only named later (opposition between blood family and the family made up of those who obey the will of God [3:31–34f.]. In Mark 6:3—"Is not this the carpenter, the son of Mary and brother of James and Joses and Judas and Simon? And are not his sisters here with us?"—the designation "son of Mary" is noteworthy, when in Matthew and Luke, both of whom attest to the virginal conception, we find: "son of a carpenter."

c) Matthew. Matthew, on the contrary, draws on Judeo-Christian tradition*, while at the same time forging an opening to the universal mission* (28:18ff.). The prologue (1–2) provides answers to the questions (K. Stendahl): "Who is the Messiah*?" "Where does he come from?" Studies of the type "The Childhood Stories in the *Haggada*" (C. Perrot), and particularly those of the childhood of Moses (R.

Bloch), are decisive in enabling us to appreciate the literary genre of these chapters.

In the book of Matthew, the introductory genealogy of Jesus Christ, son of David, son of Abraham, contains anomalies (foreign or sinful women) and comes to a strange conclusion: "and Jacob the father of Joseph the husband of Mary, of whom Jesus was born" (Mt 1:16). Matthew 1:18–25 is written from the point of view of Joseph, the just and steadfast man and who has received the mission to introduce Jesus into the line of David. The revelation* revolves around Mary's virginal conception (*see* below, 2) under the action of the Holy* Spirit, according to Isaiah 7:14 (LXX). Matthew is thus in opposition to the Ebionites, for whom Jesus was the "son of Joseph." The point being christological, Matthew 1:25 (Joseph "took his wife, but knew her not until she had given birth to a son") is not concerned with what would happen later. The episode of the epiphany is reinforced by the ancient themes of the royal star (Nm 24:17) and the Davidic messiah (Mi 5:1). While elsewhere Joseph plays a leading role, here the Magi see "the young child with Mary his mother" (Mt 2:11): it is she who is charged with introducing her son to the people. In narrating Christ's public life, Matthew removes anything that might have seemed offensive in Mark (compare Mt 12:46–50 with Mk 3:21 and 31ff.).

d) Luke, Acts. To Christians of pagan origin who are tempted to reject the Jewish heritage, Luke shows that the life and works of Christ cannot be understood without their roots in the Old Testament, which reveal the continuity of God's design despite the interference of history*. Unlike Matthew, Luke 1–2 is more interested in Mary than in Joseph. The style is inspired by the Old Testament, particularly the story of the young Samuel. A typical format connects two stories: the annunciation of Gabriel to Zechariah (1:11–20), and the annunciation to Mary (1:26–38). Differences are enhanced: thus, Mary believes while Zechariah doubts. The angel*'s message to Mary *(khairé)* seems to be a return to the prophecies inviting the "daughter of Zion" to messianic joy (Sg 3:14; Zec 9:9). Mary is hailed as the recipient par excellence of God's *kharis* (that is, of his salvific intentions). The Catholic dogma* of the Immaculate Conception (Mary protected from original sin* from the moment of her birth) would be based upon this salutation.

Mary's question to the angel, "How will this be, since I am a virgin?" (Lk 1:34), is aimed at introducing the rest of the revelation and cannot be interpreted as signifying a vow of virginity. The event is presented in two stages: the messianic royalty of the child and, given the fact of the Spirit, his divine origin. Suggestions of "an apocalypse" (Legrand 1981) have been made, as the unveiling, in a paschal light, of the divine plan of salvation.* Projecting onto the origin formulas of faith* that had come later, Luke insists on the free consent with which Mary, the "servant of the Lord," yielded to God's intervention, in this case even more astonishing than in the case of Isaac (Lk 1:37 and Gn 18:14).

The comparisons between the Visitation (Lk 1:39–45) and the history of the Ark of the Covenant* (Laurentin 1964) are too tenuous to be retained on an exegetical level. Elizabeth praises Mary's faith (1:45). Mary recites the "Magnificat," which Luke has drawn from Judeo-Christian hymnology (with an emphasis on Israel* and the expectation of imminent justice* for the poor). Marian devotion would take inspiration from 1:48: "For behold, from now on all generations will call me blessed"—Mary's faith is underlined again as a passage through obscurity (2:41–52), a quest for the meaning of events (2:19–51), and an acceptance of the Word* (8:15, 11, 28). With Joseph she is depicted as a faithful observer of the law. Simeon's prediction "and a sword will pierce through your own soul also" (2, 35) refers to the rejection of the Messiah by his own people, and would be applied to the compassion of Mary at the foot of the cross (Jn 19:25). Like Matthew, Luke avoids anything that might suggest an opposition between Jesus and his mother. After the Resurrection, Mary prays in the Cenacle with the apostles, a few women, and the brothers of Jesus (Acts 1:14). There is a correspondence between the sudden descent of the Spirit* upon the church* in Acts 2 and the coming of the Spirit upon Mary in Luke 1:35.

2. Virginal Conception

Matthew and Luke are the only New Testament authors who affirm that Jesus was born miraculously of Mary. The reading of John 1:13 in the singular *(qui natus est)* is too weakly attested to be retained. However, on numerous occasions Jesus is designated as the "son of Joseph" (Lk 3:23, "being the son [as was supposed] of Joseph", 4:22; Jn 1:45, 6:42). A number of questions arise, therefore, concerning the origin of the tradition* of the virginal conception, and its theological impact.

Agreeing in their fundamental affirmation, Matthew

and Luke nevertheless diverge too significantly in their presentation to be seen as mutually dependent. Each text needs to be explained on its own.

The milieu out of which Matthew was writing would have been familiar with the Jewish *haggada,* which knew of no virgin conception. The prophecy of Isaiah 7:14 refers to the *'alemah* (meaning a young woman, married or not) as the mother of the royal heir, to which Micah 5:2 also refers. These texts can be explained by the role played at the royal court by the queen mother (H. Cazelles). Matthew, however, refers to Isaiah 7:14 not according to the Hebrew but the LXX: *parthenos* (the reading of which was prohibited by Justin and Irenaeus* as being against Aquila's *neanis,* which they regarded as more in keeping with the Hebrew). Must it be said that the idea of a virginal conception emerged in Alexandria? Philo, commenting on the birth of Isaac, would develop the allegory of the engendering of virtues*, but the Evangelists had a real birth in mind (Grelot 1972). *Parthenos* in LXX is also used as a description for towns that have nothing exemplary about them (Is 47:1; Lam 1:15, 2:13; *see* Dubarle 1978). A direct reading of Isaiah 7:14 could not therefore have inspired Matthew's story; moreover, the point of the story is that of the conception by the Spirit, and the quotation is only of interest for the additional light it sheds on the matter. In the biblical creation* stories the Spirit's role is to communicate life (Gn 2:7; Ps 104:30). According to the physiology of the era, woman did no more than gather the seed that would develop in her womb.

In Luke's text there are no references to Isaiah 7:14, but the theme gathers force with the account of John the Baptist, who is filled from his mother's womb with the Holy Spirit (1:15). Here the Spirit is at work in the conception itself. Its intervention is indicated by a verb evoking the presence of God's glory* on the Ark of the Covenant (*episkiazein,* as in Ex 40:35; Nm 9:1, 9:22, 10:34. John 1:14 has recourse to the same typology for the advent of the Logos. This comparison shows that for the authors of the second century the Word itself took form in the womb of Mary. In any event, we cannot speculate here on the personal nature of the divine *pneuma:* a principle of life, it assures the divine origin of the child.

In the Judeo-Christian tradition to which Matthew adheres, any borrowing from pagan mythology seems unthinkable. The delicacy with which Luke treats his subject illustrates well that he is at an opposite extreme from the eroticism of Greek and Roman mythology.

Was the virginal conception, then, simply a *theologoumenon,* a theological interpretation without a factual basis, or was it an affirmation based upon the reality of things? The silence of the rest of the New

Testament would seem to favor the first hypothesis. However, it must be acknowledged that a literal interpretation imposed itself very early on in the church: Ignatius of Antioch (*To the Smyrnaeans* 1:1; *To the Tralians* 1 X, 1) was the most prominent witness of this evolution, and then Irenaeus, who developed the parallel between Mary and the virgin soil whence Adam* was formed (*Adv. Haer.* 111, 21, 10). The exegete would emphasize the unprecedented nature of the texts of Matthew and Luke and the great difficulty involved in finding a satisfactory explanation for them outside of a tradition that, in the final analysis, must be as old as Mary herself, however discreet that tradition may have been in other respects.

3. John, Apocalypse 12

a) John. John was interested primarily in the divine origin of the Logos made flesh (1:14). He does not name Mary. However, she does appear, as the "mother of Jesus," in two scenes that correspond to each other. She appears first of all at Cana, with the group of "brothers" (2:12). In this prototype of "signs" accomplished on the third day (the paschal token), she intervenes but is met with a blunt refusal (2:4). Here, as in the synoptics, Jesus marks his distance from his family. But the words Mary addresses to the servants (*see* Gn 41:55) show that the conflict has been overcome. For those who see in this story a response of the covenant of Sinai, Mary expresses commitment of the people to whom the wine of the New Covenant is destined (Serra 1978).

In 8:41, does John allude to accusations of illegitimacy brought against Jesus by the Jews? These are affirmed by Celsus and provoked the reply of the *Protevangelium Jacobi* (v. 175). Clues are very tenuous where John is concerned.

The second scene in question is the narrative of the crucifixion, the "hour" of Christ's *agape*. Only John mentions the mother of Jesus at the foot of the cross, with the beloved disciple (19:25ff.). In the verse "Woman, behold, your son" the fathers* of the church recognized a sign of filial solicitude. Subsequently, the "Behold, your mother" served to support teaching about Mary's spiritual maternity. Modern commentators, in various ways, have emphasized the symbolic nature of the scene. Would not the surprising form of address, "Woman," (*see* 2:4) justify the Eve-Mary typology? But for Justin and Irenaeus, the first instances of this linkage, it was at the time of the Annunciation that Mary repaired Eve's disobedience. If the disciple was called upon to take Mary "into his home" (and thus into the community that he had founded), was this not a call to maintain the ties with the Israel of God, represented by Mary? We know with what care John seeks to show Jesus is truly the "king of Israel" (1:49), the long-awaited Messiah.

b) Revelation 12. The sign of the Woman is the symbol of the Israel of God (Rev 12:1ff.), predestined, but nevertheless exposed to the rage of the original serpent (12:9). Genesis 3 therefore constitutes a major background element for understanding the text. Although the birth followed by the lifting up into the heavens refers to the "hour" of Easter, we cannot altogether rule out a reference to Mary, for she was present at Calvary. At the level of biblical* theology, where arguments are constructed on a basis of the various facts given in the New Testament, comparisons between Cana, Calvary, and the "great sign" of Revelation 12 suggest the establishing of a typological correspondence between Eve, the mother of the living, and Mary, the mother of the people of the New Covenant. The application of the text to Mary's Assumption came fairly late.

The overall interpretation of the above points to a "trajectory" within the New Testament where Mary is concerned. This extends from Mark to the Johannine corpus, giving a central place to Luke. To realize this deeper reading is to give legitimacy to the development of the subsequent tradition that would lead to the proclamation of Mary as *theotokos,* "mother of God." Paul's extreme discretion and Mark's reserve appear as a counterpoint; they must be given serious consideration by the theologian and serve as corrective measures against mariological deviations.

4. Brothers of Jesus

The term "brother" is subject to a great variety of interpretations. According to Old Testament usage, and that of the Eastern world, "brother" implies a person one is close to, regardless of the exact degree of blood relation. The word *anepsios* (cousin) is only found once in the entire New Testament (Col 4:10). The disciples received the title of brothers (e.g., in 1 Cor 15:6). A group who shared their origins in Nazareth was set apart (as in Mk 6:3); they never called themselves formally the "sons of Mary." Initially unbelievers (Mk 3:21; Jn 7:3ff.), they figured among the disciples after Easter (Acts 1:14). The most prominent of them, "James, the brother of the Lord," was the leader of the Judeo-Christian community in Jerusalem (Gal 1:19).

Were they the uterine brothers, half-brothers, or cousins of Jesus? At issue is Mary's *virginitas post partum* (after childbirth), an affirmation that the title of firstborn (Lk 2:7) conferred upon Jesus does not suffice to call into question. Examination of New Testament texts throws up a number of difficulties. Thus, James and Joses, "brothers of Jesus" in Mark 6:3, appear as the children of another Mary in Mark 15:40, 15:47, and 16:1. "Brother of the Lord" is an honorific title, the transposition of an original Aramaean title. One cannot conclude therefore that the New Testament obliges one to take the expression "brothers of the Lord" literally.

From the end of the second century, the *Protevan-gelium Jacobi* upheld against the Jews the idea of Mary's perpetual virginity and presented the brothers of Jesus as those born from an earlier marriage on Joseph's side. Although lacking any historical value, this apocryphal (apocrypha*) text nevertheless became widespread; it seems to be the first evidence of a belief that would come to be held in common by the church until recent refutations.

B. Historical Theology

The Marian theology* that developed from Scripture* had very modest beginnings before the fourth century, which is when it began to take shape. It continued to develop throughout the Middle Ages and was the object of dogmatic definitions in Catholicism* in the 19th and 20th centuries. Its main themes will be looked at here from a historical rather than a systematic point of view (but connections will be pointed out), with particular attention being paid to the patristic period. Doctrinal themes will be covered to begin with (virginity, sanctity and Immaculate Conception, divine motherhood, Assumption), followed by the place of Mary within piety and worship (spiritual maternity, Mary and the church*, the "mediation" of Mary and cooperation in salvation*, the Marian cult*), and concluding with the contributions of Vatican* II.

I. Doctrinal Themes

1. Virginity

The earliest Marian theology, in the second and third centuries, was wholly integrated into Christology*: the aim was to affirm the *virginal conception* of Christ.

a) In the Second Century. Ignatius of Antioch mentioned Mary with a twofold purpose: to uphold against Docetism* the reality of the Incarnation*, since Christ was truly born of woman* (*Smyrn* I, 1; *Trall.* IX, 1; *Ephes.* VII, 1), and to show that through his birth of a virgin he was not an ordinary man (*Ephes* XVIII–XIX: Christ was "of the seed of David and of the Holy* Spirit"; ibid. VII, 1: Christ was "of [ek] Mary and of God*"). *Ephes.* XIX emphasizes the humility and the silence of this unobserved birth of the Prince of the World* (see *The Ascension of Isaiah,* IX–XI). In the same way, the *Ode of Solomon* 19 (second century)

may also allude to the virginal conception and birth, if the "virgin" is not a symbolical figure.

Justin, in the *Dialogue with Trypho* (c. 150), aimed to show that Isaiah's prophecy* (7, 14, *a virgin shall conceive...*, with controversy over the term "virgin" or "young girl" depending on the Greek or the Hebrew) was fulfilled only through Jesus (*Dial.* 66). He also saw in the virginal conception a sign that Jesus was more than an inspired prophet or the Messiah* (67; see *Apology* 30): he was not born through human works, but by the will of God (*Dial.* 76) intervening in history as at the time of the Creation* (84). Justin established for the first time the parallel between Eve and Mary (*see* below, 1.c). Following on from him, Irenaeus* saw in the virginal conception the mark of the Creator himself: Mary's virginity is a reference to that of the earth, from which Adam* was made (*Demonstration* 32, see *Adv. Haer.* III, 21, 7, and 10), and it refutes Gnosticism by linking creation and salvation (*see* below, 1.c, the parallel between Eve and Mary). The twin significance of the virginal conception is found here also: it attests a true human birth (*Adv. Haer.* III, 19, 3) and is also the sign that Jesus is more than a mere man (*Adv. Haer.* III, 21, 4; *Dem.* 57). At that time there was no interest in Mary outside of Christology. Irenaeus specified that Christ truly received his flesh from Mary (*Adv. Haer.* III, 22, 1–2; *see* I, 7, 2). The *Protevangelium Jacobi* on the other hand (second century?) was entirely centered on Mary, to affirm her purity from the moment of birth and her virginity preserved until childbirth (XX, 1) and forever after (the "brothers of Jesus" were sons of Joseph from a first marriage).

The insistence during the second century on virginal conception shows that there was some doubt about it. For the Ebionites Jesus was simply a man, born of

Mary and Joseph; Jewish polemics, sometimes taken by pagans, maintained that Jesus was the illegitimate son of Mary and an unknown father (*see* Origen*, *Commentary on John* XX, XVI, 128; *Contra Celsum* I, 32). Gnostic groups viewed the virginal conception as a pure symbol (see *The Gospel according to Philip* 17). Tertullian*, out of a concern for realism, replied that Mary had lost the signs of virginity by bringing Christ into the world (*The Flesh of Christ* XXIII, 2–5; *see* Origen, *Hom* XIV on Luke, 3). He saw the brothers of Christ as Mary's children (*Against Marcion* IV, 19, 7). His virginal conception then became a proof of Christ's divinity (Tertullian, *The Flesh of Christ* XVIII; Origen, *Contra Celsum* I, 69; in the fourth century, Eusebius of Caesarea, *Demonstr. Gospel* VII, 1, 30; in the fifth century, Proclus, *ACO* I, 1, 1, 104, 3–6).

b) From the third century, with the development of Christian asceticism, there was a growing interest in Mary's virginity for its own sake. The Ps.-Justin said that through the virginity of the mother of Christ, God had wanted to show that one can do without the sexual act (*Treatise on the Resurrection* 3). Clement of Alexandria, shortly after the year 200, affirmed the belief in the virginity of Mary after childbirth (*post partum*) (*Strom.* VII, XVI, 93–94). Origen affirmed that Mary could not have coupled with a man after giving birth to Christ: she is the archetype of feminine virginity, as Christ is of masculine virginity (*Comm. Mt* X, 17; see in the fourth century, Athanasius*, *Letter to Virgins,* 86–88, and in 371, Gregory of Nyssa, *On Virginity.* II, 2, 18–25; XIV, 1, 24–30); Athanasius (ibid., 100–101) moreover attributes to Mary a role of intercessor with Christ on behalf of virgins; Ambrose* does likewise (*De virgin. ad Marc.* II, 9). Augustine*, because of Luke 1:34, even attributes to Mary a *vow of virginity* preceding the Annunciation (*On Holy Virginity* IV, 4, which initiated an entire tradition).

At the end of the fourth century Mary's *perpetual virginity* during and after childbirth (*in partu, post partum)* became virtually an article of faith, defended by Ambrose (*On the Institution of Virgins,* 35–62, with the subsequently classical image of the shut gate, Ez 44:2) and Jerome against Helvidius, Jovinian, and Bonosus, or by Epiphanius (*Panarion* 78) and Augustine against others who refuted Mary's virginity (antidicomarianites). The title "ever virgin" (*aeiparthenos)* is found in Epiphanius in 374 (*Ancor.* 119, then *Panarion* 78, 5, 5, etc.) and probably in Didymus (other passages or fragments are dubious). Mary's perpetual virginity would henceforth no longer be contested in either the East or the West. But it was a topic for discussion wherever opinions were freely voiced among the churches born of the Reformation.

In partu virginity was affirmed at the time of the Council of Ephesus* (431) on the Cyrilian side (Proclus, *ACO* I, 1, 1, 104, 3–6) and the Eastern side (Theodoret of Cyrrhus, *On the Incarnation of the Lord* 23). The acts of Chalcedon* (451) authorized the *Tome of Leo* (449); Pope Leo the Great professed it (*COD* 77, 31–33). Constantinople* II (553) gave Mary the title of "ever virgin" (*aeiparthenos/semper virgo*) in the judgment against the Three Chapters and in the second anathematization (*COD* 113, 17 and 114, 20–21). The Lateran Council of 649 did likewise in canon 3 (*DS* 503), as did the final decree of Nicaea* II in 787 (*COD* 134, 45).

c) Mary, the New Eve. A certain number of exegetes had already remarked on the parallel between Eve and Mary in Rev 12, and in the second century Justin compared the virginity of the two women, opposing disobedience and corruption (Eve) with obedience and joy (Mary). The parallel was also drawn in the *Protevangelium Jacobi* XIII, 1, but with another point of view in mind (Joseph believed that Mary, like Eve, had sinned when she was alone). It was exploited by Gnostics to show that the new Adam was spiritual and not carnal (*Gospel acc. to Philip* 83). Irenaeus developed the issue *a contrario* to show the continuity between the Old and the New Testament (*Dem.* 33; *Adv. Haer.* III, 22, 4; 23, 7; V, 19, 1; 21, 1). The comparison was also found shortly after 200 in Tertullian (*The Flesh of Christ,* XVII). It would fade somewhat for a time in favor of the parallel between Eve and the church, then resurface at the beginning of the fourth century in the works of Victorinus of Pettau, and at the end of the century in Epiphanius (*Panarion* 78, 18–19). He declared that the title of *Mother of the Living* (Gn 3:20) should apply to Mary, who engendered life, rather than to Eve, who caused death* (*see* not long thereafter, Peter Chrysologos, *Sermon* 140). It then reappeared in the fifth century (an opposition between Gn 3 and Lk 1). The parallel never gave rise to the idea that Mary was the *spouse* or *betrothed* of Christ. In particular, Genesis 2:24 and the Song of Songs are understood as speaking of Christ and the church, not Christ and Mary: with the exception of one instance in Ambrose, who does not derive a nuptial theme from it (*On the Institution of Virgins* 89 *Sq*), it was not until the 12th century (Rupert of Deutz, Honorius of Autun) that there would be a Marian reading of the Song of Songs, perhaps because the attributes of the church were extended to Mary, beginning with spiritual maternity (below, II.1). Guerric of Igny, *Sur l'assomption* I, 2–4, is a witness of the transition from Eve-Mary to Eve–the church (ibid. II, 1–4 for the Marian interpretation of the Song of Songs). Similarly, the early 11th century had seen the first Marian readings of Genesis 3:15. In the modern era, Scheeben* gave renewed development to the theme of Mary as the new Eve, spouse of Christ (see *Maria* III, 553–71). Vatican II (*LG* 56, *COD* 893) went no further than to recall the parallel between Eve and Mary by quoting the Fathers*.

2. Holiness and Immaculate Conception

a) *Faith and Mary's Doubt.* Mary's holiness is distinct from her virginity: the same authors (Origen, John Chrysostom*, Ephraim) taught Mary's perpetual virginity yet attributed failings in faith to her, or feelings of vanity. There was no unanimous position on the question until the early fifth century, even if the title of "holy" was already fairly current in the fourth century, even among those authors who thought that Mary needed to be sanctified before the Incarnation. Moreover, the notion of Mary's holiness would be slow in evolving into the doctrine of the Immaculate Conception. In the second century the *Protevangelium Jacobi* presented the Virgin as utterly holy from the beginning; the text suggests that perhaps she was conceived virginally. Her holiness was seen as a total separation from the profane world. If there were any suggestions in the legends of an Immaculate Conception, they were isolated examples.

Several passages in the New Testament have caused commentators to think that Mary was criticized for her lack of faith or for her boasting: Matthew 12:46–50 par.; Luke 1:34, 2:35, 2:48; John 2:4; the Passion* narratives. Tertullian understood Matthew 12:48 as indicating that Christ rejected his mother and brothers because of their lack of faith (*Against Marcion* IV, 19, 11–13, *see The Flesh of Christ* VII, 9). Origen (*Hom. VII on Luke,* 4) spoke of a heretic who professed that Christ had rejected Mary because she united with Joseph after his birth. For Origen, Mary did not immediately believe in the angel*'s promise (*Hom. I on Gn,* 14); she did not yet have complete faith during Jesus' childhood (*Hom. XX on Luke,* 4); she doubted during the Passion (*Hom. XVII on Luke,* 6–7), although this did not prevent her from prophesying, for she was "filled with the Holy Spirit from the moment she bore the Savior within her" (*Hom. VII on Luke,* 3). Titus of Bostra (late fourth century) interpreted Luke 2:49 (TU 21–2, 152) as a reproach from Jesus to Mary, reminding her of the virginal conception that meant that God, and not Joseph, was his father. Ephraim spoke of Mary's doubt at Cana (*Comm. on Diatess.* 5, 2–4). John Chrysostom also had little praise when commenting on the Annunciation, Cana, and Matthew 12:48 (*Hom. on Mt,* 4, 4; *on Jn* 21 (20), 2; *on Mt* 44:1f.). In the fifth century Cyril* of Alexandria wrote that Mary as she stood at the foot of the cross (*Comm. on Jn* XII,

ad Jn 19, 25), as did his contemporary Hesychius of Jerusalem, who interpreted Simeon's prophecy of the sword as referring to this, after many other meanings (*Hom. I on the Hypapante* 8). Mary's doubt regarding the angel's message could also be found, in the sixth century, in the works of Romanos of Melos (*Hymn 9 on the Annunciation* 7). In the same way, various fourth-century authors deemed that Mary needed a *purification* before the Incarnation: Hilary* of Poitiers (*De Trin* II, 26), Gregory* of Nazianzus (*Disc.* 38, 13), and Cyril of Jerusalem (*Catech.* 17, 6); Atticus of Constantinople also said as much in the early fifth century (Syriac hom. *On the Holy Mother of God*).

b) *Holiness and Absence of Sin.* Ambrose was the first to maintain that Mary was the only one whose faith did not waver at the cross (*Letter* 63, 100; *On the Institution of Virgins* 49). She was unflinching and immaculate (*Letter* 42, 4 to Sirice). The Pelagian controversy (Pelagianism*) marked a turning point. In *Nature and Grace* XXXVI (42), in 415, Augustine echoed Pelagius's words by refusing to speak of sin* in relation to the Virgin, but he specified that it was because of the honor of the Lord and through an excess of grace* that she was victorious over sin. Later, Julian of Eclanum, another follower of Pelagius who held Mary to be without sin, accused Augustine of "delivering Mary over to the devil" because of his theology of original sin* marking every birth. Augustine replied in 428–30 (*Unfinished Work against Julian* IV, 122) that "Mary was liberated from her condition (at birth) through the grace of rebirth," a somewhat unclear expression that has been variously interpreted, but that did not envisage a special exemption for Mary from the legacy of sin. The fact that the Pelagians were the first to maintain that Mary was exempt from original sin, together with Augustine's opposition, would long make it difficult for the Catholics to accept the idea of the Immaculate Conception. Again, at the beginning of the sixth century, disciples of Augustine specified that Mary had inherited "the flesh of sin" (Rom 8:3), unlike Jesus (Fulgentius of Ruspina, CChr.SL 91 A, 571–72; Ferrandus of Carthage, PL 67, 892–93); the expression "flesh of sin" applied to Mary comes from Augustine, *On Penance and the Remission of Sins,* II, 24.

c) *Toward the Immaculate Conception.* In the East the Council of Ephesus, which was held in 431 in the church of "Saint Mary," inspired homilies in praise of Mary (Proclus, Acacius of Melitene); but it must be noted that words like "incorruption" or "purity" often meant nothing more than Mary's virginity preserved through and despite the birth of Christ (Theodotus of Ancyra, *ACO* I, 1, 2, 74, 25–26; *see* Fulgentius, loc.

cit.). After this council the liturgy* became the primary place for Marian theology, particularly in the East (where homiletics and hymnody were preferred to argumentation), less so in the West (but in the period immediately after the council, in Rome*, there was the reconstruction and dedication of Saint Mary Major by Pope Sixtus III).

In 634 Sophronis of Jerusalem celebrated "Holy Mary, resplendent, of divine sentiments, free of all stain of body, soul*, and thought," and spoke of a Virgin "sanctified in her body and in her soul" (it may again be a purification before the Incarnation), "pure, holy, and without stain" (PG 87–3, 3160 D–3161 B). He contested the usual exegesis of the prophecy of the sword: at issue was Mary's pain at the cross, not a weakening in her faith. In the following century Andrew of Crete, in his *Canons* (PG 97, 1305 s.) and in his homilies for the Marian feast days (particularly the Conception of Anne), also celebrated Mary's purity without stain from the moment of her conception. In the ninth century Saint Theodore the Studite (PG 96, 684 C–685 A) evoked the absence of all sin for which God had predestined the Virgin for all eternity. Photius would echo these statements (see *DThC* 7/1, 924–25). The idea of Mary being without sin seems to have quietly taken hold in the Byzantine theological arena, although there was no actual affirmation of the Immaculate Conception and it never was the subject of a precise definition.

In the West, after a dormant period, attention was once again focused on the issue after the 12th century. The development of the feast day of the Conception of Mary (below, II.3) gave rise to debate: Bernard* of Clairvaux and subsequently Thomas* Aquinas opposed the Immaculate Conception of Mary, convinced as they were that the carnal union of the spouses must necessarily be marked by sin and would therefore pass on its legacy. This conviction was largely shared, and it explained the fact that during the Middle Ages, perhaps in the light of the *Protevangelium Jacobi,* people liked to believe in Mary's virginal conception in order to preserve her from all sin (see the confusion often encountered nowadays between Immaculate Conception and virginal conception). In the light of these objections, the Franciscans (including John Duns* Scotus) prepared the way for modern Catholic theology by affirming that Mary had been redeemed in anticipation of the merits of her Son.

The Council of Basle (in the 36th, nonecumenical session, on 17 September 1439) declared the Immaculate Conception to be "a pious doctrine in accordance with the worship of the Church, the Catholic faith, uprighteousness, and Holy Scripture" (Mansi 29, 183 B–C). On several occasions Pope Sixtus IV approved and encouraged belief in the Immaculate Conception,

and promoted the feast day of the Conception of the Virgin (Constit. *Cum praeexcelsa* in 1477, *DS* 1400; Constit. *Grave nimis* in 1483, *DS* 1425–426). The Council of Trent*, in the decree on original sin (fifth session, June 1546, *COD* 667, 21–25), declared that it did not want to include the Virgin in the decree. Clement XI prescribed that the feast should be celebrated everywhere (Constit. *Commissi nobis divinitus* from 1708). The last remaining reticence was gradually overcome within Catholicism (and given the clear affirmation that the privilege of the Virgin was a grace conferred in advance by the accomplished redemption of her Son), and the dogma* of the Immaculate Conception was defined by Pope Pius IX, after long consultation, in the Bull *Ineffabilis Deus* of 8 December 1854 (*DS* 2803): "From the first instant of her conception, through the unique grace and privilege of almighty God, the Blessed Virgin Mary was, in consideration of the merits of Jesus Christ the savior of humankind, preserved pure of all stain of original sin." The Bull insisted on the title of "mother of God" as the foundation of the Immaculate Conception (rather than on the Eve-Mary parallel, put forth by Newman*; see *Maria* III, 540–44).

We should also note the importance of the liturgical feasts as a theological locus (*loci* theologici), both in East and West. The feast of the Conception of the Virgin (below, II.3.a) logically celebrates the first moment of salvation by tracing a path from the Incarnation to the birth of the Virgin (celebrated in the East from the sixth century) and right back to her conception. Founded upon an implicit belief, this feast day brought about further dogmatic precision.

The attitude of other churches with regard to the Immaculate Conception varies. The Orthodox* Church opposes even the idea of a Roman definition and its language (see *Cath.* 5, 1284–90; *DThC* 7–1, 962–79 and 1211–14), preferring to speak of the absence of all sin in Mary, who rather than exempt from original sin was pure from the first instant. As for the churches created during the Reformation (with the exception of certain Anglican circles), they are overwhelmingly hostile to the Immaculate Conception, not only for reasons of content (the Immaculate Conception seems to allow Mary to avoid the redemption) but also because of the very principle of the "deduction" of dogma so long after the closing of revelation*, not to mention the risk of encouraging the autonomous discipline of "Mariology" within theology (a complaint also found in present-day Catholicism).

3. Divine Maternity

The theological theme of Mary's divine maternity is linked, with some justification, to the Council of Ephesus (431). The debate over the subject of the title of *theotokos* (mother of God, literally "who gives birth to God", in Latin *Deipara*) drew attention to the christological question of the communication of idioms*. Can one say Mary "mother of God," rather than simply "mother of Christ" (in his humanity)? Cyril of Alexandria defended the title *theotokos* against Nestorius (Nestorianism*). Two Christologies confronted each other over the word. Debate focused on the historical age and legitimacy of the title *theotokos*.

Before the word itself, the idea appeared very early on to attribute to the preexisting Word* the birth from Mary (Justin, *Dial.* 100), encouraged perhaps by the expression: "the mother of my Lord" in Luke 1:43. The word *theotokos* was found on a papyrus (third century?: John Rylands Library, 470). Other occurrences prior to the fourth century are very suspect. Alexander of Alexandria seems to have been the first to have definitely used the word, in a letter written around 320 (Theodoret, *Hist. Eccl.* I, 4, 54, GCS v. 44, 23, 3). The term is also found in Athanasius (PG 26, 349 C; 385 A; 393 A and B; but the *Life of St. Anthony* 36, 4 is suspect, *see* REAug 41, 1995, 157); it is found in Basil*, if the homily is authentic (PG 31, 1468 B), Gregory of Nazianzus (SC 208, 42), and Gregory of Nyssa (PG 46, 1136C, and if the homily is his, 1157B and 1176B, also with *theometor,* "mother of God"). Theodore of Mopsuestia, Nestorius's master, may also have used it (see *Maria* I, 94, n. 36). Among the Latins, Ambrose uses "mother of God" twice (*On Virgins* II, 2, 7, and *Exameron* 5, 20, 65), and twice "she who engendered God" (*Comm. Lc* X, 130, CChr.SL 14, 383 and *On Virgins* II, 2, 13), an expression that was no doubt found in Athanas (*Letter to Virgins,* CSCO 151, 59). Cyril himself did not use the expression before Ephesus.

After Ephesus the title *theotokos* took the place of honor and was frequently used in homiletics (Proclus of Constantinople, Hesychius of Jerusalem). It became part of the common patrimony, even for those of the Eastern faith who favored Nestorius: Theodoret of Cyrrhus adopted the word and added *anthropotokos,* mother of man (PG 75, 1477 A). At Ephesus, Cyril's *Second Letter to Nestorius,* which defended the use of the title, was canonized (*COD* 44, 2); Chalcedon adopted it for its definition of faith (*COD* 84, 39), as did Constantinople II in its sixth anathematization (which referred not to Ephesus but to Chalcedon, *COD* 116, 29). Divine maternity remained a christological question rather than a "privilege" of Mary; it was explained after other themes (perpetual virginity, e.g.) and could not, historically, be considered a starting point for the deduction of other privileges.

4. Assumption

The last Marian dogma defined by the Catholic Church was that of the Assumption, which concerns Mary's final destiny. Ancient tradition* offers little to go on. At the end of the fourth century Epiphanius declared his ignorance on the subject (*Panarion* 78, GCS, v. III, 462). From the fifth century on, in addition to the apocryphal writings *On Mary's Transfer,* there were allusions in homiletics to the fate of her body (*see* DECA I, 280–81). The texts (Mimouni 1995) waver between notions of dormition (Mary's body, separated from the soul and transported to a hidden place, waits uncorrupted for the final resurrection*) and of assumption (the soul is reunited with the body, which has been raised up to join Christ in glory) with or without resurrection; for, according to certain texts, Mary is immortal. Belief in dormition seems to be the most ancient, often later supplanted by assumption (certain texts have dormition followed by assumption). Assumption seems to have been called into question again in the ninth century, in the East (John Geometres and others, *see* Jugie 1944) as well as in the West (Ps.-Jerome alias Paschasius Radbertus). In the modern era, even in the East, the majority of theologians seem to have adopted assumption. But only Catholicism has defined it as a dogma, something Orthodoxy has refused to do.

In 1950, appealed to by a number of voices, Pope Pius XII proclaimed (Constit. Apost. *Munificentissimus Deus,* DS 3900–3904) that "the Immaculate Mother of God, the ever Virgin Mary, when the course of her earthly life was run, was assumed in body and in soul to heavenly glory." He argued on the basis of divine maternity for the union of the Virgin to Christ who is Life, her place in the economy of salvation, her title as the new Eve and her Immaculate Conception, and the long existence of the feast of the Dormition or of the Assumption of the Virgin were mentioned (*see* below, II.3). While he specified that by the grace of Christ the body of Mary knew no corruption, he did not reach a decision on the question of her death. As with the Immaculate Conception, this definition is not explicitly reinforced by Scripture (the verses cited, such as Rev 12, are read symbolically). The definition therefore is of the nature of a deduction with a doctrinal motivation (the body that bore Christ *could in no way* be submitted to corruption; she who was so closely associated with Christ *could not* be separated from him in her final destiny), which explains its rejection by the Protestant churches.

II. Mary in Piety and in Worship

Given the unique place held by Mary in the history of salvation, there has been much debate on her *active* role in the work of redemption and in its reception by human beings. Certain themes have emerged, some of which remain much debated: spiritual maternity, universal "mediation," "coredemption."

1. Spiritual Maternity: Mary and the Church

Several factors have contributed to the emergence of this theme: Jn 19:26 *Sq;* the theology of virginity affirming the spiritual fecundity of virgins, who have Mary as their model; the parallel between Mary and the church, which is also a spiritual mother; and finally the parallel between Eve and Mary, which holds Mary rather than Eve as the "mother of the living" (*see* above, I.1). It is difficult to determine which factor came first, or has been most decisive.

Origen outlined the theme on the basis of Jn 19:26 (*Comment. on Jn* I, IV, 23): as with John, any believer "in whom Christ lives" (*see* Gal 2:20) is the son of Mary. Ambrose saw Mary in the figure of the church (*On the Instit. of Virgins* 89, and above I.1.c, for the reading of the Song of Songs). For Augustine the church is virgin and mother (*On Holy Virginity* II, 2); and Mary, like the church (VI, 6), is the spiritual mother of all the members of Christ's body (already in Ambrose, op. cit. 98). In the 13th century the *Missal* (Q. 29) of the Ps.-Albertus Magnus speaks of Mary's suffering at the cross, which made her mother of all humankind. In the 15th century Bernardine of Siena attributed this maternity to her consent to the angel's message (*Serm. 6 On Consent,* 2). Modern Catholicism has developed the notion of Mary's spiritual maternity (Leo XIII, *DS* 3262 and 3275, who quotes Jn 19:26 *Sq*). But this theme was never the subject of a definition. Vatican II mentioned the link Augustine makes between Mary and the church (*LG* 53 and 63–65, *COD* 892–94). But Pope Paul VI, in the margins of the conciliar text, insisted on proclaiming Mary "Mother of the Church," without giving this title a dogmatic significance (*DC* 61 [1964], 1544).

2. Mary's Mediation and Her Cooperation in the Work of Salvation

The Catholic tradition has exalted the role of Mary as auxiliary to the work of her Son, insisting at times on its importance in the believer's reception of salvation (Mary as mediatrix of all graces) and at times in the granting of salvation itself (Mary's cooperation in salvation, coredemption).

a) "Mediation" From the fourth century on Mary was viewed as having an intercessory role on behalf of virgins (*see* above, I.1.b). As time went on she was recognized as having a more extensive role: Bernard of Clairvaux called her the "mediatrix of salvation" (PL 182, 333B). The *Salve regina* (c. 12th century) called her an advocate (the same notion of protection and intercession is found in the Byzantine tradition). In 1896, to account for 1 Tm 2:5 (Christ the sole mediator), Pope Leo XIII specified that Mary was "the mediatrix alongside the mediator," thus emphasizing her subordinate and nonparallel role (Encycl. *Fidentem piumque, DS* 3321). But Mary's mediation, despite 20th-century requests, has not been defined. Vatican II only mentioned this title on one occasion (*LG* 62), in a marginal way, within the framework of a series of terms expressing Mary's intercession. However, Pope John Paul II made it an important theme of his encyclical *Redemptoris Mater,* but in speaking of "maternal mediation," "participant and subordinate," being expressed through the intercession of the Mother of God (*DC* 84 [1987], 399–401).

b) Cooperation in Salvation: "Coredemption"? The parallel between Eve and Mary tends to give Mary a role in the work of salvation that is as significant as that attributed to Eve in the Fall; the preservation from all sin (original sin for Catholics) makes Mary an exception and associates her with Christ; finally, Mary's yes to the angel is, as it were, the first act of salvation. Irenaeus (*Adv. Haer.* III, 22, 4) opposes Eve, a cause of death, to Mary, "cause of salvation" for herself and all of humankind (Heb 5:9 transposed from Christ to Mary). Ps.-Albertus of the *Missal* applies Gn 2:20 to Christ and to the Virgin, "a help similar to him." The title of *coredemptrix* emerged in the 16th century and became widely used in the 17th (Carol 1950, to be corrected by Laurentin in 1951). The idea would be found in Leo XIII. Pope Pius X declared in 1904 that "by virtue of Mary's communion of suffering and willingness with Christ, she has been deemed worthy to become the one who repairs the lost world" (Encyclical *Ad diem illum, DS* 3370). Pope Benedict XV produced a sacrificial reading of the Passion: the Virgin offers her Son, and one might say that with Christ she redeems humankind (*Inter sodalicia,* AAS 10, 1918, 182; *see* Carol 1950). Logic causes that which concerns Christ's works to flow back onto Mary, since her yes is the starting point of Christ's works. Pope Pius XI used the word "coredemptrix" in 1935 in a message broadcast by radio. The magisterium* has never made a decision about this title (intentionally avoided by Vatican II and thereafter), rightly a subject of controversy because of its ambiguity (the risk of diluting Christ's singularity) and its rejection by Protestants (*see* Barth* in his *Dogmatics*). The legitimate idea is that of the grace conferred upon Mary, in order that she might cooperate through the response of her faith in a salvation of which she is the first beneficiary.

3. The Marian Cult

a) Liturgy. The first feast with a partially Marian theme was that of the *Hypapante,* the meeting between Christ and Simeon, a feast recorded in Jerusalem and in Cappadocia from the fourth century onward. It was initially held on 14 February and then 2 February. The first strictly Marian feast was that of the commemoration of Mary (or Mary *Theotokos*), most often linked with the cycle of Christmas and Ephiphany, celebrated in Jerusalem on 15 August from the fifth century onward, and on other dates elsewhere (Mimouni 1995); and imposed throughout the empire as the feast of the Dormition and the Assumption on 15 August by the Emperor Maurice shortly before 600 (ibid. 67, n. 95). The Annunciation may go back as far as the fourth century, but there is insufficient documentation to establish this as fact. The Nativity of Mary on 8 September appeared, undoubtedly in Jerusalem, from the sixth century onward; and finally the Conception of Mary (or of Anne), on 9 December, was recorded in the eighth century in the East and passed to the West through the Byzantine territories in Italy. Here it was celebrated under the name of the Conception of the Virgin on 8 December; following some controversy, it was revived in the 12th century in England or in Lyons. These feasts gave rise to liturgical texts on the Virgin. From the sixth century onward, Romanos of Melos devoted several *kontakia* to the Virgin; the *Acathist Hymn* (recited standing) dates from the same era. Moreover, in the fourth century, Eastern *anaphora* (eucharistic prayers) mentioned the Virgin (J. Doresse—E. Lanne, *Un témoin archaïque de la liturgie copte de saint Basile, Bibliothèque du Muséon 47,* Louvain, 1960).

The fairly late and gradual emergence of these feasts, all of which have a basis in the Bible or in doctrine, precludes the received notion that the influence of pagan cults might have given birth to the worship of the Virgin in Christianity, even though, here and there, the risk of making Mary a divinity became quite real (the "Collyridians" according to Epiphanius, *Panarion* 79). This led to a gradual definition of the way in which the Virgin was to be honored as the mother of God (John Damascene, *Exposition of Faith* 88, 63, Kotter II, 205) and to the distinction between the cult of adoration *(latria)* owed to Christ and the honor accorded to creatures (cult of *dulia* for the saints, where the cult of Mary is emphasized as a *hyperdulia:* Thomas Aquinas, *ST* IIIa, q. 25, a. 5). For this reason, and to be rigorous about the terminology here, believers do not "pray" to Mary, but commend themselves to her prayer: "Holy Mary, Mother of God, pray for us."

b) Devotion. It was not until the middle of the fifth century (Barré 1963) that there was seen in the West a prayer* addressed to Mary (the Eastern *Sub tuum* is alleged to be older by a whole century, according to the papyrus quoted in I.3). The major prayers and Marian chants gradually took shape during the Middle Ages, during which time the devotion of the *rosary* became widespread, associating the repetition of the *Ave Maria* with the contemplation* of the mysteries* of Christ. Marian devotion is essentially liturgical in Orthodoxy; in Catholicism, such devotion has been the subject, on several occasions, of a readjustment (from the *Avis salutaires* in 1673 to Vatican II, which encouraged liturgical over private devotion, *LG* 66–67, *COD* 897–98, not without having also encouraged the liturgy itself to become recentered on Christ by eliminating a number of Marian feasts).

Among the themes of modern devotion, that of Mary's queenship became widespread from the Middle Ages in both the East and the West (Barré 1939); Luther* was hostile to this idea. It has been promoted by the Catholic magisterium (institution of the feast of Mary Queen of the World by Pius XII in 1954, *Ad coeli Reginam, DS* 3913–17), but not been made the object of a definition.

Conclusion: Vatican II, in a tight vote, integrated the Marian doctrine into the schema on the church (instead of making it a separate document): this would be Chapter 8 of *Lumen Gentium.* For the first time a council gave a synthetic presentation of the Virgin, situating her "in the mystery of Christ and of the Church": on the one hand, a very sober biblical* and patristic theology reduced the mysteries of the life of the Virgin to their significance within the economy of salvation; on the other hand, Mary was placed within the communion* of saints and the mystical body, and her link with the church was expressed through three major terms: member, type or model, and Mother in the order of grace. After the council Paul VI returned to the demands of the Marian cult (*Marialis cultus, DC* 71 [1974], 301–9, and John Paul II devoted an important encyclical to her that was largely in the same vein as the conciliar text. Present-day theological reflection emphasizes the theme of Mary-as-Servant and the link between Mary and the Holy Spirit.

● D. Casagrande (1974), *Enchiridion Marianum Patristicum,* Rome.
S. Alvarez Campos (1970–85), *Corpus Marianum Patristicum,* 8 vols., Burgos.
G. Gharib (1988–91), *Testi Mariani del Primo Millennio,* 4 vols., Rome.
♦ DICTIONARIES: *DThC* 7/1, 1927, 845–1218 (IC).
DSp 4/2, 1961, 1779–84 (Eve-M.); 10, 1980, 409–82 (M.).
Cath. 5, 1963, 1273–91 (IC); 8, 1979, 524–85 (M.).
TRE 22, 1992, 115–61 (M.).
REVIEWS: *EtMar* 5, 1947 (holiness of M.); 6–8, 1948–50 (As-

sumption); 9–11, 1951–53 (M. and the church); 12–15, 1954–57 (M., new Eve); 16–18, 1959–61 (spiritual maternity); 19–21, 1962–64 (mariology and ecumenism).

Conc(F) 188, 1983 (mariology and ecumenism).

ENCYCLOPEDIAS: H. du Manoir (Ed.), *Maria: Études sur la Sainte Vierge*, I–VIII, Paris, 1949–71.

R. Baümer and L. Scheffezyk (Ed.), *Marienlexikon*, St. Ottilien, 1988.

STUDIES: H. Barré (1939), "La royauté de M. pendant les neuf premiers siècles," *RSR* 29, 129–62, 304–34.

M. Jugie (1944), *La mort et l'assomption de la Sainte Vierge: Étude historico-doctrinale*, StT 114.

C. Balic (1948–50), *Testimonia de Assumptione Beatae Virginis Mariae ex omnibus saeculis*, Academia mariana, 2 vols., Rome.

G. Jouassard (1949), "M. à travers la patristique. Maternité divine, virginité, sainteté," *Maria* I, 69–157.

J.B. Carol (1950), *De Corredemptione* (Franciscan Institute Publications), Rome, Vatican.

H. Barré (1951), "M. et l'Église du vénérable Bède à saint Albert," *EtMar* 9, 59–143.

R. Laurentin (1951), *Le titre de corédemptrice*, Paris.

R. Laurentin (1952–53), *M., l'Église et le sacerdoce*, 2 vols., Paris.

H. Coathalem (1954), *Le parallélisme entre la Sainte Vierge et l'Église dans la tradition latine jusqu'à la fin du XIIe siècle*, AnGr 74, Rome.

Ch. Journet (1954), *Esquisse du développement du dogme m.*, Paris.

K. Rahner (1954), "Die Unbefleckte Empfängnis," *Schr. zur Th.* 1, 223–37; "Zum Sinn des Assumpta-Dogmas," ibid., 239–52.

Coll. (1954–58), *Virgo Immaculata*, 18 vols. (Acts from the Congress of Rome, 1954), Academia mariana, Rome.

A. Wenger (1955), *L'Assomption de la T.S. Vierge dans la tradition byzantine du VIe au Xe siècle: Études et documents*, Institut français d'études byzantines, Paris.

K. Rahner (1960), "Virginitas in partu," *Schr. zur Th.* 4, 173–205.

D.M. Montagna (1962), "La liturgia mariana primitiva (sect. IV–VI). Saggio di orientamento," *Mar.* 24, 84–128; "La lode alla Theotokos nei testi greci dei secoli IV-VII," ibid., 453–543.

W. Tappolet (1962), *Das Marienlob der Reformatoren*, Tübingen.

M. Thurian (1962), *M., Mère du Seigneur, Figure de l'Église*, Taizé.

J.A. de Aldama (1963), *Virgo Mater*, Granada.

W. Delius (1963), *Geschichte der Marienverehrung*, Munich-Basel.

R. Laurentin (1963), *La question m.*, Paris; (1965), *La Vierge au concile*, Paris.

H. Graef (1963–65), *Mary: A History of Doctrine and Devotion*, 2 vols., London.

O. Semmelroth (1965), *M. archétype de l'Église*, Paris.

R. Laurentin (1967), *Court traité sur la Vierge M.*, éd. postconciliar, Paris.

R. Caro (1971–73), *La homiletica Mariana Griega en el siglo V*, Dayton, Ohio.

A. Kniazeff (1990), *La Mère de Dieu dans l'Église orthodoxe*, Paris.

S.M. Perella (1994), "Il parto verginale di Maria nel dibattito teologico contemporaneo (1962–1994). Magistero-Esegesi-Teologia," *Mar.* 146, 95–213.

S.C. Mimouni (1995), *Dormition et assomption de M. Histoire des traditions anciennes*, Paris.

B. Sesboüé (Ed.) (1995), *Histoire des dogmes*, III: *Les signes du salut*, Paris, 563–621.

J. Pelikan (1996), *Mary through the Centuries: Her Place in the History of Culture*, New Haven and London.

MAURICE JOURJON AND BERNARD MEUNIER

See also **Chalcedon, Council of; Christ and Christology; Church; Cult; Ephesus, Council of; Vatican II**

Mass, Sacrifice of the

a) Concept. The concept of the Sacrifice of the Mass is a particular aspect of eucharistic (Eucharist*) theology* that took on a specific emphasis in the work of Luther* and, correspondingly, at the Council of Trent*, where it was made the object of a special decree, *De sacrificio missae*—the title was given by the editor of the council, though it corresponds closely to the content of the document. These two factors have earned it an important place in Western theology, in the 16th century and since. Even though Luther saw in it one of the three "Babylonian captivities" of Catholic eucharistic theology, the expression "Sacrifice of the Mass" is barely attested before him—though, having once been used by the reformers, it would be constantly employed by Catholics.

b) Liturgical Tradition. The idea of the Sacrifice of the Mass is supported by two characteristics of early practice. On the one hand it is based on the early Christian practice of offering eucharists for the dead, a tradition that underwent considerable development in the medieval Latin world, particularly in the final centuries before Luther; and on the other hand it is founded on the place accorded to the sacrificial aspect in the celebration of the Eucharist and in the very text of the eucharistic prayer*. In the course of celebration, as much in the East as in the West, the faithful were allowed and encouraged to bring an offering as a eucharistic sacrifice, and this offering was considered from a standpoint already to be seen in the work of Irenaeus*: the offerings presented to God* constituted the returning to God of the gifts that he had made to mankind. Expressed in terms borrowed from the prayer of Solomon (1 Chr 29:14), this idea found a place in the Antiochian anaphorae ("we offer you these gifts which come from you," *ta sa ek tôn sôn soi prospherontes*) and thence in Roman eucharistic prayer ("this offering taken from the wealth that you give us," *de tuis donis ac datis*). The eucharistic prayers—originally that of the apostolic tradition, then those of Antioch and Roman eucharistic prayer—also included in their anamnetic sections the idea of an offering of that which one commemorates, in a conception in which the act of offering is subsumed within the act of commemoration, and in a sense constitutes part of its realism.

Taking account of these characteristics shared by eucharistic prayers as a whole, Roman eucharistic prayer is distinctive in that the sacrificial aspect occupies a more important place in it than in the others, and to some extent overshadows the role of thanksgiving for the history of salvation*.

c) Theology. Until the 13th century, theology was hardly concerned with the sacrificial dimension of the Eucharist, being content to allude in passing to Augustine*'s formula (*Ep* 98, 9) according to which "Christ* is immolated every day in the sacrament*," and the Antiochene idea of the commemoration of the sacrifice (Peter Lombard, *Sent.* IV, 12, 5). Thomas* Aquinas, who gave a new emphasis to Christ's priesthood, did initiate the distinction between Eucharist as sacrament and Eucharist as sacrifice, but was far from making it the basis of his eucharistic theology. In contrast to other theologians, such as Duns* Scotus, who held that it was the *Ecclesia* that offered the sacrifice, Thomas moreover linked the act of offering with the priest's (presbyter/priest) consecrating role: a position that led to a divergence in the theory of mass offertories, which developed and grew in importance from the end of the Middle Ages.

The 16th-century Reformation rejected any notion of a church offering sacrifice. On the contrary, the Eucharist was God's offering to the faithful: "We allow ourselves to be done good by God" (Luther, *WA* 6, 364). The church's only offering was its thanksgiving.

In 1562, opposing Luther, the Council of Trent (*DS* 1738–59) defined the Mass as a true bloodless sacrifice, including a propitiatory sacrifice for the living and the dead, and stipulated that Christ at the Last Supper had instituted both the Eucharist and the priesthood*. The conciliar document was however careful to avoid the idea (which could be attributed to medieval theology) that Christ was "sacrificed anew" in the Mass (Gregory* the Great, *Dialogues* IV, 58, PL 77, 425), whereas his sacrifice had been offered once for everybody on the cross (Heb 9:4, 9:27). It seems, moreover, that the fact that communion* with the chalice was more expressive of the sacrificial aspect of the Eucharist was not highlighted. In any event it is clear that the sacrificial aspect of the Eucharist henceforth became an increasing concern of Catholic theology—for example in the work of Suarez*, who devoted a third of his treatise on the Eucharist to sacrifice.

The texts of Vatican* II, a council that could not but be attentive to the ecumenical dimension of this question, emphasize the unity of the Eucharist and the sacrifice on the cross (*LG* no. 3), state that the priest offers the sacrifice "sacramentally" (*PO* no. 2 and 5), note the unity between the spiritual sacrifice of all the baptized and the eucharistic sacrifice (ibid.), and finally entitle the chapter in *SC* that deals with the Mass *De mysterio missae*, where one might have expected *De sacrificio missae*.

● M. Lepin (1926), *L'idée du sacrifice de la messe d'après les théologiens depuis les origines jusqu'à nos jours,* Paris.

J. A. Jungmann (1953), "Das Gedächtnis des Herrn in der Eucharistia," *ThQ* 133, 385–99.

B. Neunheuser (Ed.) (1960), *Opfer Christi und Opfer der Kirche,* Düsseldorf.

E. Iserloh (1961), "Der Wert der Messe in der Diskussion der Theologen vom Mittelalter bis zum 16. Jahrhundert," *ZKTh* 83, 44–79.

K. Rahner, A. Häussling (1966), *Die vielen Messen und das eine Opfer,* 2nd Ed., Freiburg.

J. Chiffoleau (1980), *La comptabilité de l'au-delà,* Rome.

A. Duval (1985), *Des sacrements au concile de Trente,* Paris.

P.-M. Gy (1993), "Avancées du traité de l'eucharistie de saint Thomas," *RSPhTh* 77, 219–28.

PIERRE-MARIE GY

See also **Eucharist; Luther, Martin; Mystery**

Mathematics and Theology

The nature of the reality of mathematical objects and the objectivity of mathematical statements constitute two of the deepest problems in the philosophy of mathematics. Objectivity would imply a fundamental harmony between the structure of the human mind and the intelligibility of the universe; it would imply that knowledge arrived at through mathematical theories accurately represents the nature of the world and that there is an intrinsic harmony between the nonempirical, logical worlds of the mind and the empirical worlds of experience. But there are huge difficulties with such a view, and some have even suggested that logic itself is empirical. Mathematical objects and their properties do not have the a priori status Kant believed them to have. For example, whether the angles of a triangle sum to 180 degrees depends on whether the underlying geometry is taken to be Euclidean. It is possible, in other words, to construct an internally coherent mathematical theory without supposing that any reality exhibiting the properties corresponding to that theory can be found in the physical universe. Indeed, mathematics seldom regards the physical universe as an appropriate criterion to employ in deciding upon the intrinsic interest of its theories, and once the question is asked it is not easy to say why the physical universe should be the final arbiter of "reality" except under one particular preference.

A mathematics based on number will differ from another based on space. A unit Euclidean square has a diagonal of length root-two. This geometrical representation of number is seemingly elementary. But it is impossible to write down root-two as a finite decimal, to store it accurately in any physically realizable computing device, or to draw a line of length root-two in any physical medium except by chance, and even then one could never know that one had done so. Root-two, in other words, despite being a perfectly clear and intelligible number, has a problematic status as a property of any object in the physical world whether conceived under a numerical or spatial description. Yet despite these difficulties, mathematics as an instrument of the mind seems to have afforded human beings unprecedented powers to understand, predict, and control the natural world, the realm of the senses. The philosophy of mathematics therefore takes us directly into the deepest question of metaphysics concerning the nature of and the connections between reality, discourse, knowledge, and intelligibility, questions themselves dependent on assumptions about the place of human cognition in the universe.

This description shows a prima facie similarity between the mathematical and theological enterprises. It is possible to construct countless internally consistent theologies without supposing that there is an objective reality, a god or gods, to whom they refer. To the numerous major world religions can be added a large number of variants, each with its distinctive way of speaking about a god or some kind of ultimate reality. The nature of the reality of theological objects and the objectivity of theological statements constitute two of the deepest problems in the philosophy of religion. Theology and mathematics nevertheless differ in two important respects, one empirical and one experiential.

It seems possible to arbitrate between different mathematical theories about the physical world by employing empirical criteria. For example, we know from empirical evidence and criteria of epistemic economy that certain kinds of non-Euclidean geometry afford in some sense better models of the universe under Einstein's theories. Despite ongoing disagreements about detail, there is worldwide agreement about these general principles. Neither unequivocal evidence nor such a consensus can be claimed for any theology. Einstein asserted that to the axioms of any coherent geometry we need only add one, that this particular geometry models the universe, to obtain a theory about the world. To that extent we may take any internally consistent theology and add only one equivalent assertion, to obtain a theology that describes the reality of God. Both a mathematical theory and a theology are then tried in the fire of human experience: do they afford an adequate means to describe the reality of which human beings wish to speak?

Judaeo-Christian theology also posits an active reality of which it attempts to speak. Whereas mathematics strives to represent the properties of a physical or conceptual universe that is not actively seeking to communicate its truths to the mathematician, theology supposes the opposite: that God is actively engaged in trying to communicate with human beings, among them theologians. Theology therefore leaves room for existential conviction that overrides empirical criteria and ratification by like-minded competent persons, whereas mathematics does not. In mathematics what is a truth for one person must be a truth for another, other things being equal. There is no room for opinion in mathematics because the structure of logic eliminates the possibility that anything new can be introduced into the theory once the assumptions are granted. Proofs preserve truths; they do not generate them.

The conservative, preservative nature of logical deduction forces us to acknowledge that proofs only show us explicitly what is implicit in the assumptions we grant. No proof of the existence of God can therefore do more than demonstrate that our presuppositions assume that there is a God even though we cannot see that they do so. Moreover, proof has no force: if we dislike the correctly deduced conclusion of an argument, we are always at liberty to revise our assent to its assumptions. What we are not at liberty to do and remain rational is to insist upon the assumptions and deny validly deduced conclusions.

Mathematics is concerned with the exploration of the properties of a system of conceptual spaces that can be defined axiomatically. Those properties are often immeasurably complex, however simple their axioms, and frequently surprise us. For example, the system of natural numbers $\{1, 2, 3, \dots\}$ has proved sufficiently rich to generate conjectures that remain unproved to this day. Cantor was able to show in the 19th century that the irrational numbers such as root-two, known to the Greeks, cannot be counted. This century, quite unexpectedly, Kurt Gödel showed that a formal logical system capable of generating elementary arithmetic must permit undecidable propositions, and that such systems, if consistent, cannot prove their own consistency. Alan Turing and Alonzo Church showed that certain processes are noncomputable, and there are further classes of computation that cannot be completed because the number of calculations they require will always grow more quickly than any conceivable available computing power. In chaos and complexity theory the apparently insignificant constraints necessarily imposed upon the accuracy of the measurements we can perform (such as root-two) and the accuracy to which transcendental numbers can be represented in a computer have been shown to have potentially fatal consequences for our capacity to project the evolution of nonlinear systems into the future.

In all these cases, something conceived initially in terms of essentially simple axioms has been found to have properties of unforeseen and frequently counterintuitive complexity. The mathematics that began as the subservient child of the human mind has grown up to demonstrate the limitations of the conceptual capacities of the mind that created it.

James Clerk Maxwell once said, in a remark often wrongly attributed to Einstein, that insofar as the theories of mathematics refer to reality they are not certain, and insofar as they are certain they do not refer to reality. In this he reiterated Giambattista Vico's question about whether the truths of mathematics are found or made, for a mathematics that is made is certain because it is completely under our control and neither allows nor needs any reference to an external world to verify or authenticate it, whereas a mathematics that is found is uncertain because it can never proceed without perpetually referring itself back to the nature of the reality it purports to model. Once an axiomatic deductive system is defined, in other words, so are all its properties; it ceases to be necessary to ask whether those properties are "real" because they are properties of the system. We can proceed without reference to the world. And it is possible to do theology in the same way: to set up a system of assumptions and then to see what can be deduced from them without reference to the reality of an external, independent, autonomous God.

This illustration pinpoints the kernel of a difficulty we face in all our attempts to tie together God, humanity, and the world. While we model the world using mathematics, the world must seem autonomous and mechanical, even granted the difficulties of quantum mechanics. But the autonomy arises because the deductive conceptual tools we employ are autonomous and leave no room for newness to enter the system. We compensate for deficiencies in our models by making interim adjustments. We can rationalize the need for those compensations in many ways: by acknowledging that the model was inadequate; by accepting that the initial conditions were known with insufficient accuracy; even by acknowledging that there may have been worldly or divine forces involved that we had failed to take into account. What we seem reluctant to contemplate is the possibility that the world might not be susceptible to completely accurate mathematical modeling at all, for such a concession would lead us to doubt whether we can properly understand the universe. What is certainly true is that the world does not proceed on its way by solving differential equations.

Ever since Plato formulated the relationship between the particular and the general in terms of the theory of forms, human cognitive theories have struggled to understand the relationship between the two. Mathematics, as a theory of the mind, deals most comfortably with generality; it is most comfortable when least specific or quantified, as in geometry; the more accurate we need to be in terms of specific numbers associated with particular realities, the more clumsy and inaccurate it becomes. It remains a deep question whether mathematics is therefore an appropriate metaphor to use of the mind of God. Is God a Greek mathematician, a geometer, dealing with vast generality, or is God one who deals with the utterly specific and who allows the general to emerge from that specificity as a by-product of divine consistency and benevolence? Do we make a conceptual and even a theological mistake when we assume or insist that the world be understood mathematically and therefore in terms of boundless generality? Could it be that such general laws as we can discern in the universe are the emergent properties of a world governed by the deepest possible involvement of God in the singular and the particular, and that there is no traffic from the general to the particular at all, that specific events are not instantiations of universal forms, as Plato taught us, but the universal forms, like mathematics, necessary inventions of a human mind too limited to comprehend the majesty of God's specific and singular presence in the world?

Although mathematical proof proceeds by deduction, the hypotheses that mathematics seeks to prove are the products of mathematical intuition, and that intuition is based upon such things as aesthetic sense, as Henri Poincaré stressed, and heuristic power. Without good ideas, mathematics cannot proceed, yet even with good ideas many hypotheses defy proof or disproof.

It is from the work of Kurt Gödel that some of the most pressing speculations of the relationship between mathematics and theology have arisen in recent years. Gödel was able to show that sufficiently rich axiomatic systems admit the formulation of well-formed propositions that are undecidable in the system, and that such consistent systems are unable to prove their own consistency. The first result relates intimately to the capacity of some systems to refer to themselves. Such self-reference can introduce endless logical loops of the kind seen in other philosophical dilemmas. For example, if Epimenides the Cretan asserts "All Cretans always lie," then as a Cretan he is lying; but then all Cretans do not always lie, in which case what he says may be true, and so on. Or a relativist may say that all truths are only relatively rather than absolutely true, but this appears to be a universal truth, in which case there is at least one truth that is universally true, and so the assertion of the relativist is self-contradictory. Some have seen the undecidability of Gödelian statements as indications of the inherent superiority of the human mind over computation, even as a proof of the existence of an upwardly open hierarchy of intellectual power culminating in God.

The same sorts of claims follow the consistency result: if we cannot prove consistency, then we cannot be sure that in any system to which the theory applies there are not theorems whose contradictions are also theorems. This seems to be devastating for mathematics at a theoretical level, but in practice nobody worries about it, because when we have a good proof we know that a proof of the converse will not be possible. It is only in the general and abstract case that problems arise.

Most recently mathematics has been involved in issues germane to theology over computational questions and issues in artificial intelligence and the mind/body problem. The questions boil down to whether what something is made of makes a difference to what it can compute. Turing thought not, and so envisaged the possibility of a thinking machine; others think that there must be a biological substratum to thinking, that what things are made of does have a bearing on what those things can do, and so they deny that the brain is engaged in machinelike computation.

The philosophy of mathematics engages with questions about the ultimate intelligibility of the universe, for a universe of which mathematics is the preferred conceptual instrument is only as intelligible as that instrument can render it. Unresolved problems in the foundations of mathematics, in which no universal agreement exists, persist; and logicists, formalists, intuitionists, and pragmatists continue to debate central questions about actual infinities, constructive proofs, and alternative logics, suggesting that our confidence in mathematics as a monolithic homogeneous paragon of rationality is misplaced. The innocent equation of logical and empirical realities to which mathematics and its associated sciences are prone with their predominantly naive realism serves only to blind us to the possibility that the queen of human sciences may systematically mislead us about the nature of the world.

Is there an alternative? Theology in its best manifestations seeks always to be structured and guided by the nature of its divine object. The inner structure of theology, which we suppose to be its logic, is therefore constrained by the need at all points to connect with the revealed nature of God in scripture and tradition. There has always been a tendency for the logic of theology to set up systems with an autonomous structure that then mitigate against certain of these revealed truths. There is therefore a need for theology self-consciously to acknowledge the possibility of an unsystematic nominalism if it is to be true to the nature of the revealed reality of God, for the logos of God's being may well be contrary to the autonomous logic of our rationality. If that is so, then the logic that governs the universe may also be counter to the autonomous logic of the mathematical sciences; there may well be a contingency about the world that renders it unpredictable, unsystematizable, just because it exists as the creation of a God whose logos surpasses our logic. In that case, mathematics may, precisely by virtue of its autonomy, one day prove to be the consummation of all idols, a Tower of Babel that tempts humankind to reach for knowledge that lies by its nature beyond it.

Perhaps the most important parallel between mathematics and theology concerns the question of reference, the question with which we began. The nature of mathematics means that we can conduct a coherent conversation about mathematical objects without adjudicating on the question of their existence or its nature; much the same is true of theology. One cannot suppose that the quality of a conversation entails the existence of its subject-matter without conflating empirical and nonempirical worlds, as happens in logicism; one can scarcely ignore the need to understand what it is one converses about, pretending that it is sufficient just to manipulate the symbols, as in formalism; one can sympathize with those who wish to deny actual infinities and nonconstructive proofs, as in intuitionism; and one can deplore the effective unbelief of those content merely to identify a discipline with what those engaged in it actually do, as in pragmatism. The issues confronting us concerning the kind of realism theology envisages for its God are strikingly similar to those the philosopher of mathematics envisages for its objects. Both can continue relatively happily without considering such issues, but neither has any real purpose beyond that of a pastime unless it engages with the questions of ultimate reality that such issues entail.

● H. Poincaré (1902), *La science et l'hypothèse,* Paris.
D. Hofstadter (1979), *Gödel, Escher, Bach,* London.
L. Wittgenstein (1983) *Remarks on the Foundations of Mathematics,* Ed. Rush Rhees, G.E.M. Anscombe, Oxford.
P. Benacerraf and H. Putnam (Ed.) (1984), *Philosophy of Mathematics: Selected Readings,* Cambridge.
J.C. Puddefoot, *Logic and Affirmation: Perspectives in Mathematics and Theology,* Edinburgh.
R. Penrose, *The Emperor's New Mind: Concerning Computers, Minds, and the Laws of Physics,* Oxford.
M.A. Boden (Ed.) (1990), *The Philosophy of Artificial Intelligence,* Oxford.
J.N. Crossley et al. (1990), *What Is Mathematical Logic?* Oxford.
W.D. Hart (1996), *The Philosophy of Mathematics,* Oxford.
R. Hersch (1997) *What Is Mathematics, Really?* London.

JOHN PUDDEFOOT AND IRÈNE FERNANDEZ

Maximus the Confessor

580–662

1. Life

Maximus the Confessor, the great monk-theologian, was a champion of, and martyr for, Chalcedonian Christology* at its most exacting. Only the last part of his long life is reliably documented, from the time of his presence in Carthage (Whitsun 632) and above all from his involvement in the monoenergist and monothelite controversies (634). The whole of his earlier life remains for the most part unclear and open to debate. According to the traditional *Life,* he was for the most part in Constantinople, where, on completing his education, he fulfilled various important roles in the imperial administration before entering the monastic life around 614 at Chrysopolis (Scutari) on the Asiatic side of the Bosphorus. On the other hand, a Syriac biography of Maronite origin considers him a native of the upper Jordan valley (Golan). Orphaned young, he is said to have grown up in the Lavra of Saint Chariton (Palea lavra), an important center of Origenist controversies, which would explain the importance of their refutation in his writings.

According to this theory he took refuge in Constantinople during the Persian invasion of Palestine (613–14), and in 617, at Chrysopolis, would have met the young monk Anastasius, who was to become his lifelong disciple and biographer. Around 624–26 he evidently made a long stay at Cyzicus (Erdek) at the monastery of Saint George, in the company of bishop John, whose questions would inspire his expositions of ambiguous passages in the work of Gregory* of Nazianzus, and perhaps also his *Centuries on Theology and Economy.* In 626 the Persians and Avars attacked Constantinople, once again forcing Maximus into exile. It was undoubtedly at this time that he met some Severian bishops in Crete and perhaps, in Cyprus, the priest (presbyter/priest*) Marinos, with whom he was to correspond.

Having settled in Carthage around 630 he joined the Eastern community of Eucratas, led by Sophronius, the future patriarch of Jerusalem* (634–38), who enlisted his help to refute monoenergism*. He was still there in 645 at the time of his disputation with Pyrrhus, the deposed patriarch of Constantinople. He then went to Rome*, where he gave his signature, as a monk, on the occasion of the synod* of 649, which condemned monotheism*. Returning to Constantinople—in 652, according to the Syriac *Life*—he was arrested there in 654. Exiled to Bizya (Thrace) after an initial trial, he became involved there in a dispute with bishop Theodore in the summer of 656, which led to a harsher exile at Perberis. After the patriarchal synod had exiled him to Lazica (Caucasus) and ordered the cutting off of his hand and tongue, he died on 13 August 662. Nineteen years later, the third Council of Constantinople* (681), without naming him, would canonize his doctrine of the two wills in Christ*.

2. Works

For the theologian, Maximus's most important writings are first of all the *Replies to the 65 Questions* of the Libyan monk Thalassios on scriptural texts (Q.T., PG 90, 344–785, critical edition by Laga-Steel, CChr.SG, 2 vols.) and on difficult passages of Gregory of Nazianzus and Pseudo-Dennis*; and then the *Ambigua* (Amb.) I to Thomas and II to John of Cyzicus (PG 91, 1031–1418). Taking advantage of the opportunities offered by the subject texts, Maximus treats, more or less fully, the themes that stimulate his thought. Especially important are Q.T., Prol., 21, 22, 42, and above all 60, and Amb. 7, 10, 41, and 42, in which he clarifies more particularly the main elements of his theological synthesis.

The same is true of several minor works: the *Exposition of the Lord's Prayer* (Pater, PG 90, 871–910), the *Book of Asceticism* (Asc., PG 90, 911–56), and the *Mystagogy* (Myst., PG 91, 657–718). Following a literary genre common in the monastic tradition*, Maximus delights in condensing his thoughts into short "sentences" grouped into "decades" and "centuries." Examples include the *Four Centuries on Charity* (Char., PG 90, 959–1080), evidently one of his earliest works and one of the most widely disseminated, and the *Two Centuries on Theology and Economy,* sometimes known as the *Gnostic Centuries,* which are steeped in the influence of Origen (Gnost., PG 90, 1083–176). The first 15 sentences in the huge compilation of *Five Centuries on Various Subjects,* which is largely drawn from works by Maximus, are also con-

sidered to be authentic (PG 90, 1177–86). The *27 Theological and Polemical Opuscules* (ThePol., PG 91, 9–286) deal with a wide variety of topics relating to the christological controversies provoked by Monophysitism* and monothelitism. They include patristic anthologies (15, 27), definitions of philosophical or theological terms (14, 23, 26), and an account of the procession of the Holy* Spirit (10). Likewise, some of the 45 surviving *Letters* (Ep., PG 91, 363–649) are practically treatises. One such, in the spiritual field, is Ep. 2 on charity to John the Chamberlain; others, concerning christological controversies, are Ep. 13 and 19. Finally, on the question of Christology, the most important and explicit text is the account of Maximus's discussion with Pyrrhus, the deposed patriarch of Constantinople, at Carthage in July 645 (Pyrrh., PG 91, 288–353).

3. Maximus's Synthesis

Over the course of such a diversity of works, for the most part occasional and broken up into short sections—whether the two major collections Amb. and Q.T. or the treatises of monastic character such as Asc., Pater, and Myst.—there can be discerned the main outline of a synthesis firmly constructed around a small number of technical terms grouped into pairs or triads: being, being well, being forever *(einai, eu einai, aei einai);* movement, stability *(genesis, kin sis, stasis*—a triad opposed to the triad "henad, movement, stability" of Origen's followers); substance, power, operation *(ousia, dunamis, energeia).* More fundamental still is the pairing "organizing principle, mode" *(logos, tropos).*

It is above all in Q.T. 60 and Amb. 41–42 that Maximus clearly brings out the fundamental outline of his thought, organizing and sometimes correcting the Alexandrian theology of the Logos (above all that of the school of Origen) with the help of his constant reading of the Cappadocians, Gregory of Nazianzus, and especially Gregory* of Nyssa—and also, to a lesser extent, of Evagrius and the Areopagitic corpus. He deploys both Chalcedonian and post-Chalcedonian thinking on Christ to refocus this theology on the incarnate Logos. Christ is the organizing principle of creation and of the evolution of the cosmos. It is he who gives created beings the *logoi,* which ensure their stability. He guides their development according to modes *(tropoi)*—a new concept—and by his humility assumes human nature, which he restores to its original condition and leads to its final fulfillment by bringing it to share in his divine condition *(théôsis).* Thus God becomes all in all and everything is brought to unity in a *périchorèse* (circumincession*)—a term that Maximus seems to have been the first to use with a precise christological sense—which preserves the indispensable qualities of each nature.

Maximus explains this imposing synthesis first and foremost in a monastic perspective, setting out to develop the anthropological lines of reasoning that lead naturally to its fulfillment. While his reasoning is strongly inspired by the Cappadocian texts on the nature and condition of human development, his ascetic approach is largely based on the ideas of Evagrius, though he alters the emphasis of these in order to give prominence to the order of charity (Asc. and Ep. 2).

a) Ontology and Cosmology. In keeping with the dialectical mode that had dominated Greek thought since Parmenides and Heraclitus, Maximus's ontological thinking is organized in terms of the triple aporia of the absolute and the contingent, the one and the many, and being* and development, as employed by the Christian doctrine of Creation that ensures the inalienable, though relative, consistency of the second term. Its solution is found in the acknowledged polysemy of the word *logos,* whose various senses involve reference to a certain order and an organizing principle. For the tradition in which Maximus was working the divine *logos* was that in which and by which everything that exists acquires meaning and receives existence (Col 1:16). On the one hand the *logoi* of creatures, with all their differences and diversity, are merely parts of that (Amb. 42). On the other hand, inasmuch as they are "divine wishes" (*see* Clement of Alexandria and Origen), they may assume existence by means of his creative freedom (Amb. 7).

Here development comes into play: it is a necessary characteristic (*see* Q.T. 13) of created existence and indicates the "distancing" (Gregory of Nyssa's diastema) between divine immutability* and the intrinsic mutability of creatures. For this reason Maximus rejects the order of the Origenist triad, which begins with the status of *henad* (Amb. 7). This dynamism of created existence requires at the outset a beginning (*arkhè*), which supposes a "becoming" (*genesis*) that may take the form of generation (*gennèsis*). But this movement (*kinèsis*) tends toward a completion (*telesis*), which is stability (*stasis*), or participation in God's plenitude, and may therefore be called deification (*théôsis*). The three modes of existence—being, well-being, and eternal being—are shaped by the rhythm of the triad "substance, power, operation." The first is intrinsic to every nature by virtue of its being placed in existence, the second pertains to free will, but the last can only be attained by means of a divine gift that surpasses the potentiality of nature (Amb. 65). On occasions Maximus compares them to the three days in which the Creation was completed, or to the three days of the paschal triduum (Gnost. I, 50–60); and also to the three laws (the law of nature, the written law, and the law of grace, Amb. 65; Q.T. 64); or to the threefold birth of Christ by the flesh *(logos tou einai),* by baptism* *(logos tou eu einai),* and by the Resurrection* *(logos tou aei einai,* Amb. 42). Indeed, while the ontological *logos (logos phuseôs),* being intrinsic to each nature, remains identical in itself, its modes of existence *(tropoi tès huparxeôs)* may be altered or renewed. This distinction, borrowed from the Cappadocians, comes to play a vital part in Maximus's Christology.

b) Anthropology. In the works preceding his involvement in the monoenergist and monothelite controversy (634), Maximus's anthropology deals mainly with man's becoming: his status and role in the scheme of creation, his present condition after the original Fall, and the path of asceticism* that makes possible the fulfillment of his first vocation. The keynote of this anthropology is the perfect man, Christ, the incarnate Logos. The monothelite controversy forced Maximus to take a more considered approach to the structure of the human being, especially regarding the will. He drew support for this from the writings of the neo-Chalcedonian theologians of the sixth century and, through them, from Aristotelian ideas.

Maximus's thinking on human becoming is inspired by Gregory of Nyssa's *The Creation of Man* (PG 44, 123–256), though with reservations concerning the theory of a double creation, and with an emphasis on the unity of the hypostasis in a "compound nature" of soul and body—or of intellect *(nous),* soul* *(psukhè),* and body. Since man is created in God's image and according to his likeness, it is up to him to realize this image by exercising virtues* modeled on those of Christ, who gives him by grace* the status of divine filiation* (Amb. 42; Char. 3, 25; 4, 70). In so doing, man fulfils his double role of microcosm and mediator by the union of the five divisions: between the sexes, between paradise and the inhabited earth, between heaven and earth, between the visible and invisible worlds, and between uncreated and created nature (Amb. 41).

Adam*'s free decision to turn his "rational appetite" *(orexis logikè),* neutral in itself, not toward God but toward sensual pleasure involved him in the infernal dialectic of pleasure and pain *(hèdonè-odunè),* which can end only in death*. This is the interpretation Maximus gives, following Gregory of Nyssa, for the trees in Paradise (Q.T. Prol. and 43). Adam is imprisoned in self-love *(philautia)* and passionate love of the body (Char. 3, 8, 57, 59), the source of all vice. In this field Maximus takes his inspiration from the tradition of Evagrius, particularly in Asc. and Char. The normal exercise of the will, instead of being governed by reason*, is disrupted by the disturbance of the passions of sexual desire and anger (Q.T. Prol), whence the ambiguous nature of the "gnomic will" (Pater, PG 901–3). In one of his last writings Maximus offers an analysis of the various stages of voluntary activity (ThePol. 1), which would be taken up by John of Damascus and acquire classic status.

c) *Christology.* Until recently Maximus's thought has attracted the attention of theologians largely in a christological context. This focus is justified provided that his full breadth is recognized. Indeed from the very first lines of his earliest writings (Asc. or Pater) Maximus clearly sets out the fundamental aim of his thinking, offering both a general overview (Asc. 1) and a glimpse of its core: "The request for everything of which the Logos of God, in his kenosis*, became by his flesh the author, is contained within the words of the prayer. It teaches us to appropriate that fortune of which only God the Father*, by his Son, naturally mediating in the Holy Spirit, is the true dispenser *(khorègos),* since indeed the Lord Jesus* is, in the words of the divine apostle*, the mediator between God and mankind (1 Tm 2:5). By his flesh he makes manifest to men the unknown Father; by the Spirit he leads to the Father those men who are reconciled in Him" (Pater, PG 90, 876). Q.T. (22, 28, 60, 61) clarifies the various aspects of this "mystery* of Christ" (60) (as also Amb. 41, 42, and Gnost. 1, 66–67; 2, 23, 60).

By means of his incarnation*, taking on human nature within his unique divine hypostasis, the two natures remaining distinct "without confusion or alteration" in a single "compound hypostasis"—and not, as the followers of Severus maintained, a "compound nature" (Ep. 13)—Christ, the incarnate Logos, restores man to his original condition, created in the image and likeness of God, or rather for the perfection of that likeness by the path of virtue (Q.T. 53; ThePol. 1), shaping him after his own filial condition. With this in mind, Maximus never ceased to refine his observations on the ontological status of human nature and its activities—observations that occupy an important place in the Ep. (13, 15) and above all in ThePol., and which find their most consummate expression in the discussion with Pyrrhus of 645.

The monothelite controversy forced Maximus to go deeper into the structure and operations of the will in order to recognize the proper character of Christ's human will, as distinct from the divine will to which it willingly submits. This necessity would lead Maximus, as previously stated, to specify the modes and sequences of voluntary actions (ThePol. 4, 19, 25): an achievement that represents one of his major contributions to anthropology.

● Unfinished, the edition prepared by F. Combefis (Paris, 1675, 2 vols.), was completed by the important *Ambiguorum Liber* (F. Oehler, Halle, 1857) and reprinted by Migne (PG 90–91).

A few texts of lesser importance and of uncertain authorship were published by Epifanovic (Kiev, 1917).

CChr.SG, *Questions à Thalassios* (1992), *Ambigua* (1994), *Opuscules théologiques et polémiques* (1998), *Lettres* (1998), *Questions et difficultés* (1999), Paris.

J. Touraille (trans. 1985), *Centuries sur l'amour, Centuries sur la Théologie et l'Économie, Brève interprétation de la prière du "Notre Père,"* in *Philocalie des Pères neptiques,* fasc. 6, Bellefontaine.

◆ Articles "Maxime": V. Grumel (1928), *DThC* 10, 448–59; A. Cesera-Gastaldo (1962), *LThK*2 7, 208–10; I.-H. Dalmais (1980), *DSp,* 10, 836–47.

H. Urs von Balthasar (1941), *Kosmische Liturgie,* Einsiedeln (2nd Ed., 1961).

P. Sherwood (1952), *Annotated Date-List,* Rome.

P. Sherwood (1955) *The Earlier Ambigua of M. Conf.,* Rome.

L. Thunberg (1965), *Microcosm and Mediator,* Lund.

W. Völker (1965), *M. Confessor als Meister des geistlichen Lebens,* Wiesbaden.

A. Riou (1973), *Le monde et l'Église selon M. le Confesseur,* Paris.

J.M. Garrigues (1976), *M. le Confesseur: La charité avenir divin de l'homme,* Paris.

F. Heinzer and C. Schönborn (Ed.) (1982), *Maximus Confessor,* Fribourg (Switzerland).

P. Piret (1983), *Le Christ et la Trinité selon M. le Confesseur,* Paris.

V. Karayiannis (1993), *M. le Confesseur: Essence et énergies de Dieu,* Paris.

J.-C. Larchet (1996), *La divinisation de l'homme selon M. le Confesseur,* Paris; (1998), *M. le Confesseur, médiateur entre l'Orient et l'Occident,* CFi 208, Paris.

IRÉNÉE-HENRI DALMAIS

See also **Aristotelianism, Christian; Chalcedon, Council of; Constantinople III, Council of; Gregory Palamas; Monothelitism/Monoenergism**

Mechtild of Magdeburg. *See* Rhineland-Flemish Mysticism

Mediation. *See* Mary; Salvation

Meister Eckhart of Hohenheim. *See* Rhineland-Flemish Mysticism

---

Mendicant Religious Orders

The entry on monasticism* draws attention in the High Middle Ages to the decline in power of the traditional Benedictine monasteries as assertions of Christian values. The entry on Franciscan spirituality* analyzes the personal spiritual attitudes of Francis of Assisi. Both the diminution in the spiritual power of the monasteries and the personal spirituality of Francis of Assisi do however have important ecclesiological dimensions. Institutionalized mendicancy was the way in which the church met the challenge of the rise of a society based on feudalism and mercantilism, both of which put a premium on the private property whose legitimacy in any circumstances the early church had been reluctant to allow.

The term "mendicant orders" *(ordines mendicantes)* was used in the Second Council of Lyons in 1274 of those orders that had arisen in the 13th century and lived from begging. Its canon 23 suppressed all except Franciscans and Dominicans, giving temporary approval to the Hermits of Saint Augustine and the Carmelites, both to be formally approved in 1298. The number was to grow to 17 by 1993. Begging had become redundant by the 16th century, when the Council of Trent allowed corporate possessions to the mendicant orders, which by then included the Jesuits.

The mendicants not only bore witness to newly threatened Christian values, but also undertook necessary activities beyond the competence of either the monastic or the diocesan clergy. They fulfilled the need for a clerical force that was mobile and answerable directly to the pope, at whose disposition for apostolic missions they had to hold themselves ready. Such missions included preaching, the only means of religious instruction for the majority of the faithful, and also that part of the administration of the sacramental penitential regime pertaining to sins whose absolution was reserved to the pope. They were also entrusted with rights in respect of burials and the administration of other sacraments. Preparation for such work required training, and houses of study were founded by the new orders at Paris and sometimes elsewhere, often at Oxford or Cologne.

In time the mendicant orders took on the character of urban monasteries, with a spirituality based on the love of their neighbor shown by their pastoral activity. Their university training took them to the forefront of scholastic dispute, with various specific philosophical positions and tendencies associated with each order, and they filled the need to transmit to the faithful in towns a lay adaptation of monastic spirituality based on the canonical hours of the divine office. Inevitably their independence of the hierarchy and their superior powers led to clashes with the diocesan clergy, of which one of the most notable occurred in Paris between 1250 and 1260, and epitomized in the differences between the Franciscan Bonaventure* and the Dominican Thomas* Aquinas, whose order repeatedly found it difficult to enforce adherence to Thomist theology within its own ranks.

a) Franciscans.   Known as the Order of Friars Minor (O.F.M.) since 1517, the Franciscans, also called Grey Friars (in French "Cordeliers"), split into branches, including the Minorites and the Conventual, Reformed, Observant, and Discalced Franciscans. The ideal of Francis of Assisi, whose core was the penitential following of the impoverished Jesus in humble solidarity with society's weaker members, attracted a number of companions between 1206 and 1208. Francis sought ecclesiastical approval first granted by Innocent III in 1209–10 for his band of "penitents from Assisi." It expanded with surprising speed and decided in 1215 to seek formal ecclesiastical incorporation, granted when the rule was approved in 1221 and 1223.

Its evangelical base was concretized in the three vows of poverty, chastity, and obedience, but it embraced laymen as well as clerics. All worked for their living, falling back on begging when necessary. The continuity of the young order with Benedictine monasticism was ensured by prayer* in common and by making the aim of its preaching to believers and unbelievers alike simply the furthering of the praise of God by his rational creation, which had been the motive force behind the church's earliest formal worship, and which became the overriding purpose of Benedictine life. The spirituality of the Franciscans was that which had originally been personal to its founder.

By the middle of the 13th century the order had spread throughout Europe, and in 1245–46 founded its first mission in Asia. Expansion ceased with the end of the intense urbanization of Europe around the end of the 13th century, and the order's houses, heavily dependent on the alms and patronage available in the towns, found themselves open to exploitation by the towns and their more prominent citizens, who could pay through donations for the intercessory power of the prayers of the friars, whose churches and cemeteries also conferred a certain prestige.

Internal splits occurred between members of the order who wished to remain rigorously true to the obligations laid on them by Francis's *Testament* to keep true to the original rule and those, who won, who were willing to accept papal modifications to their constitutions, made as circumstances changed. Devotionally, all branches of the Franciscans were united by a characteristic blend of devotions centering on Christ's humanity, the Blessed Sacrament, the name of Jesus, and the Virgin. Ecclesiologically, their readiness to place themselves at the disposition of the pope, notably for missions to pagan countries, again showed the church's power to react to new needs and new situations by gestating an appropriately institutionalized response. In the case of the Franciscans, that response included the establishment from the beginning of an equivalent order for women and of a lay "third" order for the married, all linked closely together by their common spirituality and devotional attitudes.

b) Dominicans.   The Dominicans, known as the Order of Preachers (O.P.) and called "black friars," were founded by papal bull in 1216 with constitutions incorporating a version of the Augustinian rule (*see* monasticism), modified to ensure retention of the contemplative element in their spirituality. Innocent III had insisted at the Fourth Lateran Council in 1215 that the necessary approval for the new group would be granted only if they chose an old rule. Their aim, specifically to bring about the salvation of souls by preaching the gospel, was confirmed by papal mandate in 1217, and extended to the whole Christian world. In other words, the Dominican Order from the beginning exclusively devoted itself to fulfilling the church's obligation to announce to the world the gospel tidings. Its monastic, penitential, and ascetic norms were subordinate to its preaching role and, like the Benedictines, the Franciscans, and others, their assumption of part at least of the church's mission gives their foundation and success fundamental ecclesiological significance.

The evangelical poverty practiced by their founder, Saint Dominic (1170–1221), and enjoined by him on his companions, was as strict as that of the Franciscans and was written into the Dominican constitutions in 1220, intensifying the young group's participation in the new testimony to Christian values required by the developments in secular Western society. Its effectiveness was increased by the importance it attached to theological learning and to the study required to achieve it. Strong links with the universities of Paris and Bologna made clear the commitment of the group to intellectual endeavor, and the nature of their apostolate required mobility rather than stability of territorial presence.

Like the other early-13th-century foundations, the Dominicans, in adapting the Augustinian rule, in fact moved away from a strictly contemplative spirituality toward one compatible with missionary life, although it is still usual to speak of their spirituality as a combination, "contemplative in action," which other groups were to take as a model. The Dominicans also found that their apostolate created a greater need for priests in their ranks than had been experienced by the more purely contemplative orders.

Dominic himself had traveled round the south of France three times before devoting himself to the existence of a wandering preacher, traveling on foot to convert the Albigenses. When joined by companions he established a first house in Toulouse and an asylum for women threatened by heresy whose inmates eventually became an order of nuns. He became associated with the anti-Albigensian crusade called by Innocent III under the leadership of Simon de Montfort, and with its instrument, the papal inquisition. The order drew heavily on the educated laity for its recruitment, which meant establishing houses in the larger towns, where even in the High Middle Ages good schools were to be found, leading inevitably to some clashes with the diocesan parish clergy. Only toward the end of the 13th century were foundations made in the smaller central European towns.

As papal preachers with special powers, however, the Dominicans were also heavily involved in preaching both the Crusades* and their attendant indulgences*, including that to which Luther* took such exception. They were to be permanently associated with the Inquisition, both in Spain, where it was a civil institution, and elsewhere. It is, however, necessary to point out that Dominican spirituality also led, alongside the missionary activity of teaching, to the contemplative heights attained by some of the Rhineland mystics, like Meister Eckhart, John Tauler, Henry Suso, and others. Many of them were Dominicans. In theology the Dominicans led an intellectually humanizing movement that regarded human reason as participating in divine rationality, so that human rational search for meaning in the cosmos was necessarily correlative to divine revelation. Often seen as a recourse to Aristotle in place of the Platonic inspiration of early Christian theology, this approach came to be known as the *via antiqua,* and was regarded as overnaturalistic

by certain followers of the Franciscan tradition, notably Ockham (c. 1285–1349), who founded the *via moderna,* based on the absolute transcendence of God above his creation. Christian moral norms were revealed and did not necessarily have of their nature to conform to the moral exigencies of rational beings.

Western society outgrew the need for a Christian witness based on mendicancy, as distinct from individual poverty. The norm was altered by allowing the orders themselves to own property and to accept endowments for pious purposes. A legal means was devised to allow the Franciscans to enjoy revenue without themselves owning the capital from which it derived. From the beginning their constitutions allowed Jesuit colleges to possess capital and to receive endowments, with only the houses of their professed fathers obliged to live from alms. As the socioeconomic foundations of society moved on, the ecclesiological functions of its religious orders necessarily changed, usually demanding the appearance of new congregations to challenge new values and new circumstances. Mendicancy in the strict sense became obsolete.

● J. Morrman (1968), *A History of the Franciscan Order from Its Origins to the Year 1517,* Oxford.
P.L. Nyhus (1975), *The Franciscans in South Germany, 1400–1530,* Philadelphia.
J.B. Freed (1977), *The Friars and German Society in the Thirteenth Century,* Cambridge, Mass.
A. Rotzetter (1977), *Die Funktion des franziskanischen Bewegung in der Kirche,* Schwyz.
D. Berg (Ed.) (1992), *Bettelorden und Stadt,* Werl.

ANTHONY LEVI.

Mennonites. *See* Anabaptists

Mercy

The Latin word *misericordia,* mercy, derives from the word describing one who is *misericors,* one whose

heart is moved by the sight of the suffering of others. This implies that mercy is applied to one of the aspects of human sensibility. However, by means of a resolute anthropomorphism*, it is very much upon God* that the Latin version of the Bible* confers this attribute. Not including the New Testament, the Vulgate employs the term 273 times, to which one must add the 137 occurrences of the verb *misereor* and the 31 uses of the adjective *misericors*: in the vast majority of cases, these different lexemes refer to the divine actor. It is therefore clearly as a divine attribute* that the Latin Bible represents *misericordia*.

It remains to be determined which Hebrew lexicon covers this family of words. Since it is necessary to eliminate the Old Testament texts that were not originally written in Hebrew, our discussion can be based on only 369 occurrences. Usage reflects three Hebraic roots: *râcham, chânan,* and *châsad*. Commentators have focused on the first root, while pointing out that the plural noun that derives from it *(râchamîm),* translated as "compassion," has as its singular *rèchhèm,* which in turn designates a woman's uterus. The biblical attribute of mercy thus discreetly presents the divine actor under a maternal aspect. Henceforth the pairing "justice*/mercy," which appears in every section of the Hebrew Bible, could be interpreted as designating a symbolic wholeness that integrates both paternal and maternal features.

In the absence of a rigorous definition of these two terms one can at least attempt to describe them. While the attribute "justice" connotes severity and an uncompromising quality, but also the transcendence of divine sanctity, that of "mercy" refers to a fundamental compassion, to the understanding kindness of a God who "knows our frame" (Ps 103:14), and who has always shown himself capable of clemency and forgiveness.

It must be noted that the pair "justice/mercy" appears in the texts of the Qumran (1QSI, 26–II, 1), and in intertestamentary literature (intertestament*) (*2 Ba 48,* 17–18). But this literature, following the example of the Bible, already has a tendency to overestimate the latter term to the detriment of the former: (*Test. Zab.* 8, 1–3).

In considering this "attribute of mercy," rabbinical literature was quick to derive, in turn, this essential ethical consequence: if the vocation of man is to imitate God, he must develop this quality within himself. Thus the Talmud states: "Since God is clement and merciful, be thou also clement and merciful" (*TB Shab,* 133 b). What is more, at the beginning of our era, Rabbi Gamaliel would even assert, in commenting on Dt 13:18: "He who shows himself merciful towards others will be treated by the Heavens with mercy, whereas he who shows no pity for his fellow man will have no right to the pity of the Heavens." Similarly, the whole Jewish people was urged, as indicated by an-

other text in the Talmud, to be "merciful and modest, and to practice acts of kindness" (*TB, Yev.* 79a).

The Islamic tradition would also examine this divine attribute. Thus, all the *surahs* of the Koran open with the *basmalah,* a formula where the root *râcham* is repeated again and again, since it is voiced in this way: *bismillâh al-Rachmân al-Rachîm,* "In the name of God, the Kind, the Merciful." Moreover, numerous commentaries are devoted to the exact difference between these two divine titles.

The New Testament had already developed all of these features. Drawing its lexicon from the Septuagint, it made great use of words derived from the roots *eleein* (to pity), *oikteirein* (to have compassion for), *kharis* ("grace*"), and *splankhna* ("entrails," but above all "compassion")—the very words that the Greek translation used to render the three Hebraic roots mentioned above.

In perfect compliance with the Jewish tradition* the New Testament also revealed the consequence, at the level of human behavior, of the revelation* of divine mercy, both in the "descending" direction ("Be merciful, even as your father is merciful," Lk 6:36) and in the "ascending" direction ("Blessed are the merciful, for they shall receive mercy," Mt 5:7). The originality of the New Testament corpus on this point consisted in its transferring the traits of divine mercy to Jesus*. To be sure, God was still described as the source of this mercy—and from time to time there were unflinching evocations of his entrails *(splankhna)* of mercy (Lk 1:78), and even of their "plurality" *(polusplankhnos:* Jas 5:11)—but Jesus also possessed this "maternal" characteristic (12 instances), as well as the "pity" and "compassion" of the one who sent him.

The church* of the early centuries would do little more than develop various notions that it had received from Scripture*. In the liturgy the call for Christ*'s mercy would be condensed into the brief formula *Kyrie eleison.* This formula, which appeared in Greek language liturgies during the second half of the fourth century, would be adopted somewhat later by the Roman liturgy, and then progressively by the entire Latin-speaking world. (It should be noted that the Latin liturgy does not translate the *Kyrie eleison* but adds to it a twin formula, also Greek, *Christe eleison.*) In the Greek world the *Kyrie eleison* constituted the response of the people to the litanies of intercession recited by the deacon*. Clearly the omnipresence of this invocation in the liturgical text polarized the attention of the faithful onto the divine attribute of mercy—at least this is what is suggested by Saint John Chrysostom* (*Homercy in Mt.* 71, 4). And even well before the fourth century, Christian authors had frequently evoked the *eleos* of God (*I Clemercy* 9,1), his *oiktirmos* (*I Clemercy* 20, 11), or his *splankhna:* "Always merciful and kind, the Father is touched by those who fear him; with gentleness and goodness, he places his grace upon those who come to him with a simple heart" (*I Clemercy* 20, 11).

In Latin the privileged term remains that of *misericordia*, whether applied to God (Tertullian*: *Paen.* 2; Cyprian*: *Laps.* 15; Ambrose*: *In Ps.* 118:8, 22) or to human beings (Tertullian: *Paen.* 1; *adu. Marc.* 4, 27; Ambrose: *Off.* 1, 11, 38). Augustine* would justify this notion in opposition to the criticism voiced by the philosophers: "The stoics, it is true, habitually blame mercy. However, how much more honorable it might have been for our Stoic to be moved by pity for a man to save him from danger, than to be troubled by the fear of a shipwreck....Then what is mercy if not the compassion of our heart for the misery of others, moving us to help them if we can?" (*Civ. Dei* IX, 5).

It was in the monastic world that the exercise of mercy would find its broadest scope. Through this virtue "beyond all virtues*" the monks could set off on the royal path of imitation of God. Among the countless illustrations one might provide of such an ideal, the following two "apothegms" might be retained, deriving as from the very earliest monasticism*, that of the Desert Fathers in Egypt. They immediately proposed what one could call a "maximalism of mercy": "A brother who had sinned was chased from the church by the priest; and abba essarion stood up and went out with him and said, 'I too am a sinner.' A brother questioned father Poemen and said, 'If I see a fault in my brother, is it good to hide it?' The old man said, 'In the hour where we hide the faults of our brother, God also hides ours; and in the hour where we bring forth the faults of our brother, God also brings forth our faults' " (*Apothegms*, Systematic collection, IX, 2 and 9).

By following the direction indicated here, one could develop the spiritual aspects of the virtue of mercy, as elaborated by the monastic tradition. All the same, the strictly theological current would not fade away, however. Where the Latin tradition was concerned it would, on the contrary, expand in two directions. Until the 13th century the primary task of theology* remained that of commenting on the Scriptures. Authors encountered therein the pairing "justice/mercy," and they would try to define each concept in terms of the other. For example, Bernard* of Clairvaux considered that the tension between them would only be resolved at the end of time: "At the time of the Judgment*, he will exalt mercy more than judgment" (*In. Cant.* 73, 2, 4). But later, mercy would disappear (*Dil.* 15, 40), no longer having any purpose. In the *Summa Theologica*, Thomas* Aquinas would mention mercy as beatitude* (Ia IIae, q. 69) and as virtue (IIa IIae, q. 30). For him it corresponded with the gift of counsel (IIa IIae, q. 52, a. 4).

The relation of justice to mercy is in the background of the debate on predestination* that followed in the wake of Augustine's work. It would thus resurface among the Carolingian theologians, in the *Cur Deus homo* by Anselm* of Canterbury, and later in the lively controversy that surrounded the Reformation. If Augustinianism* seemed clearly to favor the attribute of justice, it aroused counterreactions. It is no doubt in this perspective that one can interpret the apparition in the 17th century of devotion to the Sacred Heart, which moved rapidly from being a private devotion to one inscribed in the liturgy as a norm. Did it not counterbalance the austerity of the then-dominant Jansenist tendencies?

This last example is proof of a tendency toward "feminization," applied here to the figure of Christ. Certain mystics* went very far in this direction. Julian of Norwich, for example, an English mystic of the 14th/15th century, did not hesitate to speak of "Jesus our mother." But more often it was to the figure of the Virgin Mary* that the attribute of mercy was assigned. In the 12th century the *Salve Regina* designated Mary as *Mater misericordiae*, and after Bernard of Clairvaux a host of spiritual authors would develop, at times with a considerable lack of discretion, the evocation of this "mothering" (*In Nat. beat. Mar.* 7). Indisputably, the theme of mercy raised the issue of the "feminine in God."

Apart from a few isolated examples in magisterial texts (John Paul II's encyclical *Diues in misericordia*) or in certain spiritual writers (the "Revelation of Merciful Love" to Sister Faustine), it does not seem that the present era has developed this particular theme to any degree. And yet, philosophers and theologians have resolutely reevaluated the notion of forgiveness—perhaps within the context of "crimes against humanity," which in the 20th century have attained a global dimension. Their thoughts and ideas have contributed to a revival—although somewhat reformulated —of the theme of mercy. For example, the principle according to which "there can be no forgiveness without justice" is a direct echo of the most ancient biblical tradition.

● V. Jankélévitch (1957), *Le pardon*, Paris.
A. Gouhier (1969), *Pour une métaphysique du pardon*, Paris.
W. Haase (1974), "Großmut," *HWP* 3, 887–900.
T. Koehler (1980), "Miséricorde," *DSp* 10, 1313–28 (bibl.).
S. Breton (1986), "Grâce et pardon," *RSPhTh* 70, 185–96.
O. Abel (Ed.), *Le pardon*, Paris.
A. Chapelle (1988), *Les fondements de l'éthique*, Brussels.
D. Gimaret (1988), *Les noms divins en islam—Exégèse lexicographique et théologique*, Paris.
J.-Y. Lacoste (1996), "Pardon," *DEPhM* 1069–75.

DOMINIQUE CERBELAUD

See also **Attributes, Divine; Ethics; Grace; Heart of Christ; Imitation of Christ; Judgment; Life, Spiritual; Love; Penance**

Messalianism

a) History. In the second half of the fourth century, starting in Mesopotamia and spreading to Syria and Asia Minor, a movement called Messalianism grew up in monastic circles. The word *Messalian,* constructed from the Syriac participle of the verb "to pray," means "one who prays." The movement soon joined the list of heresies* and was condemned as such. Its first mention dates from about 370, when Ephraim and Epiphanius advised of its presence in Mesopotamia and in Antioch. Ephraim insisted that these "prayers" (those who pray) were guilty of debauchery and/or of agitation and enthusiasm (the Syriac word chosen has two meanings). Epiphanius reproached them for deviating from social norms by their allowing men and women to live together and by refusing to work. He did not, however, accuse them of doctrinal deviation.

After 380, the Messalians suffered official condemnations. The first of these condemnations seems to have been carried during the synod* held in Antioch under Bishop Flavian's guidance (therefore after 381). Along with Flavian sat not only the clerics* from Syria but also a bishop from Byzantine Armenia and another from Isauria, which seems to indicate that monks suspected of Messalianism were in those regions too. This synod decided to expel the Messalians from Syria and Mesopotamia. A little later, doubtless, another synod held in Side, in Pamphylia, in which Amphilochus of Iconium played the chief role, also condemned them, which perhaps suggests that the exiles had taken refuge in that region. In any event, at the beginning of the fifth century the controversy was centered in Asia Minor. Bishop Atticus of Constantinople (406–25) wrote to the Pamphylian bishops asking them to evict the Messalians. A synod held in Constantinople in 427 under Atticus's successor, Sisinnius, repeated this request. The following year, a law against heretics mentioned them, also calling them Euchites or Enthusiasts.

In 431 the Council of Ephesus was also apprised of this problem and anathematized the Messalians. It also condemned propositions from a work that it attributed to them, the *Asceticon,* which was doubtless made up of writings circulated under the pseudonym of Macarius the Great (and which can probably be attributed to Symeon of Mesopotamia, who was active between 380 and 390 and in 430). The *Asceticon* is a collection of texts in which the work of "Messalian" communities can still be detected today.

b) Doctrine. Heresiologists and synods accused the Messalians of two kinds of errors, doctrinal and moral. Messalian heretical doctrines were said to be: (1) that a demon* has a permanent abode in everyone's soul*, a demon that baptism* has not proved capable of expelling and that prayer* alone can evict, and (2) prayer summons the Holy* Spirit into the soul and promotes union with the celestial Bridegroom, which gives rise in the perfect ones to freedom from the passions,* to impassiveness. In addition to these doctrinal statements, the Messalians were accused of claiming to acquire inspiration from visions and dreams, of claiming to be prophets*. They were also accused of spurning work*, even work demanded by charity, preferring instead to sleep (during which time they experienced their dreams). Finally, they were accused of despising the sacraments*, the ecclesiastical hierarchy*, and institutions, as being futile for spiritual people, and of perjuring themselves, even of exhibiting sexual license—things of no moment to the perfect ones.

Some accusations about the behavior of the Messalians are doubtless only exaggerations or examples of individual instances. But what is the truth about the doctrines for which they stood reproached? Elements of these doctrines certainly appear in the works of Pseudo-Macarius, but they have been taken out of context and isolated from the overall spiritual vision that these texts offer. A terminological analysis of the *Macariana* seems to show clearly that the Messalian crisis was inspired by the collision of two different cultural worlds—the world of Syriac-speaking monks and the world of Greek-speaking bishops and theologians. Pseudo-Macarius (who wrote in Greek) had borrowed his central themes from Syriac monasticism as well as from the poetic and symbolic images and phraseology in which were expressed an intensely lived spiritual experience* (metaphors of mixture, of uninhabited regions, and of filling in). The ambiguity of this language, in which the sensory experience of grace* occupies a predominant place, and which has undeniably led on occasion to misinterpretation in Greek-speaking circles, explains the accusations of heresy brought against the Messalians.

In fact, Messalianism was a movement lacking either a leader or precise doctrines. The proper term should be *Messalian tendencies*. These tendencies continued to appear in monastic circles in the East and even in the Christian West. Egypt was affected by them, and in Carthage there were also "Euchite" monks, against whom Augustine* wrote a volume about the labor proper to monks. All the same, these tendencies show differences that are sometimes deviations. The Pseudo-Macarian works are the first witness to that. In their present state they reveal, through the revisions they have undergone, that they echo discussions in the circles that read them. In any case, their rereading and rectification by orthodox authors, as well as by the author of the *De Instituto Christiano* (who may have been Gregory* of Nyssa), show their influence, and that influence has continued to make itself felt in Byzantine monasticism.

- H. Dörries, E. Klostermann, M. Kroeger (Ed.), *Die 50 geistlichen Homilien des Makarios*, PTS 4, 1964.
- Ps.-Macaire, *Œuvres spirituelles* I, SC 275.
- ♦ J. Gribomont (1972), "Le dossier des origines du m.," in *Epektasis, Mélanges patristiques offerts au cardinal J. Daniélou*, Paris, 611–25.
- H. Dörries (1978), *Die Theologie des Makarios-Symeon*, Göttingen.
- R. Staats (1982), "Beobachtungen zur Definition und zur Chronologie des Mess.," *JÖBG* 32, 235–234.[AuQ3]
- C. Stewart (1991), *"Working the Earth of the Heart": The Messalian Controversy in History, Texts, and Language to AD 431* (bibl.), Oxford.
- A. Guillaumont (1996), "Mess.: Appellations, histoire, doctrine," "Le témoignage de Babaï le Grand sur les mess.," "Le baptême de feu chez les mess.," in id., *Études sur la spiritualité de l'Orient chrétien*, SpOr 66, 243–81.

PIERRE MARAVAL

See also **Hesychasm; Monasticism; Orthodoxy; Spiritual Theology**

Messianism/Messiah

1. Vocabulary

Today, the term *messianism* is frequently used to express expectation. In the context of politico-religious movements this expectation often applies to radical, permanent, historical change. This is a derivative exploitation and extension of a word that comes from traditional biblical exegesis*, beginning with the New Testament itself.

The Hebrew word *mâshîach* in the Old Testament, translated in English as "messiah" (and in Greek, *Christos*, giving the title of "Christ"), rarely or never refers to the eschatological savior. It means "anointed" and designates either the historical king or the high priest (six times) and, in one occurrence, (metaphorically) the Fathers (Ps 105:15). The New Testament confers eschatological value on the word by applying it to Jesus*. Further, it gives a new reading of certain Old Testament texts, granting them prophetic value in light of the event of the message and the person of Jesus. The term *messianism* is applied to these representations as a whole.

2. Problematic

Generally speaking, modern critical research eschewed this theological apologetics in favor of an approach focused on the meaning of the texts in their original political, economic, and social environment. In so doing, it gradually turned away from the traditional reading to the point of losing interest, at least temporarily, in this field of biblical* theology. We might add that the shift in current language from a personal figure (messiah) to a grouping of rather vague representations (messianism) probably contributed to that disaffection. More recent research is returning to a focus on this field, where numerous questions remain unanswered.

Is the figure of the messiah confused with the royal figure? Does it suit other personages related to "the last days" (eschatology*)? What is the connection between messianic expectation and the hope* of salvation* in general? And what about the sources and mechanism of this expectation, the "eschatological" nature of this hope? If the "eschatological" is confused with the apocalyptic*, then the only messianic text would be Daniel 7:13! And then only if the personage of the "Son of man" is recognized as a personal character, which is widely contested. The broader sense of the term has led to the notion of a "messianism without a messiah," which is, to say the least, paradoxical. In this sense "messianism" would encompass the eschatological representations of the "God* who is coming" or the "reign of God" (Kingdom* of God). These are genuine difficulties. It remains that Christian theology* has to take into account relations between the Old and New Testaments. Since the church* and Jesus himself referred to the Old Testament, it is fitting to analyze Old Testament texts that refer to a coming Savior, even if they are inchoate. In this perspective we suggest an inventory of texts that might have a relation, be it distant, with the figure of Jesus.

3. Basic Representation: The Figure of the King

The biblical messiah originates in the royal line, in particular that of David, designated as the "anointed of God" (see 1 Sm 16; 2 Sm 5:3). The institution of monarchy is the enduring framework of the complex ensemble of representations known as messianism. Other models later condensed around the royal figure, which remained the reference model. Israel* borrowed the royal institution from its Middle Eastern neighbors; as a result it is charged with an ideology partially shared with different sectors of that cultural area. In the organization of the state (city) as in that of the cosmos, the king played a central role. The royal psalms* broadly reflect that ideology. The king's mission is to ensure peace* on the borders and, to this end, subdue the nation's enemies (Ps 2 and 110). He is also the guarantor of order in society* and in the cosmos*. He must ensure shalôm—peace, social harmony (Ps 72:1f., vv. 12–14)—and also the fertility of the fields (Ps 72:6f., v. 16). The king becomes the mediator of blessing* (Ps 21:7).

This foreign ideology, riddled as it was with pagan sacralism (paganism*), was something from which Israel had to distance itself. The solution was to cast off polytheistic references and leave the historical initiative to YHWH. Deuteronomist theology sometimes refers to a specific covenant* with David (and his descendants) (Ps 89:4f., vv. 20–38). However, the solemn dynastic promise* of 2 Sm 7:1–17 that constitutes the charter of monarchy is placed at the very heart of the Sinai covenant, to avoid the dangers of an overcentralized power and safeguard divine transcendence. The king takes responsibility for the covenant and protects its interests (Renaud 1994a), but God remains master of the game. The king is altogether relative to YHWH. This is clearly indicated by the title "anointed of God" (notably in the books of Samuel), which has no equivalent in any other contemporaneous religious system. The effect of that theology was to reinforce the collective dimension of the monarchy. The Davidic king, "son of God" (Ps 2:7, a designation inherited from Middle Eastern royal ideology) embodies Israel, "child of God" (Hos 4:22, 11:1, etc.).

This double current of royal ideology and covenant theology mutually reinforcing each other crystallizes the hope of the people around the figure of David. He becomes an emblematic and paradigmatic figure, as shown in the prophetic oracles of Isaiah 7, 9:1–6, and 11:1–9 and Jer 23:5f. There is no doubt that, save rare exceptions (perhaps Hezekiah, Josiah), none of the historical kings fulfilled the ideal. The monarchy, whether in the north or the south, left memories of leaders unfaithful to their mission. And yet from one royal birth to another, one coronation to the next, hope for fulfillment of the promises was reborn. The gap between painful reality and the awaited realization did not undermine the people's hope. Far from fading, the promises were constantly reinforced, nourishing hopes for an empire that would place Israel at the center of the world (see Ps 2 and 110). This hyperbolic language was of course descended from the court rhetoric of the great empires, transferred to the petty kings of Palestine. It was also the fruit of hope in an idealized personage who would initiate an era of peace and happiness.

4. Eschatological Messianism

a) Messianism and Eschatology*. The ruin of Jerusalem and the temple*, the collapse of the royal and priestly institutions that structured the life of the community, and the deportation of the nation's elite, all these provoked a grave psychological trauma as testified in Psalm 89:39–51 and brought about a profound theological upheaval. Jeremiah declared that the covenant was broken (Jer 31:32). The institutions inherited from the past no longer functioned as sources of salvation. Israel was forced to project itself into the future. The center of gravity shifted from the past to the future, at least in certain theological currents. Jeremiah announced a "new covenant" (Jer 31:31–34). The monarchy had disappeared but not the hope attached to it, and this hope was carried over into the expectation of a coming messiah, a mediator of a stable and permanent salvation. This hope can rightfully be qualified as eschatological, even if the designation is subject to terminological debate. We consider here as "eschatological" all projection into the future, even an indeterminate future, of figures and representations of unsurpassable perfection. Already present in germ in a preexilic messianism that envisaged an ideal historical figure, this eschatological messianism flourished during and after the exile, though the time frame of this advent was not defined. The ideal figure awaited as mediator of salvation was subsequently enriched as a result of various spiritual experiences of the chosen people.

b) Survival of Royal Messianism. From the time of exile and despite the disappearance of the actual institution of the monarchy, the monarch remained an emblematic figure. Preexile prophecies were significantly supplemented (*see* Am 9:11f.; "and David their king" added in Jer 30:9 and Hos 3:5). The promise during the exile in Micah 5, 1ss refers to 1 Samuel 16, 2 Samuel 7, and Jeremiah 30:21. Envisaging the resumption of the Davidic enterprise at its source, it evokes the shepherd of Bethlehem Ephrathah (Mi 5:1) rather than the warrior king of Jerusalem*. Ezekiel takes up this pastoral figure to make the messianic descendant of David the representative of the divine pastor* and confer on him the mission of unifying the chosen people and healing their ancestral divisions (Ez 34:23f., 37:24f.). By his mediation YHWH will conclude a covenant of peace with his people (Ez 34:25ff., 37:26ff.).

The more sober figure of Solomon was superimposed on this Davidian figure. A psalm book editor entitles Psalm 72 "Solomon," though it is presented as a "prayer of David" (72:20), and he inserts in its heart the oracular section of vv. 8–11, full of Solomonian reminiscences (1 Kgs 5:1, 5:4, 10:1–13). The very name of Solomon (connected to the root *shalôm*) and the pacific nature of his reign point toward the central eschatological message of peace. Similarly, the humble messiah in Zec 9:9f., who works for peace because he destroys weapons of war*, seems to designate the new Solomon, riding on a little ass at his royal coronation like his distant ancestor (1 Kgs 1:33–40).

c) Emergence of Prophetic Messianism. It is no surprise that the community in exile, grouped around these vigilant "watchmen" (Ez 3:16f; 33:1–9) Jeremiah, Ezechiel and the second Isaiah, favored an eschatological promotion of the prophetic function and experience in the person of a mysterious Servant. Four poems of the Deutero-Isaiah (42: 1–9; 49:1–9; 50:4–11; 52:13–53, 12) trace his spiritual journey towards a most humiliating death* which nonetheless assumes an expiatory value (expiation*).

d) Traces of Priestly Messianism. With the end of exile and the reconstruction of the temple, the priesthood* regained an eminent position, due in part to the disappearance of the institutions of prophecy and monarchy. The idealization of this priesthood may have contributed to the early outlines of the messianic figure, facilitated by the fact that kings in antiquity had priestly functions. Psalm 110 is a particularly eloquent witness; Jewish and Christian communities would read into it the announcement of a messiah-priest (Heb 5:5, 5:8, 6:20, 7:1–17), though attestations of this dual function are relatively infrequent (texts identified by critics as "new readings" such as Jer 33:14–18 or Is 52:10–12). Furthermore, the name of the high priest Joshua was substituted for Zerubbabel in an oracle (Zec 6:11–15) that originally concerned the latter. And there was a desire to see in the anonymous personage (Is 61:1ff.) a priestly messiah. These details, few and far between, never ascribe to the messianic high priest the brilliance of the Davidic figure. The *Testaments of the Twelve Patriarchs* and the Essene writings of Qumran attempt, more or less skillfully, to harmonize these divergent lines and envisage the coming in eschatological times of two messiahs, one a king and the other a priest. The Psalms of Solomon remain faithful to the Davidic (and Solomonic) ideal (Ps Sal 17).

e) Messianic Hope and Expectation of the Coming of the Reign of YHWH. The modern broadened concept of messianism led to envisaging a "messianism without a messiah" that would characterize the hope of the eschatological coming of the reign of God. The concept is not a particularly satisfactory one. However, recent editors of the prophetic books have tried to articulate Davidic messianism and eschatology of the "God who is coming" in an organic synthesis—for example, in the book of Micah 4–5 (Renaud, *La formation du livre de Michée,* Paris, 1977). The effort is not without artifice and the result quite unsatisfactory. This integration works best in Psalm 2 in its eschatological reading, which tightly subordinates the function of the messiah to the exercise of a divine government in which the king is merely the agent.

5. New Testament

a) Jesus and the Messianic Claim. In the face of Jesus' miracles*, his contemporaries wondered if he might be the messiah (Jn 4:29, 7:40ff.; Mt 12:23). His disciples did not hesitate to recognize him as such (Jn 1:41, 1:45–49). Peter*, provoked by Jesus, solemnly declares: "You are the Christ" (Mk 8:29). But Jesus holds back, at least until the Passion*. He himself carefully avoids the term and imposes secrecy on those who have identified him—whether they be devils (Lk 4:41) or the Twelve (Mt 16:20)—for popular notions connected with this title were too ambivalent, charged with too much political and military hope, too closely connected to temporal agency. Jesus used the title "Son of Man" (Mk 8:31; Mt 17:9, 17:22, 24:30, 26:2, 26:24, 26:64, etc.). Originally collective (Dn 7), this figure received a properly individual meaning in certain currents of Judaism* contemporaneous with the New Testament. Derived from the apocalyptic* milieu, it was open enough for Jesus to be able to introduce into it the characteristics of the suffering servant* of YHWH (Mk 8:31, 9:12, 10:32ff.) borrowed from Is 53.

However, in an increasingly hostile context, Jesus appropriated this title of messiah shortly before his death and, on Palm Sunday (Mt 21:1–11 and par.) mimicked the oracle of Zechariah 9:9f. Ordered by the high priest to identify himself before the Sanhedrin, Jesus reverted to the title of "Son of Man" (Mt 26:63) instead of "Christ," adding that he is the one whom "you will see...seated at the right hand of Power and coming on the clouds of heaven" (see Ps 110:1). By doing this he restored the original content to the title of messiah, distinguishing it from all deviant popular representations.

b) Primitive Christian Community. In the light of the Resurrection* the primitive church forthwith applied to the risen Jesus the title of Messiah, "Christ" (from the Greek *christos*), a term that was thereafter free of all ambiguity. Jesus is the true son of David (Mt 1:1; Lk 1:27, 2:4). At Pentecost, Peter declares:"God has made him both Lord and Christ, this Jesus whom you crucified" (Acts 2:36). Moreover, the term loses its appellative quality and becomes a proper noun, a name* that designates the very person of Jesus ("Jesus-Christ"), a name that draws to itself all the other qualifications. Jesus is recognized as the true Messiah because God "anointed Jesus of Nazareth with the Holy Spirit and with power" (Acts 10:38, see 4:26f.; Lk 4:16–22; *see* Is 61:1ff.).

● T. N. D. Mettinger (1976), *King and Messiah,* Lund.
J. Becker (1977), *Messiaserwartung im Alten Testament,* Stuttgart.
H. Cazelles (1978), *Le Messie de la Bible,* Tournai-Paris.
P. Grelot (1978), *L'espérance juive à l'heure de Jésus,* Paris.
E. J. Waschke (1988), "Die Frage nach dem Messias im Alten Testament als Problem alttestamentlicher Theologie und biblischer Hermeneutik," *ThLZ* 113, 321–32.
U. Struppe (Ed.) (1989), *Studien zum Messiasbild im Alten Testament,* Stuttgart.
H. Srauss, G. Stemberger (1992), "Messias," *TRE* 22, 617–29.
Coll. (1993), *Le messie dans l'histoire, Conc.* no. 245.
B. Renaud (1994 *a*), "La prophétie de Natan: Théologies en conflit," *RB* 101, 5–61; (1994 *b*), "Salomon, figure du Messie," *RevSR* 68, 409–26.

BERNARD RENAUD

See also **Christ and Christology; City; Eschatology; History; Jesus, Historical; Kingdom of God; Priesthood; Promise; Prophet and Prophecy; Psalms; Scripture, Senses of; Servant of YHWH; Son of Man**

Metaphysics. *See* Being

Methodism

A worldwide Christian communion*, numbering 60 million members and followers in 1995, Methodism arose from the evangelical revival that occurred in England in the 18th century.

1. Origins and Institutional History
The principal founders of Methodism were the two Wesley brothers, John (1703–91) and Charles (1707–88), ministers in the Anglican Church*. Both of them, particularly Charles, opposed the idea of schism*, but the missionary and pastoral structures they put in place made a separation from the Church of England more or less inevitable (Anglicanism*), itself crippled by the demographic consequences of the Industrial Revolution then under way. These structures included the joining together of the converted, or seek-

ers, into "societies," "classes," and "bands"; traveling preachers, some of them laypeople*, who met in an annual conference; prayer and preaching meetings, alongside parish worship; the building of chapels; and the establishing of charitable institutions. In fact separation from the Church of England first occurred in America, where in 1784 John Wesley had sent a number of ministers whom he had consecrated. In so doing he was effectively laying claim to the power of administering the sacrament of order (ordination/order*) in the capacity of a presbyter*-bishop: a power that he exercised in the urgent pastoral situation in the newly independent United States—in other words, outside the political jurisdiction* of the Crown and the canonical jurisdiction of the established church.

In the United States the superintendents-general received the title of bishop*, and the Christmas 1784 conference in Baltimore led to the creation of the Methodist Episcopal Church. Methodism spread rapidly, in line with the expansion toward the West. It adapted so well to the conditions of the place and time that it became the epitome of American churches, and it enjoyed a degree of cultural influence at the same time as it lost some of its critical detachment regarding the political and ideological developments in the country. In England Methodism developed more slowly. While it established itself in every region of the country ("I consider the whole world to be my parish," John Wesley had said, *Works,* Jackson 1, 201), it remained a minority denomination, attracting mainly artisans, the middle class, and, as time went on, the professional classes. For a long time, by far the most important component of English Methodism (the Wesleyan Methodist Connexion) retained the Anglican form of the liturgy (John Wesley had passed on the principal offices of the *Prayer Book* with slight adaptations), especially for the celebration of the sacraments*: the Wesleyan movement was characterized from the outset by the revival of Holy Communion as a means of grace*. However, in reaction to the rise of a Roman-influenced Anglo-Catholicism, and also of a more confident "evangelicalism" within the Church of England, Methodism aligned itself more and more with the (other) free churches in Great Britain from the second half of the 19th century, while remaining itself autonomous.

In America as much as in England Methodism underwent internal schisms during the 19th century. In the United States "black" churches were created, of which three main ones are still flourishing: the African Methodist Episcopal (AME), the African Methodist Episcopal Zion (AMEZ), and the Christian Methodist Episcopal (CME). Leaving aside the great division between the American North and South over slavery (for

the abolition of which John Wesley had already fought), disagreements between clergy and laity on the question of authority* were the usual cause. During the 20th century Methodism largely reunited: in the United States the Methodist Episcopal Church, the Methodist Episcopal Church South, and the Protestant Methodist Church merged into the Methodist Church (1939), which in turn formed the United Methodist Church (1968) along with some communities of German-speaking origin. Since 1932 the Methodist Church of Great Britain has united the Wesleyan Methodist Church and a number of small communities that appeared during the 19th century. At the present time the United Methodist Church of the United States (8.5 million adult members, and an overall community of between 15 and 20 million people) and the Methodist Church of Great Britain (400,000 adult members, 1.2 million in total) are suffering from the general trend toward secularization*. Methodism is at its most vigorous in Africa and in some countries in Asia and Oceania, where its presence is the result of energetic mission* work in the 19th and early 20th centuries. Methodist churches also exist in central and northern Europe, where they were at first composed mainly of immigrants returning from the United States.

2. John Wesley, Spiritual Founder and Doctrinal Master

In the words of a Catholic theologian, Methodism is indebted to John Wesley "in the same way that, in the Catholic Church, a religious order or a spiritual family derives its spirit from its founder" (Frost 1980). According to a Catholic historian, in the development of Protestantism* Wesley's Methodism represents a reaction analogous to Lutheran "solafideism" (Piette 1927). How then may one characterize the thought of this man, a handful of whose writings constitute the official doctrinal basis of the great majority of Methodist churches (the first four volumes of his *Sermons,* his *Notes on the New Testament,* and, for American Methodism, his abridgement of the *Articles of Religion* [24 instead of the 39 of Anglicanism] and the *General Rules of Methodist Societies*)?

a) Catholicity of Sources. By referring to himself as *homo unius libri,* "the man of a single book," Wesley indicated his reliance on the Holy* Scriptures as a doctrinal source and criterion (*see* Article VI of the *Thirty-nine Articles*). He regarded the ecclesiastical writers, in particular those of the first three centuries, as the "most authentic commentators on the Scriptures, being at the same time the nearest to the source and singularly endowed with the same Spirit by which the whole of Scripture was given" (*Works,* Jackson 10, 484). While he continued to quote from the most important of the later Fathers*, he had less confidence in the testimonies of the post-Constantinian Church, in view of the moral and practical corruption that had entered it by way of the empire. The Apostles*' Creed, and that of Nicaea*-Constantinople*, provide the dogmatic* key to Wesley's hermeneutics*. He was an heir of the Reformation in its English form (Articles, homilies, Prayer Books) and drew on English spiritual writers of the 17th and 18th centuries (Jeremy Taylor, Thomas Ken, Henry Scougal, William Law, Nathaniel Spinckes, Thomas Deacon). He encountered continental Protestantism by way of the pietist Moravian Brethren of Herrnhut, whom he met during his travels in America (1736–38). It was under their influence that he underwent his "evangelical conversion*" (*see* c below), though he held aloof from their quietist tendencies. On another front, Wesley rejected a number of "errors and superstitions" of Roman Catholicism* (he republished the Anglican bishop John Williams's *A Roman Catechism faithfully drawn out of the writings of the Church of Rome, with a Reply thereto*) but included some medieval spiritual writers (*The Imitation of Christ*) and even some more recent ones (Pascal*, Fénelon, Madame Guyon, John of Ávila, Gregory Lopez, Molinos) in the "Christian Library" (1749–56) in 50 volumes that he produced for his ever more educated preachers and laypeople (Orcibal 1951).

b) Doctrinal Orthodoxy. Faced with the deism* and neo-Arianism* of some intellectual and even ecclesiastical circles of his time, Wesley held firm to the "Triune God" and his work of redemption. Rejecting excessive speculation on the mystery* of God*'s inner life, he affirmed the death* and the merits of the incarnate Christ* and the free action of the Holy Spirit as indispensable for leading the faithful to the Father by way of the Son (*Sermon* 55, *On the Trinity*), in expectation of the day when "there will be a deep, intimate and uninterrupted union with God; a constant communion with the Father and his Son Jesus Christ, through the Spirit; a continual rejoicing of the Three-One God, and of all creatures in him" (*Sermon* 64, *The New Creation*). Amid the prevailing latitudinarianism, Wesley insisted on the "essential doctrines," while tolerating (no more) "those opinions which do not undermine the very root of Christianity" (*Works,* Jackson 8, 340).

c) Anthropological and Soteriological Focus. The optimism of grace*—a phrase E. G. Rupp uses concerning Wesley—occupies the middle ground between Calvinist pessimism and the Pelagianism* of which the Lutherans suspected the father of Methodism. Wes-

ley himself said that "our principal doctrines are three in number: repentance, faith*, and sanctity," adding that they resembled "the porch of religion, its door, and religion itself (*Works,* Jackson 8, 472). A modern English Methodist formula has summarized Wesley's position under four headings:

1) Everyone needs redemption. Wesley's most extensive theological treatise is devoted to original sin* (*Works,* Jackson 9, 196–464). The purpose of redemption is to restore human beings to the image of God, understood in a christological sense.

2) Everyone may be saved. In opposition to the doctrine of predestination, Wesley affirmed God's desire that all might receive that salvation (1 Tm 2:5) for which Christ had paid the price. By virtue of Christ's redemptive work, every person enjoyed "prevenient grace," enabling each to respond freely in faith to the offer of the Gospel. The initial justification* was received by faith alone.

3) Everyone may know himself to be saved. Wesley describes his "evangelical conversion" (*Works,* Jackson 1, 103) in the following terms: "In the evening [of 24 May 1738], against my better judgement, I went to Aldersgate Street where a religious society was meeting. Luther*'s preface to the Epistle to the Romans was being read. At around a quarter to nine, whilst he was describing the change which God works in the heart by faith in Christ, I felt my heart strangely warmed. I felt that I had confidence in Christ, in Christ alone, for my salvation; and I was given an assurance that he had taken away my sins, yes *mine,* and that he had saved me, *me,* from the law of sin and death." This classic text of Methodist spirituality mentions "assurance," "a regular privilege of the faithful," which is manifested as an expression of the Spirit of adoption (Rom 8:15). Against the doctrine of absolute perseverance, however, Wesley teaches that God's promises* are valid (only) insofar as they are freely welcomed by faith.

4) Everyone may be saved fully ("to the uttermost"). Against the doctrine of *simul iustus et peccator* in the Lutheran sense of a permanent paradox, Wesley preached that sanctification was a real transformation that could lead from this world (in contradiction of Calvin*'s doctrine) to perfection. Without excluding the ignorance, weaknesses, and errors that still resulted from the Fall, this perfection consisted in a faultless love* of God and one's neighbor. While good

works* alone did not merit salvation*, the believer would not be finally justified without these fruits of faith (2 Cor 5:10). (This is the social significance of sanctification as conceived by Wesley, which would inspire the involvement of English Methodists in trade unions, or that of American Methodists in the campaign for prohibition.)

d) Ecumenical Openness. Without playing down Wesley's criticisms of certain Catholic doctrines and practices, the pacific tone of his *Letter to a Roman Catholic,* written in Dublin in 1749 (*Works,* Jackson 10, 80–86), must be emphasized. Calling on the one Creator and Redeemer of all mankind, he sets out in particular the faith shared by Protestants and Catholics (by way of a discussion of the Creed of Nicaea and Constantinople), as well as their common spiritual and moral aspirations. On this basis he calls for mutual charity, prayer, and assistance in all matters that "lead to the Kingdom* of God." In his *Sermon* 39 of 1750, entitled *Catholic Spirit* (*Works,* Jackson 5, 492–504), Wesley extends a hand to all those who, in terms of doctrine, worship, and morals, affirm at least "the first elements of Christ's Gospel" according to the Scriptures and offers them "unity in affection" even if "an entire external union" is prevented by differences of opinion, liturgical forms, or government*. (According to Wesley, the one "purpose of any ecclesiastical order" is to "lead souls* from Satan to God and to teach them to fear* and love him"; *Works,* Jackson 12, 80 *Sq.*)

e) A Sung Faith. Charles Wesley is the principal poet of Methodism, whereas John acted mainly as critic and publisher, although he did produce excellent translations of 30 or so German hymns. Together the two brothers provided Methodism, and to a lesser extent all English-speaking churches, with a huge wealth of hymns, rich in meaning, which mark the major feasts of the year, embellish the celebration of the Eucharist (the collection of 166 *Hymns on the Lord's Supper,* 1745), and above all trace the way of the experience* of faith (*A Collection of Hymns for the Use of the People Called Methodists,* 1780).

3. Denominational Aspect of Methodism

Methodists do not like to consider themselves a "denomination" in the Lutheran or Reformed sense of the term. A. C. Outler (1991) describes them rather as an "abortive church," an "evangelical order" in search of a "catholic environment." The institutional realities do not permit an unqualified acceptance of this description—it must be acknowledged that there exist two ways of viewing Methodism and of putting it into practice in the context of a disunited Christendom.

a) American Trend. Considering its independent constitution and its rapid expansion, Methodism in the United States quickly acquired the character of a church (church as confessional denomination), indeed of a multitudinist church in which freedom* of opinion favored theological (as well as liturgical) pluralism. In the cultural milieu of America this led to a reversal of Wesley's emphases: "from revelation* to reason*," "from the sinful man to the moral man," and "from free grace to free will" (Chiles 1965). Inasmuch as during the years 1970–90 the existence of a "Wesleyan quadrilateral" of sources or criteria for theology* was put forward, the progressives highlighted the epistemological importance of *reason* and above all of *experience* (sociopolitical and individual), while the orthodox camp emphasized the substance of the Scriptures and tradition*. As far as ecumenical strategy is concerned, the American approach has consisted in upholding a "reconciled diversity," permitting the survival of denominations in a coexistence that is marked by cooperation, but also perhaps by healthy competition on the capitalist model.

b) English Tendency. As a minority denomination English Methodism has so far retained a more strictly Wesleyan identity, due above all, on the popular level, to its attachment to Wesley's hymns, and on the intellectual level to the devotion of its theologians to traditional biblical, historical, and theological disciplines. On the ecumenical front, successive generations of Methodist theologians have contributed to the "Faith and Order" movement, and Methodist churches of the English type have participated in the founding of churches* that have come together organically in various countries or regions (Southern India, 1947; Northern India, 1971; Australia, 1977). In 1969 and 1972 the conference of the Methodist Church of Great Britain approved a plan to reunite with the Church of England, though this came to nothing.

c) Bilateral Dialogues. Thanks to the World Methodist Council, comprising 70 member churches, Methodism has pursued, and continues to pursue, bilateral dialogues with the Catholic Church (since 1967: *see* in particular *The Apostolic Tradition* of 1991 and *The Word of Life: On Revelation and Faith* of 1996), the Lutheran World Federation (*The Church, Community of Grace,* 1984), the World Alliance of Reformed Churches (*Together in the Grace of God,* 1987), the Anglican Communion (*Sharing the Apostolic Communion,* 1996), and the Orthodox churches (a document is in preparation under the direction of the Ecumenical Patriarchate*).

● *The Works of John Wesley,* Ed. T. Jackson, 14 vols., 3rd Ed., London, 1872.

The Works of John Wesley: Bicentennial Edition, critical edition, 35 vols., Nashville, 1975.

The Poetical Works of John and Charles Wesley, Ed. G. Osborn, 13 vols., London, 1868–72.

John Wesley, Ed. A. C. Outler, New York, 1964 (anthology).

Charles Wesley: A Reader, Ed. J. R. Tyson, New York, 1989 (anthology).

◆ M. Piette (1927), *La réaction de John Wesley dans l'évolution du protestantisme,* Brussels.

G. C. Cell (1935), *The Rediscovery of John Wesley,* New York.

J. E. Rattenbury (1938), *The Conversion of the Wesleys,* London.

J. E. Rattenbury (1948), *The Eucharistic Hymns of John and Charles Wesley,* London.

J. Orcibal (1951), "Les spirituels français et espagnols chez John Wesley et ses contemporains," *RHR* 139, 50–109.

J. Bowmer (1951), *The Sacrament of the Lord's Supper in Early Methodism,* London.

M. Schmidt (1953–66), *John Wesley,* 2 vols., Zürich-Frankfurt.

J. Orcibal (1959), "L'originalité théologique de John Wesley et les spiritualités du continent," *RH* 222, 51–80.

C. W. Williams (1960), *John Wesley's Theology Today,* Nashville.

F. Baker (1962), *Representative Verse of Charles Wesley,* London.

R. E. Chiles (1965), *Theological Transition in American Methodism, 1790–1935,* Nashville.

R. E. Davies, A. R. George, E. G. Rupp (Ed.) (1965–1988), *A History of the Methodist Church in Great Britain,* 4 vols., London.

F. Baker (1970), *John Wesley and the Church of England,* London.

J. Weissbach (1970), *Der neue Mensch im theologischen Denken John Wesleys,* Stuttgart.

C.-J. Bertrand (1971), *Le méthodisme,* Paris.

O. E. Borgen (1972), *John Wesley on the Sacraments,* Zürich.

C.-J. Bertrand (1974), "Le méthodisme, 'province' méconnue de la communion anglicane?" in *Aspects de l'anglicanisme: Colloque de Strasbourg, 14–16 juin 1972,* Strasbourg.

F. A. Norwood (1974), *The Story of American Methodism,* Nashville.

F. Frost (1980), "Méthodisme," *Cath* 9, 48–71.

T. A. Langford (1983), *Practical Divinity Theology in the Wesleyan Tradition,* Nashville.

G. Wainwright (1983), "Methodism's ecclesial location and ecumenical vocation," *OiC* 19, 104–34 (repr. in id., *The Ecumenical Moment,* Grand Rapids, Mich., 1983, 189–221).

J. M. Turner (1985), *Conflict and Reconciliation: Studies in Methodism and Ecumenism in England, 1740–1982,* London.

A. Coppedge (1987), *John Wesley in Theological Debate,* Wilmore, Ky.

H. D. Rack (1989), *Reasonable Enthusiast: John Wesley and the Rise of Methodism,* London.

R. L. Maddox (1990), "John Wesley and Eastern Orthodoxy," *AsbTJ* 45, 29–53.

T. A. Campbell (1990–91), "The 'Wesleyan Quadrilateral': The Story of a Modern Methodist Myth," *MethH* 29, 87–95.

T. A. Campbell (1991), *John Wesley and Christian Antiquity,* Nashville.

A. C. Outler (1991), *The Wesleyan Theological Heritage,* Grand Rapids.

W. Klaiber and M. Marquardt (1993), *Gelebte Gnade: Grundriss einer Theologie der Evangelisch-methodistischen Kirche,* Stuttgart.

R. L. Maddox (1994), *Responsible Grace: John Wesley's Practical Theology,* Nashville.

R. P. Heitzenrater (1995), *Wesley and the People Called Methodists,* Nashville.

S. J. Jones (1995), *John Wesley's Conception and Use of Scripture,* Nashville.

G. Wainwright (1995), *Methodists in Dialogue,* Nashville.

K. B. Westerfield Tucker (Ed.) (1996), *The Sunday Service of the Methodists,* Nashville.

GEOFFREY WAINWRIGHT

See also **Anglicanism; Calvin, John; Calvinism; Ecumenism; Family, Confessional; Luther, Martin; Lutheranism; Pietism; Puritanism; Quietism**

Methodist Churches. *See* Methodism

Millenarianism

a) Origins. In the strict sense of the term, *millenarianism* designates the belief in the Christian tradition according to which Christ* will return to earth with the just who have risen to reign in glory for 1,000 years. Universal resurrection* and judgment* will follow this thousand-year period, and then the end of the world will come, and the establishment of the reign of God*. This belief is based on a literal interpretation of Revelation 20:1–6.

In actual fact, the passage from Revelation is no more than a Christianized adaptation of a theme already present in Jewish apocalyptic* literature. Since the second century B.C. this literature had tended to speculate on duration, with a view to establishing the date of the coming of the Messiah*, as can be seen in the books of Daniel, Enoch, and Jubilees. In rabbinic debates, varying time spans were attributed to the reign of the Messiah. These ranged from 40 years, according to Rabbi Aqiba, to 1,000 years, according to Rabbi Eliezer ben Yose (*see*, in particular, *Pesiqta Rabbati* 1, 7; *Midrash Tanhuma*, section 'Eqev, 7b; and *Midrash Tehillim* 90, §17; *see also 4 Esdras* 7:28, which mentions 400 years). The appearance of the millennium was most frequently based on Psalm 90:4: "For a thousand years in your sight are but as yesterday when it is past, or as a watch in the night." It would seem that the author of Revelation himself subscribed to this exegesis*.

Quite obviously, it is essentially through the Book of Revelation that the millenarian idea became widespread among Christian authors of the 2nd century A.D. One must emphasize that—with the notable exception of the Gnostic current—it was adopted by all the other Christian tendencies from the most orthodox to the most dissident (provided such a distinction had any relevance in the second century). However, it would seem that the birthplace of this idea can be situated in Asia Minor. It was, in fact, from this region, in the early second century, that Cerinthus (Eusebius, *HE* III, 28, 2) and Papias (*HE* III, 39, 12) were born. If we are to believe Irenaeus*, Papias transmitted details said to originate with the Lord about the 1,000-year reign, details that had considerable similarities with other elements of Jewish apocalyptic literature (compare Irenaeus's *Adv. Haer,* V, 33, 3 with 1 Enoch 10:19, 2 Baruch 29:5, etc.). Montanus also hailed from Asia

Minor; he was the initiator in 172 A.D. of the "new prophecy,*" which bears his name—Montanism*—but, in fact, Montanism is not characterized by any particular emphasis on millenarianism. In the *Epistle of Barnabas* 15:3–5, however, one can find the equivalence between one day and "1,000 years") and, above all, Justin, in his *Dialogue with Trypho* 80:4, mentioned this theme as a normal element of Christian belief. Justin writes: "For me, and for Christians of integral orthodoxy, for as long as they may be, it is clear that a resurrection of the flesh will occur for 1,000 years in a rebuilt, decorated, and expanded Jerusalem*, as has been affirmed by the prophets Ezekiel, Isaiah, and others."

In *Dialogue with Trypho* 81:3, Justin also refers to the equivalence between "one day" and "a thousand years," and in 81:4, he mentions the Book of Revelation.

b) Developments and Debate up to the Time of Augustine. While the second century represented the golden age of Christian millenarianism, later periods would gradually abandon this consensus. To be sure, the millenarian idea was still quite widely held until the fifth century. In the note he devoted to Papias (*De viris inlustribus* 18), Jerome referred, in this regard, to Apollinaris, Tertullian*, Victorinus, and Lactantius. And at the beginning of Book 18 of his commentary on *Isaiah,* he added Irenaeus to the list. Irenaeus had, in fact, adopted the teachings of Justin on that point for his own use (*Adv. Haer.* V, 28, 3; 36, 3). In Tertullian's opinion, Jerome was referring to a lost work, *De spe fidelium,* which Tertullian himself mentioned in support of his millenarianism (*Adv. Marc.* III, 24, 3–6). The case of Apollinaris of Laodicea seems more difficult to evaluate. Basil*, in fact, reproached him with having judaizing tendencies, which were not necessarily millenarian (*Ep.* 263, 4; 265, 2). Finally, while Jerome did, advisedly, refer to Victorinus of Pettau (*Scolia on Apocalypse.* 20) and Lactantius (*Inst. div.* VII, 22.24), he could have added Commodianus (*Instructiones* I, XLV, 9) and Methodius of Olympus (*Banquet* IX, 5) to his list. On the other hand, as the *De viris inlustribus* dated from 393, Jerome could not include a certain Hilarion, whose treatise dates from 397 (*De mundi duratione* 18), nor could he refer to Gaudentius of Brescia, who was still millenarianist at the beginning of the fifth century (*Sermon* 10).

Alongside this first group of authors were others who were beginning to challenge the millenarian model, and it seems most likely that their protests were an integral part of the debate on the canonicity of the Book of Revelation. Eusebius of Caesarea mentioned the debate in writing about Dionysius of Alexandria (HE III, 28, 1–5; VII, 25, 1–8), as did Dionysius Bar-Salibi (a Syrian Monophysite from the 12th century) in writing about Hippolytus of Rome *(In Ap. Intr.)*.

As for Origen*, he overcame the difficulty by developing a decidedly allegorical reading of Revelation, thus avoiding any expressions of doubt over the literal meaning (*De princ.* II, 11, 2–3; *Com. Mat.* XVII, 35; *Com. Ct.,* prol.). Following Origen's example, Augustine* would understand the 1,000 years of the reign of Christ as referring to the time of the church* (*Civ. Dei* XX, 7), while admitting that he himself had been drawn to millenarian-

ism (see *Sermon* 259, 2). One might say that millenarianism began to fade during the fifth century. From that time on the church would consciously settle into duration.

● H. Leclercq (1933), "Ml.," *DACL* 11/1, 1181–95.
L. Gry (1934), *Le millénarisme dans ses origines et son développement,* Paris.
W. Nigg (1954), *Das ewige Reich: Geschichte einer Hoffnung,* Zürich-Stuttgart (2nd Ed. 1967).
J. Daniélou (1958), *Théologie du judéo-christianisme,* Tournai-Paris (2nd Ed. 1991).
B. E. Daley (1991), *The Hope of the Early Church: A Handbook of Patristic Eschatology,* Cambridge.
S. Heid (1993), *Chiliasmus und Antichrist-Mythos: Eine frühchristliche Kontroverse um das Heilige Land,* coll. Hereditas 6, Bonn.
C. Nardi (Ed.) (1995), *Il Millenarismo: Testi dei secoli I–II,* Rome.

DOMINIQUE CERBELAUD

See also **Apocrypha; Apollinarianism; Apologists; Eschatology; Judeo-Christianity; Montanism**

Ministry

A. Biblical Theology

a) Nature of the Problem and Principal Questions. In the beginning Jesus* addressed to the first disciples a call and a duty of service (Mt 4:21). But at what point did the disciples become ministers and their service a ministry? Was it with the institution of the Twelve; was it in the Galilean period or in the Judean period (which includes the Last Supper); was it with the appearances of the Risen One, or with the appointment of Matthias (Acts)? The mention of the "hundred and twenty" (Acts 1:15) suggests the community has a collegial role. In the Gospels* the vocabulary of ministries varies. For example, Matthew 9 and 10 use "disciples," "the Twelve," and "twelve apostles*."

The variety of titles denotes an evolution, between Jerusalem* and Rome*, starting from a specifically apostolic ministry and moving toward an "ecclesial" (E) ministry and more institutional forms: 1) in Jerusalem, the Twelve (who are "Hebrews"), the seven ("Hellenists": E), then come prophets, "elders" (*presbuteroi:* E), teachers (rabbi); 2) in Caesarea, an evangelist (Philip): his daughters prophesy; in Joppa, the

widows (Tabitha); 3) in Antioch, a pastoral triad in hierarchical form: apostle + prophet (E) + teacher (E); 4) in Ephesus, an evangelist (Timothy), the *episcopi* (E) (Acts); 5) in Corinth, the same triad as in Antioch; *diakonos* emerges (Romans, 1 and 2 Corinthians); *proîstamenos,* "president" (*see* Romans); 6) in Rome, *hègoumenos* "leader" (Hebrews).

The evolution and stabilization of ministries is explained by: 1) the situation of the Church* of Jerusalem from Pentecost to the Jewish War; 2) the growth of the church (from 60,000 c. 60 A.D. to 240,000 c. 80 A.D., a quarter of them in the province of Asia); 3) the disappearance of the apostles and of traveling ministers; and 4) the role of the Church of Rome, which replaced that of Jerusalem. A close analysis reveals several developments. The term "presbyter*" was gradually extended to all the communities. In Ephesus, *episcopus,* a term derived from civil administration, gradually achieved dominance (the function was conferred by a laying* on of hands according to 1 Tm 4:14, 5:22; 2 Tm 1:6; *see* Acts 6:6 for deacons*).

With nuances and variations, we can note the contrasts: charism vs. institution; traveling vs. localization with universality; and temporary vs. permanent ministries.

b) Before Easter. The mention of Judas as "one of the Twelve" argues for a pre-Easter origin of the Twelve. In Matthew, 11 times; Mark, 14 times; Luke, 13 times; John, 12 times; Acts, two times; they are called disciples and then apostles (12 men plus three priests; differing from the version of Qumran). The closeness of the Twelve to Jesus even before Easter is the prototype of the relationship of Jesus to the people* of God. Their being sent on a mission* had a universal apostolic meaning; Jesus acts through his apostles and hence through the whole Church. "Eleven" (Matthew; Acts), used after the defection of Judas, confirms the existence of the Twelve. The term "Twelve" is ancient, and that of apostle is posterior to it.

The ministry of the Twelve differs from the Jewish priesthood*: it is not hereditary, and there are no degrees of purity*, no canonical age, and no judgment of their colleagues (Mt 7:1–5). Seven *logia* attribute to Jesus the rejection of the institution of a hierarchy between them—, for example, Mark 9:35: "if anyone would be first, he must be last of all and servant of all." According to these *logia* the community gathered around Jesus is not to possess a structure of power analogous to that of the surrounding society (whether civil, priestly, or that of Qumran).

What role was played by the trio of Peter*, James, and John? The personal role of Peter, who received the first appearance of the Risen One (Lk 24:34), is already attested in Paul (1 Cor 15:5). The primacy claimed by James and John shows the absence of a hierarchy by rights (Mk 10:35–45) or of a *mebaqqér* (supervisor) of the Qumran type.

c) Jewish and Christian Church of Jerusalem (Acts 1–7): Hierarchy and/or Collegiality? With a dual allegiance, the apostles frequented the temple daily, and many priests serving in it became followers of Jesus. The integration of Matthias into the now institutional apostleship of the Twelve serves to bring out the bond with the Risen One, the initiative of Peter, the collegiality* of the group, the action of the Holy* Spirit, and recognition by the one hundred and twenty. According to Acts, Peter and John jointly exercise a special authority*. Various collegial authorities may be distinguished: diarchic (Peter and John), oligarchic (the "Twelve," the seven, the elders), democratic (the community: the hundred and twenty). The Judeo-Christian Hebrews practice communal ownership. The Greeks, without this type of economic organization,

are more open to female participation in ministries (Acts 21:9).

d) In Corinth. Paul moved from the Semitic world to the Hellenistic (all the provinces of Anatolia), Greek, and Roman worlds. Paul had 162 collaborators (among them 60 women). Their classification is beyond the scope of the present article.

The influence of the surrounding society is clear in Corinth. Small religious groups, Christian *thiases,* sprang up spontaneously, each a leader at its head: Paul, Apollos, Cephas, Christ (1 Cor 1:12). They emphasized personal performance; Paul rejected their ministerial fluidity.

In place of the triad of Corinthian ministries—prophecy in the Greek manner, speaking in tongues, Greek wisdom*—Paul instituted the three pastoral ministries of the apostolic triad: apostle, prophet, teacher (1 Cor 12:28). He knew the value of this, for he was himself apostle, prophet, and teacher.

To designate the ministries (G. Friedrich), Paul does not use the vocabulary current in the Greek world. Eight terms are excluded: *timè,* duty; *doxa,* dignity; *telos,* power of decision; *arkhè,* power; *bathmos,* rank; *topos,* position; *taxis,* assigned place; and finally *leitourgia* in the sense of priestly office (but *see* 2 Cor 9:12, and the verbal form in Rom 15:27). Hence, the ministry is neither a position of honor nor a post of authority, nor an institution with several grades, nor a priestly organization. In addition, Paul never uses the word "elder" *(presbuteros),* common in the Church of Jerusalem and in the synagogues.

Paul retains five words for the ecclesial ministry: 1) *oikonomia,* "administration" or "management," designates duty; 2) *exousia,* "power conferred for the building up of the community"; 3) *kharis,* "grace*," designates Paul's own apostleship, entrusted to a sinner; 4) *kharisma,* "gift for a service with a view to the common good," is almost unknown in the Old Testament and in the speech of the time; eliminates *pneumatikon,* related to inspiration; 5) *diakonia,* which Paul adopts in Corinth, designates service in the broadest sense and not a precise ministry: "gift of service" in Romans 12; "ministry of the apostle" in 2 Corinthians and Romans. The word may be qualified: "of the spirit"; "of justice*"; "of reconciliation" (2 Cor). In Romans 12 *diakonia* is associated with the gifts of teaching *(didaskalia),* of exhorting *(paraklèsis),* of presiding *(proîstamentos),* and of exercising mercy *(eleôn).* The distinction between temporary gifts and instituted permanent ministries has already emerged.

e) Marriage, Widowhood, or Celibacy of the Minister. Just one passage speaks of celibacy (Mt 19:12), and this not in relation to ministry. Only Luke mentions giving up a wife to follow Jesus (Lk 14:26, 18:29). The call of Jesus involves giving up one's home, one's livelihood, and one's possessions: "leaving all" (Lk 5:11, 5:28, 18:22). At the time of their call nothing is said of the possible separation of the disciples from their wives. Peter is married (Mk 1:30: his mother-in-law), and the other disciples may also have been. According to 1 Corinthians 9:5 all the first apostles except Paul "take along a believing wife." Barnabas the Levite must be or must have been married.

Paul arrives in Corinth without a wife and makes of his situation "outside marriage*" a gift of God (1 Cor 7:7ff.). He does not count himself among the celibates, or "virgins" (1 Cor 7:25), but among those outside marriage, *agamoi* (1 Cor 7:8, and vv. 11, 32, 34), having been married, but married no longer. Is he a widower? The fact that he cites his example next to that of widows might suggest as much. If his wife had abandoned him after his conversion* to Christ*, the "Pauline privilege" (1 Cor 7:12ff.) would be the application to others of his personal case. Without a wife, Paul is more available and can live on little. If Barnabas is also a widower, the two apostles are in the same situation.

f) Minister's Means of Existence. Only those of Paul are known to us. He is a maker of heavy cloth (sails, tents, and the like), of the same craft as Priscilla and Aquila (Acts 18:3). In Miletus he reminds the elders of the Church of Ephesus of his refusal to be a burden, of his unselfishness (Acts 20:33ff.; *see* 1 Thes 2:9). In 1 Corinthians 9:1–18 Paul explains why he does not apply to himself the rule that comes from the Lord: "The Lord commanded that those who proclaim the gospel should get their living by the gospel" (9:14; *see* Mt 10:10; Lk 10:7), although he has the right to do so (1 Cor 9:6.12).

From 1 and 2 Corinthians, Galatians, Romans, and Philippians, it emerges that: 1) the minister has the right to be provided for where he proclaims the gospel; 2) he may also receive subsidies from a church other than the one in which he is working (Phil 4:10–20); 3) he may refuse any "salary"; 4) the respective situations of Silvanus, Timothy, and Titus are not known in detail (2 Cor 1:16ff.). Manual labor, normal for a Jew, was not normal for a free Greek man. And by refusing any salary, Paul risked the exercise of a ministry that was not recognized (*see* Simon Magus against Peter in Acts 8:18–24).

g) Participation of Women in the Ministry. Does the rule of equality of Galatians 3:28 apply to the ministry? In 1 Corinthians 7, Paul mentions marriage, celibacy, separation, or widowhood, without alluding to ministry, for ministry does not depend on any of them (the celibacy envisaged in verses 25–35 does not apply to ministry). Greek society in Corinth was more favorable to a ministry of women (unmarried?) than Palestinian society. But the pagan context (priestesses, bacchantes) made the church attentive to 1) dress at worship (1 Cor 11:5); 2) restrictions already applicable to men; and 3) ecstatic experiences (1 Cor 14:34f.). The case of the couple of Priscilla and Aquila (1 Cor 16:19 ...) does not make it possible to determine whether there is a ministry for a married woman whose husband has no ministry. 1 Timothy 5 articulates the conditions for the ministry of widows (60 years old, married only once, enrolled in the church). We do not know whether Lydia (Acts) and Phoebe (Romans) were widows.

- B. Reicke (1954), "Die Verfassung der Urgemeinde im Licht jüdischer Dokumente," *ThZ* 10, 95–112 (English trans. in *The Scrolls and the New Testament*, Ed. K. Stendahl, New York, 1957, 143–56).
- L. Cerfaux (1956), *La communauté apostolique*, 3rd Ed., Paris.
- J. Jeremias (1957), "Presbyterion ausserchristlich bezeugt," *ZNW* 48, 127–32.
- N. Brox (1961), *Zeuge und Martyrer: Untersuchungen zur frühchristlichen Zeugnis-Terminologie*, Munich.
- J. Roloff (1965), *Apostolat-Verkündigung-Kirche: Ursprung, Inhalt und Funktion des kirchlichen Apostelamtes nach Paulus, Lukas und Pastoralbriefen*, Gütersloh.
- P. Schubert (1968), "The Final Speeches in the Book of Acts," *JBL* 87, 1–16.
- A. Lemaire (1971), *Les ministères aux origines de l'Église: Naissance de la triple hiérarchie: évêques, presbytres, diacres*, Paris.
- H. Merklein (1973), *Das kirchliche Amt nach dem Epheserbrief*, StANT 33.
- J. Dupont (1974), *Les ministères de l'Église naissante d'après les "Actes des apôtres,"* StAns 61.
- J. Delorme (Ed.) (1974), *Le ministère et les ministères selon le Nouveau Testament*, Paris.
- K. Kertelge et al. (1977), *Das kirchliche Amt im NT*, Darmstadt.
- M. Carrez (1980), "Les incidences des conjonctures historiques et géographiques sur la naissance et l'évolution des ministères," *Bulletin de Saint-Sulpice* 6, 29–55.

MAURICE CARREZ

See also **Apostle; Authority; Bishop; Church; Deacon; Deaconesses; Government, Church; Hierarchy; Presbyter/Priest; Priesthood; Structures, Ecclesial; Woman**

B. Historical and Systematic Theology

1. Ministry: Singular or Plural?

The New Testament offers the picture of a plurality of ministries that, with adjustments, was to persist through the first five centuries and even into the 13th, in spite of a strong tendency to emphasize the clerical and the priestly. From that time on, the ordained ministry was concentrated in the figure of the priest*, the diaconate having become a temporary order*, and the title of bishop a dignity associated with powers superior to those of priests; and if there were other ministries, they participated in or supplemented those mentioned. In Reformation churches we observe the same concentration on the ministry—which became the only one—of the pastor*; references to universal priesthood did not recover their pertinence until the revolutions of 1848. With doctrinal nuances, and at different rates, the contemporary period in both Catholicism* and Protestantism* has been characterized by a rediscovery of New Testament ecclesiology*: the people* of God (N. A. Dahl, *Das Volk Gottes,* Oslo, 1941); Christian fraternity (J. Ratzinger, *DSp* 5, 1141–67); the priesthood of the faithful (P. Dabin, *Le sacerdoce royal des fidèles dans les livres saints,* 1941; *Le sacerdoce royal dans la tradition ancienne et moderne,* 1950); the diversity of gifts and the laity* (Y. Congar, *Jalons pour une théologie du laïcat,* 1953; H. Krämer, *Theology of the Laity*); coresponsibility. These rediscoveries (also associated with egalitarian and functionalist impulses) have enriched the search for a rearticulation of the specific ministry of pastors with the plurality of other services and ministries.

2. Ministry and Service

a) Concepts. In the church* no one is exempt from serving. Every ministry must be a service if it is not to be distorted. But is all Christian service ministerial? Theology* written in German, which distinguishes *Amt* (ordained ministry) from *Dienst* (service), has more difficulty with this assertion than theology written in Romance languages or in English, where the term "ministry" is generic (ordained or not).

By entitling a report "All responsible for the Church? The presbyteral ministry in an entirely ministerial Church," the plenary Assembly of the Bishops of France (1973) wished to articulate the responsibility of all in the diversity of their ministries, while not however making the presbyteral ministry a simple service with no basis other than empirical necessity for the church to distribute the services necessary for its life. Indeed, being assigned a role in the church, even when ordination is associated with a choice, does not derive solely from the service rendered by the one who agrees to preside, but expresses structurally and symbolically (in an order that is not that of simple utility) the fact that the word and the sacraments* do not come to us from ourselves.

b) Practice. Since the 1970s, ministries without ordination have proliferated. Very few lectors or acolytes have been commissioned, a path open to men alone by *Ministeria Quaedam* in 1973. On the other hand, many Christian men and women are catechists, liturgical leaders, leaders of youth groups, and hospital and prison chaplains. Further, in a situation of a dearth of priests, and in virtue of the *Code of Canon Law,* can. 517, §2, bishops* also entrust a "participation in the exercise of the pastoral duties of a parish to a deacon*, another person who is not a priest, or a community of people." Final responsibility, in this case, lies of course with a "regulating priest, invested with the powers of a priest." But one might ask whether the ecclesiologically important distinction between ordained and nonordained ministry can thereby be preserved, especially in the long term. There are questions along these lines in *Christefideles laïci* of John Paul II (1989), no. 23; B. Sesboué, *N'ayez pas peur* (1996).

3. Ministry and Representation of Christ

According to the Reformation, the ministry instituted by God is assigned a certain role in the church: with the gospel that it preaches and the sacraments that it celebrates, it is a means of giving the gift of the Holy Spirit and faith* (*CA* 5). Protestantism, on the other hand, is classically opposed to a certain number of formulations, frequent in Catholic literature without actually having become dogma, that seem to obscure the uniqueness of the ministry of Christ*.

The priest is thus not a *mediator* between God and man, in the sense in which Christ is a mediator, and he adds nothing to the mediation of Christ. He can be a mediator only in an instrumental sense, in the acts of his ministry, as Calvin, echoing *CA* 5, says in the *Institution:* "God does his work through them, just as a worker uses a tool" (IV. 3. 1). The expression *alter Christus* has the same meaning but is used no more than *mediator* by Vatican II because it leads to confusion. As for the formula *in persona Christi* (nine uses in Vatican II), it denotes the attribution to Christ of certain acts accomplished by the priest in accordance with his ministry, and these acts must in addition be situated in the context of the invocation of the Holy Spirit (epiclesis*). But taken the wrong way, this formula might seem to favor a certain isolation of the action of priests from the action of the church, and suggest that there might be priests who are priests in and for themselves, and who are, moreover, situated above the church. Indeed, the link between ministry and church poses several problems.

4. Articulation between the Ministry and the Church
Vatican II's ecclesiology of communion* ("central and fundamental concept of the council documents," according to the final report of the extraordinary synod* of 1985) might simultaneously require and facilitate a better link between ordained ministries and the church.

a) "Absolute Ordinations." A certain number of bishops are legitimately ordained without being assigned to a church (can. 376). For Protestant theology an apostolic* succession thus detached from local churches is too individualized or too abstractly collegial to be credible. An analogous question arises with respect to priests, for whom installation in a diocese is only one possibility among others (can. 266). Almost unknown in Orthodoxy*, these practices are the symptom of a bond that is too weak between ministry and church.

b) Hierarchical Interpretation of Ministries. In Vatican II and in the 1983 *CIC,* the pope and the bishops continue to receive the name "hierarchy." This vocabulary remains suspect to Protestantism because it seems to indicate a plenitude of power such that "hierarchical" decisions would have no need to be accepted by the faithful, that it would extend to the temporal realm (indirect power), and, moreover, that it could impose, on pain of sin*, obligations in domains in which the gospel established liberty* for the Christian (*see* rejection of fasts, Lenten diets, monastic vows, and priestly celibacy by *CA* 27 and 28). Melanchthon, for example, formally rejects a hierarchy understood in these terms: "Our adversaries wish the Church to be defined as an external monarchy whose supremacy is extended over the entire world and in which the Roman pontiff must have an unlimited power that no one has the right to discuss or to judge *(anupeuthunon);* he can at will establish articles of faith...promulgate laws.... But for us, in the Church as it was defined by Christ, we must not apply to pontiffs *(non est transferendum ad pontifices)* what is said of the Church as such" (*Apology* VII–VIII).

Dispelling the misunderstanding of an identification of the church with its hierarchy is easier since Vatican II has reinvigorated the equal dignity of all Christians (*LG* 32) and their active participation in the liturgy* (*SC* 14), made presbyteral councils obligatory (*PO* 7), and recommended pastoral councils (*CD* 27). The council also wished to give new life to plenary councils and diocesan synods in which laypeople might hold a majority (*CD* 26), and in which "all questions proposed [might] be submitted to free discussion" (*CIC* can. 465). There is thus taking shape in Catholic ecclesiology a greater integration of personal, collegial, and synodal authority. The concept of hierarchy must, however, be preserved in order to express the legitimate capacity of bishops to make decisions that commit the faithful; as, for example, in councils.

5. The Person of Ministers and the Object of the Ministry
Dogmatically, the content of the ministry ought to have authority over the person of the minister. Protestant theologians (e.g., Persson 1961) nevertheless think that in Catholicism the person of the minister has authority over the object of the ministry—for example, in the case of the magisterium*, preaching*, and the Eucharist*. This unsatisfactory balance also appears when, in a situation of a dearth of priests, the conditions requisite for acceding to the ministry (E. Schillebeeckx, *Plea for the People of God*) seem to contradict the right of the faithful to the word* of God and the sacraments (*CIC* can. 213).

a) Vocation to the Ministry: System of Candidacy or of Consent? In the early church the vocation to the ministry, considered as coming from God, coincided with the church's choice. The current system of candidacy was unknown, and priests and bishops were legitimately ordained against their will (Congar 1966). In deciding a famous controversy between Branchereau and Lahitton, Pius X covered the objective conception of the latter with his authority: "What is called 'priestly vocation' consists not at all, at least necessarily and as a general rule, of a certain interior attraction on the part of the subject, or of invitations by the Holy Spirit to embrace the ecclesiastical state" (*AAS* 4. 1912. 485). However, 20 years later the Congregation of the Sacraments required of every ordinand that he swear that he "freely desires (ordination), experiences and feels that he is truly called by God" (*AAS* 22, 1931, 127). Current vocabulary ("have a vocation," "live one's priesthood"), like the vocabulary of the *CIC,* which regularly designates ordinands as candidates, thus evidences what is hardly a traditional—neither medieval nor especially modern—subjectivization of the vocation for the ordained ministry. And this subjectivization has brought about a system of volunteering that makes it more difficult for episcopal authority to bring together pastoral needs and competent people, which would more easily be possible through a system that involved a call from the church and a consent to that call.

b) Personal Status of Ministers. The personal status of ministers comes only indirectly under the heading of faith. For example, Vatican II states: "Celibacy was imposed by a law of the Latin Church.... . it is not required by the nature of the priesthood" (*PO* 16). In the case of a reexamination of this status, two theological criteria would need to be taken into account: the pastoral good of the church, superior to the status of individuals, and the correlation between church and ministry, which makes it possible to think that a universal decree would not necessarily bear spiritual fruit. Modifying or maintaining a custom that has been so highly valued would also require the spiritual involvement of the churches concerned. The question of whether Christian women can be called to the ordained ministry, novel in its present form, is more complex (woman*). Permanence of the person in the ministry is not to be confused with the permanence of the effects of ordination, as expressed through the theology of the indelible character (Council of Trent*, sess. VII, can. 9 [*COD* 685, 7–9]). Here too the object of the ministry provides a criterion for the persons: just as one "does not make oneself a priest," one ought not to decide by oneself to leave the ministry. The conjunction between the needs of the service of the gospel and the aptitudes of the person (his faith, his health, his age) will be decisive in the matter (the *CIC* [can. 401 and 538] ordinarily provides for the resignation of ordained ministers at the age of 75).

6. Ecumenical Perspectives
Long thought to be insoluble, the question of the ministry has recently undergone a clarification.

a) Diverging Perspectives. Catholics and the Orthodox do not have the same initial doctrinal emphases as Protestants. In Protestantism the ministry is a secondary preoccupation. Even if it is a part of the *esse* of the church, as implicit in the proclamation of the Word and the celebration of the sacraments, its forms and its modes of exercise are part only of its *bene esse.* Lutheran bishops, for example, are not always ordained bishops and do not always have that title. Reformed churches, for their part, ordinarily exercise the *episkopè* collectively. Almost everywhere, the ministry is linked to a synodal form of government. Ordination is not a sacrament, and the diaconate is not governed by a sacrament; the emphasis is placed on the ministry of the Word and on administrative tasks, and all "sacerdotalization." (The Anglicans have a different position on each of these points.)

In the Catholic and Orthodox churches, on the other hand, ministers are recognized to have strong personal authority. They play a decisive role in the communion among local churches and in the expression of the faith. Linked to that of the apostles*, their ministry is also a priestly ministry.

b) Convergences. These divergent doctrinal emphases could, however, be brought into unity, on the condition that the churches take more account of their actual practices and less of the theoretical explanations they offer for them. For example, no church exists without a regulated supervision of its liturgical life and without continuous leadership: ministers are called, commissioned, and ordained according to rules established by other ministers. Ministry includes preaching, teaching, presiding over the life of the church, and representing it to the outside world. We can see everywhere the existence of an *episkopè:* the right of visitation, vigilance over doctrine and over the call to the ministry, participation in ordinations, and the like. The "Faith and Constitution" Commission of the COE has developed a document (*Baptism, Eucharist, Ministries—BEM,* "Lima Document") that could be fruitful for Catholics and Protestants. Catholicism could learn from it how to supplement its highly personalized practice of the ministry through collegial and synodal bodies; and the Protestant churches could accept a greater personalization of the episcopacy while not abandoning their synodal structures.

● P. E. Persson (1961), *Kyrkans ämbete som Kristus-representation,* Lund (*see* c.r. by L. M. Dewailly, *RSPhTh* 46, 1962, 650–57).

Y. Congar (1966), "Ordinations, *invitus, coactus,* de l'Église ancienne au can. 214," *RSPhTh* 50, 169–97.

R. Gryson (1970), *Les origines du célibat ecclésiastique du Ier au VIIe s.,* Gembloux.

Y. Congar (1971), *Ministères et communion ecclésiale,* Paris.

H. Dombois (1971), *Hierarchie: Grund und Grenze einer umstrittenen Struktur,* Freiburg-Basel-Vienna.

H. Legrand (1972), "M. et caractère indélébile," *Conc(F)* no. 74, 63–70.

Commission internationale catholique-luthérienne (1981), official texts (Ed. H. Legrand, H. Meyer), *Le ministère dans l'Église,* Paris (with *excursus* by Y. Congar); (1985), *Face à l'unité,* Paris.

Commission mixte catholique-orthodoxe (1982), "Le mystère de l'Église et de l'eucharistie à la lumière du mystère de la Sainte Trinité," *DC* 79, 941–45.

F. Frost (1982), "M.," *Cath.* 10, 185–286.

P. Eicher (1991), "Hierarchie," *NHThG,* vol. 2, 330–49 (*Dictionnaire de théologie,* 1988, 287–98).

J. Freitag (1993), "Amt," *LThK3* 1, 547–50.

H. Legrand (1993), "Les m. de l'Église locale," in B. Lauret and F. Refoulé (Ed.), *Initiation à la pratique de la théologie,* vol. 3, 3rd. Ed., Paris, esp. 239–73 (and bibl. 333–42).

J. Delorme (Ed.) (1994), *Le m. et les ministères selon le Nouveau Testament,* Paris.

HERVÉ LEGRAND

See also **Baptism; Bishop; Church; Deacon; Deaconesses; Ecumenism; Hierarchy; Ordination/Order; Synod; Woman**

Minucius Felix. *See* Apologists

Miracle

A. Biblical Theology

I. Vocabulary

There is no equivalent in either Hebrew or biblical Greek for the word "miracle," understood as denoting an exception to the laws of nature* that is attributed to divine agency because it is otherwise unexplainable. The religious experience in the presence of a miracle outweighs its element of interrupting ordinary causality (*see* Bultmann [1926], *Jesus*). The universality of physical laws is no longer observed.

The Hebrew *'ôt* (78 times), "sign" (Septuagint *sèmeion*) and *môfét* (36 times), "prodigal" (Septuagint *teras*) are often associated (18 times): a miracle is a message; *môfet,* alone, can also signify "omen" (Ez 12:6–11). One will find *nifelâ'ôt* (rare in the singular), "wonders" (Septuagint *thaumasia*) or the verb *pl'*, "to make wonders"; *nôrâ'ôt* (44 times), "fearsome actions"; *gevoûrôt,* "exploits;" *ma'aséh*[AuQ7] (Septuagint *ergon*), "action," or "work," an encompassing term; *paradoxon* (Wis 5:2, 19:5; in the superlative: 16, 17), "extraordinary." The synoptic Gospels prefer *dunamis* for the miracles of Jesus*, while John favors *sèmeion* (27 times), or *ergon.*

II. Old Testament

1. Diversity of Miracles

A miracle does not necessarily come from God* (Dt 13:2ff.). Moses and Aaron before Pharoah surpass his magicians only after a long competition (Ex 7–8). Owing to their proximity within the main current of tradition, certain miracles can be grouped together. Miracles of the Moses cycle belong to the very heart of the Torah, at the point where tradition is transmitted: didactic texts (Dt 4:34, 7:19, 29:2, 34:11), catechesis* for the son (Ex 13:14; Dt 6:22; Ps 44:2, 78:1–7, 78:43, 105:5, 105:27) narrative "credo" of Dt 26:5–9 (*see* Jos 24:5). In the case of the miracle of Joshua ("Sun, stand still!": Jos 10:12b), there is no recurring motif. The cycle of Elijah and Elisha illustrates the prophetic tradition: cosmic signs (1 Kgs 18:19–46), the gift of food (1 Kgs 17:8–16; 2 Kgs 4:1–7, 4:42ff.), the healing of a pagan (2 Kgs 5), the dead brought back to life (1 Kgs 17:17–24; 2 Kgs 4:18–37), and so on. But there are no miracles attributed to the prophets* of the eighth century (except in Is 38:1–8; 2 Kgs 20:1–11) or their successors.

2. Changes in Literary Form

In the myth* of origin the irruption effect that belongs to miracles does not exist: the improbable, briefly touched upon, is continuous (Gn 2–3; *see* Mt 4:1–11, Jesus in the desert) and is not surprising. Comical flavor and naïveté color *local traditions* (a corpse brought back to life after having been quickly thrown in Elisha's tomb: 2 Kgs 13:20f.). Late legends are fantastical, detailed, and artificial in character (2 Macc 2:1–6, 3:24–34; Dn 3). On the other hand, there was nothing miraculous in either the long story of David and of Solomon, or even in the story of Joseph, however literary this may be otherwise (Gn 36–50).

3. New Interpretations

a) Change in Scale. The Red Sea parts without the help of the natural forces that were mentioned in Exodus 14:21 and 14:25: Israel* walks between two liquid walls (Ex 14:16, 14:22f., 14:29). The writer's intention is to highlight God's act of separation in Genesis 1:6–10: the savior thus presents himself as the Creator. The phenomenon of the manna is presented with many nuances: miraculous (Ex 16:26) or rather enigmatic

(Ex 16:15), natural (color, shape, consistency, taste: Ex 16:14, 16:31; preparation: Nm 11:8). According to Exodus 16:14, manna is discovered; it "falls" according to Numbers 11:9; it becomes "bread from heaven" in Psalm 105:40 (embedded in the writing of the miracle of Joshua: Jos 10:10–14).

b) Interiorization. Israel had to overcome its fear of death to cross the Red Sea (Ex 14:13f., unknown source). In order for the Jordan river to part, the bearers of the ark would have had to dare to put "the soles of the feet" (Jos 3:13) in it.

c) Rationalization. The Hellenistic period saw the simultaneous rise of a specifically apocalyptic* form of the fabulous and a new interest in the laws of physics, particularly with respect to medicine (terminology of 2 Macc 7:22b; Moses and the pharmacist: Sir 38:5: Salomon: Wis 7:20c). Song of Songs records the miracles of Exodus (plagues, crossing of the sea, manna) by recombining the same cosmic elements.

4. Disappearance of the Miracle

a) Interruption. Lamentations rise toward God: marvels are distant (Ps 74:11f., 77:11, 80:3–17, 89:50, 143:5); they belong to former days (Ps 44:2, 78:3f.; Is 51:9; Mi 7:14), to the time of the Fathers. This schema became a common concept: Judges 6:13 and 15:18 (for rabbinical literature: Hruby 1977). Deuteronomy indicates the distance between the time of the Fathers and the present time (5:3, 29:13f.). What is left of the miraculous? The relics* kept with the ark (manna: Ex 16:33f.; Aaron's staff: Nm 17:25) have disappeared. In the second century B.C. God hands over to martyrdom those who obey his law (1 Macc 2:38; 2 Macc 7). The theme of Wisdom 2:10–20 concerns the righteous possibly being killed without God intervening.

b) Series. Miracles "are lightning" (Pascal*), but they open a course of closely linked events. The crossing of the desert is interpreted as an itinerary punctuated by miracles (Ex 15:23–26, 16:1–4, 17:2–7; Ps 78; *see* Dt 6:16). Its disappearance turns a miracle into a test. It leads either to a deepening of faith* or to insatiable demands for proof, an increase in challenges: Israel in the desert "tempts" God (*nâsâh*, intensive) (temptation*). A request of God for a sign is not necessarily an occasion for divine anger (Jgs 6:17, 6:36–40; 2 Kgs 20:8; Is 7:1). But when the Israelites put God "to the test ten times" (Nm 14:22), God reveals that to test him is the opposite of "believing" (Ps 78; Nm 20:12). Each miracle only exacerbates the thirst to see God act (Ex 17:2–7) without satisfying it. For Wisdom

2:17–20, this inclination goes as far as planning to kill the righteous to "see if" God will act (Wis 1:2, 2:22c). But God will act only in secret (Wis 2:22a), a secrecy that is all the more profound when the act is decisive.

III. Miracles of Jesus

1. Continuity

a) Confirmation of the Signs. In Matthew 11:2–6, miracles are called "the works of Christ* (the Messiah*)" by the evangelist, and Jesus himself borrows from Isaiah to describe them (Mt 11:5): healing the blind (Is 42:18); the lame (Is 35:6); the deaf and blind (Is 29:18, 35:5, 42:18); the dead raised (Is 26:19), all this inaugurated by the announcement made to the poor (Is 61:1 Septuagint). The exorcisms* in Matthew 12:28 prove that the Kingdom* that was prophesied has come. The pairing "signs and wonders" (also occur in the reverse order) that evokes the miracles of the tradition* (*see* above, II, 1) appears in Acts 2:19, 7:36, 2:22, 6:8, 4:30, and 5:12 (*sèmeia kai dunameis* in 8:13). The expression, when it is used in Romans 15:19 and 2 Corinthians 12:12, serves to authenticate Paul's credentials as an apostle*.

b) Repetition of Schemas. John 6:31f. (bread/manna) refers to Moses (*see* the "desert" in Mk 6:31). And Jesus, who subjugates the winds and the sea (Mk 4:41), probably also refers to him (Ex 14:16, 14:21, 14:26f.). More than one story about the miracles of Jesus and his apostles refers, through certain details, to the miracles of Elijah and Elisha (the raising of the widow's son: Lk 7:11; *see* 1 Kgs 17:17–24; and of Jairus's daughter: Lk 8:42; *see* 1 Kgs 17:21; of Tabitha: Acts 9:36–42; *see* 2 Kgs 4:8–37). Even the miracle of the loaves in Matthew 14:13–21 and 15:32–38 is a copy of 2 Kgs 4:42ff.

2. Specific Characteristics

a) Types of Miracles. Certain miracles (known as "epiphanies": Cana, the loaves, walking on water, the miraculous catch of fish) are meant to reveal who Jesus is. As a healer (healing*), Jesus can find himself before large groups of sick people, especially in Matthew 8:16f., 9:36, 12:15, and 15:30f. The goal is social and collective. Jesus saves from sickness (15 times) or death (three times). He delivers the possessed (eight times), who are sometimes also sick (three times). In the final analysis, these acts have several dimensions: to save, or even to confirm a truth ("apothegm" [Bultmann] illustrated by healing work in Mk 2:1–12, after the pardon, 3:1–6; Sabbath* by an anecdotal marvel in

Mt 17:24–27: temple* tax.). As in the past, discernment was needed: Jesus *and* his adversaries drive out demons* (Mt 12:27; par. Lk 11:19). Jesus will condemn those who have performed miracles in his name (Mt 7:22f.). There are some counterfeits (Acts 8:9–13, 13:8).

b) Meaning. A miracle is always a sign, linked to teaching in Matthew 4:23 and 9:35; Mark 1:21, 1:27, and 6:34–44; and Luke 5:17, 6:6, and 13:10. The accounts of the principal miracles do not reveal all their symbolic impact, hidden in Mark (Lamarche 1977), and expounded upon in John. They partake of a truth* that will be revealed only later on. It should be noted that Jesus does not perform any miracles to protect himself from death and that, in the scheme of things, it does not matter if there are no miracles. Nevertheless, the miracle of the loaves does not belong to this category: a crowd, which could give Jesus political power, benefits from it (Jn 6:15).

3. New Characteristics

a) Main Features. The fact that Jesus' miracle stories have roots in the Old Testament does not lessen their originality. 1) They focus on the human body and compassion (reference to the Servant in Mt 8:16f., 9:36, 12:15). 2) Though they are not entirely free of embellishments, their sweep is reduced. We are far from the great deeds of Moses. Indeed the parallel and contrast between the "desert" of Galilee and that of Exodus, between the bread from the sky and the basket that a child brings, are part of the message. 3) The effect of communicative intensity, however, increases correspondingly: the eyes, the ears, the mouth are healed by the eyes, the ears, the mouth; the miracle worker transfers his power to the disciples; the spectators praise God. 4) The great number of demons concretizes the apocalyptic atmosphere in everyday life. 5) Jesus more than once resists performing miracles (Mk 8:11f., 9:19; Jn 4:48) and forbids their being publicized (Mk 1:34, 1:44, 5:43; Lk 8:56; Mk 7:36, 8:26; Mt 9:30).

b) Overall Narrative Movement. The beginning and end of the story shed light on Jesus' reserve. The initial appearance of the tempter provides a key to the miracles. On the one hand it establishes a link to the Exodus (Mk 1:13: "desert"; Mt and Lk: dialogue consisting of verses from Deuteronomy). In particular, Satan tempts Jesus to "test God," as Israel had done in the past (*see* above, II, 4, *b*) so that his status as "Son of God" cannot be contested by anyone (filiation) (Mt 4:16; Lk 4:12; Dt 6:16). On the other hand, Luke 4:13b

anticipates Calvary, where Jesus' miracles will be turned against him: "He saved others; he cannot save himself" (Mk 15:31; *see* " Physician, heal yourself" in Lk 4:23). The challenge will parallel Satan's (Mk 15:31): a miracle "that we may see and believe" (Mk 15:32). Matthew 27:40—"If you are the Son of God, come down from the cross!"—adopts Matthew 4:3, 4:6 words. However, the very absence of a sign has, in a certain way, become a sign: the centurion believes.

c) Miracles, Signs, Parables. For faith*, each miracle signifies more than it shows. Either the series of miracles becomes progressively more invisible or the cross invalidates the series of miracles: it can only go forward or backward. The miracles are a risky way of teaching, but an unavoidable risk. Hence the strongly underlined parallel between miracle and parable* (Mk 4:11f.: "for those outside everything is in parables"; 8:18: the blind and deaf before miracles). John clarifies the transition from the visible to the invisible when he interprets a healing as a figure of the Resurrection* (5:21), or interprets the miracle of the loaves as a figure of eternal life (Jn 6:27). His series of seven "signs" (2:1–11, 4:46–54, 5:1–15, 6:1–15, 6:16–21, 9, 11) represents an escalation. The signs, for him, create faith (Jn 2:11, 6:14, 11:42, 11:45), but this faith is not always solid (Jn 12:42f.). The cumulative effect leads to the miracle of the raising of Lazarus (perhaps a later elaboration), which triggers the murderous plan of the high priest (Jn 11:49–53; characteristic without historical impact, *see* Brown 1966). The real outcome is the summary of John 12:37–41, which firmly connects the reception given to signs with that given to parables: John 12:40 here transposes the quotation in Isaiah 6:9, used by Mark 4:12.

The "sign of Jonah" announced to "an evil and adulterous generation" (Mt 12:39), when all signs (Mk 8:12) were denied to it, could not be the Resurrection, which is invisible to nonbelievers. It could only be this sign that they could receive from the Resurrection: its announcement in the preaching* (see), as with sinful Nineveh that received for its salvation* the preaching of Jonah, who had been delivered from the abyss.

- R. Bultmann (1933), "Zur Frage des Wunders," in *GuV* 1, 214–28.
- R. E. Brown (1966), *The Gospel according to John* I–XII, New York, App. III: "Signs and Works," 525–32.
- G. Theissen (1974), *Urchristliche Wundergeschichten: Ein Beitrag zur formgeschichtlichen Erforschung der synoptischen Evangelien*, Gütersloh.
- X. Léon-Dufour (Ed.) (1977), *Les miracles de Jésus*, Paris, especially K. Hruby, "Perspectives rabbiniques sur le miracle," 73–94; P. Lamarche, "Les miracles de Jésus selon Marc," 213–26; X. Léon-Dufour, "Structure et fonction du récit de miracle," 289–353.

J.-M. van Cangh (1982), "Santé et salut dans les miracles d'Épidaure, d'Apollonius de Tyane et du Nouveau Testament," in J. Ries (Ed.), *Gnosticisme et monde hellénistique,* Louvain-la-Neuve, 263–77; (1987), "Miracle," in *Dictionnaire encyclopédique de la Bible,* Bruges, col. 833–46.

P. Beauchamp (1989), "Paraboles de Jésus, vie de Jésus," in coll. "ACFEB," *Les Paraboles, Perspectives nouvelles,* LeDiv 165, 151–70; (1992), "Le signe des pains," *LV(L)* 209, 55–67.

Y. Zakovitch (1992), "Miracle," *AncBD* 4, 845–56.

J. P. Meier (1994), *Rethinking the Historical Jesus,* vol. 2, New York–London, pt. 3, 509–1038.

PAUL BEAUCHAMP

See also **Faith; Fundamentalism; Healing; Jesus, Historical; Literary Genres in Scripture; Narrative; Passion; Resurrection of the Dead; Temptation**

B. Historical and Systematic Theology

A theory of miracle is apparently absent in the earliest Christian theology*. There are good reasons for this. The idea of miracle is indeed neither Jewish nor Christian. In the religious world of late antiquity, miracle working was common activity. The boundary between the magical and the medical had not yet been delineated, and the number of divine entities that populated the cosmos* was high enough to render banal what was later to be called "supernatural*" or "preternatural." And even though popular theology, as expressed in the Gospels* and apocryphal acts, surely betrays a taste for wonders, this penchant is absent from the more or less scholarly theology, as it is from the New Testament corpus. Isolated from contexts that give them the force of meaning and revelation*, the miracles of Jesus* undoubtedly called for an apologetic: on the one hand they were real miracles, not trickery; on the other, they were miracles of divine origin, not demonic wonders (e.g., Origen*, *Contra Celsum* II, 48 *Sq*). Above all, it was a question of meaning. The miracle could only be integrated in terms of *proof*, as a part of a whole, "the event of Jesus Christ," in which, first of all, the hopes (and the Scriptures*) of Israel* were fulfilled, and in which were also fulfilled the hopes of a paganism* that certainly did not expect another miracle worker.

It was thus within a framework rather larger than that of apologetics—the framework, that is, of a *mystical cosmology*—that Augustine approached the question of miracles. For centuries this approach provided important terms of reference. The first precise definition of miracle can be attributed to Augustine: "*Miraculuum voco, quidquid arduum aut insolitum supra spem vel facultatem mirantis apparet*" (I call miracle that which appears to have an unusual quality and that which exceeds all that which the one to be enchanted expected or could do) (*De util. cred.* 16, §34). For Augustine, however, beyond these distinctive features, the miracle is par excellence (and it is not strange that a convert to Manicheanism* saw in this the material for theological emphasis) nothing else but the totality of a creation* in which nothing is lacking to give witness to the Creator and his omnipotence (*Ep.* 137). Without ever denying the realist meaning of the Christian Eucharist* (it is, moreover, after having recalled the divine power manifested in the Eucharist that he discusses miracles in *Trin.* III, V, 11), Augustine never refuted a theological argument that made an appeal to wondrous episodes in world history. But, just as his theology of the Eucharist is first developed as a doctrine of the *figura,* of the "mode of apparition," his theology of miracle is developed in the same way as the contemplation* of a meaningful totality. Each fragment of the totality deserves the awe (*mirari, thaumazein*) with which one must praise divine manifestation. A dialectic of miracle remains possible—it is nevertheless an aesthetic of miracle that occupies the foreground, and, to one who possesses a spiritual sensibility toward the created order of things, it appears that everything deserves to be called miraculous.

The Augustinian concept prevailed over Western theology as long as there also prevailed the concept of a sacramental and diaphanous world in which all is symbolic and in which each symbol fulfills a theophanic function. It therefore dominated until, in a process that was to begin as early as the Carolingian Renaissance, a school of thought fascinated by *causes* gradually supplanted one that was concerned with signs and symbols. Aristotle's gradual "introduction" into the West, the reappearance of a philosophical urgency to which the universities would grant some independence from theology, and the resurgence of a scientific interest in the real: such factors would in the

13th century impose a worldview in which the nature of things had an intrinsic intelligibility sufficient to render obsolete the intrusion of all supernatural elements. The explanation of the immanent networks of causality henceforth replaced the contemplation of an order woven with transcendental references. From this there arose a new cosmology—and with it a new theory of miracle—in which any such occurrence appeared as an aberration, as something uncaused, an exception to the physical/metaphysical laws that govern the world. Because the world has a Cause—a God* who has the dignity of the *primary cause*—the causes that rule over the correct order of the world are themselves only *secondary causes* (Augustine already knew this very well, e.g., *Trin.* III, VIII, 13–IX, 18). The primary cause, which is not counted with the secondary causes, exercises its authority through their mediation. It is, however, not limited to manifesting itself through mediation, and it is precisely with its manifestation that it confronts us. The miracle therefore reveals the sovereignty of the primary cause in that it sets aside the causal order that the primary cause has given to the world, and inasmuch as it acts "against the very order of all created nature" (Thomas* Aquinas, *ST* Ia, q. 110, a. 4). Once this had been stated, the miracle ceased to be subjected in the first place to strictly theological inquiries: it was first of all a matter of *physical* questions (the miraculous being defined as a violation of physical laws), and the response provided by theologians was a *metaphysical* answer that utilized only one theological doctrine, that of divine omnipotence.

A theory of miracle that posited the synergy of the primary cause and the secondary causes, and the immediate operation of the primary cause suspending the regulated interplay of secondary causes, was endowed with consistency (and still has this quality) and could answer all the demands of rationalism. The use of the theory nevertheless contained a trap of which medievalists were not aware because of their great trust in the Greek physics that the Arabs had passed on to them, but which modern objectors easily spotted. Whereas both do not belong to the network of secondary causes, it does not necessarily follow that it cannot be integrated. The miracle is an exception to the laws of our physics—but it will suffice to form the idea of scientific progress to make of the miracle not a manifestation of divine lordship but only an index of our present ignorance. The medieval theory of miracle, in fact, only allowed the epistemological status of the unexplained to be defined.

It was up to the Reformers, who had great reservations about the theoretical strategies of Scholasticism*, to carry out a first critique of the appeal to miracles.

For Luther*, faith*, which is the interior miracle, is more important than healing*, the external miracle (*WA* 41, 19). Miracles belonged to the past; present miracles could only endanger church doctrine, and the only miracle was now to be found in the experience of forgiveness and faith (*WA* 10/3, 144 *Sq*). Calvin followed Luther in regarding miracles as a distinctive characteristic of the early church, and of it alone. Indeed, Protestant orthodoxy would routinely contest the appeal of modern Catholic thought to current miracles. But this same orthodoxy would later readopt the Scholastic concept of miracle as a *contra et supra naturam* event, against nature and beyond nature (e.g., Quenstedt, *Syst. Theol.* I, 671), and it would also abandon the Lutheran concept of faith as miracle par excellence.

Nevertheless, the most incisive criticism came from the development of *historical* science. The physical theory of miracles seeks to specify that one thing or another *is* a miracle. However, the major miracles of which *theology* aims to speak (above all, the miracles of Jesus) are susceptible not to the test of observation but instead to the work of memory: these are the recounted miracles. Even in the time of rationalism*, miracles could certainly happen and play a role in the life of rational human beings: thus the "miracle of the holy thorn tree" in Pascal*'s experience. But what about reported miracles? On this point, Hume posed objections that were much older than the Enlightenment. He said that the miracle story could be considered true only under one condition, namely the impossibility of attributing any improbability at all to the account given. Only the infallible account can lend credibility to the miracles of which it speaks, since the error of such an infallible account would represent an even greater miracle (*An Enquiry Concerning Human Understanding*, Ed. Selby-Bigge). And since the present experience of the world does not present us with any miracles, it is doubtful that there ever were any. Those things happen, or "occur," that *can* happen and occur. The *present* conditions of experience—the world as it is and the nature of things as they are—provide the conditions of all possibilities.

Whether tacitly or explicitly, all the hermeneutics* of historical accounts developed from the end of the 17th century up until Troeltsch made these affirmations their own. Only a certified miracle, Lessing suggested, could be "the proof of spirit and power," but we only ever deal with recounted miracles. Henceforth, the ontological status of miracle would only be that of a textual object (miracles find their true home in mythical texts), or of a product of faith. It would not be denied that miracle stories have a *meaning*. Nevertheless, throughout a long chapter in the history of thought—one that would not end until Bultmann* (although Bultmann only gave his theological blessing to a split between "meaning" and "fact," the origins of which are not theological)—it was our world, understood as our "vision of the world," that was asked to determine from which *facts* this meaning originated. Philosophical modernity and theological modernity thus come together in analogous policies of exclusion. Scholasticism tended to perceive exclusively in the miracle a miraculous fact. The kind of thinking that foreshadowed the Enlightenment and also that came out of it undoubtedly retained the idea of the miraculous fact. But this was in order to set the logic of facts (occurred facts and narrated facts, *Geschichte* and *Historie*) in opposition to the logic of miracles.

Systematic theology could not find many answers to contemporary critiques that flourished in the biblical exegesis* of Strauss's and Renan's era. Protestant supernaturalism certainly did not miss the opportunity to defend the classic theory with the help of modern terminology. Thus, F. G Süskind (1767–1829) defined miracle as "a phenomenon that belongs to the world of the senses, but is founded in a reality that is in itself supra-tangible and to which it must be linked." The Protestant 19th century also saw one R. Rothe (1799–1867) make of miracle "an element of revelation*." The most influential decisions were also the most timid. In the theory of pious consciousness that constitutes the backbone of Schleiermacher*'s dogmatic* theology, the miracle, for such consciousness, is the finite leading sometimes to the infinite*—but it is clearly noted that the finite does not, therefore, cease to belong to the network of natural causalities (*Christ. Glaube*, §47). In Catholicism, a certain J. S. Von Drey readopted a theory that had already been championed by Leibniz* and saw in miracles the action of hidden natural forces. These forces only manifest themselves in an exceptional way (theory of the preformation). Among other Catholic scholars, as divergent as J. M. Sailer, G. Hermes, and L. Bautain, a certain Kantian influence and the concern for emotional apologetics led to the marginalization of the idea of "proof by miracle." It is therefore not surprising that it was during this period that the magisterial authorities of Catholicism* first expressed themselves on the question of miracles (previously, this had only been approached in terms of canonical regulations, and by Benedict XIV to determine the need for a miracle to promote a cause of beatification or canonization). Moreover, the series of reminders (*DS* 2768, 2779, 3009), which were to be adopted again in the 20th century by the antimodernist oath (*DS* 3539) and the encyclical *Humani generis* (*DS* 3876), was less about proposing a definition than defending the possibility and the convincing force. These texts consider miracles a demonstration of divine power, without explicitly linking them to a violation of natural laws.

As the keystone of an apologetics of demonstration and proof, an apologetics that hardly questioned the status of demonstration and proof, whether in theology or in philosophy*, the miracle was bound to meet the same fate as this aspect of apologetics, which only barely survived in fundamentalist Protestantism* and in Catholic Neoscholasticism. However, it was also bound to find new meaning and a role in recent fundamental theologies. It was above all thanks to E. Le Roy and to Blondel*, after the latter had provided his specifications and outline for a method for revived apologetics (1896, *Lettre sur l'apologétique, OC* 2, 97–193), that miracle was afforded the dignity of a philosophical and theological subject in debate (Le Roy 1906; B. de Sailly 1907 and Blondel *OC* 2, 725–40) that marked the end of all purely physical definitions of the miraculous and the rebirth of *sign* thought of as the "seed of faith" (*OC* 2, 728). The influence of Blondel would also play a role in the tradition* illustrated in the 19th century by theologians like Cardinal V. Dechamps (whose influence preponderated at the First Vatican* Council) or J. H. Newman, and then in the 20th century by P. Rousselot and those who were inspired by his work. It contributed to the development of a form of understanding in which all Christian reality in particular, as it is actualized and transmitted by the church, was asked to have credibility, and in which global human experience, at once intellectual, free, and emotional, was asked to note the believable suggested by the mediation of the church.

The discourse on proof was of course reorganized. The factuality of miracle, if there are miracles (and certain phenomena like healings witnessed in the sanctuaries in Lourdes, for example, have maintained within Catholicism an interest in miraculous happenings; *see* Pius XII, encyclical *A Pilgrimage to Lourdes, AAS* 49 [1957], 605–19), is more than that of a marvel since it calls for theological deciphering that would allow its insertion in a network of significations. And in order precisely to reach these meanings, one will have to borrow in a privileged manner—probably from the theology of the Resurrection of Jesus—categories within which all other miracles can be accounted for. Thus, the miracle emerged again as a sign, and specifically as a *messianic* and *eschatological* sign. Perceiving this sign therefore requires an ability to interpret, and the interpretation is spiritual more than rational (R. Latourelle, *DSp* 10, 1281). For, although it is quite clear that there is no room for the miraculous in the "modern world," it should also be clear that Christian experience has its own world*

("world" designating a totality of relationships, prejudices and forms of behavior), the world of biblical experience, and that this world has the characteristic of remaining habitable in the discontinuity of time. Access to biblical experience, access to the Resurrection of Jesus as the mark of this experience, access to the eschatological community that transmits the kerygma of the Resurrection, the founding acts that retain the meaning of all miracles and the conditions of its recognition: retrospectively, the Resurrection of Jesus allows us to see, in the miracles recorded in the Old Testament, signs foreshadowing the Easter event, and likewise in Jesus' miracles themselves. Prospectively, it allows us to see a certain memory of the Resurrection of Jesus in the miracles of the time of the church. Perhaps theology needs no other miracles than the double event of Easter and Pentecost in order to know that Christian experience is the experience of a new age and a new world. But for a reasoning mind—believing or only borne along by a "budding faith that strives to test itself or develop" (E. Le Roy)—that accepts leaving questions open about what is possible and about God (Marion 1989), the miracle is evidence of the new order of the world. Not everyone regards the appearance of anything strange, inexplicable, or unfathomable as miraculous. It is only in the horizon of meaning opened by the Resurrection of Jesus that the miracle is recognized for what it really is. In this respect the doctrine of miracles is a footnote to that first chapter of Christian theology.

Finally, the philosophical discussion of miracles has remained alive in the Anglo-Saxon world, whether it has been under the continued influence of Hume (Gräfrath 1997) or under the guidance of Wittgenstein.

● J. H. Newman (1897), *Two Essays on Miracles,* London.
E. Le Roy (1906), "Essai sur la notion du miracle," *APhC,* 4th series, vol. 3, 5–33, 166–91, 225–59.
B. de Sailly (M. Blondel) (1907), "La notion et le rôle du miracle," *APhC,* 4th series, vol. 4, 337–61.
P. Rousselot (1910), "Les yeux de la foi," *RSR* 1, 241–59, 444–75.
J. Huby (1918), "Miracle et lumière de grâce," *RSR* 8, 36–77.
R. Bultmann (1933), "Zur Frage des Wunders," *GuV* I, 214–28.
R. M. Grant (1952), *Miracle and Natural Law in Graeco-Roman and Early Christian Thought,* Amsterdam.
C. S. Lewis (1947), *Miracles,* 2nd Rev. Ed., London, 1960.
R. Guardini (1959), *Wunder und Zeichen,* Würzburg.
L. Monden (1961), *Theologie des Wunders,* Freiburg.
R. Latourelle (1963), *Théologie de la révélation,* Paris-Bruges, 416–34.
D. Dubarle (1967), "Réflexions sur le miracle," *Approches d'une théologie de la science,* CFi 22, 77–99.
A. Kolping (1968), *Fundamentaltheologie* I, Münster, 297–314.
H. C. Kee (1983), *Miracle in the Early Christian World,* New Haven–London.
H. Fries (1985), *Fundamentaltheologie,* Graz, 276–95.
L. Pearl (1988), "Miracles and Theism," *RelSt* 24, 483–96.
J.-L. Marion (1989), "A Dieu, rien d'impossible," *Com(F)* XIV/5, 43–58.
T. L. Nichols (1990), "Miracles, the Supernatural, and the Problem of Extrincism," *Gr.* 71, 23–40.
R. Bauman (1991), "Wunder," *NHThG* 5, 286–99.
S. Slupik (1995), "A New Interpretation of Hume's *Of Miracles,*" *RelSt* 31, 517–36.
B. Gräfrath (1997), "Wissenschaftstheorie oder Ästhetik der Wunder," *ThPh* 72, 257–63.

JEAN-YVES LACOSTE

See also **Credibility; Faith; Fundamental Theology; Sciences of Nature**

Mission/Evangelization

In the broad sense, the mission is a basic characteristic of the church,* which is called upon to be the sign and instrument in the world of God*'s salvation* for all of mankind. Two major tasks are incumbent on the church as on every true believer: to testify to the gospel (evangelization) and serve man (diaconate). In a narrower sense mission means the work of spreading the faith* and founding new communities outside "traditionally Christian countries." This meaning attained increasingly special importance after the 17th century, when the Jesuits pronounced the *votum de missionibus,* a vow of readiness to be "sent on mission" by one's superiors. Furthermore, all religions that claim to be universal see themselves as missionary communities, as distinguished from tribal and national religions.

1. Biblical Foundations

In the Old Testament the idea of a God who sends envoys is found primarily in narratives* of prophetic vocation (Ex 3:10; Jer 1:7; and Is 2:3–4 and 3:4–5). With the prophets* was born the hope of a conversion of the nations to faith in the unique God (Is 2:2–4, 19:21–25, and 45:20–25, and the books of Ruth and Jonah). "Proselytes" who become Jewish are evoked in post-exilic literature (Est 8:17; Tb 13:13; and Dn 3:17–20 and 6:26–28).

The New Testament sees Jesus* first as the envoy of God among men; the Gospel* According to John bases the authority* of Jesus on this mission—he is the Son sent by the Father* (Jn 3:17, 10:36, and 17:18). Jesus is sent first (Mt 15:24) to Israel*, but his mission also has a universal dimension, which is made evident by his attitude toward outcasts and pagans, as when he shares the table of the sinners and takes liberties with Jewish dietary practices (Mk 7:15–23 and Lk 10:8). Jesus' disciples, too, are envoys, from before Easter (Mk 3:13–15 and 6:7–13 and parallels to both) bearing responsibilities similar to their master's (to announce and heal). This mandate is renewed at Easter: the Risen Lord appears before his followers to send them out on mission (Mt 28:19; 1 Cor 15:5–8; and Jn 20:21–23). However, the mission does not begin until after Pentecost, for the indispensable condition of the apostolate of the community of disciples is the gift of the Holy* Spirit. The beginnings of the church's mission is related in the Acts of the Apostles; Paul occupies a special place as the one who transmits the gospel to the pagans (Rom 11:13 and Gal 1:15–16). He saw his mission as that of a plenipotentiary envoy (Rom 1:5; 1 Cor 9:2; and Gal 2:8).

2. Historical Landmarks

The mission of the church met with rapid, spectacular success in the first centuries of the Christian era. During this period of cultural and religious distress in the Roman Empire, Christianity could take advantage of the network of Jewish communities and synagogues that served as points of departure for Christian missionaries in many cities. By the third century, and despite numerous persecutions, the church was present and active on all social levels. Christianity, which was tolerated in the empire before it became the official religion, became increasingly influential in every walk of political, social, and cultural life. The missionary extension of Christianity was methodical, apologetical, and didactic.

The most remarkable phenomenon in the fourth century was the missionary enterprise of Irish and British monks who had taken a vow of "pilgrimage" and saw themselves as envoys of the pope to the pagans. A political dimension was then added to the religious dimension of evangelization, and cultural prestige also came into play. Since this mission imposed a rather lengthy cohabitation of Christian faith with paganism*, the church developed means of cultural adaptation and accommodation well beyond the practices of the ancient church.

The Nestorian Church was the ultimate in missionary churches in the medieval East. Despite the existence of other missionary religions, this church, which had no political backing or possibility of creating a strong ecclesial structure*, developed considerably.

After the 16th century the opening of new lands stimulated renewed missionary enthusiasm for Catholicism*, especially in the Iberian peninsula, with Latin America as the major field of action. In reaction to the brutality and cupidity of the conquerors and with the intent of ensuring the survival and the evangelization of Indian tribes, the Jesuits set up missionary enclaves, called *reductions,* that remained in operation from 1610 until their expulsion from Argentina and Paraguay in 1768. The Jesuits sought to transmit the faith liberated from its traditional forms, in order to bring forth a Christianity adapted to local situations. At the same time indigenous forms of Christianity arose in India and China.

To develop the mission, Gregory XV created the Congregation for the Propagation of the Faith in 1622, and Urban VIII founded a Collegium Urbanum to train priests* for missionary work. In 1663 the *Société des missions étrangères* (Society of Foreign Missions) was created in Paris at the initiative of François Pallu (1626–84), with the double purpose of training missionaries and encouraging the formation of a native clergy in Asia. However, this native clergy did not really take shape until the early 20th century.

In the Orthodox East, the Russian missions were very active, with the support of the princes of Kiev and then the czars, notably Peter the Great (1682–1725). These missions would often start out under the impetus of a single person; the gospel would be translated into a local tongue followed by the creation of monachal-type poles of evangelization resembling small groups of fervent believers. However, when Czar Alexander I (†1825) decided to tolerate cults* other than the Byzantine Orthodox, the Russian Church had great difficulty containing the apostasy of baptized pagans.

In the Reform churches, pietism* made way for development of the missionary idea by liberating it from its traditional dogmatic and territorial bonds. When the Dutch and the Danish took over certain Portuguese colonies they set up Protestant missions focused on personal conversion*, created native churches, and favored the study of native religions. In 1795 the creation of the Mission of London opened what could be called "the great century of the Protestant missions" (K. S. Latourette), a period in which missionary development influenced the entire European continent with the creation of numerous missions. It was also a great century for Catholic missions.

Probably the most important fruit of this movement was the unitary dynamic engendered by the dissemination of the missionary idea in the different churches. An initial encounter of Protestant missionary societies from all over the world was held in Edinburgh in 1910. This climate of international collaboration was concretized in 1921 by the creation of the International Missionary Council—a decisive step in the process that led to the creation of the World* Council of Churches (WCC) in 1948. Then, in 1961, two factors favored the integration of the entire International Missionary Council into the WCC: 1) the realization that Europe and America had also become "lands of missions" (this had already been acknowledged by the founders of the "interior missions" in the 19th century), and (2) the fact that the African and Asian churches had become independent. The "overseas missions" became "missions on the six continents." Economic crisis and secularization* in Europe, along with the decolonization and emancipation of Asian and African nations, resulted in the decline of Western missions and the development of autonomous churches on all continents.

3. Theological Challenge

The theology* of missions implied a theology of non-Christian religions. This theology has been subject to significant development over the past two centuries, posing a challenge to many traditional missionary practices. At the Edinburgh missionary conference (1910) a study group that attempted an interpretation of religions concluded that they were auxiliaries of the missions in their struggle "for the liberation of souls* that are prisoners of error and perdition." The Jerusalem conference (1928) considered non-Christian religions as potential allies against secularism; the idea of dialogue and a common presence gradually prevailed, particularly when there was a need to take a stand on ethical questions. However, the WCC was never able to settle the question of salvation by other religions: "We cannot indicate any pathway to salvation other than Jesus-Christ. Nor can we set limits to the redemptive power of God" (San Antonio Missionary Conference, 1989).

The Catholic Church also asserted the exclusivity of salvation in Christ* (Vatican* II, AG 7), while acknowledging that fidelity to a non-Christian tradition could allow men to participate in salvation. The work

of the missions then became to purify "all the truth* and grace* already found among the nations, as if by a secret presence of God" (Paul VI) and bring it to perfection. This goes back to a patristic thesis in which non-Christian religions are deemed partially worthy, as "preparation" for the gospel. For believers of other religious traditions, "the salvation of Christ is accessible in virtue of a grace which has a mysterious relation with the Church; it does not formally introduce them into the Church, but brings them an enlightenment adapted to their state of mind and way of life" (John Paul II). Even if God can save outside the church, this does not dispense the church from its missionary work. For it is the missions that bring authentic liberation, opening men to the love* of Christ; and all men seek "a new life in Christ" (Paul VI). "The Church is the normal path to salvation and it alone possesses in plenitude the means to salvation" (John Paul II). Compatibility with the gospel and communion* with the universal Church are the criteria for regulating practices and doctrines while preserving its irreducible content, "the specificity and integrity of the Christian faith."

Lively debate on these same questions took place within the Reform movement. The "evangelical" current did not go along with advocates of dialogue with other religions; they feared that affirming the possibility of salvation outside the explicit confession of Christian faith replaced and discouraged evangelization.

There arose a need for redefinition of the relation between the missions founded by the Western churches and the "young churches" they created. In the 19th century, missions were generally undertaken in a "colonial" spirit that projected on a worldwide level a "paternalist" attitude consisting of "entrusting authority and control to a man meant to play the role of the father" (R. Mehl). However, from the mid–19th century, theologians stressed the need to promote an indigenous pastorate and local churches that were autonomously directed, financed, and developed. Though remnants of dependence still exist, this wish is largely fulfilled today. The Whitby Missionary Conference (1947) proposed a model of "partnership in obedience" to define this new relation that places all churches on an equal footing. The Bangkok Conference (1972–73) marked the height of demands for theological, financial, and human autonomy, including a proposal for a moratorium on interecclesial support. The only other option envisaged by the conference followed the model of the CEVAA, *Communauté évangélique d'action apostolique,* or Evangelical Community of Apostolic Action, that unites the French-speaking Protestant churches: The "ancient" and the "new" churches place their goods in common and manage them according to the "round table principle."

Today all churches agree that the missions are not meant to impose a Western ecclesial model on an international scale. They all share the problematic of acculturation. The Christian message needs to be translated to all cultural and social contexts; no particular style of ecclesial life shaped in a particular culture can claim to be its sole possible incarnation. The organisms that guarantee the unity of local churches vary, of course, according to their traditions whatever their mode of operation—federal (WCC or confessional families), communions of bishops* among themselves (in the Orthodox* movement), or colleges of bishops joined with the bishop of Rome* (in Catholicism). And they are all careful to leave room for legitimate differences.

The question of the connection between evangelization and social commitment is still on the agenda of missionary reflections in all the churches. The WCC Assembly in New Delhi (1961) affirmed that God "is at work in all the great changes of our times." The Uppsala assembly (1968) expressed the conviction that the church is called on "to anticipate the kingdom* of God by making visible here and now something of the newness that Christ will accomplish." In this perspective, the mission of the church is to encourage and accompany major social changes by deliberate commitment. In certain cases missions might even be called upon to support revolutionary-type movements. These WCC policy statements provoked a rupture with the evangelical movement, whose theological position is that the purpose of missions must be the conversion of individuals and not the transformation of society. The evangelicals believe that spiritual needs precede physical needs, and man himself is not capable of creating a just and peaceful society. Nevertheless, assemblies organized by the evangelicals in Lausanne (1974) and Manila (1989) clearly affirmed that there can be no opposition between evangelization and social action.

The question was studied anew by the WCC in Canberra (1992), bringing forth a proposition to support "intergovernmental organizations such as the United Nations Organization and the International Court of Justice that can speak in the name of the majority of peoples." At the Canberra congress particular attention was given to questions of human rights, with pointed criticism of economic systems. "The economic adjustments, imposed by managers of the 'free market system,' that asphyxiate poor, indebted countries" were rejected in the name of the gospel.

The same debate occurs within the Catholic Church, though it is seemingly less tense than the Protestant* version. Vatican II's decree on the church's missionary activity, *Ad Gentes divinitus*, did stress the social consequences of evangelization, acknowledging that the person to be evangelized is always caught in concrete social and economic situations. Notwithstanding, similar challenges (liberation* theologies, e.g.) were faced with the same urgency, and Pope Paul VI had to take a stand against "the temptation to reduce the missions [of the church] to the dimensions of a simply temporal project." Also noteworthy is the interpretation of the evangelizer, in the encyclical *Evangelii nuntiandi*, as first recipient of the gospel: No one can be truly qualified to transmit the gospel if he is not himself willing to be evangelized.

The mission calls for a new analysis of ecclesial practices with reflection on the different contexts and interreligious dialogue, and a redefinition of the connection between the word and social action. Moreover, it determines the style and content of all theology; it is "the mother of theology" (M. Kähler) as well as a "note" from the church (Barth*, KD IV/3, §72. 2). Every encounter between the gospel and a different culture brings forth a new intelligence of the biblical message and the church's mission.

• **Catholic Church**
Vatican II: Documents conciliaires (1966), Paris.
COD, 817–1135 (*DCO* II/2, 1661–2300).
Paul VI (1976), *Evangelii nuntiandi*, Vatican City.
John-Paul II (1987), *Sollicitudo rei socialis*, Vatican City
John-Paul II (1991), *Redemptoris missio*, Vatican City.

Reports from the General Assemblies
(1962), *New Delhi 1961*, Neuchâtel; (1969), *Rapport d'Uppsala 1968*, Geneva; M. Henriet (Ed.) (1976), *Briser les barrières, rapport de Nairobi 1975*, Geneva; J.-M. Chappuis and R. Beaupère (1984), *Rassemblés pour la vie: Rapport officiel de l'assemblée du COE Vancouver, 1983*, Paris; Th. Best, M. Westphal (Ed.) (1991), *Signes de l'Esprit: Rapport officiel: Septième assemblée Canberra*, Geneva.

World Mission Conferences
(1973), *Rapport de Bangkok*, Geneva; (1980), *Que ton règne vienne! Perspectives missionnaires: Rapport de Melbourne, 12–25 mai 1980*, Geneva; (1982), *La mission et l'évangélisation, affirmation œcuménique*, Geneva; (1990), "San Antonio 1989," *Informations Évangélisation 1/1990*, Paris.

Committee of Lausanne for World Evangelization
(1976), "Déclaration de Lausanne 1974," in *Au-delà des confessions*, Paris, 81–92; (1989), *Le Manifeste de Manille*, Pasadena.

Journals
International Review of Missions, 1912–70; *International Review of Mission*, 1970–; *The Ecumenical Review* 1948–.
◆ H. de Lubac (1946), *Le fondement théologique des missions*, Paris.
J. Daniélou (1946), *Le mystère du salut des nations*, Paris.
S. Delacroix (Ed.) (1956–59), *Histoire universelle des missions catholiques*, 4 vols., Paris.
R. Mehl (1964), *Décolonisation et missions protestantes*, Paris.

J. de Santa Ana (Ed.) (1982), *L'Église et les pauvres*, Lausanne.

L. Newbigin (1989), *En mission sur le chemin du Christ: Perspectives bibliques*, Geneva.

N. Lossky et al. (Eds.) (1991), "Mission," *Dictionary of the Ecumenical Movement*, Geneva, 690–96.

H. Rzepkowski (Ed.) (1992), *Lexikon der Mission: Geschichte, Theologie, Ethnologie*, Graz-Vienna-Cologne.

J.-F. Zorn (1993), *Le grand siècle d'une mission: La mission de Paris de 1822 à 1914*, Paris.

A. V. Ström et al. (1994), "Mission," *TRE* 23, 18–80.

H. J. Findeis et al. (1998), "Mission," etc., *LThK3* 7, 288–327.

Fritz Lienhard

See also **Conversion; Inculturation; Liberation Theology; Paganism; Philosophy; Salvation; World Council of Churches**

Modalism

Modalism is a modern term coined on the basis of the notion of "mode," of modality (Latin *modus;* Greek *tropos*). Under this notion are grouped various theologies that, during those centuries when Trinitarian and christological doctrines were being formulated, attempted to understand the relation of the Father* and the Son, but in a way that ended by appearing to be heterodox. Beginning with the confessions of faith* of Nicaea* and the First Council of Constantinople*, what was considered the modalist heresy took on several forms in the second and third centuries. Their common characteristic was a concern to maintain some kind of preeminence for God* the Father, something that was broadly inherited from fidelity to the one God of Judaism*. A distinction is usually made between monarchian modalism, adoptionism, and Sabellianism.

a) Monarchian Modalism. We owe the epithet "monarchians" to Tertullian* (*Adv. Praxean* 3. 1), who included Praxeas among them, contrary to modern opinion (*see* Studer 1985 and Simonetti 1993). Noetus of Smyrna, in the late second century, was perhaps the earliest representative of this manner of thinking; his disciple Epigones propagated his doctrine in Rome* in the early third century. The anonymous work *Contra Noetum* (before 213), as well as Tertullian and the *De Trinitate* of Novatian, condemn monarchianism on the grounds that, in attempting to preserve monotheism*, it does not give its proper place to the economy of salvation* or to the redemptive role of the incarnation.

Patripassianism (*see* Cyprian*, *Ep.* 73) is one of the variants of monarchianism. It maintains that "the Father suffered on the cross," but it is difficult to know

which writers explicitly affirmed what is scripturally indefensible (*see* Slusser 1982). This concept had some influence in the late second century, particularly in Rome, but also in Italy and North Africa.

b) Adoptionism. According to adoptionism the Son is merely a man adopted by God because of his merits; and, before the incarnation*, the word* of God was an impersonal power not distinct from the Father. Although Harnack saw in the *Pastor* of Hermas (apostolic fathers) the archetype of adoptionist Christology*, today scholars are more cautious (Simonetti 1993). The earliest representatives of this tendency were, in the Rome of the late second century, Theodotus of Byzantium, known as the Cobbler, and his disciples (Eusebius, *HE* V. 28. 6), another Theodotus of Byzantium, known as the Banker, followed by Artemon (also Artemas) in the third century.

Monarchianism and adoptionism were able to blend into a more highly developed whole—for example, in the two bishops Beryl of Bostra (according to Eusebius, *HE* VII. 23. 1–3) and Heraclides (according to Origen, *Conversation with Heraclides,* SC 67). Paul of Samosatus and, in the fourth century, Marcel of Ancyrus and Bishop Photinus of Sirmium may also be classified among supporters of an adoptionist brand of Christology.

c) Sabellian Modalism (Sabellianism). Assimilated by Methodus of Olympus (*Symposium* 8. 10) to a patripassian, and presented by Hilary* of Poitiers as the preeminent heretic, Sabellius was perhaps a native of Libya (Basil* of Caesarea, *Ep.* 9. 2; 125. 1). He was condemned by Callixtus in Rome around 220. Several ancient sources attribute to him the creation of the compound term *huiopatôr,* "Son-Father," to designate the one God. After 325 the ambiguity of the word *ousia,* which the Council of Nicaea used in order to define the Son as consubstantial*, *homoousios,* meant that it could be made an equivalent of the term *hupostasis,* which was how the Sabellians understood it. This cast suspicion on the doctrine of Nicaea, and the Arian front had Nicaean bishops deposed under the accusation of Sabellianism. This doctrine, in any event, revived monarchianism while also giving a place to the Holy* Spirit. By favoring the term *prosôpon* to designate the Father, the Son, and the Holy Spirit, the Sabellians emphasized appearance—the three *prosôpa* were thus only modes of the single divinity. According to other documents, sometimes attributed to the same writers (e.g., Marcel of Ancyrus, according to Simonetti), *prosôpon* and *ousia* are synonyms and the Trinity* is nothing but a single *prosôpon.* Sabellianism thus appears in the Trinitarian debates as the opposite pole to Arianism*, and it was between these two understandings that the fathers of the church developed the definitions of Constantinople I (*see* Gregory* of Nyssa, *Adversus Sabellium, GNO* II. 1).

● J. Daniélou (1958), *La théologie du judéo-christianisme,* Tournai (2nd Ed. 1991, Paris).
M. Simonetti (1975), *La crisi ariana nel IV secolo,* Rome.
V. Grossi (1976), "Il titolo cristologico 'Padre' nel antichità cristiana," *Aug* 16, 237–69.
P. Th. Camelot (1982), "Monarchianisme," *Cath* 9, col. 536–43.
M. Slusser (1982), "The Scope of Patripassianism," St. Patr. 17, Oxford, 169–75.
B. Studer (1985), *Gott und unsere Erlösung im Glauben der Alten Kirche,* Düsseldorf.
M. Simonetti (1993), *Studi sulla cristologia del II e III secolò,* Rome.

HENRI CROUZEL

See also **Adoptionism; Arianism; Christ and Christology; Subordinationism; Tertullian; Unitarianism**

Modernism

The word "modernism," which came into use in Italy and France in the late 19th century, came to refer to a crisis that confronted the Catholic Church* in the early 20th century. From the perspective of Rome*, modernism was a set of doctrinal errors born out of heterodox tendencies, but the phenomenon had a broader cultural and institutional significance. In the words of E. Pulat, it was "the encounter and confrontation between a religious past, long since set in stone, and a present that had found powerful sources of inspiration elsewhere than in this past."

From the 1880s onward, Catholics became preoccupied with adapting their church to the modern world. Many of them were aware of the gap between the teachings of the church and the nascent discipline of religious studies; similarly, a number of institutions and activities no longer seemed to meet the needs of the apostolate, in the midst of populations that had moved away from Christian practices and beliefs. The church's position and role in society was called into question over the course of the conflict that culminated, in France, for example, in the separation of church* and state (9 December 1905). By the end of the century, political power, social life, and culture were all escaping the church's control.

Freethinkers and anticlericals celebrated this turn of events, but Catholics, whether priests* or laypeople*, did not resign themselves to it. The years from 1880 to 1910 were characterized by a ferment of ideas and initiatives, which did not, however, form any general, organized movement: several participants in the crisis were isolated or went unheard, although there were networks of correspondence and friendship among them. Should the church change in response to developments in the world? Could it change? There was a diversity of answers to these questions.

a) Geography of the Crisis. In Germany, some decades earlier, liberal Protestantism* had attempted to reconcile new knowledge with the requirements of faith*. During the 1860s, this "German science" had induced Catholics to address the problem of the legitimate autonomy of university research in relation to the legitimate doctrinal authority of the church. Pope Leo XIII was well aware of the influence of Kantian thought (Kant*) and of German idealism (Hegel*, Schelling*), as well as of the low level of philosophical training provided within the Catholic Church. Following his accession, he thus revived instruction in the teachings of Thomas* Aquinas in the seminaries and universities, with his encyclical *Aeterni Patris* (4 August 1879), and supported the Catholic institutes that were founded from 1875 onward to improve the educational standards of the French clergy. In line with the pope's directives, the future Cardinal D. Mercier (1851–1926) developed in Louvain a form of Neoscholasticism that sought to integrate the progress made in physical, psychological, and social studies into the traditional expression of the faith.

In France, "progressives" *(progressistes)*, such as Monseigneur P. Batiffol (1861–1929) in the field of history or M.-J. Lagrange OP (1855–1938) in exegesis*, made scholarly advances by mastering modern methods, but did not challenge theology. By contrast, the "modernists" *(modernistes)* thought that the development of scientific culture required a sort of intellectual conversion, along with a profound revision of received ideas and intellectual work within the Catholic Church. The modernist tendency may be exemplified by A. Loisy (1857–1940), in the domain of biblical criticism, and by E. Le Roy (1870–1954), a mathematician who was a disciple of Henri Bergson. "Rationalists" *(rationalistes)*, such as J. Turmel (1859–1943) or A. Houtin (1867–1926), rejected what they saw as an illusory compromise and were prepared to renounce Catholic beliefs. Finally, those who became engaged in controversy and were then "suspected of being modernists" included the philosophers Maurice Blondel* and L. Laberthonnière (1860–1932), the historian L. Duchesne (1843–1922), and the philologist P. Lejay (1861–1920). Outside the realm of culture, the "democratic abbots," supporters of Christian democracy* and of the journal *Sillon* (Furrow) by Marc Sangnier (1873–1950), were accused of "social modernism."

France was the epicenter of the crisis, which echoed through Britain and Italy. F. von Hügel (1852–1925), an erudite layman based in London skilled in biblical criticism, religious philosophy*, and the history of spirituality, cultivated relations with other scholars, notably in Italy. He had some influence over the preacher G. Tyrrell (1861–1909), who wrote essays in apologetics, emphasized the mystical element in religion, and denounced the confusion between the Christian faith and its medieval expression. In Italy, a number of separate movements made their appearance, centered on outstanding individuals. E. Buonaiuti (1881–1946) promoted the intellectual renewal of Italian Catholicism* and the extension of the religious ed-

ucation of the masses. R. Murri (1860–1944) sought to develop cultural bases for an authentic Christian democracy and supported radical reforms within the church. A. Fogazzaro (1842–1917), heir to the political liberalism and religious reformism of the *Risorgimento,* wrote a novel, *Il Santo* (1905), in which he popularized the ideal of reform in opposition to the spirit of "immobilism."

b) Issues at Stake. According to R. Aubert (*Nouvelle histoire de l'Église* [New History of the Church], vol. 5, p. 205):

> In a matter of years, the Tridentine calm of an entire church (A. Dupront) was suddenly and almost simultaneously disrupted on a range of fundamental issues: the nature of revelation, scriptural inspiration, and religious knowledge; the personality of Christ and his true role in the origins of the church and its sacraments; the nature and function of the living tradition in the Catholic system; the limits of dogmatic development; the authority of the church's *magisterium;* the real meaning of the notion of orthodoxy; and the value of traditional apologetics.

Before the crisis erupted, Blondel had sought to face up to those who negated revelation and transcendence by proposing a "method of immanence," stating that "the human order has a part in everything but does not find adequacy in anything": the dynamism of humanity, in the full play of its faculties, calls for a superior and supernatural truth* that fulfills the truth of its nature by grace (see *L'Action,* 1893). It followed that there was a need for a new apologetics that could avoid the twin pitfalls of an apologia for dogma* independent of history ("extrinsicism") and a history independent of dogma ("historicism"). This was the goal of Blondel's *Lettre sur les exigences de la pensée contemporaine en matière d'apologétique et sur la méthode de la philosophie dans l'étude du problème religieux* (1896; Letter on the Requirements of Contemporary Thought in Matters of Apologetics and on the Method of Philosophy in the Study of the Problem of Religion). A new trend in reflection on the Catholic tradition, concerned with the future as well as with the past, developed from this point. Laberthonnière set out to conceive a theory of moral and religious knowledge that could give due regard to the role of subjectivity in the free assent of the intellect to revealed truth (*see Le problème religieux* [The Problem of Religion], 1897, and *Le dogmatisme moral* [Moral Dogmatism], 1898). E. Le Roy returned to the problem of the meaning of dogma for a scientific mind in his article "Qu'est-ce qu'un dogme?" (What Is a Dogma?, in *La Quinzaine,* 16 April 1905), reprinted in *Dogme et critique* (1907; Dogma and Criticism).

In parallel with these discussions, the application of methods of literary and historical criticism to Holy* Scripture, as well as to the history of the origins of the church, marked the beginning of the crisis in France. Some Catholic exegetes accepted many of the results of these criticisms, while rejecting any conception of the history of Israel* and the church that eliminated the supernatural. Others, such as Loisy, did not hesitate to demand a total transformation of apologetics on "the general problems posed by Scripture, the meaning of the divine truth that it expresses, and the value of the church that preserves that truth" (R. Aubert). The publication of a French translation of A. Harnack's lectures on The Essence of Christianity provided Loisy with the occasion to present a detailed synthesis of his system in his book *L'Évangile et l'Église* (The Gospel and the Church), which appeared at the end of 1902, and was backed up and explained a little later in his *Autour d'un petit livre* (On the Subject of a Little Book). According to Loisy himself, *L'Évangile et l'Église* was "primarily a historical outline and explanation of the development of Christianity, and, secondarily, a general philosophy of religion, and an attempt to interpret dogmatic formulas, official symbols, and conciliar definitions, with a view to bringing them into accord with the facts of history and the mentality of our contemporaries by sacrificing the letter to the spirit." In the course of the controversy that followed, it quickly became apparent that, in Loisy's view, revelation is merely "the awareness acquired by humanity from its relationship with God," and dogmas serve to maintain "harmony between religious belief and the scientific development of humanity." Loisy's system presupposed a set of dualities: within the philosophy of religion, between revelation and dogma; within historical criticism, between dogma and history; and, when it came to Christology*, between the historical Jesus* and the Christ of the Catholic faith.

With considerable insight, Blondel demonstrated that Loisy's positions implied dualism, and emphasized the true notion of tradition within the Catholic synthesis (*see* the series of articles, "Histoire et dogme" [History and Dogma] in *La Quinzaine*, 16 January, 1 February, and 16 February 1904). He thus took the problematic elaborated several years before to a new level.

c) Rome's Condemnations and Reactions. Loisy's "little books" were placed on the Catholic Church's Index of Prohibited Books at the end of 1903, and refutations were published by P. de Grandmaison in *Études* and by Batiffol in the *Bulletin de littérature ecclésiastique*. In Rome, the Holy Office prepared a list of errors and set out to identify the body of doctrine that underlay the positions of various writers. On 3 July 1907, it published a decree, *Lamentabili*, that cataloged and condemned 65 propositions: Loisy recognized around two-thirds of these as having been taken from his writings. On 8 September the same year, Pope Pius X issued the encyclical *Pascendi*, in which he described various modernist "figures"—the philosopher, the believer, the theologian, the historian, and others—and then reconstructed the system of errors that they had in common. This system was said to center on two fundamental errors: agnosticism*, which denies that rational demonstration can have any value in matters of religion; and "vital immanentism," which makes faith dependent on the religious feelings and needs of human beings. Tyrrell was excommunicated in 1907, Loisy in 1908, and more works were placed on the Index (notably, works by Duchesne, Laberthonnière, and H. Brémond). The teaching staffs of seminaries and faculties of theology were purged; an antimodernist oath was imposed in 1910; and committees of vigilance were established in the dioceses. In general, these repressive and preventative measures were accepted and obeyed. However, their impact was aggravated by the campaigns of denunciation against "integral Catholics" that altered the climate in the closing years of the pontificate of Pius X (1903–14).

d) Historical Process or Special Case? The modernist crisis erupted at the turn of the 19th and 20th centuries as an internal phenomenon within the Catholic Church, revealing the tensions between traditional theological instruction and progress in the sciences, criticism, and history, between the church's institutions and the new aspirations, and between the church's official position and a society that was becoming more secular (secularization*). Since the word "modernism" reappeared in the disputes that followed Vatican* II, it may be the case that, as Poulat has contended, modernism is "an authentic historical process, with the slowness" that that implies, and with a dynamism that ensures continuity despite the differences in circumstances. In *La pensée de M. Loisy* (Monsieur Loisy's Thought, p. 204), J. Guitton concludes that "modernism seems to us to be a special case of a more general system, a form of thought that will return again and again in the course of the history of Catholicism whenever the intellect seeks to base the faith on the spirit of the age, instead of integrating the spirit of the age into the faith."

● Correspondence: H. de Lubac (Ed.) (1957–65), *M. Blondel–Aug. Valensin*, 3 vols., Paris.

C. Tresmontant (Ed.) (1967), *M. Blondel–L. Laberthonnière*, Paris.

A. Blanchet (Ed.) (1970–71), *H. Brémond–M. Blondel*, 3 vols., Paris.

♦ J. Rivière (1929), *Le modernisme dans l'Église,* Paris.

R. Marlé (1960), *Au coeur de la crise moderniste,* Paris.

É. Poulat (1962), *Histoire, dogme et critique dans la crise moderniste,* Paris.

E. Poulat (1969), *Intégrisme et catholicisme intégral,* Tournai-Paris.

P. Scoppola (1969), *Crisi modernista e rinnovamento cattolico,* Bologna.

R. Aubert (1975), "La crise moderniste," in id. et al. (Ed.), *Nouvelle histoire de l'Église,* vol. 5, Paris, 200–18.

C. Tresmontant (1979), *La crise moderniste,* Paris.

A. Boland (1980), *La crise moderniste, hier et aujourd'hui—un parcours spirituel,* Paris.

G. Daley (1980), *Transcendence and Immanence,* Oxford.

D. Dubarle (Ed.) (1980), *Le modernisme,* Paris.

E. Poulat (1982), *Modernistica,* Paris.

P. Colin (1997), *L'audace et le soupçon, la crise du modernisme dans le catholicisme français, 1893–1914,* Paris.

CLAUDE BRESSOLETTE

See also **Blondel, Maurice; Exegesis; Fundamentalism; Rationalism; Secularization; Traditionalism**

Möhler, Johann Adam. *See* **Tübingen, Schools of**

Molina, Luis de. *See* **Bañezianism-Molinism-Baianism**

Molinism. *See* **Bañezianism-Molinism-Baianism**

Molinos, Miguel de. *See* **Quietism**

Monarchianism. *See* **Modalism**

Monastic Theology. *See* **Bernard of Clairvaux**

Monasticism

A. Ancient History

Confirmed by a papyrus as early as 324, the word *monakhos* ("monk") entered into literature with *The Life of Anthony* written by Athanasius of Alexandria immediately after the latter's death (356). Derived from the Greek *monos* ("unique"), the word suggests a plan for a simple life, unified by abstention from marriage* and a distancing of oneself from society* as well as by a total self-consecration to God*, who is One. After celibacy, of which the term seemed to refer initially, the idea of physical isolation took priority with Jerome (c. 342–420) (*Letters* 14, 6, etc.) until inner unification became the key idea in Pseudo-Dennis (*Hier. eccl.* VI, 1–3) and in Gregory* the Great (*In I Reg.* I, 61). With an original twist, Augustine* interpreted *monachus* as a union in charity with one's neighbor, that is, communal life (*En. Ps.* 132, 6).

a) Antecedents. The most important of the cognates is *monastèrion* ("monastery"), which designates a monk's abode. It can already be found in Philo (*De vita contemplativa* 25), applied as a sort of individual study room where certain Jewish ascetics, the "Therapists," "isolated" themselves in order to study the Bible,* the only book admitted into this sacred place.

This precedent hints that Christian monasticism had its precursors. Aside from Philo's Egyptian therapists, who lived a fundamentally solitary life while living in mixed groups, actual monastic communities, those of Essenes, described by Philo as well as by Flavius Josephus, also existed in Palestine toward the beginning of the Christian era. The Sectarians of Qumran, uncovered by recent discoveries near the Dead Sea, are also related to these communities.

While similar to their predecessors, Christian monks do not seem to have been indebted to them at all. In the second half of the third century monasticism appeared quite independently in the church*. Of course the term *monakhos* had already made its appearance around the year 140 in Thomas's evangelical apocrypha*, but there seems to be no relation between this distant Gnostic precedent and the movement that developed in orthodox circles a century later.

Where then did monasticism come from? Apart from its deep human roots, which have produced similar phenomena elsewhere (Hinduism, Buddhism), this great Christian creation was inspired above all, if not exclusively, by the Scriptures*—even if the pagan model of the philosophical life might have played a role. At an epoch when persecutions were growing rare and then ceased entirely, the monk responded personally to the evangelical appeals that had inspired so many martyrdoms. "Selling one's goods and giving them to the poor," "abandoning everything," "taking up one's cross and following Christ*": these watchwords were the source of Anthony's vocation and of that of the majority of his imitators. One has to choose between love* of the world* and love of God (Jas 4:4; 1 Jn 2:15–17, and 4:4–6). "Whosoever hates his soul* in this world will keep it for eternal life*" (Jn 12:25). Those maxims and so many other similar ones from the New Testament explain for the most part a movement, which refers to them constantly.

Other referential figures can be added: Elijah and Elisha, as well as the "sons of the prophets*" Jeremiah the celibate, the solitary, the persecuted; above all, John the Baptist, the man of the desert; finally, Jesus* himself, son of the Virgin and totally chaste, who fasted in the desert and sought solitude in order to pray. A communal model should be added to these individual examples: the primitive Church of Jerusalem* and its ideal of "communion*." All being of a single heart and a single soul, because no one owned anything privately and everything was shared mutually (Acts 4:32); such would be the ambition of the majority of the cenobitic enterprises (from *koinos bios,* "communal life") that have made their mark on the history of monasticism.

b) Origins. The first biography of a monk was therefore Anthony's. Written in Greek for Western readers, this fundamental text was quickly translated into Latin, but the only definitive version by Evagrius of Antioch, which would make its fortune in the West, wasn't established until about the year 370. A rural proprietor in the Thebaid, Anthony "converted" around the age of 20, sold his goods, spent 15 years near his village and made contact with other ascetics; then he took the plunge that made him famous. Going into the desert, he imprisoned himself in a small abandoned fort where they brought him bread twice a year. When, after 20 years his admirers' curiosity made him show himself, this man of about 55 years old impressed those who saw him by his self-mastery and by his gifts. But after an intensely influential period, when his abode in the desert near the Nile "became a city*," this lover of solitude retreated further into the "inner desert," toward the Red Sea. He died there at more than a hundred years old, mourned by everyone as the "physician of Egypt," on which he had lavished the healings* of the body and of the soul.

Anthony was the first anchorite (from *anakhôrein,* "to go into a retreat"). Among his numerous imitators, the hermit Palaemon deserves a special mention for having been the master of Pachomius (c. 290–346), the founder of cenobitism. Born of pagan parents, the young Pachomius converted to Christianity during his military service, moved by the charity that the Christians had shown him. His vocation from the start was "to serve the human race," in the steps of these charitable men. After having been initiated into asceticism* with Palaemon, he left him to make himself available to those who would come to him. After difficult beginnings marked by trials and errors, he began around the year 320 to gather monks around him whose numbers grew rapidly, so many as to populate about 15 giant monasteries. Upon his death, Pachomius left a *Koinônia* ("fraternity") in upper Egypt, grouping thousands of brothers, which, despite a serious crisis, would develop even more under his successors Orsiesius and Theodore. The Rule, or rather, the four collections of "Precepts," that he had set down in writing for this vast group, would be translated into Latin by Jerome (404) and would have its influence on several Western monastic codes of law.

c) Forms. Anthony and Pachomius created the two main types of monastic life: hermitry and cenobitism.

These two men's histories prefigure the transferals, which would constantly occur between the two forms of monasticism. Anthony's life was at first semicommunal, then completely solitary, but at the end it did include the role of a spiritual father. As for Pachomius, he offered a vast community gathered around him the relationship of a disciple to his master, which he had lived himself, one on one, with the hermit Palaemon.

This coming and going between cenobitism and anchoritism can be confirmed for the most part by two common phenomena. On the one hand, the great anchorites often attracted numerous disciples and thus engendered communities, often involuntary; this influence was sometimes understood as a call from God and the goal of a constructive search. On the other hand, the anchorites "derive from the *Coenobia,*" wrote Jerome in 384 (*Letters* 22, 35). This process, which the Western witnesses and theorists (Sulpicius Severus [c. 360–c. 420], Cassian [c. 360–435], the anonymous author of the Rule of the Master, Benedict [c. 480–c. 550]) would give the rigor of a law, is based on the nature of things: a communal apprenticeship should normally precede the solitary life.

Moreover, between cenobitism and hermitry in their pure forms lay many intermediate forms. There were anchorite colonies, of which the most famous in fourth-century Egypt were those of Nitria. The Cells and Scetis brought together monks who lived alone but who gathered together on Saturdays and Sundays for the Eucharist* and for feasts. A little later, in the East, the name "lauras" would be given to groups that were similar but who lived in closer contact with each other, since the homes of the solitaries bordered the same street *(lavra).* Another type of association of the two kinds of life was that of the hermit living near a community where he had often received his training and on which he sometimes exerted a spiritual influence while receiving its material help. Well documented in Egypt and Palestine about the year 400, this sort of symbiosis would be institutionalized by Cassiodorus (c. 485–c. 580) in Vivarium, where Mount Castellum's solitude was adjacent to the *coenobium,* and many centuries later by a Saint Romuald (c. 950–1027) in Camaldoli.

Several of these phenomena are illustrated by Benedict of Nursia's life and work. A student in Rome* at the beginning of the sixth century, when he decided to become a monk, he was given the habit by a cenobite called Romanus and settled secretly in a cave near the latter, who fed him with bread from his own ration. In an original way (Romanus's community and his abbot were unaware of the nearby young hermit's existence) that was a case of symbiosis between the two lives. After three years, the clandestine anchorite was discovered, and a monastery in the vicinity took him as its abbot. This first abbacy ended badly, but, once he had reverted back into solitude, Benedict saw dozens of disciples come to him, for whom he organized 12 small monasteries of which he retained the administrative duties: a typical example of a hermit engendering cenobitism. Finally, in his *Rule for the Monks,* probably written later at Monte Cassino, Benedict set down right from the first chapter the traditional doctrine that required a long cenobitic apprenticeship before moving on to a solitary life. Moreover, the latter life had retained a certain attraction for him as suggests his biographer Gregory of Nyssa, who reported that the abbot of Monte Cassino did not sleep in the communal dormitory but lived in a separate tower, where he used to pray alone at night.

Excluded by Basil* as contrary to the Gospels*, solitary monastic life would, however, be generally considered the height of monastic renunciation. Elijah and John the Baptist are models of it. Less naturally accepted today perhaps, hermitry's Christian authenticity was only rarely challenged in the early centuries.

d) The Goal and the Means.

According to classical viewpoint, which regards hermitry as the term of the monastic goal, monks began by purifying themselves in the *coenobium* through the "active life" before leading the "contemplative life" in solitude. Such was the schema followed in the majority of his *Institutions* and *Conferences* by John Cassian. The "active life" consisted of combating the eight main vices, following the methodical list drawn up by Evragius Ponticus (346–99) (greed, lust, anger, avarice, sadness, acidie [spiritual discouragement], vanity, and pride) in order to achieve purity of heart, the condition for entering the Kingdom*: "Blessed are the pure in heart, for they shall see God." Already, from this point, *apatheia* (mastery of the passions*) gave access to contemplation*. The battle against the vices took priority in communal life, while contemplation flourished in solitude. Another comparative schema laid greater stress on cenobitism, acknowledging its capacity for developing two major virtues*: abandonment of one's own will and absence of any thought for the morrow (Cassian, *Conf.* 19, 8).

The asceticism by which the monk purified himself especially stressed food consumption (fasts, abstinence, rationing), sleep (vigil), and the use of words (silence). Born of faith*, this asceticism led to charity. It was in order to devote himself to charity that the monk separated himself from the world. This separation, in which Basil saw a requirement imposed by God's love, led, among other signs, to wearing the distinctive habit.

A conscious and constant relation with God: this ideal of the monk is called prayer*. This prayer draws its sustenance from the Bible, read and learned by heart for two or three hours per day, then recited constantly during the periods of manual work. The monk answers and listens to the voice of God with prayer as often as possible and continuously in this way. As for the moments set aside for prayer, in Egypt there were two (morning and evening), and more in other places, where a canon of seven daily prayer periods would end by being set, this number suggested by a word of the Psalmist (Psalms 118, 164). At these day and night offices, every psalm* was followed by a silent prayer, which diminished little by little and finally disappeared.

The will to "pray constantly" (1 Thes 5:17) did not preclude work. The monk had the duty to perform it, so much as to earn his living and to give alms as to avoid idleness, the soul's enemy. On that point, Paul's injunctions and example would win out over a Syrian movement, which understood his call to constant prayer too literally. The movement of the Messalians ("Praying people") of Syria would, however, produce in Constantinople the perpetual praise performed by the Acemetes ("Those who do not go to bed"), who relayed each other in the choir day and night, and similar attempts at *laus perennis* (perpetual praise) in a few of the big Western monasteries in the seventh century.

e) Two Forms of Communal Life.

In the cenobitic environment a typical development that took its inspiration from the New Testament was frequently seen: a group of disciples gathered together around their master transform into a fraternal communion. In the first type of association, the unifying principle was each member's relation to its leader; between them, the subordinates were united only by their common relationship with their leader. Favoring the vertical and hierarchical schema, this kind of community was like a school or a troop. But often, as time passed, there also arose a concern about the horizontal relations between individuals. Thus they progressed from a school to a communion.

An evolution of this type appears in Pachomius's code of laws. Its first three volumes (*Institutia, Iudicia, Praecepta*) mentioned only obedience to rule and to superiors, while the last one (*Leges*) displayed a new concern about peace and harmony among the brothers. Similarly, the "fundamental pact" of the Egyptian *coenobium* described by Jerome in 384 (*Letters* 22, 35) implied everyone's obedience to the superiors, whose educative acts they unilaterally praised, without saying a word about fraternal relations. Taking up this bit a little later, Augustine took special care to make an explicit reference to the Church of Jerusalem (*De mor.* I, 67). Between Lérins's first two Rules, that of the Four

Fathers and the "Second Rule," just as between the two great Italian Rules of the sixth century, the Rule of the Master and the one by Benedict, similar contrasts can be seen.

This kind of law goes back to the origins of Christianity. The group of the Twelve was initially a school, where each disciple had been called or attracted by that master who was Jesus. Before he died, the latter gave to each one the "new commandment" of mutual love, whence flowed new relationships. Henceforth, the "teaching of the apostles*," which continued Christ's teaching, engendered communion (Acts 2:44). Without giving it any thought, it seems that monastic circles often followed the same process, which reflected a religious society's very nature. The primordial relationship to God and to his representatives was the first essential; then, the awareness of spiritual unity and obedience to the law of love, just as much as the experience of a difficult communal life, caused attention to be paid to the relations among the brothers.

f) The Coenobium *and Its Scriptural Models.* In the Rule of the Master, the monastery is called the "school of Christ." When Benedict picked it up again, this definition made the *coenobium* a continuation of the group of the Twelve, where Christ was represented by the Abbot. The division of many communities into groups of 10, while reminiscent of the Roman army, also looked back to the model of Israel* in the desert. The same can be said of the "houses" and "tribes" of Pachomius's *koinônia*. Basil's favorite image was Christ's body. This Pauline metaphor was also allied to the image of the community in Jerusalem, so often evoked by monastic legislators. For the Master, who hardly gave a thought to the primitive church of the Acts, the model instead was the church of his own time, since the monastery's hierarchy* was compared to the clergy. Elsewhere, and particularly in Pachomius's Rule, the monastic tradition was conceived as a replica of the great ecclesial tradition*.

g) Obedience: Its Forms and Motives. Whether he was an anchorite's disciple or a member of a *coenobium,* the monk had to obey. This obligation gave rise to many commentaries. Certain people, like Augustine, invoked texts from the New Testament that order children to obey their parents, and the faithful to obey their pastors. Others instead thought of Christ, viewed as the one obeyed through his representatives (Lk 10:16), or as the one who was obedient to his Father* even unto death* (Jn 6:38; Ph 2:14). Whether as a commanding leader or as a model of obedience, Christ gave this virtue a mystical character that goes far beyond the simple necessities of communal life.

Obedience was required first of all from the novice, who had everything to learn. But it was also commended to the more advanced monk, who through obedience renounced his own will just as Christ accepted death through his obedience. When applied to the superiors, their obedience was given to God, whom they represented. But it could also be mutual, with no other motive than humble charity.

h) Paths of Perfection. In the Benedictine Rule, which the Carolingian age would make the common charter of Western cenobitism, obedience was not viewed in isolation, but taken as one of the aspects of a general trend toward humility. From the initial fear* of God up to the perfect love that drives away fear, the monk ascended by humbling himself, according to the evangelical paradox, and this path of humility that the Master and Benedict borrowed from Cassian passed through the stages of obedience and patience, self-effacement and submission, to renunciation of speech and laughter. In this program, the two key virtues were obedience and taciturnity. The first consisted of humility in deeds; the second represented humility in speech.

i) Clergy and Sacraments. In the *Life of Anthony,* although he was a bishop, Athanasius never mentioned the Eucharist*, of which the saint seems to have been deprived for long periods. At the end of the sixth century, however, Apollonius and the anchorites who gathered around him met daily at the ninth hour to take communion before they ate, and Jerome's *coenobium* in Jerusalem keenly felt their need for a priest who could consecrate the Eucharist. In sixth-century Italy, the Master's entirely lay communities would be ministered to by those of Benedict, which included priests* and clerics*. The conventual Mass, however, would not become a daily event until much later. During the week, a simple communion service preceded the meal at the Master's, and probably also at Benedict's.

At the period when the monasteries tended to provide themselves with the clergy necessary for celebration of the Eucharist, bishops and their clerics adopted a quasi-monastic way of life. During the second half of the sixth century, Eusebius (†371) in Verceil, Martin (†397) in Tours, and Augustine in Hippo set the example for the hybridizations whose fruitfulness Jerome himself acknowledged in some of his letters. Monasticism and the clergy were also allied in the missionary enterprises of monks like Columban (c. 543–615) and so many other Irish or Anglo-Saxon islanders, whose original aim was to "peregrinate" like Abraham far from their native land.

j) From the Cell to the Dormitory. Finally, speaking again of the most common practice, we should note an important change that occurred about the year 500 in the majority of monasteries, as much in the East as in the West. From its anchorite origins, cenobitism had retained the practice of living in individual cells where the monks spent their time alone with God. Now, to remedy certain drawbacks of a moral nature, at that period cells were replaced by a communal dormitory. Communal life thus lost an element of solitary contemplation that had made it akin to hermitry. It was that integrated community life that for a long time codified the Rule of Saint Benedict, until cells reappeared at the height of the Middle Ages among the Carthusians, and later among the Benedictines themselves.

The dying days of antiquity therefore opted modestly for a monastery more concerned with transparency and regularity (disappropriation) than with meditation and leisure given over to contemplation. It was a acknowledgment that the monk was a weak being, and that cenobitism was an institution forever threatened with decadence, in line with a certain historic pessimism that was particularly evident in Benedict and that provoked an appeal on his part to the good faith of the most generous so that they might go beyond the overly lax common norms and thus come closer to perfection.

- H. Weingarten (1877), "Der Ursprung des Mönchtums im nachkonstantinischen Zeitalter," *ZKG* 1, 1–35, 545–74.
K. Heussi (1936), *Der Ursprung des Mönchtums*, Tübingen.
P. Cousin (1959), *Précis d'histoire monastique*, Paris.
P. Cousin (1961), *Théologie de la vie monastique*, Paris.
A. de Vogüé (1961), *La communauté et l'abbé dans la Règle de saint Benoît*, Paris.
D. J. Chitty (1966), *The Desert a City*, Oxford.
A. de Vogüé (1971), "*Sub regula vel abbate:* Étude sur la signification théologique des règles monastiques anciennes," *CCist* 33, 209–41.
G. M. Colombás (1974), *El monacato primitivo*, vol. I–II, Madrid.
A. Guillaumont (1979), *Aux origines du mon. chrétien: Pour une phénoménologie du mon.*, SpOr 30.
W. Dircks (1982), *Die Antwort der Mönche*, Frankfurt.
A. de Vogüé (1985), *Les règles monastiques anciennes (400–700)*, Tournai.
C. S. Frank (1988), *Geschichte des christlichen Mönchtums*, Darmstadt.
A. de Vogüé (1991–), *Histoire littéraire du mouvement monastique dans l'Antiquité. Première partie: le mon. latin*, Paris (vol. I to V published in 1998).
H. Holtze (1992), *Erfahrung und Theologie im frühen Mönchtum*, Göttingen.
A. de Vogüé (1998), *Le monachisme en Occident avant saint Benoît*, Bégrolles-en-Mauge.

ADALBERT DE VOGÜÉ

B. Theological Stakes

A well-known phenomenon in the history of religions, and a phenomenon lacking in the earliest Christian experience*, monasticism succeeded in showing an extremely pregnant theological sense. Its founding word was *anchoritism:* the monk in fact appears as a person who disappears, who abandons the city and the company of men. What he leaves or what he wants to leave bears a name that covers a theological concept, the *world*. Considered in Pauline and Johannine terms as the sphere of decadent existence, since it had compromised with sin*, the world is in fact that which is proper to flee and is nothing more than that. To break with the world is therefore an elementary Christian task: this break is nothing more than that elementary task. First of all, therefore, anchoritism should refer to a spiritual deed: the theological life lived "in Christ*" is as such victorious over the world, and as such an act of exodus and of joining an eschatological community: anchoritism's spiritual reality takes precedence over the topological reality that the monastery gives it. It

does not follow that monastic anchoritism might be a naïveté or an aberration (that it might be confusing existential distancing with spatial distancing). For if any one trait is constant in the monastic experience it is indeed the fact that the world weighs just as heavily on man in the desert as in the midst of a city. In the solitude that he finds, the monk has no privileged right to possess peace* of the soul* and of the heart.

His experience is not that of an *otium* reserved for whoever has taken leave definitively of the world: it is the ascetic experience of a labor to achieve conversion*. The paradox of the symbolic distancing that is life in the desert is thus its cruel emphasis on distances that have not been taken: the monastic experience is first of all one of temptation*.

With the proviso that that fact be acknowledged, and clearly acknowledged, it is then possible to do full justice to the monasteric plan. The negative concept of anchoritism is counterbalanced by its positive images of the "angelic life" led by those who labor at perpetual praise*. As the heir to the Greco-Roman philosopher of antiquity, the monk presents himself as the man who lives life itself, life as it deserves to be lived by a man (Balthasar* 1961). And then the organization of a monastic anthropology* that is identical to an eschatological anthropology can be seen. Logic in action is therefore a logic of anticipation. Negatively speaking, the monk is the man who refuses to incarnate historical images of man's humanity: positively speaking, he is the man whose deeds reveal a certain hold over the *final destiny* in the present time. His celibacy sets him apart from those who, in the sequence of the generations, assure humanity's history*; but it also makes him the image, in the period before death, of a complete man who transcends in his flesh the differences between the sexes (Mt 22, 30 apr., *hôs angeloi* and *isangeloi*). His silence seems like the renunciation of an eminent form of human experience, the intersubjectivity achieved in the element of language—but this silence is not dumbness, and while accusing the daily use of words of being just verbiage, it also has the role of restoring man to his most human state, his role as listener to the divine word*. The cenobite's obedience deprives him of his own will and falls under the suspicion to which are exposed all alienated behaviors; but it is also a christological reality, a kenotic deed that restores the will to a sense that it does not possess in the limits of the world, and which is its eschatological secret. The monk's poverty makes him marginal and troubling, because it stipulates that the right to poverty is more human than any right to property*; but it is also a kenotic behavior lived in imitation of God who made himself poor (2 Cor 8:9).

Lastly, the existence of a fraternal community devoted to incessant praise is the purest eschatological sign that the monastic project owns: in a period of temporary realities, the monk appears in it as the witness to the definitive, to what does not die. The life that wants to be totally liturgical is the present icon (and the only possible illustration) of an eternity within man's grasp; and communal life where the neighbor has no other identity than the theological identity of a brother proves that man's being* is a being of communion*, and proves moreover that communion is not a reality within the grasp of the world, thus suggesting ways of becoming worthy of everlasting life.

The project's "theoretic splendor" (G. Bedouelle) is undeniable; it also constitutes its paradoxical weakness. The monastic tradition* has made its own the beatitude* of the pure in heart, "who will see God" (Mt 5:8). By conceiving the ambition of attaining peace, *hèsukhia,* it also wants to share in the eschatological joys. But if the "desert" or the monastery wants to display itself as the domain of an experience in-

tended to subvert any hold over man that the world might have, and if the monk, in this sense, is among those who try to take possession of the Kingdom by force (Mt 11:12), the desire to symbolize the *final destiny* does not have the power to make real what it symbolizes. The eschatological meanings unfolded by the monastic experience cannot therefore mask that, like all Christian experiences, it has a *pre*-eschatological reality, and that the first monastic requirement is the eminently historial one of the "conversion of morals." If the monk sets himself the goal of living life itself, it must also be understood that the logic of his experience does not aim at the definitive except by being constantly at war with the weaknesses, temptations, and sins that constitute the temporary fabric. And Protestantism's objection—in which the monastery is the Pelagian enterprise of men and women trying ascetically to take possession of the good of which, by definition, is to be granted only by God—can only be answered as monastic spirituality being a spirituality of humility and of openness to grace*: "no man makes himself a monk, he is made a monk by a force which does not come from himself" (Theophanes the Recluse [1815–94]). If the monk reveals no immoderation, if the project of a *vita angelica* is neither an arrogance nor an absurdity, it is—and it is only—because the monk knows himself to be all the more a sinner in that "the work" at which he labors, *opus Dei*, is holy work. Only the humble man can assign himself the dangerous mission of symbolizing the eternal in the temporal, for only the humble man can let the sublime symbolism of his deeds judge the empirical person who performs these deeds. In the person of Anthony the Great, every candidate to the monastic experience is set the example of the shoemaker from Alexandria who prayed by repeating: "I alone shall perish, all will be saved."

In the end, monasticism's spiritual secret is its ecclesiological secret. In fact the monk tries to take leave of the world only to exist in the formal role of the being-in-the-church; and his prayer* therefore is less his own work than the church*'s work, *Ecclesia orans*. Monastic life affirms that the being-in-communion is the full realization of the being-with, of the *Mitdasein,* which describes man's relationship in the world with man. This life must also affirm that the particular monastic community itself exists only in the total communion of the whole church. The monastic project must explain itself in terms of vocation, and this vocation is the double call, of God and of the church—above all, the latter's call should not be forgotten. It is really from the church, understood in the linked and hierarchized totality of its communion, that the monk receives the mission to pray for all men, and to praise God on behalf of those who do not do so or do so rarely. Then can one understand that his entry into the ecclesial community might allow the monk to also take on, paradoxically but in a perfectly exact sense, the clothing of the apostle*.

"The institutions fully devoted to contemplation*...contribute to the greatness of the people* of God by the abundant fruits of holiness*, they attract the people by their example and procure their growth by a secret apostolic fecundity, *arcana fecunditate apostolica*" (Vatican* II, *PC*, §7).

● C. Marmion (1922), *Le Christ, idéal du moine*, Namur-Paris.
L. Bouyer (1950), *Le sens de la vie monastique*, Paris-Turnhout.
H. U. von Balthasar (1961), "Philosophie, Christentum, Mönchtum," in *Sponsa Verbi*, Einsiedeln, 349–87.
G. M. Colombás (1961), *Paradis et vie angélique*, Paris.
T. M. Cannon, G. Traub (1969), *The Desert and the City: An Interpretation of the History of Christian Spirituality*, London.

G. M. Colombás (1975), *El monacato primitivo*, vol. 2: *La espiritualidad*, Madrid.
L. Gutiérrez Vega (1976), *Teología sistemática de la vida religiosa*, Madrid.
A. de Vogüé (1977), *La règle de saint Benoît*, vol. VII: *Comm. doctrinal et spirituel*, SC 186.
G. O. Girardi (1979), *La vita religiosa: Teologia della vita religiosa*, Naples.
J. M. Lozano (1981), *La sequela di Cristo: Teologia storico-sistematica della vita religiosa*, Milan.
P. Miquel (1986), *La voie monastique*, Bégrolles-en-Mauges, 11–58.
A. M. Triacca, C. Andronikoff, et al. (1989), *Liturgie, conversion et vie monastique*, BEL.S 48, 73 *Sq.*
B. Calati (1994), *Sapienza monastica, saggi di storia, spiritualità e problemi monastici*, StAns 117, Rome.

JEAN-YVES LACOSTE

See also **Communion; Philosophy; Religious Life**

Monogenesis/Polygenesis

a) Theological and Scientific Definitions.   In the strict theological sense, monogenesis is the doctrine according to which all of humanity has its beginnings in one unique couple* created by God*. Uncontested during most of Christian history, in so much that it alone seemed compatible with the Holy* Scripture, this doctrine was questioned in the 17th century by I. de La Peyrère (1594–1676), who induced the existence of "Preadamites" from a singular reading of Romans 5:12ff. and saw the different human races* as many distinct species resulting from independent creations*. These extreme polygenetic concepts have been used as a basis for some racist theories, justifying slavery (J.-C. Calhoun, Liberty* B), then racial segregation.

At one time it was intended to distinguish a couple of theological terms (monogenesis/polygenesis) and a couple of scientific notions, monophyletism/polyphyletism (the monophyletic hypothesis attributes to a given species one evolutionary class—unique *phylum*). In fact, today this last hypothesis is often considered as a "monogenesis" on the scientific level, in so far as it gives a common "spatio-temporal cradle" to all of humanity. The theological understanding of this makes it possible to speak of monogenesis in a larger sense.

b) Data of Positive Science.   Today, the strict biological unicity of the human species is no longer contested. For 30,000 years, all human beings around the world are of the one type *sapiens sapiens*, whose monophyletic origin presently seems more than likely, even if it remains difficult to define precisely. The genetic, reproductive, and molecular unicity of the modern human is complete and without possible mixture. This was not always the case, however: during some 60,000 years, two distinct types of *Homo sapiens* coexisted, possibly without mixing, at least in Palestine (*neandertalensis* and *sapiens sapiens*, both issued from *Homo erectus*). As to strict monogenesis (one original couple), it seems difficult for science to make a pronouncement. If the essential passages were made by extremely thin "stalks," according to Teilhard's expression, one can hardly reconstitute them. Some people, however, argue that great mutations have an individual genetic beginning. Supporting this thesis, a recent study on the levels of divergence of mitochondrial (nonchromosomal) DNA transmitted purely through the maternal line has been invoked. Heavily discussed and no doubt contestable calculations have led to the conclusion of a singular origin of humanity, which would descend from an "African Eve" dating some 250,000 years. But these are, at the moment, speculations.

c) *Theological Intelligence.* To avoid all confusion, it is necessary to distinguish as much as possible the theological (theology*) question from that of the positive sciences. The Biblical data (Bible*) of the first three chapters of Genesis indicate a deep community of nature in the human species, all issued from the same act of creation proceeding from divine love*, and thus an essential fraternity and equality between all human beings—which is radically incompatible with the ideas of La Peyrère. They do not impose a strictly monogenetic interpretation (unicity of the original couple). In the Catholic Church*, the theological difficulty comes more from the transmission "by propagation, not by imitation" of the original sin*, as defined by the Council of Trent* (*DS* 1513) and recalled by Pius XII in his encyclical *Humani Generis* (1950, *DS* 3897). For Catholics (Catholicism*) this allowed the open discussion of the theory of evolution* of species—applied to the origin of the human body (*DS* 3896)—but not of the unicity of the original couple, considered as necessary for a correct interpretation of the original sin. It is rather more a matter of being warned about the possible consequences of an adventurous "conjuncture," than a clear condemnation of all types of polygenesis. It is significant that the new *Catechism of the Catholic Church* (1992) recalls with force the unity of nature and the essential fraternity between all human beings, without alluding on this point to the encyclical *Humani Generis* (*CEC* 356–61): in this respect, the question is thus open in the Roman Church as in the other great Christian confessions.

In conclusion, the most probable position to the diverse points of view evoked seems to be that of a monogenesis in a broad sense—a single evolvable *phylum* biologically incarnating the essential unity of nature today's humanity—without being able to make a pronouncement on the question of the originating couple.

- K. Rahner (1954), *Schriften zur Tehologie* 1, Einsiedeln, 253–322.
P. Teilhard de Chardin (1955), *Le phénomène humain*, Paris.
P. Teilhard de Chardin (1956), *Le groupe zoologique humain*, Paris.
T. G. Dobzhansky (1962), *Mankind Evolution: The Evolution of the Human Species*, New Haven.
A. M. Dubarle (1967), *Le péché originel dans l'Écriture*, New Ed., Paris.
B. Chiarelli (1979), *L'origine dell'uomo*, Bari.
J. Reichholf (1991), *L'émergence de l'homme*, Paris.
St. Parker (1992), *L'aube de l'humanité*, Fribourg (Switzerland).

MARC LECLERC

See also **Adam; Evolution; Race; Sciences of Nature**

Monophysitism

The term "Monophysitism" (from *monos,* "sole," and *phusis,* "nature") designates the position of those who attribute to Christ* "a single nature." But it is important to distinguish at least two types of Monophysitism. One, which was represented in particular by the monk Eutyches, implies a certain assimilation between the human nature and the divine nature of Christ, so that the divine absorbs the human rather than leaving to it its specific character. The other, although opposed to the "diphysite" language of Chalcedon* (that is, to the language of the "two natures"), recognizes in the humanity of Christ all the characteristics appropriate to a human nature. The former is contrary to Christian orthodoxy, the latter is not. Judgment must therefore be exercised between the positions that in the past were associated with Monophysitism, and this judgment continues today in the framework of the dialogue between the Chalcedonian churches and the Monophysite churches.

a) *Monophysitism of Eutyches.* By the last decades of the fourth century, Apollinarianism* had opened the way to Monophysite language by attributing to Christ "a single incarnate nature from God* the Word" (*Ad Jovianum,* in TU, 1904, 251). Certainly, a similar formula was later used by Cyril* of Alexandria with a fully orthodox meaning. But Apollinarius in fact believed that the divine Logos had replaced the human soul* or human spirit of Christ, which already implied a certain confusion between the humanity and the divinity of the incarnate Word.

Monophysitism (as a heresy*) found its most radical expression shortly before the middle of the fifth century. Its principal representative, the monk Eutyches, was at the head of a large monastery and had attained considerable influence at the court of Constantinople. He presented himself as a fierce opponent of Nestorianism* and ceaselessly repeated that it was necessary to recognize "a single nature of the incarnate Word." He was to be harshly judged by some of his contemporaries, who saw him as an ignorant and obstinate old man. But his ideas became sufficiently widespread to provoke a refutation by Theodoret in 447 in *The Beggar* (which did not, however, mention Eutyches). This was followed by the intervention of Patriarch Flavian of Constantinople, who summoned the accused monk before a synod* in 448. Eutyches, while saying that he accepted the humanity of Christ, declared that his flesh was not consubstantial* with ours; and, above all, he unwaveringly maintained the same formula: "I confess that before the union Our Lord was of two natures, but after the union of only one nature." Eutyches was then excommunicated. But he had the support of the emperor Theodosius and, in spite of the intervention of Pope Leo in his *Tome of Leo,* was rehabilitated in 449 at the tumultuous meeting that was later to be called "the robbery of Ephesus." In 451 the Council of Chalcedon* condemned Eutyches's doctrine and opposed to it the famous definition according to which Christ is "recognized in two natures, without confusion, without change…the difference between the natures being in no way abolished because of the union, the specificity of each nature being rather preserved." Eutyches had of course claimed reliance on Cyril of Alexandria, but this reference was deceptive. For when Cyril said "a single nature of the incarnate Word," he understood "nature" in the sense of individual and concrete *existence,* and his doctrine corresponded in essence with that of Chalcedon, which, in different terminology, recognized in Christ "a single *hypostasis.*" But in Eutyches the unity of nature implied the absorption of human nature by divine nature. This position, on the pretext of fighting Nestorianism, lost sight of the specific nature of the humanity assumed by Christ: it was in fact a new form of Docetism*.

b) *Monophysitism after Chalcedon.* The very ambiguity of the expression "a single nature" was the source of many conflicts in the period following Chalcedon. The supporters of Cyril remained convinced that the expression should be maintained at all costs; but while some understood it as Eutyches had, others understood it in an orthodox sense and opposed in good faith the Chalcedon language of the two natures, which appeared to them to be a concession to Nestorianism. Many monks in particular pointed out that the formula "a single nature" preserved the absolute divinity of the Savior. In addition, religious motives were joined by political and ecclesial motives, for Monophysitism was particularly widespread in Egypt and Syria, whereas Western regions and Asia Minor were dominated by the Chalcedonians. It also happened that patriarchal sees were held sometimes by Chalcedonian bishops and sometimes by Monophysite bishops, in an atmosphere often marked by confused ideas and violent passions.

In 457 the Monophysite Timothy Aelurus became patriarch of Alexandria. Another Monophysite, Peter the Fuller, became patriarch of Antioch soon thereafter and introduced into the liturgy* the expression "holy God…who has been crucified for us." In 482 Emperor Zeno, advised by the patriarch Acacius, proposed a compromise formula, the *Henotics,* which condemned both Eutyches and the defenders of Chalcedon. But this formula was rejected by the diphysites and condemned by the pope, who excommunicated Acacius (484). Monophysitism nevertheless continued to spread. It was supported by several theologians, such as Philoxenus of Mabbug and especially Severus of Antioch. The latter understood "a single nature" in the sense of "a single hypostasis" and rejected the "in two natures" of Chalcedon, which seemed to him to imply the erroneous affirmation of two hypostases. However, from 527 onward Emperor Justinian became a fervent defender of "neo-Chalcedonianism": wishing to restore everywhere the faith* of Chalcedon (two natures in one hypostasis), he tried at the same time to win over the supporters of Monophysitism by reiterating the anathemata of Cyril against Nestorius and by imposing a formula that had been advocated by Scythian monks: "The one of the Trinity* suffered in the flesh." But when his efforts failed he exiled the Monophysite bishops. One of them, James Baradeus, consecrated new bishops in the East; thus Monophysites were given the name "Jacobites," whereas the Chalcedonians were called "Melkites" (that is, "imperial"). Justinian once again tried to win over the Monophysites at the Second Council of Constantinople* in 553, and his successor Justin II in turn tried a policy of openness. But the Monophysites, despite their internal divisions, maintained or consolidated their own positions. During the debates provoked by monotheism* in the seventh century, Emperor Heraclius published a new compromise document. But the Arabs had already invaded Syria and Egypt. They accommodated the Monophysite populations, who found their domination preferable to the pressures of the empire. In any event these populations were to survive down to the present, despite a history that turned out to be often difficult and troubled.

c) Monophysite Churches Today. Monophysite churches, known as "pre-Chalcedonian," are divided into four groups: the Coptic Orthodox Church, that is, the Christians of Egypt who adopted Monophysitism; the Ethiopian Monophysite Church; the Armenian Orthodox or "Gregorian" Church, which includes the Church of Etchmiadzin and the Church of Cilicia; and the Syrian Orthodox or "Jacobite" Church, which in turn is divided into two branches, that of Syria and that of southern India.

For some years, efforts have been made toward doctrinal agreement. Meeting in Addis Ababa in 1965, leaders of Monophysite churches proposed to open a dialogue with the churches from which they had been separated. In 1971 the Syrian patriarch of Antioch, Ignatius Jakub III, signed a declaration with Pope Paul VI recognizing that their respective communities, despite divergences in language, professed the same faith with respect to the Word made flesh. In 1973 an analogous declaration was published by Paul VI and the Coptic patriarch Chenuda III; the same basic agreement was expressed again in 1984, at the meeting between Pope John Paul II and the Syrian patriarch Ignace Zacca I Ivas. Common declarations were also made by John Paul II and the Armenian patriarch Karekin I in 1996 and then by John Paul II and the Armenian catholicos of Cicilia Aram I in 1997. In addition an official dialogue has been established between the Monophysite churches and the Orthodox Church, first in Chambésy in 1985, and then in the Egyptian monastery of Anba Bichoï in 1989, and again in Chambésy in 1990 (*see Towards Unity: The Theological Dialogue between the Orthodox Church and the Oriental Orthodox Church,* Geneva, 1998).

Nonetheless, all difficulties have not been resolved, not only because the various churches must still continue their work of doctrinal clarification, but because even today they give evidence of many divergences in their liturgical and pastoral traditions.

● M. Jugie (1913), "Eutychès," *DThC* 5, 1582–1609.
M. Jugie (1928), "M.," *DThC* 10, 2216–51.
J. Lebon (1951), "La christologie du m. syrien," in A. Grillmeier, H. Bacht (Ed.), *Das Konzil von Chalkedon: Geschichte und Gegenwart,* Würzburg, I, 425–580.
R. Janin (1952), "Églises orientales," *Cath.* 3, 1464–71.
P.-Th. Camelot (1961), *Éphèse et Chalcédoine,* Paris.
W. H. C. Frend (1972), *The Rise of the Monophysite Movement,* Cambridge.
F.-X. Murphy, P. Sherwood (1974), *Constantinople II et III,* Paris.
J. Pelikan (1974), *The Christian Tradition: A History of the Development of Doctrine,* vol. II: *The Spirit of Eastern Christendom (600–1700),* Chicago, chap. 2.
L. Perrone (1980), *La chiesa di Palestina e le controvesie cristologiche,* Brescia.
J. Liébaert (1982), "M.," *Cath.* 9, 576–83.
G. Zananiri, "Monophysites (Églises)," ibid., 583–86.
M. Simonetti (1983), "Monofisiti," *Dizionario patristico e di antichità cristiane,* 2291–97.
B. Dupuy (1986), "Où en est le dialogue entre l'Orthodoxie et les Églises dites monophysites?" *Ist.* 31, 357–70.
B. Dupuy (1990 *a*), " 'La déclaration approuvée' d'Anba Bichoï (24 juin 1989)," *Ist.* 34, 137–46.
B. Dupuy (1990 *b*), "L'Église syrienne d'Antioche des origines à aujourd'hui," ibid., 171–88.
T. Y. Malaty (1990), "La christologie de l'Église copte: *Mia phusis tou theou logou sesarkomenè*," *Ist.* 34, 147–58.
P. Allen (1994), "Monophysiten," *TRE* 23, 219–33.
B. Sesboüé (Ed.) (1994), *Histoire des dogmes,* t. I: *Le Dieu du salut,* Paris, 417–28.

MICHEL FÉDOU

See also **Christ and Christology; Hypostatic Union; Monothelitism/Monoenergism**

Monotheism

I. Origin and Definition

Monotheism, defined in the *Evangelisches Kirchelexicon* as "the acknowledgment and adoration of a single God," is distinguished from monolatry (worship of one god) and henotheism (acknowledgment of the supremacy of one God). In his *Natural History of Religion* (1767), Hume declares that polytheism is more primitive, and his view has become the prevailing one.

However, Wilhelm Schmidt (1912) argues that polytheism is a degeneration from the original cult of one God. The "sense of the numinous" posited by Rudolf Otto implies an undifferentiated deity*. Mircea Eliade notes that the sky-god (necessarily single) is often considered the supreme god, although he is worshipped only in extremis.

MARK J. EDWARDS

II. Biblical Theology

1. Old Testament

The Old Testament starts with Genesis 1:1 and its differentiation between God* and the world*; and the creator and the creation*. While it does not, of course, present the background to biblical monotheism, this passage fixes the limits within which it is to be understood.

In the Old Testament, certain unrelated representations or traditions are transposed onto the one God as a result of the absolute requirements of biblical faith*. Certain divine names, such as *El Olam* ("God of Eternity*, Everlasting God") (Gn 21:33, 14:18ff., and 22; Ps 46:5f., etc.), may have been preserved because the ancient proper name *'El* could take on an appellative sense ("God") and function as a surname or attribute of the single God YHWH.

We may distinguish six aspects or levels in the historical development or the objective content of this knowledge of faith:

a) *Witness to the Unique Bond between the God YHWH and a Particular Group.* Various fundamental traditions in the Book* of Exodus (Ex 3:14f., 18:12, 19:16ff., 24:10f.) attest to the unique and reciprocal relationship between a human group and YHWH, the God "of Israel" (Jgs 5:4f.; Dt 33:2).

b) *God's Superiority over Other Celestial Powers.* Such powers (Ps 89:6ff.) are subordinated to him, honor him, and execute his wishes (e.g., Ps 29, 47, 93, and see 103:19ff.; Is 6; Jb 1–2).

c) *Contribution of the Prophets* in the Ninth and Eighth Centuries.* Elijah is already unwilling to restrict himself to defending the exclusivity of the faith (1 Kgs 18:21 and 36f.); without absolutely rejecting the existence of foreign gods, he asserts that in Israel* the one God alone is the rescuer on whom diseases and cures, life and death*, depend (e.g., 2 Kgs 1:3 and 6; see Hos 4:12ff.; Jer 2:27f.). Like the Decalogue, which is probably of a later date, Hosea links God's declaration that "I am the Lord your God" with the formulation of the exclusive relationship that results

from it: "You know no God but me, and besides me there is no savior" (Hos 13:4; *see* 12:10). The prophet Isaiah (2:17; *see* 31:3) affirms this exclusivity in the form of a universal prediction: "The pride of Men must crumble....and on this day, the Lord alone will be exalted."

d) *Legal Formulas.* The relationship between humanity and the one God is developed within the law as a principle or an injunction. Its most ancient expression is probably to be found in the "book of the covenant" (Ex 22:19), with its reference to the consequence that follows from transgressing it (the expulsion of the culprit). Here, the prohibition concerns public and visible acts (*see* Ex 34:14: "you shall worship no other god"; 23:13: "make no mention of the names of other gods"; *see also*, e.g., Lv 19:4, 26:1; Dt 13). However, the first commandment in the Decalogue (Ex 20:3; Dt 5:7) also prohibits private acts hidden from the eyes of others: "You shall have no other gods before me."

e) *Confession of the "Uniqueness" of God.* The invocation "Hear, O Israel," which was to become the crucial profession of faith within Judaism*, expresses a new interpretation of the exclusivity of the faith: "The Lord our God, the Lord is one" (Dt 6:4; repeated in Zec 14:9; Mal 2:10; Jb 31:15). However, it follows immediately that "You shall love the Lord your God with all your heart and with all your soul and with all your might" (Dt 6:5). Human conduct must be "blameless, perfect," and without reservation (Gn 17:1; Dt 18:13; *see* Lv 19:2 and Mt 5:48), turned toward God alone (e.g., Ps 51:6 and 71:16; Is 26:13).

f) *Affirmation of Monotheism at Around the Time of the Exile.* The Second or Deutero-Isaiah, the prophet of the Exile, uses phrases that unambiguously exclude the existence of any other gods: "Before me no god was formed, nor shall there be any after me" (Is 43:10); "I am the first and I am the last; besides me there is no god" (Is 44:6; *see*, e.g., 41:4, 45:5f., 45:18, 45:21f., 46:9). Nevertheless, this prophet is a herald of salvation* and consolation: he does not put forward a doctrinal system. He takes up the theme of Hosea 13:4: "Besides me [God] there is no savior" (repeated in Is 43:11). If other gods existed, it would be possible to deny his power (41:24, 41:29): "their works are nothing." In the "priestly" narrative (Gn 1), neither chaos nor the stars are envisaged as mythical entities; no domain of activity is left to any other powers apart from God. However, the existence of other gods does not seem to be fundamentally denied (Ex 12:12). In Deuteronomy, the article of faith, "The Lord is one" (6:4), is explained later: "there is no other besides him" (Dt 4:35, 4:39; *see* 32:39). It is in this sense that it was to be understood later, in the New Testament (Mk 12:32): "He is one, and there is no other besides him."

In general, then, monotheism is not the foundation of Israel's belief, but only one of its consequences. The belief functions as an absolute requirement, rather than as a "doctrine," and should be seen as involving an act of placing faith and trust in God.

Changes of period and name (Ex 6:2f.) gave rise in Israel to the hope that "all the peoples of the earth" would acknowledge the one God (1 Kgs 8:60; *see*, e.g., 2 Kgs 19:19 and 5:15; Is 19:21ff., 45:6, 45:22ff.; Sg 2:11; Ps 83:19). God's power will triumph even over death (e.g., Am 9:2; Prv 15:11; Ps 22:30, 49:16, 73:23ff.; Jb 14:13, 26:5; Is 25:8, 26:19). The possibility of a new profession of faith is already accepted in the Old Testament (Jer 16:14f., 23:7f.; *see* Is 48:20).

2. New Testament

While the New Testament continues to profess belief in the one and only God (*see* Mt 4:10), it asserts it in a new way: "No one can serve two masters" (Mt 6:24; *see* 6:32f.). "Who can forgive sins but God alone?" (Mk 2:7, *see* 10:17f. and 12:28ff.; Mt 22:36ff., 23:9, 24:36; Lk 5:11).

a) The One God and Jesus. The earliest witnesses present the first Easter as the salvific act by which God manifests himself through Jesus*. While the Old Testament generally affirms that God "kills and brings to life" (1 Sm 2:6; *see*, e.g., Rom 4:17; Lk 1:51ff.), the New Testament bears witness that it is God who "raised [Jesus] from the dead" (1 Thes 1:9f.; Gal 1:1; Rom 8:11; *see* 1 Cor 15:3f.; Lk 24:27). According to Paul, God sent his Son (Rom 8:3; *see* 5:8 and Gal 4:4) and "gave him up for us all" (Rom 8:32; *see* 4:24f., *but also*, e.g., Gal 1:4). According to 2 Corinthians 5:18ff., reconciliation is the work of God "through" or "in" Christ* (*see* Rom 3:25). John's Gospel* also says that God "sent" and "gave up" his Son (e.g., 3:16f., 7:16; *see* 1 Jn 4:9f.).

Nevertheless, as in the Old Testament, Paul is not able to make a rigorous denial of the existence of other divine powers, although in respect of such powers he maintains that "for us there is one God, the Father…and one Lord, Jesus Christ" (1 Cor 8:5f.; *see* Rom 11:36; 1 Tm 2:5f.; Eph 4:4ff.).

b) Maintaining the First Commandment. Even the christological hymn in Philippians 2:5–11 closes with a celebration of "the glory of God the Father (*see* 1:11, 4:20; Rom 15:6f.; *as well as* Lk 2:11, 2:14).

In the final analysis, Paul's hope that "the Son himself will also be subjected to him who put all things in subjection under him, that God may be all in all" (1 Cor 15:28; *see* 3:23 and 11:3) is an expression of the Old Testament expectation that "On that day the Lord will be one and his name one" (Zep 14:9; *see*, e.g., Is 2:17 and 60:19f.). The Epistle to the Romans, in its present form, ends with a doxology that reprises the word "only": "to the only wise God be glory" (Rom 16:25–27; *see* Eph 3:20f.; Jn 17:3; 1 Tm 1:17 and 5:15f.; Jude 24f.; Rev. 15:4; as well as the doxology of Our Father, Mt 6:13).

The "christological event" not only brought about a new interpretation of the first commandment but was itself interpreted in such a way that the intention of the commandment is preserved within the doctrine of the Trinity*, by which the early church attested, beyond the differences between the persons, the uniqueness and indivisibility of God.

● H. Ringgren (1963), *Israelitische Religion.*
H. Cazelles (1976), "Le Dieu d'Abraham," *Les Quatre Fleuves* 6, 4–17, repr. in *Autour de l'Exode (Études),* Paris, 1987, 53–66.
N. Lohfink (1983), "Das Alte Testament und sein Monotheismus," repr. in *Studien zur biblischen Theologie,* SBAB 16 (1993), 133–51.
G. Braulik (1985), "Das Deuteronomium und die Geburt des Monotheismus," repr. in *Studien zur Theologie des Deuteronomiums,* SBAB 2 (1988), 257–300.
J. Briend (1992), *Dieu dans l'Écriture,* Paris, 111–26.
W.H. Schmidt et al. (1994), "Monotheismus I–IV," *TRE* 23, 233–62.
W.H. Schmidt (1995), "Erwägungen zur Geschichte der Ausschließlichkeit des alttestamentlichen Glaubens," VT.S, *Congress Volume Paris 1992,* 289–314.

WERNER H. SCHMIDT

See also **Filiation; Idolatry; Knowledge of God; Paganism; People of God; Simplicity (Divine); Theophany; Universalism; Wisdom**

III. Historical Theology

1. Antiquity

Already during Homer's time, the sky-god Zeus occupied an elevated status. During the fifth century Pindar and Aeschylus carried that status even higher and made Zeus into the custodian of morality. At the time, Xenophanes already criticized the Homeric gods' immortality, positing the existence of a single (or supreme) god without anthropomorphic features. Later, Plato argues in the *Timaeus* that the goodness of the world implies the existence of a single maker, the "Demiurge," and a single paradigm, but Plato is not very clear on the relation of both to the Form of the Good*, the origin of all other essences (*Republic* 509). Aristotle identifies God with perfect actuality (*Meta-*

physics 12); this God, being free of matter, is indivisible (1075 a). Stoics regarded the Homeric gods as allegorical names for the elements or the divine powers; but the singularity of the world also implied the existence of a single God, whom they often called Zeus. In late antiquity, Isis was sometimes identified with all other divinities, while Macrobius (c. 400) argues in the *Saturnalia* that all gods are identical with Dionysus, Apollo or the Sun. Neoplatonism, after Plotinus (204–270), allowed for popular divinities to be provisionally worshipped as lower energizations of the impersonal One. Finally, imperial formulas often allude to a single divinity, and, in the second century, Celsus and Apuleius compared lower gods to the ministers of a king.

2. Judaism and Islam

Written at the beginning of the first century, Philo's treatise *De Opificio Mundi* (The Creation of the World) maintains that there are only one world and one creator. Since the Bible* does not say that God created the lower powers, even such texts as Deuteronomy 6:4—"the Lord our God, the Lord is one"—could be interpreted henotheistically. Thus, angelic intermediaries were recognized and even revered. Subsequently, Cabalists admired the existence of 10 mediating powers below the unknowable Deity *(Keter),* or even a moral duality in God. Nevertheless, Maimonides (1135–1204) made the unity of God his second principle of faith*, while Crescas (1340–1410) included it as a consequence of his existence. Monotheism, whether as a simple belief or as reflection, could lead to an interpretation of Christianity as a form of polytheism, as, for example, in the case of Saadia Gaon (b. 882), or in the *Kuzari* of Judah Halevi (c. 1075–1141), which sees Judaism* vanquishing Christianity in dialogue. Islamic monotheism is consistent: even if the Al-Ghazzali (1058–1111) distinguishes 99 names for God, the Sura 19 of the Koran denounces the Trinity*. Maimonides, while denying that Islamic dialectic could prove God's unity *(Doctor Perplexorum* I. 75), himself draws proofs from revelation* and philosophy* (II.1).

3. Early Christianity

To the early Christian apologists*, pagans appeared to be polytheistic idolaters. However, the most cited verse in martyrology is Acts 4:24, which is a prayer to the only unique God. The Fathers* did not hesitate to draw their arguments in favor of monotheism from philosophers and tragedians *(see,* e.g., Ps-Justin, *De Monarchia).* After the Peace of the Church, some thought that the unity of the empire presupposed monotheism and consequently entailed universal monolatry *(see* above all Eusebius of Caesarea's *Tria-*

contericus of 336). Augustine's *Civitas Dei* (City of God) mocks the petty deities of the Roman state and criticizes the theory that gods make use of intermediaries. Throughout this period, the development of the dogma of the Trinity had to avoid the twin pitfalls of modalism*, which denied the existence of real distinctions, within God, between Father, Son, and Spirit, and tritheism, which no one ever professed. (The tritheism detected by John Philoponus was the result of a conceptual confusion that Philoponus himself did not share.) However, Trinitarian belief was thought by some to threaten monotheism. This is the reasons for which Arius (c. 320) rejected the possibility of plurality in the Deity, and that Gregory* of Nyssa was undoubtedly not engaging in a mere exercise in style when, on the eve of the First Council of Constantinople*, he demonstrated that the three divine persons were not three gods (*Ad Ablabium,* c. 375). The continued presence of Jewish communities in the Byzantine Empire, and the confrontation with Islam, ensured that the defense and illustration of Trinitarian monotheism remained an urgent task for theologians in eastern Christendom.

The refutation of gnosis*, of Manicheanism*, and then of medieval dualisms (the Bogomils, the Paulicians, the Cathars) also had a significant effect on the affirmation of Christian monotheism. Refuting the existence of two uncreated principles, and therefore of an uncreated principle of evil*, required theologians to think about evil. This in turn led, on the one hand, to the important emphasis on the classical thesis that evil is merely privation and nonbeing, and, on the other hand, as a consequence, to a reasoned affirmation of the absolute innocence of God.

4. Subsequent Developments

The search for proofs of God's uniqueness is an important feature of medieval and modern thought. Anselm*'s definition of God as the most perfect being conceivable, "the unsurpassable" *(Monologion)* implies divine uniqueness. In his *Quaestiones Disputate* of 1266–67, Thomas* Aquinas identifies God's existence with his essence, and hence provides the conceptual means for excluding the existence of more than one god. Descartes*, in the third *Meditation,* and Leibniz*, in the *Monadologie,* infer the unity of God from his infinity and from the necessity of his being*. In Spinoza's *Ethica* (I, 14), the axiom that only one substance can exist concentrates the whole of reality, without exception, in a God that lacks any personal traits and that is synonymous with nature (pantheism*). In the writings of Kant*, the God postulated on the basis of practical reason must be the God of monotheism (but a God who cannot be defined in terms of a trinity), which is also the case for Fichte, within the framework of his philosophy on the ego. In Hegel*, by contrast, the Trinity becomes increasingly important: the life of the Absolute is a "game of love with itself," and God himself is engaged in history in such a way that he is not truly himself until it ends. Schelling* was the first to criticize this view. For the young Schelling, who defined nature as mind made visible (*Ideen,* 1797–1803), a single world implies a single God. In his later writings, his plan for a "philosophy of revelation" lead Schelling to develop a "theory of powers" aimed at linking the "economic" Trinity (God manifested as Father, Son, and Spirit) with the "immanent" Trinity (the divine life in itself). With deism* the modern period has seen a less determinate form of philosophical monotheism; by which it has even been possible to introduce certain types of theology (as with Tillich*'s description of God as the "ground of being").

The theology* of the 20th century has consecrated fruitful debate to a reexamination of Eusebius's "imperial theology," whether in order to construct a political theology that draws distant inspiration from it (Carl Schmitt) or in order to deny that it is possible (E. Peterson). However, the main focus of the most inventive currents within Protestant and Catholic theology has been on the Trinity.

The order of reasoning adopted by Scholasticism* had led to a distinction between two types of theological treatise, the "treatise on the one God" and the "treatise on the triune God," in such a way that the former could not be addressed until after the latter had been studied. Luther*'s theology contains an explicit rejection of this order of reasoning, but his asperities were quickly smoothed away. Barth*'s *Dogmatik* and Balthasar*'s trilogy constitute, perhaps, the first highly articulated ensemble capable of replacing the Scholastic program. Orthodox theology has also made a contribution to this development by permitting reflection on monotheism in terms of the *monarchy* of the Father (Vl. Lossky, J. D. Zizioulas), rather than in terms of the unique divine essence.

In addition, the 20th century has also known a radical critique of (mono)theism. In the face of this critique, it became possible to make a theological interpretation of the "death of God" predicted by Nietzsche* as implying conceptions that are themselves nontheological (such as the death of a God who possessed a "metaphysical essence," *essentia Dei metaphysica,* the death of the highest value, or the death of the God of ontotheology). Such an interpretation led to a new affirmation of God, who seeking a way "between theism and atheism," finds it, for example, in a theology of the cross (E. Jüngel) oriented toward a theology of the Trinity. Occasionally, God's unity and uniqueness have ceased to be taken as preconditions for Trinitarian discourse—on the contrary, only a Trinitarian theology can provide the conditions for its affirmation.

• Wilhelm Schmidt (1912), *Der Ursprung des Gottesidee,* Münster.
E. Peterson (1935), *Monotheismus als politischer Problem,* Leipzig.
M. Eliade (1953), *Traité d'histoire des religions,* Paris.
J. Hick (1977), *God and the Universe of Faiths,* London.
A. Kenny (1979), *The God of the Philosophers,* Cambridge.
S. Breton (1980), *Unicité et m.,* Paris.
J. Moltmann (1980), *Trinität und Reich Gottes,* Munich.
R. M. Grant (1984), *Gods and the One God,* Philadelphia.
D. Halperin (1988), *The Faces of the Chariot,* Tübingen.
P. Hayman (1991), "Monotheism—A Misused Term in Jewish studies?" *JJS* 42, I-15.
D. Sibony (1993), *Les trois monothéismes,* Paris.

MARK J. EDWARDS

See also **Angels; Arianism; Attributes, Divine; Deism and Theism; God; Trinity; Tritheism; Unitarianism**

Monothelitism/Monoenergism

Monothelitism and monoenergism are two facets of the same christological doctrine set forth at the beginning of the seventh century. After enjoying great success, the doctrine was condemned by the Lateran Council (649) and Constantinople III (681). It stated that Christ had only one will *(thélèma)* and only one way of functioning or working *(energeia)*. It raised a different question from that of Monophysitism*. For political and religious reasons, Patriarch Sergius of Constantinople (†638) elucidated the question in order to help Emperor Heraclius (†641) bring about the union of the Christians inside the Byzantine Empire, which was under serious threat from the Persians, then later from the Islamic Arabs. It was a matter of discovering a Christology capable of reconciling Monophysitic and orthodox Chalcedonian opinions. After long transactions with the bishops of both groups, the doctrines of both monothelitism and monoenergism seemed acceptable to everyone.

On the theological level, the Patriarch of Constantinople was tackling an essential christological point that until then had remained obscure, the point about Christ's human will and functioning. In fact, according to monothelitism and monoenergism, Christ possessed only a *divine* will and a *divine* way of working. In no way did the problem concern his divine will and divine way of working, for the Word* incarnate was acknowledged by all, by both the Chalcedonians and the Monophysites, as a divine person (or *hypostasis*), "one of the Trinity*," willing and working in common with the Father* and the Holy* Spirit. But, by that very fact, it had to be denied that he had a *human* will and way of functioning. To oppose Arianism*, the fourth century Fathers had stated clearly the three divine persons' unity of nature, will, and working.

During the same period, Apollinaris (Apollinarianism*) had already drew up an early form of monothelitism and monoenergism. But while the Fathers had vigorously asserted the reality of Jesus' human soul* and intelligence, they had left in obscurity the question of his will and way of functioning, which followed from that fact. Gregory* of Nazianzus is far from clear about the matter. The doctrine of monoenergism could also base itself on one of Pseudo-Dionysius*'s assertions, that in Christ could be found "a new theandric functioning *(théandrikè energeia)*" (*Letter* 4).

An early attempt at unity with the Monophysites, made in Alexandria in 633 on the basis of monoenergism, ended in failure because it was challenged immediately by the monk Sophronius, who then became patriarch of Jerusalem*. Sergius responded at once by publishing his *Psèphos* (Decree) in which he made a subtle move from monoenergism to monothelitism, by his reference to Jesus' prayer in Gethsemane, as it is recounted in the synoptic Gospels. Sliding from the hypothesis of the two ways of working to the hypothesis of the two wills, Sergius wrote (*Mansi* 11, 533 E): "We would admit two wills behaving in opposite ways to each other: on the one hand the God*-Word wanted to carry out the saving passion, but on the other hand,

the humanity within him resisted his will by opposing it. By admitting this, we would be introducing two beings who wanted opposite things, which is impious." In fact, in the Gospel text, mention is made of Jesus' human will, which seems to oppose the divine will by its refusal of the passion (Mt 26:39). But afterward, Jesus renounced that will: "nevertheless not my will, but thine, be done" (Lk 22:42). In Sergius's theology, the problem of Christ's human will is presented in moral terms: This will is not examined as a simple human faculty of willing but as a potential capacity to oppose the divine will. The key expression is "contrariety or clashing of wills." The human will possesses the (sinful) ability to oppose the divine will. Denial of Christ's human will and affirmation of a single (divine) will was the logical result of these premises. (All the same, the expression "single will" is not used explicitly in the *Psèphos*.)

At first, in 634, Sergius's *Psèphos* received unanimous approval, from the bishop of Rome*, Honorius I, as well as from the man who would later become the chief adversary of monothelitism and monoenergism, Maximus* the Confessor (Epistle 19; PG 91, 592 BC). Sergius's greatest "success" was having brought Honorius to confess monothelitism explicitly in his reply (*Kirch*, no. 1058–59): "We confess our Lord Jesus Christ's single will, for our nature has obviously been taken in hand by God, and it has been taken in hand in a state of innocence, such as it was before the fall.... The Savior did not possess a different or contrary will...and when the Holy Scriptures say: 'I did not come to do my will but to do the will of the Father who sent me' (John 5:30), and 'Not my will, Father, but thine' (Mark 14:36), they are not speaking in those terms to express any difference of will." The text leaves vague the distinction between a *different* will and a *contrary* will; if the human will is denied, it was because a clash of wills had to be denied at any price. The crisis then came to an end with the official monothelite doctrine, the *Ecthèse*, promulgated in 638 by Emperor Heraclius. Sergius, its drafter, again took up the main points from his *Psèphos*, while including in it Honorius's monothelite statement about the impiety of an affirmation of the two wills (*Kirch*, no. 1071–73): "How is it possible for those who confess the orthodox faith and who glorify an only Son, Our Lord Jesus Christ and true God, to accept two contrary wills in him? Hence, following the Holy Fathers in everything and on this point, we confess our Lord Jesus Christ and true God's single will."

The rigorous sequence of these three primary documents: the *Psèphos*, Honorius's Letter, and the *Ecthèse*, reveals monothelitism's cohesiveness and strength, but the refusal of the cup still needed an explanation. It can be said that in reality Christ's refusal sprang from his humanity without it being the expression of a will. An inframoral reality was seen in it, a "natural reaction of the flesh" provoked by fear of death*—that is the classical explanation on which Sergius fell back in his *Psèphos* and his *Ecthèse*. But the working of a true human will can also be seen in this refusal—then it amounts to an act of "opposition," which could not be attributed to Christ except by way of "rational appropriation" *(oikeiôsis skhetikè)*. This second thesis finally won out in Byzantine monothelitism (*see* PG 91, 304 AB). Like the first thesis, it amounted to depriving Christ's humanity of its engine. Deprived of will, his humanity was nothing more than a passive instrument moved by divine will alone.

From 640 onward, thanks to Maximus the Confessor's theological activity, doctrines of monothelitism and monoenergism were attacked in the West by the Roman Church and by the African churches, leading Heraclius himself to disavow the *Ecthèse* (*see* PG 90, 125 AB). Heraclius's successor, Constans II (641–68), at first upheld this doctrine in a brutal and dictatorial way. Later, realizing the extent of the disagreement, he claimed the right to impose silence on the matter by means of his *Typos* of 647 *(Mansi* 10, 1029C–1032A).

See bibliography for "Constantinople III, Council of."

FRANÇOIS-MARIE LÉTHEL

See also **Christ and Christology; Constantinople III, Council of; Maximus the Confessor; Monophysitism**

Montaigne, Michel de. *See* Skepticism, Christian

Montanism

a) History. The term *Montanist* is first attested to in the fourth century by Cyril of Jerusalem (in his *Catechesis* XVI, 8) to refer to a much more ancient group, the Phrygians, or the "Pepuzians," from the name of their city-kingdom, Pepuza; certain ecclesiastic authors use the term *Cataphrygians*. These names indicate that the birthplace of Montanism was in the communities in Asia Minor. The movement probably developed at the beginning of the second century, during the reigns of Antoninus Pius and Marcus Aurelius.

Patristic testimonies about Montanism are varied and probably tendentious. The fullest information comes from Eusebius *(HE* 5, 14, 16–19) and from Epiphanius *(Panarion* 48–49.51). The attribution to Didymus of Alexandria of a *Dialogue between a Montanist and an Orthodox Believer* remains unverified. The names Montanus, Maximilla, and Priscilla are given as those of the movement's originators, and, according to Epiphanius *(Panarion* 51, 33), the Christian community of Thyatira was entirely won over to Montanism around the year 170. Perhaps because he recognized himself in the Montanists' moral rigor, in the second half of his life Tertullian* joined their ranks, and the works that he wrote during that period made him the group's major representative in Christian Africa. However, Montanism's history, traces of which survived in Asia Minor until the beginning of the ninth century, must be put back into its original context of second-century Asian Christianity—and, in particular, the community of Philadelphia (Trevett 1989; *see* Rev 3:7–13). Ignatius of Antioch's letters and the narrative of Polycarp's martyrdom constitute important testimonies to the place reserved in the communities for discussions on authority and the role to be assigned to the prophets (*see* Ignatius, *To the Philadelphians* 5:2).

b) Doctrine. Montanism was primarily a prophetic movement, and there still exist a series of oracles attributed to Montanus and Maximilla (Labriolle 1913 *a*), of which several had been transmitted by the Fathers*. The movement's Phrygian origin and its prophetic demonstrations of an ecstatic type have led to comparisons with the cult* of Cybele (*see* Strobel 1980). However, the "new prophecy" should also be linked with the eschatological expectation held by the first generations of Christians. According to ancient sources (Labriolle 1913 *a*), Maximilla asserted that her death would herald the end of the world. The "new prophecy" found its favorite references in the Johannine Gospel and stressed the Paraclete at work in the group's prophets*. Montanus seems to have adopted the name of Paraclete, but that does not prove that he identified himself with the Holy* Spirit or with any of the three divine persons (in fact, the upholders of orthodoxy did not challenge the Montanists' Trinitarian doctrine). In any case, the refutation of the Montanists clearly suggests that at that time prophecy was a topic of debate in the communities of Asia Minor.

Montanism probably also appealed for demonstrations of the extraordinary, and Jerome pointed out the existence of a treatise by Tertullian on ecstasy (fragments in CChr.SL 2, 1334–36). Such appeals were held all the more suspect because they were accompanied by protests against a ministerial-hierarchic conception of the church. The church answered Montanism by reinforcing its episcopal structure. In a commentary on Paul's statement that "the women should keep silence in the churches" (1 Cor 14:34), Origen* criticized the role to which the Montanist prophetesses aspired and answered with a restrictive analysis of the function of prophetesses in the Old and New Testaments (fragment of a commentary on 1 Corinthians, preserved in a collection of exegetic material).

The revisions that Tertullian made about the years 207–8 to his *Adversus Marcionem* (SC 365, 368, 399) show his enlistment in the Montanist ranks. Tertullian asserted that the possibility of prophecy was always open (*Adversus Marcionem* I, 21, 5; V, 8, 12), and in answer to the Marcionite condemnation of marriage, he made his own the Montanists' insistence on the exclusive nature of marriage* (*Adversus Marcionem* I, 29, 4). This affirms his definite break with the church*, and this break is stated even more clearly in his later treatises. From then on, the church would be defined as the community of "psychics"—and, therefore, the community of those who remained rooted in sin—and Tertullian would no longer acknowledge the primacy of the bishop of Rome (*De Pudicita*, SC 394–95), contrary to the ecclesiology* he had earlier developed in his treatise on penitence.

The Montanists' moral and disciplinary prescriptions take up a lot of space in Tertullian's last writings (*De Monogamia*, SC 343, *De Jejunio adversus Psychicos*, and *De Pudicita*). In an apocalyptic context that went far beyond the Montanist group, calls to purity* and to virginity, the condemnation of second marriages, the insistence on fasting and penitence, and exhortations not to avoid martyrdom* all signaled the desire to create a community of "the pure." Its ascetic tendencies have caused Montanism to be taxed with Encratism, but such an accusation proves the extent of the difficulty of defining the specificity of a movement born in a period in which heresy* was not yet a working concept.

● P. de Labriolle (1913 *a*), *Les sources de l'histoire du montanisme,* Fribourg (Switzerland)–Paris.
P. de Labriolle (1913 *b*), *La crise montaniste,* Fribourg (Switzerland)–Paris.
E. R. Dodds (1965), *Pagan and Christian in an Age of Anxiety,* London.
F. Blanchetière (1978–79), "Le montanisme originel," *RevSR* 52 and 53, 118–34 and 1–22.
A. Strobel (1980), *Das heilige Land der Montanisten,* Berlin.
R. E. Heine (1987–88), "The Role of the Gospel of John in the Montanist Controversy," *SecCent* 6, 1–20.
C. Trevett (1989), "*Apocalypse,* Ignatius, Montanism: Seeking the Seeds," *VigChr* 43, 313–38.
W. H. C. Frend (1993), "Montanismus," *TRE* 23, 271–79.
C. Trevett (1996), *Montanism,* Chicago.

FRANÇOISE VINEL

See also **History of the Church; Millenarianism; Prophet and Prophecy; Tertullian**

Moral. *See* Ethics

Moral Theology. *See* Ethics

Moses

Traditionally, Moses was the epic hero who lived in the reign of Rameses II (1290–1224) in the late 13th century B.C. Under divine guidance he led the Israelites from Egyptian oppression across the "sea of reeds," formerly mistranslated as the Red Sea, and through the desert to "Mount Sinai," and thence toward the promised land, which he was allowed to see but not to enter. The story is related in the Pentateuch, divided by the Jews before the advent of Jesus into its five constituent books (Genesis, Exodus, Leviticus, Numbers, and Deuteronomy), but still known collectively as the Torah. The Torah was considered by Jesus and the apostles (Jn 1:45–47; Rom 10:5) to have been written by Moses, himself both the hero and the author of the epic and the law.

The Pentateuch contains at least two creation narratives, two accounts of Cain's genealogy, two combined versions of the flood story, and at least two accounts of the legal dispensations of the Jews, together with much other material in several variants, and is uncontroversially considered to be composed of different strata. A great deal of what it relates about Moses, like his abandonment in the river in a wicker basket lined with bitumen and pitch, is common to the mythology and folklore of different parts of the Middle East. The same fate is narrated of the infant Mesopotamian king Sargon who was to reign in the millennium before Moses. The deeds and stature of Moses are in part compounded of the heroic lore of non-Israelite traditions.

After the Pentateuch's narratives of the Creation and the patriarchs in Genesis, in which the story of Noah is similar to that of Utnapishtim, hero of the Sumerian epic *Gilgamesh,* Exodus is primarily concerned with the laws given to Moses for the Israelites, not only the Decalogue but also the social, moral, religious, and ritual prescriptions ordained by YHWH, with its numerous sections preceded by such phrases as "Yahweh said to Moses …" YHWH's instructions for the mak-

ing of the ark and of the tent in which it is to be housed, for vestments, sacrifices, and ritual obligations are spelled out by Moses in great detail, down to measurements and types of wood. They must reflect some record of actual rites and customs, however they originated.

The next book, Leviticus, is devoted primarily to the legal prescriptions communicated by YHWH to Moses on Mount Sinai for the Israelites and interrupts the historical flow of the Old Testament. The Book of Numbers takes up the narrative again with a sporadic account of the desert march interspersed with long enumerations, formulae, and lists. Deuteronomy enshrines a whole legal code within a long discourse by Moses, the whole preceded and followed by further speeches by Moses, and ending with an account of his death.

The religious truth of the Pentateuch as we have it is therefore far removed from straight narrative or literal accuracy. The dimensions of the law given in the Pentateuch—once short enough to be engraved on stone, according to passages like Deuteronomy 27:3 and 27:8—have clearly undergone massive augmentation, and the original religious message has no doubt been corrupted by the addition of material later than the earliest stratum. Some at least of the legal procedure attributed to the Mosaic legislation dictated by YHWH in the present text can be shown by religious, ethical, and sociological evidence to be of post-Mosaic origin, while much of it preexisted Moses and the vocation of Israel.

In the early 21st century we can be only at the beginning of the confrontation of biblical narrative with scientific archaeological investigation, which is becoming increasingly sophisticated and which might eventually produce clear evidence of what actually happened, and what relationship different parts of the Pentateuch bear to an accurate chronicle of the events that they relate. We have, for instance, no convincing idea of where Mount Sinai might have been, or therefore of what route the Israelites took to get there. Reconstruction of the life and deeds of the historical Moses is therefore bound at present to remain to some extent a matter of academic controversy and informed religious conjecture, although behind the biblical figure of Moses there does indeed seem to lurk a real religious and political leader. He appears in the Pentateuch at the beginning of what we know as the second chapter of Exodus, which gives two similar accounts of Moses' calling and is devoted to accounts of the liberation of the Israelites from Egypt, their crossing of the desert, and the establishment of the alliance with YHWH.

Exodus tells of the oppression in Egypt by the king of the prosperous, numerically increasing, and powerful descendants of Jacob, whose firstborn males were on the Pharaoh's orders to be destroyed at birth. The mother of one male of the tribe of Levi put her firstborn male in the wicker basket in the reeds of the river. Pharaoh's daughter found the infant, unknowingly had him nursed by his own mother, and adopted him as her own son, giving him the name Moses, which Exodus uncertainly claims to be connected with a Hebrew root indicating that the baby had been taken from the water. We next hear of Moses when, fleeing after killing an Egyptian for beating a Hebrew, he settles in Midian to the east of the gulf of Aqaba, where he marries Zipporah, daughter of a local chieftain.

There are parallels for the raising of foreigners at the Egyptian court, and for escape after suspicion of murder leading to the marriage of a daughter of a local chieftain, but there is no nonbiblical warrant for the oppression of the Hebrews in Egypt, or for their mass exodus. It is safest to think in terms of the expansion into a national epic, "to fit the needs of theological ideology" (Ze'ev Herzog), of the private story of at best a few families falling into a general pattern of migration into Egypt and the acquisition of power there. Nationalistic propaganda reasons can be given for later modifications of the Pentateuch material into the national epic that it has in part become, and there are anachronisms in the Genesis account of the patriarchs, which suggest reworking by a later, historically unskilled hand.

Exodus continues with God's decision to have mercy on the Hebrews in Egypt, and with the appearance to Moses, while he is tending his father-in-law's sheep, of an angel of YHWH under the appearance of a burning bush that remains unconsumed, an easily recognizable symbol of the divinity. A voice from the bush addresses Moses by name, and reveals the speaker to be the God of Abraham, Isaac, and Joseph.

Moses covers his face out of fear that he might otherwise be harmed by seeing God. God announces his plan to relieve the children of Israel in Egypt and to have them led to the land flowing with milk and honey, confiding this mission to a reluctant Moses, giving him three miraculous signs by which the Israelites will recognize in him the envoy of YHWH, and promising prodigies sufficient to force Pharaoh to release them. He identifies himself with a term derived from the verb "to be," "I am who am," and gives Aaron to Moses for support.

Exodus then contains a second, abbreviated version of YHWH's mission to Moses. This conflation and many other elements in the text suggest that whoever finally edited it was glorifying the origins of Israel's conversion to monotheism. What occurred is more likely to have been some modification introduced into the preexisting cult of YHWH, which is known to have predated God's self-revelation to Moses as "I am who am," and Exodus may well contain the mythologization of a major religious dispute in Egypt redacted from an anti-Pharaonic point of view. It is now considered unsafe specifically to connect the exodus of the Israelites with the conversion to monotheism, which may actually have come later.

YHWH hardens Pharaoh's heart and brings him to submission by means of the nine plagues, ending with the death of Egypt's firstborn. The story is told twice before Exodus moves on to the crossing of the sea of reeds, with the waters closing behind the Israelites over the pursuing Egyptians, the march across the desert, and the theophany on Mount Sinai, the Decalogue, and the alliance. The miracles, the episode of the golden calf, and YHWH's idiosyncratic behavior make a list too long and too well known to be repeated here. Dozens of naturalistic explanations have been fabricated for everything, but they have all been discredited. In view of the repetitions, the propagandist intention, the omissions, and the unexplained motivations, the historical career of Moses must remain largely conjectural.

All that is certain is that the final editors of Exodus and Deuteronomy must have been working on a text to which they accorded religious respect sufficient to leave blatant contradictions, and one through which they intended to impart a strong nationalistic and religious message. Their YHWH is vengeful and at times capricious, conscious of power but not depicted in the Moses story as omnipotent. The editors were deeply attached to the minutiae of ritual, but were not clear about ethical standards. It is not clear for what sin Moses was punished by not being allowed to enter the promised land. At times Moses himself appears to be quasi-divine. He argues with YHWH, even lectures him, when he proposes to destroy Israel after the episode of the golden calf, and obtains mercy for the people from YHWH, only himself to fly into a rage and have three thousand executions carried out by the tribe of Levi, who thereby become the priests of YHWH.

What is clear is that Moses, as depicted in Exodus and Deuteronomy, is the figure of a great religious leader, portrayed as the founder of Judaism as a religion, and acknowledged by Christians as foreshadow-ing the very different ethical and priestly status of the Anointed One. The meaning of the revelation YHWH entrusted to him is not clear, and too much mythologizing and rewriting, incorporating alien folklore, has obscured the actual details of his career, but he is certainly the founder of one of the first of the three great religions to have come out of the Middle East: Judaism, Christianity, and Islam.

ANTHONY LEVI

Mouroux, Jean. *See* Experience

Music

Music—according to what is doubtless a rather vague consensus as to its content and boundaries—is understood as the practice of singing and playing instruments, in contexts as varied as the concert hall, musical theater, worship, and so forth. The use of music in Christian worship is a fact. In order to try to understand this fact and its implications, it can be shown that an interplay of historically based constraints and resources has given rise, within the Christian liturgy*, to a special type of musical practice, defining forms, producing repertoires, and deriving the logic of its development from certain principles.

It is, nonetheless, important to note that the term *musica,* which originates in Graeco-Latin theory, was scarcely used by Christian writers until Cassiodorus (c. 485–c. 580) introduced the theory of the liberal arts into clerical and monastic circles (*Institutiones,* PL 70). Even then, however, the word denoted a science related to mathematics—a kind of cosmology of sonic, rhythmical, and numerical phenomena—far removed from the practical and spiritual realities of the church's music. Isidore of Seville (c. 559–634), in his study of the voice and of singing, was to fuse Cassiodorus's approach with that of the rhetoric derived from Quintil-ian. This fusion clearly indicates the two domains in terms of which the "effects of music"—henceforth an obligatory chapter in any treatise *De musica* (Hameline 1978)—would subsequently be considered.

1. From the Origins of Christian Music to Clement of Alexandria

There was, at the outset, no Christian Church* music comparable to the musical establishment of the Temple at Jerusalem*, still less to that of the political and social institutions of the Mediterranean cities and their public worship. There were no bodies of musicians (singers, dancers, or instrumentalists) and no musical practices codified in a repertoire and a calendar. The musical practices of the earliest Christian communities seem to have been closer to what can be seen in the context of religious brotherhoods or associations centered on mutual enlightenment and drawing on the human resources of their members, understood as charismata in the service of the community (1 Cor 14). The domestic space, extended to the members of the community, seems to have been the main forum for this, and its importance would continue during the following centuries. The role of the family, or in a wider sense household, in the development of Christian prayer* and worship, and even of certain forms of urban monasticism*, cannot be overlooked.

Even if it appears necessary to play down somewhat the direct influence of the practices of the synagogue on the liturgical choices of the first communities (Taft 1985), it remains certain that the synagogue, a place of worship with a psychologically and materially restricted space, offered some very significant models: the reading of the Holy* Scriptures and their commentary, the singing of the Psalms*, and certain styles of prayer. In any event, all authorities agree that the first Christian groups displayed a remarkable degree of activity in the field of hymnody (Perrot 1985), at times spontaneous and even improvised. As Tertullian* attests, "each person is invited to sing to God, in the midst of the assembly, a song drawn from the Holy Scriptures or from his own inspiration" (*Apol.* 39, 18). There is also agreement in emphasizing the growing importance that the nascent church would come to attach to the Psalms of David.

As it developed, however, Christianity could not help providing itself with means of expression in keeping with what it saw as its religious originality, and with the forms taken by its institutions and its social organization. For this reason, the fundamental choices that would characterize the role of music and singing in Christian worship over the first millennium can offer a key to the understanding of all that was later to occur in this sphere.

Christian music, which as yet was hardly recognized as such, but which can be supposed to have been in search of its own form of expression, was at first led to define itself in opposition to a musical art that was an integral part of paganism, and to everything in this art that seemed to corrupt morals. On this point Christians were in agreement with civic Platonism, which banished effeminate poets and musicians from the city; and they shared the reservations of the numerous contemporary thinkers who condemned the art of music as unworthy of a virtuous and upright life (Quasten 1983). The growing theological conception of a sinful corruption of human nature* was then enough to strengthen this suspicion. For example, when Augustine came to deal with concupiscence, in particular abuses related to hearing, he expressed hesitation (fruitfully, moreover) over the church's acceptance of such a frivolous and formidable art as singing.

In any event it is highly likely that the very concept of *song,* and more precisely that of *new song* (in the words of Ps 144:9), very soon appeared as a suitable term to denote what would henceforth be seen much less as a ritual or "artistic" practice than, metaphorically, as a properly Christian attitude to life and the renewal of life, as a felicitous way of living according to grace*. This metaphorical and truly innovative approach to the concept of song is clearly seen in the *Protrepticus* of Clement of Alexandria (†212), a text whose date and place of composition, in the especially cosmopolitan and multireligious context of the great Mediterranean city, correspond to a defining stage in Christianity's organization and its interpretation of itself. So, according to Clement, song is a model of an intense and joyous presence in the world, but a presence that the worship of false gods can only render illusory and deceptive. Christ*, Logos and Wisdom*, but also a true man and the singer of his Father*'s praises, therefore intercedes as he who makes possible a "new song," *kainon asma,* whose role is to convert the song of Amphion, Orpheus, or Homer to the succession of David and the prophets*. This new song, sustaining itself with hymns and psalms in order to constitute itself, is identified with a life (also new) of piety (*theosebeia*) and wisdom. Consequently, the art of music has no direct power of salvation* in itself, no more than it has the power to influence the deity. The new and musical harmony of beings must be attributed to the action of the Holy* Spirit, and song is therefore a fruit of wisdom, lit up as it were by the beatified humanity of Christ, but having a poetic reality, which cannot be separated from an ascetic dimension. And so the actual phenomenon of song, and all the musicians' art, can do no more than evoke that other song—perhaps more real in its nature of song—that is the song of the virtuous life. This reversal of perspective was to sustain the whole subsequent conception of song and *laus vocalis* ("vocal praise") that Christian moralists would develop (*see,* among many others, Augustine, *En. in Ps.* 146, 148, 149; John Chrysostom*, *In Ps.* 111; and, in general, commentaries on Ps 46 and 149).

If then we are obliged, in the absence of more precise evidence, to imagine on the basis of the *Protrepticus* a hypothetical practice of song in Christian assemblies, we should certainly emphasize the absence of any established musical organization. Clement rejects everything reminiscent of sacred theater, initiatory pilgrimage*, or Bacchic intoxication. His strong ascetic tendencies are, however, joined to a warm and imaginative impulse for hymnody, which permeates all his remarks, and suggests a lyrical, even a vocal quality.

This wisdom-centered asceticism recurs in monastic psalmody, with variants resulting from the greater or lesser strictness of the customs and rules of a community. Thus Athanasius*'s letter to Marcellinus (PG 27, 37–41) attributes a calming effect to the melodious chanting of the Psalms, which reconciles the rhythm of the soul* with that of the inspired author, and thereby prepares the heart for prayer (Dyer 1989). This theme was to have a lengthy history (Vogüé 1989).

The Christian concept, then, was characterized by three refusals. First there was the refusal of any form of song or music that might endow the art with a constraining effect on natural and supernatural forces. Then there was a refusal of any Gnostic tendency to attribute a power of illumination, and of access to the divine consciousness*, to musical forms (scales, numbers, rhythms, etc.) as such. Finally, there was a refusal of all association of musical practices with what appeared as moral dissoluteness, drunkenness, frenzy, extreme states, or trances.

2. Ethos of Song in Christian Celebration

The ritual of baptism called on the catechumen to renounce the "vanities of Satan," and these were doubtless embodied most strikingly and resoundingly in the processions that opened the often bloody games at the circus, accompanied by a multitude of fanfares, shouts, and banners. Christian writers did not hesitate to express their feelings of loathing for this sound-world (e.g., Tertullian in *De spectaculis,* ch. 10, PL 1, 642–44). Once the establishment of the church, the local prestige of the bishops*, and the development of the clergy made possible the appearance of a liturgical ceremonial of broader scope than at first, the rejection of musical instruments and the use of the unaccompanied voices of the singers and congregation gave Christian celebrations a sonic ethos that was undoubtedly more innovative than historians of music have acknowledged, and without which it is hard to imagine the appearance in subsequent centuries of the great Latin monody, Roman, Milanese, Gallican, Hispanic, and Romano-Frankish.

The key characteristics of this ethos of song, or at least of a desired and suggested ethos, are clearly evident in a sermon by Niceta of Remesiana (c. 454–85), *De psalmodiae bono* (PL Suppl. 3, 191–98), the terminology and content of which would be taken up in part by Isidore of Seville (*De ecclesiasticis officiis* I, ch. 1–10, II, ch. 11–12). Niceta was not unaware that some in both the East and the West held the singing of psalms and hymns to be pointless and "unsuited to divine religion," and confined themselves to a restrictive interpretation of the apostle*'s words, "be filled with the Spirit,...singing and making melody to the Lord with all your heart" (Eph 5:18–19)"—or, in their interpretation of the phrase *in cordibus vestris,* "in the secrecy of the heart." But the apostle spoke of singing, not of silence, and in point of fact his words refer to the union of the heart and voice. Niceta goes on to praise the psalms and canticles of the Bible, holding that for

every situation in this life, and for every age and sex, they offer a remedy made effective by the sweetness and charm of the singing in such a way that the heart cannot help being moved when it has understood that all the mysteries* of Christ are celebrated in them.

The well-known expression from Psalm 46, *psallite sapienter,* clearly indicates that one must not sing with the breath alone, but also with one's intelligence, awakened by the beauty of the song. If this is the voice of the church in its assemblies, the task of defining its characteristics can hardly be left to chance, still less to disorder. Christian simplicity cannot borrow the charm of its melodies from a vain and theatrical art. Rather, all must be in accordance with the sanctity of such a religion. Unfortunately, Niceta only indicates one feature of the realization of this program: the recommendation of singing *ex uno ore,* exemplified by the song of the three young men in the furnace (Dn 3). This insistence on *una voce* was akin to the horror of heterophony, and more generally of any vocal behavior that might evoke tumult and haste (Quasten 1983), evinced by a good many priests and monastic superiors.

When the voice was addressed to God, all booming sounds were forbidden, as Cyprian* had explained in his commentary on the Lord's Prayer (Réveillaud 1964): "The mode of speech and the demands of those who pray should betray a concern for calm and restraint. Consider that we are in the presence of God. It is important to please the divine eyes by the attitude of the body and the intonation of the voice. As much as it is the mark of an insolent man to make shouts resound, so it is proper for Christian humility to make itself heard through measured prayer." Of course this did not rule out the religious significance of groans and sighs (Armogathe 1980), nor the fervor and enthusiasm so emphatically praised by Ambrose* (*Explanatio Ps.* 1, PL 14, 924–25, *Sermo contra Auxentium,* PL 16, 1017), who in other respects was the theoretician of Christian *verecundia* (De officiis, PL 16, XVIII, 43–47).

In the organization of the musical repertoire, the Carolingian liturgists were thus obliged to distinguish different motivations and to allow song to find expression in a necessary (and theologically significant) diversity of modes of singing: the fullness of congregational psalmody sung in a moderate and flowing voice, the "artistic" and sustained (*strenua voce*) singing of the clerks in their own repertoire (particularly the soloists performing the versets), and the "secret" (*in secreto*) utterance of the priestly prayer in the canon of the mass (*see* Chrodegand, Bishop of Metz, *Regula canonicorum,* PL 89, L, 1079, taken up by the Council of Aix in 816).

3. Fundamental Questions of a Theory of Liturgical Music

In the patristic period, then, everything appears very straightforward, as though the church was faced with the open-ended task to define a music, or more precisely a musical quality of voice and singing, that would be in keeping with its worship and be able, through its performance and perpetuation, to maintain its forms (formal models and established repertoire), its principles, and its sensibility. The aim was to link the tradition* of songs to the tradition of song, understood within the church as a theological act. It is important to note, moreover, that the development and dissemination of Christian singing were not inherently tied to a particular language. Admittedly, the earliest historical languages of church music, apart from the geographical traces they left in the shape of a small number of revered and untranslated terms or formulae—such as those untranslated Hebrew terms (*amen, alleluia,* and *hosanna*) of which Augustine speaks (*De doctrina christiana* 1. 2, ch. 2)—did not fail to leave a strong influence on Christian diction, as demonstrated by the example of the psalmic verset, so alien to Graeco-Latin prosody (Gerson-Kiwi 1957).

Still more significant, however, was the character that the various languages and cultures were to impose on the musical material handed down to them. Serious attention must therefore be given to the phenomena of linguistic inculturation* (Gy 1990), invariably the joint product of a language and a religious self-awareness shaping one another at the very level of the medium of expression. Thus not only Ambrose's hymns, but also the poetic works of Paulinus and Prudentius, succeeded in reconciling the heritage of Latin poetry with the *elocutio* proper to the Christian message, in a "new song" (Fontaine 1981). And the strange melting pot in which psalmic declamation met Latin accentuation was to witness the appearance, after a slow process of maturation, of that new and still surprising musical object, the antiphon—and above all the development around it, and in keeping with the *ars canendi* proper to the institution (also new) of the *schola cantorum* (a qualified group of singers with a well-defined ceremonial status), of a systematic repertoire, the antiphonary, in which the mystery of the Christian liturgical year could be unfolded in a sonic form that was both continuous and differentiated, joining a musical hermeneutics* of the text to the offering of heartfelt and joyful praise.

A few insistent, if not essential, characteristics of Christian music can thus be identified (but *see also* Gelineau 1989 and Ratzinger 1995):

a) The involvement of singing in the individual and collective experience of faith* is essentially a matter of oral confession, as defined once and for all in Romans 10:8–10, on which the whole theology* of the voice of the church in its assemblies is based. While confessing the faith, singing permits the understanding of whatever can be expressed in it. It does so however in its own musical mode, giving the text a sonic space in which, paradoxically, its weight of meaning appears more clearly than in the pure and simple utterance of the words. Singing works in favor of clarity by lengthening diction. The *tarditas* peculiar to sung utterance had already been well expressed by Boethius* (*De Institutione Musicae,* 1. 1, ch. 12, *see* Potiron 1961). More than the ceremonial function, what is important here is the establishment of a zone of audibility peculiar to the sung action. This development may be seen from this time on as the primary role of the provision of music for liturgies. It was to open the way to later innovations, in particular polyphony.

b) The tradition of Christian singing cannot deny its Pentecostal and charismatic origins. It may be that the three terms "psalms and hymns and spiritual songs" mentioned in Colossians 3:16 and Ephesians 5:19 did not correspond to categories of singing actually in use. Nonetheless, the reference to these forms of singing offers a glimpse of a possible extension of established repertoires in the direction of forms in which art and didactic motives give way to the communication of an energy drawn from religious experience itself, to that "jubilation" (*vox sine verbis*) in which the commentators of the fourth century saw an excess and an overflowing, which both fell short of and lay beyond verbal expression (Hilary*, *Tractatus in ps. 65,* 3, PL 9, 425 and Augustine, *Sermo 2 in ps. 32,* PL 36, 283; *in ps. 99,* §4, PL 37, 1272).

c) A lyrical heritage, consisting of both psalms and hymns, is contained within the Christian Scriptures. At its heart is the Psalter, a palette containing all the feelings of the fortunate or unfortunate believer, read through the symbolic figure of Christ the psalmist (Fischer 1951). Its invitatory structure, expressed by the imperatives *cantate, psallite, magnificate, laudem dicite*—and by the place occupied in the liturgy of the hours by Psalm 95, which begins, "O come, let us sing to the Lord"—offers an understanding of what is undoubtedly the most fundamental characteristic of Christian singing: the affirmation that God is in some sense "singable," indeed cannot perhaps be adequately acknowledged if the believer does not at some time place himself in a hymnodic situation. Of course God cannot have need of praise of any kind, and nothing is more repugnant to Christianity than adulation (John Chrysostom, *5th Homily on 1 Timothy,* PG 62, 525–90 and Augustine, *En. Ps.* 134, PL 37, 1708–55). Singing is of benefit only to the singer and his audience. For them it signifies the liberality of the divine gifts, presenting itself as the (eschatological) restoration of a (protological) power of song. Singing sings the praises of God by singing its own possibility. It sings the possibility of giving praise, to which it ceaselessly repeats an invitation.

d) The figure of the cantor, or psalmist, to which Augustine so frequently alludes (also of course the title on which Johann Sebastian Bach would pride himself), appears at this time as guardian of this lyrical heritage, and as responsible for keeping the invitatory tradition in a state of sufficient vitality. In the description he gives of ecclesiastical roles, after describing the responsibilities and the art of the reader, Isidore of Seville goes on to define those of the psalmist. Unlike Niceta, several of whose expressions he borrows, he offers an outline of a theologically sound vocal ethos in *De ecclesiasticis officiis* (1. 2, ch. 12): "It is important that the psalmist be notable and distinguished for his voice and art, in such a way that he can lead his listeners' souls to give themselves over to the charm of a sweet psalmody. His voice should be neither harsh, nor coarse, nor out of tune, but resounding, melodious, clear, and dignified, a voice whose sonority and melody will be in keeping with a holy religion. It should not betray an interpreter's art, but should exhibit a true Christian simplicity in its musical display. It should not smack of the ostentation characteristic of musicians, neither of theatrical art, but should rather bring about in its listeners a real softening of the heart."

Thus the art of song properly conceived tends to produce a lifting of the resistance and heaviness of the heart, giving rise to a *compunctio,* which approaches the register of tenderness, but without weakness, since the voice must be direct, clear, and sonorous, as befits a religion that rejects theatrical effects and ostentatious music. It is fair to suppose that this program and this definition of an aesthetic of "suitability," far from playing an artistically inhibitory role, were on the contrary able, by their advocacy of a lyricism, restricted to the search for an ideal form, to open the way to an unending search for forms and to give rise to an incessant striving for approaches and solutions that, in a sense, has merged with the history of Western music.

e) One characteristic of this art—for by this time it was certainly an art—remains hard to pin down. It is expressed in the "charm" and "sweetness" (the *oblectamenta dulcedinis*) of which Isidore speaks. Everything that concerns the "sweetness of singing," the *suavitas canendi,* might be assumed to be an almost meaningless literary cliché. The interpretation of a passage by Amalarius (c. 830), nonetheless, urges us to take it all seriously. For Amalarius, who was highly influential throughout the Middle Ages (Ekenberg 1987), singing quite specifically foretells the delightful reality of the rewards promised in the contract of faith. Following Augustine, Amalarius insists, moreover, that God does not attract "by necessity but by delight"—*non necessitate sed delectatione*—which bestows on singing the privilege of announcing that love* cannot be born from constraint (Amalarius, *Liber Officialis, Opera omnia,* Ed. J.M. Hanssens, Vatican, 1948, vol. 2, L. 3, ch. 5, §6).

● B. Fischer (1951), "Le Christ dans les Psaumes," *MD* 27, 86–113.

E. Gerson-Kiwi (1957), "Music (in the Bible)," *DBS* 29, 1411–68.

E. Werner (1959), *The Sacred Bridge: The Interdependance of Liturgy and Music in Synagogue and Church during the First Millenium,* London–New York.

S. Corbin (1960), *L'Église à la conquête de sa musique,* Paris.

H. Potiron (1961), *Boèce, théoricien de la musique grecque,* Paris.

M. Réveillaud (Ed.) (1964), *Cyprien: L'Oraison dominicale,* Paris, 81–82.

O. Söhngen (1967), *Theologie der Musik,* Kassel.

J. Claire (1975), *Les répertoires liturgiques latins avant l'Octoechos,* vol. 1: *L'office férial romano-franc,* Solesmes.

J.-Y. Hameline (1978), "Histoire de la musique et de ses effets," *Cahiers Recherche-Musique,* Institut national de l'audiovisuel, 66, 9–35.

J.-R. Armogathe (1980), "*Gemitibus inenarrabilibus,* Notes on Rm. 8, 26," *Aug.* 1–2, 19–22.

J. Fontaine (1981), *Naissance de la poésie dans l'Occident chrétien,* Paris.

J. Quasten (1983), *Music and Worship in Pagan and Christian Antiquity,* Washington, 52–57.

C. Perrot (1985), "Le chant hymnique chez les juifs et les chrétiens au premier siècle," *MD* 161, 7–32.

R. Taft (1985), *Liturgy of the Hours in East and West,* Collegeville.

E. Ekenberg (1987), Cur cantatur? *Die Funktionen des liturgischen Gesanges nach den Autoren der Karolingerzeit,* Stockholm.

J. McKinnon (1987), *Music in Early Christian Literature,* Cambridge.

J.-Y. Hameline (1988), "Acte de chant, acte de foi," *Catéchèse* (Paris) 113, 31–46.

J. Dyer (1989), "Monastic Psalmody of the Middle Ages," *RBen* 96, 41–74.

J. Gelineau (1989), "Le chemin de la musique," *Conc(F)* no. 222, 157–70.

A. de Vogüé (1989), "Psalmodier n'est pas prier," *EO* 6, 7–32.

P.-M. Gy (1990), *La liturgie dans l'histoire,* Paris, 59–72.

J. M. Spencer (1991), *Theological Music: Introduction to Theomusicology,* New York.

H. Seidel et al. (1994), "Musik und Religion," *TRE* 23, 441–95 (bibl.).

H. de La Motte-Haber (1995), *Musik und Religion,* Laaber.

J. Ratzinger (1995), *Ein neues Lied für den Herrn: Christusglaube und Liturgie in der Gegenwart.*

E. Fubini (1997), *Geschichte der Musik-Ästhetik: Von der Antike bis zur Gegenwart,* Stuttgart-Vienna.

U. Taddai et al. (1998), "Musik," *LThK*3 7, 543–51.

JEAN-YVES HAMELINE

See also **Architecture; Beauty; Cult; Images**

Mystery

A. Biblical Theology

a) From the Term's Origins to Its Use in the New Testament. The word *musterion* is composed of a root (the root *muo*) and a desinence *(-terion).* The final *terion* seems to point to an original meaning that was either local or instrumental. For example: *thusiasterion* (altar, upon which sacrifices are made); *bouleuterion* (council chamber); and so forth. The root remains undetermined, even if the most probable seems to be *muo* (to close; whence "to remain silent," "preserve silence"); *see* LXX: *mustes* (initiated, masculine form; Wis 12:5), *mustis* (initiated, feminine form; said of wisdom* in Sg 8:4), *mustikos* (in a low voice; *3 M* 3, 10).

With respect to this root, *musterion* might derive from the mystery religions, where it would initially have designated the place of initiation, and then the rites and secrets, the mysteries celebrated. LXX did not invalidate this impression, for *musterion* appears above all in texts of the Hellenistic period, written therefore directly in Greek (Tobit; Judges; 2 Maccabees; Wisdom), as well as in the later books of Sirach (Sir 22:22, 27:16, 27:17, 27:21) and of Daniel, where it is a translation for the Aramaic *raz* (Dn 2:18–19, 2:27–28, 2:29–30, 2:47), but literary contexts do not confirm it either.

In the New Testament the term is almost always used as in Daniel 2, where a) mysteries are related to coming events, in particular at the end of time (*see* Dn 2:29f.) (eschatology*); b) they are divine, in the sense that they concern the eternal decisions of God*, where he alone could make them known through revelation*; c) beneficiaries of the mysteries were those whom he had chosen, and not the wise men of the world (*see* Dn 2:27f., 2:47f. LXX). These three components can be found in the New Testament, in revelations either on a precise point (Rom 11:25; 1 Cor 15:51) or on the entirety of divine decisions and their implementation (Mt 13:11; Mk 4:11; Lk 8:10; Rom 16:25; 1 Cor 2:1, 13:2; Eph 1:9, 3:9; Col 1:26; Rev 1:20, 10:7, 17:5–7). But although in Daniel 2 the revelations touch upon events that have not yet taken place, in the New Testament *musterion* designates not only future events, but also have as their primary subject Jesus Christ* (*see* 1 Cor 1–2; Col 1:27, 4:3; Eph 3:9, 5:32), whose ministry*, death* on the cross, and resurrection*, proclaimed as gospel, are unprecedented proof of the divine plan of salvation*, and which—in particular through the Resurrection—give a foretaste of the end of time.

b) Dimensions of musterion *according to Saint Paul.* By naming the divine plan for salvation *musterion,* the texts of the New Testament not only aimed to emphasize the inability of humankind to gain knowledge of it by themselves, but also indicated that once this plan for salvation had been revealed, human wisdom would remain powerless to understand it and receive it, for it was accomplished through means and events that appeared unreasonable. It was therefore not only because the divine ways had not been revealed up until then that they were a mystery (Col 1:26–27, 2:2; Eph 3:9), but also because, even when they were revealed and proclaimed, the world could not recognize them as being willed by God. This explains therefore why Paul saw the mystery of God to be exemplified by the cross of Jesus (*see* 1 Cor 1:18–24). But the cross was not the only event that aroused astonishment. Colossians and Ephesians also insist on the way in which faith* in Jesus the Son of God (filiation*) could be experienced by all cultures (inculturation*), and this Paul calls "Christ among the nations" (*see* Col 1:27) (universalism*). This presence of Christ *among the nations* is unprecedented, because pagan nations were not waiting for a Messiah, and because in the Jewish hypothesis of their conversion* to the true God, it was up to them to go up to Jerusalem*, the holy city. The fact that, with the message of the gospel, salvation would reach the Gentiles wherever they were, and that their diversity went hand in hand with a strong unity under Christ, to the degree that the church* came to be called *his body,* were all part of the mystery (Eph 5:21–23).

c) Use of the Term and Its Reasons. The Pauline usage of the term is paradoxical, in particular in Colossians and Ephesians, for the gospel must be announced to all, whereas mystery contains the notion of a secret that surpasses understanding. However, Colossians and Ephesians make them practically synonymous (the mystery is the gospel itself; Eph 6:19), and this is not by chance. In telling of newness in Jesus Christ, *musterion* in fact enabled the gospel to be proclaimed with the help of new concepts. But even as it led to new formulations within the gospel, it also provided a basis for their legitimacy. The remarks in Colossians and Ephesians about the church and its relation to Christ were not, of course, predictive. Nor were they announced as such in Scripture. But if messages such as these cannot be founded on Scripture, do they not run the risk of being invalidated and discredited? It is in this respect that the use of the term *musterion* takes on

its prime significance. For it is borrowed from Scripture—Daniel 2 was already a part of the holy books*—and, as the voice of Scripture, it signaled that Scripture had not announced everything, that at the end of time God would have new things to say. This was a paradoxical use of a scriptural term to justify the usage of nonscriptural terms (body/head, etc.)!

Even though, as a message of the unprecedented, mystery is not per se focused on the past, it nevertheless enables one to reread the past. Because it provides entry to the intelligence of the eternal wisdom of God, through the paradoxical coherence of his designs, mystery authorizes believers to (re)read Scripture on the basis of the novelty experienced and announced, and to see therein the correspondences and foundation stones for a spiritual and, above all, a typological reading (*see* Rom 16:26; Eph 5:32) (senses of Scriptures*).

Subsequently, *musterion* would be expressed through *sacramentum* (from the first African Latin translations) and would come to designate the celebrations that are now known as *sacramental.*

● G. Bornkamm (1942), "*Mustèrion,*" ThWNT 4, 809–34.
K. Prümm (1957), "Mystères," DBS 6, Paris, 1–225.
R. Penna (1978), *Il mystèrion paolino: Traiettoria e costituzione,* Brescia.
Ch. Reynier (1992), *Évangile et mystère: Les enjeux théologiques de l'épître aux Éphésiens,* Paris.
J.-N. Aletti (1995), "Sagesse et mystère chez Paul," in *La sagesse biblique: De l'Ancien au Nouveau Testament,* Paris, 267–90.

JEAN-NOËL ALETTI

See also **Apocalyptic Literature; Christ and Christology; Church; Evil; History; Intertestament; Knowledge of God; Pauline Theology; Religion, Theology of; Revelation; Sacrament; Scripture, Fulfillment of; Universalism; Wisdom**

B. Liturgical and Sacramental Theology

a) In the Churches of the Aramaic and Syriac Languages. The tradition of these churches stemmed directly from the biblical heritage of the Jewish tradition. The word *raza,* whose Persian origin has been established—*Raz* designates the secret of the major royal council of the Achaemenid and Sasanid empires, where the most important decisions were made (Dalmais 1990)—corresponds to the Greek *musterion,* and its plural, *raze,* to *musteria.* In the singular it designated ei-

ther mystery or the Eucharist*. In the plural it could be extended to the other sacramental mysteries from before the fifth century, having previously referred exclusively to the divine plans that were kept secret, then revealed, as in Daniel. The enigmatic sense of these *raze* remains, but the idea of an anticipated unveiling prevailed, even when the plural *raze* referred to the rites destined to show and to give what they concealed. The result was a certain eschatological emphasis in the liturgy*.

This cultic sense of the term is attested in the fourth century by Aphraates, Ephraem, Theodore of Mopsuestia, and then by other masters from Edessa and Nisibis. Aphraates speaks of "these mysteries, *raze*, which the saint ordered for the celebration of Easter" (*Demonstr.* XII on Mosaic Easter, SC 349, 298, §1 and 10). Given to the "first people," mysteries are no more than signs, *ata*, type, *tupsa*, figure, *dmuta, dumya, salma,* of a truth* fulfilled through the Easter of the Lord and through "true baptism*: the mystery, *raza,* of the passion* of our Savior," which he prescribed to his disciples to give. The fruit of salvation* that issues from the cross is "the sign of the mystery of life," *rushma d-raza d-hayyé,* communicated by the sacraments* (Dalmais 1990; *Diatessaron* by Ephraem XXI, 11, SC 121, 380).

For Ephraem, *raza* was combined with other words of the same semantic register to form expressions such as *braza-w-tupsa,* which designated the liturgical acts of the church. It was then the "already there" of their eschatological content that was emphasized by "often indicating a resemblance between the symbol and that which it symbolized" (P. Youssif in Dalmais 1990). After having been collected in the Torah, the mysteries were "incarnated" in Christ*, who fulfills all the symbols, in the expectation of their unveiling, but "to the point of comprising an integral part" (G. Saber in Dalmais 1990). This theology* would become more refined with Theodore of Mopsuestia (*Catechesis* and other representatives of this tradition) (Dalmais 1990).

b) In the Greek-Language Churches. Pagan mystery cults persisted from the seventh century B.C. until the third century A.D. in the Greek world and Hellenized regions. Their terminology was progressively adopted by Christians. Furthermore, their strong imprint on the Christian liturgy of the fourth century is clear, not solely in terms of language but even in the character of the ritual experience.

The shared root *mu(s)* of the related Greek terms *mustes, musteria,* in relation with the verb *muo,* which designated the act of "closing one's eyes and lips" when confronted with something that would therefore remain secret (Burkert 1987), suggested the attitude of fear that dramaturgical activity aroused: the sensation of the presence of gods and sacred silence. The mysteries of Eleusis, for example, were called *arrethos telete:* a prohibition, *aporrheta,* ensured their prestige and effectiveness. The fascination exerted by the gods required the ritual workings of the unexpected and unspeakable, *arrheton,* of the "terrible" presence, fascinating and gratifying, of an almost tangible holiness in the experience of knowledge, of agony, *pathein,* and of exaltation aroused by the initiatory ritual drama. In certain cases the mysteries were the expression of the human soul*'s religious fervor in its will to take part, from the moment of earthly life, in the mythical itinerary of the gods through the anamnestic story, through the initiatory rites and acts that constituted the sacred drama. This salutary experience of renewal was sometimes linked to a promise regarding the afterlife. The ritual symbolism that pagan mysteries practiced was more that of an initiation, *telein* and *telete,* into the divine, than that of a social link. There was no body of doctrine; nor were the followers required to repudiate the practices of shared religion. It is better therefore to speak of a cult of mysteries than of a religion of mysteries (Burkert 1987).

When the apologists of the second century developed the typological interpretation of history and of biblical writings on Philo's model, the use of the word "mysteries," *musteria* (Justin, *Dial.* 40 and 24; 44, 85, 111, 138), once again designated the events and the revealed secrets of God's plan of salvation in Jesus Christ (Justin, I *Apol.* 1, 13; *Dial.* 74, 91). But the usage in worship culminated with Justin, when he denounced pagan mysteries as the demonic counterfeits of Christian rites (I *Apol.* 1, 54; 66, 4; *Dial.* 70, 78). Tertullian*, Firmicus, the Ambrosiaster, and Augustine* would do likewise.

Melito of Sardis sang of the *mystery of Easter* (SC 123, 2), which was, for him, the event of salvation "announced in the law," the object of proclamation within the paschal Christian assembly and the ritual mystery of the New Covenant*. The technical expression of the mysteries of worship, "to accomplish the mystery entirely at night *(nuktor diatelesas to musterion),*" with regard to the ancient Easter festival according to Exodus 12:10 (ibid., 15, 16, 68, and 145 n. 95) leads one to conclude that it included Christian Easter, and its accomplishment, as a mystery, that is, as a ritual celebrated by a community of initiates bringing about through the acts they implemented the saving act of God, which took on the shape of an event.

Clement of Alexandria expressed the mysterious nature of Christianity with the help of the technical vocabulary of the ritual mysteries (*Strom.* IV, 3, 1; IV, 162, 3; V, 9–10; *Protreptique,* 12). The Gnostics appreciated the category of the mysterious, which had already enabled them to express an entire portion of the philosophical quest (Diotima of Mantinea in Plato's *Symposium,* 210 a–212 c); Clement, in the same vein (Riedweg 1987), saw in Christianity the true gnosis* (*Strom.* V, 57, 2; VI, 124, 16).

According to Origen, "the mystery of Christ is refracted through the Church, as it appears in the Scripture. It is also manifest in the sacraments" (Bornert 1966). The sacraments, *tupoi,* enabled a participation, by both designating it and by hiding it, in the truth, *aletheia,* of the mystery, of which the old covenant was merely a shadow, *skia.* Unveiled through Christ, it would not be fully manifest until its eschatological accomplishment. This revelation* of the mystery provided the basis for the typological interpretation of Scripture found in Origen. It derived from Judaism*, which also applied it to rites. Origen did the same. It is therefore probable that these hermeneutics*, identical in the case of the mysteries (divine plans) proclaimed by the biblical text and in that of the ritual mysteries that signified them, led to a generalized acceptance of the notion of ritual mysteries. Origen called Christianity in general "the *teletai* which are our own" (*Cels.* 3, 59). Julian, his adversary, saw in Christianity a new *telete* (Burkert, 1987).

Eusebius of Caesarea saw in the "mysteries of [Christ's] body and his blood" (*Demonstr. Ev.* V, 3) the best example of the fulfillment of the sacrifice* of the peoples (*Demonstr. Ev.* I, 10). *Musteria* then came to be a preferred term for the Eucharist. Expressions related to the adjective *mustikos,* "mystic eulogy," would be found, for example, in Cyril* of Alexandria.

In the fourth century the celebration of the sacraments of initiation* was provided with systematic commentary by the Fathers*, who drew on the terminology of the pagan mysteries. The categories and language of the mysteries allowed them, it would seem, to elaborate a mystagogy of the celebration, the efficacy of which became culturally possible and pastorally urgent (Ph. de Roten 1993). The risks of confusion with pagan worship were disappearing. It was now possible to validate the liturgical experience by means of a more mysterious ritual capable of inciting those who were reluctant to convert* to become baptized, and to signify more effectively the essential graces* of illumination and their source: Christ, at the right hand of the Father (Kretschmar 1970). The emphasis was placed on the simultaneously gratifying, inexpressible, and "terrible" nature of the mystery of salvation realized in the terrible and sacred mysteries of the Easter drama. Cyril of Jerusalem, Epiphanius of Salamina, Basil* of Caesarea, Gregory* of Nazianzus, and Gregory* of Nyssa are noteworthy (Ph. de Roten 1993). The most typical author in this respect is Saint John Chrysostom*: there are 66 occurrences of the vocabulary of mystery in his work, and 17 in the eight baptismal catecheses (SC 50).

Pseudo-Dionysius* distinguished the number and degree of the holy mysteries and described a Christian theurgy where they were organized in hierarchical fashion. For their part, they contributed to the union of man to Trinitarian thearchy (the very principle of deity). The central concept was that of the illumination,

which led to give to initiation the privileged dimension of contemplation. For Gregory* Palamas, the heir to Dionysius, the reception of divine light occurred through communion* with the mystery of the illuminating eucharistic body of Christ.

c) In the Latin Churches. The sacraments were also called mysteries in the Latin tradition, yet here again, it was only once the risk of confusion with the worship of pagan mysteries had disappeared (Ambrose*, Hilary* of Poitiers, etc.), but the ready transliteration of the plural *musteria* was carefully avoided throughout the first three centuries for Christian rites (Mohrmann 1952), whereas this was not the case of the singular *musterion,* which became *mysterium.* This singular *mysterium* could indeed be used without risk, for it had become a term in the common language that had a profane and general meaning—"secret," "mystery"— whereas the implications of *musteria* or *mysteria* were still exclusively cultic and pagan. Also rejected were the Latin equivalents of Greek words designating sacred acts and the cultic experience of the mystery religions (*sacra, arcana, initia,* and so on), in favor of *sacramentum* and *sacramenta,* which were unambiguous (Tertullian) (*see* sacrament*). The word "mysteries" has sometimes been used in its cultic sense in the various liturgical books that emerged after the final liturgical reform called for by Vatican* II.

Related to such semantic evolutions, and considered from the point of view of their ability to make of the celebration an epiphany of the mystery, these three traditions of the inculturation* of the Christian liturgy permit various theological emphases, as well as the emergence of derivatives (excessive allegorization, didactic moralism, and so on) and elaborations (Dalmais 1990).

d) Theology of Mysteries. In returning to a concept of Christian mystery centered on the liturgy (Schilson 1982), this theology renewed all fields of theological inquiry in the 20th century. It was this theology that was the principal initiator of a number of patristic studies of the *Musterion* in our century.

In 1921 Dom Casel (1886–1948), a monk of Maria Laach (1907) and chaplain of the Benedictines of Herstelle (1922–48), was entrusted by his abbot, Dom Herwegen (†1946), with the compilation of the *Jahrbuch für Liturgiewissenschaft* (nowadays called the *Archiv für L.*), where up until 1941 he published a series of liturgical studies (Santagada 1967, *Bibl. gen.*). His spiritual teachings from Herstelle display a theology whose style and content are truly mystagogic. The spread of his teachings to France, at the instigation of the Centre de pastorale liturgique, began in the 1940s.

This theology would have to meet the challenge of historians of the modernist period who saw in the pagan mysteries the origin of the Christian sacraments. As a result, the Jewish antecedents of Christian worship were neglected; Casel (1921) detected in these pagan mysteries—initially in a balanced fashion, and then by forcing analogies—a providential "propaedeutics" of Christian worship. Although recent research (Burkert 1987) into these mysteries has corrected such perspectives on a historical level, Casel's theological vision recalls for today the pertinence of a vision of wisdom that seeks to understand the soteriological status of religions and the rightful place of liturgy in any synthesis of Christian theology. Reference to pagan mysteries comes essentially within the method of a fundamental* theology of worship.

Casel's perspective seeks to reconcile theology, spirituality, and liturgy. He insists less on the instrumental effectiveness of the sacraments than on their relation to the paschal mystery, which they accomplish in the form of communal liturgical acts; and in emphasizing their unity, Casel seeks to restore the theology of the church-as-mystery to the forefront, in its relation with the liturgy as the full realization of that mystery. A number of forgotten truths about the sacraments have thus been highlighted once again.

● O. Casel (1921), *Die Liturgie als Mysterienfeier,* Freiburg; (1932), *Das christliche Kultmysterium,* Regensburg.

C.H. Mohrmann (1952), *Latin vulgaire, latin des chrétiens,* Paris.

C.H. Mohrmann (1954), *"Sacramentum dans les plus anciens textes chrétiens,"* in *HThR,* 47, 141–52 (also *Études sur le latin des chrétiens,* Rome, vol. 1, 1958, 233–44; vol. 3, 1965, 181–82).

R. Bornert (1966), *Les commentaires byzantins de la divine liturgie du VIIe au XVe s.,* Paris.

O.D. Santagada (1967), *"Bibliografia generale,"* ALW 10/1, 1–77.

G. Kretschmar (1970), *Die Geschichte des Taufgottesdienstes in der alten Kirche, Leit 5,* Kassel.

A. Schilson (1982), *Theologie als Sakramententheologie, Die Mysterientheologie Odo Casels,* TTS 18 (2nd Ed. 1987).

L. Bouyer (1986), *"Mystèrion," du Mystère à la mystique,* Paris.

Ch. Riedweg (1987), *Mysterienterminologie bei Platon, Philon et Klemens von Alexandrien,* Berlin–New York.

W. Burkert (1987), *Ancient Mystery Cults,* Cambridge, Mass.

I.H. Dalmais (1990), *"Raza et sacrement,"* in P. De Clerck and E. Palazzo (Ed.), *Rituels: Mélanges offerts au Père Gy,* Paris, 173–82.

Ph. de Roten (1993), "Le vocabulaire mystagogique de saint Jean Chrysostome," in A.M. Triacca and A. Pistoia (Ed.), *Mystagogie*: *Pensée liturgique d'aujourd'hui et liturgie ancienne,* conferences of Saint-Serge, XXXIXth week of liturgical studies, 1992, Rome, 115–35.

NICOLAS DERREY

See also **Liturgy; Sacrament**

Mystical Body. *See* Church

Mystical Theology. *See* Negative Theology

Mysticism

Over the course of many centuries, it is impossible to disentangle the concept and the field of mysticism from theology* in general. From Bernard* of Clairvaux (1091–1153) onward, however, a literature of mysticism took on independent existence. It frequently set itself in continuity with the patristic heritage, and in reaction against a scholarly theology that had moved further and further away from its contemplative foundations. It is fair to say that this distance became a definite break in the West in the 14th century, when mysticism as a form of knowledge definitively asserted its autonomy, as demonstrated for example by Gerson's methodological considerations in his *Théologie mystique* (1402–8). It flourished first in the countries of northern Europe (mysticism conventionally identified as primarily "speculative," that is, invoking a "mirror" of God in the soul*, alluding to 1 Cor 13:12), and then in Spain in the 16th century and France in the 17th (a more "affective" mysticism, that is, more attentive to the psychological aspects of the experience that it described). Within this framework, mysticism can be grasped in itself, and that is how it will be considered here.

I. Mystery and Mysticism

The word "mysticism" has lost all precision since Rousseau and the romantics applied it to any irrational experiences, especially those attributed to religious phenomena. We will restrict it here to its most classic Christian meaning of a perception of God* that is, so to speak, experimental, a genuine celebration of the soul at the inner coming of Christ*. It consists of "an experience of the presence of God in the spirit, through the inner joy that is given to us by an entirely personal feeling of that presence" (Tauler [1300–1361] *Sermon* XII. 1, referring to Jn 7:6). A modern commentator explains: "There we discover, experienced by the mystic with the clarity of the obvious, what each of us knows through his faith and by which he lives" (Garonne, in Cl. Moine, *Relation spirituelle* 7). What is involved then is a very particular coming to consciousness of the mystery* of Christ, and it was to evoke this that the word entered the Christian vocabulary with Clement of Alexandria (160–220). Mysticism is knowledge of the mystery, that is, knowledge that goes beyond the

letter of Scripture and the signs of the liturgy* to the very reality designated by both, and that is hidden in God (*see* Bouyer, *Histoire de la spiritualité chrétienne* I, 486–96). From this point of view, a fundamental continuity links Abraham and Moses to John* of the Cross and Theresa of Lisieux, and the latter two claimed never to say anything but what was substantially contained in Scripture and transmitted by the church*.

Let us conclude our definition of the scope of the field of mysticism with the words of its most knowledgeable French interpreter in the 20th century, H. Bremond: "Good or bad, pagans or Christians, God is in us. Or better, we are in him.... He is in us before all our actions, and from the very beginning of our existence.... He is in us as the living principle of all life, present in everything that is most myself in myself, [so that] we are all potential mystics. We become so in reality as soon as we reach a certain consciousness of God in us, as soon as we in some sense experience his presence, as soon as this contact—which is, moreover, permanent and necessary between him and us—seems palpable to us, takes on the character of an encounter, of an embrace, a sense of being possessed" *(Autour de l'humanisme).*

II. Mystical Experience in Its Raw State

Let us begin with a particularly clear description of mystical experience from the Ursuline Marie of the Incarnation (1599–1672): "In the year 1620, on 24 March, a morning when I was going about my business, which I was earnestly dedicating to God...I was suddenly halted, inwardly and outwardly.... Then, in an instant, the eyes of my spirit were opened and all the faults, sins*, and imperfections that I had committed from the day of my birth were represented to me in general and in detail, with a distinction and clarity more certain than any certainty that human industry could express. At the same moment, I saw myself entirely immersed in blood, and my spirit [was] convinced that this blood was the Blood of the Son of God, for the shedding of which I was guilty through all the sins that had been shown to me, and that this precious Blood had been shed for my salvation*.... At the same moment, my heart felt ravished from itself and changed into love* for him who had granted this remarkable mercy*, which caused my heart, in the experience of this same love, to feel the most extreme sorrow and regret that can be imagined for having offended him.... What the soul conceives in this marvel cannot be expressed.... These visions and these operations are so penetrating that in an instant they say everything and express their efficacy and their effects.... And what is the most incomprehensible, the rigor [of this arrow of love] seems gentle.... Coming back to myself, I found myself standing, stopped in front of the little chapel of the reverend Feuillant Fathers...in Tours" (*Écrits spirituels et historiques* II, 181–84).

Narratives as spectacular as this often seem to imply that mystical experience is reserved to quite exceptional, if not abnormal, individuals. Let us therefore forget the divorce between theology and mysticism and read the same irruption of the supernatural* in its most minimal manifestations: "Mystics are not supermen. Most of them do not experience ecstasy or visions.... Moreover, it may be, and I am personally almost convinced of this, that in the most humble prayer*, and even more in the slightest aesthetic feeling, there takes shape an experience of the same order that is already mystical, but imperceptible and evanescent" (H. Bremond, loc. cit.).

Even so, the exceptional intensity of the episode recounted by Marie of the Incarnation makes it possible to observe under a microscope the characteristic elements of any mystical life:

- Complete discontinuity between that experience and all others: "I was suddenly halted, inwardly and outwardly."
- Lucidity and certainty: "The eyes of my spirit were opened...with a distinction and clarity more certain"—and we should note the clarity of the memory when Marie was writing 34 years after the event, and from the distant Canada where she was to die.
- Loving and transforming presence of him who thus penetrates into the soul: "My heart felt ravished from itself and changed into love for him who had granted this remarkable mercy."
- Suspension of the flow of time: "In an instant...at the same moment...at the same moment."
- Hence the simultaneity of perceptions that the soul is accustomed to dissociate: the soul is immersed in a rapture that is at the same time sorrow, but whose "rigor seems gentle."
- And by definition, the absolute inexpressibility of this experience: "What the soul conceives in this marvel cannot be expressed."

III. Expressing the Mystical Experience

1. Mysticism and Language

We have just raised a question that has persisted since the 13th century, about the status of truly mystical texts. These claim to say inexpressible things, "things that were, are, and will be," all at once, explains John of the Cross (*Ascent of Carmel* 26. 3), for, at the root of its experience, the soul "has been united with pure intelligence, which is not in time" (ibid., 14. 10–11). Hence language in this context is subjected to extreme constraints, for "the signifier [in a language] being of auditory nature, it takes place only in time" (F. de Saussure, *Cours de linguistique générale* 103). There is therefore an irretrievable devaluation between the mystical experience and the account of it: "Human and external conversation offers to us the things of God so that we may enter into them; but in offering them to us, it degrades them in their dignity, debases and lowers them in order to make them comprehensible to the being who is clothed with the outer man" (C. de Condren, *Lettres et discours,* 1668).

Of course, any language is the articulation of eternity in time, but it is precisely that degradation that the mystic wants to remedy, for he has had the privilege of tasting things in their eternity, of contemplating them in the Word* (Jn 1:3f., according to the punctuation of Tatian [second century], adopted by all mystics), beyond language. Having become a writer, he experiences a fundamental contradiction and resolves it as well as he can only by constantly denouncing the weakness of words, putting them together in unexpected combinations intended to hold onto the vanishing presence to which they testify. In this, the mystical writer is basically a poet, whatever literary genre he may adopt, "the one who rediscovers the buried relationships among things, their dispersed similarities" (Michel Foucault, *Les mots et les choses* 63).

We should note in passing that the surprising cultural richness of mystics (Hadewijch [13th century] and Ruusbroec [1293–1381] in Flanders, Teresa of Avila [1515–82] in Spain, Francis de Sales [Salesian spirituality*] in France) finds its explanation here: approaching the unspeakable, the mystic returns language to its origin, recharging it with all the virtualities contained in the Word from which it proceeds, and shows us in turn that all language is rooted in this kind of experience.

2. Mysticism and Theology

Whatever his reason for expressing himself (linked most frequently to spiritual* direction given or received), the mystic in the end turns himself into a theologian in his attempt to name him whom he knows to be above any name. His hyperconsciousness of God leads his language into a constant process of going beyond itself by means of simultaneous affirmation and negation. God is not this *or* that, for he is eminently this *and* that and much more. Negative* and affirmative theology support one another in a continual invitation to join in pure faith him who gave himself first, beyond all reason and all speech. In the 14th century Eckhart analyzed this obligatory transcendence to its ultimate theoretical consequences: "You must love God not because He is lovable; He is above all love and all attraction of love.... You must love Him inasmuch as He is a Non-God, a Non-Intellect, a Non-Person, a Non-Image. Even more: inasmuch as he is One, pure, clear, limpid, separate from any duality. And in that One we must eternally lose ourselves: from Something to Nothingness" (*Sermon* 83).

Although negation constantly returns the theologian to the luminous origin of his knowledge, in an attitude of pure receptivity that precisely defines the *act* of faith*, it bases its impetus on the affirmative experience of previous acts of faith, crystallized in *articles* of faith, and as such available for a new transcendence: "Just as there are two acts of understanding, one called intellection of the indivisible, in which there is neither division nor composition, and which consists of the apprehension of the simple substance, and the other that we can call composition and division of propositions, so there are also two acts in the knowledge of faith. The first of these acts is the simple apprehension of the objects of faith, that is, the prime truth*; and the other is the compound knowledge of the mysteries of faith directed toward that truth" (Quiroga, *Mystical apologia,* 4. 2).

In defending the legitimacy of a contemplative theology, Quiroga (1562–1628), last champion of the great Spanish tradition against a pervasive theological rationalism*, was merely taking up Pseudo-Dionysius*, heir of Greek patristics, endlessly commented on by the medieval West, who had provided for the expression of mystical experience a structure and a vocabulary that remained essentially unchanged: "As for you, Timothy, deeply engaged in mystical contemplations, forget the perceptible as well as intellectual operations, everything that is perceptible and intelligible, everything that is not and everything that is, and raise yourself in unknowing toward union, as far as that is allowed, to what is beyond all essence and all knowledge. In fact, it is only through a free and total ecstasy outside yourself that you will be borne toward the super-essential ray of divine darkness" (*Mystical theology,* I. 1).

IV. Restoration of the Soul in Mystical Experience

1. Rectification of Language and Rectification of the Soul

All language is a revelation of spirit in matter; it unveils "silences that have taken on bodily form"

(Valéry, *Œuvres complètes* I, 624). In the silence of his experience, the mystic has found himself carried above this body of language ("the perceptible and the intelligible" of Pseudo-Dionysius) through which each one of us weaves his history in contact with a particular culture. And it is again that carnal density of language that the mystic goes through when, returning to the universe of words, he invites us through them to join in pure faith with him whom he now knows is entirely other from what he earlier imagined.

Moreover, words do not only acquire a new density in the course of this passage; they recover their true meaning, and the entire spiritual organism is thereby reoriented, departing from illusion and again becoming able to say what is. The major patristic themes provide for the most recent mysticism the anthropology* that it needs. Since man had turned away from God and turned toward the earth, these thinkers asserted, his soul had been distorted: "When man inclines toward earthly concupiscence, in a sense he bows down...." (Augustine, PL 36. 595; *see* P. Delfgaauw, *Saint Bernard, maître de l'Amour divin*). And this "curvature" of the soul due to original sin* is redressed in the very act of man's spiritual assumption: "but when he raises himself to things above, his heart grows upright" (ibid.). This is the source of all the purifications that the mystic experiences as he progresses in his illumination; just as the light of the sun reveals the spots on a window, so the light of God makes it possible to perceive one's impurities and to detach oneself from them. This image, thoroughly developed by John of the Cross (e.g., in the *Ascent of Carmel* II. 5, 6), makes it possible to understand that the process of mystical transformation is at the same time a process of purification, and that divine contact, while fulfilling Adam*'s calling to share divine life, restores him to his primal innocence: "Under the apple tree, that is where I wed you, that is where I gave you my hand and you were restored, there where your mother was violated; by the apple tree the Beloved means the tree of the cross, on which the Son of God redeemed and consequently married human nature and consequently every soul" (*Spiritual Song A* 28. 3). The theme of purification, within that of union and transformation, here ties up with the theme of the passage from the image to the likeness of God, as it was developed for example by William of Saint Thierry (1085–1148), in a founding text of medieval and modern spiritual literature: "Nowhere, indeed, is the measure of human imperfection better revealed than in the light of God's face, in the mirror of the vision of God. There, the one who, in relation to eternity, sees better and better what is lacking to him, corrects by a daily likeness all the evil he had done by unlikeness, approaching through likeness him from whom he had been removed by unlikeness. And thus an ever clearer likeness accompanies an ever clearer vision" (SC 223, §271).

2. Classic Stages of the Inner Life

This journey goes through customary stages set forth as early as Origen*, and accounts of it have engendered a spiritual topography virtually the same in all mystics, even though all of them are careful to tell us that this is only a practical guideline, and that God maintains complete freedom to elevate and restore his image in created beings following another pace and another chronology: In the various communications that God makes to souls of his gifts and his visitations, there is no certain and limited order, so that it may be said, for example, that after one process will come this other one; or, that from one level of prayer one moves to this other one (L. Lallement [1586–1635], *La Doctrine spirituelle* VII. 4, 9). In this respect, the case of Marie of the Incarnation, immersed with almost no preparation in the fullness of a total union with God, is exemplary.

With this reservation, the standard mystical journey is divided into three principal phases, corresponding to the transformation of the three zones of the personality sequentially seized by the divine presence (spiritual* life): the zone of the lower faculties (the senses), the zone of higher faculties (spirit), the connection between the two being accomplished by the imagination; and finally the summit of the soul, the place where the free and conscious act that defines the particularity of man in the image of God takes shape: "When man, through all his exercises, has drawn the outer man into the inner and reasonable man, when thereafter these two men, that is, the faculties of perception and of reason, are fully drawn into the innermost man, in the mystery of the spirit, where the true image of God is found, and when man thus gathered into himself leaps into the divine abyss in which he eternally was in his state as an uncreated being... then the divine abyss inclines itself and descends into the purified depth that is coming to him, and he gives to the created depth a higher form and draws it into the uncreated, so that the spirit is no longer anything but one with God" (Tauler, *Sermon 62*).

Mystical union properly speaking thus completes the reharmonization of the soul. Restored to its paradisal normality, it is now entirely passive, undergoing divine penetration; and also entirely active, God acting freely in it. There it leads a perfectly happy life, the "common life" of Ruusbroec, the "spiritual marriage" and "transforming union" of Teresa of Avila and John of the Cross: "When the soul has reached that state, it matters very little to it whether it is in the trouble of daily concerns or in the quiet of solitude. Everything is the same to it, because everything that touches it, everything around it, everything that strikes its senses does not prevent the enjoyment of present love. In the conversation and noise of the world, it is in solitude in the chamber of the Bridegroom, that is, in its own depths where it caresses him, converses with him, and nothing can trouble that divine exchange... . It seems that Love has taken hold of everything, when the soul made a gift of it by acquiescing to the higher part of the spirit, where this God of love has given himself to the soul, and the soul reciprocally to God" (Marie of the Incarnation, *Écrits* I, 360ff.).

V. Structure of the Soul and the Mystical Experience

1. The Soul Discovers That It Is Trinitarian

Knowledge* of God and knowledge of self thus advance at the same pace, a process summed up in Augustine's expression *noverim te, noverim me* ("may I know You so that I may know myself!" *Soliloquies* I. 2). We must follow Augustine in the elaboration of a structure of the soul that was to dominate all of Western mysticism.

Twelve centuries before Descartes*, Augustine felt surprise at thinking, and saw in that single indubitable experience the core of his religious experience, the fixed point of every certainty, if not of all of reality. What is thinking, in fact, but wishing to know? But what is knowing but recognizing what is; better still, recognizing *the one* who is? In fact, my quest is not simple curiosity, but a groping response to a vital call, a response to a person whom I will perhaps never identify, but who draws me to a place before my thought, at the same time that he gives himself to me in the dual form of knowledge and love, Truth and the Good*: "Where then did I find you so that I could learn of you, if not in the fact that you transcend me?" (*Confessions* X. xxvi [37]). The place before my thought, where I exist in God, is my *memory,* the background of my consciousness, of which the capacity to remember is only a partial actualization, and which, for Augustine, fundamentally defines thought as recollection.

The exploration of that recollection then reveals to us three centers between which all spiritual activity unfolds as an advent of him whom we perceive as the source of truth and goodness, three centers that we will identify as Father*, Son, and Holy* Spirit when "the Truth himself, having become man and speaking with men, will reveal itself to those who believe" (*De libero Arbitrio* 13. 37). This sourceless source associates us with the Father in the exercise of our memory (in the sense, this time, of the faculty of remembering). This truth that we receive from it in the knowledge that we have of it associates us with the Son in the exercise of our intelligence. And this goodness that we attain when we actively conform ourselves to this truth associates us with the Holy Spirit in the exercise of our will (*see Trin.* XIV. 7. 19). And we find again in this advent the movement from the capacity and the image of God, which every human person bears, to its actualization in the final likeness that presupposes having "put on Christ" (Gal 3:27).

2. Anthropological Vocabulary of the Mystics

For a minimal set of guidelines in the descriptions that mystics give us of their experience, here is their most common anthropological vocabulary, bearing in mind that the traditions to which they refer constantly intermingle, and that there would be little to be gained from attempting to disentangle lines of influence.

a) Summit of the Soul. Its mystical transformation corresponds to the "unitive way" (Pseudo-Dionysius), to the state of the "perfect" (Origen, William of Saint Thierry, John of the Cross), to the "spiritual man" (William of St. Thierry), to the "super-essential life" (Ruusbroec) or "super-eminent life" (Benet of Canfield, Bernières de Louvigny, Jean de Saint-Samson), and to the ""transforming union" (John of the Cross). In an ascendant view of spiritual life, mystics speak of it as the "pinnacle" of the soul (Bonaventure*, Camus), or "pinnacle of the spirit" (Hugh of Balma), as the "heaven of the soul" (Marie of the Incarnation, who also expresses it as the "higher part of the spirit"). To express the fact that all psychic activity derives from it and returns to it, they speak of it as the "spark" of the soul (Bernard, Eckhart), as the "point of the soul" (Louis de Blois, Francis de Sales, 17th-century France), or "point of the intellect" (Yves de Paris), as its "center" (Teresa of Avila, John of the Cross, James of Milan, Marie of the Incarnation, Francis de Sales, Maria Petyt, Camus, Laurent of the Resurrection), and as its "ground" (Ruusbroec, Rhineland*-Flemish mysticism, Marie of the Incarnation, Jean de Saint-Samson, Laurent of the Resurrection).

At the same time it makes up the inalienable part of the soul, the "substance" (Julian of Norwich, John of the Cross), the "essence" (Thomas* Aquinas, Ruusbroec, Eckhart, Tauler, Harphius, Benet of Canfield), seat of the "unity of the spirit" (Camus), and of the "essential unity" (Ruusbroec). To indicate that only God can accede to it, they use the images of the "citadel" (Plato, Plotinus, Eckhart), the "seventh dwelling" (Teresa of Avila), and the "chamber" (Angela of Foligno). In a more psychological register, they speak of it as "simple intelligence" (Sandeus) or "intellectual part of the soul" (Piny). It is the Greek *noûs* or the Latin *mens;* the "animus" (Augustine, Tauler), the "synderesis" (Bonaventure, Hugh of Balma, Eckhart, with an emphasis on will; Thomas Aquinas, with the twofold

aspect of knowledge and will), "intelligence and synderesis" (Gerson), "higher reason" (Thomas Aquinas), the "intellectual sense" (Richard of Saint-Victor), or again "memory" understood as the ground of the soul in Augustine. Finally, they sometimes simply call it "spirit," in the triad *spiritus, anima* (higher part of the soul), *corpus,* referring to 1 Thessalonians 5:23.

b) Higher Part of the Soul. Its transformation corresponds to the "illuminative way" (Pseudo-Dionysius), to the state of the "progressors" (Origen, William of Saint Thierry, John of the Cross), to the "rational man" (William of Saint Thierry). In Augustine it is the *memoria* as it encompasses other faculties, that is, the "higher powers" (radiating in their variety from the *mens:* Ruusbroec, Harphius), or "rational powers"—"memory," "understanding" (or "intelligence," or "intellect"), and "will"—from Augustine on and for all those who follow him. It is also found as "rational sense" in Richard of Saint-Victor, and as the pairing "reason and will" in Gerson. It corresponds to the Greek *psukhé* and the Latin *spiritus.* It appears simply as *anima* in the *spiritus, anima, corpus* triad. This higher part is the seat of the "spiritual senses," in mystical perception, with intellect paired with vision, memory with hearing, and will with the senses of smell, taste, and touch.

c) Lower Part of the Soul. Its transformation corresponds to the "purgative way" (Pseudo-Dionysius), the state of "beginners" (Origen, William of Saint Thierry, John of the Cross), to "animal man" (William of Saint Thierry). It groups together the "lower powers," radiating out in their variety from the "heart" (Ruusbroec, Harphius). It includes the "sensitive powers" (the five senses) and the "appetitive powers" (the "irascible" and the "concupiscent" forming the "natural passions*," expressed according to various divisions, notably, desire, repulsion, joy, sadness, love, hatred, fear, and so on). For Gerson it is "sensuality" (for its aspect as knowledge) and "animal appetite" (for its aspect as love). It sometimes appears simply as *anima* in contrast to the *animus* constituted by the higher powers.

The best traditional presentation of the spiritual organism can be found in the preface to one of the most read manuals of the Renaissance, the *Institution spirituelle* by Louis de Blois (1551).

VI. Authentication of Mystical Phenomena

1. Role of the Spiritual Director

We have seen that mystical rectification of the soul and rectification of language go hand in hand. This entry of God into words qualifies mystical experience as a phenomenon of revelation and of prophecy. Scholasticism* treated it as such (*see* the introduction of Thomas Aquinas to *ST* IIa IIae q. 171). This revelation (individual revelations*), private as long as the church does not officially take it into account (e.g., by giving the title of doctor to a Teresa of Avila or a Francis de Sales), may be compared for the Christian to already authenticated forms of revelation, namely, Scripture and tradition*. This comparison makes it possible for the mystic to judge the tree by its fruits in a domain in which the soul has no direct access to the source of its experience. The basic role of the spiritual director is to carry out this confrontation between revelation and Revelation, in order to invite the mystic either to follow or not to follow the inner call. In either case, it involves relying on the words of faith to reinvigorate the movement of faith, the only attitude toward salvation required of the Christian, whether or not he is a mystic. Without these words he would be at the mercy of the inadequacy of the relation between what he has experienced and what he believes he knows of God: "it is a difficult thing, full of suffering, for a soul not to understand itself in these moments and to find no one who understands it. It may happen, indeed, that God leads a soul along a very high road of obscure contemplation and dryness, on which it will seem to be lost" (John of the Cross, *Ascent of Carmel,* Prologue).

This explains the importance, emphasized by all the masters, of a competent and experienced director for the journey. It also explains the importance, from the Christian point of view, of the evangelization* of the experience, so that it may be liberated from all its false meanings and develop in correspondence to the fundamental revelation that is found in Jesus*, only Word* of the Father (*see* John of the Cross, *Ascent of Carmel,* II. 22).

2. Link with Scripture and the Magisterium of the Church

To return to spiritual* direction, there is a contribution of authentic mysticism to the tradition: in its adhesion to the revealing God that defines faith, it receives in its understanding more than any other experience "a certain impression of the knowledge of God" (Thomas Aquinas, *ST* Ia. q. 1. a. 3. ad 2). This is the creative role of contemplation in theology and preaching* (and the very word "theology" at first designated contemplation as such, before indicating its teachable result, and then only a theoretical result, when the divorce between the two was complete; *see ST* IIa IIae. q. 188. a. 6).

VII. Evaluation of Peripheral Phenomena

Faith alone qualifies Christian experience, and the lucidity of faith qualifies mystical experience. The fact remains that the mystic, Christian or not, is sometimes subject to spectacular phenomena, ranging from visions, rapture, and temporary loss of consciousness to levitation, extreme fasting, and stigmata. The variability of these phenomena, depending on time and place, indicates that none of them is essential to mystical experience. All are not susceptible to the same interpretation. Let us set out some guidelines.

- The restoration of the soul never occurs in a perfectly linear fashion. Even in the most classic journeys, its tangible zone is not definitively reorganized until that has been accomplished for its spiritual zone. This is why there are inevitable turbulences in perception, when the soul sees a union with God located high above it: "then for some there is a transport of impatience, within and without.... In this transport it happens that one perceives sublime and profitable words suggested and pronounced inwardly.... Some can then not prevent true tears from flowing.... Out of these transports and this impatience, some are on occasion drawn upward in spirit above the senses; and they perceive through words addressed to them, through images or tangible pictures shown to them, some truth...or the proclamation of things to come. This is what is called revelations or visions or the like" (Ruusbroec, *Ornament of the Wedding* II. 2).

- This kind of phenomenon is likely to become less marked in a more mature experience: "When the soul has been purified by the great number of ordeals that it has gone through, when it has life only for Jesus Christ, often all these favors are taken from it, or rather they are converted into other favors, more hidden but more precious and more excellent. It is led on a path more detached from the senses, a more spiritual path" (P. de Clorivière [1735–1820], *Considérations sur l'exercice de la prière et de l'oraison* II, 46).

- Within the union properly speaking, other kinds of refraction of the inner experience may occur in the body, either in a still disorderly form, or as a harmonious somatic expression of the experience. Levitation, for example, still belongs to a disorder, in that it reflects a certain divorce between body and soul: "Though mortal, he tastes the good of the immortal; though bound to the weight of a body, he acquires the lightness of a spirit. Thus, very often, his body is raised from the earth, thanks to the perfect union that the soul has achieved with me [Christ], as though the weighty body had become light. Not that it is deprived of its weight, but because the union that the soul has achieved with me is more perfect than the union between soul and body" (Catherine of Siena, *Dialogues*, ch. 79).

- In contrast, stigmatization (and its overtones, such as seraphic transverberation) is a complete association of the body with the same union: "Because the pains of him [Christ] whom I love come from his love, insofar as they afflict me through compassion, they delight me through kindness.... It was this love that brought the stigmata on the loving seraphic Saint Francis, and the burning wounds of the Savior on the loving angelic Saint Catherine of Siena, loving kindness having sharpened the points of loving compassion" (François de Sales, *Traité de l'amour de Dieu* V, 5).

This spectacular aspect of their experience has never been sought by mystics; all of them regret, as a lesser joy, what it may express of disorder, and they emphasize the purely accidental character of what is accidental to the union. For example, Marie of the Incarnation speaks of her own maturity: "There are no visions or imaginings in this state; what you know happened to me in the past [the vision of her Canadian mission when she was still in Tours] only had to do with Canada; all the rest lies in the purity of faith, in which, however, we have an experience of God in a wonderful way" (*Letter 263*, 888).

Thus proper course is to take no account of these phenomena, whether they take place at the beginning of spiritual life or in its full flower: "Men in this state must dominate themselves by reason, as far as possible, and await the end that God has established: thus the fruit of virtue* is kept for eternity" (Ruusbroec, op. cit., referring to beginners).

- A. Saudreau (1896), *Les degrés de la vie spirituelle,* Angers.
W. R. Inge (1899), *Christian Mysticism,* London.
H. Delacroix (1908), *Études d'histoire et de psychologie du mysticisme,* Paris.
E. Underhill (1911), *Mysticism,* London.
M. Grabmann (1922), *Wesen und Grundlagen des Mystik,* Munich.
C. Butler (1922), *Western Mysticism,* London.
A. Tanquerey (1923), *Précis de théologie ascétique et mystique,* Paris.
J. Maréchal (1924–37), *Études sur la psychologie des mystiques,* 2 vols., Bruges-Brussels-Paris.
A. Gardeil (1927), *La structure de l'âme et l'expérience mystique,* Paris.
M. de la Taille (1928), "Théories mystiques," *RSR* 18, 297–325.
R. Otto (1929), *West-Oestliche Mystik,* Gotha.
A. Poulain (1931), *Des grâces d'oraison,* Paris.
Dictionnaire de spiritualité ascétique et mystique (1932–95), 16 vols. plus charts, Paris.
Crisógono de Jesús (1933), *Compendio de ascética y mística,* Madrid.
H. Rahner (1935), "Die Lehre der Kirchenväter von der Geburt Christi im Herzen der Glaübigen," *ZKTh* 59, 333–418.
A. Stolz (1936), *Theologie der Mystik,* Ratisbonne.
J. de Guibert (1937), *Theologia spiritualis ascetica et mystica,* Rome.
Vl. Lossky (1944), *Essai sur la théologie mystique de l'Église d'Orient,* Paris.
R. C. Zaehner (1961), *Mysticism Sacred and Profane: An Inquiry into Some Varieties of Praeternatural Experience,* New York–Oxford.
B. Jimenez-Duque (1963), *Teología de la mística,* Madrid.
A. Ravier (1965), *La m. et les mystiques,* Paris.
L. Bouyer, L. Cognet, J. Leclercq, F. Vandenbroucke (1966), *Histoire de la spiritualité chrétienne,* 3 vols., Paris.
L. Gardet (1970), *La mystique,* Paris.
W. Beierwaltes, H. U. von Balthasar, A. M. Haas (1974), *Grundfragen der Mystik,* Einsiedeln.
Coll. (1977), "M.," *StMiss* 26—W. Johnston (1984), *Christian Mysticism Today,* San Francisco.
J. Colette (1986), "Mystique et philosophie," *RSPhTh* 70, 329–48.
B. McGinn (1992), *The Foundations of Mysticism,* vol. 1, New York, 265–343.
N. Pike (1992), *Mystic Union: An Essay in the Phenomenology of Mysticism,* Ithaca-London.
P. Gerlitz (1994), "Mystik," *TRE* 23, 533–92 (bibl.).
K. Albert (1996), *Einführung in die philosophische Mystik,* Darmstadt.
P. Miquel (1997), *Mystique et discernement,* Paris.

MAX HUOT DE LONGCHAMP

See also **Asceticism; Contemplation; Experience; Knowledge of God; Life, Spiritual; Prayer; Spiritual Theology**

Myth

There is no universally accepted definition of myth, but a good starting point is that of Mircea Eliade: "Myth relates a sacred history*; it relates a history which took place in primordial times." We might add that myth offers a way of experiencing the world and a model of active social integration.

a) Approaches to Myth. The Enlightenment placed myth in the sphere of the irrational. In the view of 19th-century evolutionism it represented an infantile stage of humanity, a savage or unhealthy form of language. For Tylor and J.G. Frazer, the latter being the author of *The Golden Bough,* myth was an attempt to explain the world, but one shackled by a confused way of thinking (which would be incisively criticized by Wittgenstein*). L. Lévy-Bruhl, in his early works, also insisted on the primitive character of myths and their connection with a prelogical mode of thought. According to Cassirer, on the other hand, myth had a logic, even if it was not the logic of scientific thought. For his part B. Malinowski proposed a functionalist approach, seeing myths as codifying and justifying the beliefs and practices of primitive societies, and making possible an active integration within those societies.

Nevertheless, the justification of social practices is not myth's only function. In terms of the structural analysis developed by Georges Dumézil, mythological discourses have structures in common. According to Claude Lévi-Strauss the analysis of myth is to be undertaken by seeking out its particular logic. This leads to the development of a model inspired by Saussurean linguistics, in which myths form a closed system whose meaning derives from internal relationships. Permanent structures known as *mythemes* are thereby identified. These are stable "parcels of relationships" whose combinations make possible the diversity of the narratives*. Understanding myth is thus a matter of decoding its structural organization, and this analysis enables us to grasp the work of a human intellect, which is always the same, and which gives form to content and (unconsciously) organizes it into structures that reflect oppositions and tend gradually to mediate them. This is the work of an intellect that organizes myths just as strictly as it does societies.

By focusing in this way on the semiotic organization of language, the structural approach is inevitably led to take less account of the semantics that organizes units of discourse. Lévi-Strauss doubts whether human individuals and groups genuinely have the ability to construct themselves (Piaget). They are governed more than they govern; they merely choose combinations from a closed repertoire of possibilities. In the wake of structuralism the question is therefore to discover what becomes of the truth of myth when it is approached as a discourse, as an expressive phenomenon in search of meaning and reference.

According to Ricœur, who asks this question, myth's special characteristic is the deployment of a symbolic and metaphorical language, which shatters ordinary classifications and places at the disposal of human beings a tool that allows them to express that which can only be arrived at indirectly. Moreover, since myths are narratives, the manner in which their plots are constructed allows heterogeneous collections of events to become a unified story, making overall sense. Myth thus has a role of creative production, a *poetic* function; and also a *heuristic* function—that of opening up a world for itself at the same time as it gives rise to an expansion of language within language as such *(semantic innovation).*

Considered on the level of discourse, not all myths say the same thing. From the classifying approach favored in totemic societies to the metaphorical one cultivated in the Greek or Semitic worlds, a whole varied mythological repertoire may be sorted out and typologically categorized.

According to Freud*, myth is to be classed among those creations of the collective imagination that enable humankind to cope with the traumas that mark the passage to civilization. Guilty of assassinating its father in the person of Moses, the Jewish people was impelled by its guilt to set up a religion centered on a legalistic cult, while Christianity emphasized the murder of its God* and derived from it a religion of universal forgiveness. According to Jung, on the other hand, myth derives from a collective unconscious more archaic than the personal unconscious of Freud. E. Drewermann places himself within the Jungian tradition when he considers that Christianity draws on a timeless language of imagery, as presented equally in the Bible*, in myths, and in stories. In these terms myth performs two functions, reducing anxiety and contributing to the integration of the individual. G. Theissen disputes both these points: on the one hand, Christianity as a religion is a system of historically rooted signs; and on the other hand, far from reducing anxiety it offers the means to endure it.

b) Myth and the Bible. Is the Bible a myth or a collection of myths? To answer this question we must begin by focusing on the process of demythologization that goes on in it—already noted by Gunkel (*see* Gibert 1979). The Bible, being monotheistic, abandons the theogonies of the Sumero-Semitic world. While mythological motifs do survive (e.g., Gn 6:1–2), a wholesale effort to combat polytheism is evident: in Genesis 1 the sun and moon are reduced to the status of light sources and are not named. The creation* of the world by God ensures that the gods are excluded from the universe.

If *muthos* is to be understood as a narrative entailing semantic innovation, then the Bible is close to such narratives, but the diversity of the literary genres that make up its structure tends to impose a characteristic literary style. That which gives such writing its coherence is to be found not in references to a primordial and theogonic period but in the recollection of an ostensibly historical sequence of events, that of the Exodus. This provides the motif for a history of salvation* that echoes throughout all the literary genres: the escape from Egypt, the covenant*, the gift of the law and of land. The creation narrative itself is charged with the history of salvation to come. For this reason the rabbi Rachi of Troyes (1040–1105) presented the creation of the world in terms of that of Israel*: "For the beginning, Israel, God created the heavens and the earth."

Israel's active integration into the world was achieved through the observance of the law. Of divine origin, this law was not in heaven but rather "very near you...in your mouth and in your heart" (Dt 30:14). Individual and collective behavior did not derive from a primordial past, but from a law that accompanied the people from the time of Sinai. The biblical myth, then, is not theogonic but exodic: God walked alongside his people to bring them out of Egypt (2 SM 7:7), and the founding law accompanied Israel throughout her history.

This entry into history of a saving God and the founding law may be described in terms of the cultural schemata of direct communication between the gods and history—but we should not be deceived. In fact Israel's experience initiated her into the true stability of history and the density of its mediations. The relationship between heaven and earth is mediated through the memory of the saving event and by the observance of that law that "is not in heaven" (Dt 30:12). Thus the authors of the books of Samuel and Kings show themselves capable of a genuine historiographical work that establishes relationships between facts and persons and judges the actions of the kings of Israel without indulgence.

Messianic hope*, prophecy*, and apocalyptics are all currents that would later emphasize the theme of the end. So salvation is hoped for from a future action of God. The memory of the Exodus leads on to an expectation that reuses protological and exodic images: a new creation, a new Adam*, a new law. The institutions and rites themselves are presented metaphorically in such a way as to open onto an unprecedented world: an ideal king, a heavenly temple*. The real world, its violence and its darkness, is reconsidered in terms of eschatological realities. The wisdom writings, for their part, take note of this imbalance between real and ideal history, and derive a modus vivendi from it.

In Bultmann*'s "demythologizing" project the (theological and rational) treatment of myth consists of extracting from the *muthos* an older proclamation, the kerygma, *kèrugma*. The complex written forms of the narrative-*muthos* are thus dismissed in favor of oral utterances (the first apostolic preaching) that antedate their putting into narrative form—the structure of the text now represents only an objectification and an obstacle to faith*. Studies following Bultmann, on the other hand, have led to a rehabilitation of narrative and a more serious appraisal of that which makes the New Testament a written event, in which biblical myth is not repudiated but incorporated in the shape of the Old Testament, and in which Christ's Passover* fulfils the original event of the Exodus. So the great narrative that runs from Genesis to the Apocalypse derives its unity from the plotting of a story narrated in terms of the figure of Christ. It is this plot structure that guarantees to the believer the Word* that inspires his faith.

Finally, in the work of Northrop Frye the Bible is explored as the myth—the narrative, the plot—that has acted as a source for Western mythologies (to be understood as the totality of discourses, including literature, which "explain the relationship between human beings and values"). Alongside science, which deals with our relationship with nature, myth expresses humanity's concern with the ideal construction of a world of culture. All Western cultures over the last 2,000 years find their origins in the Bible and in a Judeo-Christian tradition* that has absorbed all the other myths: the Bible is thus the "great code" that offers us a model of both space and time.

● E. B. Tylor (1871), *Primitive Culture,* London.
J. G. Frazer (1911–15), *The Golden Bough,* 12 vols., London.
S. Freud (1912–13), "Totem und Tabu," *Imago.*
B. Malinowski (1916), *Mythology of All Races,* 13 vols., Boston.

E. Cassirer (1922), *Die Begriffsform im mythischen Denken,* Leipzig-Berlin.

L. Lévy-Bruhl (1935), *La mythologie primitive,* Paris.

S. Freud (1939), *Der Mann Moses und die monotheistische Religion,* Amsterdam.

C.G. Jung, Ch. Kerenyi (1941), *Einführung in das Wesen der Mythologie,* Zürich.

M. Eliade (1957), *Das Heilige und das Profane,* Hamburg.

J. Henniger, H. Cazelles, R. Marlé (1957–58), "Mythe," *DBS* 6, 225–68.

C. Lévi-Strauss (1958), *Anthropologie structurale,* Paris.

P. Ricœur (1960), *Finitude et culpabilité II,* Paris.

C. Lévi-Strauss (1964–70), *Mythologiques,* 4 vols., Paris.

G. Dumézil (1968), *Mythe et épopée,* Paris.

P. Smith, P. Ricœur (1971), "Mythe," *EU* 11, 526–37.

M. Meslin (1973), *Pour une science des religions,* Paris.

P. Gibert (1979), *Une théorie de la légende: H. Gunkel et les légendes de la Bible,* Paris.

N. Frye (1981), *The Great Code: The Bible and Literature,* New York–London.

E. Drewermann (1984–85), *Tiefenpsychologie und Exegese,* 2 vols., Olten.

G. Theissen (1993), "Identité et expérience de l'angoisse dans le christianisme primitif," *ETR* 68, 161–83.

L. Wittgenstein (1993 post.), *Bemerkungen über Frazers Golden Bough,* in J. Klagge and A. Nordmann (Ed.), *Philosophical Occasions,* Indianapolis–Cambridge, 115–55.

PIERRE-MARIE BEAUDE

See also **Anthropomorphism; Bultmann, Rudolf; Creation; Cult; Exegesis; Freud, Sigmund; Fundamentalism; Hermeneutics; History; Holy Scripture; Literary Genres in Scripture; Narrative; Narrative Theology; Schelling, Friedrich Wilhelm Joseph von; Schleiermacher, Friedrich Daniel Ernst; Sciences of Nature; Scripture, Senses of**

N

Name

a) *Biblical Anthropology and Theology.* In the ancient Near East a name was not a mere label, alien to the reality it designated, but was mysteriously linked to that reality. To give a name to a place or person was to define the meaning or destiny. This much is clear from the conferment of names of rule upon the new Pharaoh, or even the Israelite king (*see* Is 9:5). Receiving a "great name" was consequently equivalent to "becoming powerful" or "renowned" (2 Sm 7:9; 8:13; see 1 Kgs 1:47). When God* changed Abram's name to "Abraham" (Gn 17:5) or Jacob's to "Israel" (Gn 32:29; 35:10), it marked for them the beginning of a new life.

Knowing and uttering the name of God had important implications: this invocation was found at the heart of all prayer* and defined the action of worship, since it signified the relationship of belonging and called down divine blessing* (*see* Nm 6:22–27). The Hebrew Bible* uses various terms to speak of God: Elohim (with or without an article), which is generally translated as "God"; "El" and different expressions based on this name (El Shaddai, El Olam, etc.), which can be attributed to Israel's Canaanite heritage; and YHWH, the proper name of the God of Israel, which some translations render by "the Lord" or "the Eternal." This phenomenon is exploited for theological purposes by the "priestly" author (P) or the final compiler of the Pentateuch: God is known as Elohim (*see* e.g. Gn 9:6), then he reveals himself to the patriarchs under the name of El Shaddai (Gn 17:1; 28:3, etc.),

and finally to Moses under his name of YHWH (Ex 6:2f.). Thus we receive a progressive revelation* of the God of Israel by himself.

b) *YHWH, the Name of the God of Israel.* In the Hebrew Bible the Tetragrammaton is the proper name of the God of Israel, revealed to Moses at the burning bush (Ex 3:13ff.). Moses finds himself in the presence of the angel of YHWH, who sends him to free his oppressed people. Moses then asks God: "If I come to the people of Israel and say to them, 'The God of your fathers has sent me to you,' and they ask me, 'What is his name?' what shall I say to them?" (Ex 3:13). Three successive divine answers to this question are offered. The oldest—and the only one which truly answers the question—is that of v. 15: "The Lord, the God of your fathers, the God of Abraham, the God of Isaac, and the God of Jacob" (Ex 3:15). This reply would later be commented upon by v. 14b: "Say this to the people: 'I Am' [*'èhyèh*] has sent me to you" (Ex 3:14b). This sentence suggests an etymology for the name YHWH, relating it to a form of the verb *hayah,* "to be." Finally, the famous phrase of v. 14a, "I am who I am" (*'èhyèh 'ashèr 'èhyèh,* sometimes rendered "I will be what I will be" or "I will be, yea, I will be") develops v. 14b's *'èhyèh.*

The Septuagint interprets the phrase in an ontological sense: "I am the existant" (*egô eimi ho ôn*), and this reading long prevailed both in exegesis* and in dogmatics*. It occurs in the writings of the church fa-

Name

thers*, and also in those of Maimonides, Luther*, and Calvin*; the translation of the BJ ("I am he who is"—1975 ed.) still echoes it, while the 1954 edition put the emphasis on the first person: "[...] he who am." In fact the author could not have intended a definition of God as the supreme Being*, since this type of abstract thought was not current in Israel. Moreover, the verb *hayah* does not refer to the concept of existence as such, but includes dynamism, action, and presence; the sense is rather "active being," or "being for" or "with" (*see* v. 12). In short, Ex 3:14 resounds as the commitment of YHWH's active and faithful presence in respect of his people*.

Occasionally the phrase is assumed to be evasive—God refuses to answer the question, as the parallelism with texts such as Ex 33:19 and Jgs 13:17f. may suggest; God remains ungraspable. This interpretation cannot be accepted. In the Semitic view it is knowledge of the name which ensures mastery of the other. This name (YHWH) is given in v. 15; v. 14a does not reveal the divine name, but offers an explanation of it. Moreover, the phrases based on the model of Ex 3:14a are not evasive in meaning either: on the contrary, in several cases they express an intensive sense (1 Kgs 8:60; *see* 2 Kgs 23:16; Ez 12:25; 14:23; 36:23).

The name of the God of Israel occurs in two forms: the long form represented by the Tetragrammaton YHWH and the short form YH ("Yah", Ex 15:2; Isa 38:11; Ps 94:7, 94:12) or YHW, attested in some liturgical exclamations ("Alleluia" = "Praise Yah"). The short form appears in ancient theophoric names (names whose composition includes a divine name) such as Joshua (JHW-*shua'*) and Jonathan (JHW-*natan*), and this usage continued until recent times. Moreover, "YHWH" occurs not only in the oldest texts of the Bible, but also on the stela of Mesha (Moab, ninth century B.C.), the inscriptions at Kuntillet-Ajrud (North Sinai, ninth to eighth centuries), a tomb at Khirbet El-Qom (eighth century), and the letters of Lakish (seventh century). According to conventional wisdom the short form is to be explained as an abbreviation of the older long form. However, M. Rose (1978) points out that there is no known example of the abbreviation of the name of a national deity, and sees the long form as resulting from the addition of a final *hé* as a *mater lectionis* (a letter added to facilitate reading, without the value of a true consonant). YHWH and YHW were in all likelihood no more than spelling variants, and it seems that the initial minority usage of the long form gradually won over.

Since the ancient Hebrew text is not vocalized, the pronunciation of the name ("Yahweh") has been reconstructed on the basis of the Greek transcriptions of Epiphanius of Salamis and Theodoret of Cyrrhus

(*iabè, iaouè*); this pronunciation appears to be confirmed by the wording of Ex 3:14 (assonance with '*èhyèh*). However, other older transcriptions (Clement of Alexandria, Origen*) suggest a reading of "Yahwô" or "Yahûh." The use of the short form YHW and of the theophoric names in *yehô-* or *yô-* support this.

Chapter 3 of Exodus does not introduce the use of the name YHWH—it was already known from Gn 4:26. At the same time, it is impossible to prove that the Israelites borrowed it from another people (for example the Kenites, as has sometimes been supposed). Doubtless the name goes back to a period when the semi-nomadic pre-Israelites were barely distinct from other comparable populations. This would explain why a number of peoples of the ancient East had deities bearing rather similar names: Ya(w) (Ebla), Yao (Byblos), YW (Ugarit), and Yau (Hamat). Although other hypotheses have been suggested, it appears that this divine name derives from the root *hwh/hwy*, which became the Hebrew *hayah* "to be"—an etymology that corresponds to the explanation given in Ex 3:14.

In the Septuagint, "Elohim" is translated by *ho theos*, "God," while "YHWH" is rendered by *kurios*, "the Lord," or sometimes by *kurios ho theos*, "the Lord God." This translation is revealing of the attitude of Judaism*, which from this time (especially from the third century B.C.) refused to utter the thrice-holy name in speech, to avoid disrespect. The reading '*adonay*, "the Lord," was soon preferred to "YHWH." For this reason the Masoretes added the vowels *a* (very short), *o* and *a* under the letters of the Tetragrammaton, giving rise to the hybrid reading "Jehovah," a linguistic barbarism unrecorded before the 14th century.

c) Name of Jesus. The New Testament does not use the name YHWH. When it speaks of God, it usually employs the expression *ho theos*, corresponding to "Elohim." *Kurios* also denotes God (e.g. in the expression *kurios ho theos*), but it is used too to speak of Jesus as the risen Lord (*see* e.g. Acts 2:36). While this title may not express faith* in Christ*'s divinity in an obvious way, it tends to imply it. It is the risen Christ who receives "the name that is above every name" (Phil 2:9). Baptism is initially given "in the name of Jesus Christ" (Acts 2:38), then "in the name of the Father and of the Son and of the Holy Spirit" (Mt 28:19).

● A.-M. Besnard (1962), *Le mystère du Nom*, Paris.
J. Kinyongo (1970), *Origine et signification du nom divin Yahvé*, Bonn.
M. Rose (1978), *Jahwe: Zum Streit um den alttestamentlichen Gottesnamen*, Zurich.
W. Vogels (1981), "'Dis-moi ton nom, toi qui m'appelles par mon nom': Le nom dans la Bible," *ScEs* 33, 73–92.
W.H. Schmidt (1979), "Der Jahwename und Ex 3:14", in

A. H. J. Gunneweg and O. Kaiser (Ed.), *Textgemäss.*, FS E. Würthwein, Göttingen, 123–38.

D. N. Freedman and P. O'Connor (1982), "YHWH," *ThWAT* 3, 533–54.

K. Waaijman (1984), *Betekenis van de naam Jahwe,* Kampen.

M. Rose (1987), "Jahwe," *TRE* 16, 438–41.

J. C. de Moor (1990), *The Rise of Yahwism,* Louvain.

H. Kruse (1990), "Herkunft und Sinngehalt des Jahwe-Namens," *ZThK* 112, 385–405.

R. Liwak (1994), "Name/Namengebung," III. Biblisch, *TRE* 23, 749–54.

R. Rendtorff (1994), "'El als israelitische Gottesbezeichnung," *ZAW* 106, 4–21.

H. Cazelles (1995), "Yahwisme ou Yahwe en son peuple," *in* R. Kuntzmann (Ed.), *Ce Dieu qui vient: Mélanges offerts à B. Renaud,* 13–29, Paris.

JACQUES VERMEYLEN

See also **Attributes, Divine; Being; Blessing; God; Monotheism; Praise; Prayer; Preaching**

Names, Divine. *See* Attributes, Divine

Narrative

---

1. Renaissance of the Narrative

Today a new interest in narrative has arisen, inspired by its place in the Bible* and by the historical nature of Christian faith*. For a long time narrative was neglected by a systematic theology* that reduced it to the level of an illustrated theme, and depreciated it through a historicist exegesis*, which stressed its discrepancy with the facts. Based on these viewpoints, the texts splintered into editorial layers, sources, and simple literary forms, bearers of ideas from which the history* was constructed. The final writing-up was conceived too much as an arrangement of materials showing a "theology" reduced to the motivations of such a project. Dialectic theologians (such as Karl Barth* and Rudolf Bultmann*), by insisting on the ever-current proclamation of the Word* for the principle of faith, hardly favored reflection on the narrative.

A reaction set in with Gerhard von Rad, who discussed the narrative form of the confession of faith (Dt 26:5–10) and the theological scope of the great narrative traditions in Genesis through Joshua, with the discovery of the role played by the narrative element in the texts about the covenant*. For E. Käsemann, the kerygma is not everything and the creation of the narrative on Jesus* has a theological value; Bultmann, on the other hand, excluded the pre-Easter Jesus from the domain of a theology of the Word. Then, with regard to the parables, Jüngel raised the question of a theology of language: in the parables, narrative is what permits the Kingdom* of God to accede to the level of language and to be at work in communication. More recently, literary studies on fiction and the development of narrative analysis have begun to stimulate philosophical thought. (Paul Ricoeur holds that narrativity explores human temporality.) Other studies have spurred on theological research, touching on such topics as "narrative* theology" and salvation* as experienced and recounted history. In addition, exegetic research has considered the narrative construction of biblical writings and the features of Biblical narration.

2. Narrative's Anthropological Domain

As the most widespread form of discourse, narrative clearly attests to a human ability to tell a story, and it communicates a universal love of storytelling. In a narrative, one may distinguish between the series of utterances with a beginning and endpoint, the whole story that is being told, and the narration (or narrative operation) that is implied between two points; and also between the narrator, who is the organizer of the message, and the narratee, who is the potential receiver of the message.

a) Between History and Fiction. The past, a great supplier of narrative, is always revealed after the fact and the narrative, as a work of language, enjoys a real autonomy with regard to the past, so much so that the history recounted may be fictional. "Historical" narrative and fictional narrative do not differ on account of their content but through the often implicit contract between the narrator and the narratee, who commit themselves (or not) to encounter a real-life story. The "historical" narrative goes beyond the chronicle of successive facts by linking them together according to a causal logic. It cuts to the quick of the real-life experience, shapes what it retains of it, gives cohesion to the heterogeneous, and leaves open the possibility of recounting it in another way. All narration, therefore, contains a fictional element. A fictional narrative recounts events *as though* they have happened, while the most "historical" narrative tends to recount events *as though* they have happened *as they are recounted.*

Embedded in mankind's general timeframe, recounted history detaches itself by means of a narration that is not tied to chronology, but that uses ellipses and pauses, flashbacks and anticipations. It creates moments of global transformation out of scattered incidents, integrating them according to an original "tempo." The time recounted takes on a thinkable image, and the experience of temporality is humanized (Ricoeur). The narrative pays a debt to what is no more, but which still counts (ancestors, momentous or founding events, experiences* that must be attested to, sometimes to the limits of the sayable), and which becomes a signifier in the narration's present. Individuals and collectives unfold their identity in the narrative. Simultaneously, the narration says that the past is irreversible, that it could have happened differently, and that life goes on. It attests to a freedom that endures, constructs an identity open to the future, and—faced with this freedom—constructs a form of possible existence.

b) Situation of Narration and Speech, Veracity and Truth. Through the interplay of the actors put on the stage, the narrative seems to stand alone without a narrator. And the recounted story's interest risks causing the present of the narration to be forgotten. This present is not limited to the time of the narrative's birth.

Thanks to the written form, it becomes real at the time of the reading. The stepping aside from the narrator and the listener in the text may be either a trap for readers—they forget themselves in the story and let themselves be manipulated—or it may be a piece of luck—not being involved directly, readers are in a dialogic position of listening freely to another spoken word. What is written does not abolish speech, but confers another pattern on it, favoring its otherness. It fixes its traces for the author as for the reader, and is not possessed by either of them. This type of communication is staged when an actor in a narrative begins to recount something—for instance, Jesus relating a parable*). What he recounts takes his place in order to solicit a hearing abandoned to the listeners' freedom. It seems that the wish to recount and to hear what is recounted, attested in all cultures, is rooted in the desire for the speech of the Other.

The question of the narrative's truth* splits into two parts: the first concerns the narration's past, and the second concerns the narration's present. Veracity* about the past is evaluated by historical criticism, which produces supporting arguments to establish the facts and to link them together (thus to interpret them). To that end it invokes a plausibility based on the constancy of human behavior (the logic of the same or the similar), but it may encounter the unknown, the other, the unexplained. It tends to produce another more or less probable narrative, which weighs its own veracity and does not exclude other possible narratives. This problem of veracity with regard to history (the referential dimension) does not tackle the question of the truth of the narrative as an act of language. Since the narrative's dynamic is the bearer of the words just as much for the person who constructs it as for those who reconstruct it while reading it, whether it is historical or fictional, the narration can serve or not serve the subject's truth by what is stated in it about man, his desire, and his relation with the other. In that sense, the narration, even historical narration, traces a "symbolic" course as a path of language for a subject of speech.

3. Narrative in the Bible

Narrative's eminent place in the canon* (the great narrative that stretches from Genesis to 2 Kings, almost a third of the "Writings," more than half of the deuterocanonical texts, and two-thirds of the New Testament) suits a faith founded on a historical revelation*. The narrative is composed of a story of salvation, from the "beginning" of everything to the post-exilic restoration (Hebrew Old Testament) and to the Maccabean crisis (Greek Old Testament), then from the beginning of the Gospels* to the spreading of the Word as far as Rome* (Acts). Unlike a history of modern conception, the biblical narrative covers varied literary* genres (elements of myth*, popular traditions, chronicles, and exemplary or romanticized biographies, such as those of Ruth, Esther, Judith, and Tobit).

a) Narrative in the Domain of the Word. Allied to other forms of discourse (legislative, prophetic, hymnal, sapiental, epistolary, and apocalyptic*) the biblical narrative is embedded in the wider domain of the word and under its authority. The Word is at the "beginning" (Gn 1, Jn 1). In the Hebrew canon, the Law gives its name to Genesis through Deuteronomy, which encompasses it, and the Prophets* give their names to the books of Joshua through 2 Kings, which tell their stories. The Gospels and Acts precede the Epistles, but it is the Epistles which, in the Churches'* present testify to the force of the Gospels, based on which Jesus' past becomes tellable. And Mark founded his "beginning" on the earlier word written in Isaiah (Is 40:3). Just as the prophets open history to eschatology*, the evangelic narrative orients it toward the Parousia*, and Revelation subjects it to the light of a "revelation," which it depicts in narrative with symbolic visions of a coming that is being heralded in the trials and persecutions of believers.

Thus, biblical narration places time under the impetus of an original gift, which strives toward its fulfillment. Its truth is felt in the "now" and the "soon" of a pact lived daily. This results in a form of writing that differs from the storyteller's or the historian's art, not in the way that the "religious" would differ from the "historical" or from the "literary," but through the characteristics of its enunciation, through the intent and the relation to time implied in the narration.

b) Evangelic Narration. Evangelic narration, for instance, has its roots in a living testimony that gives it, in its choice and treatment of the facts, a freedom that the historian rejects. Criticism is faced with varied documents about a social history of the origins of Christianity that refer undeniably to Jesus, but the historical figure of the latter does not emerge from them as a well-defined subject of knowledge. That fact shows that the evangelic tradition* is something other than informative, that it takes on something of the form of a liberating declaration. The Scriptures are the echo of the "eyewitnesses and ministers of the word" (Luke 1:2), resulting in the name "Gospels," which fits these writings better than the literary genre of the Hellenistic biographies. What makes people talk and narrate becomes history: the event becomes the word. So it is with Jesus. His deeds and his passion had marked those who perpetuated their memory and found their truth there.

A typical characteristic of the Gospels is the integration of short narratives into a global narrative from which they are easily detached. The narrative of the passion*, the only integrated account in the form of a sequence of several episodes that gave rise to others, has become the apex of every Gospel. Each particular narration presents itself to the reader on two levels—within its own limits, and within the global narration. Nothing is reported about Jesus apart from his progress toward death* and resurrection* (compare *The Gospel of Thomas*). His passion, death, and resurrection constitute the common source of evangelical preaching* and narration (*see* Mt 26:13), which form the passage that opens once and for all for believers onto a way of life*. The Old Testament is oriented in this direction by means of quotations, reminiscences, or evocations. Continuity follows a scriptural and not a causal or historical order. It undergoes a rupture in level that triggers a rereading in both directions. The promise* finds its realization in Jesus Christ* recounted, and the covenant sealed in the latter's body reveals what was hidden beneath the great images of the biblical narrative, and which offers to live in the social body of the Church.

4. Analysis of the Narrative

On the one hand, narrative analysis springs from literary interest in narrative art and in the Bible as literature (Erich Auerbach, Frank Kermode, Robert Alter), and, on the other hand, from the encounter in the 1960s between the morphology of the story (Vladimir Propp) and the structuralism applied in linguistics (Ferdinand de Saussure), in poetics (Roman Osipovich Jakobson), and in mythology (Claude Lévi-Strauss). They generated two main movements: narratology and semiotics. Narratology (Claude Bremond, Roland Barthes, Gérard Genette, and S. Chatman) describes the narrative sequence, the various types of plot, and the moments they link together. It notes the interferences and distortions between narrated history and narrative recounting (the narration). The narrative follows or does not follow the order and temporality of history. It can vary its vantage point (from above, from behind, or with the characters) and the narrator's position (he is omniscient, or he knows more, or he knows less than the actors, remains neutral or judges the action, delegates the speech, or takes the floor). Whether or not they are represented in the narrative, the narrator and the narratee are positions implied by narrative communication, and they are not the "real" author and reader who start the action (whence the name of the "implied" author and reader according to Wolfgang Iser). These specifications sharpen the attention paid to the text, as well as to the strategies directed at readers, with the aim of influencing them. The work's aim takes the place of the author's (Eco).

The semiotics that has taken the most interest in the Bible developed with A. J. Greimas and related researchers, including Geninasca and Zilberberg. Coupling theoretic and practical development of the texts, it tries to elucidate the linkage of the discourse (the content's form) by singling out several levels. The sequence of the actions (general grammar of the functions and the agents or fundamental roles)—which is inseparable from the knowledge of the actors and of their interpretations, their desires, affects, and emotions (the cognitive and thymic dimension)—can only be analyzed based on the figures of the actors linked together in time and space (figurative and discursive dimensions). The latter dimensions refer to the world, indicate the subject under discussion, and compose the narrated history. However, their linking together, specific to each narration, frees them from hackneyed meanings, to embark on a search that is not only for meaning, for it is a work of language and challenges in man a subject of speech divided between what can and cannot be said. Particularly in the Bible, narration often tackles a reality that resists language. Here we touch on enunciation, which tests itself through being written and read. As a trigger to the plot, it is narration, with an implied narrator and narratee. More deeply, as trigger to the discourse, it deals in them with the speaking subject confronted by the subject of the spoken word on condition of a possibility of meaning.

5. Reading and Theology of the Narrative

These analyses stimulate the reading, criticize it in the name of the text, and tend toward a global interpretation that does not limit itself to the reconstruction of a history or a didactic message. The narrative linkage and dynamic sustain an interest that goes beyond the anecdotal to ask the questions: What does this text want from me? What does it state about man, about his relations with the world and with time, with himself and with others, with desire and with speech? This anthropological dimension underlies a believer's reading: the recognition of the Other of the speech, under his biblical name, takes root in the relation of otherness that is learned through the language, the writing, and the reading. The latter can become theologal—the sparking of a dialogue, of an unfinished encounter.

The act of reading becomes a theological act, not through paraphrase or extraction of doctrinal statements, but through participation in the understanding (rather than in the explanation) at work in the narrative, up to the limits of the knowable. Theology elucidates according to its own rules not only contents, but what,

of the Word made flesh*, is at work in the narration and is borne out in the reading ecclesial body. The salvation that is recounted permits neither systematization nor objectivization outside the progress followed in a history of loss and of the new, of sin* and forgiveness, of suffering and joy. There the language confronts a reality whose resistance the biblical narrative calls to mind, while drawing attention to the resources of the figurative and of the conceptual for speaking about the interaction of man and of God, of time and of eternity*, of the ultimate and the contingent. From the narrative, theology learns to locate itself at the meeting point of absence and desire, of the provisional and of the word that endures.

- V. Propp (1926), *Morphologie du conte,* Leningrad (2nd Ed. 1969).
  G. von Rad (1938), *Das formgeschichtliche Problem des Hexateuchs,* Stuttgart.
  E. Auerbach (1946), *Mimesis,* Bern.
  G. von Rad (1957), *Theologie des AT,* Munich.
  C. Lévi-Strauss (1958 and 1973), *Anthropologie structurale* I and II, Paris.
  E. Jüngel (1962), *Paulus und Jesus,* Tübingen.
  E. Käsemann (1964), "Sackgassen im Streit um dem historischen Jesu," in *Exegetische Versuche und Besinnungen* II, Göttingen, 31–68.
  H. Weinrich (1964), *Tempus,* Stuttgart.
  (1966), "L'analyse structurale du récit," *Communications* 8.
  P. Beauchamp (1970), "Propositions sur l'Alliance de l'AT comme structure centrale," *RSR* 58, 161–94.
  L. Marin (1971), *Sémiotique de la passion,* Paris.
  G. Genette (1972), *Figures III,* Paris.
  W. Iser (1972), *Der implizite Leser,* Munich.
  R. Jakobson (1973), *Questions de poétique,* Paris.
  J. Calloud (1973), *L'analyse structurale du récit,* Lyon.
  C. Chabrol, L. Marin (1974), *Le récit évangélique,* Paris.
  H. Frei (1974), *The Eclipse of Biblical Narrative,* New Haven.
  M. de Certeau (1975), *L'écriture de l'histoire,* Paris.
  P. Beauchamp (1976), *L'un et l'autre Testament: Essai de lecture,* Paris.
  R. Barthes et al. (1977), *Poétique du récit,* Paris.
  Groupe d'Entrevernes (1977), *Signes et paraboles,* Lyon.
  A. and D. Patte (1978), *Pour une exégèse structurale,* Paris.
  S. Chatman (1978), *Story and Discourse,* Ithaca.
  L. Marin (1978), *Le récit est un piège,* Paris.
  J. B. Metz (1978), *Glaube in Geschichte und Gesellschaft,* 2nd Ed., Mainz.
  F. Kermode (1979), *The Genesis of Secrecy: On the Interprétation of Narrative,* Cambridge, MA.
  U. Eco (1979), *Lector in fabula,* Milan.
  J. Delorme (1979), "L'intégration des petites unités dans l'évangile de Marc du point de vue de la sémiotique structurale," *NTS* 25, 469–91.
  Groupe d'Entrevernes (1979), *Analyse sémiotique des textes,* Lyon.
  A.J. Greimas, J. Courtès (1979), *Sémiotique: Dictionnaire raisonné de la théorie du langage,* Paris.
  R. Alter (1981), *The Art of Biblical Narrative,* New York.
  P. Beauchamp (1982), *Le récit, la lettre et le corps,* Paris.
  A. Gueuret (1983), *L'engendrement d'un récit: L'évangile de l'enfance selon saint Luc,* Paris.
  P. Ricoeur (1983–85), *Temps et récit,* 3 vols., Paris.

L. Panier (1984), *Récit et commentaires de la tentation de Jésus au désert*, Paris.

F. Hahn (Ed.) (1985), *Der Erzähler des Evangeliums*, Stuttgart.

J.-M. Adam (1985), *Le texte narratif*, Paris.

Coll. (1985), "Narrativité et théologie dans les récits de la passion," *RSR* 73/1–2.

J. Calloud (1985–86), "Sur le chemin de Damas: Quelques lumières sur l'organisation discursive d'un texte," *SémBib*, nos 37, 38, 40, 42.

J. Calloud, F. Genuyt (1985–91), *L'évangile de Jean*, 4 vols., L'Arbresle-Lyon.

B. van Iersel (1986), *Marcus*, Boxtel.

A. Chené et al. (1987), *De Jésus et des femmes: Lectures sémiotiques*, Montréal and Paris.

J. Geninasca (1987), "Sémiotique," in M. Delcroix and F. Hallyn (Eds.), *Méthodes du texte*, Gembloux.

P. Bühler, J.-F. Habermacher (1988), *La narration*, Geneva.

J.-N. Aletti (1989), *L'art de raconter Jésus-Christ*, Paris.

J. Delorme, "Récit, parole et parabole," in ACFEB, *Les paraboles évangéliques*, 123–50, Paris.

P. Beauchamp (1990), *L'un et l'autre Testament*, vol. 2: *Accomplir les Écritures*, Paris.

J.L. Ska (1990), *"Our Fathers Have Told Us": Introduction to the Analysis of Hebrew Narrative*, Rome.

L. Panier (1991), *La naissance du Fils de Dieu*, Paris.

J. Delorme (1991), *Au risque de la parole*, Paris; (1992), "Sémiotique," *DBS* 12, 281–333 (with bib.).

O. Davidsen (1992), *The Narrative Jesus*, Aarhus.

J. Delorme (1995), "Prise de parole et parler vrai dans un récit de Marc (1, 21–28)," in P. Bovati, R. Meynet (Eds.), *"Ouvrir les Écritures" (Mélanges P. Beauchamp)*, 179–200; (1997 a), "La tête de Jean-Baptiste ou la parole pervertie: Lecture d'un récit (Mc 6, 14–29)," *in* P. M. Beaude (Ed.), *La Bible en littérature*, Metz, 294–311; (1997 b), "Évangile et récit: La narration évangélique en Marc," *NTS* 43, 367–84.

JEAN DELORME

See also **Biblical Theology; Book; Covenant; Exegesis; Literary Genres in Scripture; Jesus, Historical; Language, Theological; Myth; Narrative Theology; Time; Scripture, Senses of; Word of God**

Narrative Theology

a) Another Form of Theological Thought? Narrative* theology aims to "renew traditional theological thought by the integration of narrative forms" (Meyer zu Schlochtern 1979). Internationally, J.-B. Metz and H. Weinrich (1973) deserve the credit for proposing for discussion a number of analyses whereby conceptual and systematic thinking was enriched with new approaches focusing on metaphor, symbol, parable*, the art of rhetoric, the epic or biographical dimension, and so on. At the same time, they emphasized the experiential character taken on by the theological attestation of faith*, so that we may also speak of an "experiential" theology, proposed by J. Mouroux as early as 1952. It is important to distinguish here between the experiential and the empirical: narrative theology does not relegate theology to the empiricism of the social sciences, but rather examines it from the perspective of narrative and theories of narrative. The theoretical aspect of this new orientation has been forcefully articulated and developed by P. Ricoeur. Tradition* and history* are seen by narrative theology not so much from the point of view of the act of understanding (the hermeneutic* standpoint, as a "fusion of perspectives"), as from the point of view of narrative communication: "History tells stories" (Danto 1965). Rational communication takes place through the intelligibility of an argument whose every step is subject to logical control; but mutual understanding may still come up against insurmountable limits that the speaker can overcome only by means of narrative communication, by recounting how he reached his conceptions. This complementary function of the narrative element is most clearly seen in E. Schillebeeckx's *Jesus* (1974). Metz, in addition, emphasizes the critical function of narration understood as "dangerous memory," and conversely the need to "interrupt" the ideological narrative. For the insinuating power of the narrative act may have, like rhetoric or music*, the capacity to enchant (*see* Faye 1972). It was S. Crites (1971) who first pointed to the narrative structure of experience*. Narration, according to him, expresses "the full temporality of experience in the unity of a form." Thus history, according to Arthur C. Danto in his *Analytic Philosophy of History*, is a narrative governed by practical intention. Narrative, which transforms lived facts and events into a fund of personal experience, reinforces "experiential competence," which is based on openness, on a capacity for critical evaluation and integration, on an understanding of meaning, and on a taste for praxis (Mieth 1976).

Narrativity cannot be separated from reflexivity, which is also shown with extreme clarity by modern literature. But literature emphasizes form, presentation, symbol, and image to the detriment of the ordinary pillars of argument: concept, reasoning, and coherence. Narrative theology, on the other hand, requires that narrative and reflection be bound together in the unity of a form (see Hauerwas 1974; even earlier, Dunne 1967). According to J. S. Dunne, the task of narrative theology is "the search for God* in time* and memory," and along the way it has rediscovered the subjective witness of faith as a locus of theological reflection. It has also made a genuine exegetical contribution to the problem of the collective composition of narratives, as revealed in the observation of certain elementary schemas (see Jolles 1930). The American theologian S. McFague (1975) in particular, in a thorough discussion, has sketched the contours of a theology shaped into parables and metaphors. A number of her ideas have become part of the common heritage of theology, in particular the concern to highlight what there is in a story that goes beyond the explanatory and doctrinal propositions that constitute a skeletal image of the story in the mode of comprehension.

The classic examples are provided by the parables of Jesus*, principally in Luke (the good Samaritan, the prodigal son), which can be reduced neither to norms nor to doctrinal pronouncements. Indeed, in the first case, Jesus changes in a critical sense the lawyer's question about his neighbor, and has him ask: "Who is my neighbor?"; in the other, he establishes a relationship of unity and tension between straying and mercy that cannot entirely be transposed into a conceptual dialectic. In order to understand what is intended, it is necessary to follow the story. This can be done in various ways, depending on personal creativity, as shown for example in the Latin American catechism Vamos caminando (1979).

The theoretical debate on narrative theology largely took place in the second half of the 1960s, but it remains influential today, particularly in reflections on temporality, the formation of identity, and ethics*.

b) Temporality, Identity, and Narrative Ethics. The rediscovery of and emphasis on narrativity influenced the debate in the 1980s on "communitarianism." In theology, narrativity meant the encounter of experience, the examination of faith, and ethos in a narrative of liberation with a practical purpose ("orthopraxis"). In philosophy*, particular attention has been paid to the role of the collective and society* in the unity between the lived world* and a form of moral life attached to the virtues* (see A. McIntyre). This latter concern has also been addressed from a theological perspective, in a relatively exclusive variant of narrative theology (S. Hauerwas), and in a variant that was more open to the world (D. Mieth). The reflections of Ricoeur on "time and narrative" (1983–85) are noteworthy for coining the notion of "narrative identity," which applies to communities as well as to individuals. In a differentiated theory of mimesis, the "model nature" of narrative forms is described by the transmission, confrontation, and discovery of the self (similarly, Mieth 1976, 1977). The question of the relationships between narration and the formation of identity has also been treated by Charles Taylor. Others—in part communitarians, in part neo-Aristotelians—associate with this the paradigm of a non-normative ethics that has been called an ethics of aspiration (in contrast to an ethics of duty; see H. Kramer). The theory of the ethical model, which is rooted in the tradition of the ethics of virtue, here opens a new path to moral cognitivism. The moral theology of the Church*, through the doctrine of sensus fidelium, also accepts the importance of personal convictions, as they are lived through in practice, for the knowledge and recognition of what is just (justice*). Tensions have thus arisen in Catholic moral doctrine due to the confrontation between a Neoscholastic system of logically coherent concepts that no longer correspond to any lived reality and questions raised by the self-recognition of moral tradition and moral creativity.

● A. Jolles (1930), Einfache Formen, Tübingen.
J. Mouroux (1952), L'expérience chrétienne, Paris.
W. Schapp (1953), In Geschichten verstrickt, Hambourg.
A. C. Danto (1965), Analytical Philosophy of History, Cambridge.
J. S. Dunne (1967), A Search for God in Time and Memory, Notre Dame (1975, London).
S. Crites (1971), "The Narrative Quality of Experience," JAAR 39, 291–311.
J.-P. Faye (1972), Théorie du récit, Paris.
J.-B. Metz (1973), "Kleine Apologie des Erzählens," Conc(D) 9, 334–41.
H. Weinrich (1973), "Narrative Theologie," ibid., 329–33.
R. Koselleck, W. D. Stempel (Eds.) (1973), Geschichte—Ereignis und Erzählung, Munich.
St. Hauerwas (1974), Vision and Virtue, Notre Dame.
S. McFague-TeSelle (1975), Speaking in Parables, Philadelphia.
E. Schillebeeckx (1974), Jezus, het verhaal van een levende, Bloemendaal (as Jesus: Die Geschichte von einem Lebenden, 1975, Friburg-Basel-Vienna).
S. Simon (1975), Story and Faith in the Biblical Narrative, London.
D. Ritschl, H. O. Jones (1976 a), "Story" als Rohmaterial der Theologie, Munich.
D. Mieth (1976), Dichtung, Glaube und Moral, Mainz.

D. Mieth (1976 b), *Epik und Ethik,* Tübingen.
D. Mieth (1977), *Moral und Erfahrung,* Friburg.
J. Navone (1977), *Towards a Theology of Story,* Slough.
B. Wacker (1977), *Narrative Theologie?,* Munich.
J. Meyer zu Schlochtern (1979), "Erzählung als Paradigma einer alternativen theologischen Denkform," *Theol. Berichte* 8, Zurich-Einsiedeln, 35–70.
E. Arens (1982), *Kommunikative Analysen,* Düsseldorf.
P. Ricoeur (1983–85), *Temps et récit,* 3 vols., Paris.
R. Zerfass (Ed.) (1988), *Erzählter Glaube—erzählende Kirche,* QD 116 (bibl.).

M. C. Nussbaum (1990), *Love's Knowledge: Essays on Philosophy and Literature,* Oxford.
H. W. Frei (1993), *Theology and Narrative,* New York.
K. Wenzel (1997), *Zur Narrativität des Theologischen,* Frankfurt; (1998), "Narrative Theologie," *LThK3* 7, 640–643.

DIETMAR MIETH

See also **Gospels; Exegesis; Experience; Hermeneutics; Liberation Theology; Narrative**

Nationalism

In practice, some accommodation between sacred and secular authorities in organized societies (*see* sovereignty*) has historically always been necessary. Even where Christianity in one of its forms has been the dominant religion, the relationship between church and state has taken every possible form, from that of the theocratic state, in which civil authority has been subsumed into ecclesiastical power, to that in which sacred authority has been reduced to the status of a tool of the civil sovereign. The entry on sovereignty in this work briefly surveys the evolution of the theological theory underlying the relationship between sacred and secular authority. The present entry seeks to examine the nature of the development of the evolving theology as it can be inferred from the actual political history of the Christian West. The pragmatic attitude of the Christian churches to the rise of the large nation states of Western Europe allows important insights into the constraints behind the development of modern ecclesiology.

Theological theory followed political developments, often justifying them or pointing the way forward. From Constantine's early-fourth-century exercise of imperial authority over appointments to the Roman see, when he himself moved to Constantinople, to the investiture controversy of the 11th and 12th centuries, the theological principles at stake had been mired in pragmatic considerations and struggles for power in which popes and emperors had themselves sometimes been mere pawns. Then on 23 September 1122 it was agreed at the concordat of Worms that, following the custom already introduced into France, the emperor should renounce the right to invest bishops with the ring and crosier, symbols of spiritual authority, and should guarantee them canonical election and free consecration. Pope Callistus II (c. 1050–1124) conceded that elections to German abbacies and Episcopal sees should be held in the emperor's presence, and that the emperor should invest the abbots and bishops with the scepter, symbol of their temporal authority.

This rudimentary separation of temporal and spiritual powers respected the nature of the Church as, necessarily, a body with spiritual power to further the salvific purposes for which it was founded; but which had also in the course of time acquired buildings, lands, revenues, codes of behavior, and in general the legal structures and temporal rights and obligations for which the concordat conceded that it was in part answerable to a temporal power. Only very rarely in western Christendom, as in the papal states of later history or in Calvin's Geneva, was the spiritual power identical with the temporal one. Since it was at least arguable that the Church could no longer serve its divine purpose without temporal possessions, the regulation of the obligations of its bishops and abbots respectively to spiritual and temporal powers needed open acknowledgement and regulation. The solution was most famously established in this early concordat.

The Worms concordat did not, of course, remove further controversy, which continued to be fuelled by such matters as clerical immunity from the secular courts and ecclesiastical exemptions from taxation. In England John of Salisbury (c. 1115–80), later bishop of Chartres, witnessed Becket's murder in 1170 and developed his view of the secular primacy of ecclesiastical over civil authority that lay behind the practice of Innocent III (1160/1–1216), who ineffectively annulled *Magna carta* because it had been agreed without papal consent. In return King John handed over his domains as a papal fief.

It was the 13th century that saw the full measure of the canonists' claims that the spiritual power was prior and superior to the temporal power, but by its end Boniface VIII was being forced partly to withdraw his claims that clerical property was of its nature exempt from royal taxation. Civil authorities, especially the English kings, began more strictly to circumscribe the economic and legal rights of the clergy, while by the early-14th century Marsilio of Padua (c. 1275–c. 1342) was defending the simple subordination of the church to the state.

It was in the late-15th century that the widespread use of concordats redefined the theology of the relationship between spiritual and temporal powers by the creation of national churches. The nation states began at this date to consist of much larger units than hitherto. In Eastern Europe in the late-15th century Matthias Corvinus created the kingdom of Hungary, Casimir IV created a much larger Poland, and Ivan III brought together the Russian principalities as a single nation. On the Italian peninsula the popes absorbed the smaller independent cities into the papal state, and in western Europe Spain was unified by the merging of Castile and Aragón in 1474, while Louis XI of France took over Anjou, Maine, Provence, Roussillon, Artois, and Burgundy, finally annexing the duchy of Brittany in 1491. England was united under Tudor hegemony after the battle of Bosworth Field in 1485.

The system that was devised certainly had theological implications. Larger secular administrative burdens and Renaissance reform of non-clerical education appeared to justify the transfer of senior ecclesiastics to administrative posts, leaving their pastoral responsibilities to be fulfilled by substitutes, and the transfer of ecclesiastical revenues to charitable or educational foundations—as at Christ Church, Oxford, or at Ingoldstadt—or even to national treasuries. In 1438 the French clergy issued the Pragmatic Sanction of Bourges, upholding the right of the French church to administer its own temporal property independently of Rome, and to be granted automatic papal ratification for nomination to vacant benefices. Eugene IV protested, but in 1447 he made a similar agreement with the German Electors, although the papacy under Nicholas V won something back at the 1448 concordat of Vienna.

In Spain the crown annexed the grand masterships of the military religious orders established during the Crusades, and in 1476 the Spanish Cortes won the transfer of further legal powers to the crown. In 1482 Ferdinand and Isabella of Spain obtained an incipient right of nomination to bishoprics, which was later strengthened. From 1493 papal bulls could be published in Spain only after royal assent, and the Inquisition—in Spain a secular institution—was granted sufficient ecclesiastical jurisdiction to complete the hegemony of secular over ecclesiastical sovereignty. In France papal decrees, including in the 16th century those of the Council of Trent, remained without force until registered by the *parlements.* In England the chief justice Sir William Hussey could assert in 1485 that the king was superior to the pope within his realm.

In order to prevent clashes of civil and sacred jurisdictions, it became common practice in the early-16th century for lord chancellors already endowed with the plenitude of civil jurisdiction, like Ximenes in Spain, du Prat in France, and Wolsey in England, to be made papal legates *a latere,* giving them within their own territories the plenitude of papal jurisdiction. The closing of monasteries and the diversion of their funds in England to his Oxford foundation was set in motion by Wolsey with full papal powers to act as he did.

In the trade-offs of successive concordats, what was safeguarded was not the real power to nominate bishops or to receive ecclesiastical revenues, but the right of monarchs to exercise a widening civil jurisdiction, to name certain candidates for benefices, and often to receive ecclesiastical revenues, particularly from vacant benefices, while the right of Rome to supply all ecclesiastical jurisdiction required by nominees of national churches was safeguarded. The repudiation of Rome as the source of all spiritual jurisdiction, rather than any single unifying doctrine, was almost constitutive of the major 16th-century schismatic movements, as the unfolding of events in England makes clear. Henry VIII repudiated Roman spiritual jurisdiction and usurped the Church's ultimate teaching authority, but pursued anti-Lutheran religious policies for years after his break with Rome.

The theological implications of the European creation of national churches need therefore to be distinguished. In countries, provinces, and regions that remained in communion with Rome, the pope provided the ultimate source of all ecclesiastical jurisdiction, however much the real power to run their own ecclesiastical affairs devolved onto the nation states. In territories that broke with Rome, ecclesiastical and secular jurisdictions had both to be generated from within. With the birth of the modern world, in which countries contained citizens of different religious affiliations, it became necessary as well as normal for different religious communions to accept spiritual jurisdiction according to their own traditions.

In America the situation differed from state to state, with separation of church and state in nine of the original thirteen British colonies. The First Amendment to the Constitution subsequently prohibited the establishment of any religion and maintained the freedom of all to practice their religion. These provisions have been interpreted strictly by the Supreme Court, which has enforced the strict neutrality of the state in religious matters, thereby not only according with the dominant modern theology of church-state relations, but also creating an exemplar for it.

The existence of countries that continue to have established religions is scarcely a matter of great theological consequence, since the function of the religious affiliations and structures retained as established in such countries is, in so far as their established position is concerned, almost entirely administrative and ceremonial, as in Presbyterian Scotland or Anglican England. In neither country is there any constraint to practice the established religion or impediment to the practice of any other. The Church was disestablished in Wales in 1920, but in England the sovereign remains governor of the Church, appoints its senior officials on political advice, and still exercises widespread powers of patronage.

Some anomalies and difficulties remain in that established churches are normally in a position to exercise an influence greater than that warranted by their moral authority alone on legislation affecting the ethical norms that they profess, as for instance those concerning divorce, birth control, homosexual behavior, and modern techniques of fertilization. It can, however, be argued that the ability of established churches to exercise political pressure on legislation compromising the ethical norms to which they adhere is universally slight, and that the anomalies it entails are outweighed by the social and ceremonial contribution that the remaining established churches make to national life. The modern theology of a total separation of temporal and spiritual authorities is essentially uncompromised by the preservation of such ancient religious privileges as have been retained within modern states.

ANTHONY LEVI

Natural Religion. *See* Deism and Theism

Natural Theology

Natural theology refers to a knowledge* of God from the creatures, independently of revelation*. Natural theology underlines the relationship between the "book of nature" and the reasonable nature of man. Throughout history*, it expressed a tension between Christian claims of the universal and the historic contingencies of Christianity. In the 20th century, natural theology, a question disputed between Catholics and Protestants, showed a tendency to become a sign of two theological attitudes.

a) Pre-Christian Concept of Natural Theology. The notion of natural theology was already present among the Greeks, who did not oppose it to a *supernatural* theology, but distinguished it from *mythical* theology—that of poets, and from *political** theology, which corresponded to the official civic religion. The *physical* theology of philosophers designated the knowledge of a divine expressed within the nature of things. Augustine* borrowed Varron's distinction of three types of theology*: the *mythicon*, the *physicon*, and the *civile,* and he was the first to Latinize the expression of natural or physical theology (*see De Civitate Dei* VI, chapter V).

b) Natural Theology as Natural Knowledge of God.
Even if the presocratics were not only physicists, but in some way the first theologians (*see* Jaeger, 1947), Christian thought could only view natural theology as being, if not opposite, then at least completely subordinated to the plenary revelation of God in Jesus Christ. With Tertullian*, natural theology plays but a secondary role, but he acknowledges a natural knowledge of God that relies either on the testimony of the exterior world (*Apologia* 18, 1), or on the testimony of the soul*, which enjoys a congenital knowledge of God (*Apologia* 17, 6; see also *l'anima naturaliter christiana*). Thus Augustine, who got the expression of natural theology from Varron, especially insists on the goodness of the creation* against the gnostic—that is, the identity of the Creator and the Redeemer. The two "books," he contends—the *Liber Naturae* and the *Liber Scripturae*—should actually be attributed to the same author. This dual knowledge of God is present again in Bonaventure* (*Brevil.* II, 5.11), who asserts that the book of nature, made less legible because of sin*, has become once again legible thanks to the book* of Scriptures.

The term natural theology is not found per se in Thomas* Aquinas, who doesn't mention the book of nature either, and rejects the Platonists' work *physica theologia* as idolatrous (*Summa Theologica* IIa IIae, q. 94, a. 1 c). However, in his work *De Deo uno,* where he exposes the *praeambula fidei* ("preambles of faith"), he defends the legitimacy of the natural knowledge of God and of his main attributes* (see *Summa Theologica* Ia, q.12, a. 12). These questions *De Deo uno* represent the rational moment of the supernatural knowledge (supernatural*) of God. Faith perfects the power of reason*, as grace* perfects the power of nature*. He who adheres to God's existence by confessing the first article of the *Creed,* but who is capable of furthermore proving the existence of God, believes in a more noble manner (*De veritate.* q. 12, a. 12).

Therefore, it would be improper to talk of "natural theology" with regard to the natural knowledge of God that a theology understood as *intellectus fidei* requires for its own equilibrium. This equilibrium, however, would not be respected thereafter. By the time of the Renaissance, the first presentation of natural theology in monograph form appeared, the *theologia naturalis seu Liber creaturarum* by Raymond Sebond (1487), whom Montaigne praised (see *Essais* 1. II, chapter 12). In the 18th century, under the influence of Leibniz* and his theodicy, the *theologia naturalis* (1736–37) by

Christian Wolff, discussed in his *Special Metaphysics,* would systematize a natural theology turned autonomous—in the context of the *Aufklärung,* it would become the science of religion within the limits of understanding.

c) During the Reformation. Neither the expression nor the idea of natural theology were to be found among the Reformers. The scriptuary principle and the principle of justification* by faith alone do not lead them to exclude all natural knowledge of God. Using Romans 1:19 and 2:14, Luther* admits that natural reason might lead to some knowledge of God, whose action is manifested in nature. A correct reading of the book of the Bible* leads to a better reading of the book of nature and only reinforces faith in the creation. Calvin*, who admits a knowledge of God inherent in the human spirit, acknowledges a dual manifestation of God in creation and in the redemptive work.

d) Refutation of Natural Theology by Karl Barth. Barth violently rejects the possibility of a natural knowledge of God, as defined by Vatican* I (*DS* 1785) and he even calls the *analoga entis,* supported and illustrated by the Jesuit philosopher E. Przywara (*Analogia entis,* Munich, 1932) "the invention of the Antichrist" (*KD* I/1, preface). "The vitality of natural theology is the vitality of man as such" (*KD* I/1, 185). Thinking itself able to consider the Creator without considering the Redeemer at the same time, natural theology splits the idea of God and claims to know the true God by making an abstraction of the revelation. In fact, however, Barth contends that "one knows God through God and only through God" (*KD* I/1, 47). Not only is his position in open conflict with Catholic theology, but it also hardens the Reformers' doctrine: proof can be seen in his polemic against E. Brunner (who was trying to retain a Christian natural theology imposed by the existence of a revelation of God stemming from the creation) and in the manner with which he moved away from Bultmann* (who, by defining man as a "question of God," confirmed a necessary *precomprehension* of God).

e) Beyond the Polemic. Barth's polemic conception—natural theology understood as an attempt to subordinate the revelation to an authority foreign to its essence—in fact led to a better interpretation of Vatican I's teachings on the capacity of knowing God in the light of reason. The council* did not rule on any particular historic form of natural theology and did not claim that the natural knowledge of God must *precede* the knowledge of faith. It defended a *principle,* that of the rational moment of Christian faith, or more precisely its *transcendental* condition (see Bouillard 1957). In contemporary theology, the question of natural theology is no longer really a matter of denominational controversy, despite the brilliant exception of E. Jüngel and his (Barthian) defense and illustration of a theology "more natural" than any natural theology. Protestant theologians such as W. Pannenberg have rehabilitated a certain natural theology while Catholic theologians are the representatives of a kerygmatic theology. Natural theology is more used as a revelator between two types of theologies: theology marked by *manifestation,* which insists on the presence of God in all that is, and theology marked by *proclamation,* which denounces all attempts at idolatry* in the name of the word* of God.

● K. Barth (1919), *Der Römerbrief,* Munich (2nd Ed. 1922).
R. Bultmann (1933), "Das Problem der "naturlichen Theologie"," in *Glauben und Verstehen: Gesammelte Aufsätze* 1, Tübingen, 294–312.
E. Brunner (1934), *Natur und Gnade,* Zurich.
K. Barth (1940–42), *Die Kirchliche dogmatik* II/1 and 2, Zurich (*Dogmatik,* Genève, 1956–59).
W. Jaeger (1947), Introduction, *The Theology of the Early Greek Philosophers,* Oxford.
H. Bouillard (1957), *Karl Barth,* vol. 3, 63–139, Paris.
H. Brouillard (1960), "Le refus de la théologie naturelle dans la théologie protestante contemporaine," in coll., *L'existence de Dieu,* Tournai.
C. Geffré (1960), "Theologie Naturelle et révélation dans la connaissance du Dieu un," ibid.
K. H. Miskotte (1960), "Natürliche Religion und Theologie," *Die Religion in Geschichte und Gegenwart 3* 4, 1322–26.
G. Söhngen, W. Pannenberg (1962), "Natürliche Theologie," *Lexikon für Theologie und Kirche 2* 7, 811–17.
B. J. F. Lonergan (1968), "Natural Knowledge of God," in *A Second Collection,* Toronto (2nd Ed. 1996).
A.-M. Dubarle (1976), *La manifestation naturelle de Dieu d'après l'Écriture,* Paris.
Ch. Link (1976), *Die Welt als Gleichnis: Studien zum Problem der natürlichen Theologie,* Munich.
E. Jüngel (1980), *Entsprechungen,* Munich, 158–201.
W. Pannenberg (1988), *Systematische Theologie* 1, chap. 2, "Der Gottesgedanke und die Frage nach seiner Wahrheit", Göttingen.
W. Sparn (1991), "Natürliche Theologie," *Theologische Realenzykopadie* 24, 85–98.
O. Muck and G. Kraus (1998), "Natürliche Theologie," *Lexikon für Theologie und Kirche 3* 7, 673–81.

CLAUDE GEFFRÉ

See also **Barth, Karl; Existence of God, Proofs of; Knowledge of God; Reason; Revelation; Vatican I**

Naturalism

The term "naturalism" has a large spectrum of meanings and usages, from the fields of sciences to the figurative arts, and to literary production in general. It should be kept in mind, however, that it was originally coined by theologians. These theologians, in the atmosphere of disputes on the relationships between nature* and grace*, intended to qualify a general attitude with regards to natural and historical reality, the attitude that excludes "supernatural" realities and interventions, or does not take them into account (*see* e.g. the syllabus of Pius IX, §1–7, *DS* 2901–2907). The term's connotation is evidently negative: it is about errors that eventually must be refuted and in any case condemned; these mistakes are deemed to be caused on the one hand by an appreciation of human nature that is too optimistic, and on the other hand by the conviction that everything can be explained and founded by way of causes and natural forces.

In this light, it is only in a metaphoric way that one could speak of naturalism with regard to classical thought: indeed, if we measure them by referring to Christian theology*, any theoretical perspective and any practical behavior anterior (or exterior) to the Judeo-Christian action ("revelation*") could only be naturalist. And if, on the contrary, we speak of classical thought by following its own principles, we will realize that the connotations and spheres of application of the concept of nature vary from school to school, and especially since in many cases, nature is not at all the ultimate horizon of things, neither of speculation nor of action. In the Middle Ages, however, and more particularly in the 12th century, the reappropriation of Greek thought and the discovery of Arabic sciences by the Latin West posed the problem in terms that would be inherited by modernity. The problem that confronted all then was to understand how a model of the universe completely transparent to reason*, made up of a hierarchical series of causes (including the Primary Cause) that exerted their causality in a necessary mode and sufficed to explain the true nature of things, could reconcile itself with the idea of a world dependent of the free will of a God* who makes himself known by revealing himself. Likewise, the idea of man building his own ethics* in an autonomous fashion through the exercise of the intellect (that is to say following his own nature), and able to reach in this life a felicity in place of beatitude*, seemed irreconcilable with the main themes of Christian thought, which were the notions of sin* and grace. In the second half of the 13th century, however, a group of Christian intellectuals, professors at the faculty of arts at the University of Paris, proposed the simultaneous adoption of two models—a concord between faith* and science. Their thesis was that, in spite of appearances, the two models did not oppose each other, provided their principles and methods were rigorously distinguished: revelations and miracles* characterized faith and theology, reason and natural causes, science and philosophy*. This solution would be officially pushed back with the condemnation promulgated by the bishop of Paris, Etienne Tempier, on 7 March 1277 (Hissette 1977; Bianchi 1990; Libera 1991). Beyond the only theses concerned, it was the rebirth of a secular philosophy in a Christian milieu that the bishop and his theological counselors condemned: the emergence of a philosophy claiming its own autonomy from theology. Its proponents did not deny the existence of something superior to reason and natural causes; they even stated its possibility—but by giving up this field to theology and in recusing all interference of the truths of faith in a scientific and philosophical inquiry, they indeed posed a new challenge to theology.

The "naturalist" attitude was known for a long time under the name of "theory of the double truth*" (thus Tempier: "Indeed they say that certain things are true according to philosophy, which are not true according to Catholic faith, as if there were two truths." *Charularium Universitatis Parisiensis* I, 542). Also linked to the doctrines of the eternity of the world, of the unicity of human intellect and of the reign of necessity in moral and physical things, the "double truth," according to Renan and Mandonnet, would have been the characteristic of Averroism, often considered as the medieval beginning of all modern naturalism. A better knowledge of the texts and authors, however, showed that, if by Averroism one means a body of doctrines accepted by a compact and quite identifiable group of thinkers, then Averroism never existed (and many theses regarded as typical of Averroism do not come from Averroes). In the same way, no-one ever defended a

doctrine of double truth. Indeed, for all the medieval proponents of the independence of the philosophical, the truth of faith remained the absolute truth. It is true, though, that beyond doctrinal differences, these "philosophers" (Masters of Arts) jointly worked toward the intellectual construction of a physical and ethical world that would do without miracles or *post mortem* rewards and punishments*.

The condemnations of 1277 had deep and lasting effects on the intellectual history of Western Europe, but the model that continued to prevail was the one legitimizing a strict separation between philosophy and theology, between causes or natural laws and the miraculous intervention of an omnipotent God. From John of Jandun and Marsilius of Padua to Agustino Nifo and Pietro Pomponazzi, the philosophers would continue simultaneously to recognize the limits of a strictly rational and natural approach to the real, and to reject all foreign intervention in philosophy's principles and methods.

In the thoughts of the Parisian professors of the 13th century, a theory laden with consequences began to prevail: one could recognize the possibility of divine interventions (or even angelic, if not diabolic) infringing on the ordinary course of nature, but this did not exclude that the scientist would seek the possibility of driving everything back to natural causes, including events apparently extraordinary. This was done, for example, for visions in dreams and magical practices (Fioravanti 1966–67): Boethius of Dacia indeed reduced the firsts to being nothing but the imaginative transcription of physiological and pathological states, and Singer of Brabant stated that the *virtutes naturales* of elements and bodies (*see* soul*-heart-body) sufficed, in their diversity, to explain the second. In this way, philosophy and science always pushed back their limits, and pushed back the supernatural* toward a horizon always further away. This type of interpretation, present all through the 14th century, would multiply and strengthen near the end of the 15th and 16th centuries. Pomponazzi (*De incantationibus, de fato*) would explain the miracles, almost in the same way of Giordano Bruno, by already having recourse to exclusively psychophysical causes; he would place the highest human faculties in a system of natural forces, according to which it is useless to resort to external interventions to cause and explain each fact, not only physical, but also moral and historical, including the appearance of the great revealed religions, as well as the life and the character of their founder.

In the 16th century, this all-encompassing nature would progressively assume the characteristics of a subject that has an intrinsic force of development and self-organization. This type of natural materialism would survive Cartesian dualism, and would even inherit some of its characteristics by going from vitalism to mechanism: the matter and quantity of the movement then became the ultimate principles through which all diversity of events, not only physical but also psychological and ethical, could be renewed. An important part of the Enlightenment would support this program (La Mettrie, Holbach). From then on, the simple possibility that a being transcending nature could intervene in it could not be denied; and the belief in transcendent entities reduced itself to psychological processes that are individual or collective, completely natural and thus completely comprehensible from a rational point of view (Hume, *The Natural History of Religion*, 1757).

The varied naturalism of the 19th century (biological naturalism of Moleschott, evolutionary naturalism by Darwin) would maintain the general idea of nature as completely self-sufficient totality, fully intelligible by human reason (maybe in the terms of an indefinite progress). The totaling and metaphysical character of this idea of nature, however, would be criticized in the twentieth century in numerous trends of thought. The conviction would grow that man, the only being capable of a symbolic approach by means of language, was not reducible to his pure natural dimension. From naturalism, however, we keep the conviction that it is not acceptable, in the field of natural sciences*, to have recourse to first principles that transcend the course of this nature.

● Averroes, *Aristotelis Opera cum Averrois commentariis*, Venice, 1562–1574.

Boethius of Dacia, *Opera*, Ed. A. Otto, H. Roos, et al., *Corpus philosophorum danicorum medii aevi*, Copenhagen, 1969–.

A. Nifo, *De immortalitate animae libellum adversus Petrum Pomponatium Mantuanum*, Venice, 1518.

P. Pomponazzi, *Tractatus de immortalitate animae*, Ed. G. Morra, Bologna, 1954.

Singer of Brabant, *Quaestiones in tertium de anima, De anima intellectiva, De aeternitate mundi*, edited by B. Bazan, Louvain, 1972.

Singer of Brabant *Écrits de logique, de morale et de physique*, edited by B. Bazan, Louvain, 1974.

◆ E. Renan (1852), *Averroès et l'averroïsme: Essai historique* (*OC*, vol. 3, Paris, 1949).

P. Mandonnet (1911–18), *Siger de Brabant et l'averroïsme latin au XIIIe siècle*, 2 vol., Louvain.

F. van Steenberghen (1931–42), *Siger de Brabant d'après ses œuvres inédites*, 2 vol., Louvain.

É. Gilson (1932), "Le Moyen Age et le naturalisme antique," *AHDL* 7, 5–37 (*Études médiévales*, Paris, 1986, 19–52).

B. Nardi (1945), *Sigieri di Brabante nel pensiero del Rinascimento italiano*, Rome.

É. Gilson (1955), "Boèce de Dacie et la double vérité," *AHDL* 22, 81–99 (*Études médiévales*, 147–66); (1961), "Autour de Pomponazzi: Problématique de l'immortalité de l'âme en Italie au début du XVIe siècle," *AHDL* 28, 163–278 (*Humanisme et Renaissance*, Paris, 1986, 133–250).

G. Fioravanti (1966–67), "La 'scientia sompnialis' di Boezio di Dacia," *Atti della Accad. delle Scienze di Torino, Classe delle scienze morali, storiche e filolog.* 101, 329–69.

R. Hissette (1977), *Enquête sur les 219 articles condamnés à Paris le 7 mars 1277*, Louvain and Paris.

L. Bianchi (1990), *Il vescovo e i filosofi: La condanna parigina del 1277 e l'evoluzione dell' aristotelismo scolastico*, Bergamo.

A. de Libera (1991), *Penser au Moyen Age*, Paris.

R. Imbach (1997), *Siger de Brabant, profession: philosophe*, Paris.

GIANFRANCO FIORAVANTI

See also **Intellectualism; Sciences of Nature; Paganism; Philosophy; Revelation; Supernatural**

Nature

The concept of nature was imposed on Christian theology* from without. It does not correspond to any Hebrew term. In the Old Testament it appears only in the deuterocanonical books (Wis 7:20, 13:1, and 19:18), while in the New Testament it signifies merely the being* or normal order of things according to their origin, type, and definition (Jas 3:7). The pagans, for example, naturally follow the Law* (Rom 2:14 and 2:27) to which the Jews are bound by their birth (Gal 2:15). In Christianity, unlike gnosticism*, nature implies no negative or positive judgment. It merely serves to denote the totality of beings whom Christ* has come to save. Mankind is, of course, destined to participate in another nature, the divine nature (2 Pt 1:4), but God in his freedom is all-powerful over created nature; he can even intervene in it—for example to graft the branch of the pagans "against nature" onto the trunk of the Jewish nation (Rom 11:21–24). Moreover, the contradiction between the animate body (see soul*-heart-body) and the Holy* Spirit must finally be resolved (1 Cor 15:44), and the natural world become transparent to the Kingdom* of God (Mk 4:30–32 and 13:28–29).

The concept of nature was to play a considerable role in the patristic era, starting from the basis of a neutral definition: "Nature is nothing other than what one considers a thing to be in its kind" (Augustine, *De moribus ecclesiae,* 2, 2; PL 32, 134 b). Trinitarian and christological thought implied a distinction between the concepts of nature and person*, while the Pelagian controversy involved a confrontation between nature and grace*.

a) Nature and Person. God is unique in his nature, and the divine persons share in this same essence. According to the Cappadocians, *phusis* was equivalent to *ousia,* and the term "consubstantial*" (Nicaea* I) could be replaced by "connatural" (Basil*, *Against Eunomius* II, 580 b). It was then possible to say that God was "one nature in three hypostases" (Cyril of Alexandria, *Contra Julianum* VIII; PG 76, 904 C). In Christology*, the concept of nature gave rise above all to numerous misunderstandings. Athanasius* thought it appropriate to place the emphasis on the unity of God, who made himself flesh "in order to save men and to do them good, so that, by participating in humankind, he might enable it to participate in the divine and spiritual nature" (*Life of Anthony* 74, 4; SC 400, 324). Apollinarius spoke of Christ as an incarnation of the divine nature: "A single nature of God the incarnate Word*" (monophysitism*). For the Antiochenes, on the other hand, two hypostases (human and divine) were united in Christ to form his person* *(prosopon).* Cyril, who took up Apollinarius's formula (which he believed to be Athanasius's) and rejected what seemed to him to be a division of God, spoke of a single hypostasis and a single nature. At this time the terms had no strict technical sense. The definition of Chalcedon*, in clarifying Christology*, was to impose a rigorous definition of the concept of nature: Christ was "a single person" in which were united "two natures," divine and human.

b) Nature and Grace. The opposition between nature and grace is based on these Trinitarian and christological considerations: Christ is the Son of God by nature, while man is so by adoption (Cyril of Alexandria, *Thesaurus* XII, 189 AB). Hence, so Pelagius considered, it was necessary to affirm the goodness of human nature, its liberty*, and its power to do good* (*De natura,* 604;

see Pelagianism*) in order to give homage to the Creator. For Augustine*, on the other hand, a doctrine that considered man to be capable of good on his own accord rendered Christ's incarnation* and sacrifice* superfluous: "Man's nature was originally created without sin* and without any vice; but man's present nature, by which everyone is descended from Adam*, is already in need of the physician, for it is not in good health [*sana*]" (*De natura et gratia,* PL 44, 249; BAug 21, 248). Inasmuch as it was created, all nature was good; and consequently all evil* derived from man and was but a distortion of the good. The corruption of nature had two aspects: it was both the automatic consequence of sin and the result of divine punishment. Having sinned of his free will, man was punished by way of his own sin, and lost his power of self-mastery. So was this corruption total? Augustine's initial response is unsystematic: in the *De Natura et Gratia* he wavers between the notions of man's subservience to bad habits, a weakening of free will, and its complete disappearance. Subsequently, in his *De Correptione et Gratia,* he is inclined to defend the idea of a radical loss of liberty.

These extreme developments were not all accepted by Catholic tradition*, though the concept of "tainted nature" was taken up by the Council of Orange in 529 (CChr.SL 148 A, 55; *DS* 174), and again by the Council of Trent* (5, 239; *DS* 174). According to Anselm*, the fall of the devil resulted from his voluntary abandonment of righteous will. Paradoxically, if God did not give him the gift of perseverance, it was because he did not accept it (*The Fall of the Devil,* or *De Casu Diaboli,* ch. 3). In the 12th century, however, theology was faced with the rediscovery of the sciences* of nature (School of Chartres*; Speer 1995); and in the 13th century it encountered the Aristotelian concept of nature: a nature that formed the object of physics, that had its own autonomy and stability, and in which theology could perceive only an unchanging capacity for the receipt of grace. From this point, the opposition between nature and grace grew stronger.

For Scholasticism*, the nature created by God obeyed the laws conferred upon it by its creator (Bonaventure, II *Sent.* d. 34, a. 1, q. 3, ad 4 prop. neg.). To act against these laws would be to contravene his very decision. There was thus an autonomy in the natural order.

Then divine omnipotence* promptly appeared as another focus, external to the previous one, and theology was to hesitate between the extremes of naturalism* and the absolute exaltation of omnipotence (nominalism*). Emphasized by Luther* (*Heidelberg Dispute,* 1518, *WA* 1, 350–74), the corruption of nature was played down on the Catholic side by Robert Bellarmine* (*De Controversis Christianae Fidei, De Gra-*

tia Primi Hominis 5, 12): "The corruption of nature does not result from the lack of a natural gift, nor from the attainment of an evil state, but from the simple absence of the supernatural gift" (*see* Bañezianism*-Molinism-Baianism). The debate remains open between Catholics and Protestants, Catholic thinking being characterized by the harmony between nature and grace, while the radical corruption of nature remains an essential element of Protestant dogmatics*.

Finally, one might ask whether the concept of nature, as applied to mankind, retains its clarity and relevance, when man is a transcendent being not confined within limits assigned *a priori* (Rahner 1954).

● Augustine, *De natura et gratia* (BAug 21).
Pelagius, *De natura* (PL 48, 598–606).

◆ R. Arnou (1933), "Unité numérique et unité de n. chez les Pères, après le concile de Nicée," *Gr.* 14, 269–72.
K. Rahner (1954), "Über das Verhältnis von Natur und Gnade," *Schr. zur Th.* 1, 323–45.
S. Otto (1960), Natura *und* Dispositio*: Untersuchung zum Naturbegriff und zur Denkform Tertullians,* Munich.
F.-J. Thonnard (1965), "La notion de *natura* chez saint Augustin. Ses progrès dans la polémique antipélagienne," *REAug* 11, 239–65.
F.-J. Thonnard (1966), "Les deux états de la n. humaine, 'intègre' puis 'corrompue,' et la grâce du Christ," *in* Augustin, *La grâce*, BAug 21, 614–22.
H. Köster (1973), "Phusis," *ThWNT* 9, 246–71.
A. Speer (1995), *Die entdeckte Natur: Untersuchungen zu Begründungsversuchen einer* Scientia naturalis *im 12. Jahrhundert,* Leyden.

OLIVIER BOULNOIS

See also **Being; Grace; Naturalism; Supernatural**

Negative Theology

I. Apophaticism and Neoplatonism

1. Definition of Negation (apophasis, aphairesis)

The Greek term *aphairesis* denotes the motion of discarding *(remotio),* cutting off, or taking away something (Plato, *Critias* 46 *c*). It is the opposite of *prosthesis,* the action of placing (Plutarch, *Lycurgus* 13). It is a mathematical term: in the *Metaphysics* A2, 982, a. 28 Aristotle opposes *aphairesis* to *prosthesis* as "subtraction" is to "addition." It is also a term in logic: in Aristotles's *Posterior Analytics* (I, 18, 7) *ex aphaireseôs* signifies "by abstraction," and this sense was taken up by numerous Latin translations that render *aphairesis* by *abstractio. Aphairesis* is opposed to *thesis* as negation is to affirmation, but it is also distinguished from *apophasis* (which equally signifies negation) inasmuch as *aphairesis* denotes a movement beyond.

Latin translators rendered *aphairesis,* according to context, either by the concrete sense of "cutting off" or "suppression" *(ablatio),* or by the sense of abstraction *(abstractio)* or negation *(negatio).* Thomas* Aquinas noted the two meanings of *aphairesis,* and translated it by *remotio,* mostly in his earliest works, and thereafter by *negatio.*

1) For Aristotle the aphaeretic method was a process of separation or subtraction that led to the grasping *(noèsis)* of an intelligible form or an essence. This method of separation or cutting off is abstraction. It proceeds from the complex to the simple and from the visible to the invisible.

2) This method is represented in the work of other Middle Platonic writers such as Alcinous, who in his *Didaskalikos* (ch. 12) distinguishes four ways by which the human mind may raise itself to God*: affirmation, analogy*, transcendence, and negation.

2. Plato's Parmenides *and its Neoplatonic Commentaries*

a) The key text for any study of negative* theology is the first hypothesis of the *Parmenides* ("The One is one"), in which after asserting that "the One in no way partakes of being*, and that it does not even have enough being to be one, since immediately it would be and would partake of being" (141 *e*), Parmenides reaches this formidable assertion: "It appears indeed, on the contrary, both that the One is not one, and that the One is not" (141 *e*)—which is a negation of the hypothesis itself. The conclusion of the first hypothesis is thus the unknowable and ineffable nature of the One: "Therefore it has no name*; of it there is neither a definition, nor knowledge, nor sensation, nor opinion" (*Parm.* 142 *a*).

b) This apophaticism recurs in the Neoplatonic commentaries on the *Parmenides*, both the anonymous commentary whose author has been identified as Porphyry by P. Hadot (*Porphyre et Marius Victorinus*, Paris, 1968), and that by Proclus. It is equally to be found in the apophatic theology of Pseudo-Dionysius*.

c) For Plotinus, as for Plato, the first principle lies beyond *ousia*. Unlike Plato, however, Plotinus asks what chance we have of knowing this transcendent principle, the One, which is neither being nor thought. Only the One, the first hypostasis, is simple, whereas in the second hypostasis, the intellect, there is a duality of being and thought. It is therefore not possible to conceive of the One, but only to have a non-intellectual apprehension of it, which is a kind of mystical* experience. This experience is described in the *Enneads* in terms borrowed from the love-madness of Plato's *Phaedra* and *Symposium*. "The Plotinian mystical experience is a kind of oscillation between the intellectual intuition of the thought which conceives itself, and the amorous ecstasy of the thought which loses itself in its principle." (Hadot, *EU*, vol. 22, p. 497). Mystical experience and negative theology remain distinct, however: "It is mystical experience which is the basis of rational theology, not the reverse" (ibid.).

d) It is in the work of Damascius (c. 458–533) that the negative method becomes most radical. In his treatise *On the First Principles,* he expresses perfectly the paradox of a first principle of everything that cannot be outside everything (since then it would not be the principle), yet which must at the same time transcend everything (if it is really the first principle). These difficulties lead to a radical apophaticism: "We demonstrate our ignorance and our incapacity to speak of it [*aphasia*].... Our ignorance regarding it is total, and we know it neither as knowable or as unknowable" (*see* J. Combès's preface to his edition of the treatise *On the First Principles*, v. 1, CUFr, Paris, 1986).

II. Negative Theology and Mystical Theology

1. Apophatic Theology

a) Philo of Alexandria and the First Church Fathers. Philo was the originator of a whole school of thought concerning the incomprehensibility of the divine essence (*ousia*): "The greatest good is to understand that God, according to his essence [*kata to einai*], is incomprehensible [*akatalèptos*]" (*Poster.* 15).

The assertion that knowledge* of the divine essence is beyond the natural powers of human beings is a commonplace of the earliest Christian theologians (Justin, *Dialogue* 127, 2; Clement of Alexandria, *Strom.* II, 2; Irenaeus* of Lyons, *Adv. Haer.* IV, 20, 5; Origen, *Against Celsus* VII, 42).

b) Eunomian crisis and Its Refutation by the Cappadocians. It was, however, in response to the heresy of Eunomius, who identified the divine essence with the nature of the unbegotten (*agennètos*) and thereby denied incomprehensibility, that a Christian negative theology was really developed by the Cappadocians and John Chrysostom*. For Eunomius, the concept of the unbegotten exactly (*akribôs*) expressed the divine essence, so that the latter no longer presented any mystery*, and we knew God as he knew himself: "God knows no more of his being than do we; his being is no clearer to him than to us" (Socrates, *Hist. eccl.* IV, 7).

Basil* of Caesarea and Gregory* of Nyssa, in their respective treatises *Against Eunomius,* then demonstrated that there was no concept that exactly expressed the divine essence, since it remained unknowable, and attempted to define the properties and relations of the divine persons*. John Chrysostom, meanwhile, took up the arguments of the Cappadocians in two series of homilies against the Eunomians, delivered at Antioch in 386–87 and at Constantinople after 397, which he collected into his *Treatise on the Incomprehensibility of God.* "God's essence is incomprehensible to any creature" (IV, 6). This was as true for natural reason* as for the Bible*: the psalmist "is seized with vertigo before the infinite and yawning ocean of God's wisdom*" (Ps 138:6); Moses testifies that none see God and live (Ex 33:20); and Paul says that God's judgments are unsearchable and his ways "inscrutable" (Rom 11:33; *see also* Is 53:8).

So the vocabulary of negative theology became established. It employs New Testament terms such as invisible (*aoratos*), unutterable (*arrètos*), indescribable (*anekdiègètos*), unfathomable (*anereunètos*) and inaccessible (*aprositos*). Others come from Philo: inconceivable (*aperinoètos*), impossible to delimit (*aperigraptos*), to represent (*askhèmatistos*) or to contemplate (*atheatos*). Finally the term *aphatos*, ineffable, comes from Neoplatonism. This vocabulary is found in the Byzantine liturgy* of St John Chrysostom and St Basil, in Byzantine spiritual texts, and in the works of Maximus* the Confessor and Symeon the New Theologian.

2. Affirmative and Negative Theology According to Dionysius the Pseudo-Areopagite.

Dionysius was the first, in his *Mystical Theology*, to systematize the relationship between affirmative or cataphatic theology and negative or apophatic theology, and then to propose a rigorous theory of negation.

a) Status of Negation. Negation is defined from three points of view:

1) As the non-contradiction of affirmations and negations—there is no contradiction between negation and affirmation. This would be the case were one to restrict oneself to the realm of the existents, but it is not the case when dealing with the transcendent Cause.

2) As a surpassing of all privation. Negation is not practiced by means of privation *(kata sterèsin)* but, as is the case when speaking of the Darkness, by means of transcendence or superiority *(kath' huperokhèn)*. The Darkness is another negative metaphor for the transcendence of the inaccessible light.

   To say that negation *(aphairesis)* is not a privation *(sterèsis)* is first of all to assert that there is no privation in the Cause, which is "above privations," and thereby to assert some positivity of negation by transcendence *(huperokhikè aphairesis)*, which increases the negation. This idea would be developed later by medieval writers such as Thomas Aquinas, for whom negation, when it concerned God, was a negation of privation itself.

3) As being beyond all negation and all position. The surpassing of privation is reinforced by a surpassing of negation and position. Here Dionysius uses the term *aphairesis* in place of *apophasis*, in the opposition *aphairesis–thesis*.

b) Dual Limit of Negation. Negative theology is thus defined by a dual transcendence of the Cause, which marks its dual (lower and upper) limit.

1) The negation of privation. On the one hand, negative theology is not a negation by privation, but by transcendence; on the other hand, it is itself transcended by the Cause, which is beyond negation and position. "We affirm nothing," says Dionysius, "and deny nothing, for the one Cause is beyond all affirmation, and transcendence beyond all negation" (MT V, 1048 B). There is thus a reinforcement of negation and of transcendence: the fact of affirming something is denied, and the fact of denying something is denied. There is a progression from "neither...nor..." to "nothing."

2) The beyond of negation. What does this "nothing" mean? This is the final question of negative theology, and becomes apparent in its very transcendence. This nothing is the opposite of the beyond. It is the same to say "the Cause is beyond negation and position" as to say "we affirm nothing and deny nothing." The "nothing" means that we cannot affirm or deny the transcendent Cause as if it were a "something," nor speak of That which is above being *(huperousios)* as if it were a being *(on)*. The absolute nature of Dionysius's final assertion—"we affirm or deny nothing"—sets out the absolute transcendence of the Cause without however invalidating negative theology. God is beyond everything, but this does not imply the destruction of language. And insofar as it is still a theo-logy, negative theology is able to avoid the two pitfalls of the reduction of God to an idolatrous representation (*see* Marion 1977) and the collapse of any possibility of a discourse on God.

Thomas Aquinas showed in his critique of Maimonides that radical apophaticism destroys the very possibility of a language about God. Admittedly God remains unknown in his essence, inasmuch as he is superessential, but he cannot be totally unknown. And while "idolatry*" reduces God to the representation of a something, of a this or that, radical apophaticism destroys negative theology itself as a possible discourse on God (*see* A. Osorio-Osorio, "Maïmonides: El lenguaje de la teología negativa sobre el conocimiento de Dios," *Sprache und Erkenntnis im Mittelalter,* MM 1981; A. Wohlman, "Théologie négative et analogie," in his *Thomas d'Aquin et Maïmonide: Un dialogue exemplaire,* Paris, 1988).

c) Negation and Eminence. God is thus named, in a naming according to his eminence, as "He who is beyond all essence and knowledge," "He who is beyond everything," "He who surpasses everything," "He who is totally unknown," "He who transcends vision and knowledge," "the Ineffable," "the Cause of everything who is above everything," and "the transcendence of Him who is absolutely detached from everything and who is beyond everything."

A dual series of adjectives prefixed by *huper-* and privative *alpha* is used to describe him. On the one hand, he is beyond Being, the Good*, and the Divine *(huperousios, huperagathos, hupertheos)*, super-luminous *(huperphaès)* and super-unknowable *(huperagnôstos)*. On the other hand, he is invisible *(aoratos, atheatos)*, impalpable *(anaphès)*, ineffable *(arrètos)*, lacking intellect *(anous)*, speech *(alogos)*, life *(azôos)*, and substance *(anousios)*, and inexpressible *(aphthegtos)*. God may be referred to as Silence *(sigè)*, Tranquility *(hè-sukhia)*, or Ineffability *(aphthegsia)*. He eludes all sight and all contact, as he does all knowledge. This is why the mystic, in order to know him, must carry out a "binding" of all the operations of the senses and the intelligence: the suspension of all knowledge or the absence of all intellectual activity *(anenergèsia)*, the closing of the mouth *(aphthegsia)* and of the eyes *(ablèpsia)*, the absence of vision and knowledge *(agnôsia)*. So Moses, in penetrating the truly mystical cloud of unknowing, "shuts his eyes to all the apprehensions of knowledge and frees himself from the spectacle and the spectators."

III. Negative Theology and Learned Ignorance

1. Thomas Aquinas

Dionysius's doctrine of negative theology meets with "prudent correction" (V. Lossky) in the work of Thomas Aquinas, for whom God is not beyond being, but "being itself subsisting," *ipsum esse subsistens,* who confers upon *esse* itself the nature of the unnameable. We know that God is, the *an sit,* but not what he is, the *quid est.*

Thomas locates himself unambiguously within the Dionysian tradition when he says that we join with God, not merely as with an unknown, but actually inasmuch as he is unknown, *tanquam ignotum* or *quasi ignotum.* "The peak of our knowledge in this life, as Dionysius says in his work *De mystica Theologia,* is that 'we are joined with God as with an unknown'; this results from our knowing of him what he is not, his essence remaining absolutely hidden from us *[quid vero sit penitus manet ignotum].* Hence, to emphasize the ignorance of this sublime knowledge, it is said of Moses that he 'approached the obscurity in which God dwells' *[quod accessit ad caliginem in qua est Deus]*" *(CG,* 1. III, c. 49; see also *In Boethium de Trinitate,* q. 1, a. 2, ad 1 and *ST* Ia, q. 12, a. 13, ad 1: *In hac vita non cognoscamus de Deo quid est, et sic ei quasi ignoto coniungimus).* It is nonetheless possible to speak of Thomas's God: the *via eminentia,* endowed by Thomas with a positivity that it lacked in the work of Dionysius, enables him to develop a theo-logy.

2. Meister Eckhart

Following Dionysius the Pseudo-Areopagite, Meister Eckhart *(see* V. Lossky, *Théologie négative et connaissance de Dieu chez Maître Eckhart,* Paris, 1960, and E. Zum Brunn and Alain de Libera, *Métaphysique du Verbe et Théologie négative,* Paris, 1984) also maintains that the name* of God is at once the *nomen innominabile* and the *nomen omninominabile.* The op-position between the *poluônumon* and the *anônumon* corresponds to the two theologies, affirmative and negative, and the latter is more perfect than the former because it focuses on the ineffable nature. Eckhart also draws on Thomas Aquinas, however: the *esse innomi-nabile* is an *esse absconditum;* and in his commentary on *Cum quaeris nomen meum, quod est mirabile,* Eckhart is also conscious of how Thomas had treated it. With the *Parisian Questions,* however, Eckhart commits himself to the Dionysian view of God beyond being: defining the *esse* as the *esse* of created beings, he obliges himself to state that God, being pure intellect, is *non ens* or *non esse.* So the theologian follows an intellectual mode of ascent that forces him to leave behind created things in order to try to reach God in himself, in his "unity" *(einigheit)* or his "solitude" *(wüestunge),* two terms brought together in the German Sermon 12. In German Sermon 9, Eckhart goes as far as to deny the attribution of pure being to God: "I would be saying something equally unjust if I called God an essence as if I were to call the sun pale or black. God is neither one thing nor another." Later however, he adds: "By saying that God is not a being and that he is superior to being, I have not denied him being: on the contrary, I have exalted being in God."

In a third period, Eckhart was to return to a solemn declaration of the equivalence of being and God: *esse est Deus.* This was no rejection of negative theology, however, since being remains mysterious and hidden: *deus sub ratione esse et essentiae est quasi dormiens et latens absconditus in se ipso (Exp. in Io.,* C., f. 122*b).*

3. Nicholas of Cusa

Nicholas of Cusa set out his negative theology in the *De Docta Ignorantia* (1440), an expression he borrowed from Augustine. The crux of this doctrine is the "coincidence of opposites." Human beings are part of the world of duality; in order to raise themselves to God, however, they must attain the place where opposites are absorbed or reconciled into unity, or where they coincide in God. The divine names imposed by reason are contrasted with their opposites—for example unity and plurality, identity and otherness—but these opposites coincide in God, and it is through this coincidence that they befit God (§25). This is why "the theology of negation is so necessary... for the theology of affirmation, that without it God would not be worshipped as the infinite* God, but rather as a creature.... Sacred ignorance has taught us that God is ineffable.... We speak of God more truly through removal and negation, as the great Dionysius [does]" (Chap. 26).

4. Angelus Silesius

Silesius (1624–77) comes at the end of the great Rhineland*-Flemish mystical tradition of Tauler, Eckhart, Ruusbroec and Henry Suso, all of whom in their own way lie within the apophatic current originating with Dionysius. In the *Cherubinischer Wandersmann*, he goes even further than them in the expression of negativity, and even talks of superdeity as a way of expressing the bare and indefinable nature of the deity*: "What is said of God is not yet enough for me: Superdeity is my life and my light." One must take oneself beyond the self and even beyond God: "Whither should I strive? Even into a desert, beyond God himself"; and "If God did not wish to take me beyond God, I would know how to force him by pure love*." God is expressed by silence: "If you wish to express the being of eternity*, you must first abjure all speech."

5. Mystical Theology and Negative Theology in the Twentieth Century: V. Lossky

The apophatic current that originated with Dionysius, enriched by the Carmelite experience of the "dark night," continued up until the 17th century with the work of Cardinal de Bérulle*. However, while the Jesuits continued to write treatises on mystical theology in the 17th century, interest in these issues waned in the 18th century—there was presumably a conflict between mysticism and the Enlightenment, which aimed to dispel mystery. It wasn't until the 20th century, and the renewal of interest in mysticism within both Catholicism* and Orthodoxy*, that we could pick up the thread of the *via negativa* intrinsic to all mystical theology.

Two books illustrate this renewal: A. Stolz O.S.B., *Théologie de la mystique*, Chèvetogne, 1947, and V. Lossky, *Théologie mystique de l'Église d'Orient*, Paris, 1944. The latter situates himself explicitly within the Dionysian tradition*, and regards apophatic theology as inseparable from the mystical theology of the Eastern Church*. In his conclusion—which he was to repeat in a lecture on the Trinity* and apophasis—he shows that the Trinity, and in particular the person of the Holy* Spirit, can only be understood in terms of the apophatic approach: "The apophaticism characteristic of the Eastern Church's mystical theology ultimately appears to us as bearing witness to the plenitude of the Holy Spirit, a person who remains unknown, for all that he fills all things and guides them towards their final accomplishment." (245)

IV. The Inexpressible and Silence

Wittgenstein's *Tractatus Logico-philosophicus* presents issues analogous to those set out by Damascius. The opposition is no longer between the whole and the principle, but between language, or the world*, and its meaning: "That which is expressed in language, we can only express by language" (4. 121). Certainly, everything is not expressible; and to that which can be expressed logically, Wittgenstein opposes an inexpressible that cannot be uttered, but which can be shown. Propositions "show" the logical form of reality; what is shown, however, is not of the order of logic, but of the "mystical": "The mystical *(das Mystische)* is not 'how the world is,' but 'the fact that it is'" (6. 44). Mystical experience cannot say to itself, "Whereof one cannot speak, thereof one must be silent" (7). Not only is the meaning of the utterable unutterable, but the end of language, as of all negative theology, is silence.

● Vl. Lossky (1930), "La théologie négative dans la doctrine de Pseudo-Denys l'Aréopagite," *AHDL* 5, 204–221.

Vl. Lossky (1944), *Essai sur la théologie mystique de l'Église d'Orient*, Paris.

A.J. Festugière (1954), *La Révélation d'Hermès Trismégiste* vol. IV: *Le Dieu inconnu et la Gnose*, ch. 4, §6: "La voie de négation", Paris.

J.W. Douglass (1963), "The Negative Theology of Dionysius the Areopagite", *DR* 81, 115–24.

H.-J. Krämer (1967), *Der Ursprung der Geistmetaphysik*, Amsterdam.

J. Whittaker (1969), "Neopythagoreanism and Negative Theology", *SO* XLIV, 109–125.

H. Theill-Wunder (1970), *Die archaische Verborgenheit: Die philosophischen Wurzeln der negativen Theologie*, Munich.

J. Hochstaffl (1976), *Negative Theologie: Ein Versuch zur Vermittlung des patristischen Begriffs*, Munich.

M.J. Krahe (1976), "Von der Wesenheit negativer Theologie," thesis, University of Munich.

J.-L. Marion (1977), *L'idole et la distance*, 183–250, Paris.

P. Hadot (1981), *Exercices spirituels et philosophie antique*, ch. 8, 185–93: "Apophatisme et théologie négative," Paris.

É. des Places (1982), "La théologie négative du Pseudo-Denys: Ses antécédents platoniciens et son influence au seuil du Moyen Age", StPatr 17, 81–92.

C. Guérard (1984), "La théologie négative dans l'apophatisme grec," *RSPhTh* 68, 183–200.

H.U. von Balthasar (1985), *Theologik* II, *Wahrheit Gottes* 80–113.

M. Corbin (1985), "Négation et transcendance dans l'œuvre de Denys," *RSPhTh* 69, 41–76.

D. Carabine (1988), "Apophasis in East and West," *RThAM* 55, 5–29.

H.D. Saffrey (1990), "Connaissance et inconnaissance de Dieu: Porphyre et la théosophie de Tübingen", in *Recherches sur le néoplatonisme après Plotin*, Paris.

M.P. Begzos (1996), "Apophaticism in the Theology of the Eastern Church: The Modern Critical Function of a Traditional Theory," *GOTR* 41, 327–57.

YSABEL DE ANDIA

See also **Dionysius the Pseudo-Areopagite; Eternity of God; Jealousy, Divine; Justice, Divine; Knowledge, Divine; Mysticism; Omnipotence, Divine; Omnipresence, Divine; Simplicity, Divine.**

Neoplatonism

For a broad understanding of the nature of Plato's contribution to the development of Christian theology from the fourth century onwards (and chiefly in the West), it is necessary to consider the reasons for which Christian thought has needed in successive waves to turn for its intellectual base to what since the 18th century has been known as Neoplatonism. This was an amalgam of elements of Stoic, Aristotelian, and Pythagorean thought, and the development by Plotinus (A.D. 205–270/1) of Plato's "middle period" metaphysics. It dominated the philosophical thinking of the ancient Mediterranean world from the middle of the third century to the closing of the pagan schools by Justinian in A.D. 529.

1. Sources and Documents

a)   The most important early Neoplatonist document, synthesizing earlier Stoic, Aristotelian, and Pythagorean traditions but based on a development of Plato's metaphysics, is the *Enneads* of Plotinus, edited by Porphyry (232/3–c. 305), his disciple and biographer, only after his death. The *Enneads,* six groups of nine essays (54 developed from an earlier arrangement into 48) originally circulated for discussion among the pupils at his fashionable classes in Rome, are written in a confusing mixture of dialectic, allegory, analysis, and exegesis. They do not constitute a systematic metaphysics, but lean toward the view that all modes of being derive from a single immaterial and impersonal force, the 'One' of Plato's *Parmenides* and the 'Good' of the *Republic,* at once the source of all being and all values. All existence is related to this impersonal force by its degree of Oneness, which is higher in beings that transcend the temporal and the spatial.

The degrees of being envisaged by Plotinus were often later to be represented by a series of concentric circles denoting relative distance from the centre, the absolutely One. The descending degrees of reality move through pure mind *(nous),* within which are Plato's forms, the world soul *(psyché),* which creates time and space, and nature *(physis),* which projects the physical world. These sorts of existence are marked by increasing individuation and diminishing unity. Uninformed and unintelligible matter is the outermost circumference or boundary of all existence. Human beings possess all three major principles of reality and can attain unity within themselves in ecstasy, and even momentary identification with the One.

Plotinus had joined the Persian expedition of Gordian III in A.D. 242, and spent two years studying Persian and Indian philosophy in the East before the assassination of Gordian by his troops forced him to take refuge at Antioch, from where he moved to Rome in 245. It is to his study of oriental religion and philosophy that we owe the incorporation into his own thought of elements of the oriental doctrine of emanation against which Christian theology developed the Hebrew doctrine of creation* *ex nihilo.*

Plotinus himself had studied under Ammonius Saccas in Alexandria, and alongside his own mystical doctrine there entered into the Neoplatonist amalgam elements of the oriental modes of worship that had been easily accessible in the Alexandria of Plotinus's youth, as well as Judaic and Christian thinking, which had originated chiefly in Philo's attempts to present christianized Judaism, with its transcendent monotheistic Hebrew divinity, in acceptably Hellenistic attire to Greek-speaking pagans and the Jewish diaspora. In fourth century Neoplatonism there were therefore logically incompatible elements drawn from oriental and Jewish sources, to which were added some elements from early gnosticism (*see* gnosis*) as well as the Platonic mysticism of Plotinus.

Neoplatonism in the fourth century was neither a religion nor a coherent philosophy. Harnack is reduced to describing it as a "mood," characterized by "the instinctive certainty that there is a supreme good, lying beyond empirical experience," which is not a purely intellectual good (article "Neoplatonism" in the classic 11th edition of the *Encyclopaedia Britannica,* 1911). To this "emotional dream" which "treated the old world of fable as the reflection of a higher reality" can be ascribed the realization that "man cannot live by knowledge alone," and it continues to nurture the type of dedication that, effecting a renunciation of the world, "is never able to form a clear conception of the object of its own aspiration."

b)   This attitude and the values it sustained were transmitted to the Middle Ages not only by Augustine, who was heavily dependent on Plotinus; not only by

Origen*, and Gregory* of Nyssa, and by the Chalcidius commentary on the *Timaeus* by which Plato was himself chiefly remembered; but also in two collections of the greatest importance in later centuries, giving high Christian authority to Neoplatonist doctrines and attitudes, the *Corpus hermeticum* and the *Corpus Dionysiacum.*

The *Corpus hermeticum* is a series of treatises written in Greek probably in the second and third centuries by non-Christians living in Egypt, but in the 15th century Italian Renaissance understood as a single work and called after the first treatise, the *Poimandres (Pimander).* Its authorship was ascribed to Hermes (Mercury) Trismegistus, believed to have received it as an original divine revelation, in content homogeneous with the first five books of the Old Testament, which it was often believed to have ante-dated. Its content was thought to have been handed down through Orpheus, Aglaophemus, Pythagoras, and Philolaus (the list appears frequently and is often modified) to Plato, who was considered to have visited Egypt, where he is thought to have come into contact with the Mosaic tradition. As a result its content was thought necessarily to accord with the teaching of the Judeo-Christian revelation, since it ultimately derived from the same source.

The *Corpus Dionysiacum,* dating from the late-fifth or early-sixth century, consists of the *Celestial Hierarchy,* the *Ecclesiastical Hierarchy, The Divine Names,* the *Mystical Theology,* and ten letters all ascribed during the whole of the Middle Ages to Dionysius, Saint Paul's first convert at Athens (Acts 17:33–34), but now ascribed to an otherwise anonymous author referred to as Dionysius the Pseudo-Areopagite. This Dionysius, amalgamated by Gregory of Tours (c. 538–94) with the Dionysius sent to evangelize the Gauls, claimed to have known the apostles, to have seen the darkening of the sun at the death of Jesus, and to have been present at the dormition of the mother of Jesus. For the Renaissance, therefore, this corpus, too, linked Neoplatonism with Christianity, particularly in its teaching on the celestial and terrestrial hierarchies and on its division of the spiritual life into the three sequential categories of initiation/purgation, illumination, and perfection. For the French it had the added advantage of providing apostolic tradition and continuity for the French church, which could now trace its origins back to Saint Paul, whose doctrinal authority was thought equal to that of Saint Peter, the first bishop of Rome, giving the Gallican church parity of standing with the church of Rome.

2. Transmission and Influence

While the influence of Neoplatonism on Christian theological thinking is pervasive, enduring, and complex, there are clearly identifiable historical waves of specific recourse by Christian thinkers to Neoplatonism as contained in one or other of the three main sources.

a) Augustine's dependence on Plotinus in his anti-Manichaean* polemic, and his subsequent position for at least a millennium and a half as the father of Western theology, ensured that Plotinian Neoplatonism should provide the Christian theology of creation with its basic structure, placing the human body and soul between the angelic and the purely material creations. The image of concentric circles of being was called on implicitly or explicitly to oppose the different forms of cosmic dualism which did not cease to appear until the Renaissance. Augustine's Plotinian understanding of the body–soul relationship, which underlay his quest for the image of God in human beings, also provided the major Scholastic theologians with the basic anthropological categories that led them to distinguish cognitive and volitive activities and assign them to different human "faculties" of the soul, intellect, and will.

b) In mystical theology the Rhineland* mystics of the 14th century and their successors in the Low Countries, France, and Spain needed to have recourse to a different Neoplatonist tradition to explain mystical experiences that occurred outside the boundaries of discursive knowing. Post-Renaissance theologians such as André du Val (1564–1638), the French commentator on Aquinas, transformed what the mystics had referred to as the "high-point" of the soul *(apex mentis),* for which Scholastic anthropology did not account, into the "heart," seat of both knowledge and virtue.

c) The Italian Renaissance, as represented chiefly by Marsilio Ficino (1433–99), translator of the hermetic corpus and pseudo-Dionysius, and both translator and commentator on Plato and Plotinus, whose thought was developed by Pico Della Mirandola (1463–94), exploited the full Neoplatonist tradition finally to provide a theoretical basis for the Renaissance enhancement of human dignity. Neoplatonism allowed Ficino, and those thinkers north of the Alps like Lefèvre d'Etaples (c. 1460–1536) who relied on him, to provide a way round the Scholastic impasse in which no orthodox theology of grace could escape making God's predestinatory decrees arbitrary. Neoplatonist assumptions allowed the obliteration of distinctions between nature and grace and made emotional love between human beings potentially the first step on the ladder ascending to divine love.

c). A current of Neoplatonist exemplarism transmitted by Augustine had, even during the high Middle

Ages, provided an alternative epistemology to theories of knowledge relying on the abstraction of some essence (or "quidditas," or "haecceitas") from an external object by an *intellectus agens*. Such exemplarist theories of knowledge ultimately underlay the thought of philosophers such as Descartes* and Malebranche, who were intent on preserving an immaterial and immortal principle of knowledge in the human body–soul. When Locke riposted against Descartes the possibility of "thinking matter," he unleashed the line

of philosophical speculation that finally resulted in German idealism and Hegel's phenomenology.

Augustine's dominance, the Rhineland mystics, and the human anthropology of the Renaissance provide only examples. In the history of western theology, Neoplatonism as defined above is to be found, as Harnack saw, behind all attempts to see the good, and in particular the spiritual fulfillment of the individual, in a realm outside the knowledge in which, for Aquinas and the Aristotelian Scholastic tradition, beatitude* itself consisted.

ANTHONY LEVI

Neoscholasticism. *See* Thomism

Nestorianism

(a) From Antioch to Constantinople. Nestorius was born near the Euphrates in Syria at some time in the last 25 years of the fourth century. Having been a monk in the monastery of Euprepios, he became a priest in Antioch*, and was trained in theology at that city's celebrated school. In 428, Emperor Theodosius II appointed Nestorius as Bishop and Patriarch of Constantinople (patriarchate*), where he became prominent from the outset in the struggle against Arianism* and Apollinarianism*. The difficulties that eventually led to his deposition and exile began when he supported one of his priests who had been accused of challenging the orthodoxy of applying the title *Theotokos* ("Mother of God") to Mary*. Nestorius was concerned to safeguard the transcendental nature of the Word*, the Son of God, and to maintain without compromise the distinction between the humanity and the divinity of Jesus*. He therefore recoiled from the use of any expression that might imply "communication" of properties (or idioms*) between these two natures.

(b) Nestorius's Christology. In response to reprimands from Cyril*, Archbishop of Alexandria*,

Nestorius put forward the following exegesis of the introduction of the symbol of the *Theotokos* at Nicaea (*DCO* II/1, 115):

> You have interpreted the tradition of these holy Fathers in a superficial way and have fallen into a pardonable ignorance. You have concluded that they said that the Word, coeternal with the Father, is passible [*pathetos*]. However, this divine gathering of Fathers did not say that the consubstantial [*homoousios*] divinity is passible, nor that the Word, coeternal with the Father, was recently engendered, nor that the Word, which restored its Temple after it was destroyed, has been resurrected.

Without any warning, Nestorius moves from the concrete term "Word" to the abstract term "divinity," attributing to Cyril the notion that the events in the story of Jesus affected him because of his divinity. Nestorius then goes on (*DCO* II/1, 115–17):

> They [the Fathers] say, I believe, therefore . . . in Our Lord Jesus Christ, his Only Son. Observe how they place first, as fundamentals, "Lord," "Jesus," "Christ," "only begotten," those names shared by his divinity and his humanity, and then construct the tradition of the incarnation,

the resurrection, and the passion. In thus putting forward certain names with meanings common to both natures, their goal was to show that what concerns his filiation cannot be separated from what concerns his lordship, and that, within the uniqueness of this filiation, what concerns the two natures is no longer at risk of disappearing because of confusion.

Nestorius speaks of words shared by the two natures ("Lord," "Jesus," "Christ," and so on) as if they are simply the sum of the natures that they unite (divinity and humanity). In his explanation, these words that Nestorius says are shared by the two natures do not describe a new ontological structure that could take account of their unification in Jesus, and therefore have no formal reference to what it is forbidden to separate (*DCO* II/1, 118–19):

> In every case where holy Scripture mentions the economy of the Lord, the generation and the passion that are presented are not those of Christ's divinity, but those of his humanity. It follows that the Holy Virgin ought to be given the more precise title of Mother of Christ [*Christotokos*] rather than Mother of God [*Theotokos*].

Here too, Nestorius makes an equation between humanity and Christ, on the one hand, and between divinity and God, on the other. Each nature is assimilated to a concrete subject (*DCO* II/1, 120–23):

> It is good, and in conformity with the gospel tradition, to confess that the body is the Temple of the divinity of the Son, a Temple unified in accordance with a supreme and divine conjunction [*sunapheia*], so that the nature of the divinity appropriates that which belongs to this Temple. However, to attribute to the Word, in the name of this appropriation, the properties of the flesh in this conjunction—I mean generation, suffering, and mortality—is, my brother, either to take up the disturbed thinking of the Greeks, or to fall sick with the madness of Apollinarius, Arius, or other heretics.

Clearly, however much Nestorius feared confusion between the two natures, he was still capable of saying that that the nature of the divinity appropriates that which belongs to the "Temple." On the other hand, it is not clear how the conjunction (*sunapheia*) that is at issue in this passage can be anything other than a moral combination. Accordingly, Nestorius seems to compromise the integrity of the two natures, and to assume a duality between two concrete subjects, Jesus and the Word. In his defense, it might be pointed out that, on the eve of the Council of Ephesus*, the notions being deployed here did not have the precision and the clarity that they were to acquire two centuries later.

(c) Condemnation and Exile. At Ephesus in 431, following the reading of his second letter to Cyril (*DCO* II/1, 113–25), Nestorius was banished by the Emperor to a monastery near Antioch, and then sent into exile in Arabia, Libya, and Egypt. He wrote several texts in his own defense, notably the *Tragoedia* and the *Book of Heraclides of Damas*, of which a version in Syriac was discovered in 1895. Neither Nestorius's statements about the relationship between the two natures in Christ—their interpenetration (circumincession*), inhabitation, accreditation, or confirmation—nor his statements on the meaning of *prosopon* (the mode of appearance of a concrete nature) removed all the doubts from his somewhat clumsy thinking. He died at around the time when the Council of Chalcedon* was beginning (451), believing himself to be in full accord with the Christology* of Flavian of Constantinople and of Pope* Leo I.

(d) Syriac Tradition. Nestorius's own teachings must be distinguished from those of the Antiochene bishops* who rejected the Act of Union of 433 and gave their support to a "Nestorian" tradition in a declaration issued in 486. The Assyrian Church of the East (the Nestorian Church of the Edessa region) rejected the conclusions of the Council of Ephesus on the communication of idioms and the application of the title of Mother of God to Mary. However, as early as the seventh century the theologians of this church ceased to take anything more than some terminology and metaphors from Nestorius. On 11 November 1994, the Nestorian and Catholic Churches agreed on a declaration about Christology that put an end to the disputes initiated at Ephesus (*Ist.*, 40/2 [1995], 233–35):

> The Word of God...was incarnated through the power of the Holy Spirit by assuming from the Holy Virgin Mary a flesh animated by a rational soul, with which it was united indissolubly from the moment of conception...His divinity and his humanity are united in one person...The difference between these natures is preserved in him...but, far from constituting one thing and another thing, divinity and humanity are united in the person of the one and only Son of God and Lord, Jesus Christ, the object of a single worship. Christ was therefore not an ordinary human being whom God adopted, in order to reside within him and inspire him...but the very word of God, engendered by the Father...was born from a mother without a human father. The humanity to which the blessed Virgin Mary gave birth has always been that of the Son of God himself. This is why the Assyrian Church of the East prays to the Virgin Mary as Mother of Christ Our Lord and Savior. In the light of this same faith, the Catholic tradition addresses the Virgin Mary as Mother of God and also as Mother of Christ.

The study of the "Nestorius case" has been taken up with some enthusiasm during the 20th century, frequently with a degree of sympathy toward Nestorius, thanks to the editing of his writings, by F. Loofs and by P. Bedjan, and to research, most notably by E. Amann, L.I. Scipioni, M.V. Anastos, and L. Abramowski.

GILLES LANGEVIN

- *DCO* II-1, 112–125.
F. Loofs (1905), *Nestoriana*, Halle.
F. Nau (Ed.) (1910), Nestorius, *Le livre d'Héraclide de Damas*, Paris.
◆ L.I. Scipioni (1974), *Nestorio e il concilio di Efeso*, Milan.

A. Grillmeier (1979), *Jesus der Christus im Glauben der Kirche* I, Friburg-Basel-Vienna (2nd Ed. 1990).
A. de Halleux (1993), "Nestorius: Histoire et doctrine," *Irén* 66, 38–51; 163–78.
Coll. (1995), *La tradition syriaque, Ist* 40/1; *L'Église de l'Orient, Ist* 40/2.
L. Abramowski (1995), "Histoire de la recherche sur Nestorius et le nestorianisme," *Ist* 40, 44–55.

See also **Chalcedon, Council of; Christ/Christology; Cyril of Alexandria; Ephesus, Council of; Hypostatic Union**

"New Theology." *See* **Lubac, Henri Sonier de**

Newman, John Henry

1801–1890

---

a) Life. John Henry Newman was born in London on 21 February 1801. Having become a student at Trinity College, Oxford, in 1817, then Fellow of Oriel College and Vicar of Saint Mary's, the university parish church, he lived in that town until his conversion to Catholicism on 9 October 1845. Entrusted with founding in England the Oratory of Saint Philip Neri, he set up his community in Birmingham, where he died on 11 August 1890. In 1879 Pope Leo XIII had made him a cardinal.

Newman's output is many-faceted (literature, history, philosophy, pedagogy, morality, spirituality). The core of his theological thought is based on the statement that access to revelation* comes about after an ascent that starts from natural* theology and leads through obedience to the moral conscience* up to the plenitude of the truth* revealed in all its multiplicity: the Holy* Scripture, Tradition*, the Church*, and the sacraments*.

b) Natural Knowledge, Revealed Knowledge. For Newman, the above descriptions represent two sources of our knowledge, distinct and yet linked together in the same individual, who knows facts through evidence or from demonstration and who believes with the steadfast certainty that faith* imparts to him. What is at stake in the relations of the two types of knowledge, which must become a perfect harmony, is revealed truth, which is threatened by a hegemonic rationality. Newman's writings on this question—the *University Sermons* (1826–43) and *The Grammar of Assent* (1870)—provide a good introduction to the more theological parts of his works.

At the end of the 18th century a school of apologetics, called the Evidential School, had arisen in order to study the challenges to revealed knowledge, insofar as they were founded on the requirement of rational proof. This school's ideas, and particularly those of its chief representative, W. Paley (1743–1805), did not please Newman, for Paley admitted that the proofs of Christian truth should have the rigor of a logical demonstration: he thus reduced faith to a rational belief and demanded the abandonment of unprovable statements of faith. In the *University Sermons*, Newman created a balance between the two forms of knowledge. Firstly he showed that knowing facts and believing are two of man's equally valid abilities; and then, that the rational evidence is not as clear and the mental certainty that stems from it is not as firm as the philosophers state. Borrowing the arguments of the Anglican bishop and philosopher J. Butler (1692–1752), he applied himself to proving, with numerous examples, that belief is a generally practiced human behavior, exercised far beyond the sphere of religious doctrines.

Newman not only concerned himself with the object of faith, but also with the defense of the believer. On the latter point he asserted every Christian's right, whether or not he could give his reasons for it, to believe with the same certainty that Newman observed in his own self. It is from this viewpoint that the *Grammar of Assent* clarifies the mechanics of inference that lead to assent, the logic of the "sense of inference," that is, of the "illative sense," which those mechanisms put into play, and the transition from notional assent (assent given to notions) to real assent (assent given to the realities named by these notions).

Yet Newman did not entrust the search for religious truth to pure intellectuality. On the contrary, this search is supported by a moral disposition that serves as its foundation and directs it toward its ultimate goal. It corresponds to the appeal to the moral conscience, and requires deeds subject to its orders. These orders come from outside and from above every individual, and they imply a supreme judge of human actions*. Spurring man to go outside himself in search of the one of whom conscience is the voice, this moral conscience prepares him also to accept a revelation if one should present itself. Obeying his own conscience impels man to compare its commandments with the teachings of the gospels. Therefore, the existence of conscience is not only an argument in favor of the existence* of God: it also disposes man to acknowledge the teachings of revealed religion. In answer to the British statesman W. E. Gladstone (1809–1898), who in 1874 had publicly expressed his fears that British Catholics would no longer be loyal subjects of Her Britannic Majesty if they accepted, as was their duty as Catholics, the dogma* of Papal infallibility* proclaimed during Vatican* I, Newman gave a reminder of that authority* of moral conscience. Writing, in the name of British Catholics, *A Letter Addressed to the Duke of Norfolk* (1875; the dukes of Norfolk are the premier lay Catholics in England), he defended the primacy of moral conscience over any other authority: in every individual, conscience is "the vicar of Christ*."

c) The Relations between Holy Scripture and Tradition: Anglicanism's "Middle Way." Through his contribution to the birth of the Oxford movement, Newman wanted to work on a systematic exposition of Anglican theology that would allow Anglicanism* to be seen as a *via media* or "middle way" between Roman Catholicism and Protestantism*. For Newman, the foundation of Anglican doctrine was the apostolic and patristic doctrine contained in the creeds of faith. And in his first book, *The Arians of the Fourth Century* (1833), he explained that the Church had triumphed over Arianism* because of its fidelity to the tradition of the apostles*, that is, to the *credo* which, "in those ancient times, was the chief source of instruction, in particular for the understanding of the obscure passages in the Scriptures" (134–35). The relations between scripture and tradition form the main theme of his *Lectures on the Prophetical Office of the Church Viewed Relative to Romanism and Popular Protestantism* (1837). There Newman defines the Church's teaching task: it receives the tradition as a rule of faith and conduct which it then expounds; all the same, this tradition is always "subordinate and auxiliary," while "the Scriptures are the foundation of all proof." The expression "fundamental doctrines," borrowed from the Anglican theologians R. Hooker (1554–1600), W. Laud (1573–1645), and E. Stillingfleet (1635–1699), refers to one of the most important foundations of the *via media*, that is, the doctrines contained in the three principal ancient symbols. These doctrines can already be found in Scripture and have been clearly specified in these symbols in order to answer the heretics and to instruct the faithful: accepted "everywhere and always by everyone" (according to Vincent of Lerins's canon from the *Commonitorium*) they form the "episcopal tradition." Alongside the fundamental doctrines, other doctrines have appeared in the Church's various branches: the Roman branch, the Greek branch, and the Anglican branch. These other doctrines form the "prophetic tradition," which varies from one Church to another, and they serve to explain the episcopal tradition without having the authority to do so. At the Council of Trent* the Roman Church had imposed such non-fundamental doctrines, granting them the same authority as the ancient doctrines. Conversely, by acknowledging only the authority of Scripture and of the private judgment of each believer, the Protestants had abandoned the fundamental doctrines. And yet, explained Newman in his *Apostolical Tradition* (1836) and in *Tract 85* (1835), it is impossible to prove the great doctrines of the divinity of Jesus* by means of scriptural references which exclude the reader's referring also to the tradition that formulated them. Anglicanism is indeed, therefore, the *via media* between the extremes—that is, between the corruptions added by the Catholics, and the deficits—in other words, the losses—sanctioned by the Protestants.

His *Lectures on the Doctrine of Justification* (1838) also set out to define the Anglican position. The polemic was directed against the Protestant extremists. There he again asserted the Church's responsibility, its priestly or sacramental duty. Newman protested against the danger represented by the private feeling of being justified (justification*) by faith alone, without taking into consideration the external rituals or the obligation to live in conformity with this faith; and he gave a reminder about the role of the sacraments as instruments of grace*, as well as about the necessity for good works.

His exposition of the *via media* came to an end with his publication of *Tract 90:* the Thirty-nine Articles of Anglicanism can be understood in a Catholic sense because they are compatible with the doctrine of the Early Church. For Newman it was a matter of proving the factual reality of the *via media.* But the Oxford theologians rejected the tract and the bishops condemned it. Moreover, by extending his reading of the Fathers*, Newman became convinced that "the old Catholic truth" did not lie in the Church of England but in the Church of Rome*. Superimposing the present and former states of the Church, he perceived first of all, concerning the Monophysite* heresy, that the Church of Rome remained in his own time the same as it had been then, while the Church of England stood in the position of the Monophysites. And then he realized, with regard to the Arian crisis, that the Protestants took the same stance as the Arians had done and the Anglicans that of the semi-Arians, while the Catholics of that time believed as they still did in Newman's own day.

d) Development of the Christian Doctrine. Newman had believed for a long time that the Roman additions to primitive doctrine were corruptions. But the very direction of his thought brought him to reconsider his stance. If the additions made to doctrine were not corruptions, they ought to integrate with doctrine and explain it: in short, they should constitute its development.

At the end of 1842, having identified the principle of development as a fundamental phenomenon, he studied it first in itself and then applied it to the dogmas of the Catholic Church (*University Sermons* No. XV and *Essay on Development of Christian Doctrine*). Basing himself on the Scriptures (Lk 2:19), Newman thought that the case of Mary* illustrated the use of reason in the examination of the doctrines of the faith. The formation of the Catholic doctrines resembled an idea that is born, grows, makes progress, protects itself from deviations while feeding on other ideas, and becomes increasingly

precise as it develops. This process culminates in dogmatic statements, whose function is to expose hitherto latent aspects of the idea. In reality, things could not be otherwise once a great idea arose in the mind (moreover, Newman also showed this in the idea of a university). In order to justify the application of this principle to divine revelation, Newman stressed that, whatever might be the mystery* of God, the idea of revelation included the communication of teachings addressed to the human intellect and therefore grasped according to this intellect's laws. If ever that ceased to be the case, one could no longer speak of revelation; but if God really speaks, what he communicates can be heard and understood by man according to the law of his own mind, and understood from more than one angle.

His *Essay on Development of the Christian Doctrine* is a reworking of the philosophical analysis of development and a very thorough verification of that idea in the form of an analysis of the Roman Church's doctrines. In it, Newman enumerates the categories applicable to the development of Christianity (political, logical, historical, ethical, metaphysical) and studies the seven signs of the idea's true development: preservation of the type, continuity of the principles, capacity to be assimilated, logical progression, anticipation of the future, active preservation of the past, enduring vigor.

He then draws two consequences that historical investigation would have to verify: firstly, if Christianity corresponded to the development of the idea it would undergo such a development; secondly, if development was shown to have happened, one should expect to find an infallible authority. Development is indeed an unpredictable effect and is only recognized retrospectively; it occurs under the stress of circumstances and appeals to an authority that controls its energies and whose existence should be no surprise. This authority should not reside in each individual's private judgment, for the individual is not infallible, nor should it reside in the Anglican use of the canon of Lerins, which Newman had put to a fruitless test with regard to the *via media:* it was found at the present time, he contended, in the Catholic Church. The remainder of this work is devoted to applying the signs of true development to numerous doctrines. Newman shows how the historical continuity of doctrine resulted from a dialogue between the teaching Church and the Church that receives instruction, with both of these aspects playing their role in the preservation of the truth.

● V. F. Blehl, *John Henry Newman: A Bibliographical Catalogue of his Writings,* Charlottesville, 1978.
(1868–81), Standard Edition of Newman's works, London, Longman Green and Co.
(1955), *Sermons universitaires,* Paris and Bruges.
(1956), *Écrits autobiographiques,* Paris and Bruges.

(1961) *Letters and Diaries of John Henry Newman,* edited at the Birmingham Oratory, 31 vols., Oxford.

(1962), *Esquisses patristiques,* Paris and Bruges.

(1964), *Essai sur le développement de la doctrine chrétienne,* Paris and Bruges.

M. J. Svaglic (Ed.) (1967), *Apologia Pro Vita Sua,* Oxford (French trans. 1967)

P. Murray (Ed.) (1973), *An Essay on the Development of Christian Doctrine,* Harmondsworth.

H. M. de Achaval and J. D. Holmes (Eds.) (1976), *The Theological Papers of John Newman on Faith and Certainty,* Oxford.

I. Kerr (Ed.) (1976), *The Idea of a University,* Oxford.

P. Murray (Ed.) (1980), *Newman the Oratorian: His Unpublished Oratory Papers,* Leominster.

I. Kerr (Ed.) (1985), *An Essay in Aid of a Grammar of Assent,* Oxford.

A. N. Wilson (Ed.) (1989), *John Henry Newman, Prayers, Poems, Meditations,* London.

P. Murray (Ed.) (1991), *Sermons 1824–1843,* vol. 1, Oxford.

V. F. Blehl (Ed.) (1993), *Sermons 1824–1843,* vol. 2, Oxford.

P. Gauthier (Ed. and Trans.) (1993–96), *Sermons paroissiaux,* Paris.

♦G. Faber (1933), *Oxford Apostles,* London.

M. Nédoncelle (1946), *La philosophie religieuse de John Henry Newman,* Strasbourg.

(1948–), *Newman Studien* (18 vols. published by 2002), Nuremberg and Sigmaringendorf.

J. H. Walgrave (1957), *Newman: Le développement du dogme,* Paris.

T. Gornall (1981), "Newman," *DSp* 11, 163–81.

R. Strange (1981), *Newman and the Gospel of Christ,* Oxford.

O. Chadwick (1983), *Newman,* Oxford.

G. Casey (1984), *Natural Reason. A Study of the Notions of Inference, Assent, Intuition, and First Principles of John Henry Cardinal Newman,* New York.

P. Gauthier (1988), *Newman et Blondel: tradition et développement du dogme,* CFi 147.

O. Chadwick (1990), *The Spirit of the Oxford Movement: Tractarian Essays,* Cambridge.

S. Gilley (1990), *Newman and his Age,* London.

PIERRE GAUTHIER

See also **Anglicanism; Blondel, Maurice; Credibility; Dogma; Lubac, Henri Sonier de; Monophysitism; Sensus fidei; Vatican I**

Nicaea-Constantinople, Symbols of. *See* Creeds

Nicaea I, Council of

A.D. 325

The First Council* of Nicaea, the first of seven ecumenical councils celebrated in the early Church*, is like the matrix for all of them. The proof is the praise showered upon the Council by the Fathers of Nicaea* II (held in 787), who remarked that they were putting finishing touches to the conciliar work of the earlier times of Christianity, at the very place where God* had inaugurated the Christian era. Two representatives of the Bishop* of Rome* took part in Nicaea I, which was labeled "ecumenical" by two direct witnesses, Eusebius of Caesarea and Athanasius* of Alexandria. Considered at first to have a territorial scope, the term quickly acquired authority. Such a council legislates in the Emperor's name for all his subjects by enunciating divine truth* and law*, for which the Church stands guarantor everywhere.

a) History and Stakes. After his final victory over Licinius, on 19 September 324, Constantine wanted to organize a general meeting of the eastern episcopate at Ancyra (Ankara) in Galatia, in order to solve all the ecclesiastical disputes and crown his pacifying work.

He had underestimated the gravity of the conflict triggered five years earlier in Alexandria by the excommunication of Arius. Some personal letters of Constantine, brought toward the end of 324 by his theological counselor, Hosius of Cordova, to Bishop Alexander of Alexandria and to his priest Arius, attest his lack of knowledge concerning the dogmatic stakes. A synod* held in the presence of Hosius at Antioch reinforced the division of minds by ruling that Alexander was right. Hosius informed the emperor that it was urgent to deal with the Alexandrine matter by putting it on the agenda of the General Council he was planning to hold. Constantine sped up the preparations of the Council by holding it in Nicaea, in the immediate vicinity of Nicomedia, where he was residing. He would put the Imperial Post at the participants' disposal, and he would see that they get lodging and board at his own expense. Finally, the Council would be followed by the celebration, on 25 July, of the 20th anniversary of his accession to the imperial dignity.

In June 325, at the solemn inauguration, approximately 300 bishops were in attendance (from the 360s on, the symbolic number of 318 was to be adopted, following the number of Abraham's servants in Genesis 4:14). The Acts of that Council being lost, it is difficult to be more precise. The Emperor read a welcoming speech in Latin. Eusebius of Nicomedia, Metropolitan of the province of Bithynia, where the assembly was taking place, thanked him. Constantine himself chaired this first sitting, as well as the subsequent ones, but he left to Hosius the responsibility of conducting the doctrinal debate. Constantine intervened on several occasions and ratified the decisions made; in his capacity as *pontifex maximus* of the whole Empire, he had, in fact, the responsibility of establishing a religious peace duly controlled in the provinces that had recently fallen under his supreme authority.

All the parties in the dispute had been summoned. Arius himself was present, accompanied by his friends. Among the bishops engaged in the controversy over Arius's condemnation, it was possible to distinguish three groups. The first gathered around Alexander of Alexandria. The second group gathered around the intransigent Eustathius of Antioch; he was influencing the decision to excommunicate Arius again, on the grounds of his own conception (shared by Marcellus of Ancyra) of the *unique* Trinitarian *hypostasis,* whereas Alexander and his group had censored Arius in the name of the Origenian doctrine of the *three* divine *hypostases.* Finally, there was the group led by Eusebius of Nicomedia; it had rallied to that same Origenian tradition, but it had been more conservative and more favorable to Arius ever since the beginning of the dispute, primarily to trigger some trouble for the bishop of Alexandria.

A creed*, to which was added an anathema, was adopted on 19 June and submitted to the imperial authority by the Nicene assembly. Eusebius of Caesarea mentioned this Anti-Arian credo in his *Letter to the Church of Caesarea* (Opitz, III, U. 22), which was written as soon as the Council was over. Arius and two compatriots from Libya, Bishops Secundus of Ptolemais and Theonas of Marmarica, refused to sign. They were excommunicated, and then sent away in exile. This same Eusebius related that the Emperor recommended from the very beginning of the debates to have the word *homoousios* ("consubstantial*") inserted into the creed being prepared (U. 22, 7). Eusebius himself had, during the first sitting, presented his own profession of faith, which was in accordance with the baptismal liturgy* of Caesarea; he had done so in order to demonstrate his orthodoxy*, following the censorship he had sustained from the Antioch synod a few months earlier.

The creed of Nicaea is different from Eusebius's profession of faith; it is connected to the baptismal tradition of Antioch and of Jerusalem*. The Commission entrusted with writing its final version tried hard to formulate an acceptable interpretation, closer to the Scriptures*, of the nonbiblical attribute *homoousios,* by placing prior to it some significant explanatory notes. In Nicomedia, before the opening of the great imperial synod, Alexander of Alexandria had perhaps agreed with Hosius to resort to the "consubstantial" (Philostorgius). For all these circumstances, we have to rely, however, on mere conjectures. From the 350s on, the eastern bishops, who were hostile to the Alexandrine see, increased the number of synods intended to eliminate the controversial term from the official formula of faith. Athanasius of Alexandria had the merit of opposing, at the cost of an Episcopal ministry severely perturbed, what represented to his eyes a confusion of political matters and of the rule of faith. The cause of Nicaea ended up prevailing.

Aside from the business of dealing with the Arius affair, the Nicene Fathers had to take care of two more major stakes: the old dispute regarding the exact date for celebrating Easter and the elimination of the Melitian schism* in Egypt (Melicius, Bishop of Lycopolis, had opposed the patriarch, Peter of Alexandria, about the reintegration into the church of Christians who had apostatized during Diocletian's persecution, and had illegitimately ordained bishops). Decrees were promulgated regarding these points, as well as other aspects of ecclesiastical* discipline.

The activities of the Council were perhaps closed by 19 June, and certainly before 25 July. On 25 July, Constantine invited the whole assembly to a banquet in his summer palace, where the synod had taken place. Eusebius of Caesarea delivered there a famous eulogy, glorifying the reign of peace established by Constantine over the whole Empire; and he did so in light of his own political* theology of the divine Logos.

The Nicene formula of faith became, from the fourth century on, the central issue at stake in the doctrinal controversies. A solemn reading of that formula was delivered at the First Council of Constantinople* (381), which added to it a more elaborate mention of the article concerning the Holy* Spirit. The creed of Nicaea-Constantinople was later acclaimed in Ephesus* (431) and in Chalcedon* (451). It is still being recited in our Eucharistic liturgies.

b) Canonical Decrees. Concerning the Paschal matter, the compromise decision that was reached (a decision that did not assume necessarily the form of an actual decree) was to insist that the Churches of Rome and Alexandria reach an agreement every time their respective calculations demanded, in theory, dates that were different. The bishop of Alexandria was entrusted with the task of announcing every year the exact date for Easter.

The synodal letter which, beside an encyclical letter from the Emperor, informed the Alexandrians about all these matters, transmitted as well the particularly moderate recommendations of the Council that aimed at curbing the Melitian schism: Melitius would remain a bishop, under house arrest; he would lose his ordaining powers; the bishops, priests*, and deacons* he had ordained would keep their titles and responsibilities, as subordinates of Alexander, following a new imposition of hands.

The 20 canons of Nicaea confirm the rules in practice and eliminate the abuses. Six of them set the structures of government* straight. Canon 4 imposes a minimum of three bishops as co-celebrants in an episcopal consecration. Canon 5 approves the Metropolitan synods in spring and autumn. Canon 6 consecrates the primacy, over vast regions, of the sees of Alexandria, of Rome, and of Antioch. Canon 7 adds the privilege of honor recognized to the Church of Jerusalem, and so the ancient structure of the four Mother Churches identifying with a Petrine foundation was thus canonized. Canons 15 and 16 object to the mobility of the clergy from one diocese to another. Canons 1 (on eunuchs), 3 (on cohabitation with women), 17 (on usury), 18 (on deacons), and 19 (on deaconesses) deal with matters concerning the clergy. Four canons organize the penitential discipline, in a by-and-large lenient way. They are: canon 11 (dealing with Christians implicated in the persecution's unforeseen turn of events, the *lapsi*); canon 12 (on soldiers); canon 13 (on the dying), and canon 14 (on catechumens). Finally, canon 8 settles the question of the schismatic Novatians, and canon 9 settles the matter of the Paulinists, Christians who had remained faithful to Paul of Samosata. Canon 20 forbids genuflection on Sundays and on Whitsuntide.

● Decrees: *COD,* 1–19 (*DCO* II/1, 27–64).
Ambrose, *De fide,* prol., 3–5; 1, 18; 3, 15: O. Faller (Ed.), CSEL 78, Vienna, 1962.
Athanasius of Alexandria, *De decretis,* etc.: H.-G. Opitz (Ed.) (1934), *Athanasius-Werke* II/1, Berlin.
Eusebius of Caesarea, *Vita Constantini* 3, 6–23: F. Winkelmann (Ed.) (1995), *Eusebius I,* GCS, Berlin; *Lettre à l'Église de Césarée*: H.-G. Opitz (Ed.) (1934), *Athanasius-Werke* III, 1/2, Berlin.
Hilary of Poitiers, *De synodis* 86, PL 10, 534.
Philostorgius, *Histoire ecclésiastique*: J. Bidez (Ed.) (1913), GCS 21, Berlin.
◆ G. Fritz (1931), "Nicée," *DThC* 11/1, 399–417 (older, but still useful).
E. Honigmann (1939), "La liste originale des Pères de Nicée," *Byz.* 14, 17–76.
P. Galtier (1948), "Les canons pénitentiels de Nicée," *Gr.* 29, 288–94.
I. Ortiz de Urbina (1963), *Nicée et Constantinople,* Paris.
P. Th. Camelot (1964), "Les conciles œcuméniques des IVe et Ve siècles," *in* coll., *Le concile et les conciles,* Paris, 5–73.
E. Boularand (1972), *L'hérésie d'Arius et la "foi" de Nicée,* vol. II, Paris.
C. Kannengiesser (1978), "Nicée dans l'histoire du christianisme," *Conc(F)* 138, 39–47.
H. J. Sieben (1979), *Die Konzilsidee der alten Kirche,* Paderborn, 25–67.
A. de Halleux (1985), "La réception du symbole œcuménique, de Nicée à Chalcédoine," *EThL* 61, 5–47.
G. Alberigo (Ed.) (1990), *Storia dei concili ecumenici,* Brescia.
J. Ulrich (1994), *Die Anfänge der abendländischen Rezeption des Nizänums,* PTS 39, Berlin.
H. C. Brennecke (1994), "Nicäa I," *TRE* 24, 429–441 (bibl.).

CHARLES KANNENGIESSER

See also **Arianism; Athanasius; Consubstantial; Trinity**

Nicaea II, Council of

A.D. 787

The Second Council of Nicaea was the seventh ecumenical council*. It confirmed its entire faithfulness to the teaching of the ecumenical councils that had preceded it. By way of this faithfulness it wanted to guarantee the legitimacy of the cult* of images*. Because of the great difficulty in assessing the respective parts played by each of a variety of causes, historians give divergent interpretations of the iconoclastic quarrel and of its causes (see Brown, 1973). Possible causes include the pressure created by Islam with its conquering strength, the internal crisis of the Byzantine Empire, and the latent clash of two theologies that followed Nicaea II. It was also with Nicaea II and the reception it had that the gradual separation of Eastern and Western Christianity became clearer.

1. History

a) Iconodules and Iconoclasts (Seventh–Ninth Centuries). Nicaea II was preceded and followed by two periods of controversy over images (iconoclasm). From 692 on, canon 82 of the so-called Quinisext Council, which has been identified as the "first official evidence of a stand by the Church* in the matter of images" (Grabar 1957), forbids the representation of Christ* as a lamb, such an image resorting more to the typology of the old covenant* than to incarnation* (Dumeige 1978): "We order that Christ our God*, who removes the sins* from the world*, be henceforth painted according to his human form in the images, instead of the former representation as a lamb; thus, recognizing in him the splendor of the Word*'s humility, we will be led to remember his life in the flesh, his passion*, his salutary death and the redemption he brought to the world."

In 726, while the caliphs were intensifying their fight against the Christian images (decree of Yazid II in 723), the Byzantine Emperor Leo III inaugurated an iconoclastic policy. This first attitude triumphed at the Council of Hieria, convened in 754 by Emperor Constantine V, which was attended by 338 iconoclastic bishops*. Any type of image cult was forbidden as heretical. The decisions of Hieria thus created a *de facto* separation between Constantinople and the other patriarchates*. In response, Pope Stephen III convened at the Lateran, in 769, a synod* that condemned Hieria and thus supported the primacy of Rome*. In 786 Empress Irene convened a council, to be held at Nicaea the following year. The sessions of Nicaea II were presided over by the patriarch of Constantinople, and the five patriarchates were represented; Pope Adrian I sent two legates. The decisions of the Council provoked strong reactions among the iconoclasts, and there was a long wait until 843 for the iconophiles to prevail, at long last, thanks to Empress Theodora and Patriarch Methodius. The solemn restoration of Christ's image at the entrance of the imperial palace, on 11 March 843, marks the "triumph of orthodoxy," a festival inscribed since then in the liturgical calendar of Eastern Christianity ("the Sunday of Orthodoxy").

b) Protagonists and Stakes of Nicaea II. Some actions, including the destruction and reestablishment of images and imperial coins bearing or not bearing the image of Christ (see Grabar 1957) and some written documents marked the different steps of the crisis. The works that survived and reached us concern mostly the defense of images, because Nicaea II proceeded to destroy the iconoclastic documents. In any case, far from being a manifestation of popular piety (see Brown 1973, who challenges the very relevance of that concept for early Christianity), the crisis proved that the cult of images was state business. The Constantinian Empire had already decided in the fourth century that the cross was a good sign of its victory; the *acheiropoietae* signs of Christ (those not created by human hands) had subsequently increased in number (Grabar 1957).

From the sixth century on, the cult of the *Theotokos* experienced new growth in Constantinople. This growth came together with the encouragement given to the reverence for images and relics* (Cameron 1978). A role of intercession and of protection for the Eastern capital was in fact recognized for Mary* (this was particularly obvious during the siege of the city in 726), and the controversy regarding the images may be interpreted partly as an interrogation, more insistent during a troubled period, of the manner in which mediations between God and men can be made clearer.

Starting with the reign of Leo III, the succession of

iconophile and iconoclastic emperors and the divisions of the Eastern episcopate played a major role. A theocratic concept of power ("I am an emperor and a priest," according to a declaration attributed to Leo III —see Dagron 1996) and the emperors' interventions in matters of dogma* created conflicts between emperor and patriarch, and also between Constantinople and Rome. Within the pentarchy of the five patriarchates—considered, since the reign of Justinian I, to be of equal dignity (see Schatz in Boespflug-Lossky 1987), Rome tended to assert its preeminence. But it was the rise of Frankish power in the West, then the Carolingian Empire, that helped Roman primacy against the East and accelerated separation.

Other aspects are more difficult to assess, such as the role and the position of the Eastern monastic communities. They were rather iconophile prior to Nicaea II, as evidenced by the role of the monk George of Cyprus; but later they were divided. Under the influence of Origenism (see Schönborn 1976), iconoclastic tendencies appeared; they were interpreted also as the sign of some opposition between the city, where the seat of power was situated, and the rural areas (Brown, 1973).

2. Doctrinal Work

In order to rule on the matter of images, the horos, or final decree, relied on "the tradition* of the Catholic Church*," and the Council declared itself first as ecumenical by anathematizing the decisions of Hieria (Dumeige 1978). The horos referred then specifically to a christological declaration by Basil* of Caesarea: "the honor paid to the image goes to the prototype" (Traité du S.E., 18, 45). Then it ordered the following: "As is the case for the representation of the precious and uplifting cross, venerable and holy images, mosaics and other works of art made in any other respectable manner should be placed in God's holy churches, on holy objects and clothes, on walls and boards, in homes and on the roads; the image of our Lord, our God and Savior Jesus Christ, that of our Immaculate Lady, the Holy Mother of God, those of the angels*, worthy of our respect, those of all the Saints and the Just."

The iconodules' recourse to a christological argumentation should not lead to an increase in dogmatic dispute. The definitions of Chalcedon* are recognized on both sides, and the hypothesis of a connection between iconoclasm and Monophysitism* is as contested nowadays as that of a correlation with Nestorianism* (Desreumeaux and Dalmais in Boespflug-Lossky 1987). It is in fact the very meaning of the word icon, or image, which is at the source of the difficulties. For the iconoclasts, Christ alone is the unique and perfect image (see Col 1:15), and the divinity can be communicated through images only in the consecrated realities of the cross, the churches, and the Eucharist*. The answer given by the defenders of the images is founded on a theology of incarnation. If they state, like their adversaries, that God is aperigraptos, or "uncircumscribable," Jesus*, the Son who has come in the flesh, can be represented because he is perigraptos, or "circumscribable" (anathema 1). As a corollary, Mary, the saints, and the angels can also be represented. And to bring an end to the accusations of idolatry* made by the Christian iconoclasts and by Islam, the fathers of Nicaea II make a clear distinction between veneration (proskunèsis) and adoration (latreia). Reserved for God, adoration confesses his salvific power; on the other hand, the veneration of images recognizes that they have merely the value of signs.

When added to the erroneous translation of proskunèsis into adoratio in the Latin Acts of Nicaea II, the ambivalence of the term icon meant that there had to be a deeper, more thorough examination of this theological matter before the council could get a full reception.

3. Reception

a) In the East.   The Discourse Against Those Who Reject Images, written by John Damascene around 730, offered a first elaboration of the concept of image and of its various meanings; in the "icons," the Discourse perceived, at first, material images pertaining, as all matter does, to the grace* of the Creator. Being the first defenders of the images, John Damascene, the patriarch Germanus of Constantinople, and George of Cyprus had been anathematized by the Council of Hieria. The decisions of Nicaea II were not sufficient to put an end to the controversy. In fact, at the beginning of the ninth century, the emperors Nicephorus and Leo V were openly opposed, and the latter openly went over to iconoclasm. A council convened at the Hagia Sophia in 815 condemned the decisions made by Nicaea II and brought Hieria's decisions back into force. Faced with this second iconoclastic reaction, Patriarch Nicephorus (Antirrhetici) and Theodore of Studium offered further new expositions of the iconodulic theology (Schönborn 1976). The images had to wait until 843 to be solemnly reestablished; and under Photius's patriarchate, a council spelled out the official condemnation of iconoclasm.

b) In the West.   The reception of Nicaea II is one of the stakes in the opposition that asserted itself in the eighth and ninth centuries between the Pope and the Carolingian Empire. While Pope Adrian manifested his agreement with Nicaea II, the Council of Frankfurt, convened by Charlemagne in 794, condemned the "veneration" *(adoratio)* of images. The *Livres carolins,* composed around 791–94 by theologians from Charlemagne's entourage, defined what was to be, throughout the Middle Ages, the Western theological opinion regarding images. Quoting the declarations of Gregory* the Great, they asserted that images have a pedagogical, catechetical, and ornamental value (*see* Schmitt in Boespflug-Lossky 1987), but that Eucharist alone could act as a full memorial of the salutary incarnation. It was thus that a theological shifting took place, from image to sacrament*; it was to be of central importance in medieval Western Europe and during the Counter-Reformation.

● *COD,* 133–156 (*DCO* II/1, 298–345).

Libri carolini or *Capitulare de imaginibus,* MGH, *Concilia* II, supplement, Leipzig, 1924.

H. Hennephof (1959), *Textus byzantinos ad iconomachiam pertinentes,* Leyden.

♦ A. Grabar (1957), *L'iconoclasme byzantin: Dossier archéologique,* Paris.

P. Brown (1973), "A Dark-Age Crisis: Aspects of the Iconoclastic Controversy," *The English Historical Review* 88, 1–34.

S. Gero (1973), *Byzantine Iconoclasm during the Reign of Leo III,* CSCO, Subsidia 41, Louvain.

J. Pelikan (1974), *The Christian Tradition: A History of the Development of Doctrine,* vol. 2: *The Spirit of Eastern Christendom (600–1700),* chap. 3, Chicago.

J. Gouillard (1976), "L'Église d'Orient et la primauté romaine au temps de l'iconoclasme," *Ist* 25–54 (reprinted in *La vie religieuse à Byzance,* London, 1981).

Ch. von Schönborn (1976), *L'icône du Christ: Fondements théologiques,* Fribourg (3rd Ed. 1986, Paris).

A. Cameron (1978), "The Theotokos in Sixth Century Constantinople," *JThS NS* 29, 79–108.

G. Dumeige (1978), *Nicée II, HCO,* vol. 4, Paris.

F. Bœspflug and N. Lossky (Eds.) (1987), *Nicée II, 787–1987, douze siècles d'images religieuses: Actes du Colloque international Nicée II,* Paris.

G. Alberigo (Ed.) (1990), *Storia dei concili ecumenici,* Brescia.

G. Dagron (1993), "L'iconoclasme et l'établissement de l'Orthodoxie (726–847)," in *Histoire du christianisme,* vol. IV: *Évêques, moines et empereurs (610–1054),* edited by Ch. and L. Pietri et al., 93–166, Paris; (1996), *Empereur et prêtre: Étude sur le "césaropapisme" byzantin,* Paris.

FRANÇOIS BŒSPFLUG ET FRANÇOISE VINEL

See also **Cult; Church and State; Images**

Nicholas of Cusa

1401–1464

a) Life. Nicholas of Cusa—in Latin, Nicolaus Cusanus or Nicolaus Treverensis—was born in Cues on the Moselle. He studied philosophy* in Heidelberg (1416–17), ecclesiastical law in Padua (1417–23)—as well as mathematics, natural sciences*, and especially Aristotelianism*—returning to studies in philosophy and theology* in Köln (from 1425) under the guidance of Eymeric de Campo, who introduced him to the works of the late-medieval heirs of Albert* the Great and Raymond Lulle. On two occasions (in 1428 and 1435) Nicholas refused the chair of canon law* offered him by the University of Louvain. In 1432, during the Council of Basel*, he intervened in the political struggles that were stirring up the Church; initially conciliarist, he rallied to the Roman camp in 1437. After this he undertook important diplomatic missions, accompanying the emperor and the patriarch of Constantinople to the 1438 council of union in Ferrara-Florence. He was named cardinal in 1448, and bishop of Brixen in 1450. This led to a series of journeys of legation and inspection, notably to provincial synods* in Salzburg, Magdeburg, Mainz, and Köln. The fall of Constantinople in 1453 and the Turkish threat awakened his interest in Islam and led him to elaborate a philosophy of religion* that reconciled the different confessions. Following a disagreement with Duke Sigismond of the Tyrol, he left Brixen in 1458 to assume important functions in Rome and in Italy. He died on 11 August 1464 in Todi (Umbria).

b) Doctrines. One of the objectives of Nicholas of Cusa was to reform the life of Church* and State in the furtherance of religious peace*. In *De concordantia catholica* (1432–33) he traced the paradigm of a universal Christian order, following the schema "Spirit-soul*-body": the one Church is the place where the divine Spirit, the sacerdotal soul, and the body of believers should be in harmonious agreement. In *De pace fidei* (1453) he defended the idea of a "single religion…in a diversity of rites" (VI, n. 16, H. VII, 15, 16 *Sq*), arguing that, more than any other religion, Christianity is in a position to respond to the expectations of the various national religions. In *Cribratio Alchorani* (Critique of the Koran, 1460–61), Nicholas tried to explain the mysteries* of the Christian faith to Muslims. *De docta ignorantia* (1440) is generally considered Nicholas's major philosophico-theological work. The method of learned ignorance, by which the incomprehensible is understood in an incomprehensible way *(incomprehensibile incomprehensibiliter comprendere)*—that is, imprecisely and approximatively—makes it possible to determine the absolute maximum that cannot be surpassed; since this maximum has no opposite, it is not opposed to a minimum, but on the contrary coincides with it (*De docta ign.* I, 4, H. I, 10, 4–16). This unique reality—which actually exists *(actu)* as a maximum and which simultaneously, as a minimum, is every possible being *(omne possibile est)* —according to the belief of all peoples, is God* (ibid., I, 2, H. I, 7, 3–15). Nicholas of Cusa then deals with the universe, which he conceives of as a "contracted maximum" *(maximum contractum)* because it does not precede and does not connect the contradictory opposites, but only the contraries (II, 4, H. I, 73, 8–16); a soul cannot be attributed to it, God being himself the soul and spirit of the world* (II, 9, H. I, 95, 29–96, 4). God is at the same time the center and the circumference of the universe, a notion that deprives the earth of the central position it occupies in ancient cosmology (II, 11, H. I, 100, 10–16). Nicholas concludes by turning to Christ*, conceived as a maximum that is both absolute and contracted (III, 2, H. I, 123, 11 s).

De coniecturis (written before 1444) expounds a conjectural method of knowledge*, but Nicholas clearly forgets his own theory in speaking of the mental unity of God *divinaliter* (*De coni.* I, 6, H. III, 31, 4), that is, from the viewpoint of divine unity itself, determining it as pure negation (ibid., I, 8, H. III, 38, 12–39, 3): the Neoplatonic tetrad "God-reason-intellect-body" is carried over here into a process of emanation/return and at the same time built—a point that Nicholas was not to develop anywhere else—into the concept of *mens,* spirit, that encompasses these four unities (ibid., I, 4, H. III, 18, 3–19, 1).

All his life Nicholas of Cusa sought to shape the most appropriate idea of God possible, while keeping his eyes fixed on the trinitarian structure of the divinity. In these approaches formulated in philosophical terms, he particularly attempted to retain that which is not known to philosophers (*De venatione sapientiae* XXV, n. 73, H. XII, 71, 24–26): the Holy* Spirit. God is not only absolute possibility and absolute reality, he is also the connection *(nexus)* between the two (*Trialogus de possest* 6, H. XI/2, 7, 16–8, 17). But Nicholas (see De ven. sap. XIV, n. 40, H. XII, 39, 1 s) believed that no idea could better express God than the idea of "non-other" *(non aliud);* this non-other, against all Aristotelian logic and insofar as it defines itself by itself, is the quiddity of all quiddities. And this is the definition posited by Nicholas in 1462: the non-other is none other than the non-other (*De non aliud* I, H. XIII, 4, 29 *Sq*). In this trinitarian definition of self, the non-other is itself and therefore transcendent, but at the same time it is immanent to all that is other than it, because the other is none other than the other (Stallmach 1989).

Concerning Nicholas's numerous mathematical writings (most of them composed in the period 1445–59), one observation should be made: just as God is at the origin of the real, the human mind is the source from which numbers are born. Geometrical figures, by their symbolic nature, make it possible to illustrate the coincidence of opposites *(coincidentia oppositorum)* in God. Reason *(ratio),* the principle of mathematical content, is not able to understand exactly the imparticipable truth*, the divine essence, any more than is intellect *(intellectus),* in which opposites can agree but not coincide.

c) Reception of Nicholas of Cusa's Work. As a theologian engaged in the field of philosophy, Nicholas was especially concerned to establish the inadequacy of the "Aristotelian sect" of his time; he considered himself an innovator. He had to write an apology against Johannes Wenck de Herrenberg, who did not understand his ideas. His theory of coincidence was also criticized by Vincent d'Aggsbach, whereas it was favorably received by Bernard de Waging, Eymeric de Campo, Jacques Lefèvre d'Étaples, Gérard Roussel, Giordano Bruno, Athanasius Kircher, and Leibniz*. His ideas were afterward accommodated within a fideist perspective, or transmitted second hand; it was only in the 20th century that a critical edition of his complete works was published, stimulating an intense labor of interpretation.

d) Critical Perspectives. We will simply observe that although Nicholas of Cusa, in the context of his philosophical theology, was constantly inventing new concepts of God understood as a coincidence of opposites, and also advanced many innovative ideas in cosmology, he nonetheless remained faithful to a hierarchical model that, relative to God, excluded the thought of absolute auto-causality (*God causa sui*) and regression to the infinite. In a word, Nicholas of Cusa saw God as the cause of all but not of himself. God is infinite*, but he is also his own limit, beyond which it is impossible to go back. These are questions that a philosophico-critical theology must face today. It could lead to a new, philosophically justifiable idea of God as absolute possibility.

- *Nicolai de Cusa opera omnia iussu et auctoritate Academia Litterarum Heidelbergensis (H.),* Leipzig, 1932 ss, Hamburg, 1950–.
♦ MFCG 1–21.
  VerLex 6, 1093–1113.
  E. Vansteenberghe (1920), *Le cardinal Nicolas de Cues,* Paris.
  M. de Gandillac (1941), *La philosophie de Nicolas de Cues,* Paris.
  R. Haubst (1952), *Das Bild des Einen und Dreieinen Gottes in der Welt nach Nikolaus von Kues,* Trier.
  R. Haubst (1956), *Die Christologie des Nikolaus von Kues,* Friburg.
  P. Duhem (1959), *Le système du monde,* vol. X, Paris.
  W. Beierwaltes (1964), "Deus oppositio oppositorum," *SJP* 8, 175–85.
  E. Meuthen (1964), *Nikolaus von Kues,* Münster.
  G. von Bredow (1970), "Die Bedeutung des Minimum in der *coincidentia oppositorum*," in *Nicolò Cusano: Agli inizi del mondo moderno, Atti del Congresso...1964,* Florence, 357–66.
  G. Schneider (1970), *Gott—das Nichtandere,* BCG 4.

  K. Flasch (1973), *Die Metaphysik des Einen bei Nikolaus von Kues,* SPAMP 7.
  K. Jacobi (Ed.) (1979), *Nikolaus von Kues: Einführung in sein philosophisches Denken,* Friburg and Munich.
  D. Pätzold (1981), *Einheit und Andersheit,* Köln.
  K. Flasch (1987), *Einführung in die Philosophie des Mittelalters,* Darmstadt.
  S. Meier-Oeser (1989), *Die Präsenz des Vergessenen: Zur Rezeption der Philosophie des Nicolaus Cusanus vom 15. bis zum 18. Jahrhundert,* BCG 10.
  J. Stallmach (1989), *Ineinsfall der Gegensätze und Weisheit des Nichtwissens: Grundzüge der Philosophie des Nikolaus von Kues,* BCG, HS.
  B. Mojsisch (1991), "Nichts und Negation: Meister Eckhart und Nikolaus von Kues," in B. Mojsisch and O. Pluta (Eds.), *Historia Philosophiae Medii Aevi. Studien zur Geschichte der Philosophie des Mittelalters* II, Amsterdam and Philadelphia, 675–93.
  L. Hagemann and R. Glei (Eds.) (1993), Hen kai plèthos: *Einheit und Vielheit,* Altenberg/Würzburg.
  G. Piaia (Ed.) (1993), *Concordia Discors: Studi su Niccolò Cusano e l'umanesimo europeo offerti a G. Santinello,* Padua.
  K.-H. Kandler (1995), *Nikolaus von Kues: Denker zwischen Mittelalter und Neuzeit,* Göttingen.
  B. Mojsisch (1995), "Epistemologie im Humanismus: Marsilio Ficino, Pietro Pomponazzi und Nikolaus von Kues", *FZPhTh* 42, 152–71.
  K. Flasch (1998), *Nikolaus von Kues: Geschichte einer Entwicklung,* Frankfurt.

BURKHARD MOJSISCH

See also **Cosmos; Infinite; Knowledge of God; Negative Theology; Religion, Theology of**

Nietzsche, Friedrich Wilhelm

1844–1900

Nietzsche's self-presentation in *Ecce Homo* centers on what he sees as a veritable "crisis" in the history of thought, a crisis that imposes on him at least two tasks. One is the reinterpretation of the whole of Western history* from the perspective of nihilism. In this regard Nietzsche should be understood as analyzing an upheaval that affects our own era first and foremost. The other task is the proclamation of a new philosophy*, grounded in a new set of values and capable of being characterized as "the gay science" (to borrow the title of his 1882 book). Nietzsche is a radical philosopher because of the questions he asks, his undertaking to destroy the foundations of philosophy, and his desire to invent a new way of thinking. He remains, even today, one of the most controversial figures in the history of philosophy.

1. Nietzsche and His Image

The son of a Lutheran pastor, Nietzsche grew up in a religious and moral atmosphere permeated by a biblical and pietist spirit. From this starting point, and continuing right up to the end, he developed a merciless and ever more violent philosophical critique of religion and, more specifically, of Christianity.

Nietzsche was born in Röcken (Saxony) on 15 October 1844 and was educated in one of the best institutions of the time, the Schulpforta, before going on to study classical philology and, briefly but intensely, theology. He was appointed a professor of classical philology at the age of 25, but just ten years later he was compelled to resign. He succumbed to insanity at the age of 44 and died at Weimar on 25 September 1900, in his 56th year. During his 20 years of public activity, and in defiance of his failing health, Nietzsche displayed an exceptional intellectual fecundity. All his writings were initially received with total incomprehension, from his first published book, *Die Geburt der Tragödie aus dem Geiste der Musik* (1872, *The Birth of Tragedy from the Spirit of Music*), and his youthful critiques of the culture of his time, to the texts of his maturity—*Menschliches, Allzumenschliches* (1878, *Human, All Too Human*), *Die fröhliche Wissenschaft* (1882, *The Gay Science*), *Also sprach Zarathustra* (1883–85, *Thus Spake Zarathustra*), *Jenseits von Gut und Böse* (1886, *Beyond Good and Evil*), and *Zur Genealogie der Moral* (1887, *On the Genealogy of Morals*)—and then the vehement writings of his last period, *Der Antichrist* (1895, *The Antichrist*) and *Ecce Homo* (published posthumously in 1908). Even the way in which his ideas are formulated presents difficulties, since he simultaneously communicates them and uses esotericisms, aphorisms, and other stylistic methods to disguise them. They cry out for interpretation. "It is difficult to make oneself understood"—and perhaps Nietzsche himself did not even think that being understood was desirable.

Philosophical interpretations of Nietzsche's works have been undertaken by such thinkers as Martin Heidegger*, Karl Jaspers, and K. Löwith. More recently, however, French and Italian interpreters have adopted a new approach. Going back to the authors who preceded Nietzsche in the history of thought, they examine the structural aspects of his style in order to decipher his intentions from the perspective of a theory of culture. Meanwhile, theological studies have made it increasingly clear that Nietzsche's ideas need to be handled with subtlety.

2. Destruction as New Foundation

The destruction of metaphysics undertaken by Nietzsche—"philosophy by hammer blows"—has a clear purpose: to liberate the will from all constraints. The first discourse of *Also sprach Zarathustra*, "On the Three Metamorphoses," lays out the chain of events by which the will may be liberated from all belief in a prior truth and from all duty, and at last given over in full to the power of affirming and creating life. Hence, Nietzsche's philosophical project may be interpreted as an unconditional affirmation of humanity in respect of what is appropriate to humanity: *homo semper maior*. This aristocratic and elitist "experimental philosophy" (e.g., *KGW* VIII, 3, 288) is informed by the pathos of an individuality that is capable of giving form to the world* and is embodied in "higher exemplars" (*KGW* III, 1, 313).

To this end, Nietzsche mounts a systematic critique of language, reason*, truth*, and morality—"We do not possess truth" (*KGW* V, 1, 382)—and, finally, of religion, and of Christianity first and foremost. In other words, he criticizes everything that might constrain this affirmation of humanity or of will, whether in the name of being* (in a beyond, or in terms of a "true" world), or in the name of the good* (morality). Accordingly, Nietzsche is hostile to any form of "background world," to every naive or dogmatic belief in something beyond this Earth and this life, in a single being, self-identical and eternal, who knows nothing about becoming and the tragedy of experience. More specifically, he is hostile to any moral foundation for truth, which he interprets as the archetype for such background worlds. The Socratic figure of the theorizing man and the Platonic ideal of a "true world" are the earliest forms of this enfeebling of life that Nietzsche diagnoses and contests, although modern culture has produced many more of them. His aim is to set in train a "countermovement" (e.g., *KGW* VIII, 2, 432) in opposition to the will to self-negation and general decay, and to rediscover, through an apprehension of the Earth, the power of affirming life.

Nietzsche's most original ideas and images are expressions of his conception of a world dominated by affirmation. They include the "eternal return," the *Übermensch* ("superman" or "higher man"), *amor fati* ("love of fate"), and "Dionysus"; but, above all, there is the "will to power," conceived as the power of life desiring itself, the essence of all reality. This is not to be interpreted as a substance in the traditional sense. Indeed, this phrase indicates the distance that Nietzsche traveled—and expressed ever more clearly over the course of his intellectual development—away from his first philosophical master, Arthur Schopenhauer. For Nietzsche, the will desires itself and tends to surpass itself in desiring its own growth, which is why it is the will to power. Being more powerful is its way of desiring and of affirming itself.

3. Critique of Religion and Christianity

The critical dimension of Nietzsche's work culminates in a confrontation with Christianity. The rejection of "background worlds" leads into the theme of the "death of God." Since Christianity is "Platonism for the people" (*Jenseits von Gut und Böse*, Preface), the critique of the one is naturally a continuation of the critique of the other. However, Nietzsche's polemic becomes more radical in the writings of his last period, giving rise, in the form of a self-interpretation, to the phrase "Dionysus against the Crucified" (*KGW* VIII, 3, 58).

a) God and the Gods.

The famous statement that "God is dead" (*Die fröhliche Wissenschaft* 125), adopted not so long ago by "theologians of the death of God" (J.J. Altizer, W. Hamilton), was intended to describe the irreversible historical process of liberation from the traditional concept of God. However, Nietzsche has more than this simple observation in mind. He also seeks to confirm its legitimacy ("revaluation of values"), to show how God and religion may have been born ("genealogy"), and to justify the possibility of a different interpretation of the divine ("Dionysus").

It follows that Nietzsche's denunciation of the concept of God should be extended into a denunciation of the reactive forces that have constructed the concept. Nietzsche's "genealogical" project is intended to uncover, in the background of every system or concept, the instinct that has produced it. Behind morality and the concept of God, "genealogy" reveals the hidden intention to avenge oneself on life. God must die because he is, at least partially, connected with those reactive forces—resentment, bad conscience*, the ascetic ideal—that Nietzsche subjects to an implacable inquisition. Here the emphasis is no longer on the very existence of God, but on the power of humanity, its strength or weakness: "He who no longer finds greatness in God will not find it anywhere, and must either deny it or...create it" (*KGW* VII, 1, 28). What has been regarded until now as "divine" has entailed the "diminishing" of humanity (*KGW* III, 25).

Against the reduction of both the divine and the human that has resulted from asceticism*, and from distrust of the world, Nietzsche seeks to establish a new doctrine in which the divine retains a place, but within a new framework: that of the innocence of the world, and the complete, tragic, Dionysian affirmation of existence. Hence, Nietzsche can call for the creation of new gods, in line with his wishes. His philosophy entails a rejection of the idea of a transcendent divine subject, endowed with responsibility and "total awareness" (providence*); but it also entails a protest against commonplace forms of agnosticism* and atheism*. Between "monotonotheism" (belief in a boring God; *Der Antichrist* 19) on the one hand, and atheism on the other, Nietzsche seeks to define a polytheistic conception of existence: "In fact, only the moral God has been surpassed" (*KGW* VIII, 1, 217). In other words, in the European context God has become an abstract, Platonic/Christian deity, understood, even within the structures of language, as a negation of life in all its fullness and abyssal depths.

b) Christianity and the Church.

Nietzsche's critique of religion reaches its most concentrated expression in his attack on Christianity and the image of the priest*, the image *par excellence* of bad conscience. From Nietzsche's perspective, the devaluing of this world that is implied in the doctrines of sin*, redemption on the cross, and resurrection*, along with the moral practices of Christianity, represents "the most extravagant variation on the theme of morality" (*Die Geburt der Tragödie,* Preface, 5). Christianity has inoculated Europe with a "moral ontology" (*KGW* VIII, 1, 273); it is a religion of decadence, "an example of the alteration of personality" (VIII, 3, 98). The history of Christianity is thus a history of sin and guilt, a history of misfortune.

Nietzsche's specific target is Paul and his successors: "The Church was built in opposition to the gospel" (*Der Antichrist* 36). Yet, in praising Jesus* for his exemplary "practice" (*Der Antichrist* 35), free from resentment and moralizing, in opposition to a Church that believes in things, conditions, and effects "that do not exist" (*KGW* VIII, 3, 125), Nietzsche merely appears to avoid criticizing him. In fact, and most notably in his last period, he tags "Jesus' psychological type" (*KGW* VIII, 2, 407–08 and 417–20; *Der Antichrist* 29), and the message that Jesus conveyed, with the label of the blessed naif, the "idiot," belonging to a past age that was unaware of the reality of existence. It is true that Nietzsche eloquently contrasts Jesus' simple and radical "good news" with the subtle and vengeful "bad news" (*Der Antichrist* 39) of Paul and the Church, which promises salvation* as a reward, and he also reduces Christianity to a "simple phenomenon of consciousness" (*Der Antichrist* 39). Yet both the good news and the bad news are alike envisaged from a Protestant perspective, informed by dialogue with outstanding thinkers of the day, such as D.F. Strauss, Ernest Renan, Wellhausen, and Tolstoy. In fact, they are interconnected, since they are both infinitely far removed from the "gospel of the future" (*KGW* VIII, 2, 432), the gospel of the Antichrist, who, by contrast to Jesus and Christianity, is not content to deny reality, but creates it. The claim that Nietzsche attacked Christianity only in its distorted form cannot be sustained except by neglecting patent facts, by neutralizing his undeniable intentions, and by devaluing (above all with the intention of recuperating Nietzsche) the hostile attitude that Nietzsche intended.

4. Questions and Confrontation

Nietzsche's destructive enterprise poses some fundamental questions for a religion that has connections with metaphysics. The Christian ethics of resentment (servile and gregarious), and the dogmatic* theology that corresponds to it and precedes it, are caught up in an irreversible process of "self-overcoming" (*Zur Genealogie* *der Moral* III, 27). Nietzsche denies that this form of Christianity has any capacity or will to make a grand affirmation. By contrast he describes nihilism as the "logic, taken to its final consequences" (*KGW* VIII, 2, 432), of values and ideals that are Christian above all.

Nietzsche's philosophy also leaves certain questions open with regard to his own enterprise, over and above the possibility that it depends on what it seeks to surpass. Is the Platonism that Nietzsche hoped to overthrow incorporated into his worldview? To what extent is the figure of Zarathustra derived from the Christ* of the Gospels (as opposed to the historical Zoroaster who is Nietzsche's nominal model)? Nietzsche's philosophy demands a response from theology, an unavoidable confrontation with the thinker who presents himself as "the implacable enemy of Christianity" (*Ecce Homo*, "Why I am so wise," 7). In the end the main concern of his philosophy is to make an affirmation: he presents it as a confrontation between a Yes and a No, and as consisting in singing the song of Yes and Amen (*Also sprach Zarathustra*, "The Seven Seals"). Yet what is it that we must say Yes to? What must we recognize as the highest form of affirmation? Is it simply a matter of affirming the self, the will that is certain of itself, that extends its power and takes possession of the world by establishing new values? It is necessary to inquire whether all of Nietzsche's texts belong within the same perspective, and to wonder, for example, what exactly it is that must be loved with *amor fati*. Nietzsche does not say that the affirmation of the "eternal return" is solely directed toward the self, any more than he says that it is directed toward God. Nietzsche's philosophy, which is so often polemical, also calls for interpretation wherever it seeks to surmount its own violence. As for the polemic itself,

Nietzsche frequently uses it to raise questions that he then neglects or leaves unresolved, such as the implacable and irreconcilable nature of reality*, or the nonevangelical cult* of God, Christ, and the Church, transformed into simple instruments of authority. He thus gives believers occasion to return critically to themselves. Yet his provocation also invites those who have faith* to think more about what they hope to mean. Whatever objections may be raised to them, his iconoclastic and demystifying attacks should nonetheless provide food for theological thought, clearing a path for a deeper understanding of biblical faith in the service of a living Christian practice.

- G. Colli, M. Montinari (Eds.), *Kritische Gesamtausgabe, Werke (KGW)*, 1967– (30 vols. published); *KGW Briefwechsel*, 1975– (7 vols. published), Berlin and New York; *Œuvres philosophiques complètes*, Paris, 1967–, and *Correspondance*, Paris, 1986–.
- M. Montinari et al. (Eds.) (1972–), *Nietzsche Studien: Internationales Jahrbuch für die Nietzsche-Forschung*, Berlin and New York.

J.-L. Marion (1977), *L'idole et la distance: Cinq études*, 49–114, Paris.

E. Blondel (1980), *Nietzsche: le 5e évangile?*, Paris.

J. Figl (1984), *Dialektik der Gewalt: Nietzsches hermeneutische Religionsphilosophie*, Düsseldorf.

U. Willers (1988), *Friedrich Nietzsches antichristliche Christologie: Eine theologische Rekonstruktion*, Innsbruck and Vienna.

U. Willers (1994), "Dekonstruktive Demontage oder Analyse der Wirklichkeit? Friedrich Nietzsches Rede vom finis christianismi," in M. von Brück and J. Werbick (Eds.), *Traditionsabbruch—Ende des Christentums?*, 27–54, Würzburg.

M. Fleischer (1994), "Nietzsche," *TRE* 24, 506–524 (bibl.).

D. Franck (1998), *Nietzsche et l'ombre de Dieu*, Paris.

ULRICH WILLERS AND JÉRÔME DE GRAMONT

See also **Atheism; Freud, Sigmund; Heidegger, Martin; Marx, Karl; Paganism; Secularization**

Nominalism

I. Terminology

We can distinguish two forms of nominalism, one narrowly defined in relation to logic and theory of knowledge, and the other, more broadly, taking into consideration metaphysical, ethical, and theological matters as well.

1. Nominalism in the Strict Sense

In the strict sense, nominalism is the theory holding that there is nothing outside the human mind corresponding to general terms such as *man* or *living thing* (universals). The term *man* refers to concrete individuals, not to a universal thing like humanity, in which individual men can be said to participate. The universality of the term, the fact that it corresponds to different individuals, does not have to do with what is signified (with the *significatum*) but with the manner in which the signified is designated by the term (with the *significatio*). The universal term, therefore, derives its universality from an activity of the human intellect, which is able to form universal concepts applicable to different individuals.

This universality thus exists only in the human mind, not outside it (differentiating nominalism from realism). For a nominalist, a universal is a sign *(signum)* and not a thing outside the mind *(res)*. And because every science necessarily uses universal terms and looks for the universality of concrete phenomena, the theory implies that the object of the various sciences is not merely reality outside the mind, but that reality as it is expressed and signified by universal propositions. Nominalism thus makes a strict distinction between concrete reality (the real order of the *res*) and discourse concerning concrete reality (the rational order of *signa*). In nominalist theory, all sciences, including theology*, are conceptual constructions of reality; their structure depends on the manner in which man can know reality and on the way in which he can speak about it.

2. Nominalism in the Broad Sense

Nominalist epistemology is based on a few philosophical and theological propositions that make up nominalism in the broad sense, and the theological relevance of nominalism appears in this context. Reality is made up of different individual things, each of which exists in itself. There are no universal things, such as "humanity," that give particular things their nature and being. There is no super-individual system of *universalia ante rem* and *universalia in re* structuring and necessarily determining reality. God* can make each individual exist without another. Particular created beings thus have a direct link with God. God is not obligated to act through a series of created causes organized hierarchically. If he likes, he can intervene directly and immediately anywhere in his creation*. In his activity, God is entirely free and omnipotent. The power through which God has ordered creation as it is is called *potentia dei ordinata*. However, God might have acted differently; he might have made a different creation; this power that would have made it possible for him to act in a way other than the way he in fact did act is known as *potentia dei absoluta*.

The role played by the notion of *potentia dei absoluta* in nominalist philosophy* and theology is primarily a heuristic one. If God, *de potentia dei absoluta*, can make A exist without B, that means that A and B

are two particular things that do not necessarily depend on one another, even if in reality they always exist together. It is possible that God has ordered creation in such a way that when the words of the Eucharistic consecration are spoken, *hoc est enim corpus meum,* the bread is thereby transubstantiated, but that does not mean that these words are always necessarily required. Because of his omnipotence, God himself is able to fulfill the function of the words. This heuristic principle is applied in epistemology, in the doctrine of grace* and the sacraments*, and in morality, as well as in other areas. Neither nature* nor the economy of salvation* has an internal structure giving either of them a necessary organization. In every detail, they are determined by a divine will that depends on nothing (voluntarism*).

The question that defines nominalism in the strict sense goes back to the ancient debate on the ontological status of universals, as set forth in the *Isagogè* of Porphyry. However, it did not really take shape until the 12th century, when the term *nominales* was used for the first time. In the 14th and 15th centuries it resurfaced in a more pronounced form, in which the term *nominales* was joined by *terministae* and *moderni*. This later form of nominalism deeply influenced the intellectual climate of the time; it strongly contributed to the birth of the modern conception of the sciences and of Reformation theology. Because of its critical epistemology and its emphasis on divine will, nominalism has provoked resistance up to the present, particularly on the part of Thomists.

II. 12th Century

Twelfth-century nominalism originated in the areas of grammar and logic—that is, in areas of knowledge dealing with propositions and nouns. The vocalism of Roscelin that reduced universals to mere noises seems to have been the final harbinger of nominalism (Jolivet 1992). The influence of theories of logic and semantics was felt at the time in theology—for example with reference to the object of faith*—and in Christology*, so that it is possible to speak of theological nominalism. The concept of *nominales* is found after 1150 in some texts, where it designates contemporary thinkers in general. It is difficult to determine with certainty when this current disappeared, but it must have been in the late 12th or early 13th century, at the time of the formation of universities. In general, the sources speak of an anonymous *nominalis,* of *nominales,* or of *opinio nominalis,* and not of particular individuals, which makes identification of the theories more difficult. The sources nevertheless provide information on the content of views that were considered nominalist at the time. They concern principally the ontological status of genus and species, the distinction between language and reality, the doctrine of the *unitas nominis;* and the conceptions of logical inference. The sources also show that in the 12th century the views of the *nominales* were often contrasted to those of the *reales*. We sometimes find the expression *theologus nominalis.*

1. Genus and Species

The anonymous 12th-century treatise *De universalibus* attributes to the *nominales* the view that genera and species are only words *(vocabula)*. The argument goes back to Aristotle's *Categories,* where the naming of a first substance "states" *(proferri)* the species rather than the genus. "To be stated" is a property of words *(voces);* this is why genera and species are words (Iwakuma-Ebbesen 1992). We find an analogous view in the *Summa* of Peter of Capua (shortly after 1200), although he replaces the term *vox* ("word") with *nomen* ("name"). Peter of Capua says that, according to the nominalists, genera and species are names *(nos nominales ...dicimus genera et species esse nomina).* The work further establishes a contrast between the nominalists' view and that of the *reales* (Iwakuma-Ebbesen 1992).

The same view is set forth in the early-13th-century nominalist treatise *Positiones nominalium.* According to the anonymous author, the nominalists agree in saying that universal terms, such as *genus* and *species,* are names—*consentimus quod universalia sicut genera et species sunt nomina.* Against the *reales,* they thus demonstrate that there is nothing in reality but particular individuals—*nihil est praeter particulare* (Ebbesen 1991). Albert* the Great interpreted the nominalist argument in conceptual terms. In his commentary on Porphyry, where he deals with the ontological status of genus and species, he attributes to the nominalists the view that the generality *(communitas)* of universal terms *(universalia)* to which particular things that come under the universal term are related exists only in the intellect (Borgnet ed. I, 19*b*). The interpretation proposed by Albert exercised strong influence on later views of the nominalist argument. It corresponds to what was considered typical of nominalism in the 15th century.

2. Language and Reality

The doctrine that the order of language is different from the order of reality is also characteristic of the nominalism of the 12th century. Propositional assertions are complex verbal realities made up of simple verbal realities rather than complex things made up of simple things. For example, according to the Summa *Brevis sit* (1160) by Robert de Paris, the nominalists

distinguish the subject of a predicate *(predicatum)* from the subject of a saying *(locutio)* in such a way that only terms *(termini)* are subjects of predicates. In fact, terms are attributed only to terms. Real things, on the other hand, can be subjects only of sayings. And in fact, sayings deal with reality (Kneepkens 1987). An analogous distinction is noted in the nominalist treatise *De praedicatione,* in which the anonymous author contrasts an expression in which things are said of things *(res de re praedicari)* to one in which terms are said of terms *(terminum de termino),* and the first form of predication is attributed to the *reales.* The author, who calls himself a nominalist, prefers the second form, *nos terminum de termino* (Iwakuma-Ebbesen 1992).

3. Unitas Nominis

The theory of the *unitas nominis* is found primarily in works of the early-13th century. It states that the same event can be signified in different ways. It played a major role in the debates on the immutability* of divine knowledge* and on the immutable truth of a faith expressed at different moments in time*. The proposition *Pf* "Christ will be born" is true before the birth of Christ*, whereas the proposition *Pp* "Christ is born" is false. After the birth of Christ, the opposite is true; at that point *Pf* is false and *Pp* is true. That raises the question of whether the faith of Abraham is the same as the faith of Paul. Because the nominalists held the opinion that the content of faith is immutable, they resolved the problem by distinguishing what is signified from the way in which it is signified. The signified of *Pf* and *Pp* is identical (the birth of Christ), but the ways in which it is signified are different (the verb tenses are different).

In his *Summa,* Peter of Capua contrasts the views of the *nominales* and the *reales* on this point. He takes as his point of departure the question of divine knowledge. According to the *reales,* it is true that I exist now *(me esse),* whereas beforehand this was not true; this is why God knows now that I exist, whereas earlier He did not. The *nominales,* on the other hand, claim that the *me esse* was true from the beginning of creation *(a principio mundi),* but that earlier it was signified by the proposition *ego erit tunc* ("I will be at such a time"), and now it is signified by *ego sum* ("I myself am"). At this moment, then, God does not know any more than He knew earlier (Iwakuma-Ebbesen 1992).

Later in the *Summa,* Peter of Capua discusses the faith of the Old Testament and that of the New. He says that for the *nominales,* Abraham never believed that Christ would come *(Christum esse venturum),* for to say that "Christ will come" means even now that he will still come *(Christum esse venturum est ipsum modo esse venturum).* Abraham, therefore, believed the same thing that we believe—that is, that Christ has come *(Christum venisse),* for although that is now expressed by the proposition "Christ has come," in Abraham's time it was said that "Christ will come" (Iwakuma-Ebbesen 1992). In the *Summa* (1206–10) of Prévostin, the view of the *nominales* is presented concisely in the formulation "what is true once will always be true" *(quod semel est verum, semper erit verum);* this is why Abraham believed that Christ was born—*Christum esse natum*—and not that Christ would be born—*Christum esse nasciturum* (ibid.).

In an anonymous commentary on the *Sentences,* Peter Lombard's view—God knows neither more nor less than he has known (Tertia, Ed., 1, 293)—is compared to the nominalist argument that what is once true will always be true (Iwakuma-Ebbesen 1992). This is also the case in the *Summa aurea* of Guillaume d'Auxerre (Ribailler, Ed., 1, 181). The argument is also noted as the *opinio nominalium* in the works of Albert the Great (Borgnet, Ed. 26, 350 *b*) and Bonaventure* *(Opera omnia* 1, 740b). According to Bonaventure, this was the argument that gave the nominalists their name—*dicti sunt nominales, quia fundabant positionem suam super nomini unitatem* (Chenu 1935–36).

4. Logical Inference

In some 12th-century treatises, the doctrine of the nominalists is related to a few rules concerning logical inference. For example, the anonymous *Fragmentum Monacence* attributes to the *nominales* the view that a negative proposition cannot be deduced from an affirmative one (Iwakuma 1993). A later work, the *Obligationes Parisienses,* describes as incoherent the rule that the acceptance of a false proposition makes it possible to accept and prove any contingent thing (De Rijk 1975). Finally, the anonymous author of the treatise *De communibus distinctionibus* mentions the opinion of the *nominales* that from the impossible comes anything at all—*ex impossibili sequitur quidlibet.* According to the author, this view is opposed to that of the *reales* that nothing comes from the impossible—*ex impossibili nihil sequitur* (De Rijk 1988).

5. Theologicus Nominalis

In his commentary on Job, written in the third quarter of the 12th century, Pierre le Chantre uses the expression *nominalis theologicus* to characterize a theologian who considers only the name of Christ *(nomen Christi)* and not the thing designated by that name (the divinity and the humanity of Christ), unlike the *theologus reales* (Landgraf 1943). A sermon of the late 12th century by Hubert of Balsema also contrasts the *theologi reales* to the *neutraliter nominales vel nominaliter*

neutrales, and he makes a clearly negative judgment of these *nominales;* they are not as good disciples of Christ *(christiani)* as the *reales,* because their doctrine is without commitment and it has little value *(parum valet)* (d'Alverny 1984).

III. 14th and 15th Centuries

After the 13th century, *nominales* was no longer used to designate contemporary thinkers. It reappears in the sources for the first time in the early-15th century. These sources show that the concept of *nominales* in the late Middle Ages derived its meaning from the debate between the philosophical schools *(via nominalium* against *via realium)* of the time. The discussion focused in the first place on the ontological status of human concepts and their relation to reality. For example, in a 1403 letter, Guillaume Euvrie wrote that the *nominales* of his time reduced all the differences between divine attributes* and divine ideas to mere differences between human concepts *(humanae conceptiones).* The letter includes among the *nominales* such 14th-century thinkers as Adam of Wodeham, Gregory of Rimini, and Henry of Oyta (Pellerin 1967–68). In his *De universali reali* (1406–18), Jean de Maisonneuve, a disciple of Albert the Great, criticized the view of the *epicuri litterales* (Weiler 1968, 137), a term that his disciple Emeric of Campo transformed into *epicurei nominales* (*Invectiva* 117; see also *Tractatus* fol. 2v). These followers of Albert the Great connected the nominalist argument to the view that universals are nothing but concepts in the human mind—*universalia post rem.* William of Ockham, Jean Buridan, and Marsilius of Inghen were known as its most significant defenders. In a 1423 work, Jean Gerson identified the *nominales* with the *terministae,* apparently in connection with problems of logic—*logici, quos alii vocant terministas seu nominales* (OC 10, 127).

The situation had scarcely changed in the late-15th century. Fourteenth-century writers were those principally named, and the question at issue was always a the status of human concepts in relation to reality. The edict of Louis XI of France against nominalism (1473) mentioned the following names: William of Ockham, Jean de Mirecourt, Gregory of Rimini, Jean Buridan, Pierre d'Ailly, Marsilius of Inghen, Adam of Wodeham, Jean Dorp, and Albert of Saxony (Ehrle 1925). The nominalists replied to Louis XI's edict in 1474; in their view, with respect to divine attributes, there is a distinction between the order of language and the order of reality, and this is why the differences between the concepts of language do not always correspond to differences in reality—*illi doctores "nominales" dicti sunt qui non multiplicant res principaliter per termi-*

nos secundum multiplicationem terminorum. The *reales,* on the other hand, in the view of the *nominales,* claim that every conceptual distinction refers to a distinction in reality—*"reales" autem qui econtra res multiplicatas contendunt secundum multiplicitatem terminorum* (Ehrle 1925).

In the late Middle Ages, the concept of nominalism was thus attached to 14th-century writers, although it did not come to prominence until the 15th century. This historical fact makes it difficult to determine the precise content of "nominalism" in the late Middle Ages. But there are apparently clear correspondences among the 14th-century writers mentioned above, particularly with respect to universals and divine attributes.

1. William of Ockham

In his *De universali reali,* Jean de Maisonneuve saw the ideas of William of Ockham (c. 1300–c. 1350) as the origin of nominalism (Weiler 1968). The modern literature similarly considers Ockham as the first important representative of the nominalism of the late Middle Ages. This does not, however, mean that all of his ideas that are nominalist in character originate with Ockham himself. For example, his doctrine of the *potentia dei absoluta* is rooted in the traditions of the 13th century (Courtenay 1990), and the emphases on the individual and on voluntarism refer to passages of Duns* Scotus. Ockham's nominalism, in any event, provides important elements in the areas of logic and epistemology, and divine attributes and ethics*.

a) Logic and Epistemology. Ockham defends the idea that universals exist only in the human mind, not outside it. Reality is made up only of individuals, and universals are also individual things—signs in the human mind. The generality of the universal, therefore, has to do only with its function as a sign that can be a sign for several things—*quodlibet universale est una res singularis, et ideo non est universale nisi per significationem, quia est signum plurium* (OTh 1, 48). Human knowledge begins with the knowledge of individual things. These individual things are the object of an intuitive grasp *(notitia intuitiva)* when they are known in such a way that the knower has an immediate certainty *(notitia evidens)* of the existence or nonexistence of the thing known. This has to do with the knowledge not only of necessary truths but also of contingent truths. If, on the other hand, it is impossible to deduce from knowledge of the thing its existence or nonexistence, we are dealing with abstract knowledge *(notitia abstractiva).* And that applies to memory or conceptual knowledge, deduced from sense perception (OTh 1, 30–33).

The question of the status of intuitive knowledge led to one of the most interesting problems in the application of the concept of divine omnipotence *(potentia dei absoluta),* whether God can deceive man. In his omnipotence *(de potentia dei absoluta),* can God assume the role of an intuitively grasped object and thereby give the knower the immediate certainty of the existence of the thing known, whereas in reality the thing does not exist? In the first book of his commentary on the *Sentences,* Ockham concedes this possibility. God can do everything that a created cause is capable of doing; he can thus cause immediate certainty; and, in addition, he can bring into existence everything existing in itself *(res absoluta)* without anything else. Intuitive knowledge of a thing is an activity of the soul* and exists in the soul; it can therefore be caused by God even if the thing known does not exist (OTh 1, 37–39).

In his later *Quodlibeta,* however, Ockham speaks with more reticence and shows that there is a contradiction in God causing in man an immediate grasp of, for instance, "this whiteness is" *(haec albedo est),* if that whiteness does not exist (OTh 9, 499). Divine omnipotence is thus limited by the principle of noncontradiction (ibid., 604), and immediate knowledge of the existence of a nonexistent object cannot be produced by God. This can also be applied to the intuitive (beatific) vision* of the divine essence. In this vision, God cannot deceive man, because although he can replace any created cause by His own causality, it will always be necessary, if he wishes to cause in man the intuitive knowledge of his essence, for he himself to exist as first cause. If man knows that God exists by basing himself on an intuitive vision, it is certain that God exists (ibid., 605–06).

b) Divine Attributes. Ockham distinguishes two ways in which divine attributes—knowledge, will, and so on—can be conceived: first, as an attributive perfection really identical to God *(perfectio attributalis)* and, second, as a thing in the human mind applicable to God *(conceptus* or *nomen attributalis).* The first conception concerns reality itself, and the second the way in which man thinks or speaks about reality; and according to Ockham, the answer to the question of the plurality and the ontological status of the attributes will be different depending on whether it is a question of the reality itself or of thinking about the reality. In the first case, there are not several attributes but a single perfection, perfectly one and identical to God. In the second case, on the other hand (attribute as predicate), the attribute is not really identical to God, but only a concept or a sign in the human mind. If we are dealing with predicates, then it is possible to say that God has several attributes. Hence, plurality does not exist in God but only in the human mind (*OTh* 2, 61–62).

c) Ethics. In Ockham's ethics, there is no supreme principle intelligible in itself to man. All ethical norms have been established by the omnipotent will of God. This certainly does not mean that the moral order is entirely arbitrary. The will of God is in fact identical to his intellect and his wisdom*, and he always acts according to *recta ratio,* which means that divine law* and natural law are identical (*OTh* 4, 610; 5, 352–53).

2. Adam of Wodeham

The thought of Adam of Wodeham, in the first half of the 14th century, is related to the nominalism of Ockham in various respects. Adam, too, defends the position that universals are only signs signifying particular things in a general way—*sunt communes et universales in repraesentando quodlibet tale, licet nullum distincte* (Gál-Wood Ed., 1, 21). Like Ockham, he also defends the idea that there is a distinction, with respect to divine attributes, between the order of language and the order of reality. In God the attributes are identified with the divine essence so that they cannot be distinguished from one another. On the level of language, however, they have to be understood as signs freely established by man and attributed to God—*sunt quaedam signa mentalia vel ad placitum instituta quae Deo attribuimus per praedicationem.* Each sign is a particular thing, and this is why the attributes really are different *(differunt realiter)* on the level of language (Gál-Wood Ed., 2, 324). But unlike Ockham, with respect to the object of knowledge, Adam of Wodeham holds to the doctrine of *complexe significabilia,* a concept that strikingly corresponds to the 12th-century nominalist doctrine of *unitas nominis* (Gál 1977).

3. Gregory of Rimini

The influence of Ockham and Adam of Wodeham can be clearly seen in the *Lectura* of Gregory of Rimini (c. 1300–49). He shares their opinion on universals: they exist only in the human mind, not outside it. Gregory also claims that reality consists only of particular things. Like Ockham and Wodeham, his epistemology gives priority to knowledge of the particular over knowledge of the universal (Würsdörfer 1917). His conception of divine attributes also clearly corresponds to that of the two other nominalists (Trapp Ed., 2, 88). Finally, like Adam of Wodeham, Gregory of Rimini defends the theory of *complexe significabile* as the object of knowledge. He does this in particular in his explanation of divine knowledge. God knows things that may be signified by a single word *(incomplexe),* for example men and angels*, and he knows

things that can be designated by a collection of different words, such as "fire heats wood." Gregory calls similar connections *enuntabilia* or *cognoscibilia complexe significabilia* (Trapp Ed., 227–28). And if he speaks of *enuntabilia* and not, like Ockham, of propositions, in order to name the objects of knowledge, this is because, according to him, the object of a judgment is not a proposition but what is meant by it (Nuchelmans 1973).

4. Marsilius of Inghen

The 15th-century sources also include Marsilius of Inghen (c. 1340–96) among the most important nominalists. A comparison of Marsilius's ideas with those of the other theologians mentioned clearly shows correspondences. Universals exist only in the human mind. Humanity *(humanitas)* in general does not exist. Even abstracting from all the individual characteristics of Socrates, the humanity of Socrates remains particular—it is only the humanity of Socrates (Strasbourg Ed., fol. 3 r).

Like the other nominalists, Marsilius clearly distinguishes the order of language from the order of reality. Divine attributes are identical to the divine essence, as attributive perfections *(perfectiones attributales),* but they are distinguished from divine essence in human thought as attributive concepts—*licet enim intellectus et voluntas, intelligere et velle sint in deo omnimodo idem, tamen apud nos in mente nostra diversos conceptus de essentia dei important,* or "even though in God the intellect and the will, thought and desire are absolutely identical, in our minds they imply different concepts of the divine essence" (Strasbourg Ed., fol. 61 r).

The thought of Marsilius nevertheless contains significant differences from that of his predecessors. For example, he criticizes Ockham's doctrine of ideas and the conception of *complexe significabile* (Hoenen 1993) as an attributive concept in Adam of Wodeham and Gregory of Rimini.

5. Gabriel Biel

In 1508 the University of Salamanca established a chair of nominalist theology *(cátedrade nominales)* for the study of the works of Marsilius of Inghen and Gabriel Biel (Andrés 1976). Gabriel Biel (1418–95) was included among the nominalists along with Marsilius because his commentary on the *Sentences* was in fact nothing but an *abbreviatura* of Ockham's *Scriptum,* made obvious by the correspondences in structure and content. According to Biel, the universal exists only in the human mind; it is a particular thing that signifies several things equally; its generality exists only at the level of the signifier—*esse universale nihil aliud est quam repraesentare vel significare plures res singulares univoce* (Werbeck-Hofmann Ed., 1, 180).

Biel also follows Ockham on the question of divine attributes. He distinguishes between the attribute as a thing identified with God in reality *(res ipsa quae est perfecta)* and the attribute as a sign that can be predicated about God *(signum praedicabile de re perfecta;* Werbeck-Hofmann Ed., 1, 147–50). In the first case as opposed to the second, there are not several perfections or attributes. However, Biel clearly distances himself from Ockham in matters of ethics. In fact, he accepts the existence of an objective norm in morality. One who sins acts not only against God but against right reason* *(contra quamlibet rectam rationem).* One commits a sin* by acting against *recta ratio,* and this would be true even if God did not exist—*si per impossibile deus non esset.* The norm for action is immutable and identical for everyone (Werbeck-Hofmann Ed., 2, 612). On this point, Biel follows Gregory of Rimini (Trapp Ed., 6, 235).

IV. Historiography

The historiography of nominalism began as early as 1474 when, in response to the edict of Louis XI, the nominalists presented an outline of the history of their school. The description is highly rhetorical (Kaluza 1995), but it nevertheless had a significant influence on the later image of nominalism. Two other works also influenced that image: the *Annales Boiorum* of Aventinus in the 16th century, in which Ockham, Gregory of Rimini, and Marsilius of Inghen are considered as *antesignani nominalistarum* (Trapp 1956), and the *Historia Universitatis Parisiensis* of Du Boulay in the 17th century.

In the 20th century, we should distinguish two angles of approach to the nominalism of the 12th century. The first considers nominalism primarily as a doctrine of universals (Vignaux 1930), whereas the second emphasizes the theory of the *unitas nominis* (Chenu 1935–36). These two approaches are still present in current research, although attempts have been made to combine them (Courtenay 1991). Until the 1960s, research on the nominalism of the 14th and 15th centuries was dominated by a negative judgment: by emphasizing the *potentia dei absoluta,* nominalism had made itself fundamentally skeptical (Michalski 1969) and disrupted the synthesis of faith and reason accomplished by the Scholasticism of the 13th century (Gilson 1938). Thanks to modern critical editions of nominalist writers and studies based on new sources (Baudry 1949; Boehner 1958; Oberman 1967, 1981; Courtenay 1978, 1984; Tachau 1988; Kaluza 1988), that negative image has been corrected. It has thus been possible to bring to light the specific contribution of nominalism to the development of philosophy and theology.

● Adam de Wodeham, *Sent.*, Paris, 1512; *Tractatus de indivisibilibus,* Ed. R. Wood, Dordrecht, 1988.

Adam de Wodeham, *Lectura secunda in librum primum Sententiarum,* Ed. G. Gál and R. Wood, St. Bonaventure, NY, 1990, 3 vols.

Albert the Great, *Opera omnia,* Ed. A. Borgnet, Paris, L. Vivès, 1890–1899, 38 vols.

Bonaventure, *Opera omnia,* Ed. Quaracchi, Florence, 1882–1902, 11 vols.

Du Boulay, *Historia Universitatis Parisiensis* 1, Paris, 1665, Repr. Frankfurt, 1966.

Gabriel Biel, *Collectorium circa quattuor libros Sententiarum,* Ed. W. Werbeck and U. Hofmann, Tübingen, 1973–92, 4 vols.

Grégoire de Rimini, *Lectura super primum et secundum Sententiarum,* Ed. A.D. Trapp et al., Berlin, 1979–87, 7 vols.

Heymericus de Campo (1496), *Tractatus problematicus,* Köln; *Invectiva,* in G. Meersseman, *Geschichte des Albertismus* 2, DHOP 5, 1935, 112–212.

Jean Gerson, *Œuvres complètes,* Ed. P. Glorieux, Paris, 1960–73, 10 vols.

Marsile d'Inghen, *Quaestiones super quattuor libros Sententiarum,* Strasbourg, 1501, Repr. Frankfurt, 1966.

Peter Lombard, *Sententiae in quattuor libris distinctae,* Grottaferrata, 1971–81, 2 vols.

William of Auxerre, *Summa aurea,* Ed. J. Ribaillier, Grottaferrata, 1980–87, 5 vols.

William of Ockham, *Opera philosophica (OPh) et theologica (OTh),* St. Bonaventure, NY, 1967–88, 17 vols.

♦ J. Würsdörfer (1917), *Erkennen und Wissen nach Gregor von Rimini,* BGPhMA 20/1.

F. Ehrle (1925), *Der Sentenzenkommentar Peters von Candia des Pisaner Papstes Alexanders V.,* FS Beiheft 9.

P. Vignaux (1930), "Nominalisme," *DThC* 11/1, 718–84.

M.D. Chenu (1935–36), "Grammaire et théologie aux XIIe et XIIIe siècles," *AHDL* 10, 5–28.

É. Gilson (1938), *Reason and Revelation in the Middle Ages,* New York (2nd Ed. 1966).

A. Landgraf (1943), "Studien zur Theologie des zwölften Jahrhunderts, I: Nominalismus in den theologischen Werken der zweiten Hälfte des zwölften Jahrhunderts," Tr. 1, 183–210.

L. Baudry (1949), *Guillaume d'Occam: sa vie, ses œuvres, ses idées sociales et politiques,* Paris.

A.D. Trapp (1956), "Augustinian theology of the 14th century," *Aug(L)* 6, 146–274.

Ph. Boehner (1958), *Collected Articles on Ockham,* Louvain and Paderborn.

H.A. Oberman (1967), *The Harvest of Medieval Theology: Gabriel Biel and Late Medieval Nominalism,* 2nd Ed., Grand Rapids.

E. Pellegrin (1967–68), "Un humaniste du temps de Charles VI: Guillaume Euvrie," *BIRHT* 15, 9–28.

A.G. Weiler (1968), "Un traité de Jean de Nova Domo sur les universaux," *Vivarium* 6, 108–154.

K. Michalski (1969), *La philosophie au XIVe siècle: Six études,* Ed. K. Flasch, *Opuscula philosophica* 1, Frankfurt.

R. Paqué (1970), *Das Pariser Nominalistenstatut, Zur Entstehung des Realitätsbegriffs der neuzeitlichen Naturwissenschafts,* Berlin.

G. Nuchelmans (1973), *Theories of the Proposition,* Amsterdam.

L. M. de Rijk (1975), "Some Thirteenth-Century Tracts on the Game of Obligation II," *Vivarium* 13, 22–54.

M. Andrés (1976), *La teología española en el siglo XVI,* vol. 1, Madrid.

G. Gál (1977), "Adam of Wodeham's Question on the *Complexe Significabile* as the Immediate Object of Scientific Knowledge," FrSA 37, 66–102.

D. M. Armstrong (1978), *Nominalism and Realism: Universals and Scientific Realism,* vol. 1, Cambridge.

W. J. Courtenay (1978), *Adam Wodeham: An Introduction to his Life and Writings,* Leyden.

H. A. Oberman (1981) (Ed.), *Gregor von Rimini: Werk und Wirkung bis zur Reformation,* Berlin.

M.-T. d'Alverny (1984), "Humbertus de Balsema," *AHDL* 51, 127–91.

W. J. Courtenay (1984), *Covenant and Causality in Medieval Thought,* London.

R. Imbach (1987), "Philosophie und Eucharistie bei W. von Ockham," in E. P. Bos and H. A. Krop (Eds.), *Ockham and Ockhamists,* Nimegen.

C. H. Kneepkens (1987), *Het iudicium constructionis: Het leerstuk van de constructio in de 2e helft van de 12e eeuw,* Nimegen, 4 vols.

L. M. de Rijk (1988), *Some Earlier Parisian Tracts on* Distinctiones Sophismatum, *Artistarium* 7, Nimegen.

K. H. Tachau (1988), *Vision and Certitude in the Age of Ockham,* Leyden.

Z. Kaluza (1988), *Les querelles doctrinales à Paris: Nominalistes et réalistes aux confins du XIVe et du XVe siècle,* Bergamo.

W. J. Courtenay (1990), *Capacity and Volition: A History of the Distinction of Absolute and Ordained Power,* Bergamo.

W. J. Courtenay (1991), "Nominales and Nominalism in the Twelfth Century," in Lectionum Varietates: *Hommage à Paul Vigneaux (1904–1987),* 11–48, Paris.

S. Ebbesen (1991), "Two Nominalist Texts: 'Positiones' and a 'Categories' Commentary," *Cahiers de l'Institut du Moyen Age grec et latin* 61, 429–40.

J. Jolivet (1992), "Trois variations médiévales sur l'universel et l'individu: Roscelin, Abélard, Gilbert de la Porrée," *RMM* 97, 111–55.

Y. Iwakuma et S. Ebbesen (1992a), "Logico-theological Schools from the Second Half of the 12th Century: A List of Sources", *Vivarium* 30, 157–72; (1992b), "Twelfth-Century Nominalism Bibliography", *Vivarium* 30, 211–15.

M. J. F. M. Hoenen (1993), *Marsilius of Inghen: Divine Knowledge in Late Medieval Thought,* SHCT 50.

Y. Iwakuma (1993), "Parvipontani's thesis 'ex impossibile quidlibet sequitur': Comments on the Sources of the Thesis from the Twelfth Century," in K. Jacobi (Ed.), *Argumentationtheorie,* 123–51, Leyden.

C. Michon (1994), *N. La théorie de la signification d'Occam,* Paris.

Z. Kaluza (1995), "La crise des années 1474–1482: L'interdiction du n. par Louis XI," in M. J. F. M. Hoenen et al. (Ed.), *Philosophy and Learning: Universities in the Middle Ages,* 293–327, Leyden.

A. de Libera (1996), *La querelle des universaux,* Paris.

MAARTEN J. F. M. HOENEN

See also **Luther, Martin; Omnipotence, Divine; Realism; Scholasticism; Voluntarism**

Notes, Theological

The preservation of faith* and discipline—the pairing *fides et mores,* whose scope has expanded and contracted from age to age—has been the object of constant vigilance on the part of Christian communities ever since the time of the apostles. Through the great Eastern councils*, the patristic age laid down the key points of orthodoxy and orthopraxy by means of creeds and canons; or, more often, in the form of condemnations, the most solemn of which was the anathema, long taken to imply heresy*. Nonetheless it was not until the rise of a speculative theological science, linked to the appearance and growth of the universities and the mendicant orders, that the use of increasingly precise and numerous "notes" arose and became widespread. These notes served to indicate, positively or negatively, the value of expressions of dogma* or of the doctrine peripheral to it, which was constantly growing in volume as a result of theological conclusions extending the *revelabile.* The great Parisian condemnation of 1277 (*see also* philosophy*, truth*) already illustrates the strengths and weaknesses of a system that the teaching authority*—in the first instance the Roman pontiff—was to borrow directly from the universities. The theology* faculties of the latter, in the course of their doctoral assemblies, would continue to advance numerous doctrinal opinions that, in the cases of Paris and its college of the Sorbonne, of Oxford and Köln, and later of Leuven, Douai, Alcalá, and Salamanca, met with considerable acceptance. Thus there was a distinction between the scholarly judgments of the universities, given *doctrinaliter,* and the authoritative judgment of the organs of the magisterium*—the bishops* as judges of the faith, the council, the Roman pontiff—given *judicialiter,* with canonical consequences if *assertores* were involved and displayed obstinacy. Only the collapse of the old political and ecclesiastical regimes at the end of the 18th century put an end to this regulatory activity carried out by the great *studia generalia* of Catholic Europe, and to that of the tribunals of the Inquisition, which while operating on a penal level did not leave aside the examination of doctrines. By the 19th century only the Sacred Congregation of the Roman and Universal Inquisition, or Roman Holy Office, survived. Founded in 1542, placed at the head of all the dicasteries in 1588, with the pope* as its prefect, and given the title of "supreme" in 1907, it retains a monopoly on the pronouncing of "censures" (denoting error) and the offering of "qualifications" (denoting the relationship to revealed truth or common doctrine).

Until the last century the Church* tended to clarify dogma by the negative approach of condemnations much more than by the positive one of canons, expositions of faith, or formularies, and in consequence notes of censure—until they gradually disappeared from the acts of the magisterium—attracted the attention of theologians more than did qualifications. As far as the latter are concerned, mention should be made of the attempts at classification presented by Holden in his *Divinae fidei analysis* (1652), Amort in his *Demonstratio critica religionis catholicae* (1741), Blau in his *Regula fidei catholicae* (1780), and Chrismann in his *Regula fidei catholicae et collectio dogmatum credendorum* (1792), and by the dogmatic specialists of the Germanic world and the Roman College, which after 1870 became the Gregorian University. This scale of relationship to revealed truth was closely dependent on the work of speculative thought, which alone makes it possible to determine the scope of specific concepts such as "dogma of faith," "positively revealed," "to be believed as a matter of divine faith," "article of Catholic faith," "virtually a matter of faith," "theological conclusion," "apostolic tradition," "probable doctrine," "dogmatic fact," "morally certain," "practice of the Church," and so on. While the existence of a "hierarchy of truths*" can be recognized, applying it is an extremely sensitive matter: the idea of "faith," like the opposite one of "heresy," has only slowly assumed the character of a noetic concept, and has long included elements that would nowadays be placed in the moral or disciplinary field. This is particularly true of censures: over the centuries, especially since texts began to be disseminated by means of printing, these had been carried to a degree of complexity that from the 16th cen-

tury made the *ars notandi* a theological specialty in its own right, with veritable experts, whether university doctors, members of religious orders, or advisers and qualificators of the Holy Offices. In the course of dissecting theological writings, these experts were sometimes tempted to stray imperceptibly from the strictly doctrinal and prudential register—the detecting of heresy or various forms of error—to that of a virtuoso exercise that came closer to a critical revision of the texts.

Consideration of the principal notes of censure confirms this progressive broadening of scope: if a proposition is judged "heretical," "close to heresy," "erroneous," "close to error," or even "reckless," the normative judgment speaks for itself—even if it is not always clear, in the case of the note "heretical," that the contrary proposition is *ipso facto* to be taken as a matter of faith. But it is a much more delicate matter to apply censures to a proposition, without leaving any room for objection, when such censures are aimed at every nuance of thought and expression, every latent meaning that can be contained in texts whose construction is usually highly elaborate and that lend themselves to countless ambiguities. This refinement in interpretation, encouraged by the asymptotic nature of error, led the experts to increase the number of notes—over a hundred certified by use. They range from those previously quoted that are directly concerned with the dogmatic substance of statements, to those that principally condemn the form—such as "misleading and ill-sounding," "offensive to piety" *(piarum aurium offensiva),* "insulting to the Church," or "ambiguous"—to others that judge the effect—such as "impious," "scandalous," "blasphemous," "seditious," or "schismatic"—and to yet others, even subtler in their application, that focus on latent meanings that may be brought out by circumstances of time, place, or person, such as "suggestive of heresy," "suggestive of error," "unlikely," "false," "questionable," and so on. The most complete inventory of and commentary on notes of censure is to be found in the survey by Father Antonio Sessa (Antonius de Panormo), *Scrutinium doctrinarum qualificandis assertionibus, thesibus ac libris conducentium...* (Rome, 1709, folio). They were subsequently also considered by Du Plessis d'Argentré and C. L. de Montaigne, to name only the French.

Faced with a proliferation that was compromising the purifying role of censure and offering ample scope to *odium theologicum,* the teaching authority reacted. It went so far as to specify, in the conclusion to the decree of 2 March 1679 that condemned 65 laxist propositions, "that doctors, Scholastics, or whosoever else, should refrain henceforth from all offensive accusations... and use neither censure, nor note, nor polemical judgment against propositions commonly held in Catholic circles, as long as the Holy See has not pronounced judgment on these propositions." This prohibition was repeated by Benedict XIV in his constitution *Sollicita ac provida* of 9 July 1753. Perhaps what was needed above all was to require the censors to give reasons for their judgments. Indeed, it is the most striking feature of the note system (which has never been officially codified, remaining a purely practical procedure whose secret is now lost) that no explanation is ever given for why a particular note is applied to a proposition. Because of this, the way is left open for suspicions of arbitrariness and for endless objections on the part of the authors or theological schools concerned. This characteristic was shared with the Roman Index, which did not justify its proscriptions, but confined itself—in even the most favorable cases—to a *donec corrigatur* (signifying a work placed on the Index "until it has been corrected") without any further detail to shed light on the errors committed.

This lack of precision seems to have troubled neither the experts nor the teaching Church, in an age of rationality convinced that the meaning of a text could be condensed into a proposition without loss of substance, and that the doctrinal value of such a proposition could be unambiguously fixed. Nonetheless, difficulties soon became evident when it was necessary to go beyond the censure of categorical negations of the Catholic faith—for example Luther*'s theses and those of the Protestants—to the unearthing of errors concealed in the depths of the text. For all that the possibility of judging propositions in themselves was maintained *(absolute objective, ut jacent, ut verba sonant)*, there was often a tendency toward an examination of context *(in sensu auctoris, in sensu ab assertoribus intento)*. This in no way implied that the target was the author's personal meaning, his intimate thoughts, which God* alone knew; but rather the sense that arose from a reading of the whole text of which the propositions formed a summary, made expressive by their concision. These propositions did not have to appear word for word, *verbatim*, in the text to which they were attributed, as in the case of the famous five propositions of Jansen's *Augustinus* (*see* Jansenism*). It was enough that an examination of the writing or book in question should allow the understanding of a "proper and natural" sense that could be qualified by a theological note—positive or negative—applied to the proposition considered in its "obvious sense."

The exact application of notes of censure to each proposition gave rise to as much difficulty as the relationship of propositions to a corpus (book, theses, university course). Censure could be brought to bear *speciatim* or *singillatim*, in other words individually;

each proposition was qualified by the note or notes that applied to it. But censures could also be inflicted *globatim*, overall, the frequent comment *respective* indicating that each note applied of necessity to one or more propositions, none of which was exempt, but without specifying which one or ones. This left the reader, and especially the theologian, the task of allocating the notes. The deficiencies of this procedure, commonly used despite its (sometimes intentional) lack of rigor, became clear when 101 propositions taken from Quesnel's *Réflexions morales* were condemned by the bull *Unigenitus* of 8 September 1713: more than twenty notes of censure were applied "respectively", leading to endless quibbling over which heresy or errors should be attributed to each proposition. The court of Rome displayed more care over the condemnation of the canons of the synod* of Pistoia by the bull *Auctorem fidei* of 28 August 1794, which censured each proposition *singillatim*, one by one, and in addition referred to the Acts of the synod for the provenance of the proposition, thus forestalling any dispute over the facts.

What kind and degree of approval *(assensus)* is any believer to extend, then, to a decision that fixes, by means of notes (whether qualifications or censures), the value of a theological text or statement in relation to an author's doctrine? The collegial judgment of the universities involved a scholarly competence that called for serious consideration of the *doctrina communis* expressed by it. The same went for the pronouncements of the Holy Offices of Spain, Portugal, and Italy. In the case of the Roman congregation of the Holy Office, decrees have been given "in common form," *in forma communi*, involving the sole authority of the college of cardinals of the Inquisition and demanding complete submission; or "in specific form," *in forma specifica*, with the express approval of the Roman pontiff. In the latter form, decrees constitute pronouncements that, like any act of the ordinary pontifical magisterium, call forth a religious assent, *ore et corde*, on a par with that extended to the bulls, constitutions, and briefs that can come directly from the head of the Church and contain condemnations of points of textual dogma. The judgment of the Roman pontiff may bear the marks of a solemn pronouncement—for example *declaramus, damnamus, definimus*—but infallibility* concerning points of dogma, including decisions on theological texts, has not been defined: the First Vatican* Council left this point aside, but on the other hand distinguished between *credenda* and *tenenda*, according to whether "divinely revealed truths" or "truths related to revealed truths" were involved. While Clement XI, in the bull *Vineam Domini Sabaoth* of 16 July 1705, rejected a simple *silentium* *obsequiosum,* or mere outward deference, he did not go so far as to call for an act of divine faith, but contented himself with a reception by "inward obedience," *interius obsequendo, quae vera est orthodoxi hominis oboedientia*—a type of *assensus* confirmed by the decree *Lamentabili* of 8 July 1907, prop. 7.

In order to take account of this type of assent a number of theologians since the 18th century have proposed the idea of an "ecclesiastical faith," justified by the infallibility of the Church and not directly by "the authority of the revealing God." This has aroused strong opposition from Thomists, who maintain that points of dogma are also infallibly defined by the Church and are the object of divine faith in the same way as biblical revelation or the dogmatic definitions of the Councils or the Roman pontiffs. The analyses of P. Guérard des Lauriers, O.P., *Les dimensions de la foi* (1952, specifically excursus VIII–XI), made a decisive contribution to the clarification of this subject, even if some commentators have seen in the appeal to divine faith a danger of overemphasizing the magisterium. It is in any case "close to being a matter of faith" nowadays that the infallibility of the Church extends to that which is related to revealed truth. However, anyone who was to withhold his complete assent, *internus assensus,* to the condemnation of a doctrine advanced by theological texts, whether or not it had been evaluated by notes of censure, would not in consequence be a heretic—there being no negation of a truth directly revealed and proposed as such by the Church—but would be gravely culpable and wide open to the suspicion of heresy.

The International Theological Commission has recently called for a re-evaluation of theological notes: "It is to be regretted that the science of doctrinal qualifications has been to some extent relegated to obsolescence by the moderns. It is nonetheless useful in the interpretation of dogma, and for that reason should be revived and developed further" (*Enchiridion Vaticanum* 11, *Documenti ufficiali della Santa Sede. 1988–1989,* 1991, no 75, p. 1749).

• Fr. de Salignac de La Mothe-Fénelon (1704), *Ordonnance et Instruction pastorale portant condamnation d'un imprimé intitulé "Cas de conscience"* (*OC*, vol. 3, 1848).

H. Tournély (1726), *Praelectiones theologicae de Ecclesia Christi*, Paris.

H. Quillet (1905), "Censures doctrinales," *DThC* 2, 2101–2113.

L. Choupin (1907), *Valeur des décisions doctrinales et disciplinaires du Saint-Siège*, Paris (2nd Ed. 1928).

L. Garzend (1912), *L'inquisition et l'hérésie: Distinction de l'hérésie théologique et de l'hérésie inquisitoriale: à propos de l'affaire Galilée*, Paris.

Fr. Marin-Sola (1924), *L'évolution homogène du dogme catholique*, 2nd Ed., Fribourg.

R. Favre (1946–1947), "Les condamnations avec anathème," *BLE* 46, 226–41; 47, 31–48.

J. Cahill (1955), *The Development of the Theological Censures after the Council of Trent, 1563–1709*, Fribourg.

Y. J.-M. Congar (1956), "Fait dogmatique et foi ecclésiastique," *Cath* 4, 1059–67.

C. Koser (1963), *De notis theologicis historia, notio, usus*, Petrópolis.

A. Kolping (1963), "Qualifikationen," *LThK*2 8, 914–19.

P. Fransen (1968), "Enkele opmerkinger over de theologische kwalificaties," *TTh* 8, 328–48.

J. Schumacher (1974), *"Der Denzinger" Geschichte und Bedeutung eines Buches in der Praxis der neueren Theologie*, Friburg.

P. Legendre (1974), *L'amour du censeur: Essai sur l'ordre dogmatique*, Paris.

L. Ceyssens (1974), "Le fait dans la condamnation de Jansénius et dans le serment anti-janséniste," *RHE* 69, 697–734.

R. Hissette (1977), *Enquête sur les 219 articles condamnés à Paris le 7 mars 1277*, Louvain.

L. Ceyssens (1981), "Les jugements portés par les théologiens du Saint-Office sur les 31 propositions rigoristes condamnées en 1690," *Anton* 56, 451–67.

A. Houtepen (1987), "*Hierarchia veritatum* et orthodoxie," *Conc(F)* no 212, 53–66.

G. Thils (1982), "Notes théologiques," *Cath* 9, 1389–94.

B. Neveu (1993), *L'erreur et son juge: Remarques sur les censures doctrinales à l'époque moderne*, Naples.

G. Fragnito (1997), *La Bibbia al rogo: La censura ecclesiastica e i volgarizzamenti della Scrittura (1471–1605)*, Bologna.

Bruno Neveu

See also **Heresy; Loci theologici; Magisterium; Theology; Truth**

Nothingness

The concept of nothingness *(nihil)* or non-being *(non ens),* absolute *(ouk on)* or relative *(mè on),* is one of the key concepts in the history of metaphysics, from the *Poem* of Parmenides, Plato's *Parmenides,* or, on the

Sophist side, Gorgias's treatise *Peri tou mè ontos (On the Non-existent)* to Heidegger's* *Was ist Metaphysik?* or Sartre's *L'être et le néant.* Theology* has used the concept in a number of ways. On the one hand it has been called on with regard to questions and doctrines, often of considerable importance: most notably God*'s transcendence (that which is beyond being* has been conceptualized as non-being), creation* (conceived as *ex nihilo*), and evil* (error or sin* as participation in nothingness). On the other hand the concepts of annihilation or obliteration have been employed in order to view the dogma* of the Incarnation* in terms of the Son's kenosis*, or to consider ideas as essential as conversion* in the history of piety, or destitution in that of asceticism*; or indeed to apply the theme of "nihilization" (perhaps "the liberation of the consciousness from reality through denial") to Hell* (Augustine, *En. in Ps.* 38) or to illuminate the spiritual, rather than merely psychological, basis of suicide (self-hatred as a desire for non-being). We will mention here only those points that are not given an article of their own in this work.

Beside the scriptural references offered by the doctrine of creation, the negation of God (Ps 13:1 and 52:2; see atheism*), and the moral analysis of the emptiness and vanity of the human condition (Jb, Eccl), Christian meditation on nothingness has centered upon a small number of decisive biblical passages: Ps 41:8 (the abysses of God and of sin), Gal 6:3 and Ps 38:6 (the direct opposition in the texts of the Septuagint and the Vulgate between *substance* and *nothingness:* "[Jesus] made himself nothing, taking the form of a servant" (Phil 2:7 (exinanition, or abasement) and above all Romans 4:17 (God "calls into existence the things that do not exist"), and Jn 1:3–4 with its well-known problem of punctuation and the two main readings that the position of the caesura imply: "Without him was not anything made that was made; in him was life," or "Without him was not any thing made. That which has been made was life in him."

1. Mystical Theology: God as Cause and Nothingness

The way of negation allows theology to say what God is not: "We know not what God is, but what he is not" (Clement of Alexandria, *Strom.* V, 11). But from the knowledge of what God is not, and even of the fact that he is no known being, it does not follow that he does not exist. The impossibility of knowing God, insofar as he transcends all existence, including being (like the Neoplatonists' "One"), and even the One itself (in opposition to the Neoplatonists), does not imply that he should be characterized by nothingness—which would in any case be opposed to the letter of Ex. 3:14. The

concept of God as nothingness was therefore not necessary to the negative way or to apophasis. According to Dionysius* the Pseudo-Areopagite, while super-essentiality "has no being according to the manner of any other being" (*Divine Names* 1, 1), the way of eminence (or cataphasis) grasps the fact that the cause of all things has no part of being, but also no part of non-being (*Mystical Theology* 5). For this reason God, who transcends both that which exists and that which does not, is not in opposition to anything, even to nothing. What brought about the progression—from the view of this transcendence (represented by the oxymorons of "shadow more than luminous" or "shadowy beams") as the superessential cause, having no part of what is, to the perilous formulations that went beyond the negations and declared it to be nothingness—was the realization that the mode of unknowing was like any mode of knowledge* for God (*Divine Names* 7, 3; see also the *Ambigua* of Maximus* the Confessor, PG 91, 1232). From this point, Dionysius's commentators would take the plunge and complete this "metamorphosis of apophasis" (A. Gouhier). So John of Scythopolis wrote: "Do not consider that the divine is, but cannot be comprehended; think rather that it is not; such indeed is knowledge in unknowing" (*Commentary on the Divine Names,* PG 4, 245 c). And in the words of Maximus the Confessor: "By reason of his super-being, the name* which is most appropriate for God is non-being... The two names of being and non-being should both be strictly applicable to God, even while neither of them is exactly fitting. The first is appropriate inasmuch as God is the cause of all things, the second through the eminence of the abstractive cause of the whole being of existing things" (prologue to the *Mystagogy,* PG 91, 664 b). Among Latin authors, John the Scot Eriugena in his *De Divisione naturae* distinguished five modes of opposition between being (that which can be perceived by the senses or understood by the intellect) and (relative) non-being, and made God the first type of non-being, since it was by the excellence of his nature that he was beyond the grasp of the senses and the intellect: "The divine nature... is nothingness, it exceeds all beings not inasmuch as it is not itself being, but inasmuch as all beings proceed from it" (*De Divisione naturae* 1. II, 589 B). However, for this whole tradition of commentators on the Dionysian corpus the key point is the following: it is always the method of causality that justifies the use of the concept of nothingness to conceive of God as the supereminent cause. This doctrine would be reinforced by the mystical* tradition (Hadewijch of Antwerp, Suso, Angela of Foligno). Thus even in the context of mystical theology, what is at stake is at bottom creation and causality; hence, conversely, the importance of this theologoumenon* to the history of metaphysics.

2. Natural Theology: Nothingness and the Intelligible

a) Renaissance Cosmologies. Speculations on nothingness formed an essential part of the Christian Platonism* of the Renaissance, which took the hierarchical cosmologies of Dionysius and Maximus and added a strong affirmation of God's transcendence. The opposition between God and nothingness, "a non-being immense and infinite in its action" but from which a proof of God's existence* can be drawn (since the existence of the impossible implies that of the necessary), is the prime example of "the art of opposites" that Charles de Bovelles developed after Nicholas* of Cusa: the paradoxical *Liber de nihilo* (1510) concludes with a restatement of the most daring theses of the Dionysian tradition, in particular the one that "links the name of nothingness to God…pronouncing in mystery* that God is nothing *[nihil]*" (c. 11). However, Bovelles firmly insists on the fundamental discontinuity or incommensurability that separates every creature from the Creator, and gives this gap the name of *assurrectio.* While laying claim to the paradoxes of the "coincidence of opposites," Renaissance natural* theology was thus able to avoid overstepping the prohibition set out in the Augustinian *De natura boni:* "It is an audacious sacrilege to equate nothingness and God" (X). This prohibition was intended to counter the Manichaeans who attempted to assign the same status to the Son born of (*de*) God and the creatures made by (*ab*) him "from nothingness, that is to say from (*ex*) that which absolutely is not" (I). The idea that creatures were *de nihilo* and had been drawn *ex nihilo a Deo* (though *ex Deo* could also be employed in this context), while the "begotten" Son was *de* and *ex Deo,* was constantly asserted. For this reason the idea that the self could tend toward nothingness was to be understood on an ontic and not simply a spiritual level (Gal 6:3; Augustine*, *De civitate Dei* XIV, XIII; En. in Ps 134:6; Bernard of Clairvaux, *De gradibus humilitatis* IV, 15).

b) Protestant Metaphysics. From the moment when modern metaphysics, finding fulfillment in ontology, defined the extant as the conceivable and thus subjugated being to representation, the opposition of *ens* and *nihil* was displaced. Johannes Clauberg (1622–65), the heir to Rudolf Goclenius (1547–1628) and Clemens Timpler (1567–1624), pronounced this dictum: "The extant is everything that can be conceived (intelligible), and nothing whatever can be opposed to it" (*Ontosophia,* §4). For this reason it was the most general of concepts, absolutely indeterminate, preceding the separation of something (*aliquid,* which could in turn be divided into substance and accident) from nothing (*nihil*). In spite of being a Catholic, N. Malebranche (1638–1715) developed a comparable metaphysics: to "think of nothing" was to have "the vague notion of being in general"—in other words, to sense the "clear, intimate, necessary presence of God" (*Récherche de la vérité* III, II, 8). Kant* falls within this tradition by way of the *Tractatus philosophicus de nihilo* by Martin Schoock (1614–69), Leibniz*, Wolff's (1679–1754) *Ontologia* (§132 *Sq*), and above all Baumgarten's (1714–62) *Metaphysica* (§7)—all these were writers who considered being primarily as the possibility of being. The conclusion of the transcendental analytics in the *Critique of Pure Reason* summarizes four senses of nothing *(nichts):* 1) the void concept without an object *(ens rationis),* a simple fiction such as the noumenon; 2) the void object of a concept *(nihil privativum),* in other words the negation of reality, such as cold; 3) the void intuition without an object *(ens imaginarium),* such as pure space and time*; 4) the void object without a concept *(nihil negativum),* the contradictory. The identification of being and nothingness was asserted in turn by Hegel* in his *Wissenschaft der Logik:* "Being and nothingness are the same thing" (Ed. of 1817, §40–41), an identification that attacks the idea of God as the absolute, "being in all being-there or supreme being *(das höchste Wesen),* since these definitions express him only in terms of pure negativity or indeterminacy. Rehabilitating the theologoumenon of creation *ex nihilo,* Schelling*'s later philosophy* in turn reworks the difference between the *mè on*—the negation of a position, simple nothingness, pure indefinite possibility—and the *ouk on,* the position of negation, the Nothing (*Philosophie der Offenbarung*), which expresses the doctrine of creation and makes possible the linking of natural theology and revelation* at the outset of positive philosophy. Once again, however, this takes place by way of a notion of God, "the Lord of being," as cause.

3. The Three Nothingnesses of Mankind

In the *Miroir des âmes simples et anéanties,* Marguerite Porete (†1310) identifies liberty* (*"franchise"*) with annihilation. To know one's nothingness is, for the simple soul, neither to know nor to wish anything. The "desire for nothingness" disencumbers (*"descombre"*) it of everything (including God) and leaves it free for union with God. No longer having a will of its own, the soul no longer feels desire except through the divine will. In Rhineland*-Flemish mysticism, especially in the work of Meister Eckhart, annihilation is in the same way a condition of divinization. The return to nothingness enables the creature to attain the being that it had in God before any creation. It also entails becoming the place where divine goodness must necessarily unfold, in keeping with the Dionysian principle: the good* diffuses of its own accord. "Deep calls to deep" (Ps 42:7) was thus an obligatory scriptural reference-point (and was commented on by John the Scot Eriugena). Mention must also be made of the anonymous 14th century mystical treatise *The Cloud of Unknowing,* whose influence was considerable, and Harphius's *Theologia mystica*; and, as late as the beginning of the 17th century, *La perle évangélique* (1602) by Dom Beaucousin. Jean Orcibal has assessed the influence of the northern mystics on the spirituality of Carmel* and John* of the Cross, in whose work the concept of annihilation appears in the form of destitution: the "dark night" is the equivalent, in John's contemplation*, of the negation of everything created, its nothingness.

The influence of the *corpus dionysiacum,* which can be clearly discerned throughout the Middle Ages, was however never so strong as at the beginning of the 17th century. Its remarkable translation into French by the Feuillant Jean de Saint-François (Goulu) in 1608 was of the highest importance for the vocabulary of mystical theology. What Louis Cognet has referred to as the "abstract school" kept alive the heritage of Rhineland-Flemish mysticism, by way of Benet of Canfield's *Rule of Perfection* (1593) in particular. Bérulle* was its foremost exponent, which did not prevent him from producing an original body of work and highlighting, after Canfield and his *praxis annihilationis* (*Rule of Perfection* 3, 9), a christological understanding of nothingness. Bérulle enumerates "three sorts of nothingness: the nothingness from which God draws us by creation, the nothingness to which Adam* consigned us by his sin, and the nothingness into which we must enter with the Son of God, who annihilates himself in order to atone for us" (*Opuscules de piété,* 136).

Bérulle relies on Romans 4:17 to show that "nothingness relates to God" inasmuch as he is capable of fulfilling all his desires; and so we should imitate the "nothingness of being" from which God drew us in order to flee the second nothingness (that which Adam brought upon us) and place ourselves within the third by imitating the "annihilated state" of Jesus*: "We are a nothingness that strives toward nothingness, that seeks nothingness... that fills itself with nothingness, and that ultimately ruins and destroys itself for a nothingness. Whereas we should be a nothingness, in truth (for it befits us by nature), but a nothingness in the hand of God... a nothingness referred to God" (ibid., 111).

The concept of abnegation expresses this last sense (ibid., 132), and assigns its achievement to what Bérulle calls mystical theology (ibid., 8), by way of opposition to positive* theology and Scholastic* theology: it is abnegation that shapes the Christian's spiritual and sacrificial annihilation to the objective annihilation of Christ.

4. Anthropology: Mankind as Midpoint between God and Nothingness

The concept of nothingness has on several occasions made it possible to assign mankind a metaphysical status, no longer as nothingness but as a midpoint between God and nothingness. Man is metaphysically limited (metaphysical sickness) because his status as creature means that he participates in nothingness: theodicies from Augustine onwards explain error, and on occasions sin, in these terms. Breaking free from the problematics of mankind's *situation* in the universe of the medieval and Renaissance cosmologies, Descartes defined man's *position* for the first time (*Stellung,* Heidegger 1961): "I am as it were a middle point between God and nothingness [*medium quid inter Deum et nihil*], situated in other words in such a way between the supreme being and non-being [*inter summum ens et non ens*] that, in truth, there is nothing to be found in me that could lead me into error, inasmuch as a supreme being has made me; but... if I consider myself as partaking in some way of nothingness or non-being, that is to say as I am not myself the supreme being, I find myself vulnerable to an infinity of lapses" (*Meditatio* IV). Pascal* took note of this new problematics in his *Pensées* in order to describe man's relationship both to God and to nature: "What is man in nature? A nothingness with respect to the infinite*, an everything with respect to nothingness, a middle point between nothing and everything." What is at stake in the possibility of error is nothing less than liberty, in other words subjectivity as a matter of "leaving it to oneself" (Heidegger 1961). With *Sein und Zeit* (1927) and *Was ist Metaphysik?* (1929), Heidegger started from the analysis of anguish, the affect that most fundamentally reveals nothingness, to illuminate the intrinsic connection between nothingness and human existence: "Nothingness is the condition which makes possible the revelation of the extant as such for the *Dasein*" (1929).

It is not clear whether contemporary spiritual* theology recognizes annihilation, or whether the concept of nothingness remains relevant to present-day speculative theology. At the very least its history shows that for Christianity the attribution to God of the concept of being has never ceased to be problematical.

• Parmenides (c. 475 B.C.), *Poem.*
Gorgias (c. 440 B.C.), *Treatise on Non Being.*

Plato (c. 368 B.C.), *Parmenides.*

Clement of Alexandria (c. A.D. 200), *Stromata.*

Augustine (399), *De natura boni*; (406–407), *Tractatus in Joh. ev.*; (401–414), *De Genesi ad litteram.*

Dionysius the Pseudo-Areopagite (c. 480–500), *Divine Names*; *Mystical Theology*; *Works.*

John of Scythopolis (before 530), *On Dionysian Corpus.*

Maximus The Confessor (c. 630), *Mystagogia*; *Ambigua.*

John the Scot Eriugena (864–866), *De divisione naturae.*

M. Porète (†1310), *Le Mirouer des simples âmes, Speculum simplicium animarum,* CChrCM 69 (Turnhout, 1986).

Anon. (mid-14th century), *The Cloud of Unknowing.*

Nicholas of Cusa (1440), *De docta ignorantia.*

C. de Bovelles (1501, 1510–1511), *Ars oppositorum,* Paris; (1510–1511), *Liber de nihilo,* Paris.

Harphius (1538), *Theologia mystica,* Köln.

C. Timpler (1604), *Metaphysicae systema methodicum,* Steinfurt.

B. de Canfeld (1610), *Regula perfectionis,* Köln.

R. Goclenius (1613), *Lexicon philosophicum,* Frankfurt (new edition, Hildesheim, 1980).

R. Descartes (1641), *Meditationes de prima philosophia...* Paris.

J. Clauberg (1647, 3rd ed., 1664), *Metaphysica de ente, quae rectius Ontosophia...* Groningue (new edition in *Opera omnia philosophica,* Amsterdam, 1691, and Hildesheim, 1965), 2 vols.

M. Schoock (1661), *Tractatus philosophicus de nihilo,* Groningen.

C. Wolff (1728), *Philosophia rationalis sive logica,* Leipzig (reprinted Hildesheim 1983); (1736), *Philosophia prima sive Ontologia,* Frankfurt and Leipzig (reprinted Hildesheim, 1977).

A.G. Baumgarten (1739), *Metaphysica* (new edition Hildesheim, 1963).

E. Kant (1781), *Kritik der reinen Vernunft (Critique of Pure Reason),* Riga.

G.W.F. Hegel (1817), *Wissenschaft der Logik,* Berlin.

F.W.J. Schelling (1841–42), *Philosophie der Offenbarung,* Stuttgart, 1861.

M. Heidegger (1927), *Sein und Zeit,* Tübingen

M. Heidegger (1929), *Was ist Metaphysik?,* Frankfurt, GA 9, 103–122.

J.-P. Sartre (1943), *L'être et le néant,* Paris.

♦ E. Cassirer (1927), *Individuum und Cosmos in der Philosophie der Renaissance,* Berlin.

A.O. Lovejoy (1936), *The Great Chain of Being,* Cambridge, MA.

J. Orcibal (1959), *La rencontre du Carmel thérésien avec les mystiques du Nord,* Paris.

É. Gilson (1948), *L'être et l'essence,* Paris (2nd Ed. 1981).

J. Vanneste (1959), *Le mystère de Dieu Essai sur la structure rationnelle de la doctrine mystique du Pseudo-Denys l'Aréopagite,* Louvain.

M. Heidegger (1961), *Nietzsche,* Pfullingen, 2 vols.

L. Cognet (1966), *La spiritualité moderne,* Paris.

E. zum Brunn (1969), *Le dilemme de l'être et du néant chez saint Augustin,* Paris.

Coll. (1978), *Dieu et l'être: Exégèses d'Exode 3:14 et de Coran 20:11–24,* Paris.

P. Courcelle (1974), *"Connais-toi toi-même" de Socrate à saint Bernard,* Paris, 3 vols.

A. Jäger (1980), "Gott: das Nichts als ens realissimum," in his *Gott: 10 Thesen,* Tübingen.

A. Gouhier (1982), "Néant," *DSp* 11, 64–80.

J.-L. Marion (1982), *Dieu sans l'être,* Paris.

Th. Kobusch (1984), "Nichts, Nichtseiendes," *HWP* 6, 805–836 (bibl.).

J.-F. Courtine (1990), *Suarez et le système de la métaphysique,* Paris.

P. Magnard (1992), *Le Dieu des philosophes,* Paris.

VINCENT CARRAUD

See also **Being; Bérulle, Pierre de; Creation; Dionysius the Pseudo-Areopagite; God; Heidegger, Martin; Incarnation; Infinite; John of the Cross; Kenosis; Mysticism; Negative Theology; Platonism, Christian; Rhineland-Flemish Mysticism**

Novatianism

The Novatian schism* lastingly affected the early Church*. After the edict of Decius in late 249, requiring all subjects of the Roman Empire to honor the gods, and the ensuing wave of persecution, the Church had to deal with the question of the many *lapsi,* members of the clergy or laity* who asked to rejoin the Christian community after having apostatized. In 251, Cornelius was elected bishop* of Rome*, and with him the party of clemency won out. The correspondence on this question between Cornelius and Bishop Cyprian* of Carthage indicates the role played by the bishop of Rome in defining the attitude to adopt toward the *lapsi* (*Ep.* 49 and 50, letters to Cyprian included in Cyprian's correspondence; *Ep.* 55 from Cyprian).

Novatian was at the time an influential Roman priest whose theological works were thoroughly orthodox (he is noteworthy as the author of the first treatise on the

Trinity* in Latin), but against Cornelius and Cyprian he represented a rigid position influenced by Montanism*. With ecclesiology* and ethics* calling for the same firmness, Novatian and his disciples refused penance* for the *lapsi,* as for adulterers. In response to the election of Cornelius, Novatian also had himself elected pope by his supporters, initiating the schism. He was joined in Rome by some members of the clergy of Africa, including Novat (the two names Novat and Novatian were often confused by writers in antiquity), and both were excommunicated by a council called by Cyprian in 251. Indeed, it was their combined opposition to Cyprian and Cornelius that brought the supporters of the two men together, because Novat had at first been noted for excessive indulgence toward the *lapsi.*

The Novatian Church was then established and its influence spread in the West, in the African Church (Cyprian wrote his treatise, *The Unity of the Catholic Church,* against the Novatianists), and as far as Asia Minor. In the late-fourth century, Ambrose* of Milan attacked the Novatianists in his treatise on penance (SC 179). Like the Montanists and Donatists with whom they have frequently been associated, the Novatianists, the "pure" *(katharoi)* as they called themselves, expressed one of the recurring questions of the early Church: are the perfect the only ones worthy to be a part of the Church? The conflict also marks a stage in the development of the recognition of the role of the bishop of Rome.

● H. Weyer (Ed.) (1962), *Novatianus, De Trinitate: über den dreifaltigen Gott,* Darmstadt.
G. F. Diercks (Ed.) (1972), *Novatiani opera,* CChr.SL 4.
♦ H. J. Vogt (1968), Coetus Sanctorum: *Der Kirchenbegriff des Novatian und die Geschichte seinen Sonderkirche,* Bonn.
H. J. Vogt (1990), "Novatien," *DECA,* 1777–79.
Ch. Munier (1991), *Autorité épiscopale et sollicitude pastorale, Ier-VIe s.,* Aldershot.
M. Simonetti (1993), *Studi sulla cristologia del II e III secolo,* Rome.

FRANÇOISE VINEL

See also **Catharism; Donatism; Martyrdom; Tertullian**

Obligation

In moral theology*, the concept of a command of God* functions either to indicate the ultimate origin of moral obligation, or to determine its content, or to provide a means by which we come to know what it requires of us. It does not explain the concept of obligation as such.

a) What It Is That Obliges. For materialists such as Hobbes (1588–1679), obligation is reducible to the instinct for survival. What obliges us is the fear of pain and death*. When enlightened by prudence*, our instinct will lead us to enter into mutually advantageous contracts with other people, but whatever obligations such contracts entail, they are secondary and instrumental to the primary obligation to avoid death.

Theologians standing in the teleological tradition of Augustine* and Thomas* Aquinas also regard moral obligation as reducible but not to a nonmoral category. They hold that, beyond fearing death, human beings naturally desire to pursue good* and that the preservation of life is only one of a range of goods, which also includes such things as friendship and knowledge of the truth*. Proportionalists (proportionalism*) such as R. A. McCormick argue that our basic obligation is to realize as many goods as much as possible and, if need be, to promote some at the expense of others. Other writers (e.g., John Finnis and Germain Grisez) argue that our basic obligation is not to intend harm to any good. In either case, the binding force of obligation is reducible not only to the terror of death or to any desire but specifically to the desire to maintain and promote goods.

However, those moral theologians who stand in the deontological tradition of Kant* contend that obligation is not reducible at all: it is entirely sui generis. What binds us is not desire or inclination but sheer respect for the moral law*; or, better, what binds us is the intrinsic authority of the law, which elicits our respect. (Barth*'s emphasis on obedience to God's command may fairly be read as a theological version of this position.) For Kantians, one cannot therefore reduce moral obligation to a nonmoral desire. However, they leave unanswered the question, Why should we respect the moral law?; for them, the question is, moreover, immoral, and to ask it is simply to withhold recognition of the law's nature as an axiom of practical reason*.

Nevertheless, the question does seem a reasonable one. The fact that it is perfectly intelligible to ask of any law, What purpose does it serve?, suggests that law is not in and of itself axiomatic. Let us take two of Kant's formulations of the "categorical imperative": "Act only according to that maxim by which you can at the same time will that it should become a universal law" and "Act so that you treat humanity, whether in your own person or that of another, always as an end and never as a means only" (*Foundations,* section 2). These prescriptions are, in fact, intelligible only as specifications of respect for certain goods that they presuppose, the good of being reasonable and the good of "humanity," or, more precisely, the moral autonomy of the human individual.

b) Subjective and Objective Obligation. The distinction between the objective aspect and the subjective aspect of obligation is made most forcibly by Kant, who makes the subjective aspect crucial. "Duty" refers not so much to particular acts that we are obliged to perform as to the motive for the right or good action; and it is the motive that determines the act's moral quality. Moral goodness resides only in that principle of will that acts out of respect for the moral law, that is, out of "a sense of duty." Kant understood his theory to explain the commonsense judgment that someone who performs his objective duty (e.g., caring for his elderly parents) out of a selfish motive (greed for a legacy) deserves no credit. In order to be morally praiseworthy, we must act not only *as* duty requires but also *because* duty requires it.

Motivation also mattered a great deal to Aquinas, who argues that we should always do as our conscience* instructs, even when it is erroneous (*STh* Ia IIae, q. 19, a. 5). We should always do what we mistakenly think is right rather than contradict our moral understanding. In placing such emphasis on the subjective perception of obligation, both Aquinas and Kant signal the high importance that they ascribe to the virtue of the moral agent, although Aquinas discriminates between the subjective moral quality of the agent and the objective moral quality of his act. For him, conscience is necessarily related to the objective order of morality.

At the opposite extreme are the consequentialists, for whom all that matters is that one fulfills one's objective obligation to perform the act that will affect the greater proportion of good in a given set of circumstances.

c) Conflicts of Obligations. There are cases where prima facie obligations—such as keeping promises, telling the truth, and not harming others—are in conflict and where no one act can possibly fulfill them all. In such a case, one's obligation must be determined by which obligation is the more important. Quite how such an estimate is to be made is not clear. Of those who have posed this problem, W. D. Ross (1877–1940), refuses to admit any hierarchy of duties and places his faith in intuition (*The Right and the Good,* Oxford, 1930). Consequentialists, on the other hand, resolve the problem by acknowledging only one obligation—namely, to perform that act whose consequences are most beneficial—and by calculating which act that is. However, critics of consequentialism such as Grisez and Finnis argue that this calculation

has only the appearance of reason and that cases where meeting one obligation (e.g., telling the truth) involves failing to meet another (e.g., not harming others) should be resolved by taking as a basic obligation that of not intending harm and then applying the principle of double effect (intention*).

Some philosophers prefer to distinguish between obligation and duty. "Duty" is taken to refer to an obligation entailed by our role in an institution, a role that we may not have chosen—for example, the duties of parents toward their children and of children toward their parents. One of the contrasts, then, between duty and obligation is between what is natural and what is contractual. Another is between what is personal and partial and what is impersonal and impartial. The issue here is whether duties to family* or fellow countrymen take priority over obligations to strangers.

d) God's Reason as the Ultimate Ground of Obligation. In moral theology, the ground of obligation is located in God. If it is located in God's reason, then it will be mediated to human beings through conscience's grasp of the moral order or natural law by which God has structured created reality and that reflects the eternal law of God's own mind. Obligation will then be understood in terms of the pursuit of certain natural ends (Aquinas) or conformity to the axioms of practical reason (Kant).

Within this metaethical scheme, the commands of God in the Bible*—especially the Decalogue*—are restatements of what the created moral order requires. According to Aquinas, such restatement is necessary on account of the obscurity into which sin* casts the moral understanding. By contrast, according to Kant, whose confidence in the capacities of practical reason was supreme, revealed morality is redundant: the teaching and example of Jesus* should be measured against the norms of reason, not vice versa (*Foundations,* section 2).

e) God's Will as the Ultimate Ground of Obligation. Some theologians have preferred to locate the foundation of obligation in God's will. Our moral obligations are established by divine commands. These are found preeminently in the Bible though sometimes also in occasional utterances by the Holy* Spirit. There are several lines of argument in this type of voluntarism*: that the will transcends reason; that, since God is omnipotent, he cannot be constrained by laws and is free to command as he wills; that there is a need to account for passages in the Bible where God commands something immoral—most famously, that Abraham should sacrifice his son (Gn 22:1–19); that there is a need to disturb the complacency or rigidity of an ethical rationalism* that pretends to absolute comprehensiveness; or that there is a need to assert the importance of responsibility and authenticity against moral conformism. The first three factors inspire the voluntarist metaethic and the ethics of divine command characteristic of John Duns* Scotus, William of Ockham (1284/85–1349), and, through Ockham, of Luther*. The last two factors were the predominant influences on Kierkegaard* (*see Fear and Trembling, OC* 5, pp. 97–109) and Barth (*KD* II/2).

There are four main objections to this type of ethics. First, God's sovereignty requires him to be free only of external constraints, not of the internal order of his own reason; second, an ethics of command does not take adequate account of the first person of the Trinity*, the Father* or Creator; third, the biblical passages in which God is presented as commanding something immoral can be accounted for as expressions of a theology not yet sufficiently enlightened by Jesus Christ; and, fourth, if God can trump moral reason arbitrarily, by what criteria can we discriminate between a command of God and a wicked whim?

f) God's Commands in the Bible. Whereas Catholicism has regarded biblical prescriptions as an auxiliary means of apprehending our moral obligations, Protestants have tended to regard them as the primary means. Some Calvinists (Calvinism*) and Lutherans (Lutheranism*) have made the Ten Commandments (Ex 20:1–17; Dt 5:6–21) the basis of their ethics (e.g., the *Loci communes theologici* of John Gerhardt [1582–1637]). On the other hand, Anabaptists (e.g., John H. Yoder and Stanley Hauerwas) have thought it more appropriate for a Christian ethic to take its moral norms from the gospel* and from the example of Christ*. Barth, whose ethics shares this Christocentric focus, is wary of the moralistic and legalistic effects of attending too soon to moral prescriptions and insists that both the Decalogue and the Sermon on the Mount be interpreted in the larger context of the history of salvation*.

g) God's Commands in the Church. Counter-Reformation Catholicism saw Protestantism*'s affirmation of the right to private interpretation of Scripture as a factor of anarchy and strongly affirmed the role of the magisterium (the Church's teaching authority) in moral as well as theological matters. Under pressure from the strife kindled by Jansenism* and from the

threats posed by the Enlightenment, the French Revolution, and Napoleon, this authority became increasingly concentrated in episcopal and papal hands. According to some conservative theories of the magisterium (e.g., Grisez's), certain episcopal and papal pronouncements, interpreting natural or revealed morality, are so immune from criticism and require such deference as to carry an authority difficult to distinguish in practice from that of God himself. An alternative ecclesiology*, more Pauline*, more Protestant, and perhaps more in line with Vatican* II (*see Gaudium et Spes*), sees the Church as a community rather than a hierarchy* and thinks that the knowledge of God's commandments is disseminated by dialogue rather than by official pronouncements.

However, the process of dialogue and the exercise of authority should not be regarded as alternatives. Dialogue seldom achieves consensus, and when it is about basic moral problems, it ought not to be resolved simply in favor of majority opinion. Therefore, persons of recognized expertise and wisdom* need to be vested with the authority to make judgments and to define what the Church believes God's commands to be. Nevertheless, if such judgments are to be made responsibly, it is arguable that they will always follow honest consideration of contrary opinion and remain open to the possibility of future revision, should reason require it.

- W. A. Pickard Cambridge (1932), "Two Problems about Duty," *Mind* 41, 72–96, 145–72, 311–40.
- G. E. Hughes (1944), "Motive and Duty," *Mind* 53, 314–31.
- B. Brandt (1964), "The Concept of Obligation and Duty," *Mind* 73, 374–93.
- J. Henriot (1967), *Existence et obligation,* Paris.
- G. Outka (1973), "Religion and Moral Duty: Notes on 'Fear and Trembling,'" in G. Outka, J. P. Reeder (Ed.), *Religion and Morality,* New York, 204–54.
- O. Nell [O'Neill] (1975), *Acting on Principle: An Essay in Kantian Ethics,* New York.
- P. L. Quinn (1978), *Divine Commands and Moral Requirements,* Oxford.
- J. M. Idziak (Ed.) (1979), *Divine Command Morality: Historical and Contemporary Readings,* New York.
- J. Finnis (1980), *Natural Law and Natural Rights,* Oxford.
- P. Plé (1980), *Par devoir ou par plaisir?,* Paris.
- P. Helm (Ed.) (1981), *Divine Commands and Morality,* Oxford.
- A. B. Wolter (1986), *Duns Scotus on the Will and Morality,* Washington, D.C.
- N. Biggar (1993), *The Hastening That Waits: Karl Barth's Ethics,* Oxford.

Nigel Biggar

See also **Authority; Ethics; Law; Liberty**

Ockham, William of. *See* **Nominalism**

Olivi, Peter John (Olieu, Pierre Jean). *See* **Bonaventure; Millenarianism**

Omnipotence, Divine

---

a) Omnipotent or All-Powerful? Judaism* is founded on the memory of God*'s power: "By strength of hand, the Lord has brought you out from this place" (Ex 13:3). He can save his chosen people everywhere and do what he wants for them. Israel*'s strength lies in God (Gn 32:29), for YHWH is the only Omnipotent: From him comes the Creation*, the election*, the victory (Dt 4:32–39). This sovereign universal power is free—"he does whatsoever he pleases" (Ps 115:3; *see also* Is 46:10)—but it is a loving power (Ps 86:15–17). This power intervenes in history* and controls the planets and all the forces in the universe.

In the Hebrew Bible*, God is given the names Sabaoth—"the Lord of hosts, the God of the armies of Israel" (1 Sm 17:45)—and El-Shaddaï ("Habitant of the Mountains"; Gn 17:1), translated in the Greek Septuagint as *pantokratôr* ("all-powerful") in 170 occurrences. Thus, the divine force is presented as a free power that dominates (*kratein*) everything (*to pan*), combining the initiative of salvation* and the power that maintains the cosmos*. Numerous texts proclaim God's sovereignty over everything. "Lord, Lord, all-powerful King, the universe is in thy power, and no one can challenge thee ... for thou hast made the heavens and the earth" (Est 4:17 b). The saving power creates, preserves, and destroys. "Nothing is too hard" for God (Gn 18:14 and Jer 32:17; *see also* Lk 1:37). But divine will is not arbitrary; it yields before the power it

has granted to man (Gn 19:22). Thus, the All Mighty becomes God's proper name*: "All Mighty is his name" (Ex 15:3, Vulgate). In the New Testament, this name has a liturgical function. Hymns of praise recall the pact with God, his paternity, his reign, his eternity* (once in 2 Cor 6:18 and nine times in Revelations). There he speaks in an eschatological context, to regulate the world for Christ*'s Easter glorification.

The term *pantokratôr* occurs in the earliest of the creeds. It passes from the Old Testament to the Christian liturgy* to mean the only God, Father* of his people* and of the world*. Since all the other occurrences of the term *pantokratôr* are posterior to the Septuagint (Montevecchi 1957), it is useless to look there for a cosmological principle inherited from philosophy*. It is more worthwhile to list the varied uses of *kratein*. Followed by the genitive it means "to rein, to dominate": *Pantokratôr* equals Lord of the universe; followed by the accusative it means instead "to hold in one's power, to seize" (Mk 1:31). God penetrates to the heart of everything by means of his power. A Stoic connotation, meaning the maintenance of the world by Providence*, a comparison with Plato's demigod, preserving what he creates (*Timaeus* 41 a), and its close connections to Zeus *pankratès* ("who upholds everything"), to Jupiter *omnipotens, rerum omnium potens,* make omnipotence gravitate toward the second meaning.

For Theophilus of Antioch, God was the creator, "but he is called *pantokratôr* because he holds (*kratei*) and embraces everything (*ta panta*)" (I, 4, 64; *see Epistle to Diognetus*, 7, 2, p. 66). Omnipotence slants the generation of the Son and the creation of the world toward God's transmission of his glory* to the resurrected Christ: "In fact it is through his Son that the Father is omnipotent" (Origen*, *Princ.,* 1, 2, 10). The term thus includes the cosmic function (adopted from the Hellenic heritage) in a Trinitarian synthesis: "When we hear the name of *pantokratôr,* our thought is that God maintains everything in existence" (Gregory of Nyssa, *Contra Eunomium* 2, 126, 366). The link should thus be made between biblical omnipotence (Almightiness, power *over* everything) and philosophical omnipotence (Greek *pantodunamos, able to do* everything; Geach 1973).

The controversies over the Trinity modified its meaning: God's paternity is focused on the engendering of the Son (Filiation*), so much so that omnipotence expresses the identity between the God of the prophets*, whose name is All-Mighty, and the Father of the Lord. Since the act of creation was no longer evoked by the paternity, it was added as a development of omnipotence: "creator of heaven and earth" (Kelly 1950). Contrary to the Arians, who restricted omnipotence to the Father alone, Athanasius* gave a reminder of Christ's universal reign: "Omnipotent is the Father and omnipotent is the son" (*Letter to Serapion* 2, 611). Then omnipotence became an attribute* common to the three Persons*. The symbol *Quicumque* became its radical echo: "All powerful is the Father, all powerful is the Son, all powerful is the Spirit; and yet there are not three all-powerful persons, but a single Omnipotent one" (*DS* 75). Nonetheless, Christ *pantokratôr* remains at the center of the Byzantine churches' iconographic program (Capizzi 1964).

Latin distinguishes precisely two attributes: *omnitenens* and *omnipotens* (Augustine*, *Confessions* XI, 13, 15; CSEL 33, 290), the first, *omnitenens,* coined to translate *pantokratôr* (Pseudo-Tertullian, *Carmen adversus Marcionem* V, 9, 5, 1089 A), while *omnipotens* translates *pantodunamos* and refers to "the power to do all things"—"who is omnipotent if not he who can do everything?" (*The Trinity* IV, 20, 27; 197). But usage would give *omnipotentia* both meanings, as D. Petau would already know (1644, reedition 1885). A new problem arose from this equivocal meaning: God can do what he wills, but "he cannot die, he cannot sin, he cannot lie, he cannot make a mistake" (Augustine, *Enchiridion* 24, 96). Can he really do everything? Origen answered already: "God can do everything that he can do without ceasing to be God, to be good, to be wise." One should particularly *not* understand "that he can even do unjust things but he does not want to." "Neither can God perpetrate an injustice, for the power to commit an injustice is contrary to his divinity and to his omnipotence"—his nature entails the absolute impossibility of committing evil, and that does not depend on his will (*Against Celsus* 3, 70; 158–61). Augustine's reply soon came: "All that, he cannot do it, for if he could, he would not be omnipotent" (*Enchiridion* 24, 96, 100). Omnipotence should be seen not as an isolated attribute but as that of the good God, who would cease to be himself if he ceased to be good, immortal, and so on. "If God can be what he does not want to be, he is not omnipotent" (PL 38, 1068; see *Sermons* 213 and 214).

b) Middle Ages: Absolute Power and Well-Ordered Power. In the Middle Ages divine omnipotence was a fact held in common by all the revealed religions, including Islam (Koran 46, 32). Reacting against God's submission to Good* and considering every attribute in itself, medieval theology* demanded that divine power should be asserted as infinite* to the highest degree (Peter Lombard, *Sentences* I, d. 43, §1). Believing that God's power was limited by his goodness or his will would amount to denying him certain perfections. Countering Jerome (*Ep.* 22:5; 150), Peter Damien thought that God could make a deflowered virgin a virgin again; he could even cause it to be that something that had existed had not existed, for instance, that Rome* had never existed. Abelard stressed the necessary conformity of God's works with good, to the point of asserting that God could do only what he did do and that he could not make the world better than he made it. He was condemned, and Peter Lombard's *Sentences* criticized him severely (Boulnois 1994).

For Anselm, Christ did not sin and was incapable of wanting to sin because he did not want to, having himself placed these restrictions on himself; there were, therefore, things that God could do but that he had refused to do (*Cur Deus homo?* 2,5. 10. 17; *see* Courtenay 1984). The foundation was thus laid for a distinction between *absolute power*—what God can do, within the scope of his power taken in the strict sense, but what he does not do—and *well-ordered power*—what God has freely chosen to do and that he knows through his prescience (Pseudo-Hugo of Saint Victor, *Quaestiones in epistolam ad Romanos* q. 91, 457; Hugo of Saint-Cher, *Sentences,* Boulnois 1994).

The 13th-century authors tackled anew this purely logical opposition between pure absolute power and God's ordered autorestriction of this power. A new paradigm, often attributed to nominalism* but derived from John Duns* Scotus and interpreted by means of a political model, appeared in the 14th century: ordered power is the autorestriction of the law*; absolute power is the power to act de facto by making an exception to the law. Henceforth, absolute power changed from being an abstract concept to become an operational one that invaded every field of thought—cosmology, morality, and theology. The present order could always be suspended by a divine intervention. God could lie, deceive, and demand that man hate him. The world lost its order and God his intelligibility.

c) Modern Contemporary Period: The Sovereign and the Watchmaker.   Luther's attacks destroyed the distinction between absolute power and well-ordered power: "I call God's omnipotence not that power through which he does not do many things that he could do, but that real power by which he does absolutely everything powerfully, in the same way as the Scriptures call his omnipotence" (*De servo arbitrio, WA* 18, 718). Either God is subservient to destiny (*fatum*), just like the pagan gods, or God knows the future and is all-powerful, and in that case man can do nothing—human freedom and divine omnipotence are contradictory. Absolute power took on a political meaning and meant the absolute power of the prince. Thus, the modern period hesitates between two models of power: the absolute ruler and the watchmaker subjected to the mechanisms of existence (E. Randi 1986).

Montaigne reasserted forcefully the omnipotence of God in comparison with mathematical truths (*Essais* II, 12), and Descartes* went so far as to suggest the creation of the eternal truths. On the other hand, Giordano Bruno fiercely rejected the existence of an absolute power belonging to God that would extend further than the necessary order of nature* (*De immenso* III, 1, *Opera* I, 1, 320). For Spinoza, well-ordered power was the equivalent of God's ordinary power—that is, the necessity of nature (*Cogitata metaphysica* II, 9).

Modern metaphysics fell into the aporia of God either as the watchmaker, subservient to the order of the world (deism*), or as the arbitrary sovereign. In reaction to that, contemporary thought distrusts omnipotence. Karl Barth* gives the reminder that omnipotence is commanded by divine election. Process* theology, and H. Jonas in Jewish thought, frankly denies omnipotence. Should the baby be thrown out with the bathwater? It is perhaps enough to become sober, to remember that power is always controlled by charity and that it is allied to human powerlessness through Christ's self-abasement. That view would simply be a return to the biblical and Patristic meaning, in which God is "Lord of all," which does not precisely mean "capable of doing anything whatsoever."

● Athanasius, *Epistle to Serapion,* SC 15.
Augustine, *Confessions,* CSEL 33; *De Trinitate,* CChr.SL 50; *Enchiridion,* CChr.SL 46, 49–114.
Theophilus of Antioch, *Epistle to Diognetus,* SC 33 *bis.*
Gregory of Nyssa, *Contra Eunomium,* Ed. W. J. Jaeger, *GNO* II, Leiden, 1960.
Ps.-Hugues de Saint-Victor, *Quaestiones in epistulam ad Romanos,* PL 175, 431–514.
P. Damien, *Lettre sur la toute-puissance divine,* SC 191.
Origen, *First Principles,* Ed. Koetschau, Berlin, 1913.
[Ps.]-Tertullian, *Carmen adversus Marcionem,* PL 2, 1051–90.
◆ D. Petau (1644–50), *Dogmata theologica* I, new Ed. J.-B. Fournials, Paris, 1865–67.
K. Barth (1940), *KD* II/I, 587–685 (*Dogmatique,* vol. 7, Geneva, 1957, 243–363).
J. N. D. Kelly (1950), *Early Christian Creeds,* London, 1972³.
H. Hommel (1956), *Schöpfer und Erhalter,* Berlin.
O. Montevecchi (1957), Pantokratôr, *Studi in onore di A. Calderini e R. Paribeni,* Milan, 401–32.
P. Biard (1960), *La parole de Dieu,* Paris.
C. Capizzi (1964), *Pantokrator,* Rome.
H. Jonas (1968), "The Concept of God after Auschwitz," *Out of the Whirlwind,* Ed. A. H. Friedländer, New York.
D. L. Holland (1969), "*Pantokratôr* in New Testament and Creed," StEv 6, 256–66.
M. F. Lacan (1970), "Puissance," *VThB* 2 (1988⁶), 1060–68.
M.-A. Pernoud (1972), "The Theory of the *potentia Dei* according to Aquinas, Scotus and Ockham," *Anton.* 47, 69–95.
P. T. Geach (1973), "Omnipotence," *Phil.* 43, 7–20.
T. Gregory (1974), "Dio ingannatore e genio maligno: Note in margine alle "*Meditationes*" di Descartes," *GCFI* 54, 477–516.
K. Bannach (1975), *Die Lehre von der doppelten Macht Gottes bei Ockham,* Wiesbaden.
A. de Halleux (1977), "Dieu le Père tout-puissant," repr. in *Patrologie et œcuménisme,* Louvain, 1990, 68–89.
F. Bergamelli (1984), "Sulla storia del termine *Pantokratôr* dalle inizi fino a Teofilo di Antiocha," *Sal* 46, 439–72.
W. Courtenay (1984), *Covenant and Causality in Medieval Thought,* London.
F. Oakley (1984), *Omnipotence, Covenant and Order: An Excursion in the Theory of Ideas from Abaelard to Leibniz,* Ithaca-London.
A. Funkenstein (1986), *Theology and Scientific Imagination from the Late Middle Ages to the XVIIth Century,* Princeton.
E. Randi (1986), *Il sovrano e l'orologiaio: Due immagini di Dio nel dibattito sulla* potentia absoluta, *fra XII e XIV secolo,* Florence.
W. Courtenay (1990), *Capacity and Volition: A History of the Distinction of Absolute and Ordained Power,* Bergame.
G. van den Brink (1993), *Almighty God: A Study of the Doctrine of Divine Omnipotence,* Kampen.
O. Boulnois (Ed.) (1994), *La puissance et son ombre,* Paris.
J.-P. Batut (1998), Pantocrator, *"Dieu le Père tout-puissant": Recherche sur une expression de la foi dans les théologies anténicéennes,* thesis, University of Paris IV and Institut catholique de Paris.

OLIVIER BOULNOIS

See also **Attribute, Divine; Eternity of God; Images; Immutability/Impassibility; Justice, Divine; Knowledge, Divine; Omnipresence, Divine; Scholasticism; Simplicity, Divine**

Omnipresence, Divine

a) Concept and Definition. Many forms of presence are attributed to God* in theology*: presence ("habitation") in the soul* of the just, presence in Christ*, presence of Christ in the Eucharist* and in the Church*. The term "omnipresence" conveys an idea of divine ubiquity: the presence of the Creator, as first cause, throughout his creation*.

In Christianity this ubiquity is not, strictly speaking, defined; it appears in the notion of divine immensity (*Symb. Ath.*, DS 75): God cannot be localized (*incapabilis*) or circumscribed (*incircumscriptus*) (*Conc. Lat.* 649, DS 504, with regard to Christ according to his divinity). Vatican* I (*COD* 805, 33–34) adopted the terms of Thomas* Aquinas (*ST* Ia, q. 8, a. 2) when he comments on Peter Lombard's concept of omnipresence *per potentiam, praesentiam, essentiam,* by power, by presence, by essence (*see* infra, d.).

The 46th of the 99 names* given to God by Islamic thinkers (al-Djurdjani, Sharasthani) is the Omnipresent (*al-wasi*).

b) Sources in Scripture. The Old Testament speaks of the presence of God in creation and with his people* without making a clear distinction. God is said to be immense (Bar 3, 25), present in all parts of the world that he fills. This is noted particularly in Psalms 138:7–12, the text most often cited in theological tradition*, and carried over into line 115 of the II surat of the Koran (Nm 39; Jer 23:24; Is 6:2; Wis 1:4); his grandeur surpasses the world (Jb 11:8–9; 1 Kgs 8:27). Elsewhere, he makes a promise of his presence to the Fathers (Gn 17:7, 26:24, 28:15), to Moses (Ex 3:12, 39:4), to Joshua and the judges (Jos 1:5; Jgs 6:16; 1 Sm 3:19), to the kings and prophets* (2 Sm 7:9; 2 Kgs 18:7; Jer 1:8–19), and to humanity in the announcement of Emmanuel (Is 7:14; Ps 46:8).

The doctrine is not directly present in the New Testament; it is expressed in such a way that the divine omnipresence is limited to a presence within every human being (Acts 17:28; 1 Cor 15:28). Jesus* also makes a promise to abide with the disciples (Mt 28:20; Lk 22:30, 23:42), with those who pray in his name (Mt 18:20). He lives in those who have faith* (Gal 2:20; Eph 3:17), even if his corporeal absence is preferable (Jn 16:7). He will be all in all (1 Cor 13, 12). His presence for all believers (Rev 3:20) is not limited to any people (Col 3:11) or place (Jn 4:21). The hymnal fragment of Ephesians 4:6 is a chant about "*a unique God and father of everything who is above all, through all, and in all*"; the hymn in *Colossians* 1:15–18 is a chant to Christ "*in whom everything subsists*"; this is the scriptural text that particularly nourished the meditation of Teilhard of Chardin.

c) First Elaboration by the Fathers. The omnipresence of the first Principle was not thematized in Greek thought. The Stoicists represented a material God diffused like a fluid throughout the universe (*SVF* II, 306–8). But Plotinus's concept, directed against the Stoicists, had a stronger influence on the patristic tradition because it was compatible with the idea of the omnipresence of the incorporeal and immutable (present in a place but without movement to lead it there), that is, the omnipresence of the soul to the body and of being* to the totality of beings (*Enn.* VI, 4 and 5).

For the Fathers*, the attribution of omnipresence answered the need to keep God limitless but entailed a danger of pantheism*, which the Stoicists apparently did not resist.

The Greek Fathers (first mention in Clement of Rome, who cites Ps 138, Epistle to the Corinthians, c. 28, nos. 1–4) articulated their thought on omnipresence around the notion of divine immensity: God escapes all limits (*aperigraphos*), all measure (*ametrètos*), all location (*akhôrètos*). Origen* reviewed all the biblical expressions that assign a place to God (PG 11, 485–86 D). He argued for divine incorporeity: "incorporeal" is used in the sense of "without body" (*SC* 252, 86–97). The dialogue with the Samaritan woman (Jn 4:24) clearly shows that God is spirit. All of these themes were pursued, notably by Gregory* of Nyssa in *Against Eunomius* III (*PG* 45, 603), thereafter frequently cited. John Damascene devoted a chapter of *Orthodox Faith* (I 13, PG 94, 869) to the question. He contributed to Scholasticism* a doctrine formulated with an Aristotelian vocabulary in which corporeal place is distinguished from spiritual place, the latter being the space where a spirit is manifest; God alone, among all spirits, manifests his power in all places (852 C -853 A). The Latin tradition interpreted this as meaning that God is not circumscriptively present (like a body in a corporeal place) or definitively present (like a spirit manifest in a place) but fully present (because he contains all things in all places).

The Latin Fathers inherited the Greek determination of omnipresence based on immensity, but their thought was more strongly influenced by the Stoicist concept of corporeality. Though Tertullian*, Hilary*, and Ambrose* (PL 16, 552) all emphasized the presence of God altogether in all places (*Deus ubique totus*), they did not always eschew Stoic images of liquid or luminous fluid penetrating all things. Once freed of these images, which he had employed during his Manichean period (*Confessions* I, 2 and 3), Augustine* formulated the most developed doctrine of omnipresence given by any of the Latins. In the letter to Dardanus (*Letter* 187), which he himself called "letter on divine omnipresence" (n. 11–21), he added to the precedent themes a derivation of omnipresence from divine creative causality. Along with Gregory* the Great, he was the authority most cited by the Scholastics.

d) Scholastics. It is nonetheless erroneous to attribute to Gregory, via the *Song of Songs Commentary* (c. 5), the triad *per potentiam, praesentiam, essentiam,* as did all the medieval doctors after it was introduced by Peter Lombard (*Sent.* I, d. 37, c. 1). In fact the origin is unknown. These mysterious words, associated with diverse commentaries, constitute the most original contribution of the Scholastics, who developed the two foundations of omnipresence established by the Fathers: immensity and the causal relation between God and creatures. The former alone guarantees the substantial, eternal nature of omnipresence, while the latter connects it to the actual existence of creatures.

Hugh of Saint Victor's teaching on the creative and preservative causality of God (*PL* 176, 825 C, 826 B, 828 C) was a significant contribution to the systematization of Augustine's doctrine and is worthy of mention beside Anselm*'s speculations on the vocabulary of omnipresence (v. *Monologion* XX–XXIV). Arguing against Honorius of Autun's assertion of a ubiquity *potentialiter* but a presence of God in heaven *substantialiter* (*PL* 172, 1111 C), Anselm affirmed that the omnipresence is substantial because God is substantially identical with his power.

Thirteenth-century authors pursued this development in their commentaries on Peter Lombard. Thomas Aquinas's argument stands out because it is based on the principles of Aristotle's physics (notably CG III, 68) instead of creative action. Its most outstanding positive characteristic is the integration of divine ubiquity into metaphysics of being. The mode of presence remains the traditional one of operation: God is said to be present in all things as the causal agent because he is the cause of being of everything. But this causality does not maintain the transcendence of the cause with regard to the effect because the participation ensures a certain immanence that reinforces the notion of presence. Between his commentary on the *Sentences* of Peter Lombard and his *Somme théologique* (Ia, q. 8, a. 1–2), Thomas changed his interpretation of Lombard's triad and revived the explanation of Albert* the Great (*In Sent.* I, d. 37, a. 6). Thereafter he attached the presence *per potentiam* to divine government, the *per praesentiam* to divine science, and the *per essentiam* to the creation (and preservation).

e) Development of the Concept. Subsequent developments of the doctrine of omnipresence fit into the systematic framework of the Scholastics. It became a matter of intense debate in the Protestant movement with the ubiquity controversy (the eucharistic presence explained by the ubiquity of the risen body of Christ), which led to a long-term division between the Lutherans and the Reformed. A secular controversy in which Clarke and Newton were pitted against Leibniz* gave new life to this divine attribute, this time by questioning its attachment to space (which Newton clearly distinguished from God; *see* Funkenstein 1986).

The question of the presence (and absence) of God was carried over into contemporary theology and concretized by Barth* (KD II/1, 395–451) with a test of traditional developments on ubiquity. The localizations attributed to God in Scripture (heaven, the temple, the human heart, Jesus) should not be withdrawn, but these places are not all places of God to the same degree. Barth would seem to question the sharp distinction between different modes of presence (by nature, by grace, by union), seeing them as simply a distinction of degrees, culminating in Jesus. Catholic theology (Congar 1958) chooses to place greater emphasis on the Church, the body of Christ, as the privileged place of God.

● D. Petau (1644–50), *Dogmata Theologica*, L. III, c. VII–X (New Ed., Paris, 1865–67).
M. J. Scheeben (1873–82), *Handbuch der Katholischen Dogmatik* II, §§240–50 (New Ed., GA 4, Fribourg, 1943).
D. Kaufmann (1877), *Geschichte der Attributenlehre in der jüdischen Religionsphilosophie des Mittelalters von Saadja bis Maimuni*, Gotha.
J. Thomas (1937–38), "L'omniprésence divine," *CDTor* 33, 69–79.
K. Barth (1940), *Kirchliche Dogmatik* II/1, Zurich, 495–551.
A. Fuerst (1951), *An Historical Study of the Doctrine of the Omnipresence of God in Selected Writings between 1220–1270*, Washington, D.C.
M. Frickel (1956), Deus totus ubique simul: *Untersuchungen zur allgem. Gottgegenwart im Rahmen der Gotteslehre Gregors des Grossen*, Fribourg.
Y. M.-J. Congar (1958), *Le Mystère du Temple*, Paris.
M.-F. Lacan (1970), "Présence de Dieu," *VThB* 2, 1019–23.

J. Stöhr (1971), "Allgegenwart Gottes," *HWP* 1, 162–63.

I. Kolodziejczyk (1972), "L'ubiquité de Dieu *per potentiam, praesentiam, essentiam* selon l'ontologie de saint Thomas d'Aquin", *DT(P)* 75, 137–48.

A. Funkenstein (1986), *Theology and Scientific Imagination from the Late Middle Ages to the XVIIth Century,* Princeton, N.J.

D. Gimaret (1988), *Les noms divins en islam,* Paris.

E. Brito (1991), *Dieu et l'être d'après Thomas d'Aquin et Hegel,* Paris.

CYRILLE MICHON

See also **Aseitas; Attributes, Divine; Eternity of God; Immutability/Impassibility; Justice, Divine; Knowledge, Divine; Mercy; Omnipotence, Divine; Simplicity, Divine**

Omniscience, Divine. *See* Knowledge, Divine

Ontologism

1. The Problem

a) Concept. The word *ontologism* comes from the *Introduzione* (III, 53) by V. Gioberti (1801–52). Against psychologism, which subordinated being* to the idea and was thereby allied with relativism* and subjectivism, Gioberti claimed that his ideas had an ontological foundation. On this basis, ontologism asserts that only the intuitive knowledge* of God makes all other forms of real knowledge possible, for only God* truly is.

b) Risk of Pantheism. A doctrine of this kind might tend toward pantheism*, which led to Gioberti's works being put on the Index of Forbidden Books (1852), the prohibition against teaching seven ontologist propositions (1861), and, finally (1887), the criticism of 40 propositions taken from Rosmini (1797–1855). Were these challenges from Rome* aimed at a hidden pantheism in ontologism or at ontologism itself? Those who were called ontologists attacked pantheism in any event. Already in the 17th century, Nicholas Malebranche (1638–1715), from whom the ontologists claimed descent, had opposed Spinoza (1632–77). In

the 19th century, Gioberti criticized figures who were influenced by German idealism, such as V. Cousin (1792–1867). In the 20th century, Pantaleo Carabellese (1877–1948), the last advocate of ontologism, wrote polemics against G. Gentile (1874–1944). In fact, if ontologism remains within certain limits, it does not eliminate the plurality of consciousnesses. The thesis of the vision in God, as set forth by Malebranche, does not imply that of the vision of God or that of the identity of the principles of the intellect with the divine essence.

2. In the 17th Century

a) Malebranche. For Malebranche (*Entretiens* V), the light that illuminates the mind comes not from the nature of weak and distracted man but from the Eternal. An extension of the argument attributes an active role in knowledge to "vision in God." "The mind can see what there is in God who represents created beings, since that is very spiritual, very intelligible, and very present to the mind" (*Recherche...* III, vi). This doctrine does not deny the distinction between natural knowledge (in God, *in via*) and beatific vision (of God, *in patria*). Vision in God is not of God.

b) Gerdil. In 1748, Cardinal H.-S. Gerdil (1718–1802) gave a more "ontologist" twist to Malebranche's theses. All knowledge is an intelligible union with being. God is immediately perceived not in His ineffable essence but in His attribute* of "being." Knowing what is thus consists in knowing God in His being, which is simple and infinite*. The infinity of the divine being is the basis for His action. Human knowledge is passive. Everything in it that is active comes from God. We therefore know only in and through the Creator.

3. 19th Century

a) In Italy. According to the *Nuovo Saggio* (1830) of A. Rosmini-Serbati, we become aware of indeterminate and universal being immediately and prior to any judgment. The idea of being is fragmented into modifications that arise at the time of its application to experience*. However, Rosmini objects to a conception in the "vision in God" that is too "ontologist," like that of Malebranche. We see God not directly but rather mediated through the idea of being. (For Gioberti, on the other hand, the mediation of the idea of being is of no use, for in order to be foundational, an intuition must have something to do with the real, not with the possible.) By thus distinguishing between the idea of being and God, Rosmini in fact moves away from ontologism. According to followers of Rosmini, the criticism of 1887 (see the proposition that "in the order of the created, something of the divine, or that which belongs to the divine nature, is manifested in itself immediately to the human intellect") is a call for prudence* of thought rather than a condemnation.

b) In France and Belgium. For the *Ontologie* (1856–57) of F. Hugonin (1823–98), there are no created truths because the truth is absolute or it does not exist. We thus see all truth in the absolute—that is, in God. "Being, the law of thought, the being of truth, is God Himself substantially and not purely ideal" (I, 95). Hugonin asserts that we perceive all truth in the existence of God because we have no knowledge of His ineffable essence.

Ontologism was taught in Louvain before the Thomist revival brought about by *Æterni Patris* (1879). For the *Essais* (1860) of G. Ubaghs (1800–1875), ontologism is Christian philosophy*. If reason is defined by the totality of truths according to which each human being naturally makes judgments, and because those truths are not the work of the created being who finds them before making judgments about them, but the work of God, and finally, because those truths are God, for in God attributes are God

Himself, then reason judging reasonably necessarily judges in and through God.

c) Condemnation of 18 September 1861 (DS 1841–47). These doctrines unquestionably risked abolishing any distance between the intellect and God. The Holy Office, therefore, published a decree that spread alarm among ontologists who wished to defend the faith*. Of the suspect propositions, we note here the second and the fifth: "The being that we know in all things and without which we know nothing is the divine being" (this proposition confuses the *ens commune* and the *esse subsistens*). "Ideas are modifications of the idea through which God understands Himself simply as *ens*" (this echoes Spinozist ideas, along with elements from Rosmini).

As for the first proposition, the reason for its condemnation is not obvious: "An immediate knowledge of God that is at least habitual is essential to human intelligence, which can know nothing without it; this knowledge is the light of the intellect." Faith says that there is an immediate communication from God to the reasoning created being. Roman authority* was in this instance probably attacking the particular form of ontologism articulated by traditionalism*. This form presupposed a revelation* of God at the origin of history* and a kind of continuing historical innateness through time that would make any effort on the part of freedom and the intelligence to know God futile.

- N. Malebranche (1674–75), *Recherche de la vérité,* Paris (1964–74).
- N. Malebranche (1688), *Entretiens sur la métaphysique et sur la religion,* Rotterdam (1964–74).
- J. S. Gerdil (1748), *Défense du sentiment du P. Malebranche sur la nature et l'origine des idées contre l'examen de M. Locke,* Turin.
- A. Rosmini-Serbati (1830), *Nuovo saggio sull'origine delle idee,* Rome, New Ed. in *Opere edite e inedite,* Rome, 1934.
- V. Gioberti (1840), *Introduzione allo studio delle filosofia,* Brussels, (New Ed., Rome, 1941).
- F. Hugonin (1856–57), *Ontologie ou étude des lois de la pensée,* Paris.
- G. Hubaghs (1860), *Essais d'idéologie ontologique,* Louvain.
- ♦ J. Henry (1924), "Le traditionalisme et l'ontologisme à l'université de Louvain (1835–1865)," *AISP,* 39–150.
- A. Fonck (1931), "Ontologisme," *DThC* 11/1, 1000–1061.
- L. Foucher (1955), *La philosophie catholique en France au XIXe siècle avant la Renaissance thomiste et dans son rapport avec elle (1800–1880),* Paris, 167–95.
- M. F. Sciacca (1958), *Opere complete,* Milan.
- D. Connell (1967), *The Vision of God: Malebranche's Scholastic Sources,* Louvain.
- P. Ottonello (1967), *L'essere iniziale nell'ontologia di Rosmini,* Milan.
- F. Percivale (1977), *L'accèsso naturale a Dio nella filosofia di Rosmini,* Rome.
- P. Ottonello (1978), *L'attualità di Rosmini e altri saggi,* Geneva.
- F. Évain (1981), *Être et personne chez Antoine Rosmini,* Paris-Rome.

G. Giannini (1985), *Esame delle quaranta proposizioni rosminiane,* Genoa.

H. Jacobs (1985), "Ontologisme," *Cath* 10, 95–98.

PAUL GILBERT

See also **Aseitas; Being; Creation; Descartes, René; Infinite; Intellectualism; Nature; Rationalism; Reason; Truth**

Ontology. *See* **Being**

Ontotheology. *See* **Being**

Optatus of Milevis. *See* **Donatism**

Oratory. *See* **Bérulle, Pierre de; Newman, John Henry**

Orders, Minor

So as to distinguish them from the major or holy orders of subdeacon, deacon, and priest, for a long time Catholic theology* designated as minor orders* those lower ministries that received an ordination* of either a permanent nature or as an interim stage on the way to the reception of major orders. The early Church*, by contrast, made a clear distinction between the ordained ministries, received through the laying* on of hands (those of bishops*, priests*, and deacons*), and the other ministries, which were instituted without ordination. The oldest document concerning ordinations, the *Apostolic Tradition,* a document that might date from the first third of the third century and is attributed to Hippolytus of Rome, states the instituted ministry of widows, lectors, and subdeacons. In the year 251, Pope Cornelius listed for the bishop of Antioch the lower ministries in the Church of Rome*: subdeacons, acolytes, exorcists, lectors, and doorkeepers (quoted by Eusebius, *HE* VI, 43, 11). The overlapping of subdeacons and acolytes arose from the fact that in Rome at that time there were as many subdeacons as deacons. This overlap never happened in the East, where the only lower ministries in common use were lectors and subdeacons (with the meaning of acolyte).

During the course of the centuries, the functions vouched for by Pope Cornelius were exercised in different ways (particularly between Rome and the Frankish countries), either in a permanent way, for the service of the liturgy*, or often as steps toward a higher order, the preliminary step being, since the time of Gregory* the Great, entering clerical ranks. On the other hand, the difference between the institution of the lower ministries and ordinations, properly speaking, lost its clear distinction.

Before the Middle Ages the notion of a holy order seems somewhat imprecise in the Roman vocabulary. It was applied to the subdiaconate and to the higher orders when the marriage* of subdeacons had been forbidden at Lateran* I in 1123 (can. 21) and at Lateran* II in 1139 (can. 6). Henceforward, the subdiaconate was no longer a minor order.

The Council of Trent* attempted to adapt the minor orders for a new situation in the Church and the liturgy but without managing to carry it through (sess. XXIII [1563], reform decree, can. 17).

After Pius XII had drawn attention, through his Constitution *Sacramentum Ordinis* (1947), to the legitimate importance of the three orders of diaconate, priesthood, and episcopate and after Vatican* II had confirmed the sacramental validity of the episcopate in the context of the participation of all the laity* in liturgical roles by means of its *Motu proprio Ministeria quaedam* (1972) (*CIC* 1983, can. 1035), Paul VI replaced the idea of minor orders with that of instituted ministries, a category that was reduced to two groups (lectors and acolytes) by doing away with the other minor orders and the subdiaconate. From then on, entry into clerical ranks would be through ordination into the diaconate.

● M. Andrieu (1947), "La carrière ecclésiastique des papes et les documents liturgiques du Moyen Age," *RevSR* 27, 90–120.

W. Croce (1948), "Die niederen Weihen und ihre hierarchische Wertung," *ZKTh* 70, 257–314.

P. Jounel (1982), "Les ministères non ordonnés dans l'Église," *Not* 18, 144–55.

B. Kleinheyer (1984), *Sakramentliche Feiern II,* Ratisbonne, 61–65.

A. P. Kazhdan (Ed.) (1991), *The Oxford Dictionary of Byzantium,* articles "Anagnostes" (P. Magdalino) and "Subdeacon" (A. Papadakis).

PIERRE-MARIE GY

See also **Ministry; Ordination/Order**

Ordination/Order

I. New Testament

Like *episkopos* and *diakonos,* the Greek term *kheirotonia,* "laying on of hands" or "ordination," is secular in origin. Ordination—that is, access to a ministry* through the laying* on of hands along with a prayer in the context of a liturgy* of the Christian assembly—is attested with certainty only in the pastoral epistles (1 Tm 4:14; 2 Tm 1:6; *see also* 1 Tm 5:22). Did Jewish ordination provide a model? There is little consensus on this point because that ordination is difficult to reconstitute. In Christian ordination, the laying on of

hands falls to the *presbyterium* and is accompanied by prophetic words (1 Tm 1:16, 4:14); the assembly plays the role of witness (1 Tm 6:12; 2 Tm 2:2). Ordination confers on the ordinand a gift of the Holy* Spirit, in particular to see to the transmission of the gospel* (2 Tm 2:2; *see also* 1:14).

II. Basic Structures of Christian Ordination

No liturgy of ordination has come down to us from the second century. However, *Clement's First Letter* states that ministers are chosen with the consent of the whole Church* (1 Clement 44:3) and that they retain their position for life (1 Clement 44:3–5), and it formulates the idea of a succession beginning with the apostles* (1 Clement 42:4, 43:1, 44:2). By the middle of the third century, Cyprian* already had a precise conception of access to the position of bishop*: under the judgment* of God*, the people* and the clergy* of the local* Church contribute their votes and their witness; the consensus of neighboring bishops is also required.

The earliest ritual that has come down to us is the *Apostolic Tradition* attributed to Hippolytus of Rome. It is certainly pre-Constantinian, although it may contain later revisions, and its basic structures represent the most classic form of Christian ordination. The *Apostolic Tradition* was accepted in Syria and Egypt, and its influence can be seen in all current Eastern rituals. It also served as a model for the liturgical reform of ordinations after Vatican* II (Pontifical of 1968, revised in 1990).

For the intervening history of rites, governed principally by the Roman-Germanic Pontifical of the 10th century, modified by William Durandus, bishop of Mende, in the 13th century, and its theological interpretation, see P. De Clerck (1985). The focus here will be on the understanding of ordination expressed in current rites, which have explicitly revived the *Apostolic Tradition*.

1. Ordination as Bishop

In the *Apostolic Tradition* of Hippolytus, the ordination of the head of the local Church, the bishop, is the principal center of attention, all the more because parishes did not yet exist. Here is the text: "The person ordained as bishop should be chosen by all the people.... When his name has been pronounced and he has been accepted, the people will gather with the *presbyterium* and the bishops who are present on Sunday. With the consent of all, the bishops should perform the laying on of hands and the people watch and do nothing. All should be silent, praying in their hearts that the Holy Spirit might come down. After that, one of the bishops present, at the request of all, should lay his hands on the one who has been made bishop and pray, saying: [the text of the prayer follows]."

a) Access to the Office. (1) Meaning of the Role Attributed to the Members of the Local Church: Christians played an active role in ordination—that is, in the choice and the liturgical entry into office by the one who presided over their Church. This role was expressed in four procedures, which were integral parts of ordination: election, witness, epiclesis, and reception.

Election. Although we do not know the details of the procedure (the clergy played a special role), the principle of election by the people was clearly affirmed in both East and West. For Pope Celestine in the mid-fifth century, "no one should be given as bishop to a community that does not want him" (*Letters* 4:5), and Leo the Great prescribed that "the one who is to preside over all should be elected by all" (*Letters* 10:6). Practice went through serious vicissitudes, including the intervention of secular authorities and the monopoly of certain clergy beginning in the 13th century, but the principle remained fixed in the general law* of the Catholic Church until 1917. Paradoxically, the "election day holiday" of the British monarch reflects the same principle.

The import of the principle is clear: congregation and ordained ministers are partners and share responsibility for the Church of God, according to a structure that binds and distinguishes all and some. Vocation for the ministry is a call from God mediated by the Christians and those who preside over the Church.

Witness. The *Apostolic Tradition* 2 indicates the agreement that is necessary, which was established by voting in all later rituals; it is concerned with the qualities and abilities of the ordinand and his faith*. There remain today a questioning of the people and a profession of faith before the assembly.

The import of the principle is clear: congregation and ordained ministers are together responsible for apostolic faith; the succession of some in the ministry is rooted in the faith of all; the lists of succession prove it because they are established according to the succession in a particular church, not according to the uninterrupted chain of the laying on of hands (L. Koep, *Bischofsliste, RAC* 2, 410–15). Faithful to this view, Catholic and Orthodox Churches thus still state today that "the minister receives from his church, faithful to the tradition*, the Word* that he transmits" (Munich 1982, II, *DC* 79, 941–45).

Epiclesis. "All should pray...that the Holy Spirit might come down": The ministry is conceived as a gift of God to His Church; hence, the relation of a church to the pastor whom it elects is not that of electors to a representative. Ministry in the name of Christ* is also a ministry in the Holy Spirit.

Reception. The community of the baptized, who also have the Holy Spirit, accepts the ministry of the bishop as a gift and not as an emanation from the community, and this gift must continue to be accepted. Canon* law still requires it of priests (*see CIC*, can. 1741, §3).

(2) Meaning of the Role Attributed to Neighboring Bishops: The *Apostolic Tradition* prescribes the participation of neighboring bishops. Nicaea (can. 4, *COD* 8)

requires the participation of all the bishops in the province, three at a minimum, with the others agreeing in writing; the rule is still in force in the Catholic and Orthodox Churches. The categories describing the action of the congregation can also describe that of the bishops.

Election. They also participate in the choice of the person; their role grew over time.

Witness. Coming from churches that have the apostolic faith, the bishops present attest that the church in which the ordination is taking place, as well as its future leader questioned in the presence of the people, have the same apostolic faith.

Epiclesis. The whole assembly is the subject of the epiclesis*, but only the bishops perform the laying on of hands for this purpose.

Reception. The bishops receive the newly ordained as one of their own. As early as Nicaea (can. 5, *COD* 9, 8–12), if a Church did not accept an ordination, it was not valid; the correctness of the liturgical performance and the will of the ordinands could have no effect if they were not carried out in explicit communion* with the other local churches.

The theological import of these procedures is clear: the cooperation among neighboring churches in the ordination of a bishop shows that they are in solidarity, (partners in the service of apostolic faith), that tradition creates communion, and that succession in the ministry presupposes both. The pneumatological aspect of the procedure, finally, excludes reduction of ordination to the schema of a transmission of power and simultaneously excludes the reduction of the Church to its hierarchy*.

b) Content of the Office Conferred by Ordination. The bishop is elected, receives the laying on of hands, and enters into his duties by presiding over the Eucharist* at his own ordination, in a single liturgical continuum (*Apostolic Tradition* 4). The first millennium had no absolute ordinations (ordinations of bishops not designated to occupy a see). Chalcedon (can. 6, *COD* 90) had declared null and void any ordination of a priest* or deacon* that had not been done for a particular Church, but in 1198 Pope Innocent III contravened this rule (*Patrologia Latina* 214:68). The meaning of the rule is clear: ordination is concerned first with the Church and not the person ordained; the power received is not personal but tied to the office received, even if one of the purposes of epiclesis is to make the person suitable for the office. This constitutes a theological criterion. To think that ordination is primarily an incorporation into a college succeeding the college of apostles and that the charge of a church is secondary would be doubly mistaken; it would respect neither the

articulation between church and ministry nor the nature of powers conferred through ordination (see Yves Congar, *Ministères et communion ecclésiale,* Paris, 1971).

To set forth the content of the office of bishop, it is possible for the most part to follow the *Apostolic Tradition.* The office is:

(1) A gift intended to guide the Church in the tradition of the apostles. The Holy Spirit confers on the bishop a *pneuma hègemonikon,* the spirit "given to the holy apostles who established the Church in every land" (*Apostolic Tradition* 3). The bishop must be able to guide the Church according to the gospel, the book of which has been opened on his shoulders during ordination since the fourth century.

(2) A presiding in and for communion. The very structure of ordination is full of meaning. Elected by his Church and accepted by it to be at its head, the bishop is in a position to represent it before all others. But able to become a bishop only with the cooperation of the heads of neighboring churches, who accept him into their college, he also represents the entire Church in his own. The symbol and the task are clearly expressed: located both in his church and in the face of it, the bishop is in both senses the link between communion and the service of Catholic unity.

(3) A ministry of pastor. After the *pneuma hègemonikon,* the *Apostolic Tradition* 3 asks for the bishop the grace to be "the pastor of the flock," the classic designation of his ministry even today.

(4) A priestly ministry. In two places, the *Apostolic Tradition* 3 asks that the bishop may exercise the "great priesthood"—offering of gifts and the power to forgive sins*. This begins the development of a priestly interpretation of the ordained ministry, which applies first to the bishop and then to the priest.

2. Ordination to the Priesthood

Is the priest elected by the people? The case is not as clear as it is for the bishop. At least the bishop, in choosing the priest, must ask the opinion of the clergy and the congregation, as the current Roman ritual still indicates with the question, "Do you know if they are worthy?" Another important characteristic, found in the *Apostolic Tradition* 7 and continuing today, is that priests perform the laying on of hands on the ordinand after the bishop—they too make up a college. The ministry of the priests is described by the gift that they receive: "a spirit of grace* and counsel so that they may help to govern Thy people." No further details are given.

3. Ordination of Deacons

The deacon is apparently more directly chosen by the bishop because he is an even closer associate of the bishop than the priest. The *Apostolic Tradition* 8 prescribes that only the bishop performs the laying on of hands in his case "because he is not ordained for the priesthood* but for the service of the bishop, to do what the bishop tells him to do," and also because "he is not part of the council of the clergy, but tells the bishop what is necessary." It is asked that he have "the spirit of grace and zeal to serve the Church."

4. Other Ordinations

For the bishop, the priest, and the deacon, the *Apostolic Tradition* speaks of ordination (*kheirotonia*); for the other orders (lector, subdeacon, exorcist, and widow), it speaks of institution (*katastasis*), the first appearance of minor orders*. Does the current proliferation of ministries entrusted to the baptized call for their revitalization under different names and with different contents? The question is open.

III. Ecumenical Rapprochements and Open Questions

1. Rapprochements

A consensus is now taking shape among the Churches engaged in bilateral or multilateral dialogue on the ministries (with the exception of the Congregationalists) that recognizes the fruitfulness of the basic concepts of ordination that can be derived from the *Apostolic Tradition*: election and calling, witness, epiclesis, reception, powers involved in the office, collegiality* of ordained ministries, articulation between all and some in the apostolic and priestly ministry, and the fragility of absolute ordinations—these are the bases from which the changes necessary to resolve remaining questions are now being proposed.

2. Open Questions

a) Convergences Are Emerging on the Threefold Division of Ordained Ministries. On the one hand, Vatican II restored the deaconate as a permanent ministry and made a clearer distinction between the offices of priest and bishop while recognizing that these forms of ministry are *ab antiquo* (*LG* 28) rather than from divine law. The abolition of minor orders in 1973 also clarified the scope of the ordained ministry. According to a doc-

ument proposed for ecumenical consideration, the *BEM* (Lima, 1982, n. 25–16 and 28–31), an ecclesiological agreement on the threefold form of the ordained ministry is possible, on condition that the personal authority* of ministers be more clearly articulated with their collegial and synodal authority. The Lutherans, for example, have agreed throughout the world to restore the office of bishop on condition that its theological import be clarified. In the dialogue between Catholics and Lutherans, the document *Church and Justification* (1993) is a sign of an historic opening (n. 204, *DC* 91, 1994, 840): "The difference remaining in the theological and ecclesiological scope that should be recognized for the ministry of the bishop, connected to the historical succession, loses its acuteness when Lutherans can grant to the ministry of the bishop a value that makes restoration of full communion with the institution of the bishop desirable, and when the Catholics recognize that the ministry of the Lutheran Churches...carries out essential functions of the ministry that Jesus Christ instituted in His Church, and when there is no challenge to the status of Lutheran Churches as Churches. The difference in the importance given to the historical office of bishop is then interpreted so that the doctrine of justification* is no longer at issue, and so that the restoration of full communion in the institution of the bishop is therefore no longer a theological impossibility."

b) Connection between the Concrete Church and the Ordained Ministry Is Necessary. Agreement in this context can be reached on the mutual belonging of ministry and Church. The ministry no more emanates from the Church than the Church depends entirely on the ministry. Hence, the practice of absolute ordination (which appeared late, in the 13th century, but became common practice in the Catholic Church) seems all the more problematic in a time when the Church is seen primarily as a communion of local churches. And following a similar kind of reasoning, it is possible to agree to interpret the indelible character of ordination not as a grace given to a person for himself but as a spiritual authorization for a ministry. From this derives the fact that Churches today that practice ordination never repeat it.

c) Although the theological understanding of collegiality is not always unanimous among Catholics, it has nevertheless become an integral part of the daily life of the Church through the restoration of the importance of the structures of the *presbyterium* and through the institutionalization of conferences of bishops.

d) Whereas Protestant theology* gives the name of sacraments* only to the spiritual actions necessary for salvation* (baptism* and the Eucharist*), the Council of Trent* defined ordination as a sacrament (*DS* 1766, 1773). However, this divergence is in the process of being overcome; the designation of ordination as a sacrament was not rejected in principle in the early Reformation (*Apol. CA* XIII, 11); moreover, it can be said today that it is the bearer of grace and that it "cannot be reduced to a sort of nomination to and installation in a church office" (International Catholic-Lutheran Commission, 1981, §§32–33).

e) *The ordination of women**, practiced by all the Reformed Churches since the mid-1990s, remains a matter under discussion between them and the Catholic and Orthodox Churches.

● Hippolytus of Rome, *Apostolic Tradition from the older versions,* SC 11 *bis,* Paris, 1968.
Pontificale romanum: De ordinatione diaconi, presbyteri et episcopi, ed. Typica, Vatican, 1968.
Pontificale Romanum: De ordinatione episcopi, presbyterorum et diaconorum, ed. Typica Altera, Vatican, 1990.

♦ L. Ott (1969), *Das Weihesakrament, HDG* IV/5.
A. Faivre (1977), *Naissance d'une hiérarchie: Les premières étapes du cursus clérical,* ThH 40.
C. Vogel (1978), *Ordinations inconsistantes et caractère inamissible,* Turin.
Foi et Constitution (1982), *BEM,* Paris.
P. Jounel (1984), "Les ordinations," in *L'Église en prière* (Ed. A.-G. Martimort), Paris, 154–200.
B. Kleinheyer (1984), *Sakramentliche Feiern II, Ordinationen und Beauftragungen,* Regensburg.
P. De Clerck (1985), "Ordination, ordre," *Cath* 10, 162–206.
H. Legrand (1993³), "Les ministères de l'Église locale," in B. Lauret and F. Refoulé (Ed.), *Initiation à la pratique de la théologie,* Paris, vol. 3, 181–273.
P. F. Bradshaw (1995), "Ordination IV," *TRE* 25, 343–62.
J. F. Puglisi (1996), *The Process of Admission to Ordained Ministry: A Comparative Study, Epistemological Principles and Roman Catholic Rites,* vol. 1, Collegeville, Minn.

HERVÉ LEGRAND

See also **Bishop; Collegiality; Communion; Deacon; Epiclesis; Ministry; Presbyter/Priest; Reception; Sacrament**

Origen

c. 185–c. 250

Alongside Augustine*, Origen was the dominant figure in Christian theology* during its first five centuries. Both in his lifetime and later, he was the one theologian who aroused the strongest and most conflicting feelings. What is known as "Origenism" covers a range of doctrinal and spiritual concepts as well as a form of exegesis* that Origen initiated and that was to be developed after his time both in the East and in the West. The denunciation of an Origenist tendency at the Second Council of Constantinople* in 553 led to the condemnation of Origen himself and to the disappearance of a very large part of his work.

a) *Life.* Origen's life is relatively well known, thanks to Eusebius of Caesarea, who devoted almost the whole of Book VI of his *Historia ecclesiastica* to him. It appears he was born into a Christian family in Alexandria circa 185. He successively taught grammar, catechesis*, and Christian philosophy*. Under the influence of a patron, Ambrose, who had converted Origen to the faith*, he reluctantly agreed to start writing, although he was already more than 30 years old. After several journeys, to Palestine, Arabia, and perhaps Rome, he left the Egyptian metropolis once and for all in or around 232, having met with the hostility of the local bishop*, Demetrius. The second half of Origen's life was spent mainly in Caesarea, in Palestine, where he was ordained as a priest* and continued to teach. At the request of Ambrose, he also continued his literary endeavors. He was invited to take part in several regional councils* in order to bring back to the orthodox faith certain bishops whose Trinitarian beliefs had caused problems. In 250, during the Decian persecution, Origen was arrested and tortured. His health broken, he died shortly after, probably in Tyre.

b) *Works.* Barely one-quarter of Origen's immense literary output remains in existence, and a large number of those texts that have survived are available only in Latin versions composed by Rufinus and Jerome around the first decade of the fifth century. Setting aside his letters, which have almost all been lost, we may divide his work into two groups: his studies of Scripture, including commentaries, homilies, and "notes" (or "scholia"), and his treatises, which deal with theology, spirituality, and apologetics. In his commentaries, homilies, and, more rarely, scholia, Origen explained almost every scriptural text and returned several times to the same books of the Bible*. According to ancient testimony, he composed some 260 "volumes" (books) of commentary and almost 500 homilies. Today, there are no more than 31 volumes of commentaries, including some in Greek on Matthew and John and some in Latin on the Song of Songs and Romans, as well as 205 homilies, among which only 21 are in Greek. While the loss of some important commentaries, notably on Genesis, is to be deplored, the disappearance of his major treatises, which aroused controversy in Origen's lifetime, is even more serious. They include *On Natures, Dialogue with Candide, Stromata,* and *On the Resurrection.* Fortunately, we do possess his most important theological work, the treatise *De Principiis,* a Latin translation of *Peri Archôn,* and his massive apologetic work for Christianity, *Contra Celsum.*

c) Intended Readership and Issues Addressed. Informed by a vast biblical and philosophical culture, Origen's work is addressed primarily to Christians committed to improving themselves intellectually, morally, and spiritually. His treatises and commentaries gave him opportunities to develop a scholarly theology intended for "advanced" Christians, such as his patron Ambrose, while his homilies reveal his concern to provide edification for the community as a whole.

Origen aimed his most sustained and fiercest polemics at gnosis* and Marcionism*, but he also engaged in dialogue with Gnostics. His desire for dialogue is still more evident in his dealings with Judaism*—he learned about its methods and traditions from a Hebrew teacher—and with Platonic philosophy, to which he was apparently introduced by the Neoplatonist Ammonius Saccas, who was Plotinus's teacher.

d) Origen and the Bible. Scripture, for Origen, was the source of all wisdom* and thus became the main focus of all his work. He approached it as a philologist, a grammarian, and a theologian. His capacity for textual analysis and critical editing is illustrated by the *Hexapla,* of which only fragments remain. This was an edition of the Old Testament laid out in six columns, in which the Hebrew text, transliterated in Greek letters, was accompanied by the Septuagint and other Greek translations by Aquila, Symmachus, and Theodotion. One of the objectives of this remarkable research tool was to pinpoint the differences between the Hebrew text used by Jews and the Greek Septuagint used by Christians.

However, Origen's renown as a biblical scholar rests principally on his work as a theoretician of hermeneutics* and a practitioner of allegorical exegesis. Following in the tradition of Philo and of Clement of Alexandria*, he defended and developed a notion of the spiritual sense of Scripture* as being its fundamental meaning. Readers must receive the spirit of Christ* if they are to grasp, over and above the letter of the text, the meaning that the divine Spirit has placed within it. Origen established rules by which to reach this spiritual sense, which is always mysterious and which is related to the triune God*, to the intelligible world*, and to the end of time. One of his rules is that the Old Testament is to be interpreted by way of the New Testament, which in turn is to be interpreted by reference to the person* and revelation* of Christ. Another rule is that the interpreter must place any specific passage being studied in relation to the whole of Scripture. This approach requires rigorous attention to the words of the text and their various uses in order to distinguish their figurative or allegorical meanings, and it depends on the presupposition that Scripture forms a single entity.

Origen made the discovery of the spiritual sense the overriding objective of his interpretation, but he did not neglect research into the literal or historical sense (the history of Israel*, the acts and gestures of Christ, or testimony on the primitive Christian community). Hence, more often than not, his exegesis covers both the literal and the spiritual levels, although occasionally he refers to a third sense that he calls "moral," though he is not very specific about what it is.

e) As Theologian. The *Peri Archôn* defines and accomplishes a theological program that had no precedent or counterpart in the patristic era: that of developing, on the basis of symbols, on the faith of the Church, and on Scripture, a coherent doctrine of God, humanity, and the world. The requirement of coherence led Origen to formulate certain hypotheses that were later held against him: the preexistence of souls*; the succession of worlds, which continues until every spirit has freely accomplished its conversion* to God; and the identical nature of the initial condition and the final condition. The inclusion of these and other hypotheses points to an important characteristic of Origen's method that has often been misunderstood: his consistent commitment to research, which led him, whenever he was faced with a difficulty, to propose (rather than assert) a solution in the form of an "exercise."

Within the system that Origen constructed, the decisive roles are played by the goodness of God and the liberty* of human beings. The Fall was caused by an evil use of liberty by created spirits, but this same liberty, educated and assisted by divine providence*, will lead human beings to a constant contemplation* of the triune God.

The *Peri Archôn* also represents a significant stage in the development of the doctrine of the Trinity*, notably in the two sections on the Holy* Spirit, in which Origen emphasizes both its individual substance and its two functions, the charismatic and the gnoseological.

Origen's Christology* is complex. God the Son is both subordinate to the Father* and equal to him and exercises a multitude of revelatory and mediating functions that are indicated by the diverse epithets (*epinoiai*) that Scripture applies to him. Since before the Incarnation* he has taken on an unfallen human soul. His Incarnation is salvific in the sense that it conveys the full revelation of God and provides a model for the human will completely and freely subject to God.

f) The Spiritual. Knowledge* of God and contemplation of him are to be acquired through spiritual understanding of Scripture and imitation of the incarnate Logos. Human beings, each composed of a spirit, a soul*, and a body, are engaged in combat with themselves. The soul, the seat of free will, is subject to the passions: on the one hand, it is drawn away by the body, but on the other hand, the spirit, which is part of the divine Spirit, induces the soul to direct itself toward God. This struggle is not played out solely within each human being, for it is related to the struggle between the angels* and the demons* and, beyond them, between Christ and Satan. Asceticism*, prayer*, and the practice of the virtues* are all weapons that allow human beings to continue the fight to the point of victory. But the decisive weapon is the power, the light, and the love* that Christ, the image of the invisible God, brings to human beings when he comes to dwell and grow within them. In this way, Christ makes human beings into participants in his own character as image, and believers are gradually transformed into spiritual and perfect beings who can attain the contemplation of God through union with Christ. However, perfect vision is not attainable in this world. Origen's ideal is a mystical one (mysticism*), yet his works do not contain any clear testimony to any mystical or ecstatic experience of his own.

g) Origenism after Origen. During his lifetime and throughout subsequent history, Origen has been attacked and defended, and the *Peri Archôn* has often become the focus of controversies. The liveliest debates took place between the fourth and sixth centuries. Origen's admirers, some of them enthusiastic, others more moderate, included Eusebius of Caesarea, Athanasius*, Hilary* of Poitiers, Didymus, Basil* of Caesarea, Gregory* of Nazianzus, Gregory* of Nyssa, Evagrius, Ambrose*, Rufinus, and Jerome (in his early years). In the fourth century, two works, full of quotations, were entirely devoted to Origen: Pamphilus of Caesarea's *Apology for Origen* and the *Philocalia,* traditionally attributed to Gregory of Nazianzen and Basil of Caesarea. Origen's opponents included Methodius of Olympia, Eustathes of Antioch, Peter of Alexandria, Epiphanes, Theophilus of Alexandria, and Jerome (at a later stage).

The controversies that developed around Origen's legacy from the fourth century on are not immediately accessible. They were concerned with elements of Origen's thinking—such as the preexistence of souls, apocatastasis*, the doctrine of the resurrected body, eternal creation*, subordinationism*, and his excessive use of allegory—but they also brought in elements that were foreign to his ideas, that contradicted them, or that were falsified by some of his readers. In the West these controversies culminated in Jerome's spectacular conversion to the anti-Origenist cause around 400; in the East they culminated in the condemnation of both Origen and the Origenists in the middle of the sixth century.

Origen's thought inevitably influenced the exegetical labors and theological reflections of later centuries and was also developed within monastic circles. From its earliest stages, Egyptian anchoritic monasticism* took from Origen's spirituality such themes as asceticism, spiritual combat, and the struggle against demons. In the closing years of the fourth century, there were readers of Origen among the monks of Nitria and the Kellia, practicing a highly intellectual form of speculation that gave rise to problems because it rejected any form of piety related to material reality and any Christian use of anthropomorphism*. It was in this milieu that Evagrius (346–99) developed a theological system (*see* in particular his *Gnostic Chapters*) structured around hypotheses concerning the creation of intellects by God and the ultimate restoration of primal unity. During the first half of the sixth century, Evagrius's version of Origenism won support among the monks of Palestine: it was in order to suppress them that, in 543 and 553 (at Constantinople II), Justinian condemned a form of Origenism that was closer to Evagrius's teachings than to those of Origen himself.

The loss of the majority of Origen's writings was the direct result of this condemnation. It must be noted that Origen nonetheless continued to influence the scholarly theology of the East, both indirectly through such theologians as Gregory of Nazianzen and Gregory of Nyssa and more directly through the work of those who quite often used his commentaries in compiling exegetical sequences. In the West, throughout the Middle Ages, exegesis continued to be dominated by the Origenist principles, which had previously been used by Hilary, Ambrose, and Jerome. During the Renaissance, Origen was rediscovered for the first time, notably by Lorenzo Valla and Erasmus*, while the Reformers, in particular Luther*, displayed some serious reservations about his allegorical exegesis. More recently, in the middle of the 20th century, Origen's works, methods, and ideas have been brought to the forefront once again by theologians such as Henri Sonier de Lubac*, H. Rahner*, and Hans Urs von Balthasar*, all of whom have played a decisive role in the renewal of Catholic theology.

- Most of Origen's texts appear in GCS and SC; *see also* PG 11–17.

Exhaustive bibliography up until 1980 in H. Crouzel (1971 + supplement 1982), *Bibliographie critique d'Origène*, Steenbrugge.

• About Origen
J. Daniélou (1948), *Origène*, Paris.
H. de Lubac (1950), *Histoire et Esprit: L'intelligence de l'Écriture d'après Origène*, Paris.
H. Crouzel (1956), *Théologie de l'Image de Dieu chez Origène*, Paris.

M. Harl (1958), *Origène et la fonction révélatrice du Verbe incarné*, Paris.
J. Rius-Camps (1970), *El dinamismo trinitario en la divinización de los seres racionales según Orígenes*, Rome.
H.-J. Vogt (1974), *Das Kirchenverständnis des Origenes*, Köln-Vienna.
P. Nautin (1977), *Origène Sa vie et son œuvre*, Paris.
H. Crouzel (1985), *Origène*, Paris.
A. Monaci Castagno (1987), *Origene predicatore e il suo pubblico*, Milan.
B. Neuschäfer (1987), *Origenes als Philologe*, 2 vols., Basel.
M. Fédou (1995), *La sagesse et le monde: Le Christ d'Origène*, Paris.
T. Hermans (1996), *Origène: Théologie sacrificielle du sacerdoce des chrétiens*, Paris.
See also the Acts from international colloquia on Origen: *Origeniana* (1975), Paris; *Origeniana Secunda* (1980), Rome; *Origeniana Tertia* (1985), Rome; *Origeniana Quarta* (1987), Vienna; *Origeniana Quinta* (1992), Louvain; *Origeniana Sexta* (1995), Louvain.

On Origenism and Origen's Legacy
A. Guillaumont (1962), *Les "Kephalaia Gnostica" d'Évagre le Pontique et l'histoire de l'origénisme chez les Grecs et chez les Syriens*, Paris.
W. A. Bienert (1978), *Dionysius von Alexandrien: Zur Frage des Origenismus im dritten Jahrhundert*, Berlin-New York.
M. Schär (1979), *Das Nachleben des Origenes im Zeitalter des Humanismus*, Basel-Stuttgart.
J. F. Dechow (1988), *Dogma and Mysticism in Early Christianity: Epiphanius of Cyprus and the Legacy of Origen*, Macon, Ga.

ÉRIC JUNOD

See also **Alexandria, School of; Anthropology; Resurrection of the Dead; Scripture, Fulfillment of; Spiritual Theology; Translations of the Bible; Trinity**

Orthodox Church. *See* Orthodoxy

Orthodoxy

A. Doctrinal Orthodoxy according to the Churches

The concept of "orthodoxy"—*orthè doxa,* right opinion—was known and used outside Christianity: its Christian field of application became established as the complementary concepts of heterodoxy and heresy* were defined. Its use stems from a fundamental claim of Christian communities: to hand down words that are *true,* to *define* the meaning of these words, and finally to decide whether any given words uttered within their midst *contradict* the defined faith*. The believer's orthodoxy is thus measured by what he or she believes and confesses: the orthodox person is one who on the one hand believes and confesses what the Church* believes and confesses (*material* orthodoxy) and on the other *wants* to believe and confess what the Church believes and confesses (*formal* orthodoxy). Since only a person who engages in the literal repetition of creeds and confessions of faith or who entrusts entirely to the Church the responsibility of saying what he or she believes (*see* Brague [1981] on "blind faith") may be assured of faultless orthodoxy, error is always possible, whether it is born of ignorance (an *idiota* may say things that are *materially* heretical while at the same time fully and firmly intending to confess the faith of the Church rather than his own private choices) or of conceptual mistakes. The theologian may, in good faith, say things today that the Church's instruments of doctrinal decision—popes*, councils*, and bishops*— may tomorrow decide to be inadequate or erroneous: so, for example, a large part of Origen*'s Christology* suffers from subordinationist tendencies, even though Origen fully and firmly confessed the faith of the pre-Nicene *catholica,* whose words lacked the precision of the vocabulary that was formally adopted between Nicaea and Chalcedon. However, just as orthodoxy has two faces, objective (*fides quae creditur*) and subjective (*fides qua creditur*), so too heterodoxy may be deliberate: a person who says things that are judged materially heretical by the Church (which in so doing exercises its *munus docendi,* its teaching function) in the course of a legitimate proceeding will be found guilty of *formal* heresy in many cases if he or she persists in saying them after such a judgment.

To the concept of orthodoxy should be added that of "indifferent matters" (*adiaphora*). These matters fall into two categories: theological or quasi-theological questions that do not form part of the faith of the Church (questions of liturgical ceremonial, the celibacy of the priesthood*, and so on) and legitimate differences in the expression of the content of that faith (*see* inculturation* and theological schools). Legitimate dissent does exist, then, and has recently been fiercely debated within Catholicism* (*see* Dulles 1996)—but while its theoretical rights are clear, the limits within which they may be exercised vary from Church to Church (a given question may be an *adiaphoron* for Protestantism*, e.g., the apostolic* succession of hierarchs, while for the Catholic and Orthodox Churches it is nonnegotiable), and the exercise of this dissent raises difficult problems in terms of the ethics of Church life. In addition, moral commandments "related to revealed truths" may be so closely associated with the content of the faith (to the extent of receiving what Protestant theology* calls the *status confessionis*) that their violation gives rise to a situation of "ethical heresy" (*see* the *Bekennende Kirche* on the subject of anti-Semitism as a heresy, the World Alliance of Reformed Churches on apartheid as a heresy, and Pope John Paul II on unconditional respect for life). In Catholic circles, this is doubtless what the *CEC* means at §88 by "truths having a necessary connection with the former [i.e., the truths contained within revelation]" (*see also* §2035, which is more explicit). On the other hand, this is not what is to be understood when ecclesiastical texts refer to "morals" (e.g., in the expression *fides et mores*): in this context the word denotes the discipline of the Church, that which governs its own life, especially in liturgical matters; "morals" does not signify morality.

The use of the concept of orthodoxy obviously varies according to the faith confessed by each Church and the official procedures that each Church sets out to judge it by. In practice, these procedures are intended not so much to set out an orthodoxy in positive terms as to define its boundaries negatively; any interpretation that is explicitly not condemned is assumed to be orthodox, at least until a possible condemnation—of which the most serious form is traditionally the anathema, which is a formal notice of heresy.

1) In the Churches that describe themselves as "orthodox," doctrinal orthodoxy is judged in terms of material and formal conformity with the doctrinal decisions of the seven councils recognized as "ecumenical," from Nicaea* I to Nicaea* II (in the case of the Churches referred to as "pre-Chalcedonian," conformity with the doctrinal decrees of the first two or three of these councils), it being understood that each council ratifies some development of the doctrines and that it is the responsibility of the College of Bishops to impart the teachings of the "Fathers" and bring them up to date for every age. Moreover, an influential current in recent Orthodox theology has suggested making Palamism (Gregory* Palamas) a preferred yardstick for the Orthodox faith.

2) The Roman Catholic Church also relies on the criterion of fidelity to the Fathers and the councils (albeit that it additionally recognizes as "ecumenical" the 14 general synods* of the Western Church between Constantinople* IV and Vatican* II) but accords the bishop of Rome* considerably wider powers of doctrinal definition than are conferred on the patriarchs by the Orthodox Churches. Within the defined limits of his infallible teaching, it also grants him the power solemnly to confer the highest possible orthodoxy on statements of faith (the power of dogmatizing).

3) The Churches that originated in the Reformation vary in their criteria. The Lutheran tradition links *scriptural principle* and *denominational principle* in such a way that ancient creeds* (the Nicene-Constantinopolitan, Apostles', and Athanasian creeds) and 16th-century books of doctrine, considered as a "normalized norm," constitute a proper exegesis of the unique "normative, not normalized norm," which is the Word* of God. The Anglican tradition has also furnished itself with a denominational charter—the Thirty-nine Articles—alongside Scripture and the three ecumenical creeds; but it advances no official and normative interpretation of the articles and accepts as orthodox (or at least as not heterodox) any possible reading that does not violate the letter of them. As for the Calvinist Churches, not all have retained their 16th- or 17th-century confessions of faith in their present-day constitutions, but all live by reference to Scripture, the ancient creeds, and books of doctrine. Finally, the so-called free Churches accord to the scriptural principle alone the right of assessing sound Christian opinion but are able to maintain this principle strictly only by basing it on a theory of the inspiration of the Scriptures and, often, by extracting from Scripture "fundamental articles" on which Christianity stands or falls (fundamentalism*).

It is also noteworthy that while Catholicism has developed a very subtle set of theological criteria, orthodoxy has never become a precise theological designation within this (theological notes*). Moreover, the close link between faith as confessed and faith as lived out, between doctrinal orthodoxy and a life faithful to the Gospels, has been especially insisted on in recent theology, in which the concept of *orthopraxis* is frequently invoked to convey that it is not confessions of faith alone that make a Christian. Finally, it should be remarked that doctrinal orthodoxy is expressed within all Christian denominations by liturgical traditions compatible with the confessed faith: not only in liturgical texts but also in liturgical acts, such as the veneration (or not) of images*, blessings*, the layout of places of worship, and so on. The *lex orandi* of the Churches expresses the faith that they confess, whether explicitly or implicitly (the classic example of the latter being Trinitarian orthodoxy, which was implicitly present in Christian doxologies long before it was made explicit by a council; *see* Basil*).

● F. Lau (1960), "Orth. altprotestantische," *RGG* 3 4, 1719–30.
R. Brague (1981), "Oh, ma foi…," *Com(F)* VI/3, 74–79.
W. Henn (1990a), "Ortodossia," *Dizionario di teologia fondamentale,* 838–40.
W. Henn (1990b), "Ortoprassi," *Dizionario di teologia fondamentale,* 840–42.
J. Baur, W. Sparn, et al. (1991), "Orthodoxy," *EKL* 3, 953–76.
B. Neveu (1993), *L'erreur et son juge: Remarques sur les censures doctrinales à l'époque moderne,* Naples.
J. Baur (1995), "Orth., Genese und Struktur," *TRE* 25, 498–507.
J.-L. Leuba (1995), "Orthodoxy protestante," *EncProt* 1110.
M. Mathias, O. Fatio (1995), "Orth.," *TRE* 25, 464–97.
A. Dulles (1996), *The Craft of Theology,* new expanded Ed., New York, 105–19, "The Magisterium and Theological Dissent."

JEAN-YVES LACOSTE

See also **Heresy; Notes Theological; Race; Schism**

B. The Orthodox Church

The Orthodox Church obviously retains the general sense that orthodoxy quite quickly assumed during Christian antiquity; however, as *doxa* also means glory*, the term has been reinterpreted in such a way as to emphasize the doxological character of the Orthodox faith, its character of righteous glorification—just as in the case of its Slavonic equivalent, "pravo-slavie," *slava* (glory) is understood more than the original *slovo* (word). This faith is that of the communion* of Orthodox Churches or, in a second sense, of Orthodoxy: Orthodoxy comprises a group of Churches, mostly Chalcedonian but also pre-Chalcedonian, united under the general title of Orthodox Churches.

The Orthodox Church, like the Catholic Church, sees itself as the Church that dates back uninterruptedly to Pentecost: it therefore considers itself to be one, holy, catholic, and apostolic. From a doctrinal point of view, it was the Code of Justinian that brought together the fundamental principles of the Orthodox faith on the basis of the "four councils" of Nicaea*, Constantinople* I, Ephesus*, and Chalcedon*, supplemented by Constantinople* II and III as well as the important Nicaea* II. John of Damascus's *De fide orthodoxa* is a classic presentation of this doctrinal corpus. The gradual breach between Catholicism* and Orthodoxy saw the Orthodox Church assimilated into a conception of the Christian East, the Greco-Byzantine world. However, Constantinople, for all its unrivaled importance—known as the "New Rome" since the first Council of Constantinople and capital of the Roman Empire—was not the whole East. Besides, for over a thousand years, Catholics and Orthodox formed one single Church with varied and multiple liturgical traditions*: these two Churches "not originating in the Reformation" have much in common, as the present climate of the ecumenical movement makes all the clearer.

Besides political factors (the sack of Constantinople in 1204, the forced reintegration into Orthodoxy of the Ukrainian Greco-Catholics in 1945, and so on) and cultural (languages, liturgies*) and intellectual ones (Orthodox theology* is dominated by the major figures of Athanasius* of Alexandria and the three great Cappadocian doctors, Basil* of Caesarea, Gregory* of Nyssa, and Gregory* of Nazianzene), the separation between the Orthodox East and the West has a doctrinal and an ecclesiological cause. 1) On the one hand, the unilateral addition of the Filioque* to the Nicene-Constantinopolitan creed and above all its medieval interpretation as implying the procession of the Holy* Spirit from the Father* and Son "as from a single principle" remain unacceptable to Orthodoxy (though this does not prevent a possible Orthodox interpretation of the Filioque in the economic order and in the eternal radiance of that which the Three have in common—what the Greek Fathers* called "energies" and the Latin Fathers "communion"). 2) On the other hand, Orthodoxy accepts neither the pope*'s universal jurisdiction* nor the concept of infallibility* as defined by Vatican* I. However, Pope John Paul II's encyclical *Ut unum sint* (25 May 1995) declares that it is time to attend to the *manner* in which universal presidency should be exercized in the Church—a task that has already been begun by the COE's commission on Faith and Constitution (a commission of which the Catholic Church is a full member despite not being a member of the COE). Thus, the two main points separating Catholics and Orthodox now seem capable of solution.

Orthodoxy is made up of local* Churches in full communion with one another; they are thus "sister-Churches" under the presidency (since the break with Rome*) of the patriarchate* of Constantinople. The universal primate, like that of each local Church, is a *primus inter pares,* first among equals; each bishop* has full responsibility for his diocese. The primate encourages the maintenance of unity* and intervenes locally only if he is asked to. The basis of Orthodox ecclesiology* is territorial rather than national. While numerous Churches are more or less coincident with sovereign states, nationalism—in the sense of the identification of Orthodoxy with one ethnic group—was condemned as a heresy*, "phyletism," at the synod of Constantinople in 1872. Despite its unanimous condemnation, however, phyletism remains the chief temptation of contemporary Orthodoxy, with the result that often several jurisdictions coexist in areas where Orthodoxy is dispersed.

The local Churches are in the first place the ancient patriarchates, which together with Rome formed the "pentarchy": Constantinople (*see* at Istanbul), Antioch (see at Damascus and jurisdiction over Syria and Lebanon, a vestige of the territorial and nonnational principle), Alexandria, and Jerusalem*. The other autocephalous Churches (those that elect their own primate) comprise the patriarchates of Moscow (numerically the most important, including the provinces of Ukraine and Belarus, which today enjoy considerable autonomy), Georgia (a very ancient Church, originating in the conversion* by Nino), Romania (second in numerical terms), Serbia and Bulgaria, and the Churches of Greece, Cyprus (also ancient), the Czech Republic (Bohemia and Moravia) and Slovakia, Poland, Albania (in the process of revival), and, smallest of all, Sinai. The remaining Churches are "autonomous" (the election of the primate is confirmed by the primate of an autocephalous Church), such as those of Finland, Crete, and Japan. America's autocephalous Church (the Orthodox Church in America) is still not officially recognized by Constantinople. Finally, there are missions* in China, Korea, and several African countries.

The Orthodox liturgical tradition is a veritable patristic anthology, well served by its splendor and the force of its symbols. The Syro-Byzantine cycles (fixed and mobile) are available in their entirety to the French reader, in the translation by D. Guillaume (Rome). It may be concluded that the vitality of the Orthodox faith is due largely to the richness of its liturgy.

- J. Pelikan (1974), *The Christian Tradition. A History of the Development of Doctrine, vol. 2: The Spirit of Eastern Christendom (600–1700)*, Chicago.
O. Clément (1985), *L'Église orthodoxe*, Paris.
N. Lossky (1987), "L'Église orthodoxe," in M. Clévenot (Ed.), *L'état des religions dans le monde*, Paris.
Jean-Paul II (1995), *Lumen Encyclical*. See the biblio. of "Orthodoxy, Modern and Contemporary."

NICOLAS LOSSKY

See also **Chalcedon, Council of; Church-State; Filioque; Gregory Palamas; Hesychasm; Orthodoxy, Modern and Contemporary; Patriarchate**

Orthodoxy, Modern and Contemporary

Modern Orthodoxy can be considered the result of the fall of Constantinople (1453). At that time the great majority of the Orthodox world was under Muslim occupation. Already, from the seventh century on, the former patriarchates of the East, Alexandria, Antioch, and Jerusalem*, were under the yoke of Arab Mohammedanism. In the 15th century, the younger autocephalous Serbian and Bulgarian Churches* fell into the hands of the Turks, after Constantinople and the eastern part of the Empire. Russia, which was freeing itself from the Mongol yoke and whose political power was rising, represented the notable exception. However, despite the fall of the Byzantine Empire, Constantinople, the "New Rome" (Constantinople* I, 381, canon 3) held on to its place as the primatial see of Orthodoxy just as long as communion* was not reestablished with the first Rome*. After Russia became an empire, certain people were tempted to give it the ranking of a "third Rome," but this more political than ecclesiological opinion would never be taken seriously.

a) Attempts at Union between Constantinople and Rome. Before the Turkish invasion, Constantinople was a center of intense intellectual activity. In the 14th century, in particular, on account of an imperial policy oriented toward the reestablishment of a union with Rome, interest in Latin culture saw considerable growth, including from people such as Nicholas Cabasilas (mid-14th century). But, although in his *An Explanation of the Divine Liturgy* (SC 4 *bis*) Cabasilas proved quite exceptional by his recognition of the plurality of rites, in particular of the Latin tradition (Meyendorff 1982), he proved less so in his knowledge of Latin culture. Gathered around Emperor John Cantacuzene, a whole group in fact (Demetrius Cydones and his brother Prochoros should be mentioned) showed deep interest in the philosophical and theological Latin revival. Augustine*'s major works and Thomas* Aquinas's *Summa Theologica* were translated into Greek. Nonetheless, these Latinophile intellectuals were not opposed to Hesychasm*, as shown by Cabasilas's example. But it is true that at the beginning of the 15th century, access to the chief sources of Latin theology* did not really bear fruit, as the failure of the Council of Ferrare-Florence in 1438–39 attests.

After the aborted union of Florence and under the Ottoman occupation, contact with the Christian West did not cease entirely. To be sure, Constantinople's fall inspired in the majority of Orthodox believers a leaning toward conservatism. For this reason, in most of Orthodoxy at about this period, the Syriac-Byzantine liturgical tradition was frozen in the form in which it still exists today in traditionalist circles, which are in the majority in contemporary Orthodoxy. However, the empire's fall brought with it a phenomenon whose consequences for Orthodoxy would be important and enduring. At that time, many Orthodox believers left to study in the universities of Western Christendom. And from the 15th to the 17th centuries, instead of facilitating an authentic theological dialogue between the Greeks and the Latins, these contacts would result in what could be called the infiltration into Orthodoxy of the various trends in Western Catholic and even in Protestant Christianity.

Before we look at what G. Florovsky (1937) calls the "Babylonian captivity" of Orthodoxy, an event should be mentioned that represents another form of contact with the West and that also had long-term consequences: the Union of Brest-Litovsk of 1596. The Orthodox minority in southwestern Russia (the future Ukraine and Byelorussia and part of Poland), which belonged to the Polish-Lithuanian kingdom, suffered strong pressure from the King's Catholic Lords, who tried to assimilate it. These Orthodox believers appealed to the pope* for protection under the terms of the decrees of the Council of Florence, which recognized liturgical and canonic pluralism (in particular, the use of the Byzantine rite and the ordination* of married men as deacons and priests). Thus, it came about that six out of the eight bishops* present at the synod* of Brest-Litovsk (including the metropolitan of Kiev, Michel Ragoza) placed themselves under Rome's jurisdiction* and became "Greek-Catholics" (or Uniates, a pejorative term).

Southwestern Russia and other parts of Eastern Europe, such as Romania, are not the only places where Catholics of the Eastern rite can be found. The Near East had already had the Maronite Church since the 12th century. In the 16th century, the "Chaldean" Church was formed; later, the Syrian Catholic, Melchite Catholic, Armenian Catholic, and Coptic Catholic Churches sprung up. There is a Greek-Catholic Church in Greece and others further away, in India and in Ethiopia. The "Greek Catholic" Churches are far from being alike. Each region of the world offers an individual example, and the "problem of Uniatism," the central point on the agenda of the Orthodox-Catholic dialogue today, cannot be treated as a unified whole.

b) The Influence of Western Christianity. Alongside these questions of "union," which belong to the jurisdictional and ecclesiological fields, Orthodoxy and Western Christianity had some unusual encounters in which an Orthodoxy that was becoming "repetitive" was trying to have a dialogue with Latin theologians who held to the concepts of late Scholasticism* or those of the Reformation movements. Exchanges took place from 1570 to 1580 between Jakob Andreae and Martin Crusius, Lutheran theologians from Tübingen, and the patriarch of Constantinople, Jeremias II, who had been sent a Greek translation of the Augsburg Confession. The two parties came to a dead end, however, because they could not really understand each other. Among the points they discussed were grace* and free will, Scripture and Tradition, prayer for the dead, and the invocation of saints (Ware 1963).

Although Patriarch Jeremias II was able to counter the doctrines of the Reformation with an Orthodox criticism, that was not the case with one of his successors, Cyril Loukaris (1572–1638). Born in Crete, Loukaris studied in Venice, then in Padua, where he acquired a knowledge of Latin theology. He attended as a priest* the synod of Brest-Litovsk, where he represented the patriarchate of Constantinople. In 1602 he became the patriarch of Alexandria and in 1620 of Constantinople. Little by little, his favorable attitude toward the Church of Rome changed into an increasingly marked fellow feeling with the Churches born of the Reformation. Once on the throne of Constantinople, Loukaris fought the Catholic influence in the Ottoman Empire. To that end he used the Protestant arguments, and his *Confession* of his Orthodox faith, published in Latin in Geneva in 1629, is clearly inspired by Calvinism*. This *Confession,* whose original is in Geneva, was immediately translated into French (four times), into English, into German (twice), and finally into Greek, all in Geneva. After many vicissitudes, Cyril was strangled to death by Sultan Murad's janissaries.

The Protestant influence is clearly expressed in a letter that one of the creators of the Union of Brest-Litovsk sent to the patriarch of Alexandria, Meletios Pegas (who had studied in Augsburg). The letter says that, in Alexandria, Calvin* now stood in Athanasius's place; in Constantinople, Luther* (an allusion to Cyril Loukaris); and, in Jerusalem, Zwingli* (Florovsky 1937). Despite this tirade, the fact is that Cyril Loukaris's Calvinism was repudiated by the majority of his Orthodox brothers, notably by six local councils (Constantinople, 1638; Kiev, 1640; Jassy, 1642; Constantinople, 1672; Jerusalem, 1672; and Constantinople, 1691). In addition, it was and harshly condemned by two very able 17th-century theologians, Peter Moghila, the metropolitan of Kiev, and Dositheus, the patriarch of Jerusalem. Each of the two composed a confession of the Orthodox faith*. And this is where the Latin influences in Orthodoxy come fully to light.

Peter Moghila (1597–1647), born to a noble family in Moldavia, studied at the University of Paris and then in Poland before he became the abbé of the "Laura" of the Crypts of Kiev in 1627 and the metropolitan of Kiev in 1632. (Kiev was a prestigious town, even though Moscow had supplanted it as a primatial see since the 14th century and would become a patriarchate in 1589.) Moghila tried to raise the educational level of clerical studies, which were extremely deficient. Paradoxically, his aim was to fight the Greek-Catholic influence encouraged by the King of Poland. Obviously, the Catholics found it easy to say that Orthodoxy had converted to Protestantism in the person of its patriarch primate, Cyril Loukaris. It was to answer him that Peter Moghila composed his *Orthodox Confession* in 1640. This *Confession,* written in Latin, neglected traditional Orthodox theology and reproduced what could be found in the post-Trent Catholic catechism textbooks. On several points it adopted purely and simply medieval Western theological positions: consecration of the eucharistic gifts restricted to the recital of the institution and concept of transubstantiation, affirmation of purgatory*'s existence, and the seven sacraments*. (It was also Peter Moghila who introduced into the traditional wording of absolution, which speaks only of pardon granted by God, a second part that speaks of absolution *by the priest,* who has received a *special authority* for this purpose). Approved as it stood in Kiev in 1640, translated into Greek (with corrections concerning the Eucharist* and purgatory), the *Confession* was accepted at the local Council of Jassy in 1642, then in Constantinople in 1643. According to several historians (including Meyendorff [1960] and Ware [1963]), this document is the most "Latin" of those found among the official or "symbolic" Orthodox texts.

The *Confession* of Dositheus, patriarch of Jerusalem from 1669 to 1707, is another very systematic reply to Cyril Loukaris's Calvinist *Confession.* Born in 1641 in the Peloponnesus, from a modest background, Dositheus was placed very young in a monastery near Corinth. In 1637 he entered the service of the patriarch of Jerusalem, and in 1669 he was appointed to this see by a synod held in Constantinople. In 1672 Dositheus got his *Confession* approved by a council held in Jerusalem (in Bethlehem in fact), and this text is known most often as *The Proceedings of the Council of Jerusalem.* It is an extremely important document because not only do a considerable number of Orthodox believers still profess today an Orthodoxy close to this text but the majority of the non-Orthodox think it the most official expression of Orthodoxy.

In reality, like Peter Moghila, Dositheus was strongly inspired by the Catholic Reform and the Council of Trent*. He restricted himself to using against Protestantism the Catholic arguments on free will and grace, predestination*, the Church and the Scriptures, and the number and nature of the sacraments. He defended the thesis according to which sinners' souls* could be purified after death* (a doctrine close to that of purgatory), and, finally, he conceptualized the eucharistic conversion by identifying *metousiôsis* and *transsubstantiatio*—that is, by adopting the Scholastic conceptuality to make a technical term of Eastern theology out of a Latin notion.

The Moghila and Dositheus *Confessions* were very important. In their wake, all Orthodox theological teaching was imbued for a long time with the ubiquitous Latin influences in the textbooks used in the seminaries and the theological academies. In Russia, all theological teaching would be done in Latin until the end of the 19th century and even at the beginning of the 20th. Its considerable effect can still be seen in Russia, which is now emerging from a long period of "imposed silence," during which it had been almost impossible to acquire a worthwhile theological training. However, it can also be observed elsewhere despite various current theological revivals. And although a few individual exceptions exist here and there, it can be said that the inheritance in a degraded form of the Moghila and Dositheus *Confessions,* completed by Latin theology textbooks, shows an almost total lack of theological reflection, as George Florovsky (1937) stated forcibly. The abundant and interesting aspects of Latin (or Lutheran) theology are conspicuous by their absence. Perhaps it should be added that Peter the Great, who was not a theologian, took an interest in Protestantism, but solely from an ecclesiological viewpoint, in order to better watch over the organization of the Church in his state. It is difficult, therefore, not to speak of a decline when describing the theology of Orthodoxy from the 17th to the 19th centuries.

The 17th century would witness a schism* in Russia (which has still not been healed). The liturgical books were corrected to make them consistent with the Greek originals, which had been altered by Western influences. These corrections, undertaken by the patriarch of Moscow, Nikon (1605–81), provoked a strong reaction on the part of those who have become known in history* as the "Old Believers," who were excommunicated in 1667 and persecuted. Their most remarkable representative was Archpriest Avvakum, a strong opponent of all Western influences.

c) The Revival of the Hesychastic Tradition. Alongside these Latinizing developments, the Hesychastic tradition remained alive in monasticism*, notably at

Mount Athos, but also in Russian monasteries such as the Trinity, founded by Serge de Radonège (c. 1314–92), in which flourished a remarkable growth of iconography in the Hesychastic spirit, particularly with Andrei Rublev (c. 1370–c. 1430). Then, in the 18th century, in the middle of the Enlightenment, the renaissance of the Hesychastic tradition occurred, first at Mount Athos and then in the whole of the Orthodox world. It was spurred by the compilation of a vast anthology of texts by Fathers of the desert and spiritual writers of the fourth and fifth centuries. These ascetic and mystical texts, which focused on perpetual prayer* or the prayer of Jesus*, were collected by Nicodemus of the Holy Mountain (1748–1809) and Macarios Notaras (1731–1805), the metropolitan of Corinth, and published in Greek in Venice in 1783 under the title *Philocalia* ("Love of What Is Beautiful"). This collection's influence can hardly be overstated. Nicodemus himself was also inspired by other Western spiritual texts, particularly those of Ignatian spirituality*, which proves again the compatibility of an attachment to Hesychasm and an interest in Latin spirituality.

The *Philocalia* began to be circulated in earnest thanks to a Ukrainian, Païssij Velitchkovsky (1722–94), who, unhappy with the spirit of theological studies in Kiev, left for Mount Athos, where he grew friendly with Nicodemus and got acquainted with the Hesychastic tradition. In 1763 Païssij left for Moldavia, where a little later he became the abbot of the monastery of Neamt, a big spiritual center of more than 500 monks who under his guidance undertook to translate the Greek Fathers into Slavonic. He himself translated the *Philocalia,* published in Moscow in 1795 (five volumes). In his own spiritual direction, Païssij was something of a partisan of ascetic monasticism and insisted on obedience to a spiritual father or *starets* ("elder"). Certainly the most prestigious *starets* was the world-renowned Seraphim of Sarov (1759–1833), whose dialogue with Nicolas Motovilov made known the Hesychastic experience of the Light of Tabor. In the 16th century, Russia also experienced the classic conflict between monastic reformers who accepted gifts of land and money, such as Joseph of Volokolamsk (1439–1515), and those who would not accept such gifts, such as Nil Sorsky (1433–1508). It is worth observing that both Joseph and Nils were canonized.

In its Slavonic version, the *Philocalia* was primarily the instrument of a strong monastic revival in Russia. In particular, an important center inhabited by *startsy* (plural of *starets*) grew up from 1829 on: the famous "Desert of Optino." This center's influence went far beyond the monastic world, and no one is unaware of

the interest taken in it by writers such as Gogol, Dostoyevsky, and Tolstoy and such slavophiles as Alexis Khomiakov (1804–60) and Vladimir Solovyov* (1853–1900). Moreover, the spiritual revival did not touch only intellectual circles, as attested to by *Accounts of a Pilgrim,* a famous anonymous work written in a very popular style and imbued with perpetual prayer. In this work, the pilgrim, a simple peasant, travels with a copy of the *Philocalia,* in the edition obtained for the first time in a single volume (1857) by Bishop Ignatius Brianchaninov (1807–67). Between 1876 and 1889, another spiritual type, Theophanus the Recluse (1815–94), published the first complete (five-volume) edition of the work in Russian—and his own work and his correspondence are themselves very copious. It should be added that in the 20th century an even more ample edition (11 volumes in 1990) was produced in Romania by one of the greatest Romanian theologians of our century, Dimitru Staniloae.

d) Religious Philosophy and Contemporary Theology. Alongside the spiritual rebirth, from the middle of the 19th century, Russia witnessed a rediscovery of the fathers* of the Church in the big academies of theology, where critical editions, translations into Russian, and studies on the Fathers began to be published. This trend increased steadily until 1917. Even today, the theologians of Russia, many of whom know only Russian, use these translations. This patriotic revival was to bear fruit in the 20th century and especially abroad. However, as early as the middle of the 19th century, there sprang up a bishop-theologian who rediscovered the authentically Orthodox tradition and whose preaching* traveled beyond the Russian frontiers. He was Philaret Drozdov (1782–1867), the metropolitan of Moscow. (Peter the Great had suppressed the patriarchate, which was replaced by a synod.) Although Philaret had great respect for the Council of Jerusalem of 1672, he approved of the famous 1848 Encyclical in which the Eastern patriarchs answered Pope Pius IX's appeal "to the East." Philaret's sermons, which urged the conversion of the mind in order to contemplate the mystery*, were translated into French as early as 1866 (three volumes, Paris). The 19th century also saw important thinkers and theologians. Khomiakov and Solovyov were doubtless the most creative among them.

The man who was considered the first original Russian theologian, Alexis Khomiakov (1804–60), born into the landed gentry, was a former military man. With Ivan Kirievsky (1806–56), he became the founder of the slavophile movement and a lay* theologian. Under the obvious influence of the *Philocalia,* as well as of the rediscovery of the Fathers, he reacted against borrowing from the theology of the schools of the West and advocated a return to the sources of Orthodox tradition—that is, to a sense of the Church situated above "Romanism" ("unity* without freedom*") and above "Protestantism" (freedom without unity"). Khomiakov also reacted against German idealism (Schelling*, Hegel*), which was very influential in Russia. He wrote mainly in French, and *L'Eglise latin et le protestantisme au point de vue de l'Eglise de l'orient,* articles collected by his son, were published in Lausanne in 1872. Khomiakov coined the Russian neologism *Sobornost.* Based on the Slavonic translation of "Catholic" in the creed (*Katholikè = sobornaïa*), the word *sobor* means "synod" or "council" (also "Church"), giving rise to the idea of "conciliarity" to describe the Orthodox Church.

Vladimir Solovyov (1853–1900) provides a typical example of the birth of a Russian religious philosophy* by way of German idealism. A slavophile at first, he eventually progressed toward a more open attitude toward the West and devoted himself to a search for Christian unity (he would die in communion with the Roman Church). One of his chief contributions to Orthodox thought was the introduction of the feminine principle of "Wisdom" (*Sophia*) as the soul of the world. His Sophianism would have descendants in two great 20th-century theologians, Paul Florensky (1882–1952) and Serge Bulgakov (1871–1944).

In Russia, the end of the 19th century and the beginning of the 20th were characterized by an ecclesial activity in continuous expansion, and the preparation of a council for renovation struck many as a necessity. The Council of Moscow (1917–18) reestablished the patriarchate under Patrick Tikhon (recently canonized) and undertook a considerable renewal of Russian Orthodoxy's liturgical, canonic, and academic structures. If the persecution had not begun immediately after the Bolshevik revolution, this council would have been able to represent for worldwide Orthodoxy the equivalent of what Vatican* II represented for Catholicism*.

In Greece, too, the beginning of the 20th century saw the renaissance of a more vital Orthodoxy that was expressed in the *Zoé,* the *Sotèr,* and the *Apostolikè diakonia* movements and in the works of great systematicians, such as Christos Androutsos (1869–1935), Panagiotis Trembelas (1886–1977), and Ioannis Karmiris (1904–91).

The most productive revival of Orthodoxy in the 20th century was, nonetheless, the result of the Bolshevik revolution, which exiled the best minds among the Russian intelligentsia. The Russian exiles regrouped in Prague, where they founded a university, and then in Paris, where they started an institute of Orthodox theology (Paris, Saint-Serge, 1925). It was in these institutions that the various revivals (religious philosophy, study of the Fathers, reflections on the different aspects of liturgical life) bore their fruits.

Religious philosophy was represented in the persons of such philosophers as Nicolas Berdiaev (1874–1948), Simon Frank (1877–1950), and Nicolas O. Lossky (1870–1965) but also among the theologians, heirs to religious philosophy, such as Serge Bulgakov, who developed his Sophianism as an attempt to explain the relationship between God* and the creature, until his condemnation in 1936 by the synod of Russia (or what remained of it), a doctrinal condemnation and not, as has been said, a political one. This line of theology inspired by philosophy would show up again in Paul Evdokimov (1901–70), who was also the heir to the patristic revival.

This patristic revival itself was the creation of two amateur theologians (neither one of them had in fact studied in a theological institute): George Florovsky (1893–1973), a jurist by training, and Vladimir Lossky (1903–58), a historian of Western medievalism. Neither one had much interest in religious philosophy, and they taught that authentic Orthodoxy consisted not only of a knowledge of the Fathers but also of a way of thinking modeled on the Fathers today and for today. Their theology was adopted by such Russians as John Meyendorff (1926–92) and Alexander Schmemann (1921–83), who developed a "liturgical theology," and by Boris Brobinskoy as well as by such Frenchmen as Olivier Clément (who also inherited from religious philosophy), by such Greeks as Panagiotis Nellas (1936–86) and Christos Yannaras, and by others too, including the Englishman Kallistos (Ware), bishop of Diokleia.

The 20th century also experienced an ecclesiological renaissance focused on the idea of communion*, with Nicolas Afanassiev (1893–1966) and Metropolitan Jean de Pergame (Zizioulas). Finally, spurred by Leonid Ouspensky (1902–87), there was a revival of the theology of the icon, which spread throughout the West and was not limited to Orthodoxy alone (*see,* e.g., C. Schönborn, *L'icône de Christ,* 1976, and even *CEC,* 1992, 1159–62). A "theology" of liturgical music was also proposed by Maxime Kovalevsky (1903–88), composer, philosopher, and theologian.

A "great and holy pan-Orthodox Council" has been in preparation for several decades. The very process of its preparation is an opportunity to re-create the conciliar fabric of an Orthodoxy that has suffered greatly during the 20th century, especially from its jurisdictional divisions.

● F. Lau (1960), "Orth. altprotestantische," *RGG* 3 4, 1719–30.
R. Brague (1981), "Oh, ma foi…," *Com(F)* VI/3, 74–79.
W. Henn (1990a), "Ortodossia," *Dizionario di teologia fondamentale,* 838–40; (1990b), "Ortoprassi," *Dizionario di teologia fondamentale,* 840–42.

J. Baur, W. Sparn, et al. (1991), "Orth.," *EKL* 3, 953–76.

B. Neveu (1993), *L'erreur et son juge: Remarques sur les censures doctrinales à l'époque moderne,* Naples.

J. Baur (1995), "Ortodoxie, Genese und Struktur," *TRE* 25, 498–507.

J.-L. Leuba (1995), "Orthodoxie protestante," *EncProt* 1110.

M. Mathias, O. Fatio (1995), "Orthodoxie," *TRE* 25, 464–97.

A. Dulles (1996), *The Craft of Theology,* new expanded Ed., New York, 105–19, "The Magisterium and Theological Dissent."

JEAN-YVES LACOSTE

See also **Heresy; Notes, Theological; Race; Schism**